STURGIS'
ILLUSTRATED DICTIONARY
OF ARCHITECTURE
AND BUILDING

*An Unabridged Reprint
of the 1901–2 Edition*

Russell Sturgis *et al.*

Vol. II
F–N

DOVER PUBLICATIONS, INC.
New York

Published in Canada by General Publishing Company, Ltd., 30 Lesmill Road, Don Mills, Toronto, Ontario.

Published in the United Kingdom by Constable and Company, Ltd., 10 Orange Street, London WC2H 7EG.

This Dover edition, first published in 1989, is an unabridged and unaltered republication of the work originally published in 1901–02 by The Macmillan Company, New York under the title *A Dictionary of Architecture and Building: Biographical, Historical, and Descriptive.*

DOVER *Pictorial Archive* SERIES

Manufactured in the United States of America
Dover Publications, Inc., 31 East 2nd Street, Mineola, N.Y. 11501

Library of Congress Cataloging-in-Publication Data

Sturgis, Russell, 1836–1909.
  Sturgis' dictionary of architecture and building : an unabridged reprint of the 1901–2 edition / Russell Sturgis, et al.
      p.   cm.
  Reprint. Originally published: New York : Macmillan, 1901–1902.
  Bibliography: p.
  ISBN 0-486-26025-9 (v. 1)
  ISBN 0-486-26026-7 (v. 2)
  ISBN 0-486-26027-5 (v. 3)
  1. Architecture—Dictionaries.   2. Buildings—Dictionaries.   I. Title.
NA31.S838   1989
720′.3—dc19   89-1350
                                                          CIP

LIST OF CONTRIBUTORS

TO THE

DICTIONARY OF ARCHITECTURE

CLEVELAND ABBE, Ph.D., LL.D.
Meteorologist U. S. Weather Bureau, Washington, D.C.

WILLIAM MARTIN AIKEN, F.A.I.A.
Architect; New York. Late Supervising Architect of U. S. Treasury Department.

EDWARD ATKINSON, Ph.D., LL.D.
Economist, and President Manufacturers' Mutl. Ins. Co., Boston, Mass. Author *Mill Construction: What It Is and What It Is Not; Right Methods of Preventing Fires in Mills.*

CHARLES BABCOCK, M.A., Hon. Mem. A.I.A., Hon. Mem. R.I.B.A.
Emeritus Professor of Architecture, Cornell University, Ithaca, N.Y.

W. J. BALDWIN, Mem. Am. Soc. C.E., Mem. Am. Soc. M.E.
Expert and Consulting Engineer in Heating and Ventilation; New York.

CHARLES I. BERG, F.A.I.A.
Architect; New York.

C. H. BLACKALL, M.A., F.A.I.A.
Architect; Boston, Mass.

EDWIN H. BLASHFIELD, N.A., Hon. Mem. A.I.A.
Mural Painter; New York. Joint Author *Italian Cities;* Joint Editor Vasari.

H. W. BREWER, Hon. Assoc. R.I.B.A.
Author many papers published in the Proceedings R.I.B.A.; London, England.

ARNOLD W. BRUNNER, F.A.I.A.
Architect; New York. Joint Author *Interior Decoration.*

CARYL COLEMAN, A.B.
Ecclesiologist and Decorative Designer; President Church Glass and Decorating Co.

WALTER COOK, F.A.I.A.
Architect; New York. President Soc. of Beaux Arts Architects; President N.Y. Chapter A.I.A.

EDWARD COWLES, A.M., M.D.
Medical Supt. McLean Hospital, Waverley, Mass.; Clin. Instruc. Ment. Dis. Harvard University.

R. A. CRAM.
Architect; Boston, Mass.

FREDERIC CROWNINSHIELD.
Mural Painter and Decorative Artist; New York. Author *Mural Painting.*

FRANK MILES DAY, F.A.I.A.
Architect; Philadelphia, Penn.

CHARLES DE KAY.
Writer on Fine Art; New York. Author *Life and Works of Barye, the Sculptor.*

F. S. DELLENBAUGH.
Painter; Writer and Lecturer on American Archæology and Ethnology; New York.

WILLIAM DE MORGAN.
Keramist and Designer; London, England.

BARR FERREE, Hon. Cor. Mem. R.I.B.A., Cor. Mem. A.I.A.

JOHN SAFFORD FISKE, L.H.D.
Alassio, Province of Genoa, Italy. Writer on Fine Art, especially of Italy.

ARTHUR L. FROTHINGHAM, Jr., Ph.D.
Princeton, N.J. Professor Ancient History and Archæology, Princeton University; Late Editor *Am. Journal Archæology;* Joint Author *History of Sculpture.*

WILLIAM PAUL GERHARD, C.E.
New York. Consulting Engineer for Sanitary Works; Cor. Mem. A.I.A.; Author volume on American Plumbing in the *Handbuch der Architektur* publishing at Darmstadt and Stuttgart, Germany; and many works and articles, in English and German, on Sanitary Engineering.

ROBERT W. GIBSON, F.A.I.A.
Architect; New York; President Architectural League.

WILLIAM H. GOODYEAR, M.A.
Archæologist; New York. Professor Brooklyn Inst. of Arts and Sciences (Curator since 1899); Author *The Grammar of the Lotus; Roman and Mediæval Art; Renaissance and Modern Art.*

ALEXANDER GRAHAM, F.S.A., Mem. Council R.I.B.A.
London, England. Author *Travels in Tunisia; Remains of the Roman Occupation of North Africa.*

A. D. F. HAMLIN, A.M.
Adjunct Professor Department of Architecture, Columbia University, New York; Author *A Text-book of the History of Architecture.*

H. J. HARDENBERGH, F.A.I.A.
Architect; New York.

GEORGE L. HEINS.
Architect; New York.

GEORGE HILL, M.S., C.E., Assoc. Mem. Am. Soc. C.E., Mem. Am. Soc. M.E.
Architect; New York. Author *Office Help for Architects; Modern Office Buildings; Test of Fireproof Floor Arches.*

FRED. B. HINCHMAN.
Architect; New York. Late U. S. Engineer Corps.

WILLIAM RICH HUTTON, C.E., Mem. Am. Soc. C.E., Mem. Inst. C.E., Mem. Inst. C.E. of London.
Civil Engineer; New York.

JOHN LA FARGE, N.A., Hon. Mem. A.I.A.
Mural Painter, Artist in Mosaic and Decorative Windows; New York. Author *Considerations on Painting; An Artist's Letters from Japan.*

v

LIST OF CONTRIBUTORS

W. R. LETHABY.
London; England. Joint Author *Sancta Sophia, Constantinople;* Author *Architecture, Mysticism, and Myth;* *Leadwork, Old and Ornamental.*

W. P. P. LONGFELLOW, S.B., Hon. Mem. A.I.A.
Cambridge, Mass. Editor *Cyclopædia of Architecture in Italy, Greece, and the Levant;* Author *Essays on Architectural History; The Column and the Arch.*

ALLAN MARQUAND, Ph.D., L.H.D.
Professor Archæology and the History of Art, Princeton University, Princeton, N.J.; Joint Author *History of Sculpture.*

HENRY RUTGERS MARSHALL, M.A., F.A.I.A.
Architect; New York. Author *Pain, Pleasure, and Æsthetics; Æsthetic Principles.*

GEORGE P. MERRILL.
Head Curator Dept. of Geology, U.S. National Museum, Washington, D.C.; Professor Geology and Mineralogy, Corcoran Scientific School of Columbian University, Washington, D.C.; Author *Stones for Building and Decoration; Rocks, Rock-weathering, and Soils; The Onyx Marbles.*

W. T. PARTRIDGE.
Lecturer on Architectural Design, Columbia University; New York.

CHARLES A. PLATT.
Architect and Landscape Architect; New York. Author *Italian Gardens.*

CORYDON T. PURDY, C.E., Mem. Am. Soc. C.E.
Civil Engineer; New York. Author *Pamphlets and Reports on Construction and Fire-proofing.*

RUSSELL ROBB, S.B., M.A.I.E.S.
Boston, Mass. Author *Electric Wiring for the Use of Architects.*

W. C. SABINE.
Assistant Professor of Physics, Harvard University, Cambridge, Mass. Engineer for Acoustics, Boston Music Hall (1900).

ALEXANDRE SANDIER.
Architect; Directeur des Travaux d'Art, Manufacture Nationale, Sèvres, France.

JEAN SCHOPFER.
Paris, France. Author many articles on Architecture in American and European periodicals.

MONTGOMERY SCHUYLER, A.M., Cor. Mem. A.I.A.
New York. Author *Studies in American Architecture;* Joint Editor *New York Times.*

F. D. SHERMAN, Ph.B.
Adjunct Professor of Architecture, Columbia University, New York.

EDWARD R. SMITH, B.A.
Librarian Avery Architectural Library, Columbia University, New York.

CHARLES C. SOULE.
Boston, Mass. President Boston Book Company; Trustee Am. Library Assoc.; Trustee Brookline, Mass., Pub. Lib.

R. PHENÉ SPIERS, F.S.A., Mem. Council R.I.B.A.
London, England. Editor Fergusson's *History of Ancient and Mediæval Architecture,* Third Edition; Editor Pugin's *Normandy,* Second Edition.

DANFORD N. B. STURGIS.
Architect; New York.

RICHARD CLIPSTON STURGIS, F.A.I.A.
Architect; Boston, Mass.

ANDREW T. TAYLOR, F.R.I.B.A., R.C.A.
Architect; Montreal. Author *Towers and Spires of Sir Christopher Wren; Dominion Drawing Books.*

EDWARD L. TILTON.
Architect; New York. Late Student and Explorer, Am. School of Classical Studies, Athens, Greece.

T. F. TURNER, B.S.
Architect; New York.

HENRY VAN BRUNT, F.A.I.A. and late President A.I.A.
Architect; Kansas City, Mo. Author *Greek Lines and other Architectural Essays.*

WILLIAM R. WARE, LL.D., F.A.I.A.
Professor of Architecture, Columbia University, New York. Author *A Treatise on Plain and Curvilinear Perspective.*

H. LANGFORD WARREN, F.A.I.A.
Architect; Boston, Mass. Asst. Professor of Architecture, Lawrence Scientific School, Harvard University.

EDMUND M. WHEELWRIGHT, A.B., F.A.I.A.
Late City Architect of Boston, Mass. Author *Municipal Architecture in Boston.*

PETER B. WIGHT, F.A.I.A.
Architect; Chicago, Ill. Secretary Illinois State Board of Examiners of Architects.

The Author of ARCHITECT, THE, IN ITALY records his indebtedness for special information to the Commendatore Camillo Boito.

The Author of LAW, — to Mr. Philip Golden Bartlett.

The Author of MUSIC HALL, — to Mr. Theodore Thomas.

The Author of SURVEYING, — to Mr. Edward B. Sturgis.

PREFACE TO VOLUME II., DICTIONARY OF ARCHITECTURE

A GOOD dictionary will be good reading even if a column or a page be read consecutively; but it will be still better reading if the reader is in the mood to take a little pains and turns to one article after another, following not the alphabetical sequence of the terms, but the sequence of his own thought. This matter of the student's use of the book, briefly touched upon in the Preface to Vol. I., becomes of more obvious importance now that two thirds of the whole work is in print. There are some large general subjects which can be fairly well studied if this plan is followed; and with the appearance of the third and final volume, four months hence, these studies can be carried yet farther.

An obvious instance is that subject, the most important to us moderns of all matters of architectural history, the system of building and design of the great Empire, from 50 B.C. to 250 A.D. The building and the art of the European world since that time, and of much beyond the European world, take their origin in what was done during that epoch; and yet there is so little generally known about it, and it is so misunderstood, that all architectural thought and writing is seriously marred by this lack of accuracy. This very subject will be found treated at great length in the Dictionary. If, for instance, the reader begins with Italy, Part IX., Latium, and especially the second division of Part IX. where the city of Rome itself is treated; if then he seeks in the other parts of the article, Italy, for Roman remains, and farther in the article France, especially Part X., and in Asia Minor, the Balkan Peninsula, and North Africa; if he then studies Memorial Arch, Memorial Column, Amphitheatre, Basilica, and the technical terms referred to under Columnar Architecture, the subject will have been presented to him from several points of view. The appearance in Vol. III. of the general article on Roman Imperial Architecture and that on Syria, with Portico, Thermæ, and Tomb, may seem to complete fairly well (especially if Masonry, Vaulting, and the like be looked up) the presentation of what is known on the general subject.

The mechanical and scientific art of building may be followed up from item to item in the same easy and natural way; and the present volume gives Floor, Foundation, Frame, Framing, Iron Construction, Masonry, and Mortar, to be read with Builder, Brickwork, and the like in Vol. I.

Gas Fitting and House Drainage come here; Plumbing, Ventilation, and Warming in Vol. III., and these may be read in connection with Hotel, or with Apartment House (and with Tenement House, when it appears), or with Library, or with Hospital; for to many readers these hygienic departments are what is most important in modern building. The valuable and novel work given in Vol. I. under Acoustics, and its kindred shorter articles, receives a practical confirmation in Vol. II. by the article Music Hall; and some further help is given in Vol. III. under the caption Sounding Board.

The volume now issued contains the longest of the guidebook articles, Italy first, treated with unexampled thoroughness; France, Germany, Greece, Japan, North Africa, each written by one who knows well and loves the land in question and its monuments. Other vast regions, such as India, have received treatment less full and less minute, because of their very greatness and of their less immediate interest to students of European tradition; Farther India and Hungary, Ireland, Mexico, have proportionate space allowed them. There are articles which must be considered as continuations of those named above; thus Moslem Architecture helps greatly India and North Africa, as it will help Balkan Peninsula and Egypt in Vol. I., and Persia, Spain, and Syria in Vol. III.

R. S.

FULL PAGE ILLUSTRATIONS

F

FAÇADE. The architectural front of a building; not necessarily the principal front, but any face or presentation of a structure which is nearly in one plane, and is treated in the main as a single vertical wall with but minor modifications. Thus, if a large building presents toward one street a front consisting of the ends of two projecting wings with a low wall between them enclosing a courtyard, that would be hardly a façade, but rather two façades of the two pavilions.

With buildings which present on all sides fronts of similar or equivalent elaborateness of treatment, it is, perhaps, incorrect to speak of a façade; thus, in a great church, although the west front may be described by this term, it is inaccurate because that front would not be what it is were it presented without the flanks or north and south sides. The façade rather comes of street architecture and of buildings which have but one front considered of sufficient importance to receive architectural treatment. — R. S.

FACE (v.). *A.* To dress or finish one or more faces of a piece, member, or structure.

B. To provide with a relatively highly finished face by the application of a finer or more elaborately worked material.

FAÇADE: CATHEDRAL, CREMONA; NORTH TRANSEPT.
This, having no intimate connection with the side walls, is essentially a façade.

FACING: TWO BYZANTINE STILTED ARCHES, IN VENICE.
The rough brick work shown in *a* is covered in *b* by very thin facing of marble.

FACE MOULD. In stair building, a full-sized pattern of the inclined projection of a wreath, in sense *B*, produced by projecting the given horizontal plan vertically upon an inclined plane which corresponds to the slope of the wreath, or as nearly so as possible. If the plan of the wreath is, as usual, described on a circular arc, the face mould will be elliptical. (See Falling Mould.)

FACET. Any one of the several polygonal faces of a crystal or cut jewel; hence, any one of the faces or plane surfaces of a stone cut into like forms, as in rusticated masonry where each is dressed to a pyramidal projection. There are many examples in Italy, among them the exterior east façade of the Doge's palace at Venice and the Palazzo dei Diamanti at Bologna.

FACE WORK. That part of a masonry structure which forms the exposed or more important face, especially when constructed of better material or more elaborately worked. (See Ashlar, *B*; Face; Face Brick, under Brick; Facing.)

FACING. Any material used to face with, whether forming an integral part of a structure and built simultaneously with it as in certain methods of brick building, or applied to the completed rough structure as a veneer, as in the case of a marble dado; in this sense distinguished from Face Work. (See Ashlar; Face; Face Brick, under Brick.) (Cut, cols. 5, 6.)

FACTOR OF SAFETY. The quantity by which the numerically stated ultimate strength of a member is divided, in order to determine what force the member may resist with entire safety. Thus, in practice, an iron column is commonly allowed to support a load only one fifth the amount it would actually carry before breaking, the factor of safety thus being five. The amount of a factor of safety, as usually employed, is determined by experience and practice, but is arbitrarily assumed in any given case or arbitrarily established by law or custom. (See Strength of Materials.) — D. N. B. S.

FACTORY. *A.* A building in which factors (that is to say, agents, as of merchants or other business men) reside or conduct their business. In this sense, the term corresponds nearly to the Italian *fondaco*. In the Middle Ages, and to a certain extent in later times, the merchants of one country doing business in another required a building which would be a centre of their position as tolerated foreigners who must have some common office and place of gathering. Even in very recent times the existence of such buildings in Oriental lands is not unknown. The factory (called in French *hôtel*, or simply *maison*) of an important commercial country built in a seaport of another commercial country would often be a building of some architectural pretensions.

B (abbreviated from manufactory). A building in which manufacturing is carried on. Such buildings rarely receive architectural treatment; but some cotton mills and the like have square entrance towers and present a seemly appearance of decent construction and simple proportion. (For their structural peculiarities, which are sometimes of interest, see Slow Burning Construction.) — R. S.

FAIENCE. Pottery of coarse or dark coloured body covered by an opaque coating, such as is called enamel, which enamel may be elaborately painted. This is the proper signification, and it covers all the beautiful decorative wares of Italy from the fifteenth to the eighteenth centuries, including the richest varieties of majolica, and also the various potteries of France of slightly later epoch, such as those of Rouen, Nevers, Moustiers, and many more. These wares are often very soft, both enamel and body; but when used for external decoration, such as wall tiles and the like, the same effects of colour and brilliancy are possible with an extremely hard and enduring substance, and the greatest epochs have been marked by the production of cresting tiles, ridge tiles, finials for painted roofs, and the like, which are perfectly durable. (See Épi; Keramics; Tile.) — R. S.

FAIN, PIERRE; architect and sculptor.

In 1501–1502 Fain worked on the archiepiscopal palace at Rouen. December 4, 1507,

he contracted with others to build the chapel of the château of Gaillon (Eure, France). In 1509 he completed the portal leading from the outer to the inner court at Gaillon, which is now at the *École des Beaux Arts*, Paris. (See Delorme, Pierre.)

Deville, *Comptes de Gaillon.*

FALCONET, ÉTIENNE MAURICE; sculptor; b. 1716; d. 1791.

Catherine II. invited Falconet to Russia to make the colossal equestrian statue of Peter the Great. The *Œuvres d'Étienne Falconet, Statuaire* (6 vols. 8vo) were published in 1781.

Gonse, *Sculpture Française; La Grande Encyclopédie.*

FALCONETTO, GIOVANNI MARIA; painter, architect, and sculptor; b.1458; d. 1534.

Falconetto spent twelve years in an extensive study of the antique remains of architecture and sculpture in Rome. He also measured and drew the antiquities of Verona, Naples, and Spoleto, and later of Pola, in Istria. He settled finally in Padua, under the patronage of Luigi Cornaro, for whom he designed and built the famous palace now called Giustiniani, which bears his signature and the date 1524. Falconetto built the Porta S. Giovanni, Padua, in 1528 (signed); made the design and model for the church of S. Maria delle Grazie, Padua; and other buildings. In 1533 he began the stucco work of the Cappella del Santo, in the church of S. Antonio, Padua, which was finished after his death by Tiziano di Guido Minio.

Müntz, *Renaissance;* Redtenbacher, *Die Architektur der Italienischen Renaissance.*

FALKENER, EDWARD; architect and archæologist; b. February, 1814; d. Dec. 17, 1896.

He was a student of architecture at the Royal Academy, London, and in 1839 won its gold medal. He travelled extensively in Asia Minor, Syria, Egypt, Greece, Crete, Italy, and Russia, and in 1849 excavated a house in Pompeii. Falkener was editor of the *Museum of Classical Antiquities* during the three years of its publication. He published a pamphlet on the ancient theatres in Crete (1854), *Dædalos, or the Causes and Principles of the Excellence of Greek Sculpture* (1860), a pamphlet on the Hypæthron of Greek temples, and other works.

Obituary in *Journal of Royal Institute of British Architects*, 1896–1897, p. 149.

FALL (as of a roof, gutter, or the like). Same as Pitch.

FALLING MOULD. In stair building, a full-sized pattern of the side of a wreath. It is cut out of a thin piece of veneer, or the like, following the lines of the developed (*i.e.* unrolled or opened out) curved elevation, and is then bent around the wreath to give the actual lines of the steps, mouldings, and other parts. (See Face Mould.)

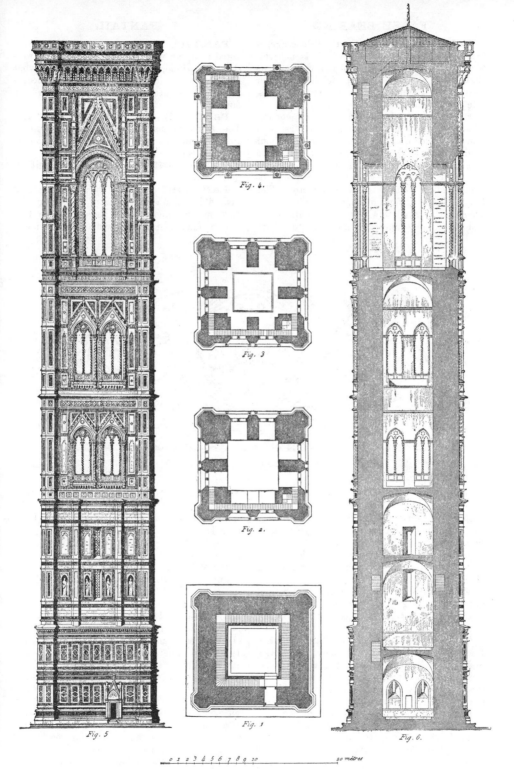

Fig. 4.

Fig. 3.

Fig. 2.

Fig. 1.

Fig. 5.

Fig. 6.

0 1 2 3 4 5 6 7 8 9 10   10 mètres

FACING: GIOTTO'S CAMPANILE, FLORENCE, COVERED WITH AN ELABORATE FACING OF
COLOURED MARBLES.

5   6

FALSE BEARING. In English usage, a bearing or point of support which is not vertically over the supporting structure below, as that which is afforded by a projecting corbel or cantilever. (Apparently an attempt to translate the French term, *porte-à-faux*.)

FAN. A contrivance for creating a current of air, either within a limited space, as in a room to which no air is supplied from without (compare Punkah), or as in the ventilation of a house, a mine, or the like, in which cases air is driven by it from without into the space to be ventilated, or from that space outward. The fans used merely for agitating the air in a room are either revolved slowly in a horizontal plane and have large vanes or wings, or are wheel-

FANE (I.). A temple, especially one devoted to pagan worship; hence, a place of worship of any kind, but in a general and somewhat poetical sense. The word *profane* is connected with this as meaning outside of (before) the fane.

FANE (II.). A weathercock; a vane. The term means originally a flag (German, *Fahne*), and in the present signification is probably confused with Vane.

FAN GROINING. Same as Fan Vaulting, under Vaulting.

FAN LIGHT. Strictly speaking, a glazed sash filling the arched head of a door or window opening, and having radiating sash bars like a fan; hence, any window occupying a

FAN LIGHT OF WOOD AND WROUGHT IRON, FROM A DOORWAY IN PARIS—RUE ANTOINE DUBOIS.

shaped, set vertically, and revolved at high speed. (For the fan used in thorough ventilation, see Ventilation; Warming.)

Plenum Fan. One which supplies a current of air by forcing it from without into the given space.

Vacuum Fan. One which causes a current of air by drawing it out from the given space.

FANCELLI, LUCA; architect; b. 1430; d. about 1501.

On the recommendation of Cosimo de' Medici, Luca entered the service of Ludovico Gonzaga, Marquis of Mantua, about 1450, and superintended his constructions for forty years at Mantua. He carried out, from the plans of Alberti (see Alberti), the small church of S. Sebastiano (1460–1472) and the more important one of S. Andrea (begun 1472). After the death of Giuliano da Maiano (see Giuliano da Maiano) he was employed by Ferdinand I., King of Naples.

Braghirolli, *Luca Fancelli in L'Archivio Storico Lombardo*, Vol. III. (1876); Carlo d'Arco, *Delle Arti e degli Artefici di Mantova.*

similar position over a door or window. (Compare Transom Light.)

FAN ROOF. A vaulted roof adorned with fan tracery.

FANSAGA, COSIMO; architect and sculptor; b. 1591, at Bergamo, Italy; d. 1678. According to Milizia, he built the façade of the church of S. Spirito de' Napolitani, in Rome. About 1626 he went to Naples, and built the façade of the church of S. Ferdinando (1628), the church of S. Theresa (Terresella, 1625), the fine façade of the Sapienza, and other buildings.

Gurlitt, *Geschichte des Barockstiles in Italien*, Milizia, *Memorie;* Sasso, *Monumenti di Napoli.*

FANTAIL. *A.* Any member or piece of construction having a form approaching that of a fan, as a dovetail or a combination of radiating pieces. Especially, a centring constructed with such pieces, and hence, —

B. One of the radial struts forming the support of the ribs in a centring, as above described.

FAN TRACERY. (See Fan Vaulting, under Vaulting.)

FAN WINDOW. *A.* The same as Fan Light.

B. Any approximately semicircular or semielliptic window upon a horizontal diameter; especially one having radiating bars or leading, like a fan in appearance. (See Fan Light.)

FANWORK. Decorative work abounding in fanlike patterns; especially Fan Vaulting, and the imitation of this and of late Lierne Vaulting, in the carved stone canopies of tombs and the like.

FANZAGA. (See Fansaga.)

FARLEIGH, RICHARD DE; architect.

Supposed to have built the spire of Salisbury cathedral, England, about 1334.

Redgrave, *Dictionary of Artists.*

FARLEY, or **FERLEY, WILLIAM**; ecclesiastic and architect.

Abbot of Gloucester from 1472 to 1498; finished the Lady Chapel of Gloucester cathedral begun by Abbot Henley between 1457 and 1472.

Winkle, *Gloucester Cathedral;* Britton, *Architectural Antiquities.*

FARM BUILDINGS. Those which are occupied by an agriculturist and his family and including all the stables, poultry houses, cart sheds, and the like, which make up the necessary provision for carrying on the work of a farm. In the United States it has never been customary to make of the farm buildings any architectural arrangement or grouping; and even in England the accidental clustering of the different structures in places found convenient at the moment has been generally the rule. Moreover, in both countries the common use of cheaper and less enduring material, such as wood, has caused the erection of barns, cribs, sheds, and the like, which have no permanent character. On the Continent of Europe the unsettled condition of the country for many centuries, and the constant possibility of attacks by a considerable force, have always led to the arranging of farm buildings around a court and with but few windows in the exterior walls, and those high above the ground. There results from this system an extremely suggestive architectural arrangement which it is easy to make effective in every way; and the much more common use of masonry has tended to make these French and German farms permanent ornaments of the country. The same arrangement and disposition carried out on a larger scale and at greater cost produces the typical manor house of the Continental nations, of which many admirable examples still exist, at least in part. One of the most attractive of these is the celebrated Manoir d'Ango, near Varangeville (Seine

Inférieure), in Normandy. (Compare Barn; Byre; Colombier; Dovecote; Stable.)

Halsted, *Barn Plans and Out-Buildings;* Denton, *Farm Homesteads of England;* Narjoux, *Histoire d'une Ferme.*

— P. S.

FARMHOUSE. That one of a number of farm buildings in which the farmer and his family reside.

FARMING SHELTER. A structure erected by American Indians near their tilled fields, where crop tenders dwell till harvest time. These constructions are of various kinds, from rude brush shelters to good houses built of stone, on the level, in cliffs, or forming small villages. Of the latter class the modern village of Nutria, belonging to Indians of Zuni, is a good example, though there is a growing tendency to occupy such villages all the year, as there is now no defensive motive for retiring to the pueblos when the crops have been gathered. Many cliff dwellings and cavate lodges were no more than farming shelters. (See Communal Dwelling.) — F. S. D.

FARNHAM, NICHOLAS. (See Ferneham, Nicholas.)

FARTHER INDIA, ARCHITECTURE OF. That of the old native states of Burmah, Siam, Anam (now more commonly called Cochin China), Cambodia, which is more or less dependent upon Siam, Lower Cochin China with Saigon as its capital, and the Malay Peninsula with the ancient town of Malacca. The European occupation of single points like Singapore, now for many years, Pulupenang and the province of Wellesley, and Burmah since 1885, all by the British, and the very extensive invasions of the eastern coast (Anam and Cochin China) by the French, have not sufficed to change the architectural question, for the building of the Europeans has not attained any peculiar importance. The same tropical climate which makes domestic architecture a thing of little account has prevented the factories and dwellings of Europeans from assuming an architectural character worthy of special note.

The French government centre at Saigon has one or two buildings of pseudo-European style; and with better taste the barracks are surrounded by broad balconies, giving them a semitropical look not inelegant. An iron bridge of great boldness spans the broad Chinese river at Saigon. The country is almost wholly within the tropics, and much the greater part of it lies between the Tropic of Cancer and the line of ten degrees north latitude; that is to say, exactly the latitude of the West India Islands. If the insular form of the latter, opening parts of the territory to the regulating climatic influence of the ocean and to the steady trade wind for much more than half the year has given to them an exceptionally favourable climate, the

climate of Farther India is diversified by mountain chains; and nothing at all resembling the great plain of Northern India, with its extreme heats of summer contrasting with a much colder winter, seems to exist, the peculiar conditions of the mountainous country alone excepted. The whole peninsula, in general, is thinly settled, for, while its superficies is about equal to the United States east of the Mississippi, the highest estimate put upon its total population is about 35,000,000. In other words, it is much more thinly settled than any of the states of Western Europe, and in this respect cannot bear the least comparison with the peninsula of India, properly so called, or the southern provinces of China.

One result of these conditions is that vast tracts of forest, with enormous trees arguing a duration of six or seven centuries, cover half the larger peninsula, and this not merely in the almost unknown interior, but within fifty miles of the sea in many places. It is in these vast forests that are found those surprising ruins which have been explored chiefly by French government missions, and which are spoken of by the French writers as the work of the Khmers. The district assigned to this ancient people is on the boundary between Siam and Cambodia, along the twelfth and thirteenth degree of latitude, and due east of Bangkok. Fragments of the ancient buildings have been brought to France, and Delaporte (op. cit.) has given a number of representations which seem trustworthy, sometimes of a building as conjecturally restored, though only in detail, the main masses remaining intact, sometimes of a measured plan, sometimes of fragments as the artist saw them. The general character of these buildings is one with that of the pagodas, stupas, and topes of India, in that they are without interiors in the ordinary sense, consisting, as they do almost exclusively, of shrines carried up into pinnacle-like masses, and larger structures in which many shrines are combined, and piled high with masses of carved stone. The shortcoming of all this work is, as a European student conceives it, in the absence of structural reasons for architectural design. Although the Oriental builder has had what few Europeans have ever possessed, a power of designing in the abstract, — of designing for monumental effect and without utilitarian significance, — there still is something lacking when it appears that vast and lofty structures of carved stone are in the forms and proportions which we see merely because they were thought to be effective in those forms and when carved with those details. The lover of highly specialized trabeated or arcuated building, with its resulting appropriateness to secular or to religious uses, feels in that work with which he has greater familiarity a satisfaction which the most magnificent

piles of the East do not afford to him. Thus much urged, there remains nothing but praise and the question of relative merit between the superb ruined piles of the forests of Cambodia, those hardly less ruined of the Malay Islands (see Malay Architecture), and the better known religious piles of India proper.

A shrewd writer has pointed out that in all the Khmer monuments the doorway, or gateway of entrance, is the important feature. With this statement should be compared the significance of the Indian gateway towers (see Gopura) and the city gates with their defences, their water steps, and their accessories (see Ghat). It is worthy of consideration, also, how far the respect shown by the Chinese for the memorial gateway independent of walls or enclosures (see Pailoo) and the Japanese torii (see Torii) compares with this disposition to adorn gateways which lead, at all events, to a covered and enclosed place of prayer and meditation. The Khmer gateway is in itself of no great size. It allows an elephant with its canopied saddle seat to pass through, and is, therefore, 16 or 18 feet high in the clear; but these limited dimensions have nothing to do with the enormous structure which is found piled upon and above the square head of the gateway. The famous temple near the city of Angkor, or Ongkor, which is called indifferently the Angkor Wat or the Nakhon Wat, is very like the Boro Buddor in Java, but larger. The platform is 600 feet square, and from this rises a slowly developing mass of steps and platforms carrying porticoes, covered corridors, and nine lofty towerlike masses only to be compared to the Buddhist temple gateways of India. Cut stone of the most massive character is the material, except that wooden ceilings, sometimes serving as tie beams, are used in places where a rounded roof having the shape of a wagon vault is found, whose structure of the corbelled or horizontally bedded pseudo-vault seems inadequately protected against thrust. The ruins of the city of Angkor (called Angkor Thom) are so lost in a dense tropical forest that exploration is of immense difficulty. Malaria of deadly kinds and abounding carnivorous and poisonous creatures make access difficult, and nothing approaching complete exploration has been carried out by any European. The city is known to contain a great palace spoken of as that of the forty-two towers, and a temple called the temple of Baion.

In Burmah, the architecture which has attracted the attention of Europeans is much more recent than the undated but very ancient buildings of Cambodia. The palaces and temples, though not wholly unlike the ancient stone pagodas, are to a great extent built of wood, which, being of enduring quality and protected by lacquer, gilding, mosaic, and the like, all which were kept in repair so long as the building was cherished, has proven as indestructible as that of the Japanese temples. At Rangoon there is indeed a monstrous pagoda commonly called the Shway Dagoon (by Fergusson, Shoëdagong), which is, indeed, of stone, and so is the magnificent and, from any point of view, beautiful tope of the temple at Pegu, the Shway Madoo (Fergusson, Shoëmadu); but the palaces at Mandelay and elsewhere seem always to have been largely of wood, and the exquisite decoration by means of gilded and lacquered ornament and mosaic of glass of many different varieties seems to have been thought sufficient as splendour for even an absolute and splendour-loving monarch. The important building known as the Queen's Monastery (*kioun*), in Mandelay, is entirely of wood, and in part has been left to show the effects of the weather, the unpainted wood acquiring a lovely gray in the equable and warm climate. Gilding, however, has been evidently an important part of the adornment and of ceremony in Burman architecture, the effect of which metallic lustre when seen investing richly modulated surfaces is far more harmonious and refined than when it is applied to such smooth rounded cupolas as those of Paris.

All these buildings are one-storied. Even when the roofs are piled high like those of the Japanese pagoda, balconies and sloping roofs succeeding one another for a height of seven or more apparent stories, there is but one floor of occupation. Balconies and galleries there may be above, but the avoidance of upper floors is so complete that the assertion is made by European travellers that the Burman sense of personal dignity forbids any one to endure the feet of other persons being above his head, and that on this account upper stories are unknown. The result of the one-story arrangement has been the development of a columnar architecture of extraordinary interest. Separate columns are not unlike Roman Doric columns in the proportions of capital to shaft and in the character of the capital, but the shafts are usually thicker in proportion to their height; they are cylindrical, and their surfaces are covered with patterns in low relief reminding one of the mosaic-covered pillars in Pompeii and the stucco-patterned pillars of the Palazzo Vecchio in Florence.

The architecture of Siam is admitted to be of less importance than that of Burmah; and that of the eastern coast is still more nearly that of a race which, though having many of the habits of a civilized people, has never undertaken great architectural labours. Throughout the peninsula the domestic architecture of the people, though, as has been suggested above, slight and of a character not apparently permanent, is yet worthy of the closest study by all interested in domestic building. The tropical residence, as suggested in the article House, is

apt to consist of little more than uprights and a roof, the walling, of whatever description, being of little consequence, and often temporary. To raise a floor above the earth and to support it on posts which are difficult for reptiles and insects to climb is to provide the extreme of comfort which the climate demands. As, however, it is not considered important to make such a dwelling stately or impressive in appearance, domestic architecture is in itself a matter of inevitable and almost unthought-of picturesque effect, while any approach to grandeur is to be had only by the great accumulation of small buildings within a fortified enclosure or upon a walled terrace.

It is unfortunate that European buildings in tropical countries are always built on European lines, or with such slight and fantastic admixture of foreign elements as spoils their character without giving them a new and independent significance. If European architects of intelligence, with power to see the possibilities of the local systems of construction and arrangement, were to try to develop the pillared and heavily roofed house of Farther India into a European dwelling or palace with offices, very beautiful results might follow. This, which is true in a special sense of Japan, with its highly organized architecture of post and beam, is applicable to the more tropical regions under consideration.

Albert de Pourvouville, *L'Art Indo-Chinois*; Delaporte, *Voyage au Cambodge*; James Fergusson, *History of Indian and Eastern Architecture*; Henri Mouhot, *Travels in Indo-China, Cambodia, and Laos*; Garnier, *Voyage d'Exploration en Indo-Chine*; Abel Remusat, *Nouveaux Mélanges Asiatiques*; Mrs. Ernest Hart, *Picturesque Burma, Past and Present* (with many illustrations); Captain Henry Yule, *Mission to the Court of Ava in 1855*; Lieutenant G. C. Rigby, *Report of a Tour through the Northern Shan States*; Captain John Harvey, R.A., *Report of the Thetta Column and Work in the Southern Chin Hills*.

— R. S.

FASCES. The ancient Roman emblem of civil authority — a number of rods bound together with an axe into a cylindrical bundle. It appears frequently in Roman and in modern carved decoration.

FASCIA. In Latin, a bandage, a strip; hence, —

A. Any one of the long narrow bands or divisions of the Ionic architrave, each projecting slightly beyond the one below, as described by Vitruvius. Hence, also, —

B. In modern usage, any similar band, as a string course or belt, or the plane face of a cornice or like member, but always a vertical surface, and broader than a mere fillet.

FAST. Any simple contrivance to be attached to a door, window, or the like, to secure it when closed. Usually, in combination, as sash fast, casement fast.

FASTIGIUM. In Latin, the crest or top of a roof; the whole roof or upper part or side of anything; especially, a roof having pediments or gables, as distinguished from one which does not affect in this way the exterior of the building. In no sense common in English usage, but originating the adjectives fastigiate, -ious, and the French *faîte*.

FAUCES (Latin plural noun, the throat, etc.). A passage, inlet, or the like; in Vitruvius (VI., 4) a passage in a house, and generally, in Roman archæology, such a passage, especially if from the atrium to the peristylium, or garden. In Mau's *Pompeii*, however, it is assumed that this is erroneous, and that the only passage properly called fauces is that from the vestibulum to the atrium. The main reason for this seems to be the general giving of Greek names to all rooms, etc., back and beyond the atrium, while the old Latin names remain to the rooms of the original house. (See plan of House of Pansa, under House.)

FAUCET. A tube or hollow plug to facilitate the discharge or passage of water or other fluid, and fitted with some contrivance by which the flow is controlled. (See Spigot.)

More specifically, in plumbing, a contrivance for allowing the outward flow of water and stopping it at will, this being usually a fixture at the end of a supply pipe for hot or cold water.

Waterspouts so small as to be evidently intended for faucets, and wrought into very beautiful representations of lions' heads, dogs' heads, and the like, are found among Roman remains. These are usually of bronze. In modern decorative art, where the fittings of the bathroom or dressing room are to be made especially elegant, silver, plain or oxidized, and silver gilt have been used, the modelling being by sculptors of ability. These last are wholly exceptional, because modern plumbing appliances are made with sufficient accuracy and completeness of finish in great quantities and at a low price. In British usage, a Tap. (See Cock.) — R. S.

Compression Faucet. One in which the valve is closed by being forced against its seat by compression applied through the handle. This is usually a screw by which, when turned, the valve is raised or lowered.

Fuller Faucet. A certain kind of Compression Faucet, the name being originally connected with a patent.

Rabbit-ear Faucet. A self-closing faucet in which a spring is compressed and the valve opened by the action of a pair of handles. These project from the faucet in the form of a V, and are shaped so as to give somewhat the appearance of a pair of rabbit's ears. They are pressed together to open the valve.

Self-closing Faucet. One containing a device which automatically closes the valve when the handle by which it is opened is released.

The device is generally a spring, which must be compressed to open the valve.

Swing Faucet. One having a horizontal biblike outlet which controls a valve by being rotated about a vertical pipe forming the inlet. The valve is opened when the horizontal arm is swung over the basin or other vessel, and is closed when the arm is turned away at the side.

Wheel Faucet. One in which the valve is operated by turning a wheel on an axis projecting from the outlet. The term is not specific, and usually applies to a Compression Faucet in which the screw is turned by a wheel attached to the head.

FAULCHOT, GÉRARD; architect.

The most important member of a family of architects employed in the city of Troyes (Aube, France). In 1577 he replaced Gabriel Favreau as *maître de l'œuvre* (supervising architect) of the cathedral of Troyes.

Assier, *Les arts et les artistes de Troyes.*

FAVISSA. An underground cellar or reservoir under a Roman temple for the storage either of water, or, more generally, of worn-out and useless sacred implements and furnishings of the temple.

FEATHER. *A.* A small projecting member worked along the edge of a board or the like, as in matched boarding. In this sense more commonly Tongue.

B. Same as Loose Tongue (which see, under Tongue).

FEATHER BOARD. Any board having a feather edge; especially, in British usage, the same as Clapboard, *A.*

FEATHER BOARDING. Feather-edged boards or clapboards, especially those intended to be applied to the sheathing of wooden buildings, each board overlapping with its thick edge the thin edge of the one below. (See Clapboard; Feather Edge.)

FEATHER EDGE. An edge formed by bevelling one or both sides of a slab, board, or the like, wholly or in part, so that they meet in a sharp arris; or, by extension, a relatively narrow face enclosed between such sloping sides when they approach without meeting.

FEATHERING. The cusping of tracery; the elaboration of tracery by means of cusps. The term is not common; introduced in the early years of mediæval archæological research, it has been generally replaced by Foliation.

Double Feathering. The subdivisions of larger cusps by smaller ones. (See Cusp; Tracery.)

FEATHER WEDGING. (See Foxtail Wedge.)

FEDERIGHI (DEI TOLOMEI), ANTONIO; sculptor and architect; d. 1490.

He built, about 1460, the Loggia del Papa, at Siena, and also, at Siena, the open chapel near the Palazzo dei Diavoli. He made the beautiful holy water basins at the cathedral. Federighi designed four important compositions in the great mosaic pavement of the cathedral of Siena (see Beccafumi). He was employed in Rome during the pontificate of Pius II. (Pope 1458–1464).

Müntz, *Les arts à la cour des papes;* Geymüller-Stegmann, *Die Architectur der Renaissance in Toscana.*

FÉLIBIEN DES AVAUX, ANDRÉ; architect and writer ; b. 1619; d. June 11, 1695.

He was *historiographe des bâtiments du roi,* and was secretary of the Académie de l'Architecture at its foundation in 1671, and published *Entretiens sur la vie et les ouvrages des plus excellents peintres anciens et modernes* (Paris, 1885), *Les Maisons royales des bords de la Loire* (first published in 1874), and other works. His son Jean François succeeded him, and published *Recueil historique de la vie et des ouvrages des plus célèbres architectes* (12mo, Paris, 1705).

Lance, *Dictionnaire;* Bauchal, *Dictionnaire.*

FÉLIBIEN DES AVAUX, JEAN FRANÇOIS. (See Félibien des Avaux, André.)

FELLOWSHIP. *A.* The position of a Fellow, one of the members of the corporation of a college, or the like.

B. A kind of scholarship ; a foundation or grant as of a certain sum of money paid annually to encourage post-graduate studies or to give opportunity for foreign travel.

The term in sense *A* formerly implied life membership and residence in a college, with a share in the revenues and in certain rights of management. As this institution gave opportunities for study the term grew to cover the sense *B.* In nearly all of the existing architectural fellowships the money allowed is to be expended in foreign travel and study. The oldest existing fellowship in architecture is the *Grand Prix de Rome,* which was founded by the French Academy of the Fine Arts in 1720, and has been offered continuously ever since. The holders of this prize, which is open only to French citizens, receive a pension from the government of eight hundred dollars per year for four years, and are given commodious quarters, rent free, in the Villa Medici at Rome, where they are expected to reside a greater portion of the time, and to pursue their studies under the immediate guidance of the resident director. Next in importance is the travelling fellowship of the Royal Institute of British Architects, which affords the holder the opportunity for a year's travel on the Continent. Besides this, several of the European governments have established travelling fellowships for architecture, but none of them are of special note. In the United States there are six architectural foundations, the oldest of which is the Rotch

Travelling Scholarship, established and endowed by the heirs of Benjamin S. Rotch in 1883. The holder of this scholarship receives the sum of one thousand dollars per year for two years, during which time he is expected to travel and study in Europe under the advice and direction of a committee appointed by the Boston Society of Architects. A so-called Roman Fellowship was established in 1894, open in competition to graduates in architecture from either Cornell University, the Massachusetts Institute of Technology, the University of Illinois, Syracuse University, Lehigh University, Columbia University, or the University of Pennsylvania, and to all American students who have spent two years in the *École des Beaux Arts.* This fellowship provides for eighteen months in foreign travel and study in Italy, Sicily, and Greece, ten months to be spent as a student of the American School at Rome, and the other eight months as may be agreed upon between the fellow and the Executive Committee of the American School of Architecture in Rome. There are two architectural fellowships in New York, both of them in connection with Columbia University, designated as the Columbia and the McKim Fellowships. The former was endowed by Mr. F. A. Schermerhorn, of New York, in 1889, the successful candidate being expected to spend at least one year in foreign study. The second fellowship was endowed by Mr. C. F. McKim, in 1890, with two prizes given out simultaneously every second year, so as to alternate with the awards of the Columbia Fellowship. There is also an architectural fellowship, established in 1893, under the direction of the architectural department of the University of Pennsylvania, the winner of which is required to spend a full year of study abroad. The fellowship idea is being worked out in a somewhat different manner at Cornell University, where a fellowship is awarded each year for two years to encourage post-graduate study. The holder is required to study at the University during eight months of each year, alternating with four months' travel abroad under the direction of the Department of Architecture. This fellowship has been in existence only since 1898. — C. H. BLACKALL.

FELT. A material resulting from the compressing or matting together of minute fibres, as of wool or fur, the fibres clinging to each other by their natural roughness or microscopic hooklike protuberances ; therefore, generally, a flexible clothlike stuff made without weaving and without the spinning of threads. The finest felt known to modern times is that made in Persia, where floor cloths an inch or more in thickness, and of considerable size, are made to replace the very costly carpets of the country. These pieces of felt are sometimes richly adorned by the insertion into the surface of fibres of various colours, the whole substance being felted together. In Europe and the United States the architectural use of felt is chiefly limited to the covering of heating pipes, deafening and lining of walls and floors, and the like ; the material, being an excellent non-conductor, tends to keep heat in, and thereby aid its safe delivery at a distant point, while at the same time woodwork is protected from ignition. — R. S.

FENCE. A structure, as of bars, posts, and the like, used to enclose fields, gardens, orchards, etc. The term is generally limited to those in common use in connection with farms and country residences of the common sort. As long as wood is plentiful there is a disposition to enclose and separate all the fields of a farm from one another and from the high road, and fences are of various kinds, as the zigzag, or worm fence, post and rail fence, etc. As wood becomes scarce and dear these disappear, and are replaced, as in England in old times, by hedges ; and as in the newly settled countries and in the present age of cheap metal working, by wire secured to light iron uprights, or by slender strips of steel twisted or not, and sometimes furnished with sharp hooks or "barbs" at frequent intervals. These common fences have the advantage over hedges in that they do not affect the landscape as much, for the hedge divides a distant hillside into parallelograms much too strongly marked, and, moreover, a hedge 6 feet high will hide miles of country from the eye of a person passing in the road. The wooden fences, moreover, assume a pleasant colour and weather beautifully, while the light iron fence is practically invisible.

(For fences made of boards set upright, planed, and finished, see Paling.) — R. S.

FENESTELLA. *A.* Generally, a small glazed opening in an altar, shrine, or reliquary, to afford a view of the relics it contains.

B. A small niche on the south side of an altar above a piscina or credence.

C. Sometimes an opening for a bell at the top of a gable.

FENESTRAL (n.). A small window, or (in old English usage) a window filled with oiled paper or cloth instead of glass.

FENESTRAL (adj.). Of, or pertaining to, a window.

FENESTRATION. *A.* The arrangement in a building of its windows, especially the more important and larger ones. In this sense fenestration is nearly the same thing as the providing of daylight for the interiors of buildings. (See Lighting.) (Cut, cols. 21, 22.)

B. The art of adorning or designing architecturally the exterior of a building by the proper arrangement and apportioning of windows and doors considered together as openings in the wall, affording spots of darkness contrasting with the lighted surface of the wall, and also affording convenient spots for concentrating ornamental treatment.

FERETORY ; **FERETRUM.** *A.* A portable shrine or reliquary in a church, to contain relics of saints or martyrs.

B. A fixed shrine for relics ; or a place in a church reserved for such a shrine.

FERGUSSON, JAMES, D. C. L., F. R. S. ; writer on architecture ; b. 1808 at Ayr, Scotland ; d. 1886.

James Fergusson was educated at the High School in Edinburgh and entered the firm of Fairlie, Fergusson and Company at Calcutta, India. He retired from business later, and devoted himself to archæological study. In 1840 he was elected member of the Royal Asiatic Society, of which, at his death, he was a vice president. In 1857 he was appointed a member of the Royal Commission to inquire into the defences of the United Kingdom. He published *The Illustrated Handbook of Architecture* (2 vols. 8vo, 1855). This book was revised and published under the title, *A History of Architecture in all Countries from the Earliest Times to the Present Day* (4 vols. 8vo, 1865–1876). In 1878 he published *The Temples of the Jews and the other Buildings in the Haram Area at Jerusalem. The History of the Modern Styles of Architecture* appeared in 1862, and a separate *History of Eastern and Indian Architecture* in 1876. In 1869 Fergusson was appointed secretary to Austin Henry Layard, commissioner of public works, and later inspector of public buildings and monuments. In 1871 he won the gold medal of the Royal Institute of British Architects. He was an active member of several commissions for the decoration of S. Paul's cathedral.

Leslie Stephen, *Dictionary of National Biography.*

FERLEY. (See Farley.)

FERME ORNÉE. A farm, and especially the buildings and gardens of a farm, treated in a decorative manner, and generally the residence of a man of means who carries on agriculture, stock-raising, or the like, for his gratification. Such buildings are not to be confounded with farm buildings of the Continent of Europe, or the small manor houses of England of the seventeenth and earlier centuries, although these may be extremely elaborate in their architectural character. Such a farm, as many of those in Normandy and northern France, was the centre of very serious agricultural and moneymaking occupations, but the conditions of the time required defensible buildings, and the spirit of the time required architectural treatment.

FERNANDEZ, GREGORIO. (See Hernandez, Gregorio.)

FERNEHAM (FARNHAM), NICHOLAS ; bishop.

The central tower of the old Norman cathedral of Durham was altered by Bishop Ferne-

FENESTRATION: PALAZZO ANGARONI-MANZONI, GRAND CANAL, VENICE.

An example of effective design, with many and large openings and little solid wall.

ham about 1241–1249. He constructed a lantern above the main arches.

King, *Handbooks of the Cathedrals of England.*

FERSTEL, HEINRICH FREIHERR VON; architect; b. July 7, 1828; d. July 14, 1883.

From 1847 to 1851 Ferstel studied in the Architectural School of the Academy of Vienna. In 1855 he won first prize in the competition for the construction of the *Votivkirche* in Vienna. After travelling in Italy, France, and the Netherlands, he returned to Vienna and finished that building in 1879 in the style of the French cathedrals of the thirteenth century. He built at Vienna the Austro-Hungarian bank, the Austrian Museum for Art and Indus-

try, and the University. In 1856 he was made professor of architecture in the *Technische Hochschule* (Vienna).

Meyer, *Conversations Lexicon.*

FESTOON. Anything hanging in a natural catenary curve; especially in classical and neoclassical architecture, the representation of a garland of flowers, fruits, and the like, hanging from two points, heaviest at the middle and lightest at the points of suspension. Such festoons are common in Greco-Roman architecture, the most celebrated instances being those on the frieze of the round temple at Tivoli. They were taken up by the later neoclassic architects and much used in the seventeenth and eighteenth centuries. The avoidance of festoons in all other styles than those named is somewhat remarkable, for the form is naturally a beautiful one and not difficult to compose. The apparent reason is the very artificial character of the bunched masses of leaves, flowers, and fruit which are generally employed ; but it is still worthy of inquiry why the natural fall and sweep of branches trained from tree to tree, or of wild vines in the forest, have never suggested anything to the sculptor of ornament. The most delicate of modern festoons are those of Michelangelo's smaller sacristy at S. Lorenzo, Florence ; they consist of laurel-like leaves forming an imbricated pattern. (See Encarpus ; Swag.) — R. S.

FIAMMINGO. The name by which Flemish artists working in Italy were usually known. (See Bologne, John ; Duquesnoy, François.)

FIBROUS SLAB. A material introduced in 1851 and used instead of wood, and also instead of plaster, for interior finish. The dome of the reading room of the Boston Museum is described as lined with it (A. P. S.). (For the use of such incombustible slabs of material, compare Staff.)

FIERAVANTI (or **FIORAVANTI**), **FIERAVANTE DEI** ; architect and engineer.

A letter of Giacomo della Quercia (see Giacomo della Quercia) dated July 4, 1428 (Milanesi, op. cit.) ascribes to Fieravanti the castle (*rocca*) of Braccio dei Fortebracci, at Montone near Perugia, Italy, and the reconstruction (begun 1525) of the right wing of the Palazzo Publico at Bologna, which had been burned in 1424.

Corrado Ricci, *Fieravante Fieravanti* in *Archivio Storico dell' Arte*, Vol. IV., 1891 ; Milanesi, *Documenti dell' arte senese.*

FIERAVANTI (**FIORAVANTI**), **RIDOLFO DEI** (**ARISTOTELE**) ; architect, engineer, and mathematician ; b. before 1418 ; d. after 1480.

A son of Fieravante dei Fieravanti (see Fieravanti, F. dei). He entered the service of Nicholas V. (Pope 1447–1455) in Rome, and moved the great monolithic columns from the church of S. Maria sopra Minerva to the Vatican. He suggested to Nicholas V. and Paul II. the transportation of the obelisk of the Vatican to the Piazza di S. Pietro, which was finally accomplished by Domenico Fontana (see Fontana, D.) in 1586. He served the Sforza in Milan and in 1467 was invited to Hungary by the King Mathias Corvinus, for whom he built bridges over the Danube. In 1472 he was in the service of Ferdinand I., king of Naples. In 1475 he went to Russia and for Ivan III. built the cathedral of the Assumption at Moscow and probably also portions of the Kremlin. He probably designed the façade of the Palazzo del Podestà in Bologna.

Malagola, *Delle cose operate in Mosca da Aristotele Fioravanti ;* Canetta, *Aristotele da Bologna ;* Amico Ricci, *Storia dell' Architettura in Italia.*

FIESOLE, MINO DA. (See Mino da Fiesole.)

FIGURE. In wood, same as Grain.

FIGURING. The process of adding to architectural drawings the dimensions of the parts shown. The mere statement on a drawing that it is to such and such a scale (as four feet to one inch) is not sufficient ; first, because the delay caused by laying a rule on the drawing is considerable, and second, because there is great possibility of error. It is customary to figure the extreme dimensions and also the minor dimensions ; thus, if the total length of a house is, over all, 102 feet 4 inches, that figure is put upon the drawing, while if there are three main subdivisions which measure respectively 40 feet, 47 feet 8 inches, and 14 feet 8 inches, those dimensions also are added, and it is the business of the draftsman to see that the addition of the three equals the larger measure. This is carried still further, and every separate room, every window, every door, every break in the wall, is figured in the same way. The form of this figuring is generally as follows : —

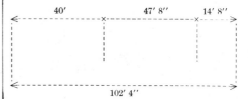

the little arrowheads or crowfeet denoting by their points the exact termination of the distance whose dimension is given. The dotted lines are usually the construction lines of the drawing carried out, as it were, to infinity, and

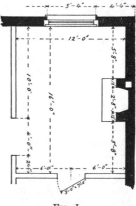

FIG. I.

marked by dots, or a special colour, as far as it may be necessary, to show exactly the limits of the figure given.

Figure I. shows this system applied to a single room in a plan of the usual sort given to workmen for their guidance. Figure II. shows a plan often followed in drawings made to show

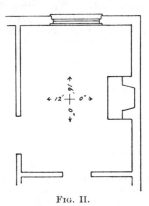

Fig. II.

to the employer ; such drawings as are included in what are generally spoken of as preliminary studies. — R. S.

FILARETE (ANTONIO DI PIETRO AVERLINO, AVERULINUS); architect ; b. about 1400 ; d. after 1465.

The surname Filarete (*phil-arete*, lover of virtue) is given by Vasari, but is not found in contemporary sources. He assisted Ghiberti (see Ghiberti) on the second gate of the baptistery. Filarete made for Eugenius IV. (Pope 1431–1447) the bronze doors of S. Peter's church at Rome (1445). Soon after the accession of Nicholas V. (Pope 1447–1455) he went to Milan, where he held the position of cathedral architect from February, 1452, to July 5, 1454. Filarete's chief work is the Ospedale Maggiore at Milan, of which the first stone was laid April 12, 1457. He undoubtedly made the plans and carried out the southwestern short side and the adjacent portions of the long side as far as the main court. He left the work in 1465. Filarete began the cathedral of Bergamo in 1457. His famous *Trattato dell' Architettura*, written for the instruction of the Duke Francesco Sforza, was begun about 1460 and finished in 1464.

Von Oettingen, *Leben und Werke des Antonio Averlino*; Von Oettingen, *Filarete's Tractat über die Baukunst*; *Annali del Duomo di Milano*.

FILIPPO DA CAMPELLO; architect. He built the upper church of S. Francesco at Assisi, finished in 1253.

Frothingham, *Introduction of Gothic Architecture into Italy*.

FILISTER (also **FILLISTER**). *A.* A rebating plane. — (N. E. D.)

B. A rebate made by a filister, as defined above ; especially the rebate of a sash bar, which receives the edge of the glass.

FILLET. *A.* A relatively small and narrow flat moulding, generally as a plain band in a group

of mouldings ; either of rectangular section, projecting, or sunk, from the general surface ; or simply a flat surface included between other mouldings.

B. A thin strip of material having more or less the form of a fillet in sense *A*.

Back Fillet. The narrow flat surface of the return of a trim or casing, which projects slightly from the surface of the wall. The term is applied to this surface even if merely a fillet in the ordinary sense, that is to say, an unbroken flat strip. — R. S.

FILLETING. Material, such as mortar, used as a substitute for flashing, at the meeting of a sloping roof with a wall. The mortar is carried up the side of the wall and over one or two courses of slates or tiles, the next course lapping over it. It is very liable to leaks from settlement and from loose slates.

FILLING. Rough masonry used for the body of a wall which has a facing of smoother and more finished material ; or for the loading of the haunches of an arch.

FILLING-IN PIECE. In a framed structure, any piece shorter than those composing the main portions and used for the shorter spans and smaller spaces ; as tail beams, jack rafters, and the like.

FILLING-IN STUFF. A species of sizing rubbed into the pores of any fibrous or porous material in order to provide a good surface for painting or varnishing. Compositions prepared especially for woodwork are called wood fillers.

FILTER. A device intended for the mechanical purification of water by straining out the solid suspended impurities in the same. Filters operate by gravity or under water pressure. Water is filtered on a large scale by means of artificial filter beds, composed of layers of gravel and sand (sand filtration). Domestic filters are either pressure filters placed on the line of main service pipes, when they cleanse the entire water supply of the house, or drinking water filters, attached to faucets or nozzles, like the Pasteur-Chamberland and Berkefeld filters which render the water practically germ free. The filtering material may be sand, gravel, charcoal, iron, quartz, porous stone, cloth, paper, porcelain, or infusorial earth. — W. P. G.

FINIAL. A boss, a knob, or a more elaborate ornament at the point of a spire or pinnacle. The finials which crown the pinnacles in Gothic churches are often of great beauty ; their position bringing their ornamental treatment against the sky and thus causing them to be less clearly seen, does not prevent them from being among the richest and most effective parts of the associated sculpture of the edifice. The term is sometimes extended to apply to the hip knob or épi and similar culminating ornaments.

FINISH. *A.* Elegance or refinement in a completed piece of work ; especially in the workmanship or mechanical excellence of the work as distinguished from its design or significance. It is to be observed, however, that in some kinds of work the significance itself depends upon high or elaborate finish. Thus, in Florentine mosaic as applied to walls, or marble inlay as applied to pavements, the intended effect is not obtained without very perfect workmanship.

B. Those parts of the fittings of a building which come after the heavy work of masonry, flooring, etc., has been done, and which are generally in plain sight and are closely connected with the final appearance of the building. The term is especially applied to interior work and often in connection with some other word forming a compound term. (See the subtitles.)

Cabinet Finish. Interior finish in hard woods, framed, panelled, moulded, and varnished or polished like cabinetwork in distinction to finish in soft woods nailed together and commonly painted. (United States usage.)
— A. D. F. H.

Hard Finish. Fine white plaster which, when used, forms the last coat of a piece of plastering.

Inside Finish. In the United States, the fittings, such as doors and door trims, window trims, shutters, door-saddles and the like, dadoes or wall lining with wood, marble, or tile; sometimes also mantelpieces and even sideboards, presses, or dressers if put up permanently. The term is most commonly used for the woodwork of ordinary dwelling houses and business buildings, but is extended to the most elaborate and permanent work. — R. S.

FIORAVANTI. (See Fieravanti.)

FIORE DI PERSICO. A marble of which pieces are found among Roman Imperial remains. There are several minor varieties distinguished by Italian adjectives, such as *chiaro* (light), *rosso* (red), etc. It is thought to have been brought from the mainland of Greece.

FIR. Same as Fur.

FIRE ALARM. *A.* A device for automatically giving notice of a considerable rise of temperature, as in a room. It is generally managed by means of electricity. (See Alarm; Thermostat, under Electrical Appliances.)

B. A bell which may be sounded as a means of giving notice of a conflagration.

FIRE ALTAR. An altar used for burnt sacrifices. The altars of antiquity were, many of them, of this kind. Where the altar is of stone and small, especially if it is decorated with sculpture, the inference may be that the substances burned would be small in quantity and symbolical or representative of the whole sacrifice; and such altars when within a house or temple may be supposed to have been used for burning incense; or, at least, not for animal sacrifices. (See Altar.)

FIRE BACK. Primarily, the back of a fireplace. The term is usually applied, however,

to the cast-iron or other metal lining frequently applied to the backs of fireplaces; sometimes of highly ornate design. Ventilating fire backs have been the objects of much experiment and invention, especially in France; they are of various patterns, usually tubular, serving to warm the cold air admitted from out-of-doors and to deliver it so warmed through registers into the room.

FIREBOARD. A board or shutterlike contrivance to close the opening of a fireplace when not in use, whether of wood or of cast or sheet metal. Called also summer piece and chimney board.

FIRE CLAY. Any clay adapted for making fire brick (which see, under Brick).

FIRE DOOR. In a furnace, stove, or the like, the doorway or opening through which fuel is supplied and the fire is tended. Also the door, usually of iron, which closes it.

FIRE ESCAPE. A contrivance for enabling persons to escape readily from a burning building; either fixed or movable. The movable and adjustable fire escapes are numerous, different patent devices competing with one another for popular favour; the ladders and other appliances used by fire departments in cities are also of this character. Fixed fire escapes are generally of the nature of a ladder or a series of ladders or stairs of wrought iron connected with landing places, such as balconies, and all arranged on the exterior of a building, connecting in each story with a window or windows, all of which are easy of access. (For dimensions, etc., see Apartment House.) The laws in some American cities require the use of fire escapes for certain buildings, such as tenement houses, apartment houses, hotels, and business buildings, and generally all buildings where more families than one, or the occupants of more offices or sets of offices than one, are liable to be exposed to the danger of fire. The significance of such laws seems to be that where one tenant may, by his carelessness, endanger the lives of other tenants the use of fire escapes is compulsory. In clubs, however, even the largest, the law does not often require their use; perhaps because but few persons sleep in such places, and also because of their quasi private character. (See Legislation.) The great frequency of fires in American cities, and the terrible loss of life which has sometimes resulted from a fire, as in a hotel or factory, have caused these laws to be very commonly enacted and fairly well enforced. At the same time, the general feeling that fire escapes disfigure a building or, at least, lower it in the scale, as suggesting a building for common and humble uses rather than elegance, has caused a tendency to resist or evade the law in all practicable ways. The only remedy for this seems to be the adoption of some system of fire escapes which shall be architectural in character, rather decorative than disfiguring to the building, and forming a part of the general design. A New York architect, and one of the chief contributors to this work, has suggested the use of balconies without ladders, but with adjustable bridges from balcony to balcony, horizontally along a front. If these bridges drop into place by their own weight, as when a cord is cut, they may be trusted, and the horizontal balconies can easily adorn rather than disfigure the building. Tile or other masonry, rather than iron, should meet the hands of those who are seeking to escape from fire.

A few houses in New York have an incombustible stair and staircase provided in a recess or compartment arranged in the exterior wall, and continuous from sidewalk to cornice. This stair and staircase may communicate only with balconies which pass along the front at the different stories, and the shaft or recessed member may be entirely without communication by doors or windows with the interior. The advantage of this over the fireproof stair and staircase within is that the former is not likely to be rendered entirely useless by dense smoke.
— R. S.

FIRE HOUSE. *A.* In the United States, in general, any building for the keeping of the fire-extinguishing apparatus of a municipal fire department. A popular, but not specific term. (See Engine House ; Truck House.)

B. Same as House Place ; in allusion to the fact that here alone was a fireplace in early times.

FIREPLACE. That part of a building which is arranged for the making of fires, as for warmth ; especially, such a provision when made for open fires of coal or wood, as distinguished from furnaces, stoves, or the elaborate hypocaust of the Romans. In this sense the fireplace is either the hearth in the middle of the room, as common in primitive times, the smoke escaping through openings in the roof (see Louver), or a part of a chimney. This latter sense is much the most common and is the ordinary use of the term fireplace, and implies a recess in the wall or chimney breast which connects directly with a flue for smoke. If, however, the conditions are favourable there need be no recess in the wall, but the smoke flue being furnished with a large hood corresponding in size to the hearth upon which the fire is made, the wall may be continuous behind the hearth, with the hood and the flue above projecting from its surface. This arrangement, which was not uncommon in mediæval times and as late as the sixteenth century, is hardly compatible with the modern use of fuel or with the modern desire to avoid all such inconvenience as might arise from the blowing about of smoke by accidental draughts. The very small rooms used by moderns make

this device, as well as the "fire on the hearth" in the middle of the room, impracticable. The fireplace is, then, to be considered as a recess or a space enclosed by two jambs or cheeks, and terminating above in the flue. The decoration of the fireplace has always been important, because that one part of the room is wholly different in its uses, and probably in its material as well, from the rest. The mantel shelf and mantelpiece, in all their forms, result from the desire felt to surround the opening of the fireplace with incombustible material, and to make use of this for a special decorative treatment ; and also from the expediency of putting one or more shelves where it is evident that no piece of furniture can be placed permanently. (Cuts, cols. 31, 32.)
— R. S.

FIREPROOF (adj.). Capable of resisting heat, such as that of conflagration ; said of a building, or a part of a building, and also of materials and fabrics. By extension, calculated to resist heat ; or capable of resisting considerable heat ; or, rarely, slow to burn. The term Slow-burning Construction (which see) has a separate technical signification.
— C. T. P.

FIREPROOF (v.). To make fireproof or fire resisting ; that is to say, to make proof against, or at least to partially protect from, the effects of great heat or a conflagration, either by a treatment, as by chemicals, of the thing to be made "fireproof," or by its protection with other materials.

The object so treated or protected is always one which is combustible or susceptible of injury when exposed to a great heat or to a fire. When fireproofed it will not so easily burn or otherwise be injured by heat, and if perfectly fireproofed the protection from injury will be complete.

Parts of a building are fireproofed when they are covered with a material which protects them from fire. Wood has been so treated with chemicals as to yield but slowly to a great heat and to burn to ashes without bursting into flame. Woods which have been fireproofed in this way have been adopted by certain naval bureaus for the interior finishing of war vessels. Textiles are also fireproofed ; and curtains properly treated for that purpose will not burn. All parts of steel frames in buildings should be fireproofed.
— C. T. P.

FIREPROOFING (n.). *A.* Material or a combination of materials intended to make buildings fireproof.

B. The art, process, or act of making buildings fireproof. In colloquial phraseology, a fireproof building is one in which at least the external walls and the floors are constructed of incombustible material. Only rarely are the words used to express their etymological meaning, that a fireproof building is proof against fire in the full meaning of the separate words.

FIREPLACE IN THE HOUSE OF JACQUES CŒUR AT BOURGES (CHER).

The whole is in cut stone; but decorative breasts were often made with plaster on wooden frames.

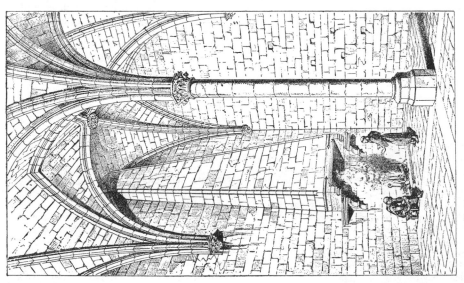

FIREPLACE IN CHAPTER HOUSE AT NOYON (OISE), c. 1250.

The hood has no side pieces below, but rests on corbels only, so that the fireplace has no recess.

It would be well if generally accepted terms had been coined for buildings, expressing, from the point of construction, different degrees of resistance to fire. Without them, circumstances and the context must govern the accurate meaning of the words.

Some of these words and expressions have, also, limited and definite meanings in certain localities, which are not accepted at all in other places. For example, "to fireproof" means, in certain localities, to protect wooden beams with incombustible material, and "fireproofed construction" is likewise made to mean a construction of wooden beams protected from fire by a covering of some incombustible material.

Buildings that could not burn have been built in all ages. Buildings have also been made in all ages and in all climates, having only a small portion of combustible material in their construction, so the idea of making the construction proof against fire is not at all modern.

Since the fall of the Roman Empire, the buildings of the Latin races and in the south of Europe have been commonly of masonry with but little use of wood. In the northern part of Europe, however, and in America, wood was more available and timber was always used more in construction. Fires were always more prevalent in London than in Paris, and it has been mainly due to this fact.

Prior to the beginning of the nineteenth century, very few buildings were built in England, or in the north of Europe anywhere, or in the United States, of which the floors and roofs did not depend upon wooden beams for their support. In many cases, however, for two centuries or more, this timber construction had been disposed of, or combined with concrete material in such a way, that fires would burn but slowly, and such forms of construction were adopted with that end in view.

The first organized effort in England, looking toward the reduction of fire losses by employing improved forms of construction, occurred about 1775, when Parliament appointed a committee to investigate the subject. Cast-iron beams and brick arches began to be used in the beginning of the nineteenth century, and were employed to a considerable extent until about 1850, when rolled beams were invented. (See Iron Construction.) About this time the attention of English architects was particularly called to the importance of changing the construction. The fire officers of London had been trying for ten years or more to arouse a sentiment in behalf of methods which would lessen the danger of fire. It was then predicted that the new rolled beams carrying brick arches would become the permanent method of making fireproof floors; but the importance of covering the soffits of the beams was not appreciated. It was ten years later, between 1860 and 1870, when such floors

had been constructed in numerous warehouses, and tried in fires that had warped and bent the iron work so that the buildings were quite destroyed, before the mistake was satisfactorily demonstrated. The construction was condemned by the fire department of London, which proclaimed that iron could never be used to make a floor indestructible by fire. It did not occur to them that the beams could be protected; but in 1866 a patent was issued to a Frenchman for an arch which was devised for this very purpose.

Flat arches made of solid clay blocks were occasionally used on cast iron beams prior to 1850, and a flat arch made of hollow clay blocks was made in 1850 for the floor of a lunatic asylum belonging to the Society of Friends, in York, England. The area covered was about 15,000 square feet. The cast beams were $4\frac{1}{2}$ to 5 feet apart. Each block was about a foot long, and the completed arch weighed 31 pounds per square foot. Except that the soffit of the arch was not below the beam, it was, therefore, in all essential respects, the same as the most modern side construction arch. Floors of that character, however, have never been popular in England, though they have been exceedingly so in America since 1870. Brick arches, beams protected with a furring, and furred ceilings, have been used in Europe to a much greater extent.

For a time after rolled beams were invented, many fireproof floors were made in England by connecting the beams with strips of wood of small size resting on the bottom flanges. They were spaced near to each other, the intervals being about as wide as the strips, and the area thus formed was covered with a filling of concrete of one kind or another, which was made to completely envelop the woodwork. Floors of this kind were used particularly in dwelling houses. These methods have been replaced in latter years by a great variety of other adaptations of concrete to floor construction which continue to be used, especially in the higher buildings.

In France the rolled beams were used as soon as they began to be manufactured. The floors were made fireproof by the use of a béton made with plaster of Paris. The beams were covered with a lacing of iron bars, hanging low between the beams, which, in turn, carried the béton. Both the bars and the beams were completely embedded and so protected. Brick arches are also used in Paris with other forms of construction.

In Germany, as in England and France, a great many inventions of fireproof floors have been patented, but few of them are in use owing to the conservatism of the authorities. That country has also had to learn to protect ironwork by the repeated destruction of iron constructed buildings in great fires, those in the warehouses of Hamburg being especially notable. A furring of wire lath and plaster known there as " Baritz " is now commonly used in Berlin and the other great cities for covering the metal wherever it is exposed. Brick arches are generally used, and hollow clay constructed arches are not used to any extent.

In America the use of both rolled beams and clay has had a greater development than in Europe. The first beams were rolled in 1854, and the first flat arches of hollow blocks of clay were made in 1873. In 1855, however, hollow blocks of clay material were used with rolled beams in Cooper Institute, New York City, each block reaching from beam to beam. The first iron beams were used in the brownstone courthouse in the City Hall Park of the same city.

The soffit tile commonly used in American practice, supported under the beams by the arches on each side, is an American invention, made in 1883. Brick arches are used to some extent, and, especially since 1890, a great variety of concrete methods of construction have been introduced. They are also being widely employed. The demand for hollow clay products, both for floors and interior wall construction, has, however, greatly exceeded that for all other materials. The capital invested and the tonnage output of such products for the different parts of the country are given in the following table : —

		OUTPUT IN TONS FOR 1897.			
	APPROXI-MATE CAPITAL INVESTED.	Hard-burned Mate-rial.	Semi-Porous Mate-rial.	Porous Mate-rial.	Total in Each Section.
East of Ohio..	$4,000,000	105,000	71,000	73,000	249,000
Ohio and westward, ...	1,200,000	23,000	33,000	36,000	92,000
South........	100,000	8,000			8,000
Total in United States.......	$5,300,000	136,000	104,000	109,000	349,000

The porous material is made of clay and combustible products, mostly sawdust, mixed in about equal proportions. The combustible material having been burned out in the kiln, the baked clay is left in the "porous" state required. The object of this is to give to the material greater fire-resisting qualities, by means of the little air cells contained in it ; and because, as has been proved by repeated experiences, it allows of an unequal expansion and contraction in the same piece, without rupture, much greater than does the hard-burned material. It allows also of driving nails directly into its mass. The semiporous material is made with much less of the combustible products. Both of these materials are used for

partitions and the like because of their greater lightness and fire-resisting qualities. The term "terra-cotta lumber" is often applied to this material.

As to their resistance to burning, buildings may be divided into two general classes, one in which the fireproof qualities are dependent upon the use of brick and stone to the exclusion of wood, and the other in which they are chiefly dependent on what are generally termed "fireproofing materials" protecting ironwork. The oldest fireproof buildings are of the massive character. Warehouses and office buildings of all kinds, and most large buildings of private ownership in America, are now being made of the lighter and cheaper steel frame construction. (See Iron Construction.) There is no sharp division between the two classes. Indeed, the steel frame construction has been evolved from the massive. The walls of the latter, thick enough and strong enough to carry all the floors adjacent to them, gradually were superseded by walls that carried no load but their own weight, and these in turn were superseded by walls which are carried from floor to floor on frames of structural steel.

The older buildings will not be seriously affected by fire because the body of the material is everywhere so heavy and substantial that fire effects cannot be far-reaching ; the newer, because the exposed materials are indestructible, and perfectly protect the steel framework from any injury in case of fire.

Probably, as a whole, the massive have been made most perfectly fireproof ; but those experienced in steel frame construction can now build equally well with modern methods, in spite of the fact that special measures for fireproofing are required to a much greater extent by these than by the massive system.

The tendency of the times is to build the massive lighter by using some of the features of steel frame construction. Division walls carrying floors are omitted, and a steel construction with partitions of fireproofing material are used instead. There is also a growing tendency to make the metal portions heavier, and, as a whole, more substantial.

The covering of the bottom flanges of beams and girders in floors should be sufficient to protect the beams from heat, even under very high temperatures. To do this, the covering must either be a good nonconductor of heat, or it must be constructed with hollow air spaces or air cells, requiring the heat to pass through more than one medium to affect the metal. To be effective, the covering must also be strong enough to endure the expansion and contraction which must occur when exposed to great heat, with the possible effect of streams of cold water. It must be such that it will preserve its integrity under the severest treatment.

Many devices for the purpose have been produced, but none of them have yet been found perfectly satisfactory. Work, otherwise admirably constructed, is often faulty in this particular, and this is true in spite of the fact that no other feature of fireproofing is more important. The covering of columns is also quite often imperfectly done, but the means at hand for that work are ample for the very best construction. But the most inexcusable fault is the construction of partitions on top of wood flooring, or with the openings framed with strips of wood so as to destroy the continuity of the fireproofing materials. In a fire, these are invariably consumed, and, in consequence, the partition of fireproof material goes to pieces ; when, if metal had been used instead of wood, they would have properly served their purpose.

The material used in the floors between beams, also in the partitions, and for covering of columns and other exposed ironwork, must not only be incombustible, but it must also be practically indestructible. If it cannot be heated without injury for a considerable time to 2000° Fahrenheit and cooled again, either slowly, or suddenly as when exposed to a stream of cold water, it certainly is not good material for the purpose. It ought also to endure this test when only one surface is heated, which means that the material must be able to withstand a marked inequality of expansion and contraction. It not only should preserve its integrity under such circumstances, but its strength ought not to be impaired.

The conditions in buildings divided into comparatively small rooms are not the same as they are in buildings used for warehouses and stores, which are often entirely without division walls. In an ordinary office building, the burning of the contents of a room must be expected to at least ruin the decorations, the plastering, and

the floor beams and their arches, and if the windows and doors are made so that an ordinary fire cannot pass through them, a fire will be confined to the room in which it originates. The building will then be fireproof so far as the effect of an internal fire of wooden fittings or

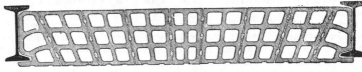

FIREPROOFING. — FIG. 1.
A floor made of voussoir-shaped terra-cotta blocks, forming a flat arch.

furniture is concerned. This standard of protection is, however, not attained by many of the new high buildings of America. A building will be fireproof in the highest sense only when combustible matter and material which can be destroyed by heat is excluded absolutely from the construction of the building. Such buildings are possible and practicable by either the steel frame or massive methods of construction.

Metal-covered doors and door frames and metal-covered sashes and window frames can now be obtained, which can hardly be detected from wood by casual observation. The windows for borrowed light, in partitions between rooms, are almost universally defective ; but it is now possible to provide them with glass that will permit the passage of light without going to pieces when exposed to a fire. (See Wire Glass.)

The destruction must, of course, be greater in very large rooms stored with inflammable materials, as in warehouses and all department stores which are open over large floor areas.

If the construction of the floors and the covering of metal is everywhere what it ought to be, the integrity of the structure will be preserved ; but there seems no way of protecting buildings of this class from very great injury, or of saving their contents from total destruction when a fire is once well started, except by dividing them some way into apartments.

It has been suggested that, while it may be very desirable, or even necessary, to have large department stores and large warehouses open over entire floors, and even from story to

FIREPROOFING. — FIG. 2.
A floor made of simpler hollow blocks than those in Fig. 1, and completed by a bed of cement in which sleepers are bedded, and by flooring nailed to those strips ; beneath, by plastering.

the woodwork used in finishing floors and walls ; but the building can be made so that the fire need not extend to adjoining apartments. If the protecting material is indestructible, if the partitions and division walls are framed everywhere with metal and are built directly upon

story, during the hours of actual use, it might be possible to devise movable screens or curtains of fireproof material for use at other hours that would effectually confine a fire in any one of the apartments so established. No such complete constructions have, however, as yet been made.

Greater reliance has been put upon systems of flooding made to work automatically. As destruction by water is as bad as destruction by fire, and as there must always remain some uncertainty in the perfect operation of an apparatus, it would seem that dependence upon some feature of construction is most to be preferred.

Protection from outside fires is, of course, quite as necessary as protection from those of internal origin. Successful construction in this respect depends upon the choice of materials for the exterior walls, upon the protection of spandrel beams and columns, and upon the window exposure. Without question, the last is the most important consideration. It is undoubtedly the greatest weakness of fireproof buildings. The glass used in exterior windows, great or small, will go to pieces when exposed to a great heat. Shutters on the outside of the window do not fill the demand, whether of iron or of wood covered with metal. On street fronts they destroy the decorative character of the building, and are not to be considered. Facing alleys and courts, and in rear walls, they are generally not closed when the building is vacated. Indeed, there seems no way to enforce their use. Interior rolling iron shutters are used to some extent. These are much more easily operated, and they may finally prove to be the solution of the problem.

The choice of materials for the construction of exterior walls and the covering of the spandrel beams and columns is also a source of weakness in a good many fireproof buildings. Granite, marble, and limestone will surely go to pieces when exposed to a hot fire. If they are used in places of great exposure, it should always be with the understanding that the exterior walls will be greatly damaged by the burning of adjoining buildings. Columns and beams in wall construction should always be covered on the outside as well as on the inside with fireproofing material of some kind that will thoroughly protect them from injury. The too common practice of covering such construction with a few inches of granite or marble, or of any kind of stone, without any other material intervening, is radically wrong, and should be prohibited by law in every large city.

Well-chosen brick are undoubtedly the best material for the construction of exterior walls, so far as their resistance to fire is concerned. A large part of the ornamental terra cotta now used to so great an extent with brickwork in the construction of façades can also be relied upon; but both the terra cotta and the brick vary in resisting qualities with the character of the clay of which they are made, and in important structures they should not be relied upon merely because they are terra cotta and brick, but because the resisting qualities of the

particular product in question have been established by experiment.

Many important buildings are so situated that there can be no great outside exposure; and, with proper protection to the ironwork, granite, marble, and other stones are as effectual for all practical purposes as any other material. The same idea should also govern their use in interior construction. There are rooms that never contain inflammable material, such as entrances and public rooms, where they may be safely used.

Steel should never be exposed, either inside of the building or out, although up to 600° heat does not materially affect its strength. Cast iron, also, should be covered when used as a part of the construction, but sometimes it may be successfully and wisely used as a protection to steel construction.

Stairs should be constructed in all large buildings with solid metal treads and risers, preferably of steel; and the use of marble or slate treads, supported on their edges by the risers, should never be permitted. In a fire a stairway is first to suffer if the flames can possibly reach it, and where the treads are made of marble alone they not only go to pieces at once but they become veritable traps, both for those who are seeking escape, and to firemen who may enter the building.

In America, dwellings, apartment houses, and tenements are not generally made of fireproof construction, and in most American cities there is no security against fire in such buildings except that afforded by the fire department. In some of the larger cities, however, the laws require very perfect construction of division and exterior walls, fire walls rising above the roof, and the like, so that fires rarely spread from one to another. In Europe, floors and partitions of such buildings are much more commonly constructed of fireproof, or at least of incombustible, materials. Metallic lath, in combination with plaster and concrete, has been used to a large extent for this purpose in all the larger cities.

The problems relating to the protection of ironwork from fire are closely related to the problem of protecting it from corrosion, particularly in spandrel construction. Though they may seem to be quite independent of each other, they are really closely allied, and any consideration of one to the neglect of the other must result to the disadvantage of the building as a whole. No method of fire protection is acceptable that does not at the same time provide, or in some way permit, of the proper protection of the metal from corrosion. Wherever iron is used in connection with concrete or plaster combinations as a part of a fireproofing material, the necessity of protection from corrosion is even yet more necessary.

While both lime and ordinary Portland cements have been recognized as conservators of iron and steel, it has been repeatedly proven by experience that not all combinations of this character are enduring, and the failure of the metal means the failure of the whole product of which it forms a part.

Although the last half of the nineteenth century has witnessed a remarkable increase in methods of construction having for their object the prevention of fire, there is yet much to be done. The time is not far distant when the use of combustible material in the construction of floors and partitions in all the greater cities of both Europe and America will be prohibited by law, except, possibly, to some extent in minor finishing, where the burning could do no harm.

The day is not far distant when some acceptable plan will be devised by which the homes of the rich and poor alike shall be made as proof from fire as the best office and warehouse buildings of modern construction.
— CORYDON T. PURDY.

FIRE REGULATOR. An automatic device to control the draft to the fire of a steam boiler, adjusted so as to be operated by the pressure of the steam.

FIRESTONE. Any stone thought to be peculiarly fit to resist great heat. Such a material occasionally used in England is described as having a large quantity of silica, and is apparently a sandstone capable of resisting even the direct effects of flame under ordinary circumstances, as in connection with an open fireplace. In the United States, some varieties of Western sandstone, generally of light brown colour, are found unusually resistant.

FIRE STOP. Any piece or mass of incombustible material used as a filling in the spaces of the framework or to close other open parts of a structure, in order to prevent the passage of fire.

FIRM (generally used in the plural). One of two rafters which form a truss; as a pair of firms. The term is local in England, or nearly obsolete. (Compare Crutch.)

FIRRING. Same as Furring.

FIRST PIECE. Locally, in Lancashire, England, the ridgepiece of a roof. — (A. P. S.)

FIRST STONE. In Great Britain, same as Foundation Stone, B.

FISCHER, KARL VON; architect; b. 1782; d. 1820.

Professor of architecture in the Academy of Munich. His most important building was the old Munich theatre, built in 1818, burned in 1823, and rebuilt under the name *Hof- und National-Teater.* (See Klenze.)

Seubert, *Künstler Lexicon.*

FISCHER VON ERLACH, JOHANN BERNHARD; architect; b. 1650; d. 1723.

Fischer von Erlach was a contemporary of

Andrea Pozzo (see Pozzo, A.), and was educated in Rome. Returning to Vienna, he began the *Schloss Schönbrunn,* the construction of which was interrupted by the death of the Emperor Joseph I., and built the church of S. Carlo Borromeo (begun 1715), the Peterskirche, the palace of the Prince Eugen, now *Finanzministerium* (1703), the Trautson palace (1720–1730), the *Hofbibliothek* (1722–1726), all in Vienna, the *Kollegienkirche* in Salzburg (1696–1707), the *Kurfürsten Kapelle* in the cathedral of Breslau, Germany (1722–1727), the Clam-Gallus palace in Prague, Bohemia (1707–1712), and other buildings. He published *Entwürfe historischer Baukunst* (1 vol., folio, 1725).

Gurlitt, *Barockstil in Deutschland;* Ebe, *Spät-Renaissance;* Löwy, *Wien vor 150 Jahren.*

FISCHER VON ERLACH, JOSEPH EMANUEL; architect; b. 1695; d. 1742.

A son of Johann Bernhard Fischer von Erlach (see Fischer von Erlach, J. B.). He completed many of his father's most important buildings, the *Hofbibliothek* (Vienna), the church of S. Carlo Borromeo, and others.

Gurlitt, *Barockstil in Deutschland.*

FISH (n.). A piece of wood or metal secured to the side of a beam or the like to strengthen it; particularly, when used to secure two timbers or the like, when joined end to end. In the latter case, two fishes are generally used on opposite sides; sometimes four. Also called fish piece and fish plate. (Compare Flitch.)

FISH (v.). To strengthen, join, or secure by means of a fish or fishes.

FISH BEAM (n.). In mechanics, a beam which bellies out, and usually on the under side. — (C. D.)

The use of this term is objectionable because it suggests a relation to the accurate term fished beam. (See Fish (n.) and (v.).)

FISH MARKET. (See Market.)

FIVES COURT. A building prepared for the game of fives, in which the balls are struck by the palm of the hand, usually protected by a glove. That which is really requisite for the play is a solid wall with slightly projecting wings, like buttresses, and usually a piece of netting at the top to prevent the balls from flying over the top of the wall. The more elaborate structure is a kind of room with only three walls, 14 feet wide and 27 feet long within the walls, but without a roof.

FIXTURE, COMBINATION. (See Electrical Appliances.)

FLAG. Any comparatively thin piece of stone suitable for paving. Most stones thus used are sandstones or mica schists which split readily into slabs.

FLAGSTAFF. A pole to which a flag is secured, and from which it floats. The term is generally confined to poles set vertically, as these are much the largest, and are placed in the most prominent positions.

In most cases, the flagstaff is merely a tapering stick painted white and capped with a sheave through which the halyards run. It is rare that any decorative treatment is attempted. There are, however, instances of this, and it is interesting to note that all designers who try to use the flagstaff in a decorative way make it much thicker than mere strength would require, and paint it in darker colours, perhaps in more colours than one. The most effective decoration connected with the flagstaff is, however, the

FLAMBOYANT TRACERY: PORCH OF S. MACLOU, ROUEN, C. 1460.

foot socket or stand in which it is set up. Any amount of rich ornamentation may be given to this supporter; the most celebrated and probably the richest instances existing being in Venice in the Piazza, and in front of the church of S. Mark. These three bronze standards are the work of Alessandro Leopardi, and were put up at the beginning of the sixteenth century. — R. S.

FLAGSTONE. Same as Flag.

FLAMBOYANT (adj.). *A.* Having to do with the late French Gothic window traceries, which are so arranged that the openings between the stone piers are no longer circles, either with

or without cusps, and triangles between the circles, but take the shape of flames. The stone

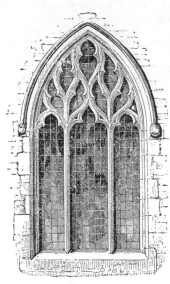

FLAMBOYANT TRACERY IN ENGLAND: SALFORD, WARWICKSHIRE, C. 1360.

piers are cut in S curves and meet at acute angles, and the general aspect of the openings may be thought to resemble flames rising either vertically or at an angle with the vertical. The term is French, but in France the significance is generally applied to that which gives out flame or resembles flame, or to what is very brilliant and shining. It is less used in a strictly architectural sense in France than in England. (See France, Architecture of; Gothic Architecture; Tracery; Window.)

B. Having to do with the French Gothic of the late fifteenth and early sixteenth centuries; namely, that which has flamboyant window tracery. As this peculiar tracery prevailed in France from the close of the Hundred Years' War until about 1495, the term serves to describe the magnificent late Gothic, of which characteristic buildings are the church of S. Maclou at Rouen, the western part of the cathedral of Tours, the cathedral of S. Pol de Léon, S. Wulfran at Abbeville, the church

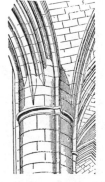

FLAMBOYANT GOTHIC: PIER AND ARCH-MOULDINGS, CATHEDRAL OF NARBONNE (AUDE), FRANCE.

of S. Riquier, not far from Abbeville, and the church of Brou at Bourg-en-Bresse. — R. S.

FLAMBOYANT ARCHITECTURE

Porch of the church of S. Maclou at Rouen. The church is one of the loveliest productions of the late Gothic style in France. It was begun very soon after the close of the Hundred Years' War, 1453, but the porch is later, probably about 1500. The carved wooden doors are of the sixteenth century; that on the left in part, at least, by Jean Goujon, about 1540.

FLAN. To splay the sides of an opening, as the jambs of a door or window. (Rare or local English.)

FLANDIN, EUGÈNE. (See Coste, Pascal Xavier.)

FLANGE. A rim projecting laterally on one or on each side of any member, usually at right angles to the general surface; as the flat upper and lower portions of an I beam at right angles to the web; a collar at the ends of wrought iron pipes by means of which they are secured together.

FLANK (n.). *A.* A lateral face of a structure; an end or side as distinguished from the front or back; a return at either side of the face of a structure or part of a structure.

B. In Scotland, a valley of a roof.
— (A. P. S.)

FLANK (v. t. and v. int.). To stand, or to be placed at, the sides or flanks; to provide with sides or flanks; as an entrance gate may be flanked by a column on each side; a court may be flanked by the wings of a building.

FLAP. *A.* One fold of a folding door, shutter, or the like; especially where two parts are hinged together, so that the door or shutter hinged to one side of an opening is itself in two parts which fold together when the door or other leaf is opened wide.

B. A hinge of which the straps, leaves, or flat plates are intended to be screwed to the side of a door, shutter, or the like; in this contrasting with butt hinge, probably an abbreviation of Flap Hinge.

Front Flap. In a folding door or shutter, the part which is in front and visible when the shutter is open and is folded back against the jamb. It is usually hinged directly to the fixed frame or jamb. (Compare Back Flap.)

FLASHING. Pieces of sheet metal covering the joints or angles between a roof and any vertical surface against which it abuts, as of a wall, parapet, or chimney, to prevent the leakage or driving in of rain water; also, such pieces covering the hips and valleys of shingle or slate roofs, or the like; or covering the joints about window frames, etc., in frame buildings. Plain flashing is continued with a single strip turned up a few inches against the vertical surface to which it is tacked or otherwise secured, and running up under the slates, tiles, or shingles to a slightly higher level. For greater security an apron, usually of lead, may be affixed to the wall above the first strip, which it overlaps; the apron being driven into the joints of the masonry protects the joint of the flashing proper. Against a brick chimney or gable parapet the sloping joint is protected by step flashing; short pieces overlapping like slates replace the continuous strip, each turned into a different horizontal joint of the brickwork. Flashings against stonework are driven into grooves cut to receive them;

in all cases the joint is cemented with common or elastic cement. — A. D. F. H.

FLAT (adj.). *A.* In painting, having little or no gloss. (See Dead; Flatting.)

B. In colour and in coloured surfaces of any substances or make, uniform, without gradation. A wash of water colour is commonly laid as flat as possible. In decorative painting of a high character, flat tints are commonly avoided because they are injurious to the general effect of the work; and gradation is very important.

FLAT (n.). One story of a building, and hence the whole, or a considerable part, of a story used as a residence. The term has been in use for many years in Scotland, where the lofty houses of Edinburgh have been let in flats. In London, where, since about 1875, the renting of separate apartments has been a custom slowly increasing, such apartments are generally called flats, and the building itself is spoken of as a "flat" house, with or without the quotation marks. Up to 1880 the only large building of the kind was the Queen Anne's mansions. In New York, which has led the other cities of the United States in the matter of apartments taking the place of separate houses, the term flat has received a local meaning expressing something rather more elegant and spacious than a set of rooms in a Tenement House, and less so than an apartment in an Apartment House. In speaking of an *appartement* of a Paris *maison à loyer* or the *Wohnung* of a German or Viennese house of the type, the word "apartment" is more commonly used, but flat would be equally appropriate. — R. S.

FLATTING. Painting with a coat of paint without gloss, presenting a dead surface when dry; usually mixed with turpentine with little or no linseed oil. Also, dabbing a still wet coat of paint with a stiff brush to conceal the usual brush marks, and to produce an even-appearing surface.

FLATTING COAT. A coat of such painting as will produce the effect of Flatting. (See Mat.)

FLAXMAN, JOHN; sculptor; b. July 6, 1755; d. December 7, 1826.

John Flaxman was the son of a moulder of plaster casts in London. In 1769 he entered the Royal Academy schools. He exhibited at the Academy after 1770. For many years after 1775 Flaxman was employed at the pottery of the Messrs. Wedgewood. About 1785–1786 he constructed the monument of the poet Collins at Chichester cathedral, and that of Mrs. Morley in Gloucester cathedral. In 1787 Flaxman settled in Rome. Returning to England in 1794, his first work was the monument to Lord Mansfield in Westminster Abbey. In 1800 he was elected a member of the Royal Academy. Flaxman designed monuments to Captain Montague in Westminster Abbey, to Sir Joshua Reynolds, Earl Howe, and Lord Nelson in S. Paul's cathedral, to the Baring family at Micheldever church, Hampshire, to Mary Lushington at Lewisham, Kent, and other works. In 1810 he was elected professor of sculpture at the Royal Academy.

Redgrave, *Dictionary of Artists;* Stephen, *Dictionary of National Biography.*

FLÈCHE. In French, a spire, large or small. In English, usually a comparatively small, slender spire surmounting and forming part of the construction of a roof, as is common at the junction of the nave and transept roofs of French Gothic churches ; and may include the lower story of the same structure with vertical walls or uprights.

FLEMISH ARCHITECTURE. That developed by the people of Flanders. This ancient geographical region has been considered for many years as divided into the three districts of French Flanders, Eastern Flanders, and Western Flanders. French Flanders is for the greater part of its extent included in the modern territory of France, but Tournai and Mons, with the country around them, form part of the kingdom of Belgium and include the cities of Ghent, Audenarde, Saint-Nicolas, and reaches to the river Schelt opposite Antwerp. Western Flanders includes the cities of Bruges, Ypres, and Courtrai, and this also belongs to Belgium. The architecture of this region is strongly influenced by that of France at almost all epochs. (See Belgium, Architecture of.) — R. S.

FLEUR–DE–LIS; –LYS. (More properly Fleur de Loys, that is to say, flower of Louis, rather than lily flower.) An ornament long associated with the royal power in France, consisting of three leaflike pointed members above and three, or one, below, a horizontal crossbar. Of the three upper ones the middle one stands erect, the two others are strongly curved outward and downward, one on either side. The lower members are treated in a similar though less pronounced fashion, but in very abstract and simple forms are sometimes united into one mass. It is stated that this ornament was first borne as an heraldic charge by Louis VII. of France, who died 1180. The escutcheon of the kings of France was afterward charged with fleurs-de-lis thickly set in diagonal order, the number being indifferent ; but in the reign of Henry IV. this was changed, and from this time on the royal shield was charged with three fleurs-de-lis, two above, side by side, and one below. The first of these arrangements is called, in heraldic language, "France Ancient"; the second, "France Modern." (See Giglio.) — R. S.

FLEURON. In French usage, a plastic semblance of a vegetable form used as the crowning feature of a decorative member, as a finial, épi, or the like.

FLEXIBLE CORD. (See Electrical Appliances.)

FLIER. One of the steps of a straight part of a flight of stairs having a tread of uniform width, and perpendicular to the general direction of the stairs ; distinguished from Winder.

FLIGHT. In a stair, a continuous series of steps uninterrupted by landings ; by extension, but improperly, any number of such series forming together the stair from one floor to another, even when landings are introduced. (See Stair.)

FLINT. An impure form of quartz, opaque or slightly translucent, and of several colours in pale neutral shades. As a building material, it is fit only for building with a great abundance of mortar, much as was customary in the Roman Imperial buildings, the resultant mass being very much like concrete, at least in its hardness and endurance. In parts of England where this stone is common, and found in masses larger than is usual elsewhere, it is customary to face walls with flints by selecting the largest pieces and those which show the smoothest face when split. Small and non-decorative buildings are those in which this material is most commonly used ; but parts of elaborate churches, such as the filling above the vaults and even parts of the face wall, where it is unbroken, are so constructed. — R. S.

FLITCH. *A.* A plank, or similar thin piece, secured to the side of a beam with which it corresponds in length and depth, or nearly so, and which it serves to strengthen ; one of several such pieces or beams secured together side by side to form a larger beam or girder. (Compare Fish.)

B. Same as Slab.

FLITCH BEAM; GIRDER. A beam or girder composed of flitches, as defined under Flitch, *A* ; usually, one constructed as described under Flitch Plate.

FLITCH PLATE. An iron plate used as a Flitch, in sense *A* ; generally, between two wooden beams, as in doubled headers and trimmers.

FLITCROFT, HENRY ; architect ; b. Aug. 29, 1697 ; d. March 5, 1769.

A son of Jeffry Flitcroft, gardener of King William III., at Hampton Court (England). May 14, 1726, he entered the office of the Board of Works, and in 1758 was appointed comptroller of the Board, succeeding Ripley. He was succeeded by Sir William Chambers (see Chambers).

Redgrave, *Dictionary of Artists.*

FLOAT (n.) (I.). A structure like a raft, but usually, in architectural usage, smoothly decked or floored. Boathouses and bathing houses, such as those maintained by clubs and the like, are often built upon floats, or have floats used as landings and docks.

FLOAT (n.) (II.). A plasterer's tool for smoothing a coat of plaster while soft, and bringing it to a true, even surface. Its essential feature is a thin blade having a smooth plane surface.

FLOAT (v.). To smooth as with the plasterer's float, or in some similar manner; said of a coat of plaster, cement, or the like, which is applied in a very soft, almost liquid, condition, so that it can readily be brought to a true and smooth surface.

FLOATING SCREED. (See Screed.)

FLOAT STONE. A stone used to grind or rub brickwork to a true curved surface, the brick having previously been laid and roughly cut approximately to the required shape.

FLOOR. *A.* The assemblage of pieces, as boards, planks, tiles, or the continuous mass of material, as cement, concrete, asphalt, which forms the lower and generally horizontal surface of the interior of a building or any part of a building; or, in like manner, the upper surface of a platform, bridge, or the like; that surface upon which we walk and place furniture, portable objects of all sorts, but generally the upper surface of a construction rather than a surface laid solid upon earth or filling between solid walls. (See Flooring.)

B. The entire horizontal structure for the support of a floor in sense *A*, together with such a floor itself. In this sense the whole system of timbers or iron beams, including girders, summers, binding beams, trimmers, headers, and ordinary joists or floor beams are included as well as the upper surface, the arrangements for deafening, and perhaps the deafening itself, and even the finish beneath (for which see Ceiling).

The simplest house floor is composed of boards laid upon and nailed to joists or beams, which rest upon the walls. If the walls are too far apart girders, or large beams, are placed to support one or both ends of the joists. The girders may rest upon walls, or upon posts or columns. In modern so-called fireproof buildings, the floors are generally supported by iron or steel beams and girders, and the surface between them is formed in various ways: by flat arches of brick or terra cotta; by slabs of concrete made in place, generally strengthened by iron bars or rods, or wires bedded in it; or bent plates of corrugated iron reaching from beam to beam, upon which concrete is placed. For bridge floors, "buckled plates" (which see) are riveted to the steel joists, and are covered with concrete and a paving of stone, wood, or asphaltum. Buckled plates are thin plates of iron or steel formed by pressure, the central portion of which is crowned or raised, forming a very flat dome, and leaving a flat margin on the edges for riveting in place. Plates may be about ⅜ inch thick, 3 or 4 feet square, and be raised in the centre 2 or 3 inches.

In the following subtitles the reference is to sense *B*, unless otherwise specially stated : —

Apparatus Floor. In the United States, the ground floor of a fire house or patrol house where is kept the fire-extinguishing, or other, apparatus and horses.

Carcass Floor. The assemblage of beams and girders in place, to receive a floor in the sense *A*.

Ceiling Floor. The assemblage of roof beams, or rafters, and ceiling joists in place, to receive a ceiling.

Double Floor. *A.* One in which large joists, called binders, binding joists, or primary joists, carry the floor joists above and the ceiling joists below.

B. A floor in sense *A*, which consists of two thicknesses of planking, the lower one being usually of rough material brought to an even thickness and carefully nailed to the timbers, its purpose being merely to give better

FLOOR IN SWISS SOLID TIMBER HOUSE; THE CONSTRUCTION AND THE FLOORING ALL REPLACED BY A SYSTEM OF STILES AND PANELS.

and more uniform support and easier nailing to the upper shell, or layer, which is usually of choice material.

Double-framed Floor. In English usage, a floor having two systems of support, the common terms being girders for the primary or heaviest timbers, binding joists, which rest on them, and the joists, or floor beams, which are carried by the latter. It is customary to specify or to state, in definition, that in such a floor the ceiling is carried by separate ceiling joists. In the United States, ceiling joists are used or omitted without much reference to the framing of the floor proper.

Fireproof Floor. One composed of fire-resisting materials carried by iron or steel beams. (See Fireproofing.)

Folded Floor. A floor in sense *A*, in which the cross joints of boards or planks are continuous, either across the entire floor or across a series of boards.

Framed Floor. One in which the binding joists are carried by still larger girders. (See Double Floor, above.)

Mill Floor. A floor of the form usual in mills. (See Mill; Slow-burning Construction.)

Naked Floor. *A.* The framing which forms the constructional part of the floor without the flooring and ceiling.

B. One in which the floor joists extend from wall to wall. — (A. P. S., under Single Frame.)

Solid Floor. *A.* One composed of joists set close and spiked together.

B. Same as Mill Floor, above.

Straight Joint Floor. A floor in sense *A*, in which the joints between the sides of the boards or planks are continuous from end to end. — R. S.

FLOOR HANGER. A Stirrup Iron; used for hanging the framed timbers of a floor.

FLOORING. Same as Floor in sense *A*, or the material prepared for such a floor. In the United States this is the general term for the material used for finishing a floor; that is, for providing the smooth and level surface upon which we walk; it corresponds with Roofing, Siding, Sheathing, and with Ceiling in its more restricted sense, *A*.

FLORENTINE LILY. Same as Giglio.

FLORENTINE MARBLE. (See Alabaster, *A*.)

FLORIATE; FLORIATED. Carved with leaves and foliage or made to resemble or suggest flowers; *e.g.* many mediæval capitals, finials, and mouldings, particularly in the fourteenth and fifteenth centuries.

FLORID. Highly ornate; extremely rich to the point of over decoration; a term applied in general to works of any style or period; but more specifically used also to characterize the art of several periods in which a style having reached its culmination has passed into a stage of excessive display ending in extravagance and decline. Such were, for instance, in Egyptian art, the age of the Ptolemies; in Greek vase decoration, the style and period of the fourth century; in mediæval art, the styles of the fifteenth century generally, in France, England, Germany, and Spain.

FLORIS, CORNELIS DE; architect and sculptor; b. 1518; d. Feb. 20, 1575.

A famous architect and sculptor of Antwerp (Belgium), and a brother of Frans Floris, the painter. Cornelis studied in Rome and was architect of the *Stadhuis* (City Hall) of Antwerp, which was finished in 1560, burned down in 1581, and rebuilt in the same style by another architect. He built the so-called *Oosterhuis* at Antwerp.

Immerzeel, *Hollandsche en Vlaamsche Kunstenaars.*

FLUE. A passage provided through solid material, as the substance of a wall, for the passing upward of smoke, or for the carrying of a draught of air upward or downward, as in forced ventilation. Flues are most commonly built solid in the brick wall and faced with plaster of some kind (see Pargetting; Parget Work); or lined with glazed earthenware pipe or similarly uniformly shaped solid material not liable to absorb gases.

FLUSH (adj.). Even with, in the same plane with, something else, whether adjacent or not; in exact alinement with the surrounding surface. Thus, a flush panel has its surface in the same plane with the surrounding frame; two piers having the same projection from a wall may be said to have their outer faces flush.

FLUSH (v. int.). *A.* In mason work, in British usage, to break or chip off from the face, as in the case of stone or brick which is too heavily loaded near the edge.

B. To come to the surface; to become flushed; said of mortar which is forced into a joint or by pressure spread and distributed in a joint until it appears at the face or bed.

FLUSH (v. t.). *A.* In laying up masonry, to fill a vertical joint or joints with mortar which is rammed or worked into the interstices until they are filled approximately flush with the surrounding surface.

B. In sewers, plumbing, and the like, to supply water, usually with great force and speed, for the purpose of cleansing.

FLUSH RIM. In the bowl of a water-closet, a rim forming a channel or tube with inlets by which the bowl is flushed from all sides.

FLUSH TANK. A box made so as to hold water and fitted with certain machinery by means of which any part of the plumbing of a house or the like can be flushed at will. The most common form of the machinery which provides for the discharge and stoppage of the water is a lever pulled from above or from below which opens a valve, which valve will not close until the lever is released. A common ball cock generally controls the automatic flow of water from the supply pipe, and fills the tank again to its original level. (Also called Flush Box.)

FLUTE. A groove or channel; especially, one of many such channels which are parallel or nearly so, and used for a decorative purpose. The most common use of this decoration is in the shafts of columns, those of Grecian and Greco-Roman origin being commonly so treated. It is customary to distinguish between the *channels* which adorn the shaft of the Greek Doric order and which are elliptical in section, and separated one from another by a common arris, from the *flutes* of the Ionic and Corinthian orders, which are circular in section, deeper in proportion, and are separated one from another by a narrow fillet. This distinction is not always maintained. (See Channel.) Flutes are used in other than straight lines in such work as the strigil ornament.

FLY. In a theatre, the space above the stage, and concealed from the front by the wall above the proscenium arch. (See Fly Gallery; Theatre.)

FLYER. Same as Flier.

FLY GALLERY. In a theatre, one of the galleries over the stage, from which parts of the scenery are hung and managed. Commonly spoken of as "the flies." (See Fly.)

FLYING BUTTRESS. (See Buttress.)

FODERA; **FODERO**. In Italian, a lining, as of a garment; hence, a casing or veneering, as of marble.

FOIL. In tracery, any one of several lobes, circular, or nearly so, tangent to the inner side

FOIL : OPENING WITH FIVE FOILS, CALLED CINQUEFOIL.

of a larger arc, as of an arch, and meeting each other in points, called cusps, projecting inward from the arch, or circle. Three such lobes make a trefoil; four, a quatrefoil; five, a cinquefoil, or quintefoil; six, a sexfoil; and a large number, a multifoil. Mere cusps on an arch produce foils only when connected by arcs, usually more than semicircles. When the foils are very small and numerous, as in Moorish arches, the arch is called a cusped arch rather than a multifoil arch. Foils are encountered occasionally in early mediæval (Romanesque) work and in late florid work, but

FOIL : ARCH WITH FIVE FOILS, CALLED CINQUE-FOIL ARCH, SALISBURY CATHEDRAL.

they characterize especially the Middle Pointed period in France, England, and Germany. (Called also Feathering; see Tracery.)
— A. D. F. H.

FOLFI, MARIOTTO DI ZANOBI; architect and engineer; b. 1521; d. 1600.

Folfi made the model for, and built, after 1549, the palace of Giovanni Uguccioni, in Florence (unfinished). There is a sketch of this famous design in the Uffizi, by Giorgio

Vasari, the younger. The building is still in the possession of the Uguccioni family.

Geymüller-Stegmann, *Die Arch. der Ren. in Toscana*; Mazzanti del Badia, *Raccolta delle Migliori Fabbriche*.

FOLIATE (adj.). *A*. Made, provided, or adorned with foils, as in mediæval tracery. When a foil is adorned with subordinate foils the tracery is said to be double foliate; if these

FOLIATED CAPITAL, CANTERBURY CATHEDRAL, c. 1177.

are again adorned with minuter foils, it is triple foliate. Tracery with cusps may be foliate even when the cusps are joined, not by true circular arcs, but by other curved outlines.

B. Made or adorned with leafage or leaf-like forms, as a foliate capital, a foliate corbel.

FOLIATE (v.). *A*. To form into leaves or leaflike shapes.

B. To adorn with foliation.

FOLIATION. The state of being foliate; foliate decoration.

FONDACO. In Italian, a factory in sense *A*.

FONDACO DEI TEDESCHI. In Venice; a very large building of about 1510, designed either by Fra Giocondo (see Giocondo), or by an unknown artist called merely Girolamo Tedesco (Jerome the German). Its large surfaces of plain wall were once covered with noble paintings by Giorgione, Titian, and others of the great school of Venetian painters.

FONDACO DEI TURCHI. In Venice; a beautiful Byzantine building which, in 1850 and thereafter, was ruinous, but still of extreme interest. It has been elaborately rebuilt, and is essentially a new building. (See Museo Correr.)

FONDAMENTA. In Italian, an embankment or quay constructed along the side of a water channel. In English usage, the term applies especially to those in Venice, which form stone-paved thoroughfares along many of the *canali*, the term being used in the names of such streets. (Compare Riva.)

FONT. A baptismal basin in which the water for the administration of baptism is con-

FONT, WITH BLACK MARBLE BOWL, STONE SHAFT, AND BASE: CATHEDRAL, LAON (AISNE), FRANCE; 12TH CENTURY.

tained, or into which it is poured, or both. The Christian Church from the first moment of its existence was compelled to determine just how the water of baptism was to be applied to the person of the neophyte, and consequently the instruments to be employed in its administration. History tells us that three methods of baptizing or touching the body with water were countenanced, viz. by immersion, affusion, and aspersion. It was not until the end of the third century that we know of a time and place being especially set apart for the administration of baptism. (See Baptistery.) In the earliest representation now in existence of a baptism, a fresco in the catacombs of S. Calixtus at Rome, the sacrament is being given by affusion or pouring; nevertheless immersion seems to have been the ordinary mode in the primitive age of Christianity. The font used in a baptistery was a large cistern, which was either sunken in the floor or raised above it. The administrator and the candidate both descended into the water; but as the Roman world became converted to the faith the baptism of adult catechumens became less and less customary, while that of children became more and more so; consequently the necessity of the administrator entering the water ceased. The fonts were made smaller,

mere bowls standing on pillars or bases of some kind, but large enough to receive a child for immersion. They were made of stone, marble, silver, lead, brass, and wood, and often lined with lead. In form they followed the variations of architecture, every style having its own; the earliest fonts were square, or square with rounded corners, resting on blocks of stone or five legs; then followed the circular form standing on four legs, the cylindrical on drums, the octagonal and hexagonal with foundations of like form. The average size of the inside of the bowl in these ancient fonts was from $1\frac{1}{2}$ to 2 feet in diameter and 1 foot deep; the bowl was covered with a flat board, hinged and held in place by staples and a lock; the opening of the bowl was almost always circular, no matter what form the exterior might be. The ornamentation varied; sometimes it was geometrical, sometimes symbolical, often heraldic, and in some cases inscriptions were employed in a decorative way. The more usual mediæval fonts consisted of three parts: a bowl, a stem, and a plinth, and each part was usually made of a single stone. The place in which these fonts stood was almost invariably near the west entrance of the church. If there was a south

FONT OF BLACK MARBLE, AT NOUVION-LE-VINEUX, NEAR LAON (AISNE), FRANCE; 12TH CENTURY.

door the font was placed to its left, and therefore nearer the west front; and this arrangement continues in modern times, except where a baptismal chapel exists. The modern font, as a

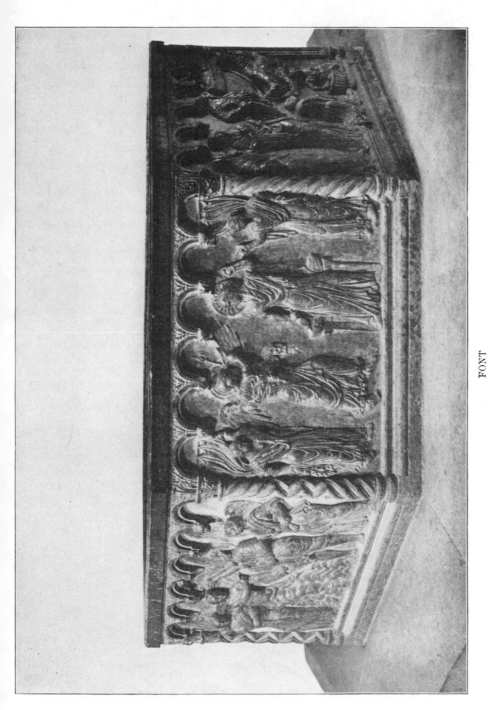

FONT

That of the baptistery attached to the cathedral at Verona. a work of the later Italian Romanesque, almost free from Byzantine influence. Its date is generally assumed as 1125. The bas-reliefs represent subjects in the life of Christ. It is cut out of a single block of marble and is about ten feet in diameter. The exterior is octagonal ; the hollow or basin within has the form of a quatrefoil.

general rule, corresponds with the architectural details of the church in which it is placed. It should be large, of good material, provided with a drain and cover, and it is well to raise it above the floor on an elevated platform with one or more steps. Its dimension is not fixed, but the following will be found in modern practice to be right : height, 3 feet 4 inches ; diameter across the top, 1 foot 11 inches, diameter of interior, 1 foot 1½ inches, and 1 foot deep.

Robert Robinson, Boston, 1817, *History of Baptism; Archæologia*, Vol. X., *Observations on an Ancient Font at Burnham;* Vol. XI., *Notices of Fonts in Scotland;* Vol. XXV., *Thomas Richman's Letters on Ecc. Arch. in France.* For illustrations of English fonts, see F. A. Paley's *Baptismal Fonts*, London, 1844.

— CARYL COLEMAN.

FONTAINE, PIERRE FRAN-ÇOIS LÉONARD; architect ; b. Sept. 20, 1762 ; d. Oct. 10, 1853.

Fontaine was a pupil of Antoine François Peyre (see Peyre, A. F.). In 1785 he went to Rome, where he was joined by Charles Percier (see Percier). He was associated with Percier in Paris, and together they were made directors of the decorations of the opera house. When Napoleon became First Consul they were made his architects, and retained that position under the Empire. Percier and Fontaine restored the châteaux of Malmaison, Saint-Cloud, Compiègne, Versailles, and other imperial residences. They restored the buildings

FONT OF STONE: ENGLISH GOTHIC, c. 1260.

of the court of the Louvre, and designed and built the Arc de Triomphe du Carrousel. They laid out the Rue de Rivoli, and built additions to the palace of the Tuileries in that street. In

1814 Percier retired from their association. Fontaine was court architect of Louis XVIII., for whom he built the Chapelle Expiatoire in the Rue d'Anjou, Paris. During the reign of

FONT OF STONE, AT URCEL, NEAR LAON (AISNE), FRANCE, c. 1220.

Charles X. he was architect to the Duke of Orléans, for whom he restored and enlarged the Palais Royal. He was chief architect of Louis Philippe. During this reign he remodelled the garden in front of the Tuileries, thus contributing to the defacement of the monument of Philibert De l'Orme (see De l'Orme, P.). Fontaine was architect in charge of the Louvre, the Tuileries, and the royal buildings until 1848. From 1831 to 1833 he was architect of the Théatre Français, Paris. In 1849 he was chosen president of the *Conseil des bâtiments civils*. (For the books published by Percier and Fontaine in collaboration, see Percier.) Fontaine published alone a *Histoire du Palais Royal*, 4to, 61 pl.

Maurice Du Seigneur in Planat's *Encyclopédie ;* Ch. Lucas in *La Grande Encyclopédie.*

FONTANA, CARLO; architect ; b. 1634 ; d. 1714.

It is not known that Carlo was related to either Domenico or Giovanni Fontana (see Fontana, D. and G.). He was a pupil of Bernini (see Bernini). He built the façade of the church of S. Marcello in the Corso (Rome, 1683), the monument of Queen Christina of Sweden in S. Peter's church (1689), the façade of the church of S. Maria in Trastevere (1702), the cupola of the cathedral of Montefiascone and the cathedral of Fulda (1696). The villa of the princes of Lichtenstein at Vienna was built from his designs between 1697 and 1700. He built the Palazzo Bolognetti (now Torlonia), Rome, 1680, the Palazzo Grimani, Rome, the Villa Visconti at Frascati, and the great portal of the Palazzo Reale at Genoa. Fontana succeeded Mattia de' Rossi as architect of S. Peter's church in the reign of Innocent XII. (Pope 1691–1700), and published his descriptive monograph, *Templum Vaticanum*, in 1694. He published also works on the Flavian Amphitheatre, on the aqueducts, and on the inundations of the Tiber. Fontana designed several fountains in Rome. His nephews, Girolamo and Francesco Fontana, assisted him in his work. Girolamo built the cathedral and fountains of Frascati.

Gurlitt, *Geschichte des Barockstiles in Italien;* Ebe, *Spät-Renaissance;* Milizia, *Memorie.*

FONTANA, DOMENICO; architect; b. 1543; d. 1607.

Domenico was born in Lombardy near Lake Como, and came to Rome during the lifetime of Michelangelo. He was a *protégé* of the Cardinal Montalto (Pope Sixtus V., 1585–1590). About 1580 he built this cardinal's villa (later Villa Negroni, Rome). When Montalto became Pope he made Domenico pontifical architect (1585). He built the lantern of the main cupola of S. Peter's church according to the designs of Michelangelo. Fontana moved the obelisk of Nero's circus from its old position to the Piazza di S. Pietro (1586). He also placed the obelisk of the Piazza del Popolo (1587) and that of the Piazzi di S. Giovanni in Laterano (1588). About 1586 he began the façade of the northern transept of the church of S. Giovanni in Laterano, Rome. He also built the Palazzo Laterano and the palace of Sixtus V. at the Vatican. The fountain of the Acqua Paola, Rome, is usually credited to his brother Giovanni (see Fontana, G.). Domenico designed the similar fountain of the Termini, Rome. He built the façade of the Palazzo Quirinale in the Via Pia (see Mascherino). In 1592 Domenico removed to Naples, and built there the Palazzo Reale.

Ebe, *Spät-Renaissance;* Strack, *Baudenkmäler Roms;* Milizia, *Memorie;* Sasso, *Monumenti di Napoli;* Falda, *Fontane di Roma.*

FONTANA, FRANCESCO. (See Fontana, Carlo.)

FONTANA, GIOVANNI; architect; b. about 1540; d. 1614.

Giovanni came to Rome with his younger brother Domenico (see Fontana, D.), whom he assisted in many of his undertakings. He was engineer and contractor rather than architect, and was especially concerned with the restoration and construction of aqueducts, laying out streets, and the like. He arranged the water-

works in the Vatican gardens and at the Villa Mondragone, at Frascati. The design of the fountain of the Acqua Paola, Rome, is attributed to Giovanni, although it is doubtless quite as much the work of his brother Domenico and his nephew, Carlo Maderna (see Maderna, C.). When Domenico went to Naples in 1592 Giovanni succeeded him as papal architect under Clement VIII. (Pope 1592–1605).

For bibliography, see Fontana, Domenico.

FONTANA, GIROLAMO. (See Fontana, Carlo.)

FONTANT, ANTOINE; sculptor and architect.

Worked at the château of La Rochefoucauld (Charente) during the second half of the sixteenth century, and his sculptured portrait, with the date 1838, is to be seen in the balustrade of the great staircase, his name being carved in an adjoining panel.

Bauchal, *Dictionnaire;* Lance, *Dictionnaire;* Michon, *Statistique monumentale de la Charente et la Rochefoucauld;* Eyriès, *Châteaux historiques de France.*

FONT COVER. A lid for a baptismal font; usually movable, and suspended above the font either by a counterpoise or by a swinging crane, to all of which apparatus a highly decorative character is generally given. The cover, or lid proper, is usually carried out in the same architectural design, agreeing with that of the font itself. In a few cases the font is enclosed at top with an immovable structure; a sort of prolongation upward of the bowl itself, but opening on one side, at least, by means of a door. (Cut, cols. 61, 62.)

FONTE, GIACOMO (JACOPO) DELLA. (See Giacomo della Quercia.)

FOOT BASE. A moulding above a plinth.

FOOTING. The lowermost part of a foundation wall, especially the wide base course, or the series of stepped courses which begin with stones or concrete three or four times as wide as the superstructure, and gradually grow narrower. (See Foundation.)

FOOTING STONE. Any stone intended for the construction of a footing; especially, a broad, flat stone for forming the base course of a foundation.

FOOT LEVEL. A pocket instrument consisting of a foot rule hinged in the middle and having a small spirit level set in the edge of one arm, and generally containing a pivoted and graduated blade by which any angle formed by the two arms of the rule may be subtended and measured; or by which may be determined the slope made by one arm with the horizontal as shown by the level.

FOOTLIGHT. One of a series of lights along the front edge of a theatrical, or similar, stage, which they light while being concealed from the audience. In the better theatres,

FONT COVER, WHICH, WITH THE FONT, IS OF BRASS; CHURCH OF NOTRE–DAME, HAL, BELGIUM.

It was cast in 1446.

these lights are (1900) being gradually abandoned, and other systems of illumination introduced by means of which the stage is lighted in a more realistic manner, avoiding the awkward appearance of shadows cast upward from below.

FOOTPACE. (See Pace.)

FOOTSTALL. *A.* The lowermost part of a supporting member, as of a pier or pillar, having generally some distinctive architectural treatment; thus the moulded footstall of a mediæval pillar corresponds to the base of a Greco-Roman column.

B. The pedestal which supports a pillar, altar, statue, or the like.

FOOTSTONE. *A.* (See Gravestone.)

B. Same as a Kneeler, when situated at the foot of the slope of a gable wall.

FOOT TABLE. (See Fractable.)

FOPPA, AMBROGIO (CARADOSSO); sculptor and medalist; b. about 1452; d. about 1526.

Caradosso was born in Lombardy, the son of a jeweller. At the court of Lodovico Sforza (Il Moro), in Milan, he was associated with Leonardo da Vinci (see Leonardo da Vinci) and Bramante (see Bramante). The charming terra cotta frieze in the sacristy of the church of S. Satiro, at Milan, was undoubtedly made by him.

Müntz, *La Renaissance à l'époque de Charles VIII.;* Bertolotti, *Artisti Lombardi a Roma.*

FORCING HOUSE. A greenhouse especially adapted to an abnormal stimulation of the growth of plants. (See Greenhouse.)

FORE-AND-AFT (adj.). Extending from the front to the rear; longitudinal. In the United States, said of partitions, or the like, which lie in the direction of the length of the typical city house, and, therefore, generally, across the beams.

FORE CHOIR. Same as Antechoir.

FORECOURT. The outer court of a large building, or assemblage of buildings. The entrance to a palace or a public building of importance is commonly through an outer court, the forecourt, which gives access to many different doorways, and which is reached from without by a gate, or gates, in an iron railing. Where the main buildings consist of a centre and two wings which advance on either side, the fourth side being closed by a railing or a wall or lower and subordinate buildings, the court within is commonly the forecourt, as there will be no outer one. Vehicles are commonly excluded from the forecourt, except the carriages of distinguished personages. (See Cour d'Honneur.)

FOREMAN. The chief of some department of a workshop or industrial establishment; especially, in the building trades, the head man among the employees and the second in command to his employer, representing him

in his absence. The term is sometimes applied to the senior or chief workman on a given job, as in the work being done upon a single building. (See Boss, III.)

FORE ROOM. The principal room of a residence; a parlour or reception room. (United States or local.)

FORK. Same as Crutch.

FORMAL GARDENING. The art and practice of landscape architecture when applied to designs of a regular and symmetrical character; that is, with little reference to natural dispositions, but rather on a geometrical plan, with straight walks, clipped hedges, carefully arranged grouping of trees, and comparatively a large amount of architectural adornment in the way of parapets, terraces, pedestals, and the like. (See Garden; Landscape Architecture.)

FORMENT (EL MAESTRO DAMIAN); sculptor and architect.

He was a native of Valencia, Spain, and studied in Italy. There is a record of payment to him on March 8, 1511, for the great retable of the cathedral of Zaragoza, Spain.

Bermudez, *Diccionario.*

FORMENTON (FORMENTONE), TOMASO; builder and architect; d. April, 1492.

In 1484 Formentone was *syndicus* of the guild of carpenters at Vicenza. He appears in records of 1489, 1490, 1491, and 1492 as superintendent of the works at the *Palazzo della Ragione* (Vicenza), afterward transformed into the Basilica (see Palladio). In 1498 he presented the model for the *Palazzo Pubblico*, at Brescia, Italy.

Magrini, *Tomaso Formenton in Archivio Veneto,* Vol. III.; Zamboni, *Memorie intorne alle pubbliche Fabbriche della città di Brescia.*

FORMERET. In French usage, a longitudinal arch of a series of vaults. In a French Gothic church of the usual type the formerets are the arches in the outer side walls and the corresponding ones along the inside of the aisles, forming part of the support of the clearstory walls.

FORNICATION. The process, or act, of covering with a vault; vaulted roofing or covering. (See Fornix.)

FORNICIFORM. In the shape of a vaulted roof or ceiling. (See Fornix.)

FORNIX. An arch or vault, especially under a building; a triumphal arch; a sally port in a wall; the classical Latin term akin to *fornus* and *furnus* (an oven), and thus to furnace, and the root word of several terms given above, signifying arched, or vaulted. In late Latin it is used for a brothel (in Rome, often an underground vaulted chamber), whence fornication in the criminal sense.

FÖRSTER, LUDWIG; architect; b. 1797 (at Bayreuth, Bavaria); d. June 16, 1863.

Förster received his training at the academy in Munich and from the architect Nobile in Vienna. He had a considerable practice in Vienna. His most important undertaking was the establishment in 1836 of the *Allgemeine Bauzeitung,* Vienna, the leading German architectural periodical.

Seubert, *Künstler-Lexicon.*

FORT. A fortified post, usually small, and often one out of many such works which together make up a Fortress. By extension, the term is applied to advance posts of a civilized government among savage or barbarous people, even if the fortifications are slight and rather formal than for real defence.

FORTIFICATION. *A.* The art and practice of making a post defensible, as in protect-

assailant approaching very near to the wall and trying to undermine it, or to effect a breach in it, or to ascend it by means of ladders, or else to force the gate. Great height of wall and elaborate preparation at top of such wall for the shelter of the defenders was therefore the primary requisite. (See Castle.) In modern times, however, no masonry is visible except in the case of the seacoast "castles" as they are called, that is to say, works intended to resist only the attacks of ships and to prevent the passing of such ships into a harbour or river mouth or the like. A modern fortress presents to the eye of the beholder from outside nothing but a series of grassy slopes; and within, the walls which rise around the enclosure of a fortified city and which belong to the fortifications,

FORTIFICATION OF ARCHITECTURAL CHARACTER: PART OF THE WORK DEFENDING THE PORTO DEL LIDO, ONE OF THE ENTRANCES TO THE LAGOON OF VENICE; 1544.

ing a city against attack or in providing a place of shelter which will enable a small number of men to hold out against the attack of a larger force.

B. A structure, or series of structures, for the purpose described above.

Modern fortification begins with the great engineers of the seventeenth century, and it has reached in our time a development which makes its study a very serious and important branch of science. Ancient fortification is more attractive to the architectural student because the results of its most skilful and scientific operations are picturesque and effective, whether in ruins or in complete repair.

It is to be observed that before the invention and considerable development of attack by means of gunpowder, the defence of the walls of a castle or city was vertical or nearly so, the

are usually the walls of barracks only, or else are unbroken smooth pieces of inside facing of ramparts and the like, having no battlements, nor openings of any kind.

(For minor and more temporary fortifications, see Block House; Palisade.) (Cut, cols. 67, 68.) — R. S.

FORTRESS. A strong place; a town or city furnished with a citadel and surrounded by fortifications, or more rarely a post fortified in an elaborate way though not having within its walls any inhabited district; a strong and extensive fortified place of any epoch.

FORUM. In Roman archæology, a public market place or open square; used in earlier ages as the one principal centre of a town. The Roman Forum (Forum Romanum; Forum Magnum) was the narrow valley between the Palatine Hill on the southwest, the Capitoline

Hill on the northwest, and the Viminal Hill on the northeast, the ground rising slowly toward the southeast to the Celian Hill. This small space could hardly be enlarged because of the rising ground on every side of it, and also because of the important buildings with which it was surrounded and which encroached upon it on every side. The temples whose ruins still remain were late edifices; but they stood on the sites of much earlier buildings, which sites were sacred and could not well be abandoned. But the building emperors seem to have been little inclined to enlarge the original forum even where that might have been done, on the northeast, but rather to have added open squares of their own which they surrounded with stately buildings and which vastly surpassed the Forum

FORUM BOARIUM. Between the Tiber and the Palatine Hill and including the temple of Vesta. Originally the cattle market.

FORUM MAGNUM. Same as Forum Romanum. (See Forum.)

FORUM OF AUGUSTUS. North of the Forum Romanum, with which it was connected by the Forum of Cæsar. It contained the temple of Mars the Avenger (Mars Ultor); and large fragments of the temple and the bounding wall still remain visible from the Via di Tor de' Conti.

FORUM OF JULIUS CÆSAR (Forum Julium). Built by Julius immediately in connection with the Forum Romanum, on the northwestern side and due north of the rostrum and the Mamertine prison. It

FORTIFICATION APPLIED TO A CHURCH: CATHEDRAL OF COIMBRA, PORTUGAL.

Magnum in splendour as well as in size. (See the names of these Imperial Fora below.) Besides those which are known to have existed, it is altogether probable that the great structures north of the Capitol, and which are associated with the names of the Antonine emperors, were also grouped around fora. The fora of other Italian cities occupy but little place in archæological study, but there were many towns in Italy, in Cis-Alpine Gaul, etc., whose names are composed with the term, as Forum Appii in Latium, Forum Cornelium, now Imola, in north Italy, Forum Julii, now Frejus, on the French Riviera. (For a similar use of an architectural term forming part of a proper name, see County Courthouse.) (Cut, cols. 69, 70.)

has not been explored on account of the superincumbent modern buildings; but it is known that it contained the temple of Venus Genetrix.

FORUM OF NERVA. Called also Forum Transitorium, because affording connection between other fora. It was built during and after the reign of Nerva, and contained the splendid temple of Minerva. The great columns called *le colonnace*, and which stand on the Via della Croce Bianca, belonged to the interior facing of the boundary wall of this forum.

FORUM OF TRAJAN. The greatest of all the imperial fora of Rome. It is generally held to include, first, the vast open space surrounded by a peristyle which adjoins the Forum of Augustus on the northwest; then the enor-

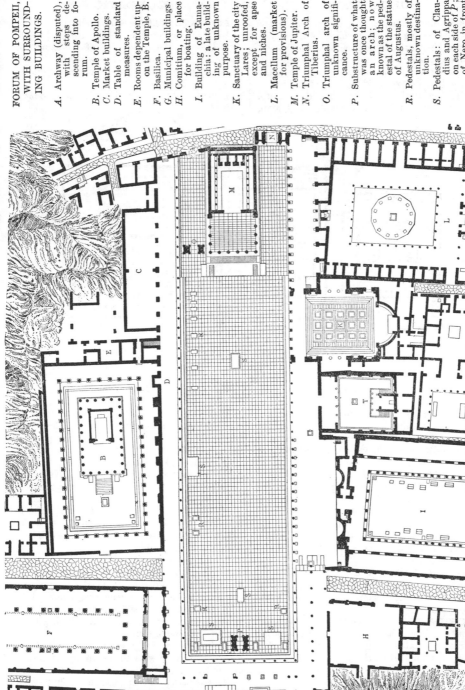

FORUM OF POMPEII,
WITH SURROUND-
ING BUILDINGS.

A. Archway (disputed),
with steps de-
scending into fo-
rum.

B. Temple of Apollo.
C. Market buildings.
D. Table of standard
measures.

E. Rooms dependent up-
on the Temple, B.

F. Basilica.
G. Municipal buildings.
H. Comitium, or place
for boating.

I. Building of Eunma-
chia: a late build-
ing of unknown
purpose.

K. Sanctuary of the city
Lares; unroofed,
except for apse
and niches.

L. Macellum (market
for provisions).

M. Temple of Jupiter.
N. Triumphal Arch of
Tiberius.

O. Triumphal arch of
unknown signifi-
cance.

P. Substructure of what
was once thought
an arch; now
known as the ped-
estal of the statue
of Augustus.

R. Pedestals, mostly of
unknown destina-
tion.

S. Pedestals: of Clau-
dius and Agrippa
on each side of P;
of Nero in front
of P; of Caligula
in front of M.

T. Temple of Vespasian.

mous Basilica Ulpia, as long as the forum was wide, and having one, or perhaps two, rounded apses at the northeast and southwest ends next the open square in which stands the still existing Column of Trajan, and which had on either side of it a library building, and, finally, farther to the northwest and toward the Capitol and the Quirinal Hill, the temple of Trajan,

FOSSATI, GASPARD; architect.

In 1847, under the sultan Abdul Mesjid, Fossati began the restoration of the church of S. Sophia at Constantinople. He published *Aya Sofia, Constantinople, as recently restored,* London, 1852 folio.

Lethaby and Swainson, *The Church of Sancta Sophia.*

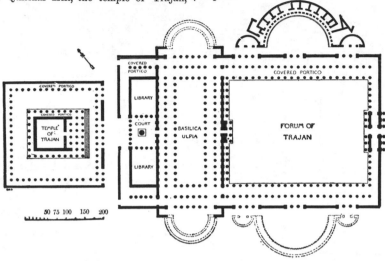

FORUM OF TRAJAN.
Restored plan, with basilica and temple enclosure. The column of Trajan is the object beneath the word "court."

with another great space around it faced by a continuous colonnade. This whole group of buildings was called by ancient writers, and with evident reason, the most magnificent thing in Rome or in the world.

FORUM PACIS. Built by Vespasian; southeast of the Forum of Augustus, with the space between them in which the Forum of Nerva was built afterward. The forum contained the temple of Peace of which no fragment is now known to exist; but the ground has not been explored, nor even the buildings upon it removed.

FORUM ROMANUM. (See definition above.)

FORUM TRANSITORIUM. (See Forum of Nerva above.)

FORUM TRIANGULARE. In Pompeii, at the southern point of the city, and west of the Stabian Gate, about 380 feet in extreme length, and situated on the verge of a low cliff which itself, with but slight additions to its height, formed the defence of the town at that point. It contained a Grecian Doric temple which is completely ruined, but seems to have been heptastyle (a very rare form) with eleven columns on the flank, and pseudo-dipteral. The forum was faced on two sides by a colonnade, and an Ionic portico at the northern end served as a principal entrance.

FOUNDATION. The base or substructure which supports a building. It is applied both to the platform, either natural or artificial, prepared for carrying the structure, and to the base of the wall or pier as enlarged to distribute the weight upon the platform. There are certain general principles which are applicable to all classes of foundations.

1. Upon the natural soils the base of the masonry must be sufficient to transmit to the subsoil no more weight per unit of area than it will bear with safety.

2. The supporting surface must be as nearly homogeneous as possible and of equal resistance throughout, in order to avoid the necessity of elaborate methods to overcome such inequality.

3. The surface must be horizontal in one or several planes, or perpendicular to the direction of the pressure upon it.

4. The centre of pressure must coincide as nearly as possible with the centre of magnitude of the base.

5. The base of the foundation should be sunk below the reach of frost, even in rock; and in important buildings of a permanent character they should go much deeper to guard against unforeseen changes of surface or other disturbing causes.

6. The soil upon which it is proposed to build must be carefully examined and tested, lest an

apparently firm ground be of little thickness and cover a soft underlying stratum. Where possible the bearing power of the ground should be ascertained, and the permanent load proportioned accordingly, and if necessary the excavation must be continued until a sufficiently resisting material is found. The excavations and experience of neighbouring buildings upon the adjoining soil form a useful guide.

The enlargement of the base of the wall or pier to distribute the load over a larger surface is termed the footing. It is usually spoken of as made in steps, but this need not be, although if made of flat stones it naturally assumes that form. To resist cross strains upon the footing, its height should be about twice its projection. If made of a single bed of Portland cement concrete, its thickness may be once and a half its projection, lest it be broken off by the reaction of the compressed earth.

The condition that the centre of pressure shall coincide with the centre of figure of the base cannot generally be fulfilled in foundations upon city lots where the wall of the building extends to the limit of the lot, and where any increase of width of base must be made on the inside of the wall. When this is done the weight is no longer evenly distributed, but is greater at the edge nearer the centre of pressure. If, for instance, the footing be made to project on the inside only of the wall, and this projection be one half the thickness of the latter, the maximum pressure upon the soil will be at the outer edge, and one-third greater than if there were no footing. With ordinary buildings on firm ground a moderate deviation is not serious. In the tall steel skeleton buildings in which great weights are brought upon the points of support, the exterior walls are carried by cantilevers which rest centrally upon piers well within the limits of the site. (See Iron Construction.)

Of the natural soils, hard solid rock, cemented and indurated gravels, partially decomposed rocks which can with difficulty be excavated with the pick, whose stability is not impaired by saturation, which are not displaced by the movement of subsurface water, and which do not move laterally under pressure, — these are treated as incompressible. Solid rock requires only to be excavated to a depth below the reach of atmospheric influences, to have soft parts removed, wide joints and seams filled up, and, if much inclined, to be made nearly level. Hard rock will safely bear any pressure that can be brought upon it by masonry. If very rough it may be levelled with a bed of concrete.

If it should be necessary to place upon rock a heavily loaded steel or iron column, with its bed-plate or without it, a special study should be made.

Partially decomposed granite and gneiss rocks, indurated gravel, etc., will bear safely 10 tons (2000 pounds each) to the square foot. They need only to be levelled, and soft loose parts removed. Coarse gravel in a thick bed will carry 8 tons. Quartzose sand at a moderate depth, protected from flowing water, can be loaded with 4 tons per square foot with a slight initial compression — a fraction of an inch. If, however, the sand is exposed to the action of flowing water, and especially to water rising from below (springs), it is very unstable, and more so if it is very fine or micaceous. These sands settle into a hard and compact mass if the flow of water can be stopped ; otherwise they are of the most intractable, and each case generally requires special treatment.

The condition of the sand must be considered in each case. In deep excavations it has already received a certain compression from the superincumbent weight, but freshly moved sand may be compressed nearly twenty per cent by ramming and flooding with water. Artificial means of preventing lateral movement due to pressure, such as sheet-piling, are rarely necessary, the resistance of the adjacent earth being generally sufficient and increasing with the depth. This fact permits the weight that can be borne by the sand to be considerably increased beyond the limit named above. Compacted sand, after a slight initial compression, yields only by lateral flow, which in extreme cases lifts the adjacent surface. The remedy for this is to increase the depth of the foundation until the lateral *resistance* is sufficient to prevent the movement.

Clay varies greatly in character. Clays suitable for making bricks, those resulting from the decomposition of the granitic rocks, are very suitable for foundations in dry places. Those coming from the feldspars — and some of the transported clays have a great affinity for water — are very soft and wholly undesirable for foundations. The former will generally bear with safety 3 or 4 tons to the square foot, but it is better to limit the pressure to 2 or $2\frac{1}{2}$ tons. It is true that buildings have been erected which bore more heavily upon their foundations than the weights here given ; but soils vary in character by infinitely small degrees, and it is impossible to define closely the limits of one variety. The pressures here given are safe for ordinary earths of the kinds described.

On soils like that of Chicago, — a soft, saturated clay, with a firm layer on top, which will bear 3000 to 4000 pounds to the square foot, and where no better material would be reached by further excavation within reasonable limits, — very wide footings may be made by the use of steel beams bedded in concrete. The weight upon each column or pier must be computed, and the area of its base carefully proportioned to the weight. Upon this area, first covered with a bed of concrete 12 to 18 inches thick, is laid a course of steel beams ; upon them, transversely, a narrower course is laid, and then, if need be, others, until the bedplate of the pier is reached. As each course of steel is laid, fine concrete is rammed between the beams. The projection of each course beyond the one above it is just what the transverse strength of the beams will permit them to carry of the pressure on the foundation or of the reaction of the soil. If beams of sufficient strength are used, more than two courses will rarely be required. The column should rest on a large rigid pedestal. It should be noted that in these concrete-steel foundations, and in all other cases where cross strains come upon concrete, that material is to be made with Portland cement, with not more than three parts of sand.

The method of wide foundations may be applied to timber platforms, where they can be used; that is, when in water or in permanently wet earth. Thick planks or timbers are laid transversely of the trench; upon these longitudinal timbers are placed, and, if necessary, other transverse and longitudinal pieces, depending on the width of foundation and strength of the transverse timbers. The longitudinals distribute the weight lengthwise of the wall. This system of timber or iron beam footings is known as grillage. The piers of a railway bridge over the Susquehanna rest upon grillages which are real pyramids of 12-inch timbers crossing each other in alternate layers, the bottom course resting on piles.

Excavations for foundations, more especially on city lots, even of moderate depth, frequently need to be supported by sheet piling or shores. It will sometimes be more economical, and much more safe for adjacent buildings, to excavate for piers or short lengths of wall, and connect them above by arches if a continuous wall is needed, the pits being filled with concrete. This method may be adopted up to depths of 20 or 30 feet if a firm substratum is found at that depth. To avoid disturbance of surrounding ground alternate piers may be made, and the intermediate holes can then be safely excavated.

If the accessible strata underlying a building are not sufficiently strong to support its weight, the following methods present themselves: (1) the surface may be compacted to a certain depth; or (2) the weights may be transmitted to a lower bearing stratum by means of piles; or if the bearing stratum is at too great a depth to be reached by piles, (3) long piles may be driven into the softer soil, which will resist displacement and support the weight by the friction of the soil upon the surface of the pile.

Timber piles are used in two ways: to transmit the weight upon them directly to a hard stratum too deep to be economically reached in other ways; or, when the hard stratum cannot thus be reached, to support their load by their friction in the earth. In the former case, if the soil is stiff enough to give some lateral support to the pile, it may be loaded with as much as the timber will safely bear. If in water for a considerable part of its length, or in a fluid ground, it must be treated as a long column, subject to bending strains. If hard ground is to be penetrated, the pile may need an iron shoe to prevent its point from being bruised and broomed. The best shoe is a cast-iron solid cone with a flat base, in which is a pin to enter the foot of the pile and hold the shoe in place. The end of the pile, cut square, has thus a firm bearing on the shoe. Care must be taken that the pile is solidly fixed for at least a part of its length. Bridge piers built on short piles through silt, though resting on hard rock, have come to grief through the *tilting* of the piles. If the pile does not reach a bearing stratum its resistance to sinking will be due to its friction in the soil. For this case there is no general rule, although formulas innumerable have been published. These aim to deduce the weight which will be safely borne from the penetration of the pile under the last blows of a ram of certain weight falling from a given height. The uncertainty of the results is due to the variable character of different soils. The rule which best applies to the theoretical conditions is that of Weisbach and of Colonel Mason (U. S. A.), which probably gives results relatively correct for the same soil. It is as

follows: the load to be borne $= \dfrac{wh}{s} \times \dfrac{w}{w + w'}$,

in which w = weight of ram, w', weight of pile, h = height of fall, and s = penetration of pile at last blow. For ordinary mixed soils of sand and clay, the results of this formula should be divided by 4 to obtain *safe* results.

But, as has been said, the relation between penetration and load varies with different soils. In some soft materials, piles which have penetrated one foot or more under a single blow, after some hours of rest have not moved at all under repeated blows. In a moderately firm, plastic soil the friction on the surface of the pile may be taken at 600 pounds to the square foot. In sand, piles are with difficulty driven with the ram or hammer. They are easily put down by means of a "water jet." This means a small pipe carried down to the point of the pile through which water is forced. The water rising along the pile loosens the sand, and the pile will frequently sink by its own weight. The efficiency of the pile driver increases more rapidly with the weight of the hammer than with the height of fall. For this reason the steam hammer is the more efficient, being a very heavy hammer with short and rapid stroke. Experience, as well as theory, demonstrates that the blow of the hammer on the sound wood of the pile is much more effective than when the head of the pile is crushed and "broomed." With the steam hammer it is possible to avoid brooming altogether by placing a steel plate or an iron cap on the pile.

The piles, being driven, are cut off at, or below, low-water level, and either capped with hard timbers upon which a floor of planks is laid, or the earth between the piles is excavated to a depth of a foot or more, and a bed of concrete laid over the whole area occupied by piles and about a foot outside and over them, upon which the masonry may be built. Sometimes, to support a column or small pier, the piles are capped with large blocks of stone. In this case a large bedplate, or base, must be used, lest the weight, coming upon the edge of the stone, may cause it to tip, and throw excessive weight on a few piles.

If piles support a wall exposed to lateral pressures, as a quay wall, some of them should be driven obliquely, pointing from the wall, and fastened to the foundation, to act as buttresses, and prevent the wall being pushed out of line.

Some earths in water are so soft that they will not hold the piles. The latter may be kept in place by a mass of riprap (loose stone) filled between and around them.

Of the different methods of consolidating soft ground, that of short piles or sand piles is the most simple. It is of no value, however, in soils soft enough to flow under low pressures. In this method short piles are driven close together, not to reach a bearing stratum or to hold by friction, but to compress laterally the mass they penetrate, and so harden it. To be of value they should cover a much larger area than the base of the foundation, otherwise it would only transmit its load to a lower stratum of the same low-bearing power. It must also extend to such depth that the underlying ground will be confined by the adjacent soil. If the ground is dry, timber piles will not be durable. They may be drawn, and the holes filled with coarse sand well compacted. A similar surface consolidation has been practised in France. A long metal cone is driven into the soil, withdrawn, and the hole filled with sand. These methods are not recommended unless for light, temporary structures. Such sand piles exert a lateral pressure upon the surrounding ground.

The wide foundation trench filled with sand or gravel is of value when it transmits the weight to a depth where it will be confined laterally.

Inverted arches are sometimes used between detached piers to transmit the load over the length of the continuous footing between them, and it is said that the whole area of a building has been covered with inverted groined arches, the piers resting on their reversed abutments. These methods are quite efficient for the intermediate piers, but the terminal, or outside piers, are supported on one side only, and the thrust of the arches tends to displace them. Special provision must be made to meet this condition. In general, such foundations are neither desirable or necessary.

The weight upon the foundations of the modern steel skeleton buildings of great height renders it necessary that they should rest directly upon the rock, or its equivalent, when the rock is some distance below the water line, as in parts of New York. This is accomplished by the use of cylinders, or caissons, sunk by means of compressed air. (See Caisson, I.) The cylinder foundations are similar to the caisson, and are put down in a similar manner by the use of compressed air. The cylinder reaches to the surface. The tube connecting the air lock is placed in the cylinder, and weight given by filling around it with concrete. The caisson has also been used, like a diving bell, in harbour works. The masonry is built inside of it, and it is raised as the masonry is built up until within a few feet of water surface, when it is lightened and floated off. Thin cylinders of steel plates have also been sunk by means of water jets applied through a perforated ring around the bottom of the cylinder. If the ground is moderately free from boulders and from old timbers, the cylinder can be sunk with great facility. But it is still full of sand or mud, as the case may be, which must be excavated from the surface, while the cylinder is kept from collapsing as the earth is removed from the inside by wooden frames at intervals. When excavated to the hard bottom, and the latter cleaned, it is filled with concrete deposited through the water; or after a certain quantity of concrete has been placed, the cylinder may be pumped out, precautions being taken against collapse.

In foundations under water, or water-holding material, if the site can be dredged or a level bed prepared either by means of piles, or on a bearing stratum, a pier or section of wall may be built in an ordinary caisson, a box with detachable sides and a strong floor. It is floated to place and sunk either by building up the masonry or by letting in water. The sides are then detached, leaving the pier resting on a timber platform. If the bottom cannot be prepared, a cofferdam is frequently resorted to. If in shallow water and clean rock bottom, posts are connected by double waling pieces top and bottom, and two enclosures of such frames surround the site and are kept in place by weights. "Sheet-piling" or planks, their lower end cut to a sharp edge, are placed between the walings and driven down on the rock so that the sharp end will fit its shape. The space between the rows is then filled with clay, gravel, or other water-tight material, after which the cofferdam may be pumped out, and the masonry laid "in the dry." If the water is deep and the bottom sand or mud, heavy piles must first be driven to support the sheeting and all parts must be proportioned to the pressures against them. The cofferdam in deep water has been to a large extent superseded by the compressed air caisson.

Where the water is not deep, a pier may be made by filling with concrete a space surrounded by a permanent enclosure of sheet piling, upon a bottom first cleaned to a firm substratum. The frame of the enclosure is made of posts with double horizontal waling pieces. These are put in place after the site is dredged and stout planks are put down between the double walings, forming a caisson to contain the concrete. The enclosure of timber and plank remains permanently. Concrete deposited through water is not so sound or strong as if laid "in the dry," but the structures built as described above have been found durable and satisfactory. Other methods of foundation under water belong to large marine works which do not concern the architect. — W. R. Hutton.

Glenn Brown, *Healthy Foundations for Houses* (reprinted from the *Sanitary Engineer*), 1 vol. 12mo, 1885, New York, Van Nostrand ; Jules Gandard, *Foundations*, translated by L. F. Vernon Harcourt, M.A., New York, Van Nostrand, 1891, 1 vol. 16mo ; George T. Powell, *Foundations and Foundation Walls for all Classes of Buildings*, New York, 1889, 1 vol. 8vo.

FOUNDATION STONE. *A.* One stone of a foundation ; or prepared for or fit for a foundation.

B. One such stone prepared to be laid with especial ceremony. (See Cornerstone.)

FOUNDRY. A building or series of buildings in which is carried on the operation of casting metal, including the furnaces for the melting of the metal. Architecturally, the building has really no character, a simple shed or open structure, like a railway station of large size, forming the chief building, to which are added in some cases separate houses for steam engines and other appliances.

FOUNTAIN. Originally, a spring or continuous supply of water, natural or artificial, and hence, architecturally, a structure or artificial setting or mounting of such a water supply ; often extensive, costly, and architecturally splendid. Fountains are of two principal kinds : (1) those which offer a basin or several basins into which the water falls, and allow the water to be taken either direct from the spout or dipped from the basin ; (2) those which are intended chiefly for decorative effect and only casually, and some-

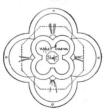

FOUNTAIN OF THE GATTESCHI, VITERBO, ITALY. PLAN.

times not at all, for the purposes of persons wishing to draw water.

Of (1) are the numerous fountains in the open squares of Italy, France, and other countries of Europe. The basin may be, as at Viterbo (built in the twelfth century), large and polygonal, with an upright shaft in the middle from which the water spurts ; of this kind are the public fountains at Salon in Provence, where they are the chief water supply for the whole town. Of this class also are those at Florence, adjoining the Palazzo Vecchio, the fountain built in the sixteenth century with a group of Neptune and Triton by Ammanati, two much smaller fountains in the Piazza dell' Annunziata, and at Rome, the great fountain in the Piazza Navona ; as are also a great number of fountains, some small and unimportant, some large and magnificent. Most of the fountains in the United States are of this kind. Where the city is large and contains many fountains besides other arrangements for obtaining water, as notably in Rome, those fountains with large round and polygonal basins are very commonly shut off with railings, and treated merely as works of art and as ornaments of the streets and squares in which they are situated. There are also those fountains in which the water springs from the face of a wall, the basin being on one side only. Of these the largest is the fountain of Trevi at Rome, but there are many others, sometimes very small, as where four fountains spring out of four opposite angle walls on the Via delle Quattro Fontane, and others very architecturally treated, as in Paris.

Of (2) are especially those fountains at Versailles which adorn the great gardens of the château and which are allowed to play on Sundays and holidays ; sometimes in their complete force (*les grandes eaux*), but more often in a reduced form, the cost being very great for each separate display. These fountains in their original form were the work of Louis XIV. at the time when the gardens were completed. At the garden of the palace of Herrenhausen, near Hanover, there are a few fountains, and one of these is of singular beauty, the stream being thrown to a height of something over two hundred feet in a single jet.

There are some fountains which partake of both of these characters ; thus the two great fountains in Rome in the Piazza di S. Pietro, where each has two basins of bronze raised above the large one on the level of the square, the water rising above the uppermost basin in a small jet and falling again over the rim of it into the larger, and thence into the great basin below. These are imitated at Munich and in other cities of Europe, the charm being always in the constant flow of water in a sheet, not very large, but pleasant both to the eye and ear. Somewhat akin to this system are those foun-

PLATE III

FOUNTAIN

That of S. Sulpice, Paris ; erected, 1847, in the square upon which fronts the church of the same name. The designer was Louis Visconti ; the four statues of Bossuet, Fénelon, Massilon, and Fléchier are by different sculptors. Attention may be called to the very unusual treatment of the pilasters in connection with the diagonal ressauts, and the heavy ribs of the roof.

tains which depend for their effect entirely on the overflow from an upper basin. Such a one is that at the Trocadéro palace in Paris, where the sheet of water is given a peculiarly beautiful effect. It is to be noted that extreme care is needed in the adjustment of such a basin to bring its edge to an exact horizontal plane, so

primal motive of decoration being almost ignored. The cistern or other water supply is completely concealed, perhaps from motives of precaution to guard its purity, and the water runs in small streams from faucets. As a contrast to these structures is to be noted the great reliance placed upon the beauty of the moving water itself, and

FOUNTAIN OF THE GATTESCHI, VITERBO, ITALY. (SEE PLAN.)

as to allow a thin sheet of water to overflow uniformly at all points.

The fountains of Constantinople and other Mohammedan cities are of a peculiar kind in that they consist each of a small closed building, polygonal or rectangular, ornamental, decorated with colonnades, arcades, niches, and cupolas, besides carving and painted tiles, but having only very small basins to receive the water; this

also its sound, in nearly all the European examples.

Some recent inventions have been employed to diversify fountains still more; thus in New York, jets have been introduced which rise high and then subside to a lower elevation at very brief intervals. (Cuts, cols. 83, 84, 86.)

FOUNTAIN OF BETHESDA. At New York, in Central Park, at the foot of the Ter-

FOUNTAIN AT NUREMBERG, CALLED SCHÖNE BRUNNEN, 1385–1395.

race. The subject is "The Angel troubling the Waters."

FOUNTAIN OF CUVIER. At Paris, near the *Jardin des Plantes ;* built in the reign of Louis Philippe on the site of an earlier one.

FOUNTAIN OF GRENELLE. At Paris, in the southwest, on the Rue de Grenelle. Designed by Bouchardon in the reign of Louis XV. This fountain has an interesting architectural disposition, emblematic of the city of Paris, and the rivers Seine and Marne, with statues of the four Seasons in niches, and symbolical bas-reliefs.

FOUNTAIN OF LOUVOIS. At Paris, in the Place Louvois opposite the National Library. It is a very graceful design of Visconti, with sculpture by Klagmann, which, though it has been carried out in cast iron coated with bronze, is effective as seen through the veil of constantly falling water.

FOUNTAIN OF MOLIÈRE. At Paris, near the great National Library, Rue Richelieu ; a wall fountain with a seated figure of Molière by B. G. Seurre, and two statues of Muses by Pradier.

FOUNTAIN OF MONTE CAVALLO. At Rome, in the Piazza del Quirinale ; famous for the colossal groups of men restraining horses ; called also Castor and Pollux. Of Greco-Roman style, probably late.

FOUNTAIN OF NEPTUNE. At Florence, at the angle of the Palazzo Vecchio, by Ammanati, sixteenth century.

FOUNTAIN OF S. MICHEL. At Paris, at the southern end of the bridge of the same name, built in 1860.

FOUNTAIN OF S. SULPICE. At Paris, in front of the church of S. Sulpice ; designed by Visconti, and built in 1857.

FOUNTAIN OF THE ACQUA PAOLA. At Rome, on the right bank of the Tiber, near the church of S. Pietro in Montorio. The basin and the other decorations are partly taken from ancient buildings.

FOUNTAIN OF THE ACQUA VERGINE. Same as Fountain of Trevi, below.

FOUNTAIN OF THE INNOCENTS. At Paris. Now near the great market (Halles Centrales) and placed in a small square. This was first built in the sixteenth century by Pierre Lescot, with sculpture by Jean Goujon ; but it was moved in the reign of Louis XVI., much altered and defaced, and the modern restoration of it is only partial. Its exquisite bas-reliefs are widely known, but the fountain as it was originally designed exists only in more or less authentic prints ; it seems, however, to have been of exquisite design, and was certainly a high, upright, vaulted pavilion, with four arches in the four sides, each flanked by pilasters, above the entablature of which rose a sculptured attic and a small cupola.

FOUNTAIN OF THE LIONS. In the Alhambra, at Granada, Spain. It stands in the middle of the court to which it gives its name, Court of the Lions. It consists of an alabaster basin, twelve-sided, and supported by twelve lions, which are very rudely carved, although their lack of realism may have some quasi-heraldic significance.

FOUNTAIN OF THE MEDICI. At Paris, in the Luxembourg Gardens, with several mythological statues by Ottin.

FOUNTAIN AT AUTUN, NOW DESTROYED ; WORK OF THE EARLY RENAISSANCE.

FOUNTAIN OF THE MERCATO NUOVO. In Florence ; that with the bronze boar, an excellent copy of the antique in the Uffizi gallery.

FOUNTAIN OF THE NYMPHS. Same as Fountain of the Innocents, above.

FOUNTAIN OF THE OBSERVATORY. At Paris, near the Luxembourg Gardens, built in 1874 ; remarkable for the group by Carpeaux of the four Quarters of the World supporting the Sphere.

FOUNTAIN OF THE TORTOISES (delle Tartarughe). In the heart of Rome, near the Tiber.

FOUNTAIN OF THE TRITON. At Rome; the work of Bernini. It stands in the Piazza Barberini, in the northwestern corner of Rome, near the Villa Ludovisi.

FOUNTAIN OF TREVI. At Rome. The termination of the ancient aqueduct, called Aqua Virgo (see Aqueduct). The water springs from an elaborate architectural façade, forming one of the walls of the Palazzo Poli; the basins in front of it are very large, and in places are accessible to all. The water is celebrated for its purity, and there are interesting popular superstitions concerning it.

FOUR COURTS, THE. A public building in Dublin, Ireland; built at the close of the eighteenth century. It is occupied by the Courts of Chancery, of Queen's Bench, of Common Pleas, etc., and many minor offices. It contains decorative and historical sculpture, and is a building of importance.

FOWL HOUSE. (See Poultry House.)

FOXTAIL WEDGE. A wedge of hard wood or metal, to secure a tenon, pin, or the like, firmly in a mortise or other hole which does not extend through the piece, by its insertion part way into the end of the tenon or pin, so that, when driven into the hole, the wedge is forced up into the tenon or pin, forcing its sides apart. When the bottom of the mortise is wider than the mouth, a tenon so wedged cannot be withdrawn, as it then forms a dovetail.

FOX WEDGE. Same as Foxtail Wedge.

FOYER. In French, a room for gatherings or meetings; especially, in theatrical language, the room of meeting for the actors, the dancers, or other persons connected with the theatre, and to which, under certain conditions, other persons, such as patrons of the theatre, are admitted. In a large French theatre, the foyer of the actors is an important and even richly decorated hall. The term in French is also extended to signify a place of promenade for the audience, as between acts, or during the long recess between two pieces. At a French opera house there will generally be three foyers, that of the singers, that of the ballet, and that of the public.

The term is used in English in any or all of the above significations, and without much accuracy. — R. S.

FRACTABLE; FRACT TABLE. A coping upon the gable wall of a building when carried above the roof to form a parapet; especially, when broken into curves, steps, or the like. Special names have been given to different portions of the fractable, according to the various outlines of the gable; a flat portion at the bottom being coped with a Foot Table; curved portions with Boltels or Bottles; a rectangular step with its copings is a Square.

FRACTABLE: THREE GABLES COPED WITH FRACTABLES; UPMARK, SWEDEN.

FRAME (I.). A structure of smaller parts brought together to form a whole; especially, in building, an assemblage of slender and relatively long pieces (see Framing). The carcase of a house, when of masonry, is not called the frame, but the skeleton of wood or ironwork put up for a building or part of a building is so designated. Frames may be composed of hollow parts, as tubes or boxes : thus, the common window frame of sliding sash windows is made of two upright boxes to contain the weights and cords, a sill below, and a head or yoke above.

Box Frame. Same as Cased Frame.

Cased Frame. A window frame for sliding sash having hollow uprights to contain the sash weights, called pulley boxes or pulley cases. These are composed of the pulley style, forming the jamb next the sash, and having at the top a pulley for each sash (usually two) ; the inside casing; the outside casing; and (except in cheap work) the back lining. These boxes form the two upright sides ; the head or yoke and the sill are secured to them.

FRAME (II.). A border prepared to enclose and isolate a picture, bas-relief, or the like. The use of the frame in strictly architectural practice is not very common, because the wainscoting, marble lining, stucco decoration, or the like, usually provides for the setting of whatever decorative panels may be inserted ; but in some styles of decoration the frame is designed especially for the work of art, and in this case it may frequently be more or less movable. In Italy, in the seventeenth century, paintings were often enclosed by extremely massive, carved, and coloured wooden frames, having 8 to 12 inches on the flat and 4 or 5 inches projection, and these often took varied forms, as oblong octagons, ovals, and the like. The picture, or other work of art, with its frame, would then be prepared for a definite place ; but was capable of being used elsewhere. In like manner, the paintings of the Venetian school, applied to walls, and especially to the large flat ceilings of palaces and neoclassic churches, were framed with wood, carved and gilded, and the whole composition of many pictures and their frames has remained in place permanently for three centuries. Something of this is seen in the movable frames which are still retained as mounts for portraits and other paintings of the same period. (For the Frame as used in Mural Paintings, see Border.)
          — R. S.

FRAME BOARD. Same as Panel Board.

FRAME HOUSE; FRAMED HOUSE. A house built by means of a framework, usually of timber and scantling. This, in modern times, is covered outside by boarding, shingling, sheet metal, and the like, and within by wood sheathing or by plaster. In the Middle Ages and in the fifteenth and following centuries timber houses throughout Europe were elaborately framed, but were not sheathed as above described. (See Black and White Work; Châlet; Half Timber; Wood Construction, Part I.)

FRAMING. Originally and properly, the putting together of parts to produce a whole ;

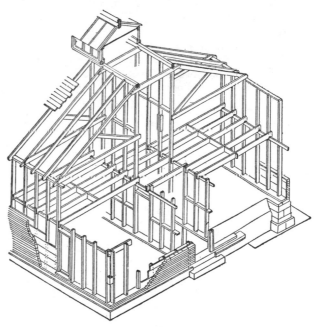

FRAME HOUSE.

The walls and partitions of studs, with interties to carry floor-beams and for stiffness ; roof of simple rafters, but with a curb enclosing the opening for a lantern. This is a German model ; and it is shown that an outer shell of brick is intended.

the making of a structure of definite form and purpose out of parts especially prepared for it. In modern building, especially the putting together of slender and comparatively long pieces, such as beams, joists, girders, posts, and the like, of timber ; or similar or corresponding parts of iron ; or both in a skeleton ; which skeleton is the essential structure of the building or part of the building. By a peculiar forcing of this signification, the term was formerly used by carpenters exclusively for the putting together of wood by means of mortises and tenons. This distinction disappears, of course, in ironwork of all kinds, and, in modern times, rarely obtains in any class of work. — R. S.

Balloon Framing. (See under B.)

Braced Framing; Full Framing. In the United States, the method of constructing wooden buildings in which the principal timbers, as posts and girts, are secured by mortise and tenon joints, pinned together and stiffened by many diagonal braces secured in like manner. Thus distinguished from Balloon Framing.

FRANCE, ARCHITECTURE OF. That of the modern state of France, as it has been since 1871. For the purposes of this inquiry, it may be divided into ten parts, namely:—

PART
I. Parisian France
II. Flemish France
III. Normandy
IV. Lorraine
V. Brittany
VI. Angevin France
VII. Aquitanian France
VIII. Auvergne
IX. Burgundian France
X. Languedoc and Provence

This region was all included in the Roman Gallia. The Roman remains found in all parts of it may be treated together, and very briefly, as the study given to them has been but superficial.

For the epoch of the earlier Romanesque architecture, we have to consider the immediate territory of the kings of France (that is, of Laon first and later Paris) separately from such great outlying states as Normandy, annexed to the crown of France in the twelfth century; Brittany, hardly one socially with the French monarchy during this period; the dukedom and the county of Burgundy, Lorraine, Poitou, Auvergne, and all the south and southwest. For the Gothic epoch, we have still to consider a number of states as independent or nearly independent of the crown, and others whose relation to the crown was constantly varying, with the result that their social condition is not necessarily the same as that of the undisputed and continuous royal dominion, and their building and decoration very different. It is not until the beginning of the Renaissance in France that the country is one in the modern sense; and even then the religious wars put off for a century the perfect unification of the kingdom, while also the boundaries were more limited than they were at a later time.

The purpose of the above remarks is to point out that the term "French Architecture," or French influence in architecture, must be used with different meanings when it is applied to different epochs of time; and, moreover, that French architecture is not altogether the same thing as the architecture of France. The buildings contained within the boundaries of the

France of to-day are those with which we have to do. These are very numerous, and their interest is very great. Even a list of the important buildings and those representative of the different styles in each district would occupy a volume. A day's walk from one small town to another may be through a country whose architectural remains deserve a month's study. In fact, France is the richest country in Europe in buildings of value to the Western student, and later than the time of the fall of the Roman Imperial dominion. It is true that the Latin and semi-Byzantine churches of Italy are not equalled by the few remains of the earliest mediæval work in France; but what there is of these earlier days and the somewhat later domed churches of the centre and southwest is as unique in every way as the Latin architecture of Italy, and is at least as important in the development of more recent architecture. In the eleventh century France takes the lead in Europe, with the noblest and richest as well as most varied Romanesque. In the twelfth century the lead is still more decided, in spite of the magnificent German round-arched cathedrals; for the Gothic art beginning about 1150 is entirely French in the strictest sense, all the other European lands having taken their primary and most of their subsequent impulses from the French royal domain. The later and the latest Gothic, that of the fifteenth century, which the French writers treat as the earliest work of the Renaissance, is still the first of its time in Europe in interest and value; and when, at the beginning of the sixteenth century, the classical feeling coming from Italy had really gained a foothold in the North, the resulting styles (those of Louis XII., Francis I., and Henry II.) are the most beautiful result of the new movement, and are beautiful and suggestive in a peculiar way. In like manner the later styles, those which followed the pacification of France under Henry IV., long remained the models for Europe in a special sense; for, in France, this style of the Decadence is preserved from lifelessness and hopeless chill, and the attempts at revival under Louis XV. and under Louis XVI. are each in its own way full of the interest which attaches to bold experiments guided by good taste.

On the whole, then, the architecture of France since the beginning of the Romanesque period is the most important for the modern student.

There remain prehistoric structures of rude stones in many parts of the country, and especially in the northwest, as in Brittany. At Quiberon and at Carnac (Morbihan) are remarkable and famous groups of rough stones; dolmens and cromlechs are numerous in the same region, and there are remarkable tomb entrances at Essé (Ille-et-Vilaine) and at Bagneux. Pre-Roman fortifications of the Gallic tribes remain at several points, as at Roc-de-Vic (Corrèze) and at the great hill near Autun, where undoubtedly stood the fortified town of Bibracte, and these fortifications are often singularly interesting as confirming and illustrating the *Commentaries* of Cæsar on the Gallic War. No remains of architectural monuments, in the proper sense, exist of any time previous to the Roman dominion. There is in the far south a Greek influence, of which there will be mention in Part X. (Provence and Languedoc); but throughout the north the remains of buildings of the first four centuries of our era are wholly Imperial Roman in character, showing less deviation from the accepted administrative type furnished by the buildings of the Imperial city than do the remains of the same epoch in North Africa or Syria (see those terms). Besides the buildings of Provence and Languedoc, there is a curious temple at Vienne (Isère); at Nantua (Ain) are the remains of a temple; and two ruins of the same kind are at Autun. Temples, like theatres, being generally built within the walls of the ancient city, are apt to be so covered by buildings of the modern town that exploration of them is extremely difficult. City gates, however, and memorial archways are often left in good condition. There are many in the south, but in the north the two

Roman gates of Autun, the Porte Noire at Besançon, the double gateway at Saintes (Charente-Inférieure), now rebuilt on another site, but with accuracy, and the splendid triple arch of Reims, are of peculiar importance. Roman aqueducts remain in part in many regions of the country, and those near Paris, especially at Arcueil, are identified with the aqueducts built or enlarged by the Emperor Julian to supply the baths of his favourite city, Lutetia, which baths are now recognized as part of the Roman construction on the south bank of the Seine, where the Hôtel de Cluny now stands. There are remains of Roman theatres at many points, and the theatre of Besançon has left fine architectural fragments; but the only structure of this kind which has been found at all complete, in the north, is that at Lillebonne (Seine-Inférieure). This has been uncovered, and partly studied and analyzed since 1840; and in the same town are remains of Roman bathing establishments and some splendid mosaics. A magnificent amphitheatre existed at Bordeaux, of which a fragment remains, and is called popularly the palace of Gallienus. At Cahors (Lot) a similar fragment is called Porte de Diane. The monument at Cussy and that at Vienne are of great interest; and hardly less important is one at Estelle (Haute-Garonne), and one near Tours. The study of Roman remains in the north of France has not, however, been carried very far. Thus, great numbers of villas have been discovered, but in hardly any instance have the plans been studied exhaustively. When such investigation has been carried on, the record of it is generally confined to some local archæological journal whose circulation is not great. It is to be noticed, however, that many of the large villas seem to have been fortified at the time of the barbarian invasions, and that in this way they passed gradually into the condition of mediæval strong castles, in which case the Roman remains have either disappeared altogether, or are deeply buried under the more modern structure. — R. S.

FRANCE, ARCHITECTURE OF; Part I.; Parisian France; that controlled from an early period by the French monarchy, but excepting Normandy, which has peculiar characteristics. No part of this region was dependent upon the Holy Roman Empire after the time of the Treaty of Verdun (843). It included in the fifteenth century the Isle-de-France, Picardy, Chartres, Vendôme, Touraine, Blois, and Orléans, the great countship of Champagne, and the dukedom of Berri, to which may be added the countship of Nevers as being more nearly akin to the royal country than to its southern neighbours, politically and socially. This great tract of country, embracing the modern departments of Aisne, Ardennes, Aube, Cher, Eure-et-Loir, Haute-Marne, Indre, Indre-et-Loire, Loiret, Loir-et-Cher,

Marne, Nièvre, Oise, Seine-et-Marne, Seine-et-Oise, Somme, and Yonne, has for its most northern towns of importance Abbeville and St. Quentin; for its westernmost landmark, Tours or Chinon; for its easternmost, Chaumont or Langres; and as marking the southernmost boundary, Nevers, or Châteauroux. It is within this region that the Romanesque architecture took that constructional form which made the growth from it of the Gothic system possible; it is here that the Gothic construction and Gothic art grew up and had its most perfect development; it is within this district that all but one or two of the most important Gothic cathedrals were built and still stand; and here the greater part of the late Gothic or

ture is in a way discoverable, if we pass in review the architectural growth of this region. There will be exceptional chapters in that history which have nothing to do with Parisian France, but those chapters do not lead on to the history of the times following.

The Romanesque architecture, as we find it within this region, ignores the cupola on pendentives and all attempt at vaulting a square by means of such a cupola (for which see Part VII.); it ignores almost wholly the pointed arch which was rather common in Aquitanian France and in Auvergne (see Parts VII., VIII.). Every effort was made to vault the churches in a way as nearly as possible like to those chambers of ancient Roman baths and other buildings, which, in the ninth and again in the eleventh century, were somewhat familiar to the inhabitants. As, however, the Roman system of building with the solid block of mortar masonry could hardly be achieved by these poor and half-organized communities, they undertook the bold task of doing what the Romans had never done, and building groined vaults with separate visible stones. These were not, indeed, what we now call cut stone; they were rather what we should call

FRANCE, PART I.: NAVE OF ABBEY CHURCH AT VÉZELAY (YONNE); 12TH CENTURY.
The semicircular transverse arches have sunk.

Flamboyant structures were erected. It is at least equal to any part of France in the value and beauty of its Renaissance châteaux, and in the importance of those few churches which we have from the Renaissance epoch. It is in Paris and its immediate neighbourhood that by far the most important late neoclassic buildings were built, those which in the seventeenth and eighteenth centuries set the pace for the development of the Post-Renaissance styles throughout Europe. The architectural monuments of this region are so very numerous and of such peculiar importance that it will be impracticable to give even such a brief and merely suggestive list of buildings as can be furnished for other districts (see Parts II. to X.). On the other hand, the history of French architec-

squared rubble or dressed rubble, no piece being larger than a man could carry on his shoulder or otherwise up a ladder, and then put into place without the aid of machinery. The vaults thus constructed were sprung from walls which were of necessity very thick and heavy, much heavier than strength alone required. The idea of a solid buttress projecting several feet beyond the wall was too bold for the timid workmen of that time; they used, indeed, a separately combined piece of masonry at the point where the vaults pushed horizontally in the most formidable way, and this piece of more carefully laid masonry they allowed to project very slightly beyond the exterior face of the wall; but this was all they tried. Under these circumstances the aisles, being narrow and also

FRANCE, ARCHITECTURE OF.   PLATE I

Front of the church of S. Gilles (Gard) ; this portal is the most florid piece   Arles, embodies all the charm of that style.   This work is probably of 1130
of Romanesque in the south of France, and, with the front of S. Trophime at   and the following years.   The church has never been completed.

low, could be vaulted without much risk, and that with square groined vaults very similar to Roman work in all except the details of construction ; but the nave could hardly be vaulted successfully in any such way, and the history of those centuries is in great measure a record of how one high vault after another fell in ruin, and took the walls with it.

It is not asserted here that it was only in this part of France that these experiments were being tried. All along the Rhine, and at Cluny in Burgundy (Part IX.), and in the south near Périgord, in the southwest, and in Provence in the southeast, the same experiment was being tried. Even in Palestine the crusading Franks developed a system of groined vaulting with cut stone ; and this, carried out under the direct influence of the splendid stone constructions of the fourth, fifth, and sixth centuries, then in perfect condition in many parts of Syria, led to a neater, fairer, and more elegant system of twelfth century building than any used in Western Europe. The reason why the Romanesque vaulting of this part of France is of such peculiar importance to us is because it led directly to the ribbed vault of the Gothic period.

This ribbed vault grows directly out of the use of the transverse arch (*arc doubleau*) and the corresponding wall arch (*formeret*). Two transverse arches and two wall arches form the outline and the frame of each Romanesque groined vault ; that is to say, of each "square" of vaulting, which vaulting square may be a parallelogram of any proportion. The builder of each vaulting square must have felt, as he sprung the transverse arches across the nave and similar

arches along the lines of the wall, whether the wall in question was built altogether beneath or beside his new arch, or was yet to be carried up, — he must have felt that if only he could spring a similar arch diagonally across his

FRANCE, PART I.: NAVE OF CATHEDRAL AT NOYON (OISE).

vaulting square his work would be half done. Without such diagonal arch he had the difficult problem of the Roman groined vault to be imitated in inferior materials and by means of a costly and troublesome centring of wood. With the possible diagonal arch, he must have felt that the problem would disappear, and that he would have nothing but triangles to vault : one triangle at a time, one piece less than one quarter the size of the vaulting square, and stayed on each of its three sides by a solid arch which he could trust. The marvel is that this, like all other bold innovations in building, should have been so slow in coming.

As to the irregularly shaped intervals left above the ring-shaped aisle which runs around the apse — the deambulatory — the difficulty of vaulting this was very great indeed ; and this difficulty also disappeared at once and altogether the moment the idea of a diagonal arch took shape. For here another improvement suggested itself, one destined to have the greatest effect upon the future history of architecture. The continuous diagonal arch came to be looked upon as two half arches, each springing from an abutment below to a keystone or boss (*clef*) at the crown of the vault. This idea once seized, and the clef made an abutment in its turn, so that each half arch became in itself an independent arch depending upon two separate points of support, one at its foot and the other at its top, anything could be done. An irregularly shaped vaulting square might have five of these half arches, or seven, or four so arranged that no two of them would form a continuous arch. The clef would be kept in place by their mutual pressure, and each half arch would stand for itself, an almost independent member.

The high vaults of the nave, of the choir, or of the transept were at once seen to be as easy as the low vaults over aisle or chapel ; but also at once it was evident to the alert and now thoroughly awakened minds of the builders of 1160 what the difficulty would be of resisting the thrust of these high vaults, and at the same time the way to overcome that difficulty. It would not do to build a huge buttress wall upon the transverse arches of the aisle, nor yet to start such a buttress wall from the foundation beyond the floor of the aisle, and thus cut the aisle into short pieces. It became evident that one more arch or half arch could be used, namely, one which would leap across the whole width of the aisle, and transport the thrust of one corner of each vaulting-square to a buttress pier built outside of the aisle, and engaged perhaps with its outer wall. This was the flying buttress, and these two great elements in building, the ribbed vault and the flying buttress, were inseparable, and together made up Gothic building. The vault dependent upon separate arches strong enough to carry its weight, which arches we call ribs, and the flying buttress carrying the thrust of one group of ribs from the abutment to any place where it might be convenient to take it up finally by the dead weight and resistance of the great mass of masonry, —

out of this combination all Gothic architecture grew.

All this took place in the Isle-de-France. Within a small district of which the city of Paris forms the centre are to be found all the very early churches in which Gothic building as above described was used frankly and without restraint. The little church of Tracy-le-Val, and that at Saint-Léger in the forest of Laigue, together with the abbey church of Morienval (all in Oise), are for us moderns the earliest monuments of the nascent Gothic art ; and in the great abbey of Saint-Denis (Seine), especially in its porch and choir, is found the first large monument in which the Gothic builders can be seen working at their ease. This abbey of Saint-Denis has been called the latest work of the Transition, and as its date is known (1140) it fixes the development of Gothic building at least twenty-five years earlier than it has been the custom to date this step in building. Louis Gonse (op. cit.), writing shortly before 1890, says without hesitation that the practice of building the vault "sur croisée d'ogives" (that is to say, on diagonal ribs) was practised in the Isle-de-France as early as 1125. The evidence for this is not exactly complete if a series of monuments of certain date is required. It is rather a safe conclusion drawn from the comparison of a large amount of circumstantial evidence. Neither the dates of the churches nor the exact time in the construction of each church when a given vaulting square was completed are ascertainable with perfect accuracy. Churches as early as the date given above and with a certain part of their vaulting dependent upon constructional ribs exist at Berri (Oise) and at La Noël-Saint-Martin (Oise), and indeed a near approach to rib vaulting is to be found in *La Basse Œuvre*, the ancient church of S. Étienne at Beauvais (Oise). In the neighbourhood of Soissons several small churches have been examined, none of which can be later than 1140, and each of which shows successful attempts at vaulting with ribs. In the neighbourhood of Laon there are similar examples. At Saint-Leu d'Esserent (Oise) is a further advance in the vaulting of the most interesting Norman church. Finally in Paris itself we have a building of known date with Gothic vaulting completely established in all the choir and the deambulatory. This is the former church of S. Martin des Champs, now forming a part of the *Conservatoire des Arts et Métiers ;* there is general agreement as to the date of the choir, namely, about 1140.

Before the twelfth century was out there were begun the Gothic cathedrals of Paris, Amiens, Chartres, Laon, Noyon, Soissons, Reims, and Meaux, all within the district we are now considering (see Cathedral), and immediately afterward were begun those of Bourges, Troyes,

FRANCE, PART I.: SENS CATHEDRAL (YONNE); INTERIOR, LOOKING EAST.

Tours, Sens, and Senlis, also belonging to Parisian France. Contemporaneously with these great buildings were begun a number of churches, now impossible to trace, besides a great number which still exist, and carried on with varying degrees of speed in all parts of this favoured region. No one cathedral and scarcely a church has come down to us completed in the style of the early Gothic art, and this because the changes in style adopted by the builders followed one another more rapidly than the walls could rise and the vaults be turned. Everywhere there are later vaults upon earlier substructures, later naves added to earlier choirs, chapels of a still later date built around these earlier choirs, towers begun at the time of the Transition, finished in the fifteenth century, and windows of early form filled with tracery of the latest Flamboyant taste. Fortunately the determination of dates is not of the utmost importance to the student of architectural art; and a design like the west front of Chartres with Romanesque porches covered with sculpture, one tower complete to its cross of the earliest Gothic taste and constituting the most beautiful mediæval tower in Europe, and one tower begun at the same time but finished in the florid style of the fifteenth century — such a composition, as it exists, is capable of giving every whit as much pleasure historically and artistically as if we had the west front as its master of the works conceived it about 1160.

The changing Gothic styles have never been treated chronologically. No one seems to have followed closely the growth of that singular spirit which refuses to accept permanently that which has formed it, which reaches out after new and perhaps less desirable things, and which wrecks in a few years every splendid conception of man — the spirit of continuity being so much less powerful than the search for novelty in all artistic tendencies. There is no opportunity here even to describe the different Gothic styles which succeeded one another in this Parisian region; it is only to be stated here that the most important monuments of the later Gothic style are the choir of Beauvais cathedral (Oise), completed about 1270, and repaired with slight alterations after the vault had fallen in consequence of the too great boldness of the structure; the famous and splendid Sainte Chapelle of Paris; the church of S. Urbain at Troyes, begun about 1270; and contemporaneous with this several civic buildings such as the Synodal Hall of Sens. All the cathedrals have much work of the middle and close of the thirteenth century, and this in the form of porches, chapels, and the like, if not in the main members of the structure. In the fourteenth century, however, there are no important ecclesiastical buildings. Nothing that can be compared with S. Ouen at Rouen is to

be found in this whole Parisian region. It is not until after the close of the Hundred Years' War that, in the fifteenth century, the Flamboyant style begins to make its wonderful record here as elsewhere throughout the north. The peculiar leadership of the central region has, indeed, passed away; its work has been done both socially and artistically in the creation of the powerful French monarchy and a masterful French leadership in architectural art. The florid architecture of Abbeville (S. Wulfran), of Saint-Riquier and of Notre Dame de l'Épine, of the north tower of Chartres cathedral, the church of S. Jacques at Paris (the tower only remaining), of the palace hall at Poitiers, and of the house of Jacques Cœur at Bourges, of Châteaudun and of the Hôtel de Cluny at Paris, vies with that of the splendid monuments of Rouen in the west, Albi and Brou in the south, and Avioth in the far northeast.

The architecture of the Renaissance took its rise of necessity with the royal influence, because they were the nobles of the court who received the Italian influence and who were prepared to push the extremely unclassical and un-Italian movement which began under Louis XII. In this reign France was prosperous and at peace, and a number of most interesting buildings were erected in that curious modified style halfway between Gothic and Renaissance, of which one wing of the château of Blois is our best example. Other buildings of this character are the Hôtel de Ville at Douai (Nord), of Dreux (Eure-et-Loir) and of Compiègne (Oise), and of Saint-Quentin (Aisne), and the bell towers of the cathedral of Tours (Indre-et-Loire). The château of Gaillon of this time has left only a few fragments and a splendid memory. Each of these was completed before 1520, except the Tours belfries, which lingered on for some years longer. Under Francis I., whose reign began in 1515, a more classical influence was soon to prevail, and yet the buildings of his reign, even in the immediate neighbourhood of the royal residence, whether at Paris, at Blois, or at Fontainebleau, are as far as possible from showing a purely classical or even a purely Italian spirit. The northern wing of the château of Blois, and the whole of the great royal hunting seat at Chambord, the château of Chenonceau, the château of Saint-Germain-en-Laye, and large parts of the château of Fontainebleau preserve this style for us. The château of Écouen (Seine-et-Oise) is enough in itself to show the more formal side of the building of this epoch. The admirable church of S. Eustache at Paris in its first conception belongs to this same epoch. This is almost the only building in which a fair attempt was made to unite non-Gothic details with a Gothic structure in any ecclesiastical building; and while the opinion is frequently expressed that this

PLATE V

FRANCE, ARCHITECTURE OF. PLATE II

Albi (Tarn); the cathedral church of S. Cécile, from the northeast. The roof is vaulted with ribs in the true Gothic manner, but the buttresses which take up the thrust of the vaults are the divisions between chapels, and the external walls are kept high and of uniform surface, apparently with the idea of making the church serve as a fortification. The walls are entirely of brick.

FRANCE, PART I.: AMIENS CATHEDRAL; INTERIOR, LOOKING EAST.

attempt was a failure in this particular edifice, such failure will not appear so evident if the building is considered by itself without reference either to the Gothic buildings preceding it or the graver classic churches which were to follow it. It was an experiment destined to have no results, but not the less interesting on this account. With the reign of Henri II., the son and successor of Francis I., the Renaissance proper in France draws to an end. The last Valois, Charles IX. and Henri III., did little work, and yet it was in their reigns that the palace of the Tuileries was built in its original shape and large parts of the Louvre as we now have it were completed, especially the western side of the square court. The château of Écouen is also in great part of this epoch. With the religious wars there was a great pause in the

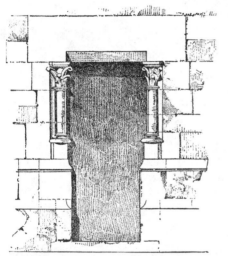

FRANCE, PART I.: CHARTRES CATHEDRAL; DOOR-
WAY, NORTH SIDE OF CLOCK TURRET.

activity of building, but with Henri IV. that manly and simple style took shape whose traces are to be found especially in the city of Paris, still intact in the Place des Vosges, and still traceable, though nearly ruined, in the Place Dauphine. The most showy building of this time is the original palace of the Cardinal Mazarin, fronting on the Rue Vivienne, and now incorporated in the great National Library.

Of the succeeding reign are the Hôtel de Sully, Rue S. Antoine, Paris, so much of the Palais Royal as remains intact, chiefly the front toward the south on the Cour d'Honneur; and outside of Paris the central part of the great château of Versailles, namely, the brick and stone edifice forming the three sides of the Cour de Marbre and distinguished by its façades in red and white from the more severe fronts immediately adjoining. The palace of the Luxem-

bourg is of this time, and the admirable church of S. Gervais S. Protais, both in Paris.

The reign of Louis XIV. was a score of years old already before the freer design of his predecessor's time disappeared. Then, as the grandiose feeling of the great king prevailed with all his ministers and employees, the stately but cold classic style superseded everything else. The colossal order was not universal; even in his favourite château at Versailles it is not used in the long façades, but, in the chapel, the disposition of a large colonnade within and of proportions similarly vast for the exterior, give to the building all the dignity of which they are capable. It is curious that the noblest buildings in this grand monarchical style came into existence, not under Louis XIV., but in the reign of his less high-minded, less serious, less dignified successor. It is then that the admirable buildings on the north side of the Place de la Concorde in Paris were built, and the dignified École Militaire on the Champ de Mars. This severe and admirable style was indeed contemporaneous with a very inferior development of the neoclassic taste, namely, the rococo style, which, however, was kept well away from the buildings of the favoured region of which we are now speaking. While the buildings last named above and the two Trianons were rising near Paris, the palaces on the Rhine and in the duchy of Lorraine were as extravagant as the loss of all classical tradition could make them. There is, however, a certain recklessness in the design of the years ending with 1775, and to correct this the reaction of the reign of Louis XVI. appeared, whose best manifestation is perhaps in the little façade on the Quai d'Orsay in Paris, once a private palace, now the home of the Legion of Honour. — R. S.

FRANCE, ARCHITECTURE OF; Part II.; Flemish France; that is to say, the small region adjoining Picardy on the north, comprising the ancient countship of Artois and the greater part of Hennegau, both of which formed a part of French Flanders in its largest acceptation. The whole country is now contained in the modern departments of Le Nord and Pas de Calais. This very small district must necessarily be separated from Parisian France (see Part I.), because the architecture of the country during the Romanesque and Gothic epochs, and still more during the time succeeding the beginning of the Renaissance, differs essentially from any French architecture properly so called. It is far more nearly Flemish than French, and far more closely akin to the architecture of modern Belgium than to that of even the most immediately adjoining French districts.

The Roman remains are unimportant, nor are there representative buildings of the round-arched twelfth century style, — a splendid baptismal font in the church of Chéreng (Nord) being the most important piece of sculpture of the time to which attention has been called.

The attractive part of the architectural history of this district is in the late Gothic buildings and in those of the established Renaissance. Thus, at Arras (Pas de Calais), a part of the old Hôtel de Ville, of which there must be further mention below, and at Saint-Omer (Pas de Calais) two fascinating churches, are of late Gothic style. At Lille (Nord) the great church of S. Maurice, a five-aisled hall church, of a type unknown in central France, is of florid Gothic except the outer aisles. The Hôtel de Ville at Douai (Nord) and its adjoining beffroi is entirely Flemish, like a building of Ghent or Courtrai ; a long building with one important story above the basement, and dormer windows in the roof, the one face broken by a very noble battlemented tower and the other by an apse-like projection containing the chapel, and which is on the axis of the tower. However modernized and even enlarged in our own time, this is one of the most beautiful of the Flemish town halls.

Of the epoch of the Renaissance there are buildings which it is hard to name apart from their still lingering Gothic feeling, or even from still existing Gothic details. Thus, the Hôtel de Ville at Cassel (Nord) has the entire lower story built with pointed arches except the entrance doorway, which, together with the important story above and the roof and its gables and dormers, is in the classical taste. The three-centred arches and the construction in materials of contrasting colour show the spirit of the years shortly before and after 1620, and the sculpture of a great frieze is apparently of the same date, while the doorway is somewhat later. The same experience awaits one who studies the Hôtel de Ville at Arras, named above, for the tower and large parts of the main building are of unmistakable neoclassic spirit, while the mass of the structure is still mediæval of the latest style ; in fact, this building comprises at once a Flemish town hall comparable to that at Audenarde, and a building of a similar class in a florid seventeenth century style, very curious and very interesting in its masses and their relation to one another. Of confirmed Renaissance style is the beautiful tower at Bergues, which, in spite of the arched panels with which its sides are slightly variegated, is as it was left by the sixteenth century, a Renaissance tower of the most interesting sort. The town gates at Cassel and at Cambrai (Nord) are fascinating bits of work of the time of Henry IV. or Louis XIII.

Of Post-Renaissance architecture there are admirable private houses in several of the cities of this department, and one or two public buildings of singular value. Such is the military hospital at Saint-Omer, at least in its present condition, which dates from 1750, after a destructive conflagration. The cities were prosperous in the reigns of Louis XV. and XVI., and much of interesting details of these times remains. Thus, to name the magnificent woodwork in the sacristy of S. Pierre at Douai is to name only one of many pieces which the traveller loves to visit. The Hôtel Colbert at Saint-Omer, and the old Bourse at Lille with the coats of arms of Philip IV. of Spain carved over its great doorways, express perfectly the Flemish taste of the seventeenth century, which, indeed, lingered on in this region until almost our own time. The very noble cathedral at Arras shows no local feeling whatever, and is as severe a classical study as if it had been designed in Italy, but this is of the first years of the present century.

Of strictly modern buildings is the Hôtel de Ville at Arras, and this, though Renaissance in design, as if particularly inspired by an ancient building occupying the same site, is to be credited to a still living architect as completely as is the new Hôtel de Ville of Paris. — R. S.

FRANCE, ARCHITECTURE OF; Part III.; Normandy; the ancient duchy, a fief of the French monarchy, but practically independent until its conquest by Philip Augustus at the commencement of the thirteenth century, from that time a part of France. The controlling population being of foreign blood, conquering immigrants from Scandinavia, gave to the social life and the arts of the country a peculiar character. The Romanesque of Normandy is radically different from that of the art of the same epoch in the provinces immediately south (see Parts VI. and VII., Angevin France, Aquitanian France), and from the royal domain at the east (see Part I., Parisian France). The conquest of England by the Duke of Normandy in the eleventh century caused a closer intellectual alliance between his Continental and his insular dominions than existed between Normandy and any of the neighbouring Continental states, and the result of this is seen in the strongly Norman character, first of English Romanesque, and then of English Gothic (see England, Architecture of; Gothic Architecture in England).

The single fact that the people of Normandy cared less for vaulting than their Continental neighbours is of great importance, because everywhere else in Northwestern Europe the question, how to vault — first, the eastern part of the choir; next, the aisles; and lastly, the high nave — was the most important architectural question of all. Throughout the early Middle Ages the effort of the northern builders was to close their churches with masonry in one form or another, and as they could not imitate the vaulting of the Roman structures, which still remained for their models, the question what to substitute for that system was the burning question; but the Normans seem

FRANCE, PART III.: CATHEDRAL OF BAYEUX; WEST FRONT FROM S.W.

to have had no such overmastering desire for the vault, and it remains a characteristic of the Norman churches that they were built very commonly with wooden roofs and without even the preparatory steps being taken for masonry roofs at a later time. Even where the aisles were vaulted there was no attempt made to raise the high vaults of the nave. This tendency was carried across the Channel; and at no time did the English builders care for the vault as did those of Central, Eastern, and Southern France. In fact, it is in England that the Norman Romanesque reached its greatest splendour, and to study it rightly the cathedrals of Peterborough, Winchester, and Saint Albans, with Waltham abbey and other of the conventual churches, especially in the north, are fully as important to the student as even the great churches of Caen.

Another marked difference in style between the Romanesque of Normandy and that of the adjoining provinces is in the comparative poverty of the sculpture in the former. The rich and significant sculpture of Poitou and Anjou — still more that of the Limousin and Périgord — is unknown in Normandy, and its place is taken by zigzags, billets, disks, and similar geometrical ornament, while the tendency toward replacing sculpture by mouldings is evident from an early date.

The two great conventual churches of Caen (Calvados), S. Étienne (*Abbaye aux Hommes*) and La Trinité (*Abbaye aux Dames*), are among the best specimens of this Norman Romanesque. The church of S. Michel de Beaucelles, also at Caen, should also be considered. The south tower of Saint-Pierre-sur-Dives (Calvados) and the famous round-arched tower of Rouen cathedral, called *Tour Saint Romain*, must be considered as among the most important architectural monuments of this character which exist in France, although the Rouen tower has lost its original crowning members. This loss is the more regrettable because the singular disposition, with very lofty and slender dormer windows relieved against the sloping pyramid of the spire, manifests itself at an early time, at least as early as the transition from Romanesque to Gothic art, and it would be of the greatest interest to be able to see what was perhaps its finest manifestation, and to trace it back nearer to its origin. The churches of Serquigny (Eure), Montgaroult and Domfront (Orne), and Secqueville (Calvados), as well as

FRANCE, PART III.: CATHEDRAL OF COUTANCES; PART OF NORTH AISLE OF CHOIR.

the fortified church of Vire (Calvados), are important monuments of this style.

When the ribbed vault was established within the original royal domain of France, Normandy, still a quasi-independent state and often at war with its suzerain, the king at Paris, was not very quick to receive the impulse; and Gothic art was forty years old (a great lapse of time in the rapid progress of that reformation) before it, then fully developed, could enter Normandy in the train of the royal armies. It is not until the late Gothic of the fourteenth, and still more of the fifteenth, century that Normandy becomes Continental in style; and at this time the English were developing their own single independent style, the national "Perpendicular Gothic," with its formal tracery and florid roofing. Thus, in the city of Rouen, the early parts of the cathedral, although built with pointed arches throughout, are hardly Gothic in spirit; they were built by reluctant hands whose masters longed for the simpler art of an earlier day;

while the high vaults, and especially the sculpture of the thirteenth century, are already French Gothic, and in the church of S. Ouen is to be found the most important French Gothic building of the entire fourteenth century. In the same town we shall find late Gothic building with all the glory of the Flamboyant style.

Some of the most attractive churches of Normandy are frankly transitional, the Gothic feeling, even that modified Gothic feeling of Normandy, contrasting with the earlier style. Such is the cathedral of Coutances (Manche), and such are parts of S. Jean at Caen (Calvados), and many smaller buildings, as the partly ruined abbey near Granville (Manche), called commonly *Abbaye de la Lucerne.* Other Gothic churches of first-rate importance are the cathedral of Séez (Orne), the cathedral of Lisieux, and the churches of Norrey and Douvres (Calvados), the church of Pont Audemer (Eure), and the ruined abbey of Jumièges (Seine-Inférieure). One monument, or group of monuments, is, however, so unique in character that it deserves to take rank even before the great cathedrals of the district. The abbey and town of Mont-Saint-Michel possess an admirable Romanesque church, which throughout the Middle Ages had vaulted aisles and a wooden central roof, but a choir of perfected Norman Gothic with vaults ; and this building, of high interest in itself, is surrounded by the most extraordinary group of cloisters, vaulted halls and chambers, staircases, gateways, and fortifications, which can be found anywhere, piled up in one small site. The disentanglement of the styles represented in this crowd of curious buildings requires the study of months, and can only be set forth, as it has been set forth in books especially devoted to the subject. (See Corroyer, op. cit.)

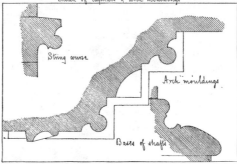

FRANCE, PART III.: CATHEDRAL OF ROUEN; DETAILS OF WINDOW IN UPPER SACRISTY.

The florid Gothic of Normandy is at one with that of France. At the close of the Hundred Years' War, about 1450, France was united as one people, and the architecture of the next half century is among the most splendid of her triumphs. At Rouen, always the capital of the duchy and the province, the lantern of S. Ouen, the tower of S. Laurent, the very interesting, though at the time unfinished, *Palais de Justice*, the north tower of the west front of the cathedral, and especially the unmatched church of S. Maclou, are all of this splendid epoch. Large parts of the cathedral of Évreux (Eure), the bishop's palace, the clock tower, or *beffroi*, and the church of S. Taurin, in the same town ; the church of Pont-l'Évêque ; that of Dives-sur-Mer ; that of La Trinité, at Falaise (Calvados); the churches of S. Germain and S. Martin, at Argentan (Orne) ; the cathedral of Saint-Lô (Manche) ; — these are but a few of the buildings of this time — buildings which vie with any of the florid Gothic architecture of central and eastern France in beauty, variety, and a true architectural sense of limitation and of restraint in the midst of the search for splendour. They are surpassed in no respect, except by two or three of the greatest churches of the royal domain, as at Abbeville, Beauvais, and Saint-Riquier (for which see Part I. of this inquiry).

The works of the classical Renaissance are very abundant in Normandy, and are of singular attractiveness ; but none of them are of very great size or cost. The small châteaux, or, as they might with greater propriety be called, the *manoirs*, of the years immediately following the expulsion of the English, are among the most attractive buildings for the student. The time, still full of memories of war and civic confusion, hardly allowed of the construction of country houses without some

FRANCE, ARCHITECTURE OF. PLATE III

Church of S. Stephen at Caen in Normandy, called le Vieux S. Étienne to distinguish it from the Abbaye aux Hommes, shown in Vol. I., pl. I. It is desecrated and has been used for many years as a storehouse, but being a historic monument is safe from destruction or serious injury. A valuable study of the more severe fifteenth century Gothic, without admixture of other styles.

means of defence, and accordingly the buildings of the manor were ranged around a large courtyard, to which they served as rampart, and from which they had their only entrance. A single gateway, more or less fortified, served as entrance to this great enclosure. The famous *Manoir d'Ango*, near Varangeville (Seine-Inférieure), is only superior to others in the variety of its buildings and the unusual amount of applied ornament; that of Boos with its remarkable towerlike pigeon house, and that of Livet (Calvados) with its timber barns and residence of brick and stone, and the unpretending little châteaux of Cricqueville, Aguessau, and Fontaine Henri (Calvados), Carrouges, La Vove, and Tessé-la-Madeleine (Orne), are all important; and there are some little manors in the Orne, as at Corday, Ronceray, and Saint-Céneri, which are of equal value with the larger buildings. The Renaissance is not without its church architecture in Normandy, as every student knows from the popular view of the apsidal chapels of S. Pierre, at Caen; but the church of S. Étienne le Vieux, in the same city (to be distinguished carefully from the abbey of S. Étienne, named above), though of less well-established classical taste and having the Renaissance details mingled curiously with those of late Gothic character, is peculiarly successful as an architectural composition. The flat roof of the choir at Tillières (Eure) and the extraordinary wooden porch of the little church at Ry (Seine-Inférieure) are unique bits of Renaissance detail like nothing else in Europe. The square tower, central in the church, or standing free, received attention during the epoch of the Renaissance, and several of the finest specimens which exist are in Normandy. Such are the central tower of S. Pierre at Coutances (Manche), the tower of the church at Mortagne, and that of the church of S. Germain at Argentan (Orne).

Of the later classical styles are the church of S. Gervasi S. Protais at Gisors, and the

ruined abbey of Bec-Hellouin (Eure); also, in the same department, the châteaux of Beaumesnil and Chambray. The north tower of Évreux cathedral should also be compared with the earlier towers named in the last paragraph. The Hôtel de Ville, at Alençon (Orne), and the prefecture of the same city are valuable pieces of street architecture, and so is, in one sense, the bishop's palace at Séez. Châteaux, in the strict sense of manor houses, not necessarily of great size, are as numerous in the style of the eighteenth century as they are of an earlier epoch; such are those of Médavy (Orne), Quilly-le-Vicomte (Calvados), Buisson-de-Mai, and Croix Saint Leufroy (Eure), — all of this interesting class. Finally, for strictly modern buildings, there are to be mentioned the château of Quesnay-Guesnon (Calvados), the Hôtel de Ville at Breteuil (Eure), and the extraordinary collection of buildings which make up the monastery of La Trappe (Orne), in which one of the most successful of modern pieces of ribbed vaulting, and its necessary accessories, is combined with severity and an absence of applied ornament well worthy of special note. (Cut, cols. 119, 120.) — R. S.

FRANCE, ARCHITECTURE OF; Part IV.; Lorraine; including parts of the ancient duchy of Lothringen (Lorraine), the duchy of Bar, the bishoprics of Toul and Verdun. The district includes the modern departments of Meuse, Vosges, and Meurthe-et-Moselle, which last is made up from the departments of Meurthe and Moselle as they existed before the War of 1871. This tract, small as it is, must be considered apart from the great region of central France (Part I.) because of its long dependence upon the German Empire and its late annexation to France. Nancy, Épinal, Bar-le-Duc, and Verdun hardly come under French influence more than the towns on the Rhine or in Westphalia until the eighteenth century. If, therefore, the less recent styles, even including the late Gothic, are so nearly French in

FRANCE, PART III.: COLOMBIER AT BOOS (SEINE-INFÉRIEURE).
See the plan and section under Colombier.

117   118

character that it requires careful study, and in detail, to differentiate them, this fact is the more interesting as showing the immense influence of French art and the wide radiation of that influence from 1050 to the rise of the time of the well-established classical Renaissance.

The early Romanesque work of this region is of extreme interest, for, although there are but

FRANCE, PART III.: WINDOWS OF THE HÔTEL BOURG-THEROULDE, ROUEN; EARLY NORMAN RENAISSANCE.

few pieces requiring special mention, they are of unusual character. The crypt of the church at Remiremont is one of these. The church at Rambervillers (Vosges), though it has some Gothic additions, shows a singularly pure and simple Romanesque style, and the church of Rollainville (Vosges) is one of the best small round-arched churches in France. The often cited appearance in Rhenish art of elements

borrowed from Byzantine sculpture is hardly notable in these churches among the hill country of Lorraine. Their sculpture is as severe and as strictly architectural in character as that of Normandy. With the Gothic epoch there appears at Épinal (Vosges) a church of the earliest period hardly past the time of transition. At Saint-Dié (Vosges) the cloister and the choir of the church, very beautiful though of mixed style, retain their unaltered Gothic character. At Pont-à-Mousson the church of S. Martin, though strictly thirteenth century Gothic in character, is most unusual in the plan, which undoubtedly recalls the plan of a primitive church. There is a magnificent Gothic font in this church, and among the curious houses of the town are traces of pure mediæval work, precious in view of the extreme rarity of domestic Gothic architecture which has not been entirely restored.

In the late Gothic epoch the choice is still greater, and the buildings more splendid. The ducal palace at Nancy (Meurthe-et-Moselle), well known through photographs and drawings, retains its very curious covered gallery of the ground story which supports, in a fashion reminding one of the street arcades of Switzerland and Italy, the principal story above, and the splendid gateway with the equestrian statue. The church of Remiremont, of which the crypt is mentioned above, and that of Saint-Nicolas-du-Port (Meurthe-et-Moselle) are, in the main, of the years following 1490; although the last named has some florid Gothic work of a still later epoch. At Avioth (Meuse) is one of the most curious Gothic monuments in Europe, a church of singularly grave and reserved design with florid tracery and two very elaborate porches, and having in addition a wholly unique chapel, small and open, a mere shelter for an altar to be used on certain occasions, and standing apart from the church, to which it is attached by a purely ornamental screen. This last of Flamboyant style, as is the little chapel.

Of the epoch of the Renaissance proper, there are some pieces of mingled sculpture and architecture fit to vie with any similar structures. Thus, the retables at Hatton-Châtel and Saint-Mihiel (Meuse), together with a wooden group in the latter church, are the undoubted work of the Lotharingian sculptor Ligier-Richier. In each instance the sculpture takes precedence of the architectural setting and, indeed, may be classed with the magnificent groups at Solesmes (Sarthe) (for which see Part VI.). At Hatton-Châtel the whole composition is magnificent, a triple disposition with deep recesses divided and enclosed by pilasters which carry a pediment; the central division arched up with a higher superstructure, the side divisions square-headed like what is called a Venetian doorway or window, and all of proportions as delicate as unusual, and invested with charming Renaissance decorative sculpture setting off the realistic groups of the three great divisions. In the little church of Étain (Meuse) there is another group by the same great artist, but less architectural in its disposition. Some of the tombs in the church of the Cordeliers at Nancy are of interest, and that of René II., the hero of the war against Charles the Rash of Burgundy, is an elaborate piece of early Renaissance screenwork and relief sculpture, as rich and varied as anything in Lombardy. The original sculptures (kneeling statue of René and statue of the Madonna and Child) have disappeared and have been replaced by modern work of some merit ; and a certain lack of harmony between this sculpture and the carved and painted shrine in which it is set up leaves the rich decoration in form and in colour more noticeable and more easy to study undisturbed. The diocese of Saint-Dié contains a great number of curious wayside crosses and churchyard crosses to which a special monograph has been devoted ; and fortunately, as their small size and remote situation would otherwise have left them nearly unknown. Some of these are of the Renaissance, and are of an origin not later than the sixteenth century whatever the style of their sculpture may be. In this, as in other respects, they resemble the calvaries of Brittany (see Part V.).

Of late neoclassic work there is much in Nancy itself. The cathedral is of the years following 1703, and in and near it are several pairs of wrought-iron gates of the utmost richness, dating from the time of the Duke Stanislaus, and well known to students for their unsurpassed splendour. In the same town, the hôtel of the marshal commanding the military district is of the eighteenth century, and fronts upon a circular esplanade surrounded by colonnades, a small but effective architectural disposition. The celebrated Adam house, the home of several sculptors, is covered with the decorative work of its former inmates ; its date is about 1720. At Épinal is a Hôtel de Ville of the eighteenth century. At Moyen-Moutier (Vosges) the most important relic of the former abbey is the church, which dates from 1766, and of about the same date is the cathedral of Saint-Dié. The church of S. Jacques at Lunéville (Vosges) and the carved stalls and ciborium in the cathedral of Verdun (Meuse) are of the eighteenth century, and all these interesting costly structures of that time remind the historical student how prosperous was this region under the reigns of the last dukes and the succeeding French administration. The great château of Bourlémont (Vosges) is practically a modern building and might be classed as of the nineteenth century, although its design is of an earlier epoch of neoclassic taste. — R. S.

FRANCE, ARCHITECTURE OF ; Part V. Brittany, which for the purpose of this inquiry, may be taken as including the modern departments of Finistère, Côtes-du-Nord, Morbihan, Ille-et-Vilaine, and Loire-Inférieure, possesses an architecture which, since the beginning of modern European civilization, has always presented many contrasts with that of neighbouring provinces. The abundance of granite rock and the comparative scarcity of other building stone is one cause of this. The separate racial character and distinctive language of the people, together with their struggles for independence of the Norman dukedom and, later, of the French kingdom, have also powerfully influenced all the civilization of the province.

Of buildings of the Romanesque epoch the most interesting is certainly at Dinan (Côtes-du-Nord), the Church of S. Sauveur. This building, of which the south flank is of the eleventh century and the portals of the west front of the same date, or hardly later, has been altered at different times so as to possess a late Gothic aisle along its north side, and a west gable of the same epoch with a splendid Flamboyant window. The tower erected over the sanctuary is, in the main, Romanesque, but with very late, even semi-classical, fittings in the upper story. The importance of the church, however, is in the earliest parts where, on the south flank, half-round engaged columns serve as buttresses, and these, together with corbels of slight projection, carry a stone cornice which, however, has been modernized. There are few Romanesque monuments of equal interest in the west of France. At Daoulas (Finistère) is a most interesting Romanesque cloister much ruined. The round church at Quimperlé (Finistère) is well worthy of study for those who have time to investigate its plan and to trace its original design, but it has been almost wholly rebuilt. At Saint-Matthieu, near Brest (Finistère), there is a very interesting church of the Transition, reminding the student of the abbeys of Yorkshire, in having pointed arches, but being otherwise completely Romanesque and without any trace of vaulting. The date given for this most interesting structure is 1160.

Of Gothic buildings there is little representing the early or the perfected thirteenth century style. There is nothing of consequence to compare with the great cathedrals or with the parish churches of the royal domain, Burgundy, Champagne, or Normandy. The cathedral of Dol, described below, is of the great thirteenth century epoch, but is very peculiar in style. Fifteenth century Gothic is, however, not rare in Brittany. Perhaps the most important monuments are the churches of Saint-Pol-de-Léon (Finistère). Here, the cathedral is a fourteenth century church with very beautiful west towers, a south transept with a splendid rose window, and an interesting interior containing much later work. This, being executed in granite, should be compared with the soft stone churches of the Paris region and the north, or, if a building of the same date is sought for, the abbey church of S. Ouen, at Rouen. It is seen here that differences of material have little weight with the ardent promoters of a growing style of architecture. Granite is found to do the same work as the softer stones, and the main difference to the builders was probably in the added difficulty of shaping and tooling the separate stones. Detail, of course, is strongly affected by hardness of the material. The small church of the Creisker or Kreizker, in the centre of the town, as its Breton name implies, has a noble central tower resting upon open arches which span the nave, and rises to a great height without buttresses or other breaks of its square prism than windows with deep jambs and arcading also somewhat emphatic. It carries a lofty spire pierced with sexfoil and cinquefoil openings and flanked by four large open pinnacles. No Gothic buildings in the northwest of France are more worthy of study than these ; there is an interesting ossuary or bone house of later date. In the same department, the little church of Rosporden is interesting, and has a spire and pinnacles of great beauty. The cathedral at Quimper, in the same department, contains admirable transition work in the interior of the nave, but the whole exterior is of the fourteenth century, except the spires of the west front, which are entirely modern, though supposed to be in imitation of the ancient ones. The flying buttress system of the choir and apse, though simple, is of great beauty of proportion. The cathedral of Nantes is an important Gothic church, more in keeping with the churches of northern France than those above named, a fact accounted for by the situation of the town on the river Loire, and accessible from Tours and the heart of royal France. The portals of the west front are much later in detail than the greater part of the structure. This church contains two splendid tombs, which are described below. The cathedral of Dol (Ille-et-Vilaine) is of singularly sombre aspect, being built entirely of gray granite. It is built in the thirteenth century style, and is one of the few instances of a very large church of the Gothic epoch almost wholly uniform in style. It is curiously like some English churches in two respects : first, in having a square east end (compare the cathedral of Laon in the district of France proper) ; and secondly, in the lowness of its walls and roof. A minor peculiarity, which results in part from this inferior height, is the steep slope of the flying buttresses, in which again a comparison may be made with English Gothic buildings.

The extraordinary massiveness of the parts and the absence of external buttresses to the aisles increase the unusual character of the exterior. There is a beautiful late Gothic church at Le Croisic (Loire-Inférieure), another at Locronan (Finistère), and others of a later date at Guérande (Loire-Inférieure), Grâces (Côtes-du-Nord), and at Dinan, where the greater part of the church of S. Sauveur, also mentioned, is of beautiful late Gothic, and where the church of S. Malo in Dinan is of the same epoch, and has a most attractive interior. The feudal castles and town halls of Brittany have great interest, and the student of military architecture should visit Tonquédec (Côtes-du-Nord), Guérande (Loire-Inférieure), Dinan, and Sucinio (Morbihan), the last of which is an enormous fortress in such condition that its plan and arrangement can be almost perfectly understood. The great fortress of Josselin must be mentioned in a succeeding paragraph, but its exterior defences are of the fourteenth century.

Interesting timber-built houses are very numerous in Brittany, and it is impossible to enumerate the towns where they can be found. Saint-Malo, Morlaix, the village of Josselin, Lamballe (Côtes-du-Nord), may be mentioned, but the larger towns, which the visitor seeks for their ecclesiastical and other monuments, contain also many of these minor buildings.

The curious Calvaries (*Calvaires*) or out-of-door monuments of the Crucifixion, though generally, in their present condition, of a much later date, belong to the Middle Ages in their origin. The one at Plougastel, near Brest (Finistère), has a platform about twelve feet high, upon which are about thirty figures of half life-size, while upon the buttresses or flanking projections are many other figures in high relief. From the centre of the platform rises a great cross, perhaps fifteen feet high above the substructure, and adorned with crossbars and corbels which carry the figures of the Marys and the other immediate attendants of the Crucifixion, while two small and less adorned uprights carry the crosses of the two thieves. The whole of this immense combination of rude architecture and ruder sculpture is intended to aid toward a clear comprehension of the Passion in all its successive stages as expounded by the Church. Similar, but often smaller, Calvaries are at Plougouver and Guimiliau, Pleyben, and Comfort, in the same department, the last of these being a modern structure erected on the site of an ancient one.

The work of the Renaissance in Brittany takes on curious provincial forms, some of which are of extraordinary interest. They should be compared with the buildings of the same epoch in eastern and southeastern Germany on account of their novelty and dashing treatment, while, at the same time, they are more elegant in design. There is clumsiness enough in the details of the church tower at Saint-Thégonnec (Finistère), but the general proportions of the tower are extremely graceful. At Le Bourg-de-Batz (Loire-Inférieure) is a very plain and severe sixteenth century tower of very graceful outline, dominating the interesting ruins of the Gothic church. At Faouet (Morbihan) is the west front of a church of mingled Renaissance and Gothic forms, rudely built in granite, and here are also an ossuary and other structures of the sixteenth century. The little church of Châteaulin (Finistère) may be studied on account of its curious towers and gables, in front of which is a small Calvary. At Kerjean, in the same department, is a curious manor house of the early seventeenth century. Of French Renaissance less abnormal and more like that of the Centre, there may be named the church of S. Armel at Ploërmel (Morbihan) where the portals are of singular beauty in the style of Francis I., and at Nantes, where the interior court of the château has early Renaissance and Transition details of equal merit. The strong castle at Josselin has a building fronting on its court which has been the favourite subject for artists. This is the well-known long façade, with one story of windows in the walls, while two-story dormers rise from the walls and project from the steeply sloping roof. There is in the cathedral of Nantes a tomb of the early Renaissance, the tomb of the Duke of Brittany, Francis II. It is one of the finest monuments of the time.

Of modern work is a very remarkable tomb, also in the cathedral of Nantes, the monument to General De Lamoricière, celebrated as the commander of the Papal armies opposing Garibaldi. This tomb is decorated by a marble recumbent statue of the dead and four bronze symbolic statues at the angles, all by Paul Dubois. Its design is by the architect Boitte; it is of exquisite Renaissance design, with a canopy supported on pilasters and columns, and is altogether one of the most important pieces of modern architectural and sculpturesque design. — R. S.

FRANCE, ARCHITECTURE OF; Part VI.; Angevin France. The small district which is designated here as Angevin France is bounded on the north by Normandy, and is situated on both sides of the Loire, including the three departments of Mayenne, Sarthe, and Maine-et-Loire. History and architectural history alike prevent the treatment of this region as a part of Brittany, or Normandy, or France proper, or other larger historical division. It is nearly conterminous with the ancient provinces of Anjou and Maine. This region, although the home of the powerful Angevin kings of Western Gaul and England, lost its political importance early in the thirteenth century, and

both before and after that time had rather suffered the architectural influence of neighbouring lands than originated anything of importance.

Romanesque architecture is well shown by a few buildings of extraordinary interest. Such are the ruins of the important abbey of S. Aubin at Angers, a building so varied in its detail, so rich in its sculptured ornamentation, and so unique in many of its dispositions that it deserves the closest study. In the same city the remains of the convent of S. Martin should also be studied; and the ancient hospital of S. Jean, the ancient Hôtel-Dieu, contains a twelfth century cloister and other Romanesque remains. The interesting church of Pré-en-Pail (Mayenne) has been restored with great completeness and has lost all its original character except in the sculptured details, as at the west door. At Cunault (Maine-et-Loire) is a very ancient church, which, as late as 1890, had been only repaired in a few places, and was still intact in all its important parts. The door is of extraordinary interest and beauty. Chemillé, in the same department, has a central church tower of a somewhat later date — Romanesque of about 1150, with an octagonal stone spire which is brought to the scale of the belfry below by means of stone dormer windows. This whole church is of importance, but the door is especially valuable. The most important piece of Romanesque work in the district is the great abbey of Fontevrault. The buildings of this establishment are used as a prison, and are kept in perfect condition; they are, also, somewhat difficult to visit with any thoroughness, but the extent and completeness of the ancient monastery and the great number of important pieces of architecture and of sculpturesque ornament make it especially necessary to every student. The church retains one of its curious early cupolas, by which it is identified as one of that series of domical churches for which see the districts of Guienne and Poitou. The kitchen of the monastery is of later date than the church, but still early, and, like the kitchen of Glastonbury, in England, is roofed by a curious pyramid. It is in this abbey that are still preserved the four precious portrait statues of Angevin kings and queens; Henry II. of England, Richard I. of England, Éléanore de Guienne, and Isabelle d'Angoulême, three of these being in soft stone, the fourth in wood. Parts of the cathedral of Le Mans are also worthy of special notice by the student of pre-Gothic architecture, especially a great south doorway with its noble statuary worthy to be compared to that of the west front of Chartres.

The most important Gothic monument of the district is the noble cathedral of Le Mans. The choir and east end of this church are unique because of the system of vaulting adopted for the aisle, which curves around the choir proper, the vaulting being arranged alternately in squares and triangles. This system, afterward followed in the cathedral of Toledo, in Spain, is practically unknown in the north, except in this one instance. The chapels, which are arranged around this east end, and radiate in the usual way, are of unusual depth, and the Chapel of the Virgin is longer than the others. The result is, for the exterior, one of the most charming choirs in France, containing the spirit of the Gothic construction carried to its highest development. The towers of this cathedral are of little importance, and, in consequence, its distant aspect is not imposing, except at the east end. In the same city the large church of Notre Dame de la Couture, though much restored within, even to the spoiling of its Romanesque choir, retains the sculpture of its fine doorway practically unaltered, and remains very picturesque in its exterior effect. The cathedral of Angers has a west front of Transition style, of which the great doorway is peculiarly interesting. The church of Évron (Mayenne) is late Gothic, with details of a singularly beautiful type. Two churches exist at Saumur (Maine-et-Loire) of which the early Gothic details are of great interest; these are S. Pierre and Notre Dame de Nantilly. There is also the chapel of a nunnery, which is a small church of great beauty. Of late Gothic buildings, one of the most effective residences in France is the building at Angers now used as the Museum, — a beautiful town house of the fifteenth century.

The Renaissance in Anjou spent its strength mainly on minor houses and small residences. Of these the Château Chemaze, though less refined in detail and in architectural treatment generally than the small buildings on the Loire and in the east of France, is of extreme interest. Saint-Ouen (Mayenne) has another château with a splendid spiral staircase of the sixteenth century, and a chimney-piece with heraldic bearings, the whole of extraordinary beauty of detail. Montreuil-Bellay (Maine-et-Loire), Mezanger (Mayenne), and Laval (Mayenne) have each châteaux of the Renaissance and of a pure and elegant style. Small houses of the sixteenth and seventeenth centuries are rather numerous in the small towns of this department, and the city of Le Mans also contains a number, one of which, bearing the sign *Tambour des Pompiers*, is of rich and florid ornamentation. The most important monument of the Renaissance in this district is, however, the singular and elsewhere unmatched array of sculpture in the little church of Solesmes (Sarthe). This church has little interest for the student except in the sculptures which fill the small north transept. In this there are groups representing the fainting of the Virgin at the Cross, the Coronation of the Virgin, the burial of the Virgin, and the Assumption, each of these consisting of many figures

associated together in an architectural framework of that curious Transition style which marks the passing into the classical Renaissance while still the Gothic spirit was strong. There are other sculptures in the church.

— R. S.

FRANCE, ARCHITECTURE OF; Part VII.; Aquitanian France; including the ancient countship of Poitou, the Limousin, and the Périgord, the great duchy of Gascogne, and such little inland states as Châteauroux and Cahors. This includes the modern departments of Basses-Pyrénées, Charente, Charente-Inférieure, Deux-Sèvres, Dordogne, Gers, Gironde, Hautes-Pyrénées, Haute-Vienne, Landes, Lot, Lot-et-Garonne, and Tarn-et-Garonne.

The geographical name, Aquitania or Aquitaine, can only be used as a general indication. During the Hundred Years' War and thereafter, the duchy of Aquitania covered the whole country from the boundary of Touraine southward to Gascony, or even included Gascony and reached the Pyrenees. After 1450 the term almost disappears from history and is replaced in part by Guienne. Its value as describing a part of France, is that from Julius Cæsar's time to nearly the end of the Middle Ages it designated what is now southwestern France, with the possible exception of the country immediately north of the Pyrenees.

Throughout this region there should be found Roman remains of great importance; but the rebuilding of churches, large villas, and city walls, as mentioned in another part of this inquiry, has caused the disappearance, or the concealment under later work, of the greater part of these remains. Drawings have been preserved of the magnificent Roman building which existed at Bordeaux until late in the seventeenth century, and of those parts of the Bordeaux amphitheatre which were not removed until about 1800.

The special glory of this district is the wonderful collection of Romanesque churches which cover the land. The large towns and the little villages alike have round-arched churches whose epoch can be ascertained with some exactness, and which succeed one another throughout the eleventh and twelfth centuries. The domical churches of Saint-Michel-d'Entraigues, Gensac, Rouillac, Saint-Amant-de-Boixe, Fléac, and the cathedral of Angoulême are all in the Charente, and besides these there are many churches which have at least one cupola, as, for instance, at the crossing of the transept and nave. No other part of France possesses buildings of this character. The most famous of all these churches with cupolas is S. Front at Périgeux (Dordogne); but this building has suffered a destructive restoration which, though it has resulted in an interesting modern church studied from a Romanesque original, has lost all its exterior character and some part of its interior authenticity. The original church has been very carefully reproduced in the plates of Verneilh (op. cit.). The ruined abbey church of Boschand (Dordogne) has kept at least two of its cupolas and the semidome of the choir, and the construction of its pendentives and the superincumbent work is easily studied.

Romanesque sculpture also is to be seen within this district in its highest development of somewhat unruly splendour. The churches named above are generally more simple ; but the façade of the churches of Saint-Jouin-de-Marnes, and Surgères (Charente-Inférieure), S. Croix at Bordeaux, and especially the wonderful abbey of Moissac (Tarn-et-Garonne), together with the above named cathedral of Angoulême, are rich in sculpture both of figure subject and floral, and are, in this respect, unique in Europe ; the only buildings comparable being those of Poitiers, named in another part of this study. One of the two or three churches in France which retain traces of the very earliest Christian building north of the Alps is at Saint-Généroux (Deux-Sèvres). Of the time of the Transition from Romanesque to Gothic are the very curious Lanterns of the Dead, or cemetery beacons as they have been called, at Fernioux and Oléron (Charente-Inférieure), at Aiffres (Deux-Sèvres) and at Cellefrouin (Charente). Some of these are in their present state evidently of the Gothic period ; but their original conception is earlier. Their slender spirelike forms are the more interesting because of the close connection traceable between them and the towers of many of the churches of the same date ; those named above, and others, as the towers of Fernioux (Charente-Inférieure), Plassac (Charente), and Trois-Palis (Charente).

The department of Charente-Inférieure on the seashore has a special class of Romanesque churches generally unrestored, sometimes simple and sometimes very rich, cared for by the State, and yet not made museums of, but still serving their purpose as places of worship. These are all basilica-like churches with roofs either vaulted or intended to be vaulted, and without cupolas ; one of the finest of them is Bassac with its magnificent four-storied tower with round arches, and topped by a conical roof. Two small and highly enriched buildings are the churches of Échebrune and Échillais. A splendid church with long transept arms and sculpture of unique character and richness is that of Aulnay. Not unlike Aulnay is Avit ; Pont-l'Abbé has one of the finest west fronts in France, admirable in proportion and extraordinarily rich in sculpture. The church of Rétaud has an extraordinary polygonal apse decorated with arcades and carving of purely architectural character, done for effect of light and shade, and almost without reference to natural forms. Finally, the great

church of S. Eutrope at Saintes has, apart from its Gothic tower, one of the most splendid unaltered Romanesque exteriors and a vaulted interior of the twelfth century carried on very massive *arcs doubleaux*. The little Hôtel de Ville of Saint-Antonin (Tarn-et-Garonne) has been made famous by Viollet-le-Duc's restoration and published drawings ; it is the only public building of this class which dates from an early period.

The Gothic architecture of this district is not so peculiarly important, nor is it so distinguished from that of other parts of France. The most important buildings are the cathedrals of Bayonne and Bordeaux, and the churches of S. Seurin and S. Michel at Bordeaux. S. Michel has an isolated tower ; and, in connection with the cathedral, though standing 200 feet away from the east end, is the famous tower Pey-

FRANCE, PART VII.: CHURCH OF S. EUTROPIUS, SAINTES (ON SEASHORE) ; FLORID ROMANESQUE CAPITALS.

Berland, named from that archbishop of Bordeaux who saw to this building in the fifteenth century. Of the Gothic epoch are the towers of the port at La Rochelle, two of them still flanking the entrance to the modern dock and the third now surrounded by made land, though this is the only one which retains its ancient spire. Nothing that has been preserved in Europe is at all of the character of these towers. They differ essentially from the mediæval military architecture which is generally cited. Of the latest Gothic style are parts of the cathedral of Auch (Gers) and of Limoges (Haute-Vienne), and there is a wonderful chapel at Ménigoute, and a church at Touars (Deux-Sèvres).

Of the earliest Renaissance are parts of the famous château of Pau (Basses-Pyrénées), identified with Henri IV. in his youth, and also parts of the château of Nérac (Lot-et-Garonne), which also was a dwelling of Henri before he could even claim to be king of France. The cathedral stalls of Auch, named in the above paragraph, are of this epoch (1520–1530), and are famous for their magnificent and florid carving. The château of Cadillac (Gironde) and that of Busson (Lot) are as important architecturally as the better-known châteaux of Oiron (Deux-Sèvres) and La Rochefoucauld (Charente); and each of these buildings is essential to the right understanding of that stately domestic architecture which made up the strength of the classical revival in France. The famous staircase of La Rochefoucauld, the work of Antoine Fontant, and the private chapel of Oiron are of peculiar interest to the student, and the manor 'of Oiron is particularly celebrated because of the inlaid pottery of the time of Henri II. which was long known by the name of this estate, and of which there are tiled surfaces in parts of the building. The jubé of the cathedral of Limoges is no longer in its original place, but is still preserved in the church and nearly complete. It dates from 1533 and is of unusual richness, a piece of associated sculpture of unique character.

Of Post-Renaissance work one of the most admirable things in this region is the church of Notre Dame at Bordeaux. This is a surprisingly successful piece of street architecture applied to a church; its front bears the date of 1707. The cathedrals of La Rochelle and Montauban (Tarn-et-Garonne) and the west front of the cathedral of Auch are of the seventeenth century, the last named structure is of peculiar importance. The famous Phare de Cordouan at the mouth of the Gironde dates, in its original form, from the reign of Louis XV.

Of modern buildings the great city of Bordeaux contains some of importance as to size and general reputation among the architects of France; but the great theatre with its dodeca-style colonnade is perhaps the only one having any particular charm. As a curious contrast to this is the little theatre at Angoulême, built at a much later time than that of Bordeaux. This is a light and graceful and somewhat fantastic building, agreeably suggestive of the purpose to which it is dedicated. — R. S.

FRANCE, ARCHITECTURE OF; Part VIII.; Auvergne; the territory once occupied by the dukedoms of Bourbon and Auvergne, and by several smaller semi-independent states, and now divided into the departments of Allier, Cantal, Corrèze, Creuse, Haute-Loire, Loire, Puy-de-Dôme. This is a hilly region, and for the most part thinly populated. There are no cities of great size, nor have there been at any time communities so prosperous or so ambitious as to erect buildings of great importance. All students of French architecture know this region as the home of the curious and beautiful variety

of Romanesque design which includes colour in external effect, and which is represented by the church of Notre Dame du Port at Clermont-Ferrand (Puy-de-Dôme), by its near neighbour, the church of S. Saturnin, with a beautiful inlaid frieze in the apse wall, by the churches at Brioude (Haute-Loire) and Issoire (Puy-de-Dôme), and by the famous cathedral of Le Puy (Haute-Loire). In these buildings there is carried to a greater extent than elsewhere the system of mosaic of coloured materials on a very large scale, the tesserae of ordinary mosaic being replaced by blocks of freestone of considerable size, and having the usual colours of reddish and grayish brown shading upward to cream colour. There are, however, many Romanesque buildings in this district of more simple style but of equally great interest. Such are the church of Châtel-Montagne (Allier), of the most stern simplicity; that of Ébreuil with its remarkable frontispiece forming a western tower of oblong section nearly as wide as the whole three-aisled church, and opened below into a vaulted porch; and at Saint-Menoux (Allier), a larger and more pretentious church, with a square central tower of fine transitional character, but with unmixed twelfth century Romanesque style throughout the greater part of its structure, although the pointed arch alternates with the round arch in the nave arcades. The church at Beaulieu (Corrèze) and the Priory church at Charlieu (Loire) are buildings of the utmost importance for their early twelfth century sculpture, in the richness, variety, and significance of which these churches rival the great buildings of Poitiers and its neighbourhood (see Part VII). The ancient church at Saint-Nectaire (Puy-de-Dôme), though much restored, has preserved its unique capitals with historical scenes and incidents, and a free treatment of costume.

The most valuable Gothic building of this region is the church of La Chaise-Dieu (Haute-Loire). It is as large as a second-class cathedral, and, next to the cathedral of Clermont-Ferrand, is the largest Gothic building in this part of France; but its height is as nothing compared to central Gothic churches of the same size, and it is singularly devoid of sculpture. In these two respects it reminds the student of many English churches; furthermore, the very severe and formal Gothic of early style, leaving large surfaces of heavy wall pierced with small lights, is, without closely resembling any English monument, akin to the style of the transitional abbeys of Yorkshire. On the other hand, the tracery, both early and late, and the treatment of the mouldings and similar details, are absolutely French. This church, situated on the highest point above the sea of any important building in France, and built of singularly hard stone, has the unique character of a mountain cathedral. The cathedral of Clermont-

PLATE VII

FRANCE, ARCHITECTURE OF. PLATE IV

Versailles (Seine et Oise) ; chapel of the Royal Château. This building was finished about 1710, after the death of its designer, Jules Hardouin Mansart, who had been for ten years the superintendent of buildings for the king. The exterior corresponds closely to the plan and interior arrangement.

Ferrand would be attractive and valuable but for comparison with the more important buildings farther north. Its modern west front will be cited below. The cathedral of Moulins (Allier) has much interesting late Gothic work, especially in the chapels disposed around the choir, and its recent enlargement must be mentioned below. The Abbey Church of Souvigny (Allier) contains long stretches of Romanesque cloister and other very early fragments combined with late Gothic vaulting, tombs, and screen-work, and tracery of unsurpassed beauty. In the church at Aubazine (Corrèze) is a very splendid Gothic monument called the Tomb of S. Stephen, that is, of S. Étienne d'Obasine, a monastic saint of the twelfth century.

The disposition to use colour in an external decoration, which has been alluded to above, appears again at a much later period in the strange tiled roofs of Moulins and Bénissons-Dieu, and in certain brick walls of the same and neighbouring towns. In each of these methods of decoration the most is made of the few simple colours obtainable, the roof tiles having more colours and more brilliant ones, and the additional brilliancy of ceramic glaze.

The hilltops of Auvergne are crowned with ruined castles of the highest interest for the study of mediæval fortification, and as picturesque in themselves and in their position as anything on the Rhine or in Carinthia. The most notable is the huge château of Bourbon-l'Archambault (Allier). As to Renaissance work, the little town of Montferrand, which forms an eastern suburb of Clermont, is rich in curious dwelling houses. Even where the greater part of the building is modernized, a doorway or even a whole façade is yet intact.

Of modern work the most important thing is the extraordinary achievement of the architect Millet, who has added a long nave to the cathedral of Moulins, and has made therein a study of Notre Dame at Paris, preserving the charm of the prototype in a way very rare in modern work. The western end of the cathedral of Clermont-Ferrand, two bays in length, and including the west front, was built by Viollet-le-Duc, but the spires have not been completed.

— R. S.

FRANCE, ARCHITECTURE OF; Part IX.; Burgundian France: including the eastern districts from Châtillon and Belfort on the north to the boundaries of Provence; embracing the country once included in the kingdom of Burgundy, the countship of Burgundy (Franche-Comté) and the Duchy of Burgundy; and including the modern departments of Ain, Côte-d'Or, Doubs, Drôme, Hautes-Alpes, Haute-Saône, Haute-Savoie, Isère, Jura, Rhône, Savoie, and Saône-et-Loire.

The Romanesque architecture of this region, though there are but few churches, compara-

tively, of great extent or elaboration, abounds in valuable material. The little mountain churches of the Hautes-Alpes and the Savoie are worthy of minute study on account of their simple effectiveness; nothing in the Tyrol or in southern Germany can surpass them in this, while they have some details of great purity. The admirable crypt of S. Laurent at Grenoble (Isère) is one of the most important pieces of Romanesque north of the Alps. At Lyons, the church of S. Martin d'Ainay has a central tower and a west tower of great value for their decoration by arcading; these towers have not been injured by the restoration which has changed the character of the church. At Saint Donat (Drôme) the church has also an admirable square tower. In fact, these Italian-like bell towers, square and plain, with arcaded belfries, are as well worthy of study as the smaller campanili south of the Alps; all students know the importance to architectural study of these unpretending structures. The church of S. Barnard at Romans (Drôme) is perhaps the richest piece of Romanesque sculpture and architecture in this region; its south porch, though much broken, has not been ruined by restoration, and is of extraordinary beauty. Larger churches are those of Embrun (Hautes-Alpes) with a porch absolutely like a Lombard porch, with the columns resting upon the backs of lions, and S. Pierre at Vienne (Isère). At Saint Paul de Verax (Ain) is a church with an early Romanesque doorway and arcade flanking it with sculptures of singular simplicity; the whole, though in the mountain region near Geneva, reminding us of the church fronts of Languedoc.

With the beginning of the Gothic building style, the differentiation of the Burgundian from the central French style begins to interest the student; but the subtle distinctions which make it up cannot be described here. The tendency is always away from the severely logical style based entirely upon its vaulted roofs and toward a reminiscence of the Romanesque variety of external treatment. The sculpture of the Burgundian Gothic churches is, though not very abundant, of peculiar value; one of the most important specimens is that admirable frieze which, taken from the jubé of the little church at Bourget (Savoie), is now built into its walls. These sculptures represent the Passion of Christ, and are narrative and descriptive to a degree not commonly reached by Gothic work. The splendid cathedral of Autun is the most important piece of transitional architecture in France, showing the almost unwilling departure from an early Romanesque type and the gradual slow acceptance of the overmastering style from the northwest. The church of Notre Dame at Dijon (Côte-d'Or) may be considered a typical piece of Burgundian Gothic; its beautiful arcaded front forms a structure as completely independent as the larger façade at Strasburg, or the west fronts of Ripon or Wells. This, in other words, is not Gothic church building, but it is admirable street architecture, carried out under the influence of the Gothic style. On the other hand, the body of the church is normal and of singular lightness and simplicity of effect. The admirable church of S. Bénigne in the same city shows, like the church last named, the local influences mainly in its west front. The plan of this church is worthy of peculiar attention by modern builders of city churches. The splendid northern doorway of the west front of the church at Semur (Saône-et-Loire) retains in good condition the most admirable thirteenth century sculpture in the east of France. All this sculpture has to do with purely secular story. There are no cathedrals of the first importance within the district, but those of Autun, Lyons, and Vienne must be included in every study of cathedral building.

Of the latest Gothic school are one or two buildings of unique character ; the famous hospital at Beaune, whose courtyard, with lofty steep roof and high dormer windows, is familiar, and the still more celebrated Church of Brou in the suburb of the town of Bourg-en-Bresse (Ain). There is also the abbey of Hautecombe, which was as elaborate once, at least in its external design, as the church of Brou itself, and even now in its rebuilt condition is attractive. As for the famous Brou church itself, the building alone without its tombs would rank with the church of S. Riquier and that of S. Wulfran at Abbeville, as of the small list of important late Flamboyant designs ; but with the tombs of princes which it includes, as a museum of fifteenth century and sixteenth century art unequalled in Europe. Such architecture as this passes by an almost imperceptible gradation into that of the Renaissance, for in France the earliest Renaissance architecture is not very strongly marked by the classical influence. The Italian example was followed but slowly anywhere outside of the immediate influence of the court at Paris. A famous and valuable instance of this peculiarity is the church of S. Michel at Dijon. Somewhat later are the two attractive buildings at Besançon (Doubs), the Hôtel de Ville and the Palais de Justice, each valuable to the modern practical student on account of the very abundant and carefully considered fenestration. The famous château of Bussy-Rabutin, near the village of Bussy-le-Grand (Côte-d'Or), has been thoroughly given in the pages of Sauvageot (op. cit.), and so has the Hôtel Vogüé at Dijon ; this last being probably the most important city house, architecturally speaking, of all the neoclassic buildings in France. There are one or two buildings of the Post-Renaissance styles which deserve especial

notice. One of these is the Château de Vizille (Isère), a building seldom mentioned by the books, but curiously valuable as a piece of bold grouping. The superb church of S. Madeleine at Besançon (Doubs), begun 1746, is a metropolitan building in everything except its situation in a small mountain town ; nothing more stately is to be found than its vaulted interior.

Of modern architecture in the district there are several town halls and *mairies* of interest, but often designed by Parisian architects. The library and museum at Grenoble (Isère) is an unusually graceful design. The most original and valuable monument of the district in recent times is the Lion of Belfort, a vast sculpture in the side of the cliff which rises above the town. It is the work of Frédéric Auguste Bartholdi, the sculptor, and the author of the colossal Liberty Enlightening the World in New York harbour. — R. S.

FRANCE, ARCHITECTURE OF; **Part X.**; **Provence and Languedoc.** In their architecture, as in their history, these two provinces have so much in common and so many points of contact, that an account of their buildings can best be given by treating them together. Throughout their whole history — up to the time of the absorption of Provence by France under Louis XI. in 1481 — the similar architectural styles of these provinces, like their common language, differed strikingly from those of northern France. The styles of architecture in that portion of Languedoc which immediately adjoins Provence were indeed identical with the Provençal styles and cannot in any way be distinguished from them. But in the Romanesque period western Languedoc has characteristics somewhat peculiar to itself and is, about Toulouse especially, more strongly influenced by the style of Auvergne than by that of Provence. The ancient Provence (including within that term the Venaissin, the domain of the popes at Avignon, and the little countship of Orange), comprised the modern departments of Vaucluse, Basses-Alpes, Alpes-Maritimes, Var, and Bouches-du-Rhône ; while the adjoining Languedoc corresponded roughly to the departments of Ardèche, Gard, Hérault, Lozère, Aveyron, Tarn, Aude, and Haute-Garonne. Ariège and Pyrénées-Orientales, approximately corresponding to the old counties of Foix and Roussillon, may be included with Languedoc. Architecturally, however, the departments of Ardèche, Gard, and about half of Hérault must be regarded as forming part of Provence, while the province of Dauphiné, especially that part of it which is included in the department of Drôme and the southern part of Isère, was under the influence of the successive Provençal styles. In Roman times these provinces formed together the Provincia Gallica, and the Roman architecture of this region, much of which is singularly well preserved, soon acquired a quality of its own, which distinguishes it from the Roman work of Italy. This is in part perhaps due to the vigorous individuality of the Gallic race, in part to the influence of the Greek colony of Massillia, the modern Marseilles, and in part to the invariable use of cut stone which is characteristic of all the styles of Provence and eastern Languedoc. In the later period of Roman art the proportions and details are crude (perhaps even more so than at the same time in Italy), but on the other hand there is in the

coarsely quarried blocks of stone the little river Touloubre, at this point nearly 40 feet wide. But the striking features of the design are the twin triumphal arches across the roadway, one at each end of the bridge. At Arles (the Roman Arelate) there are several Roman monuments of first importance. Of these the arena or amphitheatre is in an unusually good state of preservation. The exterior of this monument has arcades in two stories of the Roman arch order similar to the arcades of the Coliseum in Rome. The lower order is Doric, the

FRANCE, PART X.: CATHEDRAL OF S. NAZAIRE AT CARCASSONNE (AUDE), SOUTH OF FRANCE, C. 1320 A.D.

work of the province a robust originality of conception and a vigour of execution which compensates for this lack of refinement. Perhaps the oldest Roman monument of importance in Provence, of which anything remains, is to be found in the ruins of the temple at Vernègues (Bouches-du-Rhône), about halfway between Aix and Avignon. Its Corinthian capitals show decided Greek influence, and are refined and elegant in proportion, though somewhat over attenuated. Not far from Vernègues, at Saint Chamas, is an exceedingly interesting Roman bridge, which spans with a single arch of

upper, Corinthian, surmounted by an attic. The arena is an ellipse, 228 feet by 128 feet. The theatre is less well preserved, but contains some beautiful examples of Corinthian columns and pieces of entablature. The ancient cemetery, known as Les Aliscamps (Elysii Campi), contains a few Roman tombs. Some fifteen miles to the northeast of Arles, near the little village of Saint Remy (the ancient Glanum) are two important Roman structures: a richly sculptured triumphal arch of a single opening, of which the upper part has disappeared, and which is probably of the time of Titus or Trajan; and a tomb monument of much later date, awkward in many of its details, but of unique interest on account of its picturesque towerlike design (crowned by a circular open colonnade of squat Corinthian columns) and on account of its very perfect state of preservation. At Cavaillon (Vaucluse) is a triumphal arch, square in plan, an arch in each face, and having Corinthian pilasters on each angle ornamented with rich acanthus arabesques very refined in execution. At Carpentras, northeast of Avignon, is another well-preserved triumphal arch of late date, very wide in proportion to its height, and with three-quarter Corinthian columns at the angles. It is important because of its imitation in Romanesque times in the portal of the cathedral at Avignon. At Orange (the ancient Arausio), northwest from Carpentras, is the largest triumphal arch in Provence of three openings, and one of the best preserved Roman theatres that has come down to our day. The proscenium structure, although badly mutilated, remains to its full height. It was an elaborate design in three stories of superposed orders. Northeast again from Orange, at Vaison, there is a Roman tomb and bridge. At Fréjus, on the coast southwest of Nice, are remains of Roman baths and an aqueduct, and at Riez (Basses-Alpes) four columns of a temple colonnade still remain standing.

In Languedoc the Roman remains of importance (with the exception of a ruined bridge of three arches at Saint Thibéry in Hérault) are all in the department of Gard, concentrated at Nîmes (the ancient Nemausus) and its immediate neighbourhood. Nîmes itself possesses more examples of Roman architecture than any other city of France. Portions of the city walls still remain with two well-preserved gateways : the *Porte de France*, with a single archway between two ruinous towers ; and the richer *Porte d'Auguste* with four openings — the two central, larger, arched ; the two side openings, smaller, with lintels. But the most beautiful and most important Roman building is the so-called *Maison-Carrée*, the one almost perfect Roman temple which has remained to our day. It is hexastyle, Corinthian, of very noble architecture, and dates from the very first years of our era. It has been restored and is now used as a museum. Nîmes also has an amphitheatre in good preservation similar in style to that at Arles and of very nearly the same size. There are also important remains of public baths, including a great rectangular hall or Nymphæum ; an admirable example of the influence which the use of large blocks of stone, so abundant in the country, has exerted on all the Provençal styles. The hall is vaulted with a barrel vault in which the Roman method of using permanent centring ribs is applied to cut stone construction in a manner similar to that which they employed in central Syria, where similar conditions prevailed. Transverse arches of stone span the hall, and upon these, as centres, other arches are built of slabs resting from rib to rib. Along the sides of the hall are rectangular niches with pediments alternately triangular and segmental. Between them were Corinthian columns on pedestals (only a few remain standing), carrying the entablature from which springs the vault. These baths were supplied with water by a great aqueduct, of which there are remains in the magnificent series of arches known as the Pont du Gard, which crosses the ravine of the Gardon twelve miles north of Nîmes. At Sommières (Gard) is a ruined bridge of the time of Tiberius. Of the seventeen arches which originally crossed the Vidourle at this point eight now remain.

After the fall of the Roman Empire the ancient Provincia mainly fell under the comparatively civilized rule of Visigoths and Ostrogoths. But it is unlikely that its architectural development at this time differed essentially from that of the rest of Western Europe. In spite of the argument of Révoil, there is nothing, as Dehio has shown, which can with any likelihood be ascribed even to the subsequent Merovingian and Carlovingian epochs, save a few fortress towers such as those erected by Franks or Saracens upon the walls of the amphitheatre at Arles. The churches built at this time, of which the chronicles speak, were probably plain basilicas with piers and arches, and have practically all disappeared as a result of the invasions and destructions of the Saracens in the eighth, ninth, and tenth centuries, and the subsequent reconstructions. It is impossible therefore to trace the origin of the Provençal Romanesque style of the eleventh and twelfth centuries. But it is easy to perceive why in this romantic land, which is neither France nor Italy, but which stands midway between them, borrowing from both, there should have developed, contemporary with the literature of the troubadours, the most elegant and refined of all the Romanesque styles. These causes are to be found in the facts that no portion of the Empire outside of Italy became so thoroughly Romanized, and that this corner of Europe suffered less almost than any other from the migrations and invasions of barbarians, so that the classic character was maintained and classic traditions never quite died out. Moreover the monuments themselves were preserved. The region of the south of France, in which these monuments still exist, will be found to indicate the extent of the Provençal Romanesque style. The excellence of the building stone of the country counted for much, but the continuance of the knowledge how to use it and the proximity of good models counted for more. Structurally the great fact of the Provençal style was its being the first to develop a church building which was throughout a structure of stone. Wood is not found in the construction of any of these buildings. The constant characteristics of the style are mainly the following: The church plans consisted of a single nave or a nave and side aisles (without transepts or with transepts forming a T-shaped plan with one or three apses). These were ceiled with barrel vaults of stone, covered with sloping stone gable roofs resting directly on the vaults, roof and vault forming a single mass of masonry. The roofs frequently have pierced crestings of stone, and antefixæ are sometimes used, as on the roofs of Greek and Roman temples. The barrel vaults are generally ribbed with great arches at equal intervals. External buttresses strengthen the walls opposite each transverse arch. Longitudinal arches below the springing of the vault often connect the main piers within, forming a series of shallow niches, which lighten the walls and correspond to the nave arcades, where these exist. These niches are sometimes deepened and form a series of side chapels with barrel vaults whose axes run transversely to the single nave, as at Cavaillon and Orange. Where side aisles exist they are narrow, and the piers carrying the nave arches are large in proportion. The thrust of the barrel vault is met by very heavy walls, and in the case of the existence of side aisles by carrying these up nearly as high as the nave vault, so that there are no clearstory windows and nave and aisles are under one roof, or the clearstory is very low. The barrel vaults of the aisles are frequently ramped upward to meet the thrust of the central vault, which is often pointed to reduce the thrust. Occasionally, as in the cathedrals of Marseilles and Fréjus, plans similar to the churches of Cavaillon and Orange have groin vaults over the nave (in place of barrel vaults) abutted by transverse barrel vaults over the chapels, a scheme of construction precisely like that of the basilica of Constantine in Rome. But this scheme of construction is rare; groin vaults usually occur only over the bay of the crossing, and sometimes (even when transepts do not exist) over the bay in advance of the apse. In rare cases the dome or the cloister vaults are used over this bay. The earlier buildings and many of the later ones are almost devoid of detail; but they are nearly always very impressive from the beauty of their proportions, their constructive simplicity, their unity of conception, and their admirable cut stone masonry. The influence of such Roman constructions as the Nymphæum at Nîmes is obvious in spite of the difference in method.

The oldest post-Roman piece of building now extant in Provence, which has any architectural character, is perhaps the oratory of S. Trophimus built into the hillside beneath the impressive and picturesque monastery of Montmajour, near Arles. Dehio places it before the year

1000. The oldest certainly dated piece of Provençal Romanesque is the little Chapel of the Holy Cross (a Greek cross in plan) at the foot of the hill of Montmajour. As is proved by the inscription discovered by Révoil, it was dedicated in 1019. It shows perfect mastery of the constructive methods employed. Its builder, Abbot Rambert, carried out also the crypt, at least, of the monastery church, and may have built a large portion of the unfinished church itself, which is of the single-nave T-shaped plan with three apses. Such detail as exists, as in the apse windows, is Latino-Byzantine in character, not unlike similar detail of the same date in Italy, but showing less rudeness of conception and handling. The beautiful cloister is of the twelfth century. The church on the island of Saint Honorat-de-Lérins between Fréjus and Nice is three-aisled without clearstory. It is of two dates, of which the older portion (almost bald in its simplicity, with a very rude front) may be before the year 1000. The chapel of the Holy Trinity, in the same island, a small structure with a curious conical dome on rude pendentives over an oblong compartment, is regarded by Viollet-le-Duc and Révoil as of the seventh or eighth century, by Dehio as of the tenth or eleventh.

A very marked Lombard influence makes itself felt in the treatment of the detail of certain buildings in the department of Hérault, which probably date from the first half of the eleventh century. These are especially: the remarkable bell-tower at Puisalicon, which strikingly recalls some of the Lombard companili, and the churches of Saint-Martin-de-Londres and Saint-Guilhem-le-Désert. The former has a short single-aisled barrel-vaulted nave and east, north, and south apses with an octagonal dome at the crossing. The wall strips and arcaded cornices of the exterior, the detail of the capitals, and the profiles of the mouldings are strongly suggestive of Lombard work. Still more is this the case with the boldly designed and picturesque abbey church of Saint-Guilhem-le-Désert. This is a T-shaped basilican church, the apse of which has a bold, blind arcade, of marked Lombard character, immediately under the cornice. As belonging in part to the same group, may be mentioned the curious circular church of Rieux-Mérinville near Carcassonne. More like other Provençal buildings is the charming little church of S. Pierre at Reddes (Hérault).

A marked characteristic of the Provençal style, as it advances, is its imitation of classic detail: in part, closely following the Roman remains of the neighbourhood; in part, — especially in later examples, — showing adaptations of classic motives, which recall closely in theme and detail the Christian work of central Syria of the fourth to the sixth centuries. This influence may well have come from the pilgrimages and crusades. The similar material used would be likely especially to strike a Provençal, and Provence and Languedoc had usually close relations with the crusaders' princedom of Antioch, where lay all the central Syrian buildings which much of this work so closely resembles. But in the earliest buildings which belong to this tendency we see only imitation of the Roman work of Provence itself. The date of this conscious revival of classic form cannot be certainly determined, but the earliest example of it is probably the porch of the cathedral of Notre-Dame-des-Doms at Avignon, which Ramée and Dehio agree in placing in the last decade of the eleventh century, in other words, about the time of the first crusade. This porch is almost a reproduction, even to the treatment of many of the details, of the Roman triumphal arch at Carpentras, with variations showing Byzantine influence. The interior of this church has been much altered. It is barrel-vaulted as usual, but is remarkable for a dome inappropriately placed over an oblong bay, and carried on longitudinal squinch arches. The chapel of S. Gabriel, near Tarascon (Bouches-du-Rhône), otherwise a plain barrel-vaulted structure, has a rich portal closely imitating classic detail. In greater or less degree, the same tendency is seen in the abbey at Vaison, the church of S. Quenin at the same place, the churches of Cavaillon, S. Marie-au-Lac at Le Thor, of S. Ruf (all in Vaucluse), S. Restitut, La Garde-Adhémar, and especially Saint-Paul-trois-Châteaux (all in Drôme). Not only do the porches show the close following of classic detail, but cornices and friezes also ; and Corinthian pilasters or three-quarter columns ornament the angles of the apses. This richness of detail, however, is carefully confined to the entrances, cornices, the apse, and the cloister. At Saint-Paul-trois-Châteaux, Roman Doric pilasters and arches, forming a Roman order, are imitated with excellent effect, below the Corinthianesque entablature which forms the main cornice. Friezes of figures in the classic manner occur in the cathedrals of Vaison, Cavaillon, and Nîmes. But cathedral of Aix (Bouches-du-Rhône), a curious conglomerate of all the Provençal styles, has a portal somewhat similar in detail to that of the cathedral of Avignon. The churches of Maguelonne (Hérault) and the fortified church of Les Saintes-Maries (Gard) show similar characteristics. All these churches have strongly marked individual traits which give them charm, and in all of them is the Provençal refinement of proportion. The little church of Mollèges (Bouches-du-Rhône) is interesting from having a small belfry, imitated from the crowning feature of the Roman tomb at the neighbouring Saint-Remy. But not all the buildings, erected after this classic tendency shows itself, are influenced by it. They abbey of Le Thoronet (Var) is a

very complete example of a Cistercian monastery of twelfth century with church and cloister, chapter house and refectory, in perfect preservation. But the detail shows almost no imitation of classic remains. The sturdy proportions of columns and arch-orders in the cloister are almost Norman in their effect. The abbeys of Sénanque (Vaucluse) and Silvacanne (Bouches-du-Rhône) are similar.

The style culminates in the magnificent abbey church of S. Gilles (Gard). It was begun by Count Raymond IV. of Toulouse, one of the leaders of the first crusade, who, on account of his devotion to the saint and his abbey, preferred to be known as Comte de St. Gilles. The church was still unfinished at the outbreak of the iniquitous crusade against the Albigenses in 1209. The vaults of the nave were completed by a master builder of the north of France after 1261. The church, still incomplete, was ruined by the Huguenots at the end of the sixteenth century. The choir down to the bases of the piers, and the transepts, except the northern wall, were destroyed, as were also the vaults of the nave and aisles, save one bay of the aisles, which now serves as a sacristy. The church was revaulted between 1650 and 1655 with ugly rococo vaulting at a much lower level, and a new apse was built to the west of the crossing, so that the length of the church was reduced by about one half. The building suffered again in the Revolution. But, in spite of all these mutilations, it still remains the most magnificent fragment of Provençal architecture, and one of the most impressive of Romanesque buildings. The width of the church diminishes slightly from west to east. The stonecutting throughout is marvellously perfect even for Provence. The joints are so fine that a knife blade cannot be inserted in them, and the plinths of the columns of the ambulatory, which still remain in place, have their sides accurately cut to the curve of the apse. The spiral staircase in the north wall of the choir, with its spiral barrel vault, is a marvel of accurate stereotomy. The north wall of the transept, of most delicate detail and proportion, shows remains of the ribs (decorated with the chevron) of the vault which originally covered it. The remaining bay of the north aisle has also vaults of the twelfth century. The church has a remarkable crypt of unusual extent. Its vaulting is segmental, springing from low, fluted, rectangular piers. But the most wonderful feature of the church is the great portal of the west front. This is probably the earliest example in Western architecture of that union of the three western doorways of a great church in a single composition which afterward followed in the porches of Northern Gothic cathedrals. The motive is strikingly similar to that of the great porch of Kalat-Semaan in central Syria, from which it was probably borrowed. The figure sculpture shows clearly imitation of the Byzantine ivory triptychs, of which large numbers were imported into the West. But the Western and distinctively mediæval feeling shows itself in a certain vigour of handling throughout, and its grim humour finds vent in some grotesque heads, and in the beasts which travel along the moulding below the frieze. The couchant lions, which support the columns on either side of the central door, show that the designer was familiar with the devouring beasts in similar positions in north Italian churches. In richness and beauty of composition, and in excellence of execution, this splendid portal is hardly surpassed by any of the great Gothic porches. Immediately opposite the façade of the church is an interesting Romanesque house. Probably somewhat later in date, and imitated from the central portion of the portal of S. Gilles, is the great porch of the church of S. Trophime at Arles. The composition is somewhat more regular and even richer in its figure sculpture, which is somewhat more firmly handled. It has every evidence of being a later production by the same masters. Its single arch is slightly pointed, and it is crowned by a low gable, in this respect still more resembling the central part of the porch of Kalat-Semaan. The church of S. Trophime is older than the porch. It is three-aisled without clearstory, with pointed, ribbed barrel vault over the nave, and ramping barrel vaults over the very narrow side aisles. The piers are very heavy in proportion to the spans they carry. The choir is of Flamboyant Gothic. But of greater interest than the church is the adjoining cloister, the richest and most beautiful of all the cloisters of Provence. The larger part of it is of the twelfth century, evidently of the same date as the church porch. The round arches of this portion rest on coupled columns with richly sculptured capitals, many of which contain figure subjects. The piers are sculptured with figures of saints, precisely similar in treatment to those of the porch. The cloister is barrel vaulted. The remaining portion of the cloister is of the Gothic period, with pointed arches, and is of much less interest. The motive of the porch of S. Trophime reappears in a simpler and modified form in the porch of the church of S. Marthe at Tarascon, while that of S. Gilles, very much simplified, deprived of its sculpture, and much more northern in feeling, is found again in the porch of the incomplete façade of the church at Saint-Pons in Hérault. Similar to the beautiful cloisters of Provence is the exquisite cloister of Elne, south of Perpignan (Pyrénées-Orientales).

As already stated, the same Count Raymond IV., who began the church of S. Gilles, the culminating building of the Provençal style, built at his capital, Toulouse, the great church of S. Sernin, the central building of the Ro-

manesque of western Languedoc. It was begun in the year 1091 — twenty-five years before S. Gilles. Unlike Provence, the district of which Toulouse is the centre is without building stone, which has to be brought from a distance. It has always, therefore, made large use of brick. Like most of the buildings of Toulouse, S. Sernin is of brick with stone trimmings ; it is a great five-aisled church with boldly projecting three-aisled transepts, and with an ambulatory about its apse and radiating chapels. In this latter respect and in its constructive system it follows the style of Auvergne, having galleries over its side aisles and its central barrel vault abutted by half barrel vaults in the aisles. Its curious octagonal brick tower at the crossing in five receding stories is, in its upper stages, of the thirteenth century, with triangular, in place of arched, openings, and there are several other similar church towers in the city of the latter date. In detail, S. Sernin is quite unlike the churches of Provence, and is influenced more by the Romanesque of Auvergne and Aquitaine. At Albi the Romanesque portions of the church of S. Salvi show similar influences. But there is no evidence that the influence of these buildings was extensive in Languedoc. Most of the building that preceded the Albigensian wars has disappeared ; but the oldest part of the cathedral of Toulouse and of S. Nazaire at Carcassonne are more closely allied to Provençal work. The Albigensian wars abruptly broke off the architectural development both in Languedoc and Provence. As the result of these wars Languedoc, toward the end of the thirteenth century, was added to the royal domain of France, and the buildings constructed after this borrow the Gothic forms of the north, although applying them to the local scheme. The Romanesque cathedrals of Marseilles and Fréjus, already referred to, are reproduced in Gothic forms in the two churches erected by the orders of S. Louis in the lower town of Carcassonne, and this scheme is followed in other churches, most of which are fortified. The most splendid of these is the cathedral of Albi, which is of the fourteenth century. In this case ribbed vaults take the place of the earlier transverse barrel vaults between the interior buttresses. The church is mainly of brick with turrets opposite each buttress. It has a superb flamboyant Gothic porch of stone. The great width of the vault in proportion to the height, the absence of aisles, and the two tiers of deeply recessed chapels between the buttresses give the interior a very different aspect from that of northern Gothic churches, and this difference is increased by the Italian wall and ceiling paintings of the end of the fifteenth and beginning of the sixteenth centuries. The abbey church of S. Bertrand de Cominges

(Haute-Garonne) is similar in scheme, and both churches have very rich choir stalls and screens of the sixteenth century, Flamboyant at Albi, and of Renaissance design at S. Bertrand. The choir of the church of S. Nazaire at Carcassonne, built between 1320 and 1330, is one of the most notable Gothic monuments of Languedoc. Its rich tracery and sculpture and admirable construction are worthy of most careful study, and it continues the constructive traditions of the region in having its aisles carried to the height of the nave. But the greater portion of the later Gothic churches of Provence and Languedoc are of comparatively little interest, and differ hardly at all from such buildings in the north, as for instance the similar fifteenth century churches of Carpentras and S. Pierre at Avignon.

Of only less interest than the church architecture are the remains of city walls, fortresses, and castles. Foremost among them is the ancient castle and circuit of the city of Carcassonne, which exists complete, restored by Viollet-le-Duc. The oldest parts are Visigothic, and may perhaps rest on Roman foundations, but the greater portion of these picturesque and impressive walls dates from the twelfth to the fourteenth centuries. Very impressive, also, are the walls of Aigues Mortes (Gard), built by Philip the Bold (1272). Farther up the Rhône, at Tarascon, is the castle of King René of Anjou; and at Avignon, which on the death of Alphonse and Jeanne of Toulouse, in 1270, became the property of the popes as their share of the spoils of the Albigensian wars, still stands the great palace, or fortress, of the popes, with the perfectly preserved circuit walls of the city built by them in the fourteenth century, while across the river is the fortress of Villeneuve-lez-Avignon, built at the same period. Provence is rich in picturesque castles of minor importance, among which may be mentioned those of Simiane (Basses-Alpes), La Barrue (Vaucluse), and Les Beaux (Bouches-du-Rhône). These are of various dates, from the twelfth to the sixteenth centuries.

The archiepiscopal fortress palace of Narbonne (in Languedoc), and the cathedral, are both of the fourteenth century, and of great interest.

The Renaissance work of Languedoc and Provence is still less distinctive than the Gothic work that preceded it. The city of Toulouse is unusually rich in Renaissance work, from the time of Francis I. to Henry IV. The latter especially favoured the town, and important portions of the city buildings known as *La Capitole* were built by him, though the greatest part of it is later. Like the Gothic and Romanesque work before it, that of the Renaissance in Toulouse is distinguished by its combination of brick and stone. The stone carving is unusually rich and fanciful, if often capricious

and unreasonable. Caryatid figures in every variety of form and attitude are used in window jambs and mullions, often executed with unusual grace and refinement. The most important monuments of the time of Francis I. at Toulouse are the splendid portal of the church of La Dalbade (almost of north Italian design) and the rich gateway which leads to the enclosure of the church of S. Sernin. But the chief Renaissance monuments are the palaces, or hôtels. Of these the so-called Hôtel Du-Vieux-Raisin, or de Las Bordes, the Lycée (partly late Gothic), the Hôtel d'Assézat, the Hôtel de Caulet, and the so-called Maison-de-Pierre of the time of Henry IV., are the most important. At Avignon a number of later Renaissance buildings show stray Italian influence, if indeed they are not of Italian design. Such are the Hôtel Crillon, the Hôtel des Monnaies, and the Church du Lycée.

At Montpellier (Hérault) is a grandiose château d'eau and aqueduct and a triumphal arch and statue of Louis XIV.

Of more modern buildings, the only one which seems to call for mention is the museum at Marseilles with the great semicircular colonnade and fountain of Long-Champ, an effective composition erected by Napoleon III. Although the distinctive development of Provence and Languedoc, in their architecture as in their literature, was suddenly and violently arrested by the horrors of the religious wars and persecutions of the thirteenth century, yet none of the subsequent styles — which followed the larger development of the French nation, of which the ancient county of Toulouse then became a part — could altogether escape the romantic influences of this wonderful and too little known corner of Europe, interesting alike in its architecture, its literature, its pathetic history, and its unique and picturesque scenery.

— H. LANGFORD WARREN.

Archives de la Commission des Monuments Historiques, pub. of 1855–1872; *Archives de la Commission des Monuments Historiques*, begun in 1898, still (1901) in course of publication; Bauchal, *Nouveau Dictionnaire Biographique et Critique des Architectes Français*; Barqui, *L'Architecture moderne en France*; Berty, *La Renaissance monumentale en France*; Calliat, *Histoire de l'église de Saint Eustache*; Champeaux, *L'Art décoratif dans le vieux Paris*; Champollion-Figeac, *Monographie du Palais de Fontainebleau*; Chateau, *Histoire et caractères de l'architecture en France*; Corroyer, *Description de l'abbaye du Mont Saint-Michel*; Davie, *Architectural Studies in France*; De Laborde, *La Renaissance des arts à la cour de France*; De Verneilh, *L'architecture byzantine en France*; Dilke, *French Architects and Sculptors of the XVIIIth Century*; Du Cerceau, *Les plus excellents bastiments de France*; Ferree, *The Chronology of the Cathedral Churches of France*; Garnier, *Le nouvel Opéra*; Gélis-Didot, *Le Peinture décorative en France du XI au XVIe siècle*; Gélis-Didot, *La Peinture décorative en France du XVIe au XVIIe siècle*; Gey müller, *Les Du Cerceau, leur vie et leur œuvre ;* Geymüller, *Die Baukunst der Renaissance in Frankreichs* (forms part of the *Handbuch der Architektur*); Gurlitt, *Die Baukunst Frankreichs ;* Havard, *La France artistique et monumentale ;* Johnson, *Specimens of French Architecture ;* Lance, *Dictionnaire des Architectes Français ;* Lassus and Viollet-le-Duc, *Notre Dame de Paris ;* Lechevallier-Chevignard, *Les styles Français ;* Lenoir, *Statistique Monumentale de Paris ;* Lübke, *Geschichte der Renaissance in Frankreich ;* Macgibbon, *The Architecture of Provence and The Riviera ;* Magne, *L'œuvre des peintres verriers français ;* Narjoux, *Monuments élévés par la ville de Paris, 1850–1880 ;* Palustre, *La Renaissance en France ;* Pattison, *The Renaissance of Art in France ;* Pugin and Le Keux, *Specimens of the Architectural Antiquities of Normandy ;* Révoil, *Architecture romane du midi de la France ;* Roussel, *Histoire et Description du Château d'Anet ;* Rouyer and Darcel, *L'art architectural en France depuis François I. jusqu'à Louis XIV. ;* Ruprich-Robert, *L'Architecture Normande ;* Ruprich-Robert, *L'église et le monastère du Val-de-Grâce, 1645–*

FRANCE, PART I.: CHAPELS, 16TH CENTURY, ATTACHED TO CHURCH OF S. LAURENT, NOGENT-SUR-SEINE (AUBE).

1665 ; Rupin, *L'Abbaye et les Cloîtres de Moissac ;* Saint Paul, *Histoire Monumentale de la France ;* Sauvageot, *Choix de palais, châteaux, hôtels, et maisons de France ;* Sharpe, *Domed Churches of Charente ;* Viollet-le-Duc, *Dictionnaire raisonné de l'architecture française ;* Viollet-le-Duc, *Entretiens sur l'architecture.*

FRANCIONE (FRANCESCO DI GIOVANNI) ; wood worker (*intarsiatore*), architect, and engineer ; b. 1428.

In 1487 he assisted La Cecca in building the fortress of Sarzana, Italy. A "Franciscus Johannis carpentarius Florentinus," who in 1458 built the catafalque of Calixtus III. (Pope

1455–1458), is doubtless the same person. He was the instructor of Giuliano and Antonio da San Gallo (I.) (see San Gallo, G. and A.).

Müntz, *Les Arts à la cour des Papes ;* Vasari, Milanesi ed.

FRANÇOIS, BASTYEN (SÉBASTIEN) ; architect and sculptor ; d. about 1523.

François married a daughter of Guillaume Regnault, nephew of Michel Colombe (see Colombe, M.). In 1500 he became supervising architect of the cathedral of Tours in association with his brother Martin François.

Giraudet, *Les Artistes Tourangeaux.*

FRANÇOIS, GATIEN; architect.

A son of Bastyen François (see François, B.). He was employed first on the château of Chenonceaux. May 16, 1521, he was made *maître d'œuvre* of the king in Touraine (France).

Giraudet, *Les Artistes Tourangeaux.*

FRANK (v. t.). To frame together, as stiles and rails having moulded edges, by mitering only to the depth of the moulding, the rest of the end of the abutting piece being cut square or tenoned and joined to the other in the usual manner; said especially of the sash bars.

FRATER; FRATER HOUSE. Same as Refectory in a monastic establishment. (Sometimes fratery and fratry.)

FRATERNITY HOUSE. In the United States, a building erected for the use of some association of college students called a fraternity. Such societies are generally more or less secret; and some of them have a federal constitution with several (sometimes twenty or thirty) branches, called chapters, each in a separate college. The fraternity house is then, often, the home of one of these chapters; and may have, besides meeting rooms, a number of lodging rooms for the members, and even a common dining hall.

FRAZEE, JOHN; sculptor; b. July 18, 1790; d. Feb. 24, 1852.

Frazee was first employed as a stonecutter in Haverstraw, New York. He afterward, with Launitz, opened a marble yard on Broadway, New York City. His mantelpieces, monuments, and the like were remarkable for beauty of workmanship, especially in the lettering. His name is cut on the architrave of a window in the northern front of the old Customhouse, now the Subtreasury Building, in New York. He did not design the building, however, but superintended its construction.

Tuckerman, *Book of American Artists; American Architect*, Vol. XXXVIII., p. 80.

FREDERICKSBORG. A royal castle of the kings of Denmark; on the island of Sjaelland and north of Copenhagen. It is a very large building of considerable architectural merit, built in the early years of the seventeenth century.

FREDERIK VAN AMSTERDAM; glass painter.

Frederik van Amsterdam was a well-known glass painter of the sixteenth century in Holland. He designed the fine windows of the abbey of Tongerloo.

Immerzeel, *Hollandsche en Vlaamsche Kunstschilders*, etc.

FREEMAN, EDWARD AUGUSTUS; historian and writer on architecture.

Professor Freeman, the historian, first became known as a writer on architecture through a book of travels in Dalmatia. This was followed

by a *History of Architecture* (1849, 8vo), *An Essay on the Development of Window Tracery in England* (1850–1851, 8vo), *Remarks on the Architecture of Llandaff Cathedral* (1850, 8vo), *History of the Cathedral Church of Wells* (1870, 8vo), *Historical and Architectural Sketches, chiefly Italian* (1876, 8vo), *Cathedral Churches, Ely and Norwich* (1883, folio).

Stephens, *Life and Letters of E. A. Freeman;* Obituary in *Journal R. I. B. A.*, March 24, 1892.

FREEMASONS. (See Guild.)

FREESTONE. Any limestone or sandstone of very homogeneous structure that can be worked freely in any direction. — G. P. M.

FRENCH CURVE. An instrument used in mathematical drawing. (See Curve.)

FRESCO PAINTING (from Italian *fresco*, fresh).

Painting on fresh, wet plaster. All sorts of mural paintings, from encaustic to distemper, are indiscriminately and wrongly called frescoes. The process of true fresco painting is as follows:

Pure limestone consists of carbonic acid and lime, and is therefore a carbonate of lime. The limestone is subjected to heat, the carbonic acid is expelled, and there remains lime. If to this lime, water be added, the result will be hydrate of lime. Only a certain amount of water combines chemically with the lime. When hydrate of lime is exposed to the air, the water is expelled by carbonic acid and the result is again carbonate of lime, the original limestone chemically speaking, for mechanically the cohesion of limestone is never regained. Sand is usually mixed with the liquid lime to augment its cohesiveness. The pigments are applied while the wet plaster is drying and hardening, that is, while the carbonic acid is expelling the water. The painting must be finished before its expulsion is complete. A thin crust of carbonate of lime will then be formed over the painting and the particles of colour become encased in carbonate of lime, thus protecting it from water and moderate friction. If the painting be continued after the plaster has lost the greater part of its water, no crust will be formed and the pigments will be deprived of their natural protection. Moreover, when dry, they will exhibit chalky spots. Brick walls are the best. Those of stone are not objectionable. Both should have sufficient "key" to hold the plaster. Lathing is inferior to brick or stone for perpendicular surfaces, but under all circumstances, the wall must be dry and exempt from saline efflorescence. A limestone free from foreign ingredients yields best lime for fresco. After the lime has been well mixed with water it is poured into earthen pits and kept there for at least a year, — the longer the better. If too fresh, it will blister and flake off. When taken out of the pit the lime is again mixed with water until it is about as thick as milk, well strained, and the superfluous water poured off. It has then the consistency of cream cheese, and is ready to be mixed with the sand. No hair is to be used.

Two plasterings are necessary for fresco :

(1) The *arriccio*, or rough cast.

(2) The *intonaco*, or *scialbo*, or finishing coat.

The proportion of sand to lime varies according to the richness of the lime. Generally, the rule is two parts of sand to one of lime. The *arriccio* should be a little less than half an inch in thickness, and applied in two or three quickly succeeding coats. Its surface should be roughened to give a key to the *intonaco*. When it is thoroughly dry, it is ready for the *intonaco* on which the fresco is to be painted. After the *arriccio* is saturated with water, the *intonaco* is spread in two thin coats, the whole being about one tenth of an inch thick. Sometimes marble dust is mixed with the plaster for the *intonaco*, and, occasionally, colour, to reduce its whiteness to a middle tint. Supposing, now, that the *arriccio* is ready to receive the *intonaco*, the painter indicates to the plasterer the portion to be painted in one day, which the plasterer proceeds to cover with the *intonaco*. The corresponding portion of his cartoon is cut off and transferred to the wet *intonaco*, either by pouncing, or by passing over the outline with a style, which leaves a depression in the plaster. For delicate works pouncing is preferable. The palette for fresco is a quiet one, which, in a measure, accounts for its harmonious tones. Chalk — not lead — is used for white. The colours, when dry, appear lighter and warmer than when first applied to the cool gray plaster which ultimately dries white. To judge of their final effect, the painter tries the colours on a piece of dry umber, which immediately absorbs their moisture. It is well to prepare the whole of a needed tone at once, it being difficult to match tones in fresco.

There are two schools of fresco, the one characterized by its comparatively thin, transparent qualities, and the moderate use of impasto ; the other, by a more generous use of it. To the former school belong all the early painters from Cimabue to Raphael and Michelangelo inclusive. The other school came later, but in both schools the medium is only water. When the day's task is completed, the workman cuts away the unpainted plaster with a sharp instrument and bevels the edge. While painting a figure, it is well to paint a portion of the background at the same time to avoid hardness of contour and preserve the integrity of the outline. On the following day, the plasterer joins the fresh *intonaco* to that of the preceding day, and so on, until the picture is completed. All retouches must be made with colour tempered with size, that is, *a secco*, or dry, or when the plaster is

no longer wet. Secco is opaque, and perishable if exposed to moisture, and the less of it the better. When a considerable part of the work is unsatisfactory, it must be destroyed and repainted.

Fresco has the advantage of being cheap, lasting, and decorative in tone. It has a dead surface which is the *sine qua non* of mural painting; it may be either transparent or opaque. Vasari characterizes it as the most virile and durable of all processes. It was used by both Greeks and Romans, and it was *the* process of the early Italian and Renaissance painters. It is used in Italy to-day.

—FREDERIC CROWNINSHIELD.

FRESCO-SECCO. This is a poor substitute for fresco. When the plaster is perfectly dry, the surface is rubbed with pumice stone, and late on the day previous to that on which the painting is to be commenced, the plaster must be carefully washed with water into which a small portion of lime has been infused. The following morning the wall must be again washed. Afterward, the cartoon is fastened up, the outline pounced, and the artist commences his work. The colours used in this method are similar to those employed in true fresco. The limewater necessarily yields a very feeble protecting crust of carbonate of lime, too feeble, according to the author's experiments, to protect the pigments. But there are those who say that they have practised this method with success. (See Fresco Painting.)

—FREDERIC CROWNINSHIELD.

FRET. *A.* Same as Meander.

B. A similar ornamentation by means of right lines forming angles with one another but carried over a larger surface. Thus, certain Oriental gratings or screens made ornamental by slender lines of wood or metal breaking one another at angles are, in the sense of their decorative design, frets, but hardly meanders.

Diamond Fret. A fret or meander in which the lines form obtuse and acute angles with one another. The term is extended to mean a similar pattern in which the lines, though forming right angles with one another, are set diagonally to the main bounding lines of the border or other limited surface to which the fret is applied.

Dovetail Fret. A fret or meander with trapezoidal instead of rectangular repeats, forming a series of interlocking or counterchanged dovetails.

FRETWORK. In general, any decoration of Frets or Meanders. Hence more particularly, in modern times, interlaced openwork of wood, metal, or stone ; reticulated openwork, especially such as is intricate and composed of small units like the Arabic Meshrebeeyeh.

FRIARY. A monastery for the occupancy of a class of monks known as friars. (See Monastic Architecture.)

FRIEZE. Any long and narrow, nearly horizontal, architectural member, especially one which has a chiefly decorative purpose. Especially, in Grecian, Greco-Roman, and neoclassic architecture, that horizontal band which forms the central and usually the most important part of the entablature. In the Doric order this band is cut across by the triglyphs and is thus divided into metopes, the triglyphs having always strongly marked vertical lines, the metopes being commonly adorned with sculpture in relief or with painting. In the other orders, and in all other varieties, the frieze is a continuous band which is that part of the entablature most usually ornamented, or most richly ornamented when all receive decoration. Thus, in a Roman temple, such as the *Maison-Carrée* at Nîmes, of the Corinthian order, the frieze is filled with a richly worked scroll, rather meaningless when forming the principal feature of the entablature, but contrasting with the much smaller and less complex sculpture of the architrave and cornice.

The use of the general term frieze for the chief part of the entablature indicates its strong relation to ornamental horizontal bands generally. It is, in fact, such a band, placed above the columns from which it is separated by the simpler and more obviously constructional architrave, while it is separated also from the beginnings of the roof by the projecting cornice with its drip and the resulting deep shadow. In the Parthenon, a band of the richest and most exquisite sculpture in low relief terminates at top the plain wall of the naos, and this must have seemed to the builders the natural termination of such a wall, for it was placed so high under the roof of the pteroma that the question of its proper lighting has greatly interested modern students. The outer frieze of the Parthenon, namely, that forming part of the entablature, is divided by triglyphs into metopes sculptured in very high relief, the difference in the relief of the sculpture being obviously suggested by the difference in the direction and quantity of light received. At Assos, the Doric temple had an architrave sculptured with figures in relief, while the metopes between the triglyphs were not so adorned; it would, therefore, be not incorrect to say that the architrave of the temple of Assos by exception was turned into a sculptured frieze, while the architectural frieze above was not sculptured. The celebrated Mausoleum at Halicarnassus must have had several friezes at different heights; the enclosure of the Heraion at Gjolbaschi has one frieze on the exterior of the bounding wall near the top. The so-called Harpy Tomb from Xanthus, now in the British Museum, has a frieze at the top of the slightly sloping shaft and beneath the overhanging projection of the stone roof, which frieze is about half as high or broad as it is long on either side;

but it runs all around the small monument and seems to tie it together and give it unity and artistic purpose. The Choragic Monument of Lysicrates has a frieze of delicate sculptures of figures in action, and leaving an unusual amount of background plain, and this distribution reminds the student of the frieze of the Erechtheion, which must have been somewhat similar in effect, probably because of the plan followed of attaching to a background of one colour the figures worked in a different material.

In mediæval architecture the frieze is not a common or an important feature, except in the painted decoration of interiors. — R. S.

FRIEZE PANEL. *A.* Same as Metope.

B. In carpentry and joinery, one of the upper panels of a door or piece of wainscoting, or the like, when forming a crowning member, — generally horizontal, — above a higher panelwork or other surface; this upper row, with the framing which contains it, being considered as a frieze.

FRIGIDARIUM. In a Roman bathing establishment (see Thermæ) the cold room; that is to say, usually the large room in which was the bath of unheated water. This, in a great establishment, like those in Rome, was frequently a large swimming tank.

FRISONE (FRIXONO), MARCO (DA CAMPIONE); d. July 10, 1390.

Marco came to the works of the cathedral of Milan on March 5, 1387, the year after its commencement. Calvi (op. cit.) supposes that he designed the building. This honour seems rather to belong to Simone da Orsenigo (see Simone da Orsenigo).

Boito, *Duomo di Milano; Annali del Duomo;* Calvi, *Notizie.*

FRIXONO. (See Frisone.)

FRONT. One face of a building, or of a large member of a building, as a pavilion or the like, especially the most important face considered from the point of view of its architectural character or its visibility from without. When used in any less specific sense, the term is usually qualified. Thus, if a house stands at the corner of two streets, the side in which the entrance door is placed is commonly spoken of as the front, and the face on the other street as the end or side wall; but this side may again be called the front on such a street. (Compare Façade.)

FRONTAL. *A.* Formerly, a small pediment or like decoration over a door, window, or niche (in this sense, now obsolete; see Fronton).

B. A decorative covering for the front of an altar below the table; commonly of cloth, like a lambrequin or valence, embroidered and covering only part of the front; sometimes of wood carved and painted, sometimes of gold or silver set with gems. — A. D. F. H.

FRONT DOOR. The principal door of entrance, especially of a private house, apartment house, or other building of residence, as distinguished from the door leading to the kitchen and other domestic offices, and also from all other doors of entrance in the rear or side wall.

FRONTINUS, SEXTUS JULIUS; engineer; d. about 106 A.D.

He first appears about 70 A.D. as *prætor urbanus* under the Emperor Vespasian; 75 A.D. he was appointed governor of Britain, and was superseded in that office by Agricola in 78. In 97 he was appointed *curator aquarum*, or superintendent of the aqueducts. He was succeeded about 106 A.D. by the Younger Pliny. (See Plinius Cæcilius Secundus, Caius.) Two of his works are extant: *Strategematicon, Libri IV.;* and *De Aquæductibus Urbis Romæ, Libri II.*

Herschel, *Frontinus and the Water Supply of Rome.*

FRONTISPIECE. The principal façade, or part of a façade, of a building, especially when this is much more decorative than the rest, and is in a sense separated from it in design; more especially, a subordinate feature as a porch, a doorway treated more elaborately than the rest of the façade, and more or less as a separate composition applied to the front.

FRONTON. In French, a pediment; and by extension, any member occupying nearly the same position, either fronting a roof, or surmounting a window opening, or the like. In English usage, rare and generally confined to a pediment-shaped member crowning the architrave of an opening. (See Coronet.)

FROWCESTER (FROUCESTER), WALTER; abbot; d. 1412.

About 1400 Walter Frowcester, abbot of Gloucester, built, or caused to be built, the great cloisters of his monastery.

Britton, *Architectural Antiquities.*

FRUSTUM. *A.* In geometry, a truncated cone or pyramid; or, more accurately, that portion of any solid left between its base and a plane which cuts off the apex or upper portion parallel to its base; hence, —

B. A drum of a column, or of a pier when the section of the pier comprises one piece.

FUFITIUS (FUFIDIUS); architect.

According to Vitruvius (VII., præf.) Fufitius was the first Roman writer on architecture (*de his rebus primus instituit edere volumen*).

Vitruvius, ed Marini.

FUGA, FERDINANDO; architect; b. 1699 (Florence); d. about 1784.

Fuga was called to Rome by Clement XII. (Pope 1730–1740) to complete the works begun by Alessandro Specchi (see Specchi, A.) at the Palazzo Quirinale. His earliest independent work is the Palazzo della Consulta near the Quirinal, and his most important undertaking

the Palazzo Corsini in Rome (1732). His last years were spent in Naples. In 1781 he began the reconstruction of the cathedral of Palermo.

Gurlitt, *Geschichte des Barockstiles in Italien.*

FULBERT; bishop and architect; d. April 10, 1029.

The cathedral of Chartres, probably the fourth church erected on the site of the present building, was burned Sept. 7, 1020, during the reign of Robert le Diable, duke of Normandy. The bishop Fulbert devoted himself to the immediate reconstruction of the church. The crypt of the church was completed about two years after the conflagration. The cathedral was completed during the administration of his successor, the bishop Thierry, and dedicated Oct. 17, 1037. The towers were added after 1115. This church, with the exception of the towers which still stand, was destroyed by fire in 1194. The present cathedral was built on its ruins.

Bulteau, *Monographie de la cathédrale de Chartres;* Bulteau, *Description de la cathédrale de Chartres.*

FULL-CENTRED. Semicircular; said of an arch. Obviously a translation (partially erroneous) of the French term *plein cintre.*

FULLER, THOMAS; architect; b. 1822 (in England); d. Sept. 28, 1898 (at Ottawa, Canada).

Fuller was articled to an architect in London, and assisted J. R. Brandon (see Brandon, J. R.) in the preparation of his works on Gothic architecture. He practised in the West Indies and in Canada, and in 1863 took charge of all government buildings at Ottawa. In 1868 Fuller and Laver were chosen (by competition) architects of the capitol at Albany, New York, and held that position until they were superseded by H. H. Richardson (see Richardson, H. H.), Eidlitz, and Olmsted. In 1881 he was appointed chief architect of the Dominion Government, and held that office until 1897.

American Architect, Vol. LXII., p. 37.

FUMOIR. In French, a smoking room; especially, one in a public building or place of public resort, or the like.

FUR. To apply Furring; generally with *up, down,* or *out.* Thus, a ceiling which is suspended some distance below the joists, by means of furring, is said to be furred *down;* a roof which is carried on furring some distance above the roof beams is said to be furred *up.*

FURNACE. An apparatus by means of which a fire may be brought to a great heat, which heat may then be utilized in any way desired. Ordinarily, such a structure used for the heating of the interior of any building; in this sense, divisible into hot air furnace, hot water furnace, and steam furnace; although more commonly limited to the hot air furnace alone. Such a furnace is distinguished from **a**

stove in that the hot air, collected in a large chamber, passes to different parts of the building by means of pipes and flues, whereas a stove generally heats the room in which it stands by

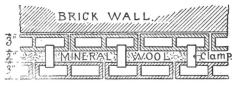

FURRING BY HOLLOW BLOCKS, AS OF TERRA COTTA, WITH DEAFENING: A VERY ELABORATE SYSTEM.
Compare the cuts under Fireproofing.

direct radiation; although some part of the heat of the stove may be diverted, and the stove become, in a sense, a furnace. (See Warming.)

FURRING. A light framework, or simply strips,—generally of wood, but sometimes of metal,—applied to walls, beams, or similar surfaces to support sheathing, plaster, or other form of finish. Its purpose is either to give a more uniform and even structure for the application of such a finish; or to form an air space behind such a finish; or to give a semblance of a constructive form, as the imitation of a vault, by means of some plastic material carried on a frame of the necessary shape. By extension, in recent times, hollow brick or tile used for such purposes.

FURRING STRIP. Any strip, generally of wood, used for furring. Specifically, in the United States, a strip of spruce, 1 inch by 2 inches in size, used chiefly in furring on the inner face of an outside wall to form an air space.

FUSAROLE. A moulding of convex rounded section, commonly carved into beads or the like; as under an ovolo or echinus, in a classic capital, or forming part of an architrave.

FUST. *A.* The shaft of a column or pilaster, equivalent to the French *fût.* (Obsolete.)

B. Locally, in Devonshire, the ridge of a roof. — (A. P. S.)

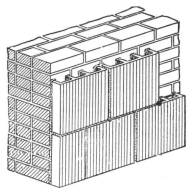

FURRING BY HOLLOW BLOCKS, AS OF TERRA COTTA: THE SIMPLEST SYSTEM.
The corrugated surface to receive the plaster.

G

GABLE. A more or less triangular-shaped piece of wall closing the end of a double pitched or gable roof. The top of the wall may be bounded by the two slopes of the roof when this overhangs; or it may form a parapet following, more or less, the slopes of the roof behind. Hence, any piece of wall of the same general shape, having a more purely ornamental purpose. The French make a distinction between the *pignon*, which is properly the enclosure of the roof at either end, and the *gable*, which is more commonly ornamental; but in English no separate term has been introduced. It is often impossible to fix the lower boundary of a gable; but also very often a horizontal band, either of projecting mouldings or of merely ornamental inlay, is carried across, usually for the artistic purpose of holding the parts firmly together in appearance. The only use of gables in classical architecture is in the pediments, and even this is rare in other than temple architecture. In the mediæval styles, however, the gable, both constructive and ornamental,

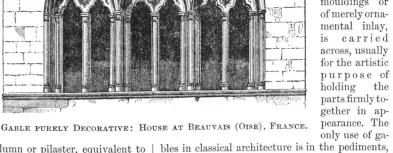

GABLE PURELY DECORATIVE: HOUSE AT BEAUVAIS (OISE), FRANCE.

GABLES OVER DOORWAYS OF PORCH, ERFURT CATHEDRAL.

large and small, is a very important item in the general decorative system. In the earlier post - Gothic styles, especially in the north of Europe, such as the German Renaissance and the Elizabethan in England, the gable, whether forming a part of the main structure, or serving as the front of the dormer, is the chief decorative feature. (For the elaborate Elizabethan gables, see Fractable.)

Stepped Gable. One whose sides have more or less the form of a continuous series of steps following the slope of the roof behind. — R. S.

GABLE BOARD. Same as Barge Board.

GABLE END. In a building having a double pitch roof, one of the end walls which terminates at top in a gable.

GABLE POLE. A pole or bar of wood laid along the edge of a roof at one side of the gable to secure the

GABLE WITH BLIND TRACERY, 13TH CENTURY; PORCH, CATHE-DRAL OF AMIENS, SOUTH AISLE.

GABLE: HOUSE OF 17TH CENTURY, AT GHENT, BELGIUM.
The pointed windows and tracery are 14th century work, restored.

thatch or shingles or roof boarding at that exposed edge.

GABLE ROOF. (See under Roof.)

GABLET. A miniature gable, usually employed as a decoration, especially in Gothic building, where it is used chiefly as a decorative form of coping, as on a buttress, pinnacle, or the like; to decorate and emphasize an arch, as in a decorative arcade, or in a church façade. (Cut, col. 165.)

GABLE WALL. *A.* Same as Gable End.

B. By extension, in the United States, any side wall of a city house of the usual type; because such houses had formerly, most often, gable roofs pitched to the front and rear, the side walls being then gables.

GABRIEL, JACQUES (I.); architect.

An architect of Argentan (Orne, France). In 1605 he contracted to build the vaults of the church of S. Germain at Argentan. He designed the Hôtel de Ville of Rouen, begun 1607, which was never finished.

De la Quérière, *Hôtel de Ville de Rouen.*

GABRIEL, JACQUES (II.); architect; d. 1686.

Jacques (II.) was a nephew by marriage of Jules Hardouin-Mansart (see Hardouin-Mansart, J.) He was the principal constructor employed at the château of Versailles, where he built the canal, reservoir, etc. In 1667 he built the establishment of the Gobelins. In 1675 Gabriel undertook the construction of the new buildings of the château of Clagny. In 1685 he began the construction of the Pont Royal.

Bouriat, *L'Architecte Gabriel* in *Nouvelles Archives*, 1876; Guiffrey, *Comptes de Louis XIV.*

GABRIEL, JACQUES ANGE; architect; b. Oct. 24, 1698; d. Jan. 2, 1782.

Jacques was the son of Jacques Jules Gabriel (see Gabriel, Jacques Jules), and assisted his father in many undertakings. At the death of his father in 1742 he succeeded him as *premier architecte* of Louis XV., and continued and completed many of the buildings begun by him. In 1745 he was made *inspecteur général des bâtiments royaux.* In 1751 he made the plans for the buildings of the École Militaire, Paris, which was built mainly by Alexandre Brongniart (see Brongniart, A.) between 752 and 1787. In 1752 he took part in the famous *concours* for the creation of the Place Louis XV., now Place de la Concorde, Paris. His plans were accepted in 1753. Work was begun in 1754 and the Place was opened in 1763. The Colonnades in the Rue Royale were not completed until 1772. Between 1753 and 1774 Gabriel rebuilt the central pavilion,

the right wing and Salle de Spectacle, of the Palace of Versailles. Between 1762 and 1768 he built the Petit Trianon in the gardens of Versailles. In 1755 he was intrusted with the restoration of the Louvre, principally the eastern portion with the colonnade designed by Claude Perrault (see Perrault, Claude). This part of the palace had never been roofed over and was much injured. About the same time he rebuilt the château of Compiègne.

Dezallier d'Argenville, *Vies des fameux architectes et sculpteurs;* Herluison, *Actes de l'état civil;* Raguenet, *Petits édifices historiques.*

GABRIEL, JACQUES JULES; architect; b. April 6, 1667; d. April 23, 1742.

Jacques Jules was a son of Jacques Gabriel (II.) (see Gabriel, Jacques, II.). In 1709 he was created *contrôleur des bâtiments* at Versailles and *architecte ordinaire du roi.* Between 1728 and 1733 he built the Hôtel Dieu at Orléans (Loire, France), and in 1727 made plans for the reconstruction of the public buildings of the city of Rennes which had been burned in 1720. In 1730 he made plans for the Palais Royal at Bordeaux (Gironde, France), which was completed in 1749. He began also the exchange and customhouse in that city, which were finished by his son Jacques Ange (see Gabriel, J. A.). In 1738 Gabriel commenced the restoration of the Hôtel des Comptes, Paris. This building, remodelled by Louis Joseph Duc (see Duc, L. J.) for the prefecture of police, was destroyed by the commune in 1871.

Lance, *Dictionnaire;* Pingeron, *Vie des architectes français.*

GABRIELIS, GABRIEL DE; architect.

Gabrielis built the palace (Schloss) at Ansbach, Bavaria, which was begun in 1713. In 1735 he was city architect of Augsburg, Bavaria, and built a chapel in the cathedral of that city.

Lessing, *Schloss Ansbach;* Gurlitt, *Barockstil in Deutschland.*

GADDI, AGNOLO DI TADDEO; painter and architect.

In 1383 Agnolo made drawings for the seven figures of Virtues on the Loggia dei Lanzi at Florence, which were executed by others. According to Vasari, the church of S. Romolo, Florence, was built from his designs in 1356. He painted frescoes at S. Croce, S. Spirito, and other Florentine churches.

Karl Frey, *Loggia dei Lanzi;* Vasari, Milanesi ed.

GAGE (and its compounds). (See Gauge.)

GAGINI, ANTONIO (ANTONELLO); sculptor and architect; b. about 1478; d. 1536.

A son of Domenico Gagini (see Gagini, D.), and the most important member of this family. An interesting work of his is the monument of Geronimo Rosso, made for the church of the abandoned convent of the Frati Minori Osservanti di San Francesco at Castroreale, near Messina (about 1506). The contract for the splendid decorations of the apse of the cathedral of Palermo was made in 1510. This work was destroyed by Ferdinando Fuga (see Fuga, F.) in his restorations in 1781. Only fragments remain. About 1515 he was commissioned to decorate in marble the tribuna of the church of S. Cita at Palermo, his most important existing work. Antonello was succeeded by his sons Giandomenico, Antonio, and Giacomo.

Di Marzo, *I Gagini.*

GAGINI (GAZINI or GASINI), DOMENICO; sculptor and architect; d. 1492.

Domenico came from Bissone, near the lake of Lugarno in Lombardy, to Palermo, Sicily, where he founded a large and important family of sculptors. He is first mentioned in a contract, dated Nov. 22, 1463, for a monument erected in the church of the convent of S. Francesco, Palermo, for Pietro Speciale (*Magnifico*). He made the beautiful sarcophagus of Antonio Grignano in the church of the Carmine at Marsala, Sicily, the sumptuous decoration of the capella of Christina in the cathedral of Palermo, and other works.

Di Marzo, *I Gagini.*

GAGINI, GIACOMO. (See Gagini, Antonio.)

GAGINI, GIANDOMENICO. (See Gagini, Antonio.)

GAI, ANTONIO DI FRANCESCO; sculptor.

May 16, 1733, Gai was commissioned to make the bronze gates of the loggietta of the campanile in the Piazza di San Marco, Venice. He made also two monuments in the chapel of the Sagredo family in the church of S. Francesco della Vigna.

GAILHABAUD, JULES; archæologist and historian of architecture; b. Aug. 29, 1810; d. April 15, 1888.

Gailhabaud was at first engaged in commerce, but after 1839 devoted himself to archæology. He formed an important collection of engravings, which was destroyed with the Hôtel de Ville, Paris, in May, 1871. Gailhabaud founded the *Revue archéologique* in 1844, and published *Les Monuments anciens et modernes*, Paris, 1840–1850, 4 vols. 4to, and *L'Architecture du Vᵉ au XVIIᵉ siècle*, 1850–1858, 4 vols. 4to.

La Grande Encyclopédie.

GAIN. *A.* The bevelled shoulder formed above a tenon on the end of a beam or similar piece, in framing. In the United States, more commonly Tusk.

B. A groove in a member or piece to receive the end of another, as by dadoing.

GAINACO, PONS DE; builder (*operarius*).

In 1265 Pons de Gainaco assisted Guillaume Artaudus in the construction of the Pont Saint Esprit over the Rhône. (See Artaud.)

De Girardot, *Ponts au XIIIᵉ siècle.*

GAINE. Anything having the shape of a sheath; hence, the lower part of a terminal or hermes where a shaft of rectangular section tapers toward the base on which it stands. The term is also, in common usage, extended to pilasters of like outline having a capital in place of a human head.

GAINSBOROUGH (GAYNISBURGH), RICHARD DE.

He was employed on the cathedral of Lincoln, England, in the fourteenth century. His tomb in the cathedral bears the incomplete date June, MCCC . . .

Britton, *Architectural Antiquities*, Vol. V.

GALBE. In French, the general outline, the exterior proportions and character, especially and primarily, of an architectural or decorative composition. Used in the same sense in English, and expressing an idea covered by no one English word.

GALILEE. In English churches, a subordinate and accessory room, usually near the entrance. The original use of the term and its derivation is uncertain.

It is generally held that there are only three galilees left in England; namely, at the cathedrals of Durham, Ely, and Lincoln; these are situated as follows : —

At Durham, across the west end; a room whose roof is supported by twelve piers carrying on round arches four walls which support the roof, which room is accessible from the north and south aisle through the square towers, which are commonly called North Galilee Tower and South Galilee Tower to distinguish them from the central tower and those smaller ones at the end of the transept.

At Ely, a porch of moderate size projecting from the tower which fills the middle of the west end.

At Lincoln, a somewhat larger porch opening into the southwest transept (that is, the southern arm of the principal or western transept) from the western side.

GALILEE PORCH. Same as Galilee, in the restricted sense given above. The term originated in the old habit of calling many halls, such as sacristies, outside chapels, rooms in the triforium, etc., by the name of "galilee," which called for the further discrimination conveyed by the compound term.

GALILEI, ALESSANDRO; architect; b. 1691; d. 1737.

Although a Florentine, much of Galilei's early life was spent in England, where Sir Christopher Wren and Sir John Vanbrugh were then

PLATE VIII

GALLERY

That of the Vatican, called Loggie di Raffaelo; described under Loggie of the Vatican. This side of the gallery consists of thirteen vaulted squares, each vault having four principal paintings of biblical subjects. The inspiration for the arrangement of the paintings came largely from the discovery in Raphael's time of ancient Roman decoration, as in chambers of the Thermæ of Titus.

practising. He appears in Rome during the reign of Clement XII. (Pope 1730–1740). His most important work is the main façade of the church of S. Giovanni in Laterano (1734). Galilei designed also the façade of the church of S. Giovanni de' Fiorentini, planned by Giacomo Sansovino (see Sansovino, G.) and built by Antonio (II.) da San Gallo (see San Gallo, A., II.). His Capella Corsini at the Lateran is especially characteristic.

    Gurlitt, *Geschichte des Barockstiles in Italien*; Ebe, *Spät-Renaissance*; Milizia, *Memorie.*

GALLAND, PIERRE VICTOR; decorative painter; b. July 15, 1822; d. Dec. 1, 1892.

    Galland was born in Geneva, Switzerland, of French parents. He first entered the atelier of the architect Henri Labrouste (see Labrouste, H.), and afterward studied with the decorator Pierre Ciceri. In 1851 he went to Constantinople to decorate a private palace. Returning to Paris, he entered upon a long period of great activity. Among his most important works in Paris are the " Preaching of S. Denis," a large picture at the Panthéon, the ceiling of the great amphitheatre of the Sorbonne, twenty-six subjects representing the " Glorification of Labor " at the Hôtel de Ville, Paris, and other works. Galland designed the diploma of the universal exposition of 1889.

    Henri Havard, *L'Œuvre de P. V. Galland.*

GALLERIA. In Italian, a gallery ; in most of the English senses of the word, especially a covered and lighted way for foot passengers, with booths and shops. The Galleria Vittore Emmanuele, in Milan, is an important structure of this sort, spacious and very lofty, opening on two important streets and upon the Piazza del Duomo, and sheltering the entrance and show windows of shops of good character. (Compare Arcade, II. ; Passage, II.)

    GALLERY. *A.* A room or hall much longer than its breadth. In old English practice the term seems to have conveyed two meanings : (1) that of a place of amusement (compare the probable derivation from " gala " or another term implying sport and gayety), and (2) that of a passage from room to room. It is to be noted that in old English and Continental houses corridors and passages were not usually provided, and that rooms opened into each other ; if, then, a gallery served as an unobstructed means of communication between a staircase and a bedroom, or the like, the term would acquire that additional meaning. Galleries in English manor houses are often very simple in architectural design ; low, plainly panelled in oak, and with flat ceilings ; but one side would be, in and after the Elizabethan era, a continuous row of windows broken by one or more projecting bay windows, and the other

side would have two or more ornamental chimney pieces. A very few richer ones exist.

    As these galleries were the common place of deposit and exhibition of family portraits, suits of armour, banners, trophies of the chase, carved and inlaid cabinets, together with chairs, settles, and tables, of greater or less richness, the transition of meaning to that given in definition *C* below was natural.

    B. A balcony or loggia used in connection with a much larger hall or room, as for the musicians who might be employed on an occasion of a festival or for divine service, or for the use of persons looking down upon the gathering in the large room. *Singing gallery* is used as the English equivalent for the Italian *cantoria*, as in the case of those which were formerly in the cathedral at Florence and are now in the National Museum of that city, and of that formerly in S. Maria Novella, Florence, and now in the South Kensington Museum. The stern gallery, poop gallery, and quarter gallery of a ship, as in the seventeenth and eighteenth centuries, were of this nature except that these projecting balconies, as they were in reality, were enclosed and housed over. They received a highly decorative treatment in the case of certain men-of-war, and artists of first-rate standing were employed to design them and the whole after end of the ship. The gallery of a church is a means of seating more persons within a tolerably short distance from the reading desk or pulpit than could be accommodated on the floor. It is usually supported on iron or wooden posts, but, with proper construction, elaborate cantilevers or brackets can be used to do this work and thus leave the floor of the church unobstructed. Such appliances are capable of being made very decorative. The gallery of a theatre is similar in purpose to that of a church, but assumes generally the form of a long horizontal curve more or less horseshoe-shaped, and is often set out of horizontal line, even in its front, in order to allow the more easily of grouping the seats so that every person in the audience can see the stage. (See Theatre.) Such galleries are often divided into private boxes. In some very recent theatres the fronts have been treated like series of bowed small balconies, one to each box. In galleries of theatres and churches the question of fireproofing or of protection against fire becomes, in recent times, of extreme importance. The problem of such protection is a very difficult one in these cases. (See Fireproofing ; also Slow-burning Construction.)

    C. A large room used for the exhibition of works of fine art or, less often, of scientific collections, instruments of precision, and the like. Such a room is spoken of generally as a picture gallery, or one used for other purposes, as a sculpture gallery, or the like. It is generally admitted that pictures in oil colour, especially large ones, should be lighted by top light. (For the admission and disposition of such light, the sections through the gallery, the relative height of walls, size of openings, etc., see Skylight.) It is to be observed that in a long and narrow room the arrangement of the side wall with the skylight above is the unit, and that everything must give way to the proper distribution of these parts.

It is, therefore, an error to try to hang pictures on the end walls. It is the side walls only which should receive the paintings for which the gallery is intended, except that the space left at the ends, after doors, etc., have been provided, may be used experimentally to place cabinets or to put up screens, as it is found expedient. The practice in the galleries of the Louvre is good in this respect. The architectural disposition should be such that the section through the gallery shows upon the end wall, so that the cove or slope or cornice at the top of the side wall should not be returned across the end walls, but should abut squarely against them. There is, of course, no difficulty in arranging this with the architectural treatment of the gallery.

A sculpture gallery is generally better if lighted from the highest part of the side wall. Perhaps the best lighting of sculpture galleries in Europe is that of the National Museum at Naples, where the light comes through the lunettes under the vaulting; but as it comes from one side only, the system is not perfect. The halls of the Central Museum at Athens are much simpler, and these are lighted by windows arranged as high as practicable above the floor and near the ceiling. The Glyptothek at Munich is lighted mainly from the side walls near their top, but with various different dispositions according to the varying architecture of the rooms of this elaborate building.

In this sense the term is used loosely for the buildings in which such galleries are included : see the sub-titles.

D. A narrow passage connected in some intimate way with the architectural design of the building. The triforium gallery of a large Gothic church is an instance; the exterior galleries of many Gothic churches belong to the same class. They are sometimes, as at Strasburg, mere balconies, very narrow and protected

GALLERY: THAT AT THE TRIFORIUM LEVEL, BELOW; THAT OF THE CLEARSTORY WINDOWS, ABOVE. CATHEDRAL OF COUTANCES; BAY OF EAST SIDE OF NORTH TRANSEPT.

by lofty ornamental parapets. In other cases they are arranged like triforium galleries, but narrow in proportion to their height and splendour.

E. An arcade or colonnade or other architectural feature, long and high but not wide or deep. This is an extension of definition D, and the structure is practically a passageway which has been obstructed by statues or the like; in other words, a possible passageway not used for that purpose but made a decorative feature. Of this nature is the Royal Gallery, or *Galerie des Rois*, at the cathedral of Amiens, or that of Paris, or that of Reims. The use of the term in Tennyson's *Palace of Art*, "Round the roofs a gilded gallery that lent broad verge to distant lands," is inaccurate because all that the description implies is a parapet. In a similar sense to this the word is applied to a very small railing of wood or metal carried along the edge of a table top, or of the shelf of a cabinet or étagère. (See Whispering Gallery.)

F. A passage outside of a building, as one which leads from one building to another; especially if somewhat architectural in treatment. The side porticoes of the colonnaded streets of Syria (see Street; Syria) were galleries, and so is the ambulatory of a cloister. The term is used, in the absence of a special one, for such structures as the covered porticoes enclosing the Piazza di S. Pietro at Rome, and for the covered way which leads from one of the gates of Bologna to the church of the Madonna di S. Luca, three miles distant and placed upon a high hill; it is also applied to the unarchitectural but long and important passages which lead from the Pitti Palace to the Palazzo Vecchio in Florence, and from the Vatican to the Castel S. Angelo in Rome. (See Corridor.)

G. Same as Galleria. — R. S.

National Gallery. In London; started 1824 and occupying the building which was begun in 1832 on the north side of Trafalgar Square. The building has been much ridiculed, but is not without a certain simple dignity in spite of its feeble cupolas. The Royal Academy occupied the eastern half of the building until 1870, when that institution was removed to Piccadilly, and the whole building was given up to the National Gallery.

National Portrait Gallery. In London; started 1856; has been recently moved to the building erected for the purpose on the northeast side of the National Gallery toward S. Martin's Lane.

Grosvenor Gallery. In London, New Bond Street; a building erected at the expense of Sir Coutts Lindsay for the exhibition of pictures; opened about 1880, but now abandoned.

Uffizi Gallery. In Florence. (See Uffizi.)

GALLETING. The use of chips of stone to increase the solidity of rubble masonry by insertion into the joints of the mortar while wet; material so used. Called also Garreting.

GALLI DA BIBIENA, FERDINANDO; painter and architect; b. 1657 (at Bologna); d. 1743.

Ferdinando was the son of Giovanni Maria Galli, a painter. The family took the name Bibiena from a little town in Tuscany. Ferdinando entered the service of Ranuccio Farnese II., at Parma. He was called to Spain by King Carlos III. At the coronation of the

Emperor Charles VI. in 1711 he went to Venice where he remained until 1716. Returning to Parma, he built the church of S. Antonio Abate. The extraordinary decorations of the double ceiling of this church were painted by him also. One of his last works was the *Teatro Reale* in Mantua. Like the other members of his family he was especially interested in the construction and decoration of theatres and in scene painting. His *Architettura Civile* was published in 1711.

Gurlitt, *Geschichte des Barockstiles in Italien;* Milizia, *Memorie.*

GALLI DA BIBIENA, FRANCESCO; architect; b. 1659; d. 1739.

Francesco was a brother of Ferdinando Galli da Bibiena (see Galli da B., Ferd.), and like him especially interested in the development of theatre construction and scene painting. He worked at Mantua, Genoa, and Naples. In this last city he arranged the triumphal entry of Philip V., king of Spain. Francesco went to Vienna where he built a great theatre. He was selected by the Marchese Scipione Maffei to build the theatre of the Accademia de' Filarmonici at Verona.

Milizia, *Memorie;* Gurlitt, *Geschichte des Barockstiles in Italien.*

GALLI DA BIBIENA, GIUSEPPE; architect; b. 1696; d. 1757 (at Berlin).

Giuseppe was the son of Ferdinando Galli da Bibiena (see Galli da B., Ferd.). He went to Vienna with his father and spent his life in the service of the various German courts. He was especially interested in theatre construction, scene painting, the decoration of processions, and the like. In 1723 he arranged an imperial fête at Prague. He built a theatre at Bayreuth, Bavaria, in 1747, and in 1750 rebuilt an opera house at Dresden, now destroyed.

Gurlitt, *Geschichte des Barockstiles in Italien.*

GALLIFA, G. DE; architect.

He directed the construction of the Capella Real de S. Agueda at Barcelona, in 1315.

Viñaza, *Adiciones.*

GALVANIZED IRON. Iron coated with zinc. The purpose of so protecting iron is to prevent rusting by keeping the moisture from its surface. It is, however, common to paint thoroughly all articles of galvanized iron as soon as they are put into place.

A. Properly, iron which has been covered first with tin by galvanic action, and subsequently with zinc by immersion in a bath.

B. In common usage, but improperly, iron which has been so coated by a non-galvanic process; having been immersed hot in a bath of zinc and other chemicals which form an alloy on the surface of the iron.

GAMBARELLI, ANTONIO DI MATTEO (ROSSELLINO); sculptor and architect; b. 1427; d. 1479.

Antonio was the youngest of five brothers Gambarelli who had a shop (botega) on the corner of the Via del Proconsolo in Florence. The others were Domenico (b. 1407), Bernardo (see Gambarelli, B.), Giovanni (b. 1417, d. 1496), and Tommaso (b. 1422). His principal work, the monument of the Cardinal Jacopo of Portugal, in S. Miniato near Florence, was ordered in 1461. According to Vasari he built also the chapel in which it is placed. Antonio designed the tomb of the Duchess of Amalfi in the church of Monte Oliveto at Naples. He was assisted by Antonio Barocci da Milano on the tomb of Roverella in the church of S. Giorgio at Ferrara (finished 1475) and by Mino da Fiesole (see Mino da Fiesole) at Pistoia, which was begun by his brother Bernardo before his death.

Von Geymüller-Stegmann, *Die Arch. der Ren. in Toscana;* Müntz, *Renaissance;* Vasari, Blashfield-Hopkins ed. ; Vasari, Milanesi ed. ; C. C. Perkins, *Tuscan Sculptors;* C. C. Perkins, *Handbook.*

GAMBARELLI, BERNARDO DI MATTEO (ROSSELLINO) ; architect and sculptor; b. 1409 (at Florence); d. 1463 (buried Sept. 23).

The surname Rossellino belonged originally only to his brother Antonio (see Gambarelli, A.). The Gambarelli were a family of stonecutters of Settignano. Bernardo first appears in 1434 in the records of the Palazzo della Fraternità dei Laici at Arezzo, of which he built the upper part ; the campanile is later. In September, 1439, he acquired a house on the corner of the Via Proconsolo, Florence, and with his four brothers established there a botega. His most interesting creation, and a very important Renaissance work of its kind, is the monument of Leonardo Bruni in the church of S. Croce in Florence, which was ordered by the consiglio of Arezzo between 1444 and 1448. The tomb of Beata Villana at S. Maria Novella in Florence was ordered in 1451. He was probably associated with Alberti (see Alberti) in the construction of the Rucellai palace, Florence, about 1450, and in Rome from that time until the death of Nicholas V. in 1455. The great apse of S. Peter's church (removed by Bramante) and extensive changes at the Vatican are credited to their coöperation. (See Von Geymüller, op. cit.) Bernardo was employed by Pius II. (Æneas Sylvius Piccolomini, Pope 1458–1464) in his transformation of the village of Corsignano into the city of Pienza. He began the church and palace in 1460, and finished them about 1462. The municipal building and bishop's palace were finished about 1463. The Piccolomini palace in Siena is attributed to Bernardo, finished after 1498.

Dr. Hans von Stegmann in *Die Architektur der Renaissance in Toscana;* Müntz, *Renaissance;* Müntz, *Les arts à la cour des papes;* Dr. Heinrich

Holtzinger, *Pienza;* Vasari, Milanesi ed. ; Vasari, Blashfield-Hopkins ed. ; Von Geymüller, article *Bramante* in *Transactions R. I. B. A.,* 1890.

GAMBELLO, ANTONIO DI MARCO ; architect ; d. Feb. 26, 1481.

May 8, 1458, Gambello was appointed *protomaestro* at the church of S. Zaccaria in Venice. He superintended the extensive reconstruction undertaken at this time, for which he is supposed by Paoletti to have made the designs and models. July 8, 1473, he was ordered by the Venetian Senate to fortify S. Servolo.

Paoletti, *Rinascimento in Venezia.*

GAMODIO (HEINRICH VON GMÜND) ; architect.

Heinrich came from Germany to Milan in 1391 and superintended the construction of the cathedral for five months. It was formerly supposed that he designed the cathedral.

Boito, *Duomo di Milano.*

GANDON, JAMES ; architect ; b. Feb. 29, 1742 (London) ; d. Dec. 24, 1823.

A pupil of Sir William Chambers (see Chambers). With John Woolfe of the board of works he published two volumes in continuation of the *Vitruvius Britannicus* of Colin Campbell (see Campbell, C.). In 1780 he designed the customhouse, and in 1786 the House of Commons in Dublin, and Aug. 1, 1795, laid the first stone of the Inns of Court in Henrietta Street, Dublin.

Mulvany, *Life of Gandon.*

GANDY-DEERING, JOHN PETER ; architect ; b. 1787 ; d. 1850.

His name was originally Gandy. He changed it to Deering in 1827 on the acquisition of an estate. He was a younger brother of Joseph Gandy (see Gandy, J.). In 1811 he went to Greece under the patronage of the Dilettanti Society, and associated himself with Lord Elgin, whose seat at Broom Hall, Scotland, he afterward built. His principal works in London were Exeter Hall, Strand; S. Mark's chapel, North Audley Street ; part of University College, and others.

Redgrave, *Dictionary of Artists.*

GANDY, JOSEPH M. ; architect ; b. 1771 ; d. December, 1843.

A brother of John Peter Gandy-Deering (see Gandy-Deering, J. P.). He was a pupil of James Wyatt (see Wyatt, James). In 1794 he went to Rome and in 1795 won the Pope's first-class medal in architecture. He was employed by Sir John Soane (see Soane, J.) and assisted John Britton (see Britton, J.) in his architectural publications. His brother, Michael Gandy, published *Architectural Illustrations of Windsor* with text by John Britton (folio, 1842).

Redgrave, *Dictionary of Artists.*

GANDY, MICHAEL. (See Gandy, Joseph M.)

GÄNÓSOTE. The smaller bark house of the Iroquois. Constructed like the Hodénosote or Long House. It contained along the side walls one berth above another, as in a ship. Eight persons could be accommodated. Dimensions were about fifteen feet by twenty on the ground and fifteen feet in height. (See Communal Dwelling.) — F. S. D.

GANTREE; GANTRY. In building, a framework, platform, or the like to support a crane or derrick.

GAOL. (See Prison.)

GARDEN. A tract of ground usually but not always open to the sky, in which plants are grown under the special care of man; distinguished from a field under cultivation by the more constant and minute care which it receives. (See the subtitles; also Landscape Architecture.)

Botanic; -al Garden. One prepared for the bringing together of plants with a view to scientific inquiry. The most celebrated in Europe is the *Jardin des Plantes*, in Paris. That of Kew near London is far more decorative, and partakes of the nature of a park; it has an enormous greenhouse. In some towns botanic gardens are made the ornamental adjuncts to a palace, or the like; especially in the tropical colonies of European powers where attempts have been made to naturalize the plants of another part of the tropical world, as when the mango and the breadfruit are brought to the West Indies.

Formal Garden. One laid out with straight paths, and regularly balanced and symmetrically planned, as distinguished from one which, to a certain degree, follows the irregularity of wild nature. Usually, and when the garden is laid out on a considerable scale of cost and display, there are terraces, perrons, or flights of steps leading from one level to another, walls with piers supporting vases, statues, and similar adornments, and sometimes the trees, hedges, etc., are clipped and brought into wholly artificial shapes. (See Landscape Architecture.)

Hanging Garden (*Horto Pensilis*). (A term taken from Pliny's *Natural History*.) One supported on vaults or arches and carried high above the streets of a town. Those of Babylon, described by Strabo and others, were of very great size, but nothing is known of their construction nor of the way in which the soil was maintained in proper condition.

Roof Garden. A covered or sheltered, but otherwise open, room or series of rooms on a city roof, enabling persons to enjoy the air. In many houses of the south of France these exist; small, usually occupying part of a story, the rest of which is wholly enclosed. In some Italian palazzi are very extensive loggie, at the top, with columns carrying the general roof, but otherwise open at the sides. In American cities some attempt has been made in this direction, both by places of resort, as restaurants, and in connection with clubs.

Winter Garden. A conservatory, especially a large one and of some pretensions; used as a place of resort during the inclement season, and sometimes so arranged that it is agreeable in the summer as well, when the glass roof, etc., is open. Such gardens are attached to palaces and large dwellings in Europe and America, and the term is extended to places of public resort, usually on the tops of city buildings, or in courts and yards covered in with glass.

GARDEN ARCHITECTURE. The design and arrangement of buildings used in gardens; all architectural structures forming parts of gardens, such as terraces, perrons, parapets, fountains, orangeries, greenhouses, and the garden fronts of large and principal buildings, such as châteaux and other country houses. This is, therefore, an important part of the general subject, Landscape Architecture. The term is in common use in German writing, and while there is a lack of logic in using this as a subdivision of the larger term, it seems better to employ it literally translated than to try to coin another.

GARDEN HOUSE. *A.* A house situated in a garden; usually a summer house, a more or less open place of shelter for temporary use. (Compare Casino; Summer House.) (Cut, cols. 179, 180.)

B. A dwelling house having a garden attached to it, especially, such a dwelling in or close to a city. Thus, Milton is said to have removed in 1652 to "a pretty garden house in Petty France, Westminster."

GARDENING. The care of gardens and the cultivation of plants therein; especially, when used without qualification, the care of ornamental plants, flowers, flowering shrubs, and the like. By extension, and because a garden in the ornamental sense applies naturally to decorative grounds of whatever extent, the designing, laying out, planting, and arranging of large and small parks, whether in connection with public or private buildings, or separately prepared for the benefit of the community. In this latter sense, the terms Landscape Gardening and Landscape Architecture are commonly employed.

GARDEROBE. Originally, a place for the safe keeping of garments, etc. By extension, in French, a latrine; used in English in mediæval archæology as garderobe tower, that in which the latrines were placed.

GARGOYLE. A water spout, especially one projecting from a gutter and intended to throw the water away from the walls and foundations. In mediæval architecture, the gargoyles, which had to be very numerous because of the many gutters which were carried on the tops of flying buttresses, and higher and lower walls, were often very decorative, consisting, as they did, of stone images of grotesque animals, and the like, or, in smaller buildings, of iron or lead.

GARNACHE, JEHANÇON; architect; d. after 1529.

About 1485 Garnache was made supervising architect of the cathedral of Troyes (Aube, France). Under the direction of Martin Chambiges (see Chambiges, M.) he worked on the towers and portal of the façade.

Assier, *Les Arts et les artistes dans l'ancienne capitale de la Champagne.*

GARNET. (See Garnet Hinge, under Hinge.)

GARNIER, JEAN LOUIS CHARLES; architect; b. Nov. 6, 1825; d. Aug. 3, 1898.

néral des bâtiments civils. He was also architect of the city of Paris for the fifth and sixth arrondissements. In the competition for the new opera house, Paris, in 1860, instituted by the government of Napoleon III., Garnier's design won fifth place in the first trial, and first place in the second. He finished the façade of the building in 1867 and the interior in 1875 (see Baudry, Paul). In 1875 he was made *inspecteur général*, and in 1887 and 1895 vice-president of the *Conseil général des bâtiments civils.* Next to the opera house, Garnier's most

GARDEN HOUSE: PAVILION, 16TH CENTURY, AT BAUX (BOUCHES DU RHÔNE).

Garnier was a pupil of Leveil H. Lebas (see Lebas) and the *École des Beaux Arts.* In 1848 he won the *Premier Grand Prix de Rome* in architecture. His *envoi de Rome* of the fourth year was a splendid restoration of the Doric Temple of Ægina, which was published by the French government in its series of *Restaurations des monuments antiques* in 1884. Garnier visited Greece, Turkey, Magna Grecia, and other Mediterranean countries, and in 1855 returned to Paris. In 1855-1856, and again in 1859-1860, he was auditor of the *Conseil gé-*

striking work is the casino at Monte Carlo, Italy. He built also in Paris the *Cercle de la librairie*, the Panoramas Valentino and Marigny, the tombs of Bizet, Victor Masse, and Offenbach at the *Cimetière du Nord.* Garnier designed the observatory at Nice and many important villas in France and in the Riviera. He published *Restauration des tombeaux des rois Angevins en Italie* (54 pls. in folio); *Le Théatre* (Paris, 1876, 8vo); *Le Nouvel Opéra* (Paris, 1875-1881, text 2 vols. 4to, plates 3 vols. folio); *Monographie de l'Observatoire de Nice* (Paris,

1892, folio); *Histoire de l'habitation humaine* (Paris, 1894, 4to). Garnier contributed a famous article on *Michel-Ange, architecte*, to the series which was published in the *Gazette des Beaux Arts* in 1876.

Charles Lucas, in *Construction Moderne*, August 13 and 20, 1898 ; Paul Sédille, in *Gazette des Beaux Arts*, October, 1898 ; J. R. Coolidge, Jr., *Notes upon the Architectural Work of C. Garnier*, in *Architectural Review*, 1898.

GARNIER D'ISLE, CHARLES HIPPOLYTE. (See Garnier d'Isle, Jean Charles.)

GARNIER D'ISLE, JEAN CHARLES; architect and landscape architect; b. 1697 ; d. Dec. 12, 1755.

Dec. 3, 1730, he succeeded Desgots as *dessinateur des plantes et parterres des jardins du roi*. As one of the architects of Madame de Pompadour he was employed with L'Assurance (see Cailleteau) to build the château of Bellevue. He designed the gardens of Crécy (Eure-et-Loir, France). At the time of his death he held the office of *contrôleur général des bâtiments du roi*. His son, Charles Hippolyte Garnier d'Isle, succeeded him in that office.

Leroy, *Dépenses de Madame de Pompadour*; Lance, *Dictionnaire*.

GARRET. *A.* Originally, and expressing its probable derivation from the French *guérite*, a watchtower, a place for a watchman, a corbelled turret, or the like ; in this sense obsolete.

B. The open space in any building beneath the roof and above the uppermost story of finished rooms. Thus, in a house with a double pitch roof, the garret is usually high in the middle ; but as the beams which form the ceiling of the topmost story are made to serve as tie beams for the roof, the height of the garret diminishes to nothing at the eaves. It is common to restrict the term to so much of this roof story as is left unfinished, excluding any rooms which may be brought into shape within this general space.

GARRETING. Same as Galleting.

GARTH. A planted enclosure ; a term connected with garden in derivation as in meaning. Especially, in modern usage, the open space of a cloister; that piece of ground which is enclosed by the ambulatories or covered ways.

GÄRTNER, FRIEDRICH VON; architect; b. Dec. 10, 1793 ; d. April 21, 1847.

In 1809 Gärtner entered the academy in Munich, and in 1812 went to Paris, where he studied under Percier (see Percier). He later travelled in Italy and Sicily. In 1820 he was appointed professor of architecture in the academy at Munich, and was at the same time director of the porcelain manufactory. In Munich he built most of the large buildings of the *Ludwigstrasse*, i.e. the *Feldherrn-Halle* (1841), the *Ludwigskirche* (finished 1845), the Library (1831–1842), the University (1835–

1840), the *Siegesthor* (1844), and the *Blinden Institut*. He built also in Munich the Wittelsbacher palace (1843), the arcades of the New Cemetery, and other works. In 1836 he visited Athens, where he built the royal palace. In 1840 he built the *Pompejanum* near Aschaffenburg. Gärtner restored the cathedrals of Bamberg, Regensburg (Ratisbon), and Speier (Spires).

Raczynski, *L'Art Moderne en Allemagne*; Seubert, *Künstler-lexicon*.

GAS FITTING (also Gas Piping). The art, practice, or trade of cutting, fitting, and putting together the pipes in buildings used for the conveyance of gas for lighting, heating, and cooking purposes.

Gas fitters form a distinct trade, though often gas piping is included in plumbers' work. In piping a house for gas, the number of gas lights and the number of gas ranges, gas logs, and gas water-heaters are ascertained first, as the estimated gas consumption governs the size of service pipe. This is put in by gas companies, and its size is 1 inch for small dwellings, while larger buildings require $1\frac{1}{2}$-, 2-, 3-, and 4-inch pipes. A shut-off is placed on the service pipe to control, from the outside, the supply of gas. Gas service and distributing pipes in buildings are made of wrought iron, which, in the best class of work, is galvanized, to prevent rusting. The pipes are cut to measure, the ends threaded, and put together with screw joints. Sockets, elbows, bends, tees, crosses, and reducing fittings are used for branches or changes in direction. The fittings should be of malleable iron, with beads, and galvanized. Joints should be tightened without gas fitters' cement, and the practice of applying cement to sand holes or leaky joints is reprehensible. It is equally bad to fill pipes with water to tighten up joints, as this usually leads to future trouble by reason of the pipes rusting on the inside. Gas piping should be tested by means of a mercury gauge and force pump, and with good material and competent workmanship pipes readily stand a pressure test of 18 inches of mercury. Leaks are found by introducing sulphuric ether, or by applying soapsuds to the joints and fittings.

Branches for side lights are made $\frac{3}{8}$ inch, branches for chandeliers $\frac{1}{2}$ inch ; in the best practice no pipe smaller than $\frac{1}{2}$ inch is used. The Table is useful in proportioning the size of risers, distributing lines, and branches : —

TABLE.

DIAMETER OF PIPE IN INCHES	LENGTH OF PIPE IN YARDS									Number of lights at 5 cubic feet per hour, gas consumption.
	20	30	40	50	60	70	80	90	100	
$\frac{1}{2}$	7	6	5	4	4	4	3	3	3	
$\frac{3}{4}$	17	14	12	10	10	9	8	8	7	
1	32	26	22	20	18	17	16	15	14	
$1\frac{1}{4}$	52	43	37	33	30	28	26	25	23	
$1\frac{1}{2}$	79	64	56	50	45	42	39	37	35	
2	150	123	106	95	87	80	75	71	67	

In gas heating and cooking : —

a ½-inch pipe supplies one gas log or cooking range, consuming 35 cubic feet per hour ;
a ¾-inch pipe supplies two gas logs or cooking range burners ;
a 1-inch pipe supplies four gas logs or cooking range burners ;
a 1¼-inch pipe supplies seven gas logs or cooking range burners, using 35 cubic feet of gas, or a proportionately smaller number of larger capacity.

Pipes are run with continuous fall toward the gas meter, to keep the system free from condensed vapour. Branches are taken up from side or top of running lines, and brackets are run up from below. Outlets must be securely fastened, and drop lights made plumb. Nipples for side and drop lights must be of exact length for the fixtures.

The gas meter, furnished by the gas company, is set in a cool place in the cellar. Where gaseous fuel is used, companies sometimes furnish a separate meter, and it is better to run special lines to outlets for gas heating or cooking. Gas fixtures are usually hung by the manufacturer, though it is better to have gas fitters do it. Chandeliers should have large supply tubes and heavy gas keys, with strongly made soldered pinstops, and all fixtures should be tested. Glass globes surrounding gas flames should have bottom openings 4 or 5 inches in diameter. Coloured and opal glass globes absorb much light. The hissing or singing of flames, caused by excessive pressure, is remedied by pressure regulators on the service pipe, or governor burners at the fixtures. These control the pressure, or flow, of gas, reduce the gas bills, and secure a better illumination. The use of gas for cooking purposes is increasing every year, and prejudice against its expense gradually disappears. Properly managed, cooking by gas is as economical as by coal, and has many incidental advantages. Heating by gas, at present rates charged by gas companies, is somewhat expensive when burners are kept lighted for many hours ; but the method is convenient and reasonably cheap where heat is only occasionally wanted.

Gas Lighting and Gas Fitting, in Van Nostrand's *Science Series.*

— W. P. GERHARD.

GAS FIXTURE. An appliance for the burning of illuminating gas in such a way as to give out light freely and safely. The term is generally applied to the brackets, pendants, lustres, and the like used indoors, rather than to the lamp-posts or the larger brackets used in streets or squares. The term " gasolier," modified from " chandelier," has been used for pendant fixtures of three or more lights, and the term " bracket " is commonly used for fixtures projecting from walls, whether they are of one or of many burners. (See Gas Lighting.)

GAS LIGHTING. The artificial illumination of interiors and of streets and public squares by means of gas flames or jets. In houses, gas lighting is accomplished by means of more or less ornamental wall brackets and chandeliers adapted for burning illuminating gas in burners or tips, arranged singly or in clusters. The gas is conducted through the fixtures in tubes, and the flow is controlled below the burner by a gas key. (See Gas Fitting ; Gas Fixture.)
— W. P. G.

GAS PIPING. The art and the process of fitting a house, or the like, with pipes for gas supply. (See Gas Fitting.)

GATCH. Plaster as used in Persia for decorative purposes. (See Chunam ; Persia, Architecture of ; Plaster ; Stucco.)

GATE. *A.* A movable barrier, hung or sliding, which closes a gateway. The distinction between door and gate is not observed ; the term " gate " carries with it (1) the idea of closing an opening in a barrier, as a fence, wall, grating, or the like, rather than an opening into a covered building ; (2) the idea of a grating of iron or a framing of timber, rather than a solid and unpierced valve or valves ; but this distinction is not always observed, as when a large and important pair of doors are called gates, as city gates. Where there are solid doors closing a doorway into a public building, and outside of these are doors of iron grating meant to shut at night, the latter are often, and properly, called gates. (Cut, cols. 185, 186.)

B. A gateway ; hardly accurate in this sense, although common, especially in composition and in proper names. (Compare Door ; Doorway.)

Balance Gate. A gate hung at each side by an axis or pivot on which it turns in a vertical arc, allowing, when open, passage underneath.

Water Gate. *A.* A gate in a dam or canal to stop or otherwise control the flow of water.

B. A gate by which access is obtained to an enclosed or separated body of water.

GATE CHAMBER. *A.* A room of any kind in a gate building, as a Gate Tower or Gate House.

B. A sunken panel, box, or recess into which one fold of a gate may be received when it is opened widely, and is not to be allowed to block the passage.

GATE HOOK. That part of a gate hinge which is secured to the immovable jamb, post, or pillar, having the form of a hook to which the gate is hung by means of a ring or staple.

GATE HOUSE. *A.* A building enclosing or accompanying a gateway of an important building ; often in ancient buildings made defensible and always containing rooms in which the gate keeper and others might be lodged.

GATE OF WROUGHT IRON, AVENUE DE VILLIERS, PARIS.

(See Gate Tower, which is another form of the same thing.)

B. A gate keeper's lodge, if forming a house by itself.

C. In hydraulic engineering, a building within which the water gates of a reservoir are situated, or in which the regulation and management of those gates is carried on.

GATEPOST. A post, usually one of two, between which a gate swings or slides. The term is extended to cover large and massive

GATEWAY: PALAZZO DELLA RAGIONE, MANTUA.

The division of the roof of the passage by the transverse arches and superimposed walls had originally the purpose of affording room for defence as by portcullis or by missiles from above.

structures of masonry as of cut stone, or even very large monoliths of architectural character.

GATE TOWER. A gate house of considerable height and size, and either fortified, or of architectural pretension. The entrances of fortified cities, mediæval strong castles, and the like, have been commonly arranged in gate towers, by means of an archway affording entrance to the ground floor of the tower, and another one leading into the tower from the court. Each of these archways allows of defensible appliances, as strong gates, a portcullis, loopholes or embrasures for archers, musketeers,

or military engines; and some gate towers are arranged so that the assailant on forcing one gateway finds himself in a court open to the missiles from above, and from which he cannot emerge without forcing another gateway or retreating.

GATEWAY. An entrance such as is intended to be closed by a gate ; hence, commonly, a passageway through a barrier, enclosing wall, fence, or the like, and in this differing from a doorway. (Cut, cols. 187, 189, 190.)

Brandenburg Gateway (Brandenburger Thor). At Berlin, a screen of columns forming a two-faced hexastyle triumphal or memorial portico, in a modified Grecian Doric style, with a bronze quadriga by Schadow on the top, through which the city is entered from the park called the *Thiergarten.* It was built at the close of the eighteenth century, the architect being C. C. Langhaus.

Golden Gateway (I.). That at Jerusalem ; a double gateway in the outer (eastern) wall of the fortified citadel, called Harem-es-Sherif, undoubtedly a restoration in late Roman times of an earlier gateway. It is a large building, with inner and outer passageways, now closed.

Golden Gateway (II.). The *Porta Aurea* at Spalato ; that which formed the gate on the land side in the outer wall of the great Palace of Diocletian.

Lion Gateway ; or Gate of the Lions. At Mycenæ, in Greece. The ancient gateway to the citadel or acropolis at the northwest angle of the triangle which it encloses. A long passage between walls of dressed stone leads to a doorway ten feet wide, which is closed at the top by a very large stone forming a lintel. This stone, sixteen feet long and eight feet high, is of a generally triangular shape, and upon it are cut the two lions of very archaic type, resting their forepaws on the top of a short column, so that they rear up, each toward the other, their backs following the sloping line of the lintel. The heads are entirely missing, and may have been of bronze. The work is of unknown date. (See Mycenæan Architecture.)

GATHERING. That portion of a channel, duct, or similar narrow enclosure which is constructed with approaching sides, by which the passage is contracted, as over a fireplace at the beginning of the flue.

GAU, FRANZ CHRISTIAN ; architect ; b. June 15, 1790, (Cologne, Germany) ; d. 1854.

Gau was naturalized as a French citizen and became a pupil of Debret (see Debret) and Lebas (see Lebas). He undertook the completion of the great work concerning Napoleon's expedition to Egypt, and also finished the third and fourth volumes of François Mazois's book on the ruins of Pompeii (see Mazois, F.). From 1831 to 1844 Gau was architect of the prisons

GATEWAY IN THE CITY WALL, PERUGIA, ITALY.
Roman imperial work, following Etruscan traditions.

189   190

and hospitals of Paris. He published *Antiquités de la Nubie* (Paris, 1820, 1 vol. folio).

Bauchal, *Dictionnaire*.

GAUDINET or **GODINTE, NICOLAS**; architect.

In 1532 he replaced Guérard Cardin as supervising architect of the cathedral of Sens. In 1535 he built the lantern of the stone tower and in 1537 the vaults near the Chapelle S. Croix.

Quantin, *Notice historique de l'Église de Sens;* Lance, *Dictionnaire*.

GAUGE (n.). *A.* In plastering, a certain definite quantity of plaster of Paris added to other plaster or mortar to facilitate setting.

B. In roofing, the exposed portion of a slate, tile, or the like, when laid in place.

GAUGE (v.). *A.* To bring to a given size or a given dimension, as thickness, or the like. The term properly signifies to test or measure (see Gauge, n.), but it is in common use as implying the rubbing, cutting, or other process which brings the object into shape. Thus, the bricks required for the voussoirs of an arch which is to be ornamental in character, especially if small in proportion to the size of the material, are commonly specified to be gauged and rubbed; that is, brought to the exact size and shape; rubbed smooth.

B. In plastering, to prepare or mix with plaster of Paris; the term meaning originally to measure the quantities, then to mix such measured quantities, finally, to mix especially those ingredients which are submitted to careful measurement. (See Gauge, n.)

Straight-gauged. Set straight by the use of the gauge, or as if by use of the gauge; said especially of a row of tiles, slates or the like in roofing.

GAUGED ARCH. An arch of which the voussoirs have been treated as described under Gauge (v.), *A.* Specifically, one built of gauged brick.

GAUGED STUFF (GAUGE STUFF). Same as Gauge (n.), *A.*

GAUGED WORK (GAUGE WORK). Plastering, such as repairing and the application of mouldings or ornaments, which is done with gauged mortar.

GAUNTRY. Same as Gantree.

GAUTHIER, MARTIN PIERRE; architect; b. Jan. 9, 1790 (at Troyes, France); d. May 19, 1855.

Gauthier was a pupil of Charles Percier (see Percier), and in 1810 won the *Grand Prix de Rome* in architecture. Returning to Paris, he was made architect of the hospitals in association with Huvé (see Huvé) in 1823, and alone in 1833. He is best known by his work, *Les plus beaux édifices de la ville de Gênes et de ses environs*, Paris, 1818–1831, 2 vols. folio.

Lance, *Dictionnaire;* Halévy, *Notice nécrologique* in *Revue Générale de l'Architecture*, Vol. XIII., 1855.

GAUZE. (See Wire Gauze.)

GAVEL. Same as Gable. (Obs.)

GAWNTRY. Same as Gantree.

GAZINI. (See Gagini.)

GEISON. In Greek and Greco-Roman architecture, the projection from the face of a wall of the coping or eaves; especially the broad shelf in front of the tympanum of a pediment and formed by the top of the cornice of the entablature below. The triangular panel may be flush with the face of the architrave of this lower entablature, or may be set farther in, making the recess for the statuary or the like so much deeper and increasing the width of the geison. In the Parthenon at Athens this projection, or the width of the geison, is nearly three feet. The term is often extended so as to imply the mass of cut stone itself which projects and forms the cornice of the horizontal entablature. — R. S.

GEMEL; GEMELLED. Coupled, especially in mediæval architecture, as gemelled arches, etc.

GEMINATE; –ED. Coupled: especially in columnar architecture, said of coupled columns in a colonnade. (Compare Accouplement.)

GENDROT, JEAN; architect.

April 24, 1463, by letters patent of René d'Anjou, titular king of Naples, then residing in France, Gendrot was created master of the works for Anjou and Maine.

Lecoy de la Marche; *Les comptes du roi René*.

GENERATOR. (See Dynamo.)

GENGA, BARTOLOMMEO; architect; b. 1518; d. 1558.

A son of Girolamo Genga (see Genga, G.). In 1538 he came to Florence and was associated with Vasari (see Vasari) and Ammanati (see Ammanati). He was employed by the Duke of Urbino at Pesaro and Urbino.

Seubert, *Künstler-Lexicon*.

GENGA, GIROLAMO; painter, sculptor, and architect; b. 1476; d. 1551.

The painter Girolamo Genga was employed as architect by the Cardinal of Mantua and the Duke of Urbino. He built the Villa of Monte Imperiale near Pesaro, and the church of S. Maria delle Grazie at Sinigaglia.

Müntz, *Renaissance*.

GENTZ, JOHANN HEINRICH; architect; b. Feb. 4, 1766; d. Oct. 3, 1811.

Nov. 10, 1798, he began the old mint in Berlin which was destroyed in 1886. In 1809 he built the first audience hall of the University of Berlin.

Borrmann, *Denkmäler von Berlin*.

GEOMETRICAL DECORATED. In English architecture, belonging to the Decorated style characteristic of the thirteenth century, and having much geometrical tracery. The term is one of many attempts at a minute and classified nomenclature which it is probably impossible to secure.

GEOMETRICAL PROPORTION. That theory of proportion in architecture which assumes the existence of a geometrical basis or system by which proportions may be determined and upon which the parts of the building may be put in the right place for producing the best effect. (See Proportion.)

GEORGIAN ARCHITECTURE. That of the reigns of the four Georges in England, namely from 1714 to 1830. The term is more usually employed for the architecture of the earlier reigns. Thus, Buckingham Palace, built under George IV., would not so often be called a building of the Georgian style as a piece of modern or nineteenth century architecture. On the other hand, the churches of S. Mary Woolworth, S. Martin's in the Fields, and Somerset House are specimens of the earliest and latest buildings which are more usually designated by the term we are considering.

Architecture of the same epoch in America has been called, generally, "Colonial," or "Old Colonial"; but some recent writers have applied the term Georgian to this also, as an expletive more accurate and more descriptive. (See Colonial; England, Architecture of; United States, Architecture of.) — R. S.

GERARD VON RILE (or **VON KETTWIG**).

The second architect of the cathedral of Cologne. In 1254 he succeeded Heinrich Soynere (see Soynere, Heinrich).

Fahne, *Baumeister des Kölner Doms.*

GERLACH, PHILIPP; architect; b. 1679; d. 1748.

A pupil of J. B. Broebes (see Broebes). His chief buildings are the church of the Friedrichs hospital in Berlin and the *Garnisonkirche* at Potsdam, near Berlin.

Borrmann, *Denkmäler von Berlin.*

GERMANY, ARCHITECTURE OF. That of the states constituting the present German Empire. If in the various lands which we call by the collective name Germany we include the eastern provinces, and also the Austro-Hungarian dominions, we shall find that it is inhabited by people of such various races, languages, manners, and religions that we might reasonably expect great contrasts in architecture; but if we except the Italian provinces of Istria and South Tyrol, this is by no means the case. Of course, here and there foreign ideas, local influences, difference of material, and personal individuality of designers exhibit certain modifications; but, as a rule, whatever is borrowed from without or originates within is welded into an unmistakable German form.

The early inhabitants appear to have commenced their architectural operations by scooping out caves in the rocks or hillsides; but it is very difficult in these works to distinguish between what has been done by nature and what by man in an uncivilized condition.

The great cave at Ettershausen, near Ratisbon, is undoubtedly a natural object, but converted into a primitive stronghold; high up, in

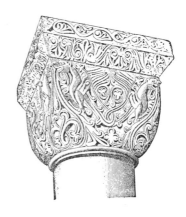

GERMANY, PART I. (THE RHINELAND): CAPITALS FROM WORK OF THE EARLY 12TH CENTURY; CHURCH AT NEUWEILER, ELSASS.

the great rock, it overlooks for many miles the valley of the Naab and its junction with the Danube.

There is a primitive class of structure, of which the rock-cut church of S. Salvator at Swäbisch-Gmünd, in Würtemberg, is a very interesting example. Here we see a precipitous rock pierced with deep-set windows at irregular intervals, and if we enter this curious structure, we find ourselves in a rock-cut chamber, its rudely arched ceiling supported upon piers, devoid of architectural arrangement, and almost dark but for the lamps glimmering before the altars. Over this is another church, or chapel, also cut out of the rock, which has been altered during the fifteenth century; it is impossible to ascertain the date of the lower church, but tradition ascribes it to a period previous to the Christian era.

There was a somewhat similar rock-cut crypt beneath the ancient church at Dietkirchen on the Lahn, but it was filled up when the church was restored a few years back.

There are in Germany prehistoric remains of quite a different character, such as the *Haupt-tempel* at Stettin, though they are not numerous.

Fragments of Roman buildings exist all over Germany. To the student of German architecture, the works to be seen at Trèves (Trier) are the most instructive. Of these the Porta Nigra is perhaps the most valuable, because it retains the whole of its original surface work. The order is Doric and the effect striking, though it is not a work of the best period; its date is not clearly ascertainable, some authorities ascribing it to the time of Augustus, and others to a period as late as that of Constantine. A certain want of refinement in detail seems to militate against the first theory, and the use of the Doric order argues strongly against the latter.

The cathedral first erected by S. Helena decidedly possesses Roman remains, notably in the large Corinthian capitals embedded in the walls. The basilica, the ruins of the baths, amphitheatre, and bridges are also Roman, as is also the elegant sculptured monument of Igel. Roman works are also to be seen at Cologne, Coblentz, Xanten, Cleves, Gmünd, Bamberg, and Augsburg. The monuments left by the Romans in Germany were sufficient to establish a style, and very remarkable are the early imitations of their works. There is, however, one element in German architecture which is far more difficult to trace to its original source, and that is the Eastern influence, which is so conspicuous in the Romanesque buildings, and which chiefly exhibits itself in churches, planned and constructed in cubes, polygons, and circles covered with domical vaults, semidomes, and lunette vaulting. The idea would seem to suggest itself that these features must have found their way up the Danube from Constantinople, or through Russia; but when we come to consider Hungary and Poland we fail to find any decided proof of this. Of course, this may be owing to the scanty remains of mediæval architecture at present existing in the southeastern states of Germany. We do certainly find round and polygonal churches in the Austrian dominions, but as buildings of a similar character are to be seen in Norway and Sweden, they cannot be regarded as proving much. It has been advanced by some writers that these Eastern characteristics were introduced from North Italy

either by way of Istria or the Tyrol, but in both of these provinces we search in vain for the required link between the Romanesque of Lombardy and that of Germany. The cathedral of Trent appears at first sight to supply that link, but unfortunately the date inscribed upon the building is 1240, so that, although it is entirely in the round-arched style, it is later than the perfected Gothic church of Our Lady at Trèves (Trier), commenced in 1227.

A suggestion has reached us that the Hanseatic League may have introduced Eastern features, but if this were the case we should probably find their influence more marked in secular than in ecclesiastical works; but this is certainly not the case. It has also been stated that one of the German orders of knights who joined the crusades may have introduced these Eastern peculiarities. Now, although there may be something in this idea, it is hardly sufficient to account for the establishment of a style of architecture. Some writers are of opinion that the Irish monks who converted several districts of Germany to Christianity may have introduced a kind of Eastern-looking architecture from Ireland; it does seem probable that they may have influenced certain forms of ornamentation, and there is a feature in the cathedral of Freising, in Bavaria, which seems to point to this. S. Columbanus and his companions are buried in the crypt where their great stone sarcophagi are still to be seen, and three or four of the columns which support the vault above them are rudely carved with snakes and lizards coiling round the shafts, which look like early Irish work. The crypt itself was built in 1160, but a careful examination of these columns convinced us that they formed portions of an earlier building.

When Charles the Great erected the minster at Aachen, 796–804, he introduced architects and workmen who erected churches in many parts of Germany, though with the exception of Aachen and a small portion of the church at Lorsch, near Worms, there are no buildings now existing in Germany which can be classed as undoubted Byzantine works, though the apse of the minster at Essen-on-the-Rhine and the western towers of S. Paul at Worms may possibly belong to that school.

During the Middle Ages the Germans borrowed ideas from the French, and it is possible they may have copied these Eastern characteristics from buildings in Auvergne or the south of France, just as, in the thirteenth century, they took their Gothic ideas from the north of France. Now, from what we have already stated, it is evident that several influences were at work which became factors in the formation of the German style of architecture, though no single influence was sufficiently powerful to account for all its characteristics.

GERMANY, ARCHITECTURE OF; Part I.; The Rhine and the Rhinelands. If we enter Germany from Holland by the Rhine, one of the first objects which attracts attention is the beautiful wood-clad hill of Cleves, crowned by its ancient castle some two miles off, but conspicuous far and wide over the great flat plain through which the Rhine flows. Here we are indeed in the land of legend and romance, for that great brick tower is the celebrated Swan Tower of Lohengrin, and the old castle has Roman fragments and inscriptions built into its walls. The neighbourhood of Cleves abounds in objects of interest ; some six miles off is the very ancient town of Xanten, said to be the site of the castle of the Nibelungs. Roman objects are constantly found here, as it was one of the most important settlements on the

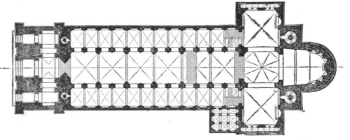

GERMANY, PART II. (THE RHINELAND): CATHEDRAL OF SPEYER (SPIRES), RHENISH BAVARIA. PLAN.

Rhine. The place is now reduced to a mere village justly celebrated for its extremely magnificent church, which both internally and externally is rich in carving and sculpture, and a perfect storehouse of mediæval works of art, stained glass, pictures, wood carvings, and ancient furniture. The west front and towers are Romanesque, but the beautiful church attached to them was commenced in the year 1263 and completed about a century later. The choir follows the plan of the church of Our Lady at Trèves (which will be described later on), but the building itself belongs to the richly developed

GERMANY, PART I. (THE RHINELAND): CHURCH AT BOPPARD, RHENISH PRUSSIA; 12TH CENTURY.

The extremely narrow nave (about 23 feet), the Italian influence visible in the nave arcade, the multifoil window openings in the vault, and the odd arrangement of the ribs in this vault, are all noticeable.

GERMANY, PART I. (THE RHINELAND): CATHEDRAL AT SPEYER; LONGITUDINAL SECTION. (SEE PLAN.)

This is typical German work, and shows the highest reach of constructional excellence of the pure Romanesque style.

school of Westphalia. It consists of a lofty nave and four aisles, supported by double flying buttresses, very like those of Cologne cathedral. The stately choir terminates in five apses. The cloister and chapter house are simpler, and built into their walls are Roman monuments and inscriptions. Few churches in Germany have so thoroughly escaped modernization. The town retains its mediæval walls and gates, which are worthy of inspection, and a museum of Roman antiquities found on the spot.

Some five miles from Xanten is another interesting old town, Calcar. The church is a plain brick building, partaking more of the Dutch than the Westphalian style; it is, however, as rich in beautiful furniture as Xanten. This remarkable characteristic is accounted for by the fact that a noble school of painters and wood carvers existed at Calcar in the fifteenth and sixteenth centuries. There is a pretty old town hall which preserves some memorials of this school of which so little is known.

The next building which claims our attention is the minster of S. Quirinus at Neuss, a noble example of the latest Romanesque style, consisting of a nave and four aisles with western transepts and a grand western tower. The choir consists of three semicircular apses radiating from a lantern. Round and pointed arches are used in juxtaposition. The church is one of those very striking ones which makes one regret that the Germans abandoned this style for the developed Gothic. Upon the richly adorned west front is the date 1209, and as this occurs near the ground, no doubt it records the commencement of the building.

We will now pass on to what may be regarded as the headquarters of German mediæval architecture, the city of Cologne.

The church of S. Maria-im-Capitol is an example of very early Romanesque, consecrated in the year 1049 and structurally little altered since; it has apsidal choir and transepts all planned in a similar way with aisles going round. S. Mary's is a very severe plain building, with square piers, unmoulded arches, and simple cross vaulting, but it has a decided Eastern character about it, which is also to be noted in the slightly later churches of the Apostles and S. Martin; but that which exhibits this characteristic in the most marked degree is the church of S. Gereon. Here no doubt it

chiefly arises from the curious manner in which the church is planned. The nave consists of a lofty polygon of unequal sides arranged so as to be longer from east to west than from north to south. The vaulting is very much domed up toward the centre, and there is a long aisleless choir built over a very ancient crypt, with genuine Roman mosaic pavements. The beautiful nave of this church was completed as late as the year 1227. The noble church of S. Kuni-

GERMANY, PART I. (THE RHINELAND): CATHEDRAL OF SPEYER; EXTERIOR. (SEE PLAN.)

bert, an example of the latest Romanesque, was erected between the years 1239–1248, the latter being a most important epoch in the history of German architecture, for in that year was commenced the great cathedral of Cologne.

Cologne cathedral is supposed to have been designed by Gerhard (Von Rile).[1] It appears most remarkable that the completion of S. Kunibert's and the commencement of the cathedral should have taken place in the same year,

[1] There is scarcely sufficient evidence to establish the surname.

PLATE IX

GERMANY, ARCHITECTURE OF. PLATE I

Cathedral of Cologne on the Rhine, interior looking east. This church is built on a thirteenth century plan, and was begun about 1245. The interior, as seen in this plate, was nearly completed in the thirteenth century, though it has undergone repair. The exterior with the towers was completed only in the nineteenth century.

as one might have thought that at least a century had elapsed between the two events ; but it is now an acknowledged fact that the cathedral is French as to its general arrangement, and the earliest portion of it a direct copy from the cathedral of Amiens. In fact the chevet and radiating chapels are almost identical in the two buildings, and as Amiens was commenced in 1220 and Cologne in 1248, to Robert de Luzarches must be given the credit for the idea. Amiens was far advanced in 1269, because that date occurs in the stained glass of the clearstory windows, and (according to Viollet-le-Duc) the exterior was quite completed in 1288 ; at Cologne, on the other hand, the choir alone was not finished until 1322.

Cologne cathedral had such an important influence on German architecture that we must attempt to realize exactly how far it was a copy of Amiens, and in what particulars the German architects departed from their French original. Kugler and other writers tell us that Gerhard erected the whole of the lower portions of the apse, but

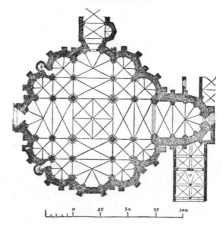

GERMANY, PART I. (THE RHINELAND): CHURCH OF OUR LADY, AT TRÈVES (TRIER), C. 1230.
Unique among Gothic churches in its plan.

after a very careful study of the building we cannot help arriving at a different conclusion. The following are our reasons for differing from such eminent authorities.

At Amiens the piers, which support the great apse, are of a very early form and look archaic for their date (1220) as they follow a twelfth century, rather than a thirteenth century, treatment. Whereas, on the other hand, the chevet and its chapels are more thoroughly developed Gothic than we should have expected from the first quarter of the thirteenth century. For instance, the tracery used in the chapel windows is formed by unenclosed trefoils (it is possibly the earliest example in Europe). Now at Cologne we shall find this peculiarity and almost every other feature of the same portion of Amiens reproduced in the chevet and chapels. Yet, when we come to examine the main apse itself, we shall find marked departures from the Amiens design. The

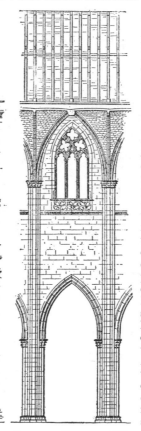

GERMANY, PART I. (THE RHINELAND): MINSTER AT FREIBURG, BADEN, C. 1275.
Two bays and part of tower, south flank ; one bay of nave, interior.

GERMANY, PART I. (THE RHINELAND): MINSTER AT FREIBURG, BADEN; WEST DOORWAY
SEEN FROM WITHIN.

most important is in the great piers, which at Cologne are far more complex in plan, with capitals and bases set out upon an octagonal outline; whereas at Amiens the square is strictly maintained and the foliage of the capital is stiff-leaved, at Cologne it is quite naturalistic; whereas at Amiens the piers and arches round the apse look like twelfth century work, at Cologne they possess every characteristic of the fourteenth century. When we come to the triforium all attempt to follow the Amiens design is completely abandoned. It would appear, in fact, that the apsidal chapels at Cologne were copied from Amiens and were probably built round the apse of the old Romanesque cathedral, and that at a later period, some time before 1322, the Romanesque apse and choir were taken down and rebuilt as we now see them. This work was probably commenced by the architect called Meister Arnold, who died in the year 1301, and was completed by his son, Meister Johann. The choir was consecrated 1332. There can be no doubt, we think, that these later architects, while retaining the ground plan of Gerhard, abandoned the Amiens design and carried out the work with a more original and national spirit.

About fourteen miles from Cologne, in a deep glen surrounded by most lovely scenery, is the sequestrated Cistercian abbey of Altenberg. This noble church should be carefully examined and compared with both Amiens and Cologne, in order that we may thoroughly understand the architectural development of the latter church. Although Altenberg was not commenced until 1235, *i.e.* seven years later than the great cathedral, yet it may be regarded as the earlier church of the two, as it was carried on steadily and without interruption. The building is about 400 feet long, much plainer than Cologne, mutilated and whitewashed all over, with a painful look of desolation about it, yet in some respects it is a nobler design than Cologne. The details of Altenberg are inspired by the local Westphalian school, hence we find cylindrical columns used in the place of piers; notwithstanding this, however, the choir and apse of Cologne were certainly influenced by those of Altenberg and were not improbably works of the same architects. Our space will not permit us to enter into a detailed account of this most beautiful church, but we must call attention to its glass, which, though it is simple grisaille and of one uniform treatment and colour scheme throughout, is so magnificent in effect as to have impressed us more than any glass we have ever seen.

Altenberg is a difficult place to get at, as there is no direct communication except by taking a carriage from Cologne, but no one should omit seeing it.

The new west front of Cologne cathedral is

somewhat disappointing, but probably the modern architect found himself bound to adhere to the old design, and no doubt he was right in doing so, for although it is certain that the mediæval architects would have modified it as it was being carried out, yet the new flèche, over the crossing, is a warning to nineteenth century architects not to meddle with ancient designs. According to ancient plans the church was to have had an open stone lantern in the centre, instead of the ugly cast-iron pinnacle which so greatly disfigures it.

Who, by the way, made the design for the west front, which now hangs up in the cathe-

GERMANY, PART I. (THE RHINELAND): MINSTER AT FREIBURG, BADEN; DOORWAY OF THE SACRISTY.

dral? It was discovered in three parts, and it is said that Zwirner found one portion beneath a beehive in a village. The name of the draftsman is, however, unknown. Perhaps it may have been Johann Von Köln, whom the Spaniards call Juan di Colonia, and who designed the western spires of Burgos cathedral for Bishop Alfonso de Cartagena between 1435–1456.[1] There is certainly much resemblance between the Burgos and Cologne spires.

Cologne cathedral is rich in ancient glass; the fifteen clearstory windows of the choir are

[1] Street's *Spain*, p. 26.

superb fourteenth century examples, and that over the shrine of the three kings in the extreme eastern chapel of the apse is peculiarly interesting, because it is Romanesque in design and belonged to the earlier cathedral. The five windows in the north aisle of the nave were executed between the years 1507–1509. Their design has been attributed to Aldegraver. The modern windows in the south aisle, though good in drawing, are totally unsuited to stained glass. There is much interesting furniture in the cathedral, especially the choir stalls, and the so-called Agilolphus Altar, a sumptuous combination of woodwork and painting executed in the year 1521. The celebrated *Dombild*, the most magnificent German picture of the fifteenth century, is by a painter named Stephen Lochner. The new work at Cologne is on the whole satisfactory, for when admiring the interior of this grand church one does not realize the fact that half of it is modern.

There are several other churches in Cologne which must be noticed. S. Severin is a large and excellent example of a fourteenth century Rhenish type ; S. Andreas, a charming Romanesque building with fourteenth century choir and a singularly beautiful narthex. The great Jesuit church is a remarkable work, for though dating 1621–1629, it is Gothic, and may be regarded as the latest successful attempt at the erection in Germany of a great church in that style. The vaulting is very ably constructed. The soffits are very concave and rest upon a network of ribs so well poised, that although the span is close upon 40 feet, the clearstory has no buttresses. The tower, though Romanesque in style, is of the same date and is a curious example of a common attempt at the revival of the Romanesque style in the seventeenth century.[1]

The *Rathhaus* at Cologne has a striking Gothic tower and a double portico which is one of the earliest examples of the classical revival in Germany, dating 1569–1571. The *Gürzenich* is a good example of an old Gothic municipal building.

The ancient domestic architecture of Cologne, which a few years back was so singularly interesting, has now almost entirely disappeared together with the ancient city walls. Fortunately, however, some of the gates have been preserved with the *Clarenthurm*, which may possibly be Roman work.

The Museum, a poor Gothic building, is said to be in the English style, though why we are at a loss to understand.

Between Cologne and Bonn is Bruhl, where there is a very graceful château erected by the Archbishop-Elector Clement Augustus between 1725 and 1740. It is a charming example of the

[1] Examples are to be seen at the abbey churches of S. Matthias, Trèves, and S. Emmeran, Ratisbon.

rococo style sumptuously decorated by Anducci and Carnioli. The staircase is magnificent and probably the best example of late Renaissance work in north Germany.

The Rhine south of Cologne is extremely rich in ecclesiastical architecture, and as no other portion of Germany presents so many interesting examples, and such magnificent ones, we shall chiefly confine our observations upon this neighbourhood to the churches. Moreover, the domestic work, though highly picturesque, is less remarkable than that of several other districts.

The minster church of Bonn is a beautiful Romanesque structure of the Cologne school ; choir dated 1175, nave, 1270, though it looks quite half a century earlier, as the arches are nearly all round ; it has three lofty spires, one in the centre and two flanking the apse.

At Schwartz-Rheindorf is a singular Romanesque church in two stories, of very elaborate architecture ; and at Heisterbach the exquisite ruined apse of a Cistercian abbey 1210–1333.

The churches of Sinzig, Salzig, Andernach, and Laach are examples of perfected Rhenish Romanesque.

Vallendar is an early basilica with a flat ceiling.

The numerous castles which add so much to the picturesqueness of the neighbourhood are not of great architectural value, for although striking in outline, they have been reduced to mere masses of masonry. Rheinfelds and Reichenberg are exceptions. De Lassaulx, quoting an old chronicle, says that the latter is in the "Asiatic style."

At Coblentz is an ancient bridge over the Moselle, close to the junction with the Rhine, which is said to be partly of Roman work, and three remarkable churches ; that of S. Castor is very early Romanesque and was built evidently for a flat ceiling. The present handsome vaulting dates from the year 1498 ; it has four towers and possesses interesting screens and monuments. S. Flarian, also Romanesque, but of a later type, contains curious stained glass. The Liebfrauen Kirche is a lofty and very graceful structure ; nave, 1529, choir, 1404–1431. It contains an interesting monument to its architect with the inscription *Anno 1420 obiit Joannes de Syry lapicida inceptor hujus chori*. The word "*lapicida*" is often used to signify an architect, though *cementarius* or *majester operum* are more common in ancient documents. This church has a feature not uncommon in Germany. The triforium is so large and important that it is used as a gallery called in Germany *Männerchor* (men's choir).

At Boppard the fine large Romanesque church has singular vaulting ; the ribs do not spring up from the capitals, but descend from a centre ring, like those of an umbrella.

Oberwesel possesses a beautiful church completed in 1321, with an exquisite rood screen and high altar. Another fine fourteenth century church with a still grander high altar is to be seen at Lorsch, and S. Werner's chapel at

shadowed which were developed in later churches. Strange to say, no cathedral in the country has suffered so frequently from fire. Six times it has been wholly or partially destroyed. The eastern choir dates between 1037–1137; the transepts and west choir, 1200–1239; the side chapels, 1260–1332; cloisters, 1397–1412. A great fire destroyed all the roofs in 1756, and one in 1793 consumed "everything that was combustible." The last fire took place early in the present century. For some time the church was used as a powder magazine, and was afterward condemned to be pulled down by the municipality. This outrage was prevented by Napoleon the Great, who, at the intercession of the bishop, had it restored to its original use. After all these vicissitudes it might well be supposed that there was little worth seeing in this great church, but, on the contrary, it is still one of the most interesting buildings in Europe.

Mayence is one of those double churches which are peculiar to Germany, that is to say, it is like two cathedrals with their west fronts

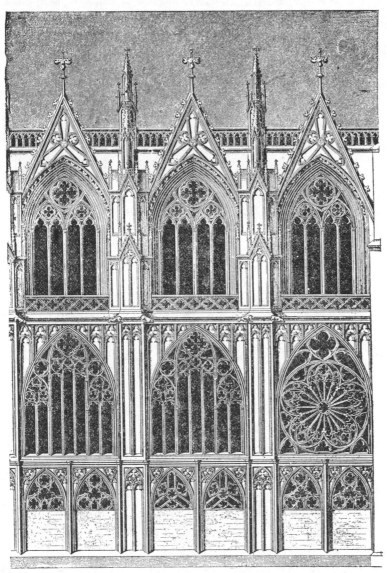

GERMANY, PART I. (THE RHINELAND): S. CATHERINE'S CHURCH AT OPPENHEIM, HESSE; SOUTH FLANK, C. 1300 A.D.

Bacharach, 1293 (now in ruins), is one of the most graceful works produced in Germany in the Middle Ages. It was probably designed by one of the architects of Cologne cathedral.

The cathedral of Mayence is to German Romanesque what Cologne cathedral is to Gothic, and in it we shall find most of the ideas fore-

removed, and the two eastern portions joined together. Thus it has apses at either end, two choirs, two pair of transepts, two crossings crowned by lantern towers, and four other towers flanking the angles. This plan of church probably originated in the ecclesiastical states, as we usually find it in the cathedrals and abbey churches of the dioceses of the prince-bishops. It is almost confined to central Germany, rarely met with in the north, and we know of no examples in Austria or Hungary.

A little way beyond Mayence is Oppenheim, where there is one of these double churches, erected for the most part in the Gothic period; choir, 1362; nave, fourteenth century. A few miles further on is Worms, with a beautiful Romanesque cathedral, all carried out in the same style, with six towers and two choirs; 1181.

Worms is a most interesting ancient city. The church of S. Paul is one of the oldest buildings in Germany, portions of which are as early as the ninth century. The Gothic church of Our Lady can only be examined internally, as the whole of its exterior is enclosed by the vineyard which produces the celebrated Liebfraumilch.

The ruins of the bishop's palace in which was held the celebrated Diet of Worms were pulled down a few years since to make room for an infants' school. A most interesting building is the twelfth century synagogue, the oldest now existing in Europe.

Mannheim is by no means an interesting place, as none of its buildings date back more than a century. The *Rathhaus*, however, is dignified, and the planning of the town may offer a hint to our surveyors how to arrange perfectly straight streets, and yet avoid those acute

Renaissance works in Germany, 1556–1559. It may, however, be doubted whether they are quite worthy of the enthusiasm bestowed upon them, though there is a picturesque charm about the whole place, which may well account for the unbounded admiration which it so frequently elicits.

GERMANY, PART I. (THE RHINELAND): RATHHAUS AT COLOGNE; EARLY GERMAN RENAISSANCE.

angles which are such awkward, inconvenient, and unsightly features in our modern towns.

A short way from the Rhine is Heidelberg, on the banks of the Necker, with its celebrated castle in a magnificent situation. The Otto Heinrich's buildings are among the earliest

To return to the Rhine, on its western bank we shall find the ancient city of Speier or Spires. The cathedral, 1030–1061 (but completed in the twelfth century), is a masterpiece of the early Romanesque style, plain but exceedingly dignified and erected on a vast scale, 474 feet long and 90 feet to the vaulting. It is the largest pure Romanesque church in Europe, and, according to De Lassaulx, the second largest church in Germany. Eight emperors are buried in the crypt behind the high altar. Spires at present belongs to Bavaria.

Strasburg is a grand old city, with picturesque ancient streets and lofty churches. The superb cathedral is the most elaborate building erected in Germany during the Middle Ages; and it is most instructive to compare it with that of Spires, as they are fairly close together, and nearly the same size. The cathedral of Spires overawes one with its stern dignity, severe simplicity, and vast solidity. Strasburg enchants by the lightness of its construction, elegance of detail, and marvellous workmanship. That style of ornamentation which consists in concealing the walls of a building behind openwork screens of tracery is perhaps carried to an excess. This is certainly the case with the tower, which assumes the appearance of a building enveloped in scaffolding, perhaps intentionally so; but undoubtedly the celebrated spire is the least satisfactory portion of the whole building. The west front, according to Kugler, was commenced in 1277, from a design by Erwin von Steinbach, and the exquisite sculpture of the doorways is believed to be the work of his daughter Sabina. The symbolical statues representing the Church and the Synagogue, on the south doorway, are worthy of a Greek sculptor of the best period. The Synagogue is much the more lovely statue of the two.

The nave looks very French in design, as the clearstory windows occupy the whole wall space, and the triforium is glazed; all are filled with the richest old glass. The walls are of a deep red stone, almost purple, and they have escaped painting or whitewash. The effect is magnificent.

The transepts and choir are much lower than the nave, and date from the thirteenth century. They are, however, of a pure and beautiful style; and one of the columns in the south transept, adorned with niches and called the Angels' Column, is a most elegant example of thirteenth century carving and sculpture. The magnificent font, pulpit, organ case, and clock are among the most elaborate examples of late German Gothic. Strasburg is full of interesting churches. The principal Protestant church of S. Thomas, which is contemporary with the transepts of the cathedral, is a singularly elegant example of thirteenth century Gothic.

At Alt Breisach is a noble church with a rich rood screen and high altar, the latter inscribed "H. L. 1526."

Some twelve miles from the Rhine is the cathedral of Freiburg-im-Breisgau, a magnificent church, with the most thoroughly beautiful spire in all Germany. The nave and western porch

are inscribed with the date 1270. The spire, which is of open tracery work, grows out of a lofty octagonal lantern, superimposed upon a square tower. The whole is broached together with pinnacled buttresses; and the composition is a perfect combination of all that is graceful and elegant, united with strength and stability. It is built of a rich rose-coloured stone. Two other small spires flank the choir. The interior is rich in stained glass and has some remarkably fine furniture, as well as a very graceful fountain, a strange object in a church, but a very pleasing one. The trade hall, opposite the cathedral, is an interesting example of secular Gothic work. The Protestant church, a large Romanesque building, is curious from the fact that it was removed from another place and rebuilt here a few years back.

GERMANY, ARCHITECTURE OF; Part **II.**; **Westphalia, Hanover, Saxony.** We must now leave the Rhine to notice certain buildings which, though situated in the Rhine provinces, are at some distance from the great river itself. We will commence with Westphalia. The city of Münster, the capital of the former powerful prince-bishopric, like all other ecclesiastical cities in Germany, is full of interest, both as to its churches and secular buildings. The great street, called *Principal Markt*, is one of the most dignified in the country. The lofty gabled houses, for the most part built of stone, have richly carved gables and are supported upon Gothic arcades, beneath which is the pavement (as in many of the Italian cities). The stately *Rathhaus* is treated in the same manner, its lofty gable adorned with open tracery and its front ornamented with elaborate niches filled with statues. The cathedral stands in a kind of close, and is for the most part thirteenth century work, consisting of a nave nearly 50 feet in span arranged in cubiform bays; it has double transepts and, as originally erected, had two choirs, but the western one has disappeared to make way for a late Gothic façade; the lower portions of the western towers date from 1174–1203, the rest of the building 1220–1260. The south porch is a magnificent example of the transition from Romanesque to early Gothic, adorned with a profusion of carving and excellent sculpture. The gable of the great south transept, *Salvator's Giebel*, 1508–1552, is a rich example of the latest German Gothic.

The churches of Münster are remarkable and with few exceptions are of that form called by the German *Hallenbau*. That is to say, the nave and aisles are of the same height without clearstory or transepts. The *Liebfrauen Kirche* is an elegant example of 1340–1346, with an exquisite tower, which together with its open lantern is 180 feet in height, and was completed in the year 1374.

The *Lamberti Kirche*, in the *Principal Markt*, is a large and very elaborate *Hallenbau*, commenced in the year 1374; its lofty doorways and open staircase in the chancel are excellent examples of Gothic detail.

The *Ludgeri Kirche* is cruciform, with an octagonal central tower crowned by a most graceful open lantern.

Paderborn, the capital of another prince-bishopric, has a remarkable cathedral with a huge Romanesque western tower, dated 1058–

earliest example of a *Hallenbau* nave in any German cathedral. The detail is thirteenth century, more like French than German work. Almost touching the cathedral is the singular little church of S. Bartholomew, which dates from the close of the tenth century, and is a perfect *Hallenbau* on a diminutive scale. The vaults are domical, saucer-shaped, but oval in plan over the aisles. They are supported by slender columns of an imitation Corinthian order, with curious capitals and entablature.

In view of these facts and much other evidence for which we have not sufficient space here, we are convinced that the *Hallenbau* church originated in Westphalia and probably in Paderborn itself, and we cannot agree with Mr. Fergusson in regarding the *Hallenbau* church as typical of southern Germany, as it is common all over the north, except on the banks of the

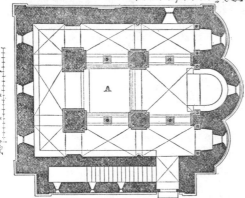

Rhine, where are very few examples.

The cathedral of Münden is perhaps the most thoroughly satisfactory example of a *Hallenbau* church, of large dimensions and dating from the commencement of the fourteenth century. It is a most noble building, both as to proportion and detail. All these Westphalian examples are better in effect than the later ones, especially those in southern Germany, because the aisles are kept up to the exact level of the nave vaulting. Whereas in the later and southern examples the vaultings of the aisles are somewhat lower, which leaves an ugly dark space above the main arches, often imparting a gloomy aspect to the whole interior of the building.

There is a very interesting and little known town in Westphalia called Soest. It possesses a Romanesque cathedral not unlike the earlier portions of Paderborn, with its huge tower built over a singular porch now used as an armoury. The church contains very early examples of wall painting and some twelfth century stained glass. All the ten or twelve churches in Soest are interesting examples of Westpha-

GERMANY, PART II.: CHAPEL OF THE CASTLE OF LANDSBERG, SAXONY.

A double chapel, with opening in floor to connect the two.

1068. The church consists of a nave, aisles, and transepts, the south one square-ended, and the north apsidal. The choir, which is raised upon a high crypt, is square-ended. The nave is internally very striking. It is the

lian architecture, from the earliest Romanesque down to the latest Gothic. The *Wiesenkirche* has an interior so rich in altars, carvings, stained glass, and ancient furniture that it is scarcely to be equalled in all Germany. The People's Altar, which, in defiance to all ecclesiastical precedent, the Lutheran possessors of the building have barbarously converted into a pulpit, stands beneath an exquisite baldacchino of stone some thirty feet high, and is flanked on either side by tall stone candelabra. Soest was formerly a Free City of the Empire, and one of the seats of the Hanseatic League, but its trade and prosperity have long deserted it, and left it the very deadest of all dead cities.

a twelfth century building, cruciform in plan, with two original towers like a little minster.

In this busy and prosperous province a good deal of new building has been going on, mostly very uninteresting and commonplace. There is, however, one very notable exception, and that is the work of Herr Guldenpfennig of Paderborn. This gentleman's work deserves notice ; it is conceived in a purely local spirit, his idea being to revive the beautiful old Westphalian architecture, adapting the fourteenth century style for churches and the sixteenth century style for secular buildings : his churches at Hoerde, Paderborn, and elsewhere

GERMANY, PART II.: CATHEDRAL AT ERFURT, PRUSSIAN SAXONY.
Choir without aisles, separated from the nave, a *Hallenbau*, by the oblong tower crowned by three spires.

One great drawback in studying German architecture is the absence of ancient villages and their churches. This is not to be wondered at, because during the Thirty Years' War the commanders on either side made a clean sweep of all villages for strategical purposes, or ruthlessly handed them over to their ill-paid and undisciplined followers to be pillaged ; and then burnt.

Westphalia, however, possesses a few village churches, though in every case the houses are modern. One of these is Wissel, near Calcar,

are more satisfactory than most modern German ones. A college and schools which he has erected at Paderborn seem remarkably well suited to an old city. His domestic work is quite what one requires in additions made to those old towns, but what strikes one as being most charming are the numerous farmhouses and buildings in the neighbourhood, which, without being in the least extravagant or eccentric, possess much of that picturesqueness which delights us in such structures of the past. Fortunately the cathedral of Paderborn has been placed in his hands, and has undergone a far more judicious and scrupulous repair than any old church in Germany.

The Moselle, which falls into the Rhine at Coblentz, bisects a province the greater portion of which, in former times, belonged to archbishop-electors of Trèves (Trier).

We have previously described the valuable Roman remains at Trèves, and its mediæval architecture is equally striking; its cathedral, a vast double-choir church with four towers, with an interior of twelfth and thirteenth century architecture, is particularly striking, and presents that large and undivided space which would be so useful for congregational purposes in modern places of worship. Close to the cathedral, with a cloister common to both, is the church of Our Lady, certainly the earliest example of thoroughly developed Gothic in Germany. Although the first impression is that of great intricacy, closer observation will discover that the plan is really simple, consisting of a Greek cross with a square enclosing the intersection in such a way as to form four smaller squares, each of which has two apses. To a certain extent, the idea is borrowed from the French church at Braine, near Soissons; and as that building was completed in 1216, and Trèves commenced in 1224, the Trèves architect probably borrowed a hint, though his idea of inverting the plan to form the western portion of the building and his treatment of the superstructure were thoroughly original, and he succeeded in creating one of the most beautiful works in Europe. The interior is exquisitely graceful; unfortunately, the succeeding architect returned to the Romanesque style, and crowned the graceful building with a heavy square tower. The cloisters show a curious attempt to convert the Gothic into a round-arched style, for although the windows have fully developed tracery, yet every light is round-headed.

The domestic architecture of Trèves is highly interesting, many of the houses dating from the fourteenth century. The treatment of their gables is peculiar and original, the chimney breasts being brought to the front, bisecting the gable, and supported upon an elaborate arched bracket. In one or two instances the front of the house is adorned by a conventional imitation of a vine in low relief executed in plaster, a style of decoration of which we know of no other examples.

In the northern portion of this Rhine province is Aix-la-Chapelle, with its cathedral, the most ancient in Germany, undoubtedly Byzantine work. The octagonal work is crowned by a gabled ridge-and-furrow dome, and internally vestiges of mosaic decoration may be traced. There is an early pulpit of silver and other curious works of art, and very ancient metal screens that are said to date from the time of Constan-

tine. The town hall is built up out of the remains of Constantine's palace.

The lovely river Lahn falls into the Rhine at Lahnstein, and is rich in castles; the most interesting ones are Hohenstein, Nassau, Stein, and Laurenberg, in ruins; Dietz and Runkel still entire and very picturesque. Weilburg is an immense structure, superbly situated, partly ancient, the more modern portions forming one of those palaces common in this part of Germany, and of which Gotha, Weimar, Ansbach, the vast unfinished palace at Cassel, and Pommersfelden, are among the best examples. These late German Neoclassic buildings are not very impressive, and are somewhat tame imitations of the French châteaux of Louis XIV.'s and Louis XV.'s times. Internally they are decorated in that poor style of rococo which prevailed in northern and central Germany, which, while possessing all the unconstructive appearance of the French ornamentation, is wanting in its refined luxury. The Germans themselves, in ridicule of its affectation and artificiality, describe it as the Pigtail and Periwig style; then, of course, in Germany, it is not combined with the graceful painting of Watteau and Le Brun or Greuze, which, of course, would redeem anything from looking commonplace. The German decorative painters of this period went to work with a heavy hand, and their "heavens" were not ethereal, but simply masses of paint. One turns with pleasure from the consideration of such works to that magnificent group which crowns the great rock almost surrounded by the waters of the Lahn at Limburg. Nothing could be more striking than the picture presented by Limburg cathedral and its environment. Standing on a great platform, inaccessible from the riverside, and crowned with seven spires, it is one of the most graceful thirteenth century churches in all Germany. The building is no less beautiful internally than externally. Very lofty, cruciform in plan, it has a large open triforium forming an upper aisle all round the building, in which the male portion of the congregation sit, the floor of the church being given over to the women. A picturesque old castle which belonged to the Knights of S. George almost touches the apse of the cathedral, while at the foot of the rock, except where it rises sheer out of the water, cluster the quaint gables and churches of the town.

Wetzlar also possesses a magnificent church which has the peculiarity of two west fronts. That which actually ends the building is of early Romanesque work, with two curious towers. Some 50 feet in front of this rises a rich unfinished fourteenth century façade, connected with the existing church by an unfinished wall on one side and a very noble tower on the other, the space between the two west fronts forming an open court. The nave is a *Hallenbau.*

PLATE X

GERMANY, ARCHITECTURE OF. PLATE II

West door of the church of S. Theobald, at Thann, in Alsace. The west portal, dating from about 1370. The sculpture crowded into the tympanums of the three arches is a remarkably early instance of pictorial work in bas-relief. The Cru- cifixion fills the left doorway, the Adoration of the Kings, the right doorway, and many different passages of biblical and legendary history are arranged in the five tiers under the great arch.

GERMANY, PART II.: TIMBER HOUSE IN MARKET PLACE, HILDESHEIM, HANOVER.

There are deep transepts and a large choir with aisles and clearstory. Internally there is a fine rood screen.

Still following the Lahn, we come to Marburg with its justly celebrated church; it is a huge *Hallenbau* of early Gothic, erected between the years 1235–1283, greatly resembling the *Liebfrauen Kirche* at Trèves. The windows are in two tiers, a somewhat uncommon treatment in a *Hallenbau*, and the tracery is all uncusped. It is full of magnificent furniture, altars, screens, and stained glass. There is a very important castle here, chiefly Romanesque, with a vaulted hall supported by slender columns, and a curious chapel. There is also a picturesque sixteenth cen-

GERMANY, PART II.: RATHHAUS AT MAGDEBURG, SAXONY; c. 1690.

tury *Rathhaus* and some excellent examples of half-timbered domestic architecture in the town.

The architecture of Hanover is of some importance, though the capital itself does not possess any remarkable examples of mediæval work; its modern buildings, however, are instructive as exhibiting in a very distinct manner the restlessness of architectural thought in Germany

during the present century. A very fine theatre erected some half a century back is in the severe Italian Renaissance style, but most of the other modern buildings in the town are in the German Eclectic style, which we shall consider more fully when we describe Munich. A remarkable reaction, however, seems to have set in, if we may judge from the new Catholic cathedral erected in memory of Von Windhorst, the last prime minister of Hanover. This building is a scrupulous revival of a fourteenth century church, and is one of the most successful and elaborately carried out attempts of the kind in Germany.

Osnabruck has a noble transition Romanesque cathedral with three massive towers, rather English-looking, a square east end, and Lady Chapel not unlike Chester. The interior, though very severe, is extremely striking and contains many objects of interest.

Brunswick also possesses a fine Romanesque cathedral, completed about the year 1227, full of objects of interest. The churches of S. Giles, S. Catherine, and S. Andrew are all valuable examples of Gothic architecture of an early character, and well worthy of study. The secular buildings are of more than ordinary value. The *Rathhaus*, in a very pure Gothic style, is one of the most elaborate secular buildings in Germany. The *Gewandhaus*, with its stately gable, is a satisfactory example of Renaissance, and shows that it is quite possible to pierce nearly the whole front of a building with windows without in any way depriving it of dignity and solidity.

Hildesheim is, without doubt, one of the most interesting cities in Europe. Every kind of architecture which is to be found in the German Empire is here illustrated. Whether we regard the remarkable antiquity of its churches, their invaluable curiosities, or its extraordinary wealth of domestic architecture, it is unique. Although its churches do not possess the splendour of those of Cologne, they illustrate an earlier epoch. The cathedral, S. Michael, and S. Gothard are all examples of the tenth and eleventh centuries, in which the

Roman basilica type has been strictly adhered to, and the imitation of Roman work is obvious. The flat ceiling, with its ancient decoration, still remains at S. Michael's. Though restored, this remarkable church, erected between the years 993–1022, is fairly perfect, with the exception of its western apse, for it was a double-choir church. A singular feature is to be observed: the sculpture is executed in artificial stone, and is of a very high order of merit; on the screens between the west choir and its aisles the figures are almost Greek in their refinement. The celebrated Bishop Bernward, who introduced this style of work into Germany, has left many examples of his art both here and in the cathedral. His followers, Bishop Azelin, who died in 1054, and Bishop Hazilo, 1079, have also adorned the churches with remarkable examples of early art. The cathedral has unfortunately been modernized internally, but its bronze doors, dated 1015, are covered with bas-reliefs which are the most valuable works of this period existing in Germany. The curious bronze column, in imitation of that of Diocletian in Rome, ornamented with small subjects in relief, the great chandelier, 22 feet in diameter, in the nave, and numerous objects in the sacristy, illustrate Bernward's artistic ability, or that of the sculptors whom he introduced from Italy. Although the cathedral is, in its present condition, neither a very dignified nor magnificent building, it would be difficult to discover one richer in works of art of every period. The font, a noble bronze casting of the thirteenth century, the fourteenth century choir stalls, and the sixteenth century rood screens are most interesting examples of their various periods. It is greatly to be regretted that a Hanoverian architect of the Eclectic school, some forty years back, rebuilt the west front, destroying the ancient forehall of this church.[1]

The third early church, S. Gothard, which from an architectural point of view is the finest, dates from 1133. It is perhaps the most beautiful church of that date in Germany, but has suffered extremely from a recent restoration. The upper portions of the choir, which were fine fourteenth century work, have been pulled down and rebuilt in imitation of Romanesque work. The stalls, which were most beautiful, with the exception of two or three, have been destroyed, and the whole ancient ritual arrangement of the building has been completely upset. A small and ugly little church dedicated to S. Margaret, though of very little interest itself, possesses a collection of most interesting church plate of very early date, scarcely surpassed anywhere in Germany.

The domestic work of Hildesheim is unrivalled in its way. The houses are for the most part built entirely of wood, and instead of the spaces

between the beams being filled in with plaster or brickwork, as is most commonly the case, here they consist of elaborately carved wooden panels. The building called the *Knockenhauer Ampthaus* is extraordinarily elaborate, and in the older streets of the town every house is a study. They date mostly from the latter part of the sixteenth and earlier years of the seventeenth centuries.

Ducal Saxony possesses several very interesting towns, especially Erfurt with its cathedral, fourteen churches, and interesting civil and domestic buildings. The cathedral and church of S. Severin stand side by side, upon a platform some 50 feet high, and are approached by stone staircases. Each has a *Hallenbau* nave, that of the cathedral poorly designed, as the aisles are much wider than the nave. At S. Severin, however, there are four aisles to the nave, whole under one great external roof. Internally, the effect is decidedly fine and very much resembles the cathedral at Zaragossa in Spain. Both of the Erfurt churches have three towers, all close together between the nave and choir, but at the cathedral a bay of the old Romanesque nave is left beneath them; there are transepts. The effect is not altogether pleasing. There are, however, two noble features about the cathedral: the lofty aisleless-choir, 1349–1353, is lighted by fifteen exquisite windows full of stained glass, and there is an exceedingly rich triangular porch at the end of the north transept. Both of these may rank among the most splendid mediæval works in Germany. The cloisters of the cathedral and the lofty stone canopy over the font at S. Severin are well worthy of notice.

Halberstadt possesses a remarkably elegant cathedral, evidently a work of the Cologne school. It is full of interesting works of art, and has the advantage of having nearly all been built at the commencement of the fourteenth century. The plan is far more like a small French cathedral than a German one. It retains the whole of its ancient fittings and furniture, among these being a very magnificent rood screen. Although the church is Lutheran, yet nowhere in Germany do we find a more sumptuous collection of church plate, priests' robes, altar cloths, etc., showing how very conservative German Protestants are. There are some fine churches at Magdeburg, especially the cathedral. In royal Saxony the most interesting mediæval work is the cathedral of Naumburg. It is one of the few double-choired cathedrals in the north, and bears a striking resemblance to that of Bamberg in Bavaria, of which it is evidently a copy. It possesses two most interesting rood screens, one having the rood below the gallery instead of above it, — the only example we have ever seen. The cathedral of Meissen has been much praised for its openwork spire, which

---

[1] It resembled the one still existing in Minden.

is, after all, a poor imitation of Freiburg-im-Breisgau.

Although Saxony contains a great number of ancient churches, mediæval buildings, castles, etc., yet they cannot be said to be remarkable for originality, and are less instructive as objects of study than those of most other parts of Germany.

Dresden is decidedly a very handsome city, but it contains no ancient buildings of any im-

will enable one to draw distinctions between the Franconian school in the north, the Rhenish in the Palatinate, the Danubian in the centre and east, the Swabian in the south and west. The river Main falls into the Rhine opposite Mainz, and presents nothing worthy of notice

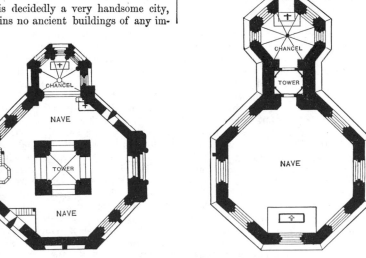

GERMANY, PART III.: OCTAGONAL CHURCHES OF WITTIGSHAUSEN, WITH SQUARE CENTRAL TOWER, AND GRÜNFELDSHAUSEN [OR GRUENFELDSHAUSEN], BOTH IN BAVARIA; SEE DESCRIPTION IN TEXT.

portance. There are only two churches that are particularly worthy of notice, the *Frauen Kirche* and the Catholic church. Both are in the rococo style. The *Frauen Kirche* is, however, an original-looking building, with a lofty stone dome. The royal palace is a not unpicturesque Neoclassic structure, with a striking-looking tower. The *Zwinger*, a vast structure of various dates, a portion of which forms a magnificent picture gallery, and the very noble opera house opposite to it, are works of Semper. The latter is one of the most beautiful buildings of its class in Europe. The architect has retained the old Roman external form, with its arcades, which have an extremely interesting effect.

GERMANY, ARCHITECTURE OF; Part III.; Bavaria, Würtemberg. The present kingdom of Bavaria is composed of a number of small states tacked on to the old dukedom which gives the name. Some of these were ecclesiastical, — such, for instance, as the prince-bishoprics of Würzburg, Freising, Eichstadt, Passau, and Spires. Others were secular states, — such as the Rhine Palatinate, Ansbach, Ottingen, Bayreuth. Others imperial cities, — such as Nuremberg, Augsburg, Ratisbon, Rothenburg, Schweinfurth, etc. This will naturally account for a certain amount of variety in the architectural schools, though they are not very strongly marked; but a careful examination

until the city of Frankfort is reached. The old part of Frankfort is picturesque, and was far more so before the fire which a few years ago destroyed the picturesque old Kraut Market and greatly injured the cathedral. The latter, with the exception of its beautiful tower, is not a very important mediæval work. It is a small fourteenth century church, to which a huge pair of transepts have been added, about the fifteenth

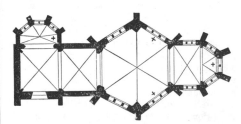

GERMANY, PART III.: CHURCH OF S. CATHERINE, AT RATISBON; UNIQUE VAULTING.

century, to make space for the coronation ceremonials of the Holy Roman Emperors. The only other mediæval building in the town of any importance is the *Liebfrauen Kirche*, a good example of Rhenish Romanesque. Although the modern parts of Frankfort are handsome, well built, and ably planned, yet there is nothing particularly remarkable from an architectural

GERMANY, PART III.: CHURCH OF S. SEBALDUS, NUREMBERG, BAVARIA; WEST END.

point of view. The only objects of special interest in this neighbourhood are the abbey of Seligenstadt, on the Main, a large Romanesque church, internally modernized, and the superb thirteenth century church of Gelnhausen, upon a little river called Kinzing, which runs into the Main at Hannau. It is a very pure example of the latest phase of Rhenish Romanesque when it began to assume Gothic tracery forms. The church has been thoroughly restored since the writer saw it, when it was in a most dilapidated condition, and one of its spires was twisted into

Pompeian house, and it is said tried to live in it. At Wertheim are the ruins of the grand castle of Löwenstein and an interesting fifteenth century church, with a singular rood screen and a very remarkable sculptured monument representing a knight in full armour holding the hands of two ladies, one of whom has rather an Eastern type of face. The story is told of a knight being taken prisoner by the Turks, and, although he had a wife at home, he "was forced to marry the Sultan's daughter." There does not appear to be a word of truth about the story, nor can

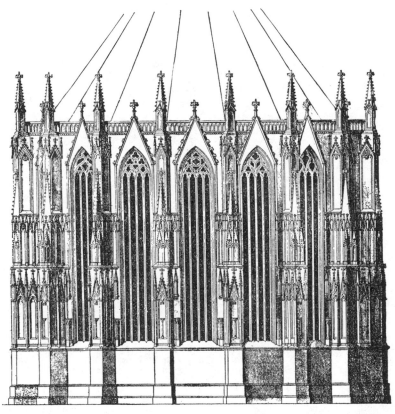

GERMANY, PART III.: CHURCH OF S. SEBALDUS, BAVARIA; EAST END; c. 1375.
The whole eastern choir is a three-aisled *Hallenbau*.

a corkscrew shape, like the celebrated one at Chesterfield, in Derbyshire (England). The Main enters the Bavarian territories close to the interesting old city of Aschaffenburg, where there is a striking old palace 1605–1618, in a style resembling English Jacobean, with five very lofty towers crowned by bulbous spires, and an early Romanesque church of the basilica type, with western transepts and cloisters surrounding that portion of the building, like the *laufgang* of a Norwegian church. There are two fine bas-reliefs in bronze, by Johann and Peter Vischer. Ludwig I. erected a villa here in imitation of a

it be ascertained who are represented on this beautiful monument, or whether in fact it is a monument at all.

The pleasant old prince-bishop's city of Würzburg, charmingly situated on both banks of the Main, connected by a mediæval bridge adorned by colossal statues, contains a cathedral and twenty-one churches. The distant views remind one of Florence. The cathedral, a vast Romanesque building with four spires, consecrated in 1189, was modernized internally in the year 1700 and covered with rococo plaster work. It must be acknowledged that this is remarkably good of its kind, and the correct anatomy of the vast figures supporting the vaulting leaves no doubt of its Italian origin. Against the piers are statues of the long line of prince-bishops who have ruled this see, the earliest dating from the eleventh century. The most remarkable, however, are those of Bishop Sherenberg, 1495, and Von Bibra, 1521, by the eminent local sculptor Tilman Rhiemenschneider, and there is a magnificent thirteenth century bronze font. At the *Neumünster Kirche*, which adjoins the cathedral, some remarkable cloisters were discovered some years back. They were adorned with sculpture of a Byzantine character. The graceful Marien Kirche, on the market place, is a *Hallenbau* of rich Gothic work, 1377–1469, its columns and doorways adorned with statues by Tilman Rhiemenschneider. The great Italian church, called the *Stifthaug*, 1679, has a finely designed dome by Petrini. The church of S. Burkard (Burchardikirche) has a Romanesque basilica-like nave of the tenth century, and a late Gothic choir which is built over the road.

There is some interesting sixteenth century domestic architecture and a very curious town hall, portions of which are Romanesque. The great palace built by the architect Baltazar Neuman is one of the finest rococo buildings in Germany. The staircase and entrance hall are magnificent. The great castle of Marienberg, which overlooks the town from a lofty rock, contains a very remarkable ancient church, circular in plan, and said to be the earliest building in this part of Germany.

A few miles from Würzburg are two very interesting village churches at Grünsfeldhausen and Oberwittighausen. The first named has an octagonal nave united by a kind of necking to a small octagonal choir, with a very elegant octagonal tower rising up between the two ; it is rich Romanesque work. The second church has an octagonal nave with a square tower in the centre supported internally upon four solid arches, and a small apsidal chancel. As nothing of the kind is to be found in the neighbourhood, it would be interesting to trace out the history of these two buildings.

The Main between Würzburg and Bamberg is almost as rich in mediæval antiquities as the Rhine. Heidingsfeld has a church partly Romanesque and partly Gothic, with a beautiful stone pulpit and tabernacle. Ochsenfurth, a remarkably picturesque town, possesses a fine Gothic *Hallenbau* church with excellent statues attached to its columns, magnificent tabernacle about 60 feet high, and a very elaborate bronze font. In the churchyard is an exquisite fourteenth century chapel with a doorway richly adorned with sculpture. The *Rathhaus*, inscribed with the dates 1498–1499, is a most perfectly preserved Gothic structure, full of ancient furniture of the same date as its erec-

tion. Dettelbach has a very curious church with two towers, one circular and the other square, connected by a bridge close to the top. It has a charming *Rathhaus* built across the street and a little river.

About fourteen miles off is the delightful mediæval town of Rothenburg, on the Tauber, with towers, walls, and gates all perfect, most interesting domestic architecture, and an extremely fine church with two curious openwork

GERMANY, PART III.: CHURCH OF OUR LADY AT ESSLINGEN; SPIRE, EARLY 15TH CENTURY.

stone spires and some magnificent altarpieces carved by Tilman Rhiemenschneider. The other churches in the town, though small, are full of ancient works of art.

To return to the Main. At Hasfurth are two very interesting churches ; one, called the *Ritters-Kapelle,* is one of the richest and most elaborate works in Germany, dated 1397 ; the exterior is covered with niches, statues, and armorial bearings.

Bamberg, another prince-bishop's city, has a singularly beautiful cathedral, which is certainly the noblest example of early Gothic work in Bavaria. It has a double choir and four lofty spires ; the eastern choir is elaborate Romanesque work, 1237 ; the western, elegant first pointed ; the towers flanking the western choir greatly resemble those of Laon, in France, though they were completed in 1274, nearly a century later than those of the French cathedral. The interior, which is very striking, is rich in carving and sculpture ; the bas-reliefs upon the screens of the eastern choir (thirteenth century) are probably the finest in the whole of Germany ; no building in the whole land is so rich in monuments. One of the earliest is that of S. Stephen, king of Hungary, an equestrian statue. In the centre of the church is the magnificent tomb of the Emperor Henry II. and Queen Cunigunda, the work of Tilman Rhiemenschneider, 1513. It is adorned with excellent sculpture executed in Salzburg marble. The western choir stalls are beautiful examples of fourteenth century woodwork. A chapel, which leads out of the south transept, has its walls literally covered with bronze bas-reliefs, the monuments of former bishops and canons of the church. The town of Bamberg is full of ancient churches, but the most beautiful of them, the *Marien Kirche*, with a very rich Gothic choir, has been atrociously modernized internally.

For domestic and military architecture Germany possesses no city equal to Nuremberg ; nowhere are there such magnificent streets, such noble houses, such walls, gates, and towers, or such a striking mediæval castle. Not the least interesting objects in this beautiful city are the vast warehouses and granaries with their stupendous roofs, often pierced by as many as six ranges of dormer windows. The houses have a peculiarity of arrangement : their flanks, and not their gables, are turned toward the street, but the roofs are adorned with magnificent dormers crowned by dwarf spires. The Nassau House, fourteenth century, has an elaborate parapet, and boldly corbelled turrets at the angles. The house called Chorlein, near S. Sebald, possesses the most beautiful oriel window in Nuremburg, 1513. The fountains are justly celebrated. The *Schöne-Brunnen*, 1385–1396, is a lofty Gothic spire some 60 feet high, adorned with a profusion of sculpture, and is certainly the most beautiful structure of the kind in Europe.

The churches are rather of the Swabian type. S. Lawrence, begun 1275, has a fine west front, nave with aisles, and clearstory ; and large *Hallenbau* choir, 1439–1471. It is a fine example of Gothic architecture, though that ugly Swabian feature, the substitution of a blank wall in place of the triforium, mars what would otherwise have been a singularly beautiful interior. All criticism, however, vanishes

when we come to examine the magnificent details, sculpture, carving, stained glass, and furniture of every description. Adam Kraft's exquisite sacrament house and Veilstross's grand sculpture of the " Annunciation " are amongst the most magnificent of the very numerous works of art in this splendid church.

The *Sebaldus Kirche* has a very fine early nave with double aisles and a *Hallenbau* choir, in the centre of which stands the noblest production of the early Renaissance school in Germany, the shrine of S. Sebald, by Peter Vischer, 1508–1519. A magnificent triple canopy of bronze forms a baldacchino over the shrine, adorned with statues of the twelve apostles and innumerable statuettes. All the churches of Nuremberg contain objects of great interest.

Ratisbon, or, as the Germans call it, Regensburg, perhaps the most ancient city in Germany, is situated at the junction of the Danube and the Regen, exactly at that point where the Danube reaches its most northern limit. Perhaps Ratisbon may be regarded architecturally as the second most important town in Germany, and is to Danubian architecture what Cologne is to the Rhine. In this most interesting town, containing a cathedral and twenty churches, we find examples of almost every kind of European architecture, both ecclesiastical and secular. The cathedral is regarded by Fergusson and other writers as the most perfect Gothic church in Germany, and, though it is of moderate size, only about 300 feet long, it would be difficult to find a more imposing and thoroughly satisfying building. The plan is one of extreme simplicity. As it rises from the ground, it consists of a nave and aisles, terminating in three apses ; at the clearstory level, however, it becomes cruciform by transepts projecting to the aisle walls, so that on plan there are neither lateral chapels nor transepts. It is of great height, 126 feet to the vaulting, and about 100 feet wide, measuring over nave and aisles. Evidently, the problem which the architect of this church had to solve was one which is of the greatest interest to the modern American and English architects. It was this : how to erect upon a comparatively small site in the heart of a city filled with unusually lofty buildings a very dignified cathedral. It is said that the celebrated Albertus Magnus was the man who overcame this difficulty, and gave the scheme for the present cathedral. He was certainly Bishop of Ratisbon when the cathedral was commenced in 1278, and was prior of the fine Dominican church when the latter was commenced in 1274. Now, although the cathedral is a very elaborate building, and the Dominican church a very plain one, the same masterly treatment and the subtle knowledge of proportion are characteristic of both buildings. The interior of the cathedral is most impressive, and the grand west front, part

GERMANY, ARCHITECTURE OF. PLATE III

Dresden : the Zwinger.   The unfinished palace of the Elector
Augustus II., built by Pöppelmann about 1720.   All that was built
is this fantastic but graceful and interesting forecourt, the most agreeable specimen in Germany of the late neoclassic, which the Germans
call *Barock*.   The building beyond on the right is the great picture
gallery, a modern building, finished 1856.

of which only dates from 1404–1486, is certainly the most magnificent in Germany. The two great towers, the spires of which have only been just recently completed, are nobly planned, and the triangular porch between them is one of the most exquisite works of mediæval times. Most of the windows are of beautiful old stained glass, and as the altars stand beneath canopies coeval with the building, there is a harmony which is not frequently met with in old churches. The cloisters, which are very extensive, do not join

that beautiful thirteenth century style of pointed Gothic which is peculiar to the Danube and its immediate neighbourhood. This style is remarkable, from the fact that, unlike all other early thirteenth century work in Germany, it has no Romanesque characteristics about it. The churches of the *Neider-Münster*, the *Ober-Münster*, and the abbey of S. Emmeran, also in Ratisbon, are early Romanesque works of the basilica type, unfortunately much modernized internally. The last named has a curious crypt

GERMANY, PART III.: ST. MICHAEL'S CHURCH, MUNICH, BAVARIA; INTERIOR OF NAVE; C. 1585.

the cathedral, and are thus more like the *camposanto* of an Italian cathedral; they are bisected by a large vaulted hall full of ancient monuments, from which two ancient chapels are entered. The larger, that of S. Stephen, is said to have been the original cathedral, and dates from the ninth or tenth century. The other one looks like a baptistery, and is thirteenth century work; both contain their original altars.

Close to the cathedral is a very remarkable thirteenth century Gothic church called the *Alte-Pfarr*. Two thirds of the area is covered by vaulted galleries, and its architecture is of

at the west end, above ground, supporting a choir and altar. There is also a very beautiful thirteenth century cloister of the characteristic Danubian school, examples of which are to be found in Austria. It is somewhat difficult to determine whether this style originated in Ratisbon, and found its way *down* the Danube, or whether it had its rise in the Austrian abbeys, and found its way *up* the Danube. (See Austrian States, Architecture of.) The Scotch abbey church of S. James is a very valuable example of a late Romanesque basilica, and has escaped alterations or modernization.

The domestic buildings are as remarkable as the ecclesiastical, many of them dating from the twelfth and thirteenth centuries. They are so lofty as to be absolute towers, and there is a remarkable feature about them which may be worthy of consideration by American and English architects who have to erect very tall buildings in cities. They are completely free from horizontal lines or features of any description ; all details, whether structural or ornamental, are vertical. There is a very interesting *Rathhaus*, chiefly fourteenth century, which retains some of the earliest tapestry we have ever seen.

Munich does not contain many valuable examples of mediæval architecture. The cathedral, which, by the way, was only made the see of a bishop at the commencement of the present century, is a vast brick *Hallenbau* more remarkable for its size and magnificent stained glass than for structural beauty. The court church of S. Michael is the most interesting Renaissance ecclesiastical building in Germany, erected between the years 1585–1591 ; it is a vast single span church with chapels between the buttresses. The great stone barrel vault of the nave is over sixty feet in span. There is some uncertainty as to the architect ; by some writers it is attributed to De Witt, called by the Italians Candido, and by others to Frederic Sustris. Munich, however, chiefly attracts attention on account of its modern buildings. German architects have here had an opportunity of distinguishing themselves such as has been granted nowhere else during the present century. King Ludwig determined to make Munich the most artistic capital in Europe, and with great wisdom he conceived the idea, not of rebuilding the quaint old city, but of erecting a new town adjoining it, a kind of "glorified suburb." Space and expense were of little or no importance, material and skilled workmen were at hand, and a school of decorative painters was established who were ready to adorn the buildings when erected with wall pictures of great excellence. Given all these favourable conditions, did the German architects rise to the occasion and is modern Munich the architectural Eldorado one has a right to expect? Two schools of thought were at work from the first, one led by Klenze, whose idea was to adapt classical styles of architecture to modern requirements, and the other by Gärtner, who attempted to invent a new style by the combination of classical, mediæval, and Renaissance. The works of the first school are exhibited in the old Pinakothek, 1826–1836, by Klenze, the Glyptothek, also by Klenze, 1816–1830, and the Propylæa, 1862, by Klenze, all very noble buildings, though especially in the case of the Propylæa almost too distinctly copies of ancient work. The other school, called the Eclectic School, produced the *Ludwigs Kirche*,

1829–1842, by Gärtner, the Library, the new Pinakothek by Voit, 1846–1853, the Maximilianeum, and the great street leading up to it. Now there is certainly no reason why a modern architect should not mix together any number of styles, provided he makes a harmonious combination of them and is master of the various elements he is dealing with, and we must ask the question, Did these German architects create harmonious combinations, and were they masters of the Romanesque and Gothic styles which they combined with the classical? Is there anything to be found in the *Auer Kirche* by Ohlmüller 1830–1839, to lead one to the conclusion that the German architects of the period had a very deep knowledge of Gothic? or in the exterior of the *Allerheiligen Kapelle* that they understood Byzantine work? and can any one find any hopeful signs for the future of a style whose most recent developments have produced the Maximilianeum and the great street leading to it? Of course the *Ludwigs Kirche* and the *Allerheiligen* Capelle have splendid features about them, but how much of this is owing to their magnificent decorations by Cornelius and Hess and to their sumptuous internal material? And even the basilica by Liebland, 1850, a great church 270 feet long, 83 feet wide, supported upon 66 columns of gray Tyrolese marble, its walls encrusted with costly marbles and frescoes by Hess and Schraudolph, could scarcely fail to be striking ; but what of the exterior where all these adventitious aids to its architecture were wanting? Can it be said to be either striking or interesting? Of course if the Eclectic School had started some forty years later, and numbered amongst its designers such Gothic architects as Professor Schmidt of Vienna, Michael Stadtz of Cologne, Guldenpfennig of Paderborn, combined with the knowledge of classical styles of such men as Klenze or Schinkel, the result might have indeed been a triumph for modern architecture, and we might have possessed a style which would equal, if not surpass, the glories of past ages.

Augsburg, the ancient capital of Swabia, is a noble city, and is to German Renaissance what Ratisbon is to the early German Gothic, and Nuremberg to later. The lofty Renaissance houses turn their great gables towards the *Maximilian Strasse*, the glory of the town, and possibly the noblest street in Europe, in the centre of which stands the great *Rathhaus*, built by Elias Holl, 1616–1620. The elevation consists of a colossal gable 147 feet broad and 175 feet high, flanked by octagonal towers crowned by ogee domes. The building is of brick, but enriched here and there by bronze work. In this same street are three very lofty towers. The Fire Tower, called the *Perlach*, close to the *Rathhaus*, was commenced 989, but rebuilt from about 40 feet to the ground by

Elias Holl in 1615; it is 226 feet high and crowned by a lantern. The church of S. Moritz on the other side of the street has a very similar tower, and that of S. Afra at the extreme end of the street has a tower 300 feet high. These towers are very Eastern in type, crowned by pear-shaped domes. They are common all over the south of Germany, Russia, and Turkey. We have been unable to discover any of an earlier date than the sixteenth century. The church of S. Afra is a fine late Gothic building, 1476–1500, commenced by Hans Luitpol and completed by Burkart Engleberger. Like everything in Augsburg it is on a grand scale, 316 feet long, 94 wide, and 100 to the vaulting. There are three magnificent fountains in this street adorned with colossal figures, sea horses, etc., in bronze, dating from the close of the sixteenth century. What strikes one so much about them is the

upon very slender columns. It is a very graceful building, and its five porches are adorned with rich sculpture. The architect was Meister Hans Steinmetz, but the upper portion of the steeple was not completed until the middle of the sixteenth century. It is, however, entirely Gothic work and the continuation of the same design. The domestic architecture of Landshut is excellent, the houses for the most part having narrow fronts and very lofty pinnacled gables. There is an elegant little Italian palace with a pretty courtyard and rooms adorned with charming panelling and parquetry. Overlooking the town from the top of a lofty hill is the castle of Trausnitz, one of the most interesting in

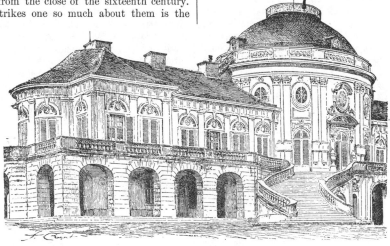

GERMANY, PART III.: VILLA CALLED SOLITUDE, NEAR STUTTGART; c. 1767.

great size of their basins and the plentiful supply of water which splashes about amongst the great bronze figures, creating quite a sea in the large pools, which are full of fish, and giving an air of freshness to this wide and very long street. The cathedral at Augsburg is a very curious church with two choirs, the eastern dating from the fourteenth century and the western, together with the nave, from the tenth century. There are grand bronze doors covered with bas-reliefs and the earliest stained glass in Europe. The older bishop's throne in the west choir, a marble seat supported on lions, is said to be Roman work. There are fine stalls, interesting furniture, and perhaps the best collection of pictures in any German church.

Landshut, another grand old city, has the houses of its principal street built over arcades. The great church of S. Martin possesses the loftiest brick tower in the world, 454 feet high. The church itself is a vast *Hallenbau*, 315 feet long and 100 feet to the vaulting, supported

Bavaria. It possesses a curious thirteenth century chapel with some interesting sculpture. The apartments on the ground floor are all vaulted in the style of the fifteenth century, but those on the upper stories were decorated and fitted up by De Witt (Candido) at the close of the sixteenth century. The stoves are beautiful examples of earthenware work and tiles.

The cathedral of Ulm is, according to De Lassaube, the third largest church in Germany, but since the completion of its steeple some few years back, it is, if measured in bulk, the second. Its great dimensions and magnificent furniture entitle it to consideration, but when the opportunity of erecting one of the largest churches in Christendom was offered to its architects, seconded by the assistance of workmen, sculptors, and stained glass painters of unsurpassed excellence, it is indeed strange that they should have produced so unsatisfactory a building. It is in every way the reverse of Ratisbon; an enormous site was available, — a town of unlimited area, by no means closely built, — and a magnificent opportunity, yet although it is double the size, the smaller church is dignified and most impressive, whereas no large church in Europe is so ill designed as that of Ulm. It has been said that it is a village church magnified to the size of a cathedral. Of course the Swabian architects delighted in simplicity of plan, but here the idea is greatly exaggerated. A great cathedral nearly 500 feet long and 144 feet to the vaulting, consisting of a nave and aisles, a western tower, and a low single-aisled choir, is an affectation of simplicity. That ugly feature, a huge blank wall in place of a triforium, is disagreeably apparent, and is all the more objectionable from the poverty of detail in the arches and the vaulting. The tower is the only portion of the building which is striking or magnificent. Its lower portion consists of an open hall, which is undoubtedly striking. The church is, however, like many of the German churches, a perfect museum of beautiful works of art. The Sacraments' house, 90 feet high, is a masterpiece of tabernacle work. The stalls, altarpieces, and stained glass are not to be surpassed in Europe. The great tower has recently been completed, but its outline is not quite satisfactory.

Stuttgart is a handsome city, chiefly remarkable for its modern architecture. The *Schloss* is a picturesque Renaissance building, 1553–1570. The new palace, 1746–1807, is not specially interesting. The theatre, which almost joins it, and the *Königsbau* are not undignified, yet, although the town is handsome, it cannot be said to contain any work of great excellence.

The picturesque little town of Schwäbisch-Gmünd is celebrated as the birthplace of two of the greatest architects of the Middle Ages, Henry and Peter Arler; of the elder brother's, Henry's, work the *Heiligenkreutz Kirche*, 1357, is a brilliant example. Henry Arler is believed to be that Enrico Di Gamodio who commenced Milan cathedral, and there is a certain similarity between the details of the church at Gmünd and the great cathedral, especially about the disposition of the niches over the doorways and the large windows round the aisles of the apse. That Henry Arler designed the celebrated Certosa at Pavia is far less likely, as we trace no resemblance to his style in that building. The younger brother, Peter, was scarcely less celebrated, and we have given notice of his works in Bohemia; he also erected the fine church at Nördlingen.

Würtemberg possesses a fair number of interesting churches, but our space will not allow of our describing them.

GERMANY, ARCHITECTURE OF; Part IV. ; the Baltic Province, Brandenburg, Silesia, and German Poland. The provinces of the German Empire on the borders of the Baltic, that is to say Schleswig-Holstein, Mecklenburg,

Pomerania, Danzig, Ermeland, and Königsberg, have an architecture which is peculiar to themselves, but which partakes of the characteristics of all the Baltic countries. Thus, there is no great distinction to be noticed between those of Pomerania and Sweden, Friesland and Gottland ; though the details are somewhat varied, yet the general resemblance is so remarkable as to point to a common origin. The material used is usually brick, but bears no resemblance to the brick construction in any other parts of Europe. In Holstein, however, Flemish influence is conspicuous, notably at Lubeck, a magnificent old town, rich in churches and domestic architecture. The *Frauen Kirche* is a most remarkable building of grand dimensions, with lofty clearstory and spire-crowned western towers. It is extremely plain externally, but the interior, though whitewashed all over, is particularly striking. The cathedral, the church of S. Catherine, and S. Jakob are also noble works, and all possess elaborate mediæval furniture and fitting. Schwerin, Wismar, Rostock in Mecklenburg, Stralsund, Anklam, Stettin, Stargard, Koslin, in Pomerania, all possess magnificent churches of this brick architecture, one peculiarity about which is that brickwork is treated almost precisely like stone. Now although it is to be admired for intricacy of detail, elegance of form, and variety in colour, it must be acknowledged that it is not equal to the treatment of brickwork in the buildings of Italy and the south of France, and for this reason there is always something unsatisfactory in art when one kind of material derives its treatment from another. Now the brickwork of the countries we have just mentioned is essentially brick in *construction*, and the detail is evolved from the special peculiarities of the materials ; but in the case of the Baltic buildings they would be more complete and fitting if the design had been carried out in stone. Whether this singular treatment of brickwork originated in Sweden, Pomerania, the extreme eastern districts of Ermeland, Königsberg, and Marienwerder, or in Brandenburg, it is impossible to determine ; it certainly appears, however, to have received its highest development in Danzig, which was geographically a portion of Poland.

A few miles from Danzig is the ancient town of Marienburg, with its magnificent castle, which was erected in the thirteenth century by the Teutonic branch of the Knights of S. John of Jerusalem who settled here in the year 1281. This vast castle covers an immense area, and is divided into three distinct buildings all within one enclosure ; the earliest portion was completed in 1309. The noble central building, resembling the keep in an English castle, and containing the knights' hall, chapter house, and chapel, was erected between 1351–1382.

This castle, the grandest in all Germany and noblest example of brickwork, was commenced while the neighbourhood was for the most part pagan. Under the auspices of the Knights of S. John rose the fine towns of Danzig, Marienburg, Elbing. Ermeland, adjoining this territory, was the see of a prince-bishop, and is still the most northern Catholic bishopric in Europe. Its capital, Frauenburg, possesses a cathedral which is a most characteristic example of this Baltic style. It is a very lofty *Hallenbau*, with four very slender gabled towers. The choir was completed in 1342. Danzig is a splendid old town, with immense gabled houses and churches. The *Marien Kirche* is a colossal building, commenced in 1343 and completed in the sixteenth century. Internally it is a vast *Hallenbau*, but externally, owing to the aisles being gabled at right angles to the nave, and there being six slender towers placed between the gables in addition to the huge tower at the west end, it presents a very imposing appearance, though, like many of the other churches in this district, it looks more like an immense town hall than a church. This secular look about the churches of northeast Prussia is very strange to the eyes accustomed to English or French churches. It probably arises from the fact that in this part of Europe alone the secular and domestic buildings were cotemporary in their inception with the ecclesiastical. In point of fact, the Knights of S. John, who were the possessors of the province, commenced their works by erecting vast residential castles, as we see at Marienburg, so that, instead of architectural development taking its initiative from churches, secular buildings originated it. This semi-secular character about the churches also exhibits itself in Brandenburg and Silesia. S. Catherine's, at Brandenburg, is a curious example, the exterior of the church being almost concealed behind pierced screens of brickwork, terminated in innumerable gables executed in glazed brickwork of various colours. At Prenzlau the eastern portion of the great church is hidden from view by a vast gabled end which is simply a masking wall, as the absolute eastern termination of the building consists of three apses, so that the plan and elevation can scarcely be recognized as belonging to the same

building. The town halls in Pomerania and Mecklenburg have these curious masking walls carried up several stories high, pierced with quasi windows opened to the sky. Although no doubt these buildings are very picturesque, the style of architecture which produces such eccentric shams cannot be regarded as grand art. This curious kind of work is also found at Posen and Silesia, though it does not hold undivided sway, as is seen from such buildings as the choir of the cathedral and the churches of S. Elizabeth and Holy Cross at Breslau, which belong to a far more dignified school.

GERMANY, PART IV.: ZEUGHAUS AT DANZIG, EASTERN PRUSSIA; c. 1605.

Although Berlin is for the most part a modern city, there are some interesting examples of mediæval work upon the island; especially, the old *Kloster Kirche*, thirteenth century, and S. Mary's, a very pleasing fourteenth century building. Before the time, however, of Frederic I., Berlin was an unimportant country town in an uninteresting locality and upon a most undesirable site, surrounded by a dead level flat — a combination of marsh and desert, with a stagnant, muddy ditch. What could have induced Prussian kings to select it as their capital surpasses comprehension, as there are no natural beauties about the place. The water supply is uncertain and insufficient, and the drainage absolutely impossible; however, not-withstanding these difficulties and drawbacks, it must be acknowledged that modern Berlin is one of the handsomest and most dignified cities in Europe; most effectively planned with great leading thoroughfares at right angles, the public buildings finely grouped together and brought strongly into evidence, either in or near to a noble street with a great double avenue of lime trees along its centre called *Unter den Linden*, which enters the town at the Brandenburg Gate, erected 1789–1792, crowned by a victory in a quadriga. The general effect of this monument is not unpleasing, although it is only of brick plastered over. The first important public building in Berlin was the arsenal, commenced by Nehering in 1685 and finished by Schlüter. It is in the rococo style, and imposing from its vast size. The royal palace, by the same architects, is a not unpleasant building, but Berlin owes its chief architectural merit to Schinkel, who erected the grand museum, 1830, with its magnificent colonnade, in the Ionic order, over 200 feet in length, and a very dignified theatre in the same severe style. Schinkel's idea seems to have been to adapt classical architecture for public buildings, and revive the Gothic for ecclesiastical. Unfortunately, like most architects of his time, his Gothic was wanting in study from ancient work, and, consequently, unsatisfactory, as may be seen from a large church which he built at Berlin.

The National Gallery, 1843–1855, by Halmhuber, is another striking and beautiful building in severe Greek style. The *Rathhaus*, 1861–1868, is a stately and imposing structure with Romanesque detail, which somehow or other does not seem to adapt itself well to the requirements of a modern public building.

The *Reichsschatzamt*, 1885–1887, is in a somewhat severely treated Italian Renaissance style, very dignified and splendidly carried out.

A considerable number of large churches have been recently erected in Berlin. The most important is the King William Memorial church in Augusta Victoria Platz. It is in the Rhenish Romanesque style, with five spires, and is certainly striking, though the interior has rather more the effect of a great hall than a church. This seems to be the general idea of a modern church in Berlin, and strangely enough has been even taken up by the Catholics, who, in the S. Sebastian church and the S. Pius church, 1893–1896, have adopted this idea. No doubt it may lend itself well to Protestant form of worship, but we cannot help thinking that the church of S. Michael, with its lofty Gothic nave and aisles and apsidal choir, is much more suited to Catholic ritual.

The domestic architecture of Berlin seems to be developing itself far more in the mediæval

and Nuremberg lines than in the severe Renaissance or classic ones. Some of the cafés recently erected are extremely elegant buildings. Berlin has always been celebrated for its statues and monuments. Rauch's monumental group and equestrian statue to Frederick the Great is equalled by few modern works and surpassed by none. The new national monument to William I., erected in 1890, is a very well-designed and striking combination of architecture and sculpture.

Kugler, *Handbuch der Kunstgeschichte*, 1856; Kugler, *Kleinschriften* (a numerous series); Otte, *Handbuch der Kirchl. Kunst-Archäologie des deutschen Mittelalters*; Müller, *Denkmäler deutschen Baukunst*; Müller, *Beitrage zur deutschen Kunst*, etc.; *Organ für Christliche Kunst*. (publication still proceeding); Chapuy, *Allemagne monumentale*; Whewell, *Architectural Notes on German Churches*; King, *Study-book of Mediæval Architecture and Art*, London, 1858; Kugler, *Pommersche Kunstgeschichte*; Puttrich, *Denkmale der Baukunst des Mittelalters in Sachsen*; Boisserée, *Denkmale der Bauk. von 7 bis zum 13 Jahrhundert am Niederrhein*; Quast, *Denkmäler der Baukunst in Ermland*; Schmidt, *Baudenkmale in Trier und seiner Umgebung*; Lübke, *Die Mittelalterl. Kunst Westfalen*; Brewer, *Some Churches in the Neighbourhood of Cleves* (paper read before the R. I. B. A., London, 1891); Grier und Gorz, *Denkmale romanischer Baukunst am Rhein*; Heideloff und Müller, *Die Kunst des Mittelalters in Schwaben*; H. W. Brewer, *Papers upon the Mediæval Architecture of Central Germany, Bavaria, and Bohemia* (published in *The Builder*, London, 1866 to 1890); Popp and Bulan, *Architektur des Mittelalters in Regensburg*; Sighart, *Die Mittelalterl. Kunst in der Erzdiocese München-Freising*; Haupt, *Backstein Bauten der Renaissance*, 1899, Frankfort a/M; Wasmuth, *Architektur der Gegenwart*, Berlin (publication still proceeding); Licht, *Architektur Deutschlands*; Förster, *Denkmale deutscher Baukunst, Bildnerei und Malerei vom Einführung des Christenthums bis auf die neueste Zeit*, Leipzig, 1855–1869; Hugo Licht, *Architektur Berlins*.

— H. W. BREWER.

GERVASE OF CANTERBURY; chronicler.

The chronicler Gervase gives an account of Canterbury during the years of his own experience, first describing the church as he knew it before the conflagration of 1174, then the events of the fire, and lastly the progress of the reconstruction. His account is printed in Willis (op. cit.).

Stephen, *Dictionary of National Biography*; Willis, *Canterbury Cathedral*.

GESSO. In Italian art, hard plaster such as is used for casts from works of art, and also as a ground for mural painting. (See Encaustic; Fresco Painting; Fresco Secco.)

GESSO DURO. In Italian art, gesso of superior quality, taking a hard finish and used for casts from works of sculpture. Bas-reliefs made of this material and usually painted for the further protection of the surface were made in considerable numbers during the sixteenth and seventeenth centuries; some of these are of very high rank as works of art, and are recognized and catalogued as such. They are often mounted in highly decorated and quasi-architectural frames, and the colour with which the plaster is painted very often imitates the ordinary colour of terra cotta.— R. S.

GHAT; GHAUT. In India, a landing place with steps and a broad quay, as on the bank of one of the great navigable rivers. There is often on the land side of the quay a piece of architectural walling with a gateway carried through it, much resembling the gates in the outward wall of a fortified city. (See India, Architecture of.)

GHEERYS, ADAM; architect; d. Dec. 10, 1394.

Architect of the dukes of Brabant. He directed in 1363, at the ducal palace in Brussels, the construction of a chapel now destroyed, and in 1376 built the château of Vilvorde.

Biographie Nationale de la Belgique.

GHETTO. In ancient cities of Europe, especially in Italy, the Jewish quarter; a district to which the Jews were confined. As the restriction lasted until very recent times, the old ghetto is often found to be full of unaltered ancient buildings, and in some cities that quarter is peculiarly interesting to students. The Ghetto of Rome, undisturbed until 1887, surrounded the so-called Porticus Octaviæ — the building named after Octavia, the sister of Augustus, and partly rebuilt under Septimus Severus. The Ghetto was therefore close to the Tiber, and lay between the theatre of Marcellus (Palazzo Orsini Savelli) on the southeast, and the church of S. Maria in Monticelli on the northwest; lying therefore due west from the Campidoglio and hardly more than one quarter of a mile distant.

GHIBERTI, LORENZO DE'; goldsmith, sculptor, and architect; b. 1378; d. December, 1455.

The earliest of the three pairs of bronze doors of the baptistery of Florence was made by Andrea da Pisa (see Andrea da Pisa). In 1401 a competition was opened for another. According to Vasari the competitors were Ghiberti and Brunellesco (see Brunellesco) of Florence, Giacomo della Quercia and Francesco Valdambrini of Siena, Nicolò Spinelli and Nicolò Lamberti of Arezzo (see Giacomo della Quercia and Lamberti, N.), and Simone of Colle in Val d'Elsa. The competitive panels of the "Sacrifice of Abraham," executed by Brunellesco and Ghiberti, are both in the Museo Nazionale, Florence. Ghiberti was successful, and began the work in December, 1403. It was finished in April, 1424. In a document of April 16, 1420, he is mentioned as associated on equal terms with Brunellesco in building the cupola

of the cathedral of Florence. He appears occasionally in the records, but had little to do with the actual construction (see Brunellesco). Jan. 2, 1424 (before the completion of his first doors), Ghiberti received a commission for another pair for the Florentine baptistery. This, the most celebrated work of its kind in existence, was finished in 1452. It is composed of ten panels in relief representing subjects from the Old Testament. In the framework are busts and figures in high relief. Ghiberti modelled also the beautiful framework of birds and foliage. The cartoons for many of the painted glass windows in the Florentine cathedral were drawn by Ghiberti. He was succeeded by his son Vittorio; and there were sculptors of the Ghiberti family in the sixteenth century. Much of our information about Ghiberti is taken from his Commentaries, extracts from which are published by Perkins in his monograph.

Perkins, *Ghiberti et son école*; Reymond, *Sculpture florentine*; Reymond, *Lorenzo Ghiberti*; Müntz, *Les précurseurs de la Renaissance*; Vasari, Milanesi ed.; Vasari, Blashfield-Hopkins ed.

GHINI, GIOVANNI DI LAPO; architect.

Ghini first appears in the records of the cathedral of Florence in 1355 as a member of the commission appointed to consider the model of Francesco Talenti (see Talenti, F.). In 1357 he was employed to lay the foundations of the first four piers of the nave. In 1358 he was associated with Francesco Talenti, and in 1364 superseded him as chief architect of the cathedral. About 1360, Ghini appears to have made a model (called *chiesa piccola* in the records) which called for five bays in the nave, and five chapels about the rotunda. Aug. 13, 1366, this model was superseded by that of the commission of architects and painters (*maestri e pittori*) according to which the church was built essentially as it stands. (See Brunellesco.) August, 1371, Ghini's name appears in the records for the last time.

Nardini, *Giovanni di Lapo Ghini ed il Duomo del 1630*; Pietro Vigo, *L'Architetto Giovanni di Lapo*; Guasti, *Santa Maria del Fiore.*

GIACOMO. Roman architect. (See Cosmati.)

GIACOMO DA PIETRASANTA. (See Pietrasanta, Giacomo da.)

GIACOMO DELLA PORTA; architect; b. 1541 at Milan; d. 1604 at Rome.

The most important of the pupils of Vignola (see Barozzio, G.). Between 1564 and 1573 he was occupied at Genoa, his principal work there being the completion of the church of S. Annunziata. After the death of Vignola in 1573, he returned to Rome and finished the church called *Il Gesù*, begun by that architect. Before his death in 1564, Michelangelo and his assistants had made a model for the cupola of S. Peter's church (Rome), and had completed the construction as far as the cornice of the drum. The cupola itself was built by Giacomo della Porta. He also built the Palazzo Paluzzi, the Palazzo Chigi in the Piazza Colonna, the Palazzo Serlupi, the Palazzo d' Este, the façade of the church of S. Maria in Monte (1579), the façade of the church of S. Luigi de' Francesi (1589), all in Rome. He was very successful in designing decorative architectural accessories. He made several fine fountains in Rome, the most important of which is the Fontana delle Tartarughe (of the Turtles), the figures of which were modelled by the sculptor Taddeo Landini. Della Porta's Villa Aldobrandini near Frascati, his last work (1598–1603), with its fine garden and casino, is especially characteristic.

Redtenbacher, *Die Architektur der Italienischen Renaissance;* Müntz, *Renaissance;* Charles Garnier, *Michel-Ange, Architecte.*

GIACOMO (JACOPO) DELLA QUERCIA (or Guercia); sculptor; b. about 1374; d. 1438.

Giacomo probably derived his name from the village of Quercia Grossa, near Siena, Italy. In 1401 he competed for the bronze doors of the baptistery in Florence (see Ghiberti). One of his most charming works is the recumbent statue on the monument to Ilaria, wife of Paolo Guinigi, in the cathedral of Lucca. The first contract for the fountain of the Piazza del Campo, the so-called Fonte Gaia, at Siena, dates from Jan. 22, 1409. It was completed in 1419. The retable of the Trenta chapel in the church of S. Frediano at Lucca was finished in 1422. About 1430 he made one of the bas-reliefs in the font of the baptistery at Siena. Another is by Donatello (see Donatello). March 28, 1425, Giacomo made a contract to decorate the great portal of the church of S. Petronio in Bologna. The bas-reliefs, representing scenes from the Creation, which he made for this door are among the finest works of the early Italian Renaissance.

Cornelius, *Jacopo della Quercia;* Sidney Colvin, *Jacopo della Quercia;* Guizzardi-Davia, *Le Sculture delle Porte della Basilica di San Petronio.*

GIACOPO. (See Giacomo.)

GIALLO ANTICO. (See Giallo Antico Marble, under Marble.)

GIAMBERTI. (See San Gallo.)

GIB. In wood framing or iron work, a metal member, usually one of a pair, for retaining two or more parts which are to be keyed together. Its form is that of a cramp, a metal strap having its ends bent at right angles to the main part. Two of them are inserted on opposite sides of the aperture or mortise prepared for the keys (wedges), so that the returned ends will fit closely to the outer faces of the connected members, which are thus prevented from

slipping or spreading when the keys are driven between the gibs.

GIBBONS, GRINLING; sculptor; b. April 4, 1648; d. Aug. 3, 1720.

The greatest of English wood carvers. Gibbons was born at Rotterdam, Holland, and probably came to England in 1667, the year after the Great Fire in London. He attracted the attention of John Evelyn in 1671, who presented him to King Charles II. and Sir Christopher Wren (see Wren). He was employed by Wren to carve the superb choir stalls and bishop's throne in S. Paul's cathedral, London. He decorated also the library and chapel of Trinity College, Cambridge. He was employed by the king at Windsor, Whitehall, and Kensington. There is a superb room by Gibbons at Petworth, extensive decorations at Chatsworth, and a throne at Canterbury cathedral. His delicate birds and flowers are to be found in very many of the great houses built in England in his time. In marble he executed the fine tomb of Viscount Campden at Exton, the font of S. Margaret's, Lothbury, and other works, all in England.

Walpole, *Anecdotes;* Cunningham, *Lives;* Evelyn, *Diary;* W. G. Rogers, *Remarks on Grinling Gibbons.*

GIBBS, JAMES; architect; b. Dec. 26, 1682 (at Aberdeen, Scotland); d. Aug. 5, 1754.

He was the son of Peter Gibbs, a Roman Catholic merchant of Aberdeen, and took his M. A. degree at Marischal College, Aberdeen. After the death of his parents he entered the service of a builder in Holland. He was discovered by John Erskine, eleventh Earl of Mar, who sent him to Rome, where he entered the school of Carlo Fontana (see Fontana, C.), surveyor general to Pope Clement XI. Returning to London in 1709, he won the friendship of Sir Christopher Wren (see Wren). The church of S. Mary le Strand was begun by Gibbs Feb. 15, 1714. August, 1721, he began for Harley, Earl of Oxford, the church of S. Peter, Vere Street, London, and a little later the tomb of Matthew Prior, in the south transept of Westminster Abbey. March 19, 1722, the first stone was laid for his famous church of S. Martin's in the Fields, and June 22, 1722, he began the "Senate House" in Cambridge. In 1723–1725 he built the church of Allhallows in Derby (except the tower). Gibbs prepared a scheme for rebuilding the quadrangle of King's College, Cambridge. Only the western side was carried out. The quadrangle of S. Bartholomew's hospital was begun by him June 9, 1730. The first stone of the Radcliffe Library at Oxford, his best building, was laid June 16, 1737. It was built from a fund of £40,000, left by John Radcliffe, M.D. Gibbs's books and drawings are preserved at Oxford. He published *A Book of Architecture contain-*

ing designs by James Gibbs, 1 vol. folio, 1728; *The Rules for Drawing the Several Parts of Architecture*, 1732; *Bibliotheca Radcliffiana*, 1747.

Herbert P. Horne in the *Century Guild Hobby Horse* for January and July, 1889; Stephen, *Dictionary of National Biography*.

GIBBS, JAMES: CHURCH OF S. MARY LE STRAND, LONDON; THE SPIRE; C. 1717.

GIBLET CHECK; CHEEK. In some British dialects a large rebate in the jamb and lintel of a doorway made to receive the door when shut, so that it shall be flush with the face of the wall, the door being arranged to open outward. (Spelled also Jiblet.)

GIGLIO. A flower-shaped ornament recognized as the special bearing or badge of the city of Florence. It strongly resembles the fleur-de-lis, but has on either side of the central spike a slender flower stalk. Its forms, also, are in a sense fixed and definite, whereas the fleur-de-lis has been used for many purposes, and in many ages and countries, and has no one form which can be positively called the correct one. It has been called in modern heraldic books Fleur-de-lis Florencé; but this is probably a recently coined term.

GILD (v.t.). To apply gilding.

GILDING. *A.* The art or practice of applying gold leaf or gold powder to the surface of anything, so as to give it, to some extent, the appearance of gold. By extension, the application of some other substance which more or less nearly approaches the appearance of gold, in this sense more properly described by another term (see Bronzing).

B. The surface and metallic appearance given by any of the processes referred to under *A*, as in the phrase, there is too much gilding in the decoration.

Much the best and most permanent method of gilding is to apply a very thin layer of pure gold, usually called gold leaf. It is, however, easy to give to a moulding or raised ornament the appearance of being solidly gilded without much use of the leaf; for the production of this effect a peculiar shade of yellowish colour is employed under the general name gold colour, and only those parts receive the actual metal which will receive and reflect the light the most strongly. Gilding is not usually a means of gaudy display or of what is called "barbaric" magnificence. To the decorator gilding is rather the universal harmonizer. If, as often happens in modern colour decoration, the use of strong and positive colours is difficult, and the designer finds his combination a disappointment to him, gold remains at his hand the most sure remedy for this lack of harmony. Moreover, the greatest artists in the use of pure and strong colour use gold with much freedom. Thus, in some of the finest Chinese enamels, it is evident that the gold line separating the small patches of colour is relied upon for a background or relief to keep the whole in place.

In gilding for decorative effect it is not the metal which is very costly (see Gold leaf); it is the necessity of going over the work at least twice, first with gold size, and afterward with the gold leaf, which has to be very carefully handled, applied, allowed to dry, and then rubbed, that the loose fragments may be removed. — R. S.

GILI, JEHAN; architect.

Gili was chosen consul of the corporation of masons of Montpellier twenty-four times before 1396. The contract which he made for the portal of the monastery of S. Firmin is one of the most interesting documents in existence on the military architecture of the Middle Ages.

Renouvier et Ricard, *Maîtres de pierre de Montpellier.*

GILLY, FRIEDRICH; architect; b. Feb. 16, 1771; d. Aug. 3, 1800.

A son of David Gilly, *Oberbaurath* in Berlin. Gilly was one of the most talented German architects of his time. His early death, however, prevented the accomplishment of any very important results. There are a few buildings in the vicinity of Berlin which are ascribed to him, but he is best known by his sketches and designs, of which there are three portfolios in the *Technische Hochschule* at Charlottenburg, near Berlin. He had great influence upon the development of the architect Schinkel. (See Schinkel.)

Borrmann, *Kunstdenkmäler von Berlin.*

GIN. An apparatus answering the purpose of a Crane or Derrick, consisting of three legs united at their tops, thus forming a tripod. A windlass is usually secured between two of the legs.

GINAIN, PAUL RENÉ LÉON; architect; b. 1825 ; d. March 7, 1898.

Ginain was a pupil of Lebas (see Lebas), and won the *Premier Grand Prix de Rome* in 1852. He built in Paris the church of Notre Dame des Champs, the library of the Faculté de Médecine, the Musée Brignole-Galiera, and other works. He was professor of architecture in the *École des Beaux Arts*, member of the *Institut*, and *architecte honoraire* of the French government and the city of Paris.

Nécrologie in *Construction Moderne*, March 12, 1898 ; Penanrum, *Les Architectes élèves de l'École des Beaux Arts.*

GINNELL. In local British usage, a passage between two buildings or the like.—(A. P. S.)

GIOCONDO (JOCUNDUS), FRA GIOVANNI; architect, engineer, and epigraphist of Verona, Italy ; d. between 1515 and 1519.

Fra Giocondo was a Franciscan monk and one of the most learned men of his time. He made a collection (begun 1477) of two thousand Latin inscriptions, which was dedicated to Lorenzo de' Medici (*Corpus Inscriptionum Latinorum*, Vol. III., p. xxvii.). He published a celebrated critical edition of Vitruvius, in 1511, dedicated to Pope Julius II. The charming Loggia del Consiglio at Verona (1476–1492) is attributed to him without documentary evidence. In 1489 Giocondo entered the service of Ferdinand I., king of Naples. After the capture of Naples by Charles VIII. in 1495, he followed the French king to Paris, and in 1497 was established at Amboise. *Jehan Jocundus, deviseur de Bastimens* is mentioned twice in *Archives de l'Art Français*, (Vol. I., pp. 108, 116). The château of Gaillon, the Pont Notre Dame, the old Chambre des Comptes, and other works in France have been ascribed to him. In

fact, however, his name is not found on the records of any important structure of the time, except the Pont Notre Dame at Paris (1499–1512) (Leroux de Lincy, op. cit.). In 1513 Giocondo was associated with Raphael and Giuliano da San Gallo in the construction of S. Peter. A design for that building, attributed to him by Antonio da San Gallo (II.), is in the Uffizi (Von Geymüller, *Les Projets primitifs*, p. 263).

Orti-Manara, *Dei Lavori Architettonici di Fra Giocondo ;* Tipaldo, *Elogio ;* Von Geymüller, *Les Projets primitifs ;* Vasari, Milanesi ed. ; l'alustre, *La Renaissance en France*, Vols. I. and II ; *Archives de l'Art Français ;* Leroux de Lincy, *Recherches historiques sur le Pont Notre Dame.*

GIORGIO DA SEBENICO. (See Orsini, Giorgio.)

GIOTTO DI BONDONE; painter, architect, sculptor ; b. about 1267 ; d. Jan. 8, 1337 (at Milan).

One of the greatest of painters, beginner of a great movement, author of important wall paintings in the Arena chapel, Padua, in the church of S. Francesco at Assisi, in the Bargello at Florence, and elsewhere. See his life in dictionaries of painters. After the death of Arnolfo di Cambio (see Arnolfo di Cambio) the construction of S. Maria del Fiore (cathedral, Florence) advanced little until 1331, when work was resumed under the care of the Arte della Lana (Wool Merchants' Guild). April, 1334, Giotto was chosen architect of the cathedral, of the new city walls, and other public works. July 18, 1334, he laid the foundations of the campanile of the cathedral, of which, at his death, he had completed the first story. The interesting series of twenty-one bas-reliefs which decorate this story were designed by Giotto, and probably executed by him with the assistance of Andrea da Pisa (see Andrea da Pisa). The remaining five are by Luca della Robbia (see Robbia, Luca della).

Karl Frey, *Studien zu Giotto ;* Selvatico, *Sulla capellina degli Scrovegni ;* John Ruskin, *Giotto and his Works in Padua ;* Harry Quilter, *Giotto ;* Guasti, *Santa Maria del Fiore ;* Reymond, *Sculpture Florentine ;* Vasari, Milanesi ed.

GIOTTO'S CAMPANILE. The bell tower of the cathedral of Florence, admittedly from the designs of Giotto, who did not live to see it completed. It is the most important piece of that late manifestation of Italian Gothic which carried with it much external decoration in coloured marbles combined with sculpture.

GIOVANNI ; Roman architect, sculptor, and mosaicist. (See Cosmati.)

GIOVANNI DA FIRENZE. (See Baccio da Firenze.)

GIOVANNI DALMATA. Giovanni Dalmata is known only as associated with Mino da Fiesole (see Mino da Fiesole) in his Roman work. Tschudi (op. cit.) ascribes to him the

Roverella monument in the church of S. Clemente in Rome, about 1476.

Tschudi, Giovanni Dalmata.

GIOVANNI D'AMBROGIO; sculptor and architect.

In 1383 he was employed to carve some of the figures designed by Agnolo Gaddi (see Gaddi, A.) for the Loggia dei Lanzi in Florence. The small northern portal of the Florentine cathedral with the Madonna and adoring angels, formerly ascribed to Giovanni Pisano, was made by him.

Frey, Loggia dei Lanzi; Reymond, Sculpture Florentine.

GIOVANNI DA MONTORSOLI. (See Montorsoli, Fra Giovanni da.)

GIOVANNI DA PISA; sculptor and architect; b. about 1240; d. about 1320.

Son of Niccolò Pisano (see Niccolò da Pisa). In 1274 he went to Perugia to superintend the construction of the fountain of the great piazza from his father's designs. The bas-reliefs of the lower story are especially ascribed to him. Between 1278 and 1283 he built the cloister which surrounds the Campo Santo at Pisa. The church of S. Maria della Spina, Pisa, ascribed to him by Vasari, was not built before 1323. Between 1302 and 1311 he made a pulpit for the cathedral of Pisa which was ruined by the conflagration of 1596. Fragments of this pulpit are now in the museum of the city of Pisa. In 1289 he began the façade of the cathedral of Siena. His design was modified by the architects of the next century. The pulpit of S. Andrea at Pistoia is one of his most important works (1303). He commenced the enlargement of the cathedral of Prato in 1317.

Supino, Il Pergamo di Giovanni Pisano nel Duomo di Pisa, in Archivio Storico dell' Arte, Vol. V., p. 65.

GIOVANNI DA PONTE; architect; b. 1512; d. 1597.

Giovanni was a pupil of Scarpagnino (see Abbondi, Antonio). In 1558 he was appointed *proto* of the reconstruction of the buildings on the island of the Rialto, Venice. In 1589 he began the construction of the bridge of the Rialto. Giovanni restored the Doge's palace after the fire of 1577, and about 1589 built the prison opposite that building.

Temanza, Vite degli architetti e scultori Veneziani; Müntz, Renaissance; Ebe, Spät-Renaissance; Milizia, Memorie.

GIOVANNI DA SIENA; architect and military engineer.

One of the leading military architects of the fourteenth century in Italy. Dec. 17, 1386, he superseded Antonio di Vicenzo (see Antonio di Vicenzo) as constructor of the bastion of S. Procolo, Bologna. In 1391 he restored the tower at Rastellino near Bologna. In 1392 he superseded Lorenzo da Bagnomarino as architect of the Castel Bolognese. About 1422

Giovanni entered the service of Niccolò d'Este at Ferrara, and in 1424 rebuilt the fortress at Finale near that city.

Corrado Ricci, Giovanni da Siena; Guidicini, Cose Mirabili.

GIOVANNI DA UDINE. (See Ricamatori, Giovanni de'.)

GIOVANNI DI BONINO D' ASSISI; glass painter.

Son of Bonino d' Assisi, one of the earliest glass painters in Italy. After 1325 he made many of the windows of the cathedral of Orvieto under the supervision of the architect Lorenzo Maitani (see Maitani). He was assisted by Andrea di Mino da Siena, Vitaluccio Luti, Tino d' Angelo d' Assisi and Tino di Biagio. Translucent alabaster was used with the glass in the windows at Orvieto. They have been much restored.

Fumi, Duomo d' Orvieto.

GIOVANNI DI STEFANO DA SIENA; architect.

The old basilica of the Lateran was ruined by fire Aug. 21, 1361. There is a letter by Petrarch to Urban V. (Pope 1362–1370) at Avignon, describing the condition of the building and urging its restoration. The reconstruction was begun at once. The architect employed was Giovanni di Stefano da Siena. From 1372 to 1389 he was supervising architect of the cathedral of Orvieto.

Fumi, Duomo di Orvieto; Rohault de Fleury, Le Latran au Moyen Age; Milanesi, Documenti.

GIRALDA. The tower of the cathedral in Seville, Spain; the name being apparently from the vane at the top, which is large and decorative (Sp. *girar*, to turn). The tower is Moorish, and 50 feet square, and was originally much less lofty than at present; the present belfry, with several rows of arcades, having been added toward the close of the sixteenth century. The figure which adorns the shaft of the vane is of bronze, and an Italian work of the same date as the belfry, about 1568.

GIRANDOLE. A candlestick with several sockets for candles, usually made into a decorative object and sometimes large and very elaborate. This method of lighting apartments was introduced in the seventeenth century. It is to be noted that there are three chief forms in which candlesticks intended for grouping many candles together are made: Lustres, or chandeliers in the usual sense, which hang from above; Girandoles, called also Candelabra, or Candelabrums, which stand on a solid base and branch out above; and, finally, wall brackets, called also by an extension of another term, either Appliques, or Sconces. Of these, girandoles are capable of the most splendid effect, and they sometimes are so permanent and massive as to form part of the architectural decoration of a large apartment. — R. S.

GIRARDINI (**GIRARDIN**) ; architect.

For the dowager Duchess of Bourbon, mother of Louis Henri, Prince of Condé, Girardini began, in 1722, the old Palais Bourbon, Paris, which was remodelled into the present Chambre des Députés. (See Cailleteau and Joly.)

Joly, *Restauration de la Chambre des Députés.*

GIRARDON, FRANÇOIS ; sculptor and architect ; b. March 17, 1628, at Troyes (Aube), France ; d. 1715.

Girardon was a pupil of François Anguier (see Anguier, F.). He studied in Rome, and on his return became the favourite sculptor of Charles Lebrun (see Lebrun). His earliest known work is the tomb of the Duke d'Épernon and his wife in a chapel of the church of Cadillac (Gironde, France). In 1690 Girardon contracted to build the great altar of the church of S. Jean-au-Marché in Troyes, which still exists. About 1699 he began the equestrian statue of Louis XIV. which stood in the Place Louis le Grand (now Place Vendôme), and was melted down for cannon in the Revolution. Perhaps his most famous work is the monument of the Cardinal Richelieu in the church of Sorbonne, Paris. Many of his works are in the Garden of Versailles.

Gonse, *Sculpture française;* Mariette, *Abecedario;* Genevay, *Style Louis XIV.*

GIRDER. Any, generally horizontal, member fulfilling the functions of a beam ; differing from a beam only as being larger or of more complicated structure, or as being used for the support of other beams. In their more elaborate framed forms, girders are not to be distinguished from certain simpler forms of trusses. (See Truss. For Bowstring, Box, Built, Compound, Lattice, Plate, and Trussed Girder, see those terms under Beam.)

Open Web Girder. Any girder of which the web is pierced, or composed of parts having open spaces between them. Usually, a small truss.

GIRDING BEAM. Originally, a beam which girds, *i.e.* holds together the walls or piers ; obsolete ; apparently the original form of girder (which see).

GIRDLE. A band, usually horizontal ; especially one ringing the shaft of a column. (Compare Annulated ; Banded Column.)

GIROLAMO TEDESCO ; architect.

In 1505 he made the model for the Fondaco dei Tedeschi in Venice, which was executed by Giorgio Spavento (see Spavento, G.) and Antonio Scarpagnino (see Abbondi).

Paoletti, *Rinascimento.*

GIRT. *A.* A small girder or the like. More specifically, in brace-frame building, the horizontal members which are framed into the posts, and some of which support the floor beams. (Compare Ribbon, and see Framing ; Wood, Construction in.)

B. Same as Fillet, *B* (rare or local).

C. The dimension of any more or less cylindrical member or piece measured around its perimeter. More specifically, the dimension of a curved or broken surface, as of a group of mouldings, measured by following its profile.

GIULIANO DA MAIANO ; woodworker (*intarsiatore*), architect and engineer ; b. 1432 ; d. Oct. 17, 1490.

A brother of Benedetto da Maiano (see Benedetto da Maiano). In ascribing the Palazzo di S. Marco and other important buildings in Rome at this period to Giuliano da Maiano, Vasari probably confuses him with Giuliano da San Gallo. (See San Gallo, Giuliano da.) His name does not appear in the Roman records. In 1468 he designed the Capella di S. Fina at Saint Gemignano near Florence. In 1472 he designed the Palazzo del Capitano at Sarzana near Spezia, Italy. May 26, 1474, he began the cathedral of Faenza, and at about this time built the palace of the Cardinal Concha at Recanati. April 1, 1477, he was elected *capomaestro* of the cathedral of Florence. Between 1475 and 1480, with Francione (see Francione), he made the wooden doors of the Sala d'Udienza at the Palazzo della Signoria, Florence. He also assisted Baccio Pontelli (see Pontelli) at the ducal palace of Urbino. In July, 1487, Giuliano was paid through the bank of the Gondi in Florence two hundred ducats for the models of the palaces of Poggio Reale and of the Duchesca near Naples. Feb. 17, 1488, he entered the service of Alfonzo, Duke of Calabria, afterward King Alfonzo II., and constructed for him these two palaces. Of the Poggio Reale, Giuliano's most important work, nothing remains except a drawing by Serlio (see Serlio).

C. von Fabriczy, *Giuliano da Maiano architetto del Duomo di Faenza;* Vasari, Milanesi ed., Vol. II., p. 467; Müntz, *Renaissance,* Vol. II., p. 399.

GIULIANO DA SAN GALLO. (See San Gallo, Giuliano da.)

GIULIANO DI BACCIO D' AGNOLO. (See Baglioni, Giuliano.)

GIULIO ROMANO. (See Pippi, Giulio.)

GIUSTO. (See Juste.)

GIVRY. (See Colard de Givry.)

GLASS. A mixture of silica and some alkali resulting in a substance hard, usually brittle, a bad conductor of heat, and possessed of a singular lustre which, as it resembles the brilliancy of no other common substance, is known by the name of vitreous or glassy lustre. The most common kinds of glass are made by fusing together some ordinary form of silica, such as sand, with a sodium salt or some compound of potassium replacing the sodium either wholly or in part, and sometimes with lead. There is no formula of universal application ; moreover, some varieties of glass contain ingredients which are kept secret by the maker, or are compounded in a way which is kept secret.

The different kinds of glass in use in architectural practice are : —

1. Clear glass in sheets more or less perfectly transparent and including ordinary window glass, plate glass, and several imitations of the latter, sometimes sold under the name of plate glass. Under this head come the various modern varieties of glass whose surface is deliberately roughened or ridged or furrowed or pressed in patterns with the purpose of reducing its transparency and allowing it to transmit light while shutting off the view of what may be beyond. (See below, Corrugated; Prismatic ; Ribbed ; Rough Plate Glass.)

2. Glass in small tesseræ or in tiles of moderate size, usually opaque and very commonly coloured. These are used for mosaic of the ordinary fashion, as in flooring and in the adornment of walls and vaults. The tiles are usually cast in one piece, in this resembling plate glass ; and it is easy to produce very interesting bas-reliefs and also inlaid patterns of great beauty, which may be complete in each tile or may require many tiles to complete the design. Such work was common among the Romans, who lined rooms with glass as freely as with marble. The tesseræ, however, are more commonly cut from large sheets by steel tools. The tesseræ are sometimes gilded, and so prepared to give to a mosaic picture a background or partial decoration in gold, by making the glass tessera in two parts, laying a piece of gold leaf between the two, and uniting the whole by heat. (See Mosaic.)

3. Glass in sheets coloured throughout its mass and used chiefly for decorative windows. (See Pot Metal.)

4. Glass in sheets, flashed, as it is called ; that is to say, coloured by means of a finer coating of deep coloured glass on one or on both sides. This device is used for colours which would be sombre if the whole substance were coloured as in pot metal. The deep reds are the colours usually so treated. This also is used for decorative windows.

Both the third and the fourth kinds of glass are modified in many ways, especially in modern times, by the addition of an opaline tinge by the use of arsenic or other chemicals. The opalescent quality, when applied to otherwise uncoloured glass, may be described as clouded with a whitish gray opacity, which, however, shows by transmitted light a ruddy spark. In the manufacture of glass for windows of great cost and splendour, it has been found that such opalescent glass, when it has received strong and rich colour in addition to the opaline quality, is capable of more perfect harmony, tint with tint, or of a more harmonious contrast, colour with colour, than if

the opaline character had not been given to it. (For glass used in decorative windows, see Windows.)

5. Glass cast in solid prisms, and in prismatic and pyramidal shapes, for the purpose of being set in metal frames and used for vault lights. (See Vault Light.)

6. Glass in the body of which some foreign substance is introduced. This may be done with purely decorative effect, as by the artists of the Roman imperial epoch in vessels of considerable thickness and mass, and this has been imitated by the modern Venetian glassworkers. Wire glass (which see below) is made on a similar plan for purposes of safety from fire.

7. Soluble glass, for which see the sub-title.
— R. S.

Corrugated Glass. That of which at least one face is ridged ; but the term is usually confined to glass which is ridged on each face, the whole substance of the glass being bent into wavelike corrugations exactly as in the case of corrugated metal, — the valley on one side forming the ridge on the other.

Crown Glass. That which is made by the blowing tube, which produces a bulb-shaped mass which, transferred to the pontil, is revolved rapidly until it suddenly opens out into a circular plate. The glass so produced is often streaky and of unequal thickness. This peculiarity, which has caused the abandonment of crown glass for ordinary window glass, has caused its use in producing partly opaque and richly coloured glass for modern windows ; but the sheets made in this way are usually of small size.

Flint Glass. A composition of white sand, potash, nitre, and a large amount of red lead, — in fact, half as much red lead as all the other above-named ingredients together, — to which mass is added "cullet," as in the case of plate glass. This glass is not used in strictly architectural work. It is very soft, and scratches easily. It has, however, extraordinary refractive power, and on this account is used for imitation jewelry of all sorts. In this way it enters into architectural decoration, not only in windows, but in the "jewelled" frames of altar-pieces and similar decorative appliances. Flint glass with a still greater amount of red lead is called strass, and is the substance commonly used under the name of "paste" for mock diamonds.

Ground Glass. Glass of which the surface has been roughened, properly by grinding, or more usually by acid, by the sand blast, or in some similar way, the purpose of the operation being to make it untransparent.

Iridescent Glass. A common translucent glass of some kind, the surface of which has received, by artificial means, an iridescence like that of a soap bubble. The ancient Roman and

Greek and other glass, especially that found buried in the earth, has an iridescence which comes from a slow process of decomposition. The sheet of glass gradually resolves itself into thin films, and the iridescence is thus a natural result like that in a metallic ore. The iridescent glass is supposed to be made in imitation of this, but it does not resemble it very strongly.

Jealous Glass. Glass depolished or otherwise finished so as to let light pass while it has lost its transparency.

Marbleized Glass. One of which the surface is marked by small irregular veins, indicating the places where the glass has been deliberately shattered by plunging into water while hot and then remelted.

Painted Glass. (See Window.)

Plate Glass. A compound of white sand, sodium carbonate, lime, and either alumina or manganese peroxide, together with a quantity—almost equal to the mass of the above materials—of "cullet," or old window glass broken up for remelting. The plate glass is then a solid casting made by pouring the melted "metal" upon a flat table of cast iron upon which a cast-iron roller of the same length as the table's width moves from end to end. The movement of the roller, which rests upon ridges at the sides of the table, fixes the thickness of the plate, and bubbles or other flaws are snatched from the semiliquid mass by pincers. The perfect evenness of the surface and the high polish, upon which, after the purity of the piece, the unequalled transparency and brilliancy of plate glass depend, are obtained by careful grinding and polishing on both sides.

Rough plate glass, used for parts of floors, is cast very thick, and its upper surface is left as it cools, — neither face being polished.

Glass of very inferior quality, and apparently made by a totally different process, is sometimes polished so as to bear a close resemblance to real plate glass; and this is sometimes sold under that name, and deceptively, and sometimes under the name of patent plate glass, or of one compounded of "plate" and a qualifying term. The great strength of real plate glass is not possessed by these imitations. To distinguish it from rough plate glass, the plate glass used for mirrors and large windows is most commonly spoken of as "polished plate"; sometimes also by other and temporary local names.

Prismatic Glass. A glass of which one surface is smooth, while the other is marked by ridges of prismatic section; distinguished from ribbed and corrugated glass by the sharp-edged character of the ridges. This glass may be so made and so fixed in windows that daylight passing through it may be refracted horizontally, or nearly so, and may in this way illuminate a very large internal space. Its use in mills in the United States has added greatly to the conven-

ience of the large rooms where many operatives work.

Ribbed Glass. That which has at least one surface ridged or ribbed. The term is usually confined to that which has only one surface so marked, to distinguish it from corrugated glass.

Sheet Glass. That produced by blowing into a cylinder which is constantly increased in size, and which is then split lengthwise by a cutter. Being then heated afresh, it falls open by its own weight, the sheet so produced being generally about 3 feet by 4 in size. It is rubbed smooth with some soft material, formerly by a piece of partially charred wood. When sheet glass is highly polished, it is sometimes called picture glass, and sometimes, when it is deceptively clear and smooth, patent plate glass. (See Plate Glass, above.)

Soluble Glass. A mixture of potash or of soda with common silica. It retains its liquid form, and is used to fix mural paintings. (See Water Glass, below.)

Stained Glass. That which is coloured either in its whole mass (pot metal) or by means of flashing, or by means of an applied stain. The only perfectly successful stain is that which gives a yellow, which, coming into use toward the close of the fifteenth century, caused a sudden change in decorative windows throughout the north of Europe. The crimson of flash glass is produced by certain oxides of copper, and by a mixture of gold with oxide of tin. Blue in many different shades, green, purple, etc., are produced by the use of cobalt, though other chemicals are sometimes combined with it. Manganese gives a dark purple glass, approaching black, which can be brought to almost complete opacity by means of the depth of colour alone, thus giving to the worker in coloured glass great results in the way of gradation. (See Silver Stain, under Stain; Window.)

Water Glass. A mixture of a soluble silicate with an oxide; therefore a liquid or liquifiable glass. It is not mixed with the pigments in painting, except occasionally for retouching, but is applied, by means of a sprinkler, to the finished picture, which has been painted with colours dissolved in pure water. In fact, it is a "fixative," and the process corresponds in principle to that of fixing a charcoal drawing. It has been much and successfully employed in Germany on interior walls. There seems to be more doubt as to its durability on exterior walls. For a full exposition of the process the reader is referred to the early pamphlet by Dr. J. N. Von Fuchs (1825) and the later work by Adolph Keim, of Munich. — F. C.

Window Glass. That which is used for ordinary windows, as in dwellings. This used to be commonly Crown Glass (which see above); but this manufacture has nearly ceased. It is now more commonly Sheet Glass; (which see).

Wire Glass. That which has a continuous network of wire enclosed in the solid mass ; a plate of this glass may bear a very great heat, as of a conflagration, without losing its consistency altogether, although its translucency may be destroyed, and it may be much cracked.
— R. S. (except for Water Glass).

GLAZE. *A.* To furnish with glass, as a window sash or a door. The past participle glazed is used more especially to describe the presence or use of glass in a place where it is not uniformly put, as a glazed door, the more common phrase for which in the trade is a sash door. On the other hand, the phrase " glazed sash " means commonly machine-made window sash with the glass in place ready for delivery, the common way of supplying both sash and glass to a new building. It is only the large lights of plate glass, as for show windows, which of late years are brought to the building without being first fitted to their sash.

B. To give (to anything) a polish or glassy surface ; in this sense rare in the building trades, except in keramics ; thus, glazed tile is commonly used in contradistinction to unglazed (*i.e.* mat or rough surface) tile. — R. S.

GLEBE. The piece of land considered as belonging for the time to the holder of an ecclesiastical benefice in connection with the Church of England. It is sometimes treated as including buildings, the house provided for the incumbent, and its appurtenances.

GLEBE HOUSE. A house provided for the occupancy of the incumbent of an ecclesiastical living.

GLEBE LAND. Same as Glebe.

GLORIETTE, THE. A casino in the gardens of the palace of Schönbrunn, near Vienna, set high on a ridge, and consisting of an enclosed central pavilion and two open arcaded wings, the whole being about 140 feet long. It was built by Joseph II. and Maria Theresa, in 1775.

GLORY. In religious art, an appearance as of light emanating from the person, which is indicated in a way often very conventional and abstract, in painting, sculpture, and decoration of different sorts. The use of this attribute seems to be of Eastern origin, and the Buddhist and other parts of Asia, since the tenth century, offer many instances of this method of distinguishing the important and most sacred personage in a composition. This term may be taken as the general one including all the special forms known by the terms Aureola, or Aureole, which surrounds the whole person ; Halo, which surrounds the head only ; Nimbus, which, in its original signification of a cloud, should be as general as glory, but is most commonly used as synonymous with halo ; and Vesica Piscis, which is the aureole, only of a special pointed, oval shape. In mediæval architectural sculpture,

the glory of any kind was often treated simply as a frame in relief, often carved with leafage, and as completely an architectural moulding or group of mouldings as the archivolt of a window ; its position surrounding a sacred personage explaining its especial significance, while its presence called attention to the figure which it surrounded. — R. S.

GLYPH. Literally, a cutting of any sort ; in its more usual sense as an architectural term, any one of many grooves, channels, flutes, or the like, usually vertical or nearly vertical. (See Diglyph ; Strigil Ornament ; Triglyph.)

GLYPTOTHECA. A building for the preservation and exhibition of sculpture. The term *Glyptothek* may be taken as a modern German modification of it.

GLYPTOTHEK. A building for the exhibition of sculpture ; the term being introduced as the name of the building erected by the care of Ludwig I. of Bavaria, 1825–1848, while still crown prince. The immediate purpose was to provide a home for the sculptures brought from the Temple of Ægina.

GMUND, HEINRICH VON. (See Gamodio.)

GMUND, PETER VON. (See Parler, Peter.)

GNEISS. A rock of the same composition as Granite, but with a more or less banded or foliated structure. — G. P. M.

GOBBO (Humpback) **IL.** (See San Gallo, Battista ; Solari, Cristoforo.)

GODDE, ÉTIENNE HIPPOLYTE ; architect ; b. Dec. 26, 1781 ; d. Dec. 7, 1869.

Godde was a pupil of Lagardette. In 1805 he was made inspector of the public works of the city of Paris. From 1832 to 1848 he had charge of the first section, which included the Hôtel de Ville, the churches, temples, cemeteries, etc. In this capacity he commenced with Lesueur (see Lesueur) the enlargement of the Hôtel de Ville and between 1838 and 1848 restored the church of S. Germain l'Auxerrois.

Lance, *Dictionnaire.*

GODEBŒUF, ANTOINE ISIDORE EUGÈNE ; architect ; b. July 31, 1809 ; d. May 15, 1879.

Godebœuf was a pupil of Blouet (see Blouet) and of Achille Leclère (see Leclère, at the *École des Beaux Arts.* In 1852 he was charged with the construction of the new buildings of the *École des Ponts et Chaussées,* Paris, and in 1859 with the construction of the *École du Génie Maritime.* From 1867 to 1873 he was architect of the *commission des monuments historiques.*

Narjoux, *Paris ; Monuments élevés par la Ville ;* Bauchal, *Dictionnaire.*

GODINET. (See Gaudinet.)

GODOWN. In Eastern countries, frequented by European travellers, a storehouse of any kind.

The term seems to be of Indian origin, and is generally stated to be derived from the Malay, although other derivations are suggested. It is in use throughout India, and in the Chinese and Japanese ports, and is applied loosely by Europeans in the East to any place of deposit. Thus, the Japanese Kura is called a godown, though improperly, for the general term, originating in ordinary farm buildings and the like, should not be applied to those much specialized fireproof storehouses.

GODROON. A convex rounded ornament, differing from a unit of Reeding in not having parallel sides and uniform section throughout. Commonly it has one end rounded and the other tapering to a point. The term is more properly used for silverware or the like than in architectural practice.

GOETGHEBUER, FRANÇOIS JOSEPH. (See Goetghebuer, Petrus Jacobus.)

GOETGHEBUER, PETRUS JACOBUS; architect and engraver ; b. Feb. 28, 1788.

He was a pupil of P. J. de Broe and at the Royal Academy of Ghent. Goetghebuer published *Choix des monuments, édifices et maisons les plus remarquables du royaume des Pays-Bas.* He built the Hôtel des Postes in the *Wapenplaats* in Ghent and other important buildings. His brother François Joseph was also an architect of note.

Immerzeel, *Hollandsche en Vlaamsche Kunstschilders,* etc.

GOING. In British usage :

A. Of a step, the horizontal distance between two successive risers. (See Tread.)

B. Of a stair or flight, the horizontal distance between the first and last risers.

GOLDEN HOUSE. (Latin, domus aurea.) A great palace in Rome, with park, larger and smaller lakes, old trees brought to the spot and great numbers of buildings ; built and arranged by Nero after the burning of Rome in A.D. 64. Its remains lie on the southern slope of the Esquiline Hill, and northeast of the Coliseum. (See account in Lanciani's *Ruins and Excavations,* Book IV, XI.)

GOLD LEAF. Gold beaten very thin. It is customary to discriminate between gold foil, which is in sheets as thick as some kinds of paper, and gold leaf, of which it may be said, following the encyclopædias, that an ounce of gold (worth about $16) may be beaten out to cover 300 or 400 square feet. The cost of gilding is therefore not largely in the value of the metal used. (See Gilding.)

GOLDSTONE; ecclesiastic and architect.

About 1450 Prior Goldstone, first of the name, built the southwest tower and porch and the Virgin chapel (Neville's chapel) at Canterbury cathedral. About 1515 Prior Goldstone, second of the name, built the central tower.

Their names are inscribed in symbols on their work.

Britton, *Cathedral Antiquities, Canterbury.*

GONDOUIN, JACQUES; architect; b. Oct. 1, 1737; d. Dec. 29, 1818.

Gondouin was a pupil of Jacques François Blondel (see Blondel, J. F.). He designed and built the *École de Médecine,* Paris, which was begun in 1769 and finished in 1786. In association with Lepère he built between 1806 and 1810 the Colonne of the Place Vendôme, formerly Colonne de la Grande Armée.

Benoît, *L'Art français sous la Révolution et sous l'Empire;* Quatremère de Quincy, *Notice de M. Gondouin.*

GONTARD, KARL VON; architect; b. 1738; d. Sept. 23, 1791.

Gontard received his training in Paris, and travelled in Italy, Sicily, and Greece. In 1764 he entered the service of Friedrich II. (Frederick the Great). He built at Potsdam, near Berlin, the offices of the *Neues Palast,* the *Freundschaftstempel* and *Marble Palace.* He built in Berlin the *Königsbrucke* with its colonnade, the two towers of the *Gensdarmen Markt* and other important buildings.

Borrmann, *Kunstdenkmäler von Berlin;* Meyer, *Konversationslexikon.*

GONZALEZ–VELASQUEZ, ALEXANDRO; painter and architect; b. Feb. 27, 1719 (at Madrid).

At the age of nineteen he painted the decoration of the theatre of the Buenretiro, Madrid. In 1752 he was made director in architecture at the Academy of S. Ferdinando at Madrid.

GOPURA. In Indian architecture, a gateway, as of a town or temple enclosure ; especially, in the writings of European students of Eastern art, a gateway tower, *i.e.* one built above the main entrance to a temple, as if to call attention to its position. (See India, Architecture of.)

GORGE. In some orders of columnar architecture, a band around the shaft near the top, or forming part of the capital near the bottom ; a fillet or narrow member which seems to divide the capital from the shaft. In those orders, such as Roman Doric, in which the capital proper is a small, thin moulding, the gorge is used to give to the capital a certain height and mass, and it may then be a band of some inches in width between two groups of mouldings, the whole forming a necking which is larger than the capital itself.

GORGERIN. Same as Necking.

GORGON. In architectural sculpture, the representation of a monster somewhat resembling a woman with huge mouth and teeth and glaring eyes. (See Gorgoneion.)

GORGONEION. The representation of a gorgon's head. In earlier work it was without serpents; in later work, with many and much involved and convoluted serpentine bodies surrounding the face. It is represented as borne upon the ægis carried by Pallas Athene, and occurs in Grecian architectural sculpture, especially of the earlier work.

GOSPEL SIDE. (See Ambo.)

GOTHIC ARCHITECTURE. *A.* That of the Goths properly so called. This is not now traceable nor to be identified except in Spain, where a very early Romanesque may be ascribed

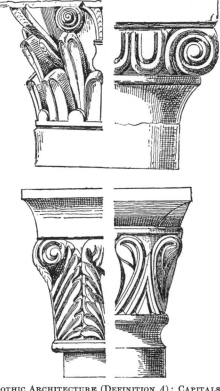

GOTHIC ARCHITECTURE (DEFINITION *A*): CAPITALS OF SPAIN BEFORE THE MOORISH CONQUEST.

to the Visigothic kingdom, before the Moorish conquest. Even of this, no complete buildings can be named, but separate capitals and some larger members are built into Moorish and other buildings. (See Bibliography under Spain.)

B. That of populations already skilled in building, but brought under Gothic rule. Of this, the most important instance remaining is that of Ravenna: the buildings erected under the rule of Theodoric (King of the Ostrogoths from 475 A.D., King of Italy from 493), and which show a peculiar modification of Latin Architecture (which see; see also Italy, Part V.).

C. That which originated in northern central France about the middle of the twelfth century, and which at the close of that century had spread

over what is now northern France; while detached buildings in England, in northern Spain, and 'on the Rhine were beginning to show its influence. In this sense, the term is an invention of the classical Renaissance, and expresses contempt. The thirteenth century was the time of complete development of the original style as described below; but in spite of very serious modifications which are often spoken of as corruptions or signs of decay, the style which may be properly called Gothic continued to prevail in France until 1500, in Germany and in Spain nearly as long, and in England until even a later date. France was always its chief centre, the architecture of no other country equalling it in dignity or beauty, in perfectly rational and logical working out of its principles, or in beauty of sculptured detail.

In Spain, however, there is architecture, probably the work of French architects, of extraordinary dignity and splendour; and in England the style was developed in a peculiar way with strong national characteristics, on a smaller scale, without the great expense of money and labour which the French buildings must have required, and yet in a peculiar way attractive. (See England, Architecture of; Gothic Architecture in England.) In Germany no general principle of growth can be found, for the architecture of the Rhineland was constantly receiving new inspiration from France, and that of the more eastern provinces varies greatly from one district to another. In Italy a style was introduced from eastern France and the Rhineland at the very close of the twelfth century. It retained there its true northern character only in the hands of its original introducers, who seem to have been the Cistercian monks; elsewhere it was modified almost out of recognition, while yet it prevailed until the introduction of classical details about 1420. (See Architecture; Neoclassic; Renaissance Architecture.)

The essence of Gothic architecture is in its vaulting. Throughout the earlier Middle Ages there was a constant attempt to roof the aisles and naves of churches in masonry, and various modifications of the Roman vault were made. (See Architecture; Romanesque; Vault.) The difficulties which were found the most nearly insuperable were in the curved aisle which was carried round the apselike end of many Romanesque churches. When, however, the idea was suggested of a rib of stone thrown in an independent arch from impost to impost, and carrying the weight of a vault which should rise from it, a solution was offered which was found to be sufficient for all the problems which might arise. Take, for instance, a plan as in Fig. 1. If a simple vault is sprung across from *A* to *C*, this will go on diminishing like a funnel as far as *BD,* and if another vault intersects it at right angles this will be a vault sprung across from

C to *D* and from *A* to *B*. This will be groined vaulting; but the result will be extremely ugly and very unsafe. To take a single instance, the point *O* where the vaults meet would be no longer the highest point of the vault, and the most ungainly effect would be produced by the rising of the groins *AD* and *BC* above the point of intersection. If, however, the point *O′*, is taken as the highest point of the vault, and independent ribs are sprung from the four imposts *A B C′ D′* to a boss or plate of stone at the point *O′*, then those four ribs divide the vault into four triangles very easy to build so long as they are built directly upon the ribs, throwing their whole weight and thrust upon their ribbed arches.

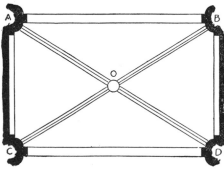

If, now, the space to be vaulted is of the usual square or rectangular form, such as is given by one of the divisions of the nave or aisle, the same system of vaulting gives us a plan generally like Fig. 2. Now, however, it appears that two of the ribs which meet at the central boss *O* may be, and generally will be, in the same vertical plane, and will, therefore, form

GOTHIC ARCHITECTURE:
FIG. 1.

Diagram of vaulting of circular deambulatory.

GOTHIC ARCHITECTURE: FIG. 2.

Plan of one compartment of a Gothic vault, *A O* being one half rib, *A O D* a whole diagonal rib; *A O D*, *C O B* forming the *croix d'ogives* and *O* the boss or *clef*; *A B*, *C D*, transverse arches; *A C*, *B D*, wall arches (formerets).

a single arch with a continuous or a broken curve. The two ribs *AO* and *OD*, for instance, in Fig. 2, form a round or pointed arch the side

271

view of which would be nearly like that in Fig. 3. This arch, however, is not absolutely complete because the two ribs meet at a boss which will be placed at *O*, Fig. 3. If, however, we take the arch at *BD* or the arch at *CD*, Fig. 3, we have a pointed arch which has no boss, or in other words, an ordinary pointed arch. This arch will have no keystone, but a joint at the apex, and in that respect the true Gothic arch differs from the pointed arch often used in Italy, and in modern times.

We have still, however, to provide against the thrust or outward horizontal or diagonal pressure of this cluster of arches. If the vaulting square which we have considered hitherto should occupy the whole width of the church, or other building to be roofed, it will be sufficient to put heavy piers of masonry at the points where the ribs of the vault have their imposts, or at or near the points *A*, *B*, *C*, and *D*, Fig. 2. This will give a result nearly like Fig. 4, the famous Sainte-Chapelle at Paris. The great piers, seen projecting from the side walls, which take up the thrust of the inside vaults by their mere passive resistance, are called buttresses.

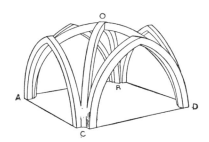

GOTHIC ARCHITECTURE: FIG. 3.
Diagram of ribs corresponding with Fig. 2.

In all vaulted buildings something of this kind has to be provided, but in the case of Roman buildings (see Roman Imperial Architecture), those great masses of material are generally within the building somewhere, and form division walls, or in some other way encumber the floor. If, however, the more usual type of church is under consideration, and the nave has aisles on either side of it, it will be necessary to take up the thrust of the high vaults of the nave by some other device; because the appearance of such great piers in the very heart of the aisle on either side would be to defeat the very object of such a building, by encumbering the internal space which is intended to be free and open. If, in a church of simple plan, as in Fig. 4, the buttresses are put outside the building; so also they needed to be in the more complicated plan, if the scheme of the Gothic builders was to be carried out. The result was a system like that shown in the right-hand half of Fig. 5: an arrangement overhead, by which the thrust of the

272

great vaults over the nave was carried through the air across the width of the aisles and thrown upon the buttresses, which are seen outside of the aisle walls. This system of carrying the thrust horizontally, or nearly so, and far overhead, was adopted almost at the beginning of the Gothic period; for, indeed, the chief characteristic of the Gothic architecture is its extraordinary logic and deliberate reasoning out of point after point, the needs being always met by new devices, and those devices treated as decorative features. The flying buttress, which resulted from this necessity and this resolute way of meeting it, is shown in its general scheme in Fig. 5. It will be seen from these diagrams that all that is really essential is the carrying of the bar of stone along a certain line which represents the thrust of the vault; or, at all events, the providing of the mass of stone in that place and along that line, although, of course, a larger and heavier mass might be used which would disguise the true nature of the construction. This, however, the Gothic builders never did. Their flying buttress is a sloping bar or stay of stone put where it is most needed, and held in place by the simple device of an arch underneath it. (See Flying Buttress, under Buttress.)

The full Gothic plan, as shown in Fig. 6, is a mere development of the diagrams given above, the curve of the aisle at the chevet (see Deambulatory) being constructed nearly as in Fig. 1. The plan is, indeed, capable of considerable variety; thus, it is not essential that all the vaulting squares or all the piers should be of the same size. The diagrams, Figs. 2 and 3, show what is called quadripartite vaulting, and, in Fig. 6, the similar lines of the nave and aisles show the same kind of vaulting, but the system called sexpartite vaulting might also be used.

It has been said above that the arch at AC in Fig. 2 and in Fig. 3 would be a plain pointed arch without a boss. This kind of arch became, then, the natural form for an opening

toward the outer air, such as a window, or an opening from bay to bay within the church. The exterior aspect, then, of the Gothic church soon became notably a long row of such pointed arches alternating with large buttresses project-

GOTHIC ARCHITECTURE: FIG. 4. THE SAINTE-CHAPELLE FROM THE SOUTHWEST; 1243–1247 A.D.

ing boldly between them. In like manner, the interior became a forest of slender stone piers, engaged like pilasters or detached like columns, with pointed arches rising from them. The characteristic pointed arch became a beloved feature of the decorative designer, as well as a necessary part of the construction, and many arches were built in this way to span openings which did not need so strong a closure. Thus, in the interior view of a large church there is no necessity for the pointed arches over the small openings of the triforium, but the pointed arch very soon became a matter of course and was used everywhere, as in arcades or the like. Another peculiarity of the matured Gothic is the complete disappearance of the wall in all important places; for, as the roof of stone is entirely carried on pilasters and piers supported vertically, and the thrust of the vault is taken up by the buttresses (with or without flying buttresses to carry the thrust to the buttress), so there remains no longer any duty for the wall to fulfil. The glass of the windows, therefore, with the slender stone tracery which held it in

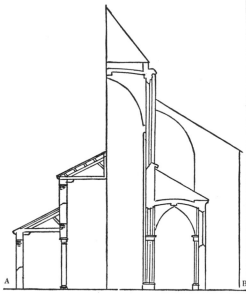

GOTHIC ARCHITECTURE: FIG. 5.

A, half section of early basilica with tie-beam roofs; *B*, half section of Gothic church with vaulting and flying buttresses. Both buildings on the same ground plan.

place, was allowed to fill the whole space beneath the pointed arch, except that a low, very thin wall was built beneath the sill of the window, having no utility except to afford a less fragile means of enclosure at the lower level where injury was to be feared. Hence arose the familiar saying, which is not wholly incorrect, that a Gothic church was a roof of stone with a wall of glass. Although a Gothic church is much more than that, it is that also; and its builders enjoyed the novelty that they had in their hands so much that every effort was made through long lapses of time to diminish the size of the stone uprights and to increase the general appearance of lightness, openness, and apparently impossible piling of weight and mass upon

slender uprights. This is a principle of designing exactly as admissible as the putting of lightness upon weight; grandeur, grace, and diversity of proportion can be obtained in either way. The Gothic builders, having chosen their principle of design, followed it out with a boldness never before seen in the history of architecture, and produced a style which, more than any other style, or perhaps more than all combined, gives a seemingly infinite variety, with a uniform and unvarying principle of construction and design.

The love of the pointed arch brought with it a love for the steep upward sloping line, and a strong verticality of design. Thus, the wooden roof which was put as a mere shell or mask above the stone vault in order to keep the rain from it, was made unnecessarily steep because the style had grown in that direction, while the steep roof was of course, no worse, or even a little better for its purpose, having no real fault except its great cost, and the surface exposed to the action of the wind. It is, however, a mistake to suppose that the great relative height of the Continental Gothic churches was merely matter of verticality of design. Fig. 5 shows the aisle with its sloping roof above its vault, and the nave rising high above the aisle roof so as to have a large clearstory window. This clearstory window determines the height of the nave roof; and if the architects wanted a great volume of light poured in at these large windows, they had to make the height of the clearstory very great. The matter of proportion also was to be considered, and the side view of this double row of arches open below and filled with windows above was an important consideration. If, for instance, the width of the aisle were 12 feet, the nave would be nearly twice as wide; and the piers which separate the aisle from the nave would need to be at least 16 feet high to the tops of their capitals, for even this would make the neckings of these capitals only 13 feet from the floor. But from this height everything else results, and it will be found that, with the width of aisle we have supposed, the height of the nave vault from the floor to its crown would be 61 feet, and the height to the ridge of the roof would be 82 feet. If, now, the church is doubled in its horizontal dimensions, and the nave is made 50 feet wide, we have a height of 127 feet to the crown of the vault and 171 feet of total height to the ridge of the roof, which is very nearly that of the great French cathedrals of the thirteenth century. In other words, it was no *tour de force* which the Gothic architects were engaged in, but the carrying out of their simple and obvious principles of design, which they fearlessly followed wherever they might lead.

The decoration of the Gothic structure is chiefly derived from skilful and elaborate stone cutting, including sculpture, and this stone cutting is of two kinds : first, the repetition in a decorative way of forms which were once purely constructional ; and, secondly, of forms suggested by visible nature, of plants and animals.

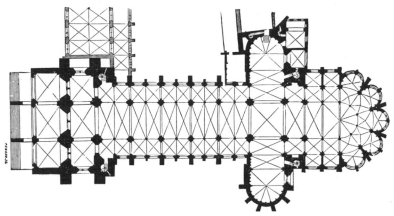

GOTHIC ARCHITECTURE: FIG. 6. CATHEDRAL OF NOYON (OISE), FRANCE.
Transept peculiar in having two rounded ends.   Elaborate vaulting of deambulatory and apsidal chapels.

gested by visible nature, of plants and animals. The second kind of decoration was a direct inheritance from the Romanesque work out of which the Gothic architecture had grown. But the first kind came of that intense love for the style which they had invented, peculiar to the Gothic builders. Thus, in the sculpture which is put upon the outside of a gable, like that of the transept of Notre Dame, there are little arcades and tracery suggested in the stonework, and there are also pieces of very rich sculpture of natural form in great variety and abundance. It seems to many persons that the first of these two styles of decoration was carried too far, and for the solidity and dignity of the building. Less of such ornamentation as this, with even more of sculpture of natural form, would be welcome to such critics. It is noticeable, however, that no other system of architecture had ever included much attention paid to external sculpture except in the reliefs of the Egyptian pylons, and this was hardly architectural sculpture, but rather carving put upon a wall as a convenient place for its exhibition. Greek decorative sculpture was very limited in the number of its parts and in its application, the sculptures which now excite our wonder having been almost free from architectural character. The Gothic builders were, therefore, without examples before them of a sculptural decoration applied freely to the exteriors as well as to the interiors of buildings, and their feeling may well

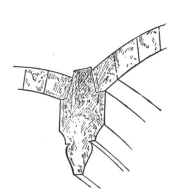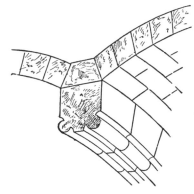

GOTHIC ARCHITECTURE: FIGS. 7 AND 8.
Relation of rib to shell of vault.

the constant succession of blind and open traceries, arcades, moulded bands and cornices, pinnacles resting upon open cages of light stonework, too numerous, too varied, and too fanciful have been that the building would better carry off the abundant wealth of representative sculpture which was put upon it, if this sculpture had an elaborate and highly wrought framework of sculpture without significance or reference to nature.

Gothic architecture was originally ecclesiastical almost altogether. Few buildings except churches required the vaulted roof upon light supports. The interiors of the great castles of the time were, indeed, vaulted in imitation of the churches, but in these cases the vaults were supported by such ponderous masses of wall that the Gothic principle disappeared altogether. Dwelling houses, in the cities especially, in the later times, were often beautifully adorned with the external features of Gothic architecture, but their floors would generally be made of wood, and each room was then covered by the flat under side of the floor above. Large houses of assembly, such as the Synodal Hall of Sens, were, indeed, vaulted much as the churches were.

The discovery of the Gothic principle of construction was contemporaneous with an unprecedented growth in the art and practice of architecture, and buildings were multiplied all over the land in every prosperous country of Europe. The number of churches built between 1175 and 1250 is something incredible. The building of the great cathedrals is a chapter in European history which is entirely unique (see Church Building). For the structures themselves which still remain in Europe and can still be studied, reference must be made to the articles on the architecture of the different countries in which Gothic architecture prevailed, — England, France, etc.

Gonse, *L'Art gothique;* C. H. Moore, *Development and Character of Gothic Architecture;* Ungewitter, *Lehrbuch der Gotischen Konstruktionen;* Thomas H. King, *The Study Book of Mediæval Architecture and Art;* Von Essenwein, *Die romanische und die gothische Baukunst* (forms part of the Darmstadt *Handbuch,* 2d Pt., Vol. IV., 1st and 2d divisions deal with military and domestic architecture: all published); Viollet-le-Duc, *Dictionnaire Raisonné de l'Architecture Française,* 10 vols.; Edward S. Prior, *A History of Gothic Art in England;* G. E. Street, *Some Account of Gothic Architecture in Spain,* and *Brick and Marble in the Middle Ages;* and in the general bibliography the works by Schnaase, Kugler, Lübke, Gailhabaud, G. T. Scott. (See also bibliographies under England, France, etc.)

There are many monographs and treatises on the Gothic architecture of separate towns and provinces; also very many volumes of plates without text, or with but little text, such as Richard Norman Shaw's *Architectural Sketches from the Continent;* Nesfield's *Specimens of Mediæval Architecture chiefly selected from Examples of the 12th and 13th Centuries;* R. J. Johnson, *Specimens of Early French Architecture;* W. Galsworthy Davie, *Architectural Studies in France.*

— R. S.

GOTHIC ARCHITECTURE IN ENGLAND. In speaking of English Gothic it has been customary in England to divide it into four more or less arbitrary divisions.

First, the traditional, covering the period between the Norman Romanesque, and that marked by the general adoption of the pointed arch, from 1140 to 1200.

Second, the early English, the first true Gothic period, covering roughly the time from 1200 to 1300.

Third, the decorated, from 1300 to 1400.

Fourth, the perpendicular, from 1400 to 1550.

The names are not altogether fortunate, nor is it possible to fix the dates which bound any one of the above styles. It seems best, therefore, to speak of centuries rather than styles.

All the phases of Gothic up to 1350 began and had their most perfect fulfilment in France. There Gothic was solely concerned with the problem of the vault and its supports. Incidentally the wall was obliterated, and they studied the filling of the space. In discussing English Gothic it will be unnecessary to touch upon those features whose history belongs to the general development of Gothic, and attention will be concentrated on the points which are essentially English.

The English were never attracted by the vault problem, and, although there is abundant evidence that the principles of the vault were understood, they were not looked upon as essentials. Therefore the sense of a building enclosed by walls was never lost, and wood frequently took the place of a stone vault. Both were probably due to the long duration of the early types, Saxon and Norman, which made so much of wall surface, to the lack of ambition or the abundance of wood, and to the wide influence of Cistercian simplicity. The thirteenth century showed, as essentially English features, the great length, the transepts and double transepts, and the square east end with its group of lancets. The west fronts were not logical end walls of a great building, but screens, used as at Wells to form a frame for sculpture. The isolation of England and its comparative peace enabled domestic work and the semidomestic buildings of the monastery almost to keep pace with the ecclesiastical work. Thus an element of simplicity, almost of domesticity, was introduced. As the thirteenth century saw the culmination of the logical Gothic of the Île de France, so did it see the best English work. The English level was not so high, but both earlier work and also much of the later work vie with that of the most perfect time in beauty and interest.

The early fourteenth century marked the abandonment of the simplicity of the thirteenth, and the adoption of profuse ornament. More especially was it marked in England by the multiplication of ribs in the vault, and divisions in the window which formed tracery of great beauty. The cleric character of English work as contrasted with the laic Continental work, produced many beautiful buildings, in the chapter houses, dormitories, halls, and refectories of the great abbeys. All of these show a knowledge of Gothic principles and a purely English treatment, modified in various localities by mason craft, or local material.

With the end of the fourteenth century England had advanced far away from Continental lines, and the movement which began about 1350 developed rapidly into a purely English style. Towers and spires, which, owing to the long low lines of the buildings were always favourite features in England, were brought to great perfection in the fifteenth century. Domestic work, which was now becoming more prominent, was influenced by this last phase of Gothic well into the seventeenth century.

The only constructional feature of this period was a logical development of mason craft.

As soon as the rib became a fixed feature in the vault, the English began to plan a means by which to simplify the many curves which the varying length of the ribs seemed to demand. The outcome was the system generally adopted and which led eventually to the fan vault. The diagonal rib, being the longest, was taken as the basis, and this was composed of two curves, the one the curve of the wall rib, the second a curve of greater radius, the two together producing the four-centred arch. All the other ribs were portions of this fixed curve.

Then a still further step was taken in the direction of mechanical production. Taking a square compartment, the ribs were made not only of the same curve but of the same length, so that all the ribs stopped at a fixed height and at a fixed distance from the springing. This resulted in a fan-shaped vault. The wall rib and the transverse rib alone reached the central lines, and a space was thus left which was filled with flat blocks, as in the vault of Gloucester cloisters, or with great pendants, as in Henry the Seventh's chapel. Moreover, the filling between the ribs was no longer a vault, but was a slab of stone reaching from rib to rib.

However wonderful, and in a way beautiful, this work appears, it must ever remain a mechanical *tour de force*, in no way to be compared with the best French vaults, which speak in every line and stone of the intelligent hand of the artist.

The four-centred arch, first devised to meet the exigencies of the diagonal rib, became, when the arches were all identical, the curve of the wall rib, and then of the window opening. Thus it grew to be the keynote of the later perpendicular work. — R. CLIPSTON STURGIS.

GOTHIC REVIVAL. The attempt during the nineteenth century to restore Gothic architecture to the position it held in the thirteenth and fourteenth centuries, as being the only style

in use, and lending itself alike to buildings of all classes. In the absence of general acceptance, the movement became more exclusively a matter of church building, in which it had, indeed, originated. It was understood by the earliest revivalists that the architecture of the Middle Ages was primarily that of churches; but it was also understood by them that the style created as an ecclesiastical style was extended into buildings of all kinds, even into fortresses, just so far as the conditions, site, plan, and structure allowed. Thus, a small house could not be Gothic in the strictest sense, as having none of its rooms vaulted; and a fortress could not be Gothic in the strictest sense, because even the ribbed vaults of the halls and corridors were retained by enormously thick walls, instead of by buttress and flying buttress without the aid of walls, which were replaced by great spaces of glass. The revivalists, therefore, were of different minds, some being strongly led toward ecclesiological conclusions, and trying to re-create what they esteemed to be the only proper architecture for Christian churches; while others were minded to restore the conditions of the thirteenth century in all those things which were compatible with modern improvements.

The revival took shape in France, Germany, Belgium, and the Netherlands, as well as in Great Britain; and at a later time its doctrines were accepted by architects in the United States. The brick church in the Au suburb of Munich (see Ohlmüller) was built about 1837, and about the same time S. Clothilde (which see, under Church) was built in Paris from the designs of F. C. Gau and Theodore Ballu (see those names). These were typical of original work on the Continent; but there was little of this compared with the great amount of work done in the way of restoration and consequent addition to the great cathedral establishments. Thus, when Notre Dame of Paris was in the way of being restored, a large building, intended for vestries, chapter house, and the like, was built on the south side of the church, and carefully planned in the style of the church itself, this being, therefore, just so far original as that it was a modern house carefully studied in detail from the great example before it, while its plan, and even its general outline and mass, were entirely modern. This building, however, designed by Viollet-le-Duc, is one of the most perfect specimens in existence of the revival of an ancient style. The restoration, often ruinous, of great buildings carried with it also a great deal of study of mediæval sculpture, and the principles and practice according to which it was carried on. It was soon discovered that the production of the enormous amount of excellent sculpture, still existing or already destroyed, of France and the neighbouring countries, had been possible only under a state of society and a condition of the working mason and stonecutter such as was no longer in existence, or even within reasonable possibility of revival. Still, other serious attempts were made to educate, at least, a certain number of stonecutters in the line of Gothic decorative carving. (See Gothic Architecture; Sculpture.)

In England, however, the enthusiasm excited was much greater than elsewhere, the number of advocates and practitioners was also greater, and the results were, for a time at least, promising. In 1836, when the Houses of Parliament (see Westminster Palace) were undertaken, the terms of competition required that the building should be designed in the Gothic or Elizabethan style. All over England parish churches were repaired, restored, or rebuilt in what was intended to be pure Gothic architecture; but here again difference of opinion and of practice was seen, and while some were busily engaged in studying, moulding, and reproducing, as closely as possible, forms and details of a given epoch, in the style of which their church or town hall was to be erected, others were studying Italian Gothic, with its effects of polychromy, and French Gothic, with its freer treatment and richer sculpture, and were engrafting these foreign elements of architectural effect upon the English stock. What was called at one time Victorian Gothic was, indeed, characterized essentially by the introduction of many Italian features, such as the alternate colouring of the voussoirs of arches, the introduction of bands and patterns of brickwork into external and internal wall surfaces, and a general simplicity of mass, relieved by such colour effects as these and by sculpture very freely introduced.

In the United States, the building of the church of the Holy Trinity in Brooklyn, about 1845, and of Trinity church in New York, about 1847, marks the earlier introduction of the movement. Churches of certain Christian sects were from that time on commonly Gothic in their general character, while other religious bodies chose, rather, a round-arch mediæval style. The most carefully studied piece of Gothic church building in America is, perhaps, Trinity chapel, on West Twenty-fifth Street, New York City, the work of Richard Upjohn, who was also the architect of Trinity church. In civic buildings, the most remarkable structure was certainly the National Academy of Design, in New York City; in which an attempt not matched for thoroughness, except in one or two English buildings, was made to revive Gothic sculpture according to its supposed mediæval methods and processes.

The result of the Gothic revival has been this: that in Great Britain and in the British colonies churches are still commonly built in some form of the Gothic style. Some of these build-

ings are admirable in design, and William Butterfield, one of the earliest masters of revived Gothic (see church of All Saints, under Church), has built two important churches in Australia; while Pearson's design for the cathedral, though not wholly carried out, is a remarkable achievement. Also, there still appears, at intervals, a domestic or civic building equally mediæval in character. The larger public buildings of the last thirty years have been, however, almost exclusively neoclassic in character, and the majority of private houses more nearly classical than Gothic in their design. In the United States a strong influence of French academic teaching has been felt, and there are but a few architects who still retain a preference in their work for mediæval forms. This fact of the strongly neoclassical influences of France carries with it the statement that the study of Gothic architecture has almost ceased in that country, in spite of the influence of Viollet-le-Duc and his powerful contemporaries. Still, the buildings of certain ecclesiastical and monastical establishments are built in some form of Gothic; and the much more common practice of vaulting in France makes the French modern Gothic much more nearly mediæval in character than any except the very few monuments in England. The architects who produced these buildings are, however, a small class apart. (See Architect, The, in France; France, Architecture of.) In Germany, although the great majority of the buildings are neoclassical in character, Gothic architecture in some form is still used for special ecclesiastical undertakings and for some important civic buildings. The votive church in Vienna, by H. von Verstel, finished in 1879, is ranked as one of the two or three most perfect reproductions of mediæval art; but the new *Rathhaus*, in the same city, built by F. Schmidt a few years earlier, is an unsuccessful attempt to adapt the style to a building for public business. — R. S.

GOUJON, JEAN; sculptor and architect.

As Goujon appears first in Normandy, it is supposed that he was born there. It is not known that he ever studied in Italy. He is first mentioned in a contract dated Aug. 9, 1541, for two columns supporting the organ loft of the church of S. Maclou at Rouen (see Castille, Colin). The two sculptured wooden doors in the porch of this church are always ascribed to Goujon without evidence, except such as is derived from their style, — in this case very convincing. A third door on the side of the church is later, and may be by another hand. From about 1542 until 1544 he was associated with the architect Pierre Lescot (see Lescot) and the sculptors Laurent Regnauldin and Simon Leroy in the construction and decoration of the choir screen (jubé) of the church of S. Germain l'Auxerrois, Paris. The jubé was destroyed in 1745. The records of this work have been preserved, and two of its bas-reliefs by Goujon are now in the Louvre. About 1544 he became architect to the Constable Anne de Montmorency, and was associated with Jean Bullant (see Bullant) in the decoration of the château of Écouen. The chimney-piece by Goujon at Écouen is extremely fine. In the dedication of Jean Martin's translation of Vitruvius, published in 1547, for which Goujon drew many plates, he is mentioned as architect to the king, Henri II. After this time, and probably until his death, he was occupied in association with Pierre Lescot in making the splendid sculpture on the façade of the Louvre at the southwest angle of the old court. The pairs of figures about the œils-de-bœuf over the doors are especially fine. The contract for the music gallery, supported by four caryatides in the lower hall of this building, one of his most famous productions, was made in 1550.

The so-called Fountain of the Innocents, in Paris, was originally a loggia built at an angle of the old cemetery of the Innocents (see Fountain of the Innocents) on the corner of the Rue Saint-Denis and the Rue aux Fers, Paris. June 10, 1786, the cemetery was suppressed. The fountain, with Goujon's bas-reliefs, was rearranged in the square which replaced the cemetery.

Goujon's decorations of the château of Anet date from about 1553 (see De l'Orme, P.). Of these, the most important is the group of Diana with a stag, which is now in the Louvre. The sculptured decoration of the Hôtel Carnavalet, Paris, is attributed to Goujon by Sauval. After 1562, Goujon's name disappears from the meagre records of the works at the Louvre. He was probably a Protestant, and it has been supposed, without proof, that he was killed in the massacre of S. Bartholomew (Aug. 24, 1572). A "Giovanni Goggeon francese, intagliotore di rilieve," who died in Bologna, Italy, between 1564 and 1568, is supposed by Montaiglon (op. cit.) to have been the great French sculptor.

Gailhabaud, *Jean Goujon, architecte et sculpteur*; Montaiglon, *Jean Goujon*; Reveil, *Œuvre de Goujon*, text by Pottier; Berty, *Les Grands Architectes*.

GOURLIER, CHARLES PIERRE; architect; b. May 15, 1786; d. Feb. 16, 1857.

A pupil of Alavoine (see Alavoine) and Huyot (see Huyot). In association with Biet, Grillon, and Tardieu he published *Choix d'édifices projetés et construits en France dupuis le commencement du XIX siècle* (Paris, 1825–1850, 3 vols. folio) and *Des voies publiques et des habitations particulières*, Paris, 1852, 8vo.

Maurice du Seigneur, in Planat's *Encyclopédie*.

GOUST, L.; architect.

Goust was appointed inspector of the works at the Arc de Triomphe de l'Étoile, Paris, under Chalgrin (see Chalgrin), whom he succeeded as architect of the building after his death in 1811. From 1813 to 1823 work on this monument was interrupted. From 1823 to 1830 it was continued by Goust in association with Huyot (see Huyot).

Lance, *Dictionnaire*.

GOVERNMENT ARCHITECT. *A.* (In French, *Architecte du Gouvernement*.) One who has been employed on public work. Apparently, the term is retained after the work is done, and is employed as an honorary appellation, if not by the bearer of it, then by his publishers or those who may write of him, and serves as a means of giving professional rank.

B. In America, the supervising architect of the treasury department, in whose hands is the designing and supervising of the greater part of the buildings erected by the government of the United States, except in cases where, by general or special law, local architects are employed to carry out special buildings.

GRADIENT. The slope or divergence from the horizontal of a street, path, or the like, usually described as 1 in 10, 1 in 17, etc., the "one" signifying the vertical rise; but also described as so many in the hundred or thousand, the round numbers applying to the horizontal measurement. A moderate gradient of a carefully laid out street or of the approach to a bridge is 1 in 25 to 1 in 35; of a railroad, 85 feet in 1000.

GRADINE. In Italian, a step; hence, in English writing on Italian art, the superalter, a raised shelf set above the altar and at its back, usually as long as the mensa, one third or one fourth as wide, and having the front closed in. This front is, then, frequently adorned with paintings, and this narrow row of pictures is called the predella.

GRÆCOSTASIS. In the Roman Forum, a platform or tribune, so called because the ambassadors from the states of Greece (as later of other foreign powers) were supposed to stand there during certain ceremonies held in the Forum, in which there was speaking from the rostra near at hand. Recent explorations have uncovered what is thought to be the later rostra, and beneath and within this is a platform with a rounded front which has generally been thought the original græcostasis. According to this theory, the platform was not in use under the Empire.

GRAEL, JOHANN FRIEDRICH; architect.

Grael built the *Sophienkirche*, in Berlin, in 1734.

Borrmann, *Denkmäler von Berlin*.

GRAFFITO. In Italian, a scratching or incising upon rough material, as a plastered wall; the term is applied especially to the ancient scratched inscriptions which have been of value to modern archæologists. (See also Sgraffito.)

GRAIN (n.). The fibres of wood taken together; the fibrous or strongly marked longitudinal texture of wood in which the sheaves of the sap vessels, all running one way, cause a marked distinction between the character of wood if cut crosswise or lengthwise of the log. Blocks for wood engraving are cut across the grain, but in nearly all other careful workmanship the end grain is avoided, and a perhaps excessive care is shown by modern carpenters and joiners never to allow this end grain (that is to say, the texture of the wood as shown when cut across) to be seen. Even in wood when cut in the direction of the grain, that is, lengthwise, there is a difference in the adhesiveness of the parts. According as a log is cut into parts in the direction or nearly in the direction of the radii of one section of the log considered as a circle, the wood will be found tougher and less liable to split. It is well known that a log allowed to dry naturally will be found checked, or divided deeply by checks. (See Check.) If, then, parts are taken out of a log in such a way that the broad surfaces of these parts go in the direction of these checks, those parts will have little or no tendency to split. Advantage is taken of these circumstances to saw wood quartering, as it is called (see Quarter, v.), the wood specially treated in this way being oak, on account of the open character of its grain. The term is used also to indicate the pattern or veining caused by the irregularity of the arrangement of the sap vessels and fibres. This, in some woods, is of great beauty, and it often happens that a knot, a part of the root, or even one of those curious warts or protuberances which are sometimes found projecting from the trunk of a large old tree, contains wood of a very beautiful pattern. The finest and most precious pieces of this kind are commonly sawed into thin veneers, which are then used by gluing them to thicker pieces of inferior wood. (For the imitation of grained wood, see Grain, v.) — R. S.

GRAIN (v.). To produce, by means of painting, an imitation, more or less close, of the natural grain of wood. The process is chiefly one of wiping, with a cloth held firmly upon the end of a stick, narrow bands in freshly laid paint; these bands showing light in contrast with the darker and thicker paint left on either side. If, for instance, paint of the colour of walnut is laid over a lighter priming, a skilled grainer will use his wiping tool with greater or less pressure, as he wishes to produce broader and paler or narrower and darker stripes.

These stripes, kept close together and nearly parallel, constitute graining of the simplest kind. But the process in the more elaborate patterns is similar to this. Graining is not now fashionable, the tendency having been of late years strongly toward painting of a more purely decorative sort, so that graining is in a sense despised, even by persons of not very critical habits in decorative art. As late as 1860, however, it was very common both in England and America, and there exist in our libraries books on the art and practice of house painting in which the art of graining is insisted on as one of considerable importance. In the decoration of Abbotsford, for instance, grained imitation of ancient wood is used in close juxtaposition to the ancient wood itself brought from destroyed or ruined buildings. — R. S.

GRAIN ELEVATOR. A building with appliances for receiving grain in large quantities from railway cars or other carriers, weighing, storing, and delivering to cars or vessels. It contains a receiving hopper into which the grain drops when discharged from the railway car, an elevator formed of buckets, or cups attached to an endless band, by which it is raised to the top of the building and discharged into a garner, from which it flows through spouts to a weighing machine. Thence it is transported to bins for storage by conveyor belts, or directly into railway or shipping spouts. The storage bins are deep and narrow pockets, constructed of timber and plank 12 or 14 feet square, and from 40 to 80 feet deep. They are usually without ventilation, but some have perforated tubes running through the centre. The elevators are supplied with all the necessary machinery and appliances to save time and labour. There is usually a movable "marine" leg for unloading grain arriving by water. This is a flexible box containing elevator belts which raise the grain from the vessel's hold. The capacity of the modern grain elevator varies from half a million to three or four million bushels. The floating elevator is similar in principle to the one described, but much smaller. It has a movable leg for unloading and loading vessels, and is fully equipped with all modern machinery. It is used for transshipment, but not for storage.

The exterior of the grain elevators are plain, but the arrangements for lighting, etc., often produce a picturesque outline, and they rise high above the houses of the city.

— W. R. HUTTON.

GRANARY. A place for the deposit of grain in large quantities. In modern times a purely general term. (Compare Grain Elevator.)

GRAND STAND. A platform arranged for spectators at a race-course, a ground for athletic exercises, and the like; especially such a stand when roofed and treated architecturally.

GRANDJEAN DE MONTIGNY, AUGUSTE HENRI VICTOR; architect; b. July 15, 1776; d. 1850, at Rio de Janeiro.

A pupil of Delannoy and Percier (see Percier) at the *École des Beaux Arts*. In 1799 he won the *Premier Grand Prix d'Architecture*, with Gasse. About 1814 he went to Brazil and erected at Rio de Janeiro the Palace of the Fine Arts, the Exchange, and other important buildings. Grandjean de Montigny published *Recueil des plus beaux Tombeaux executés en Italie pendant les XVᵉ et XVIᵉ siècles* (Paris, 1813, folio), and *Architecture de la Toscane*, in association with Auguste Famin (Paris, 1815, folio).

Benoit, *L'Art française sous la Révolution et l'Empire*; Maurice Du Seigneur in Planat's *Encyclopédie*.

GRANGE. Originally, a granary; hence, a farmstead; the buildings of a farm taken together. The term was used at first in a special significance of a group of buildings connected with the agricultural department of a monastery, a large manor house, or the like, but it does not appear that the term was long limited to this signification. With Shakespeare and other writers of the reign of Elizabeth the term is common in the sense of a farming place of any kind.

GRANITE. A massive igneous rock consisting essentially of quartz and orthoclase feldspar, but usually carrying mica, hornblende, or other minerals in addition. Hence, known as mica granite, hornblende granite, etc.
— G. P. M.

GRANJA, LA. A country palace of the kings of Spain, situated in the mountains about fifty miles from Madrid and 4000 feet above the sea. The palace was built by Philip V. in the first half of the eighteenth century.

GRAPERY. A greenhouse especially adapted to the cultivation of grapes, either with or without artificial heat; in the latter case the house is called a cold grapery. (See Greenhouse.)

GRAPPIN, JEHAN (I.); architect and sculptor.

A son of Robert Grappin. He worked with his father on the church of S. Gervais et S. Protais at Gisors (Oise, France) until his death. His name disappears from the accounts of the building in 1547, and was replaced by Pierre Monteroult.

(For bibliography, see Grappin, Robert.)

GRAPPIN, JEHAN (II.); architect and sculptor.

Son of Jehan Grappin (I.). He worked at first under Pierre de Monteroult at the church of S. Gervais et S. Protais at Gisors (Oise,

France). In 1562 he became himself supervising architect.

(For bibliography, see Grappin, Robert.)

GRAPPIN, ROBERT; architect and sculptor; d. about 1537.

In 1521 Robert appears as supervising architect (*maître de l'œuvre*) of the church of S. Gervais et S. Protais at Gisors (Oise, France). After 1537 his name disappears from the accounts of the church. (See Grappin, J., I.)

Marquis de Laborde, *Gisors, documents inédits*; Palustre, *Renaissance en France*.

GRASS HOUSE. The permanent dwelling of the Wichita American Indians and of others of the same stock, the Caddoan. It is a dome-shaped structure of poles thatched with grass and banked with earth at the bottom. A square framework of 8-inch logs is built within the area formed by a circular trench. Poles are then planted in the trench and brought together across the top of the log frame and firmly bound in place by elm bark. Smaller poles are then attached horizontally from ground to top, and upon the structure thus formed a thatch of grass is laid, overlapping in courses, shingle fashion, from below up, the rods fixing each layer of grass to the frame being covered by the succeeding layer. A smoke hole near the top is left as usual in redskin houses of this class, while at opposite sides are doorways, with doors made of a frame of rods covered with grass. This is the "straw house" of Coronado's Quivira. (See Earth Lodge; Tipi; Wickyup; also p. 131, *American Anthropologist*, N. S. 1, 1899.) — F. S. D.

GRATE. Originally and properly, a grating; in ordinary usage, that form of grating which is used to retain fuel in place while the air which supplies combustion passes freely upward from below between the bars. In this sense, especially, (1) a basket-like receptacle of bars such as is used in an ordinary fireplace; sometimes hung by rings or sockets upon hooks built into the jambs, sometimes supported on feet, and in this latter case often called basket, or basket grate. Soft or bituminous coal is more commonly burned in grates of this last-named form. (2) The bottom, or floor, of a fire room or fire box in a furnace or stove of any sort. In this sense, usually and normally flat and placed horizontally, but often arranged to revolve, to drop at one side while remaining supported on a pivot, or even to fold upon itself; these devices being for greater convenience in dumping the fuel when it is desired to clean the grate and start a fresh fire. — R. S.

GRATING. A structure of bars held together by cross pieces of any sort, or similar bars crossing one another in at least two directions, or, finally, of bars arranged in some more elaborate pattern. In this sense the term is equally applicable to a frame made of thick bars or beams of wood, and to a lighter and slender structure, as of metal. This is the generic term, and grate, grille, grillage are used in special senses. Gratings of wood are used to admit air and light, or to allow of vision through an obstacle, while at the same time ingress or egress is prohibited, or, when placed horizontally, an opening is made safe against persons or things falling into it accidentally. This is its most common use in building. The openwork partition across the parlour of a convent or the visitor's room in a prison is called by this name, although frequently the bars are wide apart and may even reach from floor to ceiling without cross pieces. In this sense the term approaches in signification the terms Palisade; Stockade. — R. S.

GRÄTZ, HANS VON. (See Niesenberger, Hans.)

GRAVE MONUMENT. The structure raised upon or near a grave to mark its place, and usually to record the name, etc., of the deceased. The simplest form is the heaped-up mound of earth covered with sod. This was often, in old English graveyards, held in place by a light net or lattice of osiers which were allowed to decay before being removed. The addition of a gravestone of any sort seems to have been in Christendom the more usual step to take in the way of a more permanent memorial; but in many parts of Europe it has been for centuries customary to erect small crosslike memorials of wood or of wrought iron, and upon these is often placed some tablet or frame within which perishable memorials, such as an inscription on paper, can be preserved for a time. On some of these tablets are placed usually very small paintings of souls in purgatory; and it may be added that a similar memorial acting as a cenotaph is often placed as near as possible to the spot where the person has been drowned, killed by robbers, or by accident; the purpose in each case being to request the prayers of the passer-by. Grave monuments in the open air were seldom more elaborate than this, previous to our own time of elaborate and extensive cemeteries; at present it is not uncommon to set up a monument of considerable height and elaboration and frequently of many thousand dollars' cost at, or near, the grave in such a cemetery. The obelisk, column, or other shaft, or the still more elaborate tombal structure so put up sometimes serves as a memorial of the graves of a number of persons, as those belonging to the same family. — R. S.

GRAVE MOUND. Same as Barrow.

GRAVESTONE. A stone marking a place of burial; the simplest form of tomb; often called tombstone. It is but seldom that a memorial slab (the simplest form of cenotaph) is called by this name.

Among the Greeks, graves in the open air were marked by upright stones carved sometimes into the shape of pillars of circular section, sometimes into flat slabs decorated on one side, or on both, and often adorned by an ornamental crown (compare Stele), and sometimes by a piece of sculpture, a statue, group, figure of a beast, or an imaginary monster, or an imitation of a funeral vase, sometimes of great size. At the cemetery on the western side of the ancient city of Athens, gravestones have been found of extraordinary beauty. One is a sphinx and another is a siren, each of these being symbolical of death (on the Xanthian tomb in the British Museum harpies are carrying away spirits of the dead); another is carved with a low relief of a lion, and with rosettes of great beauty; another bears three vases in low relief, and it is understood that this means that the persons commemorated died unmarried; another is the sculptured semblance of such a vase "in the round," and adorned with exquisite sculptures in very low relief; several have a portrait of the deceased with certain attendants, the function of which last personages is not well understood. Under Stele the two most magnificent of these gravestones are described. Similar monuments exist in different museums of Europe. It is not quite settled how far these stelæ are strictly gravestones, and how far they are set up in convenient places, as we put up slabs in churches without the supposition that the grave is near. (See Cenotaph.)

Graves not within any building are commonly marked either by one very large stone, covering practically the whole grave, and inscribed with names, etc., on the upper surface, or they have a larger headstone and a smaller footstone. In the first case, the slab is not unfrequently mounted upon a low substructure of brickwork, or the like. A variant of this form is when the stone is not merely a slab having the two large faces parallel, but is cut with an upward slope, forming a ridged roof-like cap or cover for the grave. This form may be further modified by being cut to the semblance of a cruciform roof, — two ridges crossing one another at right angles, each ending either in two gables or in two backward slopes, as in a hipped roof. This last-named form is capable of decorative treatment, for the ridge may be adorned by the semblance of a cross as long and as wide as the whole stone, and this may again receive floriated and other ornamentation.

In the second case, the headstone nearly always receives the greater part of the inscription and the ornament, and the side turned toward the grave is apt to receive more than the reverse side.

(For other forms of memorial put up at the grave, see Grave Monument.)

Among Mohammedans, the rule of their religion limits grave monuments to simple brickwork; but this is interpreted with some liberality, and the *tarkibeh* is an oblong, rectangular structure not unlike an altar tomb, but very simple, and having an upright stone called a *shahid* at the head and another at the foot. That at the head has commonly a curious knob or finial at the top, which is carved into some semblance of a turban or other headdress. In the crowded cemeteries near Constantinople, the *tarkibeh* seems to be omitted or reduced to a very small size and sunk deeply in the earth.

— R. S.

GRAVEZANDE, ARENT ADRIANS-ZOON VAN; architect.

He was city architect of Leyden, Holland, and built the *Mare Kerke* in that city in 1639, the oldest domical church in Holland.

Galland, *Holländische Baukunst.*

GREAT–HEAD. (See Grosseteste.)

GRECIAN ARCHITECTURE. That of the Grecian people in the mainland of Greece, the islands, and the colonies previous to the complete establishment of Roman dominion, about 100 B.C.

The architecture of ancient Greece in its PREHISTORIC PERIOD (3000–1500 B.C.) reflects the nomadic character of its wandering tribes. The use of perishable materials, the absence of organic construction and of a fixed style, characterize these early efforts; and yet the one example which best illustrates the building art of this period, the second of the nine successive settlements which occupied the site of ancient Troy, exhibits many features which linger throughout the entire history of Grecian architecture. The typical form of a rectangular building preceded by a porch was now established, and the specifically Grecian love of symmetry shown in the repetition of the porch at the rear of the building. Similarly the gateway of this Trojan city and that of the courtyard of the palace consisted of two porches set back to back, a form which was subsequently elaborated into the imposing Propylæa of the Acropolis at Athens. Various architectural details — such as antæ or terminal pilasters — and some decorative designs — such as rosettes and spirals — were already in use in this period, but columns and the gable roof seem to have been absent.

The period which followed has been called the MYCENÆAN AGE, because the Acropolis and tombs of Mycenæ have furnished the most representative examples of the civilization which followed the prehistoric age. The limits of the period, though still in dispute, are by the best authorities placed at 1500 B.C. to 1000 B.C., though in some quarters this civilization may have been begun earlier than 1500 B.C., and it

was too strongly and widely established to have ended everywhere at as early a date as 1000 B.C. The centre of this civilization, judging from the magnificent remains at Tiryns, Mycenæ, and Argos, was apparently in Argolis, but it left substantial traces to the north as far as Thessaly, to the east as far as Troy, to the south in Egypt, Cyprus, Crete, and many of the Greek islands, and to the west in Sicily and Italy. Its strongly fortified palaces indicate established centres of monarchical government, with types of architecture so strongly marked as to become fixed for centuries. These types follow along the lines of Grecian architecture of the previous period, but show more advanced construction, with decorative forms of more pronounced Oriental character. The building sites were more carefully levelled, the strongholds surrounded by compactly constructed walls of massive quadrangular or polygonal blocks. The palaces

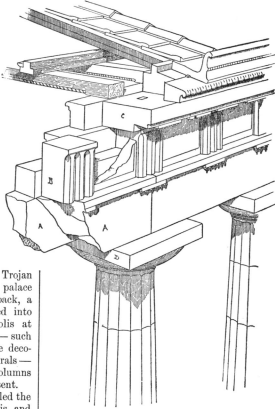

GRECIAN ARCHITECTURE: CONSTRUCTION OF A DORIC BUILDING.

A, Epistyle or architrave, in this case two stones in depth. *B*, Triglyph; the metopes are between the triglyphs, and this whole horizontal band is the frieze. *C*, Cornice. *D*, Abacus of the capital.

seem still to have had flat clay roofs, although the conical false vaults of the beehive tombs indicate the possibility that domical construction may have been used in the building of houses. The column was now employed as a supporting member in the palace porches and in the arcades of the courtyards; but it was not yet a characteristic and distinguishing feature. A peripteral Mycenæan building did not exist. At Troy, where the sixth city corresponded in date to the settlements at Mycenæ and Tiryns, the non-columnar type of architecture still survived, notwithstanding the great advances which had been made in stone construction. Even in Argolis, stone columns seem not to have been used. The columns were of wood, and, judging from the stone copies of columns upon Mycenæan tomb-façades, were decorated with channellings or sheathed with ornamental plates of bronze.

complex character, seems to indicate that Mycenæan architects, no less than those of Egypt, Babylonia, and Assyria, utilized all the resources of colour and decorative design to adorn the façades of their buildings. This decoration had little or no relation to the architectural construction. The abundant use of spirals and rosettes show it belongs to the same family or ornament represented at Troy in the preceding period. The painted and sculptured walls of the palaces and beehive tombs show an enlarged acquaintance with Egyptian ornamental motives, while in some cases, like the painting of the bull and its trainer at Tiryns, there is an independence of treatment indicating that in painting as in architecture the Mycenæans were no mere copyists of Oriental art.

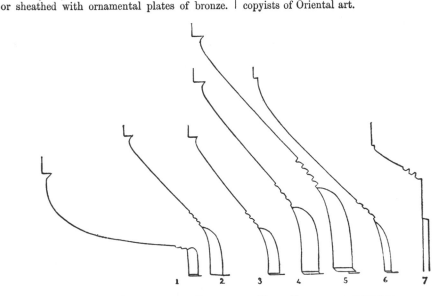

GRECIAN ARCHITECTURE: PROFILES OF DORIC CAPITALS, AS FOLLOWS:

Nos. 1 and 6, early capitals found on the Acropolis at Athens. No. 2, Athens; so-called Temple of Theseus. No. 3, Athens; Propylaia. Nos. 4 and 5, Athens; Parthenon. No. 7, Cori (Southern Italy); so-called Temple of Hercules.

The tomb-façades and some small objects of industrial art suggest that Mycenæan columns diminished in diameter from summit to base, but this impractical feature could not have existed long, even if it were attempted by Mycenæan architects. The capitals of columns consisted of one or more cushion or torus mouldings, a species which may have served as a prototype for the early Doric capital. Upon the columns rested the entablature of wood, decorated with a frieze which, in some cases at least, foreshadowed the triglyphs and metopes of the Doric order. The palace walls, usually constructed of sun-dried brick, were covered with stucco and painted; the cement floors were also ornamented with incised and painted designs. The façade of the tomb of Atreus near Mycenæ, which is a veritable marble mosaic of

The DORIANS and IONIANS brought to an end the Mycenæan civilization and established gradually new forms of art, following in great measure the traditions already established on the soil of Greece. The new civilization was democratic in character, and buildings representative of the interests of the people, such as the temple, the theatre, the gymnasium, made the strongest demands upon the architects; fortified palaces of the kings were now objects of the past. Even private residences were for a long period unimportant. The new civilization was at once more religious and more intellectual. The temple became eminently the standard and type from which other buildings drew their inspiration, and religious sculpture dominated all other forms. The intellectual character of Dorian and Ionian art is exhibited not only in its subject-matter, but also in its technical perfection. Architecture became now as never before a field in which artists sought to arouse intellectual emotion through refinements of form and harmonious proportions.

In the construction of the walls of buildings, stone and marble largely replaced the sun-dried brick of the Mycenæan period, but reminiscences of brick construction survive even in these walls of stone. Thus the small blocks of which the walls are composed are unnecessarily set upon a high surbase which now serves a purely ornamental purpose. The regularity of brick construction also survives in the use of blocks of uniform size laid in parallel courses with joints set in alternate bond. Flat wooden roofs covered with clay seem to have been first employed, their eaves being protected by cornices of terra cotta. When roofing tiles were invented, perhaps in the eighth century, the peaked or gable roof made its appearance and became the typical Grecian roof. So universal was its use that a Grecian temple without a gable roof would seem a solecism.

It may have been the introduction of the gable roof which led to a second feature of the religious architecture of this period, that is, the peripteral character of its temples. The Grecian temple seems incomplete until surrounded by columns. The cause which led the Dorians and Ionians to build peripteral temples is still obscure, but certainly this feature of their architecture became as marked a characteristic as the gable roof. So small a portion of the entire structure as the capital of the column has been used from the time of Vitruvius to the present day as the chief element in distinguishing the so-called "orders." All this results from the fact that the column, which in the Mycenæan period was subordinate, was now the predominant element in Grecian architecture. (See Columnar Architecture; Greco-Roman Architecture.)

Besides the gable roof and surrounding columns, there is a third characteristic feature of Doric and Ionic temples: the stepped base upon which the building reposed. Foundations above the ground level were hardly necessary on the hard soil of Greece; hence, this base is apparently of foreign origin. But neither Egyptian nor Mesopotamian prototypes offer a ready explanation. The normal temple base was a *tribasmos;* that is, the superposed rectangular platforms of which it was composed were three in number. Variations from this standard were, however, by no means uncommon. A temple without a base would have appeared to the Greeks of this period like a statue without a pedestal.

The eminently sculptural sense of the Greeks is evinced in their architecture still further by their use of painted and carved decorations, and by very delicate refinements in the use of curved

surfaces. The earlier temples, made of rough stone or brick, with cornices overlaid with terra cotta, were uniformly covered with a thin layer of stucco, and painted. Prehistoric Grecian and Mycenæan, as well as Oriental, example established this practice as traditional, and it was too useful in giving uniformity to crude material or faulty construction to be easily set aside. But parallel with the development of sculpture, architectural painting was confined more and more to the imitation or emphasizing of sculptural decoration. As compared with a Mycenæan façade, such as that of the tomb of Atreus, a Doric or Ionic façade depended less upon the kaleidoscopic effects of colour and more upon the clear presentation of its structural and sculptural parts. Thus the capitals of columns, the triglyphs, the cornices, and mouldings were emphasized by colour; more important still were the masses of red or blue, which formed the background for the gable sculptures, the sculptured metopes, and continuous friezes. In its fully developed form the Grecian temple was not merely a shrine for the statue of the divinity within, it was also a framework for its external sculptures.

The external sculptures of the temple consisted of groups, usually of free standing figures, in the triangular gables; of compositions in high relief for the Doric, and in low relief for the Ionic, frieze. Capitals and mouldings made also demands upon the sculptor's chisel. The subject of the external sculptures was not always directly related to the divinity of the temple. The principal or eastern gable was frequently filled with a tranquil group, while the western presented a more active or violent scene. The metopes required a series of simple compositions, like the labours of Herakles, while the unbroken Ionic frieze demanded a procession or a combat involving many figures.

The substitution of curved for horizontal and vertical lines and surfaces was a refinement of building in special accord with the plastic sense of the Greeks of the best period. The temple base, the architrave, and the upper and lower lines of the metopes were not perfectly horizontal, but slightly convex, and the columns were not constructed with a rectilinear but a curved profile. This refinement was so delicate that these curved lines and surfaces long escaped observation, but since attention has been called to them, similar phenomena have been discovered in Egyptian obelisks, columns, and architraves, and it has been shown that the practice was carried into Christian architecture by Byzantine Greeks and Italian architects long before the Renaissance. The motive which guided the Greeks in their use of curved lines or surfaces is not altogether obvious. It is difficult to prove that this was done either to correct an optical illusion, as was held by Vitruvius, or for the sake of producing a perspective illusion, as suggested by Professor Goodyear; it seems more likely that the Greeks found in this device a means of avoiding the mechanical impression likely to be produced by straight lines and surfaces, and

divinity and for the deposit of votive offerings, hence the sunlight which streamed through the entrance doorway was sufficient for the purpose. Windows therefore were unnecessary. There is no evidence that clearstory windows, which seem

GRECIAN ARCHITECTURE: ANGLE OF AN IONIC BUILDING; ONE CORNER CAPITAL AND TWO
COMMON IONIC CAPITALS.

The broad band in each capital would be decorated by anthemions in a rich building.

of giving to their buildings a more plastic external form. (See Refinements in Design.)

Grecian temples were generally of moderate proportions. They were not halls of worship, but shrines for the protection of the statue of a

to have been employed in the Mycenæan palace, occurred in the Grecian temple; and it is most improbable that hypæthral devices of any sort were employed in the normal temple. A flat-roofed building, especially a large hall of columns like the Telesterion at Eleusis, may have been lighted by an *opaion* in the roof, and possibly some of the Greek colonies in the Alexandrian period may have had domical temples with an hypæthral opening like that of the Pantheon in Rome. But such cases have little or no bearing on the case of the rectangular, gable-roofed temple of classic times.

In the arrangement of the temple plan, the Dorians developed the rear to resemble the front of the temple, producing thus a bifacial type, whereas the Ionians generally adhered to the unifacial plan. In the erection of temple walls and columns the Dorians gave to both a slight inward slant, whereas the Ionians made them vertical. In their columns the Dorians at

GRECIAN ARCHITECTURE: DETAIL OF AN IONIC BUILDING; NORTH DOORWAY OF ERECHTHEUM, ATHENS.

In reference to style, Grecian architecture of the classic period may be most conveniently considered as either Doric or Ionic. It is not yet possible to establish an Æolic type of architecture, and the traditional Corinthian was no more than a slight variation of the Ionic. The Doric and Ionic had many elements in common. They are branches of the same stock. But they differ also in many particulars besides the capital of the column.

an early date discarded the base, which the Ionians retained and developed. The typical Doric shaft tapered toward the top, had a relatively strong entasis or curved profile, was provided with twenty elliptical channellings separated by sharp arrises, and in height ranged from four and a half to six and a half times its lower diameter. The Ionic shaft tapered less, had a slighter entasis, was enriched by twenty-four semicircular channellings separated by flat fillets, and in height ranged from eight and a half to ten lower diameters. A more marked distinction occurs in the capital. The Doric capital seems to have been moulded upon Mycenæan prototypes, its principal member, the echinus, being originally rather flat and having a rounded profile. In the sixth century the echinus became proportionately higher and had a strong profile with a curve resembling a parabola, while in the late fifth century the profile of the echinus was almost rectilinear. Its decoration consisted of carved annuli or flat bands at the base of the echinus, occasionally of carved floral or geometrical design at the neck of the capital, and sometimes of painted ornament on the echinus itself. The crowning member of the capital was the abacus, usually a cubical block, the value of which was to break the abrupt transition from echinus to architrave. The less monumental examples of Doric capitals exhibit many variations of the normal type. The Ionic capital consisted of three parts, the neck, the volute or scrolls, and the abacus. The neck was occasionally distinctly marked by carved ornament, but usually appears as a thin echinus moulding, ornamented in part with carved or painted eggs and darts, and in part concealed from view by the scrolls. The volutes form the characteristic member of the Ionic capital. In the archaic examples the volutes on the face of the capital seem to spring from the shaft like the petals of an Egyptian lotus and between them is figured a somewhat flattened palmette. By the fifth century the palmette has disappeared, the volutes no longer rise from the shaft, but are united by waving lines. In the Alexandrian period the lines which unite the volutes are more nearly horizontal and straight. The abacus in all periods was relatively thinner than in Doric examples, and its faces were frequently covered with an egg and dart or leaf ornament. While the front of an Ionic capital appears as a conventionalized lotus flower, the side view has little apparent connection with the front, and presents the appearance of a scroll of parchment held together by a central ribbon. Such a capital was applicable to the temple *in antis*, but was adapted with difficulty to the peripteral temple. A special capital for the corner had to be constructed with rather awkward diagonal volutes.

Doric and Ionic buildings differed also in the entablature. The Doric architrave presented in part an unbroken surface, whereas the Ionic was divided vertically into three parallel and horizontal bands. Above the architrave the frieze in the Doric order was divided into triglyphs and metopes, the triglyphs being apparently a reminiscence of the ends of the ceiling beams, and the metopes the spaces between the beams, which were closed and decorated with painted ornament or relief sculpture. In the Ionic order the frieze was an unbroken member, ornamented by a continuous band of painted or sculptured ornament. The ends of the ceiling beams are not forgotten altogether in the Ionic order. They appear above the frieze, structurally their proper place, but they are diminished in size and appear as a decorative moulding known as the dentils. The other mouldings differed in the two orders. The Dorians had a preference for mouldings of simple or strong profile, decorated with severe ornament; the Ionians made their mouldings of more delicate profile and with more graceful ornament.

The Grecian orders of architecture were well adapted to buildings of a single story and of moderate size, especially when constructed of white marble. The attempt to apply them to buildings of large dimensions usually ends in failure, for columns cease to be pleasing when magnified or multiplied beyond a certain normal limit. White marble also lends itself best to this style of architecture, the glory of which lies in refinements of form and proportions and in sculptured ornament. — ALLAN MARQUAND.

Stuart and Revett, *The Antiquities of Athens;* Stuart and Revett, *Antiquities of Athens and other Monuments of Greece;* Chandler, Revett, and Pars, *Ionian Antiquities, published with permission of the Society of Dilettanti; Unedited Antiquities of Attica, comprising the architectural remains of Eleusis, Rhamnus, Sunium, and Thoricus, by the Society of Dilettanti;* Cockerell, Kinnard, Donaldson, Jenkins, and Railton, *The Antiquities of Athens and other places in Greece, Sicily;* Texier, *Description de l'Asie Mineure;* K. Bötticher, *Die Tektonik der Hellenen;* F. C. Penrose, *An Investigation of the Principles of Athenian Architecture;* L. Lohde, *Die Architektonik der Hellenen;* P. F. Krell, *Geschichte des dorischen Styles;* E. Blocht, *Die Griechisch-Dorische Architektur;* A. Choisy, *Études épigraphiques sur l'architecture grecque;* V. Laloux, *L'Architecture grecque; The Journal of Hellenic Studies.*

GRECO-EL. (See Theotocopuli.)

GRECO-ROMAN ARCHITECTURE. An architecture of the beam and column, the lintel being used pure and unmixed by the Greeks, but forced into union with the arch by the Romans. Its elementary type is the Order, a primary composition or unit of composition, consisting of the column and its load, the entablature, and executed, as a rule, in stone. When these two parts had been evolved and shaped, as they were early by the Greeks, into definite and permanent forms, they constituted the Order. They hardened into types, — at first into two, the Doric and Ionic, — not immutable indeed, but subject to small variations of proportions and of adjustment of mouldings and the like, yet distinct and fixed as species of animals and plants. Of the two parts that made the order, the upper (the entablature) consisted of three members: the architrave, the beam or lintel that spanned from column to column; the frieze, a low belt of wall, plain or decorated, borne by the architrave; and the cornice at the top, which ordinarily crowned the composition, uniting a wall with a roof, and consisting of an overhanging slab supported by mouldings, or by brackets reënforced by mouldings.

The columns had their prescribed capitals, and except in the Greek Doric, their bases. Their continuous support was in some buildings a simple platform, as in the Greek temples, in others a basement consisting of a strip of wall with base and light cornice mouldings, which is sometimes accounted as part of the order, and which by the Romans was often cut into detached pieces called pedestals, one under each column. So shaped, the orders were the direct embodiment of the simplest idea of building construction next to a plain wall — a beam supported on posts. Based upon them, classical architecture was in idea strictly trabeated, and even the arch added by the Romans did not change the artistic intention, although it greatly changed the actual construction, until in later hands it revolutionized the forms. The characteristics of classical architecture, by natural development from the forms of the orders, are broad simple masses and straight lines, horizontal and vertical, the horizontal predominating, the vertical subordinated. It owed its singular charm as much to the consistency with which these characteristics were preserved and to the breadth, harmony, and repose which were gained by them, as to the beauty of proportions and details that we find in the Greek examples, won by centuries of persistent refining of the same forms.

The purest form of classic architecture was the Greek. It was as strictly a trabeated architecture as the Egyptian, and fixed the types of classic building from the beginning, and for all subsequent ages. It was small in scale and its types were few and simple, as were its requirements. The life of the Greeks was out of doors; towns were small and compact, their houses were insignificant, in narrow streets crowded about the central market place, where were accumulated their public buildings, and especially the temples, conspicuous and chief among the buildings as the churches in mediæval towns. Their architecture was essentially public architecture; its central and primal type the temple, a rectangular hall or cella, faced at one end or both, or entirely surrounded by an order arranged in a colonnade, and covered by a pitched roof with a pediment at each end. These few elementary forms, invented in the evolution of the temple — the order, the colonnade, the pediment, and the pitched roof — with the rectangular plan, sufficed in all their buildings, from which visible curves and oblique angles were severely

banished, except for an occasional round building, tholus or exedra, and the curved seats of the theatres and stadia, which, being sunk in the ground and without walls or roofs, are hardly to be called buildings.

The primitive life of the Greeks was a life of religion and warfare, and their religion was intimately concerned with their wars. Their architectural study was lavished on their temples, and the forms evolved for these were consecrated by tradition. Half a dozen different schemes of plan were devised, to suit different arrangements of the colonnades (see Temple), and two distinct types of order, — the Doric, used first in Hellas, the Ionic, first in the Asiatic colonies; these once determined, though not with all the scheduled minuteness which Vitruvius prescribes for the Romans, yet by fixed tradition, were held to with a persistence that precluded any considerable modification of type in the form of entablature or column, capital or moulding. The types once chosen, the Greeks never showed any desire to change them; generation after generation went on refining and readjusting their elements till they reached a delicacy and elegance of line and proportion that no architecture has equalled. No change of scale altered the relation of parts, or disturbed the simplicity of the composition. A large temple was only a small temple of the same class magnified; a small order was, as it were, the photographic reduction of a large one. The order thus made inviolable became the whole substance of their architecture, standing alone and covering practically all the building to which it belonged, with nothing above it, and under it only a platform or a basement wall. It was too rigid to lend itself easily to combinations; it was scarcely used in more than one story. The use of the lintel or beam forbade wide spacing in stone architecture, and so limited the size of the orders; the habits of the Greeks and the moderate size of their communities did not call for large buildings; their great gatherings were in the open air; buildings for the shelter of the public were long galleries, called stoas, or halls divided into comparatively narrow aisles. The only large buildings were the temples of a few of the great colonial cities, and in the greatest of these the chamber or cella, encompassed by colonnades, hardly exceeded 40 feet in width. So the single order sufficed for, or limited, all their buildings, and hence the harmony and the elegant simplicity of their architecture. Hence, too, the absence of complexity in the plans and combinations of their buildings so far as we know them by their remains.

The architecture of the beam is naturally also that of the column, the column being only a beam set on end, and Greek building was distinguished by the prevalence of colonnades: the temples were girt with them; they surrounded the agoræ or markets; they extended in long stoas or porticoes against the hillsides, and from one public building to another; they divided the larger halls and the cellas of temples into aisles. This led to a great multiplying of vertical and horizontal lines and right angles, — the horizontal lines always terminating the composition excepting in pediments or gables, — and to a conspicuous expression of repose and stability which was increased by the habit of rigid symmetry in the arrangement of parts. It also led to the subordination of the wall surface, which in their important buildings, being in a great degree hidden behind the colonnades, became a secondary element in the architectural effect; so that there is hardly any style except the developed Gothic in which the architectural members are so prominent and the wall surface so surbordinated as in the Greek. The Greeks, living in a country of wooded hills and marble mountains, built only in stone, roofing their buildings with wood. Like the Egyptians, they knew the arch and occasionally used it; like them, they rejected it from their important architecture. Imported from barbarous countries and built of brick, a despised material, it was put to inferior uses, building of drains and the like, and hidden under ground.

The Romans were the natural inheritors of the architecture of the Greeks, the architecture of the lintel and the order, both through the Etruscans, and immediately from the Greeks. Being a hard-headed, practical people, apt for war and dominion, but not for culture, they contentedly accepted their art, first from the conquered Etruscans and then from the conquered Greeks, whose superiority in so subordinate a matter they were ready to accept for what it was worth. So they took their architecture unquestioningly, and with it the tradition of the supremacy and inviolability of the orders. For them the order was still the embodiment of what was most stately and sacred in building. They were faithful to tradition in preserving the ancient form of the temple as the Etruscans and the Greeks transmitted it to them, using only the single order for it, and rejecting the arch, except that in some few late instances the interior was vaulted. They sometimes expanded the cella till it took in the width of the colonnades, preserving the order engaged or embedded in the side walls of the cella, as we still see in the temple called the *Maison Carrée* at Nîmes, — a treatment for which the Greeks had given them an example in the great temple at Agrigentum. They liked to raise the columns above the platform on a basement, while they kept the general outline of the temple unchanged and retained the traditional porticoes and pediments at the ends. To the end, wherever they wanted monumental architecture, the single order, magnified to the full

dimension that was called for, was the substance of their design. But they were too practical, inventive, and independent to confine themselves to such simple use of the orders as sufficed for the Greeks. As they grew powerful, their requirements outran their traditions, strong in the beginning. Not essentially a religious people like the Egyptians and the early Greeks, after the republic was ended, as they grew more powerful and domineering, they made their architecture, like their empire, worldly and secular. Their temples ceased to be their most important buildings. Palaces, baths, theatres, amphitheatres, far exceeded them in size and splendour. The two orders of the Greeks were not enough for their need of variety, and they invented three more. They piled them on each other in their theatres and amphitheatres: in the Septizonium, the great barrack of Septimius Severus, there were seven stories of them, we are told.

The Romans had no prejudice against the arch. As architecture they had inherited it from the Etruscans, who, building in stone, had used it monumentally, of which we may still see examples in the city gates of Volterra, Falerii, and Perugia. They must have used it early, perhaps independently, for ordinary building; for Rome was built in an alluvial region, and in the days of her poverty brick was probably her usual building material, as we infer from its abundant later use and from the well-known boast of Augustus that he found her a city of brick, and left her a city of marble. It is difficult to build freely in brick without the arch. We first find it in the ruins of Mesopotamia, an alluvial country devoid of building stone, as if it were the child of the bricklayer. It was too serviceable to be set aside; and evidently its nobility and dignity when used on a grand scale impressed the Romans, for it was the form they persistently chose for monuments of triumphal arches with which the emperors, from Augustus down, besprinkled Italy. Indeed, as trabeated architecture, born among the sacerdotal Egyptians, carried to its finest type by the pious earlier Greeks, may be taken as a symbol of religious domination, and was always consecrated to the building of temples, so the architecture of the arch may be called symbolic of civic and warlike dominion, — an architecture of palaces and of buildings for display. The Assyrians and Romans, warlike, aggressive, domineering, and ostentatious, were its patrons. For the Romans, as their empire gained on the world, and under their rule cities grew populous and wealthy, and filled with such great public buildings as were unknown before, the arch was found their best servant. It gave so much flexibility to their style, adapting itself to every increase of scale, bearing any burden, and by the concurrent introduction of curved lines brought so much variety into the plans of buildings, so

PLATE XII

GRECO-ROMAN ARCHITECTURE

The temple at Nîmes in southern France known as *La Maison Carrée* and the most perfectly preserved of all temples of the Roman Imperial epoch. These buildings were more closely imitated from Grecian forms than any others erected by the Imperial builders.

much splendour of effect into the exteriors, that a practical, sumptuous people like the Romans could not but make the most of it. Accordingly they made the arch the constructive basis of most of their civic architecture ; but, working always in deference to Greek art, they could not give themselves up to a purely arched style, and they set to work to use the order and the arch together. With this combination they enormously increased the magnificence of their buildings. They piled arcades on arcades, and orders on orders, making their theatres and amphitheatres great monuments which have never been equalled. Their palaces and baths were vast complexes of courts, corridors, porticoes, halls of every variety and contrast of shape and size. Their streets and squares were lined with miles of colonnades, arcades, temples, and lofty palaces. Perhaps there never has been such an accumulation of architectural magnificence as there was in imperial Rome. The whole heart of Rome was not a mass of streets, like any modern city, but a great congeries of open squares bordered by galleries colonnaded or arcaded, and communicating freely with each other, so that one might walk for half a mile through forum after forum, among temples and basilicas, exedras, porticoes, triumphal arches and columns, and a whole population of statues. The Palatine Hill was covered close with enormous palaces, whose intricate plans and sumptuous decoration are the wonder of the modern explorer.

The Romans have been much blamed because, having borrowed the architecture of the orders from the Greeks, they did not maintain its purity. It is true that they did not succeed in combining the arch and the order without prejudice to both ; that they used the orders in ways that did not suit them, and made changes in their proportion and decoration that robbed them of the exquisite purity which the long elaboration of the Greeks had wrought into them, making them mechanical and common in comparison. The Romans were not artists in form, as the Greeks were ; but it is unfair, in comparing, not to recognize that their architecture is, after all, a much greater intellectual achievement than the Greek. Its problems were far more complex and difficult than those of the Greek, its conceptions grander, its combinations more inventive and interesting. The Romans were incapable of Greek grace and refinement ; but their work shows fertility of invention and free command of resources which are not seen in the Greek. The Greek types, we have seen, were few and simple, complete, and obdurate to modification, inapt for combination. Two orders of different scales would not accommodate in any part. We see how in the Doric temples the ceilings of the pteromas are laid on without adaptation to the colonnades.

In the Erechtheum at Athens, the only somewhat complex Greek building that remains to us, the great parts, though put together with care for harmony of masses, are absolutely without interadjustment. Except for some continuity in the base mouldings, there is no sign of thought in fitting the parts together beyond chopping them off and laying one against the other as they come. The habit of cumulative design seems to have been foreign to the Greeks ; of Roman architecture, as would appear, this was the strong side, and it is doubtful whether anything has surpassed the majesty of its great combinations. The vault, which the Romans inherited with the arch from the Etruscans, and its natural counterpart, the dome, gave enormous value to these combinations. They used few forms of vault, — the barrel vault, plain and annular, the groined vault of equal intersecting cylinders, the spherical dome and half dome, — but these gave variety and dignity before unknown to their interiors. They covered spaces which, so far as we know, the Greeks had not dreamed of covering, and handled their vaulting with a boldness and security that even the Gothic builders hardly surpassed : the dome of S. Peter's has less span than that of the Pantheon, though it is hung higher ; its great nave is but a yard wider than that of the basilica of Constantine.

Abuse has been poured upon the Romans for neglecting to design an architecture to suit the arch, and for studying instead to ally it with the order. But it is difficult to see why they should have done otherwise. Having received from their earliest days a consecrated type which was to them the noblest of building forms, and having in use also a subordinate form, — the arch, — too serviceable to be neglected but of capacities not yet developed, when they began to build on a great scale and for great effects they naturally did not discard the first and set themselves to deduce an architecture from the second alone. The natural course was to use both together until in the end that one prevailed which was fittest to survive, and this they did. Their problem was, and they could hardly escape it, to combine the arch and the order. If we examine their solution impartially we shall be more inclined to confess their skill than to accuse them of dulness. The Roman way of combining the two forms was in idea to build the wall, pierced by its arch or series of arches with piers between, and then overlay it with an order, giving one intercolumniation to each arch. They set the columns on pedestals, diminishing their height and the preponderance of their entablature, but rather awkwardly increasing their stride. They bound the parts together by carrying the base mouldings of the pedestals round the piers ; surrounded the arch with an archivolt which echoed the architrave of the entablature, and was the form previously used to border square openings ; they added an impost moulding to receive the archivolt, which gave the pier an analogy to the columns without making it less a part of the wall. Finally they set a keystone at the crown of the arch to receive the overhang of the entablature midway between the columns. This not only gave the arch an apparent structural relation to the entablature, but, what was artistically more important, it bound the two parts of the composition together at the top, as the base mouldings bound them at the bottom. This keystone, which so used is perhaps the best detail contributed by the Romans, has been sorely misunderstood and misused by later builders. That the order and the arch, embodiments of opposing principles of construction, should make a perfect union was not to be expected ; but to the Romans the combination was perhaps inevitable, and at least their composition is artistically skilful and effective, if it is irrational in that the order appears to be doing the supporting work of the arch. The problem, indeed, was probably solved by Greek brains, for the Romans, we may remember, did no work but that of administration ; their work was done for them by freedmen and slaves, — that is, by conquered foreigners and their children. The workshops of Rome were full of imported workmen and artists, mainly Greek. It was enough for the Romans to prescribe and administer their architecture.

That part of the order which was really apt for combination with the arch, the column, had been immemorially joined with the entablature ; to separate them involved the disruption of the order, and for three hundred years it was not thought of. The pier was the natural support of the arch, which was but a hole in a wall, and two archways which adjoined left a pier between them. To replace this pier by a column and readjust the bearings was a matter of contrivance and difficulty ; the Romans never attempted to detach the column from the entablature, or to find any other support for the arch than its pier. The forced alliance between arch and order lasted throughout the classical period. But at the end of this period the vault showed the way. The lunettes of the groined vaulting over a high clearstory, as in the Baths of Diocletian, or the Basilica of Constantine, left between them a narrow pendant which called for a special support. A vaulted roof could not, like an archway, be set under an order ; it must rest upon it. Here was the natural position for a single column, and the Romans were used to single columns standing in front of their triumphal arches and carrying each its block of entablature, broken forward over it. Column and entablature were not to be separated ; they were taken together and set under the pendant of the vaulting, as against the triumphal arch.

This arrangement, often copied in modern imitations of classic architecture, still shows in the transept of the church of S. Maria degli Angeli at Rome, which was the great hall of the Baths of Diocletian. The lesson of this was obvious, but it was reserved for the progressive eastern provinces to apply it. The palace built for the same Diocletian to live in after his abdication, now transformed into the town of Spalato in Dalmatia, is the oldest building we know in which the block of entablature is omitted and arches bear directly on the columns, while elsewhere in the same building we see the normal combination of the Roman arcades ; and in the Basilica of Constantine, built at about the same time, the treatment of the Baths of Diocletian is repeated. This basilica was the last great building of imperial Rome, and there is no indication that in it the order was ever divided. The change seen at Spalato was a beginning of the growth of the mediæval styles. The union of the column with the arch has never since been set aside. Its survival when classic architecture was revived in the Renaissance was the most conspicuous difference between the new classic and the old. Its history in the interim belongs to Romanesque and Byzantine architecture.

If the arch was the ready servant of the Romans in construction, they found the order — or made it — scarcely less serviceable in design. Their genius for administration shows itself as clearly in their buildings as in their polity. They raised up a body of well-trained engineers, who did an enormous amount of skilful building throughout the empire, as the remains of their works witness, to our astonishment, at this day. There are many indications that their great buildings were in charge of engineers more than of artists. The character of the design as well as the construction seems to show that the chief concern was to develop such a system for both that when the general scheme of a great building had been devised by the engineers or master builders, trained designers could carry it out to a result which could be prescribed in advance by rules and formulæ. They dealt in masses of masonry, arches, walls, and piers on an enormous scale, building so solidly that they could build fast, and like the Pharaohs, by armies of unskilled workmen. The Greeks had been in their smaller way far nicer constructors : their buildings were wrought throughout of cut stone, fitted together like cabinet work. The buildings of the Romans were piles of rough bricks and concrete ; they overlaid them with an architectural envelope, stately, elaborate, and finely enough wrought to satisfy their not very exacting taste. It was possible to do this on a great scale with an architecture which had been disciplined into a rigid system of proportions and decorations, where every form was definitely prescribed, and the small details were repeated in absolute uniformity by the hundred or by the rod. If we may trust Vitruvius, this was the rule under which Roman architecture was brought. None could have submitted to it so easily as the architecture of the order; none could have furnished so facile a basis for it as that of the Greeks, in which the conditions of harmony, effectiveness, and a minutely ordered system were already secured. That the Greek forms suffered under such unsympathetic handling, that they were cheapened by mechanical iteration, was inevitable; but we must not refuse the Romans the credit that is really theirs, of having embodied in them many noble conceptions and grand combinations of which the Greeks had not dreamed. — W. P. P. LONGFELLOW.

Ch. Chipiez, *Histoire critique des origines et de la formation des ordres grecs*; A. Baumeister, *Denkmäler des klassichen Altertums*; *Antike Denkmäler, herausgegeben vom Kaiserlich Deutschen Archäologischen Institut*; Ch. Chipiez, *Le Système modulaire et les proportions dans l'architecture grecque*; *Bulletino dell' Instituto archeologico*; *Archäologische Zeitung*; *Revue Archéologique*; *American Journal of Archæology*; Vitruvius, *De Architectura* (Gwilt's translation); B. de Montfaucon, *L'Antiquité expliquée et représentée en figures*; F. Mazois, *Les ruines de Pompei*; Ch. Texier, *Description de l'Asie Mineure fait par ordre du gouvernement français de 1833 à 1837, etc.*; J. Overbeck, *Pompeji in seinen Gebäuden, Alterthümern und Kunstwerken*; *Archives de la commission des monuments historiques publiées par ordre de son excellence M. A. Fould*; F. Reber, *Geschichte der Baukunst im Alterthume*; H. Nissen, *Pompejanische studien zur Städtekunde des Alterthums*; J. Uchard, *Architecture de Pompei — ordre ionique — Revue gén. de l'arch.*, 1860; *ordre Corinthien — Revue gén. de l'arch.*, 1862; G. E. Perrot, G. and J. Delbet, *Exploration archéologique de la Galatie et de la Bithynie* (*Rev. gén. de l'arch.*, 1874); Ch. Normand, *Essai sur l'existence d'une architecture metallique antique, etc.*, *Encyclopédie d'arch.*, 1883.

GRECQUE. A meander; especially one of the simplest kind, the lines of which make right angles with one another and are few, and arranged in one sequence.

GREECE, ARCHITECTURE OF. That of those lands which are now occupied by people of Greek race and traditions, chiefly the modern kingdom of the Hellenes.

The architectural history of Greece proper and the adjacent islands may be divided into periods coinciding with its political history as follows:

    I. Prehistoric Period to First Olympiad, 776 B.C.
    II. Early Period to Persian Wars, 500 B.C.
    III. Classic Period to Decline of Athens, 400 B.C.
    IV. Late Period to Roman Conquest, 146 B.C.
    V. Roman Period to Constantine and Christianity, 325 A.D.
    VI. Byzantine Period to Fall of Constantinople, 1453 A.D.

    VII. Turkish Period to Independence Declared, 1830 A.D.
    VIII. Modern Period to 1898.

The beginning of Period I. is lost in the mists of antiquity. The most remarkable ruins are found in the Argolic district at Tiryns, Argos, and Mycenæ, and in Bœotia at Orchomenos. These elucidate and confirm many Homeric descriptions, and bear witness to a vigorous and artistic civilization. The massive fortification walls indicate a state of society resembling feudal Europe in the Middle Ages, while the beautiful pieces of jewellery, the swords inlaid with gold and silver, the vessels of precious metals, and many other relics of skilled workmanship found by Dr. Schliemann at Mycenæ give us glimpses of the life of an artistically refined people. The surpassing loveliness of the scenery and the facility of intercourse with Oriental countries naturally served to stimulate the early artistic development of the people near the Argive Gulf, and Herodotus tells of the commercial attractions offered by this section to the Phœnician traders. At Tiryns there is a ruined palace with accessories, surrounded by massive fortification walls referred to in the *Iliad*, II., 559. Dr. Dörpfeld's restoration enables us to picture all (the propylæa, megaron, bath, colonnaded courts, women's apartments, etc.) which composed this royal stronghold. Tiryns occupies a low rocky hill rising from the Argive plain about one mile distant from the gulf. Its oblong shape of nearly 1000 by 300 feet is enclosed by walls which to Pausanias rivalled in wonder the Egyptian Pyramids, and tradition asserted to be the work of Cyclops. The original exterior height of the walls was probably 65 feet; their thickness varied from 16 to 57 feet, in parts honeycombed with galleries, chambers, and stairways. Two varieties of local limestone were used in blocks, of which some measure 6 to 10 feet long by 3 feet wide and high. The stones were laid up roughly in courses with beds more or less dressed, and in a clay mortar which has been partly removed by the action of lizards, rats, and rain. The galleries and chambers, honeycombing the thicker walls, have a noteworthy roof construction, peculiar to this period in Greece, which consists in a gradual convergence of the horizontal layers of stones, and resembles a rough vault in appearance but not in principle. We find this construction again in the sanctuary of Hera Teleia, Mt. Ocha, Eubœa; in the "beehive" tombs at Mycenæ and elsewhere, and in the corbelling used to relieve the door lintels of this period. The gates and doorways had rebated stone jambs with wooden doors, secured by heavy wooden bolts let into holes in the jambs; at Mycenæ is a typical example, the "Lion Gate," which derives its name from the two lionesses whose headless bodies are carved on the stone slab filling the triangular tympanum formed by the lintel and sides of the relieving corbels. This piece of sculpture is, architecturally, most appropriate both as to design and position.

The propylæum at Tiryns is a prototype of the noble portal on the Athenian Acropolis; while the Megaron, or Great Hall, seems an incipient temple with its porch *distyle in antis* and its main roof supported on interior columns. The general plan at Tiryns furthermore reveals a picturesque irregularity combined with a skilful disposition of the main parts typified in later times by the Erechtheum. The architectural transition, therefore, from the Mycenæan age to that of Pericles is a natural sequence, although several centuries intervened.

The columns supporting the Megaron roof were four wooden pillars on stone bases, surrounding a circular hearth of nearly 11 feet diameter. This arrangement of the hearth illustrates the passage in the *Odyssey* (VI., 304), where Ulysses is directed by Nausicaa to the queen. The smoke from the fire escaped through an opening in the roof, which may have been elevated over the hearth like a clearstory supported on the four pillars. All of the Megaron floor except this hearth is of lime and pebble concrete, polished and decorated with rectangles and squares formed by incised lines, and painted alternately blue and red. The lower portion of the house walls was built of rubble stonework laid in clay mortar, and plastered; the upper portion of sun-dried bricks. The plastering consisted of a coat of clay and another of lime smoothed and painted while still fresh. In painting, the colours used were white, black, blue, red, and yellow. The vestibule of the Megaron was decorated with a beautiful frieze of alabaster and blue glass and a wainscot of wood. The axis of the Megaron coincides with that of its large forecourt, and is parallel and adjacent to that of a smaller court and hall belonging to the women's apartments. Similar arrangements for the men's and women's apartments of this period are found at Mycenæ and Troy.

Another interesting feature at Tiryns is the bathroom, which had a monolithic floor 10 feet by 13 feet by 2¼ feet thick, and weighing twenty tons. This gigantic limestone block is polished and sloped to drain the water. A painted fragment of a terra-cotta bath-tub was found with thick rim and two handles.

About eight miles north of Tiryns is a foothill of Mt. Eubœa commanding the Argive plain, and once sacred to Hera. A Cyclopæan wall of large boulders, more ancient in appearance even than the Tirynthian walls, supports a terrace partially paved with irregular flat stones, and upon which once stood the Heræum, probably the oldest peripteral temple in Greece of which

there are any remains. It was built chiefly of wood, and its destruction by fire is mentioned by Pausanias, II., 17.

About two miles farther north lies Mycenæ, whose walls show stones tooled and fitted in ashlar courses and polygonal masonry. But of chief architectural interest here are the beehive tombs, whose counterparts are also found in Attica and Bœotia. The largest of the eight at Mycenæ is the so-called *Tholos of Atreus*, or Tomb of Agamemnon, excavated by Dr. Schliemann. An approach or *dromos* 115 feet long and 50 feet wide leads horizontally to a great circular subterranean chamber built in the hillside. The walls of the *dromos* are built of large squared blocks. The doorway to the chamber is 17 feet 9 inches high and 8 feet 1 inch wide at top and 8 feet 9 inches wide at bottom. Each doorpost was decorated with a half column of dark gray alabaster. The shafts tapered downward, and were ornamented in relief with spirals in zigzag bands. Over the lintel a triangular space was left similar to that over the Lion Gate. This triangular space, measuring about 10 feet on the sides, was filled up with slabs of red porphyry laid horizontally and adorned with rows of spirals. The passage leading from the doorway into the great chamber is 18 feet long, and is roofed by two enormous slabs beautifully cut and polished, of which the inner one is 3 feet 9 inches thick, 27½ feet long, 17 feet broad, and weighs approximately 130 tons. The great beehive-shaped chamber measures 50 feet in diameter at the floor and 50 feet high. It is built of tooled breccia blocks smoothed and well fitted on the inside, and laid in horizontal courses, gradually converging until the apex is covered by a single stone, which, however, is not a keystone, since the dome is not constructed on the arch principle. Heavy stones are placed on the outside to keep the horizontal courses in position. Bronze nails and nailholes in the wall indicate that bronze rosettes or similar ornaments were used for decoration. On the north side of the beehive chamber a doorway opens into a smaller dark chamber 27 feet square and 19 feet high, entirely cut out of the rock.

Our Period II. directs the attention more to religious architecture. The separate states and colonies formed by earlier migrations are unified by the Olympic festivals and Delphic oracles, so that we find the same type used for the old Heræum at Olympia, the Hecatompedon at Athens, and for the temples at Corinth, Ægina, and Delphi. It is the ancient megaron developed, with the principal addition of an enclosing colonnade, or peristyle, and built of finer material and with greater artistic skill; the statue of the deity, the oracular fire, or tripod, occupies the position of the old hearth. Forms formerly executed in wood are now built of stone or mar-

PLATE XIII

GREECE, ARCHITECTURE OF

The ancient Cathedral or Metropolitan church of Athens; a curious piece of mediæval Byzantine work dating, as is generally thought, from the time of the Latin conquest and the foundation of the French dukedom of Athens early in the thirteenth century. The building is in great part composed of ancient sculptured fragments. It is very small, measuring only 28 × 40 feet outside, and its cruciform clearstory is carried on six piers so that there is hardly room for a congregation.

ble. Architectural terra cotta (mouldings, roof tiles, antefixæ, etc.) are found at various sites, but of similar patterns, as though having emanated from one central manufactory. At Olympia, the treasury of Gela had a stone cornice encased with terra cotta. The institution of religious festivals and games concentrated a wealth of architecture in certain favoured cities. Each city of importance built a treasury at Olympia, Delphi, or elsewhere, in which to deposit reconnaissant gifts and trophies. The games required the gymnasium, stadion, palæstra, and bouleuterion; the accompanying sacrifices necessitated the temples, altars, porticoes, and stoa, while to the heroes of the hour were erected statues and tripods until the sacred grounds became fairly crowded with the various ornaments.

Our "classic" period (III.) is the culminating era. The successful repulse of the Persians had sent a wave of exhilaration throughout Greece which stimulated effort and inspired thought. With true artistic instinct the architects limited their efforts to developing and refining the old forms. Athens had been chief in repelling the Persian invader, and also stood foremost in the activity which ensued, with Argos second. Artists had developed apace with the rapid growth of wealth and refinement, and, as in the times of all good art, the architects, sculptors, and painters interlocked arms or were embodied in the same individuals.

The octastyle Parthenon on the Athenian Acropolis represents the perfect Greek temple. Penrose (*True Principles of Athenian Architecture*) discovered by careful measurement that its design embodied the most subtle curves. (See Refinements in Design.) The general type of temple, however, continued to be hexastyle; the Zeus temple at Olympia and the Hera temple at Argos both contained chryselephantine statues of the deity similar to the Athena figure in the Parthenon; the statues in the Parthenon and Zeus temple were both executed by Pheidias; the Hera statue by his brother sculptor, Polycleitos. Everywhere we find great activity; Ionian influences are bearing fruit, as shown by the Nike temple, the Erechtheum, and the interior columns of the Propylæum at Athens and of the Apollo temple at Bassæ. We find Doric temples at Megalopolis, Tegea, Epidaurus, Athens, Eleusis, Rhamnus, Sunion, Delos, and Delphi, whose ruins tell their history more or less clearly. The polygonal masonry at Rhamnus is a spiritual link with the early work of Mycenæ.

Other buildings besides temples had been perfected. Next in beauty, and at times rivalling them, were the stoas, — colonnaded buildings devoted to various uses. The Poikile, or painted stoa, of Athens's market place, was painted by Polygnotus; the stoa Basileus, where the archon

sat in judgment, was a prototype of the Roman basilica. The Lesche at Delphi was a lounging or club room famous for its frescoes by Polygnotus. The stoa of the Athenians at Delphi, the Echo Colonnade of Olympia, and the stoas at the Argive Heræum, at Epidauros, Thoricos, and Oropos repay careful study.

Religion and athletics were associated in Greece. Gymnasia and stadia at Athens, Megalopolis, Delos, Olympia, Delphi, Isthmia, and Nemea equalled the temples in importance. The gymnasium type consisted of a peristylar court, from which opened rooms for baths and exercises, both physical and intellectual. Under Roman influences the scope of the gymnasium was extended. The stadion was an oval race track 600 feet long, with seats for spectators.

The theatre, originally only a circular space like the modern Greek threshing floor, had developed with the drama, and its design may be traced at Mantinea, Argos, Epidauros, Sicyon, Athens, Thoricos, Delos, Eretria, Megalopolis, and Delphi. Dr. Dörpfeld has lately published his views controverting Vitruvius and other authorities regarding the arrangements of the Greek stage.

Gateways and propylæa, resembling the early one at Tiryns, are found at Athens, Eleusis, Olympia, and Delos.

In our "late" period (IV.), the artists, incapable of advancing farther, began to copy. We see the cause in the political conditions. The southern Greeks were conquered by the less refined Macedonians. Athens was no longer the chief centre, the successors to Alexander had made their capitals at Alexandria and Antioch. The Hellenic spirit which leavened the world became diluted. From giving, Athens began to receive. She was adorned, still, by buildings, but only through the munificence of Philohellenic princes and nobles from foreign parts. Architecture became thinner, both in sentiment and design, as shown by the Zeus temple at Nemea, and the Gateway of Athena Archegetis at Athens. In the last period the artist was honoured; now it is the donor. Attalos II. of Pergamon built a stoa in Athens, and that prepares us gradually for the final domination of the Romans. The choragic monument of Lysicrates introduces a new and beautiful note amidst generally decreasing harmony. It serves as a type for the Corinthian order, of which we find other interesting specimens in the Tholos at Epidauros and the Philippeion at Olympia, all circular structures, and in the doorway of the octagonal Clepsydra, or Tower of the Winds, in Athens.

Before leaving this period, it would be well to dwell a moment on the temple construction. Indigenous architecture is influenced by the local building materials. In Greece, wood was originally used for column and entablature.

Stone was gradually substituted, retaining and petrifying the traditional wooden forms; the stone epistyle was originally a wooden girder; the triglyphs were beam ends; the metope slabs filled the spaces once open between the beams, wherein probably stood votive gifts represented later by the metope sculptures; the guttæ were nail-heads; the cornice soffit showed the rafter's slope. A wooden entablature permitted greater intercolumniations than were admissible with stone. The old Argive Heræum had wood pillars of 2 feet diameter, spaced $11\frac{1}{2}$ feet on centres. With the introduction of stone, the intercolumniation was decreased by setting the columns nearer together, or by increasing their diameter, or both. The old Heræum at Olympia illustrates the gradual substitution of stone for wood. The early column capital had a broad abacus and echinus designed for the greater support of the epistyle. In time these and the column were better proportioned and massiveness yielded to grace. In the later period an over-refinement and attenuation produced weakness, a worse architectural fault than excess of strength.

The stone columns were usually built of several drums fastened together with wooden dowels and revolved on their beds until the grinding made close joints. To facilitate this operation, several knobs were left on the stone drums when dressed at the quarry, and these were tooled off when the channels were cut at the building. At Delos (Apollo Temple) and at Eleusis (Portico of Philon) the channels were never finished. In early work sixteen channels, and even fourteen (Argive Heræum) were not unusual, but in the best period Doric columns had twenty channels and Ionic twenty-four flutes. The stone columns were often given a thin coat of lime plaster and painted an orange yellow. When marble was used, its smooth surface rendered the plaster unnecessary.

The members of the entablature were also painted, chiefly in reds, blues, and yellows. The cyma and other mouldings, when not carved, were decorated with stencil ornaments of the anthemion and other conventionalized types. The stones of the entablature were raised into position with ropes and tackle. In earlier work, holes for this purpose were cut in the top of the stones; later, on the sides; and again lewis holes were made. The stones were fastened together with bronze and iron clamps, whose form is one indication of a building's age. The clamps of the best fifth century period had the form of a double T (Dr. Josef Durm, *Die Baukunst der Griechen*). Various marks were used by the Greek masons for centring the columns and numbering the stone courses. Early roof tiles were of terra cotta until Byzes, of Naxos, 580 B.C., invented tiles of marble (Pausanias, V., 10). The temple was incomplete until the sculptor had supplemented the architect's work by filling the pedi-

ments and metopes with compositions to the glory of its deity.

The early naos or cella was long and narrow, its width doubtless regulated by the roofing ability of the builders. Gradually the cella was widened and two rows of interior columns aided in supporting the roof, recalling the Tirynthian Megaron. Later expansion of this construction led to the seven rows of columns in the Telesterion at Eleusis, whose similitude to the Hypostyle Hall at Karnak made it an appropriate sanctuary for the Egyptian-like Eleusinian mysteries. The cella or naos was preceded by a pronaos, which is found in the ancient megaron, and continued in the Byzantine church as the narthex. Behind the cella was the opisthodomos, a storeroom for valuables.

The Doric temple was usually hexastyle and peripteral, with twelve or more columns on the sides. A unit of measurement reigns throughout the fifth century temples at the Argive Heræum and at Olympia, which equals 0.326 metres, or $12\frac{3}{4}$ inches. The columns of the Argive temple were spaced ten units apart, except at the angles, where they were nine units; the triglyphs two units wide, and the metopes three units square.

The krepidoma of the Doric temple consisted usually of three steps. On the top one, or stylobate, the columns were placed, their positions indicated by masons' X marks on the stones, and a small hole at the junction of the cross to insert one leg of a compass for describing the circle and laying out the diagram on the stylobate for the channels of the columns. The stone without the circle was then cut away to a lower level, leaving the projection to mark the column's position. An incline or ramp made an easy ascent to the entrance for the sacred processions.

The orientation of the temple was usually such that the rising sun, at the time of year of the festival most sacred to its deity, would shine into the main entrance. At Bassæ is an exceptional arrangement; the main axis of the temple is north and south, while the side door admits the eastern sunlight.

Our Period V. shows Greece under the yoke of Rome, a condition less to be deplored since the Grecian states had proved their inability for self-unification, and Rome's political protectorate enabled the Greek artistic spirit gradually to revive, or at least to be preserved from utter extinction. As the riches of the world poured into Rome, the demands of luxury attracted the people who alone possessed the art instincts capable of catering to their political masters, to whose vulgarity we must attribute the frequent exhibitions of perverted taste.

The Roman buildings in Greece worthy of note are but few, and their ruins usually overlie earlier Greek work. A small circular temple 23 feet in diameter dedicated to Rome and

Augustus confronted the east end of the Parthenon. On the south slope of the Acropolis Herodes Atticus dedicated an odeum to his wife and at Olympia he built an exedra. At the Argive Heræum are remains of a building whose hollow floor and wall construction resembled that of the baths at Pompeii ; the upper floor, supported on small piers about 2 feet high and 2 feet apart on centres, was constructed of large tiles laid on the piers, over which was spread concrete and finally a mosaic or tile pavement. The air, warmed in a furnace room, percolated under the floors and throughout special hollow tile lining in the side walls. These wall tiles were coated with plaster which was probably painted while still fresh. At Olympia are ruins of Roman thermæ and of a house attributed to Nero, while throughout Greece are traces of Roman aqueducts and walls.

Hadrian's era of affected eclecticism transported and confused the styles of all countries ; the arch in Athens which marks the quarter built by Hadrian and the huge Corinthian columns of the Olympeion, though grand, are discordant elements in the city of Athens.

The Byzantine period (VI.) finds Greece still but a province of the vast Roman empire, an empire now rapidly disintegrating. This period derives its title from Byzantium (Constantinople), where is found its most beautiful type, S. Sophia. It is limited from the reign of Constantine, 325 A.D. to 1453, when Constantinople fell before the Mohammedan conquerors.

The architectural elements which compose the Byzantine style had, however, been gradually assembling for centuries before the time of Constantine, and are traceable in early ages to Egypt, Assyria, and Persia. The chief characteristic of this style is the dome, supported on pendentives springing from a square or rectangular plan. Monasteries, convents, small churches, and chapels are found throughout Greece often occupying sites originally sacred to the pagan cult, but as examples of Byzantine architecture they are small and unimportant. (See Byzantine Architecture.)

During the Turkish period (VII.) from 1453 to the War of Independence, 1831, Greece lay prostrate under Mohammedan rule, almost dead to the world. Her art was stationary.

These four centuries may be passed over quickly, as there is nothing of special interest in the Turkish fortresses, mosques, or minarets to warrant delay.

The modern period (VIII.) begins with the successful expulsion of the Turk. It is a period of hopeful anticipation rather than one of especial achievement thus far. The latent Greek spirit has not had time to recuperate after centuries of oppression. Modern architecture in Greece is not indigenous. Austrians and Germans have designed most of her buildings, of which the royal palace, the Zappeion, the National Museum, Academy of Science, university, and Dr. Schliemann's house, all in Athens, are most noteworthy.

The type of the villagers' house in Greece to-day can differ but little from that of ancient times. A yard or court is enclosed by high walls except such spaces as are occupied by the dwelling, stables, and outhouses. The building material is sun-dried or mud brick. An exterior stone stairway leads to the second story of the house, which, like the ground floor, usually consists of but one room.

Henry Fanshawe Tozer, *Lectures of the Geography of Greece* ; Henry Fanshawe Tozer, *The Islands of the Ægean* ; Joanne, *Guides — Grèce, I, Athènes et ses environs* ; Joanne, *Guides — Grèce, II, Grèce continentale et Îles* ; and other guidebooks. A. Couchaud, *Choix d'Églises Byzantines en Grèce*, 1842 ; Auguste Choisy, *L'Art de bâtir chez les Byzantins*, 1883 ; *Gazette des Beaux Arts*, 1897, Article on Mistra by Lucien Magne ; R. W. Schultz and S. H. Barnaby, *Byzantine Architecture in Greece* (not yet published).

— EDWARD L. TILTON.

GREENHOUSE. A building of which the roof and some, at least, of the sides are glazed sashes, contrived for the protection and growth of exotic and tender plants incapable of enduring the open air during the colder months of the year ; to afford to native plants the advantage of perpetual summer through the inclement season ; or to force the growth of flowers, fruits, and vegetables. In order to obtain the conditions of temperature necessary to these purposes, greenhouses are generally provided with artificial heat and means of ventilation. They are the adjunct of gardens, and, according to their especial functions, are distinguished as conservatories, which properly are for the preservation of tender plants, whether potted or bedded ; hothouses, or forcing houses, where a higher temperature is maintained with the necessary degree of humidity ; orchid houses, provided with tropical heat ; warm and cold graperies. There are also many specific subdivisions, such as palm houses, orangeries, rose houses, etc., including glazed buildings of many sorts for the growth of specific market produce. Greenhouses to accommodate flowering and ornamental plants in general are provided with ranges of open shelving for pots, approximately corresponding with the slope of the glazed roof, whether single or double, with a shelf or bed of soil for propagating purposes against the outer wall, and a narrow passage between. The old custom of setting the glass in wooden frames with putty is now in good work superseded by framing the glass in metal sashes contrived with gutters to carry off the water of condensation, as in the system known as the Rendle System.

The form and height of greenhouses are subject to many variations according to use; for lofty tropical plants they are built with greater height, and often with curvilinear roofs, domes, pavilions, and transepts of decorative character.

When attached to, and forming part of, a dwelling house, the greenhouse becomes a place rather for the display, than specifically for the preservation and growth, of ornamental and flowering plants, and has a decorative character adapted to its position as an element in a general architectural scheme. When so placed it is, by common but strictly incorrect usage, called a conservatory; and when considerably enlarged, so as to occupy a court with a glazed roof, it becomes properly a winter garden (jardin d'hiver), where not only potted and tubbed, but bedded, plants are displayed, with fountains, statuary, and other decorative adjuncts. (See Conservatory; Forcing House; Grapery; Hot-house.) — H. Van Brunt.

GREENLAND, ARCHITECTURE OF. The modern structures are the Danish houses of European pattern adapted to the extreme cold, and the huts of the Eskimo. In the line of ancient architectural works are the remains of stone churches and other buildings of the early Norsemen. At Katortok the walls of a church still stand almost entire. The masonry is not coursed. (See Iglu; Iglugeak; Snow House.) — F. S. D.

GREEN ROOM. Same as Foyer, in the sense of a place of meeting of the actors in a theatre; the original English word for such a room, which, however, was generally a very poor and plain room originally hung and furnished with green, though no particular reason for that custom is alleged.

GREETING HOUSE. A reception room or place of meeting connected with a church or convent in early Christian times. — (C. D.)

GREMP, HANS. (See Hans Von Strasburg.)

GREPON. A council house of Nicaragua Indians.

GRIFFE. In French, a claw; but by extension, a spur or projection; in English, a spur projecting from the round base of a column and filling a part of the triangle formed by the projection of the square plinth below. The primary use of this is to give the column a broader base and to diminish the amount of the cutting away of the solid stone. The griffe, however, is often used for elaborate ornamentation, being carved into vegetable or even animal form. Its use is chiefly confined to mediæval styles.

GRIFFIN. In decorative art, an imaginary creature compounded of lion and eagle. The more common representations show lion's paws, eagle's wings, and a head furnished with a hooked beak. In Greco-Roman art these creatures occur in sculptured friezes on marble urns,

and the like, but they are more effectively used in Italian Romanesque art, where admirably designed creatures of this sort are used for the supports of the columns of church porches.

GRIGI, GIOVANNI GIACOMO; architect; d. Sept. 15, 1572.

The son of Guglielmo Grigi (see Grigi, G.). In 1550 he succeeded Scarpagnino (see Abbondi) as *protomaestro* of the Scuola di S. Rocco, Venice. May 22, 1567, with a Magistro Andrea della Vecchia, he contracted to build the church of S. Giorgio Maggiore at Venice according to the designs of Andrea Palladio (see Palladio).

Paoletti, *Rinascimento in Venezia*, Vol. II.

GRIGI, GUGLIELMO DI GIACOMO, of Alzano ("Guglielmo Bergamasco," Temanza); architect and sculptor (*lapicida*), in Venice; d. 1550.

Grigi's most important work is the charming Capella Emiliana at the church of S. Michele in Isola near Venice. He assisted in the construction of the Procuratie Vecchie, the church of S. Andrea della Certosa (destroyed), the choir of the church of S. Antonio, and the Scuola di S. Rocco, all in Venice, and the Palazzo della Ragione in Vicenza.

Paoletti, *Rinascimento in Venezia;* Müntz, *Renaissance;* Temanza, *Vite*.

GRILLAGE. A grating or structure of timbers laid horizontally side by side and crossed by others, and so on for several thicknesses, the whole being intended to carry a foundation on

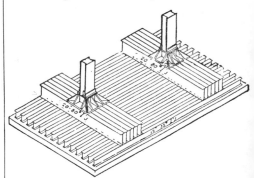

GRILLAGE OF STEEL I BEAMS, WITH TWO IRON BOX-COLUMNS AND THEIR SHOES.

piling or on soil not otherwise fit to receive it. By immediate transference to new material, a similar structure made of bars of iron or steel, such as rolled rails. (See Foundation; also illustration of Crib.)

GRILLE. In French, a grating of any sort, especially of light ironwork, such as a gridiron, or a grate of a fireplace. Architecturally, in French, and by adoption in English, a defence of metal, usually wrought-iron bars, high enough and close set enough to prevent the passage of a body, and serving in this way to enclose a courtyard or the grounds around a public building; or to fill up the place between two masonry piers, or between two pavilions of a building. The term in English is generally restricted to something rather elaborate and architectural in character. In this sense the word is used sometimes for a metal window guard, even when the opening is small. It is customary also to use the term as synonymous with gate when a doorway is closed by a swinging or sliding grating instead of a solid door. — R. S.

GRILL ROOM. A room in a restaurant, hotel, or club where it is supposed that the chief entertainment afforded is broiled meat, such as chops, steaks, etc., served promptly at tables placed near the fire used for the broiling.

GRIMALDI, FRA FRANCESCO; architect.

Grimaldi's first work in Naples was the convent and church (1590) of S. Apostoli. In 1608 he built the fine Capella del Tesoro at the cathedral, Naples. He built the church of S. Maria degli Angeli at Pizzo-Falcone near Naples. The reconstruction of the church of S. Paolo Maggiore, Naples, was accomplished from his designs after his death.

Sasso, *Storia de' Monumenti di Napoli;* Gurlitt, *Geschichte des Barockstiles in Italien;* Ebe, *Spät-Renaissance.*

GRIMUHALDUS; architect.

The crypt of the cathedral of Sutri, Italy, is signed by him: *Grimuhaldus presbyter accolyta.* It was built in the twelfth century.

Frothingham, *Roman Artists of the Middle Ages.*

GRISAILLE. Painting in monochrome, especially in rather delicate gray. By extension, any flat ornamentation which is devoid of effects of colour; thus, ornamental windows composed of uncoloured but rough and not perfectly transparent glass set in lead sash are commonly said to be *en grisaille.* The term is generally used as a French word.

GROIN. The arris formed by the salient between two intersecting vaults. In the most common form of vaulting with groins the vaults which intersect one another are simple barrel vaults, and each groin, beginning at the spring in a solid angle usually of ninety degrees, increases in obtuseness of angle as it ascends, and, where the vaults are of equal height, gradually passes into nothing, the surfaces being practically continuous at the crown of the vault. (See Vault.)

GROIN ARCH. A piece of arched construction forming in some way the angle between two simple vaults. The term has no accurate significance, and is applied erroneously to the

diagonal rib of a ribbed vault, and also to the whole of a groined vault taken together. The only sense in which it can be rightly used seems to be in the series of larger and more carefully dressed stones laid as voussoirs in the angle between intersecting arches in which stones the groin is worked.

GROINED VAULTING. (See Vault, and Groin Vault under Vault.)

GROIN: VAULTS WITH GROINS; DORSETSHIRE, C. 1110.

GROINING. Properly, the meeting of simple vaults, such as barrel vaults, at an angle so as to form a more elaborate structure. (See Groin Vault, under Vault.) By extension, the building of groined vaults generally.

Underpitch Groining. The groining and also the groined vaulting resulting from the intersection of a larger and higher vault by smaller ones. It is generally assumed that the larger and the smaller vaults spring from the same plane and have the same, or nearly the same, shape, viz., of semicircular section; the smaller vaults will then intersect the larger one but will not reach above its haunches.

Welsh Groining. Same as Underpitch Groining.

GROIN POINT. A groin in the strict sense given above; a mason's term to designate the actual arris.

GROIN RIB. The diagonal rib in a ribbed vault occupying the place where a groin might be constructed; an erroneous expression, as a ribbed vault is not groined.

GROOVE. A narrow continuous sinking, usually of the same width and depth throughout. Grooves are worked on the edges of boards and planks for the purpose of making tongued and grooved flooring and sheathing.

GROSE, FRANCIS; antiquary; b. about 1731; d. May 12, 1791.

Grose published in 1773 the first number of his *Antiquities of England and Wales*, and completed the work in 1787 (London, 4 vols. folio). The *Antiquities of Scotland* was published in 1789–1791 (London, 2 vols. 4to). The *Antiquities of Ireland*, begun by him, was published after his death by Dr. Edward Ledwich (London, 1791–1795, 2 vols. 4to). The *Military Antiquities* appeared in 1796–1798 (London, 2 vols. 4to).

Stephen, *Dictionary of National Biography*.

GROSSETESTE (GREATHEAD), ROBERT; Bishop of Lincoln; d. 1253.

Robert Grosseteste, Bishop of Lincoln, is supposed to have built, or to have caused to be built, the transept of the cathedral of Lincoln, England, to have completed the nave, and to have carried the central tower (rood tower) to the beginning of the upper story.

Pegge, *Robert Grosseteste;* Storer, *Cathedral Church of Lincoln*.

GROT. Properly, a cave; in architecture, a piece of rockwork in which a cave is simulated.

GROTESQUE. *A.* Properly, having to do with a cave or caves; hence, rude, not according to system or the canons of art, wild, irregular, confused.

B. By extension, in describing ornament which is of a new or unexpected character, akin to the original use of Arabesque, fantastic and unclassed. The monsters and the exaggerated human and animal forms of mediæval sculpture are often called by this term, and so are the strange creatures, half human and half animal, and the scrollwork in which a part of the body of a man or a beast emerges from a flower; which the Renaissance artists inherited from the Roman imperial painting.

Used as a substantive in each of these senses.
           — R. S.

GROTTO. Same as Grot.

GROUND (I.). Anything used to fix a limit or to regulate the thickness or projection of the more permanent or of exterior finished work. The term is generally used in the plural; thus, grounds in ordinary building are pieces of wood secured to the jamb of a doorway, as in a brick wall, or to the base of a stud partition, to stop the plastering at the edge and to determine its thickness, and to these grounds the wooden trim may be nailed, or the grounds may be removed. Also, any strip secured to a wall, and more or less embedded in the plaster, to furnish a nailing, as to secure a wooden mantel, heavy trim, or the like. — D. N. B. S.

GROUND (II.). *A.* In painting, the surface of uniform colour upon which ornaments and the like are relieved, corresponding nearly to Background in relief sculpture, and to the French *champ*.

B. (Used attributively) having to do with the ground or background; thus, ground colour is the colour used for the ground as in definition *A*.

GROUND FLOOR. Properly, that floor of a building which is most nearly on a level with the surrounding surface of the ground. By extension, same as Ground Story.

GROUND STORY. That story of a building the floor of which is nearly on a level with the surrounding surface of the ground. The term should be limited to such a story when its floor is not more than two or three steps above or below the sidewalk in a city, or the courtyard, greensward, or the like, nearest approaching it, in the country. Thus, in the case of a house with a high stoop, as in many American cities where the principal floor is seven feet above the sidewalk, and the floor of the basement story is five feet below it, there is properly no ground story.

GROUPED. Standing in close proximity to one another but not in contact; said of columns when more than two are brought near together, especially in the case of the compound piers of Gothic architecture, where a large central column or pier has small shafts set a few inches from it, as especially in Salisbury cathedral. Such a pier is described as consisting of grouped shafts. (See Clustered Column.)

GROUPING. *A.* The act of arranging buildings or parts of buildings in a definite way, and for architectural effect.

B. The state of being grouped or arranged.

C. A group with reference to the nature of the assemblage or the greater or less merit of the artistic effect produced. The simplest grouping is that where two buildings or two important wings, pavilions, or the like, resembling one another closely, are set in a sort of pairing. Thus, on the Campidoglio at Rome, the two buildings whose design is ascribed to Michelangelo, one occupied by the Capitoline Museum and the other called the Palace of the Conservators, are set face to face, with the width of the square between them. This group, however, may be considered as made up into a triple group either by considering the Palace of the Senator as forming a third member, or even by reference to the equestrian statue of Marcus Aurelius which is halfway between their fronts; or the whole layout of the square, with the three buildings on three sides and the important and celebrated statue in the middle, may be considered together as a group of four parts. So, in the case of the two towers of Notre Dame looked at from the west; they may be considered together as a group of two united by a much smaller central division, or the very strong horizontal divisions of the façade may be considered as more important than the vertical divisions made by the towers, and the front may be taken all together as a group of three principal parts, of which only the upper part is divided into a group of three.

This possibility of looking at any group from several different points of view has produced extreme vagueness in the common discussions of the subject. Fancied resemblances between a smaller architectural object, as a member of a building, and a much larger structure, as an entire building, are also introduced into the discussion. Thus, in the case of our lofty tower-like business buildings erected since 1880, it is assumed that the comparison to a column or pillar is safe and is complete; and it is asserted as a positive rule of design for such structures that they should be divided into a base, a high and comparatively plain shaft, and a crowning structure which is likened to a capital. If, however, these buildings are compared to the finest steeples in existence, a different system of grouping at once appears, namely, the division into vertical wall and high and slender roof, with perhaps an intermediate member which, if it exists, may be much smaller than either the upper or the lower part just described, or may be as large and prominent as, for instance, the roof or spire. If, then, one should take a tower-like twenty-story building which had been previously divided into a group of three parts as above suggested, and if to that were added four or five stories more in the way of a rooflike or spirelike pavilion, the group would be at once changed and the inadequacy of the previous arrangement would appear, for the new group of four parts would be far more effective than the old group of three. So in the case of horizontal grouping. It is a good general principle to have a central feature, and many a simple house front with one or two windows or groups of windows in each story may be saved from disorderly insignificance by a very small but well-placed feature, as a niche, a panel with inscription, or the like. On the other hand, the immense variety of the possible groupings in such cases, and still more in the case of large and varied buildings with many pavilions, towers, separate roofs, and the like, is so great that hitherto the makers of rules of architectural design have generally avoided the subject. The book named below is a serious attempt at reducing to order the various theories upon this subject, and of providing a possible working basis for further study.

John Beverly Robinson, *Principles of Architectural Composition; an attempt to order and phrase ideas which have hitherto been only felt by the instinctive taste of designers.* New York, 1899.

— R. S.

GROUT. Mortar made thin for pouring into the interstices of a masonry wall; for spreading over a bed of concrete to form a smooth finish; and for other similar purposes where the use of stiff mortar is unpractical.

GRÜBER, BERNHARD; architect; b. 1806.

Grüber studied painting and architecture at the academy of Munich, Bavaria. He was employed on the restoration of the cathedral of Regensburg, Bavaria, and in 1842 went to Prague, where in 1844 he was appointed professor in the Academy of Art. A list of his works is given in Wurzbach (op. cit.).

Wurzbach, *Biographisches Lexikon.*

GRÜNBERG, MARTIN; architect.

After March 24, 1699, he was royal director of buildings at Berlin, Prussia. He built the *Kölnische Rathhaus,* and the *Garnisonkirche,* and began the Friedrichs Hospital, all in Berlin.

Borrmann, *Denkmäler von Berlin.*

GRÜNE GEWÖLBE (The Green Vaults). In Dresden, Germany, the ground floor chambers of the royal palace; so called from the original colours of the decorations, and containing a vast collection of costly decorative objects. The vaults themselves are not of importance.

GUARD BAR. Any bar serving as a protection or means of security; especially, a slight parapet, as set above the sill of a window, and secured commonly to the jamb on either side, thus permitting persons within to lean upon it in comparative safety while looking out of the window. It commonly consists merely of a single bar, but is often a quite elaborate structure, and may project from the face of the wall so as to enclose a considerable space above a wide sill, as is common in Italian residences.
— D. N. B. S.

GUARD CHAMBER. Same as Guard Room.

GUARD HOUSE. *A.* A building, as in a fortress, a prison, or the like, in which the guard is stationed. Its purpose is the same as that of the Guard Room.

B. Locally, or perhaps anciently, the term retained in certain districts for a jail or place of confinement.

GUARD ROOM. A room in a fortress or the like, usually near the entrance gateway; large, permanent, and intended for the use of the guard for twenty-four hours, for the night, or the like. As it is from the guard, so chosen and separated from the rest of the military force, that the sentinels are taken, and as the term of sentry duty is always brief, the larger part of the guard is generally free from immediate duty and may find shelter in the guard room.

GUARINI, D. GUARINO; architect; b. 1624 (at Modena, Italy); d. 1685.

Guarini was a Theatine monk who carried the baroque style in Italy to its extreme development. In 1674 he became the court architect to the Duke Carlo Emmanuele II. of Savoy. He served also his successor, the King Vittorio Amadeo I. His most extraordinary buildings are the domical church of S. Lorenzo and the sanctuary (also domical) of the Madonna della Consolata, both in Turin. He built about 1657 the mortuary chapel of the house of Savoy at the church of S. Giovanni (Turin). Buildings were erected from Guarini's designs at Lisbon and Prague. He built the Theatine church of S. Anne on the Quai Voltaire, Paris, which has been destroyed. Guarini was a speculative writer on philosophy and mathematics. His last work was an *Architettura civile*.

Gurlitt, *Geschichte des Barockstiles in Italien;* Ebe, *Spät-Renaissance*.

GUDGEON. *A.* The stationary portion of a simple wrought-iron hinge, forming a pintle or eye to hold the movable leaf, which is usually a band or strap. It has a flaring end which is secured in a masonry jamb, or a plate or strap which may be bolted or screwed to the woodwork. (See Hook and Eye Hinge, under Hinge.)

B. In certain parts of Great Britain, a member in the framing of a roof. Its exact character and place vary with locality.

GUÉRIN, CLAUDE; builder (*entrepreneur*) and architect.

Guérin was one of the first constructors employed on the chapel of the Valois at Saint-Denis, near Paris. After 1571 he built the Hôtel de Soissons under the direction of Jean Bullant (see Bullant).

De Laborde, *Comptes des bâtiments du roi;* Bauchal, *Dictionnaire*.

GUEST HOUSE. *A.* In a large establishment, such as a convent, especially in the Middle Ages, a building prepared for the use of strangers.

B. A place of public entertainment ; an inn.

GUGLIA. In Italian, a building or part of a building, having the shape of a pyramid, obelisk, or pinnacle. Any building having a generally upright and slender form, when not easily classified under some other technical name ; thus, a small pagoda or tope, or a monument of undescribed architectural character, or an elaborate German stove of enamelled earthenware may be said to be a guglia or of guglia form. (Also Aguglia.)

GUGLIELMO, FRA. (See Agnelli, Guglielmo.)

GUGLIELMO DA MARCILLA. (See Marcillat, Guillaume de.)

GUILD. Formerly, and to a limited extent in modern usage, an association of merchants, artisans, or mechanics, both employees and masters, of the same trade or similar trades, organized for mutual protection, advancement, and the instruction of apprentices bound over to the association ; and also for benevolent pur-

poses, as in providing for destitute members, bearing the expenses of burial, and the like.

There is very little information regarding *hetairies* or associations of craftsmen among the Greeks : one evident fact is the considerable amount of individual freedom allowed to the architect[1] as compared to his condition under Roman rule.

Rome. In ancient Italy the colleges of craftsmen were organized at an early date, — perhaps even in the kingly period, — but were discouraged by the first emperors as dangerous institutions. Hadrian himself an amateur architect — decided not only to recognize them, but to organize them under strict government control, enrolling in them the mass of the working population and using them as an important part of the huge administrative machine. In return for exemption from military service and taxation, the members of these colleges (*collegia*) were obliged to give their expert services to the State for a small remuneration, the amount of which was determined by the State. A tariff for such services was issued by the Emperor Diocletian. The following further restrictions were placed on individual liberty : (1) No member was allowed to change his occupation ; (2) the occupation was made hereditary, the father teaching it to his sons ; (3) no member was allowed to change his residence, transferring from the *collegium* of one city to that of another, and any one violating this rule was brought back by force ; (4) apparently no one who did not belong to such a *collegium* was allowed to exercise any manual occupation. Hence the craftsman's condition involved : compulsory public service ; hereditary occupation ; obligatory membership of some college. When we add to this that the ordinary labour under the direction of these master craftsmen (aside from their own assistants) was secured by forced *corvée*, and that the materials for construction were furnished by the State, which received lumber, bricks, stone, and lime as tax in kind, we can understand both the rapid erection and the immense number of Roman public monuments. On the other hand, the craftsmen were allowed to work by contract for private individuals.

Each *collegium* had its meeting house and office called *schola*. It had a president under whom was a secretary, and the members were subdivided into groups of tens (decuries) and hundreds (centuries), each group being regularly officered as if it were a military organization. Regular instruction in the various branches seems to have been given at the *schola*, and sometimes a stipend was attached

[1] Throughout this article the word "architect" is used in its etymological sense as master builder or master of the works, without reference to the modern profession.

to the teaching. The Theodosian Code says, "Architects enjoy immunity so that they may the more easily teach the practice of their art to their children." The number of colleges connected with construction was considerable, owing to the Roman tendency to specialize. The builders of scaffolds and constructors of centres, the marble cutters, marble incrusters, hewers of timber, and quarryers, each had their separate organization. This specialization was carried still further within the college itself. Thus, among the stone masons and wall builders, one set worked on foundations, another on walls, and still another on arches and vaults.

Thus heredity and subdivision of labour made for immobility of style and methods.

Besides the imperial laws affecting all corporations throughout the empire, some of which are preserved in the *Codex Theodosianus*, each corporation had its special regulations about such matters as membership requirements, fees, meetings, religious ceremonies, artistic and technical standards, aid to poor artisans, funeral services, etc. Thus far detailed information on most of these points is scanty. It is certain that both citizens and freedmen belonged to the colleges; the remaining inscriptions point to a predominance of freedmen over citizens in the case of the architects.

Owing to enforced residence and differences in their private standards, local schools were developed in various parts of the empire. It is, however, evident that the restrictive laws were enforced only in Italy — especially in Rome. In the East an antique Greek liberty was encouraged, and after the seat of power was transferred to Constantinople the restrictions were practically dropped; they found no place in the laws of Justinian, though the associations of artisans in Constantinople were already becoming troublesome.

Byzantium. The condition of the colleges in the Orient in the matter of organization appears to have varied but little from the time of Justinian to the present day. At the head of each was and is a proto-magister, assisted by a secretary. Though the corporations were local their members travelled periodically, singly or in bodies, enjoying the hospitality of and offering their services to brother guildsmen in other places. In their individual freedom and in other ways the Byzantine were far more closely allied than the Roman associations to our mediæval guilds. In Antioch, Alexandria, Milan, and especially Ravenna the colleges continued to flourish during the early Byzantine period, and in Rome itself they survived all vicissitudes until the end of the Middle Ages, though their name was changed from *collegium* to *schola*, from their place of meeting. Taken

as a whole the *scholæ*, as distinguished from clergy and nobles, represented the people, and wielded great power.

Lombardy. When the Lombards devastated Italy (end sixth century), they did not entirely extinguish these associations within their new territory; and when the Lombards turned to civilization they called on the guilds for architects and granted them privileges. This is shown by the Lombard laws, issued in 643 by Rotari, and in 742 by Luitbrand. Here the master architects are called *magistri commacini*, their responsibilities defined, and a maximum tariff of prices set for different kinds of work, in faint imitation of the Roman regulations. The companions or colleagues of these *magistri*, themselves not yet passed masters, are also mentioned. Such master masons are spoken of in other Lombard documents of Lucca, Toscanella, etc. As they could hold property and make contracts they were evidently not slaves, as the mass of Romans certainly were under the Lombards. Though at first of Roman descent, the *magistri commacini* soon admitted Lombards to membership in their associations. They built in either of two manners — the *Gallic*, or wood construction, and the *Roman*, or stone and brick construction.

A great deal of nonsense has been written by grave authorities on these *magistri commacini;* chapters and even volumes have been based on the supposition that Commacinus means "a native of Como," and that this region was so specifically the centre of the revival of architecture under the Lombards as to give its name to the profession of architect; master from Como = architect. Such a fact would be without a parallel, and is, besides, an etymological blunder. The word *com-macinus* is from the same stem as *macio*, the common late Latin word for stonemason, with the addition of the collective prefix, and may also be connected with the current Byzantine word for practical architect, *mechanicos*.

Middle Ages. The multiplication of lay artists in Italy as soon as the arts were patronized, in the eleventh and twelfth centuries, proves the activity and existence, in many parts of Italy, of the Commacine associations, and the records show that they travelled great distances. Compared with the rest of monk-ridden Europe Italy shows, then, only an infinitesimal percentage of monastic as compared with lay architects. Some of the mediæval guilds that then sprang up were modelled directly, like those of Venice, on Byzantine originals; others in Lombardy and Rome went back to classic models; while the Tuscan, latest of all, were based on Lombard models. In one respect Roman tradition ruled quite generally, — the transmission of occupation in the same family. This can best be studied in the signed monuments of the Roman mediæval school, where a family can be traced through four or five generations (families of Paulus, Ranuccius, Laurentius), and each family could keep a large workshop in which the various branches of decoration as well as construction were taught and practised. In this particular — the practice of several branches of art by a single artist — these associations differed fundamentally from the ancient Roman.

These Italian guilds, as they increased in membership and developed in artistic methods, found it necessary to reduce to writing their statutes and regulations, which may at first have been handed down orally. This was done during the thirteenth and fourteenth centuries, in every city of any size and artistic spirit (Venice, Pisa, Lucca, Florence, Siena, Perugia, Bologna, etc.). The guild was very careful to guard its reputation by stringent requirements of artistic integrity and thoroughness, and regulated even the maximum number of apprentices for each master, and the quality of the material used, as well as the methods for settling all disputes.

Freemasons. In the flood of literature on the modern Freemasons, the attempt has often been made to connect their mysterious signs and symbols and their vows of secrecy with the mediæval guilds, and their origin has even been carried back to ancient times through the *magistri commacini*. While there is no proof of such connection, there is a certain analogy interesting to examine. In the first place, there is both literary and monumental evidence for believing that in the architectural revival early in the eleventh century the Italian *commacini* took a leading part, erecting in the Rhenish province, in Burgundy, and in Normandy monuments that were in a style different from anything then known in France and Germany, and which served as models to native artists. This fact is not sufficiently recognized. In the rest of Europe the artistic field had been occupied exclusively by monks since before the Carlovingian period. It is therefore probable that the impulse given by these incoming Lombard artists to the practice of architecture by the laity led to the formation of guilds of lay artists in Northern Europe, where they came into existence, certainly long after Italy was honeycombed by them, toward the close of the twelfth century.

As to the element of secrecy and mystic signs in connection with the guilds, it seems purely mythical, and the idea is due probably to the following circumstances. Of all crafts that of architecture — as Vitruvius contends — had always been supposed to require the broadest as well as the deepest knowledge. When the crafts were at a low ebb, even the modicum of

geometric and static knowledge preserved by the architects of the decadence must have seemed remarkable. In the time of Charlemagne it is evident that Vitruvius — as Eginhard shows — was still used, and even for those incapable of understanding him some equivalent knowledge was generally transmitted orally or in writing from one generation to another, within a limited group. This monopoly or patent was held as a valuable secret. But the secrecy was then and afterward purely professional — not political or anti-religious. Then the strange or mythical animals and symbols carved on so many churches are supposed to be part of masonic mystery; it has long since been demonstrated that these weird productions have a symbolic meaning, taken straight from those popular mediæval fables, the *Bestiaries*, whose origin is even attributed to St. Augustine. Finally, there are signs cut in mediæval monuments which receive the same interpretation. These are really of several classes : (1) quarry marks, which usually disappear on finished monuments, and the like of which have always been in use since early Egyptian times ; (2) builders' marks, which are often so cut as to be visible after the structure is completed, and originally made in order to indicate the exact position of each block or member ; (3) masons' signatures, monograms, or conventional marks, which we find occasionally on ancient monuments, and very frequently in Byzantine architecture. Evidently there is nothing special to Freemasonry in all this.

There remains but one point, the secret watchwords, signs, or grips by which the " brother " was recognized. It has often been shown how closely the different lodges of an art association were bound together, and what frequent relations the lay architects, as great travellers, must have had with lodges in other cities, which were bound to give them help and hospitality. The inference of the use of secret signs for purposes of recognition is obvious, but not proven until their use in Germany in the fifteenth century.

There is no sign that the Italian local lodges of architects ever joined in a confederation ; but this was the case in Germany, where the lodge of Strasburg, doubtless the oldest and founded from France in the thirteenth century, was made the supreme lodge in the fifteenth century, with authority over the others throughout Germany. In northern France and Flanders the guilds acquired even more power than in Germany. Probably it was in Germany, however, where the fight with the nobles and clergy was more difficult, that the associations of artisans had recourse to those secret methods that have given colour to the pretensions of Freemasonry, though their laws and statutes received approval and were published (1563). With the preponderance of the individualism of the Renaissance, the importance of the associations gradually waned in Italy, and was practically extinct there in the sixteenth century. Their continuance was largely *pro forma*. During the seventeenth century, with the cessation of their usefulness came the transformations that made them seem dangerous to public order, and led to the coercive measures of the eighteenth century throughout Europe, which gave Masonry its stamp of secrecy. — A. L. FROTHINGHAM, Jr.

GUILDHALL. A hall for the meetings of the controlling members of a guild, association of artisans, or merchants, or persons associated together without primary religious purpose ; an institution originating in England in the earlier Middle Ages. The separate halls of ancient guilds in London are known by other names (see Company Hall, under Hall). In modern times, a municipal building is commonly called guildhall, as in Bristol, York, Plymouth.

The Guildhall, especially so called, is in London, on King Street, and is a municipal building, deriving its name probably from the custom of permitting the different guilds to hold meetings in it ; for its purpose has always been connected with the municipality itself. The present structure was partly built after the Great Fire in 1666, and then wholly rebuilt in 1789 in a fantastic Gothic style, but in 1866 restorations were begun, a new open timber roof constructed, and the front brought to more strictly archæological correctness. — R. S.

GUILLAIN, AUGUSTIN ; builder and architect ; b. Jan. 4, 1581 ; d. June 6, 1636.

A son of Pierre Guillain (see Guillain, P.). He was associated with his father, and in 1613 replaced him as director of the public works of the city of Paris. At the old Hôtel de Ville, Paris, he built the pavillion on the left behind the Pavillon du S. Esprit.

(For bibliography, see Guillain, P.)

GUILLAIN, GUILLAUME ; builder (*entrepreneur*) and architect ; d. after 1582.

Guillaume Guillain married a Pierette Chambiges, who is supposed to have been a daughter of Pierre Chambiges (I.) (see Chambiges, Pierre, I.), and appears to have succeeded him about 1544 as *maître des œuvres* of the city of Paris. With Jehan Langeois, he engaged to build the châteaux of Saint Gemain-en-Laye and La Muette, according to the contract which had been made with Pierre Chambiges (I.), Sept. 22, 1539. Between 1555 and 1568 he received large payments for the construction of that portion of the Louvre which was designed by Pierre Lescot (see Lescot). In 1578 he assisted at the deliberations relative to the Pont Neuf, Paris.

Berty, *Topographie, Louvre et Tuileries ;* Palustre, *Renaissance ;* De Laborde, *Comptes des bâtiments du roi.*

GUILLAIN, PIERRE ; builder (*entrepreneur*) and architect.

A son of Guillaume Guillain (see Guillain, G.). He was associated with his father, after 1575, in the direction of the public works of the city of Paris, and in 1578 in the deliberations relative to the construction of the Pont Neuf. April 20, 1582, he succeeded his father. From 1594 until after 1600 Guillain was associated with Pierre Chambiges (II.) (see Chambiges, Pierre, II.) and others in the construction of the western half of the Grande Galerie of the Louvre and the adjacent parts of the Tuileries.

Berty, *Topographie, Louvre et Tuileries ;* Herluison, *Actes de l'état civil ;* Vachon, *Hôtel de Ville.*

GUILLAUME DE MARCILLAT. (See Marcillat, Guillaume de.)

GUILLAUME DU CHÂTEAU ; abbot and architect.

Guillaume was abbot of Mont-Saint-Michel (Manche, France) from 1299 to 1314. He rebuilt his monastery, which had been nearly destroyed by lightning in July, 1300.

Corroyer, *Abbaye du Mont-Saint-Michel.*

GUILLOCHE. An ornament composed of curved lines usually intersecting with one another, differing from a fret or meander which is composed of straight lines. As the French term *guilloche* has no such exact and limited meaning, so the English term is often used for any ornament composed of interlacing lines, bands, ribbons, or the like. (Also guiloche.)

GUINAMUNDUS, GUINAMOND ; monk and architect.

In a manuscript of the monk Genoux, at the Bibliothèque Nationale, it is recorded that Guinamundus, a monk of the monastery of Chaise-Dieu, made the monument of S. Front, first bishop of Perigueux, at the cathedral of that city, in the year 1077.

Branche, *L'Auvergne au moyen âge ;* Chennevières, *Archives de l'art français.*

GULA. A moulding or group of mouldings having a large hollow, as a cove or cavetto. The term is used also as synonymous with Ogee.

GULIMARI DA PIPERNO, PETRUS ; architect.

According to an inscription, Petrus and his sons, Morisu and Jacobus, built the church at San Lorenzo, now Amaseno, Italy, finished 1291.

Frothingham, *Roman Artists of the Middle Ages.*

GUMPP, GEORG ANTON ; architect ; b. 1670 ; d. 1730.

Gumpp was one of the most important architects of the baroque style in Germany. His best works are the S. Jacobskirche (1717–1724), the S. Johanniskirche (1729), the Landhaus (1719–1728), the Turn und Taxis palace, all at Innsbruck in the Tyrol.

Gurlitt, *Geschichte des Barockstiles in Deutschland.*

GUNAIKEIOS ; GUNAIKONITIS. Same as Gynæceum.

GUNDULF ; ecclesiastic and architect ; b. about 1024 ; d. 1108.

Born in France, and became about 1060 a monk of the Abbey of Bec. In 1077 he was appointed Bishop of Rochester, England, by Lanfranc (see Lanfranc). He built, or caused to be built, the cathedral of Rochester. Of his work, a part of the crypt, a part of the west front, and the tower on the north side remain. For William the Conqueror, he built the Great White Tower in London.

Bayley, *Tower of London ;* Storer, *History of Rochester Cathedral ;* Wharton, *Anglia Sacra ;* Britton and Brayley, *Memoirs of the Tower of London.*

GUNTER'S CHAIN. A chain, each link of which is composed of a steel bar with a small ring at each end, the bars having a fixed

GUTTER: MODERN CHURCH OF S. JEAN-BAPTISTE DE BELLEVILLE, PARIS.
Metal gutter on stone wall-cornice.

length and larger subdivisions being marked by pieces of brass of a recognized form secured at every tenth link to the rings which join the links. Until recently this was the implement always used in Great Britain and the United States for measuring land; each link was 7.92 inches, so that the whole chain of 100 links was 66 feet long, and so that 100,000 square links were equal to an acre.

GUSSET. A triangular piece of metal to serve as a brace in the angle formed by two intersecting members of a framework, either to stiffen the connection, or as a support of one of the members.

GUTTA. In Grecian Doric architecture, one of a number of small circular ornaments in low relief which are cut on the under side of the mutules and the regulæ. (See Entablature.)

GUTTÆ-BAND. Same as Regula in a Grecian Doric entablature.

GUTTER. A channel, trough, or like contrivance to receive and convey away water; whether in connection with the roofs of a building, or forming part of a pavement, roadway, or the like. When used on a building it may either form part of a roof-covering turned up and supported along, or near, the lower edge of the slope; or it may be in the form of a trough of metal or wood hung from the edge of the roof; or it may be part of a masonry structure below, in which case perhaps of cut stone and forming part of the cornice or serving itself as the crowning feature.

Arris Gutter. A gutter or eaves trough of V-shaped section, and hence showing an arris underneath.

Fillet Gutter. A narrow gutter on the slope of a roof against a chimney or the like, formed of sheet metal turned over a fillet of wood. — (A. P. S.)

Parallel Gutter. A gutter constructed with decided, deep, parallel sides, as distinguished from one formed merely by the sloping sides of a valley, or brought about by the meeting of a roof with a wall or the like.

Parapet Gutter. A gutter constructed along the lower edge of a sloping roof and concealed by a low parapet formed by carrying up the side wall. Common in England, but a poor form of construction, inasmuch as the greater part of the gutter lies over the ceiling below instead of over the street.

GUTTER BOARD. A board, or, in recent times an iron slab, to bridge over a gutter, as along a curb, so as to form an easy slope for the passage of vehicles from the roadway upon the sidewalk or into a building.

GUTTER HOOK. A light iron hook or strap used to hold in place the upper edges of a metal gutter; or perhaps to support the gutter.

GUTTER MEMBER. The exterior or front of a roof gutter when considered as a member of the external architecture, as the topmost moulding of a cornice or a member crowning the cornice. In Greek temple architecture, the cornice along the eaves was crowned by such a moulding, which formed the outer face of an earthenware gutter. In some modern styles, the gutter, usually of metal, is elaborately adorned and becomes an important feature in the design, because terminating the wall with a very ornamental band.

GUTTER PLANK. Same as Gutter Board.

PLATE XIV

HADDON HALL, DERBYSHIRE, ENGLAND

Part of the garden front. The bay windows and battlements are of the the plan and the general character of the structure date from the reign of reign of Elizabeth ; the parapet of the terrace is comparatively modern ; but Edward IV. It is uninhabited and unfurnished, but kept in order.

GUTTER SPOUT. A water spout leading from a roof gutter, either as a gargoyle or in the way of a pipe led to the ground or to another roof.

GWILT, JOSEPH; architect and author; b. Jan. 11, 1784; d. Sept. 14, 1863.

Joseph was a son of George Gwilt, surveyor of the County of Surrey, England. In 1801 he entered the school of the Royal Academy, London. He had a good practice as architect and held the office of surveyor in succession to his father from 1807 to 1846. In 1816 he visited Rome. Gwilt is known by his books, *A Treatise on the Equilibrium of Arches*, (8vo, 1811), *Notizia Architectonica Italiana* (8vo, 1818), *Sciography, or Examples of Shadows with Rules for Their Projection*, (8vo, 1822), an annotated edition of Sir William Chambers's *Treatise on the Decorative Part of Civil Architecture* (1825), a translation of Vitruvius (1826), and the *Encyclopædia of Architecture, Historical, Theoretical, and Practical* (8vo, first ed. 1842), reëdited by Wyatt Papworth, in 1876.

Stephen, *Dictionary of National Biography;* Obituary in *Builder*, Oct. 3, 1863.

GYMNASIUM. *A.* A place for physical exercise, as (1) among the ancient Greeks, a public place more or less official and governmental in character in which the young men were duly exercised. (2) In modern times, a large and high room, sometimes forming a building by itself, and treated architecturally, but always arranged for the reception of gymnastic apparatus, such as vertical and horizontal bars, ladders, swinging ropes, trapezes, and the like. (See Palæstra; Stadium.)

B. In Germany, and elsewhere in imitation of Germany, a high school. In the German cities, the *Gymnasium* is the school for classical studies and those branches which are akin to these, and is opposed to the *Real Schule*, which is the school for mathematics and scientific training generally; the one being considered as the preparation for the university, the other as the preparation for the polytechnic school, the school of engineers, or the like.
— R. S.

GYN. Same as Gin.

GYNÆCEUM; GYNÆCIUM. *A.* In Greek archæology, that part of a large dwelling which is devoted to the women, hence, the family rooms as distinguished from the more public rooms where the master and his soldiers or male dependents commonly lived.

B. In modern times a haram; the living place of the women in a dwelling of any nation or epoch.

C. In ecclesiology, that part of a church occupied by women to the exclusion of men, as in early Christian practice, and still to a certain extent in the East.

GYNÆCONITIS. Same as Gynæceum.

GYNAIKEIOS. Same as Gynæceum.

GYPSUM. Hydrous sulphate of lime. (See Alabaster.) — G. P. M.

GYRATION, RADIUS OF. A quantity entering into the formulas for the strength of columns. It is equal to the Moment of Inertia of a surface divided by the area. (See Moment of Inertia.) — W. R. H.

H

HABERSHON, MATTHEW; architect.

In 1842 he went to Jerusalem to arrange for the erection of the Anglican cathedral which was built from his designs. Habershon published *The Finest Existing Specimens of Ancient Half-timbered Houses in England*, (London, 1836, folio).

Arch. Pub. Soc. Dictionary.

HACHURE. In architectural drawings, same as hatching; also a line or system of lines used in hatching.

HACIENDA. In Spanish America the chief house on an estate or very large farm, and hence and more often, the estate itself as a whole. — F. S. D.

HACKING. The breaking of one course of stone in a wall into another course of a different height; especially, in a case where a course of larger stones is interrupted and the course is continued with smaller pieces. It appears that two courses of smaller stones need not correspond exactly to another course of larger stones, but that hacking more nearly approaches building which is known as Random Coursed Work.

HADDON HALL. A great country house in Derbyshire, England, now unoccupied. Celebrated for its unaltered Elizabethan character and for its beautiful formal gardens.

HADRIAN'S MOLE. The great mausoleum of Hadrian at Rome; now, Castel S. Angelo.

HÆMATINUM. In Latin, red; used absolutely as representing the phrase *hæmatinum vitrum*, red glass; in this sense, the term has been applied to Roman glass of deep red colour, as in the fragments of tile which have been found.

HAGIA SOPHIA, MOSQUE OF. (See Church of S. Sophia, under Church.)

HAGIASTERION; –IUM. In ecclesiastical history, something very sacred; a sacred place; probably, in most cases, the baptismal font.

HAGIOSCOPE. In ecclesiological usage, an opening through a wall or pier, as in a church, and pierced in such a direction that a person in the aisle or transept can see the altar. Called also Squint, and more rarely Loricula. Openings of this character are not uncommon, but it is not certain that they were originally intended for the purpose mentioned.

HA-HA FENCE. A barrier made by a retaining wall at a place where the ground level is changed. From the upper side this barrier or enclosure will be invisible or hardly seen ; a desirable result sometimes in landscape architecture. Written also Haw-Haw.

HAIKAL. In Arabic, a sanctuary ; a holy place. Used by writers on the archæology of the Levant for a shrine of a Christian church in the East.

HAIKAL SCREEN. The screen of a sanctuary ; in Eastern Christian churches, of other sects than Greek, that which corresponds to the Iconostasis. (See Choir Screen and references.)

HALFPENNY, JOHN. (See Halfpenny, William.)

HALFPENNY, JOSEPH ; draughtsman and engraver ; b. Oct. 9, 1748 ; d. July 11, 1811.

He was clerk of the works to John Carr (see Carr) during his restoration of the cathedral of York, England. Halfpenny published *Gothic Ornaments in the Cathedral Church of York*, (1795–1800), *Fragmenta Vetusta, or the Remains of Ancient Buildings in York*, (1807), and other works.

Stephen, *Dictionary of National Biography.*

HALFPENNY, WILLIAM ; alias Michael Hoare ; architect.

He is known by his numerous practical works on architecture : *Multum in parvo, or the Marrow of Architecture* (1722–1728, 4to), *Practical Architecture* (London, 1730, 12mo), *Perspective made easy* (1731, 8vo), *Modern Builder's Assistant* (1742–1751, folio), and

other works. He was assisted by John Halfpenny.

Stephen, *Dictionary of National Biography.*

HALF-RELIEF. Sculpture in relief, between bas-relief and alto-relief ; a term of no accurate or precise value.

HALF TIMBERED. *A.* Composed of timber so far as the framing is concerned, the spaces of which framing are then filled in with masonry in some form ; this is the more usual meaning given to the term, but certain British authorities claim that such building as this is really whole timbered, the filling in by means of masonry having nothing to do with the construction in timber.

B. Having the lower story or stories of masonry, such as stonework, and the upper stories, or perhaps only the walls of the gables, framed of timber. This definition is given by those writers who object to the use of the term in the sense *A.*

In building done in wood according to either definition, the timbers show on the outside, and are usually arranged so as to form a somewhat ornamental pattern. In this respect the buildings of some parts of the continent of Europe, such as Normandy and northwestern France in general, and large parts of Germany, are found more stately in design than the English examples ; with more sculpture and with a beautiful system of proportion. On the other hand, this system of building lasted long and was popular in England ; the patterns of the framework itself were elaborate ; and many valuable examples remain, even of stately country mansions, built in this way. It is a reasonable theory that during the reigns of James I. and Charles I. and the Restoration, country houses built by residents of London or nobles connected with the court were built of masonry according to the revived classical theories brought from Italy and France, while those built by proprietors who resided in the country were built according to the traditional methods with much use of timber. The filling of the spaces between the timbers was done sometimes with brickwork or rubblestone masonry (compare Nogging ; Brick Nogging) and sometimes by means of stout oak laths plastered on both sides. In case there were two sets of laths, one at the outer and one at the inner side of the wall, each set plastered on each side, there was obtained a very warm and solid filling. (See Wood, Construction in, Part I.) (Cuts, cols. 345, 346 ; 347 ; 349, 350.) — R. S.

HALL. *A.* A room very large in proportion to rooms for sleeping or for family or individual use ; a covered and enclosed place of gathering. In speaking of the great thermæ of the Romans, the tepidarium, usually an oblong in shape, is commonly called a hall, and in like manner we speak of the halls of Assyrian palaces; while the Egyptian temple interiors, crowded with columns, are called hypostyle halls, as those at Karnak. So those mediæval churches which have the aisles and nave of nearly the same height are called hall churches (Hallenkirchen) to distinguish them from churches of the more usual type, and the great

portant part of the mediæval dwelling. The disposition of the College Halls at Oxford and Cambridge gives still a good idea of what the halls of Manor Houses were in the times of Elizabeth and later. Such a hall is to be thought of as low and long, simple in plan, and lighted from side windows; but there are exceptions. Thus, at Wallaton (Nottinghamshire),

HALF-TIMBERED HOUSE, MORETON OLD HALL (CHESHIRE), c. 1590.

building at Sens, called by the French *Salle Synodale*, is called in English a Synodal Hall. In English domestic building, the hall was the only important room in the early Middle Ages; there the lord, his family, and all his retainers, dependents, and serfs, met at meals, and here alone could they find shelter and warmth. Even later, as private bedrooms and sitting rooms became more numerous (see Bower; Closet; Solar), the hall remained much the most im-

built by John Thorpe, the hall rises high above the other buildings in imitation of mediæval castle keeps; and is lighted by windows very high above the floor. It was common, as early as the fourteenth century, to cut off with a screen that part of the hall in which were the doors leading to the open air, in order to give more warmth and privacy; and these screens are still a marked feature of the College Halls named, and also of those Company Halls in

London which have retained their original features.

In recent times, the term hall is applied to a large room used for lectures, political meetings, concerts, and the like, and such a term as Concert Hall is differentiated from the term Theatre as signifying a square-cornered room without galleries, or with galleries in one tier only, and not arranged with a stage and appliances for scenery. Such a room, used in a small town or village, as a place for gatherings of many kinds, lectures, entertainments, and the like,

HALF-TIMBERED (DEFINITION B) HOUSE IN HILDESHEIM, NEAR HANOVER, GERMANY.

often receives the name of Town Hall, which name is extended to the building which contains it. (See definition B.) A similar use of the hall was common in manor houses on the continent of Europe, but as the need of fortified dwellings lasted longer there, the fortresses of the fourteenth and fifteenth centuries include very large halls, of which the outer walls are generally made by the curtains of the fortification. (See Castle.) And these halls were sometimes two, three, or four in number, serving evidently as shelter for the garrison, which was in these cases so numerous that the lord

could not expect to have it all under his own eye. In this way, the signification of the term is extended to imply any very large room except when it is so long and narrow as to become a gallery.

B. A building erected with the chief purpose of supplying a hall in sense *A.* Thus, a building containing a large concert hall, with many rooms for other purposes, will take the common name of Music Hall. The most important structure in which the term is used in both senses in England is the celebrated Westminster Hall.

C. At the English Universities, a college; the term being used in combination in the names of certain institutions, the organizations of which differ somewhat from those of the colleges commonly so called.

D. Part of the compound name applied very loosely to buildings not necessarily halls in any of the above senses. Thus, a separate building of many American colleges is so called, as Massachusetts Hall.

E. In British usage, a manor house, and in this sense forming part of the names of many such buildings, as Haddon Hall.

F. In recent times, the room into which the outer doors open when it is large enough to be more than a mere vestibule. Thus, in a country house, if the entrance door opens directly into a room large enough, or a passage wide enough, to contain some furniture, as a settle, table, and the like, that room or passage is the hall. It is an error to speak of the room in which the stair is contained as a hall. The proper name for that is the staircase; but a modern misuse of that term has caused the use of the terms Stair Hall and Stairway Hall. In small houses, however, it often happens that a single space 6 or 7 feet wide and 25 feet long, or of about that magnitude, serves as hall and passage, and also contains the stair. (Cuts, cols. 351, 352; 354; 355, 356; 357, 358; 359, 360; 362.)
— R. S.

Albert Hall. Properly, the Royal Albert Hall, in Kensington, London; a building for musical and other festivals, finished in 1874, and, like the Albert Memorial, named from the Prince Consort. It provides for an orchestra and chorus of 1200 persons, and an audience of 7000; the exterior is not without interest, having a frieze of some decorative effect; and the iron roof is remarkable.

Carnegie Hall. (Properly, Music Hall.) In New York; built at the expense of Andrew Carnegie, from the designs of William B. Tuthill, aided afterward by H. J. Hardenbergh.

City Hall. In the United States, a public building for the transaction of the municipal business, or some part of it; especially, for the executive branch of the city government. (Compare Broletto; Hôtel de Ville; Palazzo Publico.)

HALF-TIMBERED HOUSE AT BEAUVAIS (OISE), FRANCE.

FIG. 1.—HALL OF OAKHAM CASTLE, RUTLANDSHIRE, 12TH CENTURY; INTERIOR. (SEE FIG. 2.)

FIG. 2.—HALL OF OAKHAM CASTLE, (SEE FIG. 1.)

Cloth Hall. An exchange for cloth merchants; that at Ypres, in Belgium, is an extraordinary and valuable piece of civic Gothic. The building of Eumachia, in Pompeii, was probably a cloth hall.

Company Hall. The large room used by a society or association bearing the name in which the word company occurs; hence, the whole building containing such a room. The term is used especially for certain important buildings in London, which are still the property of the ancient companies of merchants, mechanics, etc., dating from the Middle Ages. There are twelve Great Companies, and five or six others which are not so notable; the most important buildings of the Great Companies are Mercers' Hall, in Cheapside, built immediately after the Great Fire; Fishmongers' Hall, near London Bridge, rebuilt in 1831; Ironmongers' Hall, in Fenchurch Street, built 1748; but each of the Great Halls is worthy of study.

Faneuil Hall. In Boston, Massachusetts; built in 1742; called the "Cradle of Liberty" from the early meetings of Revolutionists which were held there. It is of what would now be called old Colonial or Georgian architecture, but is not of elaborate design within or without.

Guild Hall. (See Guildhall.)

Hypostyle Hall. One having many columns. The term is rarely applied except to one of a very few great monuments of antiquity. That of Karnak, in Egypt, among the ruins of the ancient Thebes, is 175 feet long from door to door, on the main axis of the group of temples and courts, and nearly 340 feet wide, and is crowded with columns, 12 larger (over 60 feet high) and 122 smaller. Its decoration within and without is extremely rich and varied. It was built by Ramses I., Seti I., and Ramses II., about 1400 to 1300 B.C., kings of the 19th Theban Dynasty.

Moot Hall. In English archæology, a place of judgment; hence, in recent times, a hall for debate, especially when occupied by a society whose purpose is discussion of questions of the day, such as is sometimes called a moot court.

S. George's Hall. A public building in Liverpool, Lancashire, England; built about 1854, the architect being Lonsdale Elmes. It is about 400 feet long, with a very elaborate Corinthian peristyle, and contains law courts and a great hall 169 feet long by 74 wide, in which are given musical and other entertainments. It is an important architectural monument, and one of the least faulty buildings of the middle of the century.

Servants' Hall. In a large residence, a room set apart for the general use of servants, commonly serving also as their dining room.

Town Hall. A large central building in which the business of the town is transacted, and which generally includes a hall for public assemblies, and a clock tower, with numerous offices. The Flemish town halls are treated under Belgium and France (Part II., Flemish France), also under Cloth Hall. (Compare City Hall; Village Hall.)

Trade Hall. A public hall in a city for the general business and meetings of merchants and manufacturers; also for incorporated trades.

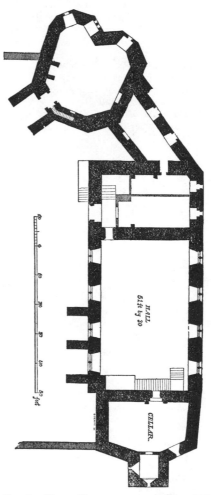

FIG. 3.—HALL: PLAN OF THAT OF STOKESAY CASTLE, SHROPSHIRE. (SEE FIG. 4.)

Village Hall. That building of a village which serves a purpose similar to that of the town hall of a larger community.

Westminster Hall. In London; a building 290 feet long inside, containing one single enormous room with but very small accessory structures, the span between the walls being nearly 68 feet and the roof in one single span built of oak without tie-beams, the most important piece of mediæval woodwork existing. It rises at the ridge to a height of 92 feet. It has never been seriously injured or restored, but was repaired judiciously in 1820. The building as it now stands was built by Richard II.

HALLAN; HALLAND. In the dialect of Scotland and the north of England, a partition, as in a cottage, often a solid one without openings of any sort as when used to separate the part of the cottage occupied by the family from that used as a cowhouse. The N. E. D. defines the term as meaning especially the partition between the door and fireplace which shelters the room from the draught of the door. (Called also Speer.)

HALL CHURCH. A church with aisles but without clearstories, the interior of which is a hall of approximately uniform height throughout. (See Hallenbau.)

HALLE AU BLÉ. (Wheat Hall or Corn Hall.) In Paris; a circular building, dating

He was *Bauinspektor* at Nürnberg, Bavaria, and in 1810 went to Greece, where he was associated with C. R. Cockerell (see Cockerell, C. R.) in his excavations at Ægina and Phigaleia. It was through his agency that the sculpture of the pediments of the temple of Athena, at Ægina, were secured for the Glyptothek, in Munich.

Seubert, *Künstler-Lexicon.*

HALLES CENTRALES. In Paris, the central market house, built from the designs of Louis Pierre Baltard about 1860. It is one of the earliest modern light structures of iron and glass, and is still a model of arrangement and structure; probably the finest market house in Europe.

HALLET, STEPHEN. (See Thornton, Dr. William.)

HALL HOUSE. *A.* In local British usage, the principal room of a farmhouse.

FIG. 4.—HALL: EXTERIOR OF THAT OF STOKESAY CASTLE, SHROPSHIRE. (SEE FIG. 3.)

from 1766, with twenty-five arched doorways leading to a great rotunda. The roof, in form of a cupola, is the earliest important piece of iron work applied to building. (See Iron Construction.)

HALLE AUX DRAPS. Same as Cloth Hall (which see, under Hall).

HALLENBAU. A building resembling a hall in its construction or plan; especially in German church architecture, a church whose aisles are carried to a height equal or nearly equal to that of the nave, so that there will be no clearstory, and so that the whole interior shall appear as a large hall divided by two (or more) ranges of columns carrying arches.

HALLENKIRCHE. A Hall Church. (See also Hallenbau.)

HALLER VON HALLERSTEIN, KARL; architect; b. 1774.

B. By extension from the preceding definition, the principal building of a farm.

C. Same as Hall, *E.*

HALL OF THE ABENCERRAGES. In the Alhambra at Granada, Spain; a not very large chamber opening out of the Court of Lions.

HALL OF THE COLUMNS. A pillared room forming a part of the Tzapotec ruins of Mitla, in Oaxaca, Mexico. It contains a row of six round stone columns through the middle, longitudinally, each 9 feet 4 inches in circumference and about 12 feet high. (See Mexico, Architecture of, Part I., Precolumbian.) Viollet-le-Duc has made a study of the restoration of the building containing this hall. — F. S. D.

HALLWAY. A hall serving as a passageway; a corridor or entry. Apparently confined to the United States.

FIG. 5.—HALL CALLED SALLE DES MORTS, OURSCAMP, NEAR NOYON (OISE). (SEE FIG. 6.)

HALO. That form of the Glory which is represented around the head alone. (See Aureole; Glory.)

HALVE; HALVE TOGETHER (v.). To join, as two pieces of wood, by cutting away each one for part of its thickness, so that each fits into the other. The faces forming the joint need not necessarily be parallel with the outer faces, nor need they be plane surfaces.

HAMILTON, SIR JAMES, OF FYNNART; architect; d. August, 1540.

A natural son of James, first Earl of Arran and master of the works to King James V. of Scotland. He built the northwest portion of Holyrood House, Edinburgh, and was employed on the castles of Edinburgh, Sterling, and Rothesay, all in Scotland.

Arch. Pub. Soc. Dictionary.

HAMILTON, THOMAS; architect.

In 1820 he designed the memorial to Robert

HAMMAM. A Turkish bath; especially, an establishment in a European city for bathing in the Oriental way by sweat rooms, manipulations, cold plunge, and the like. (Written also Hummum.)

HAMMER. In Stonedressing, same as Axe (II.).

HAMMER-DRESSED WORK. Stone masonry, the faces of which have been shaped and brought to an approximately smooth surface by means of the hammer alone. (See Stonecutting.)

FIG. 6. — HALL CALLED SALLE DES MORTS, OURSCAMP, NEAR NOYON (OISE). (SEE FIG. 5.)

Burns at Ayr, Scotland, and April 28, 1825, laid the first stone of the High School, Edinburgh (Grecian Doric). He had a large practice in Scotland.

Builder, Vol. XVI., p. 146, and Vol. XVII., p. 243.

HAMLET. *A.* In Great Britain, a village of little consequence, especially a village which does not in itself constitute a parish, and has therefore no parish church.

B. In some of the United States, the official designation of certain villages.

The term is sometimes used, perhaps erroneously, in the sense of a farmstead, — that is to say, of a group of buildings standing isolated in the country and belonging to a single establishment.

HANCE. In Great Britain, the curve of shorter radius which adjoins the impost at either side of a three-centred, four-centred, or similar arch. By extension, a corbel at either end of a lintel of a door or window opening, and this because the corbel and the lintel taken together approach the form of a many-centred curve. The term seems to have been originally equivalent to a lintel, and then by confusion with the word Haunch to have gained its meaning as given above. It is probably obsolete or obsolescent.

HANDLE. (Of a door, draw, or the like.) (See the technical terms Knob; Lift; Pull.)

HAND-RAIL. The top bar of a parapet when made of slender pieces of material, as a balustrade. Generally, the horizontal or inclined piece of material upon which rests, or is likely to rest, the hand of a person going up or down stairs, or leaning upon the parapet. In staircases between solid walls the hand-rail is often a cylinder of small diameter secured to the wall and serving merely to aid a person in ascending the stairs. Elsewhere it is often a very massive bar, and if of stone may have a section of two hundred square inches.

HANGER. In the building trades, any contrivance, fixed or movable, for the suspension of any structure or member. Usually, in combination.

Beam Hanger. A contrivance serving the purpose of a stirrup, but more elaborate and of better finish.

Door Hanger. A hanger for the support of a sliding door, especially such a door when hung from above. The meaning of the term is usually extended to mean the entire apparatus for such purpose, including the track or rails from which the door may be supported.

HANGER BOARD. (See Electrical Appliances.)

HANGING (I.). A piece of material used for covering and decorating the wall of an apartment; originally, tapestry or some kind of textile fabric hung to hooks, hence the name. In modern times, more commonly in the plural, as Paper Hangings, hangings of silk, and the like.

HANGING (II.). The art or process of securing in place a door, casement, or shutter, by means of hinges, or a sliding sash or the like by means of counterpoise and cords, or sliding doors when these are supported from overhead or from the side by means of sheaves or rollers of any kind.

HANGING BUTTRESS. The semblance of a buttress, usually having the upper part, the weathering, etc., like other buttresses of the same building, and put in to carry out the sequence; supported, however, upon a corbel or in some similar way, and not firmly based upon the ground. Such an addition might be of use as enabling a greater weight of masonry to be applied at the haunches of an arch above; but of course is not a buttress in the proper sense.

HANS VON BERCKHEIM (HANS AMMEISTER); architect.

Hans von Berckheim was architect (*Werk Meister*) of the city of Strasburg in the first half of the fifteenth century. He built the public granary of Strasburg, a part of which still remains.

Gérard, *Les Artistes de l'Alsace.*

HANS VON STRASSBURG (HANS GREMP); bell founder.

The great bell of the cathedral of Strasburg (Alsace, Germany) which weighs nine thousand kilogrammes and is only rung on the most important occasions, bears the date July, 1427,

and the name *Magister Joannes de Argentina ;* that of Overnai, one of the finest in Alsace, the date 1429, and that of S. Adelphe de Neuwiller the date 1431, and the name *Meister Hennin von Strassburg.* All doubtless refer to the bell founder, Hans von Strassburg.

Gérard, *Les Artistes de l'Alsace.*

HANS WINLIN. (See Erwin, II., von Steinbach.)

HANSE. Same as Hance.

HANSEN, HANS CHRISTIAN; architect; b. April 2, 1803; d. May 2, 1883.

A. Passage.
B. Gateway.
C. Small Watchtower called the Horse Leads.
D. Modern Gateway.

GROUND PLAN

FIG. 7.

A. Fireplace.
B.B.B. Lockers.
C.C. Seats in the windows
D. Drain.

FIG. 8.

FIG. 7. — HALL (DEFINITION *E*) : GROUND PLAN OF HOUSE CALLED YANWATH HALL, WESTMORELAND. FIG. 8. — PLAN ON LARGER SCALE OF UPPER STORY OF TOWER IN FIG. 7.

A brother of Theophilos Hansen (see Hansen, T.). In 1831 he won a stipend at the academy in Copenhagen which enabled him to travel in Italy and Greece. He was made court architect at Athens. Hansen designed the university at Athens and in association with Schaubert and Ludwig Ross (see Schaubert and Ross) rebuilt the temple of Nike Apteros on the Acropolis, putting into place the ancient blocks of marble, which had been recovered when the Turkish fortifications were destroyed.

La Grande Encyclopédie.

HANSEN, THEOPHILUS; architect; b. July 13, 1813 (at Copenhagen); d. Feb. 17, 1890.

Hansen was educated at the academy of Copenhagen. In 1838 he visited Italy and Greece and practised for eight years in Athens, building at this time the observatory near that city. Reaching Vienna in 1846, he was associated with Ludwig Forster (see Forster, L.) in conducting the *Allegemeine Bauzeitung*, and built the Waffen Museum of the Arsenal and other buildings in a mediæval style. He again went to Athens in 1860–1861 to build the Academy, one of his most successful works. In the reconstruction of the city of Vienna (begun in 1857) Hansen built the Exchange (1869–1875), the Academy of Fine Arts (1874–1876), and the Parliament House (1883).

Niemann and Feldegg, *Theophilos Hansen;* Farrow, *Recent Development of Vienna.*

HAPSE. Same as Hasp; an old form now rare.

HARAM. In countries inhabited by Mohammedans of civilized town life, that part of a dwelling which is appropriated to the females. The term is a transliteration of the Arabic, and has passed into English as the common name, but different terms are employed in different countries; thus, in India the term is *zenana*. In Cairo the larger houses are so arranged that there is an inner court for the haram, in which cases the arrangement of the rooms about that court is not unlike that connected with the outer or men's court.

HARD FINISH. (See Plastering.)

HARMANDUS; architect.

On the upper part of the old tower of the cathedral of Chartres (Eure-et-Loire, France) is inscribed the name Harmandus and the date 1164. Harmandus is supposed to have been the architect of the old tower.

Gonse, *L'Art Gothique.*

HARDOUIN–MANSART, JULES; architect; b. April 16, 1646 (at Paris); d. May 11, 1708 (at Marly).

Jules Hardouin was the son of Raphael Hardouin, *peintre ordinaire du roi* and Marie Gauthier, a niece of François Mansart (see Mansart, N. F.). He added his grand-uncle's name to his own and was known as Hardouin-Mansart, frequently signing himself Mansart. He studied architecture with François Mansart and Libéral Bruant (see Bruant, L.). While assisting Bruant in the construction of the Hôtel de Vendôme, Paris, he was presented to the king, Louis XIV., who requested him in 1672 to design the château of Clagny for Madame de Montespan. In 1674 he was commissioned to enlarge the new château of Saint-Germain-en-Laye (finished under Henri IV.; but destroyed in 1776). Oct. 22, 1675,

Hardouin-Mansart was appointed *architecte du roi* and later *contrôleur général des bâtiments du roi.* In 1675 he was admitted to the Académie de l'Architecture. His name appears for the first time in the accounts of the palace of Versailles, Feb. 26, 1677. He was occupied with that building during the remainder of his life. At this palace he built between 1679 and 1681 the great southern wing. He finished in 1684 the Grande Galerie, overlooking the park in the central pavilion, and the garden façade of the central pavilion. Between 1684 and 1688 he built the great northern wing, thus completing the entire length of 580 metres. He built the grand stairway, and in 1698 began the beautiful Orangerie. The chapel of the château was begun in 1696, but was not finished until 1710 (after Mansart's death) by Robert de Cotte (see Cotte, R. de). In 1683 he commenced the château of Marly. In 1685 he approved the plans of François Romain for the Pont Royal (see Gabriel, Jacques, II.). In 1686, he was appointed *premier architecte du roi*, and in the following year sold the office of *contrôleur général des bâtiments du roi* to his grand-nephew, Jacques Jules Gabriel (see Gabriel, J. J.). In 1688 Mansart built the two wings of the Grand Trianon in the Park at Versailles, which were afterward connected with a colonnade by Robert de Cotte. He continued the work of Libéral Bruant at the Hôtel des Invalides, building the portal of the church in 1693. He designed the dome, which was well under way when he died, but was not finished until 1735. Mansart was assisted in his work by Robert de Cotte, who succeeded him as *premier architecte* in 1708, by Charles Daviler, and by Cailleteau called L'Assurance (see Cailleteau).

HARDOUIN–MANSART DE JOUY, JEAN; architect; b. 1700.

Jean was the son of Jacques Hardouin-Mansart, *conseiller au Parlement*, and grandson of Jules Hardouin-Mansart (see Hardouin-Mansart, Jules). A legacy of forty thousand livres was left by Colbert (d. 1683) to rebuild the façade of the church of S. Eustache in Paris. The old portal, built by Charles David (see David, Charles) was torn down in 1733, and the new façade begun the following year by Jean Hardouin-Mansart. After much interruption it was completed in 1788 by Pierre Louis Moreau.

Jal, *Dictionnaire;* Du Seigneur in Planat's *Encyclopédie.*

HARDOUIN-MANSART DE SAGONNE, JACQUES; architect; b. 1703.

Sieur de Levy and Compte de Sagonne, a younger brother of Jean Hardouin-Mansart de Jouy (see Hardouin-Mansart de Jouy). He was created member of the Académie and *architecte du roi* in 1735, and between 1742 and 1754 built the important church of S. Louis (cathedral) at Versailles. He built also in

Languedoc the monastery of the Dames de S. Chamont and the Abbaye Royale de Prouilles.

Du Seigneur in Planat's *Encyclopédie;* Raguenet, *Petits Édifices historiques.* Duchesne, *Notice historique sur Jules Hardouin-Mansart;* Guiffrey, *Comptes des bâtiments de Louis XIV.;* Sauvageot, *Palais, châteaux, hôtels et maisons de France;* Michel Hardouin, *Château de Clagny;* De Laborde, *Versailles ancien et moderne;* Dussieux, *Le Château de Versailles;* Gavard, *Versailles, Galerie historique.*

HARD PAN. Clay more or less firmly compacted with gravel or sand approaching Conglomerate in structure and hardness. It can generally be loosened with the pick.

HARDWARE (as used in building). (See Builders' Hardware.)

HARDWICK HALL. An ancient English manor house near Mansfield, in Nottinghamshire. It is of the reign of Elizabeth, and very little altered. It is habitable, partly furnished, and contains some exquisite works of art.

HARLEMAN, KARL, FREIHERR (BARON) VON; architect; b. 1700; d. 1753.

A pupil of Tessin (see Tessin, Nicodemus, I.); he continued the construction of the royal palace at Stockholm, Sweden, begun by that architect. He was royal architect and held various offices at the Swedish Court.

Füssli, *Allgemeines Künstler Lexikon.*

HARNESS. The straps, bolts and other contrivances by which a bell is suspended from its stock. By extension, the entire apparatus by which a bell is hung and tolled.

HARRISON, HENRY G.; architect; b. 1813; d. 1895.

He designed several important buildings in New York City, and became prominent in connection with the architectural schemes projected by Mr. A. T. Stewart for Garden City, Long Island. Of the proposed buildings only the cathedral, designed by Harrison, was carried out.

Obituary in *American Architect,* Vol. XLIX, p. 97.

HARSDORF, CASPAR FREDERIK; architect; b. 1735; d. 1795.

Educated in France and Italy, and was chief royal architect at Copenhagen, Denmark, and director of the Academy of Sciences in Stockholm, Sweden. He built the propylæa of the royal palaces in Copenhagen and other important buildings.

Weilsbach, *Nyt Dansk Kunstner Lexicon.*

HASENAUER, KARL, FREIHERR (BARON) VON; architect; b. July 20, 1833; d. Jan. 4, 1894.

He was educated at the Collegium Carolinum in Braunschweig, Germany, and at the academy of Vienna, and travelled in Italy, France, and England. In 1854 he won first prize in architecture at the academy of Vienna. He won also second prize in the competition for the new

façade of the cathedral of Florence. In association with Semper he designed at Vienna the Museums of Art and Natural History, built between 1872 and 1884, and the new Imperial Palace. He designed also the Hofburg theatre at Vienna. He published *Das K. K. Hofburgtheater in Wien* (1890, folio).

Farrow, *Recent Development of Vienna;* Meyer, *Konversations-Lexikon;* Hasenauer, *Hofburgtheater in Wien.*

HASP. A fastener for a door, lid, or the like, usually in the form of a plate or bar of metal hinged at one end, and with a slot or opening to receive a staple. A padlock, or in default of this a pin of wood or the like, being passed through the staple, the door, etc., is held fast.

HATCH (n.). A rough door; the original signification being connected with the idea of grating or crib work, but in general use having equal application to that which is solid and uniform in surface; especially, —

A. A heavy door filling the lower part of a doorway; either completed by a second heavy door above (see Dutch Door), or shut when the larger or more permanent door is opened, as when business of some kind is to be done across and above this lower door acting as a barrier or counter (see Buttery Hatch).

B. A door in a nearly horizontal position; in this sense like Trap, except that it conveys the idea of a much larger opening to be filled by the door in question. The hatches of ships are not hinged, but are lifted off and put on again so as to cover the Coaming, or in some cases are made to slide; but in architectural practice a hatch is usually hinged, and is often secured by a counterpoise, or is held in some way to avoid falling heavily when allowed to close.

C. By extension, the opening closed by a hatch. In this respect, exactly resembling the use of gate for gateway, door for doorway, and the like. — R. S.

HATCH (v.). To cover or partly cover with closely drawn lines. (See Hatching.)

HATCHING. Drawing by means of small and numerous lines laid close together. In freehand drawing, hatching may be used to produce effects of rounding and to distinguish shades from shadows, and the like. In architectural drawing, it is more commonly used to distinguish the cut or sectional parts from those shown in ordinary projection. (Compare Hachure.)

HATFIELD HOUSE. An ancient English manor house in Hertfordshire, England, the greater part built in the reign of James I. It is inhabited by its owner, the Marquis of Salisbury, and is full of architectural interest.

HATHORIC. Having to do with the Egyptian goddess Hathor. Used especially of capitals in the later architecture of Egypt characterized by masks of the goddess.

HATHPACE. Same as Estrade or Dais in the sense of a raised platform. In this sense, probably derived from corruptions of *haut-pas* and *hault-pace;* by confusion with Halfpace, whose origin moreover is doubtful, a landing or platform on a staircase.

HAUNCH. That portion of indefinite extent which is included between the crown and the abutments of an arch.

HAUSSMANN, GEORGES EUGÈNE, baron ; administrator and politician ; b. March 27, 1809 (at Paris) ; d. Jan. 11, 1891.

The family of Baron Haussmann came originally from Cologne, Germany. He was educated at the Collège Henri IV., Paris, now Lycée Condorcet. He sided with Louis Philippe in the revolution of 1830, and May 22, 1831, was made *secrétaire général* of the préfecture of Vienne, France. He was promoted to various *sous-préfectures.* Haussmann was a supporter of Louis Napoleon who, as President of the Republic, appointed him to the préfecture of the Var, January, 1849. Haussmann assisted Napoleon III. in the *Coup d'État* of Nov. 7, 1852, and on Jan. 23, 1853, was appointed *Préfet de la Seine.* He held that office for sixteen years and accomplished a complete transformation of the city of Paris. He remodelled the sanitary system of the city, destroyed old quarters, annexed suburbs, laid out boulevards and wide streets, created parks and public gardens. Under his patronage, also, several monumental works on the history, archæology, and architecture of Paris were prepared and published, such as *Histoire générale de Paris* (see Berty, Adolphe), *Paris dans sa splendeur* (3 vols. folio), *Promenades de Paris* (2 vols. folio, 1867–1873), and other works. He was removed from office at the commencement of the ministry of Émile Olivier in January, 1870, and devoted the remainder of his life to the preparation of his Memoirs.

Haussmann, *Mémoires.*

HAW–HAW FENCE. (See Ha-Ha Fence.)

HAWKSMOOR, NICHOLAS ; architect ; b. 1661 ; d. 1736.

At the age of eighteen he became the scholar and domestic clerk of Sir Christopher Wren (see Wren) and was employed by him from 1682 to 1690 as deputy surveyor at Chelsea Hospital, and after 1705 as deputy surveyor at Greenwich Hospital, London. He assisted Wren in the construction of S. Paul's cathedral from June 21, 1675, until its completion. Hawksmoor was associated with Vanbrugh (see Vanbrugh) at Castle Howard, 1702 to 1714, and at Blenheim Palace, 1710 to 1715. At Oxford he designed the library of Queen's College, 1692, and the two towers of All Souls' College, both of which buildings have been

ascribed to Wren. Jan. 6, 1716, he was appointed surveyor to the committee in charge of the construction of churches in the city of London, and designed several churches for them, the best being those of S. Mary Woolnoth, 1716–1719, and S. George Bloomsbury, 1720–1730. He was made surveyor of Westminster Abbey at the death of Wren, and completed the towers. His excellence lay in his attention to details and thorough knowledge of construction.

Blomfield, *Renaissance Architecture in England;* Birch, *London Churches;* Wren, *Parentalia;* Britton and Pugin, *Public Buildings of London.*

HAYA, RODRIGO DEL ; sculptor and architect.

In 1575 Haya made the statues of S. Andres and of S. Matias in the cathedral of Burgos, Spain. In 1577, with his brother Martin, he commenced the great retable of that church.

Bermudez, *Diccionario.*

HEAD. *A.* In general, the top or upper member of any structure ; the top or end — especially the more prominent end — of a piece or member.

B. A roofing tile of half the usual length, but of the same width ; for forming the first course at the eaves.

HEADER. Any piece or member which is laid in a direction transverse to a series of other similar members which abut against it. Specifically, —

A. In the framing of a floor or roof, the piece which is framed into one or two trimmers, and which in turn supports the tail pieces.

B. In brickwork, and more rarely in building with cut stone, a piece of material, as a brick, having its length placed across the wall and serving to a certain extent as a bond. (See Bond ; Brickwork ; Stretcher.)

HEADING (n.). That which forms or serves as a head, or as a header, or a combination or series of either.

HEADING COURSE. A course of headers in a brick wall, or the like. In ordinary brick building in the United States, four or five courses of stretchers alternate with one heading course ; in Great Britain, every alternate course is usually a heading course.

HEADPOST. A post or stanchion at the head of a stall ; *i.e.* the end at the manger. (Compare Heelpost.)

HEADROOM. The clear space allowed above a flight of steps or a floor, platform, or the like, so that a person passing will have abundant room. The space should be sufficient to remove all sense of annoyance from the nearness of the floor or flight of stairs above. Thus, where stairs are arranged, one flight above another, 7 feet in the clear vertically is the least space that should be allowed. As soon as a stair and its surroundings assume some architectural character, the headroom must be much greater than this, and its proper distribution is an important consideration in planning. By extension, the term is loosely applied to any space allowed vertically for a given purpose ; as when an attic room is said to have 4 feet headroom at the low side nearest the eaves.

HEADSTONE. (See Gravestone.)

HEADWAY. Same as Headroom.

HEALING. Roofing; the covering of a building by any system; local in parts of Great Britain.

HEARSE. Originally a grating of any kind, as a portcullis at the gate of a fortress, or a fence around and perhaps above a tomb ; in this latter sense either temporary and intended for the display of burning candles, drapery of rich stuffs, and the like on occasions of ceremonies ; or of iron as a permanent protection. By extension in the sixteenth century and later, a temporary structure of wood, canvass, and the like, set up as part of the display at a public funeral, as of a prince. It was arranged like a temporary triumphal arch in the streets to receive banners, heraldic devices, and the like. It is by an extension of this meaning that its modern significance of a wheeled car has come in. Also Herse. (Cut, cols. 379, 380.)

Altar Hearse. A framework built above or around an altar, and intended on certain occasions of ceremony to be covered with hangings and to carry lighted candles. — R. S.

HEART BOND. (See under Bond.)

HEARTH. A piece of floor prepared to receive a fire ; whether in the middle of a room, as in primitive times, and in buildings of some pretensions — the smoke being allowed to escape through openings in the roof ; or, as in later times, the floor of a fireplace in the modern sense. The hearth of ancient times was sometimes raised above the floor, and then had often a low rim around it ; and sometimes sunk beneath it, forming the bottom of a shallow pit. In either case it might be fitted with certain permanent holders for wood representing the dogs or andirons of later times. Some cooking hearths, as in Pompeii, are raised a foot or more above the floor, and are built of masonry, with an arched opening at one side in which fuel might have been kept. The hearth, then, includes properly the entire floor from the back lining of the fireplace to the outermost edge of the incombustible material. In builders' usage, however, it is very often customary not to include in the term the rougher flooring, as of hard brick, which is enclosed between the actual cheeks of the recess made in the wall or chimney breast. According to this custom, the hearth, or, as it might be called, the outer hearth, is usually a slab of slate, soapstone, marble or other fairly resistant material, which

is placed outside of and beyond the fireplace proper. The mantelpiece in modern usage generally rests upon it, as do the fender and the front feet of the basket grate, or other fittings. A flooring of tile sometimes replaces the slab of stone. Whatever the material of the hearth, it is usually supported upon a flat arch of brickwork which often is built between the trimmers of the floor below. (See Trimmer Arch, under Arch.)

HEARTING. Masonry forming the interior or body of a wall, pier, or the like, as distinguished from the facework. (Compare Backing ; Filling.)

HEARTWOOD. The wood formed at the interior or " heart * of a tree. It is quite free from sap, — the more so as the tree becomes older, — of finer and more compact and even grain, and therefore harder. It is usually considered better for general use than the outer portion of the trunk which contains the sap, and is, hence, known as *sapwood*. The latter has comparatively little strength and is more liable to rapid decay.

HEATHER ROOFING. A variety of thatch.

HEATING. (For heating of water, see Boiler ; Plumbing ; Range : for heating of interiors, see Warming.)

HEATING, ELECTRIC. (See Warming.)

HECATOMPEDON ; - DOS. Something measuring 100 feet ; a Greek term applied by the ancients to the Temple of Pallas Athene at Athens. Much discussion has been given to the question which building was intended and where the measurement was to be taken. The soundest opinion seems to be that it refers to the actual cella or naos of the Parthenon, and that the measurement of that building, outside the walls, is 100 Attic feet.

HECATONSTYLON. A building having one hundred columns. — (C. D.)

HECK. *A.* A hatch or trap.

B. A fastening for a door. — (A. P. S. ; C. D.)

HEEL. *A.* A moulding called *cyma reversa;* a local builder's term.

B. That part of an upright post or of a rafter in the sloping part of a roof which rests upon the sill or plate.

HEELPOST. *A.* A post or stanchion at the free end of the partition of a stall.

B. A post to receive the hinges of a gate ; either a part of the gate, or the stationary support to which the gate is hung.

The term appears to have no certain meaning, unless in the sense of definition *A.* (Compare Headpost.)

HEGIAS OF ATHENS ; sculptor.

The first master of Phidias (see Phidias). An inscription bearing his name has been found on the Acropolis at Athens.

Collignon, *Histoire de la Sculpture Grecque;* Overbeck, *Schriftquellen.*

HEIDELOFF, KARL ALEXANDER VON; architect, painter, and engraver; b. Feb. 2, 1788; d. Sept. 28, 1865.

In 1822 he was appointed professor at the *Polytechnische Schule* in Nürnberg, Bavaria, and custodian of the monuments of that city. Heideloff is best known by his books, *Ornamentik des Mittelalters*, 1838; *Bauhütte des Mittelalters in Deutschland*, 1844; *Kunst des Mittelalters in Schwaben*, 1855; and other works.

Seubert, *Künstler-lexicon*.

HEINRICH SOYNERE or **SUNERE**. (See Soynere.)

HEINRICH VON GMUND. (See Gamodio.)

HEINRICH VON ULM; architect.

Two architects of this name appear in the history of the construction of the cathedral of Ulm, Germany. Heinrich, the elder, was doubtless the earliest architect of the church (begun 1377). A second Heinrich appears in 1387. They probably belonged to the same family as Ulrich and Mathias Ensingen (see Mathias and Ulrich von Ensingen), who worked on the cathedral in the fifteenth century.

Pressel, *Ulm und sein Münster*.

HELICAL LINE. The central or determining line of a helix or spiral, such as a volute, corresponding to the axis or straight line upon which an ordinary building or detail is constructed.

HELICED. Decorated with helices, such as volutes.

HELICOGRAPH. An instrument for drawing a spiral (helix); consisting of a wheel carrying a pencil, and working on a shaft which is cut into the thread of a screw. As the shaft is turned about a pivot at one end, the wheel constantly approaches (or recedes from) the pivot.

HELIEIUM. A building or enclosure dedicated to the sun considered as a divinity. (Also Heleion.)

HELM, WILLEM VAN DER; architect.

He was probably a pupil of Pieter Post (see Post, Pieter). He built the Waard Kerke in Leyden, Holland, and several important gates in that city.

Galland, *Holländische Baukunst*.

HEM. The slightly raised rim of a volute of an Ionic capital, forming a border and following the spiral of the curve.

HEMICYCLE. Same as Hemicyclium. That of the *École des Beaux Arts* at Paris, a room of generally semicircular shape serving as a hall for ceremonies, has the curved wall decorated by a celebrated mural painting, the work of Paul Delaroche. In the new buildings of the Sarbonne, Paris, the large lecture room has the wall behind the speaker only slightly curved,

concavely, but this also is called hemicycle. It is covered by a noble painting by Puvis de Chavannes.

HEMICYCLIUM. In classical archæology a more or less nearly semicircular structure in the sense of an exedra of the simpler form; that is to say, a long and curved bench or seat of permanent character. By extension the term applies to a hall or portico fitted with such seats.

HEMIGLYPH. The half channel which forms a chamfer on each vertical edge of a triglyph.

HEMITRIGLYPH. In some modifications of classical architecture, a half or large portion of a triglyph at a point where the frieze is suddenly cut across, as at a reëntrant angle.

HENHOUSE. Same as Poultry House.

HENRI DE BRUXELLES; architect.

Henri came originally from Flanders. In 1382 he won the competition for the choir screen (jubé) of the cathedral of Troyes (Aube) France. This work was begun April 22, 1385, and finished in 1388. It was destroyed in 1793.

Assier, *Les arts et les artistes dans l'ancienne capitale de la Champagne*.

HENRI DEUX ARCHITECTURE. In French, that of Henry the Second, the second king of the completed Renaissance, who reigned 1547 to 1559. The style known as *L'Architecture Henri Deux* is that of the French Renaissance properly so called, and is of the greatest purity. The classical Renaissance was not perfectly established in France until this reign, for during the preceding reign, that of Francis I., much of the mediæval feeling remained in existence.

HENRI QUATRE ARCHITECTURE. In French, that of Henry the Fourth, the king whose title was finally recognized by all parties about 1598, and who died 1610. The style known as *L'Architecture Henri Quatre* appears complete at the close of the long anarchy of the religious wars; it is strongly differentiated from the pure architecture of the French Renaissance (see Henri Deux; Renaissance). The style is firm, spirited, rational, but devoid of especial charm; a style of severe utilitarianism, as far as that was possible in an age when the traditions of decorative art were still fresh. The best-known buildings are those of Paris, as, especially, the house fronts on the Place des Vosges and the Place Dauphine, but also large parts of the Palace of Fontainebleau, such as the Galerie des Cerfs and the Cour du Cheval Blanc. The long gallery of the Louvre on the water front connecting the old Louvre with the palace of the Tuileries was continued under Henri IV., but the alterations extending even to complete rebuilding have changed the character of the design; moreover, the greater part of this work

PLATE XV

HENRI DEUX ARCHITECTURE

A private house in Orléans (Loiret), called the house of Diane de Poitiers and known to have been built about 1550. The building is now used for a museum of local antiquities. The conditions of the early French Renaissance — the artists doubtful of the classical orders and uncertain how far to modify their designs to conform to them, while the details are all of exquisite delicacy — are well shown in this design. The treatment of two projecting corners with very different use of columns is very curious.

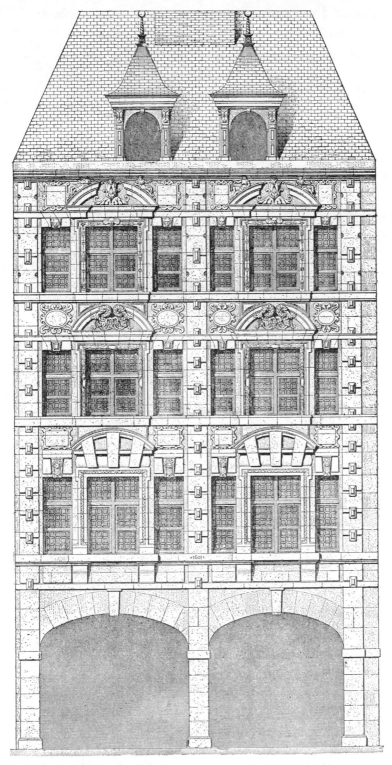

HENRI QUATRE (STYLE OF): HOUSE AT ROUEN, RUE DE LA GROSSE-HORLOGE.

was carried out during the next reign, that of Louis XIII.

HENRY DE ESTRIA (HENRY OF EASTRY); ecclesiastic and architect; d. 1331.

Henry was elected prior of the cathedral of Canterbury, England, in 1285. According to the *Obituary* of Canterbury (*Anglia Sacra*, Vol. I., p. 141) "he decorated the choir of the church with most beautiful stonework delicately carved." This work is mentioned more specifically in his *Register*. These notices refer undoubtedly to the fine enclosure of the choir, much

HENRI QUATRE (STYLE OF): FAÇADE, PART OF THE PLACE DAUPHINE, PARIS.

of which remains. The north doorway is still perfect.

Willis, *Canterbury Cathedral;* Wharton, *Anglia Sacra.*

HEPTASTYLAR; –STYLE (adj.). *A.* Having seven columns; said of a portico.

B. Having a portico of seven columns at one or at each end; said of a building such as a temple. (See Columnar Architecture.)

HERÆUM (Greek Ἡραιον: Heraion). A temple or sacred enclosure dedicated to the goddess Hera or Here. That at Olympia in the Morea, Greece, is most celebrated.

HERALDRY. The art and science of the herald; the only branch of which at all connected with architecture is the determination and marshalling of arms. (See Achievement; Arms; Escutcheon.)

HERCOS. In Greek, a fence or enclosing wall.

HÉRÉ DE CORNY, EMMANUEL; architect; b. Oct. 12, 1705; d. Feb. 2, 1763.

Supposed to have received his training from Germain Boffrand (see Boffrand, G.), and was made architect in ordinary to Stanislas I., King of Poland, and Duke of Lorraine. At Lunéville (Meurthe-et-Moselle), France, then a city belonging to the duke, he built the towers and the tribune of the organs of the church of S. Remy, the Hôtel des Carmes, and many other important buildings. At Nancy (Meurthe-et-Moselle), France, then the capital of Duke Stanislas, he built the church of Bon Secours, the convent of the Minimes, and the important constructions of the Place Royale (now Place Stanislas), commenced in 1751, which include the Hôtel de Ville, the episcopal palace, the Hôtel Alliot, the theatre, the Collège Royale de Médecine, the Hôtel Jacquet, and the Arc de Triomphe. Héré de Corny published *Recueil des plans et élévations des châteaux, jardins, et dépendances que le roi de Pologne occupe en Lorraine*, Paris, 1753, folio; *Plans et Élévations des bâtiments de la place Royale de Nancy*, etc.; *Recueil des fondations et établissements faits par le roi de Pologne*, Lunéville, 1762.

Lepage, *Archives de Nancy;* Du Seigneur in Planat's *Encyclopédie.*

HERLEWIN; abbot of Glastonbury; d. 1120.

He destroyed the old church at Glastonbury, England, and laid the foundations of the new and much larger building.

Dugdale, *Monasticon*, Vol. I., p. 4.

HERMES. In Greek archæology, a figure having the head, or head and bust, of a god resting upon a plain, blocklike shaft. It is supposed that the use of these figures is of very remote antiquity. By extension, and especially at Athens, any four-cornered pillar finished at top with an indication, however slight, of a human head; such figures were considered as inviolable on account of their use in marking boundaries of landed property (called also Term; Terminal Figure; see also Gaine).

HERMITAGE, THE. A palace of the Czars of Russia; built by Catherine II., and connected with the Winter Palace, at Saint Petersburg. It is celebrated for its great picture gallery, library, and collection of Greek vases, arms, and other works of art.

HERMODOROS; architect.

Hermodoros of Salamis built the temple of Mars in the region of the Circus Flaminius in Rome. This temple was probably founded by

PLATE XVI

HENRI QUATRE ARCHITECTURE

A building of private ownership with apartments to rent, built in the reign of Henry IV., and forming a part of the interesting Place des Vosges. The front given in the plate forms the end of the narrow Rue Birague which enters the open Place through the archway in the middle of the façade, but the front on the Place is similar. This work, in red brick and white stone, is characteristic of the epoch and style of the succeeding reign (Louis Treize), which retains many of its features.

Brutus Gallæcus in the year 139 B.C., and contained a statue by Scopas (see Scopas).

Brunn, *Geschichte der griechischen Künstler.*

HERMOGENES; architect.

An architect of Asia Minor who is mentioned frequently by Vitruvius without any indication of the precise time in which he lived. His temple of Diana at Magnesia is mentioned by Vitruvius as an example of a pseudodipteral temple, a style of building which he is supposed to have invented. He wrote descriptions of this building and of the temple of Bacchus at Teos.

Vitruvius, Marini ed.

HERNANDEZ, GERÓNIMO; sculptor and architect; b. about 1586; d. 1646.

He was born at Seville, Spain, and was a pupil of Pedro Delgado. He made a statue of S. Geronimo in the cathedral of Seville and numerous retables of the Spanish churches.

Bermudez, *Diccionario.*

HERNANDEZ (FERNANDEZ), GREGORIO; sculptor and architect; b. 1566; d. 1622.

Hernandez made the great retable of the cathedral of Plasencia, Spain. An extended list of his works in sculpture is given by Bermudez (op. cit.).

Bermudez, *Diccionario.*

HEROÖN. (See Heroum.)

HEROUM Greek (ἡρῷον; Heroön). A building or sacred enclosure dedicated to a hero, that is to say, to a person more than an ordinary man, whether considered as a demigod or not. Hence, by extension, a tomb or cenotaph, as when dedicated to a personage of great dignity. In this latter sense, used both in Latin of the classical period and in the Greek of the Byzantine empire.

HERRERA, FRANCISCO (EL MOXO); painter and architect; b. 1622 (at Seville, Spain); d. 1685.

A son of Francisco Herrera the elder, painter and engraver. He studied in Rome. At the death of his father in 1656 he returned to Seville, Spain, and after painting several pictures for the cathedral of that city, went to Madrid. In 1681 he was made supervising architect of the Alcazar, Pardo, Campo, and Buen Retiro at Madrid.

Stirling-Maxwell, *Annals of the Artists of Spain;* Bermudez, *Diccionario.*

HERRERA, JUAN DE; architect; b. about 1530.

The favourite architect of Philip II. of Spain. He studied philosophy at Valladolid, Spain, and visited Brussels and later Italy. After the death of Juan de Toledo (see Toledo, Juan de) whose associate he was, he succeeded him as architect of the Escorial. He designed the church of the Escorial, the cathedral of Valladolid, and the bridge of Segovia. In 1597 he published illustrations of the Escorial engraved by Pedro Perret.

Stirling-Maxwell, *Annals of the Artists of Spain.*

HERRINGBONE (adj.). Diagonal in arrangement; set diagonally; said of many small members closely succeeding one another, and usually set at forty-five degrees with the general direction of the row, and at right angles with the members of the adjoining rows. Thus, in a wall built of thin stratified stones, such as slate of certain qualities, the stones in successive rows may be laid alternately sloping upward from left to right and from right to left. In

HERRINGBONE PATTERN.

an ornamental floor short lengths of plank are often laid in this way.

HERRINGBONE BOND. (See under Bond.)

HERSE. Same as Hearse. (Cut, cols. 379, 380.)

HEXAPARTITE. Same as Sexapartite, as applied to vaulting.

HEXASTYLAR; HEXASTYLE (adj.).
A. Having six columns; said of a portico.

B. Having a portico of six columns at one or at each end; said of a building such as a temple. The majority of the larger Grecian Doric temples are hexastyle. (See Columnar Architecture.)

HEXAPROSTYLE. Having a portico of six columns in front; that is, hexastyle at one end and without columns along the sides.

HEXASTYLOS. A hexastyle building (Vitruvius).

HIERACOSPHINX. An Egyptian sphinx of the kind which combines the head of a hawk with a lion's body.

HIEROGLYPH. A figure usually or frequently representative of some object, as an animal, a weapon, a utensil, or the like; or else a simple zigzag, circle, parallelogram, oval, or similar conventional representation of a well-known object too complex to be readily represented; standing for a sound as a syllable, and in this way forming part of an inscription. The term signifies "sacred cutting," and originated in the belief that the Egyptian figure writing, to which was first applied the name hieroglyphic, was exclusively religious in character. Such writing differs from Chinese syllabic writing in that each figure represents something, and is not a merely conventional mark; and in decorative and ornamental work it requires to be enclosed in a decided frame in order to avoid a scattered and dislocated look. It is probably much easier to make a statelier and effective design of a series of Chinese characters or of Arabic letters than to use hieroglyphs successfully in the same way; but the Egyptian use of the last-named

HERSE: OVER A TOMB AT MONASTERY OF NONNBERG, NEAR SALZBURG, AUSTRIA.

method of writing shows how much can be done in this latter way by an artistic people. (Compare Cartouche.) — R. S.

HIEROGLYPHIC. *A.* Expressed in hieroglyphs, as a sentence or passage.

B. Consisting of hieroglyphs, as an inscription of an Egyptian obelisk or pylon, or a Mexican or South American temple.

HIERON. In classical, especially Greek, archæology, a holy place of any kind, especially a temenos; that is to say, the sacred enclosure of a temple or shrine. The hieron of Asklepios at Epidauros, that of Zeus at Olympia, that of Apollo at Delphi, and that of Hera at Argos were celebrated in antiquity for the crowd of interesting buildings, monuments, statues, and other works of art which they contained, and each of these has been more or less thoroughly explored by modern archæologists.

HILDEBERT; monk and architect; d. 1023.

In 1020 Hildebert, the second abbot of that name, began for Richard II., Duke of Normandy, the Romanesque church of Mont-Saint-Michel (Manche), of which the transepts and four bays of the nave still remain. He was chiefly occupied with the enormous substructure of the building. Instead of cutting away the crest of the rock, he constructed an immense plateau even with the crest, a part of the mass being occupied by crypts and subterranean chapels.

Corroyer, *Description du Mont-Saint-Michel.*

HILL FORT. A rude defensive post occupying the summit of a hill or a strong position among hills, as, in antiquity, those which grew to be the citadels of important towns; and, as in India, the works of native tribes. Especially, an earthwork of North American Indians encircling the summit of a bluff or hill. Fort Ancient, in Warren County, Ohio, is a good example. — F. S. D.

HINDPOST. Same as Heelpost, as in the partitions between stalls in a stable.

HINDU ARCHITECTURE. That of the styles of building in India which prevails the most widely throughout the peninsula, and shows the least influence of foreign conquerors. In this sense it might be considered to include the Buddhist and Jaina as well as the later ones, but not the Mohammedan architecture of which the great centre is at Agra. According to a more strict definition, the term would exclude the Buddhist and Jaina buildings as well as the Mohammedan buildings, and would include only that architecture which has taken shape since the almost complete expulsion from India of the Buddhist religion in all its forms. It seems evident that no accurate use of the term exists as applied to architecture. (See Buddhist; Dravidian; India, Architecture of; Jaina.) — R. S.

HINGE. A connection used to attach and support a member or structure so that it may be movable as about a pivot; as a door, sash, table leaf, or the like. The movable member may be hung by means of the hinge to a fixed support as a frame or jamb, or to another movable piece.

WROUGHT-IRON ORNA-MENTAL HINGES OF CHURCH DOOR, SINZIG.

In its common form, a hinge consists of two flaps or leaves of metal, each of which has one edge bent about a pin, wholly or in part; such a portion, or both together, forming the knuckle. The pin thus forms a pivot about which one flap is free to turn when the other is permanently secured. The simplest form of hinge may be formed by a hook permanently fixed, as the stationary member, and a ring secured to the movable member. — F. B. H.

Blind Door Hinge. A hinge designed especially for a blind door; usually one of a pair of double-acting hinges on the principle of the "hook and eye" hinge. The special feature of the device is in the lower hinge, of which the pin projects from an inclined lug upon which the shank of the eye travels; the inclined plane causing the door to remain at right angles to the jamb when undisturbed, or to return to such a position by gravity when opened and released.

Butt Hinge. Any form of hinge in which the leaves are applied to the edge or *butt* of the frame or to the face of the jamb and to the *butt* of door, sash, or other swinging member, so that when closed the leaves fold back upon each other; thus distinguished from hinges intended to be applied to the faces of the jambs and other members; as flap hinges, strap

HINGE: SWISS WROUGHT-IRON WORK OF SEVENTEENTH CENTURY.

hinges. Many forms of hinges may be used in either way, and the placing of such a hinge might be described as set as a flap, or as a butt.

Cross-garnet Hinge. A strap having the form of the letter T; the crosspiece forming the stationary member, the long stem being the movable flap. The latter has sometimes also a crosspiece corresponding to the stationary flap.

Double-acting; — Action Hinge. A hinge so arranged that the door or other valve to which it is attached may swing on both sides of the jambs. Such a hinge is usually in the form of a butt hinge fitted with springs by which the valve is automatically closed and held in the plane of the opening.

Dovetail Hinge. A strap hinge with both leaves flaring from the pin in the form of a Dovetail.

Fast Joint Hinge. One in which the pin is permanently retained in place by the flaps; so distinguished from loose pin and loose joint hinges. Usually a Butt Hinge. (See Heave-off Hinge.)

Flap Hinge. The ordinary form of hinge, usually with both leaves applied on the surface. (See Butt Hinge.)

Floor Hinge. A double-acting hinge secured to the floor or sill and forming a vertical pivot on which a door may turn, the head of the door having a single pivot to correspond.

Garnet Hinge. (Same as Cross-garnet or Crosstail.)

Gate Hinge. A form of flap hinge in which the knuckle is supported by a lug projecting from the surface of either flap, often with a contrivance similar to a rising hinge so that the gate or shutter will remain fixed when swung out.

Gravity Hinge. A hinge designed to close a door or the like automatically by the action of the force of gravity. Commonly a Rising Hinge. (See also Blind Door Hinge.)

Heave-off; Lift-off; Loose Joint Hinge. One in which one half of the knuckle forms a part of each flap, the upper one being removable from the pin, so that the shutter or door can be readily removed. Usually a Butt Hinge.

H Hinge. (See Parliament Hinge.)

Hook and Band Hinge. A modification of the Hook and Eye hinge with the shank of the eye formed into a strap, for securing to the face of the door or other valve.

Hook and Eye Hinge. A primitive form of hinge consisting of an eye worked upon the end of a spike and resting upon a hook or pin worked on the end of a similar spike; the spikes being driven respectively into door and frame.

Lift-off Hinge. (See Heave-off Hinge.)

Loose Joint Hinge. (See Heave-off Hinge.)

Loose Pin Hinge. (Usually, Loose Pin Butt.) One in which the pin is not secured to either flap, so that it is readily withdrawn, so that the door, etc., can be easily unhung.

Parliament Hinge. A form of strap hinge with leaves enlarged so that when the hinge is open it has the general form of the letter H.

Pew Hinge. A small butt hinge of iron or brass with a rising joint, projecting from one to two inches from the face of the door; as its name implies, it is for light doors. The hinge lifts the door slightly as it is opened so as to clear obstructions on the floor, and enables it when wide open to fold back against the wall over all projections so as to lie in a plane parallel with the plane of the opening.

Pivot Hinge. A double-acting spring hinge swinging on pivots let into lugs on the jamb plate.

Reënforced Hinge. A patent strap hinge with two thicknesses of metal surrounding pin and extending on leaves.

Rising Hinge. A form of gravity hinge so constructed that when the door to which it is attached is opened the door is lifted somewhat from the floor so as to pass over a rug, carpet, or other obstruction, and will also have a tendency to close itself. The use of thresholds or saddles in doorways makes this device less essential. Hinges for blinds are sometimes so constructed in the United States that they rise only in process of opening or shutting and fall back into normal place not only when they are fully closed but fully open. This device is intended to take the place of ordinary fastenings used to prevent the blind from being blown by the wind when opened back against the outside wall. Usually a Butt Hinge. A common form has the joints of the knuckle oblique so that, when turned, the moving flap rises on the other.

Screen Hinge. A form of a Butt Hinge so arranged that the leaves of a screen may fold on either side of each other.

Setback Hinge. A hinge which, in opening the door, blind, shutter, or casement to which it is attached, lifts it slightly and drops it again when fully opened so as to prevent it from swinging in the wind.

Shutter Hinge. (See Gate Hinge.)

Single Action Hinge. Similar to Double Action, but allowing the door to swing one way only.

Skew Hinge. One having the joints of the knuckle oblique as described under Rising Hinge.

Spring Hinge. A hinge fitted with some form of spring, generally a coiled spiral of steel, to cause it to shut automatically.

Strap Hinge. A simple and primitive form of hinge, with two long leaves, one made fast to the frame and the other to the door. The leaves are often ornamentally treated by foliation or incised patterns; and such hinges of wrought iron received much consideration during the Middle Ages and formed important parts of the decoration of doors.

T Hinge. A modification of the Strap Hinge, with one long leaf and one narrow one, the latter being made fast to frames too narrow to receive a long leaf, and set perpendicular to the long leaf. (See Garnet Hinge.)

Turnover Hinge. A hinge of any sort so made or so set that the door, or casement, which it carries can be swung back flat against the face of the wall, or piece of furniture. Almost always a Butt Hinge.

Water Joint Hinge. A hinge so contrived that its action will not be, to any extent, impaired by the action of rust. Usually a simple hinge for gates, cellar doors, and the like, having its two parts joined by interconnecting loops or eyes. — F. B. H.

HINGING POST. A post or similar upright member, to which a door or the like is hung by its hinges. (See also Hanging Stile, under Stile.)

HIP. A sloping salient angle in a roof, where the slope of the roof changes direction, the other by a hip ; or the bevel which must be given to the end of a rafter, so that it will conform to the oblique construction at a hip.

HIP KNOB. A vertically projecting pinnacle, ending in a finial, ball, or similar feature, and situated at the end of the ridgepole in a hipped roof. The hip rafters meet at that point, and sometimes in their framing require a central vertical piece, of which the hip knob is the natural decorative termination. The hip knob is, however, more commonly a mere ornament of the form called for at that place, and sometimes forms part of the metal or pottery covering of the end of the ridge.

HIPPODAMUS ; sophist and engineer (*architektonos*).

Hippodamus was probably from Miletus in

HIP: ROOF WITH FOUR HIPS, NEUKIRCHE, SWITZERLAND, 1734.

and one plane cuts or intersects another. Thus, in a double pitch roof, where there are no gables, and where the ridge is shorter than either of the wall plates which run parallel to it, the roof falls back at a slope above the end walls, (which would otherwise be gable walls), and at either end two hips are formed. (See the compound terms which follow. For roofs built with hips, see Hip Roof, Hipped Roof, under Roof.)

(For roofs in which the hip is not carried all the way from the ridge to the plate, but is shorter, so that a truncated gable results, see Jerkin Head.)

HIP BEVEL. The angle between the two slopes of a roof which are separated one from

Asia Minor. According to Aristotle (*Politics*, VII., 10, 4), he was the first to pay attention to the proper arrangement of cities. He laid out the Piræus (the port of Athens) with wide streets radiating from the central Agora, and built the city of Rhodes in the form of a theatre. He planned the new city of Thurium in Magna Græcia, 440 B.C., with streets crossing at right angles. His principles were adopted later in many important cities, such as Halicarnassus, Alexandria, and Antioch.

Brunn, *Geschichte der griechischen Künstler.*

HIPPODROME. *A.* In Grecian archæology, a place provided for horse racing, chariot racing, and the like. It is probable that none was ever as large and elaborate as even a Roman third-class circus, and the majority of them were probably very simple and temporary in their construction, natural hillsides being used as far as possible to provide sloping arrangement of seats.

B. In modern times, a kind of circus, distinguished by a long and narrow arena replacing the ordinary Ring. There have been but few hippodromes in this sense, and those which have existed, as in Paris, and, for a few years, in New York, have been distinguished by more serious contests, better riding, and a closer imitation of classical entertainments than the modern circus can offer. — R. S.

HIP ROLL. Same as Hip Moulding.

HIRSVOGEL (HIRSCHVOGEL), AUGUSTIN; glass painter, enameller, potter, engraver, etc. ; b. 1503 ; d. 1569.

A son and pupil of the elder Veit Hirsvogel (see Hirsvogel, Veit), and one of the most versatile of the German artists of the sixteenth century. He painted eleven windows in the chapel of S. Rochus in Nuremberg, Bavaria, from designs by Albert Dürer (see Dürer). He invented improvements in the processes of glass making, and was a skilled enameller, draftsman, engraver, musician, potter, stonecutter, and mathematician. He designed numerous fine earthenware stoves, of which there are examples in the Museum at Nuremberg. His stoves were widely imitated.

Friedrich, *Hirschvogel als Töpfer;* Seubert, *Künstler-lexicon.*

HIRSVOGEL, VEIT, the elder; glass painter ; b. 1461 ; d. 1525.

In 1495 he was appointed *Stadtglaser* at Nuremberg. He made four important windows in the S. Sebaldus Kirche in that town. His son Veit, the younger, was also glass painter. (See Hirsvogel, Augustin.)

Seubert, *Künstler-lexicon.*

HISPANO-MORESQUE. Having the characteristics of the Mohammedans in Spain and of their work. The building and the ornamental arts of the Spanish Moors were much in advance of their fellows who remained in Africa. (See Moorish Architecture.)

HISTORICAL MONUMENT. A building so important from its architectural character or historical associations as to be registered, cared for, and partly controlled by the state or municipality — especially in France, one of those put under the direction of the *Commission des Monuments Historiques.*

The soil of France is covered with monuments that tell the history of the architecture of that country. The Dolmens and the Menhirs mark the prehistoric period ; then follow the triumphal arches, temples, aqueducts, amphitheatres, reminders of the Roman epoch ; then, after the Roman period of transition, comes the French

architecture, properly so called, springing into existence spontaneously in the different provinces, and producing masterpieces everywhere ; finally, we find the delicate architecture of the Renaissance, and the styles of Louis XIV., Louis XV., and Louis XVI. At the present time we have to add to all this wealth of art the monuments, megalithic, Roman and Arabian, of Algeria and Tunisia.

Unfortunately, for more than two centuries, indifference, ignorance, and even scorn for the edifices of the Middle Ages, still more than the action of the weather and revolutionary troubles, have destroyed or allowed to perish a number of valuable monuments.

It has been given to our century to understand that to preserve these edifices was to make the past live again to the profit of the present and of the future.

As early as 1790 and 1792 a commission was organized, and expenses were authorized for the purpose of preserving the monuments of the past. But it was not until 1830 that the National Legislature associated itself with a movement which took place at that time, and voted, for the first time, a credit of 80,000 francs, subject to the direction of the then existing *Direction des Beaux Arts.*

The grant of a regular credit led to the nomination of an inspector general, Ludovic Vitet, who should occupy himself with looking up those edifices having need of immediate care.

He filled this office during two years. His successor, Prosper Mérimée, inspired the architects with a new ardour, and very soon the National Legislature, understanding the importance of the office that had been created, raised to 120,000 francs, and then in 1837 to 200,000, the amount of the sums allowed for the preservation of historic monuments. It then became necessary to have the employment of this sum directed by a commission. This was the first Commission of Historical Monuments. It was composed of eight members, Messieurs Vatout, Lepprevost, Vitet, De Montesquiou, Taylor, Caristie, Duban, and Prosper Mérimée, of whom the first-named was president and the last-named secretary and inspector general.

In 1839 the sum was raised to 400,000 francs. The commission was reorganized. The Minister of Fine Arts became its president, Vitet and Mérimée were elected vice-presidents, and five new members were appointed. The commission occupied itself at once with collecting all the documents necessary for appreciating the architectural worth of the monuments of each department, regarding them from an artistic and historical point of view. It was very soon ready to make the first classification, and to appropriate judiciously the resources they had at their disposal. The object it had in view, above all others, was to aid in the restoration of the edifices which remain as the types of an architecture, and which mark the greatness and the decadence of an epoch. It applied itself also to the undertaking of complete restorations, and put aside for that purpose considerable sums of money in order to obtain satisfactory results.

At the present time the classification of the historic monuments is made according to the following regulations : —

FRANCE :

1. Megalithic monuments.
2. Antique monuments.
3. Monuments of the Middle Ages, the Renaissance, and of modern times.

ALGERIA :

1. Megalithic monuments.
2. Antique monuments.
3. Arabic monuments.

The number of monuments classified in the list amounts to more than 2000. Unfortunately, this classification does not place the edifices under shelter from mutilations, and even from demolitions. The present state of the legislation does not give to the commission any means of exacting respect for its decisions ; and while Italy, Greece, Spain, Denmark, Sweden, and Norway have been able to take the precautions necessary for preserving their artistic wealth from all attack, the law in France has as yet done nothing to protect against the relentless hand of man monuments which have stood firm against the action of Time.

Still, it can be said that in spite of the difficulties and obstacles met with by the commission on its way, it has been able to preserve for France some specimens of architecture of every epoch from the earliest historic times down to the present century. It has been able to discover the processes of the ancient builders, determine the methods employed by them, and define the principles according to which must be executed every restoration worthy of that name.

The credit allotted to the commission that we have seen to be in 1839, 400,000 francs, was carried to 600,000 from 1842 to 1847 inclusive ; raised in 1848 to 800,000 francs ; in 1855 to 870,000 francs ; then in 1859 to 1,100,000 francs, a sum which has not been augmented since that time.

It is proper to say that the credit of 1,100,000 francs is only a Fund for Aid. The concurrence of the local administrations is indeed often demanded as a condition for the assistance accorded by the commission, and nearly all the parishes possessing historical monuments contribute unhesitatingly to their restoration. It is thus that the government, with a credit of 1,100,000 francs, is able to have executed each year work amounting to about 3,000,000 francs.

In 1848, 1852, 1860, 1871, the commission was subjected to various alterations. At present it is composed of forty members chosen from among the high functionaries of the fine arts, and directors of museums, architects, painters, and archæologists. It is aided in its work by forty architects, who charge themselves with seeing that all things are properly done, and who are elected after having passed a special examination. Among them may be mentioned P. Boeswilwald, De Baudot, Daumet, Formige, Gout, Lisch, Simil, Suisse. Among those who are no longer living may be recalled the venerated names of E. Boeswilwald, Labrouste, Laisne, Lassus, E. Millet, Questel, Viollet-le-Duc.

Outside of the interest that is attached to monuments that have been saved from ruin, these restorations form, as a result, skilful and intelligent workmen. The work is, indeed, very varied, and requires a thorough acquaintance with the divers systems of structure, and the ignoring of all routine. Every day new problems are declaring themselves, and every day the task of the master and of the workman varies.

The architect, also, obliged to put himself in close relation with the workmen whom he directs, and to instruct each one, must act with absolute precision and leave nothing to chance.

The work of restoration of any of the classified monuments is only authorized by the government after an examination by the Commission of Historical Monuments, of the estimates, plans, and drawings showing the state in which the edifices are found to be, and the reparations they require. In the archives of the commission is a collection of the drawings of these works, executed by the best architects of this century, and they form to-day a collection of the highest interest, which includes faithful souvenirs of the edifices which it has not been possible to save.

Not wishing these precious documents to remain unknown and almost inaccessible, the commission has undertaken the publication of its most remarkable drawings. It has been directed in its choice by the impartiality that has always guided it, and it has sought to collect in this work every style and every school.

The first series, composed of 4 volumes in folio, including 43 monographs, and 237 plates, is completed. The second is (1899) in course of publication. — ALEX. SANDIER.

HITTITE ARCHITECTURE. That of a confederacy of tribes constituting, with Egypt and Babylonia, the third great power of the ancient world before c. 1000 B.C. Their monuments are found throughout Asia Minor and Syria, where they were politically supreme, and these in the style commonly called Pelasgic or Cyclopean by the Greeks. As the Greeks termed Pelasgians the early Asiatic colonists who brought civilization to the islands and to

Greece proper, and as these emigrants came from Hittite lands, it would seem as if the Pelasgians were Hittites. This explanation is confirmed by recent discoveries. From its broader use, however, the term Pelasgic seems preferable, to include both Eastern and Western branches of the style. Hence Hittite architecture is treated under the heading Pelasgic.

— A. L. F., Jr.

HITTORFF, JACQUES IGNACE; architect; b. Aug. 20, 1793; d. March 25, 1867.

Hittorff was born at Cologne and naturalized as a French citizen. He was a pupil of Charles Percier (see Percier). Between 1819 and 1823 he visited England, Germany, Italy, and Sicily. After 1825 he built with Lepère the church of S. Vincent de Paul, Paris. About 1831 he was architect of the Parisian prisons. In 1833, as the result of a competition, he was made architect of the Place de la Concorde, the Champs Élysées, and the Place de l'Étoile. In the Place de la Concorde he built the pedestal of the obelisk, placed the statues of the cities of France, and completed the decoration, lamps, fountains, etc. From 1844 to 1866 Hittorff was architect of the Column of the Place Vendôme, Paris. The Neo Grec movement received much help from him; and the church of S. Vincent de Paul is often spoken of as a monument of the style; (but see Neo Grec). In 1864 he was made general inspector of the *Conseil des bâtiments civils.* He won a first-class medal at the exposition of 1855. In association with Zanth (see Zanth) Hittorff published *Architecture Moderne de la Sicile* (one vol. folio, Paris, 1835), and *Architecture Antique de la Sicile, recueil des monuments de Ségeste et de Sélinonte* (text one vol. 4to, plates one vol. folio, Paris, 1870). He published alone *Restitution du Temple d'Empedocle à Sélinonte; ou l'Architecture polychrome chez les Grecs* (text 4to, atlas folio, Paris, 1851).

Normand, *Notice historique de Hittorff* in *Moniteur des Architectes* (1867); *Notice Nécrologique* in *Revue de l'Architecture*, Vol. XXV., 1867.

HOARD; -ING. A wall or close fence made of planks; usually rough and temporary, as in cities, to enclose ground not built upon. The term seems not to be common in the United States. The use during the Middle Ages of temporary wooden galleries and parapets at the top of fortress walls has involved the reintroduction of this term as a kind of translation of the French *hourde*, which is thought by some to be originally an English word altered by French writers.

HOARE, MICHAEL. (See Halfpenny, William.)

HOB. *A.* The horizontal upper surface of the masonry filling on either side of a grate in a fireplace. The term, as well as the thing itself, is English and of the eighteenth century.

Old fireplaces arranged for burning wood were readily adapted for the use of coal by building in a dwarf wall of masonry, in the middle of which was set a grate with space left below for the access of air. The two small spaces on the top of the dwarf wall were convenient for setting things that had to be kept warm, and each of these was a hob. According to the N. E. D. the term signifies the whole piece of masonry.

B. In recent English usage, "the iron plated sides of a small grate on which things may be set to warm."

HOBAN, JAMES; architect.

He was a native of Ireland and settled in Charleston, South Carolina, before the Revolution. July, 1792, he came to Washington and was employed on the public buildings there for more than a quarter of a century. His plan for the President's mansion (the present White House) was accepted, and this building was built by him. He rebuilt it after its destruction by the British in 1814. He superintended the construction of the old Capitol from the designs of Dr. Thornton (see Thornton).

Howard, *Architects of the American Capitol.*

HOD. A box for carrying building materials, especially mortar; usually shaped like a trough and with a pole secured to the bottom. The trough or box being set upon the labourer's shoulder, the pole serves to steady and balance the load. Hods are now usually raised to the scaffolding by machinery of some kind. (Compare Hod Elevator.)

HOD ELEVATOR. A contrivance for raising a large number of loaded hods at one time. One of the forms is an endless chain resembling somewhat a flexible iron ladder; this serves for the workmen to use in ascending, or, when set in motion, for carrying up the hods. (See Hoist; Lift.)

HODÉNOSOTE. (See Long House.)

HOF. In German, originally a court in the sense of an open yard, and hence, exactly as in English, a court in the sense of an establishment kept up by a sovereign or great noble. In common use as a prefix, connected with the court or government. Thus, *Hofkirche*, a church connected in one of several ways with the palace, but not usually the palace chapel. *Hoftheater*, a theatre maintained wholly or in part by the government, and considered as being under the special patronage of the prince.

HOGAN (ho-gawn). In the Navajo and Apache languages, a house. (Written also hogun, for the latter.) — F. S. D.

HOG-BACKED. Cambered; applied especially to the ridge of a roof, which, if not somewhat so raised in the middle, is apt to look as if it sagged, and is also apt to sag in reality in the course of a few years.

HOIST. An appliance for raising passengers or materials to a height, as to a scaffold or within a building to an upper floor. In its simplest form it is merely a tackle operated by a horse or by hand. In its more elaborate forms, as when operated by steam, it is not to be distinguished from an elevator, except, possibly, as being rougher or as having simpler machinery or lower speed. The two terms are often used as synonymous.

HOISTING MACHINERY. (See Crane; Derrick; Elevator; Gin; Hod Elevator; Hoist.)

HOISTWAY. The vertical passage or channel through which a hoist of any kind ascends. Thus, in buildings, it is commonly provided that the hoistway, or the clear space carried through the floors from top to bottom, shall be enclosed with solid partition or with gratings to prevent accidents. (See Elevator Shaft, under Shaft.)

HOLDFAST. An implement for securing anything in place, or which when secured itself to a solid structure makes easy the fixing of other more movable parts to it. Many different forms of hook, bolt, spike, etc., have received this name at different times. The A. P. S. Dictionary describes one as common in Great Britain which is a wrought-iron spike with a shoulder intended to secure a shelf, bracket, or the like.

HOLL, ELIAS; architect; b. Feb. 28, 1573 (at Augsburg); d. 1636.

In 1600–1601 he visited Venice, where he learned the elements of Renaissance architecture. In 1602 he was appointed city architect of Augsburg, Germany. The city derived its principal architectural characteristics from the buildings erected during the next twenty years largely from his designs. His chief work is the *Rathhaus*, begun Aug. 25, 1615.

Leybold, *Das Rathhaus der Stadt Augsburg;* Meyer, *Selbstbiographie des Elias Holl;* Rudolph Kempf, *Alt-Augsburg.*

HOLLAND, ARCHITECTURE OF. (See Netherlands, Architecture of.)

HOLLAND, HENRY; architect; b. about 1746; d. 1806.

He designed Claremont House, Surrey, England, for Lord Clive, and directed the construction of Battersea Bridge, London, etc. His chief work was the reconstruction of Carlton House, Pall Mall, London. This palace was begun in 1788, and destroyed in 1827. In 1791 he designed Drury Lane Theatre, London, for R. B. Sheridan.

Stephen, *Dictionary of National Biography;* Richardson, *The New Vitruvius Britannicus;* Wilkinson, *Londina Illustrata.*

HOLLAND HOUSE. A private residence in Kensington, London, built originally in 1607, and, it is thought, from the designs of John Thorpe. It belonged to the first Earl of Holland, a partisan of Charles I., who was beheaded in 1649. It has had a singular history, but in spite of alteration, retains much of its original

character, and has splendid and unaltered gardens.

HOLLAR, WENCESLAS; engraver; b. 1607 (at Prague in Bohemia); d. March 28, 1677.

The famous engraver Hollar was brought to England by the Earl of Arundel in 1637. His engravings of cathedrals and other important buildings are especially fine, and his views of cities are of extreme value.

Redgrave, *Dictionary;* Walpole, *Anecdotes;* Parthey, *Wenzel Hollar*, Berlin, 1835.

HOLT, THOMAS; architect; d. Sept. 9, 1624.

He was a native of York, England, and a carpenter. He is supposed to have come to Oxford about 1600, when Sir Thomas Bodley was beginning his New Schools. Holt is credited with the design of these buildings, especially the great tower, the façade of which is decorated with the five orders superimposed.

Blomfield, *Renaissance Architecture in England;* Wood, *Antiquities of the University of Oxford.*

HOLYROOD PALACE. In Edinburgh; the ancient residence of the kings of Scotland. In great part rebuilt in the reign of Charles II., but containing a few of the ancient rooms.

HOLY WATER BASIN. (See Bénitier; Pila; Stoup.)

HOLZSCHUHER, EUCHARIUS KARL; architect.

In 1616–1619 he built the façade of the *Rathhaus* in Nuremberg, Germany. This building had been begun in 1340, and enlarged by Hans Beheim in 1521–1522.

Wolff-Mayer, *Nürnberg's Gedenkbuch;* Festing, *Gang durch Nürnberg.*

HOMESTEAD. In Great Britain, and generally in literature, the whole group of buildings forming a residence, especially a country residence, as a farm or small manor house, together with the land they occupy; a general term for the buildings and land forming the home of a family. In the United States, and also in Canada, a piece of land considered adequate for the support of a family settling upon it, and as such, limited to 160 acres by several acts of Congress, especially the "Homestead Act," passed in 1862. Such pieces of land (one-quarter of a square mile) might be taken up free of cost by actual settlers, and by laws of the United States and of certain states were exempt from seizure in process of debt.

HONDURAS, ARCHITECTURE OF. (See Central America, Architecture of.)

HONEYCOMB WORK. Primarily, any kind of decorative work forming a pattern with a reticulated mesh resembling or suggestive of a honeycomb. Particularly a system of decoration widely used in the Moslem styles of architecture upon pendentives, corbelled-out masonry, and niche heads, and consisting of an intricate combination of minute brackets, inverted pyramids, and tiny squinches successively projecting row over row; the aggregation of niches and hollows, of geometric forms, producing the suggestion of a broken honeycomb. This work, which is more commonly called Stalactite Work, is sometimes wrought in stone, but more often in plaster; and in interiors is richly painted and gilded. It is a conspicuous element in the architecture of Cairo, North Africa, and of the Spanish Moors; slightly less so of the Persian and Turkish architecture, and is hardly at all found in that of Moslem India. (See Moslem Architecture; also special articles on the Moslem styles named above.) — A. D. F. H.

HONEYSUCKLE ORNAMENT. Ornament of anthemions of the form common in Greek decorative sculpture.

HONNECOURT, VILLARD DE. (See Villard de Honnecourt.)

HOO, WILLIAM DE; prior.

Chosen prior of the cathedral of Rochester, England, in 1239, and built or caused to be built the choir of his church.

Wharton, *Anglia Sacra*, Vol. I., p. 393.

HOOD. A rooflike canopy over an opening, especially over a fireplace. In particular: —

A. In mediæval and later architecture, a structure of masonry or of plaster work held by a frame of wood or the like, which is entirely secured and protected by the plaster, and projecting from a wall above a hearth. The flue for the smoke passes upward from the top of the hood, and is generally concealed in the wall. Such hoods are sometimes carried on projecting cheek pieces or jamb pieces, so that the fireplace is partly enclosed on three sides. They were also sometimes carried on long corbels projecting

HOOD OVER DOOR; CUT STONE SUPPORTED ON CORBELS; SYRIA, 5TH OR 6TH CENTURY.

from the wall, or on light columns, one or more on either side.

B. In modern usage, a light pyramidal or conical covering as of iron suspended over the

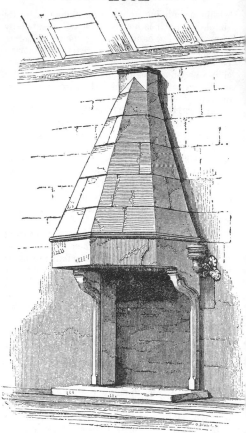

HOOD OVER FIREPLACE IN THE HALL, MEARE, SOMERSETSHIRE.

furnace of a laboratory or the like, or even a cooking range, either hung free from the ceiling or supported on light uprights or set against the wall, as the furnace, etc., stands free or has one side engaged. The use of such a hood is mainly for ventilation; sometimes very important to prevent disagreeable or noxious smells from pervading the building. A flue and special provision for the circulation of air in the flue are therefore necessary. (Cuts, cols. 395, 396, 397, 398.) — R. S.

HOOD MOULDING. (See Dripstone.)

HOOK. A member, usually of metal, of which a part is bent at an angle or to a curve so that, when secured in place, the free portion can, by means of the bend, serve for suspension, attachment, or security. In its simpler form it may be merely a bent wire which can be screwed or driven into a wall.

Chimney Hook. A large hook, generally of wrought iron, secured to the masonry inside of a fireplace or chimney, for suspending utensils or provisions over the flame or in the smoke.

(Compare Crane, which may be considered as a more elaborate form.)

HOOK AND BUTT. A form of Scarf Joint (which see, under Scarf).

HOOKE, ROBERT; physicist, astronomer, and architect; b. July 18, 1635; d. March 3, 1703.

This celebrated philosopher and physicist was a cotemporary and rival of Sir Christopher Wren (see Wren). Sept. 19, 1667, he exhibited a model for rebuilding the city of London after the Great Fire of 1666, which was not adopted, but secured for him the appointment of city surveyor. He designed, in London, Bethlehem Hospital, Montague House, burned in 1686, the College of Physicians, and, in 1691, Alderman Aske's hospital in Hoxton.

Stephen, *Dictionary of National Biography*.

HOPPER. In building, anything having the shape of a hopper of a mill ; *i.e.* a funnel-shaped or reversed hollow conical or pyramidal object of any sort, or something approximating to that shape. Thus, in simple appliances for ventilation, a hopper casement is a piece of sash having a slope outward and upward, allowing air to enter at the top ; and the term is still applied when such a piece of sash is hinged at the bottom and allowed to swing outward at pleasure. It has

HOOD OVER DOOR OF AYRAULT HOUSE, NEWPORT, R.I.

side pieces, so that when opened the air passes at the top only. By extension, but erroneously,

HOOD OF 12TH CENTURY FIREPLACE, BOOTHBY PAGNEL, LINCOLNSHIRE.

the term is applied to sloping objects whose smallest part is at the top, as a ventilating Hood.

HOPPER CASEMENT. (See under Hopper.)

HOPPER HEAD. A hopper-shaped catch-basin at the head of a water leader.

HORIZON LINE. (See Horizontal Line.)

HORIZONTAL CORNICE. Same as Geison ; a term used to distinguish it from the raking cornice of the pediment above.

HORIZONTAL LINE. In a perspective drawing, a line across the picture representing the horizontal plane which passes through the eye of the spectator ; the trace of that plane on the picture plane. Called also horizon line.

HORIZONTAL PLANE. In Projection, one of the planes to which the vertical lines of projection are carried, and upon which the horizontal projection is set down. Plans of stories are drawings of such projections.

HORLEMAN, BARON CHARLES; architect ; b. Aug. 24, 1700 (at Stockholm, Sweden); d. Feb. 9, 1753.

From 1728 to 1753 he superintended the construction of the royal palace in Stockholm, and designed many public buildings in the Italian style.

Arch. Pub. Soc. Dictionary.

HORN. *A.* Something projecting, usually of small size, and tapering more or less toward a point. One of the four angles of a Corinthian abacus is in this sense a horn; and the term may be applied to one of the strong-stemmed projections terminating in leaf form which were characteristic of thirteenth century Gothic sculpture. (French *crochet*.)

B. A volute like that of an Ionic capital, for which the more extended term ram's horn would seem to be more appropriate.

C. One of the corners of the Mensa of an altar.

HORN CENTRE. A small disk, originally of transparent horn, with three minute pointed legs, to be placed on a drawing at the centre of a required circle or arc, to protect the paper from injury by the point of the compasses.

HOROLOGIUM. A building intended to contain, or support, a timepiece; whether this be a sundial, a water clock as in the so-called Temple of the Winds at Athens, or a clock with works and a dial.

HORSE. *A.* A beam or scantling supported horizontally by a pair of legs at each end, the tops of each pair uniting with the horizontal piece, and their feet spreading so as to form a broad stable base.

B. A handbarrow with four legs, usually about two feet high, so that the handles come easily within the workman's reach.

C. A portable platform supported on two brackets and arranged so as to be hooked to the sill of a window, and to provide standing room outside the wall for carpenters, glaziers, and the like. Several movable devices receive this name, but have hardly a close connection with building. (See Builders' Jack, under Jack.)

D. Same as Horse Block.

HORSE (v. t.). To cut (a piece of lumber) into a peculiar shape. In this sense, limited to one or two special members of a building; thus, a horsed string of a flight of stairs is one which has been sawed alternately horizontally and vertically so that the upper edge shows a series of right-angled projections to which may be secured the treads and risers which are to form the steps. The string of a stair so treated is said to be horsed or horsed-out, as distinguished from ploughed or ploughed-out; and the same terms are used for the completed stairs.

HORSE BLOCK. A solid block, as of stone, or a platform, set near a door or elsewhere for persons wishing to mount on horseback or enter a vehicle. At some doorways of modern houses such a platform is constructed in the width of the flight of steps leading to the level of the doorsill, corresponding in height to three or four steps, and projecting past them outward to about the line of the lowest riser. This may be arranged where vehicles as well as horses can be drawn up close beside it.

HORSEGUARDS. In London; the building of the army administration of Great Britain.

It stands between Whitehall and St. James's Park, and was built by William Kent and John Vardy about 1742 in what was considered the Palladian manner, though it is not a columnar building nor decorated with pilasters.

HORSE-OUT (v.). Same as Horse (v.).

HORSESHOE. (Used attributively.) Having the form and somewhat resembling a horseshoe, as a horseshoe arch; or suggesting the idea of that form; this being very often remote enough from the actual curved shape. Thus, the great double staircase in one of the courts of the Palace of Fontainebleau has always been called the Horseshoe Staircase, and a similar name is given to a perron in the new Louvre, although in neither case is the actual plan very suggestive of a horseshoe.

HORTON, THOMAS DE; abbot; d. 1377.

He commenced building the cloister of the cathedral of Gloucester, England, in 1351. He built also the north transept of the cathedral.

Winkles, *Gloucester Cathedral*; Britton, *Cathedral Antiquities*, Vol. V.

HOSPICE. In French, a resort for travellers; usually one maintained by monks or connected with a religious or charitable fraternity. It is the Latin term *hospitium* modified (see the passage concerning the derivation of these terms at the beginning of the article Hospital; see also Hospitalium). The word in French means also a kind of almshouse, but in this signification has not been adopted in English.

HOSPITAL. (From the Latin *hospes* (gen. *hospitis*), which, like earlier forms of the word in other languages, meant both host and guest; hence the word *hospitalis*, a guest; *hospitalia* and *hospitium* were used for the place in which a guest was received as an inn or lodging house. Through the French *hostel*, and *hospital*, which later became *hôtel* and *hôpital*, the like words with distinctive meanings came into the English language.)

A building for the care of the sick, or for surgical operations and the subsequent care of those who have undergone them.

In the gradual development of the ideas which have found expression in provision for the care of the sick, since the beginning of the Christian era, the forms of construction of hospitals in more modern times have been largely influenced by their association with religious interests. The monastic institutions took on the character of places of entertainment and refuge for both the well and the sick; thus the earlier hospitals that were constructed solely for the sick maintained a distinctive architectural character, and were large and strongly built, enclosing open courts. A few ancient examples remain, in European countries, of hospitals which owe their preservation to the interesting monumental character of their architecture; and the monastic influence is still seen in some of even the most recent examples in which architectural effects are given undue prominence. The mediæval idea appears to have been to collect in large halls as many patients as possible; this rendered supervision easy, while it conformed with the desire of philanthropic founders and builders to produce imposing exterior effects. The great hospital at Milan for 3,500 patients is an existing example; and the old Hôtel Dieu of Paris consisted of an extraordinary aggregation of wards added to wards in a many-storied building. The old S. Thomas Hospital of London, of later date, was of like character.

The crowding of the sick and wounded together in large buildings, with wards inadequately ventilated and lighted, was the cause of a terrible mortality; the medical profession, more than a century ago, appreciated this, and strongly condemned and protested against such hospital construction. This had little effect in Europe, but with the experience of the War of the Revolution this country was saved from such extreme errors; and even then the military surgeons declared the superiority of huts and barracks. Before the middle of the present century John Howard in England proposed small wards with large opposite windows, and that water-closets should be outside the wards; and surgeons refused to operate in unhealthy hospitals. In Paris the Lariboisière was the first example of a pavilion hospital of any importance; it was completed in 1854, avowedly upon the principles promulgated by the Academy of Sciences in 1778. But later the new Hôtel Dieu, completed in 1876, although a very costly pavilion hospital, is one of the worst examples in modern times of many-storied buildings; there was great opposition to it by the medical profession of Paris.

It was the experience of the civilized world in the third quarter of this century that has largely caused the remarkable change in the methods of caring for the sick and wounded. In the Crimean War the mortality in the badly drained and ventilated and overcrowded hospitals at Scutari rose to .427 of the cases treated, while in the rough wooden huts above Balaclava it was under 3 per cent. The lesson of the war was that not only is a proper allowance of cubic space necessary, but there must be free movement of air. Dr. de Chaumont wrote, "For many diseases, especially the acute, the merest hovels with plenty of air are better than the most costly hospitals without it." Florence Nightingale said, "It may seem a strange principle to enunciate, as the first requirement of a hospital, that it shall do the sick no harm."

The American Civil War, followed by the Franco-Prussian War, emphasized the experiences which seemed to establish the principle that all constructions for the care of acute medical and surgical diseases should be temporary, and so cheaply built as to make it practicable to destroy them and build anew every twelve or fifteen years. A number of examples of this idea in hospital construction were built prior to 1875, particularly in America, France, and Germany. The substantial, permanent hospitals were then regarded with regret for their cost, and as only to be tolerated; and as requiring great care to correct their evils. It was believed that the high rates of mortality in such hospitals were due to defects of construction; and that, as the well are made sick by "crowd-poisoning," so the sick placed under like influences are all the more surely hurried to their death. These evil conditions were characterized as due to "hospitalism" and "hospital influence," and certain "hospital diseases" were recognized. It was proved by these experiences that the safety of the sick and wounded from the infectious influences of hospitalism could be prevented by separating them more from each other, giving them ample air-space and a sufficient supply of pure air in one-story buildings, and by maintaining cleanliness.

The architectural requirements of a hospital, under the influences just described, had thus become reduced to very simple terms for their practical adaptation to the essential purpose. The student of the subject, in order to understand the reasons for the great apparent change of opinion in these matters, during the last twenty-five years, in the minds of those who are best informed, needs only to recognize the influence of the remarkable progress in medicine. As the "germ theory" of disease became established it explained more precisely what the real hospital requirements are, and then it was revealed how to meet them. The principle of cleanliness was found to require not only the exclusion of morbific germs from wounds, but it meant also purity of hospital atmosphere. It was found that septic bacteria in the excreta from the bodies of the sick could be destroyed by antiseptics, and that aseptic methods being employed in surgical operations and in the dressings of wounds, no poisonous influences were permitted to exist in the hospital, or were not generated there. It became evident that extreme simplicity in the forms of the buildings, or their destruction in a few years, was no longer required, but that almost any hospital can be kept free from infectious influences.

The problem of construction then assumed a more definite form. It was found that hospital buildings of a durable and comfortable character were not only permissible, but better in all respects, than the temporary structures which had certain inevitable defects. While the one-story pavilions are still the best for the infectious diseases and surgical cases in their acute forms, the majority of the inmates of a large hospital may be properly placed in two-story buildings, and exceptionally in a third story, provided that the arrangements for insuring the air supply and ventilation are adequate and effective, and that the buildings themselves are sufficiently separated from each other, and of moderate size. These forms of construction all require careful regard for simplicity of the interior finish, to render wall surfaces as non-absorbent as is practicable, to make it easy to keep them clean, and to prevent the lodgment of dust. The perfection of modern plumbing permits also the more convenient arrangement of lavatories and water-closets, without resort to extreme measures for isolating them from the wards. The principles of construction here implied are now generally accepted with modifications and adaptations to the various requirements of large and small hospitals, according to their general or special character, and the circumstances of their location. The soundness of these principles is manifest in the continued evolution of improved forms as the special requirements become better understood in different cases. Those principles that should govern the building of hospitals demand first that they should serve the best interests of the sick. Even under the best conditions conflicting indications are involved, as between the advantage of the isolation of each sick person from all others, and, on the other hand, a proper economy in the humane care of many who need it — a consideration which demands that they shall be aggregated in considerable numbers. In the problem of hospital construction certain principles have come to be accepted as axioms which should keep within the limits of suitability even a proper desire for the pleasing architectural effects that greatly contribute, in their place, to the salutary influences of the hospital. The general principles having been stated, the purport of these axioms may be given in a specification of the requirements of good hospital construction. Taking a general hospital of average size as a type of all, the following subjects are to be considered.

1. Location and site, — water supply and drainage. 2. Foundations and materials. 3. Construction of wards and their service rooms. 4. Construction of administration, operating, and service buildings. 5. Size of hospital and arrangement of buildings. 6. Heating, ventilating, and lighting. 7. Furniture and fittings.

1. *Location and site, — water supply and drainage.* The questions arising here are hygienic and economic ; the first relate to the aspect with reference to exposure, to sunlight, and the prevailing winds as to their being favourable or the contrary, and to the conformation of the ground favouring good drainage. The

site should be somewhat elevated, with a dry, gravelly, or sandy soil. If there is an underlying and uneven stratum of clay it should be carefully drained ; and unhealthy surroundings should be avoided. The ground area should average not less than 300 square feet per bed in a city, and some authorities prescribe two or three times that amount when it can be had. Economic considerations are involved with reference to an urban or suburban site, — ease of access for patients and physicians, and cost of land. In a city, a whole square is desirable, that there may be sufficient space to allow a distance between the hospital and the highest surrounding buildings of at least twice their height. The indications as to a good water supply and proper sewerage are obvious.

2. *Foundations and materials.* In laying foundations they should be damp proof, with special care to intercept the flow of ground water, in order that the basement spaces may be kept dry ; and the construction should permit them to be well ventilated. The basement story should be 6 to 8 feet high, and the first floor should be 5 feet, if possible, above grade ; if too high it invites the danger of being used for storage, which is inadmissible under the wards. Hospitals intended to be permanent are best for most localities and climates when built of durable materials, — brick or stone, or both together, — thus requiring little repairing, and comfortable in all seasons. Hollow walls plastered directly upon their inner surface avoid spaces that harbour dirt and vermin, and mitigate the effects of extremes of temperature. For fireproof construction very satisfactory results are gained by using thin vitreous tiles, in connection with brick walls, to form the shallow arched supports of ceilings, floors, stairways, etc., in the old Roman fashion, to the exclusion of all wood framing. The use of terra cotta lumber for partitions is well known, and for thin walls, gaining economy of space, expanded metal lathing upon iron supports has been employed.

The fact that there is perflation of a large quantity of air through the walls of a house suggests that they may become saturated with organic matter filtered from the air. Great stress has been laid upon the need of rendering inner surfaces impermeable ; but there appears as yet nothing more serviceable, under the more ordinary circumstances, than well-painted plastered walls which can be washed with soap and water ; there is less objection to this with the use of modern aseptic methods in the care of the sick. When there is reason for it, as in wards for infectious diseases, operating rooms, toilet rooms, and the like, the whole, or lower half, of the walls may be lined with Keene's cement to be painted ; or use may be made of slate, marble, plain or hammered glass, and enamelled brick or tiles. Forms of these may be had for bases, chair rails, and to construct hollow curves for corners between walls or where they join the floors and ceilings. For the latter, metal plates are coming into use. There should be a minimum of woodwork.

Floors of hard pine are generally satisfactory, in temperate climates, in wards and rooms for the sick; such floors can be kept clean easiest in most places by the use of wax and paraffin dressings. In the attempts to provide an impervious flooring, asphalt and granolithic cement have been used in operating theatres and accessory rooms, and in such places as out-patient departments, lavatories, etc.; but after some use such floors have required painting. The later use of terazzo flooring and that made of cubes of marble laid close together with still less of a cement surface, have been more satisfactory. When there is a long stretch of these surfaces, the inevitable cracking has been prevented by division lines sometimes marking them off in panels, or in a corridor by cross stripes of a different coloured marble. In all floors where they join the walls, the material of one or the other should be worked to form a hollow curve.

3. *Construction of wards and their service rooms.* The unit of construction is the hospital ward. Its size may vary for small or large hospitals and for different classes of patients, twenty to thirty-two beds being within the limits of safety and suitable for convenience and economy of service. Wards of four to ten beds, or single rooms, are necessary for special cases or in small hospitals. Wards for patients with acute infectious diseases, or serious surgical cases, are best placed in a separate pavilion of one story. Exceptionally, pavilions may be two-storied; and in a large hospital, a few proper cases may be selected for a third story.

Long wards with opposite rows of windows and beds were formerly considered best; but wards that are square, octagonal, or round in form are found to be excellent, generally having a chimney, vent shaft, and fireplaces in the centre of the ward. The width of oblong wards should be from 24 to 30 feet. When the heads of two opposite beds are placed 18 inches from the walls, a clear space of 12 feet is left in the centre of a ward 28 feet wide. A linear wall space of $7\frac{1}{2}$ feet gives a floor area of 105 feet per bed; and a ward for twenty-four beds would be 90 feet long; a height of 12 to 14 feet at the centre of a slightly arched ceiling is ample, and these dimensions will furnish an air space per bed of 1470 cubic feet. Some surgical wards may have a window to each bed, but ordinarily it is allowable to place two beds between each pair of windows. These should have an area equal to 25 or 30 square feet for each bed, with sills 2 to $2\frac{1}{2}$ feet from the floor; and double windows are advisable in cold climates.

One or two small rooms for separation of patients from others should be attached to every large ward. The service rooms proper are a dining or serving room with food lift; a scullery or duty room; a small day room with adjoining toilet room for head nurse; rooms for linen and patients' clothing; and a broom closet. The lavatory and bathroom may open directly upon the corridor; and the former may be arranged as a lobby to the water-closets; all these rooms should be well lighted. Sun rooms are often placed on the southern exposure of wards, having broad windows, or, if practicable, glass roofs and panelled removable sides. A broad connecting corridor between buildings is sometimes thus utilized.

4. *Construction of administration, operating, and service buildings.* The administrative part of a hospital contains the business offices, rooms for residence of officers and servants, storerooms, and rooms for nurses, where there is no special house for them. This building may follow ordinary forms as to interior construction, except that simplicity should prevail. The service buildings, which are wholly or in part detached in large hospitals, include the kitchen, laundry, boiler house, etc.; convenience and economy of service should be studied here, with strict regard for the requirements of light, air, and cleanliness. In small hospitals, the kitchen may be within the administration house, provided it has an ample ventilating chimney, to the efficiency of which a smoke flue from an adjoining boiler or furnace room may contribute.

The operating theatre, with a few accessory waiting and etherizing and apparatus rooms, constituting a separate building, though conveniently connected with others by a covered way, has been a common arrangement; an out-patient department is sometimes included, or the latter is also separate in a large hospital. A more recent practice is to associate with a smaller operating theatre a number of rooms for special surgical work, with the required waiting rooms and those for sterilizing and storage of dressings, instruments, etc. The elaborate use of metal, porcelain, marble, and glass in all these rooms has been indicated. The aseptic character of such construction has seemed to justify the addition of a number of rooms in the same building for the after treatment of operative cases.

A pathological laboratory should be an adjunct of every modern hospital of any importance; a properly constituted building may contain also the autopsy or post-mortem room, and the mortuary. These apartments may have connections with the main buildings of the hospital. Every hospital should have a completely detached disinfecting house, equipped with apparatus for subjecting infected clothing to the heat of steam under pressure.

5. *Size of hospital and arrangement of buildings.* It is the rule that every hospital must be enlarged as its benefits are appreciated and as the population which it serves increases; the estimate was made in 1867 that there should be four hospital beds for every one thousand inhabitants of London. In American cities one-half as much general hospital accommodation would be ample. The natural growth of every hospital should be provided for when it is founded; allowance should be made for ground space, to permit the addition of pavilions and special service buildings. An administration building, made large enough to be at first the residence of officers, nurses, and others, even including patients, may be used later more exclusively for official purposes.

The administrative and service departments being conveniently centralized, the pavilions containing wards should be arranged with special care to gain their exposure on three sides to sunlight; service rooms may be placed on the fourth or northerly side. The axis of a long ward should lie near a meridian line or to the west rather than to the east of south, if that position is more expedient. The rule for the distance between buildings is twice the height of the highest one. Much depends upon the contour of the ground, the approaches, and other considerations that must be carefully studied before any plan is begun.

6. *Heating, ventilating, and lighting.* The first two of these topics are inseparable; there should be adequate provision for the escape of impure air to let the fresh air in. It is a cardinal principle that there should be an abundant air supply warmed by indirect radiation, for which steam heat is the most controllable for a large hospital. The inlets may be near the floor, in the outer wall near or under a window; the outlets should open into vent ducts, both near the floor and ceiling, the upper ones having valves to close them. Vent ducts should lead to a warmed vent shaft, or to a chamber in the loft of considerable size where the holding of a body of warm air, before its escape through the ventilating openings above, tends to determine the upward flow. With heat in these vent shafts and chambers, a more efficient extraction system is constituted; after the provision for that system is made, a propelling fan to control the inflow of fresh air may be added to constitute the plenum system. No single ventilating duct in the form of a chimney flue leading upward directly to the outer air can be depended upon. These general principles should be carried out by the experts in these matters, who should be consulted.

The artificial lighting of hospital wards is made easy by the modern perfection of electric lighting; and the deterioration of the air by burning gas is avoided.

7. *Furniture and fittings.* In the planning of hospital wards, structural considerations should have regard, as far as necessary, to the principles of simplicity in all furnishings, fixtures, and fittings. The movable articles of ward furniture are now made almost entirely of metal, painted or enamelled, or fitted with glass, as table tops for example; in like manner the fixtures of the toilet and bathrooms should be of materials impervious to absorption of organic matter. The plumbing fixtures should be exposed as completely as possible; it is a good rule to keep the wastes and traps of water-closets above the floor, or to place traps below the ceiling in the room below, the object being not to permit these or pipes of any kind to run laterally in the space under the floor. In some cases, a pipe shaft $(2 \times 2\frac{1}{2}$ feet$)$ has been used for ventilating such rooms, and made to convey all the perpendicular runs of pipes, — for hot and cold water, steam, etc. Into these shafts they can be led laterally from the room.

There are still to be considered small hospitals in communities where large ones are neither practicable nor necessary, and special hospitals of different kinds. A point of special interest concerning these is the growing demand for serviceable and inexpensive buildings in small towns and villages. A great advance has been made within a few years in devising satisfactory forms of construction suitable to such circumstances. Some single buildings, and small groups of them suitably arranged, have been planned and built with admirable success.

In the construction of hospitals for special diseases it is always possible to make a practical adaptation of the accepted axioms, the strictest extremes not always being required. The great institutions for the insane present problems for special study, concerning which there are changing views as well as differing needs and circumstances.

The subject of hospitals has a peculiar interest in that the best structural results are to be gained through a recognition of the fact that requirements are combined of which the best knowledge is held by experts in two professions and in neither singly. The history of hospital construction proves that its evolution is on the truest lines when the combination of knowledge and experience on all sides of the complex problem leads to logical results. — EDWARD COWLES.

Chelsea Hospital. For invalided soldiers; built by Charles II. and in part from the designs of Sir Christopher Wren. It is an interesting building, in great part of red brick, and encloses three quadrangles, one of which is large and stately in effect. The growth of London has caused it to be included now in a densely built section.

Cottage Hospital. One for a small community, as a village or small town, or for a special

PLATE XVII

HÔTEL

Court of the Hôtel Carnavalet in Paris. A building of the French centuries. The sculptured figures of the four seasons are of the school of Renaissance originally designed by P. Lescot, but associated with the Jean Goujon. The building is now used as a historical museum of the

form of disease, or depending upon a separate small foundation, which in disposition, plan, and design may be thought to resemble a cottage or several cottages rather than the more elaborate public building.

Greenwich Hospital. For invalided sailors and other men who have served in the British navy. It was founded by Charles II. but was built chiefly by Mary II. and by her husband, William III., from the designs of Sir Christopher Wren. The growth of the town has brought this hospital and the beautiful park attached to it close to the built-up region of Southwark.

Pavilion Hospital. One in which the wards occupy separate buildings, connected with one another by narrow and well-ventilated corridors, if at all. One in Berlin has twenty-eight beds in each ward; the wards occupy each the whole of one story of a pavilion, and the pavilions are wholly detached and removed from one another by six times their width and five times their height. One in Nuremberg, with pavilions only two stories, or wards, in height, with steeply sloping roofs above, has the pavilions sixty-eight feet apart, and also wholly unconnected. A recently accepted design for a public hospital at Wiesbaden has larger buildings, with smaller wards; two in each story of each building; but these buildings are very widely distributed over a large park-like piece of ground, and have absolutely no intercommunication except by the out-of-door paths. S. Thomas Hospital, in London, built about 1870, has much larger wards and four stories of them in each pavilion; but these pavilions are separated from one another by one and a half times their height; although, from the river, certain tower-like additions to the fronts make them seem broader and therefore nearer together. In this case an ambulatory only one story high connects them at one end, but at the other end they are attached to a long stretch of buildings which are taken up by the administration, the anatomical theatre, and the like. It is a compromise between the systems of separate and of attached pavilions. Johns Hopkins Hospital, in Baltimore, has pavilions separated from each other by nearly twice their width, so far as the wards are concerned, but each pavilion is broader where the private rooms and the lodgings of the attendants are situated, and at this part they are connected by covered galleries. A not unsimilar arrangement exists in the Hôpital de Lariboisière in Paris. The distinction between even the least successful of these and the regular building completely enclosing square or rectangular courts is obvious, and is of admitted importance.

Some pavilion hospitals have a certain number of circular or polygonal pavilions. There are two at Johns Hopkins Hospital and in the Child's Hospital at Bradford there is one pa-

vilion two stories high, about sixty-eight feet in external diameter and containing in each ward twenty-eight beds arranged in a circle, their heads to the wall. The advantages of the circular pavilion are obvious; it is only a question whether they are counterbalanced by greater disadvantages, as, for instance, in the considerable loss of space. — EDWARD COWLES.

Snell, *Charitable and Parochial Establishments;* Galton, *Healthy Hospitals;* Degen, *Der Bau der Krankenhäuser;* Husson, *Étude sur les Hôpitaux;* Burdett, *Hospitals and Asylums of the World;* Kuhn, *Krankenhäuser* in *Handbuch der Architektur;* IV. Part, 5, 1; Klasen, *Grundrissvorbilder von Gebäuden aller art;* F. Oppert, *Hospitals, Infirmaries, and Dispensaries;* Narjoux, *Monuments élevés par la Ville, édifices sanitaires.*

HOSPITALIUM. *A.* In Roman archæology, a guest chamber (Vitruvius, VI., 10).

B. In a Roman theatre, one of the two entrances reserved for strangers, that is for actors representing personages supposed to arrive from foreign cities (Vitruvius, V., 7).

HOSPITIUM. In Roman archæology, a guest chamber, or, by extension, a place such as an inn, where strangers were habitually entertained.

HOTEL. A building arranged for and adapted to the purpose of lodging, feeding, and caring for the wants of travellers, persons without domicile, or those desiring a temporary or permanent place of residence which shall not entail effort or responsibility, beyond a pecuniary one, on their part.

The modern hotel should not only afford ample means of furnishing lodging and food to those seeking those necessities, but such privacy, comfort, luxury, or means of entertainment as may be secured in a private domicile, and in addition every means of carrying out the domestic, public, or social functions of life. Further, it should afford means of offering diversion or amusement to those abiding under its roof, and may also present opportunities for the transaction of business within its walls; although shops should not be incorporated within the scheme, except in so far as they contribute to the daily actual needs of the guests — as might be maintained of a barber, hairdresser, newsdealer, or ticket agent.

In plan a city hotel should — where possible — be a parallelogram, either square or with the width and length within the proportion of two to three, and if practicable all sides should front upon streets or open spaces. The courts, lighting and ventilating rooms not upon the fronts, should aggregate at least from one-fifth to one-sixth the total area covered; the main or central court should comprise one half of this open area, and may be unroofed and form a driveway or entrance, as in the Grand Hôtel at Paris; be roofed with glass at the top as in the Kaiserhof at Berlin; or be roofed with glass part way of its height as in the Waldorf-Astoria at New York. The first treatment is only possible where space can be spared, but is not economical; the second impairs the proper ventilation of the rooms opening into the court; while the latter has been found to possess the greater advantages. The ground floor should be upon the level of the main avenue upon which the building fronts, or raised but slightly above it, the main entrance being upon the principal front. A covered portico should protect this entrance and a driveway, pass under it, which may be extended into the building and out again, although this feature is not essential and has some objections. One or more private entrances should be provided for those desiring to avoid the publicity of the main entrance, and to reach those portions of the house devoted to amusement or public entertainments. The main entrance should open upon a spacious and imposing hall, decorated and embellished in a rich and sumptuous, although severe, manner, to impress the visitor with the sense of the comfort, luxury, refinement, or cheer which are to be found within the walls. This apartment, variously termed vestibule, foyer, hall, rotunda, etc., according to its shape or size, should be regarded as of great importance, as it is the heart of the building from which all life springs and to which it returns; in size large enough to accommodate a multitude of arriving and departing travellers, and at the same time to admit of intercourse between those lodging in or visiting the house. This apartment in some more modern houses has been curtailed so as to allow only space for arrivals and departures, the other accommodations being found in reception rooms, cafés, smoking rooms, etc., but the arrangement has not been found altogether successful; on the contrary the tendency is to enhance the importance of this apartment, making it a place where guests of both sexes may assemble.

The setting apart of rooms for men or women is being abandoned, and all rooms are for use of both alike, the only restriction being that in one or more dining or reception rooms smoking is not permitted. This has led to the adoption of glass partitions or screens, dividing or forming the various public apartments, and admits of greater freedom in social life, less exclusiveness and fuller opportunity to view the life and movement going on within the house; privacy being found in the more retired drawing-rooms located in the upper stories.

The dining rooms should be bright and cheerful, both as to light and decoration; being used by day as well as night, it is essential that artificial light be not wholly relied upon; a luxurious and quiet air should pervade them rather than that of grandeur or size. The treatment of a portion of the space set apart for dining as a garden, using plants, flowers, fountains, etc.,

has become general, and is a marked feature of improvement.

The café for men is an advance upon the smoking room of old houses, as offering greater comforts and accommodation, while conversation, reading, or newspaper and writing rooms, to which may be added a library, are necessary adjuncts to, and should form a part of, the modern house, as they do in all representative American hotels.

The kitchen of a modern hotel being one of its most important features, the greatest judgment should be exercised in its arrangements and disposition. The dining room, café, restaurant, etc., necessarily spreading over so great an area, centralization is absolutely required, and separate stairways or passages for each room to be served should be provided; easy access meaning quick service, which is a *sine qua non* of modern living. Where dining rooms are more than one story above the kitchen, they are reached by two or more quick-running lifts, controlled from the kitchen, but where such dining rooms are large or important, it is not unusual to have a separate kitchen contiguous to same. Kitchens should always be finished in materials easily kept clean, such as marble or tiles for floors and walls, and access should be given to the public for inspection, as tending toward improved discipline in the service, and confidence or interest in the patrons.

The staircases, owing to the adoption of elevators, have become a secondary means of reaching the upper stories, and less importance is given to their size and decoration; they should exist, however, as a means of communication in case of panic, or as a reserve should elevator service be crippled. From the ground floor to the next above, or possibly to a third story, the staircases should be ample, easy, and well placed, as these are more used than to stories above, and form important decorative features.

The elevator service should consist of a sufficient number of quick-running electric or hydraulic lifts, having commodious cars, each capable of carrying ten or more passengers; in a building of more than ten stories, one such lift should be provided for every one hundred and fifty guests; the speed at which they can be most successfully run has been found to be about 450 feet per minute. Freight and servants' lifts — the same machine answering for both purposes — should be provided in one-fourth the proportion named for guests.

The stories forming the lodging portion of the house should be divided into rooms varying in size and arrangement, viz.: single chambers or bedrooms; suites, two or more connecting rooms, generally parlour, bedroom, and bathroom (or simply bedroom and bathroom); and apartments, sets of rooms cut off from the main corridors by private door and anteroom, embracing parlour, dining room, several bedrooms, bathrooms, and pantries. The extreme of comfort is too often intrenched upon by reducing the size of the guests' rooms to supply a greater number, but the plan cannot be too strongly deprecated, although the cost of the land upon which the house stands usually leads to its adoption ; this can only be overcome, where ground space is restricted, by adding to the number of stories ; the rooms in upper stories are lighter and less noisy than those nearer the ground level, hence are more desirable.

A marked feature of luxury in modern hotels is the number of bathrooms and their fittings ; there should be at least one of these connecting with every two chambers, and, for important suites of apartments, each chamber should have its own bathroom. All bathrooms should have a window opening upon the outer air, and in no case should bathrooms open upon shafts which give ventilation to other rooms.

In the design of the façades, the serious problem of taking care of the multitude of windows can only be met by a proper disposition of masses and a carefully studied outline, leaving the windows to be disposed with a symmetrical arrangement as far as practicable, but not emphasized as features of the design ; the roof should help largely to give character and dignity, but should not waste room in the plan by eccentric angles or too great a recession from the perpendicular ; wholly extraneous constructions for ornament simply are to be avoided ; the structure being monumental from its size and orderly handling rather than from individual features of too evident assertiveness.

One feature of the modern hotel is that which provides vast, luxurious, and commodious apartments for entertainment and amusement, such as ball rooms, concert and lecture halls, banquet rooms, and suites where weddings and other social functions may be held. These, while not forming a necessary part of the hotel proper, are valuable adjuncts. These rooms are usually placed on the first story above the ground floor, and are reached by special entrances, private staircases, and elevators, and should be so arranged that two or more entertainments can take place at the same time without conflicting with each other, and without disturbing or encroaching upon the privileges of the regular guests. The dining room or restaurant capacity of the modern hotel is generally beyond the limit required for the guests lodging within the house, so as to accommodate transient guests who desire to dine or to take their meals without lodging.

Another extraneous feature of the modern hotel, but sometimes added, is the roof garden. Utilizing the entire roof of the structure and laying out the same to simulate a garden, with walks, shrubbery, and vine-covered trellises,

illuminated at night, an attractive space is gained for dining and light entertainments, such as concerts, etc., in temperate and fair weather. This necessitates abundant or extra elevator service, as the regular service would not be adequate for the purpose. — H. J. HARDENBERGH.

HÔTEL. In French (the term being continually transferred to English in connection with special appellations, or otherwise), a building larger and more costly than other buildings of the same general class, or distinguished from them by peculiarities of use. The word seems to have had a more general application during the sixteenth century and before that time, implying in old French any building in which men lived or followed their vocations ; since then, the change has been wholly in the direction of limiting it to the more sumptuous buildings ; as follows : —

A. A large dwelling for a single family ; and in the cities (as most families live in apartments in large houses containing many apartments) especially a house built for the occupation of one family only. In this sense it is applied retrospectively to large buildings of the Middle Ages (see the following titles).

B. In special cases, the public edifice in which the business of a governmental department, or the like, is carried on. In this sense, often apparently signifying still a place of residence ; thus, the Hôtel des Finances or Hôtel du Ministre des Finances is in name as well as in fact the residence of the minister as well as the business place for his many assistants and clerks. It is less easy to explain the term Hôtel des Monnaies — the Mint of Paris.

As in Italy it is often said that a palazzo is merely a house with a great door into which a carriage can drive, so it is said in Paris that a hôtel is merely a house with a *porte cochère*. The infrequency of the use of *palais* and the inapplicability of *château* to the city house leaves no word but hôtel for the many important structures which are hard to classify otherwise. (Cuts, cols. 415, 416, 417, 418.) — R. S.

HÔTEL BOURGTHÉROUDE. At Rouen, in Normandy ; a building in the latest Gothic, with remarkable bas-reliefs on the wall of the entrance court.

HÔTEL CARNAVALET. In Paris, east of the Hôtel de Ville. The building is of the sixteenth and seventeenth centuries, partly the work of Pierre Lescot, and completed by F. Mansart. There are sculptures on the principal front and on the court which are attributed to Jean Goujon, and are of importance. The building has been adapted for use as a museum, and has lost part of its original internal character, but is still worthy of study.

HÔTEL DE BOURGOGNE. In Paris ; of which only one tower remains (now often called *Tour de Jean sans Peur*). It was the

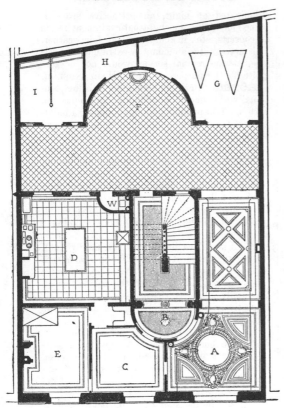

FIG. 1. — HÔTEL: PRIVATE HÔTEL, RUE CIMAROSA, PARIS;
PLAN OF REZ-DE-CHAUSSÉE, OR GROUND STORY.

A. Vestibule of *porte cochère* with passage to court.
B. Vestibule to staircase, two steps above *A.*
C. Porter's room, or office.
D. Kitchen.
E. Bedroom of porter, or office.
F. Court.
G. Carriage house.
H. Harness room.
I. Stable.

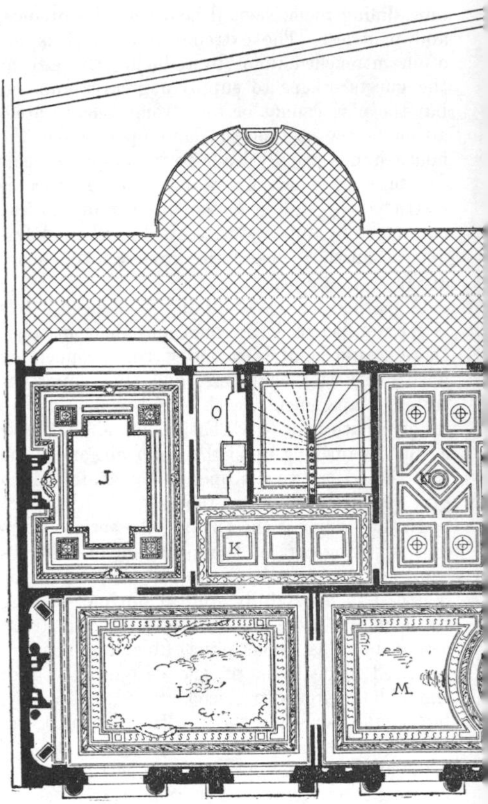

FIG. 2. — HÔTEL: PLAN OF PREMIER ÉTAGE, OR F
STORY ABOVE GROUND STORY. (SEE FIG. 1.)

J. Dining room.
K. Landing place.
L, M. Drawing-rooms (salons).
N. Salon, or library.
O. Service room (butler's pantry).

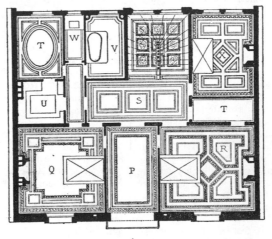

2ᴹᴱ ÉTAGE

FIG. 3. — HÔTEL: PLAN OF DEUXIÈME ÉTAGE, OR SECOND STORY ABOVE GROUND STORY. (SEE FIG. 1.)

P. Private sitting room.   *R.* Bedroom (master of the house).   *T.* Dressing room.   *V.* Bathroom.
Q. Bedroom (mistress of the house).   *S.* Landing place.   *U.* Closet.   W. W. C.

Paris residence of the Dukes of Burgundy down to the time of the fall of the independent power of those princes with the death of Charles le Téméraire.

HÔTEL DE CLUNY. A large dwelling house in Paris, built for the city residence of the abbot of the great monastery of Cluny, and now

finest and best preserved pieces of developed Gothic architecture applied to a civic building which still remain. It has been restored for the purposes of a town hall, but without serious injury to its pristine character.

HÔTEL DES INVALIDES. In Paris, a great hospital and asylum for invalided soldiers ;

FIG. 4.—HÔTEL: FAÇADE. (SEE FIGS. 1, 2, 3.)

occupied by a museum of mediæval and more recent art. The building was built toward the close of the fifteenth century, and remains generally unaltered ; one of the most beautiful late Gothic civic buildings existing.

HÔTEL DE JACQUES CŒUR. In Bourges, France. The building is one of the

founded by Louis XIV. ; the building was finished in 1675. It stands on the south bank of the Seine at the head of the great open *Esplanade des Invalides*. There are but few old soldiers living there at present, and a large part of the building is occupied for museums and similar public purposes. (For the church adjoining, see church of S. Louis, under Church.)

Peran, *Description historique de l'Hôtel Royal des Invalides;* Granet, *Histoire de l'Hôtel Royal des Invalides.*

HÔTEL DES MONNAIES. The Paris mint; an interesting building of the eighteenth century, on the south bank of the Seine near the Pont Neuf. Its special interest for visitors is the museum of coins and medals, historically and artistically of the first importance.

HÔTEL DES VENTES (more properly *des Ventes Mobilières*). In Paris, a public building in which nearly all auction sales are conducted, and famous therefore on account of the magnificent works of art and great collections which have been sold in its rooms. The present building is in the Rue Drouot, and is often called Hôtel Drouot. It is of no special architectural importance.

HÔTEL DE VILLE. In France, a building in which is located the central

HÔTEL DIEU. In French, a hospital; especially one of those in certain cities where the building and the establishment have resulted from a gift of charitable people in former times. Those of Paris, Lyons, Beaune, are particularly celebrated.

HÔTEL DROUOT. (See Hôtel des Ventes.)

HOTHOUSE. A greenhouse in which a high temperature is maintained.

HOTON, WILLIAM DE; master mason. Oct. 1, 1351, William de Hoton, mason, son of William de Hoton, also a mason, succeeded Thomas de Patenham as master mason of the cathedral of Durham, England.

Browne, *Church of S. Peter, York.*

HOUDON, JEAN ANTOINE; sculptor; b. March 20, 1741 (at Versailles); d. July 16, 1828.

Houdon was a pupil, first of Michel Slodtz (see Slodtz, M.), and afterward of Pigalle at the *École des Beaux Arts.* He won the

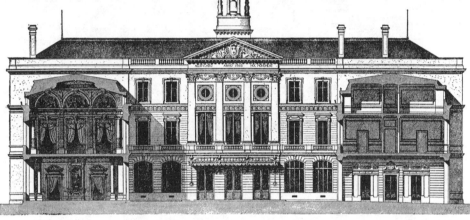

HÔTEL DE VILLE, CAMBRAI (NORD), FRANCE.

authority of a municipality. Several very important buildings, ancient and modern, are commonly called by this name, but they are never mentioned without geographical indication afforded by the name of their cities, and, therefore, do not need mention here. That of Paris, built in part under Henry IV., destroyed in 1871 by the Commune, and rebuilt with great splendour in our own time, is occasionally mentioned without the name of the city.

L'*Architecture,* series of articles on *Mairies et Hôtels de Ville;* Calliat, *Hôtel de Ville de Paris avec une histoire de ce monument;* Lacroix, *Histoire de l'Hôtel de Ville* in Hoffbauer, *Paris à travers les Ages;* Vachon, *L'Ancien Hôtel de Ville de Paris.*

HÔTEL DE VOGÜÉ. In Dijon, Burgundy. A beautiful city house of the sixteenth century, with two admirable façades, one on the court of entrance and the other on the garden.

Grand Prix de Rome in 1761 at the age of twenty. During his stay in Rome he made the famous statue of S. Bruno in the portico of the church of S. Maria degli Angeli. Houdon's best work is in portraiture. Of his portrait statues, perhaps the most important is the superb Voltaire of the Théâtre-français, Paris. Houdon was his own bronze founder, and was without a rival in that art. In 1785 he visited America with Franklin, and made the statue of Washington at the capitol in Richmond, Virginia.

De Montaiglon et Duplessis, *Houdon,* in *Revue Universelle des Arts,* Vol. I.; Gonse, *Sculpture Française;* Benoît, *L'Art français sous la Révolution et l'Empire.*

HOUSE. A dwelling; the term being usually restricted to those dwellings which have some elaboration; excluding Cabin, Cot, Cottage in its original sense, Hut, Iglu, Shack,

HÔTEL DE CLUNY, PARIS.

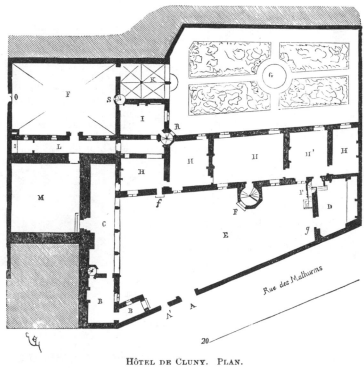

HÔTEL DE CLUNY. PLAN.

Shanty, Tipi, Wigwam, and the like. Buildings inhabited by many families are generally called by some compound term of which the word house or dwelling forms a part; as Apart-

the climate is fairly warm, with but a short winter, the house is almost invariably built direct upon the ground, without cellar or substructure of any kind. At the present time

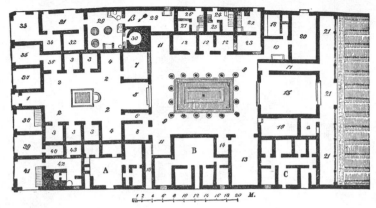

FIG. 1.—HOUSE: PLAN OF THE INSULA IN POMPEII, CONTAINING THE HOUSE OF PANSA WITH SIX OTHER DWELLINGS AND SEVERAL SHOPS.

1. Fauces, or entrance passage.
2. Atrium, with impluvium in centre.
3. Cubicula, or of unknown purpose.
4. Alæ of atrium.
5. Tablinum.
6. Andron, sometimes called fauces, leading from atrium to peristyle.
7, 8. Sitting rooms opening on peristyle.
9. Peristyle with large impluvium.
10. Passage leading to posticum (back door).
11. Alæ of peristyle.
12. Cubicula, or unexplained.
13. Probably dining room.
14. Closet.
15. Œcus.
16. Room with floor raised above peristyle, like that of the œcus.
17. Passage leading to garden.
18. Back kitchen or closet.
19. Kitchen.
20. Room leading to street, with separate door, probably for housing a wagon.
21. Colonnade of the garden.
22, 23. Ground floor of separate dwelling with second story.
24, 25, 26, 27. The same.

ment Hotel, Apartment House, Boarding House, Communal Dwelling, Lodging House, Long House, Tenement House. The term implies permanent rather than temporary residence (for which latter see Hotel; Inn).

Where the dwelling is of one large room which may or may not be divided temporarily or otherwise by low screens, it is often called by the local name, as in the case of the very large structures of Fiji, Samoa, and other islands of the Pacific; especially New Zealand. Where the local name is not used, the term hut is often

excellent houses are built in the cities of tropical South America with the principal rooms set immediately upon the ground, which has been previously dug out and filled in again with specially prepared and hard-rammed earth or sand, and this covered with a pavement of some kind. The inclination of the ground is often followed, so that it is not unusual to find the open courtyard, where the family dinner table is set under an awning in an especially breezy corner, higher in level than the reception rooms; and the stables may be still higher on the hillside, con-

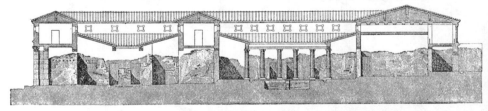

FIG. 2.—HOUSE OF PANSA, POMPEII; LONGITUDINAL SECTION. (SEE PLAN.)

The shaded parts of the drawing show the existing walls; the superstructure being restored from remains of the building found on the site.

applied to such buildings as this. At the same time, the distinction between these and the early house of the most civilized peoples of the Mediterranean world is not very great. Wherever

necting perhaps with another street. This is in the trade wind region, within the tropics; and outside of this belt of equable warm weather, and even within it as Northern European influ-

FIG. 3. — HOUSE AT MOUDJELEIA IN SYRIA, OF ROMAN IMPE-
RIAL EPOCH, SHOWING WELL THE ARRANGEMENT OF THE
ROMAN COUNTRY HOUSE IN A QUIET PROVINCE.

these additional appliances seem to
be required.

We know little of the private
house in Egypt, in Mesopotamia, or in
Greece. The ruins that have been
explored are generally those of royal
palaces ; and the resemblance between
those and the smaller house of the
same epoch is very difficult to trace,
for it depends largely upon the social
position of the inferior. Thus, we
have little information even for the
Roman dwelling as to the sleeping
place of the numerous household
slaves ; and we can only infer by comparison with modern experience that
many of them slept in any corridor or
hall of the house during the colder
weather, and out of doors, under the
roofs of porticoes, and the like, during
the summer time. The dwelling house
of the Greeks is known to us chiefly
by the appearance, in Roman dwellings of a later time, of features which
we take as being Greek in origin,
either from tradition or by strong inherent probability. The disposition
to build around the open court, which
still exists in the Mediterranean lands,
in other subtropical and in all tropical
countries, was universal in Greece and
in Italy. The Roman atrium, whether
at first roofed solidly, or with an open
louver like the megaron of the early
palaces, was, in historic times, usually
open in the middle, with a cistern
below to catch the drippings of water from the

ences prevail, the houses are apt to have their
principal rooms raised above the ground. This
is sometimes done by means of uprights, as of
wood, or built of brick, upon which the lower
floor is supported and between which the ground
is left open except as some grating or lattice-
work keeps away intruders. In all these respects the habits of Egyptian, Assyrian, and
Greco-Roman antiquity may be seen revived.

The original Roman house consisted of the
atrium alone, in which was the family sleeping
place, cooking place, and place of habitation generally. The additions to the house in the way
of small closets for sleeping places (see Cubic-
ulum) a separate eating room (see Cenaculum ;
Triclinium) and the like, were made gradually,
exactly as, in our own times, the house of a
settler in a new country will consist of one room,
with perhaps a garret in which one can sleep.
In the Roman house of later times, many of the
dispositions of the plan are apparently traditional remains of the simple, early plan ; thus,
the alæ (see Ala) seem to be the window recesses of the atrium, although the windows were
abandoned when the open compluvium was introduced. The warmer the country, the less

FIG. 4. — HOUSE AT S. YRIEIX (HAUTE-VIENNE) ;
14TH CENTURY.

partial roof. (See Atrium ; Cavædium ; Compluvium ; Impluvium.) As larger houses were built, other courts were added, and this in city as well as in country, until much later times. Thus, a second and larger atrium, often called by the generic name peristylium, with a large cistern in the middle which was made decorative, was surrounded by the rooms of the family, while the

was usually accompanied by a portico along one side at least. The larger houses of Pompeii, although in the heart of a close-built town, are not different in character from villas in the country, except that the courts and especially the gardens are smaller (see plan, House of Pansa). In all these houses the second story is of minor importance, nor is its exact disposition nor its use thoroughly well known in any one instance. (See Cenaculum ; Pergola.)

On the other hand, it is known positively that the houses of the city of Rome were often four or five stories in height. The more splendid houses, such as that one recently brought to light near what is called the gardens of Sallust, contained at least three stories of somewhat large and stately rooms. The houses which were built in the more crowded parts of the city for the dwellings of the poorer classes are little known, but it is evident that they were lodging houses, or, as we say in America, tenement houses, not wholly unlike the modern examples. The emperors, and especially Ha-

FIG. 5. — HOUSE OF 1485, NOW CALLED HÔTEL DE CLUNY, PARIS.
The wall on the right separates the street without from the court, upon which open the doors and stairways of the house, as shown.

original atrium, now treated as an outer court, was accompanied by the rooms of the porter and other dependants, and sometimes by a shop or several shops ; which might be occupied by the proprietor, who sold there the fruits of his estates, exactly as is still done in the palazzi of the Italian towns, or which might be rented to others. Beyond the rooms surrounding the peristylium there was, where practicable, a still larger open space, treated as a garden, but this

drian, issued very positive edicts about the housing of the people of the city, and to a certain extent similar regulations seem to have been put in force for the other cities of the empire.

All of this modernization — all this serious study of social problems and attempt to solve them — was brought to an end by the rapidly approaching decline of the imperial system. In the modern epoch, beginning with the Middle Ages, several curious phenomena appear, which probably had their counterpart in antiquity, though traces of it are lost. Thus, it is known that the earlier country houses of England and of Germany were habitually built with the barn and the residence in one, so that

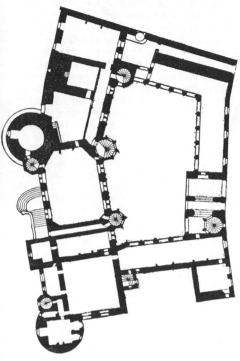

FIG. 6.—HOUSE OF JACQUES CŒUR, AT BOURGES.
PLAN.

The entrance is by the two openings on the right, the wider passage being for vehicles. The chapel is above these passages. Entrance to the rooms of residence is by the three spiral stairs on the court. The round towers on the extreme left are those of the old city wall against which the house was built.

one roof covered, and one four-square building enclosed, the stalls for horses, the stalls for cattle, the great storage place for hay and other fodder and that for grain, the cooking place, the separate accommodations, if any, of the master's family, and the places of safe keeping for whatever valuables he might possess. Houses of this character still exist among the larger châlets of Switzerland. A great barn floor might run through the centre of the building, lengthwise; on each side of this were stalls, perhaps horses on one side and oxen and cows on the other, while above these were the lofts for fodder and the like. At the end of the barn floor was the fireplace; and the fire, burning on an open hearth, without a flue, sent its smoke through all parts of the building, thus protecting the human inmates to a certain extent from the inconveniences of the presence under the same roof with them of the cattle

and matters kept in storage. Insects and the like would hardly be of much annoyance, and stable smells were hardly to be feared where everything was impregnated with a constant odour of wood smoke. At a later time the master's bedchamber was put up behind the hearth, and the point is made in ancient documents that from his bedplace he could see all parts of the interior. The further advance of the demand for comfort and for some display is seen in the building of a separate room for the mistress of the household (see Bower), and at a later time of a separate room for the sleeping place of the other women of the establishment; these having originally slept in the lofts or in special parts of them on one side, while the men occupied the other. The twelfth century had come before the country house in northern Europe had fairly separated itself from the barn and stable. Then appears the house of the lord of the soil, in which the great hall (see Hall) is the only important room. In this the master and his family ate at the same long table with the whole household; or, at least, on a table raised upon a platform and immediately connected with a lower table. A building of this importance would have a Solar (which see) and a Bower, and outhouses in considerable abundance, so that the opportunities of shelter for the dependants were not far to seek. The smaller house, that of the freeholder of no large means, would consist of a Hall and nothing else beyond a chamber in the roof, in all respects resembling a modern English cottage

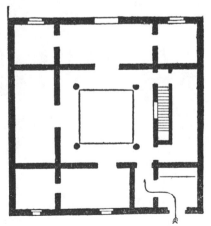

FIG. 7.—HOUSE: TYPICAL PLAN OF ANCIENT MOORISH DWELLING, PREPARED BY C. UHDE FOR COMPARISON WITH MODERN PLAN. (SEE FIG. 14.)

of the smaller type. The development from this to the large country house of the time of Queen Elizabeth is direct and simple; nor has there been any interruption in the natural evolution of the dwelling even to the present day, except where the deliberate adoption of a plan, supposed classical or in some way authoritative, has forced an otherwise undesirable arrangement of the rooms.

In the cities the difference between the house of antiquity and that of the mediæval and modern epochs is more marked. The house of the thirteenth century in a German or French town would occupy as little ground as possible, because of the crowding natural to a walled city, constantly growing in wealth and in population, but unable to expand beyond the ring of its defences. Such houses still exist; and those of the fifteenth century, built on the same plan, are not uncommon. It is usual to have a small courtyard which divides the house into a front building on the street and a back building, the two being connected by a narrow covered way, which in the upper stories may be enclosed, and serve even as a place of storage or as a sleeping place for dependants. The courtyard would contain the well; and the staircase usually was a corkscrew or spiral occupying but little room and placed in an angle of the court. It might then be more or less enclosed; in a house of some pretensions, especially in a Northern town, the staircase would become a solid round tower with a roof of its own. The rooms of the front building would be lighted from the street and from the court; the windows on the street being generally smaller, and those of the lower stories very small and strongly guarded with wrought-iron gratings. By the beginning of the fourteenth century this distinction partly disappears, and the house fronts from that time are extremely varied and beautiful, with windows of considerable size. This is especially the case in cities where great and continued prosperity and the absence of internal warfare gave the householder confidence. Thus, in Venice, even from the twelfth century, the water fronts are exquisitely graceful and fantastic, with great numbers of windows — the whole front being opened up as completely as in our modern residences. The back building, which took its light only from the court in most instances, was still sufficiently open and airy to be entirely pleasant. Even at this day one can hire a room in a German town house of the fourteenth century with no windows except those on the open gallery looking on the court, and can be entirely comfortable. The town house even of a very wealthy resident, such as that splendid fifteenth century mansion of Jacques

Cœur at Bourges, is hardly different in character from the smaller house described. Thus, in the mansion last named, the chapel is built above the entrance gate, and on each side of it are rooms, both on the ground floor and above; while opposite the entrance and across a courtyard larger in proportion to the greater size of the establishment rises the main house with three staircase towers, each one connecting with rooms on three stories besides the garret. Here again there is a well in the court, and here also partly enclosed and covered galleries connecting the front buildings with the rear ones; the main difference being that, as here the house was built against the inner face of the city wall, the main rooms are lighted only or chiefly from the court, to which, therefore, special pains was given to make it sunny and airy. (See, in addition to the references above, Ala; Andron; Fauces; Gallery; Hall; Œcus; Solar; Tablinum; Vestibulum; and the terms denoting modern subdivisions of a house.) (Cuts, cols. 433, 434; 435, 436; 437, 438; 439, 440.) — R. S.

Fig. 8. — House in Bruges, c. 1565.

The Gothic forms and details keep their hold on domestic architecture throughout the century.

Basement House. In New York and other American cities, a house of which the principal entrance is into the story below that of the principal drawing-rooms, as most common in London. There are assumed to be three kinds of these, viz. : —

First, English Basement House, which type has been in use since 1840, but has never been very common. In this it is usual for an office or reception room and the dining room to occupy the story of entrance, the kitchen to be in the cellar or sub-basement, and a cellar for the furnace, fuel, stores, and the like, to occupy the space in front of the kitchen. The front door of such a house was seldom more than three steps above the sidewalk.

story where the front door was contained only the same rooms as in the English Basement House. The chief use of the high stoop was to allow of a subcellar, or, in other words, of two stories below the sill of the front door.

Third, The American Basement House, which

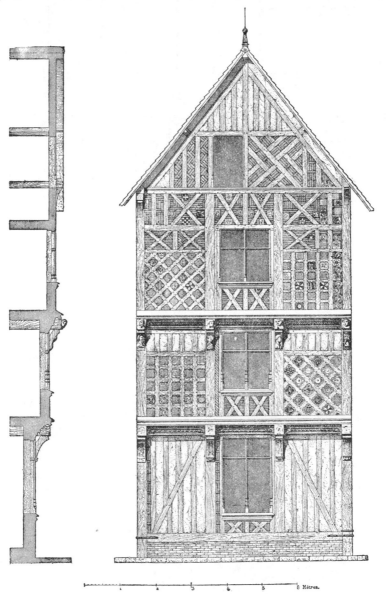

FIG. 9.—HOUSE AT BEAUVAIS, C. 1540.

Good example of the French Renaissance in its simpler manifestations.

Second, The French Basement House, which type was introduced about 1864 or 1865. In this there was a stoop as high sometimes as that of the high-stoop house proper, but the

type was introduced about 1880. In this the kitchen and other domestic offices, and the entrance vestibule with the foot of the main stairs, occupy the ground story.

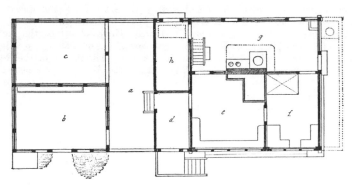

FIG. 10.—HOUSE NEAR FISCHENTHAL, SWITZERLAND; 17TH CENTURY. PLAN. (SEE EXTERIOR.)

a.
b. } Storage for grain and fodder, stable, etc.
c.
d. Vestibule, from which the door on the right leads to the house; that on the left to the barn at a, by means of a slight descent.

e. Living room, with great pottery stove in upper right hand corner and fixed bench under the windows.

f. Bedchamber, with fixed bedplace and, near the window, work bench and turning lathe.
g. Kitchen.
h. Store house for wood, with trap door to room above, where provisions, etc., are stored. The arrangement of the story above is very similar, with the addition of the gallery on the right, which in this instance is partly enclosed.

FIG. 11.—HOUSE NEAR FISCHENTHAL, SWITZERLAND. (SEE PLAN.)

Church House. A parish building for meetings, festivals, and the like.

Earth House. A prehistoric subterranean chamber; a local name in Scotland. These are especially numerous in the northeast. They resemble somewhat the Tholos of Atreus at Mycenæ, being beehive-shaped, of stone, and heaped over with earth, forming low mounds above the general grade (called also Pict's House).

Hanse House. Same as Guildhall.

High-stoop House. In New York and some other American cities, a house furnished with a stoop, having from six to twelve steps, and with the drawing-rooms, dining rooms, etc., in the story to which the front door at the

farms. The house is, then, the most important mansion in a country neighbourhood, especially in England, and often has a park dependent upon it. (See Country House; Seat, and subtitle Country Seat; also Château.)

Pict's House. Same as Earth House (see subtitle above).

HOUSE (v.). To frame, or to put together two members by the insertion of one into a recess, groove, or the like, formed in another. The term is more applicable to such a connection when of considerable relative extent, and especially when of the full thickness of the inserted member, rather than when formed by means of a comparatively small tenon or tongue.

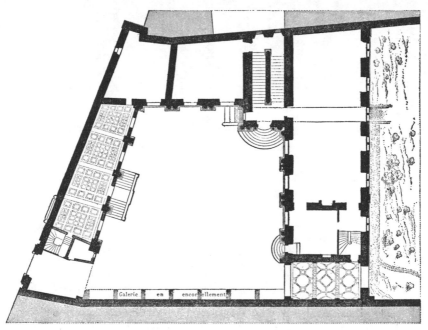

Fig. 12. — House called Hôtel d'Assézat, at Toulouse. Plan.
See Accouplement, illustration, and Arcade, illustration, for parts of court front.

head of the stoop gives immediate access. This type of house may be considered as a direct successor to the small and simple village houses which had, of course, no pretence of a story of drawing-rooms removed from the entrance; the chief difference being in the placing of the kitchen in the story below that of the entrance, in New York, while in Philadelphia, Baltimore, and other cities, the kitchen generally occupied a back building (see L), and in Boston a modification of the English Basement House was used (see Basement House above).

Manor House. A house occupied by the lord of a manor, which — formerly a landed estate of which parts were held by persons in a peculiar way, serving and dependent upon the lord — is now little more than property rented in

Thus, Dado (v.) is almost equivalent to house (v.), while an arrangement by mortise and tenon would hardly be called housing.

HOUSE BOAT. A large flat boat upon which is erected a dwelling sufficient for residence. In the rivers of China, Burmah, and parts of Hindustan such structures have been used for the dwellings of families for many years. In China the word is used also for boats used by European families on river journeys. In England and the United States they are used for residence in pleasant weather and as a place of summer resort. The boat may be moored in a lake or in an unfrequented reach of a river.

HOUSE DRAINAGE. The arrangements for the removal of sewage and water from

FIG. 13.—ROW OF SMALL HOUSES, RUE D'OFFREMONT, PARIS.
The extreme neatness of the plan is noticeable.

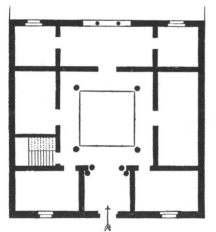

FIG. 14.—MODERN HOUSE AT CORDOVA. PLAN TO
BE COMPARED WITH FIG. 7.
The square court (patio) with four columns is a feature almost
universal in Mediterranean lands at all epochs.

buildings, comprising a system of drain, soil,
and vent pipes, the plumbing fixtures with
traps and appurtenances, and in some cases the
pipes for the removal of storm water from roofs,
yards, courts, and areas.

Fig. 1 shows the manner in which the drainage of a house should be arranged in accordance
with modern principles of sanitation. The
main house sewer is connected with the sewer
in the street; the house drain is carried above

the floor of the cellar, and provided near the
front wall with drain trap and fresh air inlet.
It receives, by means of Y-branches, the vertical
soil and waste lines, also the pipes intended for
the removal of rain water, and branches from
areas and yards.

Vitrified stoneware pipes are used for the
main outside house sewer to within a few feet
of the foundation walls; under special conditions iron sewer pipes are used. The diameter
of the house sewer depends upon the number
of plumbing fixtures in the building, except
where it receives rain water, when the size
of the lot to be drained and the rainfall govern
its size. In Greater New York, for instance,
sizes of house sewers are determined upon the
basis of a rainfall at the rate of 6 inches per
hour, and of a house sewer running nearly full,
with a velocity of at least 4 feet per second.

Table I. gives the areas of lots drained by
different sizes of pipes:—

TABLE No. I.

DIAMETER OF PIPE IN INCHES.	Grade of Sewer 1/4 Inch per Foot.	Grade of Sewer 1/8 Inch per Foot.
4	2,000 sq. feet.	2,500 sq. feet.
5	3,000 " "	4,500 " "
6	5,000 " "	7,500 " "
7	6,900 " "	10,300 " "
8	9,100 " "	13,600 " "
9	11,600 " "	17,400 " "

HOUSE DRAINAGE: FIG. 1.

It is not always necessary to provide for extreme amounts of rainfall. Generally small houses are readily drained by 4-inch sewers, 5-inch sewers answer for a large city house, and 6-inch sewers are required only for large buildings. For buildings covering a wide area it is better to provide two or more 6-inch sewers. The smaller the pipe, the larger must be the inclination given to secure a velocity of flow preventing deposits. Table II. gives suitable rates of inclination for pipes of different diameter: —

TABLE No. II.

2-inch pipes to have			fall of	1 in	20
3 "	"	"	"	1 "	30
4 "	"	"	"	1 "	40
5 "	"	"	"	1 "	50
6 "	"	"	"	1 "	60
8 "	"	"	"	1 "	80
10 "	"	"	"	1 "	100

The comparative smoothness of the inside of house drains has an influence upon their discharging capacity. Smooth vitrified pipes deliver more water than rough cast-iron pipes. Table III. gives the discharge in United States gallons per minute of smooth vitrified and of rough iron pipes of different diameters, and at various grades, running full: —

TABLE No. III.

VITRIFIED PIPES.				IRON PIPES.				
	Diameter in Inches.				Diameter in Inches.			
Rate of Inclination.	4	5	6	8	Rate of Inclination.	4	5	6	8
	U. S. Gallons per Minute.					U. S. Gallons per Minute.			
1 : 10	271	505	840	2138	1 : 10	253	472	787	2012
1 : 20	192	358	596	1521	1 : 20	179	334	558	1426
1 : 30	157	293	486	1236	1 : 30	146	274	456	1156
1 : 40	135	252	420	1061	1 : 40	127	236	394	998
1 : 50	122	227	377	966	1 : 50	114	212	353	903
1 : 60	111	206	344	887	1 : 60	103	193	322	824
1 : 70	103	192	318	808	1 : 70	97	179	299	760
1 : 80	95	179	298	760	1 : 80	90	168	279	713
1 : 100	86	160	266	681	1 : 100	79	149	249	634
1 : 200	60	112	189	475	1 : 200	57	106	176	444

Where sufficient fall cannot be obtained, flushing arrangements should be provided. House sewers should have tight joints to prevent leakage and contamination of the soil under and around habitations, or the pollution of the drinking water in wells in the country.

Two cardinal principles applying to all inside house drainage arrangements are: —

(1) All waste matter capable of being transported by water must be removed completely as soon as produced.

(2) The air of the street sewer and of the house pipes must not be permitted to enter the building through the outlets of fixtures.

It is better to carry house drains exposed

above the cellar floor, and plumbing fixtures in the cellar should be avoided. Drain, soil, and waste pipes should be of heavy iron pipe, either cast-iron plumbers' soil pipes or heavy screw-jointed wrought-iron pipes. Cast-iron pipes above the cellar floor are left uncoated, for the tarring covers up sand holes and other defects, while wrought-iron pipes are protected against rust by asphalting or galvanizing. The advantages of a screw-jointed soil and waste pipe system are rigidity, permanent tightness of the screw joints, and fewer joints as the pipes can be used in longer lengths. In larger buildings the screw-jointed system with recessed drainage fittings is now preferred, but it is also applied in the best modern dwelling houses.

Junctions and connections are made with Y-branches, for right-angled connections impede the flow and create stoppages. Changes in direction are made under 45 degrees, and no short quarter bends are used. Cleaning hand holes are provided at traps, bends, junctions, and upper ends of lines.

To prevent pressure of air, soil and waste pipes are extended full size up through the roof, and no pipes above the roof should be smaller than 4 inches. Soil and waste lines are carried straight to the roof and have proper fittings to receive branches from fixtures on the different floors. Pipes above the roof are extended at least 3 feet, their outlets being left open and unobstructed.

To induce a circulation of air through the pipes, the system is provided with foot ventilation at its lowest point. When the drain is trapped before connection with the house sewer, circulation is obtained by a fresh air pipe on the house side of the trap carried out of doors to a place remote from windows and from the air supply of the heating apparatus. Where street sewers are constructed in accordance with a well-designed plan, and are amply flushed and ventilated, and where house plumbing is tested to secure absolute tightness, main traps and fresh air inlets may be omitted, and the soil pipe system will receive air from the ventilating manholes on the street sewers.

Lead waste pipes, of weight as per Table IV., are used only for short branches connecting fixtures with the soil and waste lines.

TABLE No. IV.

DIAMETER OF PIPE IN INCHES.	WEIGHT IN POUNDS PER LINEAL FOOT.
1¼	2
1½	3½
2	5
3	6
4	8

Where practicable, fixtures should have separate connections to the vertical lines. Table V. gives the sizes of soil and waste pipes and of lateral branches from fixtures : —

TABLE No. V.

	INCHES.
Main soil pipes for dwellings	4
Main soil pipes in large buildings of more than four stories, in tenement houses, factories, schools, hospitals for insane	5
Waste pipes in dwellings	2
Waste pipes for buildings of more than four stories	3
Branches for water-closets	4
" " slop sinks	3
" " pantry and kitchen sinks	1½-2
" " bath tubs	2
" " spray, douche, or needle bath	3
" " foot tubs, sitz tubs, bidets	1½
" " one wash basin	1½
" " row of wash basins	2
" " set of laundry tubs	2
" " each tub	1½
" " one urinal	1½
" " row of urinals	2

An essential requirement of a system of house drainage is the safe trapping of plumbing fixtures. By this is meant the application of a suitable device under the waste outlet which permits waste water to flow off while it interposes a barrier against the return of soil pipe air. (See Trap.) To be self-cleansing, traps should not be larger than the branch waste pipe as above given. The simplest form of trap consists in a pipe bent in the shape of the letter U, and holding a certain depth of water forming a water seal. Atmospheric and other influences tend to destroy the seal. An abnormal pressure in a soil or waste pipe may force the seal by back pressure; sudden and quick discharges of water through a soil pipe create a suction behind the water column, and exert a siphoning effect on the traps. During prolonged disuse of a fixture the water seal is lost by evaporation, and the seal may also be destroyed by capillary attraction. Mechanical traps with floating balls, flap valves, checks, heavy balls, etc., have been devised as an additional protection, but these are only partly effective, and become more or less foul. Some water-seal traps, like the D trap, bottle trap, round or drum trap, are open to the same objection. The common S or P traps keep much cleaner, but under certain conditions are particularly liable to siphonage, and, to prevent this, so-called "back air" pipes are attached near the upper bend and on the sewer side of the trap, and carried to the roof in the same manner as soil pipes, or enter these above the highest fixture. With fixtures on several floors, this leads to a double pipe system, which increases the cost, complicates the system, nearly doubles the number of pipe joints, and establishes air currents over the water seal tending to destroy it, except where fixtures are in daily

use. The "back air pipe" system also offers opportunities for dangerous "bye-passes." (See Bye-pass.) Some water-sealed traps, called non-siphoning traps (like the Sanitas, Puro, King, Ideal, Hydric traps), are shaped with a view of retaining a seal when siphonic action takes place, and their seal is made deeper than usual. Where non-siphoning traps and water closets with deep water seal are used, special "back air pipes" can be dispensed with, provided fixtures are located close to a ventilated soil or waste line. Long branches should be

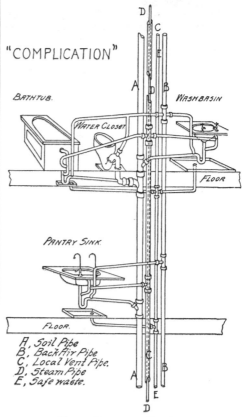

"COMPLICATION"

A. Soil Pipe.
B. Back Air Pipe.
C. Local Vent Pipe.
D. Steam Pipe.
E. Safe waste.

HOUSE DRAINAGE: FIG. 2.

extended to the roof, and trap vents omitted. This improved system is far superior to the one commonly required by rules and regulations, for the present tendency involves too much complication. Comparison between the two methods (see Figs. 2 and 3) shows the superiority of the simpler system advocated by the best authorities. Municipal plumbing regulations should be revised, and make it optional with the architect or owner which system to choose.

A feature of modern work is the accessibility of all parts. Wooden enclosures around water-closets and other fixtures are no longer used. Pipes and traps remaining exposed can be made sightly by being made of superior metal or by better finish. It is a fallacy to suppose that nickel-plated brass piping is essential for sanitary work. Where possible, water-closets should be separate from bathrooms. The fixtures are made quick-emptying to flush the trap and waste pipe, and flushing cisterns are fitted up over water closets, urinals, and slop hoppers. (See Plumbing.) Refrigerator wastes and cistern overflow pipes, safe drip pipes, and steam drips are disconnected from the drainage system, and discharge with open mouth over a trapped water-supplied sink.

In many cities plumbing is now governed by regulations and watched over during construction by city inspectors. All work is tested to guard against defects in material or workman-

"SIMPLICITY"

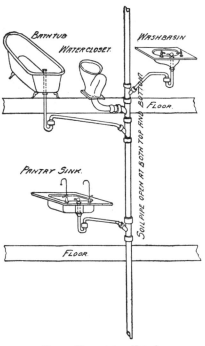

HOUSE DRAINAGE: FIG. 3.

ship. The waste pipe system in new buildings is tested under hydrostatic pressure by closing all outlets before fixtures are set, and filling pipes with water. The completed work is again tested by an oil of peppermint test or a smoke test. Such tests are also useful in the examination of the drainage arrangements of old dwellings. Of late years house drainage has become such an important factor in the interior equipment of buildings as to render it desirable or preferable for architects to leave the subject to be dealt with by educated and skilled civil

and sanitary engineers. (See Sanitary Engineering.) — W. P. GERHARD.

W. Paul Gerhard, C.E., *Sanitary Engineering of Buildings*, Vol. I., large 8vo, 454 pp. (W. T. Comstock, New York), Vol. II. in preparation; *American Plumbing Practice*, published by *Engineering Record*, 1897; *Plumbing and House Drainage Problems*, from the *Sanitary Engineer*, 1885; Corfield, *Sanitary Construction of Dwellings*, 1880; W. Paul Gerhard, *House Drainage and Sanitary Plumbing*; George E. Waring, *How to Drain a House; Methods of Sewage Disposal*; W. Paul Gerhard, *Die Hauskanalisation, Prinzipien und praktische Winke für eine rationelle Anlage von Haus-Entwaesserungen, eine bauhygienische Skizze*; J. Bailey-Denton, *Sanitary Engineering*; Coleman, *Sanitary House Drainage*; Frederick Colyear, *Treatise on the Modern Sanitary Appliances*; A. Fergus, *The Sewage Question, with Remarks and Experiments showing the Inefficiency of Water Traps*; Baldwin Latham, *Sanitary Engineering*; W. Paul Gerhard, *Amerikanische Haus-Entwaesserungs-Anlagen*, Bd. X., *der Fortschritte der Architektur*.

HOUSEKEEPER'S ROOM. In a large dwelling house, the room appropriated to the woman who acts as head of the female domestics and generally as manager. It is held in Great Britain that this room should be the parlour of the upper servants, thus separating them from the Servants' Hall; while the housekeeper has her own lodging elsewhere. In smaller establishments the term denotes merely the housekeeper's private lodging of one or two chambers.

HOUSEMAID'S CLOSET. A closet provided for the storage of brooms and the like, and usually fitted with a sink and water supply for various cleansing purposes.

HOUSE MOVING. (See Shoring.)

HOUSE OF CORRECTION. A prison of a certain class, its exact nature varying according to the law and custom of the community in which it is established.

HOUSE OF JACQUES CŒUR. (See under Hôtel.)

HOUSE OF LUCRETIUS. At Pompeii; peculiar in having had three stories for a part, at least, of its extent. There were a great number of paintings in the house and the floors were beautifully paved in marble mosaic. The paintings are mainly in the Naples Museum. Called also the House of the Musicians (*delle Suonatrici*).

HOUSE OF PANSA. At Pompeii; discovered 1811; occupies the whole of an insula, except that a number of shops and three smaller dwellings open on three streets, but do not connect with the interior. The plan is, therefore, peculiarly interesting. Mosaics and paintings were found in the house, and are now mostly in the Museum at Naples. (See plan, cols. 423, 424.)

HOUSE OF THE FAUN. At Pompeii; probably the most magnificent house discovered in the town before the House of Vettius. It occupied a whole insula, and contained when it was discovered, about 1830, large mosaics both of floors and walls, which are now to be found in the Naples Museum.

HOUSE OF THE MUSICIANS. *A.* In French architecture, a dwelling house in Reims (Marne) of the fourteenth century for the greater part of its front, and having between the windows of the principal story five statues of men playing on instruments of music, each seated in a niche.

B. Same as House of Lucretius.

HOUSE OF THE TRAGIC POET. At Pompeii; discovered 1824. A small house beautifully adorned with paintings which are now in the Naples Museum. This house had in the pavement of the vestibule a representation of a chained dog, and the inscription, *Cave Canem.*

HOUSE OF VETTIUS (or of the Vettii). At Pompeii; one of the most recently discovered of those buildings (about 1890); it is perhaps the most stately in its arrangement of all the Roman houses known, except the Villa of Herculaneum.

HOUSE OUT. To cut out, or to form a groove or recess for the insertion of a piece as described under House (v.).

HOUSE PART. Same as House Place.

HOUSE PLACE. The common sitting room of a family and their dependents; the Hall of the simple country house, in which in early times the only hearth or fireplace was situated in the house place. (Compare Fire House.)

HOUSE RAISING. (See Raising, and for full treatment of the subject, see Shoring.)

HOUSING (n.). *A.* A groove, recess, or the like, cut or formed in one piece, usually of wood, for the insertion of the edge or end of another, as described under House (v.).

B. Any light, houselike structure, as for a temporary shelter.

HOVEL. Originally, a cattle shed, a lean-to, or roughly built shelter. By extension, a poor hut; poetical and literary.

HOVELLING. The process and the result of carrying up a chimney shaft so high that the openings for the smoke may be in the sides and the top may be roofed over solidly. This device, which should be much more commonly used than it is at present, has been familiar to builders for centuries, and is peculiarly valuable where high buildings or lofty trees interfere with the currents of air and cause ordinary chimneys with their apertures at top to smoke. Many chimneys which are found to smoke might be cured in this way, instead of having the unsightly cowls and chimney pots set upon them; and the resultant forms are often very beautiful. (See Chimney.)

HÜBSCH, HEINRICH; architect; b. Feb. 9, 1795; d. April 3, 1863.

Educated at Heidelberg, Germany, and in 1817–1824 travelled in Italy and Greece. In 1827 he was appointed architect and inspector of buildings at Carlsruhe. Hübsch published *Die altchristlichen Kirchen* (1862–1863); French translation, *Monuments de l'Architecture chrétienne.*

Seubert, *Künstler-Lexicon.*

HUERTA, JEAN DE LA. (See Jean de la Huerta.)

HUGH OF LINCOLN, SAINT; bishop of Lincoln; b. about 1135; d. 1200.

The son of a Lord of Avalon near Grenoble, France, and brought to England by King Henry II. to build the Carthusian monastery at Witham. In 1186 he was made Bishop of Lincoln in England, and built the choir, called S. Hugh's Choir, of Lincoln cathedral, one of the earliest specimens of Gothic architecture in England. Some of his work still remains in the choir, which has, however, been much rebuilt. It is probable that the entire cathedral was built according to his scheme. He was not himself an architect, but employed others, especially Geoffrey du Noyer (see Geoffrey du Noyer).

Parker, *On the English Origin of Gothic Architecture;* Parker, *S. Hugh's Choir in Lincoln;* Edmund Sharpe, *Lincoln Cathedral.*

HULTZ, HANS; architect; d. 1449.

Hans Hultz of Cologne finished the spire of Strasburg cathedral in 1439. His epitaph with the date 1449 still exists. There undoubtedly was an earlier Hans Hultz of Cologne, who worked on the cathedral of Strasburg after 1355.

René Menard, *L'Art en Alsace-Lorraine;* Gérard, *Les Artistes de l'Alsace.*

HUMMUM. Same as Hammam.

HUNG (verbal adj.). Secured in place as described under Hanger and Hanging; especially, secured in such a way that the object so secured is free to move within certain limits; thus, a door or shutter is hung when it is secured by its hinges to the jamb or doorpost, and the sliding sash of a window is hung by means of cords which pass through a pulley and are secured to weights. (See Hanging.)

Double Hung. Doubly supported, as a sliding sash which has a cord, pulley, and weight secured to each of the stiles at the outer edge.

Single Hung. Secured to one side or at one point only, as a sash which is hung by one cord, pulley, and weight. This plan is followed where a window is divided by a mullion which for any reason is to be made as slender as possible. A solid mullion being put in place, the two sliding sashes are each hung on the outer edge alone, the single weight being heavy enough to counterbalance the sash. It is usually necessary to insert rollers of some kind in the other stile of each sash to prevent their binding or sticking.

HUNGARY, ARCHITECTURE OF. The same causes which have deprived Austria of so much of its ancient architecture have, as might have been expected, worked still greater havoc in Hungary. Its heaviest misfortune, however, was the fact that from 1541 to 1689, Buda and the greater portion of its Danubian provinces were under Turkish rule, and while the Turks destroyed and mutilated Christian buildings, they left few examples of their own architectural skill. The three baths and tombs of Gulbaba at Buda and a few ruined forts here and there form a poor exchange for the interesting churches and buildings shown in the *Nuremberg Chronicle* as existing in the year 1403. In addition to the Turks, other destructive agents were at work, and an idea of what some Hungarian towns have passed through may be gained from the history of Komorn, which was besieged by the Turks 1543, 1574, 1589, 1663, visited by earthquakes 1762, 1822, 1851, partly destroyed by fire 1767, 1768, 1848, 1854. Pressburg was scarcely less unfortunate, as it was besieged twenty times in three centuries, and nearly destroyed by earthquake several times, the last being about ten years back. There are extensive remains of Roman constructions in Hungary, but the only mediæval work of importance is the beautiful cathedral of Kaschau, a building of small dimensions, erected upon a plan copied from S. Victor at Xanten; commenced in 1324. It possesses a rich Gothic façade all well preserved. There is an interesting miniature cathedral of early pointed Gothic work at Saint Jak between the Danube and the Drave, with a very rich western doorway and two towers. A very pure Romanesque church with good carving and sculpture exists at Horpacz and another at Lébény, dated 1202.

There is a district in Transylvania called Sächsisch Siebenbürgen, which in 1143 became a German settlement. The churches here are curious imitations of German Romanesque, though most of them were not commenced until long after that style had been abandoned in Germany itself.

Some of these buildings are as late as the middle of the fourteenth century, the church of Sächsisch-Reen (or Regen) has the date inscribed, 1330, but exactly resembles ordinary German twelfth century work.

The best mediæval building in this district is the cathedral of Karlsburg, an elegant example of late Romanesque.

The fifteenth and sixteenth century churches are fortified and sometimes surrounded by regular castles.

There are a few round churches in Hungary, but they are unimportant.

Some of the cathedrals, such as Fünfkirchen, Bartfeld, Buda, Pressburg, Leutschau, and also the abbey of S. Martinsberg, have Gothic "shells," but so much mutilated and modern-ized as to be of little value. Some of the ancient castles are interesting.

The Renaissance work is not very remarkable; the great palace of Prince Esterházy at Eisenstadt, 1683, is perhaps the finest.

Hungary is by no means wanting in good modern architecture. The great new cathedral of Gran is a stately Italian building, and that of Erlau, by the Hungarian architect Hild, is a fine cruciform building with a dome and three porticoes supported by columns 50 feet high. Internally it is almost entirely lined with costly marbles.

The modern architecture of Pesth will bear comparison with almost any German city; the Donauzeile, the Calvin Platz, and the Andrassy Strasse present striking groups of secular buildings, and the Kettenbrücke is one of the most successfully designed suspension bridges in Europe.

Amongst the most satisfactory buildings are the *Akademia*, the National Museum, the Royal Opera House, and the strikingly designed pavilions of the Andrassy Strasse, all in the Italian Renaissance style.

The portion of Poland which was taken by Austria at the time of those various iniquities called the "partition of Poland" is by no means interesting from an architectural point of view, with the exception of the ancient city of Cracow,[1] which in general appearance bears a resemblance to Prague, though inferior to that beautiful city; but its churches are superior to those of Prague, as they retain objects of greater interest. The fine choir of the cathedral is fifteenth century work. The chapels which surround the church contain most magnificent monuments, and there is a rich throne of red marble, a very fine work.

The Jagellow chapel contains superb sculpture, both Gothic and Renaissance.

The Frauenkirche contains, perhaps, the noblest high altar in all Germany. It is by Veit Stross, 1472–1484, with a colossal statue of the Madonna and Biblical scenes in carved wood. The choir stalls are elaborate works of the same date.

The cloth hall is a fine late Gothic building, and the Florian's-Thor an interesting example of ancient military architecture.

Mittelalterliche Kunstdenkmale des Oesterreichischen Kaiserstaates; Ernst und Oescher, Baudenkmale des Mittelalters im Erzherzogthum Oesterreich; Allgemeine Bauzeitung (about 30 vols.); A Magyar Mérnok Egyles Heti Ertesitöje, Budapest; Myskovszky, Kunstdenkmale des Mittelalters und der Renaissance in Ungarn. (And see Bibliography Germany, Architecture of.)

— H. W. Brewer.

HUNT, RICHARD MORRIS; architect; b. Oct. 21, 1828; d. July 31, 1895.

[1] Annexed to Austria in 1846.

His early training was received at a private school in New Haven and at the Latin School in Boston. At the age of fifteen he went abroad with his family and settled in Geneva, where he studied architecture and drawing with Samuel Darier. In 1848 he entered the *École des Beaux Arts* in Paris under the direction of Hector Martin Lefuel (see Lefuel). For several years Hunt travelled about Europe, visiting also Asia Minor and Egypt. In 1854 he returned to Paris and rejoined Lefuel, who had succeeded Visconti (see Visconti) as architect of the extension of the Louvre and Tuileries undertaken by Napoleon III. He was appointed inspector of works and had charge of the details of the *Pavillon de la Bibliothèque* in the new Louvre. In 1853 Hunt came to America and was associated with Thomas U. Walter (see Walter), who was then occupied with the extensions of the capitol in Washington. He afterward established himself in New York and opened an atelier for architectural students, where many prominent architects received their training. Hunt was for many years the best-known architect of America, although his practice did not include many public monuments of importance. Among his principal works are the Tribune building and the Lenox library in New York, two buildings at West Point, the National Observatory in Washington, the Administration building of the World's Fair in Chicago (1893), the Fogg Museum at Harvard University, " Marble Hall " (a residence) at Newport, " The Breakers " (a residence) at Newport, the houses of Mr. W. K. Vanderbilt, Mr. F. W. Vanderbilt, Mr. E. T. Gerry, and Mr. John Jacob Astor in New York, " Biltmore House " (a residence) at Asheville, North Carolina. In 1888 he was elected president of the American Institute of Architects, and in 1893 received the gold medal of The Royal Institute of British Architects. He was honorary and corresponding member of the *Académie des Beaux Arts* of the Institute of France (1882), and chevalier of the Légion d'Honneur.

Van Brunt, *Richard Morris Hunt* in *American Architect*; Barr Ferree, *Richard M. Hunt* in *Arch. and Building*, Dec. 7, 1895; Montgomery Schuyler, *R. M. Hunt* in *Arch. Record*, 1895, Vol. 5.

HUNTING BOX. A building intended as a temporary residence for a person interested in hunting, as in Great Britain. Room for guests is always provided, and the term includes stables, kennels, and outhouses. Hunting in the strictly English sense with a pack of hounds is meant; but in other parts of the world the word is used for a house employed by persons interested in any kind of sport which consists in the pursuit of wild creatures. In this sense, same as Shooting Box.

HUNTING SEAT. A hunting box of special importance and dignity.

HUNTING TOWER. A building erected on high ground or at the junction of different roads, from which persons could see some part of the progress of a hunt.

HUSTINGS. In Great Britain, the temporary structure put up for the purpose of conducting an election and providing a platform for spectators, places for the voters (polling booths, as they are called in Great Britain), and offices. The details of barriers to regulate the order of access to the poll, and the like, vary at different times and in different places. Structures of the kind are not used in the United States. (See Booth.)

HUT. *A.* A rough and plain habitation; often a temporary shelter for soldiers, and which may be built to replace a canvas tent when the camp is more permanent and when the weather is cold; often merely a dwelling for poor people. The term, however, differs from Cot in not necessarily implying small size; a hut may be very large, and may shelter many persons.

B. A rustic cabin, or similar slight structure, commonly used as a summerhouse, or for some other subordinate purpose. The word is most often used in combination with a geographical term, — as Dutch, English, Swiss, — as in each case the peculiar character of the national architecture is assumed to be preserved.

Cossack Hut. A decorative hut, as in the adornment of a garden or park; a building exclusively of logs covered with bark. — (A. P. S.) (Compare Log House; Rustic Work.)

HUT RINGS. Rings or circles of earth apparently marking former sights of huts or wigwams in the United States, especially in the Mississippi Valley. They are from 15 to 50 feet in diameter. — F. S. D.

HUVÉ, JEAN JACQUES MARIE; architect; b. April 28, 1783; d. Nov. 22, 1852.

He was a son of Jean Jacques Huvé, architect of Louis XVI. He was a pupil of his father and of Charles Percier (see Percier), and won the *Grand Prix de Rome* in 1770. He was attached, first as director and afterward as inspector, to the works at the church of the Madeleine, Paris, then being transformed into the Temple de la Gloire under the superintendence of Vignon (see Vignon). In 1828 he succeeded Vignon as architect in chief of this monument, which he finished. The interior decoration especially was carried out under his direction. About 1817 Huvé replaced Viel as architect of the Parisian hospitals, of which he built many of the most important.

Lance, *Dictionnaire*.

HUYOT, JEAN NICOLAS; architect; b. Dec. 25, 1780; d. Aug. 2, 1840.

Huyot was the son of a builder (*entrepreneur*). He began the study of architecture at the school of design in the Rue de l'École de Médecine, and afterward entered the atelier of Antoine

François Peyre (see Peyre, A. F.) who employed him in the restoration of the château of Écouen. In 1807 he won the *Premier Grand Prix de Rome.* He made in 1817 an extended tour in Mediterranean countries, visiting Constantinople, where he designed several buildings. In Egypt he attempted a new classification of the monuments and a restoration of the ancient city of Thebes. Huyot made a special study of the topography of Athens. In 1822 he was appointed by the *Institut* to a professorship in the history of architecture. In 1823 he was charged in association with Goust (see Goust) with the completion of the *Arc de Triomphe de l'Étoile,* at that time raised to the spring of the arch. He presented a scheme introducing four columns on each side. The ministry preferred, however, the original design of Chalgrin (see Chalgrin). On the retirement of Goust in 1829 Huyot assumed superintendence of the work until 1832, when he was superseded by Abel Blouet (see Blouet). The entablature and the decoration of the vault of the arch were at this time completed.

Ch. Lucas in *La Grande Encyclopédie;* Lance, *Dictionnaire;* Benoît, *L'Art français sous la Révolution et l'Empire.*

HYDRAULIC JAR; SHOCK. Same as Water Hammer.

HYLMER, JOHN; architect.

By indenture dated June 5, 1507, John Aylmer and William Vertue, freemasons, agreed to construct the vaulting of the choir of S. George's chapel, Windsor, England, before Christmas, 1508.

Britton, *Architectural Antiquities,* Vol. III., p. 35.

HYPÆTHRAL. *A.* Without a roof; said of a building or part of a building.

B. Having a part unroofed; said of a building, as a temple, in which a court of considerable size is left uncovered, as described under Hypæthros, *B.* This is said by Vitruvius of the Temple of Olympian Zeus at Athens, which is the only building he names after saying that there was no such structure in Rome. The account is full of uncertainty, for, while his description of a " dipteros " is accurate so far as is known of the temple at Athens, Vitruvius has stated before that the hypæthros is decastylos, that it has ten columns, and not, as the Athens temple has, eight, in the front. In other words, the account given by the Latin author is brief, and apparently ill-considered, and while it assumes to describe a hypæthral temple in general, is yet evidently given of one particular building which the author had in his mind. Thus, it would not do to assume from the passage in Vitruvius that all temples which had an open court and were therefore hypæthral, were necessarily of the rare form known as decastyle, or of the rare form known as dipteral.

C. Having to do with a building, or buildings, which are without roofs in whole or in part. The " Hypæthral Theory " held by some modern writers on architecture is in general that the temples of the Greeks and Romans, having the naos or cella enclosed with solid walls without window openings, must needs have been lighted by something of the nature of a skylight, or, as two influential writers have asserted, by a kind of clearstory. Neither of these propositions would be in accordance with any theory properly called hypæthral, for that concerns only the question of an entirely open court with, as Vitruvius says, colonnades around it. This theory is taken, however, as implying the necessity of some light from above admitted to the closed shrine of the temple; and those who object to it set up the contrary theory that in nearly all cases the only daylight admitted was that from the great open doorway, aided, on certain occasions, by lamps. Thus, while it is said that the sanctuary in the Parthenon or in the Temple of Zeus at Olympia must needs have been brightly lighted in order to display the superb statue of the presiding deity, the answer is that in the climate of Greece the light, coming in through the great eastern doorway, 12 or 13 feet wide, reflected from the marble pavement of the pteroma and of the naos itself, and from the shafts of the nearer columns, would light up the statue in a way quite in accordance with the ideas of the priests in charge. It is to be remembered that, while a modern student of fine art would at once demand that the roof be taken off in order that he might see every minute detail of the design and every process of the construction of the chryselephantine statue, the worshippers asked for no such lighting as that, and the priests would hardly have desired it. Moreover, the very object of brilliant and varied polychromy applied to sculpture is the more perfect display of the sculptured forms. The question of the colouring and of the visibility of the frieze on the outside of the Parthenon cella is as difficult and as elusive as the present question of the visibility of the statue within. In either case full experimental evidence is unproducible. The probability is that, while here and there a very large temple was arranged as described in Vitruvius (III., 1) with a court, upon which we may suppose the cella opened, the majority of temples were left without any daylight except that which came through the doorway. It is noticeable too that, even where the central court existed, the doorways opening upon it may have been the only means of lighting the enclosed chambers on both sides. We are still without evidence of the use of windows in the great period of Greek architecture.

As for Roman temples, there is no objection to the assumption that there were windows in the cella wall whenever needed, but, except in certain temples of Syria, it cannot be asserted that such windows were in use. The great vaulted halls of Roman baths and palaces seem to have been lighted by large windows or groups of windows filling the lunettes under the vault; and in this manner it is possible that the temple of Venus and Rome near the Forum, and the temple of Jupiter at Baalbek, each roofed with a great wagon vault, were lighted, but in this case the external portico may probably have been hypæthral for a part, at least, of its extent. The fact that the Pantheon, with its very large interior, is lighted through an oculus in the centre of the dome, and in no other way except by the doorway of entrance, and that shutters were arranged for diminishing this light at pleasure, indicates a certain unwillingness among the Romans to open windows of the usual sort into their great halls, for whatever purpose designed. It seems probable that all attempts at giving daylight to interiors among the Greco-Roman builders were as much in the nature of experiments tried in given cases, as that of the Pantheon; and that no system was generally in use of increasing the amount of light above that coming through the door. — R. S.

Bötticher, *Hypäthral Tempel auf Grund des Vitruvischen Zeugnisses;* Clarke, *The Hypæthral Question.*

HYPÆTHROS (adj.). *A.* In Greek (used by Roman writers), open to the sky; uncovered by a roof. In Vitruvius (V., 9) the term is applied to walks between porticoes and amid vegetation. Hardly in use in English (see Hypæthral).

B. Used absolutely, an uncovered or unroofed or partially unroofed building, but in Vitruvius (III., 1) the term is applied to a temple of one particular class, which is described as Decastyle and Dipteral with the middle part unroofed, and as having a kind of peristyle two stories high in the middle, this apparently enclosing the open space. Here again the word is hardly in English use; the space may be called Hypæthral Court.

HYPÆTHROS (n.). A hypæthral building, or one having a hypæthral opening (Vitruvius).

HYPÆTHRUM. In late Latin, an unroofed building or part of a building.

HYPÆTHRUS. Same as Hypæthros; the Latin form.

HYPEROON; –OUM. In Greek architecture, apparently an upper story. It is the word used in the Acts of the Apostles, xx. 8.

HYPERTHYRUM. A part of the architrave of a doorway, apparently confined to the top of the door (Vitruvius, IV., 6). It is sometimes translated lintel, sometimes frieze.

HYPOBASIS. A lower base, or the lowermost division of a base (compare Hypopodium).

HYPOCAUST; –UM. A chamber for the reception and generally for the distribution of heat. Apparently, in Greek and Greco-Roman writing, any kind of stove or furnace, large or small, but used by modern archæologists especially for the continuous flues beneath the floor and within the walls of some Roman buildings by means of which the rooms appear to have been warmed.

HYPOGÆUM; –EUM. A building below ground, or that part of a building which is underground; used by ancient writers apparently for any cellar, but by moderns chiefly for a rock-cut tomb, or the like.

HYPOPHYGE. A hollow curve, especially that at the top of a classical shaft where it increases a little in thickness below the necking of the capital; a modern term coined to correspond with the Vitruvian term Apophyge (which see).

HYPOPODIUM. A lower podium; the basement or lowermost story of a podium when this is high and divided architecturally into several parts.

HYPOSCENIUM. In a Greek or Greco-Roman theatre, an important part of the structure of the Skene or part appropriated to the actors. The term is generally used by modern archæologists for the wall supporting the front of the stage, and which was often decorated.

HYPOSTYLE. Having large and numerous columns; columnar in a special sense, as having the roof supported by columns in several rows; said especially of one of several great halls of Egyptian and other antiquity (see Hypostyle Hall, under Hall).

HYPOTRACHELIUM. In classical architecture, a member between the capital proper and the shaft proper, perhaps a part of one or the other, and perhaps a third member, the exact signification being doubtful. (Compare Gorge.)

I

I BAR; I BEAM, etc. (See under the nouns.)

ICE HOUSE (I.). A building for the storage of ice; generally of timber, lined on the outside and inside, the hollow space so formed being filled with sawdust, sometimes with a pit underneath and drainage. For private use these structures are often partly or wholly underground, and are made large enough for a year's supply. For public use they are often of considerable extent, and are built on the borders of a lake or stream, from which the ice crop is obtained. The upper parts of such buildings are connected with the water level by an inclined plane, traversed by two endless chains connected at intervals by bars, which catch the blocks of ice and carry them to the place of storage, where they are distributed and packed by various mechanical apparatus and made ready for shipment. The term is also applied, but not correctly, to cold storage places and large refrigerators. — H. V. B.

ICE HOUSE (II.). A building made of ice. Such buildings have been erected for the amusements of the court at Saint Petersburg, where they have been put up on the frozen Neva. The first one of which we have record was a pavilion of some size lighted with candelabra and elaborately furnished. The use of frozen snow by the Eskimo as a building material has given rise to the not very accurate use of the term for the huts of those people. (See Iglu; Iglugeak; Snow House.)

ICHNOGRAPHY. The tracing of ground plans; representations of sites or plots on horizontal planes. — (C. D.)

ICON. An image, especially a portrait or likeness of something. In common usage, a sacred picture such as those which are made in Russia and other countries where the Greek Church prevails; but properly, any sacred representation when the term is used in connection with Eastern art (Levantine or Greek). Thus, it is proper to say that the icons of the iconostasis are in modern times usually painted, but were in ancient times often inlaid or even carved.

ICONOGRAPHY. The study of that branch of art which consists largely of portraits or of imaginary portraits, and other representations of sacred significance. In architecture, especially, the study of those religious pictures, sculptures, inlays, etc., which have representative significance.

ICONOSTASIS. In the Greek church a screen between the sanctuary and the body of the church; usually in one plane only; a wall built from side to side of a sanctuary and having three doorways. The term signifies image-bearing, derived evidently from the habit of covering the screen with paintings. It appears to be a general rule in the Greek Church to conceal from the laity the altar itself and the celebration of the mass.

In a Coptic church a screen conceals the three altars, as in the Greek church it conceals the single altar. The term for Egypt, as used in Butler's *Coptic Churches*, is Haikal Screen or sanctuary screen. Mr. Butler mentions seventh century examples of which the icons are of ivory inlaid in the woodwork.

The doorways mentioned above are commonly filled by curtains which are dropped at the time of the celebration of the mass. In ancient times these seem to have been uniformly filled with solid doors, as is still the case among the Coptic churches. There are, however, more variations of the type, both ancient and modern, than is generally assumed. Thus, in some existing

churches, there is an outer and an inner solid screen, the inner one opening into the sanctuary proper but still having three doors in all the well-known instances. Whether the name iconostasis is equally applied in ritual usage to both the outer and the inner screen does not appear. The essential characteristics of this Eastern form of chancel screen are, then, its height, its solidity, its being covered with paintings, or, in the most ancient examples, with inlays, and its being employed to shut off entirely from the congregation the view of what is going on within the sanctuary. — R. S.

ICTINUS (IKTINOS); architect.

Mentioned by Varro as one of the seven greatest architects of Greece, and employed during the administration of Perikles at Athens. He built the Parthenon, which was finished about 438 B.C. (see Phidias). Associated with him on this building, Plutarch mentions Callicrates; and Vitruvius, Carpion, otherwise unknown (Vitruvius, VII., præf. 12), stating that Ictinus and Carpion wrote a book on the architecture of the Parthenon. Vitruvius and Strabo mention Ictinus as one of the architects of the temple of Demeter and Persephone at Eleusis. Ictinus built also the temple of Apollo Epicurius at Bassæ. (See Cockerell, C. R.)

Plutarch, *Life of Perikles*; Pausanias, *Description of Greece*, translated by Frazer; Vitruvius, Marini ed.; Michaelis, *Der Parthenon*.

IGLOOYAH. Same as Iglugeak.

Peary, *Northward over the Great Ice*, II, 427; L. M. Turner, 11th An. Rep. Bu. Eth., p. 223.

IGLU. (Also written igloo and by Dr. Boas igdlu.) Among the Eskimo (Esquimaux) the generic term for house. They build several different kinds of house, according to locality, materials available, and the season. There are also workshops made by digging out a rectangular hole in a snowbank and covering the top with poles and skins, and there are in some villages larger houses of snow or of wood and turf used for assembly purposes and for dancing. The houses are built near each other in irregular scattering villages, and always face south. (See Karmang; Kaggi; Iglugeak; Tupek; Snow House.) Permanent winter houses are built of wood and whale ribs, where these materials can be obtained, and covered with earth, so that from without they have the appearance of little hillocks, the earth covering sloping off gradually into the ground. The entrance is through a long low passage lying below the floor level, the house then being entered through a hole in the floor, exactly the reverse of the custom of the Pueblos, who enter through a hole in the roof, indicating that these matters are the result of environment and expediency. The entrance passage is about 25 feet long and 4 or 5 feet high. The interior consists of one room nearly square (about 10 × 14 feet), with a raised bench for a bed running across the entire side opposite the entrance. In the roof there is a window made of translucent seal entrails sewed together, and above this is a ventilating hole. Sometimes several families occupy one of these houses. There are variations of this type, which is the one in use by the Point Barrow Eskimo, but the general scheme is the same. Sometimes fires are built in the houses, the window in the roof serving as a smoke outlet; but the common method of heating and cooking in winter is by means of soapstone lamps filled with seal oil. In the Mackenzie region the winter houses are similar to the one described, but their ground plan is of the shape of a cross, the arms forming alcoves, or wings, to the central room. Two houses are often built adjoining. As soon as warm weather comes these houses are abandoned for the tent, as they become wet and uncomfortable. Dall states that the Aleuts, who are of the Innuit stock, once built large communal houses without doors, entered Pueblo fashion from the roof through hatchways, descent to the floor being made by a notched log. These houses were divided by partitions of stone, wood, or matting into small chambers, open toward a central room, each accommodating one family. Aleut houses were also of sods laid up to form walls and roof. (See Barabara and Yourt.)

— F. S. Dellenbaugh.

IGLUGEAK. (From the Innuit (Eskimo) *iglu;* house.)

The Eskimo (Esquimaux) dome-shaped snow house. When the Eskimo has no permanent iglu for winter use, or when out hunting, or when visiting another village, he builds a domed structure of snow, therein constructing the only true arch made by any aborigines of the West-

IGLUGEAK: GROUND PLAN; EXTERIOR WITH SECTION OF ENTRANCE; AND LONGITUDINAL SECTION.

ern hemisphere. For the best results, snow must be deep and compact enough to permit homogeneous blocks to be cut out with the snow knife, an implement of bone, shaped like a short sword; or with a stiff steel saw when this can be obtained. A proper site being selected on some deep drift, a small block is removed as a beginning, and in the excavation thus started the builder works, rearing the circular walls

around him, the bottom of the excavation made by the removal of the blocks, finally forming the floor of the finished house. The blocks are about 8 inches thick, 24 inches high, and about 2½ to 4 feet long. One man can build a small house alone except fitting the last block; but generally two work together, one cutting blocks and the other fitting them in place, supporting the upper ones on his head while adjusting them. The first block set is of a wedge shape, the point toward beginning, thus forcing the second course to mount without a break, upon the first, and making the line of blocks continuous from start to finish by giving them a spiral trend. The advantage of this device is increased strength, and ease of construction, because there is no actual beginning of new courses, and each block laid has at once a firm support on two edges, enabling the builder to incline it inward to approach the centre. The builder " breaks joints " as he goes. The circumference is decreased regularly. The end joints of the blocks are slanted, so that the end of the new block laps over the end of the last one; and as the incline toward the horizontal grows greater, so also does the bevelling or slanting of the edges, the better to sustain the fresh blocks. Into the last opening a key block is fitted, binding the dome firmly together, and thus it stands till warm weather comes, when it is abandoned for the tent (see Tupek).

When the spiral of blocks is finished, the joints and openings are filled with fragments of blocks or with crushed snow, till the walls are perfectly tight, only a small hole being left at the top for ventilation. No smoke outlet is needed, as heat and light are obtained from seal oil lamps.

During winter journeys, a snow house may be built for a camp, about 5 feet high and 7 feet diameter, in about two hours. The permanent snow houses are made 10 or 12 feet high and about 15 feet diameter. The entrance is usually through two or three small vaults, connected, though in some localities this entrance is little more than a trench with an arched top. Doorways are about 2¼ to 3 feet high. Above the entrance a window is usually placed and fitted with seal intestines or with pieces of fresh-water ice. Much light comes through the snow itself. In the ordinary house there are generally two families. When more than two families join, they build a double house, that is, two domes near each other with a common entrance; and sometimes there are three or four domes around a central chamber with a common entrance. The beds are generally placed on raised benches of snow across the rear of the hut. The lamps stand on each side of the entrance.

In some places the house is lined with skins attached to the walls and top by small ropes

passed through and toggled outside. This is to prevent the drip from the inner surface falling on the occupants. The lining also enables the temperature within to be maintained at a higher point, the layer of cool air between the skins and the snow walls preventing melting. (See Iglu; Karmang; Kaggi; Snow House.)
— F. S. DELLENBAUGH.

I H S. A change into Roman letters of the Greek characters I H Σ (iota eta sigma, or i, long e, and s). These three letters with a bar over them form the common abbreviation of the name IHΣΟΥΣ, "Jesus." The tradition in the Italian churches is that S. Bernardino of Siena, who died in 1444, and was the founder of the Observant branch of the Franciscans, introduced the custom of distributing little tablets upon which these sacred letters were inscribed, (See under Monogram other symbols of the kind.)

ILLUMINATION. (See Lighting.)

IMARET. In the Turkish empire, an inn for Mohammedans only, and usually depending upon a foundation which provides lodging and other aid gratuitously.

IMBREX; (pl. **IMBRICES**). *A.* In Latin, a bent or curved tile approaching in form a half cylinder, either for making pipes, gutters, etc., or for covering the joints of roof tiling. (See Tile and subtitles.) Hence,

B. One of the scales or subdivisions of imbricated ornament.

IMBRICATED. Covered with or consisting of a pattern as described in Imbrication.

IMBRICATION. A covering as of a surface with a pattern resembling overlapping scales. The original significance is a tiling in which rounded forms occur, such as are made by the overlapping edges of imbrices (see Imbrex). But the term is extended to include all patterns which seem to resemble overlapping scales, and even such scales themselves, as in the pods of plants, or the skins of fish. Considered as an ornamental pattern the character of the lines and surfaces may be almost anything which can be associated with scalework.

IMPASTO. In Italian, the surface of painting and the combining of pigments which produces that surface; used commonly in English to express the technical quality of the painter's workmanship.

IMPERIAL. A kind of roofing slate; the term being often used absolutely.

IMPLUVIUM. *A.* Same as Compluvium, *i.e.*, the hypæthral opening so arranged that rain water flows through it into the space below.

B. The cistern or tank in a Roman atrium, courtyard, or garden; the receptacle for the water flowing through the compluvium from the roofs. This tank was often made very decorative, and its borders were a favourite place for the busts, small bronze statues, and the like,

with which the residence of a wealthy Roman in later times was commonly adorned.

C. The open or unroofed space below the hypæthral opening, whether filled or partly filled by a cistern or not. The Latin word, meaning simply that which is rained upon, easily lent itself to these different significations; *B* is much the most common in modern usage. — R. S.

IMPOST. The uppermost part of an abutment; that part from which an arch springs direct. As in the case of the haunch and crown of an arch, so it is impossible to fix the exact limits of the impost. It often happens that a single stone contains within itself at once the impost and the first or lowest part of a haunch. (See Abutment.)

IMPOST BLOCK. A member which gives direct support to one side of an arch, or to the adjoining parts of two arches; as in many wall openings in Italian mediæval and neoclassic work where that member is worked into the semblance of a capital; and in the heavy abacus of a Byzantine capital in some early Italian buildings.

IN–AND–OUT BAND; BOND. (See under Bond.)

IN ANTIS. (See Antis; also Anta.)

INBOND (adj.). Bonded, or forming a bond, across or in the body of a wall; as in the case of headers. Composed largely or entirely of headers, or through stones. (Compare Outbond.)

INCA ARCHITECTURE. That of the pre-Columbian inhabitants of Peru and neighbouring countries. (See South America, Architecture of, passages concerning Peru.) — F. S. D.

INCANTADA. The ruins of a late Roman building in Salonica, Turkey in Europe. It is generally in the Corinthian style, and its purpose is not perfectly understood. Only five columns remain with their entablature, above which rises a low attic with engaged figure sculpture. The work appears to be of the second century A.D. It was published in Stuart and Revett's *Antiquities*, Vol. III.

INCAVO RILIEVO. (See Relief.)

INCINERATION. The reducing to ashes of any substance, all that is not left in that form being driven off in gaseous form. (See Crematory.)

INCISED WORK. That which is done by cutting into a surface. This, if carried through the piece of metal so as to be open on both sides, is usually called pierced work, also by the French term À Jour; more rarely by the Italian term A Giorno. Lettering of any sort cut into the metal is properly called inscription; and a piece of lettering an inscription. The term "incised work" is then limited in practice to decorative sculpture in which a flat surface is adorned with a pattern sunk beneath it, or with a pattern left in relief, while the background is cut away. If this pattern is rounded and modelled into sculpture, it becomes relief. If the pattern, or the cut away parts which surround the pattern, are filled in with some other material, the term used is generally "inlay" or "inlaid work"; but it is also said that a pattern is incised and then filled in with mastic, or other soft material. (Compare Incrustation.) — R. S.

INCLINATION. Slope of any kind; especially in building that which has to do with decorative effect as contrasted with Batter, which is the slope of walls made thicker at the base for strength, or in a fortification for defence; and slope which is more commonly applied to a roof or ramp of a staircase. Thus, the axes of a Doric column in Greek work are found to have been generally inclined to the vertical (see Refinements in Design), and in mediæval work, walls and pillars are continually set with an incline. The angle of inclination is that which a roof, a ramp, or other essentially sloping member makes, either with the horizon, that is to say, with the horizontal plane, or with a vertical plane. It is rare that this is estimated by builders in terms of mathematical science, as in so many degrees and minutes. More commonly it is estimated by the horizontal dimensions compared with the vertical dimensions. Thus a carpenter will say that the inclination of his roof is three (horizontal) to two (vertical). — R. S.

INCRUSTATION. The covering of anything with an outer shell or "crust."

A. The covering of a whole surface with such a material, as when a wall of brick is entirely concealed with marble slabs or with mosaic.

B. The adornment or diversifying of a surface by partial covering which is, however, of considerable proportionate size. Thus, a brick wall may be adorned with incrustations of marble covering a fourth or a sixth of its whole surface, and the term would not be used for the mere inlaying of a few narrow bands. A metal box is said to have incrustations of enamel, or to be adorned with incrusted enamels, when the enamels themselves are somewhat elaborate compositions and are affixed as entire works of art upon the surface. — R. S.

INDENTATION. The diversifying of a surface, an arris, a moulding, or the like, by depressions or hollows; usually in a series. Ornamentation by this means is usually confined to early and barbarous work, but the beautiful Venetian mouldings are practically a series of indentations, and the edge of a slab of marble, or a board, as the shelf of a bookcase, or the like, is often ornamented by one or more series of notches which may be varied in size, in order, or in place.

INDIA, ARCHITECTURE OF. That of the great peninsula bounded on the north by the Himalaya mountains, and reaching from the lower Ganges on the east to the frontiers of Afghanistan on the west.

The history of architecture in this region presents many difficult problems, especially as to its origins and early periods, owing to the scarcity of dated inscriptions, and the almost total lack of historical statement in the classic literature of India. The multitude of petty states in what is really a continent rather than a country, the minglings and overlappings of religions and races, the paucity of authentic documents, and the successive invasions and conquests, have made impossible any broad and simple treatment of Indian history, either political or artistic. It is therefore impossible in the limits of a dictionary article to give a continuous and connected survey of Indian art as a whole, and only the most salient characteristics and most important monuments can be set forth, of the several styles which have prevailed in the great peninsula.

The natural divisions of the art, as of the civilization, of India follow religious lines. They comprise (1) the Buddhist styles; (2) the Jaina styles; (3) the Brahman styles; (4) the Mohammedan or Indo-Moslem styles. Each of these is more or less capable of subdivision along geographical lines, and there are frequent minglings and overlappings. This subdivision becomes of prime importance only in the case of Brahman architecture, which comprises the Northern Brahman, Central or Chalukyan, and Southern or Dravidian styles. The earliest of the four great divisions to develop was the Buddhist, and the Indo-Moslem was the last; but the Buddhist overlaps both the Jaina and Brahman styles, and these the Indo-Moslem.

General Characteristics. Despite the confusion of races and religions in India, certain common traits characterize all its non-Moslem styles, and are found to some extent even in Moslem buildings: peculiarities hard to explain when we consider the lack of unity in race, religion, language, and character of the people. First of all should be mentioned a predilection for minute and profuse ornament, covering every part of the architecture, without regard (except in Moslem buildings) to any controlling architectonic or structural lines. This ornament is almost exclusively of carving or sculpture, executed with extraordinary indifference to cost or labour. The second noticeable characteristic is the multiplication of horizontal bands and lines, giving an appearance as of stratification even to towers and minarets. A third characteristic is the indefinite reduplication and multiplication of the same motive, which is often itself a miniature of the tower or other construction of which it is a part. Lastly, it should be observed that in Hindu design generally, the dominant masses and chief features of a building are in no wise evolved out of structural requirements, but are purely artistic creations, in which fancy and tradition both have had a share. They are amazingly picturesque, and often produce an impression of grandeur quite out of proportion to their actual size; but one searches them in vain for evidences of that logical reasoning-out of the design, that intimate relation between the practical requirements and external form, which in Western art is regarded as essential to the highest excellence. In this respect, however, the Moslem buildings follow the Western standards, even when built by Hindus with Hindu details; if less picturesque than the Jaina and Brahman temples, and less profusely ornamented, what they thus lack is often more than made up in the monumental dignity of their larger scale, simpler masses, and elaborate settings of terraces, platforms, and approaches.

Another singularity of Indian architecture is the almost complete absence of that very important element of architectural grandeur — internal spaciousness. The impression of vast unencumbered space produced by the interior of the Pantheon or of the church of S. Sophia, or that of majestic loftiness which one experiences under the vault of Amiens or the dome of S. Peter, was never attempted by the builders of India. Vast areas were covered by the Dravidian temples and by the Mogul palace-groups, but with such small intercolumniations and low ceilings that the result, however rich and surprising, misses the effect of spaciousness.

Origins. Of the original sources of the styles of India nothing is known. The earliest buildings and ruins reveal, as in Egypt, a style already in possession of ample resources, and this is no less true of the so-called Jaina and of the Brahman styles than of the Buddhist which preceded them. The suggestions of an Egyptian origin which some drew from the caverns and Dravidian gopuras are fortuitous resemblances, due to a certain likeness of conditions, and vanish on close scrutiny. It is clear that much of the detail in all the pre-Moslem styles originated in a wooden architecture, which has itself long ago disappeared. The pyramidal stepping of the dominant masses, and the placing of temples and shrines on terraces and platforms, may perhaps be traced to Mesopotamia by way of Persia, whose art has always had more or less influence on that of India, and is conspicuous in the Mogul period. In northwestern India, in Gandhara and the Vale of Kashmir, Greek influence is plainly observable in early Buddhist art; but it never spread into central and southern India, and some of the supposed Greek details in the

northwest are rather Byzantine than classic in date and character. In spite of these exterior influences, the architecture of India is preëminently original, unlike that of any other land.

Buddhist Architecture. Nothing in Hindu civilization is more extraordinary than the absolute dearth of remains of the ancient Vedic ages, from the first Aryan invasion of northern India in the third millennium B.C. down to the time of King Asoka, 272 B.C. Meanwhile Buddhism had arisen, dating its origin from the nirvana of Sakya Muni (Gautama Buddha) about the beginning of the fifth century B.C. During the next two centuries the new religion gathered strength, and was practically supreme in India from the time of King Asoka (272–236 B.C.) until the seventh century A.D. All the monuments of Buddhist architecture in India belong to this period. As has been said, the origin of the style of these works is much debated, all the formative and transitional phases of the style having disappeared, leaving us not a single ruin or record of their existence. The strongest evidences of foreign origin or influences are seen in the Greek character of the drapery of early Buddhist statues, and in the Persian character of the bell capitals of many piers and columns, surmounted by lions or bulls couchant.

The earliest Buddhist buildings were doubtless of wood. The caverns are full of reminiscences of wooden construction, and the oldest of them were even partly finished in wood, a fact inexplicable except on the theory of the previous habitual use of wood in structural work. But no vestiges remain of the transition from wood to stone in monuments of stone imitating the slender proportions of wooden posts and beams; in no Buddhist design is there any hesitancy or lack of resource in carving and piling of stone.

Buddhist Structural Monuments. Those in India proper consist wholly of memorial columns and shrines. The columns, or lâts — isolated shafts occurring chiefly in the northwest provinces and in Ceylon — betray in their bell capitals, surmounted by lions or other beasts, the influence of Persian art, and in some of the ornaments, such as the bead-and-reel and honeysuckle, a Greek influence which may be traced to the Hellenism of the neighbouring Arsacid monarchy which succeeded the Seleucidæ in Bactria. Most of them are very old, dating as far back as the time of Asoka. More important are the shrines erected to preserve the precious relics of Buddha. These are of two kinds: stupas or towerlike structures, and topes or circular dome-shaped piles. Of the former, the only important example is the famous Buddha Gaya tower in northeastern India, marking the spot where Buddha attained Nirvana. It dates from about 500 A.D., with important restorations by Burmese pilgrims in the fourteenth century, and again by the British in recent years. It is not, like western towers, a hollow edifice of many stories internally, but a practically solid pile over a small shrine-chamber upon a broad platform, and its nine retreating stages are not true stories, but merely divisions of the external design. The horizontal stratifications, the multiplied repetitions of the same motive, the tapering of the whole, and the peculiar ornament at the top, are noticeable features. It is 160 feet high, and 60 feet square at the base.

The topes are circular stone tumuli of large size, with domical tops surmounted each by a tee or model of a shrine or reliquary. Richly sculptured stone rails surround the topes, evidently imitated from wooden railings, with one or more monumental gateways, or toranas, consisting each of two uprights crossed by two or three transverse bars, all covered with minute sculpture. The gateways suggest strikingly the wooden torii of Japan and pai-loos of China. The topes occur in groups in northern India and Ceylon; the little kingdom of Bhopal is especially rich in these groups, of which the best-known is at Bhilsa. Here is the Sanchi tope, the most ancient and celebrated of all. It dates from the third century B.C. and is 106 feet in diameter and 56 in height; but its especial glory is not its size but the remarkable sculptures of its rail and toranas. Its dimensions are far exceeded by some of the later topes: the Mani-kyala tope in the Punjaub is 127 feet in diameter; the Sarnath tope, with a richly ornamented basement, is 128 feet high, and the great topes at Abayagiri and Jetawana in Ceylon are each 360 feet in diameter. At Barhut and at Amravati in the Dekkan are carved rails and toranas belonging to topes which have wholly disappeared; the last-named dates from the closing period of Buddhist art in the seventh century A.D.

There is extant in India proper hardly a single monument of Buddhist structural art other than columns and shrines. Ceylon possesses a few scanty remains of structural temples, and there exist in Gandhara (northwest India) the foundations of several *viharas*, or monasteries, whose superstructures have disappeared. These were probably of wood, like the palaces of Patna described by Megasthenes the envoy of Seleucus; and there were no doubt many chaityas or temples of the same material, of which not even the foundations remain.

Buddhist Cave Architecture. It was in the rock-cut viharas or monasteries and chaityas or temples that Buddhist architecture in India most strikingly expressed itself. These, owing to geological conditions, are restricted to certain definite areas, especially numerous in the Bombay Presidency, northern Ghats, and Vindhya mountains. The most important of the cave-groups are those at Ajanta, Ellura, Karli, Kanheri, Nasik, and Bagh; and caves of more or less importance exist also on the island of Salsette, at Bhaja, at several points in Orissa, and in Behar; besides hundreds of others of less note at various places too numerous to be here mentioned.

Viharas. The Buddhist monasticism was the earliest in history, long antedating that of Christendom, and the earliest of the rock-cut cells in India are those excavated by Buddhist monks 250 B.C. While there are many single cells, the majority of the viharas were real monasteries, with groups of cells around a large central pillared chamber. The largest of these viharas, that at Bagh for instance, have elaborate plans with a variety of chambers, colonnades, and porches. The columns are of massive proportions, but often covered with elaborately carved and minute detail, and the chambers are often adorned with sculptures in relief and sometimes with frescoes, as at Ajanta. The central chamber at Bagh is 96 feet square, its colonnade 220 feet long. The Jogeswari at Salsette is nearly as large. The Durbar cave at Salsette, the Nahapana at Nasik, the Dehrwara at Ellura, Cave 16, and the Zodiac cave at Ajanta, are famous among many others.

Chaityas. Still more interesting architecturally are the chaitya halls, likewise cut in the rock, to serve as halls of worship or temples. They resemble the abbey churches of mediæval Christendom not only in being adjacent to the monasteries, but in being designed with a high arched nave, lower side aisles, and a semicircular apse serving as the sanctuary, around which the side aisle is often carried as an ambulatory. In the apse stands a domical shrine, or dagoba, modelled like a tope with its tee. The fronts of the oldest chaityas, like that at Bhaja or at Kondane, now entirely open, were once closed with façades of wood, for which the mortise-holes still exist. The great chaitya of Karli (100 B.C.) still retains in place a part of its teakwood screen. The later chaitya fronts were carved in the rock, in imitation of the wooden fronts, in several stories of simulated arches, columns, and railings. Wooden ribs fitted to the rock ceilings, and decorative imitations of them in rock, are further evidences of the ligneous origin of this architecture. The columns resemble those in, and in front of, the viharas; bell capitals and minute carving characterize most of them. Besides the three chaityas above mentioned there are three fine ones at Ajanta, the Viswakarma at Ellura, important examples at Nasik, Bedsa, and Kanheri, and less notable specimens at many other places.

With the seventh century begin the Dark Ages of India; the ninth and tenth centuries are historically a blank. Buddhism waned, and before the dawn of the eleventh century Jainism had appeared and spread over India. The origins of this religion are wrapped in obscurity, but owing to its affinities with Buddhism, many regard it as simply a divergent phase of that faith.

Jaina Architecture. Although Jainism is so closely related to Buddhism, its architecture resembles that of the Brahman far more closely than it does that of the Buddhist faith. Brahmanism and Jainism so long existed side by side, and their structural requirements were so much alike, that there is in many cases no appreciable difference of style between contemporary temples of the two religions. Both the Brahmans and Moslems borrowed from the earlier Jaina temples certain features and details to use in their own, and the later Jaina temples, at Khajurao and Gwalior for instance, are quite indistinguishable from the Brahman. It is therefore unreasonable to classify all Jaina temples as Jaina in style, and this makes it almost impossible to define the limits of the style.

So far as there is a Jaina style, it is — unlike the Buddhist — preëminently a structural style. The arch and dome with horizontal joints, the column with bracket arms or struts, the effective plans, the lofty sikhras, or turrets, — all denote a constructive skill and artistic taste of a high order. The Jaina temples consist usually of a sanctuary surmounted by a lofty tower (sikhra), and one or two mantapas, or porches, the whole standing in a court surrounded by small cells, each surmounted by a small sikhra or a dome, and containing a seated figure of a Tirthankhar or saint. The sikhra always tapers upward in a convex curve, and terminates in a bulbous or melonlike ornament called the amalaka. The porch, often of great size, is roofed by one or many domes, carried on one, two, or three stories of richly carved bracketed columns, the upper ones rising above the surrounding roofing to serve as a clerestory. The domes, having horizontal courses, exert no thrust and require no abutment; the result is a singular lightness and openness of columnar design. The columns are minutely ornamented, and often exhibit that multiplication of horizontal lines which characterizes Hindu buildings so generally. The same stratification marks the lower portions of nearly all the temples, and is seen even on towers like those erected at Chittore by Sri Allat (900 A.D.) and Kumbo Rana (1440) as Towers of Victory.

The oldest of Jaina temples is supposed to be that of Vimala Sah on Mt. Abu (1032), a beautiful structure of white marble, only exceeded in richness and perfection of sculptured decoration by the ruined temples of Banka and Sasonka, at Nagda, near Oudeypur, and by those of the brothers Tejpala and Vastapula on Mt. Abu (1192). The same brothers erected, in 1177, at Girnar, on the west coast, an elaborate triple temple, having three vimanas about a common porch. A hundred years later the Neminatha temple was built at the same place, with an elaborate double porch; but this is far surpassed by the great temple at Sadri, with its superb mantapa roofed with twenty domes, covering the whole area of the court and sheltering five shrines, one in the centre and four near the corners. The four chief domes are carried by three stories of columns, and the largest is 36 feet in diameter. This magnificent temple was built by Kumbo Rana, about 1440. The exterior effect of its twenty domes and its five sikhras is marvellously picturesque. The Parswanatha and Karli temples at Khajurao; the great temple groups at Girnar and Parisnath; the Panchalinga Deva temple at Huli, the ruins of Jaina temples at Somnath, Gyraspore and Amba, with many others, display the same general characteristics as those described. Of others, as the Teli-ka-Mandir and Sas Bahu at Gwalior, it is uncertain whether they were built for Brahman or Jaina worship. In southern India the style is essentially different from that of the north, and some of the Jaina temples there recall Nepaulese and Thibetan structures imitated from wooden edifices. At Sravana Belgula is a Jaina temple with a domical Tirthankhar cell and pilastered walls, Dravidian rather than Jaina in style.

The Mohammedan conquests and the multiplication of mosques, composed chiefly of materials from Jaina temples, led to a mutual interaction between the two styles. The Jaina temples of the sixteenth to the nineteenth centuries display the pointed and cusped arches, broad eaves, fluted and bulbous domes of the Mogul style, and the sikhra becomes less important in mass, as in the temple-groups of Muktagiri, Sonaghur, Ahmedabad, and Delhi. Many of modern temples are extremely picturesque in mass and rich in detail, and native artists, left to themselves, are still capable of excellent work.

Jaina caves are to be seen at Badami, Ellura, Amba, and a few other places, but they are few in number, and seem to have been cut rather to rival the Buddhists than to meet any real need. The earliest dates from 579 A.D., at Badami; the finest is the Indra Subha at Ellora (c. 750), with an elaborate porch and forecourt.

Brahman Styles. The Jaina and Brahman religions existed side by side for centuries in India with comparatively little friction, and with no sharp ethnic line of division. Both the Hindu and Mogul rulers not infrequently erected temples to both religions in the same city; and as there was no fundamental difference in their requirements, it is not surprising to find Brahman and Jaina temples so alike in style that it is hard to say to which faith any one belongs. So also of the two chief sects of Brahmanism, — the Vaishnavite and Saivite, — their temples are not distinguishable otherwise than by the subjects of their sculptures.

Northern Brahman Style. There is, indeed, more difference between the Brahman temples of northern, middle, and southern India, than between northern Brahman and Jaina temples; the chief distinction between these being the absence from the Brahman temples of the surrounding courtyard with its Tirthankhar cells, and of the open domical porches of the Jaina style. The Brahman temples of northern India generally consist of a sanctuary, or vimana, under a lofty and nearly solid sikhra, an antarala, or inner vestibule, and a jagamohan, or porch. The whole plan, internally and externally, is broken into as many rectangular steppings as possible, making innumerable vertical breaks. Over the porch is a stepped pyramidal roof, set cornerwise; and the sikhra, with a convex taper like the Jaina examples, and like them crowned with the amalaka, or broken into innumerable minute surfaces by almost countless reduplications of small models of itself, arrayed in rows both vertical and horizontal. Nothing can well be imagined more illogical and unstructural, and at the same time more picturesque and sumptuous, than these singular structures. They unquestionably impart to temples of moderate size a dignity quite beyond that of their actual dimensions. Thus the Kandarya Mahadeva at Khajurao (1000 A.D.), the most magnificent of all Saivite temples, measures but 116 by 60 feet on the ground, with a sikhra 120 feet high; yet it produces a remarkable impression of size and loftiness. Even the little temple at Barolli (eighth century), with a total length of 45 feet, appears anything but trivial. But there appears nowhere any effort after effects of internal grandeur. In the largest of all northern Brahman temples, that of Bhuvaneswar (650 A.D.), although its total length is nearly 300 feet, including the two later-built antechambers, the largest floor space measures less than 39 feet each way; that, namely, of the vimana. The importance of the temple is often further enhanced by numerous subordinate structures, dance-halls, shrines, and columns; *e.g.* the temple of Jagganatha (Juggernaut) at Puri in Orissa.

Among the oldest examples of this style are three likewise in Orissa: the Parasurameswara and the Mukteswara of the sixth century, and the Great Temple at Bhuvanneswar of the seventh. The Black Pagoda at Kanaruk, assigned by Fergusson to the end of the ninth century, is very simple in plan, but exhibits completely the characteristics of the style, although in a ruinous state. Its vimana occupies

a square of 60 feet, and is one of the largest in North India: that of the Jagganatha temple measures 73 feet. At Khajurao is an extraordinary group of Jaina, Vaishnava, and Saivite temples, among which the Kandaraya Mahadeva is the most remarkable. The lower part of this edifice, with its strong horizontal lines, and the deep shadows of its open porches, gives unity and vigour to a design covered with a marvellous intricacy of minute carving. To such an edifice it is impossible to apply the canons of Western art.

The temple of Munder Gobino Deojee at Bindrabund near Agra in 1592 is of exceptional design among Brahman fanes in having no sikhra over its small vimana, and in its magnificent cruciform jagamohan, or porch, measuring 125 by 105 feet, covered by a true pointed vault elaborately groined and decorated at the crossing. There are two stories of pointed-arched windows; and the whole design appears to be the work of some foreign architect, perhaps Persian. A group of small temples, all in ruins, in the beautiful vale of Kashmir, also deserve mention for their singularities of design, betraying the long-lingering traditions of Bactrian or perhaps of Sassanid-Byzantine art. They have pyramidal roofs penetrated by steep dormers or pediments over trefoil-arched openings, and are surrounded by enclosing walls with small cells. In Nepal the Brahman temples betray an affinity with Thibetan and Chinese structures, with multiplied hipped roofs like pagodas.

Brahman civil architecture, though less important than the religious, has produced some admirable works, such as the sacred Ghats or landing-places on the Ganges, and the palaces of Gwalior, Deeg, and Bandelkhand. These palaces are all of later date than the Moslem conquests, and are so permeated with the spirit of the Mogul architecture as to belong as much to the Indo-Moslem styles as to the Hindu. The use of the arch in these buildings is a radical departure from Hindu traditions.

Brahman caves exist in several of the great cave-groups of India. The most important are at Badami, Ellura, and Elephanta, with others less notable at Patna, Ankai-Tankai, Talaja, and Sana. Of the seventeen at Ellura the Dumnar Lena is the finest, its cruciform plan measuring 150 feet each way; but it is surpassed in elegance by that at Elephanta, an island in Bombay harbour. A noticeable detail in these caves is the design of the massive pillars with amalaka capitals. At Dhumnar is a complete monolithic temple cut from the rock by excavating a pit or court around it; but this achievement is far excelled by the celebrated Kylasa at Ellura, which, though classed by Fergusson among Dravidian monuments, may as properly find mention here. The court or pit in this case measures 270 by 150 feet, with a colonnade on three sides, and on the front an elaborate porch or mandir with flanking columns. The temple proper consists of a columnar mantapa and a sikhra with five small chambers about it. The whole was cut from the rock in the ninth or tenth century A.D., and finished with the most elaborate detail, which recalls both Dravidian and Chalukyan models.

Chalukyan Architecture. This name, derived from a dynasty which reigned from the sixth to the tenth century in the western Dekkan, has been applied to the Brahman architecture of a broad zone comprised mainly between the Narbadda and Kistnah rivers. It differs from the Jaina and northern Brahman in substituting for the sikhra a less lofty pyramidal structure over the sanctuary, usually on a star-shaped plan, and in covering the porch with a still lower stepped pyramid, starting from projecting eaves. The vertical walls are more important than in most northern temples; the lower part is deeply stratified and richly sculptured, and the upper part profusely adorned with pilasters, niches, and statues. Light is admitted through elaborate perforated stone screens set between columns of baluster outline with innumerable horizontal mouldings. The whole stands on a broad platform, and in general plan resembles the Jaina temples. Sometimes the shrine is double or triple, connected by a common porch, and the Saivite temples are preceded by a porch or shrine for the sacred bull Mandi.

The most important Chalukyan temples are those at Bailur, Hamoncondah, Buchropully, near Haidarabad, Somnathpur, in Mysore province, and Hullabid. That at Buchropully is the oldest, dating from the tenth century. The Bailur temple has an extensive porch of forty columns, and measures 120 by 84 feet; its perforated stone screens are especially fine. The Great Temple at Hullabid is, however, the most magnificent; it is a double temple, preceded by two mandi shrines, and measures, excluding these, 200 by 100 feet. It is perhaps the most superbly sculptured temple in India, and especially remarkable for its fine bands or friezes of animals, each band over 700 feet in length; and for the marvellous execution of all its details, in which it surpasses many larger and grander edifices. It dates from the thirteenth century.

There exists not far from Hullabid a group of Chalukyan temples in a peculiar style approaching the Dravidian, with pilastered walls and no sikhra. The Kalesvara at Bagali and the triple-shrined Venngopalasvami at Magala are examples of this local style. There are no caves of Chalukyan style, nor any civil monuments of importance. The style died out under the destructive Mohammedan invasions of the fourteenth century, having lasted about three hundred years.

Dravidian Style. The portion of the peninsula south of the Kistnah on the east and of Bailur on the west is known as the Dravida Desa. In this region there was developed at some unknown period, probably not before the tenth century, a distinctive style, whose complete flowering in the great temples of Chillambaram, Sri Ringam, Madura, and other examples, belongs to the centuries subsequent to the fourteenth. Though marked by many of the characteristics which are true of the Jaina and Northern Brahman buildings, the Dravidian temples differ from them absolutely in conception and planning.

The Dravidian plans vary greatly, even in general scheme, but they cover in all cases a vast extent of ground, and by their successive enclosures, each with its huge pylons or gopuras, suggest the temple groups of Egypt, such as Karnak. But whereas these are massive and simple in detail, the Indian examples are marvellously rich in their minute enrichments of carving. There is invariably a temenos, or enclosure, with a wall pierced by a gate in each face, and towering over each gate a lofty truncated pyramid or gopura covered with innumerable bands of sculpture and carved ornament. Successive enlargements have in some cases surrounded the earliest enclosure with one or more outer walls, each with its gopuras. In the inmost enclosure is the shrine or temple proper, with smaller shrines about it. In the outer courts are a sacred tank, and a vast pillared "Hall of 1000 Columns," called by Fergusson the *choultrie*, though this use of the term is not universally accepted (see Choultrie). Mantapas more or less elaborate, and long columnar corridors of one or three aisles, are features of many of the temples. But these elements are, as it were, thrown together, with no unity of conception; high and low, big and little, huddled or scattered, as the case may be, in utter disregard of their endless possibilities of cumulative effect. The great halls and long-drawn corridors are deficient in height and in contrast, and lead to nothing; the shrine or sanctuary is in many cases insignificant; and the lofty gopuras, with their sumptuous decoration, by their very loftiness emphasize the lack of grandeur within the enclosure. Yet there is so much of picturesqueness, variety, and splendour in these temples, and they are so vast in extent, that they never fail to inspire both amazement and admiration, in spite of their deficiencies.

The largest of these temples is that of Sri Ringam, near Tanjore. Its outermost enclosure measures 2500 by 2800 feet, and one of its sixteen gopuras covers an area of 130 by 100 feet, and, if completed, would be 300 feet high. The effect of the sixteen gopuras is extremely picturesque, but they are not parts of a well-ordered whole. Some of the great corridors of this temple are fine, though all too low. The temple of Chillambaram is smaller — 1000 feet square — but better arranged ; its inmost enclosure is one of the oldest of Dravidian temples (1004 A.D.), but its best portions date from the fifteenth and seventeenth centuries, the temple and porch of Parvati, and the Hall of 1000 Columns. The Ramisseram temple is chiefly an aggregation of corridors. The great temple of Madura is remarkable for its beautiful three-aisled choultrie of Tirumulla Nayak, built in the seventeenth century. At Tanjore is the oldest of Dravidian temples, dating from about 1000 A.D., if recent reports of inscriptions in it are to be trusted ; the chief feature being the magnificent pagoda over the sanctuary, — a steep stepped pyramid, ending in a dome and finial. Beside it, in the enclosure which it dominates, is the beautiful shrine of Subramanya, a magnified jewel-casket, with a low pyramid and dome over the sanctuary, and with walls decorated with pilasters and niches and ranges of statues in a manner recalling both the Renaissance and Gothic styles of the West. This shrine is of the fifteenth or sixteenth century. The most remarkable gopuras are at Combaconum and Tarputry ; but nowhere is sculpture treated with such bold waywardness of imagination as in the porches of the temples of Vellore, Vijanagar and Perrore, in which horses, bulls, monsters, and human figures are combined, and executed with extraordinary force and perfection of workmanship. In many buildings of this style slender auxiliary shafts to the piers, stone brackets, and overhanging eaves exhibit clearly the wooden origin of the details.

It was apparently not till after the Mogul conquests that the Dravidian rajahs erected important palaces. Those they then built copied the cusped arches and radiating vaults of the Moslems, e.g. that at Madura. The throne room of the latter is of imposing scale, and suggests the design of a Gothic church with Saracenic details. Most of the palaces were not single edifices, but more or less scattered aggregations of halls, passages, pavilions, and arcades, e.g. the ruined group at Vijanagar.

Except for the triumphantly successful Kylas at Ellura, which is not indisputably Dravidian, the only rock-cut monuments of this style are a few incomplete monolithic shrines called raths, at Mahavellipore, dating from the seventh century. It might, perhaps, be proper, therefore, to class these with the Kylas and the ruined temple at Pattadkal (Purudkul), which it closely resembles (c. 750 A.D.) as constituting an early Dravidian style, quite distinct from the later style of the temples at Madura, Tanjore, and Sri Ringam.

Indo-Moslem. (For the general characteristics of this style, see article Moslem Architecture.) A detailed account of all the various phases of Indo-Moslem architecture for the

seven centuries that have elapsed since the capture of Delhi by the Ghori sultans in 1193, is impossible in a short article, and even the enumeration of the really important monuments erected by or under the Moslem rules is out of the question, so great is their number. The chief subdivisions are as follows : —

(1) The Pathan style of North India (1193–1554), with monuments at Old Delhi and Ajmir, including the Kutub mosque, the impressive tower known as the Kutub Minar, the tomb of Altamsh, and the mosque at Ajmir.

(2) The Sharki style at Jaunpûr (1394–1476), chiefly exemplified in three great mosques, having imposing arched frontispieces like pylons, without minarets, in front of their domes ; the Lal Darwaza, the Jami Masjid, and the Ataladin mosque.

(3) The Ghujerati style (1398-1572) at Cambay and Champanir, Ahmedabad, Mirzapur, and Sirkejm, in some respects the most artistic and also the most prolific of the Indo-Moslem styles, especially under Ahmed Shah and Mahmûd Begurra (1411–1443, 1469–1511). In the mosques, pavilions, tombs, tanks, and palaces of this style, the application of Jaina and Brahman details to Moslem arched buildings is peculiarly successful.

(4) The Bengali style (1203–1573) at Gaur and Maldah, whose most important monument is the Adinah mosque at Maldah.

(5) The Bahmani style at Kalburgah and Bidar (1347–1525), represented by the Great Mosque at the former place and the ruined Madrasa (College) at Bidar (1478).

(6) The Bijapûri style (1489–1660), decidedly Persian in character, and remarkable for the extraordinary domes of the Great Mosque (Jami Masjid), and Tomb of Mahmûd (c. 1570–1600), both at Bijapûr, these being almost the only buildings in India in which interior grandeur is attempted on a vast scale and successfully attained.

(7) The Mogul style (1494–1707), which grew up in the wake of the Mogul Conquerors — Baber, Humayun, Shere Shah, Akbar, — and covered northern India with imposing monuments, in which the Persian influence is paramount and Hindu details almost disappear. Delhi, Agra, with its now ruined palace-suburb of Fathpûr Sikri, Secundra, Lucknow, Jonagur, and other cities, are adorned with these sumptuous monuments, in which the bulb-dome, the smooth round minaret, the cusped arch, and inlays of precious stones and *pietra dura*, take the place of the Hindu carving, the banded and stratified columns, bracket capitals, and panelled ceilings of the earlier mosques. The style culminated under Akbar, and then declined, until under Aurungzebe, in 1707, the Mogul Empire went to pieces, and its art sank to a very low level. Besides these styles, one might enu-

merate several other local phases of Moslem architecture of minor importance ; but all Indo-Moslem buildings may be divided into three general classes : (a) those in which Jaina and Hindu details predominate, as in the Pathan and Sharki styles, and in the mosques of Cambay and Champanir, of Kathiawar and Kach ; (b) those in which true domes and vaults and cusped or foliated arches predominate, with a touch of the Persian taste, as at Bijapûr, Kalburgah, and Bidar ; and (c) the Mogul buildings in which nearly every trace of Hindu forms has vanished, and stately settings of buildings and groups of buildings upon lofty terraces, with imposing surroundings, slender minarets, and great gateways, take the place of the smaller scale and far richer and minuter ornamentation of the earlier styles. This style culminated in the palace groups of Delhi and Fathpûr Sikri, the Pearl Mosque at Agra, and the Jami Masjid at Delhi, and in a remarkable series of royal sepulchres, including those of Mohammed Ghaus at Gwalior, of Humayun at Delhi, and of Akbar at Secundra ; but none of these is as widely known as the Taj Mahal, the tomb of Shah Jehan (1650), and the most beautiful of all sepulchres whether or not deserving of the extravagant praise it has received. Its beauty is greatly enhanced by its architectural environment of terraces, gates, minarets, and mosques, and by the beauty and costliness of its materials. In architectural grandeur it is surpassed at Bijapûr ; in the interest of its detail, by the buildings of Ahmedabad and Cambay. There are, besides these great tombs, hundreds of smaller tombs in Moslem style, of Jaina, Brahman, and Moslem origin, scattered through India, each with a dome supported by columns or pointed arches, and almost always of great beauty.

Modern Styles. The modern British buildings in India have rarely been successful architecturally, except where the largest possible freedom has been given to native design. The Hindu artists, whether Jaina, Brahman, or Moslem, have by no means lost their skill, and though their own modern mosques and temples and tombs are inferior to the best work of past ages, they are not without decided merit and artistic interest. The Jainas continue to erect temples with lofty sikhras over the Tirthankhar cells and vimanas, and to use bracket columns with great elegance, skilfully working into their designs many Moslem details, including the bulb dome and the pointed cusped arch enclosed in a rectangle ; as at Sonaghur in Bandelkhand, at Sutrunjya, and in the great Hutti Sing temple at Ahmedabad. The temple of Scindiah's mother at Gwalior (c. 1870), the Golden Temple at Amritsur, the tomb of the Nawab of Jonagur, and others about it, the palace at the same place, all exemplify the

capabilities of modern Hindu architects in a very favourable light ; and there have also been erected a number of colleges and administrative buildings by native architects, for the British administration in India, which are very creditable works. (See Ceylon, Architecture of ; Farther India, Architecture of ; Moslem Architecture ; also Dagoba ; Ghat ; Gopura ; Pagoda ; Sikra ; Stupa ; Tope ; Vihara ; Vimana.)

Two books stand in the first rank for popular reference : Fergusson's *Indian and Eastern Architecture*, which, in spite of some arbitrary classifications and now discredited judgments, still remains the most complete and scholarly single volume on the subject ; and Le Bon, *Les Monuments de l'Inde*, a more popular and superficial work, but rich in beautiful collotype illustrations of monuments of all the styles. The chief mine of information on the arts of India is the Government's *Archæological Survey of India*, in many volumes, issued from time to time, including many monographs on special districts or classes of buildings by such authorities as the late General Cunningham, Cole, Burgess, and Hope, and well illustrated. Other works are : Sir Lepel Griffin, *Famous Monuments of Central India ;* Cunningham, *Mahabadhi, or the Great Buddhist Temple at Buddha Gaya ;* DeForest, *Indian Domestic Architecture and Indian Architecture and Ornament ;* Fergusson, *Illustrations of the Rock-cut Temples of India ; Illustrations of Ancient Architecture in Hindostan ;* Fergusson-Burgess, *Cave Temples of India ;* Griggs, *Indian Photographs and Drawings of Historic Buildings ;* Jacob, *Jeypore Portfolio of Architectural Details ;* Le Bon, *Les Civilisations de l'Inde ;* Ram Raz, *Essay on the Architecture of the Hindus ;* and in the *Transactions of the Royal Institute of British Architects*, many articles by William Emerson, William Simpson, Sir Richard Temple, and others. — A. D. F. HAMLIN.

INDIAN ARCHITECTURE. *A.* That of the various divisions, or stocks and tribes, of the American aborigines or Red Indians. (See the references under Aboriginal American Architecture ; Amerind Architecture.)

B. That of the peninsula of India, as described under India, Architecture of.

INDRIOMENI, MARCUS GRECUS ; mosaicist, *magister musilei.*

Marcus worked in Venice in 1153, probably on the decoration of the church of S. Marco.

Müntz, *Les artistes byzantins.*

INFIRMARY. *A.* A place prepared for the sick or convalescent ; usually not a separate building, like a hospital, but a room or a series of rooms in a dwelling or an institution where many persons are employed.

B. Same as Dispensary, *i.e.*, a place for giving advice and remedies to patients who are not resident.

INFREGLIATI. (See Battista di Cristofanello.)

INGELRAM ; architect.

In the Chronicle of the Abbey of Bec, Normandy, France, it is written that Richard de Saint Leger, Abbot of Bec, wishing to build a

PLATE XVIII

INLAY

A pair of columns from the cloister at Monreale near Palermo in Sicily. The capitals are of exquisite Italian twelfth century work, but the shafts with the deeply recessed pattern were the background of the inlay which made them remarkable. All this was done in what we now call Cosmati work; namely, a minute mosaic in very formal patterns, and largely of glass, set deeply in sinkings cut in the marble.

new church at the abbey, confided the conduct of this work to Ingelram, *maître de l'œuvre* of the cathedral of Rouen. Nothing more is recorded about him. It appears from this document that Ingelram designed the third cathedral of Rouen, that which is now standing. The second was burned in 1200.

Deville, *Revue des architectes de la cathédrale de Rouen;* Gilbert, *Cathédrale de Rouen.*

INGLE CHEEK. A cheek or jam of a fireplace. (Scotch.)

INGLE NOOK. A place by the fire; a corner of a fireplace, as when in old-fashioned houses the opening of the chimney was much larger than needed for the andirons and the logs upon them, and there was space on either side where persons could sit or things be put for drying; hence, in modern usage, and inaccurately, a place near the fire, arranged with a seat or the like.

INGRES, JEAN AUGUSTE DOMINIQUE; painter; b. 1781; d. Jan. 14, 1867.

The famous painter Ingres made the cartoons for the windows of the chapel of S. Ferdinand in Paris and of the Memorial Chapel at Dreux.

Chesneau, *La peinture française au XIXᵉ siècle.*

INÍTI (in-neé-tee). The Dakota (Indian) name for Sweat Lodge. Also called inítipi and iníwokeya. As pi is a regular plural termination, iní-tipi is doubtless an error as used by whites in the singular. Derived from *ani*, to take a vapor bath, and *ti*, a house. Literally a vapor bath house. (See Sweat Lodge, under Lodge; Tipi.) — F. S. D.

INLAID WORK. Decoration by inserting a piece of one material within an incision or depression made for it in another piece of material. The term is usually confined to a combination in this way of hard materials; as black marble in white, or, as in some marble pavements in Florentine mosiac, etc., of many different coloured materials on a plain background; but it is extended to mean incised work filled with paste which becomes hard after a little while. Inlays in wood, if Italian in their design or their origin, are called Tarsia or Intarsiatura. Surfaces made up of many small parts fitted together are properly mosaic, no matter how large the pieces are, because in this case, as in the fine mosaics of a vault, there is no continuous and solid background in which the other pieces are inlaid. A patch of mosaic may, however, be inlaid upon a larger surface. — R. S.

INLAY. Same as Inlaid Work; the general term. (Cuts, cols. 483, 484; 485, 486.)

INN. Originally, a residence; the place where one lives; the *indoors* as compared with *out-of-doors.* In modern usage, a house for the temporary accommodation of travellers; especially a simple or old fashioned one as contrasted with a hotel.

The word in the original sense is now used only for a very few establishments, as the Inns of Court and the Inns of Chancery in London. In these, the term retains its original meaning as a place of residence.

INNS OF CHANCERY. In London, nine institutions which are connected with the four Inns of Court. Clifford's Inn, Clement's Inn, Lyon's Inn, belong to the Inner Temple; New Inn and Strand Inn belong to the Middle Temple; Furnival's Inn and Thavies's Inn belong to Lincoln's Inn; Staple Inn and Barnard's Inn belong to Gray's Inn.

INNS OF COURT. In London, four important institutions, entitled The Middle Temple, The Inner Temple, Gray's Inn, Lincoln's Inn, providing lodgings, lectures, a free table, and other conveniences to students of the law; and in modern practice to others as well, all of whom pay regular dues. These inns have the sole right of admitting persons to the bar, that is to say, to practice as barristers, the English custom being to distinguish sharply between attorneys and barristers. Each inn is incorporated and is independent of all others. Each of these institutions has some interesting buildings, though there is no general or systematic grouping of these buildings, nor any unity of design preserved among them. They are the very attractive growth of succeeding centuries. Thus, Middle Temple shares with the Inner Temple the control of Temple Church, and has also a very splendid hall, built in the reign of Queen Elizabeth with an open-timbered roof of great beauty. Middle Temple Library is also an attractive building of the nineteenth century with a roof studied from that of Westminster Hall. — R. S.

INSERTED COLUMN. Same as Engaged Column, rare.

INSTITUT, PALAIS DE L'. The official home of the *Institut de France*, in Paris, on the south bank of the Seine opposite the Louvre. The building is low and not large in its parts, but covers much ground. It was designed by Louis Levau, and built by him and other architects, named Pierre Lambert and François D'Orbay, and finished in 1662. The original purpose of the building was as a special college founded by Cardinal Mazarin.

INSTITUTE. In England, a great society of which the full name is Royal Institute of British Architects; in other countries and in British cities, many societies have names evidently derived from the above; as in Ireland, The Royal Institute of Irish Architects; in Australia, The Institute of Architects of New South Wales; in the United States, The American Institute of Architects, first founded in 1857, but not at first a general body embracing chapters in the different cities. (See Societies of Architects.)

INLAY WITH MARBLE OF DIFFERENT COLOURS; FRONT OF S. MICHELE, LUCCA.

INLAY: BLACK AND WHITE MARBLE; PAVEMENT
OF BAPTISTERY, FLORENCE; C. 1200.

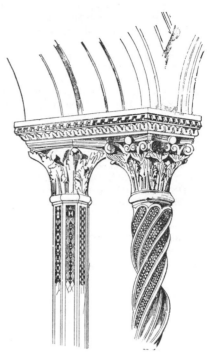

INLAY WITH GLASS TESSERAL (COSMATI
WORK) SHAFTS OF COLUMNS; CLOIS-
TERS OF S. JOHN LATERAN, ROME.

INLAY: BLACK AND WHITE MARBLE; PAVEMENT, CHURCH
OF S. MINIATO, NEAR FLORENCE; C. 1350.

INLAY: SWISS; 17TH CENTURY.

485   486

INSTRUCTION, THE, OF THE ARCHITECT. (See Architect, The, in England; in France; in Italy; and School of Architecture.)

INSTRUMENT ROOM. In an institution of learning, a hospital, an observatory, or similar scientific establishment, a room set aside for the safe keeping of the delicate instruments of observation, delineation, etc., which require to be kept from dust and injury. It is usual to line the walls of such a room with glass fronted cases.

INSULA. In Roman archæology, a block in a town; thus, in the discoveries at Pompeii each separate space bounded by four streets is called an Insula, whether it contains one house or many.

INSULAR. Standing alone; connected with no other structure, so as to be visible on every side; said of a building. The more usual word is Detached. (Compare Insula.)

INSULATED. *A.* Same as Insular.

B. Kept apart, as an electric wire, from other conducting bodies.

INSULATING JOINT. (See Electrical Appliances.)

INSULATING TUBES. (See Electrical Appliances.)

INSULATOR. (See Electrical Appliances.)

INTAGLIATURA. In Italian art, same as Incised Work; very general and including engraving, chasing, and similar arts.

INTAGLIO. Incised work of any sort, especially engraving in fine stones. In English the term is but rarely used in a more general sense.

INTAGLIO RILIEVO. (See Relief.)

INTARSIATURA. Same as Tarsia; the term carrying with it the idea of the process and the art of inlaying in general.

INTAVOLATA. The cyma at the top of a cornice; rare.

INTER. The Latin preposition and adverb signifying between; used in English in many compound words, each of which expresses the relation of the spaces between members in a series to the members themselves. Thus, interjoist is the space between two joists; intercolumn, the space between two columns, meaning thereby their shafts; and intercolumniation the same thing as intercolumn, but with the added meaning of the whole art of spacing columns with relation to the thicknesses of their shafts.

INTERAXIAL. *A.* Coming between the axes; said of a member which is left between the main lines of composition and is in a sense disregarded, it being held that the symmetry or sequence of the greater features which are distributed upon the axes makes it possible to put in minor details as convenience demands.

B. Based upon the axes, especially upon a double series of axes forming right angles with each other; said of a system of planning. Erroneous or forced in this sense.

INTERAXIS; INTERBALUSTER; INTERCOLUMN. (See Inter.)

INTERCOLUMNIATION. *A.* The space between the shafts of two adjacent columns.

B. The ratio of the diameter of a shaft to the space between two shafts.

An intercolumniation is usually considered the distance in the clear between the lower parts of the shafts; sometimes, however, it is taken as the distance from centre to centre of columns. Ordinarily, it is described in terms of the diameter or semidiameter taken at the bottom of the shaft, though its absolute dimension may of course be used. The term, though not necessarily limited to classic styles, is chiefly employed in describing classic colonnades. (See Columnar Architecture.)

The terminology of the subject is derived from Vitruvius (Book III, Ch. 2), who describes five kinds of temples, as follows: Picnostyle, with columns set $1\frac{1}{2}$ diameters apart; systyle, 2 diameters; eustyle, $2\frac{1}{4}$, with a central intercolumniation of 3 diameters; diastyle, 3 diameters, of which he says the architraves often fail through being too long; and finally, aræostyle, a wide spacing with architraves of wood.

Upon this statement, Palladio, Scamozzi, Sir William Chambers, and others have constructed sundry rules for the spacing of columns, all of which authoritative treatment of the subject may be found in Gwilt's *Encyclopædia of Architecture*, article "Intercolumniation."

The Vitruvian rules may have had some application to Roman buildings; how little bearing they had upon the work of the Greeks may be seen from the following table: —

ORDER	PLACE	BUILDING	INTER-COLUMNIATION IN TERMS OF THE DIAMETER OF THE SHAFT	LENGTH OF ARCHITRAVE, BEARING TO BEARING	AUTHORITY
Doric	Cadacchio		$2\frac{5}{8}$	2.28 m.	Dr. Josef Durm.
"	Selinus	Temple C.	$1\frac{3}{4}$	4.46 m.	*Die Bau-*
"	Athens	Theseion	$1\frac{3}{4}$	2.61 m.	*kunstder*
"	Athens	Parthenon	$1\frac{3}{4}$	4.26 m.	*Griechen*
"	Athens	Propylæa (central opening)	$2\frac{5}{8}$	5.43 m.	(p. 104).
				DISTANCE FROM CENTRE TO CENTRE OF COLUMNS	
Ionic	Priene	Temple of Athena Polias.	$1\frac{3}{4}$	7.33 ft.	The *Antiquities of Ionia*, Vol. IV.
"	Teos	Temple of Dionysos.	$2\frac{1}{4}$	10.70 ft.	
Corinthian	Athens	Temple of the Olympian Zeus.	$1\frac{9}{10}$	18.24 ft.	Penrose's *Principles.*
"	Rome	Temple of Marcus Aurelius.	$1\frac{3}{4}$	3.94 m.	Villain, *Le Temple de Marc-Aurèle.*

In none of the above, nor in the many additional Doric examples given by Dr. Durm, do the Vitruvian spacings, $1\frac{1}{2}$, 2, $2\frac{1}{4}$, or 3 occur. The statement that the architrave frequently fails in a diastyle (3 diameter) intercolumniation is seen to be thoroughly illogical when we realize that if the diameter of the column is small the architrave might actually be shorter

INTERDUCES. Same as Intertie.

INTERFENESTRATION. *A.* The space between two windows.

B. The art of disposing windows and, by extension, doors and other openings. (Compare Fenestration; Intercolumniation.)

INTERFILLING. Filling, as with masonry or plastering on lath, spaces between timbers

INTERLACE: INTERLACED PATTERNS FROM THE ALHAMBRA, GRANADA, SPAIN.

than in a picnostyle arrangement when the diameter is very great.

The rules for equal spacing of columns ignore the fact that in Grecian Doric the positions of the columns depend usually upon the divisions of the frieze. In this order the axis of the column falls in line with the middle of the triglyph, but at the angles this correspondence cannot exist, and the spacing of metope and triglyph being constant, it follows that the corner intercolumniation is less than the others. The rules also ignore the beautiful optical refinement of a gradually widening space from angle to centre, as seen in the Parthenon and other buildings.

It is hardly to be conceived that, at a time when art was free from the taint of archæology, artists would have attempted to perfect their designs by an artificial system of modules and minutes, or would have permitted themselves to have been governed by a set of rules as to the ratio of column diameter to intercolumnar space. — FRANK MILES DAY.

INTERCUPOLA. *A.* The space between two cupolas. (See Inter.)

B. The space between the two shells of a cupola; especially in the few cases in which this member is built of solid masonry, as in S. Peter's at Rome, or the cathedral at Florence, the space between the inner and the outer shells often being utilized for staircases and the like.

INTERDENTIL; –DOME. (See Inter.)

of a frame, or the like. (See Black and White Work (I.); Half Timbered.)

INTERGLYPH. The space between two of the grooves or cuts, as in a triglyph; usually, a flat surface below which the groove itself has been sunk.

INTERJOIST. The space between two joists, as in a floor. (See Inter.)

INTERLACE (v. i.). To cross and recross, as if woven; said of different cords, bands, withes, or the like, or of a single piece of flexible material returning upon itself. By extension, to seem to interlace, as of a sculptured ornament resembling a band crossing and recrossing itself, or of several bands seeming to cross one another, first above, then below. (Cuts, col. 491.)

INTERLACING ARCADE. Same as Intersecting Arcade (which see, under Arcade).

INTERLACE: INTERLACED ORNAMENT, CANTERBURY CATHEDRAL; CRYPT.

INTERLACING ARCH. More properly, Interlacing Archivolt; one of several which seem to cross one another and produce a continuous interwoven pattern, as in an intersecting arcade.

INTERLACING ORNAMENT. (See Strap Ornament.)

INTERMODILLION. The space between two modillions, as in an architrave. (See Inter.)

INTERLACE: INTERLACING ARCHIVOLT, CANTERBURY CATHEDRAL; C. 1120.

INTERMURAL. Built between walls; said of something not commonly so placed, as a stairway. Intermural stairways are treated with great effect in Italian palazzi, the largest

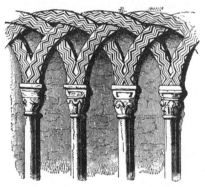

INTERLACE: INTERLACING ARCHIVOLT, CHURCH OF S. JOHN, DEVIZES; C. 1160.

of them being, perhaps, the Scala Regia of the Vatican. In the Ducal Palace at Venice there are two, the celebrated Scala d'Oro and the Scala dei Censori. The term is extended to apply to stairways of which the enclosing walls are pierced with arches, so as to be very open. Fine examples of these are numerous through-

out Italy, those of Genoa being especially showy and attractive.

INTERMUTULE. The space between two mutules, as in an architrave. (See Inter.)

INTERPENETRATE. To penetrate reciprocally each the other; in architecture, said of mouldings so worked in solid stone that one moulding, or group of mouldings, seems to pierce another and to appear again on the other side of it. This decoration is much used in the latest Gothic architecture. (Compare Stump Tracery, under Tracery.)

INTERPILASTER; INTERQUARTER. (See Inter.)

INTERSECTION. Same as Crossing.

INTERTIE. In framing, especially in carpentry work, a piece, usually horizontal, between uprights, such as studs, or in the slope of a roof between the rafters, or forming the lower member of a system of trussed framing, as in supporting a partition over a wide opening. The intertie may be at once a strut and a tie, and by its means two adjacent struts or rafters brace one another mutually.

INTERTRIGLYPH. The space between two triglyphs in a Doric frieze. Called also Metope.

INTONACO. In preparation for fresco painting, the final smooth coat of plastering upon which, while wet, the colour is applied by the artist. (In Italian, also *Intonico, Scialbo*.)

INTRADOS. *A.* The inner face of an arch or vault generally forming the concave under side, or soffit.

B. The line in which the surface above defined intersects the face of the arch.

INVALIDES. (See Hôtel des Invalides; church of S. Louis.) (Cut, cols. 493, 494.)

INVERT. An inverted arched construction, as the bottom of a built drain or sewer; an abbreviation of Inverted Arch or vault.

INVERTED ARCH. (See under Arch.)

INWOOD, CHARLES FREDERICK. (See Inwood, William.)

INWOOD, HENRY WILLIAM; architect; b. May 22, 1794; d. 1843.

The eldest son of William Inwood (see Inwood, William). In 1819 he visited Greece, and returning to England, assisted his father in the construction of S. Pancras New Church, London. Inwood published *The Erechtheion at Athens, Fragments of Athenian Architecture*, etc. (London, folio, 1827; republished by A. F. Quast, Potsdam, 1843.)

Stephen, *Dictionary of National Biography*.

INWOOD, WILLIAM; architect; b. about 1771; d. 1843.

His best-known work is S. Pancras New Church, London, built between 1819 and 1822. He was especially assisted by his sons Henry William (see Inwood, H. W.) and Charles

Frederick. He published *Tables for the Purchasing of Estates . . . and for the Renewal of Leases held under Corporate Bodies.*
    Stephen, *Dictionary of National Biography.*

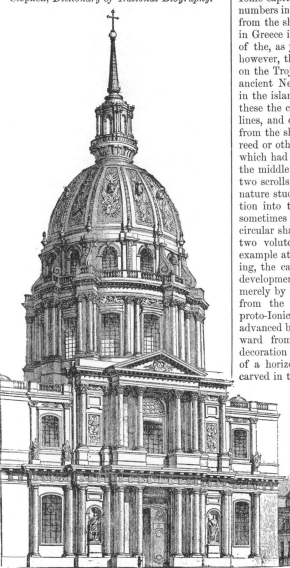

IONIC ORDER. One of the five orders recognized by the Italian writers of the sixteenth century. The order is of Greek origin, although it received a greater development on the shores of Asia Minor, a country inhabited by the Ionian Greeks, than in the mother land itself; yet the earliest existing buildings which are assuredly of this style are of the main land of Greece, and of the great islands which have always been closely connected with it. This remark applies only to the fully or partially developed Ionic order, for what are called proto-Ionic capitals have been found in considerable numbers in the non-Greek lands farther removed from the shores of the Mediterranean as well as in Greece itself. The most important instances of the, as yet, imperfect Ionic capital are still, however, those found at Athens, in some ruins on the Trojan plain, thought to be those of the ancient Neandria, at Naucrates in Egypt, and in the islands of Delos and Lesbos. In all of these the capital is almost devoid of horizontal lines, and consists of two volutes which spring from the shaft, as if the designer had studied a reed or other succulent stem of circular section which had been split for a short distance down the middle and rolled away from the centre in two scrolls. In some cases, this appearance of nature study is made stronger by the introduction into the design of a strongly marked and sometimes double band which surrounds the circular shaft just above the separation of the two volutes. In others, as in a well-known example at Athens, covered with brilliant painting, the capital has gone a step farther in its development, and is a solid block adorned merely by the appearance of two scrolls treated from the same common centre. All these proto-Ionic capitals tend to overset the theory advanced by some archæologists, reasoning backward from the developed capital, that the decoration by volutes came of the adornment of a horizontal block, the ends of which were carved in this easy and obvious way. The perfected capital is, indeed, not wanting in strongly marked horizontal lines, and even those of earlier times than that of the highest development, as perhaps of the sixth century B.C., like one recently discovered at Delphi, show a very strongly marked flat table, the ends of which only are worked into the volutes. This flat table being supported by an ovolo moulding, forming a complete circle and resting upon the shaft, and adorned with very large oves, needs nothing but the refinement of its parts to make it the perfected capital of the Erechtheum. This refinement was more needed in the Ionic capital than in some others, because the form is in itself somewhat irrational, and suggests in a disagreeable way the oozing out of a more plastic material under the superincumbent weight. Thoughts of this kind disappear when the highly wrought design of the fifth century capital is studied. The fluting of the shaft does not appear in the earliest examples; but, in those which seem to be of the fifth century, like that of Delphi mentioned above, there are channels like those of the Doric columns, but more numerous, and in the fifth century these are succeeded by the well-known flutings, twenty-four in number, and separated by narrow fil-

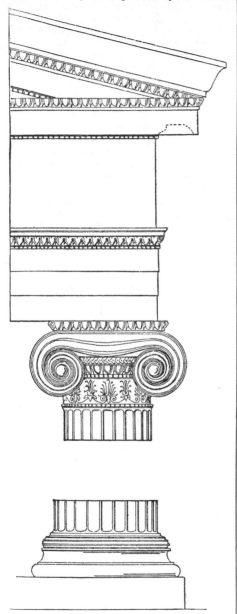

ORDER OF THE ERECHTHEUM, ATHENS, GREECE.

lets instead of meeting at the sharp arrises, as in the channels named above. The base underwent fewer important changes during the period of which we can judge, for the practice of fluting horizontally the large torus of the

base came in at a very early epoch, and this remained the most important characteristic of the order after the volutes of its capital. When the Ionic shaft is set upon the Attic base (which see under Base), it loses much of its

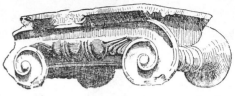

IONIC CAPITAL LYING ON THE ACROPOLIS, ATHENS.

distinction. The bases of the little temple of Nike Apteros at Athens (which see under Temple) seem to combine the two ideas, the combination of flutes resting upon a part, at least, of the Attic base; and a somewhat similar attempt was made in the famous Erechtheum. The flutings and the arrangement of the base are of peculiar importance to students, because the Corinthian order when it began was, in the main, the Ionic order with a newly invented capital. In connection with the Ionic order there are some beautifully imagined ornamental devices in less common use. Thus, the pilasters which are used with the Ionic column are sometimes of singular beauty, having simply fluted shafts with a capital consisting of a band of anthemions, with egg and dart mouldings above, and a base with rich flutings and sometimes a kind of guilloche adorning the torus. Moreover, it is in connection with this order that the most perfect instance of the caryatid occurs, namely, in the Erechtheum at Athens. The entablature and the other parts of the temple seem to have been the subject of thought

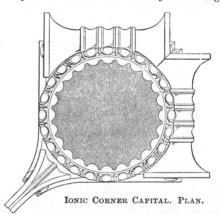

IONIC CORNER CAPITAL. PLAN.

and study as careful as that given to buildings of the Grecian Doric order. The frieze, having no triglyphs, is sometimes adorned with a continuous band of figures, those of the Erechtheum having been planted on and made of different material, so as to show some contrast of colour, even without the use of painting and gilding. The frieze of the temple of Nike Apteros, above alluded to, was also adorned with figures on a very small scale. Ionic temples were numerous on the Grecian shores of Asia Minor and Syria. The most curious instance of the introduction of the order in a place which seems incongruous is the well-known portico of the Propylæa of the Acropolis at Athens. There, while the outer colonnades on both sides are pure Doric of a perfect type, the columns which front upon the continuous passage of the roadway through the portico from west to east are Ionic; but of necessity their entablature is very far removed from the full perfection of the order. — R. S.

IRELAND, ARCHITECTURE OF. That of the island called Ierné and Hibernia by the Greeks and Romans, and Erin by the Irish themselves, which, lying in the extreme west of Europe, has preserved vestiges of architectural forms which have almost disappeared from Europe elsewhere. In her own Gaelic she has handed down curious records of the methods used by builders in osier, wattle, wood, and stone. In early times stone was chiefly confined to fortifications called dun, rath, or lis, and even then the material was apt to be found in subterranean or submural vaults, rooms, or passages, built rudely of selected stones, little, if at all, shaped with the hammer. These were mere refuges in case of war, or vaults for storage of valuables. In the west of Ireland, however, where wood was always scarce, one finds primitive forms of architecture like the clochans, or beehive huts, of the Arran and other islands, rude stone shelters without a trace of chimney, or even fireplace, yet not without design, and showing a certain skill in their making. Clochans are round or oval and of different sizes, made by laying stone on stone spirally and progressively, each course overlapping the lower until a narrow central space can be closed with a broad flat stone. (See Iglugeak.)

The beehive hut seems to have been used by monks and solitaries during the Middle Ages, but it reaches back far beyond Christian times. Radically the same construction, with approach and side wings, is found in such royal burial places as Newgrange-on-the-Boyne, in the east of Ireland. The type is the Eskimo subterranean lodge approached by a long, low hallway covered with earth. At Newgrange most of the rude slabs used to line the approach to the central vault are picked over apparently with a stone implement, in designs of rounds, spirals, lozenges, etc. But these designs antedate the tomb, for they continue round behind the slabs, and, moreover, show the signs of weathering. The inference is unmistakable that they were

taken from some field of stone pillars like that of Carnac, in Brittany.

The early Irish did not use mortar; their stone buildings have commonly disappeared, because, when once abandoned, the stones were immediately carried away for other uses. The great mass of the people lived as the ancients did, down to this century — in wicker and wood huts and cabins, usually round in shape. Farmers of a higher grade had several huts in an enclosure of earth or stone; owners of large herds could afford a separate hut, or detached room, for the women. The more or less fantastic description of the palace at Tara is really that of a country seat with its several rooms not yet assembled under one roof, for the banquet hall, prison for hostages, kitchen, doctor's house, dog kennels, etc., were separate. Tara may never have existed, but such a distribution agrees with the primitive method of early Europe. The more important buildings may be realized as circular huts of good size with one door and a few small openings, which, in later ages, were sometimes glazed, but at first closed by a shutter or covered with parchment. Rich men placed over the entrance to their walled precinct a *grienan*, or sun chamber, in which glass was used when that became accessible. Roofs were of thatch, rarely shingle, and only in case of churches, lead or slate. A fire burned in the middle of the round house. Although mortar was not used, whitewash was used on the outer wall of forts and houses. A kind of stucco was common; it was often modelled in designs, and painted. Such decoration was used in the famous early church at Armagh, so often plundered and ruined.

The tendency to build separate huts, rather than rooms under one roof, held on after Christianity had affected the customs of the people, and explains the fact that the early churches, whether of wood or stone, were generally accompanied by an oratory and a belfry quite separate, and by themselves, as we see at Ardmore, near Youghal, and many other places. It accounts for the persistence of the detached round tower, so characteristic of early Irish ecclesiastical architecture.

The ancient Irish have handed down no distinctive architecture except the beehive huts and round towers. The latter, as we find them, are strictly ecclesiastical, but represent in stone the watchtowers of wood or wicker erected by the pagan Irish in their rath, dun, or lis, to serve as an outlook for marauders, a citadel in event of a surprise. They are small, but very beautiful and finished pieces of stonework. Their derivation from the wicker round hut — basketwork on a big scale — can hardly be doubted; the oldest specimens not restored in the crenellated Norman fashion repeat in their sharp conical tops the old cone-capped huts, and many reveal the original main lines of the framework of osier. As the centre of the largest usage of round towers in Ireland, it is reasonable to suppose that such few examples as the Continent affords were built under Irish influence after Irish missionaries had invaded Great Britain and the Continent. The existing examples do not go back beyond the ninth century ; they must have been used as much for towers of refuge as signal towers against sudden raids by the plunderers from the Baltic, and locally, to guard against the pagan Irish. Petrie has left an epoch-making work on round towers. O'Curry and, later, Margaret Stokes and Lord Dufferin, have added much to our knowledge of these interesting belfry refuges. We can readily imagine that before bronze bells came into use a sonorous stone was struck from the top of a round tower. Our word " clock " is a Keltic word, meaning "stone."

The peculiar Keltic cross found chiefly in Ireland, but also in Great Britain and the Isle of Man, is, in all likelihood, a combination of Christian cross and pagan sun circle, which the halo round the heads of Christ and the saints in religious pictures from Byzantium or Rome would naturally suggest.

Towns, in our sense of the word, scarcely existed in Ireland before the tenth century, when the Danes, so called, — Germanic, Finnic, and Slavic heathens of the Baltic, — overran the country, and founded Dublin, Wexford, Waterford, Cork, Limerick, and Galway. Londonderry, Belfast, and Kilkenny, were later creations. The nearest approach to a town was such a temporary town of huts as grew up when some famous fair was held ; accounts of many of these important assemblages are found in Irish literature. Small and simple, but very charming, remains of oratories, chapels, baptisteries, refectories, and churches are scattered over Ireland, testifying to the powerful impress of the Norman-English and Norman-Welsh who conquered Ireland piecemeal one century and a half after the seizure of Great Britain by William the Conqueror. A sparing use of sculpture lends to what survives a peculiar touch of reserve, and the solidity and small size of the remains add to their effect as they appear in the bare Irish landscape. In the mediæval remains one finds an early Romanesque, but almost no Gothic of the highest sort ; nor are there many examples of the architecture that is called Saxon because found in England. Ireland was too poor and disturbed to follow the rest of Europe during the great period of Gothic art, and erect cathedrals.

Imposing and even beautiful buildings of more modern times are not lacking in Dublin. Eastward toward the sea rises the Customhouse (1794), built from designs by James Gandon, a

handsome classical structure 375 by 205 feet with lofty porches and a dome 125 feet above ground. The front on the river has statues of Plenty, Industry, Mercury, and Neptune ; on the north, statues of Europe, Asia, America, and Africa, while other decorations are found without and within its two courts. Earlier (1776) is the date for the Four Courts, the famous place of forensic displays. It cost $1,000,000, and is perhaps the most striking building in Ireland. It was designed by Cooley and finished in 1800 by James Gandon. The dome indicates a circular central hall 64 feet wide, decorated with statues of celebrated Irishmen of the robe, with bas-reliefs and other sculptures. The general post office with its Doric pillared porch (1815) and the lofty Doric fluted column of Nelson's Pillar are worth seeing, together with O'Connell's monument, begun by Foley and finished by Brock, having a colossal figure of O'Connell on the apex and ninety or more symbolical bronze figures high up on the shaft. The old Parliament House, now the Bank of Ireland, is especially interesting. Built in 1729 from designs by some unknown artist, it has no little dignity and charm. Within, the House of Lords has been little changed ; it has an east entrance with porch of Corinthian columns. That of the Commons has been altered for the bank ; it still shows an octagonal interior of fine proportions. The University, founded in 1595, has few indications of great age ; the various buildings belong to the end of the last and beginning of the present century, or later. There are four quadrangles, the principal entrance being from the Square opposite the Bank. The finest building is the Library, 210 feet long ; the first quadrangle has a notable belfry with some pretensions to elegance. Christ Church cathedral, founded in 1038 by a Danish King of Dublin, rebuilt in recent years by Street in "transition Gothic," has a good square central tower, Norman decorated entrance, and a flying bridge across the street. S. Patrick's cathedral, founded in 1190, has been extensively ruined and restored. It has a noble Gothic interior and a tower at the northwest corner (1370) rather unfortunately restored with a tall spire. A Doric modern Catholic cathedral, begun 1816, and the City Hall, built in 1779 for a Royal Exchange, are other noteworthy structures.

The church and city hall and many old merchants' houses in Kilkenny, Limerick, and Galway are picturesque ; Wexford with its crumbling old fortifications, Youghal with its ancient chapel and Sir Walter Raleigh's house ; the palace at Lismore belonging to the Duke of Westminster ; the remaining portions of the old fort at Athlone, now part of the military arrangement ; S. Laurent's gate at Drogheda ; ruins of monasteries on islands in Lochs Killarney, Derg, Erne, and Key ; the old fort at

Limerick; Dunluce ruins on the north coast; Ardfert, Aghador, Clonfert, Muckross, Clonmacnoise, Adare, Sligo, and other abbeys; Armagh, Derry, and Downpatrick cathedrals; Enniskillen, Malahide, Blarney, and other castles, — are of interest to architects and lovers of the picturesque. — CHARLES DE KAY.

Dunraven, *Notes on Irish Architecture;* Petrie, *Ecclesiastical Architecture of Ireland anterior to the Anglo-Norman Invasion;* Stokes, *Early Christian Architecture of Ireland;* Wilkinson, *Practical Geology and Ancient Architecture of Ireland;* Keane, *Towers and Temples of Ancient Ireland.*

IRON. *A.* A metal which in practical use is approximately pure only in the form known as wrought iron. This is peculiarly malleable and has the remarkable quality of being susceptible of welding, that is, of uniting one piece to another, when both are heated to a certain high temperature and are then hammered together. Cast iron contains much carbon; this, in the form in which the melted metal flows from the melting furnace, is called pig iron, the term cast iron being reserved for that which has been remelted and cast in moulds for special purposes. As compared with wrought iron, this is brittle and not malleable, and it is not susceptible of being welded. Until recently, ironwork in architecture was limited to these two forms of the metal; cast iron was found to have a great resistance to superincumbent weight, and made admirable columns, especially when cast in thin shells, cylindrical or prismatic in outward section, and having a comparatively large hollow core. Wrought iron, on the other hand, was singularly tough, tenacious, and capable of bearing a very great tensile strain; it was, therefore, fit for ties of all forms. It was also perfectly well adapted to support vertical pressure, and at a time when the American cities were being filled with façades of cast iron, similar structures on the continent of Europe were being made of wrought iron almost exclusively, the uprights being formed of plates bolted together much on the principle of hollow built beams. Steel, which has less carbon than cast iron, is to a certain degree malleable and capable of being welded; its peculiar value is, however, in its capacity for being tempered by means of which a very high degree of hardness can be reached. By recent processes of manufacture, steel has been made easy and cheap of production, and its use for rolled beams, built beams, built columns, and the like, is superseding the use of wrought iron and of cast iron. (See Cast Iron; Plate Iron; Wrought Iron.)

B. Any small or subordinate member of cast or wrought iron. In this sense, used in combination; and very often with the article, as an Angle Iron (which see); a channel iron, which is a small member similar to a Channel Beam (which see under Beam); and many similar phrases. — R. S.

Cavity Iron. A small iron anchor for tying together the parts of the masonry on opposite sides of a cavity wall. (See Hollow Wall, under Wall.)

IRON CEMENT. A composition especially prepared for filling the joints, holes, and other small openings which hold water and cause oxidization. It is therefore not a cement in the usual sense, but is a paste only. The largest part of its substance is composed of iron borings or filings, which must be clean and fresh without oxidization; this powder is held together by a glutinous or adhesive paste, for which there are many formulæ.

IRON CONSTRUCTION. Construction by framework of members of iron or steel, or of both. In referring to the general construction of buildings, the term means especially such a system of framing constituting the supporting members, as columns, girders, floor beams, or the greater part of them, the metal frame being either left exposed or covered as in Skeleton Construction.

Although the reduction and manufacture of wrought iron was one of the earliest of the arts, it does not appear as a material of construction until late in the eighteenth century. It was, indeed, largely used in the shape of ties and anchors, and its abuse in these forms gave cause for the remark of Vignola that "a building should not be held together by strings." Cast iron was first used about the end of the fifteenth century, but it was not applied as a structural material until late in the eighteenth. Both cast and wrought iron were used for minor constructions, as grilles, and stairways.

The formation of iron plates by passing them between rollers dates from 1783. The double Tee or I section, the patent of 1844, was for a plate rolled with a flange on one edge and a Tee iron riveted to the other edge. In 1854 Fairbairn remarks that it is probable that rolled I beams of less than 12 cwt. could be delivered from the rolling mills, but apprehending some difficulty in manufacturing one so large he suggests two forms (see Fig. 1), which would lessen

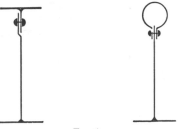

FIG. 1.

gests two forms (see Fig. 1), which would lessen the difficulties of manufacture, as there would be only one flange to be rolled.

The first iron construction of which we have record was the bridge over the Severn at Coalbrook Dale, Shropshire, England. This is a cast-iron arch of five ribs of open panels, having a span of 100 feet and a rise of 45 feet. It was completed in 1776.

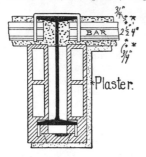

The Wearmouth bridge, Durham, England, built in 1796, was an arch also of cast iron. Its span was 200 feet and the rise 34 feet, very flat as compared with its predecessor.

It was probably designed by Thomas Paine. The spandrils are filled with circles between verticals.

Thomas Paine, the author, interested himself in the design of iron bridges, and invented a "new system of bridge construction." He submitted to the Academy of Sciences at Paris a project for an iron arch of 400 feet span, which the committee reported to be simple, solid, and suitable. He urged upon the architects of London the use of segmental arches of low rise, instead of the semicircular or "full centre" form, but his views were not accepted by them. He built a model rib in London as large as the shop in which he worked would permit. It had a span of 90 feet and a rise of 5 feet. The curve was a reversed catenary, following the lines of a chain suspended against the wall of the shop. The depth of the arch was 2 feet 9 inches at the crown and 6 feet at the ends. When the centre was set up the work was commenced at the crown and carried toward the abutments. He remarks that stone arches sometimes break down the centring by their weight; this, on the contrary, transmitted less weight as the arch increased in thickness; so much so, that, before it was completely finished, the arch "rose of itself off the centre the full thickness of a knife blade from one abutment to the other." He constructed a model in wood of an arched bridge of 400 feet span, intended to cross the Schuylkill at Philadelphia, which was to be carried on thirteen ribs, corresponding to the original thirteen states of the Union.

Influenced by the idea of designing a bridge which would be a model for crossing the great rivers of America, Paine doubtless expended both time and money, and applied some mechanical knowledge to the project, but we do not know enough of his theory or of his methods to call him the inventor of iron bridge building. There are indications that the excessive flatness of his arches was for the purpose of facilitating the approach to them by keeping them low, regardless of the increased thrust.

The *Pont des Arts*, over the Seine at Paris (1803), consisted of five arches of wrought-iron bars carrying a floor for foot passengers only.

Of strictly architectural constructions, the first was the dome of the *Halle au Blé*, now the *Bourse du Commerce*, of Paris. The timber dome of this building having been burned in 1802, a commission appointed to advise on its reconstruction recommended a dome of masonry. The Minister of the Interior requested a special report on one of wrought iron, an innovation without precedent at that time. The report declared (1) that wrought iron might be used as a constructive material. That its ductility, which promoted its expansion and its high price, prevented it from being used alone. (2) That cast iron, being less liable to expansion, and for equal weights cheaper, was preferable, but that it could not be used so thin as wrought iron, and that the excess of weight would make it nearly as expensive as wrought iron. The commission, therefore, recommended that both kinds be used, each in the place for which it was best fitted, and this recommendation was adopted. The dome was completed in 1812. Its interior diameter is 128.8 feet, and it is formed of fifty-three cast-iron ribs 23 inches in depth at the base, and 13 inches at the base of the lantern. The ribs were cast at Creusot in 1809, in lengths of about $16\frac{1}{2}$ feet; the metal was $2\frac{3}{4}$ inches thick

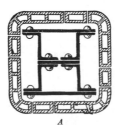  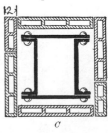

IRON CONSTRUCTION : THREE FORMS OF COLUMNS ENCLOSED BY FIRE-PROOFING OF TERRA-COTTA BLOCKS.

A, Z-bar column ; *B*, a special form composed of four quadrantal bars of iron ; *C*, channel-beam column.

at the base, and three panels are cut out of the ribs leaving narrow inner and outer ribs, connected by radial pieces. The ribs are connected by radial plates bolted to them, which form circular ties or struts, according to their position, parallel to the base of the dome. It was covered with plates of copper fastened to a lattice of wrought-iron bars. About 1887 it was altered into the *Bourse du Commerce.* The covering was removed and up to about 45° was filled in with hollow brick and covered with slates on wood laths. Above 45° it was filled with glass. Of the masonry only the inner wall of the ring — that upon which the dome rested — and the Astrological Column of Catherine de' Medici were allowed to remain, the old column, hollow and serving as a tower, having been built into the outer wall, actually forming a part of it. Upon being stripped the

was 9 feet. The beams and columns were designed by Boulton and Watt.

This first mill was the type of those which succeeded it up to 1820. At that time Fairbairn made experiments on this form of beam, which brought about some changes in the proportions of web and flanges from those previously in use from the designs of Boulton and Watt. In 1824 the experiments of Hodgkinson were commenced, which have been the basis of all designs for cast-iron beams and columns up to the present time.

Borgnis (1823) mentions that "for some years past the Russians have used cast iron to make columns and entablatures. There are in Saint Petersburg and Moscow several monuments decorated with orders of architecture of very large size made of cast iron."

About 1854 the Bogardus Building in Centre Street, New York City, was constructed. The entire exterior was of cast iron. The floor was carried on cast-iron girders supported by columns of the same material. The depth of the hollow piers and the attached columns gave stability to the wall, which, with the cornices at each story, was little more than a heavy frame for the openings. Other buildings were erected in the same manner, but the greater number of "iron fronts" were mere fronts to brick buildings.

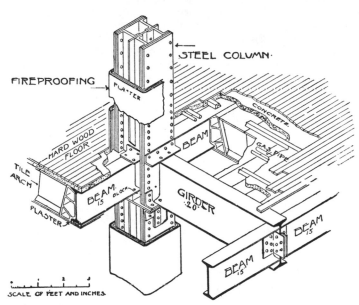

SCALE OF FEET AND INCHES.

IRON CONSTRUCTION OF A FORM COMMON IN SO-CALLED SKELETON BUILDING.

The column, formed of 4 Z bars and plates, carries girders and beams of the usual I section. The iron work is all to be encased with fireproofing.

dome was found to be in excellent condition, and to have been designed and built with the greatest care and good taste. Upon calculation it was found to be perfectly strong and stable. Bellanger was the architect; Brunet, contractor; and Crétet, Comte de Champernol, the minister who caused to be made the studies for an iron dome.

In 1801 a "fireproof" cotton mill was built in Manchester, the floors of which were carried on cast-iron columns and beams. The building was 42 feet wide by 100 feet long, of seven stories. Two rows of columns lengthwise 14 feet apart were connected by beams of inverted **T** section (**⊥**), which carried the brick arches of the floors. The span of the latter

Wrought iron had been used for bridges in the form of plate and tubular girders, and about 1853 began to be used for floor girders in mill buildings. These were generally plate beams; **I** beams of sufficient size had not then been rolled in England.

A light **I** beam (double **T** of the French) was at that time largely used for floors in France, and a triple **I** beam, 12 inches deep, having a flange at the middle of its depth, was used as a girder. **I** beams and deck beams 8 inches and 9 inches deep were rolled in America early in the fifties.

From 1850 to 1860 cast-iron girders and columns were in general use in England for supporting the floors of mills, factories, workshops, warehouses, and public halls. Cross-shaped stanchions were sometimes substituted for hollow columns. The ribs of these were stiffened with transverse flanges 'at two points in their height. The joists were of cast iron supporting brick arches. The beam conformed to Hodgkinson's rule, the bottom flange having six times the area of the top flange. The details of cast-iron columns and floors in the United States followed English practice. In the years succeeding 1851 iron construction was largely developed in Europe, and especially in France. The Crystal Palace of London (1851) gave the impulsion. In this many, if not all, the frames and girders, as well as the columns, were of cast iron. The *Palais de l'Industrie* of the Paris Exposition of '55 consisted of a central nave, covered by an arch of 161 feet span, and two lateral naves of 80 feet. The structure measured 830 × 355 feet inside, and the entire interior was of cast and wrought iron, perhaps the largest and boldest use in architecture of the latter material up to that time. The arches of the roof were of wrought-iron latticed frames. The columns were of cast iron, and the galleries separating the naves were carried on cast-iron arches. The height to the top of the central arch was 107 feet. Of wrought iron 2500 tons were used in the construction, and 4500 tons of cast iron.

The *Halles Centrales* (central market) of Paris (1854) is a very large, handsome, and appropriate structure, composed of a series of pavilions, covering together 323,000 square feet of ground. They are built of cast-iron columns, connected by arches of the same, which carry the latticed wrought-iron rafters of the roof. A brick wall 8 feet high in a line with the columns, surrounds the structure, and the openings above this are filled with persiennes, or slats of roughened glass which admit light and air, and exclude the sun, snow, and rain. The exterior columns are spaced about 20 feet and 28 feet high. The two large pavilions, 180 feet square, have each a clearstory over the central portion 100 feet square. The roof is carried by latticed beams of wrought iron, which cover a width of 40 feet from the exterior line of columns to those which carry the clearstory. The superstructure contains 380 tons of cast iron in columns and arches, 1400 tons of wrought iron, and 35,000 plates of roughened glass.

The dome of the Capitol at Washington must not be overlooked. Except that of the *Halle au Blé*, it is the earliest of the large iron domes, having been built between 1850 and 1861. It covers the central rotunda of the building, the walls of which date from 1792. The diameter of the rotunda is 94 feet, and this is the inner diameter of the dome. The extreme diameter at the base is 135½ feet. At the top of the masonry wall, 95 feet above the ground, a series of iron brackets, 50 in number,

are bedded in the masonry and project 10 feet from it. These carry the peristyle, and from them is suspended the stylobate formed of cast-iron plates, supported by open frames of the same material. Resting on the masonry wall are the main supports of the dome in the form of deep piers (6 feet 6 inches), corresponding to the columns of the peristyle, and perforated with arches, forming an interior gallery in which the stairways are placed. The framework above this is composed of nearly rectangular open ribbed panels of cast iron, which rise in a nearly straight line to the base of the tholos, outside of which the curve of the dome is supported by a light cast-iron framework. The cast-iron shell forming the stylobate is 25 feet 6 inches high from the roof of the original building. The peristyle is 34 feet high, and has a diameter of 123 feet. The next section has a diameter of 104 feet. The exterior diameter of the base of the cupola is 88 feet and its height 45 feet. Above this is the tholos, surmounted by the Statue of Liberty. The top of the statue is 218 feet above the balustrade of the masonry building and 287½ feet from the ground. There is an inner dome, with an opening 40 feet in diameter, through which is seen the painting on an upper spherical surface, lighted by windows in the story above the colonnade. The entire structure is of cast iron, chiefly in panels, fastened together with bolts and cast-iron plates.

The church of S. Eugène, completed in Paris in 1855, forms a new departure in ecclesiastical architecture by the substitution of wrought and cast iron columns and arches for the stone pillars and vaults of the Middle Ages. The church is 163 feet long over all, and 83 feet wide inside. The principal nave is 33 feet wide, and 77 feet high to the centre of the pointed arched ceiling; two lateral naves are 16¼ feet wide, and 50 feet high, and two aisles contain narrow galleries 8 feet wide. The style is approximately an early pointed form. The outer walls only are of masonry. The columns of the nave, 12 inches in diameter, those of the galleries, the gallery fronts, and the arches which support them are of cast iron. The transverse diagonal and longitudinal ribs of the vaulting are of wrought iron I beams; the vault surfaces are of two thicknesses of tiles laid flat and breaking joint, which rest upon the curves forming the intrados of the braced iron arches. The extrados, or the upper side of these arches, takes the shape of the roof, and is covered with a lattice of iron bars, upon which the roofing tiles are laid. The novelty consists first in the use of iron in place of stone for the interior supports; the construction of the vaulted ceiling and the roof upon the lower and upper members of a braced arch, leaving an air space between; the omission of the wooden roof generally needed to protect the stone vaulting; and of flying buttresses, which

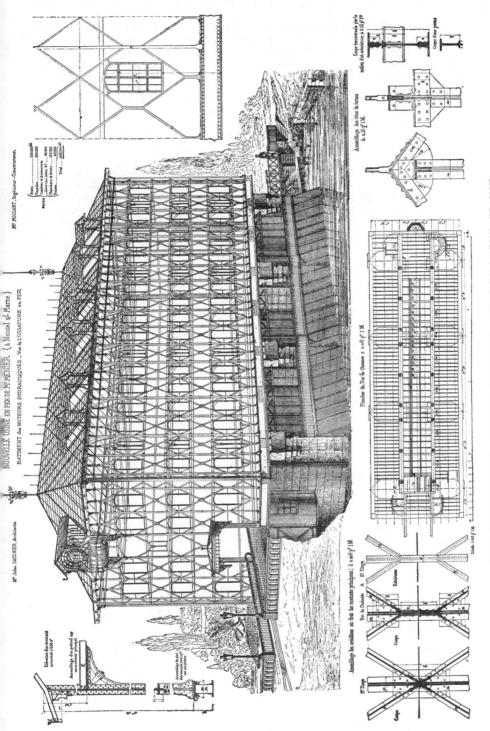

NOUVELLE USINE EN FER DE Mᵐᵉ MENIER (à Noisiel s/ Marne.)

BATIMENT des MOTEURS HYDRAULIQUES .—Vue de L'OSSATURE en FER

Mʳ Jules SAULNIER, Architecte.

Mʳ MOISANT, Ingénieur-Constructeur.

IRON CONSTRUCTION: FACTORY AT NOISIEL, SEINE ET MARNE, FRANCE.

Decorative treatment of iron framework.   The spaces between the members of the skeleton shown were filled with brick and tile in ornamental patterns, the construction thus being a modern fireproof elaboration of the half-timbered method.

are not needed to take up the thrust of the iron arches.

The iron dome of the church of Val-de-Grâce, in Paris, built in 1863–64, has a diameter of 58 feet and a height of 31 feet. It is composed of 16 ribs, each 13 feet deep, and 4 angles, $2\frac{8}{10}$ feet × 2 feet 8 inches × 36 inches. The ribs rest in cast-iron shoes bedded in the masonry, and at the crown abut against a hollow radial cone of plate iron 2 feet 6 inches in diameter. It is surmounted by an octagonal campanile $11\frac{1}{2}$ feet in diameter and 32 feet to the base of the 8-foot cross.

The metallic framing and decoration of the nave and dome of the church of S. Augustine, one of the more important churches of Paris, built in 1872, is of interest as construction. The style is intermediate between Byzantine and modern Renaissance. The ground upon which it is built is narrow in front and widens to the rear. The building is therefore in plan a nave 51 feet wide with lateral chapels, deeper as the lot widens, and terminates in an irregular octagon, the sides of which are of 22 and 51 feet alternately. The long sides correspond to the four grand arches which carry the pendentives and the dome. From the corners of the shorter sides rise triple connected columns of cast iron, upon which also these rest. The pendentives are formed of wrought-iron ribs which support a circular gallery, and a drum 16 feet high decorated with pilasters. The ribs of the inner dome start from these pilasters and unite in a ring 20 feet in diameter. The ribs are I beams 18 inches deep at the base and 14 inches at the summit, the webs of which are exposed for their whole depth and are decorated with zigzags, the flowers of wrought iron attached by rivets. The surface of the inner dome is composed of cast-iron plates riveted to the back of the ribs, and supported also by Tee irons riveted to their outer surface. These plates, as well as those which form the surfaces of the pendentives and of the arches, are cast with ornamental patterns in relief. The outer dome is also built with wrought-iron ribs composed of four angle irons connected by a latticed web. Upon the ribs are nailing strips of wood to which the roofing slates are fastened. The transverse arches of the nave are also formed of wrought-iron ribs of I section. The spandrils are vertical surfaces, running up to the ceiling. They thus form transverse ribs, and longitudinal iron beams resting upon them divide the ceiling into three panels, and carry flat arches of hollow bricks over which is a timber roof. The height under the inner dome is 164 feet. The nave from the dome to the door is 145 feet long and 77 feet high. The cost of the building was $1,000,000. If it had been of masonry throughout the cost would have been doubled.

In 1872 the chocolate factory of M. Menier at Noisiel was rebuilt on an iron frame filled in with bricks — a veritable skeleton construction. It is composed, above the foundation, of vertical I beams from foundation girders to roof frames, connected by a system of horizontals in T irons showing on the inside, and of diagonals of I beams with unequal flanges showing on the outside, forming together a surface of lozenges and triangles, which are filled with brickwork of ornamental design. Some of the lozenges contain the window frames. The building is about 36 feet wide, 130 feet long, and five stories high.

The buildings of the Vienna Exposition of 1873 were chiefly remarkable for their extent, there being but few types or forms of construction. The Central Hall was covered by a conical roof (or dome) 400 feet in diameter. The central gallery, 84 feet wide, was over 3000 feet in length, although its perspective was interrupted at its entrance into and exit from the great hall by its division into three arches, and from this long gallery thirty-two transverse halls, having light on both sides, formed the alcoves for the different articles exhibited.

The original design for the gallery of machines of the Paris Exposition of 1878 was an ordinary roof truss with tie rod, resting on wrought-iron supports. When placed in De Dion's hands for computation the side supports and the roof truss were combined into one curved latticed beam without tie rod, following the original outline of the section, and was anchored to the foundation on both sides — a perfectly rigid form. The span was small, about 80 feet.

The roof of the gallery of machines of the Exposition of 1889 was, on the contrary, an arch of large dimensions, the span being 375 feet, 160 feet high, and in length 1360 feet. Instead of being rigidly fixed to the foundations it was connected to them by hinged joints, and the two halves of the arch met in a hinged joint in the centre of the crown. At the time of its construction it was by far the largest arched roof existing. It has been exceeded a few feet by the roof of one of the buildings of the Chicago Exposition, imitated from it. It is constructed entirely of wrought iron, latticed between the two flanges. The immense ribs are 70 to 80 feet apart, and are connected by latticed beams or purlins. The arches are about 13 feet deep near the ground.

The work was let to two contractors who adopted different methods of erection. One of them put first in place the heavier lower half of the rib, the foot as it was called, weighing forty-eight tons; then the upper part of thirty-eight tons was raised to its position. The other half had meantime been put in place, and the ribs met at the top after five hours' work of eighty men. The other contractor built mov-

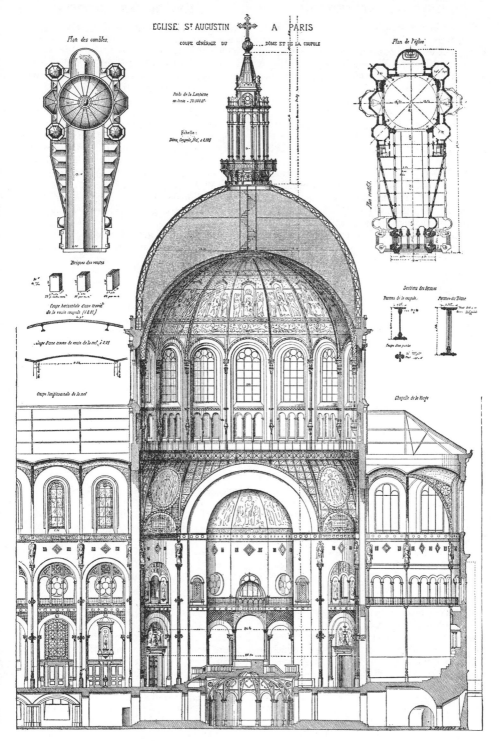

IRON CONSTRUCTION: CHURCH OF S. AUGUSTIN, PARIS.

The iron work, including vault ribs and vaulting shafts, is visible, and vaults and domes of hollow brick;
the whole made ornamental with painted decoration.

able scaffolding for the support of the ribs, which were handled and put in place in small parts, not exceeding three tons in weight.

The vestibule to the building is covered by a dome about 100 feet in diameter, of iron, and covered with glass.

The Eiffel Tower is too well known to require description. Its novelty was perhaps its principal attraction. Its height was 984 feet. Happily, the intention to build a somewhat similar tower, 1000 feet in height, at Chicago, in 1890, was abandoned.

The latest phase of metallic construction is the steel skeleton structure. The steel columns and girders make the frame of the building, and must be in themselves and in their connections strong enough to resist all the forces that may come against it. The exterior is enclosed with stone, brick, or terra cotta, and all parts of the interior are made of fireproof material, or covered with it, as a protection against fire. (See Fireproofing.)

In this, as in all other framing in iron or steel, the parts and their connections may be designed in various ways. In the best practice the columns are continuous, and are designed to offer easy connections of the girders and other horizontal parts. The **Z** column and a pair of latticed channels are usual forms.

Cast-iron columns are not generally used in the best constructions. When used, the ends or end plates are "machined" to faces exactly at right angles to the axis of the column, to cause them to bear evenly, and to stand vertically, one upon another, without shims.

The girders are **I** beams, either rolled or built of plates and angles, and are securely fastened to the column, sometimes by a pair of angles to the web; sometimes resting on and riveted to a bracket on the column. In this case the top flange also is held to the column by an angle iron. The floor joists are rolled **I** beams resting upon the girder, or riveted to its web by a pair of angles. The floors, resting upon the lower flanges of the joists, are flat arches of hollow brick or terra cotta, the brick next the beam being made to cover the lower flange of the beam as a protection against fire. Or the floor may be of concrete, strengthened by means of iron rods, or wires, or sheet metal bedded in it. Upon this the nailing strips for the wooden floor are bedded in "cinder" concrete, made of cinders, with a little lime or cement.

The main partitions rest upon the girders, others rest upon the solid floor. They are made of hollow brick, terra cotta, or concrete; sometimes of a light frame, covered on both sides with a wire netting, and plastered.

The lower flanges of the floor beams are protected from fire by the form of the hollow brick

skew back, which rests against them, extends below them, and is moulded with a recess for the flange. If the floor is of concrete it is carried below the beam, and covers it. Columns may be protected with thick tiles (3 inches), leaving an air space between them and the column, keyed to place and to each other, and each piece wired to the column with copper wire. As the outer walls are mere enclosures, and have no more weight to carry than their own, they may be very thin, frequently not more than 8 to 12 inches thick, and they may rest for each story upon a steel beam independent of the wall below. They are sometimes stiffened with steel angles, built into the masonry. The front walls are generally heavier and more elaborate.

In buildings of great height, so lightly constructed, the pressure of the wind is an important element, and must be provided for by the rigidity of the connections of the girders to the columns. If the beams and girders merely rest upon and are riveted to flat plates on the tops of the columns, knee braces, or some similar stiffening, may be necessary to carry the wind stresses to the foundations.

When *deep* floor girders are rigidly connected to the posts they form a very stiff joint, and if carried throughout the building may take the place of any other form of wind bracing. Diagonal rods in the panels formed by the floor girders and the posts give the greatest rigidity, but they interfere with windows and doors, and often cannot be used. Knee braces cause bending moments in the columns and the girders, although the latter are usually so deep as to be little affected by them.

In the design of a steel skeleton building the arrangement of the columns, both of the outer walls and of the interior distribution, must be first laid out upon a general plan, keeping in mind the girder connections which, with the columns, form the ossature of the building. A plan must be made of each floor, and the area carried by each column and girder be computed. Then, beginning at the top, the weight of the roof, with its load of snow or wind, is first computed. This is borne by the columns of the top story, and they are proportioned accordingly. The columns of the story below must bear the load coming to them from the columns of the top floor, together with the weight of the upper floor and its live load, and this method must be followed on each column from the roof to the foundation.

The load thus ascertained, which includes the weight of the column and of the fire protection around it, therefore represents the vertical load borne by the columns, and the foundation must be proportioned accordingly.

The arrangement of the iron and fireproof covering in the exposed fronts can only be made after the architectural drawings are completed, with horizontal and vertical sections of all cornices, window heads, and reveals, showing also the terra cotta or stone trimmings. The iron must be nowhere exposed; the terra cotta must, if possible, rest upon the iron, or some part of it must do so, leaving the rest suspended. It is held in place with hook bolts.

The merit of this method of construction resides in the fact that walls and partitions do not appreciably increase in thickness with the height of the building. That the material being of great strength may be carried to great height, and the concentration of the load on points, facilitates the construction of the foundations in difficult ground.

Foundations for exterior walls are ordinarily built upon the property lines, and the necessary widening of the base to increase the bearing surface must be made on the inside of the wall. Hence unequal pressures upon the base, and sometimes settlements. It is especially necessary that the weight should come centrally upon the ground on which it rests, when the latter is easily compressible. In the soft clay of Chicago, overlaid by a harder crust, foundations are generally made of a cribwork of iron or steel rails bedded in concrete, upon which the weights must be placed centrally to avoid unequal compression of the soil. They cannot therefore be placed at the building line. In New York especially the foundations of many of the higher buildings are carried to rock by means of caissons sunk by the aid of compressed air, and these also cannot be placed upon the building line. These various reasons have led to the construction of the side walls in many cases, upon cantilevers, upon the ends of which the columns rest. In this construction a very strong steel beam extends across the building from side to side, supported on the centres of the foundation piers which they cross, and the columns rest on their projecting ends. Steel beams connecting these columns at each story support the brick walls of the outside. Sometimes when the foundation cannot be placed centrally under the column it is built as near to it as possible. The steel beam rests upon the centre of the foundation, and its projecting end carries the column, while the other end of the beam is anchored down to a block of masonry to prevent the beam from tilting upon the foundation. This is cantilever construction. It is not in itself desirable. It is better, where the conditions permit, to build the foundations under the columns or walls; but it is a valuable method when the other cannot be realized.

The facility with which modern buildings of iron or steel can be erected, and the great height to which the materials must be raised, have led to marked developments in the form and arrangement of the erecting machinery. Steam hoisting engines are indispensable. At one time a rec-

tangular platform was in vogue, having a fixed derrick at each angle, which derricks together commanded the whole area of the building. When one floor was finished, the platform could be raised by its own machinery to the floor level above. A good arrangement is a large fixed derrick, which can lift all materials from the ground and place them within reach of small derricks, fixed or movable, which set them in place. This also can be raised from story to story by its own hoisting gear.

The practical part of iron and steel construction consists in the design, in the execution of the work in the shops, and the erection.

In the design of a structure of iron or steel, simplicity is a great merit. The parts are to be arranged to transmit all stresses to the foundations in the most direct manner possible. Columns should stand accurately over those below them, and their ends planed, to transmit the pressures from one to the other over the whole bearing surface. All loads are transferred to the columns in the most direct manner, and by the columns to the foundations. The connection of the girder or floor beam to the post (column) may be made in different ways, but always with a view to support and stiffen the latter. All parts are designed for ease of construction and facility of erection and connection.

If the column is of cast iron, it is cast with brackets and lugs for the support and attachment of the beams. The floor beams may rest upon the girder, but it is more common to attach them to the web of the latter, in order to reduce the thickness of the floor. The parts must be proportioned to the loads to come upon them. The limits of stress allowed in different materials are usually fixed by the building laws of the different cities. They should not ordinarily exceed one half the elastic limit of the material (see Strength of Materials). For wind pressures of thirty pounds to the square foot over the exposed surface of the building two thirds of the elastic limit may be permitted. Parts in compression should be continuous, the abutting surfaces being planed to an even bearing; all parts should be accurately fitted. Rivet holes should be punched or drilled so that they will match when the parts are brought together. Riveting in the shop is done by machines, and the pieces are put together in the shop in as large parts as can be conveniently handled on the ground, in order to save hand riveting in erection. It is important that sufficient rivets be used, not only to take the direct shear at connections, but that due to bending in plate girders.

The material now in general use for the frames of metal structures is medium steel, having a tensile strength of about 60,000 to 66,000 pounds to the square inch. This is used to give rigidity to shallow foundations, in columns, floors, roof trusses, girders, and arches. Cast iron, in addition to its use in short blocks, is still extensively adopted for columns, and suitable for arches, domes, etc., more especially in parts exposed to the weather, and where great durability is desired.

William H. Birkmire, *Architectural Iron and Steel; Skeleton Construction in Buildings; Compound Riveted Girders; Planning and Construction of High Office Buildings;* J. K. Freitag, *Architectural Engineering;* E. Brandt, *Lehrbuch der Eisen-Constructionen mit besonderer Anwendung auf den Hochbau* (Berlin, 1876, 1 vol. 4to); Guy Le Bris, *Les Constructions Métalliques* (1 vol. 8vo).

— W. R. HUTTON.

IRONING ROOM. A room connected with a laundry, private or public, and intended especially for the ironing of linen that has been washed. There are no special requirements for it except a flue for the ironing stove and abundance of light. The mangle, which in its earlier form was a machine occupying a good deal of space, is often put in a separate room.

IRONWORK. (For the constructive part, see Iron Construction; for ornamental ironwork, see Metal Work.)

ISABELLE, CHARLES EDWARD; architect; b. Feb. 24, 1800; d. May 1, 1880.

Isabelle was a pupil of Leclère (see Leclère), and at the *École des Beaux Arts* from 1818 to 1824, and between 1824 and 1828 visited Italy. In 1828 he was inspector of the works at the Madeleine, Paris. In 1834 he won first prize in the competition for the Hôtel des Douanes at Rouen. He built the *École des Arts et Métiers* at Angers between 1855 and 1877, and the *École des Arts et Métiers* at Châlons between 1845 and 1880. Isabelle is especially known by his *Édifices circulaires et les dômes* (folio, Paris, 1855). He published also *Parallèle des Salles rondes de l' Italie* (folio, Paris, 1863).

Bauchal, *Dictionnaire.*

ISACOUSTIC CURVE. *A.* A line or surface connecting points in a room having the same acoustical property, particularly that of the intensity of sound issuing from a particular point. (See Acoustics.)

B. The curvature of a bowled floor of an auditorium, so designed that the apparent elevation of each auditor above the auditor immediately in front of him, as viewed from the speaker's position, shall be the same. Thus applied, however, the term is a misnomer, for such an arrangement of seats does not necessarily give equally good hearing. — W. C. S.

ISAIE DA PISA; sculptor and architect.

A sculptor who flourished in the reign of Pius II. (Pope 1458–1464) in Rome. Porcello in his poem, *Ad immortalitatem Isäie Bisani Manuorum celatoris,* mentions among his works the tomb of Eugenius IV. (Pope 1431–1447) at the church of S. Salvatore in Lauro, Rome, and the triumphal arch of the Castel Nuovo at

Naples. In this latter work he was associated with many other sculptors (see Desiderio da Settignano; Giuliano da Maiano; and Paolo Romano).

Müntz, *Les Arts à la cour des papes.*

ISENBERT DE XAINTES (SAINTES); architect and engineer.

Isenbert appears to have built the bridges at Saintes and La Rochelle (Charente-Inférieure) in France. In a letter of King John of England, dated 1202, he is described as "master of the schools of Xaintes," and recommended to the mayor and citizens of London as qualified to continue the construction of London Bridge which was begun about 1176 by Peter of Colechurch (see Peter of Colechurch).

Thomson, *Chronicles of London Bridge.*

ISIDORUS OF MILETUS; architect.

He was employed with Anthemius of Tralles in the construction of the church of S. Sophia at Constantinople (532–537 A.D.). Another Isodorus of Miletus, probably his nephew, is mentioned by Procopius (op. cit.) as engaged in erecting important works on the banks of the Euphrates.

Procopius, *Of the Buildings of Justinian.*

ISOCEPHALOUS (adj.). Having the heads nearly on a horizontal line; said especially of human figures in a frieze or band, as a painting or bas-relief. Rarely extended to arches in an arcuated construction when for any reason the crowns and not the springing lines are brought nearly to a horizontal plane.

ISODOMUM. Same as Greek Masonry (which see under Masonry). The term signifies of equal make, and is applied properly only to such stonework as is laid in courses of equal height.

ISOMETRIC; ISOMETRICAL PERSPECTIVE; — PROJECTION. (See under Projection.)

ISTRIA, ARCHITECTURE OF. That of Istria, a peninsula at the head of the Adriatic Sea, forming part of the province of the coastland (*Küstenland*) of the Austrian dominions. It contains two important towns, Parenso and Pola, and also the town of Rovigno. At Pola there are Roman Imperial remains of extraordinary interest, though the town is modern, and the ruins are cared for merely as curiosities without having received much close investigation. The amphitheatre has its exterior in admirable preservation. Much of the bounding wall remains, and if the seats and the inner structure have disappeared, this very fact points to a most unusual peculiarity in the structure of the building, to which full attention is called in Jackson's book mentioned below. Beam construction of wood replaces, to a certain extent at least, the vaulting of Italy and Gaul, and the stone seats were carried upon this.

PLATE XIX

ITALY, ARCHITECTURE OF. PLATE I

Florence, Loggia dei Lanzi, the gallery on the southwest side of the Piazza della Signoria. This building is the type of that exquisite round-arched mediæval style of which the Italians might have made an earlier and more original Renaissance but for the overmastering influence of the northern Gothic. The building was completed about 1375. It is on a very large scale, with a total height of 70 feet.

The theatre has almost wholly disappeared. The city walls can be traced, and there are two Roman temples, one of which is almost perfect and is a beautiful Corinthian building of the time of Augustus. The celebrated memorial arch of the Sergii has but a single archway, and is not elaborate in design or in sculptured decoration. Three of the ancient gateways are traceable, of which one, the Porta Gemina, or double gateway, has some value. The cathedral of the town was largely rebuilt in the fifteenth century, but traces of very early work remain. Other churches, such as S. Michele and S. Maria in Canneto, have been destroyed; it appears that the rebuilding of the town has been accompanied by wanton removal of nearly all that was most interesting.

At Parenso there remains a cathedral which is, architecturally speaking, a basilica of singular richness in Byzantine detail. It is one of the most interesting churches in Europe, because of this mingling of styles. The atrium is preserved, and to the westward of it is the baptistery with the bell tower at the west side of that again. At the east end is an apse, and a curious vaulted sacristy standing on the north side of the eastern end has its own triapsal eastern termination of very extraordinary character. Rovigno has no single building of architectural importance except the cathedral, which was built in the eighteenth century. In all the three towns named there is, however, Venetian street architecture in great abundance, although sometimes in detached details.

At Fiume is a Roman memorial arch, but built into the neighbouring houses so that it can hardly be studied. At Trieste, which is the chief Austrian seaport of the Adriatic, there is little to see except the fragments of Venetian work and the very curious cathedral. This appears a five-aisled church with regularly placed chapels and subsidiary buildings. It appears to have resulted from the throwing into one church of a basilica and a Byzantine church which stood side by side on nearly parallel lines.

T. G. Jackson, *Dalmatia, The Quarnero and Istria* (Oxford, 1887); P. Kandlar, *Il Duomo di Trieste*, and, by the same author, other books published and unpublished, including a guidebook for Parenso and one for Pola, and some manuscripts, cited by Jackson in the book above mentioned; Stuart and Revett, *The Antiquities of Athens*, Vol. IV; which volume has 34 plates with the context devoted to Pola.

— R. S.

ITALIAN ARCHITECTURE. That of Italy; more especially that of any style assumed to have taken its origin in Italy. The term is used carelessly with the especial significance of a neoclassic style of great severity and of systematic design and fixed proportion, as if of the Italian sixteenth century. Thus, if a writer uses the term in describing a modern

building erected in England or elsewhere, it would imply the existence of a design free from the graceful irregularity of the Italian Renaissance proper, that is to say, the architecture of the fifteenth century (see Classicismo; Neoclassic Architecture; Renaissance; also Renaissance Architecture), and the presence of that formality found in the work of Palladio, Vignola, Sansovino, and their successors, also of Bernini and Maderno and the other employers of the colossal order. A design based upon S. Peter's church at Rome or the buildings of Palladio at Vicenza would be Italian in this limited and more nearly accurate sense, while one based upon the Florentine palaces of Brunellescho, Alberti, or upon the works of Bramante would not be so styled. — R. S.

ITALIAN GARDEN. A formal garden of a character imitated from, or suggested by, the villa gardens of the sixteenth and seventeenth centuries in and near the greater Italian cities. (See Landscape Architecture; Villa.)

ITALY, ARCHITECTURE OF. That of the continental part of the kingdom of Italy, together with the republic of San Marino. For the purpose of this inquiry it may be divided into fourteen parts, namely: —

I.	Piedmont.	VIII.	Umbria.
II.	Liguria.	IX.	Latium.
III.	Lombardy.	X.	Abruzzi and Molise.
IV.	Venetia.	XI.	Campania.
V.	Emilia.	XII.	Apulia.
VI.	Marches.	XIII.	Basilicata.
VII.	Tuscany.	XIV.	Calabria.

All this region is rich in ancient architecture, architectural sculpture, mosaic, and in portable works of art of durable material; also in painting of epochs, beginning with the thirteenth century and with a few remains of early painting. Here are Italian pre-Roman structures of great interest, not always thoroughly understood as yet, but included among these are Etruscan and Oscan remains of unique value to students. The Grecian architecture of Italy is of peculiar importance (see Parts XI. and XIII.). For buildings of the Roman state and the Roman dominion previous to 100 B.C., Italy is the only country in which to search and study; but for buildings of the Imperial epoch the less generally destroyed or defaced structures of North Africa, Syria, Dalmatia, and southern France are destined to prove even more instructive. At the same time the historical buildings of the city of Rome, for which documentary as well as internal evidence is to be had, are the foundations of our knowledge of this most important epoch in building — the root and stem of all modern European architecture. Latin architecture can be studied only in Italy. Byzantine architecture cannot be studied complete without the buildings of Ravenna and the scattered traces of Eastern influence in the territory of Venetia, including the city of Venice (Part IV. of this inquiry). Italian Romanesque of other than Byzantine type antedates the Romanesque of Northern Europe, and, so far as the existing monuments are concerned, is the apparent source and origin of such Northern work, except in so far as Byzantine art affected that of Northern Europe. Italian Gothic, although constructively a feeble echo of the Northern styles, is yet a charming art, investing its constructions with a wealth of carved and painted expression of artistic thought different from, and in some respects superior to, contemporary work in the North. With the dawn of the classical revival, about 1420, begins the epoch in which Italian graphic and plastic art obtained easy mastery over Europe, and the architecture of the Renaissance existed in Italy as an independent creation nearly a century before it had any echo in the North. Of all this epoch much remains in almost perfect preservation. Of the later classic styles (see Neoclassic; Post-Renaissance; Renaissance) Italy has much which even to this day holds great influence over designers among all peoples of European descent.

There is, therefore, no country in Europe in which so wide a field of art exists as in Italy, nor any country in the world in which so many styles, each representative and peculiar, are to be seen and studied, side by side. — R. S.

ITALY, ARCHITECTURE OF; **Part I.**; **Piedmont** (Piemonte); comprising the modern *provincie* of Torino (Turin), Cuneo, Alessandria, Novara. Piedmont has never been a centre of architectural influence. It has received rather than bestowed. It would, however, be wrong to suppose that in art the region had no life of its own; it gave its peculiar stamp to what

it borrowed, and its reputation of poverty is due rather to ignorance on the part of the outside world than to want of riches in itself.

With the exceptions of a triumphal arch at Aosta, and another at Susa, the monuments of Roman rule in the ancient patrimony of the house of Savoy are interesting rather to the archæologist than to the architect. One might be tempted to make further exception in favour of the remains of the theatre and amphitheatre also at Aosta, or of the Palazzo Madama at Turin, — a sort of confused epitome of the architectural history of the city, mixing foundations and portions of wall of a Roman city gate with constructions of the fourteenth and fifteenth centuries, and ending with the baroque façade designed by Juvara (1718), that corresponds with nothing within but the vast and splendid staircase of the same architect. But these and the Roman bridges and fragments of building found here and there are not of the first importance.

Of the architecture of later times several general observations may be made.

1. It is a brick architecture with, on occasion, free use of stone in capitals, columns, and voussoirs; and courses, etc., in rare cases, as in the little church of S. Secondo at Cortazzone, or in S. Nazzaro at Montechiaro d' Asti, which is an almost entire stone construction. In general, Gothic ornamentation is in terra cotta. This is often of extreme richness, and sometimes, as in the curious façade of the church at Chivasso, contains representations of the human figure of large size and great beauty.

2. The almost complete separation of Piedmont from Lombardy in matter of architecture. In Romanesque times the great single-gabled façade, universal in Lombardy, is entirely wanting in Piedmont; both then and throughout the Middle Ages the façade follows the outline of the respective roofs of the nave and of the aisles. It may here be remarked that the union of cupola with basilican nave (not peculiar to the Romanesque of Piedmont) was continued through the Gothic period.

3. Piedmont had no part in the return to classic forms that toward the end of the fifteenth century enriched the neighbouring Lombardy with so many splendid works. The duomo at Turin (finished 1498) is almost a!one as an example of the Renaissance proper, and even this, though designed by a Florentine, Meo del Caprina, imported for the occasion by the Cardinal Domenico della Rovere, is inside but a Romanesque church with classic details. It had no influence on the architecture of Turin or of the surrounding country. Matteo San Michele came into Piedmont about 1528, and executed several works (tombs, doorways); at Vercelli, the exquisite court of Casa-Momo only needs to be in Florence to be admired by all

the world; but these, and a half dozen other monuments of the epoch, scattered over so wide a space, are lost among their pseudo-Gothic contemporaries. A great proportion of the Gothic churches, and pretty well all the houses whose terra cotta framed windows and doors are still the boast of so many towns of Piedmont, in their present shape, at least, date from the fifteenth century (Mondovī, Novara, Garessio, Tortona, Costigliole, Revello, etc.).

4. So far as Piedmont obeyed an outside impulse, this came to her from France, as was indeed natural considering the intimate relations of the countries. The choir of S. Giovanni at Saluzzo (1472) is simply a bit of flamboyant architecture, more thoroughly French than anything else, probably, in Italy. It may be said, by the way, that the sculpture in this choir is of great beauty, and also that it contains a tomb of Ludovico II., Marquis of Saluzzo (1504), one of the rare examples of the early Renaissance. Two others, a doorway and a tomb, are in the chapter house of the church. Also, the cathedral at Saluzzo carries the side aisles around the apse of the choir, a French arrangement most rare in Italian Gothic, though less infrequent in churches of the Renaissance and later. Then the Gothic churches in the district about Turin, beginning as far south as Saluzzo, and extending north as far as Aosta, and from Pinerolo to Chivasso, have all of them an extraordinary detail which I believe must be a simple exaggeration of a feature common in French architecture. The central doorway, recessed, is surrounded by several alternating rolls and bands of rich terra cotta ornament (rarely colonettes). The extreme outer bands, arrived at the springing of the arch, part from the others, and, describing two sides of a triangle, meet in an acute angle high upon the façade — so high that in one case, at least (at Inverso), they cut through the lines of the roof and form a pinnacle above. This is evidently a representative of the gable above French doorways. At Chieri, in one of the churches of this group, this feature is of pierced stone, and suggests strongly that above the central door of the north transept at Rouen. In others, a rose window embraced between the pyramidal lines gives an approach to the same design. The size of this gable, especially as the other details are of modest proportions, makes it the predominant feature of the façade. At Chivasso and elsewhere it seems the only feature, and separates this group of church fronts from all others in Europe. If you make acquaintance with it in a woodcut, ten to one that it strikes you as barbarously ugly. But in reality, as the terra cotta ornaments are often fine, as they are united with colour (mosaics or frescoes; in one case, Rossano, the whole façade within and without the triangular frame is one co-

lossal play of colour, amidst which a S. Christopher mounts from above a side door almost to the roof), you soon find that these fronts have a charm of their own. Other churches of the group are at Cirié, Buttigliera Alta, etc.

Among Romanesque churches, the cathedral at Casale Monferrato is the one best known. Dating from 741, it was rebuilt 1107. Though the aisles are narrow, the number of them, five, with the addition of side chapels, gives an imposing effect of width and variety. There is a cupola at the transept intersection, and the whole was of great beauty till an unintelligent restoration spoiled its character. One feature, however, remains uninjured, the magnificent vestibule, extending at the full height of the church across its entire width, and so open to the rest that the aisles seem a continuation of it. Its vaulting system is, so far as known, unique in church architecture. Two immense arches cross the vestibule in each direction, and stand out boldly against a deep background of flattish vaulting thrown from top to top of their walls, the corner compartments alone approaching somewhat to ordinary forms. This system, simplified, was frequently employed until quite recent times in private houses in Piedmont.

Three very small but beautiful Romanesque churches, Montechiaro and Cortazzone, near Asti, and Cavagnola, near Chivasso, together with the large abbey church of Staffarda, near Saluzzo, and the extremely curious and interesting Sagra di S. Michele, near Avigliana (Turin), are left undescribed only from want of space; but there is still another partly Romanesque (apse and façade), partly transition, which cannot thus be passed over, the little abbey church of Vezzolano, high among the hills between Chivasso and Asti. In its present state it dates from about the middle of the twelfth century. The front is of mingled brick and stone, has a beautiful doorway, and above it arcades with colonettes in stone that suggest the churches of Pisa, only that the arrangement here gains in variety by means of an interesting double window with sculptures, breaking the lines of the arcades. It is one of the most charming of Romanesque façades. After its promise of three aisles, one is surprised on entering to find but two, the place of the south aisle being occupied in its first bay by a chapel, in the rest of its extent by one side of the cloister. The most remarkable feature of the interior is a sort of gallery (of 1188) in gray stone, and supported on five arches of the purest Gothic style, that crosses the nave between the first and second bays. Above its arches are two rows of sculpture, the lower representing the prophets and patriarchs of the Old Testament, the upper the evangelists and the death and assumption of the Virgin. It probably served either as pulpit or gallery for singers.[1]

Piedmont preserves four baptisteries of Romanesque architecture, at Novara, at Asti, at Biella, and at Agrate-Conturbia, between Novara and Arona, — all of them, with the exception of Asti, consisting of an octagon supporting a cupola, and having niches, round or square, on all sides. Novara, dating from the fifth, and partly rebuilt in the twelfth, century, has antique columns in the angles. That of Biella (ninth century?) is of brick; that of Agrate, apparently of the same age, of stone. At Asti, the octagon cupola, supported on squat columns, with cushion capitals, is surrounded by a polygonal or circular aisle. It is probably of the eleventh century.

The cathedral of Novara retains traces of its Romanesque period, and the nave columns, with the mosaic pavement, are antique; but the general aspect is due to a restoration, in 1862, by Count Antonelli, architect of the surprising cupola of S. Gaudenzio at Novara, and of the Mole Antonelliana at Turin.

The Gothic churches are in their present state mostly of the fifteenth century; that of S. Andrea, at Vercelli, on the whole the finest in Piedmont, of 1219, that of Asti, of 1348. Those of the fifteenth century, besides the peculiarities already named, have in general high nave arcades, supported on piers flanked by four half columns, with cushion capitals, or low, almost Doric ones, surrounded by foliage, scanty, but of fairly good execution, no triforium, low clearstory, square vaulting spaces with ribs, and the system of lighting familiar in Milan cathedral. Usually there is a transept, and the choir and side aisles (separated by walls from one another) end each in a half octagonal apse. The principal churches of the group are the cathedrals at Saluzzo, Chieri, Pinerolo, Alba (with massive and original west front, and semioctagonal chapels projecting on the sides), with the churches of Ciriè, Buttigliera Alta, Revello, etc., not forgetting Sant' Antonio di Ranverso (near Avigliana), probably the most beautiful of them all. The cathedral of Asti is of a finer type. It is what the Germans call a "hall church" (see Hall Church), and the supporting piers take the form of a cluster of columns. The vaulting ribs have been concealed in the interest of the rococo painting that covers all the vaulting. There is a fine portal on the south side. The church of S. Andrea at Vercelli, that Professor Freeman and other Englishmen have liked to fancy was inspired by English models, has been shown by M. Enlart[2] to have submitted to French influence wherever it is not distinctly Italian. The east end is strikingly like that of the cathedral at Laon, otherwise the outside would, by itself, place it among the noblest of Italian Romanesque churches.

The hills of Piedmont are still crowned by multitudes of mediæval castles, some in ruins, many still inhabited. The original construction, in these cases, is either marked by successive additions and changes, or has been more or less, generally less, judiciously restored. There are regions especially rich in ancient seats. About Ovada are twelve or fifteen, of which the most important are Silvano d' Orba (interior), San Cristoforo, Montaldeo, Lerma, Mornese, Roccagrimalda, Tagliolo (in part well restored by Alfred d'Andrade). Near Saluzzo are Verzuolo (a noble exterior in perfect preservation), Manta (good restoration of part), Lagnasco (dilapidated, rich decoration inside). There are many others about Casale; and, in the Val d' Aosta, Verres — a huge square of admirable construction, in ruin — the most picturesque (also in ruin, though preserving its court and some rooms with decoration) is Fenis, and then, admirably restored, Issogne, in latest Gothic (1480). Galliato, near Novara, is still an imposing mass, and Gaglianico, near Biella, is as charming for the artist or poet as it is interesting to the architect. The cities of Piedmont abound in ancient houses, though, almost without exception, the façades have been shamefully defaced; sometimes a single window, surrounded with rich terra-cotta ornaments, alone reveals the former beauty of the house. The mediæval village in the park of the Valentino at Turin is therefore of real service to the student of the architecture of the country, In it are reproductions of the most remarkable Gothic houses scattered among the cities of Piedmont, — Bussoleno, Alba, Cuorgnè, Avigliana, Chieri, Pinerolo, Mondovì, etc. The work was designed and executed by archæologists, artists, and architects, the most competent of the country. The whole is solidly done, and the village has, from the beginning, been inhabited. It contains also a castle, which is not the reproduction of any one, but a representative castle, having been made by the fusion of elements from two or three of the castles of the Val d' Aosta, principally Fenis, with occasional details from others.[1]

In addition to such works of the early Renaissance as have been already mentioned, the charming Casa Silva at Domo d' Ossola should not be forgotten, nor the Casa Cavassa at Saluzzo, this latter being as much the latest expression of Gothic as the herald of a new art. The entrance door or doorway and the balustrade in the court are gems of the early Renaissance. In the sixteenth century the parts of

[1] Compare *Emporium* (magazine of Bergamo) Natale, 1896, for a very good illustrated account of Vezzolano.

[2] *Origines françaises de l'Arch⁰ Goth⁰ en Italie*, Paris, 1894.

[1] Compare Frizzi, *Il Borgo ed il Castello medioevali in Torino*, Torino, 1894.

Piedmont nearest to Lombardy participated to some extent in the architectural activity of their neighbours.

Pelegrino Tibaldi has left various examples of his work, at Vercelli (duomo), Novara (S. Gaudenzio), Varallo (on the Sacro Monte), etc. The chapels upon the sacred mountains of Varallo, Orta, Crea, are many of them of pleasing architecture. Tradition ascribes one at Orta to Michelangelo. At the end of the century (1596) Vitozzi built the imposing sanctuary at Vico, near Mondovi. The cupola, a fine work, was added by the Turinese architect Gallo, in the next century. Turin itself seems to have awakened to architectural life in the seventeenth century, and the city still bears the impress of that time. It is the city of the " barocco." The genius of such men as the Counts Carlo and Amedeo Castellamonte (father and son), the padre Guarini and Juvara, has not only made the style respectable, but has shown that it is capable of a picturesque force worthy of high admiration. — JOHN SAFFORD FISKE.

ITALY, ARCHITECTURE OF ; Part II. ; Liguria ; occupying the whole coast from the French frontier to Tuscany, and comprising the two modern *provincie* of Genova (Genoa) and Porto Maurizio.

Liguria is a mere strip of coast, and its architectural history is, in large measure, simply that of Genoa. There is, however, an early history in which the country was independent of the city, or depended upon a greater one, — Rome. There are traces of Roman civilization at almost every step along the shore between the Var and the Arno, abundant in many places, as, *e.g.*, Ventimiglia (Albium Intemelium of the Romans) and Albenga (Albium Ingaunum). At the former, among others, are the remains of a theatre, at the latter, a fine bridge in a good state of preservation. At Albenga is also an early Christian baptistery (fifth century ?), in plan like that at Novara, an octagon with antique columns in the corners supporting arcades and cupola, niches alternately round and rectangular in the sides, fragments of mosaic and a tomb, probably of the eighth century, covered with Byzantine interlaced patterns.

Romanesque architecture in this region is a combination of elements from Pisa, on one side, and southern France on the other, and its monuments in Genoa do not differ greatly either in style or in importance from those of the provincial towns. By far the greater number of churches of this period have been so changed in later times as to show little or nothing of the original structure. Those that remain are, for the most part, of the basilican form, with a transept and cupola, columns, either antique, or built with blocks of marble alternately black and white and having capitals imitated from the Corinthian. Façades are of the simplest

form of Romanesque, in Genoa often in layers of black and white, in the country of a uniform gray, generally in well-squared stone. The towers were also simple, and, more frequently than either in France or in Tuscany, have for decoration the courses of little arches on brackets that are characteristic of Lombard and Rhenish Romanesque. Some of the later ones (*e.g.* S. Giovanni di Prè at Genoa) are crowned by an octagonal pyramidal spire with four corner pyramids, a disposition not uncommon in France.

Romanesque churches in Genoa are : S. M. di Castello (eleventh century ?), with antique columns, S. Donato (twelfth century), both well restored ; S. Cosmo, S. Stefano, and S. Tommaso, of each of which only the façade[1] and tower are preserved. S. Siro, formerly cathedral, was entirely remodelled in 1576 and S. M. delle Vigne in 1586, retaining of the original construction only a rude cloister (twelfth century ?). S. Giovanni di Prè (with an apse at each end, owing to a change of orientation when the church was repaired in the thirteenth (?) century) has piers instead of columns. To the west of Genoa the very interesting church of S. Paragorio (ninth century ?) at Noli also has piers, a high crypt, and traces of a narthex at the west end. It has been very carefully restored. That at Castello d' Andora, near Alassio, is in large part of the transition period. Others, more or less well preserved, are at Diano Castello (two, one of which is modernized inside, while the other, a simple oratory, has a painted wooden ceiling of the fifteenth century), at Torazzo (a Greek cross in plan) and Montegrazie (good construction and fine porch) both near Porto Maurizio, at Taggia (a charming town full of remains of all periods), and at Ventimiglia (a cathedral with barrel vaulting to the nave, as in many churches of southern France, no clearstory, Gothic portals to the façade, and an early Christian baptistery under the sacristy). Aside from these there are, as in all parts of Italy, many churches of this, as of the Gothic period, so transformed in the seventeenth or eighteenth centuries that little remains — an apse, a campanile, a few capitals, or monuments — to show what they were originally.

What the smaller Gothic churches of Genoa, like S. Matteo, once were, can probably be divined in S. Andrea at Levanto, as well as anywhere. Here, as at Monterosso and Cogorno (Lavagna), the dispositions of the façade as well as its structure in layers of black and white marble, are much the same as at S. Matteo or S. Stefano. That at Lavagna may be taken as a type of the rest. Its flat surface is relieved only by two *lisene* (shallow, pilaster-like projections) at the angles, and marking the division between the nave and the aisles, by a slight

[1] The façade of S. Stefano is Gothic.

prominence of the central doorway, and by a series of little arches bracketed out under the main gable and the half gables of the aisles. The aisles are scantily lighted by two round windows (elsewhere by long and narrow ones) and the nave by a rose. This church has a fine tower with a spire like that of S. Giovanni di Prè. In the other churches the tracery of the rose window has been removed, except at Monterosso, where it is of a richness unequalled on the whole Riviera. At Levanto the façade has suffered much from alterations, as has also the inside, which, however, retains its black and white columns, its high pointed arcades, its transept with piers and engaged columns, and everywhere, except in the choir, allows the ancient construction to be easily made out. Several of the group, like S. Siro at San Remo, have been disfigured inside by rococo renovations. S. Matteo at Genoa, renewed by Montorsoli (1543), has perhaps gained by the change. It has a fine cloister with double columns.

The one splendid church of the period is the cathedral, S. Lorenzo, at Genoa. It is, however, such a conglomerate of different styles, that the nave and the façade alone give it the aspect of a Gothic church. The cloister of two stories is Romanesque, as are the columns of the nave and two beautiful portals, one of which, with its upper story and its two supporting columns quite detached from the background, recalls the porches of Lombardy. The façade of black and white marble has three portals of French character, and the original plan was in harmony with these. But only one tower was finished, and its upper two stories are plainly of the early Renaissance. The corresponding tower ends at half its height with a Renaissance loggia. Inside, the nave of black and white marble has what at first glance appears a lofty triforium, but it opens also into the side aisles (as at Modena), which reach to the clearstory. This is modern and without character. Eastward from the transept (inclusive) is by Galeazzo Alessi (1567, the cupola), and Pennone (the too gorgeous choir). In the north aisle, the chapel of S. John the Baptist (1451–1496) has a charming front of the first Renaissance mingled with Gothic details, suggesting in some of its forms the *Porta della Carta* of the ducal palace in Venice. The interior is adorned with statues and reliefs by Matteo Civitali, a Madonna, and S. John Baptist by Sansovino, and other sculptures by Giacomo and Guglielmo della Porta. The most noteworthy civil structure in Gothic is the ancient bank of S. George, recently restored by A. d'Andrade. Remains of Gothic construction are numerous in the towns of Liguria; windows, doorways, a tower, or traces of an arcade give interest to a building otherwise reduced to vulgarity. There are towns like Noli, where half at least of the houses are still evidently mediæ-

val, and which abound in interest for the architect and the artist.

The early Renaissance is but scantily represented in Genoa. Wandering about in the streets in the centre of the city, one sees here and there a sculptured doorway opening into a vestibule of charming picturesqueness. The Palazzo Centurione, near S. Matteo, is surrounded by houses of the fifteenth century of a mixed style in which Gothic elements predominate. In fact, Genoa was so little affected by the early Renaissance movement, that it is a surprise to find upon the hill at the back of Final Borgo, halfway between Genoa and San Remo, a lovely little edifice that bears outside a striking resemblance to the Portinari chapel of Michelozzo at the church of S. Eustorgio in Milan. It unfortunately serves as a receptacle for wood for an ignorant peasant. The commission for the preservation of ancient monuments can only guarantee it against utter ruin. In fact, throughout the Renaissance period, Lombard influences were strong in Liguria, from the early doorways of Genoa to the Baroque, when some of the finest palaces were the work of Lombard architects.

But if the fifteenth century be meagrely represented, and chiefly by fragments, the sixteenth has left in Genoa such a wealth of palaces as can hardly be matched elsewhere. Great part of these are in the long street that, under several names, leads from the railway station to the Piazza Carlo Felice, and are the work of a small group of architects. Giovanni Antonio Montorsoli (1563) built the Palazzo Andrea Doria, just a little out of the line of the street named. The garden façade is the richer and more picturesque part; the garden itself, once the very ideal of an Italian garden, has mostly disappeared under the encroachments of the modern commercial city. Inside, the decorations of Pierin del Vaga, the pupil of Raphael, are still preserved. Giovanni Battista Castello da Bergamo (1569) built the Palazzo Carrega, now Cataldi, — a typical Genoese palace. Castello was architect also of the Palazzo Imperiali (Piazza Campetto), as rich in ornament as any of the Baroque period, and coöperated with Montorsoli in the interior of S. Matteo. Another Lombard was Rocco Lurago (1590 ?), whose great work was the Palazzo Doria-Tursi, now used by the municipality, the façade of which building foreshadows the coming Baroque in an exuberance of detail that is rather rich than elegant or correct, but which is certainly of great effectiveness. The court is one of the finest in a city where beautiful courts are exceptionally numerous. Finer yet, and indeed one of the most remarkable of Europe, and reminding one of the noblest architectural perspectives of Paolo Veronese, is the court of the University by another Lombard, Bartolomeo Bianco (about 1623). The palace is built against a hillside, and the way that the eye is led on from one level to another, up to the topmost arcades against the sky, is a stroke of genius. The façade is not of equal value. The Palazzo Filippo Durazzo is also by B. Bianco, and the Palazzo Balbi (Via Balbi) by him together with P. A. Corradi. Other palaces of various periods are : the Palazzo Raggio, with a charming fountain in the court ; the Royal Palace, which has nothing outside to recommend it beyond its size ; but the court, with the view of the harbour framed by a composition of arches, seen from the main doorway, is of great beauty ; the Palazzo Spinola, Palazzo Negrotto, and the Palazzo Durazzo on the Via Balbi.

We have left till the last the architect who, more than any other, contributed to the present aspect of Genoa, Galeazzo Alessi of Perugia, a pupil of Michelangelo (1512–1572). Nearly the whole of the Via Garibaldi (Via Nuova) is by him, — the Cambiaso, Parodi (Lercari), Spinola, Giorgio Doria, Adorno, Serra, and Brignole-Sale palaces. Although none of these is equal in richness and beauty to the Palazzo Marini at Milan, by the same architect, though none has a court to rival that of the University, yet this group of palaces, as a whole, not only puts Alessi at the head of the architects who have embellished Genoa, but ranks high among the most noteworthy of Italy. They with the others, by whomsoever designed, have certain features in common. The artists in general have known how to adapt themselves to the narrow streets of Genoa. The façades have few projections, none that hinder the eye from taking in the whole, a reserve that has the additional advantage of giving its due importance to the cornice, — above which is no attic. The vestibules are of a beauty and variety not to be equalled elsewhere, and occasionally the changing levels of the ground have stimulated the architects to procure effects of rare picturesqueness. In no other city are there so many noble staircases as in Genoa, and they are usually so arranged (not only in Genoa, but throughout Liguria) that they form an important feature in the view of the court or vestibule obtained from the doorway. The façades were not always ornamented with rustication or with pilasters or sculpture, but were frequently covered with painting of figures as well as of architectural details. The painted architecture is to this day a peculiarity of the Genoese coast.

Alessi was also the author of a large number of villas in and about Genoa, — Villa Pallavicini delle Peschiere, V. Spinola, V. Lercari, V. Doria, V. Grimaldi, and V. Scassi (these last five at Sampierdarena),[1] V. Cambiaso, at San Francesco d' Albaro, and, in the same suburb of Genoa, the Villa Paradiso by Ceresola. The

[1] Or San Pier d' Arena, a suburb of Genoa.

cupola of the cathedral is also his, and S. Maria di Carignano is considered his master work in religious architecture as well as one of the triumphs of the Renaissance. The exterior, however, for which he is not responsible, can hardly be entitled to much praise, and the interior, a reproduction on a small scale of that of S. Peter as designed by Bramante and Michelangelo, is injured, in the judgment of the writer, by the coarseness of the pilasters, by the cold, dead white that everywhere covers it, and by the huge statues of the most abominably sprawling rococo, in niches of the great piers supporting the dome. These seem to dwarf and contort the whole church. Notwithstanding the excessive gorgeousness of the new decoration, the interior of SS. Annunziata (Giacomo della Porta, 1587), a basilica with cupola, is much more satisfactory. Other interesting churches of the baroque period are S. Ambrogio, S. Siro, and the Madonna delle Vigne. The last two have columns in couples, as has also the church at Finalmarina, said to have been designed by Bernini. Most of the churches of the Riviera, of whatever date originally, now wear the aspect of the seventeenth or eighteenth century. Many of them, for all their lack of purity in details, produce a fine effect of spaciousness and dignity. — JOHN SAFFORD FISKE.

ITALY, ARCHITECTURE OF ; PART III.; **Lombardy** (Lombardia); containing the eight modern *provincie* of Bergamo, Brescia, Como, Cremona, Milano (Milan), Mantova (Mantua), Pavia, and Sondrio.

Lombardy has preserved very few monuments of ancient architecture. Excavations at Milan (Mediolanum Insubrum of the Romans) often reveal remains of buildings dating, some of them, from before the Christian era. The earliest found are in the region of the Piazza della Scala, and many others in the streets surrounding the Piazza del Duomo show the centre of the ancient city to have been identical with that of the modern. But the so-called columns of S. Lorenzo are the only really considerable work left above ground. These are sixteen in number, of the Corinthian order with a central intercolumniation wider than the others. The plan of the church of S. Lorenzo is of the third or fourth century, and whether it was originally the principal hall of the Thermæ of Maximian, or was an early Christian construction, it is equally Roman and noble in design.

At Brescia the museum of ancient art is housed in a triple temple (with a portico in common) built about 72 A.D. and dedicated to Jupiter, Juno, and Minerva, according to some ; according to others, to Hercules. The cellæ are shallow, and preserve in part the incrustation of the walls in fine marbles, and in one of the three, the mosaic pavement (restored). The portico consists of four pilasters and ten columns rising from a stylobate of 3 metres in height, all of marble. The order is Corinthian, and of the best style and workmanship.

In S. Salvatore at Brescia we have an example, probably unique in Lombardy, of a church of the eighth century, a very simple basilica with a single apse, columns with shafts of various lengths and diameters, a crypt under the east end, and a timber roof. The sculptures are perhaps the best of this period in Italy. Cattaneo assigns to the same century the crypt of the Duomo Vecchio, also at Brescia.

There are indeed many churches in Lombardy popularly ascribed to this period,

recently been restored. The last three have also interesting baptisteries, as has S. Vittore at Arsago, near Gallarate, a church coeval with S. Vincenzo in Prato.

There were exceptions, though rare, to the basilican plan, as, _e.g._, S. Tomaso in Limine at Almenno near Bergamo, a round church with surrounding aisle and gallery, similar in plan to the cathedral of Charlemagne at Aix-la-Chapelle. Also the tiny church of S. Satiro at Milan, a Greek cross with apses at the extremities of three arms, in curious harmony with the adjoining (fifteenth century) transept of Bramante (?); and S. Lorenzo, which, under its present aspect of late sixteenth century architecture, still preserves the plan and dispositions of the great hall of the Thermæ of Maximian.

Of the Byzantine ornamentation of the early churches there are abundant remains in museums and in the churches themselves. The interlacings of grooved bands, the conventional roses, palms, lilies, birds, vines, are such as were common to Greece and Syria as well as to Italy. Capitals were frequently clumsy imitations of the Corinthian. The decoration of the apse by a series of niches above the springing of the half cupola contained the germ of those galleries under the roof that were the glory of the twelfth century architecture, not only in Italy, but also in the lands beyond the Alps.

The boundaries of Lombardy architecturally speaking exclude Como and the large district subject to its influence, but include Parma, where is perhaps the most complete monument of the style, and extend eastward from its great strongholds in Milan and Pavia to Verona and Bologna, where however is felt the neighbourhood of Venice and Ravenna.

ITALY, PART III.—LOMBARDY: CHURCH OF S. AMBROGIO, MILAN. PART OF CROSS SECTION THROUGH NAVE AND AISLE; 11TH AND 12TH CENTURIES.

as, _e.g._, the Duomo Vecchio just mentioned, a round church now known to be of the twelfth century, while S. Vincenzo in Prato at Milan, declared by Dartein to be of the eighth century, and by antecedent writers to be of the sixth or earlier, is probably of the ninth. The church of Agliate (at Carate Brianza) is of the ninth or tenth century. Others are S. Pietro al Monte at Civate, near Lecco, and S. Vincenzo at Galliano, near Cantù. All are plain churches of the basilican type with columns, and have

If, however, the Duomo of Parma be the most finished of Lombard monuments, the mother church is that of S. Ambrogio at Milan. Its age is still the subject of contests, since recently L. Beltrami [1] returned to the opinion, supposed to be no longer tenable, that it dates in its entirety (barring cupola) from the ninth century. Were that the case, S. Ambrogio would be the mother of all the Romanesque churches in Europe, and the history of the style would need to be in large part rewritten; but it is generally held that the

[1] _Ambrosiana, Scritti varii publicati nel XV centenario della morte di S. Ambrogio_, Milano. 1897.

apse alone with certain fragments incorporated in the later constructions dates from the ninth, while the nave is of the eleventh, and the atrium of the twelfth century.

The interior impresses one as broad, low, massive, and crepuscular. There is no clearstory. The piers are alternately greater and smaller, — two bays of the aisles equalling in length one of the nave, — and have clustered about them

the cathedral at Pisa and S. Miniato at Florence; its following is more numerous and of greater consequence. Its atrium is the twelfth century descendant of those attached to the early Christian basilicas of Rome; and the façade, under one huge gable, is of the form constantly repeated even in the Gothic churches of the same region. In S. Ambrogio, however, this gable follows the lines of the construction,

ITALY, PART III. — LOMBARDY: CHURCH OF S. MICHELE, PAVIA. ONE BAY OF NAVE; 11TH AND 12TH CENTURIES.

pilasters and half columns corresponding to the several divisions of the vaulting. Though not an example of the full development attained by the style, though the forms are heavy and the vaulting tentative, the essential features of Romanesque architecture are to be found here, treated with mastery and with full consciousness of their significance. Thus S. Ambrogio in its rudeness is, in a way, a more important monument than its beautiful contemporaries,

and has not the defect that it had in later churches of being a mere mask.

S. Eustorgio, also in Milan, has been so often made over that, till the recent restorations, it was difficult to recognize it as of the same epoch. With barrel vaulting are S. Celso (a mere fragment), S. Babila, and S. Sepolcro, with a gallery and a vast crypt.

Pavia is of more importance than Milan to the student of Romanesque architecture, in that it has preserved more churches, and the progress of the style from its earliest to its latest development may be seen in three of its monuments. S. Michele, the oldest, is higher than S. Ambrogio, with galleries, a clearstory, a transept, and a cupola that formed part of the original plan, altogether discrediting the opinion long maintained of its extreme antiquity. S. Pietro in Cielo d' Oro shows further advance, the vaulting shafts of uniform section and height proving the intention from the beginning to make an equal number of vaulting bays in nave and aisles. S. Teodoro, admirably constructed, almost Gothic in part, has a cupola in which appears, perhaps for the first time, a system of superstructures such as later produced the splendid examples of Chiaravalle and S. Andrea at Vercelli.[1]

Such examples as the cathedrals at Cremona and Parma show the Lombard style in the fulness of its development. Each has a triforium (in the former continued across the transept); the vaulting in both is hexapartite, slightly later in date than the rest. The latter has the best designed façade to be found in this style, with two noble towers almost adjoining it (only one completed). The view of the apses, owing to a slope of the ground which leaves the crypt entirely exposed, is unusually imposing in its great height. The essential features of the Romanesque in Lombardy are those of the style elsewhere; that is, while preserving the ground plan of the Latin basilica, it substituted for columns piers with engaged columns or pilasters, answering to the several parts of the vaulting to be sustained. The features distinguishing it from the style of other regions are mainly in the façade. At first, when the nave and the aisles were nearly of the same height, the single gable for all three was inevitable; but afterward, when the aisles were relatively low, the retention of this form caused the wall, often pierced with empty windows, to appear awkward and meaningless. The galleries following the line of the gable (sometimes also in horizontal bands), the rose window of the centre, the buttresses marking the division of nave and aisles, sometimes taking the form of half columns with capitals supporting nothing (S. Michele at Pavia, the duomo of Casale, and that of Piacenza), sometimes of plain piers, the summits of which coincide with the line of the roof and are covered with tiles (S. Teodoro, S. Pietro in Cielo d' Oro at Pavia), — all these are essential peculiarities of these fronts. A great feature is the main entrance, which eastward from Milan

[1] A family likeness marks the façades of all these churches : above the doors several double arched windows, above these one or more single ones, and a gallery following the line of the gable. One finds the same dispositions in the Gothic church of S. Francesco.

and throughout the Emilia is preceded by a porch, often of two stories, the two columns of which are supported on the backs of lions, generally of remarkable character. The finest of these entrances, attached to S. M. Maggiore at Bergamo, is, however, of Gothic work. The cupola above the transept crossing was in Lombardy more than elsewhere an essential part of Romanesque architecture, and had generally the same form, — an octagonal drum with galleries and a low roof. The separation of the tower, or towers, from the church is rather Italian than Lombard, while specially Lombard are the independent baptisteries, either round or polygonal, which continued to be built even till the fourteenth century, long after baptism by immersion was given up.

Other influences, probably German or Burgundian, shaped the architecture of the province of Como. The interesting church of S. Abondio at Como, with its constructive façade and its two graceful towers incorporated in the main edifice, looks more like a Burgundian than an Italian church. It is typical of the Romanesque churches of the considerable region that looked to Como for its models, and, like them, is built of stone instead of brick. A word may be added as to S. M. del Tiglio at Gravedona. It is a small quadrilateral with three apses, one on each of the sides, except the west, where is a singularly graceful tower. Its careful construction, its proportions, its originality, are enough to class it among the gems of mediæval art.

The Cistercian church of Chiaravalle, near Milan, and its offshoot at Morimondo, near Abbiategrasso, both of the thirteenth century, exemplify the tenacity with which Italy clung to the round arch even after adopting the pointed one. The cathedral at Milan, on which so many Northern architects, French and German, coöperated, remains still unmistakably Italian and Lombard. A distant view of its forest of pinnacles is wonderfully effective, otherwise the outside appears poor and thin. Inside it is more successful. The spacing of the pillars according to the Northern system, the five aisles, the great area covered, and the height unite with the peculiar lighting to form a perspective that rivals in impressiveness the noblest of any land.

The Gothic churches of Lombardy commonly followed the Romanesque in respect to the broad façade with little of relief and the huge gable. At Pavia the Carmine, one of the best, and S. Francesco ; at Mortara, S. Lorenzo ; at Monza, the cathedral (inside mostly modernized) and S. M. in Istrada ; at Lodi Vecchio, the abbey of S. Bassano ; at Cremona, S. Luca, the transept façade of the Duomo and the superb Torrazzo ; at Bobbio, S. Columbano ; at Salò, the cathedral ; at Milan, S. Marco (the façade only),

PLATE XX

ITALY, ARCHITECTURE OF. PLATE II

Lombardy, Mantua, church of S. Andrea. This church was designed by Leon Battista Alberti, and was begun a little before his death, 1472. Its façade is undoubtedly wholly of his design, and follows a scheme which he used elsewhere of a Roman triumphal arch. The tower is Italian Gothic and about fifty years earlier than the present church. It is built entirely of brick.

— are all remarkable as good examples of the Como type.

Three great castles of the Visconti Sforza domination remain at Milan, at Pavia, and at Vigevano. The first, still in course of restoration, is a noble example of Gothic semi-palatial, semi-military architecture, with additions of the earliest Renaissance. The other two are equally interesting.

The most notable municipal buildings (Broletti) of this period are at Bergamo, Brescia, Como, and Monza. Except that at Brescia, each consists of an open ground floor, the arcades of which sustain a single story with a balcony from which the people might be addressed, and a tower. Another public building constructed on the same system is the fine Palazzo dei Giureconsulti at Cremona. In one of the most interesting corners of Milan, the Piazza dei Mercanti, is the plain Gothic Palazzo della Ragione, at present Corn Exchange, with, toward the south, the Loggia degli Osji of 1315. In the Ospedale Maggiore (at Milan) by Filarete (1457) the façade is a delightful nondescript resulting from the imposition of the Gothic style upon a Renaissance architect. The great court, dating from the seventeenth century, is by F. M. Richino, and one of the smaller courts is ascribed to Bramante.

Of the time of the Renaissance, and one of the earliest works of the new art, is the Portinari chapel by Michelozzo (1462–1466), in the church of S. Eustorgio at Milan. It is a charming work, and typical of the whole period it introduces.

In Lombardy, differing in this from Tuscan practice, an exuberance of fancy at times covered the construction with a wealth of ornament. And yet the façade of the Certosa of Pavia is not only one of the decorative masterpieces of Italy and of the world, but may be also called the best-conceived façade of the fifteenth century. There were a great number of artists engaged upon it, but the chief were Amadeo (or Omodeo), and, for the upper part, Cristoforo Lombardo.[1] Amadeo was also the architect of the Cappella Colleoni at Bergamo, a work of extreme richness, but a design inferior to that of the Certosa.

The great figure of the Renaissance in Lombardy was Bramante, who, coming to Milan about 1472, adapted himself to the materials and the plans that he found, and was responsible directly, or indirectly, for many of the most characteristic monuments of the epoch. He continued the use of terra cotta, which readily lends itself to abundance of ornament, and he preserved the Romanesque octagonal cupola with its galleries. He worked in the line of healthy development, and it is largely owing to him that the Renaissance in Lombardy was

[1] Beltrami, *La Certosa di Pavia*, 1895.

marked by a lightness, grace, and charm that were nowhere surpassed. In the common speech, the style is still called *Stile Bramantesco*. Ascribed to Bramante himself are the façade of the church at Abbiategrasso, — the only work as to the authorship of which there is no dispute, — the germ of the Nicchione of the Vatican, the nave, transept, and baptistery of S. M. presso S. Satiro, the eastern portion of S. M. delle Grazie with cloister and sacristy, the fragmentary cloister called La Canonica at S. Ambrogio, and, near by, a court of the military hospital, all at Milan, the loggia of the castle at Vigevano, and S. M. di Canepanova at Pavia. This last derives from the exquisite sacristy at S. Satiro, as do a number of churches by Bramante's pupils : S. M. Incoronata at Lodi (Battaggio and Dolcebuono), S. M. della Croce at Crema (Battaggio), S. M. di Piazza at Busto Arsizio (Lonati, perhaps from drawings by Bramante ; the most beautiful of the group), and its follower, S. Magno, at Legnano. (One may add the east end of the churches at Cannobio and Saronno and the grandiose fragment that is the cathedral of Pavia (Rocchi).)

By Bramante's pupils are two beautiful churches in Milan, S. M. presso S. Celso and S. Maurizio, both by Dolcebuono, and at Como the eastern part of the cathedral, by Rodari and C. Solari, with occasional aid from Bramante.

Two churches of Alberti, at Mantua, have been of the greatest consequence in the history of art : S. Sebastiano, now ruined ; and S. Andrea, a single aisle with chapels, transept, cupola of the eighteenth century, and choir terminated in an apse, notwithstanding all meddling, still one of the most beautiful churches in Italy. The two have served as models from the time of their construction till now, the first, moreover, being the first Renaissance church in the plan of a Greek cross. Cremona contains several very interesting buildings of the early Renaissance, such as the church of S. Sigismondo, the Palazzo Trecchi, the Palazzo Raimondi, the court of the Palazzo Stanga, the cloisters of the Umiliati, and the tiny octagon chapel of Cristo Risorto. At Brescia is the exquisite church of S. M. dei Miracoli and the famous Municipio, begun in 1508 by Formentone, but carried on by Sansovino and Palladio.

Of latest neoclassic are remarkable, at Milan, S. Vittore, the baroque façade of S. M. presso S. Celso, and the beautiful Palazzo Marino, all by Alessi ; the Palazzo dei Giureconsulti (now telegraph office), and a court of the Arcivescovado, by Pellegrini ; at Mantua, the palaces of Giulio Romana ; several palaces at Milan, Cremona, and elsewhere are typical of the florid styles that reigned from the declining Renaissance till the last quarter of the eighteenth century. The Palazzo Belgioioso (Milan, 1777) marks a return to a severer taste. The Arco della Pace, by Cagnola (1804–1838), is a striking example of the classicism of Napoleon's time.

The architecture of to-day is on a level with that of other European countries.

— JOHN SAFFORD FISKE.

**ITALY, ARCHITECTURE OF; Part IV.;
Venetia** (Venezia, called also Il Veneto); comprising the seven modern *provincie* of Belluno, Padova (Padua), Rovigo, Treviso, Udine, Venezia (Venice), Verona.

The semibarbarous tribes occupying this province before Roman rule have left no works of architecture. Under the Romans, in the third century, Verona was a great architectural centre. There are: (1) remains of a theatre; (2) a memorial double arch, or city gate, Porta de'

ITALY, PART IV. — VENETIA: CHURCH OF S. FOSCA, TORCELLO; EAST END.

Borsari, built by Gallienus about 265 A.D.; (3) a similar double gateway, Arco de' Leoni; (4) part of a stone bridge over the Adige; (5) the famous arena, or amphitheatre, built under Diocletian, next to those of Pozzuoli, Rome, and Capua the largest in Italy (diameters, 506 and 403 feet), and in fine preservation. During the Christian centuries before Charlemagne, the western part of the province followed the basilical style, as shown in the little church of S. Giovanni in Valle and S. Stefano at Verona (with apse ambulatory). The eastern seaboard was semi-Byzantine; the same style was followed as at Ravenna (see Italy, Part V.), Grado, and Parenzo (see Dalmatia and Austria-Hungary). In the middle districts we find Lombard influence. S. Maria della Valle, at Cividale, with its cross vaults and colossal Byzantine sculptures, combines both styles, as do

S. Pietro at Civate and the baptistery at Heraclea. Aside from primitive parts of S. Giacomo di Rialto, S. Zaccaria, and other churches in the city of Venice, the earliest remaining Byzantine building in the lagoon is S. Fosca at Torcello, substantially a Greek cross, with a central dome on a square base with drum supported by eight Corinthian columns, with tunnel and cross vaults. Its stilted arches, especially in the external porticoes, and its ornamental brickwork are typical of the Byzantine style that was to rule Venice until the fourteenth century. At the same time the Venetian Byzantines preserved the elongated basilical type for their larger churches, such as the cathedral of Torcello (1008), the cathedral of Murano (twelfth century), the earlier S. Mark of Venice (eleventh century), and S. Simon Grande in Venice. With the modern roof and columns a superb decoration was combined, borrowed direct from Constantinople: exquisite mosaic pavements softer in colouring and design than those of the Roman school; marble incrustations; figured mosaics; patterns in brick and marbles; ornaments in low or flat relief; and a style of carved capital so varied and masterly as to surpass anything else in mediæval Italy. A comparison between the cathedral of Torcello, with its plain strips as the only decoration, and that of Murano, with its open gallery around the apse (second story), not only shows the progress in richness during the eleventh and twelfth centuries, but the introduction of broad Lombard arches and profiles, as in the external decoration of S. Mark at Venice. The church of S. Mark is unique; although purely Byzantine in its scheme, construction, and ornament, it has no existing Byzantine prototype, and was not imitated even in Venice. Its plan of a Greek cross with immense plain piers and arches supporting five domes; its total absence of internal mouldings; its stately upper galleries with their screens; its complete scheme of religious mosaic pictures; its sculptural details,— point to its erection by artists from Constantinople. The political dependence of Venice at that time on the Eastern Empire was matched by the Byzantine character of its manners, customs, and art. In civil architecture, a style more akin to S. Fosca at Torcello than to S. Mark prevailed. The Byzantine palaces of Venice (tenth to the thirteenth centuries) first followed the Oriental plan of a structure around a court on which opened the main hall (*liagò*); but after the fire of 1112 a more Western arrangement prevailed, of placing the main hall directly on the canal or the street, preceded usually by a portico. In the monumental, but much restored, Fondaco dei Turchi (now Museo Correr) the façade is divided into two stories, each with a central portion and two wings.

On the lower story are ten open arcades in the centre, eighteen on the second story. The arches are stilted, and the archivolts plain and flat. The principal surface decoration was of circular, polygonal, or arched slabs carved in relief or incrusted, let into the wall over and between the windows. During the course of the twelfth century more relief ornament was introduced to relieve the flatness of the surfaces. The Dandolo-Farsetti (with coupled columns), Businelli, Bazizza, and Loredan palaces are early, and about contemporary with the Fondaco. A little later (about 1100) are palaces at Murano (Barbini), and the church of S. Maria Formosa and SS. Apostoli. Among the best examples of the later Byzantine type are the Priuli-Zorzi, Falier, Molin, and Andriolo palaces. During three centuries (tenth to twelfth), the school had created a simple but effective type of tower, massive, and rising to a great height, without openings until the summit is reached. Such are those of the cathedral of Murano, the cathedral of Torcello, and of S. Samuele, S. Zaccaria, and S. Mark, in Venice. In these towers the Lombard style exercised more influence than in any form of Venetian architecture.

In the rest of Venetia there is but little connection with the styles current in Venice itself during this period, both because Venice had not yet attempted to extend her sway inland, and because the close contact with Byzantium was there lacking. On the contrary, in the western section, which was alone architecturally productive, with its centre at Verona, the influence of Lombardy was paramount. Padua alone, from its nearness to Venice, mingles Byzantine and Lombard forms, as Venice does, but with predominance of the Lombard element. Thus, the early baptistery with a circular dome tower on a square plan is a Byzantine scheme carried out in Lombard style. A little later, the old cathedral, now S. Sophia, interesting for its early apse ambulatory and its

ITALY, PART IV. — VENETIA: CHURCH OF THE FRARI, (S. MARIA GLORIOSA DEI FRARI), VENICE.

vertically striped brick façade, the earliest in Italy, has still a few Byzantine traces in its brick ornament, as also have the few remaining parts of the Palazzo del Podestà. The crowning Romanesque monument in Padua is the Communal Palace (Palazzo della Ragione). This building (1209–1284), with its elaborate external galleries (1306), differs from the Lombard type in its use of shafts instead of piers. It is remarkable for its immense second story hall, the largest in Italy (about 270 feet), with its arched wooden roof. Finally, the church of S. Antonio, begun about 1237, is a combination of Byzantine plan and scheme with Lombard forms, varied by the subordinate Gothic forms then being introduced. The Oriental element of domes and minarets is the only fine part of this monumental structure, whose details are very inferior, the material being common brick.

The third centre of the province was Verona. Here the Lombard scheme was adopted, but without vaulting and with local characteristics. Proto-Romanesque churches are S. Giorgio in Valpollicella (eighth century), S. Pietro in Castello, and S. Lorenzo. The two latter are remarkable for their alternation of columns and piers, which feature connects them with Germany, as do also, perhaps, the round towers of S. Lorenzo. The reader may compare, also, S. Vitale of Ravenna. Besides these second-rate churches, Verona has the grandest Romanesque church of North Italy, S. Zenone (eleventh and twelfth centuries). It excels in the symmetry of its façade, similar, but superior, to that of Modena cathedral. Its impressive interior has, alternately, grouped piers and columns, and is spanned by heavy transverse arches like S. Prassede, at Rome. The usual perspective effect is reversed : the descent from outer doorway into nave, and from nave into open crypt, is an almost unique composition. The combination of dark brown stone and brick, both inside and outside, is remarkably successful. All details are careful and good; the sculpture should be compared with that of the cathedral. The Veronese churches have figured sculpture used soberly, but well. Their towers — from that of S. Zenone to that of the Scaligers — are impressive and well composed. Now, as later, Verona stands for constructive surface decoration, in opposition to the incrusted work of Venice. A typical cloister is that of S. Zenone, which should be compared with those of S. Stefano, at Bologna; a typical baptistery is that of the cathedral. As a whole, the Veronese school of the eleventh and twelfth centuries is one of the best characterized and most artistic in Italy.

Nowhere in Venetia did Gothic forms take root at an early date. In Venice itself the strength of Byzantine tradition resisted its introduction by the Franciscans and Dominicans until toward 1300. It first made itself felt in church architecture, especially in two typical buildings, S. Maria Gloriosa dei Frari and SS. Giovanni e Paolo, whose scheme was in part followed in S. Stefano, S. Maria dell' Orto,

style, created a type unsurpassed both in composition and detail. The transition between the two styles is illustrated in the palace of the Corte del Remer and in that at the *traghetto* SS. Apostoli. The ogee arch (see Accolade, and the cut of Verona Window, under Cusp), already used decoratively for the archivolts, became the most common form of constructive arch, after the usual pointed arch. The use of incrustations and inset panels gradually gave place to open tracery, increasing in richness in the fifteenth century. The general scheme of the palace, with its wide central sec-

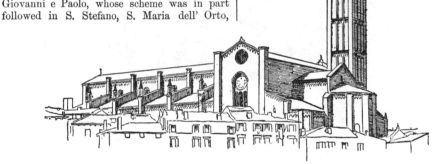

ITALY, PART IV. — VENETIA: CHURCH OF S. ANASTASIA, VERONA; 13TH CENTURY; CAMPANILE OF 15TH CENTURY.

S. Gregorio, the Carmine — all churches of the fourteenth century. In this Venetian group the façades are badly composed and poor in detail, except for an occasional good portal (*e.g.* S. Stefano and the Frari); only the rich eastern choirs, with their polygonal chapels and good window tracery, so rare in Italy, redeem the exteriors. In fact, the exteriors of the choirs of the Frari and SS. Giovanni e Paolo are the most successful of their class in Italy. The interiors of these two churches are remarkably fine, superior to those of the Florentine school; the supports are lofty, slender round columns (compare Orvieto cathedral), carrying bold, broad, pointed arches; both nave and aisles are covered with quadripartite brick vaults, and the comparative height of the side aisles gives the hall effect so agreeable to Franciscan and Dominican architects. The ornamentation is sparing, and not as good in its way as the earlier Venetian work.

It was in civil architecture that the Venetians, only slightly modifying their Byzantine

tion and two wings, remained the same, but the structures, instead of the usual two stories, had three, and, finally, often four, stories. The central "fenestrato" was gradually combined into a single mass of interlaced marble tracery of marvellous delicacy and richness, the main arches being sometimes pointed (fourteenth century), sometimes round (fifteenth century), often with trilobated cusps. In the arrangement of the various stories there were, as before, two types: one in which the ground floor was given up to storerooms and service rooms, with the piano nobile immediately over it (Palazzo Foscari); the other where the ground floor was the most highly decorated and the principal floor (Ca d' Oro). Another division is into palaces without courts, and those with wide, open courts and monumental stairways, uncovered or covered (Palazzi Bembo, Soranzo, Sanudo, Ferro). The development of window tracery at corners (Palazzo Friuli), but especially in the centre, was unique (as in Palazzo Cicogna, P. Giovanelli, P. Facanon), sometimes mingled with graceful sculptures ("Palace of the Four Evangelists"), or with capitals as beautiful as those of the Byzantine period (Palazzo Bernardo), or charming openwork balconies (Palazzo Contarini-Fasan).

The most colossal and elaborate production of this civil architecture is the Ducal Palace, erected during the fourteenth and fifteenth centuries. Its two main façades are both pure Gothic in detail; the lower part of that facing the sea and the six neighbouring arcades on the piazzetta are the earliest (1310–1360); then comes the rest of the lower arcades of the façade on the piazzetta and the whole of the second story. The rebuilding in the fifteenth century (1424) involved, probably, the whole of the present third story, which originally receded, and now forms the only blot on the palace, crushing, with its plain heaviness, the delicate strength of the two lower stories, which are among the most perfect examples of decorative and figured design in Venice. The Porta della Carta (1440–1443), in the palace, next to the church, is the best example of the latest rich Gothic work just preceding the transition to the Renaissance. The checker and tapestry surface pattern in colour, used here and on the third story, remind one of the earlier façade of S. Maria di Collemaggio, at Aquila. (See Italy, Part X.)

It was during the period of the fourteenth and early fifteenth centuries that Venice, through its new position as a land power, first exercised a predominant artistic influence throughout present Venetia and northward into present Austrian territory. This resulted, for the first time, in a certain conformity of style, less apparent in religious, perhaps, than in secular buildings. Aside from the fact that a frequent use of arcaded streets in Padua gives its palaces sometimes a certain resemblance to those of Bologna, all the principal cities of Venetia follow the palatial type of the capital with occasional Lombard modifications, including substitution of brick and terra

cotta structural facings in place of the Venetian marble veneer. Such palaces are seen at Padua, Verona, Treviso, Udine; but without the water front, for which the type was created, they lose greatly in charm. Neither have they the Venetian clear-cut delicacy.

In church architecture, Verona excels Venice in its S. Anastasia, one of the most successful Gothic churches in Italy, and having much in common with the Frari, which it preceded. At Treviso, the church of S. Niccolò (1303–1352) was a simpler replica of the Frari, but with wooden roof instead of vault, and the type was repeated there at S. Francesco (1306). There is a similar imitation at Vicenza in S. Lorenzo and S. Corona. It is curious that Verona was at the same time erecting churches like S. Fermo, which were perfectly Romanesque in their forms, but built according to the new scheme of a single wide hall nave made fashionable by the new monastic orders (Dominican and Franciscan). In Venetia, the use of this type of church led to the adoption of a peculiar form of vaulted wooden roof, — wagon roof or simple pointed roof, — because easier to manage than the stone vaulting so poorly understood in Italy. Fine examples of such roofs are at S. Zeno and S. Fermo at Verona, the Eremitani at Padua (with which the Palazzo della Ragione should be compared), S. Stefano and S. Giacomo dall' Orio at Venice. Of public civil architecture, Udine has a public palace built in the Venetian style (fourteenth to fifteenth centuries), but almost on a Lombard scheme, with lower open hall (ten columns in front and five columns on the side) and with an alternation of marble in the facing.

With the advent of the Renaissance, Venetia came under the almost exclusive influence of the Lombard school, modified, however, by local conditions, especially in Venice. Tuscany hardly affected Venetia at all. Venice contains some interesting transitional works, such as S. Zaccaria, whose choir with ambulatory (1456) is still almost pure Gothic, while the nave, a few years later, combines a Gothic triforium with Renaissance arcades, and the façade (about 1485) is in pure early Renaissance. The limitations of space and insecurity of foundations prevented now as previously the development of such grandiose types of architecture as are to be found elsewhere, and forced architects to rely upon beauty of detail and symmetry. The scheme of the palaces remained substantially the same, with added height and usually an additional story. The first steps in the new style in religious architecture were somewhat uncertain and characterless (S. Maria Formosa (1492); better than this S. Michele (1466–1482), and S. Giovanni Crisostomo (1497), but a consistent, pure and artistic style was established by the so-called Lombardi family of artists from Lugano under the leadership of Pietro Lombardo. They were, however, rather decorators than architects. This style ruled from about 1480 to about 1520. An ecclesiastical gem is the exquisite church, S. Maria dei Miracoli (1480–1489), followed by S. Fantino (1501) in purest early Renaissance. The Fraternities or "Scuole" at once employed the new architects, as in the Scuola di S. Giovanni Evangelista (1481), with its superb doorway and inner court, and that of S. Marco (1485–1495) (now forming part of a great hospital), which has one of the most significant façades for early Venetian Renaissance, whatever may be its artistic shortcomings. At the same time the palaces in the new style were more successful, inasmuch as they demanded almost nothing of the constructive and schematic faculties which were lacking in the Lombardi. The standard bearer is the Palazzo Vendramin-Calergi (1481), by Pietro Lombardo or Moro Coducci; then the Palazzi Manzoni-Angarani, Contarini, Grimani, Dario, — all on the Canal' Grande, and elsewhere the Palazzi Trevisan, Zorzi, and Malipiero. With the dearth of monumental portals, that of the Palazzo Vendramin is the more admirable; the Palazzo Contarini smacks of Bramante; the Palazzo Zorzi has exquisite capitals and mouldings; the Palazzo Minelli has a unique tower staircase. Almost immediately after 1500, columns began to replace pilasters; there were more light and shade and constructive quality and less decoration. The later Lombardi (e.g. Sante), Scarpagnino, Bartolommeo Bon, and especially Guglielmo Bergamasco, were the leaders in this transition to the middle Renaissance, when religious architecture was pushed even more into the background. Perhaps its only ecclesiastical work of moment is the hexagonal domed chapel of S. Emiliano (1530) attached to the church of S. Michele (Venice), which has been compared for its beauty to Vignola's and Bramante's *tempietti* in Rome; the façade of the Orfani (1494–1524)

is also charmingly decorative. To this style belong some important public and civil structures; the Scuola di S. Rocco (1517–1550; the façade a *chef d'œuvre* of composition and detail, and having fine halls); the Procuratie Vecchie; the Fondaco dei Tedeschi; the Palazzo dei Camerlenghi, and, most of all, the court of the Doges' Palace, where the part adjoining the Giants' Staircase (left) is the finest piece of work. In private architecture the best type is that of the Corner-Spinelli Palace.

The later neoclassic architecture begins with Sansovino's works; first, on the Canal' Grande, a transitional building from the early style, the Palazzo Corner dalla Ca' Grande (1532), with its sumptuous courtyard; then the Libreria Vecchia (1536), regarded as the most beautiful civil structure in Italy, and the building which first opened the eyes of the Venetians to the possibilities of such architecture, not as a mere decorative echo of Roman work, but as an original system founded upon it. The Doric and Ionic façade has twenty-one arcades on the piazzetta and three on each side, opening into the portico, a magnificent stairway, and a large hall. Sansovino's classic style ruled Venetian architecture even after his death, as in the work of Scamozzi (e.g. such as the Procuratie Nuove, and the completion of the Libreria). By Sansovino himself were also the Zecca, the Scala d' Oro in the Doges' Palace, S. Francesco della Vigna, and several less successful churches, and the Fabbriche Nuove di Rialto.

In 1550, however, Sammicheli produced a masterpiece in the Grimani Palace, which surpasses in grandeur anything in Venice, and which has the only monumental hall in the city. After Sansovino two men were rivals in Venice, — Scamozzi and Palladio. The former lacked originality, and Palladio's transcendent talent finally gave him undisputed sway. Palladio's greatest works of ecclesiastical architecture are in Venice, and in them he still holds to Bramante's latest type, partly as modified by San Gallo. Palladio's façades were of a more rational type than those of the early Renaissance, with better use of the gable, with only one instead of several orders, and a greater dignity of design. Heavy memberment, both inside and out, was the predominant characteristic, and with this an extreme simplicity in ornament. The standard-bearer is S. Giorgio Maggiore (1566–1610), a Latin cross ending in semicircles and with three naves; the grouping is finer than anything of an earlier time in Venice; but the Redentore (1577–1592) is considered by some critics an improvement upon the same scheme, with but a single nave and also with side chapels. The noble, if too regular, Palladian style long preserved Venice from the barocco. It is singular that Palladio should not have erected any palaces in Venice, but his inability to take advantage of limited spaces probably precluded his doing so. In the seventeenth century the leading Venetian architect, Baldassare Longhena, began by following the severe classic models before finally adopting the deliriums of barocco. His first manner appears in the dignified Palazzo Rezzonico ; his later in the grandiose Palazzo Pesaro, one of the sights of Venice. In the picturesque masses of S. Maria della Salute, with its great dome and singular plan, Longhena combines Palladian and barocco, while at the Scalzi (1649–1689), he has thrown off all classic restraints. Aside, perhaps, from Sardi, the only architect of note after this was Massari, in the eighteenth century, whose attempt at a hybrid style combining the current fashion with earlier examples was a monumental failure, as seen in the church della Pietà, in the Gesuati church called S. M. del Rosario, and in the Palazzo Grassi.

The city of Padua is of little interest for the Renaissance except for some works of a native architect, Falconetto (1458–1534) ; but the two other principal cities of the province each stand for the work of one of the most prominent architects of the Renaissance — Verona for Sammicheli (1484–1559), and Vicenza for Palladio (1508–1580). Before then Frà Giocondo (1435–1575) did some of his best work in Verona, his native city. Reference to the biographies of these artists will be sufficient. Both cities were so fortunate as to escape the

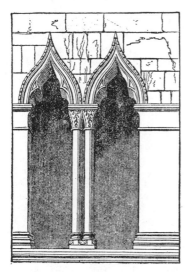

ITALY, PART IV. — VENETIA : TWO WINDOWS OF TYPICALLY VENETIAN FORM.

barocco contagion. It must be noted that, before the time of Palladio, Vicenza had some good early Renaissance works (the Episcopal Palace and several private palaces). In the

region more under the immediate influence of Venice we find its style prevalent. At Belluno this is shown by the early cathedral (1517) by Tullio Lombardo, and the Palazzo dei Rettori,

ITALY, PART IV. — VENETIA : AISLE WINDOW, S. ANASTASIA, VERONA.

from the plans of Gandi, a Venetian (1496) ; at Cividale by the cathedral, rebuilt by Pietro Lombardo (like S. Zaccaria) ; at Treviso by the cathedral, the Madonna delle Grazie, and other works of the Lombardi, whose activity extended throughout the northeastern section. Palladio himself built at Udine. In nearly the whole of the province the painting of the façades of palaces and houses, so little used in Venice, was most popular until the barocco period. — A. L. FROTHINGHAM, JR.

ITALY, ARCHITECTURE OF ; Part V. ; Emilia, comprising the eight modern *provincie* of Bologna, Ferrara, Forlì, Modena, Parma, Piacenza, Ravenna, Reggio.

Inhabited first by lake dwellers and then by Gauls, there are no pre-Roman monuments in Emilia except at the few Etruscan settlements. One of these, at Marzabotto, near Bologna, is a complete small Etruscan city, evidently built at one time, according to a regular plan, in the fifth century B.C., and showing what a purely Etruscan town was, uninfluenced by previous settlements or topographic irregularities. When the Roman conquest began, strong colonies were established and great public works undertaken. The basilica of Hercules (?) in Ravenna, the theatre in Parma, the ruins of Velleia, are of minor importance compared to the three remaining monuments at Rimini (Ariminum). These are the great five-arched bridge of travertine on the Flaminian Way, 236 feet long, erected early in the reign of Augustus; the contemporary memorial arch to mark the end of that Roman road, in severe style, and one of the earliest memorial arches in Italy; and the much later amphitheatre (diameter 393 and 298 feet) of brick with marble seats.

For early Christian and Byzantine art this district is important, containing Ravenna, Rome's rival, with an unbroken series of monuments from the fourth to the seventh centuries. These are of two classes, concentric and basilical, and form a distinct and important art school, mediating between East and West. Of *concentric* buildings there are (*a*) the octagonal baptistery of the cathedral (about 400 A.D.), one of the completest productions of early art, with original decoration of mosaics, stuccoes, marble veneer, and architectural detail; (*b*) derived from it, but with exedras projecting, the later baptistery of the Arians (about 500); (*c*) contemporary with the above, the weird mausoleum of Theodoric, a decagonal structure with a dome of a single immense slab, a derivative of the imperial Roman mausolea; finally, (*d*) the church of S. Vitale, a prime work of Byzantine domical construction (about 530), with a central dome supported on eight piers that frame niches opening on a deambulatory of octagonal plan with irregular cross vaults. Related to this group is the mausoleum of Galla Placidia, a tunnel-vaulted Latin cross with central dome, also preserving its original mosaic and carved decoration. Of *basilicas* there are three groups: the earliest, built under the Roman emperors, such as S. Francesco and S. Agata (fifth century); the group built for the Arian rite, under Gothic rule, such as S. Spirito and S. Apollinare Nuovo (about 500); and those built by the bishops under Byzantine dominion, such as S. Stefano and S. Apollinare in Classe (sixth century). They are all substantially in one style, varying strongly from the Roman. The exterior of their apses is polygonal; they never use the architrave, but always the arch, and never use the gallery over the aisles; their columns appear to have been quarried for the buildings, not taken from classic structures, and between the capitals and the fall of the arch is the Byzantine cushion, seen in Rome only seldom. These Ravenna basilicas far surpass those of Rome in the extent of their remaining mosaic decoration, and even more decidedly in examples of church furniture, such as ambones, altars, altar canopies, confessionals, and sarcophagi, all of a consistent style. Many examples still extant throughout Emilia, the Marches, part of Lombardy, and the whole upper Adriatic shore, show that the school of Ravenna ruled widely up to its fall at the time of the Lombard invasion in the seventh century. Nothing notable is extant for the ensuing three centuries.

For the Romanesque period, aside from such famous monasteries as Bobbio, Pomposa, and Nonantola, there were two main groups, northwestern and southern. The northwestern group was perhaps the most important branch of pure Lombard architecture. The cathedral of Parma (about 1100) is an advance on S. Ambrogio of Milan and S. Michele of Pavia, and, though not in Lombardy, is the most superb and complete work of Lombard architecture; its like, on a smaller scale, is the cathedral of Borgo San Donnino. The façade of the cathedral of Piacenza is the logical development toward elegance of that of Parma. Somewhat apart are the two important cathedrals of Modena and Ferrara — much alike in their scheme of exterior decoration, far richer and more highly finished than pure Lombard works, and showing possible Tuscan influence. At Modena the basilical church was planned for a wooden roof (vaulting added later), whereas all the rest were cross-vaulted, and Modena has alternate light and heavy supports. The heavy façade of Ferrara is unlike anything else in Italy, and belongs partly to the Gothic period. A very original church is S. Antonino, at Piacenza, with its open three-storied lantern tower at the intersection, its columns instead of piers, its advanced cross-vaulting, and its added unique porch with single lofty pointed arch. In nearly all these churches the crypts are monumental and well preserved, the façades show a progressive development of the porch idea, the vaults a gradual heightening, the details an increasing delicacy, and the composition a growing unity. Toward the close there is a decided Tuscan influence modifying the Lombard scheme.

The style of the southern section is far simpler, with a predominance of the square pier and an absence of detail; for example, the old cathedral of Carpi, S. Maria in Porto, at Ravenna, the church of Pomposa, and a number of other primitive Benedictine structures.

There are some fine baptisteries in the north; that of Parma is the most monumental in Italy, a polygon covered with a dome masked by a straight outer wall. Fine campanili are those at Parma (cathedral), Forlì (S. Mercuriale) and Pomposa. Of the high towers connected with civil palace fortresses, the most noted are the leaning towers of the Asinelli and Garisendi palaces at Bologna. Unique in this region is the picturesque group of ecclesiastical structures at Bologna, called S. Stefano, with its primitive cross-vaulted Lombard church of SS. Pietro e Paolo, its concentric Romanesque pointed church of S. Sepolcro, its interesting early cloisters, and smaller churches and chapels. The great fortress at Fontanellato gives the local military type.

Gothic architecture took a firm hold in Bologna and other northern parts earlier than elsewhere in Italy. The Cistercians introduced it, as usual, in such primitive structures as Chiaravalle d' Arda near Piacenza. But it gained ground in the cities as soon as the mendicant orders had adopted it in their type churches of S. Francesco (1236–1245) and S. Domenico at Bologna; these churches approach the early French cathedral type more closely than any other churches of the order, and were copied more or less exactly in later churches throughout this region and even beyond, as in S. Antonio of Padua (see Part IV.). Their most unusual feature is the choir with radiating chapels, adopted for such Cistercian churches as Clairvaux, Pontigny, and S. Martino near Viterbo. S. Giacomo Maggiore, and the Servi at Bologna, S. Francesco, and S. Maria del Carmine at Piacenza are copies of this vaulted and radiating choir type. At the same time the Franciscans used the basilical type with wooden roof elsewhere in Emilia, as at S. Francesco at Parma (1230–1250), and the cathedrals of Modena and Reggio, which have heavy square or round piers. The churches of S. Andrea and S. Tommaso at Parma should be compared in this connection. But the plan for the grandest Gothic church in Italy is that of S. Petronio at Bologna, in which Andrea Manfredi in 1390 followed the earlier type at S. Francesco on a colossal scale. Only the nave is finished. Its superb choir was never carried out.

Emilia excelled in civil Gothic. The commercial and other public palaces at Bologna, Ferrara, and especially Piacenza, are fine in composition and proportions. That of Piacenza (1281) combines pointed arcades below with triple round-arched windows above, and it is unexcelled in its rich use of brickwork and terra cotta combined with red and white marbles. It set the type for many later structures of the kind. The Loggia dei Mercanti at Bologna (c. 1400) is an example of late Gothic, coeval with S. Petronio. Bologna also contains numerous Gothic houses and palazzi (e.g. the Palazzo Pepoli) of interesting design, some of them with pointed arcades over a street gallery, and projecting second story. Throughout the Middle Ages brick was used almost entirely in all constructions, faced only very seldom with marble.

There were few native Renaissance architects. Bologna remained a Gothic stronghold until late in the fifteenth century. Similarly the early Renaissance style lasted longer here than in Lombardy, Tuscany, or Rome, because of lack of initiative. The one monument of national importance for the primitive Renaissance is S. Francesco at Rimini (1446–1455), a Gothic church remodelled by L. B. Alberti; had it been finished, with its central dome, it would have been one of the triumphs of the style. Its exterior is the most classic and symmetrical adaptation of the Roman arcade, largely inspired

by the Arch of Augustus at Rimini itself. The interior is completely sheathed with a rich decoration in relief carried out by Agostino di Duccio, one of the most notable efforts of Renaissance interior decoration — as rich as the exterior is chaste (compare the Malatesta Library at Cesena, by Matteo Nuzio, 1452–1465). The province also possesses one of the finest works of Giuliano da Majano, the cathedral of Faenza (1474–1486), a sober development of Brunelleschi's S. Lorenzo at Florence, with low domes and a combination of columns (aisles) and piers (nave). Hardly anything else of importance was built in the province until nearly 1500. Then, early in the sixteenth century, native artists begin to follow Florentine models, and centres of Renaissance are established at Bologna, Ferrara, Parma, Piacenza. The Palazzo dei Stracciardi, by Francia, at Bologna, dated 1496, marks the beginnings of this movement; it is more decorative than architectural. Ferrara was somewhat earlier under local architects, Rossetti and Tristano, whose S. Maria in Vado, S. Francesco, and S. Benedetto are partly mediæval in their interiors, but of pure Renaissance in their details, usually with domes and lines of side chapels. But Bologna soon took and held the lead, producing a superb series of palaces, beginning with the Palazzo Bevilacqua (1481), with a brick columnar court, and a façade of carefully faced stone with exquisite and rich details, arched two-light windows, and a beautiful cornice. It is one of the few palaces whose lower story is not obliterated to make way for the street arcade. In general this use of arcades gives a peculiar character to the Bologna palaces. Still, for composition, wealth, and perfection of detail, nearly always in brick and terra cotta, these street fronts cannot be excelled. Usually the courts have a second story with double the number of columns. The arch is almost invariably used in the windows. Gaspare Nadi and Andrea and Jacopo Marchese of Formigine were the foremost local architects. Both Rome and Florence influenced the school. Vignola himself executed his earliest works in Bologna before becoming Michelangelo's pupil in Rome. Some of the foremost ornamentists of the Renaissance (especially in terra cotta) were developed in this Bolognese school. A more regularly classic style appears in such buildings as the Palazzo Malvezzi-Medici, and an approach to the barocco in the works of Terribilia who became the architectural leader of Bologna about 1575. Meanwhile Ferrara was also developing a special style of palace, best exemplified by the Palazzo dei Diamanti (the present picture gallery), built by Rossetti, with its facing of facetted stone and good details and windows. The arabesque ornamentation of the Palazzo Roverella is also characteristic of the school (compare Palazzo dei Leoni) but the Scroffa-Calagnani Palace reminds one of Bologna in its remarkably fine court. Transitional to the barocco are the churches of the Jesuits (1570) and of S. Paolo (1577) by Alberto Schiatti of Ferrara. It remained for Pellegrino Tibaldi, Michelangelo's pupil, to introduce the barocco style into Emilia. The first instance in Bologna is the present University building. His son Domenico continued this style after his father's departure from Bologna (Magnani and Fioresi palaces, Episcopal Palace, Dogana Vecchia, S. Maria del Soccorso), but adapted himself with unusual facility to varying architectural problems. A few other noted Lombard or Tuscan architects worked in the province without making much local impression ; such were Palladio (at the Villa Fanzolo near Castelfranco), Peruzzi (at Capri), Sammicheli (at the Villa Soranzo, Castelfranco).

— ARTHUR L. FROTHINGHAM, JR.

ITALY, ARCHITECTURE OF ; **Part VI.** ; **The Marches** (Le Marche), comprising the four modern *provincie* of Ancona, Ascoli, Macerata, and Pesaro-Urbino.

The open character of this region, free to influences from Emilia on the north, Umbria on the west, and Apulia on the south, kept it in touch with varying styles. It also led to the disappearance of the earlier work. No Pelasgic ruins remain. During the Roman Empire it flourished more than most of Italy, as the monuments attest. Besides numerous ruined buildings on the sites of Helvia Reciva, Asculum, and Urbs Salvia, there remain : (1) the Arch of Augustus at Fano, to which the second story, so fashionable in late arches, was added by Constantine ; (2) the Arch of Trajan at Ancona, on the quay of the port, slenderest and most elegant of Roman memorial arches.

This district has little of the Early Christian, Byzantine, or Carlovingian periods. As usual the proto-Romanesque buildings are the Benedictine monasteries, such as Rambona and S. Maria di Chiente, some with columns, others with plain square piers and usually with wooden roofs (ninth to eleventh centuries). The cathedral of Ancona is one of the significant architectural landmarks of Italy, an interesting combination of the Byzantine and Romanesque. The plan, that of a Greek cross, and central dome are Oriental, but the decoration is mainly Italian, though some of it undoubtedly follows Byzantine models in niello and basket work, and some Byzantine capitals are used. This combination of styles is not unique ; but is shown in other contemporary (eleventh to twelfth century) structures such as S. Maria di Porto Novo, and at Monte Conero. On the other hand, the majority of Romanesque churches, even in Ancona, show no Byzantine traces. The rich façade of S. Maria della Piazza shows the influence of Spoleto, with Tuscan arcades (compare that of S. Pietro).

In this province also the Cistercians planted the first seeds of Gothic, at Chiaravalle near Jesi, before 1200. In Jesi itself the brick church of S. Marco, with octagonal piers supporting low pointed arches, and with two aisle bays to one nave bay, cross-vaulted, shows how the mendicant orders transformed the style. The principal cities, which show scant traces of Romanesque, — such as Pesaro, Fano, Recanati, Fermo, and especially Ascoli, — have a rich series of Gothic churches, mainly built, as usual, by the Dominican and Franciscan orders. They are mainly of the vaulted type of the North — not of the Tuscan and Umbrian wooden roof type. The most important example is S. Francesco at Ascoli (1262), in the same general class as S. Maria Novella at Florence, and S. Maria sopra Minerva at Rome, a three-aisled hall church with octagonal pillars ; but it follows the type of square masking façades (compare the Abruzzi churches, Italy, Part X.), and with a high dome over the intersection, reminiscent of Byzantium. (Compare the cathedrals of Ancona and Pisa.) Similar in every way is S. Francesco at Fermo, perhaps a copy. A similar combination of dome and cross vaults is at S. Maria, also at Ascoli. Even in the fourteenth century the Cistercian type found followers, as in S. Maria della Misericordia (about 1350), though here the plan of a Greek cross and a central dome are combined with the cross vaults. Ancona furnishes some good late Gothic in the Loggia dei Mercanti and S. Francesco, by Giorgio da Sabenico (about 1450) which show that this province was rather late in in adopting Renaissance forms.

The Marches were as eclectic during the Early Renaissance as before. By Giuliano da Majano are several works at Recanati (Palazzo Venier, S. Domenico, S. Agostino) and a considerable part of the cathedral of Loreto (1479–1486), including the side aisles and their chapels. Luciano da Laurana executed the Prefect's Palace (about 1465) and the castle at Pesaro, and the main part of the masterpiece of Early Renaissance in the province, the famous Ducal Palace at Urbino. By Francesco di Giorgia are the Communal palaces at Jesi and Ancona. Thus Florence, Venetia, and Siena sent here their architects. The earliest Renaissance church in good preservation is probably S. Bernardino dei Zoccolanti near Urbino (about 1450), a tunnel-vaulted single nave, with a dome in the centre resting on four columns. Later types of churches are illustrated by S. Maria Maggiore at Orciano, a simple concentric domed structure with cross vaults, and S. Maria delle Grazie at Sinigaglia, a single tunnel-vaulted nave with elongated choir, both of these by Baccio Pontelli (1491–1492). The strange cathedral at Loreto, though largely built at this time, is mediæval in plan, was carried on by prominent Renaissance architects, and from its importance exercised considerable influence on local Renaissance. For decorative work, as in the Santa Casa, by Bramante, it also holds, with the palace at Urbino, the highest place in the district. Bramante's work at Loreto included the fine apostolic palace. His influence was felt in other parts, as at Camerino (Madonna delle Carceri) and Matelica (S. Rocco), small examples of the chaste Middle Renaissance. To the same style — a little more advanced — belong some works by Girolamo Genga at Pesaro (S. Giovanni Battista, the Palazzo della Rovere, now the Prefecture, and the Villa Imperiale) and at Sinigaglia. Cola dell' Amatrice came from the Abruzzi and reproduced the projected (1575) façade of S. Peter's for the cathedral of Ascoli. But Lombard influence seems to have been small. The cold scientific successors of Michelangelo — such as Vignola and Palladio — did not work here. Neither did the barocco style produce any important monuments.

Briefly, this province never developed any characteristic school nor produced any salient series. — ARTHUR L. FROTHINGHAM, JR.

ITALY, ARCHITECTURE OF; Part VII.; Tuscany; comprising the eight modern *provincie* of Arezzo, Firenze (Florence), Grosseto, Livorno (Leghorn), Lucca, Massa-Carrara, Pisa, Siena.

The southwest part of Tuscany is notable for Etruscan monuments from the proto-Etruscan and Pelasgic remains of the ninth–eighth centuries B.C. at Vetulonia, Populonia, and Russellæ to the developed Etruscan of Volterra (see Etruscan Architecture). The cruder civilization of the rest of the province seems to have no early architectural history; no Greek colonies, therefore no Greek influence. Under the Roman Empire Tuscany had little monumental importance; examples of the usual kind are a finely preserved and early theatre, with a diameter of 220 feet, and baths with three main halls at Fæsulæ (Fiesole); at Lucca an amphitheatre for about eleven thousand persons, and with axes of 400 and 310 feet. This barrenness lasted until the Lombards made Lucca the seat of an important duchy. Here flourished, in the seventh and eight centuries, more than elsewhere, the association of master masons called *Magistri Commacini*. (See the account of these workmen under Guild.) But their churches were nearly all replaced by later mediæval buildings. The beginnings of communal liberties gave the impulse, in the eleventh century, first at Pisa and Lucca, then at Florence, Pistoja, and Siena. These Tuscan schools gave new life to the early Christian style of basilica, which they adopted and modified, making for it, for the first time, an artistic exterior thoroughly in harmony with the interior. The earliest phase of the Pisan school appears at

S. Pietro a Grado, a plain basilica without transept, of one kind of stone, and without any ornament or detail except pilaster strips and false arcades (about ninth and tenth centuries). There is, as yet, no individuality. Then at S. Cecilia (about 995) the influence of budding Lombard art is seen. Finally, the Pisan type, in its simpler and monochromatic manifestation, emerges at S. Frediano; at the cathedral, in its more ornate and polychromatic character; while S. Paolo a Ripa (also at Pisa) shows in its earlier parts the former, and in its later the latter, characteristics. The cathedral of Pisa is, architecturally, one of the most important buildings of mediæval Italy; it is the first of the great cathedrals, and founds a style as much as did S. Sophia at Constantinople. Its architects adopted the plan of the largest Christian basilicas, the **T** cruciform plan with five aisles, adding the great central dome from Byzantine models, the gallery over aisles also from Byzantine (or possibly Lombard) originals, and, from the same source, a system of alternate light and dark courses of marble incrustation. The free arcades in superposed galleries on the façades, and the blind galleries elsewhere, were almost an original creation, though not unknown to Byzantine art. The system thus elaborated at the Pisan cathedral during the eleventh century was perfected in symmetry and simplicity in the later baptistery and campanile, and set the pace throughout a large part of Tuscany. With time the antique features (*e.g.* in the capitals) gave way to Romanesque details. The generality of Pisan churches are, of course, much simpler. Many do not use polychromy except sparingly. Only S. Paolo a Ripa has an important dome (also interesting pointed arches in nave). The free galleries on the façade often become false galleries, and their numbers are reduced; the galleries over aisles are omitted.

Lucca followed Pisa almost exactly. There is every gradation, from the puritanic severity of S. Frediano to the gorgeousness of S. Michele and the cathedral. The length of the **T** transept in Lucchese churches is remarkable; none of them (except S. Maria in Corte Orlandini) have more than a single apse. The interiors are plainer and more monochromatic than at Pisa, but the proportions of the nave arches are very symmetrical — wider than at Pisa, perhaps from Lombard influence. The Lucchese showed their Lombard blood also in the superiority of their sculptured decoration, both figured and decorative, over that of Pisa, as at S. Giusto, S. Cristoforo, S. Giovanni, and the cathedral. There is little relief ornament in Italy as clear cut and effective. In the details also of the marble inlay of figures and patterns at S. Michele and the cathedral there is more care and effectiveness than at Pisa.

ITALY, PART VII.—TUSCANY: CATHEDRAL OF LUCCA; SOUTH TRANSEPT, LOOKING ACROSS NAVE.

While ancient structures, especially at Rome, but even outside of Italy, were plundered to supply the columns for these churches of Pisa and Lucca, some structures were erected without them, and in several instances — especially in country churches, such as Barga and Pieve di Brancoli — there were square piers in place of columns; this is the case in Lucca itself, at S. Cristoforo. The Pisan-Lucchese school extended throughout western and southern Tuscany, from the borders of the Roman States (cathedral of Grosseto) to Liguria (cathedral of Genoa), with an important centre at Volterra (cathedral) and a fine example at Massa (cathedral).

During the eleventh and twelfth centuries the Florentine school cannot compete with the Pisan-Lucchese in monumental character, owing to more backward political development; but in elegance, sense of proportion, and combined delicacy and richness, it surpasses it. It also adopted a different system of polychromatic decoration, and used it more systematically. The church of SS. Apostoli (ninth century) in Florence shows the earliest style, depending entirely on the early Christian basilica (S. Pietro a Grado), and the stage immediately preceding the adoption of polychromy is exemplified by the cathedral of Fiesole (about 1028). The marble polychromy was not in horizontal courses, as at Pisa, but in geometric and architectural figures — rectangles, polygons, lozenges, circles, arcades, rosettes. There are no decorative sculptures, as at Pisa and Lucca; no arcaded galleries. In other words, this school has none of the elements in common with Lombardy which are possessed by the other school. The connection with classic and early Christian art, however, was far closer, with the occasional addition of the Carlovingian crypt (Fiesole cathedral, S. Miniato, near Florence). Eschewing all assistance from sculptured and architectural details, it relies entirely on coloured flat surfaces, whose strong contrasts are extremely effective. The imitation of classic details in channelled pilasters, oves, dentils, Corinthian capitals, and architraves in place of arches, is so marked as to constitute a proto-Renaissance that paved the way for Brunellesco. These elements are especially prominent at S. Miniato (about 1060 –1100), the cathedral of Empoli (about 1020–1093), and the Florentine baptistery.

A middle school, partaking of the peculiarities of both Florentine and Pisan-Lucchese, centres at Pistoja and Prato, where polychromy was used both in courses and in patterns. The cathedral of Prato, with its superb heavy columns and wide stilted arches, is uniquely masculine, and reminds one slightly of Toscanella. Interesting churches at Pistoja are S. Andrea, with a well-preserved interior, and S. Giovanni, S. Bartolommeo, and the cathedral, with fine façades.

In the south there is no unity where Pisan influence did not extend. Siena has no fine Romanesque churches, as its importance commenced in the thirteenth century, though there are minor churches in its vicinity (Betleemme, Val d' Orcia, Corsano) of a plain semi-Lombard style. At Arezzo (Pieve) a clumsy attempt is made at the use of rows of external open galleries, but without polychromy.

As far as the general characteristics of the province are concerned, façades were sometimes decorated with mosaics (S. Miniato, near Florence; S. Frediano at Lucca). Porches are usually absent; neither the single porch over each portal, as in Lombardy, nor the unbroken porch across the façade, as in Rome and further south, are used. Almost the only exceptions are the porches of the cathedrals of Pistoja and Lucca, flush with façade with triple arcade — both late works of the thirteenth century. Towers are seldom used by the Florentine, constantly by the Pisan-Lucchese school. They are not usually connected with the church, but, as in Lombardy, stand on the right of the façade, and follow its style, monochromatic or polychromatic. They usually have battlements, but sometimes spires, and are neither as heavy and scantily lighted as the Lombard, nor as ethereal and widely windowed as the Roman towers. The round tower of Pisa is an exception, not only in its shape, but in its use of free encircling galleries. The baptistery was as important a unit as in Lombardy. Except for the unusual square example of S. Giovanni at Lucca, they are circular or polygonal, and always domical. They adhere closely to the decorative features of the churches, — galleries, polychromy, sculpture, — but sometimes the decoration is wholly, as at Florence, or in part, as at Pisa, a later addition. The exterior is never built up vertically, as sometimes in Lombardy (Parma), but substantially follows the shape of the dome. The Florentine baptistery exceeds in importance all others; its imitation of the Pantheon and the classic quality of its interior details are of extreme interest. The Pisan baptistery approaches it in value only in its exterior. Other good examples are at Pistoja (semi-Gothic) and Volterra. The concentric form was also sometimes used in churches of the Holy Sepulchre type, such as that of S. Sepolcro, Pisa. In general, the Tuscan Romanesque is the least structural and most pictorial and symmetrical in the peninsula. The architectural decoration in polychromy and sculpture extends harmoniously to all details of church furniture, such as choir screens (Barga, near Lucca; S. Miniato, near Florence), baptismal fonts (Pisa), pulpits (Florence, S. Lorenzo; Pisa, Campo Santo; Barga, cathedral; Pistoja, S. Giovanni and S. Bartolommeo; Volterra, cathedral), and sepulchral monuments.

Prototypes of the coursed polychromy are such Byzantine churches as S. Demetrius at Salonica (Turkey), Mistra (Greece), S. Nicodemus at Athens (Greece), Mons-tes-Koras (Constantinople); prototypes of the pattern polychromy are the sixth century interior of the cathedral of Parenzo (Istria), and the eleventh century façade of the cathedral of Amalfi — both kinds being Byzantine in origin. Compare elsewhere the

between the monastic and the cathedral and other secular churches, the former innovating, the latter maintaining many traditional forms. The religious orders introduced into Tuscany the wooden-roofed hall church of single nave, usually with vaulted transept and square apsidal chapels, derived from the Cistercians. They range from the simplest type with no chapels, such as S. Francesco, Arezzo, and with

ITALY, PART VII.— TUSCANY: NAVE OF S. M. NOVELLA, FLORENCE.

cathedrals of Altamura, in Apulia (see Italy, Part XII.), and Le Puy (in the south of France) (see France, Part VIII.).

The Tuscan cities were behind the Umbrian and Emilian in accepting Gothic forms, partly because the Tuscans did not as enthusiastically adopt monastic orders. Consequently there are almost no Cistercian prototypes or Dominican and Franciscan vaulted churches of the first generation. There is a sharp distinction

cross vaulting only in the apse as in S. Caterina, Pisa; through the type with vaulted transept and four-side chapels, as S. Francesco at Pistoja; to the type of larger church with roofed transept and more numerous side chapels, such as S. Francesco at Pisa, S. Domenico, and S. Francesco at Siena. A combination of this wooden-roofed hall type with that of the three aisles is S. Croce, in Florence, by Arnolfo del Cambio, the highest expression of Tuscan monastic architecture. This entire series had the greatest influence on the development of Renaissance interiors. It has very little that is specifically Gothic, mainly certain decorative features. It is simple and unattractive in comparison with the preceding Romanesque. The richer, vaulted, three-aisled type, has at least one Cistercian protagonist, the monastic church of S. Galgano, near Siena, a pure specimen of transitional Burgundian Gothic which strongly affected Sienese architecture, especially the cathedral. In Florence, S. Trinità (about 1250) and S. Maria Novella (about 1278) best represent the early vaulted type in three aisles, and are comparable to S. Anastasia at Verona and the earliest Gothic churches in Venice. In the Pisan and Lucchese district there was hardly any change from the old Romanesque forms throughout the Gothic period. Beside the little use of vaulting, the round arch was still used quite generally in the most important openings, when the pointed forms were confined to subordinate and decorative parts. Such are the Campo Santo at Pisa and the cathedral of Lucca, the most important works of this region — remarkable for symmetry and beauty of detail. In general the era of important structures here was now past, and the little gemlike structures of S. Maria della Spina at Pisa, and S. Maria della Rosa at Lucca, are characteristic, maintaining the old polychromy and elaborate decoration in face of the monastic severity, with such Gothic additions as gables and pinnacles. The noble round-arched style was to find its highest development in the Siena and Orvieto cathedrals. Siena is transitional from Pisan Romanesque (façade; lower part Pisan; upper part Gothic). The combination of colour and form in its pinnacled façade, similar to an enamelled shrine, was carried to its ultimate form in the later façade of Orvieto. From the slight use of vaulting these churches are in a different class from such as S. Maria Novella at Florence. The close of the Florentine development is marked by the cathedral of Florence, where the heavy grouped and very widely spaced piers resemble those of S. Petronio at Bologna. Its construction carries us to Brunellesco and the opening of the Renaissance. Yet it cannot compare either in proportions or details to such contemporary works as the cathedral of Lucca.

Porches had no place in Tuscan churches at this time, but towers of great charm were built, for the first time, by the Florentine school, in monochrome construction; usually with spires when for churches (as in S. M. Novella); and often with battlements when for civil structures (as in the Bargello). Giotto's Tower, in Florence, is as unique for its century as was the Leaning Tower of Pisa, and continued the polychromatic system. Civil architecture for the first time became prominent in the thirteenth century with communal development. The public buildings surpassed in importance even those of Lombardy. Though mostly with pointed details, they have little that is Gothic, and are sombre compared with similar Northern work. A large central court and a high bell tower are usually features of the largest. The Palazzo Vecchio, at Florence, and Palazzo Pubblico, at Siena, are the most impressive; while the Bargello, at Florence, is artistically the most perfect. Poppi, Pisa, Pistoja, San Gimignano, Montepulciano, Orvieto, Massa, and other Tuscan towns have good examples. The type varies from the Northern also in not having an open hall below. Civil constructions of other kinds, such as the Loggia dei Lanzi, the Or San Michele (now a church), and the Bigallo, at Florence, the Loggia degli Uffiziali, at Siena, the Palazzo Vescovile (Episcopal Palace) at Orvieto (see Italy, Part VIII.), gave varied scope to architectural effort. The Loggia dei Lanzi is one of the most perfect creations of round-arched Gothic. A similar style is followed in private palaces, such as Palazzo Guinigi at Pisa, P. Tolomei, P. Saraceni, P. Salimbeni, and P. Buonsignori at Siena, and a number at Florence.

The unusual prominence of secular, as compared to monastic, artists in Tuscany made it easier for the new Renaissance style, founded by Brunellesco, to obtain currency. (See Renaissance Architecture; and the articles on Brunellesco, Michelozzi, Giuliano da Maiano, Alberti, Martini, Francesco di Giorgio, and Gambarelli — all Tuscans.) For the history of the Early Renaissance is not only almost purely Tuscan (except, e.g., Luciano da Laurana), but is bound up in the personal styles of these few leaders. The lack of a fixed type at the beginning is shown in Brunellesco's work, his basilical church types of S. Lorenzo and S. Spirito not entering into the Renaissance fibre as did his exquisite Pazzi chapel (Greek cross), which gave Bramante his type, his cloister of S. Croce, so much copied by Michelozzo, and his palazzi, Pitti, Quaratesi, and Guelfo, whose heavy bossed type was splendidly developed in Michelozzo's Riccardi palace, and received its crowning form in the Strozzi palace (1489); while Alberti, in his turn, was creating a more classic palatial type, forswearing in the Palazzo Rucellai the heavy bossed work for a lighter vein with engaged pilasters, to be followed by Rossellino in the two Palazzi Piccolomini at Pienza and Siena. In all the evolution the inner court holds its place as of equal importance to the façade, as it does in Rome; while in Venice it is eliminated. Notwithstanding Alberti's superior genius, Michelozzo and his style reigned almost supreme in Florence until the close of the fifteenth century. That there was in these earliest architects no intolerance toward the Gothic style is shown, *e.g.*, by Brunellesco himself in his dome of the cathedral at Florence, by Alberti in his façade of S. Maria Novella, by Francesco di Giorgio, and in such composite buildings as the Misericordia at Arezzo. Outside of Florence the new style showed itself quickly at Prato in the Madonna delle Carceri, at Pisa in the University, at Cortona in the church of the Madonna del Calcinajo, at Pienza in the cathedral and palazzo, at

most in the use and development of figured and decorative sculpture in works of church furniture, such as screens and parapets, fonts, pulpits, holy water vessels and tabernacles for the holy oils, ciboriums, fountains, tombs, and shrines. Even when the Tuscan architects were also sculptors, they forebore on principle to marry this sculpture more closely to their architecture.

The sceptre passed from Florence with the rise of Bramante and the great Lombard movement just before 1500. Only Giuliano and

ITALY, PART VII.—TUSCANY: NAVE OF CATHEDRAL OF FLORENCE.

Pescia, at Arezzo. But the most important centre outside of Florence was Siena, where a type of palace was developed as imposing as that of Florence, for example the Palazzi Nerucci and Spannocchi, and where there are some interesting transitional churches, S. Maria degli Angeli, dei Servi, dell' Osservanza; and such classic gems as Federighi's chapel (Palazzo del Diavolo).

In church architecture the greatest variety prevailed: in plan (T cross, Latin cross, Greek cross, concentric plan), in method of covering (open rafters, flat caisson, tunnel vault, groin vault, dome), in architectural memberment (columns or piers, architrave or arches). It was not until the sixteenth century that any unity was to be evolved. Only in certain general principles was there agreement: mainly in flatness of surface, elimination of colour, reduction of ornament, and progressive purification of line. Incidental structures, like campanili and baptisteries, were suppressed. The reaction of this puritanism was to come mainly from Lombardy at the very close of the fifteenth century. But, on the other hand, the Florentines were fore-

Antonio San Gallo upheld her reputation as in S. Maria Maddalena dei Pazzi; they built also la Madonna delle Carceri at Prato (Greek cross and tunnel vaults by Giuliano); S. Biagio at Montepulciano, a development of the same type; and the cathedral of Cortona. Their works, though not yet free from a certain tentative quality, are yet far more developed in construction and composition than most earlier works. What they were doing for Tuscan church architecture, Simone Pollajuolo ("Cronaca") was doing for the palace type, giving it greater refinement and symmetry, as in the Palazzo Guadagni, in Florence, and carrying the same principles into his churches. But works of the first rank are not numerous in Tuscany in the sixteenth century. Baccio d' Agnolo shows the same delicate sense as Cronaca, but with several original features as in the Palazzo Bartolini, in Florence, and in his villas (Castellani at Bellosguardo); his style was continued by his sons and pupils. This brings us to the works of Michelangelo—especially the Medici Chapel (1520–1524), and the Laurentian Library (1523–1526)—in which he expressed the same central ideas of *bravura* and striking contrasts as in his later and more colossal Roman works. In the beginnings of the barocco style which followed, the most prominent place in Florence was held by Bartolommeo Ammanati, whose work is excellent when he is at his best, as in the cloister of S. Spirito, the Pitti court, and the Ponte S. Trinità, for he kept himself free from barocco excesses. At the same time Vasari was maintaining simplicity in his extremely well composed and dignified buildings — such as the Uffizi palace and the Abbadia at Arezzo (tunnel vaults), in which the Florentine columnar tradition was continued as against the Roman style of the pier. In the rather commonplace monuments (after c. 1575) there was still in most cases a good taste that shunned either all or part of barocco characteristics, and made of Florentine palace architecture at least an organic development of some five centuries. Even in church architecture the old traditions were at times preserved, as in S. Felicità (1736). But the Tuscan contribution to the history of Italian architecture at this time was insignificant.

— ARTHUR L. FROTHINGHAM, JR.

ITALY, ARCHITECTURE OF; Part VIII.; Umbria; occupying a position in the centre of Italy and consisting of the single *provincia* of Perugia. The earliest architecture was that of the Sabines (south) and Umbrians (centre, north), about 1000–600 B.C., before the Etruscan invasion, in the same polygonal style as in Latium and Samnium. Cities and citadels had limestone walls, architraved gateways, vaulted wells, three-stepped shrines. Spoletium (Spoleto) and Ameria preserve their circuit of walls, of the third period with worked faces. More primitive constructions are near Reate, and other Sabine sites, *e.g.*, Amiternum. The finest vaulted polygonal structure is the well hall near Frasso.

Certain Umbrian cities near the east bank of the Tiber were influenced by the neighbouring Etruscans to build in squared regular masonry; such were Tuder, Vettona, and Arna, the last substituting tufa for limestone. Etruscan in their art were Volsinii (Orvieto) and Perusia (Perugia) in Etruscan territory west of the Tiber. Their gates were arched (Porta Marzia, Arco di Augusto, at Perugia), and in their necropoli the chamber tombs were architectural, something unknown among Umbrians and Sabines. The small archaic block-built and false-arched tombs of Volsinii (sixth-fifth centuries) and the larger rock-cut, flat-roofed, or gabled tombs of Perusia (fourth-third centuries) are important. The true vault was known, witness the tomb near Perugia called "Tempio di San Manno," with central tunnel vault intersected by a lower one on each side — probably the finest pre-Roman work of its kind, the lineal

descendant of similar structures of seventh-fifth centuries in Etruria, as at Cortona. At Perugia the Volumnii tomb is the finest, in size and decoration, with seven chambers off a gabled hall — the ultimate development of the single-chambered tomb of the eighth century. The theatre at Iguvium (Gubbio), for 15,000 persons, has this interest that the *cavea* (112 m.), base of *scena*, and lateral *plateæ* are Umbro-Etruscan, while the rest seems an Augustan restoration.

The abandoned ruins of Ocriculum and Carsulæ, and the still inhabited Interamna (Terni), Hispellum (Spello), and Spoletium (Spoleto) contain groups of Roman buildings; few are in good preservation. The Corinthian hexastyle temple of Minerva (Augustus) at Asisium (Assisi) stands foremost in purity and preservation. It rose 6 metres above the forum and was approached by a double stairway passing between its travertine columns resting on pedestals. Smaller, less pure, but more picturesque was the temple on the Clitumnus (Antonines?), near Trevi, a tetrastyle in antis, slightly changed into a church. Some memorial arches and city gates are at Spoletium (Augustus) and Hispellum, both single and triple; a ruined arch at Carsulæ is attributed to Trajan; none is decorated with sculpture. Almost all Umbrian cities had both theatre and amphitheatre; remains still exist in nearly every case. The amphitheatre at Interamna (Terni), in fair preservation, seated about 10,000 persons (diameter 96.50 m.). The Flaminian Way, which intersected the district, preserves many bridges, mostly dating from Augustus. Most important is the bridge over the Nera near Narni.

This region is unusually important for early Christian architecture. The basilica of S. Pietro dei Casinensi, Perugia, is akin to the basilicas at Ravenna; its three aisles are separated by eighteen marble columns. Perugia also contains a most interesting early Christian concentric structure, S. Angelo (fifth century?), where the dome is supported on columns and encircled by an aisle. The sixteen marble and granite columns of various styles and dimensions are Roman. Fifteen windows are cut in the polygonal dome, which is supported by eight arches rising above the aisle roof.

The more florid school at Spoleto is best represented by the church of the "Crocifisso" (S. Agostino), richer than its contemporaries in Rome or Ravenna. Its heavily carved doorways and windows are unique, and the interior, on account of its dome and architraves, is effective. Twenty beautiful Doric columns, supporting rich architraves, separate the aisles, and at the end a triumphal arch, flanked by engaged Ionic columns, opens into the octagonal dome over the transept, whose pendentives end in four sculptured marble bases resting on a rich cornice. Several other churches in and near

Spoleto retain traces of the same fifth century style. As Spoleto became the capital of a Lombard duchy, we find traces there of Lombard architecture (sixth to seventh centuries). The churches of S. Giuliano and Ferentillo, both attached to monasteries near this city, are typical, in their plain basilical style, relying for decoration upon frescoes, using open wooden roofs, and barren of sculpture or mouldings. Even the Byzantine sculptured patterns used in furnishing churches elsewhere were not current in Umbria.

In its mediæval architecture Umbria did not develop a positive provincial style, but varied in different sections according to geographical affinities, often employing the styles and craftsmen of Tuscany, Lombardy, or Rome. There was no revival, as elsewhere, during the eleventh century. Such churches as S. Maria in Pensola, at Narni, — unique for its free flat arches (elsewhere used as brick discharging arches over an architrave), — S. Lorenzo and S. Andrea at Orvieto, S. Vittoria near Monteleone Sabino, the cathedral of Todi, are plain basilical structures, on a larger scale than in the preceding centuries. The cathedral of Narni appears as an exception, with its richer mosaic and sculptural decoration, proving the coöperation of Roman and Lombard artists.

Early in the twelfth century comes an infiltration of Lombards employed for important buildings, such as the cathedral of Assisi, and S. Ponziano, the old cathedral of Spoleto. The symmetrical façade at Assisi, with its rich wheel window (about 1140), is better composed than most contemporary works in Italy. The façade at Spoleto has rich fantastic sculpture inspired by the symbolic Bestiaries, well known in Lombardy ; the arrangement of the animal reliefs is more symmetrical than at Pavia, reminding us of the cathedral of Verona.

Architecture was further modified toward 1200, (1) by the influx of Cistercian monks with better constructive methods ; (2) by the overflow of the Roman decorative school. Cistercian influence came partly from the monastery of the Tre Fontane, Rome, and so far tended to grandiose, tunnel-vaulted structures, such as the churches of S. Michele and of S. Silvestro (1195) at Bevagna and S. Pastore near Rieti (1255).

The gorgeous mosaic decoration of Rome, requiring long training, was used especially in the southwest of the province. At Narni (cathedral), Orvieto (S. Andrea and cathedral) and Spoleto (cathedral) are mosaic pavements, pulpits, columns and cornices. The most striking work by these Roman or Romanized artists is the cloister at Sassovivo, near Foligno, completed in 1229 by Petrus de Maria "in the Roman style," as he himself calls it in his inscription. It is a simple reproduction of the contemporary Lateran cloister in Rome. Equally Roman is the church at Lugnano near Narni. Its columnar porch reproduces those in Rome, and its little crypt is not vaulted, but ceiled with marble slabs supported by marble beams on twelve slender columns.

The earliest town halls were built as the Gothic style was being adopted. The finest, also the latest, is at Gubbio, built in 1332 by Angelo of Orvieto, also the author of a simpler and more rustic palace at Città di Castello. Aside from its striking high-arched basement and its picturesque position, the palace at Gubbio is a simple round-arched structure, with one large hall. Of earlier date but inferior preservation are the town halls at Foligno, Narni, Spello, and Todi. The only building comparable to that at Gubbio is one at Orvieto, by a contemporary of Angelo.

Gothic forms were introduced almost simultaneously by the Cistercians and the newly founded Franciscans. The Cistercians in Umbria, less in touch with France, did not abandon the Romanesque as soon as in the Roman province, and their Gothic was more redolent of Italian provincialisms. Two Cistercian structures are especially interesting, Monte l' Abate and S. Giuliana, both near Perugia (thirteenth century). At Monte l' Abate the church is a lofty hall, of a single nave divided into three bays by bold-ribbed cross-vaults. The cloister is heavy but symmetrical, with small narrow pointed arches on marble colonnettes, remarkable in preserving intact its upper story of similar arcades. But the later S. Giuliana is frankly Tuscan in its best-preserved portion, the cloister with polygonal parti-coloured piers and wide pointed arches.

Contemporary are the earliest Franciscan churches. The Franciscans borrowed elements from the Cistercians, such as square apses and cross-vaulting. The vaulted hall church with single nave became a favourite monastic scheme in Umbria, and spread south through the Abruzzi, east through the Marches, and elsewhere. Umbria, the birthplace of the Franciscan order, set the type for Franciscan architecture. The hall type was used in S. Francesco at Assisi (1228), of three bays with bold-ribbed cross-vaults. It was better suited than the three-aisled scheme for preaching to large audiences, the main object of Franciscan and Dominican churches. Fra Filippo da Campello, who completed S. Francesco at Assisi, also built S. Francesco at Gualdo Tadino on the same plan, and S. Chiara at Assisi. The hall form was given to Franciscan churches at Terni (1265) and Trevi, which, while unvaulted, has, like Assisi, a lower church. The church at Gubbio (about 1290) is an instance of the three-aisled scheme, a Latin cross, with twelve octagonal piers. Other churches were built by the Franciscans

PLATE XXI

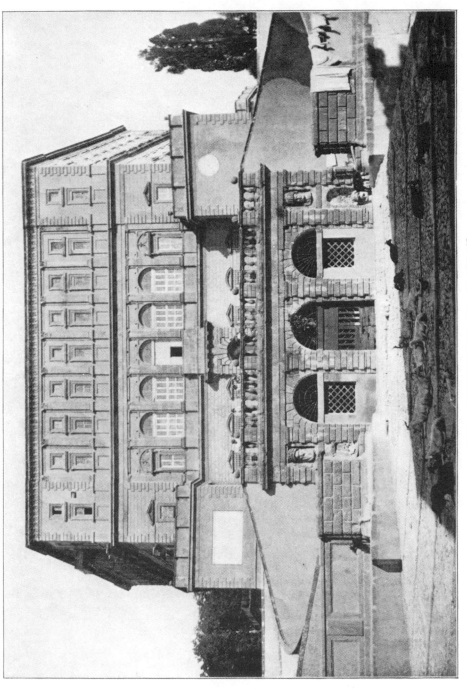

ITALY, ARCHITECTURE OF. PLATE III

Palace of Caprarola, pentagonal in plan, near Viterbo in Latium. It was built during the reign of the Pope Paul III., in the middle of the six- teenth century, and is one of the very few buildings which are known to have been designed and carried through by Vignola.

(thirteenth to fourteenth centuries) at Acquasparta, Amelia, Cascia, Città di Castello, S. Gemini, Montefalco, Monteleone, Narni, Orvieto, Piediluco, Rieti, and Todi. In comparison the Dominican order makes a poor showing.

During the fourteenth century the most grandiose Gothic churches were built. Such were S. Fortunato at Todi, S. Domenico at Perugia, and that gem, the cathedral of Orvieto. In S. Fortunato (founded 1292; completed 1465), the upper end was the work of the fourteenth, the lower of the fifteenth century. The six piers of the nave consist of eight engaged shafts, and their clear lines and slender proportions are admirable. The detail of façade and interior is exquisite, and in symmetry and approach to Northern Gothic this church is superior to most Tuscan, Bolognese, and Venetian rivals. S. Domenico at Perugia, begun in 1304, was on a similar grandiose scale, but is rebuilt, and late Gothic is represented in Perugia by the cathedral. The cathedral at Orvieto is one of Italy's best-known churches. Its brilliantly coloured and richly sculptured façade is like an enlarged enamelled reliquary, and its simple interior, with round arches on high columns, wooden roofs to nave and aisles, with vaulting only in transept and choir, is less connected with the Gothic than the basilical style, and finds its place more naturally among Tuscan than Umbrian monuments.

The Gothic period is illustrated by numerous examples of civil and private buildings. The most sumptuous of the town halls is that at Perugia, the centre of quite a group of smaller buildings of its class, like the " Udienza dei Notari " (1446), showing the prevalence of Gothic here, principally in the hands of Lombard masters, until after 1450. The two palaces at Orvieto might be attributed to the round-arched Gothic.

So priest-governed a province would not easily innovate, and the Renaissance style did not prevail until the sixteenth century, although it appeared sporadically between 1450 and 1500. Foremost is the Ducal Palace at Gubbio, built by Laurana in the same style and perfection of detail as his famous palace at Urbino. Unique is the earlier façade of S. Bernardino at Perugia (1461), with its mass of figured sculpture. The earliest prevalent style, however, was the severe and elegant style of Bramante, exemplified in the cloister of S. Francesco at Amelia and S. Maria delle Lacrime, near Trevi (1487). One of the earliest complete Renaissance churches is the sanctuary of the Virgin of Mongiovino, near Panicale, from the designs of Rocco da Vicenza, about 1510–1520. It is a Greek cross with central dome, and two of its four façades (north and south) have admirable doorways. Near Todi, the church of S.

Maria della Consolazione, 1508–1597, is also an admirably designed example of a Greek cross with central dome, each arm ending in a polygonal apse. The exterior is highly decorated, with lower rows of Corinthian pilasters and an upper line of the Ionic order, with a skilful decorative grouping of windows and niches. To complete the use of the orders, the entire interior is Doric, with a sculptural decoration including statues in niches and relief panels. Of contemporary civil structures the most remarkable are the stately Vitelli palaces at Città di Castello, and the exquisite Arroni palace at Spoleto with sculptures in the style of Sansovino. Of later neoclassic architects the following are represented: Vignola in the Palazzo Buffalini at Città di Castello, the castle at Norcia, and the Palazzo Fiorenzi at Perugia; San Gallo in the Citadel of Perugia; Galeasso Alessi in S. Caterina and other works at Perugia, the interior of the cathedral of Assisi, the Palazzo Mazoli at Città della Pieve; Bernini in the cathedrals of Spoleto and Terni. The decadence of the small Umbrian communities during the sixteenth century brought the development of architecture to a close. — A. L. Frothingham, Jr.

ITALY, ARCHITECTURE OF ; Part IX. ; Latium (**Lazio**) ; consisting of the single *provincia* of Rome (Roma). The monuments of the capital are described separately, after the rest of the *provincia*.

There are in the extreme north a few Etruscan cities (see Etruscan Architecture) some of which were previously inhabited by a Hellenic population ; such were Veii, Tarquinii, Nepete, Sutrium, Vulci, Pyrgi, nearly all architecturally interesting, while the rock-cut tombs in the necropoli of Castel d' Asso, Norchia, and Bieda are unique for façades and ground plans. Falerii is not Etruscan. Its temples are Italo-Hellenic (fourth century) with columns *in antis*. Throughout the rest of the province the " Pelasgic " remains of Cyclopean and polygonal building are thickly dotted at intervals of every few miles, and are architecturally the most extensive, well-preserved, and varied of this style in existence. Such are especially at Norba, Signia, Cora, Setia, Aletrium, Ferentinum, Circeii, Artena. (For details see Pelasgic Building.) There should be noted, also, temples at Satricum, Norba, Alatrium, dating from the ninth to the fourth centuries B.C., the bridge at Cora, gates at Norba, Aletrium, Signia, gallery at Signia, subterranean vaulted passages and vaulted and domical cisterns and repositories at almost every site. Local architectural traditions remained unbroken till the fourth century B.C. ; Roman colonies during this and subsequent centuries modified them. The terrible destruction during the civil wars of Marius and Sulla involved the wiping out of many cities. Some were reconstructed by Sulla in late republican style. Notable for the pre-Sullan age are the following: In the prehistoric age, the plan of Antemnæ, giving type of the Roma Quadrata of Romulus; of the early republican age are the so-called monument of the Horatii and Curiatii, at Albano, the magnificent emissary of the Alban Lake, and the city wall of Falerii with its towers and gates, the most magnificent speci-

thian hexastyle, prostyle, Attic bases, admirable details); Sibyl at Tibur-Tivoli (Doric tetrastyle, prostyle, of porous travertine, connected with the following); Vesta at Tivoli (Corinthian circular peristyle of eighteen columns, ten remaining, cella of tufa reënforced by travertine, columns of travertine)—both these temples of exquisite style and finish; Fortune, at Præneste (now Palestrina) (most colossal construc-

ITALY, PART IX.—LATIUM OR LAZIO: RESTORED VIEW OF TEMPLE AT CORA; ABOUT 80 B.C.

This building is unique in style, a modified Grecian Doric of singular delicacy. See profile of capital under Grecian Architecture, and doorway below.

men of military architecture of this period in Italy; in the middle republican age, the bridges and viaducts of the Via Appia, perhaps also the amphitheatre at Sutrium.

This region is unique, and more important than Rome itself for existing monuments of the Sullan age of the Republic. Among the temples are: Juno at Gabii; Hercules at Cora (Doric tetrastyle, prostyle, of porous travertine, stuccoes, with bases to the columns and bold and pure details); Castor and Pollux at Cora (Corin-

tion of Sulla's time, many parts preserved). These buildings approach more closely the pure Greek style than any imperial structures. Among contemporary civil structures are the beautifully preserved theatre at Tusculum, the earliest of the suburban villas, especially around Tusculum, in the Alban hills, and the earliest of the numerous mausoleums lining the roads from Rome, such as the so-called monument of the Scipios near Albano. Of course monuments of the imperial period abound, especially near

Rome, and mostly of the best style. Beginning at the south, Terracina (Anxur) has the temple of Rome and Augustus, with one of the finest preserved marble revetments to its cella columns used in the church; also Trajan's port; the colossal arched and vaulted substructures of the temple of Jupiter, above the city, nearly 500 feet long, one of the best-preserved and extensive Roman works of its kind; and the finest line of tombs along an ancient road, except, of course, those of Rome and Pompeii. At Piperno-Privernum there are the city gate, — for its use of piers in place of columns, and that of S. Alexander, both near the capital; while at Sutri is a rock-cut church with square piers, flat arches and vaults, parapets, and seats, all rock-hewn, unique, and probably of the time of Constantine. There are no important early Byzantine or Carlovingian monuments. The Romanesque and Gothic periods are represented by numerous important works which may be studied in the following classes: secular, religious, monastic, military, civil. In no other Italian province is there such a numerous and

ITALY, PART IX. — LATIUM : DOOR IN THE TEMPLE OF HERCULES AT CORA.

perhaps republican, — and other ruins; at Tusculum the amphitheatre; at Bovillæ the circus; at Tivoli the villa of Quintilian; other villas at Tusculum; superb groups of aqueduct arches around Tivoli; Hadrian's villa at Tivoli; the villa of Livia at Prima Porta; the ruins of Ostia; the ports of Claudius and Trajan at Porto; amphitheatres at Nepi and Bolsena; the theatre at Ferentium, near Viterbo; the port and Baths of Trajan at Civitavecchia (see Imperial Roman Architecture). Any architectural study of the Roman suburban villa is necessarily based upon the numerous superb examples in this province.

Early Christian art is represented by such suburban basilicas as that of S. Sinforosa, unique varied body of monuments. The series of military works is unique. In most of Italy the subjection of the nobles to the free communes precluded there the erection of fortified castles. But the Roman nobility preserved its preponderance. The strongholds of the Crescenzi and of the families of Vico, Orsini, Colonna, Cætani, Anguillara, Conti, and many others were not only erected in Rome itself, where nearly every trace of them has vanished, but throughout the province in every village and at every point of vantage. They are very little known. Borghetto, near Grottaferrata, is an almost perfect example of the tenth century. So also Marozza. Later come the castles of Maenza, Sermoneta (with fine *maschio*), Torre Caietani, Olevano, Soriano. Towns like Gallese and Toscanella undertook communal fortifications. Monte San Giovanni, in the panicky Neapolitan border, and Viterbo, the papal refuge in the thirteenth century, both have superb fortresses of the Gothic age. More famous is the Orsini castle at Bracciano. An interesting combination of fortress and palace is at Arsoli. For the reasons given above there are not the more peaceful types of palaces of the nobles such as were current in Tuscany, Lombardy, and Venetia. All feudal architecture was military up to the Renaissance.

Civil architecture has a multitude of examples. A large part of the existing houses in some towns are still mediæval in all parts of the province. Of the few towns that enjoyed communal liberties, unhampered by nobles, several have left communal palaces of the Gothic period. That at Anagni (twelfth to thirteenth centuries) has some beautiful early Gothic windows and an immense vaulted passage leading to the square. That at Piperno (about 1200) surpasses all others in size, symmetry, and preservation. It is in the early Cistercian Gothic; its lower floor consists entirely of an immense hall, vaulted, and opening on the square and streets through pointed arches; its three upper stories have rows of mullioned, pointed windows. Other communal palaces are at Montefiascone, Toscanella, Viterbo, Corneto. Of great interest is the episcopal palace at Viterbo, bold, and heavily buttressed toward the declivity and with an exquisite Gothic loggia (1267) on the square.

Of the civil architecture of the middle classes, the houses at Cività Castellana (twelfth to fourteenth centuries) are fair examples. Viterbo has the most artistic houses in the northern, Alatri and Ferentino in the southern, part of the province. At Viterbo, the house next to the cathedral tower, the Casa Poscia with its famous balcony, the thoroughly mediæval quarter of S. Pellegrino, with its palaces of the Alessandri and the Gatti, form an unsurpassed group in round-arched style, although dating from the thirteenth century. At Alatri, the Jacovacci (now Communal Palace), Lepori, and Gottofredo palaces are very extensive early Gothic structures in a style abounding throughout this and the neighbouring towns, introduced by the Cistercians. More than one town lies abandoned and untouched since the Middle Ages; such is Ninfa, below Norma. Monastic architecture was also prolific. Of the early Benedictine there is a little left at Farfa, Soracte, Mentorella, Monte Amiata, generally only secondary monuments, such as S. Andrea at Ponzano. The one exception is Subiaco, founded by S. Benedict, the buildings of whose two monasteries — S. Benedetto and S. Scolastica — date from the eleventh, twelfth, and

thirteenth centuries. Especially interesting are the colossal, pointed arched substructures of S. Benedetto (eleventh century; the porch of Eastern origin), the older cloister of S. Scolastica with its pointed arcades of the eleventh century (Eastern), the beautiful later cloister by the Cosmati, and the maze of vaulted churches and chapels in several stories at S. Benedetto, covered with precious frescoes of the twelfth to fourteenth centuries. The Greek basilicas are represented by Grottaferrata with its Byzantine monuments (tenth to eleventh centuries). Then, in the middle of the twelfth century, come the Cistercians. First with large tunnel vaulted churches, as at S. Maria di Falleri (about 1140), then with groined, vaulted structures, as at Valvisciolo (near Sermoneta), with its plain pointed church, its round-arched, delicate, colonnetted cloister and chapter house (about 1170), and Ceccano; then with a combination of wooden roof, groined and ribbed cross vaults and tunnel vaults, as in the most wonderful of Cistercian monasteries, Fossanova, built by the French monks themselves, in almost pure Burgundian style (church, cloister, chapter house, refectory, dormitories, hospital, chapels, storehouses). Following Fossanova, which represents the passing into primitive Gothic, come Casamari (1203–1217), with almost as varied a group of buildings, but less purely French, S. Martino al Cimino, and others. (See Cistercian Architecture, under Monastic Architecture.) The Dominican order has left but few important structures; the Franciscans a somewhat larger number. S. Francesco at Viterbo (1236) is a boldly built church with ribbed cross vaults, the largest of the order in the province. S. Francesco at Vetralla, at Corneto, at Alatri, are all of secondary interest.

Aside from this monastic architecture with imported features, the province had a variety of styles. Some very early works there are of proto-Romanesque, or rather, ante-revival. Such are S. Elia, near Nepi, a simple basilica of tufa with columns, eleventh century, and less important examples at Leprignano, Fiano, Ponzano, Acquapendente. About 1100 a monumental revival takes place, showing itself in different styles during the twelfth century. At Corneto, S. Maria di Castello is unique for its superb, large, cross-vaulted interior with piers. At Toscanella the churches of S. Maria and S. Pietro, with their low columns supporting wide round arches, their wooden roofs, and special style of decoration, also stand apart from any other Italian Romanesque churches. In the same town are S. Maria della Rosa and S. Silvestro, secondary constructions in the same style. Viterbo, the third important centre in this northern group, has a number of very important Romanesque churches of the twelfth and thirteenth centuries — the cathedral, S. Giovanni in Zoccoli, S. Maria Nuova, S. Sisto, S. Andrea, a group difficult to surpass. They are all basilical, columnar, with wooden roofs; S. Sisto has a choir with heavy piers and tunnel vaults, evidently later (end of the twelfth century). The cathedral is the masterpiece, with very fine columns and a monumental tower. The type of interior is of high columns and narrow arcades. At Montefiascone, near Viterbo, is the very original, irregular church of S. Flaviano, a double church with heavy grouped piers and ribbed cross vaults in the lower church, opening by the large central well to the less interesting upper church, in its way as unique as Corneto and Toscanella churches. Hitherto, no works of the official Roman lay school of architects has been met, though traces of their work in details, such as portals and windows, are found throughout this northern group. But this lay school of the Cosmati and their colleagues ruled nearly everywhere else, even in some of the monasteries. Its remaining masterpieces are the cathedrals of Città Castellana and Terracina (1150–1200), with their grandiose architraved porches interrupted in the centre by a single archway. More primitive are the cathedrals of Ferentino and Anagni (about 1100), the latter a structure with piers and cross vaults. Apparently, the Roman artists collaborated at times with Lombard or other constructors, themselves executing most of the decorative details. Subordinate structures are the cathedrals of Nepi, Sutri, Velletri, and in the churches mentioned above and elsewhere there are always extensive crypts (eleventh to twelfth centuries) which have been preserved even when the churches have suffered. Closest of all to the basilical style of Rome are the small churches of the towns in the Alban hills. Interesting Romanesque arched porches are at the cathedral of Piperno, the cathedral of Nepi, and S. Erasmo at Veroli. Good campanili are at Frascati, the cathedral of Velletri, Subiaco, Città Castellana, Tivoli — all of the Roman type. This is varied by elaborate surface decoration in the superb example at Terracina.

The most beautiful Gothic and pointed monuments have been described above; a number of beautiful cloisters remain, especially a group at Viterbo (S. Maria ai Gradi, S. Maria della Verità, S. Maria del Paradiso), all of the thirteenth century and closely following French models; those also at Fossanova and Subiaco. Of Gothic churches modelled on the monastic some few are important, especially in the southern group. Such are the cathedrals of Sezze and Sermoneta, S. Lorenzo Amaseno, S. Maria Maggiore at Alatri and at Ferentino.

Not the least interesting of the smaller mediæval products are the monumental fountains in the centre of squares. The finest of these are in Viterbo. Two interesting works illustrate the last days of Gothic: the monumental and very artistic Vitelleschi palace in Corneto, begun in 1436, the finest building of its class in the province, with a rich courtyard; the famous little octagonal chapel of Vicovaro, built about 1450 by Domenico da Capodistria, a mixture of Gothic and Renaissance.

The advent of the Renaissance coincided in the provinces with its predominance in Rome — last quarter of the fifteenth century. It showed itself less in churches than in palaces. The style of Bramante and of the Cancelleria is shown in many small palaces in the Alban towns and especially Tivoli and Marino. . A fine example is the Colonna palace at Genazzano with its court of two stories of colonnades. An interesting adaptation of Brunellesco's type of S. Lorenzo is seen in S. Maria della Quercia at Viterbo (1470–1480). Early Renaissance palaces are the Chigi at Viterbo, like the Florentine rustic type, and parts of the Vitelleschi palace at Corneto. To this time also belongs S. Christina at Bolsena. Bramante's pupil Sammicheli built (1519) the cathedral of Montefiascone, with fine octagonal dome. A fine work by San Gallo is the Colonna palace at Gallese — half fortress, half palace, with Doric portico. At Civitavecchia the colossal and masterly fortress is in various parts by Bramante, Michelangelo, and San Gallo. Guiliano da San Gallo built for Julius II. (1483–86) the castle at Ostia, of considerable importance in military engineering. Antonio da San Gallo built in 1494 the castle of Città Castellana, pentagonal with three lines of defence and an octagonal keep; also the fortresses of Montefiascone and of Nepi (1499), the latter an imposing work. To this time — by whom is uncertain — belong the superbly arranged fortifications and dependencies of the great monastery of Grottaferrata.

But the Renaissance architect with really important works in the province is Vignola, who can be best studied here. Churches by him are at Bolsena (Isola Bisentina?) and S. Oreste (S. Lorenzo); palaces at Soriano (Albani), Bomarzo (Orsini), Nepi (municipal palace), Bassano (Giustiniani palace and villa). The fine Farnese castle (octagonal) at Capodimonte is ascribed to him. But the masterpiece of his career is the famous Farnese fortress palace at Caprarola, of octagonal plan (1559) and circular interior with vast subterranean portico and five stories, ingeniously arranged and beautifully decorated. The grounds and casino ("Il Palazzuolo") were also designed by him. The Villa Lante, at Bagnaia near Viterbo, should be compared with this. The neighbourhood of Viterbo has other works by him, including monumental fountains (Viterbo, Ronciglione).

After a few works by Pirro Ligorio (Tivoli, Villa d'Este) and Giacomo della Porta (Arsoli, S. Salvatore); Frascati, Villa Aldobrandino, a superb scheme, — we reach the barocco style. By Bernini are the Pallavicini palace, church and villa of S. Pastore, and the church at Ariccia. By his pupil Mattia de' Rossi are the cathedral and Pamphili palace at Valmontone. By Carlo Maderna the papal palace at Castel Gandolfo. Finally may be mentioned the dignified church SS. Trinità at Viterbo (1727).

The architectural history of the city of Rome during the twenty-six centuries since its foundation is represented, though unequally, by existing monuments in all its phases.

Rome ; Kingly Period. The age of Romulus and of *Roma quadrata* has left some fragments of soft tufa walls and some wells and cisterns on the Palatine, sufficient to show that the primitive Romans followed the Etruscan use of a quadrangular plan for the city, and of squared blocks of tufa (2 feet wide and thick), in regular courses, for its walls; while, on the other hand, they adopted the Latin method in the construction of vaulted underground chambers and passages. The "Tullianum," or lower part of the Mamertine prison, originally a spring chamber with a conical false vault formed of projecting courses, is next in date. The softer tufa was used at first. A second type comes with the Tarquins and Servius Tullius, for whose constructions the harder tufa and the true arch, tunnel vault, and dome are adopted. The colossal drains, some of whose passages measure 10×14 feet, are constructed in both fashions, of false vault and true barrel vault. The true vault is used in the upper Mamertine chamber and in the cistern at the *Scalæ Caci.* The Cloaca Maxima is the most noted of the sewers. The most important and extensive work is the wall of Servius Tullius around the seven hills, with its monumental *agger.* What its gateways were like we may judge from the arch of the so-called " Porta Fontinalis," from the small arches still remaining in the wall on the Aventine, near the Baths of Caracalla and the railway station, but best of all from the double round-arched city gates of Ferentinum in Latium, which are contemporary. Of the temples, only some of the platforms and a simple cella on the Palatine remain at the *Scalæ Caci.*

Rome ; Republic. The splendid constructive age of the Tarquins was followed by a retrogression during the first century and a half of the republic. Even the rebuilding after the burning by the Gauls (390 B.C.) was not seized as a monumental opportunity. But later, in the fourth century, the Greeks began to drive Etruscan architecture out of Rome. Campania, the extreme southern colonies, Sicily,

Asia Minor, Greece proper, were the successive agents. Of the ensuing transformation of Rome by basilicas, porticoes, arches, and temples little remains, as almost everything was superseded by imperial structures. The following are the best remaining works: First, the aqueducts, as representing purely Latin-Roman utilitarian architecture ; of the Appian (313 B.C.) and the Anian (272 B.C.) there is little above ground ; but of the Marcian (144 B.C.) a fine section of peperino arches is preserved. The Fabrician bridge (62 B.C.) is built of peperino and tufa, faced with blocks of the harder travertine, which was coming into use for the protection of surfaces. Second, a few temples illustrating the pure Greek style then introduced before it was contaminated by Roman peculiarities. Of the group of three connected temples near the theatre of Marcellus, that in the centre is an Ionic hexastyle peripteral (except at the back) ; that on one side is the same, and is perfectly peripteral ; while the third, and smallest, is of similar form, but its order is Tuscan Doric. These three temples — called by Lanciani temples of Piety, Hope, and Juno — formed one side of the Forum Olitorium, opposite the Porticus Minucia, built in 110 B.C., remains of whose Doric travertine columns still exist. All three are built of travertine and peperino, except the central temple, which is entirely of large travertine blocks. Some of the columns of each are still standing. The architectural details and proportions of the Ionic temples of the late Republic are best shown by the temple of Fortune in the neighbouring Forum Boarium (built in 214 B.C.). It is tetrastyle prostyle with a pseudo-peripteral cella, having five engaged and two free-standing columns on each side. It stands on a high podium (8 feet) of travertine, and is reached by a staircase along the whole front. The cella is of tufa, but the engaged columns at the corners and the six free-standing columns of the portico are of the harder travertine. The whole surface was originally covered with a hard stucco (*opus albarium*) with painted decoration, which concealed these differences of material. The decoration of the frieze was modelled upon it in the same hard marble dust cement or stucco (garlands, candelabra, ox skulls) ; on the cymatium of the cornice the foliage is interrupted by lions' heads. This scheme of a high podium and a pseudo-peripteral cella is more Italian than Greek, but the architect was probably a Greek working under Roman ritual traditions. There are two further ruins of republican temples on the Palatine : (1) Temple of Cybele (192 B.C.), with numerous beautiful fragments of stuccoed travertine and complete foundation walls ; (2) temple of Jupiter Propugnator (?), 44 metres long and 25 metres wide, probably a peripteral octastyle with stuccoed tufa columns.

Finally, of the civil constructions that exemplify the combination of the pure Roman constructive forms (aqueducts, bridges, gates) with the pure Greek forms (temples) the only well-preserved example is the so-called Tabularium, which occupies the front of the saddle of the Capitoline, on the side of the Forum. It is one of the finest remaining monuments of any age in Rome, and the only one that belongs to the civil administration of the Republic. It is a superb example of *opus quadratum* of peperino blocks $2 \times 2 \times 4$ feet, in alternate courses of headers and stretchers. The façade on the forum still has an open arcade framed by engaged Tuscan columns with shafts of peperino and capitals and architrave of travertine. This was originally surmounted by a second story of the Corinthian order, of which many fragments remain below. Here, then, we have the earliest preserved example of the framing of the Roman arch by the architrave supported on engaged columns, which became the permanent and universal Roman order in civil structures, and passed from it to the Renaissance. The combination may have been used earlier, in some of the basilicas and porticoes of the forums, but these have been completely destroyed. The Tabularium was the repository of the archives of the Roman state. Its interior is still in remarkable preservation, with walls of tufa or concrete, framing two stories of vaulted halls, corridors, and arcades, and a perfect system of staircases. Vaulted porticoes connected it with the Forum, and allowed convenient passage from one Capitoline peak to the other.

To summarize, the changes in Roman architecture under the Republic include the increasing use of the harder peperino and travertine beside, or in place of, tufa ; the introduction, at the close, of artificial marble surfaces ; the greater use of concrete ; the supersession of Etruscan by Greek art in the temples ; and the combination of Greek forms for decorative uses with old Latin constructive forms in civil architecture.

Empire. (For a systematic treatment see under Roman Imperial Architecture ; for special classes of buildings, see that article, and also special articles under the headings Amphitheatre ; Coliseum ; Thermæ, etc.) Here the principal existing monuments will merely be enumerated chronologically. Augustus and his friends attempted to reconstruct Rome systematically with a view to making it a beautiful city. What he accomplished is indicated in his testament. He favoured the use of marbles instead of stuccoed surfaces, and patronized Greek artists and a chaste ultra-refined style. There remain parts of the Basilica Julia (33–29 B.C.), of the temples of Jupiter and Juno surrounded by the Porticus Octaviæ (32 B.C.), of the imperial Mausoleum (27 B.C.), of the theatre, Marcellus (13 B.C.), the Altar of Peace (9 B.C.), the

temple of Castor and Pollux (7 B.C.), the Forum of Augustus, with the temple of Mars Ultor (2 B.C.), the temple of Concord in the Forum (10 A.D.), parts of several aqueducts (Porta S. Lorenzo, Aqua Julia, Aqua Virgo), and perhaps a few undated monuments, such as the familiar circular temple in the Forum Boarium. Nothing remains of his beautiful buildings on the Palatine, but near their site is the contemporary so-called " House of Livia," unique in Rome as giving the arrangement and decoration of a rich private house of the early Empire.

The Augustan style is distinguished by restraint as to size, delicacy, and low relief of ornament and perfect execution. In elaboration of plan and in constructive mastery, as well as in the combination of sculpture with architecture, it was to be surpassed in the ensuing century. Even in so extensive a building as the theatre of Marcellus, the entire travertine surface was covered with hard white stucco, and the details are far more delicate than the corresponding later work in the Coliseum. The details of the Corinthian temple of Mars Ultor and of the temple of Concord are among the most beautiful in Roman art ; but the most perfect remaining gem of this reign is the commanding temple of Castor, three of whose Corinthian columns are still standing with their rich entablature of Pentelic marble. This temple is a peripteral octastyle, with eleven columns on the sides. It stands on a superb podium, twenty-two feet high, lined with Pentelic marble. Its rich cornice is supported below each column by wide pilasters with single base and cornice artistically contrasting with the richness of the superstructure.

After the death of Augustus there was a temporary lull extending almost to the extinction of the Julian line with the death of Nero. At the same time, a transformation of ideals was taking place, with a tendency toward the colossal and the rich in plan and decoration. Sculptural decorations, for example, passed from the use of a single plane of figures, in a relief, to a double and finally a triple plane. The reigns of Tiberius and Caligula were distinguished by imperial palaces on the Palatine, and the climax of magnificence was reached in the Golden House of Nero, which absorbed so large a part of the area of Rome and some of whose chambers are still extant under the baths of Trajan and Titus, which were built over part of them. In better preservation are the extensive substructures of the temple of Claudius. On their west side there remain two rows of arches of the heavy bossed rustic work favoured at this time. Little remains of Nero's colossal scheme for rebuilding Rome after his conflagration. Building on a large scale began again under the Flavian emperors, under Vespasian to repair the enormous damages of Nero's fire, and under

Domitian after the fire of Titus. Vespasian's Forum and temple of Peace has few traces left ; there is but little left visible of the baths of Titus, but the Coliseum partly compensates for their loss (see Amphitheatre ; Coliseum ; Roman Imperial Architecture). Domitian's far greater activity has left traces in the temple of Vespasian, the Forum Transitorium, and the Flavian palace on the Palatine. Comparing the best of this work with that of the Augustan age, the details are still well done, but in higher relief and more massive, as well as less purely Greek. Greco-Roman art is being consolidated, with losses and gains. The temple of Vespasian is a Corinthian hexastyle prostyle, with squarish cella (as is the case in most Roman temples). Its interior was decorated, like that of the Augustan temple of Concord, with rows of columns set on a projecting dado along the walls. These walls are of travertine, lined outside with Pentelic marble and inside with Oriental marbles. The entablature is overloaded with ornament, some of which is so minute or so hidden as to be ineffective when in position. The same heavy richness is shown in the remains of the Forum Transitorium, with its temple of Minerva, finished by Nerva. Certainly Greek artists were still responsible for most of the work, but they were swayed by less refined canons of taste. The arch erected to Titus by Domitian is the earliest arch extant in Italy with sculptural decoration. The palace of Domitian remained always the section of the imperial residence, with state apartments comprising throne room, chapel, and basilica, all most exquisitely decorated.

An even higher artistic level was reached in the succeeding reigns of Trajan and Hadrian, whose building activity fully equalled that of Augustus, and under whom Roman architecture reached its highest perfection, not only in construction and arrangement, but in effective decoration. Under Trajan it was bolder ; under Hadrian, more polished, but less instinct with life. The Forum of Trajan and his baths, the Pantheon, temple of Venus and Rome, temple of Neptune, and mausoleum of Hadrian, are the principal remaining monuments. Trajan's Forum was considered the most wonderful group of buildings in Rome, in its size, grouping, and wealth of decoration. It was the work of the Greek Apollodorus, Trajan's master architect and engineer. The temple of Venus and Rome was enclosed in a temenos decorated on all four sides by a columnar portico, and was Hadrian's masterpiece. The "Neptunium," or admiralty building of Rome, rebuilt by Hadrian, consisted of an open square bounded by a colonnade with halls (Portico of the Argonauts), with a colossal temple of Neptune in the centre. The grouping corresponded to that of the imperial fora. Eleven of the im-

mense Corinthian columns of the north side of the temple still stand in the Piazza di Pietra, with their portion of the cella wall and the spring of the heavy coffered barrel vault that covered it. The sixteen columns of the peristyle corresponded in number to the provinces of the empire, and to make the admiralty national, the temple's rich substructure was decorated under each column with a statue representing each province and a trophy or panoply ; several of these remain, with sections of the superb cornice. The use of the barrel vault instead of the ceiling over the cella is interesting and characteristic of the second period of imperial architecture. During the latter part of his reign Hadrian appears to have departed from Trajan's purer ideals, and to have indulged in love for the colossal. Both emperors, however, were leaders in a pure Hellenic revival that characterized all phases of culture, and much that was considered Augustan is now referred to them.

The subsequent decadence was almost immediate. Antoninus Pius and Marcus Aurelius continued, it is true, their predecessors' traditions, but while the architectural scheme remained similar, the execution and taste were inferior. This is shown in the temple of Faustina and in the arch, column, and temple of Marcus Aurelius. The temple of Faustina is a Corinthian hexastyle prostyle in an unusual state of preservation. Its columns are of the fashionable Cipollino, and its frieze of white marble has a beautifully executed decoration of griffins, candelabra, vases, and floral patterns. Another terrible fire under Commodus, in 191, devastated the forum and led to another burst of architectural activity under Septimius Severus and Caracalla (193–217), who undertook the rebuilding of entire quarters under the guidance of a special plan of the city engraved on marble slabs. Although so productive, the style of this period is in full decadence. The lamentable change can be seen by comparing the arch of Septimius Severus with that of Titus or of Constantine-Trajan (see below). The Stadium of the Palatine, the Palatine Aqueduct, the palace with its gigantic substructures and the Septizonium, the Arch of the Goldsmiths, the temple and atrium of Vesta, the Templum Sacræ Urbis, the Baths of Caracalla, the Amphitheatrum Castrense, a police station, the restoration of several aqueducts, — of all these structures something remains. Most of these are at present, however, mere masses of masonry. The Baths of Caracalla are an exception. They are among the best preserved and most important Roman ruins ; their influence on Renaissance art was extraordinary ; and even now, when shorn of their decoration, they are vital for a study of Roman constructive methods and an appreciation of the wonderful ability shown in elaborate grouping and composition. Three immense halls in these baths are famous — the frigidarium with its flat ceiling, the tepidarium (170 × 82 feet) covered with the three most colossal groined cross vaults constructed by Roman art, and the laconicum or calidarium originally with a dome (?) 116 feet in diameter. Certain parts are of subsequent date. Considering the colossal scale, the size of the details, the richness and profusion of the marble revetments, this structure is to Roman art what S. Peter's is to Renaissance art, and like it, with a large element of barocco.

Except for the temporary flush under Aurelian (temple of the Sun) whose reign was dignified by the building of the magnificent city walls, architectural nullity corresponded to political ineptitude until the time of Diocletian (see Arch of Gallienus). This reorganizer of the Empire has left us one important work, the Baths (306 A.D.), whose tepidarium was transformed by Michelangelo into the church of S. Maria degli Angeli. They were on an even more colossal scale than those of Caracalla, but show a great decadence in taste if not in constructive ability. The triple cross vaults of the tepidarium are substantially the same in both. A similar system of vaulting with the addition of six immense abutting barrel vaults was used, soon after, in the basilica begun by Maxentius and finished by Constantine. This use of vaults in a basilica had not before been at all common, and had never been used on such a scale.

Compared with the hall in the Baths of Caracalla the proportions are clumsy. This building is, however, significant of the fact that until the very day of the triumph of Christianity vaulted constructions on a large scale were understood. Constantine's triumphal arch shows one thing by the symmetrical incorporation of older material; that even if sculpture and decoration were then in a pitiable state of collapse, the superiority of the art of Trajan was appreciated. What the undiluted style of this time was is probably shown by the so-called arch of Janus. During the course of the fourth century, the temple of Saturn and the Porticus Deorum Consentium were rebuilt in the style they now show. Here classic Roman art ends, and also all use of vaulting except for small domes, for about a thousand years.

Rome; Early Christian. The early Christian catacombs (second to fourth centuries) are of no architectural import, except for an occasional crypt or chapel (Papal Crypt, S. Callisto), but above their entrances chapels (SS. Sisto e Cecilia, S. Sotere) and even churches (S. Generosa, S. Petronilla) were built during the third and fourth centuries. Shortly after the triumph of Christianity (312) under Constantine this emperor transferred the capital to Constantinople. This

hastened Rome's architectural downfall. There being already a superabundance of civil structures only new buildings for the new cult were required. These took the form of basilicas and sometimes of concentric structures. (See Baptistery; Basilica; Latin Architecture; Round Church.)

Rome is unique in having no break between the early Christian and mediæval periods. Its ecclesiastical architecture remained substantially unaltered for a thousand years; only methods of decoration changed. The customary type of basilical church in Rome was a construction of thin brick walls, unfaced and plain on the exterior; on the street a portico leading into a square or oblong colonnade court on which the church opened. Its façade followed the outline of the nave and two aisles into which its exterior was divided, ending in a single apse and covered by a wooden roof. There were no galleries above the aisles and no transept. Outside there was no system of architectural details, such as cornices, arcades, free or engaged columns or pilasters; inside there were no mouldings. The internal decoration was entirely of colour; marble incrustations below and mosaics or wall paintings above. After the sixth century, on account of liturgical changes, the atrium tended to disappear and the churches to be placed on the streets. Of course, there were exceptions to this scheme. A few churches have, like the Byzantine churches, galleries over the aisles; such are S. Lorenzo, S. Agnese, S. Cecilia, SS. Quattro Coronati; but they were built when Rome was subject to Byzantine influence between 550 and 850, and were used either for the female part of the congregation or for nuns. The few existing hall churches, as S. Pudentiana, S. Balbina, are evidently unwilling deviations caused by the use of an ancient structure not easily convertible into nave and aisles. There were also a very few cases where five aisles were used; this was only in the earliest and largest basilicas, such as S. Peter (now replaced by the great church S. Pietro in Vaticano), and S. Paul without the walls. The same may be said of the use of the transept, with little or no projection in plan, though its use is a little more general; as in S. Peter, S. Paul, S. Croce, S. Maria Maggiore, S. John Lateran; there is even one example of its later use, with some projection, at S. Prassede (817–824); and, of course, it is more frequent in the latter Middle Ages, *e.g.* at S. Crisogono, S. Bartolommeo all' Isola (eleventh century), and SS. Vincenzo ed Anastasio, twelfth century. Then, as a deviation from the single apse at the beginning of the Middle Ages, the custom was introduced of flanking the central apse with two side apses opposite the side aisles (earliest example, S. Maria in Cosmedin, ninth century), as at S. Clemente (twelfth century) In the matter of the supports of the basilical interiors, there were no exceptions to the use of columns. These columns were of different orders and origins. Tuscan-Doric was seldom used; only one example remains, S. Pietro in Vincoli; fifth century. Ionic was quite common, especially with the architrave, as at S. Maria Maggiore. Corinthian and composite (S. Paul, S. Sabina, etc.) were the most used. This was natural, because the orders enjoyed this relative popularity under the Roman Empire, and a large part of the columns used in the Christian churches were taken from imperial buildings. In regard to the forms above the columns, Rome employed both the architrave and the round arch. Except for a very few examples, such as the church of the Nativity at Bethlehem (Syria), the Roman basilicas are the only churches where the antique architrave was continued. At first it predominated, being used at S. Peter's (fourth century), S. Maria Maggiore (fifth century), S. Lorenzo (sixth century), and S. Martino ai Monti (sixth century). But the use of arcades, introduced probably from Ravenna, where they were universal, after a while drove out the architrave. S. Paul's basilica begins it in the fifth century, and is followed by a host of others, so that in the ninth century S. Prassede is the only representative of the architrave. It is true, Roman mediæval artists revived it, as they revived much that was primitive, and used it at S. Maria in Trastevere (twelfth century), S. Lorenzo (thirteenth century), and other churches and a host of porches. One explanation of the increasing favour of the arch in Rome is that it allowed a greater intercolumniation, which became necessary with the growing difficulty of securing a large number of columns of one size and style, preferably from a single antique structure, for the new churches. Finally, in a few churches the internal colonnade is interrupted at intervals by piers, which divide the church into sections, for ritualistic reasons. At S. Maria in Cosmedin, every group of three columns is thus isolated by piers dividing the church into three sections : the upper (apse) for the upper clergy — bishop and presbytery — with the altar in the centre ; the middle (choir) for the minor clergy — readers and singers — with the pulpits and choir screen ; and the lower for the congregation — originally for the catechumens only, while the baptized members occupied the aisles. At S. Clemente only one pier is used, to divide the entire clergy from the congregation. The piers at S. Prassede are not liturgical but architectural ; they support transverse arches which divide the church into separate compartments, as, later, in Romanesque architecture. The windows in all churches were simple semicircular openings, unsplayed, filled at times with glass, but usually with thin slabs of marble pierced with holes of different shapes, often grouped in patterns (S. Lorenzo, S. Prassede, S. Martino, SS. Vincenzo ed Anastasio). The pavements

were of marble mosaics, which were usually, during the early period, of very simple patterns in black and white, and developed into elaborate geometrical designs only in the Middle Ages. Wall mosaics were afforded only in the richer churches, where their rich colouring harmonized with the architecture better than any other decorative system. It is the merit of early Christian art to have invented and developed this art. In the more modest churches it was used in the most sacred part, the semicircle and face of the apse ; it then extended to the triumphal arch at the opening of the nave and to the walls of the nave over the columns (S. Maria Maggiore) and even to the interior of the façade (S. Sabina), but these latter cases are rare. Only in the Middle Ages did mosaics appear on the outside of the façades (S. Peter, S. Paul, S. Bartolommeo all' Isola, S. Maria in Trastevere, S. Maria Maggiore).

Besides the above points of unity with variations, there are great differences in style and execution to be considered historically. The largest and most sumptuous basilicas were built between 315 and 450 with imperial assistance, and when the Papacy was comparatively wealthy. Of the papal basilicas, S. Paul, built about 400 under the influence of Ravenna, exists largely in facsimile since the fire of 1822, and S. Maria Maggiore (about 420), representing the purely local style, is alone approximately intact, with its impressive lines of columns and its decoration of figured mosaics. Although much smaller, the almost contemporary church of S. Sabina, with its superb channelled Corinthian colonnades, its unique marble incrustation, and its mosaics of the fifth century, its closed porch, and its unique carved wooden doors, is even more representative. Soon after was built one of the most symmetrical Roman churches, S. Pietro in Vincoli, with its unique series of channelled Doric columns.

During this first stage, — that of the fourth and fifth centuries, — very little damage had been done wilfully to classic structures. No temples had been converted into churches and only a few of the civil structures, — most of them being kept in repair until the end of the reign of Theodoric (526). Of course there were exceptions, especially where buildings were abandoned. The real spoliation began in the fifth century with the imperial edicts against paganism. The Templum Sacræ Urbis became SS. Cosmas and Damian ; the Senate-House became S. Hadrian ; a hall of the Sessorian palace became S. Croce ; the basilica of Junius Bassus became S. Andrea in Cata Barbara ; the Corn Exchange became S. Maria in Cosmedin, etc.

The churches built directly after the ruinous Gothic wars (533 to 552) show traces of two changes : (1) the decadence of the local school,

PLATE XXII

ITALY, ARCHITECTURE OF   PLATE IV

Venice, Libreria Vecchia, or the old Library of S. Mark, the building which faces the ducal palace on the other side of the Piazzetta. It was built by Sansovino about 1536. The design was copied by later architects and carried along the south side of the great Piazza, and to this part a third story was added long afterwards; but the interesting part of the building consists of only seventeen arches fronting eastward on the Piazzetta and the three on the south front toward the Molo.

and hasty, careless work; (2) the introduction of Byzantine influence. S. Lorenzo (about 580) has architraves and columns made up of superb antique bits that do not match, and its galleries above are thoroughly Byzantine in scope as well as in the capitals, and cushion-like plinths above them, and the balustrades. At S. Maria in Cosmedin, built for Greek monks, is the only instance of the Byzantine closed narthex. After the reorganizing rule of Gregory the Great, a revival came in the seventh century under Greek popes and Byzantine art. The best preserved example is S. Agnese (about 626), with its Byzantine gallery and apse-mosaic (S. Sabba, SS. Quattro Coronati should be compared with this). At this time, in 608, took place an event interesting in Rome's ecclesiastical annals, the conversion of the Pantheon into a Christian church, with imperial permission, thus inaugurating a new inroad on antique structures. The basilicas of this time (sixth to eighth centuries) and until the beginning of the ninth century were small in size and built with modest resources; the arch was almost always used and the columns were placed farther apart. The church furniture was simpler: the early Christian form of decoration in straight lines and classic ornament was superseded by the basket work, open-work, and low relief patterns, the Oriental hieratic birds and animals of Byzantine art, which continued until the eleventh century (S. Maria in Cosmedin and many others).

A revival took place under Carlovingian patronage, especially under Paschal II., as shown by SS. Nereo ed Achilleo, S. Cecilia, S. Maria della Navicella, and especially S. Prassede, which is the most complete monument in Rome of the Carlovingian age — original in its architectural features and unsurpassed in its mosaics. Before the middle of the ninth century, however, a decadence set in, exemplified in S. Marco, which continued unbroken until the close of the eleventh century. For about two centuries art was dead in Rome, in the midst of a general decadence and degradation.

When under Hildebrand and other vigorous popes of the close of the eleventh century art and reform revived hand and hand in Rome, a new city had to rise from the ashes of Robert Guiscard's fire (1084). Rome had for a long time been a city of monasteries, with Greek monks in the lead. Now the laity predominated, and a new school of lay artists sprang up, organized a guild divided into families such as those of Paulus, Ranucius, Laurentius, Vasalectus, Andreas, etc., where art knowledge and tradition were handed down from father to son. These men broke away from the Carlovingian style and originated an art made up of two main elements: (1) architectural forms and pure architectural decoration reproducing

exactly the earliest Christian basilicas of the fourth and fifth centuries, with the addition of a purer and more abundant architectural ornamentation copied from classic models; (2) a system of internal ornament in mosaic patterns developed from Byzantine originals, to replace the previous sculptured patterns, in the decoration of every part of the interior except the upper walls, applied to pavements, screens, parapets, altar fronts, altar canopies, pulpits, paschal candlesticks, sepulchral monuments, etc.

The earliest complete work of this proto-Renaissance is also its most thoroughly representative, S. Clemente (1099–1112), whose internal arrangements, especially in the choir, with parapet, ambones, candlestick, seats, etc., are the stock example, even for the early Christian period. Then followed the rebuilding of SS. Quattro Coronati, S. Bartolommeo, S. Maria in Cosmedin, S. Crisogono, and many others in the first half of the twelfth century. The masterpiece of this early period is the interior of S. Maria in Trastevere, which is — barring S. Lorenzo — the finest mediæval interior in Rome. Here and at S. Lorenzo the reproduction of the classic is so perfect that the columns and capitals have been supposed to be antique, but they are the work of the mediæval sculptors whose ability to reproduce this with perfection is shown in hundreds of cases in and out of Rome, where the material cannot possibly have been an antique legacy. Other contemporary works are S. Francesco Romana, S. Maria in Ara Coeli, S. Giovanni a Porta Latina, S. Cosimato, S. Giorgio al Velabro, and SS. Giovanni e Paolo.

There is far more of architectural composition and decorative sense than before. Subordinate entities are developed, especially: (1) towers, (2) porches, (3) cloisters. In all these the Roman school had a style specifically its own, and equalling in value, if not surpassing, that of any other Italian mediæval school. The towers are of brick, and rise independently near the façade. They are square, with flat top surmounted by a low roof; they consist of a high, solid base surmounted by from two to seven stories of arched windows, increasing in number and lightness toward the top, the lower ones having one or two openings separated by piers, and the upper ones two or three openings separated by colonnettes. These towers may be considered the lightest and best proportioned in Italy. The most beautiful are those of S. Cecilia, S. Maria in Cosmedin, SS. Giovanni e Paolo, and S. Pudentiana; other fine examples are at S. Giovanni a Porta Latina, S. Lorenzo in Lucina, and S. Giorgio al Velabro. Rome is full of them; in many cases they are all that remain of a mediæval church that has been destroyed by the Renaissance and barocco vandals. The towers at S. Maria Maggiore, with their more pointed roofs, show Gothic influence, and close the series.

The porches with which the architects of the twelfth and thirteenth centuries covered the whole lower part of the façades had been unknown to previous periods. They consisted of unbroken architraves supported on rows of columns, always of the Ionic order, and took the place of the earlier atria. Their style is simple and their proportions unusually good. An early example is that of S. Giorgio al Velabro; one with rich inlaid work is that of S. Cecilia; the largest remaining example is S. Lorenzo, outside the walls; others are at S. Lorenzo in Lucina, and SS. Vincenzo ed Anastasio.

Finally, the cloisters come very close to the churches in interest. There is a steady, rational development of a type beginning with the heavy arcades on stumpy single shafts, as at SS. Vincenzo ed Anastasio (about 1140) and S. Lorenzo outside the walls (about 1150), somewhat modified at S. Cecilia (about 1175), through the slenderer but still perfectly plain shafts and lighter arcades at S. Prassede, S. Cosimato, and S. Sabina, to the rich, perfectly balanced, and thoroughly artistic culmination at S. John Lateran and S. Paul. In these last works the Roman artists joined the round-arched colonnade on twin columns of varied designs to the ornamental mosaic work which they had made their specialty. They had already done this somewhat in some of the porches, but not to so great an extent. The innumerable geometric patterns were worked into every surface, flat and curved, so that every part of the cloister glows with colour.

This mediæval Roman style spread beyond the city; many of its extra-Roman monuments are described under Lazio. There are very few monuments in Rome where any different artistic ideas are expressed. One of these is the church of SS. Vincenzo ed Anastasio, where the Cistercian monks introduced square piers instead of columns, and attempted to cover the nave with a tunnel vault, as was their custom in Burgundy.

Rome; Gothic. The Gothic style, having been introduced into Italy by the Cistercians, who never built in the cities, and having been then adopted by the Dominicans and Franciscans, it was associated with the monastic orders, and the strong school of lay artists in Rome itself were not easily led to adopting it in place of their favourite classic type, notwithstanding the fact that it was in the province of Rome that the finest of the monuments of primitive monastic Gothic were erected. Only in the last quarter of the thirteenth century did it really make its appearance in Rome, and even then almost entirely by the hands of foreign monks. After the earlier Dominican chapel at S. Sisto,

the Sancta Sanctorum chapel and the disfigured S. Maria in Ara Cœli, comes S. Maria sopra Minerva, the only complete Gothic three-aisled church in Rome, built apparently by Fra Sisto and Fra Ristoro, the architects of S. Maria Novella (1280) in Florence, in the same style. Its piers and ribbed cross vaults seem out of place in Rome. Very soon after this the departure of the papal court to Avignon brought all artistic activity in Rome to a close, just as the adoption of Gothic forms in all ornamentation gave a token of the probable approaching Gothization. In the turmoil and poverty of the rest of the fourteenth century and well into the fifteenth century, hardly anything was done.

Rome; Renaissance. Although, through its ruins, Rome was the source of Renaissance architecture, it did not itself produce any architects. A century of desolation had killed the local school. Even after the final return from Avignon (1414), and the end of the schism, papal poverty and continued civil strife deferred the renovation of the decaying city, until the pontificate of Nicholas V. (1447–1455). Therefore, although Brunellesco and Alberti got their inspiration in Rome, the city contains no monuments of the earliest Renaissance. Second-rate Florentines and Lombards built the bulk of the earlier works (1450–1500). They found a large part of the monuments of ancient Rome in substantial preservation; the present ruin is largely the work of the fifteenth, sixteenth, and seventeenth centuries. Nearly all the Renaissance churches and palaces of Rome were built up of antique material, even to their lime, which was made from antique statues. These two causes account for the specific character of the Roman "school," even though its members all came from other provinces: (1) daily contact with classic ruins and consequent closer reproduction of their style than elsewhere; (2) influence of the coarse texture of the native stone — especially travertine — unsuitable for the elaborate and finished decoration elsewhere prevalent.

The first important work extant is the immense Palazzo di Venezia (1455 and 1466), built by different hands. Its grim battlemented exterior is imposing and unique, an echo of mediæval fortresses. Its main court and the portico of the adjoining church are early examples of piers with engaged columns — Tuscan-Doric below and Corinthian above — a scheme adopted from imperial buildings. The octagonal piers of its smaller court are relics of Tuscan Gothic now first imported to Rome and repeated elsewhere, as in SS. Apostoli, S. Pietro in Vincoli, SS. Nereo ed Achilleo. The inferior artists in Rome before 1500, such as Meo del Caprina, Giacomo da Pietrasanta, and Giovannino dei Dolci, built such churches as S. Agostino (1479–1483), S. Maria del Popolo,

S. Pietro in Montorio, with façades modelled largely on Alberti's of S. Maria Novella (1470). Their style was heavy and devoid of character and sharpness. Only S. Agostino has an interesting interior with high cross vaults and a dome on circular drum. The sculptural decoration — on account of the crude material mentioned — was limited, though a few portals, such as those of S. Cosimato, S. Agostino, S. Maria del Popolo, and S. Spirito, have some fair details. Still a very productive school of sculpture, led by Florentines like Mino da Fiesole, and Lombards like Bregna, produced in marble works that contributed largely to interior decoration, such as altarpieces (S. Gregorio, S. Maria del Popolo, S. Silvestro in Capite, S. Maria della Pace); sepulchral monuments of many types (as in S. Salvatore, S. Cecilia, SS. Apostoli, S. Sabina, S. Maria del Popolo, S. Maria Maggiore), and several varieties of church furniture. In other branches of decoration, there was a survival of mediæval Roman traditions (*e.g.* mosaic pavement of Sistine chapel; Cosmati monuments by Paulus).

Except for the symmetrical hospital of S. Spirito (1473–1482), with its campanile of mediæval type, the monotony of dulness was not broken until the building, by a genius not yet identified, of the Cancelleria palace (1486–1495), a design formerly attributed to Bramante. It heralds the Middle Renaissance. The Florentine rustic work is here discarded; all heaviness disappears; the profiles are crisp and delicate. The framing of apertures by architrave and supports is transferred for the first time to the façade of a palace. Variety is obtained by not applying this system to the lower floor and by giving flat-topped instead of round-headed windows in the upper floor. The general effect is of symmetry and supreme elegance. The court shows the last use of columns in Rome; henceforth piers are to be the rule. The columns are in two stories of open galleries surmounted by an overhanging third. The effect of this palace was incalculable. It set the style for civil architecture in Rome during a generation (Palazzo Giraud Torlonia — in some ways more perfect, — Palazzo di Bramante, Casa Turchi), and this is best shown in neighbouring towns like Tivoli, less reconstructed since than the capital.

A new period was ushered in by Bramante (1444–1514), who came to Rome in 1499. The influence of Rome upon his style transformed it so that he became, when nearly sixty, and after a long career in northern Italy, the founder of the middle Renaissance style. His first known work in Rome, the round tempietto at S. Pietro in Montorio (1500–1502), is considered to be the first work breathing in every part the pure spirit of antiquity. It became a model for the "purists." Then followed the court of S. Maria della Pace (1504), equally original, though not so careful in details, with its two-storied open gallery — Ionic below and Corinthian above — so criticised because of the double number of supports in the upper gallery, where the intermediate columns rest above the keystone below. The interior of S. Maria del Popolo (1509) gives a faint idea of what Bramante could have done had he carried out his plans for S. Peter, and is full of interesting effects and details. Bramante's supremacy in Rome was shown by the commission to build S. Peter's and remodel the Vatican. He connected the papal palaces with the Belvedere by two parallel galleries (400 feet long) enclosing a superb court, whose effect has been since ruined by the building of the Library and Braccio Nuovo. There were two Doric stories beneath the gallery proper. Bramante also planned the façade toward S. Peter, but completed only one out of the three loggias. His style was characterized by elegance and lightness, the elimination of all unnecessary detail, and the subordination of minor parts. His influence long survived him. His plans for S. Peter were the greatest mine for architects for half a century, and inspired many Roman churches. Among his closest followers was Raphael (S. Eligio, Palazzo Caffarelli, Palazzo dell' Aquila), whose most notable works were the fascinating and harmonious Farnesina palace (1509–1511) and the Villa Madama, so epoch-making among Italian villas. Baldassare Peruzzi's wonderful Massimi palace (1535) is perhaps the last work in Rome to preserve intact Bramante's serene and delicate simplicity (compare Palazzo Ossoli, Palazzetto Spada, court Palazzo Altemps). Another pupil of Bramante, Antonio da San Gallo, at times followed him, though less perfectly (chapel S. Giacomo, Palazzo Baldassini, Banco S. Spirito), but also developed quite a different style, especially in the Farnese palace (1534), the most colossal and imposing of Roman palaces. It is pronounced by some the *chef d'œuvre* of the Roman Renaissance, notwithstanding its evident faults of composition and the heaviness of some details, mitigated by the superb cornice and upper story added by Michelangelo. Like the Cancelleria in the previous generation, so the Farnese palace served as a model for many Roman palaces; for example, the Lateran. With his robust style, the substitution of semicolumns for pilasters, the enlargement of details, the increase of reliefs, San Gallo prepared the way for Michelangelo and the scientifico-academic school of the late Renaissance. In the matter of external decoration the middle Renaissance had been even more chary than the earlier style; merely sculptural motives were entirely abandoned, and even those purely architectural were sparingly used. But with interiors it was different: here stuccoes and painting largely took the place of marble relief ornament, and were more closely married to the construction. Here also classic art furnished the models in the tombs and palace chambers and halls, especially those newly discovered in the baths of Titus, which were adapted by Raphael and Giovanni da Udine (Loggie); this new style of ornament was termed grotteschi (grotesques). One exception to the general rule was the Palazzo Spada (about 1540), where statuary and a relief decoration of figures, fruits, and flowers were used on the exterior.

Michelangelo's late architectural activity is now shown, besides S. Peter, mainly by the Capitoline square, which he planned and partly carried out (Palazzo del Senatore). This is no place to discuss Michelangelo's dominant part in the building of S. Peter and his abandonment of Bramante's scheme of the Greek cross. He founded a school which developed into the barocco when its extravagance was untempered by his genius. Some of Michelangelo's coöperators were men who led a school of technicians, logical and cold. Its best Roman representative, Vignola (1507–1573), produced a harmonious masterpiece in the villa of Papa Giulio, with its semicircular pillared hall, its court with open portico, and its restrained use of rustic effects. More fantastic and airy was the Villa Pia, in the Vatican gardens (1560), by the architectural dilettante, Pirro Ligorio. These two are among the few remains of late Renaissance villas in Rome. The palace of the Villa Medici, built soon after, is a fine combination of the grandiose palatial style with lighter garden architecture. In religious architecture, Giacomo della Porta and Vignola combined to produce in the Gesù church a type logically correct, but uninteresting, which was quite generally followed at the close of the sixteenth century. An important exponent of civil architecture was Ammanati, whose Collegio Romano, with an interesting court (1582), and façade of the Ruspoli palace (1586) are above the average.

Barocco. Whatever self-restraint had been observed was thrown off by the protagonists of the so-called Barocco style. Its principal Roman representatives, Giacomo della Porta (1541–1604) and Domenico Fontana (1543–1607) established the type of broken lines, of illogical and incongruous grouping of details, of striking and weird effects, and of details and ornaments colossally disproportionate to the architectural frame. Rome is full of their work. The greatest effort of the school was the façade of S. Peter by Maderna and the colonnades flanking it by Bernini. The latter are unusual for simplicity and skilful perspective; their unacademic deviations from horizontals obtain fine effects. Unfortunately, the

worst side of the school is shown in the interior decoration of S. Peter, and the façades of S. Ignazio and S. Andrea della Valle show the influence of that example. After such comparatively correct work in the façades of S. Luigi dei Francesi, the Gesù, and S. Susanna, the lowest stage of degradation is reached in the style of curved-line façades typified by Borromini, as in S. Carlo alle Quattro Fontane. However, the reaction came in the end, as shown in the dignified façade of the Lateran (1735). — ARTHUR L. FROTHINGHAM, JR.

ITALY, ARCHITECTURE OF; Part X.; **Abruzzi e Molise**; comprising the four modern *provincie* of Aquila degli Abruzzi, Campobasso, Chieti, Teramo.

Here are the highest peaks and the loftiest tableland in Italy: a civilization higher than in mountainous parts in the south (*e.g.*, Calabria), but still slow in adopting architectural novelties. The primitive Marsi and Peligni built here in polygonal style: many ruins of their cities exist of various styles and periods, some extremely primitive; for example, Alba Fucentia, Atessa, Ansedonia, Æsernia. The period of Roman dominion was not so prolific, owing to the decay and impoverishment it brought with it everywhere; but the ruins at Amiternum, Bovianum (theatre and temple) and Corfinium should be noted. Of the early Christian period there is almost nothing. Exceptions are an early church and catacombs at S. Vittorino, near Aquila, and the basilica at Alba Fucentia, with superb antique Corinthian columns from the temple which it replaced. The Carlovingian period has left nothing important in its monasteries. The region was midway between the Lombard influences in Umbria and the Byzantine in Campania, and untouched by either. The Romanesque revival affected it late; not until the twelfth century did the Benedictines and Cistercians erect here important monuments, and even later did the civic revival also lead to the building of interesting churches in the cities, most of which did not attain their highest development until the thirteenth and fourteenth centuries. Primitive Romanesque is exemplified in the upper church at S. Vittorino (1179); the more decorated but neat S. Giusta at Bazzano (twelfth century), also near Aquila, with square piers and an exterior divided by engaged colonnettes supporting architraves. The Benedictine style is best represented at S. Clemente di Casauria (twelfth century), a basilical columnar church, and at S. Maria di Moscufo, of similar style and date. There are a number of Benedictine examples of an exceedingly primitive Romanesque style — sometimes with columns, sometimes with square piers (tenth to twelfth centuries). Primitive Lombard decoration in low relief was current (Alba, Rosciolo, Capestrano, Carsoli) during the eleventh and twelfth centuries. In the thirteenth century the two currents — Romanesque and Gothic — were active contemporaneously, in different parts of the province, the Romanesque, strangely enough, lasting until the early fourteenth century in this and the decoration show Lombard influence. The Roman school has also left important traces of mosaic work and decorative sculpture (Rocca di Botte, Alba Fucentia, Teramo, etc.) in the twelfth to fourteenth centuries. Important remaining monasteries

ITALY, PART X.—ABRUZZI: CHURCH AT SANTA MARIA D' ARBONA, NEAR THE ADRIATIC; C. 1210 A.D.

the north parts (Aquila), whereas the south was more influenced by the Angevin Gothic of Campania (Solmona, Tagliacozzo). The important churches of both styles are nearly all monastic: few important cathedrals. Stone, not brick, is the favourite material. Vaulting is used more freely than in most parts of Italy; are at Ocre, Casanova, Carpineto, S. Pelino, with tunnel-vaulted and cross-vaulted churches and contemporary vaulted monastic buildings, all in developed thirteenth century Romanesque. At S. Pelino, Trasacco, and at the churches of S. Benedetto (near Pescina) is seen the influence of both late Romanesque Apulia and the school of Aquila. In general the Romanesque structures are in poor preservation — either abandoned or restored — except such as Pianella, Moscufo, and especially S. Giovanni in Venere and Casauria, which are among the most important of the style in Italy; and certain other Benedictine monasteries. At Aquila itself the rebuilding of the city after 1276 gives the date of the bulk of its churches, all in a late Romanesque with decoration in part identical with that of their Gothic contemporaries : such are S. Marco, S. Pietro, S. Agnese, S. Maria di Paganica (1195), S. Maria del Carmine, S. Giusta, and S. Silvestro. What calls for especial comment in S. Maria di Collemaggio (1287–1494) is its unique façade, an immense false square-topped front with three rose windows and portals inlaid with coloured marbles so as to resemble a colossal tapestry. These Aquila façades are square and faced with marble, usually of two colours, and should be compared with those at Celano. The finest portal of this region is the colossal round-arched portal of S. Francesco at Solmona. Interesting late Romanesque houses — semi-Norman — are at Carsoli, Tagliacozzo, Sgurgola, Avezzano, and Teramo.

The province has one monument to represent primitive Cistercian Gothic — S. Maria d' Arabona (or d' Arbona) (about 1210) — in the same style as Fossanova, but with ribbed cross vaulting. Solmona, Tagliacozzo, Chieti, Rosciolo, Teramo, Lanciano, Termoli, all have Gothic churches. The simple Umbrian type of hall church with single nave is shown in S. Domenico at Teramo, a primitive brick church, with square Cistercian apse, and five pointed transverse arches supporting a wooden roof. Here at Teramo, at Atri, and elsewhere near the coast, brick is preferred to the stone used farther inland. The best-preserved Gothic church in this section is the cathedral of Atri, built under Angevin influence, and of the thirteenth century. In the same city are other Gothic churches (especially S. Domenico).

Aside from churches and private houses, there are some beautiful mediæval fountains, especially at Aquila; a remarkable aqueduct at Solmona, with lines of pointed arches, unique as a mediæval reproduction of the Roman type; a superb castle at Celano, late Gothic of about 1450, with two-storied court, pointed arches below and round above, and an imposing battlemented exterior; some old city gates, such as the Gothic rustic "Porta di Napoli" at Solmona. Two buildings illustrate the transition from Gothic to Renaissance. At Aquila, S. Maria del Soccorso (about 1450) is still largely mediæval in scheme, but with Tuscan proportions and details. At Solmona the palace of SS. Annunziata (about 1450) is a rarely symmetrical combination of extremely rich late Gothic

and Renaissance details in its portals and windows. In the same town the Tabassi palace has equally rich late Gothic details tending to the Renaissance, similar to work farther south.

Of frankly Renaissance churches there are very few, as the cities of Abruzzi declined rapidly in the sixteenth century. A good early example is S. Bernardino at Aquila, with an artistic façade by Cola dell' Amatrice (1525–1542) in three stories of grouped columns — Doric, Ionic, Corinthian — supporting architraves in the characteristic form of a screen façade. Simple Doric façades of S. Francesco and the Locanda del Sole at Aquila are contemporary. Of the various fortresses in this region the best preserved and most notable (besides Celano) is that of the Orsini-Colonna at Avezzano (1490), a parallelogram, with keep and corner towers differing from the earlier Celano type in that the towers are circular, not square, and projecting instead of receding.

Aquila also has some examples of barocco, as at the Anime Sante and S. Agostino, as well as many palaces (Alfieri, Quinzi, Torres, etc.), where the style is rather chaste.

— ARTHUR L. FROTHINGHAM, JR.

ITALY, ARCHITECTURE OF ; Part XI. ; Campania ; comprising the five modern *provincie* of Avellino, Benevento, Caserta, Napoli (Naples), Salerno.

There is a limited number of important "Pelasgic" ruins, especially in the north, as at Arpinum (the modern Arpino), Atina, and Casinum (the modern San Germano), while in the south they are sometimes merged in Hellenic course constructions, as at Consilinum and Velia (latest polygonal), where is found a unique Hellenic use of bricks. There are magnificent remains of pure Hellenic architecture in the city walls, gates, towers, and other civil structures of Pæstum, Cumæ, Velia, etc. In religious architecture there is nothing significant (fragment early temple of Pompeii) outside of the superb temples of Pæstum, described under Sicily. The Hellenistic Campanian style is shown by the latest temple of Pæstum and the earliest architecture of Pompeii (walls and gates, Greek temple, basilica, Greek baths). Cities such as Capua used for the sheathing of all architectural forms the terra cotta plaques on wooden ground so general in Etruria. These Campanian monuments explain the transition from Greek to Roman architecture. The adaptation of Alexandrian Hellenism is best shown in Pompeii by a chain of works beginning before the coming of the first Roman colony under Sulla, and ending with the destruction of the city in 79 A.D. — about 150 years. It was in the generation before Augustus that the bay of Naples began to be developed architecturally. Puteoli and Baiæ became favourite watering places, and witnessed some of the greatest efforts of Roman art up to the Antonines, as also did Capua and Beneventum. The amphitheatres at Puteoli, Capua, and Casinum are among the largest, earliest, and best preserved. The theatres of Pompeii, Herculaneum; the triumphal arch of Trajan at Beneventum, with its perfect sculptures; the reservoirs of Bacoli; the circular baths of Baiæ; the temple of Serapis at Puteoli, and those of Pompeii; the tombs of Gaeta ("Torre d' Orlando"), Itri ("Cicero's tomb"), and Pompeii,—are all remarkable examples of their class. No description of the different types of public and private structures of Pompeii can be here attempted. (See Pompeian Architecture.)

There was no particular style in the early Christian monuments, either in such concentric monuments as S. Giovanni in Fonte at Naples (octagonal dome on square plan), the important church of S. Maria at Nocera (two concentric rows of columns with dome and vaulted ambulatory) similar to S. Costanza at Rome, or in such basilical structures as at Nola. But with the introduction, by conquest and immigration, of two new elements,—Lombard and Byzantine, —two parallel modifications of early Christian architecture went forward from the seventh to the eleventh centuries. At S. Germano (Monte Cassino) the plain columnar basilical type is represented by S. Salvatore, with its high columns, placed close and supporting narrow round arches, its wooden roofs, and three apses without transept; while the square Byzantine plan enclosing a Greek cross is used in S. Maria delle Cinque Torre, where a wooden roof surmounted by one central and four corner towers replaces the Byzantine domes. Both date from about 800. Another combination of the basilical and Byzantine schemes appears, soon after (about 860), at S. Giuseppe in Gaeta, a basilica of five bays, with a central dome on a short drum, and pendentives supported by pointed arches, the cruciform nave and transept being tunnel vaulted. Even more Byzantine, with square plan, is the old cathedral of Capri, with central dome, Greek cross marked by tunnel vaults, cross vaults in the four corner bays; with which should be compared the Cattolica at Stilo (Calabria) and earlier parts of Lecce (Apulia). This style was connected with the political Byzantine ascendency in this province. At the same time the plain basilical style was continued by the Lombards, and especially the Benedictine order. This is shown as late as the middle of the eleventh century by a series of churches, the most important being S. Angelo in Formis, founded by Monte Cassino; no transept, three apses, columnar nave, wooden roofs, which should be compared with S. Pietro, near Caserta. Its open porch of five pointed, stilted arches on columns is an innovation due to the Orient. After this the porch becomes a common feature of Benedictine and

other churches of this region, but with three arcades, of which either the central one is pointed and the others circular (cathedral, Sessa) or *vice versa* (Casauria), though sometimes all are circular (cathedral, Amalfi). In the eleventh century the architectural situation became still further complicated by the introduction of two new elements — the Norman and the Mohammedan. The antecedent Byzantine and Lombard elements were, however, not eliminated, but developed and enriched. The artistic intimacy previously existing with Calabria extended to Apulia, and the same characteristics appear in all these provinces. In Campania the greatest centre was Amalfi, which had in its hands the Eastern trade, and through which the new art influences were introduced. The conquest by the Normans led to the use of French forms at Aversa (cathedral) where they first settled; its choir with deambulatory and radiating chapels is even earlier (1070) than Acerenza and Venosa; but the dome is Byzantine, and the rows of decorative columns remind us of the Pisan school. At the same time the Lombard-Benedictine artists were sometimes using the basilical form with a substitution of square piers for columns, as at S. Clemente di Casauria and S. Domenico, Sora. The old columnar style, however, continued the favourite form even for the semi-Byzantine style (old cathedral, Gaeta, "Vescovado" at Aquino, Ravello, Scala, Salerno, Amalfi). When we reach the beginning of the twelfth century both the pure Norman and the undecorated Byzantine styles have been abandoned and two schools divide the province: Sicilian Oriental and the Lombardo-Norman Oriental. The Sicilian style, formed under Norman rule, with its preponderating Eastern characteristics, reacted on the mainland. S. Reparata, the old cathedral of Naples, has the characteristic pointed arches in the nave; S. Giovanni in Venere is in plan like Monreale or Cefalu, with a choir like a Byzantine church and a basilical nave and aisles, but with piers in place of columns. At the same time Mohammedan influences continued to come to Amalfi direct, — not through Sicily, — and produced results even more brilliantly decorative, in a style that spread to Salerno, Ravello, and other smaller places such as Scala and Minuto. So decorative, in fact, that in some cases, as in the Ruffolo palace at Ravello, the architectural outlines are floral, not structural. Stilted, horseshoe, and pointed arches; the interlacing of arcades; alternation of different coloured materials; the use of incrustations, — these are some of the elements introduced. This school does not develop architectural mouldings or decorative sculpture in relief, but through the inland commerce of such towns as Ravello, some of its characteristics, such as the dome, and the use of different coloured materials, passed to cities of the interior, even throughout Apulia.

Typical example, S. Maria di Gradillo at Ravello, with a central dome reproduced at Caserta and in Apulia, and a square tower like those of Sicilian churches. On the other hand, the inland school compounded of Lombard and Norman with Oriental elements was largely formed in Apulia (see Part XII.). Certain special features were at first used in Campania, such as the columnar court or atrium in front of the church, not elsewhere seen, as at the cathedrals of Capua (about 1070) and Salerno (about 1080) ; but these were soon given up in favour of triple porches, as at the cathedral of Sessa (about 1103), or for perfectly plain façades. The Lombard style was strongly entrenched at Benevento, where the cloister of S. Sophia, with its heavy forms and primitive ornament, is in great contrast to the Oriental looking cloisters of the region of Amalfi with their stilted and pointed arches. The church of S. Sophia itself — perhaps of earlier date — is an interesting circular edifice with double deambulatory, the inner one vaulted with elliptical and circular domes, the outer with cross vaults, a semi-Byzantine development of the early Christian type of S. Maria at Nocera. The Beneventum cathedral itself in its Lombard features recalls Spoleto. But the Romanesque style, harmoniously combining the heterogeneous elements and giving them a national flavour, begins to show itself (1103) in the cathedral of Sessa with three apses, and sixteen columns dividing the aisles ; and even better in that of Caserta Vecchia (finished 1153), where there is a most interesting combination of horseshoe, pointed, and round-headed arches, a superb dome with interlaced arcades and a later square tower by the façade like those of Gaeta and Amalfi cathedrals — all of thirteenth century, with octagonal upper story flanked by corner pinnacles. We do not find the developed phases corresponding to the Apulian style of the late twelfth and thirteenth centuries, largely for three reasons : the persistence of Mohammedan artistic influence, local decadence, and the Angevin conquest. Such works as the cloister of S. Domenico, Salerno, are Oriental in the thirteenth century. The most important work of civil architecture of this school is the Ruffolo palace at Ravello, more important than even the royal palaces near Palermo, from which it differs completely, being built, like a monastery, around a great open court with two stories of arcades. Its high walls, broken by gates at the four corners and with a crowning tower ; its broad vestibule, leading to a square hall surmounted by a beautifully decorated pointed dome ; its graceful, fantastic loggia of many colonnettes supporting intertwining lines of ornament, — form a most original and picturesque scheme and best typify the entire Campano-Arabic style.

Throughout the province a system of internal church decoration had been used consistently,

that of ornamental mosaics. While it differed from Sicily in not developing figured mosaic composition (exception at the cathedral, Salerno), it excelled both the Sicilian and Roman schools in the application of mosaic patterns to church furniture. The pulpits, paschal candlesticks, choir screens, altar fronts at Cava (monastery), Salerno (cathedral), Sessa (cathedral), Ravello (cathedral and S. Giovanni), Scala, Capua, Gaeta, Fondi, Benevento, form the richest and most perfect series known.

With the Angevin conquest the centres of art ceased to be Amalfi, Salerno, and Benevento. Naples, the new capital, was filled with churches and castles in a new style that broke completely with old traditions. The French dynasty put French architects in charge of many of the new structures and favoured also the advent of the Tuscans. Oriental and Lombard traditions vanished. The wrench was violent and the new growth never thoroughly acclimated. The foreign invasion was, as usual, assisted by the Franciscans and Dominicans. At Naples the cathedral, S. Lorenzo, S. Martino, S. Domenico, S. Maria Incoronata, S. Chiara, were all Angevin structures (end of the thirteenth and beginning of the fourteenth centuries), but most of them have been much mutilated by restoration. The French design is evident in the choir of S. Lorenzo, with its deambulatory copied from Gothic models. S. Chiara, is a good instance of the single nave hall church, with which the cathedral of Albi should be compared. It is interesting to note that most of the French artists employed were from the south of France, where Gothic was less pure and imperfectly used. External decoration was extremely meagre and confined mainly to the doorways. Internal decoration was no longer of mosaics, but of sculpture, after the Tuscan fashion, and there is a riot of sepulchral monuments unparalleled except at S. Denis and Westminster. This hardly concealed the architectural poverty. Outside of Naples very little was done, owing to the increasing decay of local prosperity. Artistically the province was henceforth dead. An increased richness of Gothic sculptural decoration preceded the adoption of Renaissance forms in Naples, which came with the Florentine Benedetto da Majano and the Lombard Pietro di Martino, called by the new dynasty of Aragon. The highly decorative triumphal arch of Alphonso and the Santangelo and Como palaces (1455–1488) are the earliest important remaining works, and are based on Florentine models, as are the cloisters of SS. Severino and Sosio, and the Galbiati palace and church of S. Maria della Stella, built early in the sixteenth century by a Calabrian artist. The *chef d'œuvre* of civil architecture of this school was the Palazzo Gravina (1513–1549), by a Neapolitan, with heavy bossed work on lower story, smooth walls with Corinthian pilasters above, surmounted by busts in medallions. At the same time the church of S. Maria delle Grazie (1517–1524) combines the simple scheme of Alberti (triumphal arches) with an extremely rich ornament, which this southern school was but too prone to adopt from the Lombards and develop. Until this time (after 1500) the old Gothic ornament had been at least in part retained. There is nothing notable of the early or middle Renaissance in the province. Only in the late Barocco period should be mentioned the following: the Palazzo Reale at Naples, by Fontana (1600); the later royal palace and park at Caserta, by Vanvitelli, with its famous stairway; and the colossal masses of the Carthusian monastery at Padula (seventeenth century).

— ARTHUR L. FROTHINGHAM, JR.

ITALY, ARCHITECTURE OF; Parts XII. and XIII.; **Apulia**, comprising the three modern *provincie* of Barri, Foggia, and Lecce; and **Basilicata**, comprising the single *provincia* of Potenza.

The numerous Pelasgic ruins in the interior of this province have never been described. Of the various early Greek cities founded on the coast the only well-preserved ruins are those at Metapontum, whose temples are described under Sicily. Neither the Roman nor early Christian periods have left notable monuments. The Byzantine colonization of the ninth to tenth centuries, combined with the progress of art among the Lombard settlers, gave the first impulse. Apulia was like Calabria in not having strong basilical traditions; neither did the Benedictine order and its style obtain any hold. But little trace is left of the early Byzantine churches such as are found in Calabria and Campania previous to the Norman conquest (middle eleventh century). Perhaps the cathedral of Otranto (tenth to eleventh centuries) fairly represents one phase of this art, a columnar basilica with three apses and without projecting transept; its crypt extends under the entire church with four rows of columns and cross vaults, and is the prototype of such crypts as that of S. Niccolò, Bari. Of the square Byzantine plan with central dome a few small examples remain, such as three primitive churches at Trani — S. Antonio, S. Giacomo, and S. Andrea. S. Basilio at Troja (about 1019), though a Latin cross, is a Byzantine church with dome, tunnel vaults in aisles, and cross vaults over nave.

The Normans brought in French methods; these are exemplified in some of the earliest churches erected after their conquest; the abbey church of SS. Trinità at Venosa, and the cathedral of Acerenza. These churches are, with the cathedral of Aversa, the only Romanesque representatives in southern Italy of the thoroughly French arrangement of the choir, with cross-vaulted deambulatory and radiating apsidal chapels, and their primitive style is almost purely Norman; both date from the middle of the eleventh century.

But even before this the Romanesque style of the province, compounded of Byzantine and Lombard elements, was assuming shape and was not radically modified by the Norman conquest — only stimulated. The first centre of this style was Bari; the second, Trani. The resemblances to Lombardy are striking. The churches have no porches (Ognissanti at Trani only exception); the pilaster strips and blind arches that form the external divisions remind us of Verona; there are usually galleries over the aisles; and sculptured decoration is preferred to mosaics. The figure sculpture is Lombard, while the foliated sculpture is partly Byzantine and as fine in its way as that of Lucca. From Byzantine and Arab sources come the domes, the pointed, stilted, and horseshoe arches often used, though not predominating, and a use of tunnel with cross vaulting, though this may come partly from France (Périgord and Provence). In symmetrical use of sculptured decoration, the Apulian school surpasses all others. The doorways, and especially the windows, are marvels of contained richness. From the simple beginnings very early in the eleventh century at Bari, until the richest developments of the thirteenth century at Altamura, there is a logical sequence. It can be studied in such details as the rose window, which is at first a mere *oculus* (cathedral, Trani) in the top of the gable, or is not used at all (cathedral, Bari), through the middle stage of simple wheel windows with rich carved mouldings — the outer resting on colonnettes — (cathedral, Bitteto), to the richest type with elaborate openwork stone tracery filling the window (cathedral, Troja). The general form of the façade also changes. It at first follows the shape of the roof, with central gable and two wings only slightly slanting, the triple division being strongly marked, but during the twelfth century the gable slant becomes ever steeper and the division weaker (Troja, Ruvo). Square screen façades were also used, especially where Byzantine influence was strongest (Barletta, Foggia, Siponto). As in nearly all the southern districts, the material used was stone — not brick. Wooden roofs were used for the wider spaces, and cross vaults usually for the narrower ones, except where the influence of France or Byzantium was strong. It was seldom that the French plan of two towers on the façade was used (cathedral, Bari), and this symmetrical arrangement was replaced by the customary Italian scheme of a single detached or semidetached tower. They were slenderer, usually, than the Lombard type. In general, the Apulian school holds a position midway between the Lombard and the Tuscan, — disregarding the important Byzantine element. There is not much use made of different coloured marbles on a large scale, as in Tuscany, though it appears very prominently in the great cathedral of Altamura (thirteenth century). The cathedrals of Bari and Trani are the most colossal Romanesque structures of the South. S. Niccolo at Bari approaches them very closely. The development of the aisle gallery in these churches gives them great richness; to this are added, at S. Niccolò, Bari, great transverse arches.

One of the peculiarities at Bari, and elsewhere, is the obliteration of the curved apsidal outline by an outer flat wall, which allows of small chambers between it and the three apses. The external effect is thus the same as in such a church as SS. Niccolò e Cattaldo, Lecce, which has no apses. Usually columns are used; sometimes their uniformity is broken in the centre of the nave and at the transept by a pier, or there is an alternation (Altamura). Sometimes piers are used entirely in the churches with heavy — especially domical — vaulting. The plans vary almost *ad infinitum;* from a basilica without transept (cathedral, Ruvo) and a long-armed Latin cross (cathedral, Troja), to types like S. Pietro in Galatina, with a single nave, at the end of which is an octagonal chapel for choir, and at the sides long parallel passages opening into narrow aisles. At Molfetta and Lecce there are schemes similar to the semi-Byzantine churches of Périgord with their groups of large domes. These domical churches constitute an interesting separate group, in which, though the decoration is Romanesque, as in the rest, the scheme is borrowed either from Périgord or direct from Byzantine art. S. Sabino at Canosa has five domes, three over the nave and two over the arms of the transept, resting on plain piers. The cathedral of Molfetta has the three nave domes but no transept domes; the same is true of S. Maria Immaccolata at Trani. In such cases the side aisles are extremely narrow. This rich type is not at all a development of the earlier Byzantine churches in this region with tunnel vaults in the cross, cross vaults in the corners, and a central dome, in a square plan. Neither is it earlier than the Romanesque type we have been describing, but contemporaneous — if anything later, in origin. An interesting variant in the systems of covering is at S. Pietro in Galatina, where the single nave is composed of three bays with bold ribbed cross vaults. The plan recalls S. Gereon, Cologne. At the same time (eleventh century) there were rustic churches with square piers instead of columns, and prismatic capitals, showing that a pervasive local style was not yet formed (S. Michele, and SS. Trinità, Potenza), and did not spread everywhere until the twelfth century.

The Hohenstaufens, succeeding the Norman dynasty, encouraged, especially, military and civil architecture, and several such monuments of great distinction still remain. At Lucera is a great fortress built for the Emperor Frederick II. in 1223, by Arab engineers, from a type copied from Byzantine originals, but otherwise unknown in the West. Of Manfred's later fortress of Manfredonia the superb mole remains; but the castle itself is a reconstruction by Charles of Anjou — a high, massive, square "donjon," with round towers at the corners, surrounded by an outer wall following its outline.

The Angevin revolution came just as all the Apulian cities appear to have completed their great sustained effort of architectural upbuilding, so that there was little scope for new work. Still, a few works emerge. The rock church of Monte S. Angelo, built about 1270, has one of the boldest and purest Gothic interiors in south Italy, with a single cross-vaulted nave; and the slightly later cathedral of Lucera (1302), by a French architect, built with wooden roof.

With local decadence and a superabundance of public buildings the period of the Renaissance found even less to do, and exercised itself — often with great delicacy of detail — principally in private architecture. Such houses still exist at Andria, Bitonto, Bitritto, Barletta, Corato, and other places.

Spanish architecture had an undoubted influence under the viceroys, but was not productive.

Of barocco architecture Lecce has the largest number of buildings of various classes: S. Domenico and the cathedral. The hospital and the château of Cavallino should be compared with the cathedral of Gallipoli.

— Arthur L. Frothingham, Jr.

ITALY, ARCHITECTURE OF; Part XIV.; Calabria; comprising the modern *provincie* of Catanzaro, Cosenza, and Reggio.

This region corresponds roughly to the ancient Bruttii, more subject to ruinous earthquakes than any region in Europe. Consequently, few works of architecture remain intact. Also, its isolated and mountainous character keeps it outside architectural movements. Even what it possesses is little known. There are some important polygonal pre-Hellenic ruined sites. Pure Hellenic remains exist at Cosentia (ramparts near the modern Cosenza), Hipponion (extensive walls and theatre near the modern Bivona), Velia (numerous ruins of city), Caulonia, Locri, Croton. The temples at Locri and Croton are still important, and of the best period. That of Croton (temple of Hera) is nearly contemporary with the Parthenon, and is about unique in southern Italy for its gable sculptures and its optical refinements of horizontal and vertical lines. The temple at Locri is unique in south Italy, of the Ionic style. Under the Romans the province declined, by extermination. It revived only through re-colonization by Byzantines in the ninth and tenth centuries. Then Rossano became the monastic capital of a province essentially monastic. Byzantine architecture radiated from here, e.g. to Grottaferrata. To these two centuries belong a number of small, but pure, Byzantine, churches. At Rossano is S. Mark, a Greek cross with tunnel vaults, inscribed in a square, with low domes at the corners and a higher dome on drum at intersection. At Santa Severina is the baptistery of the cathedral, resembling in arrangement S. Vitale of Ravenna : circular plan, central dome on octagonal drum, supported by eight columns connected with outer walls so as to form ambulatory, divided into eight hemicycles. The student should compare with this the domical chapel of S. Philomena, also at Santa Severina, a small Greek cross with high central dome. At Stilo is another church of similar severe simplicity : a Greek cross inscribed in a square, treated like S. Mark, Rossano. A combination of this with the later Norman style is shown in the abbey church of S. Maria del Patir, near Rossano, where the primitive apse and choir, with three small domes, is joined to a later columnar basilical nave and aisles with pointed arches. Here the mosaic patterns on outside of apse and the zoölogical figured mosaic pavement are both interesting.

The political capital under Norman rule was Mileto. The complete destruction of this city, with its magnificent Norman monuments, by the earthquakes of 1783 is typical of what befell the monuments at different times nearly throughout Calabria. The engulfing of the superb Norman monastery of S. Euphemia, near Nicastro, in the earthquake of 1638, without leaving a trace, is also typical. But few traces of Norman building are left in Calabria ; partly because, owing to size, they were more easily thrown down than small Byzantine structures.

There was but little architectural activity during the Gothic period of the Angevin kings. The cathedral at Cosenza preserves this style in part ; its façade, the columns of its interior, and its fine crypt remain. To the same Gothic period belongs the portal of S. Francesco. There are grand ruins of the celebrated monastery of S. Stefano del Bosco, near Mileto, and in the same region those of S. Domenico Soriano and of the Certosa of S. Bruno. There is absolutely no monument of the Renaissance worth mention. — ARTHUR L. FROTHINGHAM, JR.

Anderson, *The Architecture of the Renaissance in Italy* ; Blanc, *Histoire de la Renaissance artistique en Italie* ; Boito, *Architettura del Medio Evo in Italia* ; Burkhardt, *The Civilization of the Renaissance* ; Cameron, *Roman Baths* ; Cattaneo, *L'Architettura in Italia* (English ed., *Architecture in Italy*) ; Cellesi, *Sei Fabbriche di Firenze* ; Cicognara, *Le Fabbriche più cospicue di Venezia* ; Dartein, *Étude sur l'Architecture Lombarde* ; Rohault De Fleury, *Monuments de Pise* ; *La Toscane au moyen âge* ; *Le Latran au moyen âge* ;

De Martha, *Archéologie Étrusque et Romaine* ; De Rossi, *Musaici cristiani delle chiese di Roma* ; Durm, *Die Baukunst der Etrusker* ; *Die Baukunst der Romer* (in the Darmstadt *Handbuch der Architektur*) ; Enlart, *Origines françaises de l'architecture gothique en Italie* ; Essenwein, *Ausgänge der klassischen Baukunst* (in the Darmstadt *Handbuch der Architektur*) ; Gauthier, *Les plus beaux édifices de Gênes* ; Geymüller, *La Renaissance en Toscane* ; *Les projets primitifs pour la basilique de St. Pierre de Rome* ; Geymüller (Society of Saint George), *Die Architektur der Renaissance in Toscana* ; Gruner, *The Terra Cotta Architecture of North Italy* ; Gutensohn und Knapp, *Denkmäler der christlichen Religion*, published later as (Bunsen) *Die Basiliken christlichen Roms* ; Lanciani, *Ancient Rome in the Light of Modern Discovery* ; *Pagan and Christian Rome* ; *Forma Urbis Romœ* (maps) ; Laspeyres, *Die Kirchen der Renaissance in Mittel Italien* ; Lenormant, *La Grande-Grèce, Paysages et Histoire*, 3 vols. ; Letarouilly, *Édifices de Rome Moderne* ; *Le Vatican* ; Mau, *Pompeii, Its Life and Art* ; Mazois, *Ruines de Pompeii* ; Middleton, *The Remains of Ancient Rome* ; Montigny et Famin, *Architecture Toscane* ; Mothes, *Die Basilikenform bei den Christen*, etc.; *Die Baukunst des Mittelalters in Italien* ; Müntz, *La Renaissance en Italie et en France à l'époque de Charles VIII.* ; *Histoire de l'art pendant la Renaissance* ; Norton, *Historical Studies of Church Building in the Middle Ages* ; Okely, *Development of Christian Architecture in Italy* ; Ongania (publisher), *Basilica di San Marco in Venezia* ; Osten, *Bauwerke in der Lombardei* ; Palladio, *The Works of Palladio* ; Perkins, *Historical Handbook of Italian Sculpture* ; Reinhardt, *Palast-Architektur : Genoa* ; Reymond, *La Sculpture Florentine* ; Salazaro, *Studi sui Monumenti dell' Italia Meridionale* ; Strack, *Baudenkmäler Roms des 15–19 Jahrhunderts* (a sequel to Letarouilly) ; *Ziegelbauwerke des Mittelalters . . . in Italien* ; Street, *Brick and Marble Architecture of Italy* ; Tosi and Becchio, *Altars, Tabernacles and Tombs* ; Tuker and Malleson, *Handbook to Christian and Ecclesiastical Rome*, 4 parts ; Von Presuhn, *Die neueste Ausgrabungen zu Pompeii* ; Von Quast, *Die altchristlichen Bauwerke zu Ravenna* ; Willis, *Remarks on the Architecture of the Middle Ages, especially of Italy.*

— R. S.

ITINERARY PILLAR. A pillar serving as a guidepost at the meeting of two or more roads, and, more especially, one having the distances to different cities inscribed upon it. The term is generally limited to such pillars in classical Roman usage, and this because of the Roman itineraries or official descriptions of the roads through a province or a section of the empire, upon which chartlike records the pillars were clearly marked.

IVARA. (See Juvara.)

IVRY, CONTANT D'. (See Contant d'Ivry.)

J

JACÁL. *A.* An American Indian hut or wigwam.

B. A method of constructing walls of a house by planting poles or timbers in the ground, filling in between them with screen-work and plastering one or both sides with mud or adobe mortar; a favourite style in Mexico for poor people. A similar system was used in the valley of the Lower Mississippi and in some of the Indian buildings now in ruins in the Southwest. Examples have been noted in southwest Colorado where a kind of wicker-work was built on top of a wall and plastered on both sides with mud. In the Salado valley, Arizona, many thin walls were made in this manner, while the thick ones had two rows of wickerwork connected by transverse braces,

JACOBEAN MANOR HOUSE, BRAMSHILL (SURREY); 1609 A.D.

the intervening space being filled with rammed mud, and the other surfaces of the wicker being plastered. (See Pisé; Wattle and Daub.)
— F. S. D.

JACK (n.). In building, an apparatus for raising, lowering, or sustaining a part of a build-ing; consisting, in its usual and simplest form, of a vertical screw which is raised or lowered when turned in a fixed nut, and the top of which supports the given load. (See Jackscrew.)

Builders' Jack. *A.* Sometimes, same as Jack, above.

B. A small staging or platform hung or bracketted from a window opening.

Hydraulic Jack. A modification of the hydraulic press. By means of this instrument weights far beyond the power of the ordinary jackscrew can be moved.

Hydrostatic Jack. A variety of Hydraulic Jack, the term being adopted by the inventor to describe his invention.

Window Jack. Same as Builders' Jack, *B,* above.

JACK (adjectival term). Inferior; second-ary; the noun used attributively and generally in composition. Terms compounded with jack are often coined on the occasion to explain the idea of smaller size or secondary posi-tion, and this extemporaneously by men unfamiliar with the refinements of lan-guage. Few of the many terms so pro-duced are of permanent interest (for those few see the special nouns).

JACKSCREW. A short steel or iron screw with appliances for turning it, used for raising a heavy weight, — a Jack of the simplest kind.

JACOB VON LANDSHUT; archi-tect; d. about 1509.

He became architect of the cathedral of Strasburg in 1495, and built the chapel and portal of S. Lorenz at the cathedral before 1505.

JACOBEAN ARCHITECTURE. That of the reign of James I.; or, by extension, that of the period covering the reign of the Stuart family and the brief interval of the Commonwealth. This covers roughly the seventeenth century.

Up to the beginning of this century the domestic work of England had devel-oped slowly on natural lines, corresponding to the needs of the people and the desires and ambitions of their artists, who were taught in the school of the ecclesiastical architecture of their time. After this time it began to be affected more and more by foreign ideas, Italian and French. For a century England had been using the orders and so in a way trying to keep in touch with the march of affairs in Italy; but it was not until the educated architect appeared that the orders were sufficiently understood to be used with accuracy. From this time on there was a marked change in planning and in con-struction. For the first time in England's his-tory the architect appears; and, with his advent, the skilled mechanic, who could interpret and carry out the surveyor's sketch, began to disap-pear. In this lies the interpretation of the suc-cesses and failures of Jacobean and later work. There was more knowledge needed to design, and less knowledge to execute.

Classic knowledge, which had hitherto but modified detail, now made itself felt in the plan and the elevations. The square house took the place of the old forms, the oblong auditorium replaced the three-aisled church. Both were in harmony with the times and the general sentiment of the English people ; but it was an English people in whom it is difficult to recognize those who made England famous under Elizabeth.

Inigo Jones, working indifferently in the fast failing Gothic or in the new classic, marked the early phases of Jacobean. In both styles he showed himself a master ; but his Gothic is not better than that of his less well-known predecessors, and his classic would hardly have placed him in the first rank in Italy and France.

Wren, who is by far the most marked figure in the period, was a man of great ability and great reserve. Hampered by limited knowledge, by multiplicity of interests, and by an enormous quantity of work, he yet produced buildings which in dignity, simplicity, and good proportion stand fairly unrivalled. Wren was always distinctly English, and he laid the foundation of all that was best in the Queen Anne and Georgian times.

Jacobean work was founded on the Italian work of Palladio, who represents the closing phases of the great Italian Renaissance. It gave England classic plans and classic laws, but in so doing it led the way to a time when the science of architecture killed all the more vital qualities. — R. Clipston Sturgis.

JACOPO. (See Giacomo.)

JACQUES ; architect ; d. about 1295.

The first architect known to have been employed on the cathedral of Troyes (Aube, France) was named Jacques. He probably worked on the building as early as 1270.

Assier, *Les Arts et les Artistes de Troyes.*

JACQUET, JEAN ; architect.

According to Sauval, the brothers Jacques, Jean, and Mathieu Jacquet were among the most skilful builders in Paris in 1530. Jean, a son of Mathieu, was architect of the church of S. Gervais, Paris, from 1580 to 1603.

Sauval, *Antiquités de la ville de Paris ;* Palustre, *Renaissance en France.*

JADE. (See Nephrite.)

JADEITE. A variety of pyroxene somewhat resembling nephrite, and used for similar purposes. — G. P. M.

JAIL. (See Prison.)

JAINA ARCHITECTURE. That of a religion in India which seems to have been a variety of Buddhism, but which remains more influential in the peninsula of India than Buddhism itself. The appellation Jaina or Jain is given to a class of buildings which are scattered over the whole peninsula, and which are thought to be of a time later than the Buddhist buildings, though the date has not been fixed authentically. (See India, Architecture of.) Also written Jain. — R. S.

JALOUSIE. A structure of slender uprights and crosspieces, either a lattice, or, more usually, a set of louver boards, the whole so arranged as to admit air freely and a subdued light, while excluding the view of persons outside. A window may be filled with these slats, or a balcony enclosed by them on every side. Some panels may swing on hinges, while others are fixed. In tropical climates, town houses are often completely enclosed with jalousies for all above the ground story ; and these wholly replace walls and glazed windows for at least a part of the external enclosure. Sometimes, also, glazed sash are inserted in the wall of jalousies, for the purpose of affording more light and some view out of doors during heavy rains, when the hinged panels can hardly be opened.

By extension, the term is applied to movable window shades, and especially to those which are made of slats pierced for cords, and movable upon them so that by pulling the cords the slats can be turned easily at different angles, and can also be brought together at the top so as to leave the window unobstructed. (Compare Venetian Blind, under Blind.) — R. S.

JAMB. One of the lateral upright surfaces of an opening ; hence, also, a piece forming, or intended to form, the side of an opening. In thick walls, the door jamb is often richly panelled ; in the Middle Ages, the jambs of doorways in very heavy walls were commonly splayed with a stepped section and enriched with mouldings and jamb shafts.

JAMES, JOHN ; architect ; d. 1746.

He succeeded Nicholas Hawksmoor as clerk of the works at Greenwich Hospital in 1705, was appointed master carpenter of S. Paul's church in 1711, and in 1716 assistant surveyor at the same church. His best design is the church of S. George, Hanover Square, London. James published in 1708 a translation of the treatise on the Five Orders, by Claude Perrault (see Perrault, C.), and in 1710 a translation of the *Perspective* of Andrea Pozzo (see Pozzo, A.). He published also *The Theory and Practice of Gardening,* which gives the methods of his day.

Blomfield, *Renaissance Architecture in England.*

JAMI MASJID. Same as Jummi Musjid.

JANUS. *A.* An ancient Italian god, represented with two faces looking in opposite directions, and supposed to preside over the beginning of everything. His temple, so often alluded to in literature, appears to have been a very small structure, probably of bronze, consisting of little more than the two doors on opposite faces of the structure, which doors were open during time of war.

B. By extension, any temple of Janus, or building dedicated to Janus ; especially Janus Quadrifrons, a building having four faces. Such buildings, forming almost cubical masses, and pierced with four archways or by two barrel vaults crossing one another in the middle and continuing from face to face, were not uncommon in the city of Rome. These appear to have been akin to the arched, and probably vaulted, structures which connected the great colonnaded streets of the Syrian cities, Antioch, Gerasa, Palmyra. Some of those in Rome are stated to have been used for shelter only, but their size was not great, and they could have formed only a part, perhaps the central part, of the shelter referred to. Only one remains in condition. It is that which belonged to the Forum Boarium, and near which is the church of S. Giorgio al Velabro. It is known that this once had another story. Janus (pl. Jani) is the name given to a four-faced building of any sort; probably by abbreviation from the full term *Janus Quadrifrons.* — R. S.

JAPAN, ARCHITECTURE OF. That of the modern state of that name, but chiefly of the southern islands, as Yezo has little permanent building.

Previous to the coming of the first Buddhist priests from Korea in 552 A.D., in the reign of the Empress Suiko, we know nothing of the architecture of Japan. At this time the islands lay in almost complete barbarism, and whatever attempts at building were made were only such rude and unarchitectural efforts at shelter as were characteristic of a race made up of a mingling of Tartar and Malay blood with the primitive stock.

Owing to the persistence of type that obtains among the Japanese, traces of this primitive mode may yet be found in the modern Shinto temples, where the projecting ends of the original crossed rafters at the roof ridge and the transverse timbers once used to hold the ridge thatch in place still remain grotesque attempts at ornament and the preservation of tradition. The original thatch has given place to *hinoki* bark, and details from the architecture of Korean Buddhism are omnipresent; but the true Shinto shrine still remains small and simple, built of natural wood, without coloured decoration, and rarely with the roof tiles, so essential a part of Korean and Chinese architecture. Such approaches to architectural composition and decoration as exist are directly traceable to the new religion that in the middle of the sixth century came from India to China, and thence through Korea, to lift a race from barbarism to the highest levels of civilization.

Shinto, the rude pantheism of a savage people, had in itself no element which made for the development of the race; and, therefore, art was non-existent, yet the racial characteristics that marked the inhabitants of this cluster of islands were peculiarly vital and receptive; impulse alone was wanting, and this impulse came when, in the year 593, the regent, Prince Shotoku Taishi, converted to Buddhism, sent to the Korean court for Buddhist priests and monks, architects, scholars, artists, and teachers.

The architectural style introduced at this time, already very perfectly developed in China, was at once seized upon by the Japanese and made their own. In their hands it preserved a greater fidelity to original principles than was to be the case in the land of its birth; and though it was to be moulded and adapted to the needs and ideals of another people, expressing with the utmost delicacy the shades of a varying civilization, it was yet to remain a united, consistent, ethnic style.

It has received slight consideration hitherto; it was too aloof from Western ideas and methods, too essentially Asiatic, to compel much sympathy from Western minds, yet it must be credited with all those characteristics that a definite architectural style demands. Europe has evolved its schools of building from the exigencies of its chosen material — masonry. China and Japan have varied the material, but they have produced a style as definitely architectural and national as any of the West. There can be no doubt that the Chino-Japanese architecture is the most logical and completely developed wooden style the world has known, and in its system and details it is as perfect an outgrowth of its medium, as scientific and elaborately developed, as is any of the stone styles of Europe.

Nor is the fact that wood instead of masonry was the chosen material of China and Japan to be used as an argument against the dignity of the style, for there is no revealed law that places one material above another in nobility. Athens and France created the perfect styles in stone, China and Japan created the perfect styles in wood; that is the chief difference between them.

In spite of the fact that they were built of wood and that thirteen centuries have passed since their erection, three of the first architectural works of this great Buddhist mission still remain, unchanged in all essential respects, the Hondo, Go-ju-to, and Tu-mon of the monastery of Horiuji at Nara. This monastery was the centre from which was to go forth the extraordinary influence that within the space of a century was to change a barbarous people into a civilized nation. The buildings were begun in the year 593 by Korean architects, in the fully developed style that for many years had expressed in China the extraordinary refinement and delicate civilization that raised her at this time to a height that probably had no rival elsewhere. Korea had but recently felt the spiritual and intellectual influence of China, and it is quite probable that the art which she in turn handed over to Japan was in many ways inferior to that of the great centre of Oriental culture. This can never be known,

PLATE XXIII

JAPAN. PLATE I

Pagoda of Yakushiji near Nara. Built 680 A.D., by Japanese architects. Unique example of design. The struts giving additional support to the roofs are modern. The ancient construction, entirely of wood, is partly explained by the cuts of the Horiuji pagoda, given in the text.

for every vestige of contemporary architecture has vanished from China itself, and what we can learn of its nature must be acquired from these inestimably precious buildings in Japan.

The art of China in the sixth century was the result of a curious amalgamation of influences. Hellenic art, passing into Asia Minor, and there becoming corrupted, had travelled through Persia to India. Here it found a native style struggling to express the qualities of a new and powerful religion. Indian architecture, and more particularly Indian sculpture, were keenly affected by this new influence; and when, later, Buddhism swept into China, the artistic impulse that accompanied it, while essentially Indian, was yet powerfully tinged with Hellenic tradition. Here in China it became still further modified by local tendencies, and once more in Korea it suffered an accession of indigenous qualities, so that when at last it reached Japan it was a microcosm of Orientalism vitalized and made potent by the dominating spirit of Buddhism.

This progress is clearly seen in the sculpture of India, China, Korea, and Japan during the first six centuries of the Christian era, and in the ruined wall paintings of the Hondo of Horiuji where the Indian influence is paramount; it is the less conspicuous in architecture, the only certain trace of classicism remaining being the entasis of the columns at Horiuji, — a refinement never adopted by Japanese architects themselves.

Apart from these classical traditions and the possible but unknowable influence of Korea, this first architecture in Japan is undoubtedly Chinese in every particular, and it is only what could have been expected from a nation that had reached the high standard of culture that at that time characterized China. As we see it at Horiuji it is a finished style, both structurally and artistically; the development of each of the three buildings is simple and logical; it is a system of concentrated loads, the entire structure being supported on a number of columns tied together with massive girders, and mortised in such a way that neither pins nor nails are necessary. The outer range of columns is filled in with a screen wall of wood or plaster. Ornamental detail is almost wholly lacking; instead of being dependent on this for effect, the buildings are beautiful and architectural solely because of the subtlety of their proportions, their dignity of composition, the amazing refinement of line, and the vitality of the omnipresent curves that characterize them.

This last quality, the marvellous combination of curved lines, is the most powerful element that goes to the making up of the general impression of almost unique beauty that is inevitable when one studies this work at Horiuji, or, indeed, any of the early architecture of Japan; for the delicate feeling for curved lines first brought by the Korean builders persisted with almost no diminution to the end of the eighteenth century. Neither description nor photograph can give an adequate idea of this dominant characteristic, and it can only be fully appreciated on the spot. These curves are to be found in nearly every portion of the work: in the contours of the brackets, in the outline of the columns, in the chief rafters of the interior that extend from the outer to the inner series of columns, supporting the roof, and, above all, in the roof itself. This last feature is, of course, of far greater prominence and importance than is the case in any other architectural style, and its lines, mass, and composition have received profound study until it has reached the limit of development. It is quite possible that it is reminiscent of the ancient tents of the nomadic tribes of Asia; but the theory that its great weight and vast size were made necessary by seismic conditions is hardly plausible, since neither China nor Korea are peculiarly earthquake countries, while the region around Nara and Kyoto, to which the new architecture was confined for a thousand years, is comparatively free from this destructive influence.

Whatever its origin, the Chinese, Korean, and Japanese roof remains the greatest glory of the style, and is a most remarkable composition of curved lines. Practically every portion of it is curved, — ridges, hips, gables, eaves, — and all the varying curves flow into each other, grow out of each other, until they form a whole that is powerful, impressive, dignified, yet light, delicate, graceful. The curves are not mathematical; they are as free and instinct with life as those of Gothic architecture. The manner in which the line of the widespread eaves sweeps upward at the ends with a keen, supple curve to join with the more vigorous curve of the hips that go soaring aloft to join the subtly concave line of the ridge, is one of the greatest triumphs of architecture.

The monastery of Horiuji consists of a group of buildings standing in a large court enclosed by a cloister, open on the inside, but closed in without. Beyond the main court lie various shrines and subordinate temples with their courts, the abbot's residence, and a street of houses for the priests and monks. The main court is entered through a two-storied gate supported by twenty columns. The general dimensions of the gate are: length, 40 feet; width, 28 feet; height to ridge, 52 feet. Just inside the gate stand, on one side, the Hondo, or main temple; on the other, the five-storied pagoda. The Hondo is 47 feet long, 36 feet wide, and 58 feet to the ridge; it is supported on twenty-eight columns, 7 and 11 feet on centres, and 13 feet high; the height of these col-

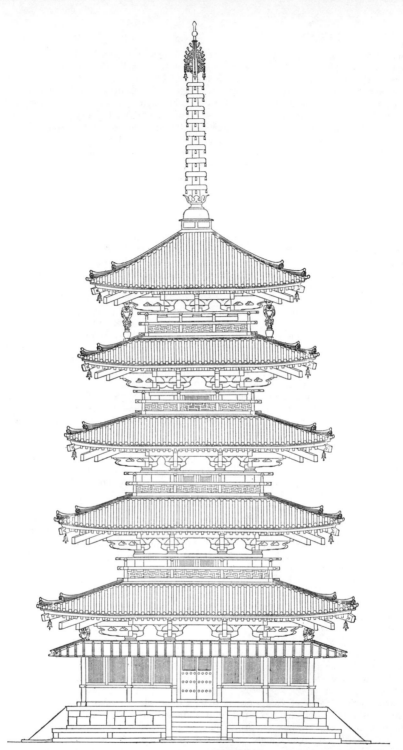

GOJU–TO, OR FIVE-STORIED PAGODA OF THE MONASTERY OF HORIUJI, NEAR NARA.
THE WORK OF KOREAN ARCHITECTS; LATTER PART OF 6TH CENTURY, A.D.

Covered gallery of the lower story is modern; also the grotesque figures supporting the fifth roof. This and the following text illustrations are scale drawings by Japanese draughtsmen. The characters on the reference lines give dimensions.

627   628

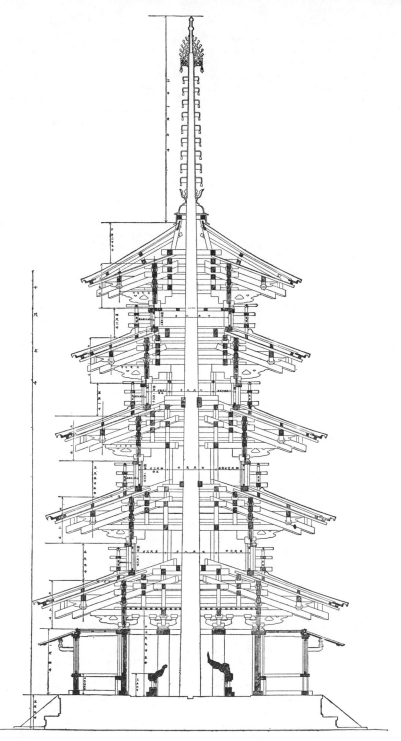

SECTION OF PAGODA AT HORIUJI.

Showing subtilty of proportions, and relation between heights of stories and projections of roofs; also the elaborate but powerful construction. The central mast is found in all Japanese pagodas.

umns is 6 diameters. The finished interior is only 23 feet high, the rest of the structure being an intricate network of beams, ties, brackets, and braces. The pagoda is 23 feet square at the base, and the total height is 110 feet. The proportioning of the roofs and the heights of the stories is very subtle, and is as follows : first story, from grade to eaves, 20 feet ; width of spread of roof, 50 feet ; second story, height from eaves to eaves, 13 feet 6 inches ; width of roof, 44 feet ; third story, height, 13 feet ; width of roof, 41 feet 8 inches ; fourth story, height, 12 feet 6 inches ; width of roof, 37 feet ; fifth story, height, 11 feet 6 inches ; width of roof, 33 feet 6 inches. All these buildings rest on a flat foundation, and the supports are not imbedded in this, except the central mast of the pagoda, which is dowelled in. The tradition that Japanese pagodas are enabled to resist the shock of earthquake by means of a huge beam that swings like a pendulum, is a fiction that has no basis in fact.

These three buildings, gate, temple, and pagoda, are the only portions of Horiuji that belong to the original work ; but there is no doubt that the rest of the group, including the great cloisters, the drum towers, and the minor shrines and temples, though comparatively modern, follow with substantial accuracy the lines of the original buildings. This faithful copying of the destroyed model is characteristic of Japanese work, and therefore we may be reasonably certain that in looking at much that is of admittedly recent date we have yet before us what is, to all intents and purposes, the original design.

In the year 646 the little three-storied pagoda at Hokiji was built, and also the very similar one at Horiuji. These are practically identical in style with the work at Horiuji, and were undoubtedly built by Korean architects ; but at Yakushiji is a pagoda of three large and two intermediate stories, so startling in its originality, so daring and revolutionary, so unlike anything we know of in China or Korea, that one is tempted to believe that it is the work of a Japanese architect. It is a three-storied pagoda, but the stories are very high, and between each of the main roofs is introduced an intermediate roof with a smaller spread. The relation of the eaves to each other in point of height, the spread of the different roofs, the varying size of the stories of the tower proper, the delicate composition of the curves, make up a remarkable example of the most consummate architectural composition. It is startlingly original and daring, but at the same time completely successful. It is as good an example as exists of the unique instinct for perfect composition that is the most salient characteristic of Japanese architecture. It would be impossible to change a line, a curve, a mass,

and achieve any improvement over what has been done. It was erected in the year 680, only a century after the coming of the Korean mission, and it would be hard to believe that in a hundred years a barbarous race could so develop as to be able to produce such a consummately original and perfect work as this, were it not for the undoubted fact that it *did*, as is proved by the superb sculpture of just this time, which is undoubtedly the work of Japanese artists. So far as we know, this matchless pagoda was without a prototype or subsequent rival. Nearly all of the work contemporary with it has perished, the only examples remaining being small and insignificant. In sculpture, the first impulse from Korea had exhausted itself, and the same is probably true of architecture, at least so far as temples were concerned ; for during the time in which the court resided at Nara, viz., from 724 to 784, the first civilization of profound religious conviction changed slowly to a gorgeous formalism, paternalism in government became a splendid imperialism, and by the end of the century the court of Nara was a centre of ignorant luxury. No trace of the palace architecture remains, though it must have been notable, and we are compelled to come down to the second period, that of Kyoto, for any indication of its nature.

In all the work of this first epoch we find certain essential characteristics. The construction is always frank and direct, the composition simple, the ornament, either in colour or carving, sparse and carefully placed. The slope of the roofs is low, and the curves are long and delicate ; the cornice lines are never broken, and the ridge is slightly concave ; the curves of the brackets are exceedingly subtle and delicate. At Horiuji, the vertical proportions are a little heavy ; but at Yakushiji the last vestige of this is gone, and the work is light, graceful, aspiring. In every case the scheme of colour is simple : white for the plaster, red oxide of lead for the wood, yellow for the end wood wherever it appears, and grayish green for the roof tiles.

With the transferring of the capital to Kyoto begins the second period of Japanese civilization, and therefore of Japanese art. The Korean impulse had exhausted itself and the ultimate result was not satisfactory. A new incentive was necessary ; and this came directly from China, and is closely connected with the name of the Mikado Kwammu, who first made Kyoto the seat of government. At this juncture the many students who had gone to China to seek the truth at what was then the fountain head, returned filled with the inspiration of the more esoteric Buddhism that was taught there, and impressed with the spectacle of an elaborately organized governmental system, and a court and aristocracy founded on the most

PLATE XXIV

JAPAN. PLATE II

The Ho-o-do or Phœnix Hall of Byodo-in, Uji near Kioto. Pleasure pavil-ion of the Fujiwara Shoguns; eleventh century. One of the few existing period of Japanese art. The interiors were enriched with carving and colour of the most elaborate and delicate sort, with paintings of religious subject and delicate culture. Almost immediately the old patriarchalism of Japan was abandoned, a complete system of highly organized government took its place, and learning, culture, refinement, and manners became the basis of aristocracy. The sculpture of the first period yielded to painting, and in architecture the purest Chinese models were followed, while architectural decoration, abandoning the austerity of the Korean style, became amazingly rich and splendid. Almost no religious architecture of this time remains, though undoubtedly in the gates of many of the Kyoto temples we can recognize more or less accurate copies of the original work. The octagonal shrine, Nan-endo of Kobukuji at Nara, is an eighteenth century copy of the original building of this time, while the curious San-ju-san-gen-do at Kyoto dates from its very last years. None of these buildings indicate any marked deviation from the first style, though were any large temples of the second period still standing we should probably be able to see the direct influence of the pure Chinese model; but in the Ho-o-do of Byodo-in at Uji we find a most perfect example of the architecture of this time, and, as well, one of the most beautiful structures to be found anywhere in the world. Built in the year 1052 as a kind of palace pavilion, it still shows, in spite of its defaced condition, the nature of the palace architecture that marked this golden age of Japanese civilization. It consists of a central shrine with its dependencies: a long, one-storied anteroom approaching it from behind, and still longer two-storied galleries reaching out on either hand and terminating in small square pavilions rising above the gallery roofs; from these pavilions short galleries or porticoes project toward the front. The shrine is of the regular temple plan, and is noticeable chiefly because of the singularly delicate curves of its roof and the beauty of its superb ceiling with the supporting columns, tie beams, and brackets that here reach the climax of classical development. The galleries are unique; they consist of a double colonnade of cylindrical shafts supporting a railed gallery bracketed out beyond the line of columns; the roof is carried by a second series of much shorter columns and projects far over the gallery. The corner pavilions are crowned by a third story, square, with a widespread roof and a railed gallery below. In subtle grace, perfection of curves, refinement of composition, this structure touches the highest point in Japanese architecture. The simplicity of outline and small number of parts that marked the Korean work at Horiuji have given place to a lavish elaboration that yet is quite equally classical and dignified. In the interior traces yet remain of the superb decoration that was so characteristic of this period of the Fujiwara. The central shrine is a perfectly

proportioned room covered by a coved ceiling resting on brackets that develop from the supporting columns. Fine and satisfying as it is in design, it must have been a thing of wonderful beauty when it was first constructed, for then it was inlaid with elaborate patterns in silver, ivory, and mother-of-pearl. From this building we can form some idea of the extreme beauty that characterized the palace architecture of the period, not only in Japan, but also in China. In Kyoto has recently been constructed a Shinto shrine in honour of the Mikado Kwammu, which is supposed to follow with complete fidelity, though with smaller dimensions, the design of one of the great Fujiwara palaces, and here we find the same classicism of form and composition with frank simplicity of construction that mark the Ho-o-do, together with that multiplication of parts and richness of imagination that is absent from the Korean work at Horiuji.

Of the domestic architecture of this time we know nothing, except that it was of the simplest form, for the basis of the aristocracy was culture, and in their devotion to the Chinese ideal the nobles housed themselves in modest dwellings that were simply cells or studies. In the Korean or Nara period Japan had been filled with temples; in the Chinese or Kyoto period the greatest architectural monuments were the imperial palaces, and with the exception of the fragment at Uji these have utterly perished.

To this epoch of culture succeeded two centuries of civil conflict and martial activity, during which the dynasty of Fujiwara shoguns fell, and was succeeded by that of the triumphant Ashikaga. Moritomo had transferred the shogunate to Kamakura, and in the middle of the fifteenth century the intercourse with China, interrupted for two hundred years, was resumed. At this time the Ming dynasty in China was striving to restore the almost incredible glories of the Sung dynasty that had made Hangchow the apex of world civilization in the twelfth century. It was for China a time of mystic philosophy, of the religion of meditation, and of splendid pictorial art. For some years Buddhist priests had been coming thence to Japan bringing the new gospel according to the Zen sect, a peculiarly lofty phase of Buddhism; and now, with peace temporarily established, their work began to show its results. A new epoch that may be called the Kamakura period set in, and, though painting was the favourite mode of artistic expression, architecture received a new accession of vitality, and indeed reached the last phase of greatness before the first trace of decay showed itself under the Tokugawa shoguns. Two sets of buildings are most characteristic of this period, the Zen temples and the palace pavilions of Kyoto.

THE HONDO AT HORIUJI (END ELEVATION); SAME DATE AND AUTHORSHIP AS THE PAGODA.

The covered gallery of the lower story and the dragon supports of the main roof are modern additions. Note development of pure and flowing lines in the roofs.

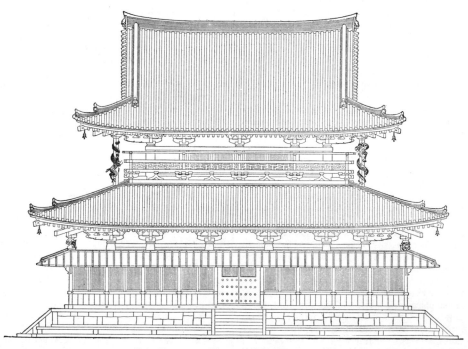

THE HONDO AT HORIUJI (SIDE ELEVATION).

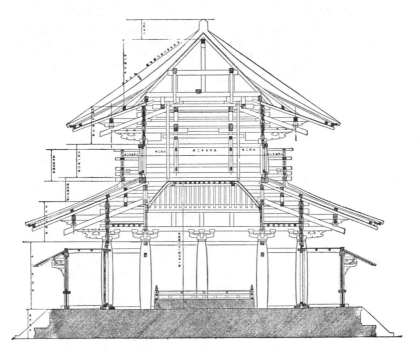

THE HONDO AT HORIUJI (CROSS SECTION).
The entasis of columns is found only in this temple.

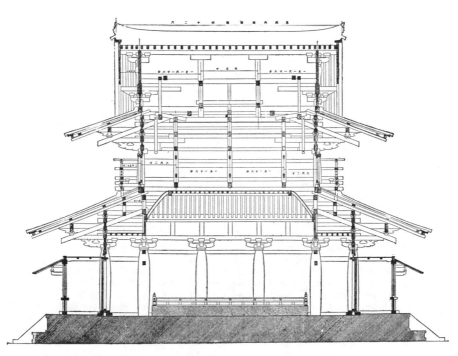

THE HONDO AT HORIUJI (LONGITUDINAL SECTION).

In the former we immediately see certain deviations from the old types. The arrangement of the group of temple buildings is different ; there is seldom a pagoda, and the temple and preaching hall stand one behind the other in the centre of the main enclosure ; libraries, schoolrooms, and monastic buildings surround this enclosure, and oftentimes open cloisters connect them with the central temples, dividing the entire space into three great courts ; minor courtyards, with shrines and schools and priests' houses, sometimes continue the composition on either hand in complete bilateral symmetry. In many cases the plan is vast and imposing, but in almost every instance so many of the buildings have been burned that little idea can be gained of the original design. The gigantic monastery of Obaku-san, between Uji and Kyoto, though dating from the middle of the seventeenth century, is perhaps the most complete example in Japan of the great Zen temple. Daitokuji in Kyoto is of the Ashikaga period, but many of the buildings have been destroyed, and those that remain are weatherworn and ruinous. The low and often long temples of the Korean style give place in the Zen architecture to buildings that are nearly square and very lofty inside. A central space reaches high into the roof, which rests on widely spaced columns, often of great size. One, and sometimes two, aisles surround this central area, and small shrines, chapels, and altars are grouped at the chancel end. In the temples of the Nara period, the whole centre of the building is occupied with a great platform, sometimes square and sometimes round, on which are grouped the images of Buddha, with those of many Bodhisatwa, and of the Shi-tenno, the four warrior spirits or archangels ; but in the Zen temple the centre is clear and the altar and shrine are in a species of sanctuary at the rear. The temple itself is raised on a low stone terrace, and the floor is also of stone slabs set diagonally. Plaster is seldom used, all the work being of wood, and the roofs rise in a steep and wonderfully graceful curve. The rafters are square in section, instead of round, as in the work of the Nara period. The system of bracketing is becoming more and more elaborate and complex, but carving is still almost wholly absent. This is the type of architecture that became fixed in Japan and persevered until the Tokugawa régime, when it burst into such unexampled exuberance and luxury.

Of the palace architecture of this time we have still the fragments at Ginkaku-ji and Kinkaku-ji at Kyoto. As both these delicate little structures were originally but garden pavilions, it is possible that they do not exactly represent the more dignified work of the time ; but they certainly bear a close resemblance to the Chinese palaces, as they are preserved to us in the screens painted by the great artists of the age. From these sources we gather enough in the way of suggestion to justify us in concluding that the dilettanteism that manifested itself in the fifteenth century was already showing itself in the architecture of the end of the fourteenth. The power and grandeur and dignity of the Fujiwara or Kyoto style has given place to a lightness and slender grace that is at least charming. Originally, Kinkaku-ji was entirely covered with gold leaf, and in this luxurious innovation we find the beginnings of the riotous splendours of the Tokugawa. Kinkaku-ji was built about the end of the fourteenth century by the Shogun Yoshimitsu ; it is three stories in height, and is surrounded by open verandas. The two lower are of the same size, and form one motive, being covered by a delicately curved roof of hinoki shingles ; the third story is much smaller and has a curving hip roof ; each floor is divided into several rooms of small size. Ginkaku-ji was built in 1479 by Yoshimasa, and is modelled after Kinkaku-ji, though it is much smaller ; as the former was covered with gold leaf, so was the latter to have been covered with silver, but the sudden death of Yoshimasa prevented this.

The last decade of the sixteenth century witnessed another revolution. During the whole of the century, the daimyo had been increasing their power and threatening the dominion of the Ashikaga shoguns, and when the seventeenth century began the Ashikaga were overthrown. Iyeasu had founded Yedo, Hideyoshi had conquered Korea and invaded China. The reign of this astounding adventurer was a carnival of war and conquest, and when, five years after his death, the Tokugawa dynasty was founded in 1603, it came to rule over a nation finally emancipated from all serious Chinese influence. The organization of the civil state was an elaborate and chivalric feudalism ; the Mikado had become an impotent and invisible fiction.

Twenty-five years after the death of Hideyoshi Japan was, by decree of the shogun, closed to the world, to remain so for 225 years.

It was a great period of industrial development and steadily progressing civilization, unhampered by wars or foreign complications of any kind. The Tokugawa feudalism was one of the most elaborate and perfect of which we have record, and under it government was, on the whole, well administered, and a sound industrial system developed. One fatal error was made by the founders of the dynasty, otherwise so notably judicious and far-seeing. Unwilling to endure a rival power in the state, not only was Christianity, at that time numbering hundreds of thousands of converts, utterly destroyed, but Buddhism was violently antagonized, and in its place a revival of Confucianism attempted, an empty system of ethics unvitalized by any religious element. The attempt was successful in a measure, and ultimately led to the revival of Shinto, while Buddhism, out of favour with the nobility and the knighthood, fell back upon the support of the peasantry, with the inevitable results.

As a consequence of this sequence of events, pictorial art rapidly severed itself from its old religious ideals and became secular, and even realistic, while architecture, cut off from Chinese influence and answering to the demands of the new society with all its ostentatious magnificence, burst into a riot of unparalleled decoration. The development of the industrial arts made possible a degree of splendour hitherto unattainable, and for the future, until the opening of the ports sounded the death knell of the real civilization of Japan, architecture was to be merged in decoration, losing little by little its early structural quality.

One curious reaction took place in the shape of a third recrudescence of the Chinese type just at the time of the closing of Japan in the seventeenth century. Obaku-san, near Uji, already referred to, is the great monument of this last attempt at a restoration of the classical style, and it came as a protest against the almost barbaric richness of the work of Hideyoshi's time. Complete as it is in plan and imposing in design, it is yet weak and inferior in detail, and shows very clearly how self-conscious and affected an imitation it was of the Chinese type. By this time, however, the monumental civilization of China was collapsing, and in all probability the architecture of the seventeenth century had also suffered an answering degradation and lost its original vitality, so that Obaku-san represents, not so much a falling off in Japan, as a similar tendency in China itself.

This last flicker of classical influence was purely sporadic, and quite impotent to stop the triumphant progress of the luxurious style already formulating itself at Nikko in the shrine of Iyeasu.

In the presence of this bewildering piece of reckless ornamentation, one is apt to be blinded by its extravagance to the actual shortcomings of its architecture; but once strip it of its carving, its lacquer, its gold leaf, and polychromatic decoration, and compare it in detail with the work of the Korean period, or even that of the Fujiwara and Ashikaga, and it is easy to see how great has been the fall. The roofs are heavy and even clumsy in their curves, the roof ridges and ribs have become enormous, coarse, and meaningless, the bracketing is fantastic and irrational in its intricacy and has lost the last structural excuse. Above all, the following of the lines, the curve composition as it were, is no longer inevitably good. In the

work of the Nara and Kyoto periods one may view a building or group of buildings from any point and find that there is not a discord, a lack of rhythm, anywhere. Under the Tokugawa this is no longer true, and one is constantly shocked at some rough grouping of curves, some violent discord in the composition of line.

It is quite true that many of the temples of this period, like the Hongwanji at Nagoya, are tremendously imposing, more so in size and general effect than any of the earlier structures, and occasionally, as in the same temple, there is almost no fault to be found with the composition or the curves, but too often size is the only reason for admiration.

Leave out the question of pure architecture, and the Nikko shrines, together with those of Shiba and Uyeno in Tokyo, are marvels of exquisite art. The decoration is masterly, the dramatic and pictorial effect triumphant; but it is the triumph of unmitigated splendour, of prodigal decoration, not of consummate architectural achievement.

Throughout Japan the majority of temples that now exist date from this period of the Tokugawa shogunate. None of them approaches in gorgeousness Nikko, Shiba, and Uyeno, but many are vastly greater and more dignified. In all of them, however, one can trace the progressive coarsening of detail and loss of sense of perfect curvature until they reach the final point of degradation in the contemporary Shinto shrine, Shokonsha, and the main temple of the monastery of Zojoji, both in Tokyo. Internally, the Tokugawa temples are less susceptible of adverse criticism, many of them, like Chion-in and Nishi Hongwanji in Kyoto, being models of religious grandeur and solemn splendour. In this respect, as examples of interior decoration, the Nikko shrines and those at Shiba may be placed beyond criticism. Every period in Japan has had its fitting artistic expression, sculpture, architecture, religious, historic, and *genre* painting, and decoration; and the last is the true manifestation of the Tokugawa régime.

Of the secular architecture of this period we have many existing examples, all, as was to be expected, characteristic of the dominant feudalism. The great castles of Himeiji, Kumamoto, Nagoya, and Hikone are magnificent representations of the feudal establishments of the daimyos; and it is most regrettable that their palaces in Tokyo, where they were compelled to live a portion of the year, have been destroyed, nothing remaining but the great gates and surrounding barracks. The arrangement of these yashiki varied but little: a hollow square, often very large, was formed by the great barracks for the daimyo's retainers; these barracks rose from the street line and were usually two stories in height, covered by low pitched roofs of tiles, with the heavy ridges and angle rolls with their clumsy terminals, so characteristic of the last stages of Japanese architecture. This nagai-ya, or "long house," was usually covered with black or blue-gray tiles, about 18 inches square, set diagonally, the joints being covered by great rolls of cement. The second story was of plain plaster; the windows were protected by heavy vertical bars of wood, set angle-wise, and in many cases these massive gratings projected some distance from the wall. In the centre of the principal façade was the great gate, used only by the daimyo or by guests of equal station; these gates were the most elaborate and stately portions of the entire group of buildings, and are of two types : the first a single line of gigantic columns of wood, square, and capped and bound with bronze or iron, supporting a massive system of huge beams that bore the tiled roof. On either side were porters' lodges and rooms for the guard, usually very rich in design and forming a part of the whole composition. The second type was one which took the place of that already described, in case it should have been destroyed by fire, for because of some superstition or prejudice the original gate could never be restored on the same lines. These substitute gates still retained the flanking guardhouses; but the main roof was omitted, and the enormous posts, with the equally massive crossbar, acted no longer as supports, except for the ponderous gates studded with big bronze bosses. These gateways were, undoubtedly, the finest architectural achievements of the modern period, and in many cases were wonderfully powerful and admirable in design.

Inside the quadrangle of barracks came a second, for the accommodation of the domestic officials of the household, and, finally, in the centre of all was the daimyo's yashiki, a plain, one-story building, huge in extent, but very simple. A forest of square wooden columns, arranged on a unit of 6 feet, formed the frame of the structure, and sliding screens of rice paper, or solid screens gorgeously painted and gilded, filled in the space between the posts, forming rooms of various sizes. In certain specified places the walls were of solid plaster ; but this was unusual, except around the place of honour, where were the two alcoves, called tokonoma and chigai-dana, in the chief rooms. Around the greater part of the house was a narrow gallery, called the yen-gawa, which, by its projecting roof, served to protect the rice paper screens, or shoji, that formed the outer walls of the house. The principal rooms, jo-dan and ge-dan, were often of great size ; the former was raised a step above the latter, and at the end were the tokonoma and chigai-dana, where the picture for the day, and a choice selection from the treasures of the daimyo, were exposed. On one side of the upper room, where the lord sat

in state, were two doors of the most gorgeous workmanship, through which the daimyo came from his anteroom. Around these two rooms ran the iri-kawa, or corridor, from 6 to 9 feet wide, forming, in fact, a portion of the state apartments, though of less honour than the jo-dan or even the ge-dan.

In the Japanese house there is no distinction between parlour, dining room, and bedroom, so a repetition of the group of rooms already described, together with reception rooms, kitchens, baths, and rooms for the taking of tea, made up the entire yashiki.

In the palaces, particularly those of the Mikado, the decoration was often gorgeous beyond description, gold, black lacquer, carved wood, coved and coffered ceilings, and splendid wall paintings, making up a whole of extraordinary richness ; but in the palaces of the daimyo much greater simplicity was the rule, and the wood was usually left with a natural satiny surface, while the ceilings were of plain boards of delicately grained wood, the whole effect being one of marvellous simplicity, reserve, and refinement.

In the country castles of the nobles there was a still greater degree of simplicity, the daimyo usually having near by a more domestic dwelling on the lines of the Tokyo yashiki, the castle being principally a refuge in case of attack. Many of these castles still remain in an almost complete condition, Himeiji, in particular, being a most noble structure. If the site were level, vast walls of stone curved upward from a wide moat, crowned by tiled and plastered parapets ; enormous barracks stood within ; and in the midst rose the great keep, three or five stories in height, each story somewhat smaller than the one below, the roofs curving outward in noble lines, and the topmost roof rising high in air, terminating, perhaps, in gilded dolphins. These keeps were built of enormous timbers, the walls being filled in several feet thick, with wattles and clay, and covered outside with fine white plaster. Sometimes they were plain and ungraceful, like Nagoya, but often they were wonderfully imposing, and withal graceful, like Himeiji, or, better still, Hikone, the castle of the great Ii Kamon-no-Kami.

I have dwelt at length on the arrangement of the yashiki, for with allowances for the difference in station of the respective owners, it is practically a type of the contemporary domestic architecture of Japan. The system of construction is the same, and the arrangements of the rooms very similar, except that the state corridor is often absent, and the jo-dan and ge-dan have become modest apartments of eight or ten mats in size, and serve as parlour, bedroom, and dining room, as the case may demand. (See Mat Room.)

In a Japanese house, all the rooms except the baths and the kitchens are floored with thick mats of rice straw; these mats are 3 feet by 6 feet in size, and the dimensions of a room are such that its floor may always be exactly covered by a certain number of mats. The rooms are arranged usually on one, or at most two, floors, and with very little reference to the effect of the exterior, which is nearly always, however, picturesque and interesting in composition. In houses of the better class there are usually two or three enclosed courts planted with bamboo, shrubs, or dwarf trees. The posts which form the skeleton of the house and support the heavy tiled roof rest on large stones sunk in the earth; the floor is raised some 2 feet above grade, and the whole space beneath is open, the ground being covered by a layer of smooth cement. The interior of a modern Japanese house of the better class is beyond question the cleanest, freshest, airiest, most refined and delicate affair that the ingenuity and artistic sense of man has ever created.

It is only in domestic work that the traditions of true architecture remain; European styles are now popular, and the results of the attempts at adapting them to Eastern conditions are not encouraging.

So far as one can see, the period of good architecture is over in Japan. The native attack on Buddhism two centuries ago was the beginning of the end, the restoration of Shinto was its continuation, and the acceptance of Western civilization was its consummation. For thirteen centuries it has developed as civilization progressed, each period perfecting some special quality, until it reached its climax of decorative splendour under the first of the Tokugawa shoguns. It is now a dead style, a thing of the past, and, with all other manifestations of art in Japan, must forever remain so unless some utterly unforeseen revolution brings back the ideals and principles of a great but now misguided people. — RALPH ADAMS CRAM.

Daly, *Les Temples Japonais* in *Revue de l'Architecture*, Vol. 43, 1886, and Vol. 44, 1887; *Japanese Society, Transactions and Proceedings;* Morse, *Japanese Homes and their Surroundings;* Anderson, *Pictorial Arts of Japan;* Conder, *Landscape Gardening in Japan;* Conder, *Domestic Architecture in Japan* and *Further Notes on Japanese Architecture,* printed in *Transactions of the Royal Institute of British Architects,* 1886–1887; McClatchie, *The Feudal Mansions of Yedo,* Vol. VII., Pt. III., *Asiatic Transactions.*

JAQUEMART. A figure, usually of metal, the arms of which move by clockwork at certain hours, and which, with a mallet or the like, strikes the hours, the quarters, etc., upon a bell. These figures are generally in pairs, one on each side of a bell, but this apparently for mere symmetry, or to make a somewhat more imposing group.

JARDIN ANGLAIS. Literally, an English garden; the term used in French for a piece of ground laid out in an ornamental way with some supposed imitation of natural scenery, and with winding, rather than straight, paths, and the like. (Compare English Garden, the name of the park in Munich.)

JARDIN CHINOIS. Literally, a Chinese garden; a piece of ground laid out in an ornamental fashion with what passed in the eighteenth century for Chinese taste, with trees clipped in odd fashion and little bridges crossing narrow canals.

JARDIN, NICOLAS HENRI; architect; b. March 23, 1720; d. 1802.

In 1791 Jardin won the *Grand Prix de Rome* in architecture. In 1754 he was called to Denmark by King Frederick V., and was made professor of architecture at the Academy of Copenhagen. In that city he continued the royal church (a domical building in marble), which was begun by the architect Eigtved (see Eigtved) in 1749. He completed only the lower story and the eastern portal. After lying unfinished one hundred years its completion, in modified form, was undertaken about 1875 by the architect Meldahl (see Meldahl).

Lance, *Dictionnaire;* P. Johansen, article on *Copenhagen* in *Blätter für Architectur und Kunst Handwerk* for Aug. 1, 1895.

JARMAN. (See Jerman.)

JASPER. (See Chalcedony.)

JAWBOX. In parts of Scotland, a wooden trough set outside of a window, as in a town house. Slops thrown into this were conveyed to the ground by an outside pipe, or a gutter and leader.

JAWHOLE. In Scotland, a sink of any kind. A place for pouring out or carrying away slops; from the Scotch verb, *jaw,* to pour out. In architecture, used sometimes instead of Jawstone and Jawbox.

JAWSTONE. In Scotland, a convenience similar to a Jawbox, but cut out of stone.

JEAN DE CAMBRAI; architect and sculptor.

Jean de Cambrai was the chief pupil of André Beauneveu (see Beauneveu), and one of the best sculptors of his time. He made for the Duke Jean de Berry a mausoleum similar to that designed by Claus Sluter (see Sluter) for the Duke Philippe le Hardi, at the Chartreuse at Dijon. This work, with its sculpture, was not finished until about 1457. Fragments of it are in the museum at Dijon.

Champeaux, *Travaux d'Art exécutés pour le duc de Berry;* Gonse, *Sculpture française;* Gonse, *L'Art gothique.*

JEAN DE LA HUERTA; sculptor.

Huerta came to Dijon (Côte d'Or, France) from the little village of Daroca, in Aragon, Spain. March 23, 1443, he contracted to build the monument of Jean Sans Peur, now at the museum of Dijon. He abandoned the work in 1457. It was completed by Antoine le Moiturier (see Moiturier). The design of this monument has been attributed to Claus de Werve (see Werve, C. de).

Chabeuf, *Jean de la Huerta*, etc. ; Lami, *Dictionnaire des Sculpteurs français.*

JEAN DE PARIS. (See Perréal, Jean.)

JEAN DE SOISSONS (JEAN DE DAMAS) ; architect.

Jean de Soissons was a pupil of Martin Chambiges (see Chambiges, M.). February 15, 1509, he went to Troyes (Aube, France), and undertook the construction of the portal and towers of the cathedral from designs by Martin Chambiges. December, 1516, he was made *maître de l'œuvre* of the cathedral, under the supervision of Martin Chambiges, and in 1519 assumed entire direction of the works.

Assier, *Les Arts et les Artistes dans l'ancienne capitale de la Champagne ;* Bauchal, *Dictionnaire.*

JEAN (JEHAN) D'ORBAIS. (See Orbais, Jean d'.)

JEAN WINLIN. (See Erwin, II., von Steinbach.)

JEDDING AXE. In parts of Great Britain, a mason's axe, or hammer. (See Axe.)

JEFFERSON, THOMAS ; statesman ; b. April 2, 1743 ; d. July 4, 1826.

Thomas Jefferson, third President of the United States, was much interested in art, especially architecture. He was intimately associated with the construction of several private and public buildings of importance, and it is probable that much of the actual design and superintendence of these works were due to him. About 1770 Jefferson began the mansion at Monticello, Virginia. In 1784 he was appointed minister to France, and made use of the opportunity to improve his knowledge of architecture. He returned to Monticello in 1787, and completed his house. Jefferson was doubtless the chief architect of the buildings of the University of Virginia, which was established in Charlottesville, Virginia, in 1818. During his official residence in Washington he was largely concerned in the erection of the national Capitol. (See Thornton and Latrobe.)

John Keenan Peebles in *American Architect,* Vol. XLVII., p. 30.

JEHAN. (See Jean.)

JERKIN HEAD. The truncated portion of a jerkin-head roof. (See that subtitle under Roof.)

JERMAN (JARMAN), EDWARD ; architect ; d. 1668.

He built the second Royal Exchange in London in 1669, on the site of the structure erected for Sir Thomas Gresham (d. 1579) in 1569 ; his building was destroyed by fire in 1838.

Blomfield, *Renaissance Architecture in England.*

JERRY BUILDING. Poor and slight building in houses and the like ; familiarly associated with small houses run up in long rows in the neighbourhood of London. Rare in the United States.

JESSE. Used for Tree of Jesse, Stem of Jesse, or Jesse Window, or Jesse Candlestick, an abbreviated appellative of any sculptured or other representation of the genealogical descent of Christ, as given in S. Matthew, Ch. i., or S. Luke, Ch. iii., and with allusion to Isaiah xi. 1. The purpose of the composition being to insist upon the royal ancestry, the figure of David is made prominent. (See the subtitle, and the next term.)

Tree of Jesse. A picture or carved representation of a genealogical tree which springs from a figure of Jesse, father of David, and bears, either in branching divisions or in a single stem, figures of David and others of the line of descent to Christ. One in a window of Dorchester church, Oxfordshire, England, is engraved in Britton's *Architectural Antiquities,* Vol. V. ; the fourteenth century tracery is diversified by waved branches which cross the lights, and the central mullion is partly carved into a semblance of a tree trunk, which takes its root in a recumbent figure. The branches do not bear figures ; these, twenty-four in number, are relieved upon the mullions. In the cathedral of Laon (Aisne), France, the central western doorway has the figures of the personages in the arched mouldings of the door-head, but the tree is not strongly marked. A similar arrangement exists in the central portal of Amiens cathedral, but the tree, or vine, is more emphasized. The Tree of Jesse is a favourite subject of the glass workers of the twelfth to the sixteenth century.

JESSE WINDOW. One in which the Tree of Jesse is represented in the design of the coloured glass ; or, more rarely, in the stone tracery. (See Jesse, and subtitle.)

JESUAT ARCHITECTURE. That of a mediæval monastic order of that name, which was suppressed in the seventeenth century. It is not strongly distinguished from other styles of its time. The order was not, at any time, very powerful, and the centuries during which it flourished were not those in which the great traditions dominated the fine arts. The church, or oratory, of the Virgin of the Rosary, in Venice, fronting on the canal of the Giudecca, is called also the church of the Jesuat Fathers (*i Gesuati*).

JESUIT ARCHITECTURE. That of the order of the Jesuits, which was founded in the sixteenth century. Beginning its great career of activity at a time when architecture was in a state of decadence, this organization produced an architecture noted for two things only : a marked change in the plan of churches, and a tendency toward florid and overwrought work. The first of these two changes consists mainly in the reduction of the size of the choir and an opening up of the church so as to admit of a large congregation; this, because the special aim of the order in its church service was direct appeal to the people by preaching. With perhaps the same purpose of fitting the church interiors for a popular congregation, recourse was had to great splendour of ornament. The church at Rome called *Il Gesù* is famous in this respect, and although the interior of this is earlier than most of the famous churches of the order, having been decorated between 1580 and 1600, it is characteristic of the style. The church is vaulted in a dignified way, and has a good cupola; its walls and piers are in large part lined with delicate inlay of marble; and the pulpit, the high altar, and even the minor altars in the chapels are adorned with this rich coloured facing and with twisted columns and delicate, if not tasteful, sculpture. The Jesuit church at Cologne-on-the-Rhine was erected during the first half of the seventeenth century. Several other important churches exist in Germany, which are characterized by this same florid system of decoration. They are generally of the seventeenth century, and their style is rather a modification of an earlier one than a natural development. The church of S. Ignazio, at Rome, was finished about 1685, with three aisles, a nave 60 feet wide, and an imposing façade. S. M. dei Gesuiti, at Venice, is of 1720, and this is as late a date as can be given to any Jesuit building. In this respect, and in its development and history, the style is radically different from the Italian barocco or the French Louis Quinze, or even the late German *Barokstil* of the eighteenth century. It is a mistake to use the word Jesuit for those monuments of the latest neoclassic art. (Compare Barocco Architecture; France, Architecture of; Germany, Architecture of; Louis XV. Architecture.) — R. S.

JETTY. *A.* A pier projecting from the land into a piece of water, to allow vessels to land passengers and freight, or to serve as a breakwater. The term is used in landscape architecture for such a pier when of small scale and on the margin of an ornamental lake, or a river treated as part of a park.

B. An overhanging portion of a building, especially a story overhanging the one below, as is common in mediæval houses.

JEWISH ARCHITECTURE. (See Synagogue; Syria.)

JOCUNDUS. (See Giocondo, Fra Giovanni.)

JOGGLE. A projection, as a tongue or shoulder, formed on a piece, or member, which it serves to unite to another adjoining, either by the insertion of the joggle into a corresponding notch or recess, or by its overlapping a simi-

lar projection on the adjoining piece. Hence, a separate piece, as a dowel or key, used for the same purpose by its insertion into the aperture formed by two adjoining recesses. In the latter connection the term is more commonly restricted to masonry.

The term is not very definite, and is extended to include various methods of such joining and decorative and structural projections for which there are no more specific terms. Thus, the stiles of a window sash may extend below the rail, to afford greater support for the tenons of the latter, these downward projections being called joggles. Again, the term is applied, in default of a more accurate one, to such pieces of stonecutting as enable stones to hold one another in place, so that one cannot drop without being broken or breaking its neighbours. Thus, the lower part of Smeaton's lighthouse tower, on the Eddystone rock, was built entirely

JOGGLE : HOOD OVER FIREPLACE, THE LINTEL BUILT OF STONES MUTUALLY SUPPORTING ONE ANOTHER BY JOGGLES ; 14TH CENTURY ; EDLINGHAM CASTLE, NORTHUMBERLAND.

of stones dovetailed together and further secured by joggles, and in like manner the elaborate polychromatic masonry of some mediæval, and many Moslem, buildings has many curved archivolts and flat arches used to replace lintels which are composed of stones cut with joggles.

JOGGLE BEAM. A wooden built beam, the component parts of which are secured together by means of Joggles. (See Scarf.)

JOGGLE PIECE; POST. Any vertical member of a truss, as a King-post, having one or more shoulders, or Joggles, each of which receives the end of a brace.

JOHANN; architect; d. about 1330.

A son of Arnold (see Arnold of Cologne), the third architect of the cathedral of Cologne, he succeeded his father in 1301. He finished the choir in 1322.

Fahne, *Baumeister des Kölner Domes.*

JOHN OF PADUA; architect.

In a grant of Henry VIII., dated June 30, 1544, there is mention of John of Padua and his " good and faithful service in architecture and in other inventions in music." A list of buildings attributed, without evidence, to John of Padua is published in the *Architectural Publication Society's Dictionary*, among others the portico of Charlecote House, Wiltshire (1558); Holdenby Home, Northamptonshire; Wollaton House, Nottinghamshire.

Rymer, *Fœdera*, XV., 34; *Arch. Pub. Soc. Dictionary.*

JOHNSON, A. E.; architect; b. 1821 (in England); d. 1895.

He was a pupil of Sir Gilbert Scott (see Scott, G.) and Philip Hardwicke. In 1852 he went to Melbourne, Australia, and obtained an extensive practice. Among other works in Melbourne he built the General Post Office and the Church of England Grammar School, and remodelled the Customhouse. He was diocesan architect, and had charge of all the public buildings in the Melbourne district.

Journal, Royal Institute of British Architects, 3d Ser., Vol. II., 1894–1895.

JOHNSTON, FRANCIS; architect; d. March 14, 1829.

He erected many important buildings in Dublin, Ireland. In 1824 he commenced, at his own expense, the erection of the building of the Royal Hibernian Academy, which he presented to that institution. He held the office of architect of the Dublin Board of Works.

Redgrave, *Dictionary of Artists.*

JOINERY. Joiners' work; the interior fittings of dwellings, etc., dadoes, door trim, and the like. The term would be more appropriate for the entire decorative woodwork of interiors than for cabinet work, but has nearly become obsolete, at least in the United States. (See Cabinet Making; Carpentry; Inside Finish, under Finish; Trim; Wainscot.)

JOINT (n.). The place at which two parts, or pieces, meet, and sometimes unite; the surfaces so brought together considered collectively; also the space between two such faces, which may or may not be filled with a cohesive material to unite the two parts; hence, the mass of cohesive material so placed. Any two pieces brought into more or less close contact form a joint between them. A wall built of stones without the use of mortar is said to have dry joints; that is, that the interstices, or spaces between the stones, are not filled with mortar. An architect's specifications may call for joints of stonework to be dressed in a certain manner, which requirement would apply to the faces which it is intended to bring into contact. (See Bed.) Again, it may be required that brickwork is to be laid in certain mortar with $\frac{3}{8}$-inch joints, such stipulation referring to the thickness of the mass of mortar between the bricks. Again, two timbers may be framed by a mortise and tenon joint, the term in such case being applied to the several contiguous surfaces, together with the parts immediately connected. In connecting lead pipes end to end, the solder forms a homogeneous mass completely enveloping the butting ends, the whole assemblage being known as a wiped joint.

Joints having specific compounded names derived from their formation or mode of connection (as, *e.g.*, dovetail joint) are not defined here, as their meaning is self-evident from the use of the attributive term. — D. N. B. S.

Abutment Joint; Abutting Joint. *A.* In carpentry, one formed where the end of one piece of wood is made to abut against the side of another, the grain of the respective parts being at right angles, or approximately so. The actual connection may be made in various ways.

B. In iron construction, the joint between two compression members whose axes are continuous, or nearly so.

Beaking Joint. One formed by several Heading Joints coming together in one continuous line; especially used in connection with the laying of floor plank.

Bed Joint. In masonry, one formed at the beds of two adjoining stones, and, therefore, horizontal, or nearly so. Among masons, commonly known specifically as " bed," as distinguished from the " joints," which are more or less vertical.

Bevel Joint. In general, any joint in which the meeting ends or edges are cut obliquely or with a Bevel, whether the joined pieces meet at an angle or in a continuous line. Specifically, same as Mitre Joint below, but usually restricted to mean such a joint when the pieces do not meet at ninety degrees.

Blown Joint. One formed in lead or other soft metal by means of the blowpipe, as, in plumbing, between lead pipes which are not subject to much pressure.

Bridle Joint. A joint for uniting the end of a timber with the side of another; the former having a deep groove or recess cut across the end so as to leave two projecting equal tongues, like tenons. These fit into recesses or notches cut in the edges of the second timber, leaving a ridge. A common method of securing the foot of a rafter to a tie beam. — (Riley.)

Butt Joint. Any joint formed by two Butts, *i.e.*, by pieces meeting end to end. More frequently used in carpentry than in other trades. (Compare Abutment Joint; Heading Joint.)

Compass Joint. A joint between two members, of which a part, usually circular, laps over, and is closely fitted to the similar part of the other, a round pin or pivot passing through both parts. In practice, as in the making of drawing instruments, one member has two nearly circular disks, separated from one another, and enclosing between them the single disk in which the other member terminates ; or one member has three disks, which enclose between them the two disks with which the other member terminates. If properly adjusted and smoothly planed such a joint allows of great uniformity of movement, the parts of the compass, or other utensil, moving one upon another freely and with equal pressure or firmness of grip at whatsoever angle they are adjusted.

Coursing Joint. The continuous joint between two *courses* of brick or stone masonry ; any horizontal joint as distinguished from a vertical or Heading Joint.

Dog Ear Joint. One formed at the corners of a trough or dish-shaped receptacle made from a sheet of metal. The edges of the sheet being turned up, the triangular portion left projecting at the corner is bent back against one of the sides and soldered, or otherwise secured.

Drip Joint. In metal roofing : —

A. A method of connecting two sheets so as to form a drip across the slope of a roof and prevent rain water from entering the joint.

B. A joint formed by overlapping the edges of adjoining sheets, the portions so joined being bent downward to form continuous channels following the slope of the roof. It has a form the reverse of a Roll. — (E. H. K.)

Faucet Joint. Same as Spigot and Faucet Joint (which see, under Spigot).

Feather Joint. A joint made by inserting a feather edge of one piece into a mortise or groove of another.

Flange Joint. One in which the two joined members have each a Flange, which are secured by bolts or rivets passed through the two. The term is especially used in connecting wrought-iron pipes whose extremities have perforated flanges or collars, by means of which they are bolted or riveted together, end to end.

Flat Joint. (As used in masonry, see Point, I.)

Flush Joint. Any joint in which the surfaces of the two joined pieces are Flush. In masonry, specifically, a Flat Joint. (See Point, I.)

Folding Joint. Any joint between two members which by means of it can be folded one upon the other, as for the flap or leaf of a Pembroke table ; specifically, a rule joint arranged for this purpose, or (where a narrow bearing and great stiffness are required) a compass joint.

Foliated Joint. A joint made by two overlapping rebated edges, showing a Flush Joint on each face. A form of joggle.

Gauged Joint. (As used in masonry, see Point, I.)

Heading Joint. One formed at the meeting of a header, or a heading, with the transverse piece or pieces.

Hick Joint. (As used in masonry, see Point, I.)

High Joint. (As used in masonry, see Point, I.)

Hook and Butt Joint. A form of Scarf, in which part of the thickness of the timbers forms a Butt Joint, the remainder being interlocked by one or more hook-shaped notches.

Joggle Joint. In cut stone, or the like, a joint between two blocks which fit one into the other by a joggle.

Key Joint. (As used in masonry, see Point, I.)

Knuckle Joint. (See Knuckle.)

Lap Joint ; Lapped Joint. One formed by lapping the adjoining pieces with little or no interlocking or framing. Thus, in sheet-metal work, such a joint is commonly made by simply overlapping the edges of two sheets without bending, and soldering them flat. In framing, the ends of two timbers are sometimes overlapped longitudinally and merely bolted together, or perhaps secured by keys and straps. (See Scarf.)

Mason's V Joint. (See Point, I.)

Match Joint ; Matched Joint. One formed by matched boards.

Mitre Joint ; Mitring Joint. One formed by two pieces meeting at an angle, the meeting ends or edges being equally bevelled so that the plane of the joint bisects the angle between the pieces. The term is commonly restricted to mean such a joint when the bevels are at forty-five degrees, thus making an angle of ninety degrees between the two pieces when joined. (See Bevel Joint, above.)

Peen Joint ; Pien Joint. In a stone stair, the joint between two steps which are secured by a pien check. (See Check.)

Pig Lug Joint. Same as Dog Ear Joint.

Pin Joint. One in which the meeting parts overlap, and are pierced to receive a pin. The common joint used for connecting the chords with the braces in American iron trusses.

Pipe Joint. A joint so made in connecting the ends of two lengths of pipe, that the interior is left of full size and even, and the joint is secured against leakage. Common examples are the Wiped Joint for lead pipe and the usual connection of iron pipe by means of hubs, with or without screw threads. (See Coupling ; Plumbing.)

Plumb Joint. In sheet-metal work, a joint made by merely lapping the edges and soldering them together flat.

Prop Joint. Same as Rule Joint.

Ring Joint. A flange joint formed at the meeting of two circular flanges, as in securing wrought-iron pipes end to end.

Roll Joint. In sheet-metal work, a joint formed by rolling the edges of adjoining sheets together and then flattening the roll.

Rule Joint. A joint between two leaves or flaps of equal thickness, either or both of which is movable about the joint. One part has a half round and fillet which fit a cove and fillet on the other, the pivot (usually formed by a hinge) being at the common centre. This is the usual way of jointing a leaf of a table to the fixed top.

Rust Joint. In metal work and plumbing, an inferior joint made by a mixture of iron filings with chemicals which produce rapid oxidation of the iron, so that the parts are thus rusted together.

Rustic Joint. In masonry, a joint formed in Rustication.

Saddle Joint. In a weathered course of masonry, as a coping or sill, a joint formed between two adjoining stones whose ends are cut higher than the surface of the weathering between. These projections at the ends are usually sloped or rounded away from the joint and toward the weathering, so as to shed water from the mortar.

Shove Joint. In bricklaying, a mortar joint formed when putting a brick into its place by shoving it over a full bed of mortar, so that some of the mortar is forced up into the interstices between the brick and the adjoining parts of the masonry. The method is advocated as a means of obtaining well-filled joints.

Slip Joint. A joint by which two parts are more or less connected while they are free to move, one along the other. Especially, such a joint between two masonry walls which allows the heavier wall to settle without affecting the lighter one.

Spigot Joint. One formed by the insertion of the spigot end of a pipe into the mouth or hub of another. (See Spigot.)

Splay Joint : Splayed Joint. In woodworking, a joint between two surfaces which are splayed with relation to the adjoining surfaces ; especially applied to the meeting rails of vertically sliding sash. No absolute distinction can be made between this and a bevelled joint.

Struck Joint. A mortar joint in facework dressed or finished with a pointer or striker. (See Strike, v.)

Tabled Joint. In cut stonework, a bed joint formed by a broad, shallow channel in the surface of one stone, into which fits a corresponding projection of the stone above or below. — (Riley.)

Water Joint. *A.* A joint through which water will not leak, as in the framework of a water gate, the gate of a canal lock, or as the junction of two pipes, etc.

B. Same as Drip Joint, above.

Wiped Joint. In connecting the ends of lead pipe, a joint made by the insertion of one into the other and securing the two together by

a mass of solder applied with a cloth with which it is wiped around the juncture, which is finally covered and concealed by a more or less spherical mass of the solder. In joining two ends of the same caliber, one is pared to a conical shape to be inserted into the other, which is reamed out to receive it. — D. N. B. S.

JOINT (v.). *A.* To form a Joint ; to construct with a joint or joints.

B. To prepare the edge or surface of a piece of material which it is intended to join with another, as by planing or rubbing, to insure close contact.

C. To finish the exposed portions of a Joint, especially, in Masonry, to embellish the mortar joints at the face of a wall by cutting grooves or otherwise shaping the material. (See Point, I (v.t.) ; Strike.)

JOINTER. Any tool for jointing in either sense of the verb joint ; or for finishing or embellishing a joint.

JOINTURE HOUSE. In England, a dwelling which by legal disposition attending a marriage is made the property, for a certain time, either of the married couple, or more especially of the woman, in case she survives her husband. Not to be confounded with Dower House.

JOIST. *A.* Any beam intended primarily for the construction or support of a floor, ceiling, or the like, and horizontal or nearly so. By extension, a sleeper as used for the support of a wooden floor over a masonry or fireproof floor.

B. Locally, in the United States, a stud or piece of scantling about three inches by four inches in size. (For the various kinds of Joist, see the terms under Beam.)

Split Joist. A piece of scantling as defined under Joist, *B*, but of half the size.

JOLY, EDMOND JEAN BAPTISTE THÉODORE RENÉ; architect; b. April 7, 1824; d. Sept. 25, 1892.

Architect of the *Chambre des Députés* (Palais Bourbon), Paris. In 1844 he entered the *École des Beaux Arts*, and in 1865 succeeded his father as architect in charge of the *Chambre des Députés*. (See next term.) In 1871 he was charged with the installation of the *Assemblée Nationale* at Bordeaux and later at Versailles.

Charles Lucas, in *Construction Moderne*, Oct. 1, 1892.

JOLY, JULES JEAN BAPTISTE DE; architect; b. Nov. 24, 1788, at Montpellier; d. Feb. 8, 1865.

Jules de Joly entered the *École des Beaux Arts* in 1808 and won the *Prix départemental* in 1815. In 1821 he was made architect of the Palais Bourbon, which he reconstructed for the *Chambre des Députés*. In 1840 he published his important monograph *Plans, coupes, élévations et détails de la restauration de la Chambre des Députés.*

Charles Lucas, in *La Grande Encyclopédie;* Bauchal, *Dictionnaire.*

JONES, INIGO; architect; b. July, 1573; d. June 21, 1652.

He was christened at the church of S. Bartholomew the Less, London, July 19, 1573, as "Enigo Jones the sonne of Enigo Jones." His artistic inclination developed early, especially in "Landskip Painting." A picture at Chiswick is ascribed to him. He went to Italy about the end of the sixteenth century, probably at the expense of the Earl of Pembroke, and after passing several years at Venice was invited to Denmark by Christian IV., brother-in-law of James I. of England. Jones returned to England before 1605, and from that time to 1613 was employed in arranging a brilliant series of masks and entertainments for the court. Two volumes of his costume designs are at Chiswick. To this period have been ascribed, without much reason, the garden front of S. John's College, Oxford, and other works in a mediæval style. From 1610 to 1612 he was Surveyor of the Works to Henry, Prince of Wales. In 1613 Jones made another visit to Italy and again in 1614. His copy of Palladio's *Architettura* with manuscript notes, at Worcester College, Oxford, bears the date Jan. 2, 1614. In 1615 he returned to England to become the King's Surveyor of Works. In 1618, for Charles I., Jones planned an immense palace at Whitehall to extend 950 feet along the Thames and 1280 feet from the river to S. James's Park. Of this design an unimportant part of one court was built and still stands, the famous Banqueting House. Jones served on the commissions for the renovation of old S. Paul's cathedral, and in 1633 began the façade with the splendid Corinthian portico which was one of his favourite works ; destroyed 1666. Lindsey House, built for Robert Bertie, Earl of Lindsey, still remains in Arch Row, Lincoln's Inn Fields. It was the beginning of a large scheme of improvement undertaken in 1620, which was never carried out. George Villiers, Duke of Buckingham, employed Jones to build the Water Gate of York House, which still stands. The church of S. Catherine Cree, London (1628–1630), is ascribed to him without documentary evidence. The porch of S. Mary's at Oxford is also ascribed to him. Jones's additions to Somerset House were destroyed in 1775. Shaftesbury House, Physicians' College, London, and other important works have disappeared. Ashburnham House in Little Dean's Yard, Westminster, remains. He designed the villa at Chiswick, the façade of Wilton, the Ionic bridge at Wilton, and other works. The little monument to his "Ancient poor friend," George Chapman, the

poet, is in the yard of the church of S. Giles-in-the-Fields, London. About 1631 he began for Francis Russell, fourth Earl of Bedford, famous piazza and church of Covent Garden, London. Inigo Jones was a Royalist in the Civil War and was captured at Basing House, October, 1643. He was buried in S. Bennett's church, Paul's Wharf, London, June 26, 1652. Many of his drawings of unexecuted schemes remain at Chiswick, in the British Museum, and elsewhere. In 1620 Inigo Jones was commissioned by the king to write an account of Stonehenge, which he supposed was a Roman ruin, and left notes on the subject which were published by John Webb in 1655.

Blomfield, *Inigo Jones* in *Portfolio,* 1889 ; Horne, *Inigo Jones* in *Century Guild Hobby Horse,* October, 1886 ; Belcher-Macartney, *Later Renaissance Architecture in England;* Loftie, *Inigo Jones and Wren;* Cunningham, *Life of Inigo Jones;* Kent, *Inigo Jones, Designs;* Campbell, *Vitruvius Britannicus.*

JONES, OWEN; architect and ornamental designer ; b. Feb. 15, 1809 ; d. April 19, 1874.

Son of Owen Jones (1741–1814), a Welsh antiquary. He studied at the Royal Academy, London. In 1830 he visited France and Italy ; and in 1833, Greece, Egypt, and Constantinople. In 1834 and again in 1837 he went to Granada, Spain, and made numerous drawings of the Alhambra. In 1851 he was appointed superintendent of the works at the Great Exhibition in London, and 1852 designed the Egyptian, Greek, Roman, and Alhambra courts at the Crystal Palace. Jones published *Plans, Elevations, Sections, and Details of the Alhambra* (2 vols. folio, 1842–1845) ; *The Illuminated Books of the Middle Ages* (folio, 1844) ; *The Polychromatic Ornament of Italy,* 1846 ; *The Grammar of Ornament* (folio, 100 plates, London, 1858, 2d ed., 1865, 112 plates).

JORDAN, ESTEBAN; sculptor, painter, and architect ; b. 1543 ; d. 1603.

He was probably a pupil of Berruguete (see Berruguete) and studied in Italy. He made the altar of the church of the Magdalen at Valladolid.

Bermudez, *Diccionario.*

JOSS HOUSE. In the semi-English language of traders in the East, a Chinese temple. The term "joss," meaning a divinity, seems to be a mispronunciation by the Chinese of the Portuguese word *deos.*

JOST, THOMAS; bell founder.

His known works were dated between 1470 and 1480. In 1782 one of his bells, called the *Rathsglocke,* or bell of the council, still existed in the cathedral of Strasburg. Another is now at the parish church of Saverne in Alsace.

Gérard, *Les Artistes de l'Alsace.*

JOUR. In French, primarily the day ; hence, daylight, and used in the sense of an opening for the admission of light. In English, used in such compounds as abatjour, à jour.

JOURDRAIN, ABBOT. (See Chambers, Thomas de.)

JUAN DE BADAJOZ; sculptor and architect.

Juan designed and, about the year 1537, directed, the execution of the plateresque work of the cloister of S. Zoil de Carrion de los Condes, Spain. He was architect of the cathedral of Leon, Spain, and completed the principal façade of the monastery of S. Marcos in that city.

Bermudez, *Diccionario historico*.

JUAN BAUTISTA DE TOLEDO; architect.

Studied in Rome, especially under the influence of Michelangelo Buonarroti (see Buonarroti). He was recalled to Spain by Philip II. His most important work is the palace of the Escorial which was begun by him in 1563 and finished by Juan de Herrera (see Herrera, J. de). He built the façade of the church of Descalzas Reales at Madrid, and other important works.

Seubert, *Künstler-lexicon*.

JUBÉ. In French, primarily a pulpit, reading desk, or ambon. In later usage, the screen at the western end of a choir, and separating it from the nave or crossing. The change of signification is evidently caused by the use of some part of this screen as a platform from which to preach to the laity. Some jubés, even of recent date, have projecting balconies fit for that purpose. Magnificent ones of late Gothic style exist in Belgium, and there are in France some of still later date, of which a marked instance is that of the cathedral of Limoges, dating from the sixteenth century, but now removed and set up in another part of the church. (See Choir Screen and references.) — R. S.

JUDAS. A small opening in a door of entrance, as to a dwelling, for the purpose of seeing a would-be visitor before opening the door. Also, in the door of a prisoner's cell, arranged so that the warden can see the prisoner. (Compare Vasistas.)

JULIO ROMANO. (See Pippi, Giulio.)

JUMEL, ROBERT; architect; d. about 1523.

In 1504 he became superintending architect of the church of S. Gervais et S. Protais at Gisors, France. In 1523, which was probably the time of his death, he was superseded by Robert Grappin (see Grappin, R.).

De Laborde, *Gisors;* Palustre, *Renaissance*.

JUMMA MUSJID. In India, the principal mosque of a town. That at Delhi, of red sandstone with cupolas of marble and standing on a high terrace, is of the Mohammedan epoch, finished in 1648. That of Agra is at Fatehpûr Sikri, outside the fortress where the other important buildings are situated, built of red sandstone with bands and other inlays of white marble, and finished about 1644. That at Bijapur has never been finished. It dates from 1560 and is of colossal size, with a great cupola and several minor ones. Other remarkable examples are at Cambay, Champanir, Ahmedabad, and Janupûr. Written also Jami Masjid. — R. S.

JUMP. An abrupt change of level in masonry, as in the base of a foundation wall, or a course of stonework which is adjusted to a slope by an occasional step. (See Step.)

JUNCTION BOX. (See Electrical Appliances.)

JUSTE, ANTOINE (ANTONIO DI GIUSTO BETTI); sculptor and architect; b. about 1479; d. September, 1519.

The oldest of the three brothers Juste, Italian sculptors in France in the early sixteenth century. He was probably the chief author of the monument of the Bishop Thomas James at Dol, Ille-et-Vilaine, France, although the name of Jean is inscribed upon the work. He appears in the records of the château of Gaillon in 1508–1509 (Deville, op. cit.). Antoine was undoubtedly associated with the other members of his family in the construction of the monument to Louis XII. at Saint-Denis, although there is no record of that fact.

Deville, *Comptes de Gaillon*. (See also Juste, Jean.)

JUSTE, JEAN (GIOVANNI DI GIUSTO BETTI); sculptor and architect; b. 1485; d. 1549.

Jean Juste was the most important member of a family of Italian sculptors which appears in France in the early part of the sixteenth century. The investigations of Gaetano Milanesi have shown that the family name was really Betti, and that they came from the village of Saint Martino a Mensola, near Florence, Italy. Giusto Betti had a son, Andrea, whose three sons, Antoine (see Juste, A.), André, and Jean, appear to have been brought to France to make the monument of Thomas James, Bishop of Dol, who died April 5, 1504. The name of Jean Juste appears in an inscription on this monument. In a book by Jean Brèche (ad *Titulum Pandectarum*, Lyons, 1556), he is mentioned as the author of the monument to Louis XII. in the church of Saint-Denis, near Paris. Jean was probably assisted in the construction of this monument by the other members of his family. (See articles above.)

Anatole de Montaiglon, *La famille des Juste;* A. de Montaiglon, *Noveaux documents sur Jehan Juste et Juste de Juste* in *Nouvelles Archives;* De Laborde, *Comptes des bâtiments du roi*.

JUSTE, JUSTE DE (GIUSTO DI ANTONIO GIUSTO); architect and sculptor.

Juste de Juste was a son of Antoine Juste (see Juste, A.). He was associated with the other members of his family in the construction of the monument of Louis XII. in the church at Saint-Denis, near Paris.

(For bibliography and family history, see Juste, Jean.)

JUTTY. Same as Jetty.

JUVARA (IVARA), FILIPPO; architect; b. 1685 (at Messina); d. 1735 (at Madrid).

Juvara was a pupil of Carlo Fontana (see Fontana, C.). His work, although done in the Baroque period, is marked by simplicity and much classical refinement. His life was spent mainly in the service of the dukes of Savoy, at Turin, Italy. Juvara's chief monument is the monastery of the Superga near Turin, which shows the influence of contemporary French practice. The Villa Stupinigi, near Turin, was probably designed by him. Many villas in Piedmont were built by him. One of his most characteristic works is the façade of the Palazzo Madama, Turin, 1710, with its fine stairway. He continued the construction of the ducal palace at Lucca, begun by Bartolommeo Ammanati (see Ammanati). At Mantua, Juvara built the cupola of the church of S. Andrea, designed by Leon Battista Alberti two centuries before. Juvara's last years were spent in Spain and Portugal.

Gurlitt, *Geschichte des Barockstiles in Italien;* Ebe, *Spät-Renaissance;* Milizia, *Memorie.*

K

KAABAH. The central shrine of the Mohammedan religion, standing in the heart of Mecca and in the courtyard of the great mosque. It is a perfectly plain, nearly cubical mass, which, at certain times, is concealed by a black cloth cover, which fits it closely.

KAGGE; KAGGI. An Eskimo assembly house. It is usually about 15 feet high, and 20 feet in diameter, built of snow after the style of an Iglugeak. (Also see Assembly House.)

KAGSSE. Same as Kagge.

KAHRI JAMI (more properly Kahiré Djami or Kahrije Dshami, as in the German authorities cited). In Constantinople, originally, the church of a great monastery dating from the fifth century, the church itself of the twelfth century, with later additions. It is famous for the mosaics with which the interior is lined, and in their character and arrangement there is visible a strong resemblance to those of S. Mark's in Venice. The building remains in use as a Greek church.

Von Hammer, *Constantinopolis und der Bosporus;* Salzenberg, *Baudenkmale von Constantinopel.*

KAILAS TEMPLE. At Ellora; a rock-cut temple of great size and elaboration of detail. A plan and small view are given by Fergusson. Called also Kylas.

KALAMIS. (See Calamis.)

KALLIKRATES. (See Callicrates.)

KALLIMACHOS. (See Callimachos.)

KALSOMINE. A liquid mixture for colouring plastered walls, consisting of glue, chalk, and water coloured with pigment. Commonly called water colour. Only one coat can be applied. If it is desired to change the tone or repaint the wall surface the first coat must be washed off, so that in the end it often proves an expensive process. If an excess of glue is used the colour scales off. The slightest moisture destroys it. Also written Calcimine.
— FREDERIC CROWNINSHIELD.

KAMPEN. (See Campen.)

KANACHOS. (See Canachus.)

KANG. In Chinese building, a structure somewhat like a German stove of the simpler pattern ; a mass of simple masonry within which a fire is kept burning while the exterior serves to lie upon by night or to sit upon by day, as in old German houses, the mass of masonry being so considerable that the heat of the exterior never becomes excessive.

Doolittle, *Social Life of the Chinese.*

KARLSBRÜCKE. A bridge at Prague, in Bohemia, built during the fourteenth and fifteenth centuries, and noted for its remarkable towers of defence, which have kept their picturesque appearance, and are among the most marked attractions of the city. The buttresses of the bridge are ornamented with statues and groups of ecclesiastical subjects, but these are all much later than the structure.

KARLSKIRCHE. At Vienna. (See church of S. Carlo Borromeo, under Church.)

KARMANG. The permanent winter house of the central Eskimo. Its walls are usually of stone and whale ribs, and, partly, the sides of the excavation that forms its basis. The site is usually a slope, and the entrance is cut for 15 or 20 feet into this slope, gradually rising to the floor of the Karmang, which is a trifle higher than the end of this passage. The passage is covered with large stone slabs. Over the entrance to the main house that is to be a whale rib is fixed, arch up, to which a number of poles are lashed, their other ends resting on the wall. Over these poles and the rib sealskins are stretched, then a thick layer of the little shrubby plant, andromeda, is laid on, and over all another thickness of skins is stretched. The fastenings are usually heavy stones. The arch of the whale rib is filled in with translucent seal intestines for a window. The interior of the house is arranged after the ordinary Eskimo fashion (see Iglu ; Iglugeak). The frame is sometimes made entirely of whale ribs, and sometimes the walls are all above ground, with an entrance of snow. Written also Qarmang.

Dr. F. Boas, *6th Annual Report of the U. S. Bureau of Ethnology;* Turner, *11th An. Rep. Bu. Eth. ;* and other papers in these Reports. — F. S. D.

KARRIGI. Same as Kagge.

KASHGA. An Alaskan Eskimo house used as a sort of town hall. Similar to a Kiva in its use. — F. S. D.

KASHIM. An Eskimo assembly house. (See Assembly House.) Written also kashimi. — F. S. D.

KAYATA. The smallest lodge of the Klamaths. (See Latchash.) — F. S. D.

KAYSER, KARL; d. Sept. 2, 1895.

An architect of Vienna, Austria, who went to the city of Mexico, and was employed by Maximilian, Emperor of Mexico, in the reconstruction and restoration of palaces there. After the death of Maximilian he returned to Vienna, and modernized several mediæval and baroque palaces.

Nekrologie in *Kunstchronik,* Oct. 24, 1895.

KEEL. A moulding, of which the profile resembles the cross section of the lower part of a ship's hull, showing the keel and bilges. Similar to Brace Moulding.

KEEP. Same as Donjon.

KEEPER'S HOUSE. On a British estate, the dwelling provided for a gamekeeper.

KEEPER'S LODGE. Same as Keeper's House, except that in the case of a royal park the building may become of considerable size, and may be used for other than merely game-protecting purposes. (See Lodge.)

KEEPING ROOM. The sitting room, as of a family, as distinguished from a room used for ceremony or entertainment. This term, apparently local in modern England, is used throughout the northern United States, especially outside of the large towns.

KEG HOUSE. A saloon, or bar, where wines and liquors are kept in small varnished kegs instead of glass bottles. This kind of saloon was in vogue on the plains about the time of the building of the Union Pacific Railway. — F. S. D.

KELDERMANS VAN MANSDALE, ANDRIES; architect; b. before 1488.

With his son Anthonis he built the old church of Bergen Op Zoom, Holland. In 1454 he began the great tower of the Lievensmonsterkerk at Zieriksee, Holland, which was never finished. He built also the city halls of Veere and Middleburg.

Galland, *Holländische Baukunst.*

KELDERMANS VAN MANSDALE, ANTHONIS; architect; d. 1512 at Mechlin (Malines), Belgium.

A son of the preceding. He was associated with his father in the construction of the town hall at Middleburg, Holland, and other important buildings. In 1497 he was made architect of the Liebfrauenkirche at Veere. With him were associated his brothers, Matheus and Rombout (see below).

Galland, *Holländische Baukunst.*

KELDERMANS VAN MANSDALE, MATHEUS; architect and sculptor.

Born at Mechlin, Belgium, the son of Anthonis Keldermans. In 1478–1479 he worked on the Porte de Bruxelles at Mechlin, and in 1487–1498 on the church of Notre Dame at Antwerp. His work is in the last period of the Gothic style.

Biographie Nationale de Belgique.

KELDERMANS VAN MANSDALE, ROMBOUT; architect.

Born at Mechlin, Belgium, the son of Anthonis Keldermans. In 1515 he was made *maître des maçonneries* of the city of Mechlin, and executed numerous important works at the palace of Marguerite d'Autriche in that city. He erected numerous important buildings in Belgium.

Biographie Nationale de Belgique.

KELTIC: Cross of Muredach, Monasterboice, Ireland, of the Type known as Keltic Cross, and bearing Keltic Decorative Sculpture.

KELTIC (adj.). Belonging to the people who formerly inhabited, almost exclusively, the whole of Western Europe, and whose monuments are found especially in France and Great Britain. (For the more elaborate and decorative works, see Ireland, Architecture of; Scotland, Architecture of; for the rough stone monuments, see Megalithic, and references.)

KEMP, GEORGE MEIKLE; architect; b. 1795; d. 1844.

He was apprenticed to a carpenter, and made a careful study of Gothic architecture. Kemp designed, in 1838, the monument to Sir Walter Scott, in Edinburgh, and was engaged in its erection when he died.

Bonnar, *George Meikle Kemp.*

KEMPTEN. (See Andreas von Kempten.)

KENNEL. *A.* A doghouse, whether a wooden boxlike structure 4 or 5 feet long, for a single dog, or an elaborate building carefully planned and arranged for lodging a large pack. The most important kennels are those provided for fox hounds in England and boar hounds in France. They have to be planned like elaborate stables, with yards for exercising, washing, and brushing, separate compartments for dogs that are sick, or thought to be, a separate yard and shelter for puppies, and a special kitchen connected with a feeding house and with a place for the storage of food. One establishment in England is given as being 400 feet long.

B. In England, a gutter, as in a paved street, or in a stable or cowyard.

KENT, WILLIAM; painter, architect, and landscape gardener; b. 1685 (in Yorkshire); d. April 12, 1748.

He went to London in 1704, and in 1710 to Rome. Returning to England in 1719, he became a *protégé* of Lord Burlington (see Boyle, Richard). He assisted Lord Burlington, and built Devonshire House, Piccadilly, and the Horseguards, Whitehall; and altered and decorated the great country houses of Stowe, Houghton, and Holkham. Kent was successful as a designer of gardens, his most important work being the park at Stowe.

Blomfield, *Renaissance Architecture in England;* Blomfield, *The Formal Garden in England.*

KEPHISODOTOS. (See Cephisodotus.)

KERAMICS. *A.* The art and industry of making objects of baked clay.

B. Objects made of baked clay taken collectively.

The arts of baked clay applicable to architecture are of two sorts; in one the clay surface, whether flat or modelled, is left without glaze or polish of any kind. (See Brick; Stoneware; Terra Cotta; Tile.) In the other, which forms the subject of the present article, the processes of the potter are employed.

The most common forms of earthenware in use in architecture are floor, roof, and wall tiling, the last having for its primary object the

protection of buildings by an indestructible surface, capable of resisting the effects of weather and changes of temperature. The glazed or enamelled face which offers most opportunity for the characteristic colours of pottery in decoration is less durable under friction than bodies

KERAMICS IN ARCHITECTURE: CLOISTER OF SAN STEFANO, BOLOGNA.

The arches and the superstructure of brick of two colours, cast to shape, and of small tiles.

of a semivitreous fracture (such as porcelain or stoneware), and consequently less adapted for floor tiling than for walls or roofs. When used for this purpose on ordinary earthenware bodies, the floor is slippery so long as the glaze retains its freshness, and as soon as it is worn down by use the soft substratum offers little resistance, and in any case its decoration is quickly destroyed. The majolica pavements of the Italian Cinquecento offer extreme instances of this, as in the floor of Raphael's Loggie in the Vatican, and the church of S. Maria del Popolo in Rome, as also in churches at Bologna, Parma, Venice, and Siena, dating from 1480 onwards. The floor tiles depending for hardness on a glazed surface that have stood the test of time best are those made on the Spanish or Spanish-Moorish system, in compartments filled in with thick coloured glazes, just as the enamel fills the compartments of Cloisonné ware. These tiles of the sixteenth and seventeenth centuries were an article of export, as we find them in Italy, especially in Genoa, and elsewhere. The tiles in the Mayor's chapel at Bristol are of this class.

In the mediæval floor tile the soft lead glazes have disappeared, except in very sheltered positions, leaving the incised patterns exposed to the wear of feet, so that in many cases only the harder clay is left. Tiles of this class have been called Norman tiles, as they are more frequent in Normandy than elsewhere, and of much earlier date. The earliest known, probably, are those from the palace of the dukes of Normandy, built within the precinct of the abbey of S. Étienne at Caen, and in England those from Castle Acre, Norfolk, of about the end of the thirteenth century. There is a very fine example in the chapter house at Westminster, probably of a rather later date.

The practice of inlaying patterns (of which the foregoing are instances) is of a very great antiquity, as Egyptian examples exist of 1200 B.C. in which the coloured glass, sometimes called porcelain, forms an inlaid pattern. Nevertheless, it is only in modern times that the system has reached mechanical perfection in the so-called encaustic paving tile, — an ill-applied name, having no connection with the manufacture, which depends for its success on the even hardness of the bodies employed.

Glazed Roofing Tiles. These are universal in China, and in Persia are an important element of external decoration. In Europe they are somewhat uncommon, except in Germany and France. A notable example exists in the thirteenth-century church of S. Stephen at Vienna, the high pitched roof being completely covered with lozenge-shaped tiles coloured and glazed. In France mediæval examples are found, as in the church of Bénissons-Dieu (Loire), in S. Martin-des-Champs, Paris, and at Dijon. In roofs of a later period we find the *épis* or small pinnacles of seventeenth-century châteaux covered in with glazed earthenware, which is also used on the ridges and angles.

Wall tiling as a means of colour and decoration is of the highest antiquity. In the British Museum are a number of glazed tiles from the palace of Rameses at Tel-el-Yehûdiyeh in the Delta, decorated with processions of captives, ornamental work, and the names and titles of the monarch. These are of about 1400 B.C., and are therefore older than the frieze from the palace of Susa, found by M. Dieulafoy, and now in the Louvre. This is more properly brickwork, resembling the glazed bricks of the walls of Nineveh and Babylon (1200 B.C.), and belongs to the later Assyrian period. The continuity of the art in Persia may be assumed from the resemblance of the materials to that of those employed later, of which the earliest known are the hexagonal and star-shaped tiles, decorated with lustre, found in the ruins of Rhè or Rhey (Rhages), south of the Caspian Sea, a city destroyed 600 years ago. From this time to the climax of the art under Shah Abbas (1600 A.D.) the record is continuous. It reached its greatest splendour in the centuries following the Arab Conquest, and spread through the countries under Mahommedan rule in Asia and Africa, and thence to Spain, where the latest effect of its influence is to be found in the Alhambra, which, if not actually the work of Persians, is the direct outcome of the introduction of Persian art by the Moorish successors of the Khalifs of Cordova. As decorative results the geometrically designed Alhambra tiles bear no comparison with the Oriental Persian work, which still remains without a rival in Western Europe.

The so-called Damascus tiles are of the Persian type, and from this source probably the mosques of Cairo were supplied. The Rhodian variety, distinguished by the introduction of a bright iron red colour not found in the same perfection elsewhere, is supposed to have been made at Lindus by the descendants of Persian prisoners transported there by the crusaders.

In China coloured tiles are largely used in exterior work, the colours being varied in private houses according to the rank of the occupant. The celebrated tower of porcelain at Nanking, destroyed by the Taepings in 1853, was so called because the lowest of its nine stories was covered with glazed brick, either of a coarse porcelain or faced with a white slip. The eaves over the balconies were roofed in with green tiles, and the window jambs of glazed porcelain modelled in relief.

In Europe tile work in architecture has never equalled that of eastern countries in importance. But the keramic art has passed into fresh phases, as in the case of the glazed sculpture of the Italian Cinquecento. The knowledge inherited from the Arab civilization of Spain was certainly communicated to Italy, and came in contact with the Renaissance in the work of Luca della Robbia, who has been credited with the independent rediscovery of the white tin glaze on which the character of his work mainly depends. The question of this rediscovery has provoked much discussion. But the real interest of his work lies in the fact that it is the only example of the union of a great original school of sculpture with a development of colour in keramics. This development was nevertheless limited, and the defect of the work is in the crudity and opacity of some of the tints. But the skill shown in the use of limited means is an earnest of what would have resulted had his successors inherited the spirit in which he worked. His art disappears early in the sixteenth century, but his name is still applied to similar work, as undertaken in our own times. (See Robbia Work.)

Methods of Manufacture of Tiles. These may be divided into (1) wire cutting from wet clay; (2) moulding; (3) stamping from wet dust. In the first the tiles are cut, one at a time, on a gauge, or in quantity, by wires placed across the mouth of a pressing machine or pug mill. In either case the necessary wetness of the body affects the shape of the tile when dry. The same is in a measure true of moulding, though less in proportion to the dryness of the clay. It is, however, much slower. In the third process the tile may be said to be formed ready dried, the damp dust that is pressed into a mould containing so little water that the tiles may be carried direct to the oven. They are more fragile in this state than when made from wet clay, and in some cases cannot be fired in a block, each tile requiring to be supported independently. As the body is at least as dense, this points to a difference in the molecular structure, and may account for the great susceptibility to frost sometimes apparent in tiles of this class.

The methods of colouring and glazing tiles are substantially identical with those employed in pottery. The range of colour available for decoration is really much more extensive, owing to the semimosaic character of tile work. It is in fact possible to employ in the same scheme of colour a number of results of processes which would be impossible on a single plaque. So great a choice of materials often proves in unskilful hands rather an embarrassment than an advantage. The tile painter's resources may be said to be coextensive with the whole range of coloured silicates, and to contain analogues of every known mineral colour employed in painting, as well as one or two (notably the ruby of copper) which approach the splendour of vegetable dyes. To these should be added the various applications of pure metal possible in pottery, and the peculiar lustres of copper and silver; however, the difficulty of producing these with certainty must always be an obstacle to their employment.

Gold, though so important in the decoration of pottery, has been little used in the keramic work of architecture. In mosaic work proper the effect of the small tesseræ is enhanced by the distributed tint of the joint, the right proportion of this to the whole surface being an essential of success. In tile design the actual size of the joint is a negligible consideration. But the shape of the tile itself is the basis of the ornament painted on it, in any architectonic treatment, although in purely pictorial decoration it may be concealed. The decoration may consist of an inlay of plain coloured tiles, or may be painted over a tile surface irrespective of the jointing, which in this case is usually hidden as much as possible, often perhaps more than is necessary. The Spanish tile of the sixteenth century is probably the best example of the first class of work; while the Dutch pictures, usually in blue monochrome, and often covering a large surface of tiles, are the extremest limit of the second. The finest work is to be found between these two extremes, as in the early Persian work before mentioned, in which a coloured and lustred decoration combines with the tile form, the result being insurpassable in richness.

It is a task which still remains open to the artist to make a satisfactory use of the whole of the resources of the keramic art in architecture. The use of external glazed work is on the increase, the apprehension formerly entertained that the glossy effect on buildings would be unpleasant having yielded to experience. As a fact, the reflection out of doors is less perceptible than under a roof and is not seen at all at certain angles. The effects of colour in modern works are certainly inferior to their ancient prototypes. Possibly the commercial necessity for the rapid transaction of business is responsible for this, at least as much as artistic incapacity. (For modern attempts at architectural decoration in keramics, see Polychromy; Sculpture; Stoneware; Terra Cotta.)

— WILLIAM DE MORGAN.

The works cited in any Bibliography of Pottery and Porcelain may be consulted, as Prime, *Pottery and Porcelain;* Deck, *La Faïence;* Fortnum, *Descriptive Catalogue of Maiolica, South Kensington Museum;* and Borrmann's book named below. Consult also Amé, *Les carrelages émaillés du moyen âge et de la renaissance;* Brenci and Lessing, *Majolika-Fliesen aus Siena, 1500–1550;* Jacobsthal, *Süd-Italienische Fliesen-Ornamente;* Dieulafoy, *L'art antique de la Perse;* Borrmann, *Die Keramik in der Baukunst* (forms part of the Darmstadt *Handbuch der Architektur*); and the articles by Professor Marquand on the works of the Della Robbia family. The books on architectural decoration contain much about tile pavements and the like.

KERB.   Same as Curb.

KERF.   Same as Curf.

KEXEN.   Among the northern American Indians, a symbolical pole. (See Canada, Architecture of.)

KEY.   *A.* An instrument for fastening and unfastening a lock; capable of being inserted or withdrawn at pleasure, and when withdrawn, leaving the lock incapable of being opened or shut except by violence. The principal parts of an ordinary key are as follows: —

Bow — the enlargement at one end of the shank whereby the key is turned by the fingers. *Bit* — the lug at the end of the shank which fits into the lock and raises the tumbler and turns the bolt of the lock. The bit is cut and grooved to fit itself to the various wards and levers of the lock. *Shank* — the shaft connecting the bow and bit.

In the East, keys are commonly of wood, and a series of metal pins set into the wooden bar of the key can be adjusted to holes on the lock, thus raising tumblers and allowing the latch to be withdrawn.

The metal keys of the Middle Ages and the succeeding centuries were often the medium of exquisite decoration, not merely in the graceful and picturesque proportion of the parts of the key proper, — bit, shank, and bow; but also in the way of delicate chasing and even elaborate inlay of other materials than iron. Locks and keys of extraordinary beauty have been preserved when the wooden chests which they were made for have disappeared, and these are among the jewels of our collections of ornamental art. — R. S.

B. A wedge, or a tapering piece or member, used singly, or in pairs, as a means of drawing two parts together and tightly securing them when it is forced into an aperture prepared for the purpose; or as a means of holding two members or surfaces apart; hence, a member for a similar purpose, whether so shaped or not, designed for insertion into recesses in two or more adjoining parts, and commonly secured in place by wedges or keys of the specified form. Thus, a key may be used instead of a cleat for

KEY (IN SENSE B): WEDGES OR PINS HOLDING IN PLACE THE FRAMING OF A SWISS TIMBER HOUSE.

securing together a number of boards edge to edge; and will be itself formed of a tapering board forced into a corresponding groove cut across the assembled boards; the cross section of such a key and its corresponding groove has usually a dovetail shape, flaring inward, for greater security. A common use of keys is in heavy framing, as in forming a scarf joint, or assembling the parts of a truss. For the last purpose, a key is commonly of iron, and known as a cotter, and used in connection with a gib, or gibs.

C. In plastering, or similar work, that part of the plastic material which enters into the interstices, or clings to the rough surface, of the backing or prepared support; and by its adherence sustains the coat of mortar, or like material. Thus, the first coat of plaster applied to lathing forms a key when pressed through the spaces arranged for it; and this coat being "scratched" or roughened enables the next coat to form a key. — D. N. B. S.

Blank Key. A key before the bit or other part is finished or shaped to fit any particular lock.

Change Key. One fashioned to fit but one of a set of locks, as distinguished from the Master Key which controls the entire series.

Desk Key. A reversible key as commonly used for the locking of the top of a desk; usually small and of simple form.

Extension Key. One with a "telescope" shank, the shank of the bow working in the cylindrical shank of the bit. Used as a Sliding-door Key.

Flat Key. One fashioned entirely from a flat strip of metal. A form commonly used for latch keys and the like, because convenient for carrying.

Folding Key. A key with a joint in the shank allowing the bit to fold back upon the bow.

Latch Key. A key to open a latch, in the modern sense of that term. (See also Latch Lock, under Lock.)

Master Key. One so fashioned that it will lock and unlock all of a particular set of locks, each differing slightly from the other. (See Change Key.)

Night Key. One for opening a night latch. (See Latch and Latch Lock, under Lock.)

Reversible Key. One having two similar bits, one on each side of the shank, permitting the key to be inserted in its lock either side up, and operating the lock by a half turn of the key.

Skeleton Key. An instrument, usually a slim strip of metal, used for picking locks.

Sliding Door Key. One fitted for the lock of a sliding door, the shank being so arranged by means of a joint, or "extension," that the bow may be turned close to the countersunk escutcheon and clear the jamb strips of the sliding door pocket. — F. B. H.

KEY, LIEVEN DE; architect and sculptor.

An architect who practised in Leiden and Haarlem, Holland, toward the close of the sixteenth century. His chief work is the Renaissance façade and stairway of the Stadhuis or Town Hall of Leiden. He built the *Ondemannenhaus* and the tower of the church of S. Anna at Haarlem.

Galland, *Holländische Baukunst.*

KEYHOLE. A hole for the reception of a key, in any sense; more specifically, the aperture by which a key (*A*) is inserted into a lock.

KEYSER (KEISER), HENDRICK CORNELISZOON DE; architect and sculptor: b. May 15, 1565; d. 1621.

One of the most important Dutch architects. He was a pupil of Cornelis Bloemaart (see Bloemaart) and studied in France. He established himself with Bloemaart at Amsterdam in 1591. July 19, 1594, he was appointed sculptor and architect to the city of Amsterdam, and in this capacity had general supervision of the artistic work done by the city. De Keyser made the cartoons for the windows in the church of S. John at Gouda, Holland, which were presented by the city of Amsterdam. He made the monument to Erasmus in the Groote Markt at Rotterdam, and the monument to William, Prince of Orange, in the Groote Kerk at Delft. He built many of the ornamental gates in the fortifications of Amsterdam. De Keyser built also the court of the East India House and the Exchange at Amsterdam. At Hoorn, Holland, he built the Hoogerbeets monument, and the front of the Oosterkerk, 1615. His son Pieter de

PLATE XXV

KHAN

Two views of the interior court of one between Bagdad and the ruins of Babylon, that is to say, in the narrow tract of flat land between the great rivers, Tigris and Euphrates, and properly called Mesopotamia. The niches roofed with four-centred pointed arches when on the ground level are stables ; when on a slightly higher level are lodging-rooms, — these being the sole accommodations for beast or man. Pieces of stuff hung upon ropes afford such privacy as is to be had.

Keyser succeeded him and finished many of his works.

Immerzeel, *Hollandsche en Vlaamsche Kunstschilders;* Kramm, *Holländische Baukunst.*

KEYSER, PIETER DE. (See Keyser, Hendrick.)

KEYSTONE. A key or wedge of stone; in general, the same as voussoir. The term is usually restricted to mean a voussoir at the crown of the arch, — coming thus in the middle of the archivolt, — although any voussoir may be considered as a key, especially the last one placed, which thus *keys* the whole system together.

KEY UP (v.). To raise slightly a structure built of, or secured by, keys, by forcing the keys into the prepared spaces. Thus, in an arch, the last voussoir, serving as a key, may be shaped slightly too large and then be driven into place, by which process the entire arch ring is crowned up higher, even to the extent of raising it entirely from the centring. A similar operation is frequently performed at the base of a settled wall which is to be underpinned.

KHAN. A caravanserai; especially one of the Turkish empire. It is usually a place of shelter merely, without further provision for travellers. When built by a rich man for a charitable motive, as is common, the courtyards of the larger khans have some architectural pretensions, the separate chambers being vaulted and open toward the court with flights of steps of solid masonry leading to an upper story. The outside wall is plain, and generally without openings, being intended for protection against sudden attacks, and the gate is strongly secured.

KHMER. (See Kmer.)

KIBLAH. (Arabic; a thing adored, or looked to with reverence.) The sacred point toward which praying worshippers look; with the Moslems, the Kaaba at Mecca. The mihrab in a mosque is supposed to mark the direction of this.

KINGBOLT. A rod or long bolt taking the place of a king-post.

KING CLOSER. (See under Closer.)

KING POST. (See under Post.)

KING ROD. A vertical tie rod serving the purpose of a king-post.

KIOSK; KIOSQUE. *A.* In the Levant, a summer palace, a pavilion, or place of temporary resort. (See the subtitles.)

B. A small and usually open building used for subordinate or temporary purposes. In this sense, the term is applied to Oriental summer houses and garden houses, in Paris to the booths in which newspapers and the like are sold, and generally to a roofed pavilion for musicians, a place of shelter in a public park, or the like.

Bagdad Kiosk. In Constantinople; a fine piece of Turkish architecture, dating from the beginning of the sixteenth century.

Chiuli Kiosk. At Constantinople; a fine specimen of Turkish architecture, thought to have been built in the middle of the fifteenth century, but decorated, and lined and faced with painted tiles at a somewhat later time. It is now used to contain part of the collection of the Imperial Museum of Antiquities, and has lost much of its beauty.

Yildiz Kiosk. Near Constantinople, on the European shore of the Bosporus; a pavilion belonging to the Sultan of Turkey and used by him for stately entertainments. As the present Sultan (1900) resides here for the greater part of the time, the name of the palace has passed into the newspapers as equivalent to the Turkish court and government.

KIOUM. In Burmah, a Buddhist monastery. (See Farther India, Architecture of.)

KIRK. A place of Christian worship, especially in Scotland. The term is the Lowland Scotch form of the word "church."

KISHONI. The uncovered shade erected by the Moki Indians in their fields. Cottonwood saplings are set up in the ground, forming a slight curve, with convex side toward the south. Brush is then laid with stems upward all around the outside to a height of six or seven feet, and fastened by bands of small cottonwood branches, tied to the uprights by means of withes.
— F. S. D.

KISI. A kind of construction where poles are set up and layers of brush fastened upon them. (See Kishoni.)

KISTVAEN. Same as Cistvaen.

KITCHEN. A room intended for the preparation and cooking of food. The kitchen is usually located in the basement of city houses, and in the basement or in a semidetached wing on the ground floor of country houses. The plan of locating the kitchen on the top floor of the house, to avoid the cooking smells pervading the entire house, though followed in some modern club-houses and the like, is open to objections. A kitchen should be roomy, conveniently planned, yet not too large, for this increases the labour of cooking and dish-washing operations. Essential requirements are plenty of light, good ventilation, and absence of superfluous woodwork. The walls should be waterproofed several feet in height, either oil-painted or lined with glazed tiles or marble, or faced with enamelled brick. Floors may be oiled or varnished, or covered with linoleum or oil cloth. White or coloured tile flooring is desirable, particularly at the sink, and sometimes at the range and the hot-water boiler. Windows on opposite sides of a kitchen afford cross ventilation; they should always have screens to keep out the flies. A family kitchen should contain a good-sized brick-set or portable coal range (called in England "kitchener"), with or without charcoal broiler; and often a hot-water boiler placed near the range, either vertically or horizontally, though some recently built houses have instead of the hot-water boiler a steam-heated tank placed in the cellar. For use in summer time there should be a small gas range (or else a combination gas and coal range); an open sink, of generous size, preferably of iron or earthenware, with hot and cold water faucets and with drain board; a kitchen dresser with bottom closets, cupboards, drawers, shelves, and glass doors; one or two kitchen tables and some chairs form the outfit. The range should have one or two ovens, a water back of proper proportions to heat the water in the boiler, and a ventilating hood to remove cooking odours and to assist in keeping the kitchen cool. The range is either set between brick jambs or flat against

hotels (see Hotel) some cooking is done by steam. Such kitchens contain not only large, so-called hotel ranges with several fires, and generally standing free on all sides on the floor, but also special roasters and broilers, steam roasting ovens, steam cookers for boiling meat, vegetable and oatmeal kettles. The fixtures are generally double-jacketed iron or tinned copper vessels, with steam and water supply connections and draw cock for emptying. In hospitals and public institutions where there are not so many different kinds of dishes, but large quantities of one kind to be done, steam cooking is quite usual, and offers many advantages. Other appliances for large kitchens are bread and pastry ovens, heated by steam or gas; gas toasters; warming closets and carving tables,

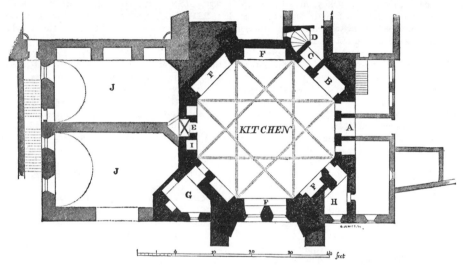

KITCHEN OF THE ANCIENT MONASTERY, DURHAM, ENGLAND; 14TH CENTURY.

A. Entrance.
B. Chimney for smoking meat, etc.
C. Passage to deanery.
D. Stair to roof.
E. Doorway, now closed.

F F. Fireplaces.
G. Scullery.
H. Storeroom.
I. Cistern.
J. Buildings, now removed.

The room is vaulted by means of intersecting ribs which support a flat roof, surrounded by a battlemented parapet.

the chimney breast. Adjoining the kitchen there should be a pantry for the storage of food, and also a storeroom or closet for the copper, iron, and earthen pots, pans, kettles, dishes, and the plates. Sometimes there is adjoining the kitchen a special scullery with sink, where meats and vegetables are prepared for cooking. Kitchens of small dwellings and apartments contain also the washtubs, but a separate laundry is preferable. (See Laundry.)

Kitchens for large institutions are generally placed in a separate building, located centrally, and sometimes connected by underground conduits with the various buildings. Sometimes kitchen and laundry are combined under the same roof. In the larger kitchens of modern

and one or more sets of self-feeding heavy copper urns tinned inside, for coffee, water, milk, and tea.

The floors of such kitchens are cemented, asphalted, or tiled, and provided with floor drains. The walls are finished in hard plaster and oil paint, or lined part of the height with glazed tiles, or bricks. Efficient general ventilation is necessary; the steam cooking kettles have special copper vent flues for the removal of vapours. One or more sinks for drawing water and washing pots, pans, dishes, and kettles are provided; these should always have drain boards. Wooden sinks are neither durable nor sanitary; sinks are either of galvanized iron or of earthenware; the drip boards of slate or soapstone, or wood lined with planished copper. Larger kitchen buildings have special sculleries with sinks for washing cooking dishes and pans, for preparing meat and vegetables, etc. A pantry located between the kitchen and the dining room has serving tables, carving boards, and sinks for washing the table ware. Modern hotels often have a large dish-washing machine for washing plates, cups, saucers, etc. — W. P. GERHARD.

Kitchens of tropical climates are arranged and fitted up with a simplicity which might be studied with advantage; for it is evidently not a gain to employ large and very costly appliances involving the consumption of large amounts of fuel. The greater part of the cooking in warm climates is done out of doors by arrangements imitating as nearly as possible the primeval fire in a roughly built hearth of stones, with a pot slung from a tripod of sticks; and the tablelike cooking apparatus with small openings in the side for introducing the nozzle of a bellows, and a large opening at top for the gridiron, frying pan, or pot, imply the use of fuel as compact and as clean as charcoal. A modification of this is visible in modern gas-cooking appliances. This matter of fuel is largely the deciding influence in the arrangement of a kitchen. The ancient "Abbots' Kitchens" of English and French mediæval convents are not different, except in size, from the usual kitchen of the well-to-do family at that time; that is to say, the cooking is supposed to be done in front of a large wood fire.

The oven for the baking of bread and the like is hardly a part of the kitchen proper; often it opens into a separate room, and it is heated separately.

The modern French kitchen is not usually large, and in many elegant Parisian apartments it is very small, not exceeding 10 by 14 feet, the French cooks having always objected to large rooms on account of the unnecessary number of steps required. On the other hand, in very large establishments, a serving room may adjoin the kitchen, and separate rooms will be provided for sweets, salads, tea, and coffee. (See Still Room.)

The following appliances are used in kitchens, but they will not all be found except in the most extensive plants.

Range; as described above, though the French model differs greatly from that most common in the United States.

Oven; anciently heated by a wood fire which was cleared away before the material to be baked was introduced, but which is now kept hot by a very small fire in a bed at one corner.

Pastry Oven.

Roasting fireplace with spits, which may be used with coal or charcoal if a cover is used; (see next item).

Broiling Stove; of which the ideal form seems to be that used in American grill rooms for oysters, chops, and the like.

Dutch Oven; for roasting in front of a fire not so large nor so hot as in an open fireplace; this, however, is movable.

Boilers or Cookers; that for vegetables; that for soup; each of which is often fitted with a steam jet by which the contents may be heated in a few minutes.

Stewing Stoves.

Bain Marie; like a very large shallow pan with water of the requisite temperature, in which saucepans and the like are kept with dishes partly prepared, or ready for serving.

Carving Table; on which the dishes are kept hot by steam.

Plate Warmer or Hot Closet; which may include a special place for silver, and the like, and may be so large that a considerable stock of utensils is kept hot permanently.

Cook's Closet; which is a dresser which the cook may keep under his own control.

Dish-washer; which in some establishments is run with soap and water heated to a very high temperature by the use of steam, so that crockery is cleansed without handwork of any sort, and also dried, immediately, by its own heat.

Dresser.

Serving Tables.

Robert Kerr, *The Gentleman's House;* Stevenson, *House Architecture;* Daincke, *Koch-Einrichtungen* in the *Handbuch der Architektur,* Part III, vol. 5; F. Colyer, *Public Institutions, their engineering and sanitary appliances;* also any large and thorough Cook Book, such as Gouffé, *Livre de Cuisine.*

KITCHEN COURT. In a large country house, a courtyard which gives light and sometimes access to a kitchen and adjacent offices. There is always a door in the outer wall; the purpose of the wall being to keep from the guests the view of the doors and principal windows of the offices. In American country houses the feature is rare, and it is more usual to "plant out" the kitchen by arrangement of trees and shrubbery

KIVA (*A kee-vah*). (From the Moki (Moquis) *kibva* or *kee-bva*.)

A chamber in a Pueblo village constructed for an assembly room, for religious observances, for a men's dormitory, and for a general lounging place for male members of the gens, clan, or society owning it. The best modern specimens are probably those of the Moki, which are rectangular. At Taos and at some other places there are round ones. Those discovered thus far in the ruins of the Southwest are generally round. Where possible, the kiva is separately built in a court and usually partly, or wholly, below the general level. In cliff regions, clefts and crevices are utilized where they extend below the surface. In Zuñi, and some other places, kivas are part of the village proper, being merely rooms on the ground that can be secluded. The kiva is entered through a hatchway in the centre of a raised part of the flat roof, descent to the floor being gained by means of a ladder. A seat formed by a low wall runs along one or both sides, and at the ends there are similar wall projections, about the same height, generally used as shelves. In the chief kiva of Walpi a wooden door exists closing the entrance to another underground room of a more secret character, said to communicate subterraneously with houses near by on the surface. The kiva floors are neatly paved with large irregular slabs of stone and at the sides there are often anchored wooden attachments for the primitive looms used by the men in weaving. Some kivas contain a *sipapû* or mystic perforation, 2 or 3 inches in diameter, through a slab of wood or stone set in the floor over a corresponding mystic hole 8 or 10 inches square, the perforation being closed by a sacred movable wooden plug. One third of the floor is usually raised about 10 inches above the rest, and this portion of the kiva is generally narrowed about 15 inches on one or on both sides, forming a kind of chancel, though the opposite end where the sipapû is situated is the most sacred portion during ceremonies. Near the edge of the raised floor, and upon it, rests the foot of the entrance ladder inclining toward the sipapû. Immediately under the hatchway, which serves also as a smoke outlet, is the fireplace, a shallow depression. On winter nights the heat is kept at a high point, the men lying about almost nude. The walls are of laid-up stone even where the kiva is completely rock-bound, and they are plastered with adobe mortar and finished smoothly with a coat of whitewash prepared from gypsiferous clay. There is no decoration, though a suggestion of it is found in some ruins. The roof is built in the same way as those of the houses, and resembles them except in having the raised square part, 5 by 7 feet in the middle, which is about 2 feet above the remainder. There may be any number of kivas in a village but one always is the chief, or *moñ-kiva*. It is this which contains the sipapû mentioned above. Oraibi has thirteen kivas. The dimensions are fixed by no rules and average about 13 feet wide, 27 feet long, 9 feet high in the middle, raised part of the roof and 6 or 7 at the ends.

The term is used by Powell as including the Assembly Chamber of American Indians generally. (See Communal Dwelling; Estufa.) For exact details and drawings, the student is referred to the paper on *Pueblo Architecture* by Victor Mindeleff, *Eighth Annual Report of the United States Bureau of Ethnology.*

— F. S. DELLENBAUGH.

KLAUS (NICOLAS) VON LOHRE; architect.

Klaus was architect of the cathedral of Strasburg for several years before or after 1400. He probably preceded Ulrich von Ensingen (see Ulrich von Ensingen) and worked on the upper part of the façade.

Gérard, *Les Artistes de l'Alsace.*

KLENZE, LEO VON; architect; b. Feb. 29, 1784; d. Jan. 26, 1864.

Klenze studied at the University and at the Academy of Architecture in Berlin. In 1803 he went to Paris to study with Durand (see Durand) and Percier (see Percier) and in 1805 visited Italy. In 1808 he was appointed court architect of King Jerome of Westphalia. In 1816 he became court architect at Munich, Bavaria, and began in that city the Glyptothek, his most important building (finished 1830). Among his many works in Munich are the Schloss Pappenheim, the Leuchtenberg Palace, 1818, the Hoftheater, rebuilt 1823–1825 from the plans of Karl von Fischer (see Fischer, K. von), the new façade of the Residenz, the southern building called Königsbau in imitation of the Palazzo Pitti in Florence, the Pinakothek, 1826, the Allerheiligen-Hofkirche, 1826, the Odeon, 1826, the Propylaën, and other works. Klenze built also the Walhalla near Regensburg. In 1834 he went to Athens and made designs for the restoration of the Acropolis which were not executed. In 1840–1850 he built the Hermitage in Saint Petersburg, Russia.

Fr. Pecht in *Allgemeine Deutsche Biographie;* Raczynski, *L'Art Moderne en Allemagne.*

KMER ARCHITECTURE. That of the ancient people of Cambodia (which see under Farther India).

KNEE. *A.* A curved or bent member of metal or wood for use as a bracket or as a brace to stiffen two parts of a structure which meet at an angle. It is generally applied at the interior of the angle. The decorative effect of ancient roof trusses of the simpler kind, and of the overhangs or jetties of timber houses, is due largely to the curved knees connecting the other members. There is no absolute distinction between knee and brace, except that the former extends well into the angle, commonly filling the space up to the apex; in timber work, however, a knee is properly formed of a naturally bent piece of wood, the grain following a curve which makes it peculiarly adapted to fit into a reëntrant angle, as in the construction of wooden ships. (See mention under Design, II.)

B. A stone cut to an angle, — generally a right angle, — to fit a sharp return; as at the corner of a label; making the angle of a merlon; or the like.

KNEELER; KNEESTONE. *A.* A more or less triangular stone at the slope of a gable wall ; cut so as to have a horizontal bed while the outer face may conform, wholly or in part, to the slope of the gable. The term Footstone is commonly applied to a single such stone form-

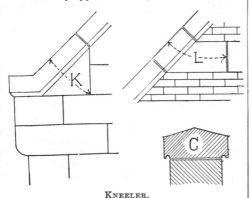

C. The stone coping of a gable shown in section.
K. Kneeler at spring of gable.
L. Kneeler at high level, preventing too great a pressure diagonally upon K.

ing the lower end of the coping on the slope and serving to resist the push of the more commonly sloping stones above. (See Bargestone ; Skew Corbel.)

B. Same as Knee, B.

KNEIPE. In German, popular usage, a tavern ; but in student slang, much influencing common usage, a drinking room, the term being connected more or less closely with ideas of comparative freedom of restraint and perhaps excess. The word *Kneiperei* means the resorting to such a room for drinking and festivity.

KNOB. A rounded projection ; in architecture sometimes a piece of utility, as when furnishing the handle to a door lock, or door latch, and sometimes an ornament. (Compare Boss and Finial.) In this latter sense the term implies generally the termination of a slender and isolated member (see Hip Knob, under H).

KNOBBING. In stone cutting, a preliminary process ; usually the mere knocking off of pieces projecting beyond the required dimensions. Called also Knobbling ; Skiffling.

KNOBBLING. (See Knobbing.)

KNOBELSDORFF, HANS GEORGE WENCESLAUS ; architect ; b. Feb. 17, 1699 ; d. Sept. 16, 1753.

Knobelsdorff entered military service, and in 1729 was quartered in Berlin, where he became interested in the work of Andreas Schlüter (see Schlüter) and others. In 1736 he travelled in Italy and, returning to Berlin, was appointed overseer of buildings to Friedrich II. (Frederick the Great). He built the Opera House in Berlin, the palace of Sanssouci near Potsdam, and the new wing of the palace at Charlottenburg. Knobelsdorff laid out the Thiergarten in Berlin

and the Lustgarten at Potsdam. He painted excellent portraits and landscapes.

Allgemeine Deutsche Biographie ; Borrmann, *Denkmäler von Berlin.*

KNOCKER. A contrivance, generally of metal, to be attached to the outside of an outer door to enable a visitor to announce his presence by means of a knock or light blow. Its essential part is a hammerlike, pivoted arm which is raised and allowed to fall against a plate.

KNÖFFEL, JOHANN CHRISTOPH ; architect ; b. 1686 ; d. 1752.

Knöffel built the Brühl palace in Dresden.

Gurlitt, *Barockstil in Deutschland.*

KNOLE HOUSE. In Kent, England. A magnificent seat, the main house dating from the reigns of Henry VII. and Henry VIII., and the furniture, which is rich, varied, and in great quantity, dating almost wholly from the seventeenth century, at which time also the interior of the house was partly modified in the taste of the time.

KNOCKER OF BRONZE, FROM A PALAZZO AT BOLOGNA ; 16TH CENTURY.

KNOT. A. Same as Knob ; an ancient form.

B. In ornament, the semblance of the tying together of cords, whether this is in flat carving as in interlaced work or Strap Work (which see), or in the carving of two or four shafts of a compound pier, these being cut out of a single block and treated as if each shaft had been flexible and so intertwined with the other or the others.

KNOTTED COLUMN; KNOTTED PIER. A pair or a group of shafts treated as described under Knot.

KNOT WORK. Ornament in relief, resembling interlaced work. (See Knot.)

KNUCKLE. In a hinge, a projecting cylindrical portion making connection between the flaps. It is formed by parts of the respective flaps bent alternately around a pin which forms a pivot.

KNULLING. A convex rounded moulding of slight projection, consisting of a series of more or less elaborate and fantastic members separated by indentations; somewhat intermediate between the egg and dart and the bead and reel.

KOECK VAN AALST, PIETER; painter and architect; b Aug. 14, 1502.

Studied in Italy, and on his return established himself at Aalst, Holland, as architect and painter. He translated Vitruvius and Serlio into Dutch.

Immerzeel, *Hollandsche Kunstenaars.*

KONAK. A large Turkish mansion, either in the city or country. A konak for use in the summer season, especially one by the waterside, is called a Yali. The difference between them is very nearly that between the mansion and villa. — A. D. F. H.

KONISTRA. In Greek, an arena; that is, a place covered with sand or dust. Commonly, in archæology, the orchestra of the Greek theatre; but as the plan and disposition of the orchestra is greatly in dispute, it is used sometimes for the whole enclosure and sometimes for a limited part of it.

KORA. Same as Cora.

KOREA, ARCHITECTURE OF. That of the great peninsula between the Yellow Sea and the sea of Japan, and considered, sometimes, as independent, and sometimes as a dependency, of the Chinese empire.

As in the case of China, we are compelled to fall back on Japan for indications of the nature of the first architecture of Korean civilization. Purely Chinese in its first estate, it was almost immediately transmitted to Japan before it had been materially modified, and in the temples of Horiuji we can find the only indication of the earliest architecture, since nearly every vestige in Korea has been swept away. It is claimed that certain of the ancient monasteries in the Diamond Mountains date back to the earliest period; even that the oldest of all, the monastery of Chang-an-sa, was " restored " to its present condition A.D. 515. This is manifestly inaccurate, and in all probability the thirteen-storied pagoda in Seoul, built in the twelfth

century, is one of the oldest of existing structures. The sculptures of this pagoda are either copies of much earlier work, or have been removed to their present position from their original sites. In style they are markedly Hindu, and therefore of the earliest period.

Nearly all the Buddhist temples in Korea were destroyed at the time Confucianism became triumphant over the Buddhism that had civilized the people; only one remains in Seoul, and apart from those in the Diamond Mountains, already referred to, Buddhist temples are hardly to be found.

The existing architecture is confined almost wholly to the royal palaces, and is seen in the form of gates, tombs, and halls of audience. None of these dates back more than three centuries, but they all show a much smaller diversion from the original type than is the case in China. The curves of the roofs, the spacing of columns, the general proportions, are still good, and only in detail do they fall short of the Japanese work of the Ashikaga period. The use of stone is most noticeable. While in Japan this material appears only in the foundations, in Korea it is used for lofty terraces, great flights of stairs, the lower stories of gateways, and for the columns that support the great roofs. In the Hall of Audience in the " Mulberry Palace " in Seoul the supporting shafts are all of stone, and are nearly 3 feet square.

The great gateways are perhaps the finest architectural works that now exist. The " South Gate " of the palace in Seoul is one of the best of its class, and is of really extraordinary dignity; the lower story is of dressed stone, and is pierced only by one semicircular arched opening. The superstructure is in two stories, finely proportioned, and with roofs of splendid curvature. This use of stone gives to Korean architecture a certain power and solidity absent from the more delicate work of Japan.

Contemporary domestic architecture is primitive; by law, private dwellings may be only one story in height, and they are of the rudest description, wattles and clay being the common building materials.

Korean architecture is simply reminiscent; the oldest and best is entirely destroyed, and there is none of to-day; what lies between is but a more or less accurate rendering of tradition. —R. A. CRAM.

Lowell, *Chosing, the Land of the Morning Calm.*

KOROEBOS. (See Coroebus.)

KRAFT (KRAFFT), ADAM; sculptor and architect; b. about 1455; d. about 1507.

Adam Kraft was probably born in Nürnberg, Germany. Nothing is known of his early education and training. No work can certainly be ascribed to him before 1490, when he appears employed upon the seven crosses (stations in the journey of Christ bearing the cross to Calvary) which lead up to the crucifixion, made also by Kraft, in the churchyard of S. John at Nürnberg. He made the monument of Sebald Schreyer outside the church of S. Sebald in Nürnberg (1492). Kraft's most important work is the Gothic tabernacle, or house, of the sacrament in the church of S. Lorenz in Nürnberg (1493–1500). He made, about 1502, the monuments of Volkamer and Groland in the church of S. Sebald.

Wanderer, *Adam Krafft und seine Schule ;* Daun, *Adam Kraft ;* Bergau, *Adam Kraft in Dohme Series ;* Neudörfer, *Nachrichten von Künstler und werkleuten von Nürnberg.*

KRANNER, JOSEPH; architect; b. June 13, 1801, in Prague, Bohemia; d. Oct. 20, 1871.

Educated at the Polytechnikum in Prague, and travelled in Germany, France, and Italy. Kranner assisted Von Ferstel (see Ferstel) in the construction of the Votivkirche in Vienna, and in 1861 was made cathedral architect at Prague.

Seubert, *Künstler-lexicon.*

KREMLIN. In Russia, a fortified enclosure, a citadel; used in English almost exclusively for that of Moscow, which has a perimeter of nearly a mile and a half. The brick walls are of such thickness and height as to be formidable in the way of mediæval fortification. There are three very interesting and lofty towers at the gateways, as well as some smaller ones, and a great number of churches and chapels are contained within the wall, among them the cathedral of the Annunciation, dating from the fifteenth century, and the cathedral of the Assumption, of a still earlier date. There is also a palace of the Czar, which was rebuilt about 1840, though some of the old structure was left intact, and is interesting for its semi-Oriental decoration. — R. S.

KREPIDOMA. Same as Crepidoma.

KRIOSPHINX. A sphinx having a ram's head. (See Sphinx ; also written Criosphinx.)

KRISMANN. (See Chrismann.)

KRITIOS. (See Critius.)

KRONBORG. A royal castle of the kings of Denmark at Helsingör (Elsinore) on the Sund, or narrow deep-water strait, between Denmark and Sweden. It was built in the early years of the seventeenth century.

KRUBSACIUS, FRIEDRICH AUGUST; architect; b. 1718, at Dresden; d. 1789.

He was educated under the architects Longuelune (see Longuelune) and Von Bodt (see Bodt). In 1776 he was appointed *Oberhofbaumeister* in Saxony and professor at the Academy of Arts in Dresden. He built the Schloss Otter-

wisch and the Steuerhaus in Dresden, and in 1740 published *Betrachtung über dem Geschmack der Alten in der Baukunst.*

Seubert, *Künstler-lexicon ;* Schuman, *Barock und Rococo.*

KUN, HANS ; architect.

Kun was a son-in-law of Ulrich von Ensingen (see Ulrich von Ensingen), and succeeded him as architect of the cathedral of Ulm, Germany. He held that office from 1417 to 1435.

Pressel, *Ulm und sein Münster ;* Grüneisen-Mauch, *Ulm's Kunstleben im Mittelalter.*

KURA. In a Japanese city, a fireproof building two or more stories high, used as a place of deposit for the valuable possessions of a family. It is built with a frame of wood or bamboo, which is covered thickly with mud and plastered, the frame being entirely protected by the solidity and mass of the material which covers it. In order to secure the permanence of this covering, pieces of bamboo are secured to the larger timbers, and ropes with coarse fibre and rough, bristly surface are tied from piece to piece of the frame. The mud is applied slowly, in layers, much as paint is applied in Western countries, but with a much longer time allowed to elapse between coats, so that it is often said that a year or more is required for the erection of a good kura. The roofs are very thick, and are covered with tiles. If there are any windows, these are very small, and are closed by sliding or hinged shutters of great thickness, and it is said that wet mud is kept at hand, by means of which the joints of these shutters are stopped up when a conflagration is raging in the neighbourhood. In such a kura the paintings, porcelains, lacquers, carvings, and the like, belonging to a well-to-do family, are kept permanently stored. These, or some of them, are brought out on occasions of ceremony, or when visitors are expected whose taste is known to lie in the direction of works of art ; or two or three pieces at a time for the enjoyment of the possessor.
— R. S.

KURHAUS. At a German health resort, a building which serves as a place of reunion for the frequenters of the place. Hence, in general, a building containing supper rooms, gaming tables, and other conveniences for amusement, but generally at a town where mineral springs and the like are to be found, and where the primary idea is the recovery of health.

KURSAAL. A large room for social gathering in a Kurhaus ; hence, by extension, same as Kurhaus.

KUTUB MINAR. (See Minar.)

KYLAS TEMPLE. Same as Kailas Temple.

L

L. *A.* A piece of pipe or a bar making a
right angle with another. (Compare Elbow,
II., *B.*)

B. A subordinate part of a building projecting from the main structure at right angles,
giving to the whole the shape of the letter L.
Hence, in local United States usage, any small
extension or wing, however situated.

LA BARRE. (See Barre, Eloy de la.)

LABEL. A hood moulding which extends
horizontally across the top of an opening, and

LABEL: DOORWAY, CLOISTER OF S. GREGORIO,
VALLADOLID, SPAIN.

(Compare cut under Doorway, viz., that of Coombe Church ;
and under Dripstone.)

returns vertically downward for a short distance at each end. (See cut under Doorway,
Fig. 4.)

LABELYE, CHARLES ; architect.
Came to London to design the bridge across
the Thames at Westminster. The first stone of
this work was laid Jan. 29, 1739, and the last,
Oct. 26, 1746. It was replaced in 1861 by the
present structure, designed by T. Page, C.E.

Arch. Pub. Soc. Dictionary.

LABORATORY. Originally a workshop for
chemists, whether for the preparation of chemicals or for the more delicate scientific experiments. By extension the term is applied to

other scientific workshops, but hardly to rooms
or buildings in which work is done according to
the more familiar and mechanical methods.
Laboratories in the great colleges are divided
into those for qualitative and those for quanti-
tative analysis, not because there is any objection to the two classes of work going on in the
same large room, but because the students of
the one subject are commonly of a different class
or under a different immediate direction than
those of the other. The general requirements
of a laboratory are abundant light, a very perfect and elaborate system of ventilation, both
general and applied, to the separate furnaces and
the like, and a careful arrangement of the space
afforded, which should not be greater than the
proposed work of the laboratory seems to make
necessary. As in the kitchen, it is a great mistake to have the distances within the laboratory
too great. — R. S.

**LABORDE, ALEXANDRE LOUIS JO-
SEPH, COMTE DE** ; archæologist ; b. 1774
(at Paris) ; d. 1842.
Son of Jean Joseph, Marquis de Laborde, a
famous French financier. Alexandre served in
the Austrian army after his father's death, and
returned to France in 1797. He travelled in
England, Holland, Italy, and Spain, and was
created count of the Holy Roman Empire in
1810. He published *Itinéraire descriptif de
l'Espagne* (Paris, 1809, 5 vols. 8vo and atlas);
Voyage pittoresque et historique en Espagne
(Paris, 1807–1818, 4 vols. folio) ; *Description
des nouveaux jardins de la France et de ses
anciens châteaux* (Paris, 1808–1815, folio);
Versailles ancien et moderne (Paris, 1839–
1840, 4to).

Vapereau, *Dictionnaire des Littératures ;* La
Grande Encyclopédie.

**LABORDE, LÉON EMMANUEL SIMON
JOSEPH, MARQUIS DE** ; archæologist and
art historian ; b. June 13, 1807 (at Paris) ; d.
March 26, 1869.
A son of the Count Alexandre Louis Joseph
de Laborde (see Laborde, A. L. J.). He was
educated in Göttingen, Germany, and travelled
in Asia Minor, Syria, Egypt, and Arabia Petræa.
He was secretary of the French embassy in
Rome under Chateaubriand, was made *conservateur* of the *Musée des antiquités du Louvre*
in 1831, and later *directeur général* of the
archives of the empire and member of the *Académie des inscriptions et belles lettres* (1842).
He published *Voyage de l'Arabie Pétrée* (1830–
1833, folio); *Les ducs de Bourgogne* (1849–
1851, 3 vols. 8vo) ; *La Renaissance des Arts
à la cour de France* (1850–1855, 8vo) ;
Athènes aux XVe, XVIe et XVIIe siècles
(1855, 2 vols., 8vo) ; *Le Parthénon* (1847 ff.,
unfinished) ; *Voyage en Orient, Asie Mineure,
et Syrie* (1837–1862, 2 vols. folio) ; *Glossaire
Français du moyen âge* (1872, 8vo); *Les*

Archives de la France pendant la Révolution (Paris, 1866, folio); *Les Comptes des bâti-ments du roi* (1878–1880, 2 vols. 8vo).

Vapereau, *Dictionnaire des Littératures; La Grande Encyclopédie.*

LABOUR AND NAILS. The service rendered by house carpenters when the greater part of the materials is found. A builder may even contract for the labour and nails required in a building. It appears that by extension the term is applied in Great Britain to other work than that of the carpenter.

LABRADORITE. Labrador rock; a variety of feldspar possessing a beautiful bluish iridescence. Little used in America, but extensively utilized by the Russians. Found in Labrador and Russia, and Fingspong, Sweden. A less iridescent variety is quarried under the name of Ausable granite near Keeseville, New York State. — G. P. M.

LABROUSTE, FRANÇOIS MARIE THÉODORE; architect; b. March 11, 1799; d. December, 1885.

A pupil of Vaudoyer (see Vaudoyer), Hippolyte Lebas (see Lebas), and of the *École des Beaux Arts.* He won the *Premier Grand Prix de Rome* in 1827. Returning to Paris, he was made architect of the *Bibliothèque de l'Arsenal.* In 1845 he succeeded Franz Christian Gau (see Gau) as architect in chief of the hospitals of Paris, and in 1876 was made *archi-tecte honoraire de l'assistance publique.*

Notice *sur Théodore Labrouste* in *Rev. Gén. d'Architecture,* vol. 45, 1886; Bauchal, *Diction-naire.*

LABROUSTE, HENRI PIERRE FRAN-ÇOIS; architect; b. May 11, 1801; d. June 24, 1875.

A brother of the preceding. He studied with Vaudoyer (see Vaudoyer) and Lebas (see Lebas), entered the *École des Beaux Arts* in 1819, and won the *Premier Grand Prix de Rome* in 1824. His *envoie de Rome* on the temples of Pæstum was published by the French government in 1884. In 1832 he was made inspector of the works at the *École des Beaux Arts* under Duban (see Duban). Between 1843 and 1850 he built the Bibliothèque S. Geneviève, Paris. From 1855 to 1875 he was architect of the *Bibliothèque Nationale,* completed there the improvements begun by Robert de Cotte (see Cotte, R.), and built the great reading room and the façade on the Rue Richelieu with the pavilion on the corner of the Rue des Petits Champs. Labrouste was made *inspec-teur général des édifices diocésains* in 1857, and *inspecteur général du conseil des bâti-ments civils* in 1865. In 1831 he opened an architectural school (atelier), which produced many prominent architects.

Bauchal, *Dictionnaire; Notice Nécrologique* in *Rev. Gén. de l'Architecture;* Penanrun, *Les archi-tectes élèves de l'École des Beaux Arts.*

LABRUM. (In Latin, a contraction of *lava-brum,* a bathtub.) In Roman archæology, one of the stone bathing tubs, of which many exist in the museums of Italy. They are sometimes made of very precious material, hard granite or porphyry, and have a little carefully chosen ornamentation.

LABYRINTH. *A.* In Grecian archæology, a complicated building, with many corridors and rooms, through which it was difficult to find one's way. The term also is applied to a cave. The Labyrinth of Egypt is described by Herodotus and Strabo, but the ruins as they exist near the ancient Lake Mœris, in the province of Fayoum, show no trace of the splendour of the buildings as they describe them, though as yet they have not been thoroughly explored. The Labyrinth of Crete, in which Minotaur was confined, is perhaps wholly mythical. The Labyrinth of Lemnos is mentioned by Pliny as similar to that in Egypt, but much smaller. The Labyrinth in the tomb of Porsena at Clusium was apparently merely the tomb itself — but a building so large and of such unusual character for a tomb that the term was applied to it in admiration.

B. A maze of any description. In modern times, generally a fantastic arrangement of lofty and thick hedges in a garden, as at Hampton Court, where it is somewhat difficult to find one's way to the centre.

C. A drawing or other representation on a flat surface of a maze, so elaborate that, even with the whole plan before him, the student is puzzled as to the right course to follow to reach the centre. In architecture such labyrinths are inlaid in the pavements of churches of the Middle Ages, where they are sometimes thirty feet or more in diameter. They were supposed to be emblematic either of the difficulty and uncertainty of the Christian's progress through this world, or they were, as some think, of purely mystical meaning, connected with some legend now lost and held traditionally by the masons. It has been remarked that they contain no religious emblems whatever. They were very numerous in the Middle Ages, but a great number of them have been destroyed when the pavements were relaid. — R. S.

LACING. (See Lattice.)

LACING COURSE. A course of brick or tile, or several adjacent courses considered collectively, inserted, perhaps, at frequent intervals, in rough stone or rubble walls as a bond course; frequently an easy method by which much dressing and fitting of perpends is avoided.

LACKER. Same as Lacquer.

LACONICUM. In Roman archæology, the hot room or sudarium of a thermal establishment.

LACQUER. Properly, a substance made of lac, that is to say, of the substance sold as

gum-lac, stick-lac, seed-lac, shell-lac or shellac; but by extension applied also to a varnish made in Oriental countries from the sap of certain plants. Persian, Indian, and Chinese lacquers are hardly of importance in architecture. Japanese lacquer is chiefly made from the tree *Rhus Vernicifera*. Lacquer ware made with this material is well known in the shops, the finest pieces being of very great value to collectors and to students of Oriental art; so that a box a few inches in length may bring several hundred dollars in public auction. Such lacquer is applied to the decoration of temples and other public buildings in Japan much as paint is used among European nations, but the perfect surface, permanent gloss and delicate colour of the lacquer gives it a peculiar charm. (See Japan, Architecture of.)
— R. S.

LACUNAR. (In Latin, an abbreviated form of *lacunarium*, from *lacuna*, a gap, an opening.) *A.* A ceiling adorned by sunken panels (see Caisson, II.), but usually a horizontal one; also, any under surface so adorned, as the soffit of a projecting cornice, the under side of an epistyle, or the like.

B. A single panel forming part of such a ceiling. In this sense, much more common in English. The lacunar, then, is the same as a caisson, but applied to a horizontal surface, and not to a cupola or vault.

LACUSTRINE DWELLING. Same as Pile Dwelling.

LAG. In a centring composed of two or more parallel ribs, a cross piece connecting such ribs and supporting the voussoirs. (See Centring.) Usually in the collective form lagging.

LAKE DWELLING. (See Pile Dwelling.)

LAKE VILLAGE. (See Pile Dwelling.)

LALYE, MICHEL; architect and sculptor. Nov. 5, 1532, Lalye succeeded Martin Chambiges (see Chambiges, M.) as architect of the cathedral of Beauvais, Oise, France. He finished the vaulting and the southern portal. April 24, 1534, he made the first proposals for the erection of an immense spire at the intersection of the choir and transept of the cathedral. This extraordinary work was designed and carried out by his successor, Jean Wast (II.). (See Wast, Jean, II.)

Desjardins, *Histoire de la cathédrale de Beauvais.*

LAMBERT (LAMPRECHT), JEHAN (JEAN); bell founder.

At the city, now village, of Deneuvre, near Baccarat, Meurthe-et-Moselle, France, there appeared at the end of the fifteenth century, one Lambert, a founder of bells, whose works were widely distributed in Alsace and Lorraine. He came from Antwerp in the Low Countries about 1470. According to the custom of the

time he set up his furnace, moulds, and machinery in the yard of the church which was to be supplied, and cast his bell in full view of the people. The big bell (*bourdon*) which still hangs in the *Kappelthurm* at Obernai, Alsace, Germany, was cast in 1484. It is richly decorated in relief. In 1479 he refounded *la Muette*, the big bell of the cathedral of Metz, Lorraine. There are bells by Lambert also in Alsace.

Gérard, *Les artistes de l'Alsace.*

LAMBERTI, NICOLÒ DI PIERO (surnamed Pela); sculptor and architect; d. about 1420.

According to Vasari, Nicolò was a pupil of a Sienese sculptor named Moccio, at Arezzo, Italy. He made at Florence two statues of prophets for the Campanile, and began the decoration of the southern portal of the cathedral called Porta della Mandorla (1402–1408), continued by Antonio di Banco and his son Nanni d'Antonio di Banco (see Nanni d'Antonio di Banco). Called sometimes Nicolò Aretino.

Vasari, Milanesi ed.; Müntz, *Renaissance.*

LAMBETH PALACE. In London, on the southern bank of the Thames; the official residence of the archbishop of Canterbury. The buildings are of many different epochs, from the thirteenth to the sixteenth centuries, and some are of importance.

LAMBREQUIN. A decorative member; a band usually horizontal and more or less fringed, lobed, or notched on the lower edge. In upholstery, the usual meaning is a short broad curtain covering the rings and rod or other fastening at the top of long curtains, such as those for a door or window. In keramics, the band around the top of the body of a richly decorated vase, as in many of Chinese porcelain. These significations mark the two extremes of the common and the more remote meaning of the term; it is applicable to any similar stripe, band, cornice (in the limited sense *D*), and the like, but strictly as a piece of ornamentation.

LAMB'S TONGUE. A moulding of considerable projection as compared to its width, and symmetrical; its section having a tapering tonguelike shape. The term appears to be of loose meaning and is applied by carpenters especially to such a moulding as worked on a sash bar, and hence to a moulding of one-half such section. In the United States, sometimes an ovolo or quarter-round, followed by a fillet, as worked along the edge of a board.

LAMOUR, JEAN; ironworker; b. 1698; d. 1771.

The name Lamour appears frequently in the accounts of Stanislas I. (Leczinska), king of Poland and duke of Lorraine and Bar for the years 1757 and 1758. He built the great grilles (iron gateways) of the Place Royale at Nancy, Meurthe-et-Moselle, France.

Michel, *Recueil des fondations du roi de Pologne.*

LAMP-POST. Originally, a slender post, as of wood, set up to carry a lamp, as in a street or any outdoor place of resort. By extension, the upright used to support at the proper height above the ground a gas burner or electric lamp, as in the streets of a city.

The artistic design of lamp-posts gives trouble to Western designers because of the lack of skill of the modern European world in the design of objects which have not a constructional or utilitarian basis for such design. It is probable that a Chinese or Malay, and still more a Japanese, would find it easy to make a suitable structure for this purpose; but the moment the European designer abandons his very slender hollow pillar of cast iron he goes astray, and nothing can be much uglier than the more elaborate lamp-posts of Paris or New York. It is noticeable that, as in the case of the flagstaff, the tendency of the designer is to make the upright much heavier than necessary; but this in itself is not to be deprecated. The recent efforts of designers for electrical fixtures seem to point in the right direction; these, when made for interiors, are sometimes sufficiently intelligent, and promise good future results. — R. S.

LAMPRECHT. (See Lambert.)

LANCE, ADOLPHE ÉTIENNE; architect; b. April 8, 1813 (at Littry, Calvados, France); d. Dec. 24, 1874.

Lance was a pupil of Visconti (see Visconti) and Abel Blouet (see Blouet). In 1850 he was made inspector of the works of restoration at the church of S. Denis under Viollet-le-Duc (see Viollet-le-Duc). In 1854, as architect of the diocesan edifices, he was charged with the restoration of the cathedral of Sens, Aisne, France, and had charge of that building until his death. He was associated with Victor Calliat (see Calliat) in editing the *Encyclopédie d'Architecture,* and published *Excursions en Italie* (1 vol. 4to, Paris, 1863). He is best known by his *Dictionnaire des architectes français* (2 vols. 8vo., Paris, 1875).

Ruprich-Robert, *Notice Nécrologique* in *Rev. Gén. de l'Architecture,* Vol, XXXII., 1875; Bauchal, *Dictionnaire.*

LANCET. *A.* Same as Lancet Window (which see under Window).

B. One light shaped like a lancet window of a large traceried window. In this sense the word is used by artists in stained glass; as

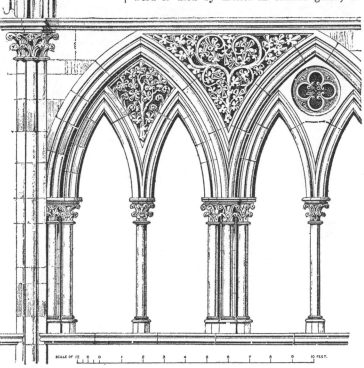

LANCET: TRIFORIUM OF CHOIR, LE MANS CATHEDRAL.

Two lancet arches beneath an equilateral arch, the concentricity of the arcs showing how the lancet is an arch whose two centres are brought near together.

a cartoon for one of the lancets of such a window.

LANCET STYLE. That style of Gothic architecture which is distinguished by the use of the lancet arch, as the Early English. (See under Arch.)

LANDING. *A.* That portion of a floor, or a confined floor space, immediately adjoining or connected with a staircase or flight of stairs; it may be either the floor space meeting the foot or top of a flight, or a platform introduced in the length of a flight. (See Pace; Stair.)

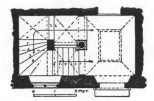

LANDING: FIG. 1.

The arrow above points up-stairs, and the figures denote the risers; 1, 2, 3, fliers, 5, 6, etc., winders. The arrow below points down stairs, and 1 is the top riser of the lower flight. (See the view, Fig. 2.)

B. Any structure, or part of a structure, at the water's edge, at which persons or goods can be embarked or disembarked. In this sense often landing place.

LANDING: FIG. 2. (SEE FIG. 1.)

LANDINI, TADDEO. (See Giacomo della Porta.)

LANDO DI PIETRO; goldsmith, sculptor, architect, and engineer; d. 1348.

At a meeting of the Consiglio della Campana, Aug. 23, 1339, it was decided to enlarge the cathedral of Siena by treating the existing church as a transept and building a new nave. In 1339 Lando di Pietro came from Naples, where he was employed on important undertakings, to superintend the work. Construction was interrupted by the great plague of 1348, in which Lando perished. In 1357 a great part of the new work was taken down, leaving the church in its present condition.

Norton, *Church Building in the Middle Ages.*

LANDSCAPE ARCHITECTURE. The disposition of open ground in a decorative way, either in connection with a dwelling house or other building, or with special reference to the beauty of the resulting park or garden itself. The term was usually landscape gardening, but this has seemed to express too exclusively the choice and care of the plants themselves, and insufficiently the lay-out and disposition of the grounds. Neither term was in use much before the close of the eighteenth century.

The landscape architecture of Europe, during the Middle Ages, was confined to the laying out of walled gardens, not very great in extent, and those were naturally formal in plan. The same feeling governed the English designers of the sixteenth century, and led them to plant gardens closely conforming to the square lines of the house. The garden stopped at a terrace wall, an invisible ha-ha, or the like, and beyond that were the unaltered hill and valley and naturally grouped trees of the park; at least, in a large place. Even in modern English houses of the middle of the nineteenth century, a time of naturalistic gardening, a terrace was often reserved and set with flower-beds in regular patterns, while immediately beyond the terrace the lawns and clumps of trees were of a generally natural or informal arrangement. On the continent of Europe the influence of the Italian villa was strongly felt; but the advantage of this disposition was more visible in a hilly country like Italy than it was afterward when similar formality was used in laying out the flat and sandy plain of Versailles, or in the smaller places which more or less closely resembled Versailles. In these great formal gardens there is little shade; little grass in proportion, large as the separate grass plots may be; a general disposition to accommodate great crowds on special occasions, and but little thought for the person who would be quiet and alone. These considerations, together with the growing interest in romanticism in art and literature, led to the movement toward informal or natural gardening in the nineteenth century. The spirit had, however, existed at an earlier date, and the English garden at Munich is an admirable instance of what could be achieved, even in the last quarter of the eighteenth century. The London parks (Hyde Park, Regent's Park, etc.) often surprise strangers by their extreme irregularity and abandonment to wild nature, even the grass of the extensive unsheltered patches, made desirable by the climate, being so little cared for that these tracts can hardly be called lawns. They are, therefore, not much intersected by paths and the like, these being laid down only on the lines naturally taken by foot passengers going from gate to gate. The Bois de Boulogne in Paris is much more of a wood, as its name implies, having but comparatively few unbroken surfaces of open grass, and the Bois de Vincennes is not unlike this last. All of those great tracts of country are left, with but little reserve, to the free access of the public. The pleasure grounds of gigantic country places, like Chatsworth, show a combination of the natural and the formal system, for many acres of park adorned chiefly by the numerous large and ancient trees, standing singly or in almost unmodified natural clusters, surround gardens which are much more formal, and approach even the elaborateness of some Continental pleasure grounds.

In the United States, the example of A. J. Downing, who died in 1852, and that of Frederick Law Olmsted, led strongly in the direction of close adherence to the irregularity of nature. Thus, a lawn was assumed to be naturally grass-grown soil improved ; trees were assumed to be in their natural places, but cared for, preserved from the attacks of insects, and thinned out on occasion to allow of better and freer growth ; if a fine old tree is on a plot, no matter how irregular in aspect or how prominent in its position, much would be sacrificed to preserve it ; the soft and perfect lawn should not be carried over the exposed roots of the large tree, nor should it be cut away in a circle around it, but, as is expressly stated more than once, is brought judiciously up to the roots and allowed to disappear among their prominences.

At present, 1900, there is a movement in favour of the formal garden, which seems to have been set on foot by architects of classical predilections. Some of the gardens laid out during the last few years, sometimes under the name of Italian gardens, sometimes with greater freedom than would allow of that appellation, are very beautiful in design ; and the question will be for the future to 'ecide whether the greater pleasure and recreation is to be got from these or from the more naturalistic treatment of the ground. The unquestioned possibility of producing designs of extraordinary beauty in the formal garden is to be urged on one side ; the desire of the citizen or hardworked man, even of a country town, to have as much as possible of free nature, or of a semblance of free nature, around him is to be weighed on the other side. — R. S.

Robinson, *Garden Design and Architects' Gardens;* Parsons, *Landscape Gardening;* Platt, *Italian Gardens;* Blomfield, *The Formal Garden in England;* *Architecture chinoise jardins,* in *Revue gén. de l'arch.,* 1859 ; Hartwig, *Die Anlage von Lustgebeiten und Blumengärten,* Weimar, 1861 ; Hughes, *Garden Architecture and Landscape Gardening,* London, 1886 ; Ernouf, *L'art des jardins,* Paris, 1868 ; Abel, *Garten-Architektur,* Wien, 1876 ; Weichardt, *Motive zu Garten-Architektur,* Weimar, 1879 ; André, *L'art des jardins;* *Traité général de la composition des parcs et jardins,* Paris, 1879 ; Neitner, *Gärtnerisches Skizzenbuch,* Berlin, 1883 ; Robinson, *The English Flower*

Garden: Style, Position, and Arrangement, London, 1884 ; Hampel, *Die Moderne Teppichgärtnerei,* Berlin, 1887 ; Milner, *The Art and Practice of Landscape Gardening,* London, 1890 ; Kaufmann, *Der Gartenbau im Mittelalter und während der Periode der Renaissance,* Berlin, 1892 ; Vacquet, *Le Bois de Boulogne architectural,* Paris, 1860 ; Robinson, *The Parks and Gardens of Paris: A Study of Paris Gardens,* London, 1879.

LANDSCAPE GARDENING. (See Landscape Architecture.)

LANDSHUT, JACOB VON. (See Jacob von Landshut.)

LANFRANC ; archbishop of Canterbury ; d. 1089.

The great Lanfranc, counsellor of William the Conqueror, was made archbishop of Canterbury, August 15, 1070. He caused to be rebuilt the cathedral of Canterbury, burned in 1067. Lanfranc's Norman cathedral was itself burned in 1174.

Wharton, *Anglia Sacra;* Willis, *Canterbury Cathedral.*

LANGEVELT, RUTGER VAN ; b. 1635 in Holland ; d. 1695 in Berlin.

He was trained in Holland and France, and in 1678 became court painter and architect to the Elector Friedrich Wilhelm, of Brandenburg. He was made director of the Academy in Berlin, and in 1678–1687 built the church in the Dorotheenstrasse and other important buildings in Berlin.

Allgemeine deutsche Biographie.

LANGHANS, KARL GOTTHARD ; architect ; b. 1733 in Schlesien (Silesia), Germany ; d. 1808.

He designed the *Regierungs Gebäude* in Breslau, Silesia, and in 1774 was called to Berlin. His reputation rests mainly upon the *Brandenburger Thor* (see Brandenburg Gateway, under Gateway), in Berlin, built in imitation of the Propylæa at Athens, between 1789 and 1793. He built also in Berlin the *Herkulesbrücke,* 1787, and the Colonnade in the Mohein Strasse. About 1789 Langhans designed the Schloss theatre and Belvedere in the park at Charlottenburg.

Borrmann, *Denkmäler von Berlin;* *Allgemeine deutsche Biographie.*

LANGHEMANS, FRANÇOIS ; sculptor and architect ; b. March, 1661, at Mechlin, Belgium ; d. 1720.

Langhemans made the great altar of the abbey of Grimberghe, Belgium, and the monuments of Pierre Roose in the church of S. Gudule, at Brussels. In 1716–1717 he restored the façade of the Palais du Grand Conseil at Mechlin.

Biographie Nationale de la Belgique.

LANGLEY BATTY ; architect ; b. 1696 ; d. March 3, 1751.

He was the son of a gardener, and practised

the profession of landscape gardening. He made an attempt to arrange Gothic architecture under five orders, and organized a school mainly for the training of carpenters. Langley is best known by his extensive series of practical works on matters pertaining to architecture, such as *Practical Geometry applied to Building, Surveying, Gardening*, etc., 1726; *New Principles of Gardening*, etc., 1728, and the like.

Stephen, *Dictionary of National Biography;* Walpole, *Anecdotes.*

LANTERN. In architecture:—

A. Any structure rising above the roof of a building and having openings in its sides by

LANTERN (DEFINITION *B*) OF CUT STONE, WITH WICKET OF WROUGHT IRON; CHÂTEAUDUN (EURE-ET-LOIR), FRANCE.

B. A structure for surrounding and protecting a beacon or signal light, as on a lighthouse, having sides of glass held by the slightest

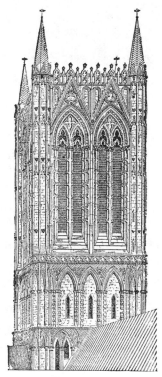

LANTERN (DEFINITION *A*): CENTRAL TOWER, LINCOLN CATHEDRAL.

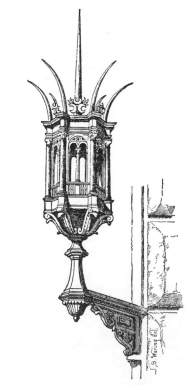

LANTERN (DEFINITION *B*) OF BRONZE; EXTERIOR OF PALAZZO STROZZI, FLORENCE.

which the interior of the building is lighted. By extension, such an architectural feature whether serving as a means of lighting the interior or not. The tower built over the crossing of a cruciform church is often so called, especially when open, and light rather than massive, as that above the octagon at Ely cathedral (of wood), and that of S. Ouen at Rouen, though of stone and very large. The uppermost large member of a cupola is so called: that of Florence cathedral is very large and heavy, about 80 feet high above the curve of the cupola.

framework practicable. Also written Lanthorn. (Compare Bracciale; Bulkhead.)
— D. N. B. S.

LANTERN LIGHT. A structure similar to a lantern in sense *A*, but much smaller and, generally, merely a framed structure built upon a roof as a skylight. A more elaborate form of Bulkhead Light.

LANTERN OF DEMOSTHENES. Same as Choragic Monument.

LANTERN OF THE DEAD. A slender, towerlike structure erected in a cemetery to contain a light which shines through openings constructed about the top, and frequently provided with an altar at the base. Such towers were common in France, and interesting specimens still remain, many of them having been erected in mediæval times.

LANTERN TOWER. *A.* A tower having the form of a lantern in sense *A*.

B. A tower for carrying a lantern in sense *B*.

LAP. In roofing, clapboarding, and the like, the extent to which one board, slate, length of building paper, or shingle, covers the one next below it; or, in some cases, the extent of overlaying beyond the nailing of the piece below.

LAPIS LAZULI. A hard, tough, and compact rock of a rich azure blue colour, mottled with gray, and with a vitreous lustre. Of a very complex chemical nature. Occurs in granular limestone and syenitic rocks, but only in small masses, and is quite expensive. Commercial sources, Persia, Siberia, and China.

— G. P. M.

LAPO (JACOPO TEDESCO); architect. Lapo is an abbreviation of Jacopo. He began the Palazzo del Podestà (now Bargello), in Florence, in 1250. Vasari is mistaken in supposing that Lapo was the father of Arnolfo di Cambio. He was more probably his associate. (See Arnolfo di Cambio.)

Vasari, Milanesi ed., Vol. I., p. 279; Rohault de Fleury, *La Toscane*.

LAQUEAR. Same as Lacunar, *A*.

LARDER. A storeroom for provisions, especially meat, game, and the like. Formerly in British country houses, a place of considerable importance and frequently one of a series of such rooms.

LARMIER. A drip, especially when forming a somewhat elaborate member, as in a cornice, water table, or the like.

LASSURANCE. (See Cailleteau.)

LASSUS, JEAN BAPTISTE ANTOINE; architect; b. March 19, 1807; d. July 15, 1857.

Lassus was one of the chiefs of the modern Gothic school in France. He was a pupil of Lebas (see Lebas) and Henri Labrouste (see Labrouste), and entered the *Écoles des Beaux Arts* in 1828. Influenced by the general romantic movement led by Victor Hugo, he devoted himself entirely to the study of Gothic architecture, especially that of the period of King Philippe Auguste. From 1841 to 1849 he was associated with Duban (see Duban) in the restoration of the Sainte Chapelle, Paris, and after 1849 had charge of that building. He built the spire (*flèche*) and cleared away the buildings from the south side of the chapel. In 1841 he won a gold medal in the competition for the tomb of Napoleon I. In 1845 he was associated with Viollet-le-Duc (see Viollet-le-Duc) in the restoration of the cathedral of Notre Dame, Paris, and in 1848 succeeded E. H. Godde (see Godde) as architect of the restoration of the church of S. Germain l'Auxerrois, Paris. Lassus was appointed *conservateur* of the buildings of the diocese of Paris in 1849, and of the dioceses of le Mans and of Chartres in 1852. He restored the spires of Chartres cathedral. Lassus designed much ecclesiastical furniture, bronzes, and the like. He contributed frequently to the *Annales Archéologiques* (see Didron). In 1837 he was chosen to direct the illustration of the *Monographie de la cathédrale de Chartres*, published under the direction of the *Ministère de l'Instruction Publique*. He prepared an edition of the *Album* of Villard de Honnecourt (see Villard de Honnecourt) which was completed after his death by Alfred Darcel, and published by the French government.

N. M. Troche, *L'Architecte Lassus;* A. Darcel, *Lassus, Architecte.*

LAT. In the Buddhist architecture of India, a slender upright pillar, the term being generally confined to monoliths, as distinguished from built towers even if not larger (see Stamba). Lats exist near several groups of ruins and in some ancient cities; and they have often been moved, exactly as the obelisks of Egypt were moved in Roman Imperial times, and set up in connection with newer monuments. Among lats is to be reckoned the famous wrought iron pillar of Delhi, 16 inches thick, and of unknown length, as all but about 40 feet is buried. It dates from about 350 B.C., but bears inscriptions of several later epochs.

LATCH. Originally and properly, a form of door bar which is permanently secured to the door by a pivot at one end, the other end being free to fall into a slot or hook, out of which it must be raised to allow the door to open. There is also, generally, a projecting member near the edge of the door beneath the bar which is thus prevented from falling when the door is open. In its primitive form such a latch was raised from the outside by a string passing through a hole in the door, which string was drawn in when security was desired; and later by a short lever passing through the door beneath the bar and working on a pivot. This is essentially the construction of the modern so-called thumb latch (see below). In modern times, the meaning of the term is extended to include spring locks designed especially for outer doors. (See Latch Lock, under Lock.)

Night Latch. One intended primarily for use at night; usually, a form of Latch Lock (see under Lock).

Thumb Latch. A latch as described in the general definition above; the outer end of the lever terminating in a flat or concave plate so adjusted that the thumb presses upon it easily while the fingers grasp an independent curved handle below. — D. N. B. S.

LATCHASH. Among the Klamaths, a lodge, whatever the material of its construction, and also, in general, a house. (See Kayata; Stinash; Tchish; also Lodge.)

Gatschet, *Klamath Dictionary*, Vol. II., Part 2; Contributions to *North American Ethnology*, *U. S. Geological Survey*, s. v. *House.*
— F. S. D.

LATCH BAR. A door or window bar, the ends of which, when in place, are inserted in holes in the jambs, and its withdrawal prevented by an arm like a latch pivoted near one end. The arm being raised, that end of the bar is pushed into its hole until the other end can pass the opposite jamb and be inserted to a properly adjusted depth. The latch is then turned down, its end coming against the first-mentioned jamb, so that the bar cannot be moved in either direction.

LATERAN. Originally in Latin, *Lateranus*, the family name of a branch of a great Roman gens; by extension, belonging to or forming part of the mansion and gardens of this family on the Cælian Hill, near the southeastern extremity of Rome, and in later times, to the buildings erected upon the same site. The Lateran Basilica, or church of S. Giovanni Laterano, is a very ancient church, which has been repeatedly altered, having especially a late neoclassic façade turned toward the east. This has been for many years the cathedral of the Bishop of Rome (the Pope), and, therefore, the central church of the Roman Catholic world; S. Peter's being a parish church, or, from another point of view, the principal chapel of the Vatican palace. The Lateran palace is a very large structure whose ground floor rooms are now used for the exhibition of antiquities, divided into two principal classes, those of Christian antiquity, under the name of *Museo Christiano*, and those of pagan antiquity, under the name of *Museo Profano*. Each of these contains treasures of ancient art not elsewhere to be matched. On the Lateran Hill there is also the ancient baptistery of Constantine (which see). — R. S.

LATH. A strip of wood, generally quite thin and narrow, but often approaching a batten or furring strip in size; a number of which are intended to be secured to beams, studs, and such members for the support of

tiles, slates, plaster, and similar finishing materials.

Counter Lath. *A.* An intermediate lath or batten interposed between a pair of Gauge Laths (see Gauge Lath, below).

B. One of a supplementary set; as when laths are nailed across others used as furring.

Gauge Lath. In roofing, one of a number of laths placed by accurate measurement so as to support a tile or slate at the proper points, as at the nail holes.

Metallic Lath. A preparation of metal, usually wrought, rolled, or drawn iron, to receive plastering by having openings which give a good key or hold to the plaster, and which is also capable of being secured to woodwork

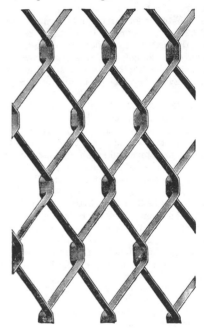

LATH: FIG. 1.

Metallic Lath, made of sheet metal cut and bent so as to produce a fabric with meshes not unlike woven wire.

or metal work in the construction. The most common form has heretofore been a coarse wire netting with the mesh of $\frac{3}{4}$ of an inch or thereabout, and this is commonly called wire lath. Many recent inventions are in the market, generally consisting of thin plates of metal in which openings are cut, the strips which are cut from the openings being left attached by one or two edges and forced into a different plane. Good three-coat plaster upon a solid and well-secured surface of metallic lath has been found to have exceptionally good powers of resistance to fire.

Wire Lath. (See Metallic Lath, above.)

LATHING. *A.* Laths collectively, or material used as a substitute for laths.

B. The operation and the result of securing laths in place for the reception of plaster, tiling, or other finish.

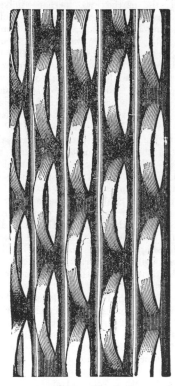

Metallic Lath, made of sheet metal cut and corrugated, and the curved parts forced into projection.

LATIN ARCHITECTURE. The early Christian architecture of historic Europe. It is reasonably called Latin, because it was the architecture of the Latin Church, and was developed among the Latin races of Italy. From Italy it passed into those provinces which remained longest to the Western Empire, — into Gaul, Germany, and probably into Spain, and even Britain. Beginning with Constantine, it held its place from the fourth century to the eighth; and only in the ninth began to give way to the Romanesque, which grew up under the impulse of the Teutonic races, and which, displacing it, was the architecture of the Western Church from the tenth century till the end of the twelfth. To trace its beginnings is difficult. The earliest Christians must have held their meetings in any modest rooms which were at hand; and, before they built for themselves, probably appropriated whatever available buildings they could acquire. When they built, they must at first have built such buildings as they saw about them.

The earliest distinctly Christian buildings were the churches, and the earliest churches which we

know were of the time of Constantine. They were of the form which we call basilican, consisting of three aisles, or rarely five, separated by columns. The middle aisle, which is the nave, was higher and broader than the others, and always ended in a round apse which bowed outward from the wall at the rear of the church. In large and important churches, where room was needed for a great number of the clergy and other privileged persons, a transept was interposed between the end of the nave and the apse. This was a great cross hall as high as the nave, against which the nave and side aisles abutted, and in its farther wall, opposite the end of the nave, was set the apse. Great arches opened into the transept from the ends of the nave and aisles and into the apse; the arch between the nave and the transept has been called the triumphal arch. The upper part of the nave, which we call the clearstory, towering above the side aisles, was lighted by a row of arched windows over their roofs. Similar windows lighted the walls of the aisles, and there was a door in the front end of the nave and of each aisle, farthest from the apse. Nave, transept, and aisles were covered with flat ceilings, or open-timbered roofs. Of this type were the three great churches built in Rome by Constantine, or after his death, those of S. John Lateran, S. Peter, and S. Paul outside the walls, the first and greatest buildings of the newly proclaimed official Church. They were enormous churches, of nearly the same size, some two hundred feet by three hundred and fifty, larger than any of the temples of Greek or Roman architecture, or than any of their Christian successors except the present church of S. Peter, and a few of the largest Gothic cathedrals. They had all double aisles each

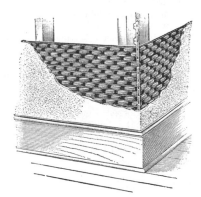

The metallic Lath, Fig. 2, shown in place, with steel corner strip.

side of the nave, transepts that projected somewhat beyond the walls of the aisles, and a single apse opening from the transept opposite the end of the nave. The earliest basilicas fronted the east, according to Oriental usage, though it was not long before this early custom was reversed for liturgical reasons, and the churches were faced westward. Unfortunately, no one of these churches survives in its original form. S. Peter's basilica was pulled down in the sixteenth century to make way for the modern church which occupies its site; S. John Lateran has been hopelessly remodelled and modernized; S. Paul's was burned at the beginning of this century, but has been rebuilt on the old plan. All the three had in front large open courts, called atriums, surrounded by arcaded galleries. Before the doors of each, occupying one gallery of the atrium, was an open porch which crossed the front of the church, and was called the narthex. In the middle of the atrium, to which with the narthex, the catechumens, penitents, and others who were not in full standing in the church were restricted, was a large basin for ablutions, under a canopy. The nave and aisles were occupied at services by the body of the faithful, the raised transept was reserved for the clergy and the privileged, the presbyters of the church sat on a circular bench about the wall of the apse, with the bishop enthroned in the middle of the arc. In front of the apse was set the high altar, which covered and consecrated the vault containing the body of the tutelary saint, and was sheltered under a sumptuous canopy, being the holiest part of the church. These buildings represented the developed ideal for Christian churches in their time, and were the models from which, with more or less variation, all the other church buildings of the Western Church were in that day copied. (See Basilica.) It is probable that the type had been evolved before Constantine's day, and not in Rome, where till that time churches must have been unimportant, but in the East, where the Christians, free from severe persecution till Diocletian's time, had grown wealthy and numerous, and had built many and costly "temples," as the writers of that day call them. Eusebius's description of the church built by Paulinus, Bishop of Tyre, before Constantine, shows that its form was essentially that of the first great Roman churches; it is hard to doubt that it followed the type of those that had just been destroyed in the persecution under Diocletian, and that it shows the prototype of those of Constantine.

Naturally, the early Christian Churches of the West did not all embody the basilican type with the completeness of the three great examples we have described. Most of them had but a single aisle each side the nave, and some small churches had none, the double aisles being extremely rare. Some had three apses at the ends of the aisles. The transept was apparently almost unknown in the East, and in the

West many of the smaller churches were without it. In many cases the atrium has disappeared, and it is likely that in many it was omitted; the narthex was perhaps universal, as the apse unquestionably was. Two of the earliest churches in Rome, S. Lorenzo and S. Agata, both outside the walls, have an upper gallery, or aisles in two stories, a peculiarity of the churches in the East, where the upper gallery was reserved for women; both of these were conventual churches. A conspicuous variation, and one which is significant of the duration of classical traditions in Rome, is that in several of the Roman basilicas the columns which divide the aisles carry the classical entablature, though in most they carry plain arcades. All the evidence shows that this use of arcades borne directly on the columns is of Eastern origin, appearing to us first in Diocletian's palace at Spalato. It seems clear that to the people of Rome, more conservative at that time than the Orientals, the classical entablature was more dignified and honourable than the simple arcade. In the old basilica of S. Peter, while plain arcades were used to divide the double aisles, the nave was bordered with colonnades bearing entablatures. So the arcade was banished from the great basilica of S. Maria Maggiore, built by Pope Liberius in the second half of the fourth century, and from various churches built in Rome at different times from the fourth century to the twelfth.

The Latin type is not properly cruciform. The nave and transept do not interpenetrate or cross each other, but the transept is an independent hall, as it were, set across the nave and aisles, which abut against it. The church is a **T** rather than a cruciform church, though the types are not kept absolutely distinct, and there are many later churches which are compromises between the two. The influence of this Latin type lasted in parts of Italy even through the Gothic period, as may be seen in the great churches of S. Croce and S. Maria Novella at Florence, and in many others. It is most visible in southern Italy and the Adriatic shore, where Byzantine influence lingered long, and in the States of the Church.

The great basilican churches in the East have disappeared, and most of the smaller; but it would seem that they were numerous. Those that remain are noticeable for the lack of transepts, which was doubtless characteristic of the Eastern basilicas. Even the great churches of that type in Ravenna built under the influence of the Eastern Empire — S. Apollinare in Classe and S. Apollinare Nuovo — have none. The basilica at Bethlehem, built, we are told, by Constantine, or his mother, Helena, is practically Roman — a doubled-aisled basilica with transepts, and has the Roman peculiarity of lintels instead of arches along the nave and between the aisles.

Another family of Latin churches was round or polygonal, and often surrounded by an aisle. The form that grew out of this by the addition of four arms of a cross naturally led to a square centre, over which a dome was set almost from the beginning. This was naturally a favourite form for sepulchral chapels, — of which early examples remain at Rome in S. Sinforosa and in the little early chapels of S. Sisto and S. Sotere in the cemetery of Callistus, — and for adjuncts to larger churches. The shape of the Greek cross is of so general occurrence in all kinds of buildings that it is hardly worth while to search for its origin. Its use in the early churches perhaps grew out of its application to tombs — in the catacombs, for instance, by the addition of niches or arcosolia on three sides of a square chamber, of which there are innumerable examples, and in Oriental tombs. A striking example is the mausoleum of Galla Placidia at Ravenna. As soon as the use of this form on a great scale was made monumental by the establishment of the dome on pendentives over a square central area, it became the characteristic and favourite type for Byzantine churches (see Byzantine Architecture). It also, in the Renaissance, became the fruitful parent of churches of a new type, of which the modern church of S. Peter at Rome is the crowning example.

The Latin basilicas were slightly built, mostly of brick, where brick was to be had, as in Italy, with high clearstory walls carried on light arcades, and were an easy prey to accident or violence. They were covered with wooden roofs, sometimes open beneath and sometimes ceiled, and no attempt was made to vault any parts but the apses, which were always covered by half domes. Architecturally they were as plain as possible, with no ornamental features whatever but the columns, which were uniformly taken from older Roman buildings, for even before Constantine's time a rapid decay had set in upon the arts, and the stone carvers in the West soon grew pitiably incapable. The churches in Ravenna almost alone show some attempt at a simple ornamentation in brick of the lines of the exterior. The round churches were more substantial, but equally plain. The use of central domes required substantial masonry; to stay them securely the surrounding aisles were vaulted, and they alone preserved the traditions of the vaulting, which became the leading feature of the subsequent Romanesque. Their solidity is still displayed in the churches of S. Costanza at Rome and S. M. Maggiore at Nocera, in the baptistery of Novara, and others. The only adornment of the early churches was in their altars and the surrounding furniture, which were lavishly enriched, and in the pictorial decoration of their surfaces. The chief of this was mosaic, which began at Constanti-

nople, spread to Ravenna, and became the one artistic achievement of Rome, where in Italy it centred. It was applied first to the apses; in the richer churches it was spread over the inside walls, and in a simpler ornamental form over the floors. When mosaic could not be had, or was too costly, painting was habitually substituted; the interiors were brilliant with Bible stories and legends of the Church. In many this decoration overflowed upon the outside, and the fronts, usually smoothly stuccoed over, were covered with mosaic or painting; several churches in Rome and the cathedral at Parenzo are examples.

— W. P. P. LONGFELLOW.

Allmers, *Die altchristliche Basilika als Vorbild des protestantischen Kirchenbaues;* Dehio, *Die kirchliche Baukunst des Abendlandes;* Gutensohn und Knapp, *Die Basiliken des christlichen Roms* (afterward published as plates to Bunsen's work on Rome); Hübsch, *Die altchristlichen Kirchen nach den Baudenkmalen und älteren Beschreibungen;* Kreuser, *Der christliche Kirchenbau,* Bonn, 1851; Messmer, *Ueber den Ursprung die Entwickelung und Bedeutung der Basilika;* Mothes, *Die Basilikenform bei den Christen der ersten Jahrhunderte; ihre Vorbilder und ihre Entwickelung;* Mothes, *Die Baukunst des Mittelalters in Italien;* Osten, *Die Bauwerke der Lombardei vom 7–14 Jahrhundert;* Quast, *Die altchristlichen Bauwerke von Ravenna vom 5 bis 9 Jahrhundert;* Quast, *Ueber Form, Einrichtung und Ausschmückung der ältesten christlichen Kirchen;* Rahn, *Ueber den Ursprung und die Entwickelung des christlichen Central und Kuppelbaues;* Richter, *Der Ursprung der abendländischen Kirchengebäude;* Stockbauer, *Der christliche Kirchenbau in den ersten 6 Jahrhunderten;* Watkins, *The Basilica or Palatial Hall of Justice and Sacred Temple, and a Description of the Basilican Church of Brixworth;* Zestermann, *Die antiken und die christlichen Basiliken nach ihrer Entstehung.*

LATRINA ; LATRINE. A place for human defecation; especially one established on a large scale, or in a public place, as in a school, barracks, etc. Often in the plural. (Compare Privy; Water-closet.)

LATROBE, BENJAMIN HENRY; architect; b. 1762; d. Sept. 20, 1820.

The son of the Rev. Benjamin Latrobe, superintendent of the Moravians in England. He entered the Stamp Office in London in 1783. He afterward studied architecture and built several residences in England. In 1796 he emigrated to Virginia and met President Washington. He was appointed engineer to the state of Virginia. He afterward went to Philadelphia, where he undertook the superintendence of the water supply. By letter of Thomas Jefferson (see Jefferson), dated March 6, 1803, Latrobe was appointed surveyor of public buildings in Washington with the especial charge of the Capitol. He was directed to retain the main features of the design of Dr. Thornton (see Thornton), but nevertheless made very considerable changes. In 1806 his general conduct of the work was defended by Latrobe in a letter to members of Congress (see Bibliography). Work on the Capitol was suspended in 1811, and on Aug. 24, 1814, the building was burned by the British. Feb. 15, 1815, Congress authorized President Madison to borrow $500,000 for the completion of the Capitol, and on April 20 of that year Latrobe was reappointed architect of the building. He resigned his position Nov. 24, 1817. Between 1811 and 1815 he was interested in steamboat navigation at Pittsburg. On his retirement in 1817 he went to Baltimore, and in 1820 to New Orleans.

Glenn Brown, *History of the United States Capitol;* Bulfinch, *Life of Charles Bulfinch;* Howard, *Architects of the American Capitol;* Latrobe, *A Private Letter on the Public Buildings of the United States.*

LATTICE. A system of small, light bars crossing each other at regular intervals. In modern country houses this is often made of laths, or light slips of wood forming regular square or lozenge-shaped openings. In Oriental work, as in the houses of Cairo and other levantine cities, the projecting windows are filled with very elaborate lattices. (See Meshrebeeyeh.) A similar filling for windows was once common in England, replacing glass, and shutting out much of the snow and rain. A lattice painted red was the sign of the tavern. The term is extended to cover glazed sash in which the sash bars form square or lozenge-shaped openings filled with pieces of glass of the same shape.

Also, in recent times and in composition, a large structure of similar form. Thus, an iron girder having a web composed of diagonal braces is commonly known as a lattice girder. A distinction is sometimes made, in iron construction, between latticing and lacing: the former applying to a double diagonal system of bars crossing each other ; the latter restricted to mean a single series arranged in zig-zag. — R. S.

LAUFGANG. In German, a Gallery in sense *D* or *E* ; an ambulatory ; a deambulatory.

LAUN, BENEDIKT VON. (See Benedikt von Laun.)

LAUNDRY. A room, or a group of rooms, or a separate building, where all operations incidental to washing and ironing clothes and linen are carried on ; often a commercial establishment, or a public washhouse, in which laundry work is performed.

In small houses and flats kitchen and laundry are combined, a set of washtubs being supplied with hot water from the kitchen boiler (see Kitchen) ; the tubs generally have covers which can be used as a kitchen table.

A domestic laundry is, in city houses, usually located near the basement kitchen, and in country mansions on the ground floor of the service wing. It usually contains a set of from two to four fixed washtubs, with rubber roller wringer ; a laundry stove with flat top for the wash boiler, and with places to heat the flatirons ; a laundry boiler, and sometimes a drying closet, or a combination laundry stove and clothes dryer (see Drying Room). Sometimes a special copper boiler, set in masonry, with grate and with flue connection, for boiling the clothes, is used, and provided with vapour pipe to remove steam and odours. There should be room for one or two ironing boards ; the flatirons are sometimes heated on gas heaters. Larger house laundries sometimes include a hand washing machine and a hand-power mangle. In modern pretentious apartment houses a general laundry is often provided for tenants, either in the basement, or on the top floor. Basement laundries are objectionable on account of noise, drainage difficulties, and laundry odours. When located on the top floor, special precautions are required to guard against damage to ceilings by accidental overflows.

The laundry of a modern large hotel is fitted up with washtubs for washing by hand, besides a complete outfit of improved laundry machinery. Modern public institutions, such as hospitals or orphan asylums, are still more complete in their laundry appointments. Often a special laundry building of one or two stories is erected, and subdivided into rooms corresponding to the principal laundry operations. The rooms are generally so placed in relation to each other that the wash passes from one room to the next in the regular order of the operations, thereby avoiding unnecessary transportation and systematizing the entire work. Here the general wash is assorted, while that from infected patients is kept entirely separate and sent to the disinfecting chamber. The large wash room where the clothes are soaked, boiled, washed, rinsed, and blued or starched contains the washtubs of earthenware, or other non-absorbing material, for the hand washing of the smaller pieces ; the large power washing machines in which the wash is soaked, boiled, soaped, and rinsed ; the wringing machines and the centrifugal hydro-extractors. From the wash room the clothes are taken to the drying room and dried by steam on horses sliding on wheels within a heated chamber (see Drying Room). When the clothes are ready to receive the finishing operations, after being blued or starched, they are sent to the ironing room. Here the larger pieces are placed in large power mangles or calendering machines, while cuffs, collars, and shirts are finished by special ironing and polishing machines. In buildings of two stories the finishing operations are generally performed on the upper floor, which is connected with the wash and drying rooms by means of clothes elevators. The receiving and assorting room should have a water-tight floor, with means for flushing ; the floor should be cemented, asphalted, or tiled, and graded to one or more floor drains. The walls are finished in hard plaster and oil paint, cemented, or tiled. The same finish is required for the large wash room. Both rooms require good ventilation, to remove odours of soiled linen and steam vapours. In large laundries special exhaust fans are provided. Plastered and wooden ceilings are undesirable for the wash room; brick arches or metal ceilings are better. Both rooms require ample light and sufficient floor space to insure order and cleanliness. The drying chambers must be built fireproof, and provided with exhaust flue to remove superfluous moisture. Filters should be installed for filtering water when necessary.

Special attention should be given to the disinfection of clothes or bedding of infectious disease patients, which is done by steam in cylindrical chambers. The disinfecting room is divided into two parts, one to receive the soiled linen, the other for the linen when disinfected, a solid partition being placed between them.

In modern laundries hand washing is almost entirely superseded by steam and machine washing. The machines require steam and water connections and large-sized waste valves which discharge into open troughs or gutters. In the machines the soaking, the washing with soapsuds, and the rinsing of the wash is accomplished. The first drying of the wash is done by steam wringers having two rubber-covered rollers, between which the clothes are passed under pressure, or by the centrifugal wringers or extractors. These are large-sized baskets of tinned copper, with perforated sides and double bottom, swiftly revolving in an outer metal case; by this means one-half of the water of the wet clothes is extracted. The subsequent drying by steam is accomplished quickly in the large drying chambers. The ironing of smaller pieces is done by hand. All work which is blued but not starched is pressed by mangles, as described above.

For bibliography see that for Kitchen; also *Laundry Management — Handbook for Use in Private and Public Laundries*, London, Crosby, Lockwood & Co.; *Steam Laundries and Public Health*, London, Sanitary Pub. Co.; Grothe, *Wäscherei, Reinigung und Bleicherei*.

— W. P. Gerhard.

LAURANA, LUCIANO DA. (See Luciano da Laurana.)

LAVA. Any volcanic rock which has been poured out on the surface of the earth rather than injected in the form of dikes and bosses.

— G. P. M.

Lava is used for building in the neighbourhood of Mt. Vesuvius, at Volvic, in Auvergne, and in the neighbouring towns, such as Clermont-Ferrand, and Montferrand (see France, Part VIII.), and elsewhere in Europe. Vases and sculptured ornaments of different kinds are made in the vicinity of Naples, from lava of many

different colours; and gas burners are fitted with tips of lava in the United States and elsewhere. A system of outdoor painted decoration is entitled Lava Painting, or Painting upon Lava, and it appears that for this purpose the natural lava is employed, the character of the work depending upon the process employed, which is not made public. — R. S.

LAVACRUM. A bathtub; a late Latin term equivalent to Labrum.

LAVATORY IN THE CLOISTER OF THE CHURCH OF S. ALEXIS, ROME.

The decoration in mosaic is of the general character of Cosmati work.

LAVATOIRE. Formerly, in an ecclesiastical establishment, a trough or bath for washing the bodies of the dead. The usual form appears to have been that of a stone slab, hollowed out to the depth of a few inches and provided with an outlet for the waste water.

LAVATORY. *A.* A room or apartment for performing ablutions; also a basin or fix-

LAVATORY IN THE ABBEY OF S. DENIS; NOW IN THE ÉCOLE DES BEAUX ARTS, PARIS.
The water spirted from the spouts between the heads.

ture, either portable or stationary, intended for washing.

B. In modern plumbing work, a "set" wash-basin. (See Basin; Lavatoire; Lavoir.)
— W. P. G.

LAVER, AUGUSTUS. (See Fuller, Thomas.)

LAVOIR. In French, in general, any place for washing. As understood in English, especially a place arranged on a river bank, or the like, for washing clothes and linen. Such places are common in the western and southern parts of the Continent, where they afford often the only facilities for such washing which are possessed by large numbers of the people. The essential features are a platform on which the worker kneels and from which a sloping board, or inclined plane, extends into the water to accommodate the articles to be scrubbed. The better sort have a roof covering a considerable part of the bank, and projecting over the water; and the space so covered is often partially enclosed. (Cut, cols. 717, 718.) — D. N. B. S.

LAW CONCERNING ARCHITECTURE AND BUILDING. That which is recognized by the courts. This may be written in codes and statutes (*lex scripta*) as general on the Continent of Europe; or may consist of the principles derived from decisions of the courts, ren-

dered, followed, and developed as times and conditions change (*lex tradita*) and known as the Common Law, as general in Great Britain and the United States; or, finally, it may consist of the latter body of law modified in detail by special statutes relating to particular subject-matters. Either body of law may be specially applied in special localities, or in respect to matters, by the rules or orders of special authorities which derive their powers from general law of either kind. Such special authorities are the Ministers of the Interior, or of Education and Worship, or of Fine Arts, of nations, the departmental bureaus or commissions established by the state, or the municipal authorities to whom special power may have been given.

This body of law, so far as of special interest to builders, may be divided as follows: —

A. That which regulates the transfer of land or buildings, either permanently or for a time. Of this only the leasing of property concerns the architect or builder. (See Lease.)

B. That which prescribes how money may be raised on land or buildings without transfer, as in the case of mortgage, whether recorded and made accessible, as in some modern communities; or, as in ancient Greece, identified with the land by the erection of stelæ set up within

Echelle de |—————|—————|—————|—————| metres
0   1   2   3   4

Plan

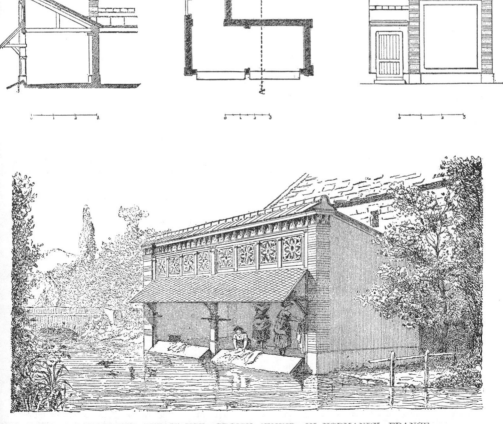

LAVOIR FOR PUBLIC USE; CROISY (EURE), IN NORMANDY, FRANCE.

the boundaries of the plot mortgaged ; or, as is frequently the case, left unrecorded and causing infinite inconvenience in case of subsequent transfer. This concerns the architect and builder only as explaining one of the modern ways of building with but little disturbance of other investments. The same scheme carried further, under the general name of Building Loan, enables the speculative builder to put up dwellings or business buildings and sell them, taking great risks, but using little money of his own. The result of this is to aid greatly those who would have homes of their own, while, on the other hand, the character of the buildings is kept down in solidity and in artistic merit ; the building loan arrangement especially tending to discourage all thought or care for design, because the building which is run up quickly for sale to the first comer must be kept free from novelty of appearance.

C. That which determines the rights and duties of owners of buildings or of parts of buildings. This is divisible into : —

(1) Provision for the partial use of streets and highways, for parts of buildings or otherwise, as in towns, by owners of private property.

(2) Provision for joint action of several owners in building or in the use of land in connection therewith. Of chief interest here are Party Wall arrangements, and easements for Right of Way, or for "light and air," or for restrictions as to the use or character of buildings. By Right of Way is meant the privilege to use a certain path through private property ; or to traverse a certain field or plot of ground, as when this affords the only means, or a necessary additional means, of reaching the plot occupied by the other owner. This may be permanent or temporary. The law recognizes the existence of an ancient right by which, if a piece of property be left open for free transit for a certain length of time, the right of such transit becomes fixed forever ; and legislation has been enacted defining and limiting this possibility. In the absence of such legislation very curious controversies have arisen in Great Britain, where the owner of a large estate has wished to put a stop to what seemed to him trespass, while the occupants of neighbouring dwellings insisted on their time-honoured privilege. In the United States, agreements for the granting of these rights have been rather in the way of selling a piece of property more advantageously by means of this privilege going with it.

(3) Provision for restrictions, as where a piece of property is sold subject to a restricted right of building upon the plot of ground. This restriction, usually the result of private agreement, is recognized by the courts so long as the conditions remain unchanged ; but a cer-

tain elasticity of treatment has marked judicial decisions in cases where the uses of the property in that neighbourhood have changed. Thus, if the houses of a row are set back six feet from the lot line by agreement, and this with the purpose of benefiting the neighbourhood as a place of residence, the courts have refused to maintain this when the neighbourhood has evidently passed into the condition of a place for business buildings, shop fronts, and the like.

(4) Provision for the prevention of public nuisances or injuries to health ; as when a law limits the height of buildings, or the amount of the lot which may be covered by a building. (See Legislation.)

(5) Provision for the safety of occupants. This in all matters of special interest to builders is largely the subject of Legislation (which see).

(6) Provision for quality of building, as in Building Laws of all sorts, and in precautions against the spread of fires (see Fireproofing ; Legislation).

(7) Provision against the disfiguring of a street or square by architectural designs assumed not to reach a certain level of excellence (see Legislation).

(8) Provision for compensating those injured in person or property by the carelessness (negligence) of builders or owner, in Specification (which see, especially definition B) or construction. This is one branch of the law of "negligence" determined in Great Britain and the U. S., chiefly by the common law, but in France a matter of special legislation and the only means used for insuring good and sufficient work. In France the criminal as well as the civil law is invoked in case of accident; and the architect whose building falls is compelled to prove his own absence of negligence, being still amenable to suits for damages. (See Architect, The, in France.)

(9) Provision for limiting the number or prescribing the qualifications of builders or architects (see Legislation).

D. That which regulates the bargains between the builder or architect and his employer. This is a branch of the ordinary law of contract.

E. That which insures their compensation to the furnishers of labour and material by giving them special claims on the property (see Lien), which, according to the legal status, may or may not have preference over mortgages.

— R. S.

NOTE. — In this and other papers touching the legal aspects of building, the writer has had the aid of Mr. Philip Golden Bartlett, which he acknowledges with gratitude.

LAW COURTS. Properly, the Royal Courts of Justice, in London ; a vast agglomeration of buildings, designed by George Edmund

PLATE XXVI

LEANING TOWER

That of S. Giorgio dei Greci in Venice. This tower was begun in 1587 and, according to the traditions, settled unevenly, so that it reached its present angle of inclination within a few years. When was set plumb. The front of the church is of 1570. The enclosing wall of the court with its different openings is interesting. The doorway on the left opens into the narrow Fondamenta dei Greci.

Street, and finished in 1882. The great central hall, which serves as a passage, place of waiting, etc. (see Salle des Pas Perdus) is a very important piece of modern Gothic with a fine vaulted roof.

LAWN. An open, grass-covered space, generally a smooth, well-kept, more or less level field with few or no shrubs, trees, or plants. (See Landscape Architecture.)

LAY. In British usage, in plastering, the first or rough coat.

LAYARD, AUSTEN HENRY; archæologist, diplomatist, and writer on art; b. March 6, 1817 (in Paris) ; d. June 5, 1894.

In 1842 Layard visited the ruins at Nimroud and conceived the idea of making excavations there. At this time he fell in with Flandin and Coste (see Flandin ; Coste) then engaged in their Persian explorations, and with Botta who was contemplating the excavations at Khorsabad. In 1845 he began the excavations at Nimroud, where he discovered in two years four great palaces. He published the results of his first expedition in *Nineveh and Its Remains* (2 vols. 8vo, London, 1849) ; and the *Monuments of Nineveh, from drawings made on the spot illustrated in 100 plates* (London, 1849, folio). The results of a second expedition undertaken for the trustees of the British Museum, were published in *Discoveries in the Ruins of Nineveh and Babylon* (London, 1853, 2 vols. 8vo), and *Second Series of the Monuments of Nineveh* (London, 1853, folio). After 1880 he lived in Venice and gave much attention to Italian painting.

Obituary in *Journal of Royal Institute of British Architects*, 1893–1894, p. 592.

LAYENS, MATHIEU DE ; architect.

He established himself at Louvain, Belgium, in 1445, as *maître des maçonneries* of that city. He designed the Hôtel de Ville at Louvain, the finest late Gothic building in Belgium, of which the first stone was laid March 29, 1448. It was finished in 1459.

Biographie Nationale de Belgique.

LAYER BOARD. Same as Lear Board.

LAY OUT (v.). To draw, describe, plot, or mark the profiles or outlines according to which a structure, or a part, is to be worked or erected ; whether such operation consists in drawing to scale on paper ; staking out on the ground ; outlining on a board in full size, the shape for a workman to cut ; or any similar process. (See Drawing ; Plot ; Stake Out.)

LAY STALL. A public place for the temporary deposit of refuse, manure, garbage, and the like, prior to their final removal.

LAZARETTE ; LAZARETTO. Same as Lazar House.

LAZAR HOUSE. A hospital for those afflicted with contagious diseases of very dangerous character ; perhaps originally the same as the French *ladrerie*, which is generally considered a hospital for lepers only. The establishment of such shelters for the hopelessly sick and those afflicted with diseases which were considered dangerous to the whole community was, during the Middle Ages, of a somewhat indiscriminate and unscientific character, one formidable disease being confused with another. The terms "lazar house" and "lazarette," derived from the story of Lazarus in the New Testament, are primarily without accurate signification.

LEAD. As used specifically in architecture, — a small slender sash bar of lead used in decorative glasswork. (See Glass ; Window ; and for leadwork in general, see Metal Work.)

LEAD, EFFECT OF WATER ON. (See Plumbing.)

LEADER. *A.* Same as Flexible Cord, under Electrical Appliances.

B. Specifically, in architectural use, a pipe for the removal of roof water. (See Conductor, B. ; Drainage.)

LEADING. The process and the result of executing any work in lead, specifically, a system of lead sash bars to receive glass. (See Glass ; Window.)

LEADS. In British usage, lead roofing ; a roof or roofs covered with lead. Used collectively, especially of flat roofs and decks.

LEADWORK. (See Metal Work.)

LEAF. One fold of a door or shutter. (Compare Valve.)

LEANING PLACE. Same as Allège. — (A. P. S.)

LEANING TOWER. A tower, usually detached and slender for its height, which overhangs its base on one side. Such towers are often found out of the true vertical. Owing to the disproportion between weight and area of support, slender towers are peculiarly exposed to those accidental deflections from the perpendicular which are common to buildings placed on marshy or otherwise treacherous soil, or which have poorly constructed foundations. On this account, leaning towers which are known to have stood in an unchanged and pronounced inclination for a number of centuries, are commonly regarded as natural wonders, but are generally assumed to have been affected by accident or carelessness. In the effort to account for the stability of such towers the theory of original and intentional construction has been occasionally invoked. Notably is this the case with two leaning towers in Bologna and one in Pisa, all of the twelfth century. Those of Bologna belong to the type of fortress towers common in the cities of mediæval Italy. They stand in close proximity to one another and near the centre of the city. Both are square, plain, brick buildings. The *Torre Asinelli* (1109), is 323 feet in height and 4 feet out of perpendicular. The *Torre Garisenda* (1110) is 157 feet in height and 10 feet out of perpendicular. It is probable, however, that this tower was once much higher. Its inclination is first mentioned in the fourteenth century in Dante's *Inferno*, Book XXXI., I., 139: "As seems the Carisenda to look below its slant when a cloud goes over it," etc. It has not changed sensibly within a hundred years. The various peculiarities of construction arguing purpose have been described by Alidosi and Leandro Alberti. Their arguments have found very general but not absolutely universal acceptance. Among the sceptics is Mothes; see his *Baukunst des Mittelalters in Italien* (1884).

The campanile of the Pisa Cathedral was begun about sixty years later than the Bologna towers (1174), and it is the belief of some Italian authorities that these suggested the construction of its even more venturesome obliquity, amounting to nearly 13 feet in a height of 179 feet. A remarkable feature of this tower is that the lean of each successive story above the first is slightly less than that of the story preceding. The lines of the tower thus show a return curve straightening toward the perpendicular, the curve being produced by a series of slight rectifications in the position of the columns which form the surrounding galleries. Each successive gallery is also slightly higher on the leaning side. The measurements for this lifting up of the seven stories of the tower on the leaning side are as follows, in centimetres, beginning above the first story: .03; .04; .07; .15; .08; .11; .38. (The last measure applies to the steps which support the top story.) These facts have been interpreted by Rohault de Fleury, *Monuments de Pise* (1866), and by Mothes, from whom these measurements are quoted, as arguing a separate and distinct settlement for each successive story of the tower corresponding to the measures quoted above, which are thus assumed to represent the correctives applied to a gradual settlement which took place *during construction*. A farther settlement of eighty centimetres, after completion, is assumed by these writers to account for the existing lean. This theory is an elaboration of that of Vasari (sixteenth century), who supposed the change in the direction of the tower to begin above the third story, and who consequently described the first assumed settlement as having taken place when the tower was about half finished. Other authorities, among whom Ranieri Grassi and Ricci are most prominent, have interpreted the same facts as arguing an original and purposed construction. From their point of view the supposed correctives were simply means to increase the stability of an original and constructed lean. The following additional arguments for such an intention are among those quoted by Grassi, *Descrizione Storia e Artis-*

tica di Pisa (1837). The spiral stairway, whose cylindrical walls form the body of the tower, is built with increased height on the sides of the lean, and with decreased height on the sides opposite the lean; thus throwing a greater weight of masonry on the side opposed to the lean. The steps of the stairway have not the full inclination which the position of the tower would lead one to expect if that inclination had been accidental. A window on the lower story opening into the well formed by the cylindrical wall containing the stairway is horizontal and not inclined. This is also asserted by Grassi of the apertures left in the walls for the scaffoldings. Gaspare Scotti, an Italian author of the seventeenth century, was the first modern writer to call attention to the law of statics which insures the stability of a leaning building whose parts are firmly bound together, and whose centre of gravity does not project beyond the limits of the supporting foundation. A knowledge of this law would have enabled the builders of this tower to erect it with absolute security of permanent stability in its present position. The question of intention is thus left to a balance of probabilities. An appeal might be made to the eccentric corkscrew-shaped spire at Gelnhausen, and to the constructive rocking minarets of Persia, described by Dieulafoy.

There are two other leaning towers at Pisa, the campaniles of S. Michele dei Scalzi and of S. Nicolà, the latter a work of Niccolò Pisano. Constructive facts arguing intention have been quoted for this latter by Grassi and by Goodyear (*Architectural Record*, Vol. VII., No. 3). The latter has also observed that the leaning Torre del Pubblico at Ravenna "is built on both the leaning sides with a batter, and that the brick masonry is all manifestly of one date and of homogeneous construction. This batter must contemplate a reënforcement in the side of the lean, belonging to the original construction, and seems to make out a clear case of intention." The campanile of S. Mark's at Venice leans slightly. That this obliquity existed in the sixteenth century is known by one of Tintoretto's paintings in the Doge's Palace. A recent examination by Mr. C. H. Blackall proves that the foundations have not settled, a fact also mentioned by Vasari. The campaniles of the churches of S. Giorgio dei Grechi, of the Frari, of S. Stefano, and of S. Geremia, all at Venice, are considerably out of plumb. There are also leaning towers at Burano, Padua, Este, Rovigo, Ferrara, Modena, Cologne, Leeuwarden, Langres, Caerphilly in Wales, Bridgnorth in Shropshire, Corfe Castle in Dorsetshire, and Nevianski in Russia; and towers with a very slight inclination are not uncommon. The leaning tower of Zaragoza, called the Torre Nueva, dating from the sixteenth century, was octagonal and built of brick, with elaborate ornamentation of the same material. It overhung its foundation about ten feet. It was taken down in 1892.

The best summary of the literature on the Leaning Tower of Pisa is furnished by Ricci, *Storia del l'Architettura in Italia.* The most instructive surveys and sections of this tower are found in Cresy and Taylor, *Art of the Middle Ages in Italy* (1829), but their measurements for the heights of the stories have been replaced by those of Mothes, as quoted. The section given in the atlas of *Les Monuments de Pise* by Rohault de Fleury should also be consulted.

— WILLIAM H. GOODYEAR.

LEAN-TO. In the United States, a small extension to a building with a roof that has but one slope, and therefore appears to lean against the main house. Also any similar building constructed against some other object, as the shelter sometimes made by Indians by laying poles against a fallen tree trunk. — F. S. D.

LEAR BOARD. A board along the lower edge of a sloping roof next to the gutter (also Layer Board).

LEASE. A document by which property in land or buildings is let to a tenant for a fixed time. Leases of land for purposes of building are for long terms, and provide for the disposition of the building at the end of the term, as by its reverting wholly to the owner of the land or as by its sale to him at a valuation. It is often asserted that the practice of building dwellings and the like upon leased property, as in cities, tends toward slightness of construction and a generally low grade of work, because the person who puts his money into the building feels perhaps too strongly that it is not his absolute property. In towns where the custom prevails the results seem to justify this view (see Law.) — R. S.

LEBAS, LOUIS HIPPOLYTE; architect; b. March 21, 1782; d. June 12, 1867.

Lebas was a pupil of the elder Vaudoyer (see Vaudoyer), of Charles Percier (see Percier), and of the *École des Beaux Arts,* Paris. In 1806 he won the *Second Grand Prix de Rome.* From 1806 until 1808 he served as a soldier in Italy. He was appointed inspector of the construction of the Bourse, Paris, in 1811, built the monument to Malesherbes in the Salle des Pas Perdus of the Palais de Justice, Paris, in 1822, and designed the church of Notre Dame de Lorette, Paris, in 1824. In 1831 he was made *architecte conservateur* of the fourth section of the monuments of Paris, which comprised the *Pont Neuf,* the *Institut,* the *Bibliothèque Mazarin,* and the *École des Beaux Arts.* In 1840 he was appointed professor of the history of architecture at the *École des Beaux Arts.* For many years he conducted the most important private architectural school in Paris. Among his

pupils were the two Labrouste (see Labrouste) and Charles Garnier (see Garnier).

Notice Nécrologique in *Rev. Gén. de l'Architecture;* Bauchal, *Dictionnaire.*

LEBLOND, ALEXANDRE JEAN BAPTISTE; architect; b. about 1680; d. 1719.

Leblond was the son of a painter. He received his first training in that art, and afterward turned his attention to architecture. In 1716 he went to Saint Petersburg on the invitation of Peter the Great. For him he built the palace of Peterhoff, and designed its gardens. Leblond published *La théorie et la pratique du jardinage* (4to, Paris, 1722), and other works.

Dezallier d'Argenville, *Vie des fameux architectes.*

LE BOUTEILLER. (See Bouteiller.)

LE BRETON. (See Breton.)

LEBRUN, CHARLES; painter and architect; b. Feb. 24, 1619; d. Feb. 12, 1690.

In 1648 he founded, with the assistance of the Chancellor Seguier, and under the auspices of Cardinal Mazarin, the *Académie royale de peinture et de sculpture,* of which he was director until 1683. In 1660 he was made director of the manufacture of tapestries for the Gobelins by Colbert. In 1666, under the patronage of Louis IV., he established the *Académie de France* in Rome. As *premier peintre* to Louis XIV., Lebrun exercised almost absolute power over the artistic undertakings of that monarch. He was, above all, a decorator. He designed and decorated the Gallery of Apollo at the Louvre, which, however, was not completed until 1848–51 (see Duban). At Versailles he decorated the Grande Galerie, the Salon de la Paix, the Salon de la Guerre, and the great stairway. He was also employed at the château of Marly.

Henri Jouin, *Charles Lebrun et les arts sous Louis XIV.;* Merson, *Charles Lebrun* in *Gazette des Beaux Arts,* 1895; Genevay, *Style Louis XIV.*

LECLÈRE, ACHILLE FRANÇOIS RENÉ; architect; b. Oct. 29, 1785, at Paris; d. Dec. 23, 1853.

A pupil of Jean Nicolas Louis Durand (see Durand) and Charles Percier (see Percier). In 1808 he won the *Premier Grand Prix de Rome.* While in Rome he made a famous restoration of the Pantheon. In 1815 he opened an architectural school (atelier) in Paris, which developed many prominent architects. Leclère built many residences in Paris, and restored many châteaux in the provinces. He was appointed *inspecteur général* of the *Conseil des bâtiments civils* in 1840.

Lance, *Notice sur Leclère.*

LECTERN. Originally a high sloping desk standing in the middle of the choir, often accompanied by a pair of tall candlesticks, and used as a rest for the service book, from whence the

LECTERN OF BRASS, CHURCH OF NOTRE DAME, AACHEN (AIX-LA-CHAPELLE), RHENISH PRUSSIA.
Fig. 1, plan ; Fig. 2, large scale detail of one corner of triangular centrepiece ; Fig. 3, large scale detail of one of the buttress towers.

hebdomadrius reads or sings certain portions of the canonical hours, the antiphons, and lessons. It can be either fixed or movable, and sometimes the desk is double; if so, it is made so as to revolve. Lecterns came into use at an early date, and were made very precious with costly materials, gold, silver, marble, and mosaics. Pope Leo III. (795–816) gave one to S. Peter's church at Rome, made "of the purest silver." During the present century lecterns of brass, with the desk resting on the outspread wings of an eagle, have been introduced very generally in the cathedrals and parish churches of the English Establishment and of the Protestant Episcopal Church in America. They are placed beneath or just outside of the chancel arch, to hold the Bible from which the lessons of the day are read to the congregation. (Cut, cols. 729, 730.) — CARYL COLEMAN.

LECTORIUM. The place in a Christian church from which parts of the Scripture are read. Hence, by extension, same as Lectern.

LECTURE ROOM. A hall or large room arranged to accommodate an audience and to furnish proper conditions for addressing it orally. In colleges, the term is applied to a room occupied by a professor or assistant, who imparts instruction therein and uses it also, on occasion, for examinations or ordinary recitations. Lecture rooms in colleges often are so small as to accommodate a class not exceeding twenty students; but it is more common to arrange them for a much larger number of persons. The disposition of the benches or chairs varies greatly; it is often temporary, and may be altered at will by the professor to whom the room is assigned; thus, the same room 24 feet square, or thereabout, will at one time have benches arranged along its walls, accommodating, in this way, as many as forty students without setting the benches two deep; and at another time the same number of benches may be arranged in four rows in the middle of the room. Lecture rooms for public audiences are generally built large enough to accommodate at least three hundred persons seated. It is not

LECTERN, AT ANGLE OF MARBLE PULPIT, CHURCH OF S. BARTOLOMEO, PISTOJA, TUSCANY; c. 1520.

LECTERN OF CARVED WOOD, CHURCH OF S. MARIA, IN ORGANO, VERONA.

The two-faced reading desk revolves; see end elevation. The whole is adorned with inlay and delicate carving.

729 730

common to build the floor with a slope nor to raise the speaker's platform more than 2 feet above the floor. The modern demand for a magic lantern and a large screen upon which to throw its pictures should be met by the reservation of a space to accommodate the lantern at such distance from the screen as the instrument requires, and without seats behind it, whose occupants could not see properly the speaker or the screen. There are a few halls accommodating a thousand or more persons each, and in these the floor may have the isacoustic curve and the stage may be raised 5 or 6 feet above the floor in its immediate vicinity. Galleries also are used where a large audience may be expected. (See Acoustics, § *Enclosed Auditorium;* Auditorium (I.), *A;* Seating Capacity.) — R. S.

LEDGE. *A.* A relatively small projecting member or moulding, as a stop bead, a fillet.

B. A member of wood fulfilling the functions of a cleat, but frequently much larger. Thus, the cross pieces at the top and bottom of a batten door are known as ledges, as also the much larger members performing a similar function in a partition or sheet piling.

LEDGED DOOR. See under Door.

LEDGED PARTITION. A partition constructed of vertical boards, which are secured at top and bottom by horizontal ledges.

LEDGER. In general, any member intended to occupy an incumbent position. Often in combination. More specifically : —

A. One of the longitudinal horizontal timbers of a scaffold, secured to the uprights and supporting the putlogs.

B. A flat stone used as the top or finish of a structure, as of a tomb.

LE DUC. (See Duc, Gabriel le.)

LEEWAN. In Mohammedan countries : —

A. The raised part of the floor of a room upon which persons may sit or lie, especially in the case of a reception room in a house. The addition of a mattress and cushions to this makes of it a deewan. Apparently, by extension, as from the furnishing to the room, and farther, to similar, though larger, rooms : —

B. A chamber or hall opening upon a court ; an open arcade of any sort, even in a mosque.

Lane, *The Modern Egyptian.*

LEFUEL, HECTOR MARTIN ; architect ; b. Nov. 14, 1810 ; d. Dec. 31, 1880.

Lefuel was trained in architecture by his father and Jean Nicolas Huyot (see Huyot), and won the *Premier Grand Prix de Rome* in 1839. In 1845 he was appointed inspector of the works at the *Chambre des Députés,* Paris, and in 1853 architect of the château of Fontainebleau, where he built for Napoleon III. the new Salle de Spectacle in the right wing. In 1854 he succeeded Visconti (see Visconti) as architect of the buildings connecting the

Louvre with the Tuileries. Lefuel made important changes in Visconti's designs. He finished the inner fronts of the buildings enclosing the Place du Carrousel, and remodelled, from his own plans, the Grande Galerie of the Louvre from the Pavillon Lesdiguières to the Pavillon de Flore. Between 1860 and 1870 he remodelled the Pavillon de Flore itself (see Carpeaux), and between 1871 and 1876 the Pavillon de Marsan. He was made *Inspecteur général des bâtiments civils* in 1866.

Maurice du Seigneur in Planat's *Encyclopédie.*

LEGEAY, JEAN.

In 1732 Legeay won the *Grand Prix* in architecture. He was called to Berlin in 1754, and became architect to the king, Friedrich II. (Frederick the Great). He designed the palace of Sans Souci, and other buildings in and near Potsdam, near Berlin.

Dussieux, *Les Artistes français à l'étranger;* Lance, *Dictionnaire.*

LEGISLATION CONCERNING ARCHITECTURE AND BUILDING. That part of the law existing in such matters which is the result of legislative action.

Under the term Law the whole body of regulations concerning this matter is given in brief analysis : that which has been especially the subject of legislation in modern times consists chiefly in the following :

(1) *Easement.* The need of agreements between owners of adjoining plots of ground has led to careful legislation with respect to certain easements, such as Right of Way. By an easement in this sense is meant the privilege granted by one owner of property to another. Thus an agreement by one party to leave open a certain space on his own ground, upon which space windows of the adjoining property may look, or a permanent right of way across one person's property from the public road to the neighbour's property, is an easement ; and the exact conditions of this have been most carefully treated by the statute makers of different countries.

(2) *Streets.* Whereas in the Middle Ages and later streets were very irregularly surveyed and aligned (see Alignment), and seem to have been kept open merely for passengers, sometimes on horseback or in vehicles, sometimes on foot only, and without other considerations ; modern statute law is careful of light and air and forbids the overhanging of the public way by upper stories or by balconies beyond a certain very limited width (see Street Architecture), or by oriel windows, and still more carefully the projection of bay windows which start from the ground. When such bay windows are allowed, it will be found to have occurred generally through the consent obtained from neighbours, or by the action, generally claimed to

be irregular or illegal, of public officials. On the other hand, the most carefully organized cities allow a certain projection upon the public way for steps leading up to a door above the sidewalk or down to an area. (See Area; Courtyard; Stoop.) So in Paris there seems to be a very large liberty given for the use of the marquise of glass (see Marquise), its transparency being supposed to prevent its becoming a nuisance. The enforcement of such statutes has tended to detract greatly from the picturesqueness of some ancient towns. Thus in the south of France, cities which have been characterized by the great number of overhanging upper stories are now devoid of them; but this has been a popular change in most cases, and the visitor is asked to sympathize with the inhabitants who have in this way gained a clearer street and a freer daylight for their front windows.

(3) *High Buildings.* In modern cases of very lofty structures it has been noted that a twenty-story business building may be thought useful even to the owner only so long as the neighbours do not erect buildings of the same height. It is often stated that no community could endure streets lined entirely by buildings of a height exceeding 200 feet and often reaching 300 feet. Moreover, it has been noted that the number of possible occupants of these buildings, taken collectively, would be more than the width of the streets in the given sections of the town would allow to pass freely to and fro. In other words, that section of the town would be overbuilt. Moreover, it is noted that very high buildings shut out sunshine from their neighbours to an unreasonable degree. Danger from fire in the upper stories is of less moment, because other legislation can provide for that. For all these reasons it is proposed to limit the heights of buildings by legislation, but this has been achieved only in one or two cases. A somewhat similar case arose not long since in one of the Eastern cities of the United States, where a building already very high was built with an unusually broad cornice overhanging the street, and it was held by the neighbours that this cornice obstructed their light and the ventilation of the street in a quite unnecessary way. It was found, however, that, under the existing statute, great difficulties arose in the way of prevention or removal of such nuisances. It has been held that owners have a claim against the community, if height of buildings is limited.

(4) *Tenement Houses.* There exists legislation with regard to the occupancy of lots by buildings likely to be crowded with occupants. Thus the tenement houses of the Eastern cities of the United States may be built over only a given part of the lot occupied, 25 per cent or thereabouts being of necessity left entirely uncovered

by buildings. The discussion now going on (1900–1901) concerning model tenement houses may lead to the adoption of a more general and comprehensive law applicable to all cases. Details of the plan are also likely to become the subject of legislation, as when the proportionate number of places where water can be drawn, the number of slop sinks, and other conveniences are fixed by law.

(5) *Safety of Life.* The safety of occupants from sudden disaster has also been the subject of legislation, and especially so in the matter of the Fire Escape (which see).

(6) *Requirements of Good Building.* The quality of the building, the thickness of walls, the use of iron instead of wood, and the protection of that ironwork from the heat of a conflagration have all been elaborately provided for (see Fireproofing). All the above conditions are treated together in certain codified bodies of law, especially as part of the charter government of some cities, published under the name of Building Code, Building Law, or the like. Some of these codes are now several decades old, others are of very recent establishment, though these perhaps always replace earlier and generally inferior ones.

(7) *Registration of Architects.* The decision who is and who is not an architect in the proper sense of the word, and of who is and who is not a competent builder, has generally been left to ordinary practice and the choice of individuals, the courts interfering only when some abuse arises. This is the view still taken in France, where under the very exact and formidable legislation concerning the results of bad building or bad planning, the mere act of undertaking a building as architect or builder is free to any one. (See Architect, The, in France; Law Concerning Architecture and Building.) On the other hand, it is proposed now, 1901, in the cities of the United States, to hold examinations for architects and to bring about a complete registration of those who may be thought worthy to be allowed to practice. The professional architect being required to take out a license, or at the least to become one of a limited number of registered architects, may be thought to be put on the same ground as members of what are called the three learned professions. This would have the good effect of reminding the public that the architect is *ipso facto* a taught and equipped man, and not, as the public think him, a mere business agent, who takes orders, and who sees to spending his owner's money honestly. It would also tend to make architects feel that they must be such taught and equipped men. Engineers are and are known to be highly trained men: the profession is a new one (only 120 years old) and therefore has been organized on modern lines; but the architect as succeeding, but not replac-

ing, the ancient master builder (see Architect; Guild; Magister) occupies an anomalous position, and is now neither artist, nor builder, nor professional man.

Even if the examinations at first established should prove to be trivial, the step would be in the right direction. Gradually the community would learn to choose for the direction of building only able men. All this is strongly urged by the advocates of the registration plan.

On the other hand, the probability is urged of a strong tendency in these examinations toward merely practical considerations, and those of a somewhat low order, and therefore of a tendency away from artistic advance. A reduction of all architectural practice to considerations of solidity of building alone would tend to make of the architect an engineer, and one of low grade because not taught scientifically. It is true that the artist is born but not made ; still, what our schools of architecture need is not more influence of a formal and tangible kind, such as can be tested by examinations, but more artistical influence ; more pressure put upon the student to make him ambitious for fine designing, and not merely for the passing of future examinations admitting him to a lucrative profession. Architecture suffers from its nature as halfway between fine art and a very unintelligent kind of practical business in materials and patent fittings ; it is a pity to have the State set up a standard which will discourage its better side. There is always the chance, moreover, that the best design will come from the previously unknown man, one who may be unable to pass the examination in mechanical and technical subjects, unless so slight as to be derisory. All this is urged by those who would see the French plan followed.

As yet only one of the states of the Union has adopted the examination system, and nothing of the kind is thought to exist in Great Britain. While, in Continental Europe, France has her practice perfectly well organized and logical, and various edicts have been issued in other countries than France, and various requirements, as of graduation from certain institutions for the obtaining of a certain degree, have prevailed, the subject is still so far in an unsettled state that American publicists have not felt inclined to go to Europe for guidance in the matter.

(8) *Regulation of Artistic Design.* The possibility of obtaining better designs, or at least of avoiding very bad designs in the buildings and monuments of a town, has been considered, and there exist in some American cities commissions established by law, whose business it is to prevent the putting up of buildings unworthy of their place. Monuments, fountains, statues in parks and streets, are the natural subjects of the interference of these commis-

sions, and public buildings may be thought to come within their scope, though as yet little has been done to overrule the architect who designs or the committee who chooses a design. Private buildings, on the other hand, are difficult to control, nor is there any reason to think that the interference of the public authority would advance the cause of good architectural art. — R. S.

LEGISLATURE, HOUSE OF. The building in which a legislative chamber, or two or more legislative chambers, are accommodated. The hall provided for the seating of the Senate, House of Deputies, or the like, is not of any very special character, and ancient buildings prepared for a totally different purpose have been used for the meetings of such a body without serious inconvenience; but the provision for galleries in which the public can witness debates, for committee rooms, and other business rooms, including private offices for the presiding officer, the chairman of certain important committees, and other officials, the arrangement of a library, which often has to be very large, writing rooms, parlours in which members can see visitors, a post office, refreshment rooms, and the like, is all extremely elaborate, and has been found difficult to bring to a perfectly satisfactory result.

Some legislative buildings have very peculiar provisions, and the differences between them are marked. Thus, the House of Commons in London (see Westminster Palace) has seats for only about two-thirds of its members, the assumption being that not more than that number will be present at any one time ; while, on the other hand, the House of Representatives at Washington has not merely a seat, but a desk, or writing table, for each member. These two Houses afford another marked contrast, namely, in the matter of galleries for the public. While in the House of Representatives there is a great gallery accommodating about twenty-five hundred persons, and of absolutely free access, except when the galleries are " cleared," on occasion, by the vote of the House, the accommodation for strangers in the House of Commons consists of two very small galleries, each as long as the width of the House, or about 45 feet, and which are accessible only by a Speaker's order for the lower one, and an order from a member of the House to the upper one. A comparison among the newly erected " palaces " for the legislatures of the German Empire, Austria-Hungary, Belgium, Italy, and Greece would show many distinctions almost as marked as the above.

LEIGHTON, FREDERICK [Lord] ; painter and sculptor ; b. Dec. 3, 1830; d. Jan. 25, 1896.

Leighton went to Rome as a boy of fourteen. His principal teacher was Steinle, of Frankfort,

Germany. He was elected academician in 1869, and president of the Royal Academy in 1878. Lord Leighton's work as a mural painter is represented by *The Arts of War* (1872) and *The Arts of Peace* (1873) in the South Kensington Museum, the decoration of a music room in New York City, the frescoes of the *Wise and Foolish Virgins* in the church at Lyndhurst, England, 1866, and other works. About 1882–1883 he collaborated with Professor Poynter in designing a scheme of decoration for the dome of S. Paul's cathedral. As a sculptor Lord Leighton is best known by his *Athlete struggling with a Python* (1877) and the *Sluggard* (1896).

Rhys, *Sir Frederick Leighton*, 4to, 1895 (3d edition, 8vo, 1900, entitled *Frederick, Lord Leighton, His Life and Works*); Crowninshield, *Mural Painting;* Obituary in *Athenæum*, Feb. 1, 1896.

LE LORRAIN, ROBERT. (See Lorrain, Robert le.)

LEMERCIER, JACQUES; architect; b. about 1590; d. June 4, 1654.

Jacques is supposed to have been a son of Nicolas Lemercier (see Lemercier, N.). He studied in Rome. About 1617 he built the old château of Louis XIII., the small building of brick and stone which forms the principal façade of the Cour de Marbre at the palace of Versailles. In 1624 Lemercier was commissioned by Cardinal Richelieu to continue the construction of the old court of the Louvre. He built, adjacent to the wing erected by Pierre Lescot (see Lescot) on the western side, the pavilion called Tour de l'Horloge, and the building next to this pavilion on the north, thus completing the western side of the old quadrangle. The Tour de l'Horloge, with its famous caryatides by Jacques Sarrazin (see Sarrazin), may be considered the best example of his work. In 1629 he commenced the palace of Cardinal Richelieu, Paris, which was afterward transformed into the Palais Royal (see Louis, L. N. V.). Of this there remains only a gallery of the second court, which is decorated with marine emblems. In 1629 also he was commissioned to build the college of the Sorbonne, founded by Robert de Sorbon in 1252. His famous church of the Sorbonne was begun in 1635. In 1631 he began the château of Richelieu in Poitou, now nearly destroyed. He commenced in 1633 the church of S. Roch, Paris, completed by Jules Robert de Cotte and his son (see Cotte, R. de). In 1633 also he succeeded François Mansart (see Mansart, Fr.) as architect of the church of Val de Grâce, Paris, which was then built to about 10 feet above the soil. Lemercier carried the walls to the spring of the vault (see Muet, Pierre le, and Duc, Gabriel le). Between 1639 and 1641 he built the first Salle de Spectacle of the Palais

Royal. He built the famous stairway of the Cour du Cheval Blanc at Fontainebleau.

Ruprich-Robert, *Église du Val de Grâce;* Quatremère de Quincy, *Les plus célèbres architectes;* Babeau, *Le Louvre;* Baldus, *Monuments principaux de la France;* Hoffbauer, *Paris à travers les âges;* Berty, *Topographie, Louvre et Tuileries;* Bourassé, *Les résidences royales.*

LEMERCIER, NICOLAS.

Nicolas succeeded his father, Pierre Lemercier (see Lemercier, P.), as architect of the church of S. Maclou at Pontoise (Seine-et-Oise, France) and of the church of S. Eustache in Paris. In the latter building he worked mainly on the nave, which is inscribed with the dates 1578 and 1580. (See David, C.)

For bibliography, see Lemercier, Pierre.

LEMERCIER, PIERRE; architect.

The founder of an important family of French architects and the earliest architect of the great church of S. Eustache in Paris, the first stone of which was laid Aug. 19, 1532. The interesting adaptation of Renaissance details to Gothic forms which characterizes this building originated with him. Sept. 25, 1552, he was commissioned to finish the high tower of the church of S. Maclou at Pontoise, Seine-et-Oise, France. His work at Pontoise and Paris was continued by his son, Nicolas Lemercier (see Lemercier, N.). The architects of S. Eustache were of the same family, and preserved the unique style of the building throughout. The façade is later. (See Hardouin-Mansart de Jouy, J.)

Trou, *Recherches sur la ville de Pontoise;* Palustre, *Renaissance en France;* Calliat and Leroux de Lincy, *Église Saint-Eustache.*

LE MUET. (See Muet, Pierre le.)

LENDTHALL, JOHN; architect; d. September, 1868.

April 7, 1803, he was appointed clerk of works at the Capitol in Washington, under Benjamin Latrobe (see Latrobe). He was killed by the falling of an arch in the staircase hall.

Glenn Brown, *History of the United States Capitol.*

LENGTH. (For lengths of buildings, etc., see Size.)

LENGTHENING BAR. A bar for lengthening a leg of a compass by the insertion of one end into the standing part, and the insertion of one of the detachable points at its other end.

LENOIR, ALEXANDRE ALBERT; architect and archæologist; b. Oct. 21, 1801; d. Feb. 17, 1891.

A son of Marie Alexandre Lenoir (see Lenoir, M. A.). He was a pupil of the architect François Debret (see Debret) and secretary of the *École des Beaux Arts* in 1862. Lenoir united the old Palais des Thermes, Paris, with the Hôtel de Cluny, and established there the Mu-

sée de Cluny. He published *Architecture Monastique* (2 vols., 4to, Paris, 1852–1856) and
the *Statistique monumentale de Paris* (1861–
1867, folio, text 1 vol. 4to, plates 2 vols.
folio).

    La Grande Encyclopédie.

LENOIR, MARIE ALEXANDRE; archæologist; b. Dec. 26, 1762; d. June 11,
1839.

Lenoir was a pupil of the historical painter,
Doyen. He was placed in charge of the magazine established by the revolutionary government for the storage and sale of confiscated
property. This depository, the old monastery
des Petits Augustins, where is now the *École
des Beaux Arts*, he made the nucleus of a
museum, which was opened to the public Aug.
10, 1793. March 30, 1796, his collection received the official title *Musée des Antiquités
et Monuments français*. During the *Terreur*
Lenoir was obliged to act with great vigilance
and courage. Bonaparte and Josephine took
great interest in the *Musée des Monuments
français*. Eight thousand francs annually were
assigned to it under the Empire. Lenoir's
main purpose was the preservation of monuments which were especially associated with
the history of French art and of the French
people. He saved in this way much of the
best work of the Mediæval and Renaissance
periods. He preserved also numerous chronicles and documents, public and private. The
modern archæological movement in France derived its principal impulse from his efforts. By
decree of the government of Louis XVIII.,
dated Dec. 18, 1816, it was ordered that the
works collected by Lenoir should be returned
to their original owners. The tombs of the
kings of France were carried back to the church
of S. Denis, and various monuments to the
churches of Paris. This dispersion was accomplished with haste and disorder, much
property was destroyed, and many monuments
abandoned in the cloisters and garden of the
deserted monastery. Among these were the
great portal of the château of Anet and some
superb architectural decoration from the château of Gaillon, near Rouen, which were rearranged by Duban (see Duban) in the court of
the *École des Beaux Arts* when that building
took the place of the old *Petits Augustins*. Between 1792 and 1816 Lenoir published not
less than twelve editions of the catalogue of
his museum, and in 1800 his *Musée des Monuments français* (Paris, 5 vols. 8vo). Folio
books with plates were also devoted to this
museum.

    Courajod, *Alexandre Lenoir;* Allou, *Notice
sur Alexandre Lenoir;* Benoit, *L'Art français
sous la Révolution et l'Empire;* Marquis de Laborde, *Les Archives de la France pendant la Révolution;* Renouvier, *Histoire de l'Art pendant la
Révolution.*

LENORMAND, LOUIS; architect; b.
1807 (at Versailles); d. Jan. 12. 1862.

Lenormand was attached at first to the
works at the church of the Madeleine, Paris.
In 1838 he was made architect of the *Cour de
Cassation*, and held that office until his death,
when he was succeeded by Louis Joseph Duc
(see Duc, L. J.).

    Ch. Lucas, in *La Grande Encyclopédie.*

LENORMANT, CHARLES; archæologist:
b. June 1, 1802 (at Paris); d. Nov. 24, 1859,
(at Athens, Greece).

He went to Egypt with Champollion in 1828,
and took part also in the expedition to the Morea
(see Blouet). In 1839 he was made a member
of the *Académie des Inscriptions*, Paris, and in
1848 professor of Egyptian archæology at the
Collège de France, Paris. He published *Musée
des Antiquités Egyptiennes* (1842, folio);
Le Trésor de numismatique et de glyptique
(1834–1846, 20 vols. folio), illustrated under
the direction of Paul Delaroche by the process
invented by Achille Collas; *Élite des Monuments céramographiques* (1844–1861, 4 vols.),
in coöperation with De Witte, and other works.

    La Grande Encyclopédie.

LE NÔTRE (LE NOSTRE), ANDRÉ;
painter and landscape architect; b. March 12,
1613; d. Sept. 15, 1700.

Le Nôtre was born at the Tuileries, Paris,
his father being superintendent of the garden
of that palace. He was educated in the atelier
of the painter Simon Vouet. In 1637 he was
appointed by Louis XIV. to succeed the elder
Le Nôtre at the Tuileries. He was made, in
1658, *contrôleur général des bâtiments et jardins*. His first important work was the laying
out of the park of Vaux-le-Vicomte. At Vaux
the classic features of the formal garden and
park, terraces, grottoes, labyrinths, and the like
appear in France for the first time in their developed form. Louis XIV., pleased by the results obtained at Vaux, confided to Le Nôtre
the direction of all the works of the park and
gardens of Versailles, Trianon, and Saint-Germain-en-Laye. At Saint-Germain he made the
famous terraces leading to the new château.
He laid out also the gardens of the Tuileries,
Clagny, and Fontainebleau. Le Nôtre designed
the park of Chantilly for the Prince de Condé,
the park of Saint-Cloud for the Duc d'Orléans,
and the park of Sceaux for Colbert. In 1678
he visited Italy. The parks of the villas Pamphili and Ludovisi and the Vatican gardens in
Rome are ascribed to him. He is credited
with the parks of Saint James and Greenwich
in London. Of all the artists employed by
Louis XIV., Le Nôtre was the one to whom the
king became personally most attached. He created the art of *jardinage* in France.

    Lambert, *Histoire littéraire du règne de Louis
XIV.;* Genevay, *Style Louis XIV.;* J. F. Blondel

and Patte, *Cours d'Architecture;* Pfnor, *Le Château de Vaux-le-Vicomte;* Mangin, *Les Jardins;* André, *L'Art des Jardins.*

LEOCHARES OF ATHENS; sculptor.

He coöperated with Bryaxis (see Bryaxis), Scopas (see Scopas), and Timotheos (see Timotheos) in the decoration of the mausoleum at Halicarnassus in Caria. His name is found in several inscriptions at Athens. After the battle of Chaironeia (338 B.C.) he attached himself to the court of Philip II. of Macedon. A marble statuette of Ganymede in the Vatican is supposed to be a copy of an original by Leochares.

Löwy, *Inschriften Griechischer Bildhauer;* Collignon, *Histoire de la sculpture Grecque;* Duruy, *History of Greece.*

LEONARDO DA VINCI; painter, sculptor, architect, and engineer; b. 1452; d. 1519.

Leonardo da Vinci was a pupil of Verrocchio (see Verrocchio). In 1483 he settled in Milan and began the equestrian statue of the Duke Francesco Sforza. Many sketches for this work have come down to us, but the actual form which it assumed is uncertain. The model, nearly 8 metres high, was finished in 1493, and still existed in 1501. It is not known when Leonardo's most celebrated picture, the "Last Supper," in the refectory of the church of S. Maria delle Grazie, Milan, was begun. He was still working upon it in 1497. Very little of the original painting is now to be seen. He left Milan in 1499 at the fall of Lodovico Sforza, and entered the service of Cesare Borgia as engineer. After the fall of Cesare in 1503 Leonardo went to Florence, and was commissioned by the Gonfaloniere Piero Soderini to paint a picture of the battle of Anghiara for the hall of the Council at the Palazzo Vecchio. The central group of horsemen fighting has been preserved to us in a sketch by Rubens and an engraving by Edelinck. (For the companion picture, see Buonarroti, Michelangelo.) In 1515 he went with the king, François I., to France, and spent the last years of his life at the little manor of Cloux, near Amboise. Leonardo left numerous architectural drawings and notes among his manuscripts, but no practical work in architecture can now be attributed to him.

Jean Paul Richter, *The Literary Works of Leonardo da Vinci;* Müller-Walde, *Leonardo da Vinci, Lebenskizze und Forschungen.*

LEONI, LEONE; sculptor, medallist, goldsmith, and architect; b. about 1509 (at Arezzo, Italy); d. July 22, 1590.

Leoni appears to have worked at first in Venice. Like his enemy, Benvenuto Cellini (see Cellini, B.), he was a man of violent temperament. He was imprisoned in the galleys for murder, but was liberated by the great admiral, Andrea Doria, at Genoa, and was placed in charge of the imperial mint at Milan. He

became the preferred sculptor of the Emperor Charles V., at one time having his atelier in the imperial palace at Brussels. The greater part of his life was spent at Milan. His palace at Milan, built by himself, is famous for the colossal half-length figures of its façade. (See Telamon.) One of Leoni's finest works is the statue of Terrante Gonzaga at Guastalla, Lombardy.

Eugène Plon, *Leone Leoni et Pompeo Leoni;* Casati, *Leone Leoni d'Arezzo;* Vasari, Milanesi ed.

LEONI, POMPEO; sculptor; d. 1610.

A son of Leone Leoni. He finished many of his father's works at Madrid, which bear the signatures of father and son. He designed the monument of the Grand Inquisitor, Don Ferdinando de Valdes, at Salas, near Orviedo, Spain, and the mausoleum of the Princess Juana, daughter of Charles V., at the convent of Descalzas Reales at Madrid. His name is especially connected with the important sculpture of the Capella Mayor of the church of S. Lorenzo at the Escorial, the architectural setting for which was designed by the architect Juan de Herrera (see Herrera, J. de). The retable of this chapel is a structure in three orders adorned with colossal statues of the Evangelists and other saints which were begun by the elder Leoni. The two monuments of Charles V. and Philip II. are especially the work of Pompeo, and are remarkable for their splendid groups of kneeling figures.

Eugène Plon, *Leone Leoni et Pompeo Leoni;* Müntz, *Renaissance.*

LEOPARDI, ALESSANDRO; sculptor, architect, and goldsmith; d. sometime between June, 1522, and March, 1523.

His name first appears signed to a document dated June 25, 1482. Feb. 27, 1484, he was appointed by the Council of Ten in Venice special designer at the mint. Aug. 9, 1487, he was banished from Venetian territory for five years for forgery. He went to Ferrara, and probably entered the service of the Este family. At the death of Verrocchio (see Verrocchio) the great equestrian statue of Bartolommeo Colleoni was turned over to his pupil, Lorenzo de Credi. As Credi was unable to complete it, the Venetian government recalled Leopardi. He finished the statue and cast it before Aug. 11, 1492. It is not clear how much of the work is due to Leopardi. The inscription, ALEXANDER LEOPARDVS V. F. OPVS, is found on the saddle girth. The superb pedestal is undoubtedly his work. The famous monument to the Doge Vendramini in the church of SS. Giovanni e Paolo is attributed to Leopardi by Temanza (op. cit., p. 114). Müntz supposes that he was assisted in this work by Tullio Lombardo (see Lombardo, T.). Paoletti attributes to him at this time the two *Mori*, or figures which strike the bell on the clock tower

(Torre dell'Orologio) of the Piazza di S. Marco. Before Aug. 15, 1505, he made and placed in position the bronze bases for the masts in front of S. Mark's. According to a memorandum of the Council of Ten, dated Nov. 22, 1509, Leopardi at that time fortified the city of Padua (during the war of the League of Cambray). February, 1521, he was called to make a new model for the church of S. Giustina at Padua (see Andrea Briosco). He took up the construction of that building in 1522, just before his death. (See Baldoria, op. cit.)

Paoletti, *Rinascimento in Venezia*, Vol. II. ; C. C. Perkins, *Italian Sculptors;* Marco Testolini, *Ricerche intorno ad Alessandro Leopardi;* Temanza, *Vite dei Architetti e Scultori Veneziani;* Baldoria, *La Chiesa di Santa Giustina di Padova.*

LE PAULTRE. (See Lepautre.)

LEPAUTRE (LE PAULTRE), ANTOINE; architect and engraver; b. Jan. 15, 1621; d. 1691.

Antoine was a brother of Jean Lepautre (see Lepautre, J.). He built between 1646 and 1648 the church of the abbey of Port Royal, Paris. His chief work is the Hôtel de Beauvais, in the Rue Saint-Antoine, Paris, of which the cour d'honneur and the grand stairway remain in their original condition. Lepautre designed the Hôtel des Gardes at Versailles and built the two wings of the château of Saint-Cloud. He was a member of the Académie Royale d'Architecture at its foundation in 1677. In 1652 he published his *Œuvres d'Architecture.*

Mariette, *Abecedario;* Guilmard, *Les maîtres ornementistes;* Jal, *Dictionnaire critique;* Lambert, *Histoire littéraire du règne de Louis XIV.*

LEPAUTRE, JEAN; architect, draftsman, and engraver; b. June 28, 1617, or 1618; d. 1682.

A brother of Antoine Lepautre (see Lepautre, A.). He was apprenticed to a cabinet maker named Adam Philippon, for whom he engraved a series of twenty-six plates from drawings which Philippon had made in Italy. The rest of his work is done from his own designs. The most important of his engravings are collected in the *Œuvres d'Architecture de Jean Lepautre* (3 vols. 4to., Paris, 1751).

LEPAUTRE, PIERRE; architect, draftsman, and engraver; b. 1659.

A son of Jean Lepautre (see Lepautre, J.); he was brought up as an engraver and draftsman. Pierre Lepautre was the principal draftsman employed by Jules Hardouin-Mansart (see Hardouin-Mansart, J.) in the construction of Versailles, Marly, and the other royal palaces. He published *Les Plans, profils et élévations des ville et château de Versailles* (Paris, 1716, large folio).

Mariette, *Abecedario.*

LEROUX, JACQUES; architect; d. 1510. In 1480 Leroux replaced Ambroise Harel as

supervising architect of the church of S. Maclou at Rouen, Seine-Inférieure, France, and Nov. 18, 1494, he succeeded Guillaume Pontifs as architect of the cathedral of Rouen. In 1506 he completed the Tour de Beurre, at the cathedral, from his own designs.

Deville, *Revue des architectes de la cathédrale de Rouen;* Deville, *Tombeaux de la cathédrale de Rouen.*

LEROUX, ROULLAND; architect; d. 1527.

Roulland was a nephew of Jacques Leroux (see Leroux, J.). He was associated with his uncle in his work on the Tour de Beurre at the cathedral of Rouen. April 24, 1509, he presented a new plan on parchment for the portal of the cathedral of Rouen, which he built with the assistance of many sculptors, especially Pierre Desobeaulx, who carved the great bas-relief of the "Tree of Jesse" in the tympanum of the main door. In 1516 he made the plans for the mausoleum of the Cardinal d'Amboise in the cathedral of Rouen, which was finished in 1525. Oct. 4, 1514, the central wooden spire of the cathedral was destroyed by fire. Leroux designed a new spire, of which he completed the first story. (For the history of this spire, see Becquet, Robert.)

Deville, *Revue des architectes de la cathédrale de Rouen;* Deville, *Tombeaux de la cathédrale de Rouen.*

LESCHE. In Greek archæology, a place of social gathering, perhaps a club-house (literally, "talking place"). There seem to have been many buildings called by this name in Grecian lands. The most celebrated is that of the Cnidians (people of Knidos) in the sacred enclosure at Delphi ; it is described by Pausanias (X., 25), and alluded to by Plutarch and other ancient writers. The recent excavations have uncovered what are admitted to be the ruins of this building ; and of these a brief description is given in Mr. Frazer's book. Pausanias described at length the paintings by Polygnotus in this building.

J. G. Frazer, *Pausanias's Description of Greece.*

LESCOT (L'ESCOT), PIERRE; architect; b. about 1510–1515 ; d. 1578.

Lescot was equivalent in the old French to l'écossais, "the Scotchman." Pierre is supposed to have belonged to an ancient Parisian family of this name which was probably of Scottish origin. He was born at about the same time as Jacques (I.) Androuet Du Cerceau, Philibert de l'Orme, and Jean Bullant (see each of those names). In Jean Goujon's epistle to the readers, published in Jean Martin's translation of Vitruvius in 1557, Lescot is called "Parisien." He was Seigneur de la Grange du Martroy and Seigneur de Clagny, was created Abbé commendatoire de Clermont, and, Dec. 18, 1554, canon of the cathedral of Notre Dame, Paris. The details of his life are known mainly from the poetical epistle which was addressed to him by the poet Ronsard. Lescot was the earliest architect to develop the use of the pure classic orders in France. His first known work was the rood-screen (jubé) of the church of S. Germain l'Auxerrois, Paris, which was built between 1541 and 1544. The sculptural decoration of this work was by Jean Goujon, Laurent Regnauldin, and Simon Leroy. He was also associated with Jean Goujon in the construction of the fountain of the Nymphs. He is supposed to have made the plans for the Hôtel Carnavalet, Paris. Lescot's greatest work is the wing of the Louvre palace which is situated on the western side of the old quadrangle at its south-western angle. This building was projected in 1540 by François I., but the building was not begun until 1546. Lescot was occupied with this building until his death. Palustre (op. cit., Vol. II., p. 112) supposed that the chapel of the Valois at S. Denis (destroyed) was designed by Pierre Lescot.

Berty, *Les Grands architectes français;* Berty, *Topographie du Vieux Paris;* *Louvre et Tuileries;* Palustre, *La Renaissance en France;* Marquis de Laborde, *Comptes des bâtiments du roi.*

LESUEUR, JEAN BAPTISTE CICERON; architect; b. Oct. 5, 1794; d. Dec. 25, 1883.

A pupil of Percier (see Percier) and the *École des Beaux Arts.* In 1819 he won the *Premier Grand Prix de Rome.* In 1835 he was associated with E. H. Godde (see Godde) in the enlargement of the Hôtel de Ville, Paris. From 1850 to 1852 he had entire charge of that building. Lesueur published numerous practical works on architecture.

Bauchal, *Dictionnaire.*

LETAROUILLY, PAUL MARIE; architect; b. Oct. 8, 1795; d. Oct. 27, 1855.

Letarouilly came to Paris in 1814, entered the atelier of Charles Percier (see Percier) in 1816, and in 1819 joined the first class formed at the *École des Beaux Arts.* In 1819, also, he served as inspector of the works at the Odéon theatre, Paris. After a prolonged sojourn in Italy he returned to Paris and was appointed inspector of constructions at the Ministère des Finances under Hippolyte Destailleur. He is best known by his two great works on Rome, *Édifices de Rome Moderne* (text one vol. 4to., 1868, plates three vols. large folio, Paris, 1868–1874), and *Le Vatican et la basilique de Saint Pierre.* At the time of his death only the plates of this work were ready for publication. These were put in order by A. Simil and published in 1882, Paris, three vols. large folio. No text was ever issued.

Penanrun, *Les Architectes élèves de l' École des Beaux Arts;* Ch. Lucas, in *La Grande Encyclopédie.*

LE TEXIER. (See Texier, Jean le.)

LET IN (v.t.). To insert; to secure together or attach in place by insertion in a recess. (See Countersinking; Dado; House; which are the more specific terms for such a process.)

LETTER (v. int.). To write, draw, or stamp letters or lettering (see Letter, v. t.); also to design the forms of letters, numerals, or signs of any sort which may be copied by others.

LETTER (v. t.). To add letters to, furnish with letters or lettering in the sense of description, titles, legends, etc. By extension, to furnish with numerals, as well as ordinary lettering; as when a drawing is said to be lettered in the sense of having all its terms and measurements given upon it.

LETTER BOX. (See Box; Chute.)

LETTERING (n.). The art and practice of making or designing letters, numerals, etc.; also, in a general sense, the letters and signs so made or designed.

The art of making written characters beautiful or interesting has lost much since the use of printing became general, because in all such cases, the need of quantity, quickness, and small cost tends to cause fine and careful design to be forgotten. Moreover, when the letter or other sign is not drawn afresh by hand, each time, the charm of natural variety is gone. The early printers and typefounders tried to overcome this in part by having, in one font, several different forms of the same F or S, and also characters for the words "and," "the," etc., and for such couples of letters as *ss, st, th*; so that with three forms of *s* and its compounds there would appear in a printed page a half dozen different shapes of the letter. This, however, was but a feeble attempt to preserve the artistic charm of manuscript.

This charm is one with that found in inscriptions on stone, engravings on metal, paintings in different media and on different surfaces, and prints from specially made engravings or stamps. Thus, in a Japanese street of shops, the signs are truly decorative, instead of being eyesores; in Moslem building, the quotations from the Koran are in harmony with the patterns and colours around; in a Florentine mural tomb the inscribed or raised letters in marble or bronze are of exquisite design, and in perfect keeping. The Orientals have an advantage in the beauty which it is easy to give to the forms of their letters or ideographs; and the Russians of modern times have a Byzantine tradition of Greek shapes possible to give to the modern Russian characters, which they use cleverly. Still, even the plain Roman letter of ancient incisings in marble, fifteenth-century manuscripts, and sixteenth-century title pages printed from engraved plates, is capable of wonderful variety and unlimited refinement.

The above deals mainly with the uses of lettering in solid and permanent work; much of non-architectural character might be compared with this, but even the lettering of mechanical drawings has some importance, and interests many draftsmen. — R. S.

LEVAU (LEVEAU), LOUIS; architect; b. 1612; d. October, 1670.

The son of Louis Levau, general inspector of the buildings at the château of Fontainebleau. About 1650 he built his first important work, the Hôtel Lambert de Thorigny on the Isle Saint Louis, Paris. For Nicolas Fouquet he built the château of Vaux-le-Vicomte, between 1653 and 1660. In 1655 he succeeded Christophe Gamart as architect of the church of S. Sulpice, Paris, and was himself superseded at that work by Daniel Gittard in 1670. In 1656 Levau succeeded Jacques Lemercier (see Lemercier, J.) as *architecte ordinaire du roi*, and continued the works at the Louvre. He completed the northern side of the old quadrangle and rebuilt a large part of the southern side, making a new façade upon the river. This front was afterward rebuilt by Claude Perrault (see Perrault, C.). Levau also designed a façade for the eastern front which was never executed. In 1664 he began to remodel the Tuileries. He rebuilt the central pavilion, removed the grand stairway, and replaced the circular cupola by a larger square one. He destroyed the pretty roofs of the side wings with their dormer windows (lucarnes), and built a story in the Corinthian order with an attic in their place. (See De l'Orme, Philibert.) He also rebuilt the upper part of the pavilion designed by Jean Bullant (see Bullant, J.) and completed the Tuileries by building the Pavillon Marsan on the north. In 1662 Levau began the palace of the Collège des Quatre Nations, called also Palais Mazarin (now Palais de l'Institut), opposite the centre of the southern side of the Louvre quadrangle on the other side of the river. In 1664 he commenced the church of S. Louis-en-l'Ile, Paris, which was continued by Gabriel le Duc (see Duc, Gabriel le). To the old château of Louis XIII., at Versailles, he added a front court with two pavilions and an orangerie.

Dezallier d'Argenville, *Vie des fameux architectes;* Jal, *Dictionnaire;* Hoffbauer, *Paris à travers les âges;* Pfnor, *Château de Vaux-le-Vicomte;* Vitet, *Le Louvre;* Maquet, *Paris sous Louis XIV.*

LEVEE. Same as Dike, the term being employed especially in the Southern states of the United States as along the Mississippi. It is apparently the use, originating in the French city of New Orleans, of the French word *levé* or *levée*, meaning raised or heaped up, as a bank of earth.

LEVEL. (See Surveying.)

LEVELLER. Anything intended to bring about a level — *i.e.* a horizontal — surface; any contrivance by which the upper surface of a structure may be brought to a horizontal or nearly horizontal plane. Especially in stone masonry, a stone of the proper dimension to make up a difference in height between two adjoining stones, so as to produce a level bed for the next course above; also a flat stone for making a level bearing, as in a footing course.

LEVELLING. (See Surveying.)

LEVELLING ROD; STAFF. (See Surveying.)

LEVER BOARD. Generally the same as Louver Board. The distinction is, however, sometimes made that a louver board is permanently fixed, whereas lever boards are pivoted and arranged in a series to be adjusted simultaneously at any angle by means of a mechanical contrivance operating on the principle of the lever, as the slats in a shutter of the usual type.

LEWIS. An instrument intended to be inserted in the top of a stone as a means of attachment in raising and lowering, thus doing away with the necessity of a sling passing around the stone. In all of its forms it holds the stone by means of keys or wedges fitted to a dovetailed recess.

LEWIS, THOMAS HAYTER; architect; b. 1818; d. December, 1898.

He was a student at the Royal Academy, London, and won its gold medal. He assisted Sir William Tite at the Royal Exchange, London. In 1854 he designed the Alhambra in London. In 1860 he was elected general secretary of the Royal Institute of British Architects. In 1864 he succeeded Donaldson (see Donaldson) as Professor of Architecture at University College, London, and superintended the enlargement of its buildings. Lewis contributed many articles to the *Transactions* of the R.I.B.A., and wrote works on *Justinian's Buildings, The Holy Places of Jerusalem, Byzantine Sculpture,* and other books.

Nekrologie in *Kunstchronik,* Dec. 22, 1898; Tavenor Perry in *Journal of Royal Institute of British Architects,* Jan. 14, 1890.

LEWIS ANCHOR. (See Lewis Bolt, under Bolt.)

LEWISSON. Same as Lewis.

LIABILITY FOR ACCIDENTS. In building, the principle that some one, either owner, builder (in the sense of chief contractor or undertaker of the work in some other form than by contract), superintendent, foreman, or chief in some capacity is responsible for injuries done in the process of erecting a building. In the United States this responsibility is commonly fixed (subject always to general law) by the terms of the contract for building. Thus the printed forms of contract kept on hand by some architects in large practice prescribe very minutely the conditions under which such responsibility exists and claim for injuries may be made. In the United States, however, as in Great Britain, this responsibility is usually a matter of common law, and the agreements described above depend upon this law of decisions as fixed by the courts rather than upon statute. In France, and generally on the Continent of Europe, the reverse is the case, and statute law can be appealed to in all cases. (See Architect, The, in France ; Law.) — R. S.

LIBERGIER (LE BERGER), HUGUES ; architect; d. 1263.

Libergier built the beautiful church of S. Nicaise at Reims, Marne, France, which is preserved to us only in an engraving of the seventeenth century. The monument of Libergier is in the cathedral of Reims.

Viollet-le-Duc, *Dictionnaire*, Vol. I., article *Architecte*.

LIBON; architect.

According to Pausanias, Libon, a local architect, built the temple of Zeus at Olympia. It is not known precisely at what time this work was done. (See Phidias.)

LIBRARY. A permanent collection of books ; hence, in Architecture, any place provided for the keeping and arrangement of a collection of books, for continual public or private use. The library of the private house may be a single room or set of rooms, the walls lined with shelves or separate cases standing on the floor, according to the number of books and the amount of space available. The library of a club, a literary society, or the like, may, in the same manner, be a room or set of rooms in a building occupied by the society. In these cases the library, as such, has no special architectural character, but the cases themselves may be of interest as works of decorative art or of ingenious construction.

Information as to the library buildings of antiquity is meagre. The clay tablets which constituted the literature of Babylonia and Assyria were stored on shelves in upper rooms of temples and palaces. The papyrus rolls of Egypt were shelved in rooms of palaces, temples, and tombs until the time of Ptolemy Philadelphus, in the third century B.C., when we have the earliest mention of separate library buildings. There is no record of such buildings among the ancient Greeks ; but, in Rome, Asinius Pollio built the first public library, 25 B.C. ; and Augustus built libraries about the year 37 B.C. Books or rolls of manuscript were arranged on the shelves of closed bookcases (*armaria*), 4 or 5 feet high, set against the walls, with occasionally a bookcase in the middle of the room.

With the fall of the Roman Empire, the libraries of the classical period were scattered or destroyed. The Mohammedan princes appear to have gathered large libraries, — that at Cairo numbering 1,600,000 volumes, the one at Tripoli 3,000,000.

During the early centuries of the Christian era literature was kept alive by the ecclesiastics. Libraries were slowly gathered in cathedrals, and also in monasteries, especially by the Benedictine order. They were at first so small that a single room, or oftener part of the cloisters, held all the books and all the readers. The library at Durham, in the north of England, is thus described by a chronicler : "The north syde of the Cloister . . . was all fynely glased from the hight to within a litle of the grownd and in every wyndowe iii Pewes or Carrells, wherein . . . the Monks dyd resort. And in every carrell was a deske. . . . And over against the carrells against the church wall did stande great almeries (or cupbords) of waynscott all full of bookes."

In the tenth century A.D., princes and nobles had caught from the clergy the love of books, and began to make collections. In the fourteenth and fifteenth centuries the great universities assumed the lead in literature, and started libraries. During this period there is little or no record of library buildings. Library rooms grew larger as books accumulated. The books of monasteries were removed from the cloisters to separate rooms, or suites of rooms.

The revival of learning in the fifteenth century, and the invention of printing, gave an impulse to the formation and growth of libraries, and led to the erection of separate library buildings. In 1433–1434 Cosimo de' Medici built in Venice the library of S. Giorgio Maggiore, and twenty years later restored and enlarged the library of S. Marco at Florence, — the predecessor of the Laurentian library, whose present building Michelangelo designed in 1515. The Libreria Vecchia at Venice (see Library of S. Mark) was built in 1571 ; the Vatican Library at Rome in 1588, and the Bodleian at Oxford in 1597.

During these centuries, and indeed down to the middle of the nineteenth century, the prevalent types of interiors were such as have survived in the Vatican, and in the Bodleian. The library of the Sorbonne, about 1640, was 120 ft. long by 36 broad. That it might be more safe from being burned, there was sufficient "interval" around it. Long and narrow rooms, with transverse cases, appear characteristic of this period. An engraving of the University of Leyden library, published in 1600, shows a rectangular room with floor-cases, lighted by high windows above the cases.

In 1740 the circular and central reading room, so often adopted in later libraries, appeared in the Radcliffe library, Oxford.

In America, the first building to be used for library purposes was that of the Loganian Library in Philadelphia (occupied in 1745), — a plain, square, one-story brick building like the typical country schoolhouse. The second was the Redwood library at Newport, Rhode Island, completed in 1750. It consisted of a main room 37 × 26, and 19 feet high, with two small wings used as offices. This building is still used as a library.

The first type of library architecture evolved in America appeared about one hundred years later in the erection (1837–1841) of Gore Hall, the library of Harvard College. A churchlike interior was adapted to library uses by shelving the bays as alcoves, and breaking their height by a gallery. This survival of mediæval arrangement, allowable if at all in a college library, was copied in subsequent libraries of different scope. The Boston Athenæum, a proprietary or club library, completed in 1849, followed the interior plans of Gore Hall. The Astor library of New York (1850–1853) developed the system of alcoves and galleries into tiers running from floor to ceiling around the walls of a large and lofty room. This plan of interior, followed in the first building of the Boston Public Library (1855–1858), in the Peabody Institute at Baltimore (1858–1861), and later in the public libraries of Cincinnati, Detroit, and other cities, is the one spoken of in the discussions of 1875–1885, as the "conventional plan."

The era of modern library progress, of library science, and library architecture, dates in England from the passage of the Public Libraries Act of 1850, and in the United States from the Boston Public Library Act of Massachusetts in 1848. The American Library Association was formed in 1876. Its annual meetings brought together the leading librarians of the United States, and constant conference gradually unified their views as to the interior arrangement of library buildings, so that architects, within the last ten years, have, for the first time, had definite and controlling conditions presented to them for architectural expression. The principal difference among librarians has been in regard to the stack system (see the Summary, Section II.).

The plan of a library varies as it is small, or large, growing, or complete ; as it is proprietary, collegiate, reference, or circulating ; and as it is specialized in any direction — as law, theology, or science.

Certain essential conditions for all libraries have been endorsed by the American Library Association, as follows : —

(1) A library building should be planned for effective and economical administration of the special work to which the library is devoted.

(2) It should be planned with a view to its available income, lest the cost of caring for too elaborate a building should cripple the proper work of the library.

(3) No essential convenience of arrangement should be sacrificed for architectural effect.

(4) It is wise not to build too much in advance of present needs, but to provide opportunities for future enlargement in each department as may be required.

(5) If a library can occupy a separate building, the problems of light and growth will be simplified. Where a museum, or art gallery, or lecture room is to occupy the same building, a separate wing or separate floors should be assigned to the library.

(6) There should be ample natural light in all parts of the building.

(7) Rooms for the use of the public should be grouped so as to insure complete supervision with few attendants. Administration rooms should be grouped according to processes of library work. The librarian's room should be the centre of the system. Communication by bells and speaking tubes or telephones should be arranged between the working rooms.

(8) Simplicity of decoration should prevail in working rooms ; and public service rooms should not be so decorated as to attract sightseers to the annoyance of readers.

Where libraries are wholly for reference use (consultation of books on the premises), conditions are simpler than where delivery for home use must also be provided for. Nearly all libraries, however, have both functions.

In a village one room will hold all the books usually available. A well-lighted, centrally situated room, shelved around the walls at a convenient height, and simply furnished with chairs and tables, will serve for library quarters. Such a room, containing 400 square feet, with three shelves running breast high around three sides, and with tables in the centre of the room, will accommodate twenty readers and 1500 volumes. If shelved from the floor to the height of easy reach it will hold 3500 volumes. When a library reaches this latter size, however, its use usually demands more rooms or a separate building. Its requirements then include : —

Storage of books ; cataloguing, preparation, and repair of books ; issue and return of books for home use ; reading of books (reference use) in the library ; care, lighting, and heating of the building.

The rudimentary form for a small library is a one-story building, with dry and well-lighted basement, and with three rooms opening together on the main floor, or one large room divided by glass screens into three compartments, namely : —

A book room (called in England "book store") ; a room for study, or the use of reference books, called the reference room ; a room for newspaper and magazine reading, generally known as the reading room. The last two are sometimes combined ; but when there is to be serious study or investigation it can be pursued more satisfactorily if separated from the stir and noise of lighter reading. From a desk at the junction of these rooms one attendant can serve and supervise all three. The basement will provide for heating and storage, and for toilet rooms. Two small rooms in the angles for cataloguing, committees, and private study, and a separate space in front of the desk for delivery, will thoroughly complete the accommodations of a small town library.

As a library grows these rudimentary divisions still prevail, subdivided according to special needs, such as

Separation of books: as under art; music; patents; public documents; duplicates; bound newspapers; etc. Separation of work: trustees; librarians; cataloguers; delivery; janitor; unpacking; binding and repairs; stores; etc. Separation of readers: children; women; newspaper readers; special students.

Perhaps the greatest difficulty in planning a library lies in providing for growth. The experience of the last twenty-five years shows that vigorous management usually brings expansion quicker and greater than is expected. Where this expansion will first come it is difficult to foresee.

As to storage of books. A book room with one tier or height of wooden floor cases (sometimes called a " one-story stack ") will be amply sufficient, whether the public are to be excluded from or admitted to the shelves, until over 25,000 volumes are to be shelved. Until this stage is reached the question of metallic shelving and the stack system need not even be considered. The late Dr. Poole contended that a stack was never needed, and was an avoidable evil. (See Summary, Section II., and also mention of the Poole Plan, Section IV.) The stack is generally accepted as inevitable, in some form and to some extent, in very large libraries. The " open shelf " idea, however (admission of readers to the shelves), now coming rapidly into vogue, is swinging the pendulum back toward floor shelving and alcove plans, and is modifying the arrangement of the stacks themselves.

There are two contrasted plans possible for a large library, one having a central stack, with reading rooms on all sides; the other, a central reading room with radiating stacks. The Library of Congress combines both these ideas. In either plan, however, it is difficult to provide for growth in the interior department. In the new building of the New York Public Library the main reading room is to be over the stacks, and can be extended *pari passu.* As a general thing in libraries of medium size the stacks project from the rear of the main building.

College libraries, being intended for the use of a small community of students, require different treatment from public libraries, especially in the grouping of seminar rooms and special

collections. Examples of carefully studied arrangement are the libraries of Pennsylvania University, Philadelphia, and of Cornell University at Ithaca, New York. The former has a stack of peculiar form, with a glass roof and an interesting use of alcoves in the reading room for departments of study. The Cornell Library has a feature worthy of imitation by all large libraries in an entrance lobby, enclosed by glass partitions, where all the public rooms can be seen, and the spectacular treasures of the library can be inspected by casual visitors without disturbing attendants or readers.

Features in which library buildings need special study and treatment may be summarized as follows : —

SUMMARY.

I. *Shelving and Bookcases.* No shelf should ever be beyond reach of a person of medium height, standing on the floor, about 6 feet 9 inches. This means that wall shelving, floor cases, stack tiers, and galleries must not be over 7 or $7\frac{1}{2}$ feet high.

Shelves should be of uniform length throughout a library, movable and interchangeable. The best length for a shelf is somewhere from 30 to 36 inches, whatever will divide evenly into the available spaces. Longer shelves are apt to sag when loaded. As hardly five per cent of the books in a circulating library exceed $7\frac{1}{2}$ inches in width, 8 inches will be sufficient depth for the ordinary shelves. Ten inches between shelves is ample allowance for octavos or smaller volumes; 12 inches for quartos, 20 inches for folios. It is assumed that all folios more than 20 inches high will be laid horizontally in cases made for the purpose. Sliding shelves on rollers for unusually large folios are provided.

Bookcases are either wall cases (shelving of single depth built against a wall), or floor cases (double shelving, open on both sides, and set across the floor).

When closely ranged, floor cases should be not less than 3 feet apart. If public access is allowed, 3 feet 6 inches is better. Transverse aisles are needed every 12 or 15 feet, and around the ends of the cases. If these are planned to be the same width as the standard length of shelves, they can be opened anywhere by removing a tier of shelving. Wall cases should be perpendicular, if possible, both to the windows (for light) and to the delivery desk (for supervision). No doors of any kind are used in modern bookcases, except where rare books are to be kept locked up.

To calculate full capacity, allow for books of ordinary size in a circulating library 10 volumes to the running foot of shelving, and for folios and quartos 6 to the foot. In a reference library the allowance should be 8 and 5, respectively. For practical capacity, leaving spaces here and there for growth by subjects, allow 7 volumes to the foot.

II. *Stack.* A stack room is a high, bare room, filled from wall to wall with floor cases perpendicular to the sides of the room, divided by decks or floors into stories 7 to 8 feet high. Cases in high stacks are always, in low stacks almost always, made of iron or steel. The shelves are either of wood, of sheet iron, or of iron grating. The Harvard stack has aisles only 2 feet 4 inches wide; but 2 feet 6 inches is the least width used elsewhere, and 3 feet is better, for light, ventilation, and administration. Large stacks have from six to nine stories, but the ordinary number is less. A common form has three stories, the middle story level with the delivery floor. Another arrangement is to break stories, having one stack deck $3\frac{1}{2}$ feet above the delivery floor, another $3\frac{1}{2}$ feet below, so that two decks are accessible by short flights of steps. In high stacks, the other stories of the library are sometimes made 14 or 15 feet high, so that every second tier of the stack comes on the level of a floor.

The dimensions, and many of the conditions specified under the head of shelving, apply also to stacks. (For lighting of stacks, see Section XI.) The material for stack floors or decks may be wood, marble, or perforated iron, but opaque glass appears to produce the best results. If solid floors are used, a space about 4 inches wide is usually left between floor and shelving on each side for the passage of light and air. This opening is sometimes protected by wire netting, or by a step projecting from the lower shelf.

The material of early stacks was gas-pipe framework with wooden shelves. There are now several patent iron or steel stacks on the market.

Large stacks require pneumatic tubes and mechanical carriers for the speedy delivery of books.

The capacity of a stack can be roughly calculated by allowing 25 volumes to every square foot of floor space on each deck or story. Thus, a 30×40 stack, three stories high, would hold 90,000 volumes.

III. *Alcoves.* These are not out of place in libraries for social or scholarly use, where readers have free access to the shelves, and where there is ample floor room.

An alcove 8 feet wide will barely accommodate a small table and two chairs, with room for passing on each side. If an alcove has a wide or double window, another bookcase may be set in the centre to increase book capacity, when needed.

IV. *"Poole Plan."* This plan, already mentioned, ignored the stack and alcove arrangement alike. It contemplated a collection

of departmental libraries and reading rooms under one roof, instead of one huge reading room with a many-tiered stack. This building would include administration rooms and one general reading room of moderate size, on the ground floor, and as many fireproof rooms above, to be entered from corridors, as might be required by the extent and scope of the library. This is an ideal plan for scholars, and its fundamental principles have more or less influenced all modern reference libraries; but the plan, as a whole, has been followed only in the Newberry Library in Chicago.

V. *Galleries.* These should be avoided, as being inconvenient in use and wasteful of room. If it becomes necessary, however, to shelve high walls from floor to ceiling, it is better to break the height by galleries about 7 feet apart than to use ladders. A gallery should be wide enough to allow stooping to the lower shelf, or carrying armloads of books. The railing should be of light ironwork, waist high, and from the top rail occasional rigid or folding shelves should project outward, to hold books in course of handling. If the room be large enough to allow space and light, wider galleries permit the use of tables near the books.

VI. *Delivery Room.* This is usually separate from the reading room, and is used exclusively for books which are to be taken away from the building. The delivery desk should be proportioned to the work to be done, with allowance for growth; 42 inches is a good height (or 36 inches, with movable desks 6 inches high). The top should be 2 or 3 feet wide, and not less than 12 feet long (6 feet for delivery, 6 feet for return). It should project on both sides, and have compartments beneath for books and supplies, with a cash drawer for fines, and drawers for records of issue. Space is needed in front of it, with seats for those who are waiting for books. Where the public are admitted to the shelves, it is usually through gates or passageways at the ends of the delivery desk, where visitors will be under close supervision in coming and going. The length of delivery counters, which will be noted in English plans, is due to the use of "indicators," large bulletin boards so divided into small numbered compartments as to indicate at a glance whether any book is in or out of the library. This device is not used in America.

VII. *Reading Rooms and Work Rooms.* Less room is required in a magazine reading room than in a reference room; 16 to 18 square feet are usually allowed for each reader in the former, and 20 to 24 square feet in the latter. There is general agreement that the reading room should not be more than 16 feet high; better 10 or 12 in small, and 14 to 15 in large, libraries.

VIII. *Librarian.* The librarian's room ought to be near the centre of the working system, accessible to the public and the staff, communicating by bell and tube or telephone with all departments. It need not be large or lofty. If space can be spared, a main room and an anteroom are better than one large room. It is convenient to have the vault for records open from the librarian's room. In large buildings, the librarian and staff need a private entrance.

IX. *Catalogues.* The room or rooms for cataloguers should be as quiet and as well lighted and ventilated as possible, and should be near the books, near the delivery desk, and near the card catalogue. The card catalogue, consisting of cards arranged in trays or drawers, is a universal feature of American libraries. The "tray" system (covered wooden trays set side by side at the usual height of a delivery desk) requires too much room for ordinary use. The general form is a cabinet, with narrow drawers in tiers. Formerly these drawers were fixed, so that one user obstructed access to a whole tier; but they are now made removable, and can be taken out for consultation. The cabinet itself does not require much space, but room must be left near it for chairs and tables. It should be near the delivery desk, so that the attendant can supervise and assist those who are using it. If the cabinet can form part of a partition between the delivery room and the cataloguer's room, the drawers, which in this case will open at either end, can be more easily used by the cataloguers.

X. *Bulletin Boards.* Wall space (or a screen) is needed near the delivery desk, for announcements, lists, etc.

XI. *Admission and Supply of Light.* Square-topped windows, reaching quite to the ceiling, diffuse light through the top of a room, and throw it farther across the floor. North light is best, or whatever exposure gives a maximum of light with a minimum of direct sunshine. Side light is considered to be better than skylight. Light-coloured or glazed walls and ceilings reflect and increase the light. In stacks there should be as much window area on both sides of the stack as good construction will allow. Piers should be opposite bookcases, windows opposite aisles. Even in the most open of stacks, with perforated or glass "decks," light from skylights will not penetrate effectively more than two tiers downward, and side light not much more than 20 feet across.

For artificial light, electricity is best, both for readers and for books. In reading rooms the best results are obtained from lamps near the ceiling or above the cornices, for general illumination, with low reading lamps on each table, wired from the floor, to be turned on and off as needed. In book rooms or stacks, a bulb attached to a flexible cord, to be hung up when not in use, and moved by hand in front of the books when light is wanted, is serviceable.

If gas must be used, sunlight burners will give diffused light, and side lights or table burners, local light. Gas injures bindings, and its use should be avoided if possible. Green shades on table and desk lights protect the eyes of readers.

XII. *Flooring.* This should be noiseless, warm to the feet, and easily cleaned. Resonant wood does not answer the first requirement, nor marble either the first or the second. In the Library of Congress, the workrooms are floored with a "carpet" of boards laid on masonry. In the Congregational Theological Seminary, Chicago, narrow strips of maple, nailed to sleepers laid in cement, form the flooring. English authorities recommend oak blocks laid in concrete, levelled and planed.

For floor coverings, the general testimony is that corticene fills all three requirements, and also wears well. Carpets and matting hold dust, and are objectionable. The best floors for libraries of moderate size would seem to be wood wholly or partly covered with corticene.

XIII. *Stairs.* The spiral staircases formerly much used in libraries are now discountenanced as very inconvenient. All stairs should have straight flights and square landings. Staircases in stacks or galleries should be at the end nearest to the delivery desk. A very grave fault in a library is to bring a stairway up through the floor of a reading room. Another bad fault is placing stairways where they separate working or reading rooms.

XIV. *Elevators and Lifts.* A book lift from the unpacking room to the cataloguing room is a convenience for even the smallest library; and such lifts are necessary in a stack. Passenger elevators in large libraries render upper stories available for public use.

XV. *Heating.* Steam pipes in floor trenches are hard to clean. If run under or behind shelving they injure books. In a stack room they are best when hung on brackets along the walls. Hot water indirect radiation gives the best heat for readers and books.

XVI. *Fire Precautions.* Every library should have a fireproof vault or safe for records, manuscripts, and books which could not be replaced. Construction of the building should be fireproof or slow burning. In large libraries the heating and lighting plants may well be placed in a detached building. If these precautions are taken, it is generally held that there is no need of shutting off the book room from the rest of the library by fireproof walls or doors.

Boyden, *Public Libraries* in *R. I. B. A. Journal,* 1899; *United States Bureau of Education,*

Circulars of Information, *Construction of Library Buildings*, 1881 ; Foster, *Planning of a Library from a Librarian's Point of View;* (in *Brochure Series*, 1897, Vol. III.) ; Soule, *Points of Agreement among Librarians as to Library Architecture* (in *Brochure Series*, 1897, Vol. III.) ; Jackson, *Libraries of the Middle Ages* in *R. I. B. A. Journal*, 1898 ; Burgoyne, *Library Construction, Architecture, Fittings, and Furniture;* Poole, *Notes on Library Construction;* Louise B. Krouse, *Reading List on Library Buildings; Suggestive Plans* for the New York Public Library Competition (for a list of forty-three rooms or groups of rooms needed in a very large library, with an estimate of the space and shelving required for each room).

— CHARLES C. SOULE.

Bodleian Library. An ancient library at Oxford, England, occupying buildings erected in the early years of the seventeenth century, chiefly at the cost of Sir Thomas Bodley. The architecture is a curious mixture of late Tudor Gothic with classical details, rather French than Italian in their style.

Congressional Library. In Washington, D.C. ; a large building erected 1895–1897 for the library of the United States Congress, which had been housed in the Capitol. The building occupies much ground and encloses four courts. It is very richly adorned with mural paintings and decorative sculpture. The architects were Smithmeyer and Pelz, to whom succeeded Edward Pearse Casey, who controlled most of the interior decoration.

Laurentian Library. (That is to say, the Library of S. Lorenzo.) A building in Florence forming part of the group around the church of S. Lorenzo. The collection of manuscripts is of the greatest importance and celebrity. The principal library room was built from the designs of Michelangelo and finished while he was still alive, about 1540. The vestibule was completed by Giorgio Vasari at a later date. The very rich and beautiful fittings of the library are of the style of the epoch ; the library room itself is dignified and stately, and, without expressing great novelty of conception, is the work of a master. It is to be noted that this is one of the earliest of those buildings in which the single order (in this case of pilasters raised upon a high dado) is trusted as sufficient for the decorative effect of the whole. The very large order afterward used in S. Peter's church at Rome, and which then became common throughout Italy, finds its origin in such designs as this of the library. Additions have been made in modern times, and the circular reading room is a useful appendage. — R. S.

Medicean Library. (See Laurentian Library, above.)

Radcliffe Library. An ancient library at Oxford, England, occupying a building finished in 1749 ; the work of that Gibbs who designed S. Mary le Strand, in London. It is a circular building with an aisle surrounding a central nave, which latter is crowned by a dome, while the aisle is roofed flat ; much in the style of the chapel at Versailles.

LIBRARY OF ARCHITECTURE. A collection of books especially appropriate to the uses of the student of architecture, either in practice or in theory. The number of books of this character has increased enormously of late years, this being caused partly by the facility of accurate and full illustration which is afforded by photography and partly by the increase of the archæological spirit among practising architects, as well as among scholars, and partly, also, by the willingness of many modern draftsmen to take their ornament and even their disposition of masses almost entirely from ancient examples.

The books of an architectural library cannot be classified with any accuracy, but they may be said to be of three classes : —

(1) The books treating of mathematics and other scientific preparation for the study of architecture.

(2) The books treating of the history and theory of architecture in elaborate texts, with illustrations used only for the better comprehension of the text by the reader.

(3) Books in which the representations of buildings and parts of buildings are the most important part, the text serving only as an explanation.

To these may be added, of course, atlases, dictionaries, encyclopædias of manufactures and of engineering, and such works which the student of architecture must refer to often ; also guidebooks, many of which, though intended for travellers, are full of valuable information for the student, and such books of travel and residence in foreign countries as contain information about buildings there.

Some great public libraries have set aside special architectural departments, the books contained in which are not allowed to be taken from the building, and are often arranged in a room apart, and to be consulted under special regulations. (See the description and special libraries under Library ; also Seminar Room.) The most valuable architectural library in London is that belonging to the Royal Institute of British Architects. The South Kensington Museum has a remarkable architectural library. At the Soane Museum, in Lincoln's Inn Fields, is a most valuable collection of architectural drawings, including many by Piranesi, and others by Bramante, John Thorpe, and others. There are also here some very valuable models. At some of the institutions devoted in England to the advancement of art and literature minor libraries of architecture exist, or at least compartments or divisions devoted to the fine arts. Such institutions are the Fitz William Museum at Cambridge ; the Taylor Building and Randolph Galleries at Oxford ; Ruskin's school at Sheffield. The greater libraries, of which that of the British Museum is much the largest (as it is second only in extent to the National Library at Paris), contain large numbers of books upon architecture and the allied arts. The special architectural libraries of the Continent of Europe are to be looked for in connection with great schools of architecture, industrial art, engineering, and the like, which are supported by the government of every important state. The largest and best-selected architectural library in America is that founded by Mr. Samuel P. Avery (see Avery Architectural Library).

— R. S.

LIBRARY OF S. GENEVIÈVE. (See Bibliothèque de S. Geneviève.)

LIBRARY OF S. MARK. In Venice. Built from the designs of Jacopo Sansovino in 1536, but continued by Scamozzi fifty years later. There are twenty-one arcades fronting on the piazzetta, and facing the ducal palace ; and of these, the twelve most northerly are generally assigned to Sansovino, the rest, with the three on the south facing toward the sea, to Scamozzi. The building is small and shallow, having but one library room of moderate size, and a number of small office rooms, and it is no longer used for the purpose of a library ; but the exterior is of extraordinary beauty. Nowhere in Italy or in Europe is there a better piece of the developed neoclassic architecture.

LIBRERIA DI S. MARCO. Same as Library of S. Mark.

LIBRERIA VECCHIA. Same as Library of S. Mark.

LICENSING. (See Legislation.)

LICH GATE. A covered gate at the main entrance of a churchyard, usually protected by a spreading gable roof. In England previous to the Revolution it was the custom to have the friends of the deceased carry the corpse to the churchyard, and on reaching the gate to rest the corpse there until the arrival of the officiating clergyman ; hence the gate was roofed in order to afford them shelter from the sun and rain. Lich gates originated thirteen hundred years ago or more, fell out of use, but are now being reintroduced. They were generally built of wood ; therefore there are very few, if any, now in existence that are over four centuries old. The most ancient gate in England is that at Bray in Berks, which bears the date 1448.

James Barr, *Anglican Church Architecture*, 1846 ; Walter Field, *Stones of the Temple*, New York, 1873 ; *The Ecclesiologist*, Vols. I. to XXII., 1842–1861.

— CARYL COLEMAN.

LICH STONE. A stone at the entrance to a churchyard, intended to receive a bier. (See Lich Gate.)

LIEN. The right granted to the builder and to all mechanics, labourers, and material men,

to keep some hold upon a piece of property upon which they have worked or for which he has furnished material. This is recognized by law, and has been the subject of carefully considered statutes. The Mechanics' Lien, as it is commonly called, enables a mechanic to secure readily a legal hold upon the property until his claim is paid or has been adjudged excessive. In some states of the United States this takes precedence of mortgage, in others it comes next after all mortgages. — R. S.

LIERNE RIB. In Gothic vaulting, any small subordinate rib inserted between the main ribs, more often as an ornament than for constructive reasons. This accepted indefinite English meaning of the term differs from that given by the French writers to the same word, which is specifically applied by them to a short rib sprung between the apex or clef of the vault

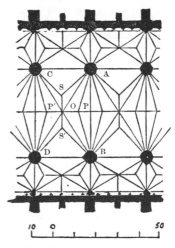

LIERNE RIB: PLAN OF VAULTING; NAVE OF LINCOLN CATHEDRAL.

and the junction of two tiercerons, — these latter being ribs springing from the piers between the ogives and the arcs doubleaux or the arcs formerets. Thus, in the diagram, AD, BC being the ogives and O the point of crossing or apex of the vault, CS, DS' are tiercerons, OS and OS' are liernes. According to English usage these last four are all liernes.

LIERNE VAULTING. Vaulting in which are used Lierne Ribs, whether in the English or French signification.

LIFT. *A.* Any attachment or mechanical device for raising and lowering. Generally used in combination, as transom-lift.

B. In British usage, the same as Elevator in the general sense, including also Dumbwaiter.

LIFTING JACK. Same as Jackscrew.

LIGHT. In architecture, — *A.* The volume of daylight received in a room, corridor, or the like. The term is often used in composition, as in the subtitle Borrowed Light. By extension, a similar volume of light from an artificial source; as a closet may have a borrowed light from a room lighted by electricity.

B. An opening or medium through which daylight may pass, as a pane (called generally by glaziers and carpenters a light) of glass. More especially the opening between two mullions or window bars in a decorative window, the glass of which is commonly in irregular or other small pieces, hardly called lights in this case.

C. An artificial source of light; a means of providing light, as in the compound or qualified terms gas light, electric light. Thus, in arranging for the lighting of an interior (see Lighting), it may be stipulated that ten lights be ranged along the cornice on either side.

D. The manner or the nature of the illumination received by a picture or other work of art, or by a wall or ceiling considered as the medium for the display of such work of art. Thus, it may be said that there is no good light for pictures on the east wall.

Angel Light. In a decorative window, one of those lights (definition *B*) which are or may be adorned by stained or painted glass representing angels, as, in some English Gothic windows, one of several smaller openings in the window head in which figures of angels are commonly inserted.

Borrowed Light. A light (definition *A*) which is received from another room or passage, which itself is lighted directly by windows or the like; thus, in ill-planned houses it is not uncommon for certain rooms to take their only daylight across a corridor, the window of the room being perhaps directly opposite a large window in the outer wall of the corridor.

Bull's-Eye Light. A small opening intended to be filled by a single bull's-eye, the effect being that the magnifying or refracting power of the lens formed by the bull's-eye diffuses light more than if admitted through an opening of the same size glazed in the ordinary way.

Vault Light. A light (definition *B*) prepared expressly for underground rooms, cellars extended under streets, and the like, often called, though erroneously, vaults (see Vault). The vault light is usually an arrangement of prismatic or lenticular glasses in a metal frame, this arrangement being covered by one of many patents, or introduced and pushed by one of many firms of manufacturers. In modern cities large horizontal surfaces, as the floors of areas or the whole series of treads, platforms of entrance, and even large sections of public sidewalk, are composed entirely of the upper surface of such vault lights. — R. S.

LIGHTHOUSE. A building used to carry, in a high and exposed position, a powerful light which can be seen from a distance. The term is used, almost exclusively, for those towerlike buildings maintained on the seashore, either to warn vessels away from dangerous reefs or shoals, or to guide them into a harbour entrance or up a channel. The lights used for these latter purposes are relatively small, and the houses are not always high. Two lights in range, showing the main course of the channel, need not generally be seen more than ten miles away. On the other hand, such lights are distinguished from one another very carefully by their character as revolving lights, flash lights, intermittent lights, and also by their colours; and in like manner the buildings themselves are given some peculiarity of structure or colour. Lights on an open coast are sometimes of the highest possible illuminating power, so as to be seen and recognized as far away as the curvature of the globe will permit. Thus, on the south coast of England, advantage is taken of the chalk cliffs, and towers are erected, as at Beachy Head, Dungenness, the Needles, Portland Bill, the Lizard, etc., some of which are among the most powerful in the world. The light on Navesink Highlands, southwest of Sandy Hook and near the entrance to New York Bay, is 250 feet above tidewater, and can be seen forty miles at sea.

The towers are rather subjects for the engineer than for the architect, and there has been as yet but little attempt to give architectural character to the modern government-built and scientifically managed lighthouse. This was not so in earlier times, when the distinction between engineering and architecture had not been established, and when every building was thought worthy of artistic treatment. It is evident from ancient writers that the lighthouse of Alexandria in Egypt was an architectural structure of importance. Many Roman lighthouses are known to have existed; the ruins of some are still traceable, and others disappeared in quite recent times. None of these still exist as architectural works of interest except that at Corunna (La Coruna) in Spain. The tower at the entrance to the port is certainly a Roman structure, restored and repaired rather than rebuilt in more recent times. It is 363 feet high, and if the guide-books are right in saying that its light can be seen only twelve miles at sea, this must come of a very feeble lamp or refractor. The Middle Ages proper were hardly likely to undertake important enterprises of the sort, but small lighthouses existed and are still traceable, or are recorded in existing drawings, at La Rochelle, at Marseilles, at Aigues-Mortes, and other places. The tower at Genoa is a valuable design of the sixteenth century, and of this epoch is the magnificent building on an isolated rock at the mouth of the Gironde, where vessels have to pass to reach the port of Bordeaux. This splendid building is recorded to have been built by Louis de Foix in the reign of Henry II. of France, but its design as given by the authorities cited below was rather that of a somewhat later period. It has now been radically altered by the substitution, for its old cupola, of a much taller conical shaft. (The reader is referred to the Dictionary of Architecture of the Architectural Publication Society; plates taken from Belidor, *Architecture Hydraulique*, and Reynaud, *Mémoire sur l'éclairage et le balisage des Côtes de France*.) The famous Eddystone Lighthouse was first built by a private philanthropist in 1696; and this, which was destroyed by a storm, and its successor, which was burned, had each some architectural pretension. The tower of 1757 is the famous one built by Smeaton; and this, like more modern lighthouse towers, had no more architectural character than that given by a rather agreeable hollow curve to the tower. Smeaton's building lasted until 1882, when a new building on another part of the reef was completed. Some modern lighthouses are open skeletons of ironwork. Such a tower was that at Minot's Ledge on the coast of Massachusetts near Cohasset, but this was carried away by a storm, and a stone tower was erected in its place. — R. S.

LIGHTING (I.). In architecture, — *A*. The admission of daylight into interiors of buildings.

B. The providing of artificial light for a surface, as a wall or ceiling, or for a room, corridor, staircase, or the like.

Lighting by daylight may be through the walls or through the roof or ceiling. Lighting in the last-named way (see Skylight) is much easier than through the walls, because the amount of daylight received through an opening of a given size in the roof or ceiling is much greater than that received from the wall. Windows and walls admit light sometimes directly from the sky, but still more generally light reflected from surrounding objects, as the ground, trees, and, in the city, buildings on the other side of the street. The first object of every person engaged in providing windows for a room should be to carry the heads of those windows as near to the ceiling as practicable, because the upper part of each window will admit vastly more light than the lower part, the exact proportion varying, of course, with the conditions in each case. This obvious and simple method of making our interiors pleasant is contradicted and opposed by the architecture of almost every style, and also by the practice of the people in almost every country. Thus, the round, and still more the pointed, arch takes away nearly half of the best part of a possible window, substituting opaque spandrels for translucent surfaces. College buildings in a modern Gothic style have been justly blamed for the exclusion from lecture rooms, laboratories, and the like, of the light which might have come through the heads of square windows had these been used instead of

pointed windows. The same charge lies against arcades with semicircular heads.

Moreover, the necessary decorative disposition of interiors is generally thought to involve the leaving of much solid wall above the window heads and below the ceiling, this space being sometimes used by moulded cornices, sometimes by painted friezes, or the like, and always considered necessary to stately effect. In private houses the windows, even as provided, are usually curtained in such a way that not more than one-quarter or one-third of the lighting space provided is allowed to serve. It is rare, even in modern times and with modern ideas of decorative furnishing, that curtains are made so that they can be drawn away with perfect ease and

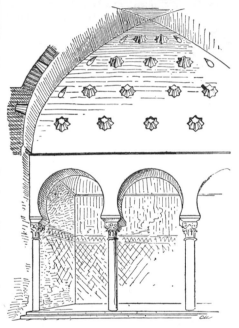

LIGHTING OF A BATH IN THE ALHAMBRA BY STAR-SHAPED OPENINGS IN THE VAULT; SEE SECTION AT LEFT.

celerity, and it is rare that they are so drawn; in fact, curtains may be recognized as the chief difficulty in the way of good lighting in all our domestic decorative scheme. When there is question of providing light in any special way, as the strong illumination of a wall upon which valuable pictures are to be hung, the difficulty of contending with established customs is still more obvious. Thus one may look through the carefully built mansions of a great city without finding more than here and there an interior wall even fairly well lighted for the reception and display of works of art.

These considerations are of importance when the external fenestration is under consideration. All designers know the value of comparatively unbroken wall space ; and their own desire to use fewer or smaller windows, but in the right places, are continually overruled by the owner, who must have more and larger openings. If, then, due consideration could be given to the subject, in advance, and windows enough, but not too many, used, better and simpler interiors, as well as nobler exterior effects, might result.

In the lighting of rooms which open on small courtyards, light shafts, and the like, these being opened to the sky and the light received from them being not therefore properly Borrowed Light (which see under Light), the difficulties are still greater. These are the conditions of the hypæthral openings (see Hypæthral ; Hypæthros) ; but the hypæthral temple, whatever its real nature, must have been extremely simple in its arrangement and the light admitted in the most obvious way, as between the columns of an inner portico, as, indeed, Vitruvius seems to assert. Inasmuch as in such a case light will nearly all be reflected from below or from the walls around, various devices have been resorted to, — as the making of all the walls of such a courtyard white, or nearly white, and providing them with a glazed or glossy surface. Enamelled bricks are much used in such cases, and in a mild climate cheap wall tiles could be used equally well. A number of devices in the way of portable reflectors have been used, intended to throw light into windows either by intercepting that which is falling from the sky immediately above, the reflecting surface being placed at the proper angle, or by the placing of similar materials at the sides of windows to receive light coming in from a side opening or space not walled in. It has also been proposed, and in one or two cases attempted, to build the walls of such courtyards constantly retreating, each story behind the next lower story, modern appliances in the way of iron construction being used to make such constantly receding wall structures safe and solid. Thus, if the wall of a second story retreats four feet from the line of the wall below, increasing the width of the courtyard by so much, the wall of the ground floor may be entirely of glass and its upper part may be rounded off or built at a slope, so that a part of this enclosing glass surface partakes of the nature of a skylight. The same plan may be followed through every story of a high building, much space within being thus sacrificed, but the space which is utilized being much better lighted.

In lighting by artificial means, the ideal arrangement would seem to be the admission of the artificial light from those wall surfaces or ceilings through which the daylight is allowed to pass. Thus, if gas or electric lights are arranged around and close to a window opening, the light by night will come from the same source as that by day and the problem of arranging the interior will be greatly simplified. It is, however, frequently the case that the room in question is not well lighted by day, the daylight being admitted by one or two windows at one end of a long room, and in such a case it might well be thought that advantage should be taken of modern appliances in the way of artificial illumination to make the light by night more diffused and general than by day (see Lighting (II.) ; Electric Lighting).

The important question of the lighting of works of art, either absolutely fixed, as in the case of mural paintings or carved friezes or panels, or, though portable, not likely to be moved on account of their size or their occupying a position intended to be not often changed, is complicated by the considerations of interior effect, as has been stated above. If, for instance, a large window be arranged in the wall facing due north, and the walls at right angles with this and running north and south are to be adorned with paintings or other works of art, it will be found that the window may easily be too near the corner of the room, and the light therefore received at an angle too acute with the surfaces of the works of art to be seen. If the pictures are framed, as movable pictures are always, the case is still more serious, because every projection of frame or shadow box will throw a shadow upon the surface, and this will increase the inevitable bad effect of light shining so steeply upon a painting as to exaggerate the threads of the canvas, if they are partly visible, or the projecting masses of paint common in the works of many artists. In the case of sculpture the effect is still more obvious, for though nothing is more disastrous for reliefs than illumination from a point opposite them (behind the spectator), as this tends to efface all light and shade and to make shadow impossible, yet the lighting at too great an angle with the surface causes all minute refinement of surface to be lost in a general darkness of shadow. The same difficulty arises in the case of artificial lighting. Thus, a large and very important ceiling painting in New York is lighted by electrical lights so near the plane of its surface that it is never properly seen. When these lights are extinguished and the picture is lighted only from below, the illumination is naturally insufficient ; and the remedy would be the lowering of the uppermost lights to the distance of at least eight feet below their present position. — R. S.

LIGHTING (II.) ; **ELECTRIC LIGHTING.** The electric current is made use of to produce light of two varieties. The arc light (see Arc Lamp, under Electric Appliances) is ordinarily of either about 1200 or about 2000 candle power in the direction of greatest illumination. The incandescent light is produced by forcing a current of electricity through a carbonized filament having a comparatively high resistance.

The current in passing through the resistance generates heat, and the current is made sufficiently strong to heat the filament to the necessary degree of incandescence. The filament is enclosed in a glass bulb from which the air has been exhausted. These incandescent lamps are made of various powers, but are ordinarily of 16 candle power.

The arc light, on account of its great intensity, high candle power, and low cost per candle power, is well adapted for street lighting and for the illumination of large enclosed spaces, but the nature of the light makes it ill adapted for general indoor use. The incandescent light is softer; it is practicable to produce the light in small quantities so that the distribution may be uniform and the light thus less obtrusive; there is no combustion and hence no vitiation of the air; the lamps may be so connected to the supply wires that the lamps may be to some extent portable; and since the heated filament is entirely enclosed the lamps may be in places not allowable with lamps likely to ignite inflammable material.

Arc lamps, with the exception of the recently adopted "constant potential arc lamps," are connected "in series" or "in tandem." That is, all the lamps in a circuit are connected so that the same current passes through each. If the circuit is broken at any place all the lamps will go out. With this system the current is kept constant, and if more lamps are added the pressure at the generator must be increased to overcome the added resistance. To cut out any lamp it is necessary first to make a bypath round the lamp to preserve the continuity of the circuit, and then the connection to the lamp may be broken. There are advantages in this method of distribution, but it is best adapted to lamps that are all lighted for the same period of time.

Incandescent lamps and "constant potential arc lamps" are connected "in multiple" or abreast. That is, they are connected in between two supply wires and are independent of one another, each receiving at its terminals the full pressure of the system. The pressure at the generator remains the same whether few or many lamps are lighted, but the circuit is greater or less according to the number of lamps that are lighted. This multiple or constant pressure system allows the use of a safe and convenient pressure, and since each lamp is independent all appliances and wiring arrangements are comparatively simple. (See Wiring, Electric, under Electrical Appliances.) — RUSSELL ROBB.

LIGHTNING ROD. A rod, wire, or strip of metal running from a point above the roof of a building to the earth so that it will carry off electric discharges from the clouds, and thus prevent discharges from passing with destructive effect through the building itself. Authorities

are now agreed that lightning rods do offer protection, and that even imperfectly constructed rods may be better than none. General agreement has not been reached, however, as to the best method of protecting a building. Recent developments in electrical science have shown more plainly that currents of electricity starting suddenly are very unlike steady currents in their action and effect, and these newer views have greatly influenced ideas of lightning protection. Lightning discharges are not confined to what are ordinarily looked upon as conductors, and they do not always choose metallic paths. Disturbances are produced by induction even in places separated from the path that the discharge takes, and discharges sometimes jump from the path provided, to water-pipe or gas-pipe systems, or to other masses of metal. Early rods were very large, had elaborate terminal points, and were insulated from the building. It is now agreed that there is little or no advantage in having rods larger than one quarter of an inch in diameter, and not only are they not insulated from buildings, but they are often connected to metal cornices and other masses of metal coming near the rods. In the simpler cases of protection it is thought sufficient to run even ordinary galvanized telegraph wires along ridges and eaves, up over all chimneys and down all corners to earth connections. It is best to have a number of terminal points distributed about in exposed places. External masses of metal like gutters and spouts should be thoroughly connected together and to the lightning conductors. The conductors should be of the same metal throughout, should have as few joints as possible, and these unavoidable joints should be made with great care. There should be as few turns and bends as possible. A good earth connection should be provided and preferably more than one. The earth connection should be in permanently moist earth, and to insure this it is best to dig until damp soil is reached, place coke in the bottom of the hole, and bury in the coke a ground plate of metal having a substantial soldered connection with the lightning conductor. Beyond these simpler rules opinion is more divided because some precautions that are undoubtedly of advantage for certain reasons may lead to unforeseen accidents. It is probably best to connect the rods to the water-pipe system outside the building with a connection that is substantial and well soldered; to connect the rod to all masses of metal near which it passes; and to connect the water pipes and gas pipes to each other where they come near together in the building. — RUSSELL ROBB.

LIGORIO (LIGORI), PIRRO (PYRRHO, incorrectly **PIERO**); architect, engineer, and archæologist; d. after 1585.

Pirro Ligorio was a Neapolitan architect who entered the service of Paul IV. (Pope 1555–

1559), and was probably employed on S. Peter's under Michelangelo (see Buonarroti). He continued the construction of the Belvedere at the Vatican, and commenced during the reign of Paul IV. the famous villa of the Vatican gardens which was finished under Pius IV. (Pope 1559–1565), and from him received the name Villa Pia (finished 1561). Ligorio saved the vault of the Sistine chapel by building buttresses and strengthening foundations. He built the Palazzo Lancellotti in the Piazza Navona, Rome. Sept. 1, 1564, he was associated with Vignola (see Barozzio, G.) in the superintendence of the construction of S. Peter's church. In 1568 he entered the service of Alfonso II. d'Este at Ferrara, where he died. The manuscripts of his intended work, *L'Antichità di Roma*, came into the possession of Emmanuele I., of Savoy. Thirty volumes are still in the library at Turin ; others are in Naples, at the Vatican, at Windsor, the Bibliothèque Nationale at Paris, and elsewhere. Ligorio's manuscripts contain numerous important drawings of antique monuments which have disappeared. They contain also thousands of inscriptions (3000 from Rome and vicinity alone) which are deliberately forged or falsified. These inscriptions have drifted into the various compilations, to the perpetual annoyance of scholars and epigraphists (Henzen, op. cit.). Those which are printed in the *Corpus Inscriptionum Latinorum* are marked with an asterisk.

Raoul-Rochette, *Notice historique sur Pirro Ligorio* in Jules Bouchet, *La Villa Pia ;* Middleton, *MS. notes by Pirro Ligorio ;* Henzen, *Zu den Fälschungen des Pirro Ligorio ;* Letarouilly, *Vatican.*

LIME. The oxide of calcium ; most frequently found combined with carbonic acid forming limestone, or with sulphuric acid forming gypsum. All calcareous cements have lime as their base. When carbonate of lime is calcined the carbonic acid is thrown off and lime is obtained ; commonly known as caustic lime, or quicklime. If then it be mixed with its equivalent of water, it slakes, — that is, it throws out great heat, swells to two or three times its original bulk, and subsequently falls to powder, — it has become a hydrate of lime, commonly known as slaked lime. Its affinity for carbonic acid is restored, it absorbs it from the atmosphere and gradually hardens. For use as a mortar in building, sufficient water is added to make a paste, and this is mixed with two or three times its bulk of sand. The hardening of lime mortar is due almost entirely to the absorption of carbonic acid from the air.

Hydraulic Lime. That made from calcareous rocks containing from 12 to 30 per cent in the aggregate of silica, alumina, iron, and magnesia, their hydraulic quality being derived chiefly from the two first. When calcined at a low temperature the product will slake, and they will set and harden in water in periods varying from one or two days to five or six months, depending on the proportion of clay contained. Limestones, containing 30 to 50 per cent of clay (silica and alumina), yield the light or Roman cements. They are merely calcined, while the cements containing a large proportion of silica are burned to incipient vitrification, and are very heavy. The hydraulic limes are not used in the United States, the light cements taking their place. (See Cement.) — W. R. HUTTON.

LIMESTONE. Any rock composed essentially of carbonate of lime. (See Dolomite.) — G. P. M.

LIMEWASH. Same as Whitewash.

LINEAR PERSPECTIVE. (See Perspective.)

LINEN CLOSET. A closet serving the purpose of a small linen room.

LINEN PATTERN. A carved design, common in late Gothic and sixteenth-century woodwork, and supposed to represent a loosely folded cloth. The usual form suggests a square cloth like a napkin folded accurately with deliberate decorative purpose ; hence, called often napkin pattern.

LINEN ROOM. A room set apart for the care and safe keeping of bed and table linen, towels, and the like ; fitted up with shelves, and, in large establishments, perhaps containing one or more clothespresses.

LINEN SCROLL. Same as Linen Pattern.

LINHAY. — An open shed for cattle ; local English.

LINING. Material used to cover the interior of anything ; hence a member forming the back or internal face of a structure. Seldom used except in special combinations ; as jamb lining, window back lining. (See Sheathing.)

LINING PAPER.
A. In general, same as Sheathing Paper.
B. More specifically, in paper hanging, a paper used to cover walls underneath the decorative hangings.

LINING PEN. Same as Drawing Pen *B* (which see under Pen).

LINO DI CAMAINO. (See Tino di Camaino.)

LINTEL. A beam or the like over an opening, which carries the weight of the wall above it. It may be of wood, of iron, or of stone. The bearings of its ends on the jambs of the opening must be sufficient to prevent injury from pressure to the material, either of the lintel or of the jamb ; and if the opening is very wide,

LINTELS CUT TO THE SEMBLANCE OF A CONSTRUCTIVE ARCH ; KHERBET HÂSS, SYRIA.

it may be necessary to consider also the strength of the foundations under the jambs, upon which the entire weight above the opening must come. — W. R. H.

Safety Lintel. A wooden lintel placed behind a lintel or arch in the aperture of a door

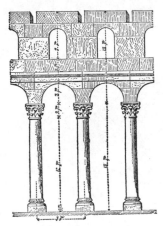

or window; usually having a discharging arch above.

LIP. A rounded overhanging edge or member, especially when curving outward and downward, as a spout or drip.

LIPPI, ANNIBALE; architect.

Lippi built the Palazzo Salviati alla Longara and the Palazzo di Spagna in Rome. His chief work was the completion in 1590 of the Villa Medici, Rome, begun in 1550. This building is now the seat of the French Academy in Rome.

Gurlitt, *Geschichte des Barockstiles in Italien;* Ebe, *Spät-Renaissance;* Baltard, *Villa Medici à Rome.*

L IRON. Same as Angle Iron.

LISENA. In Italian, a pilaster; perhaps especially one of those used in Romanesque architecture and not belonging to one of the classic or neoclassic orders.

LIST (I). The rough edge, with or without bark, of a board as sawn from a log.

LIST (II), (pl. Lists). The enclosure or border of anything; hence, in the plural, the temporary barrier separating from the spectators a tilting ground, or place for athletic sports of any sort, as well as the place set apart for a judicial combat. Lists were put up on all occasions of jousts, tournaments, archery practice, and the like, during the Middle Ages and the fifteenth and sixteenth centuries, and the term is often applied to the ground itself so enclosed.

LIST (III). Same as Fillet. Also written Listel.

LIST (v.). *A.* In Great Britain, to bring to a uniform thickness, or, more especially, a uniform width.

B. In the United States, to cut off (from boards or lumber) the list or rough edge or face beneath the bark.

LISTEL. Same as Fillet.

LITANY DESK. A kneeling bench with a low desk or bookrest placed at the head of the nave before the chancel door or gate, and used in the Church of England and in the Protestant Episcopal Church in America by the clergyman or clerk when reciting the Litany. — C. C.

LIVING ROOM. In a dwelling in the United States, a room for the general use of the family. In a dwelling for the poorer classes, as a tenement, it may combine the offices of a kitchen, and, to a large extent, a family sitting room; although there may be a small parlour as well. In houses of a better sort it will frequently be used as a dining room and parlour; while in many private residences the name may be given to a sitting room, or hall habitually used by the inmates at large; there being, perhaps, also a parlour or reception room. (See Parlour; Reception Room; Sitting Room.) (Cut, cols. 775, 776.) — D. N. B. S.

LIWAN. (See Leewan.)

LOAD. That which has to be carried or supported; as, a column may be strong enough to carry a load of twelve tons.

Dead Load. (See under D.)

Live Load. That part of the load, as upon a roof or floor, which is not permanent and essential: as snow upon a roof, merchandise, or a crowd of people on a floor.

Wind Load. Same as Wind Pressure.
— W. R. H.

LOBBY. A small room of communication, as between the entrance doors of a house and the hall or passage within, or from a larger hall or passage to a chamber to which it serves as a kind of anteroom. It is a general term, and may be applied to almost any such part of a building. Thus, if the word "vestibule" in a Roman house be properly applied only to the recess outside of the doors, the fauces or short passage within may properly be called a lobby. (Compare Antechamber; Anteroom; Dégagement; Vestibule; Vestibulum. See also Loggia.)

LOCK. A contrivance for fastening and unfastening at will a door, casement, chest, drawer, or the like, usually one of which the essential part is a bolt shot and withdrawn by means of a removable key. Door locks have usually a Latch as well as the bolt moved by the key. Locks for safes and strong rooms are sometimes of extraordinary complication, and many rival inventions have at different times demanded the attention of builders, resulting in a system of defence against burglarious attacks, which amounts almost to perfect security so far as the lock is

LIVING ROOM IN WEALTHY PEASANT'S HOUSE, FRANCE.
Permanent or standing bed-places ; chimney breast and mantel carried on corbels : a modern design.

concerned.　Locks of this sort sometimes shoot bolts in all four directions, and are frequently operated without keys, thus avoiding the necessity of a keyhole into which an explosive may be forced.

Burglar Alarm Lock.　One connected, usually by means of electricity, with a gong or other means of sounding an alarm when the bolt is tampered with.

Combination Lock.　One in which the bolt can be drawn only when a certain arrangement of the external parts, as of three rings with letters on them, has been made.　Thus, if there are three lettered rings, a combination of letters perhaps forming a word may be carried in the mind or in a note-book, and when that combination is made by bringing the rings into a certain relation to one another the handle can be turned, and the bolt withdrawn.

Crossbolt Lock.　One in which the key shoots two bolts at the same time in opposite directions, — an arrangement easy to make by means of a short lever.　This is useful for doors of bookcases and similar pieces of furniture ; the bolts shooting at top and bottom at the same time hold the stile of the door straight, and prevent its "winding" or warping with heat and use. (See Espagnolette.)

Cylinder Lock.　One of which the essential feature is a cylinder into which falls a series of tumblers, preventing the cylinder from being turned until the tumblers are pushed out by the insertion of the proper key into the cylinder.　This

is a Flat Key, or a modification, with its edge serrated or notched to fit the ends of the series of tumblers, which are thus pushed aside when the key is inserted into the end of the cylinder. The latter can then be turned and the bolt shot. This lock is one of the safest of recent key-locks, its security lying in the arrangement of the series of tumblers, of which an almost infinite number of combinations can be made.

Dead Lock.　A door lock having a bolt actuated by a key only, or by a key on one side and a knob on the other, thus distinguished from a knob lock, which has a bolt actuated from either side by a key and a latch or catch actuated from either side by a knob. (See Lock.)

Drawbolt Lock.　One in which a bolt or latch, ordinarily movable by means of a knob or the like, can also be held by locking with a key, and can only be withdrawn when the key is used to unlock it.

Extension Bolt Lock.　Same as Cross Bolt Lock.

Knob Lock.　(See Dead Lock.)

Latch Lock.　A lock designed especially for an outer door, as of a suite of offices, a front door, or the like, and therefore taking the place of a latch, properly so called.　Usually a spring lock, *i.e.* one of which the bolt is automatically shot by a spring, and can only be operated from outside by a key.　Such a lock has also usually a device by which the bolt may be retained and the action of the spring prevented, as during the hours in which the door is in frequent use.　Such a lock, when designed or adapted especially for night use, is commonly known as a night latch.

Mortise Lock. One specially arranged to be sunk in a mortise in the edge of a door or sash. It has usually an edge plate, which is set square or diagonally with the sides of the box of the lock, according to the angle made by the edge of the stile in which the lock is to be entered.

Rim Lock. One in which the " case " is secured against the face of the stile of the door, as distinguished from a mortise lock, which is let into and concealed by the wood. The case is ordinarily secured by screws, so that the lock can be readily removed. It is therefore usual to place such locks on the inside of the apartment or closet. If on the outside, clinched nails or bolts should be used, passing through the door. When it is desirable to make the builders' hardware decorative, as in the rare cases in which all pieces are designed expressly for the building in hand, it is common to choose rim locks. Admirable examples exist of the artistic treatment of such locks in wrought-iron, and it is not difficult to use fine designing even for the brass or bronze boxes, their rims and flanges, and the bolt heads which secure them.

Time Lock. One in which a clockwork attachment is used to open the door or to withdraw the bolts, so that the door can be opened at a time previously determined, and set by the clock of the lock. Such a lock may be arranged to have no keyhole whatever, and to be practically proof against attack by explosives.

Tumbler Lock. A form of lock in which the bolt is controlled by tumblers or levers which are raised by the bit of the key.
— F. B. H.

LOCK (v.t.). To provide with locks, and, by extension, with other builders' hardware, as when a firm contracts " to lock " a house.

LOCK BOX. A small box or locker in a public or quasi-public place, as a club, arranged for the locking up and safe keeping of a person's private articles. Especially, in the United States, such a box for private use in a post office, for receiving mail matter. It is open at the back for access by the post office employees, and closed at the front by a door provided with a lock for the accommodation of the lessee of the box.

LOCKER. Any comparatively small compartment intended to be habitually locked as a more or less safe depository for smaller articles of any kind. The term is generally restricted to mean a permanently fixed structure, a receptacle forming part of the general construction of a room, as a chest formed by a window seat, a small cupboard for clothes, as in a gymnasium.

LOCKHOLE. Same as Keyhole.

LOCULUS (pl. loculi). In a Catacomb used for a burial, or Columbarium, one of the recesses

used when large enough to receive a dead body with or without a coffin, and when smaller to receive the cinerary urn. It was customary to close the mouth of the loculus with a slab of stone or with masonry.

LOCUTORIUM. A place for conversation; especially the parlour of a monastic establishment.

LODGE. Primarily, a small house ; a hut or cot. Hence, in special meanings : —

A. A tipi, tent, wigwam, or other structure of the American Indians, the term being applied indiscriminately.

B. A subordinate building, or one dependent upon a large establishment ; as, in a large country residence, a building at the outer gateways (called often gatekeeper's lodge ; porter's lodge) serving to accommodate those who see to the opening and shutting of the gates, and the admission of persons or vehicles. It sometimes has the character of a small pavilion with some relations of architectural design to the principal mansion on the estate. The keeper's lodge on a large estate is assumed to be the dwelling of the gamekeeper, but this official hardly exists out of the British Islands. In royal parks in England the lodge is often a house of considerable pretensions ; and such buildings are occasionally granted by the crown to persons of great distinction, as permanent residences ; thus, Lord John Russell, afterward Earl Russell, occupied Pembroke Lodge, at Richmond Park, by special permit of the Queen, from 1847 until his death in 1878.

C. A meeting room, or set of rooms, as for a society. The term is used in this sense mainly by secret, benevolent, or political societies ; for neither in Great Britain nor in the United States is it the common term for the meeting room of literary, artistic, or convivial associations. — R. S.

Cavate Lodge ; Cavated Lodge. An American Indian dwelling wholly or partly excavated in a cliff, mountain, or hill. Four localities are known where cavate lodges are numerous : along the Rio Grande, between Santa Clara and Cochiti, New Mexico ; along the San Juan River and its tributaries, in the region surrounding the intersection of the boundaries of New Mexico, Arizona, Utah, and Colorado ; in the San Francisco Mountain region, Arizona ; and in the valley of the Rio Verde, Arizona. In these districts the number of cavate lodges reaches the thousands. They vary somewhat in the different localities, but the general features are similar. Some have rooms open to the air, some are walled up in front, and some clusters are entirely within the rock, a thin wall being left between the outer room and the face of the cliff, or mountain. Tillable lands are usually in the vicinity, and also remains of other forms of dwellings.

The Verde group is the most extensive. The average size is two or three rooms. Some clusters extend directly back into the cliff a considerable distance, in one instance reaching 47 feet from the outer face of the rock. Rooms are both oblong and circular, the oblong averaging about 10×17 feet, and the circular about 8 feet diameter. The largest circular room is 25 feet diameter. Ceilings are about 7 feet high. No chimneys have been found in the Verde group, the doorway being the only opening of any kind between the interior and the outer air, and the firepit, therefore, being placed near it. The rooms of each cluster communicate through low, narrow passages, but there was usually no connection between different clusters. The floors were brought to a level by filling in hollows with adobe mortar, and they were frequently traversed by low ridges of clay for a purpose not understood. There are many small rooms, evidently for storage, and nooks were formed in the walls, probably for closets or cupboards; and there are also depressions at the rear of some rooms that appear to have been reservoirs. No adobe brick have been found. The formation is an extremely soft, friable, purple-gray sandstone.

The San Juan group occurs in a soft, friable shale lying between harder strata that form, respectively, the floor and the roof. At one extensive group there are three stone ruins on the brink of the cliff above, one rectangular and the others circular, which seem to have been part of the village, and were probably lookouts and posts of defence, as well as serving for other uses. The circular structures were double walled.

The Rio Grande group occurs in a pumice and volcanic ash easily worked. The ceilings follow the average, being from 5 to 7 feet high. Doorways are irregularly oval. Near Santa Clara there were fireplaces in some of the lodges, and certain rooms had been used as shelters for sheep, goats, and donkeys, thus establishing their modern character. Here many caves had a stone front part built on, the beams resting in holes in the cliff.

The San Francisco group occurs in volcanic cinder cones. These cinders are soft and friable. The rooms are 10 or 12 feet in diameter, and 6 to 10 feet high. The arrangement is similar to the Verde — a large central chamber with smaller ones opening off. (See Communal Dwelling; Kiva; Notched Doorway, under Doorway; Pueblo.) — F. S. DELLENBAUGH.

Communal Lodge. A tipi or tent among the Dakota Indians, where the unmarried men dwelt together. There was one for each gens. (See Communal Dwelling.) — F. S. D.

Dancing Lodge. A form of the Medicine Lodge, such as the temporary building constructed by the Sioux for the sun dance. It is composed of two concentric circles of forked poles set in the ground about the sun pole, the inner one being 2 or 3 feet higher than the outer. A light roof of tent poles and saplings covers the space between the two rows of poles; but that within the inner row is left open to the sky, as the devotees are required to see the sun all the time. The outer wall is made of leaves and branches. (See also Assembly House.) — F. S. D.

Dirt Lodge. Same as Earth Lodge. (See Communal Dwelling.)

Earth Lodge. A lodge, in sense A, covered with earth. Not confined to any special tribe or locality. Most tribes constructed houses in several different ways. Amongst the Omaha and Ponka Indians the earth lodges were principally for summer use; while amongst the Navajo Indians the earth lodge, or Hogan, is for winter use. The Mandan earth lodge was one of the best constructed. (See Communal Dwelling.) — F. S. D.

Ghost Lodge. A tent, or tipi, erected among the Sioux Indians by parents who have lost a son, to shelter a lock of his hair, which is enclosed in deerskin and suspended within the lodge from a tripod of sticks. This lock represents the ghost or spirit of the departed. When travelling the ghost lodge is taken along, and on camping is the first to be set up. It is maintained in this manner till the final burial of the lock of hair, which is considered the real parting with the deceased; and this may not take place for several years. — F. S. D.

Medicine Lodge. A lodge, in sense A, erected for and devoted to ceremonial observances. Among the Menomini-Algonquin, the house built for the Mita-wit, or Grand Medicine Society. This structure is termed "mitawikomik" or "mitawikiop" (Ojibwa, midé wigiwam; Ottawa, mité wikomik), and is constructed by the medicine women appointed for this special work. Poles are planted in two rows about 20 feet apart for a distance of 70 feet, and then bent over and tied to each other so as to form a long arbour with an arched ceiling. This frame is then covered with rush mats and birch bark. The Navajo Medicine Lodge is a low moundlike structure composed of piñon or cedar logs set on end with an inclination toward each other, and covered with mud. A passage about 3 feet wide and 5 feet high leads to the entrance, and there is a smoke hole at the top. The diameter at the base is about 25 feet, with an interior height in the centre of about 8 feet. It is similar to the ordinary winter house, or "Hogan." These two examples and that given under Dancing Lodge, above, exhibit the usual forms of these lodges. (See also Mystery Lodge, below.)

               — F. S. D.

Mystery Lodge. A lodge, in sense A, for ceremonial purposes. Its function is analogous to that of the religious side of the Kiva. (See Dancing Lodge, Medicine Lodge, above.)

— F. S. D.

Sweat Lodge. A structure built by American Indians with no opening other than a small entrance, for the purpose of producing, by means of hot stones upon which water is poured to make steam, profuse perspiration in the occupant. It is resorted to for purification before ceremonies, and also as a remedy for disease. The construction differs in different tribes. It is generally very small; but in some districts, as in northern California, it is nearly as large as the assembly house of the tribe. Among the Sioux it is frequently large enough to allow a number of persons to enter at the same time. In Mexico called Temascale. Not to be confounded with Estufa, which is entirely different. (See Estufa and Kiva.) — F. S. D.

LODGING HOUSE. A house having rooms to rent, either singly, or in small suites, each containing a parlour and one or two bedrooms; food being sometimes furnished, or at least cooked and served. It thus differs from an apartment house in the usual sense, in which each suite is arranged with the full complement of rooms necessary for a complete dwelling.

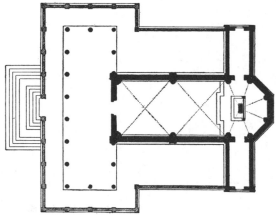

LOGGIA: FIG. 2. — CHURCH OF S. MARIA DELLE GRAZIE, NEAR AREZZO, TUSCANY.

With loggia much wider than façade of church. The outer wall has been removed.

In the United States the term is generally applied only to a low class of house in which single rooms are rented by the day or week and in which board is not furnished. In Great Britain the name is given even to a house in which the wealthier classes may rent furnished rooms and, usually, have meals served. — D. N. B. S.

LOFT. Originally, any upper floor, especially one immediately under the roof. In modern times, —

LOGGIA: FIG. 1.—HOUSE AT REFADE, SYRIA; 6TH CENTURY.

Front on court, with loggia in upper story.

A. A platform, staging, or gallery within a large room or hall, or occupying only a small part of the interior of a building.

B. In the United States, any upper floor, as in a warehouse, when intended to be used more or less as one large workshop or storage place, and, hence, open throughout without elaborate finish.

LOG CABIN. (See Log House.)

LOGGIA (pl. Loggie). In Italian architecture, a roofed structure open on at least one side and affording a protected sitting place out of doors; commonly a prominent part of a building and forming a porch or gallery, but not infrequently an independent structure serving as a public shelter.

The loggia is a frequent and important feature of the architecture of the Italian palazzi, and, less frequently, of the public buildings and open squares; but the term is hardly to be used in connection with such colonnades and like structures as are intended to serve certain positive purposes, e.g. an ambulatory, or covered passageway. In its application to private residences, it corresponds very closely to the veranda of the country houses of the United States; but the word, in its adopted English sense, is restricted to mean a subordinate, partially enclosed space forming a room open to the air, but still contained within the body of the building. — D. N. B. S.

LOGGIA DEGL' INNOCENTI. At Florence; the covered gallery and arcade of the hospital dedicated to the Holy Innocents, that is, the children killed by the order of Herod. Each spandrel of the arcade is adorned by a large circular medallion representing a swaddled baby, each one in a different attitude and with a different expression, the figures in white enamel on blue enamel ground, the whole the undoubted work of Luca della Robbia.

LOGGIA DEI BANCHIERI (DE' BANCHI). At Siena; a building of 1570, the design of Alessi. It is an open vaulted hall 60 feet wide by only 90 feet long, with two fronts

LOGGIA DEI LANZI, FLORENCE.
The interior without the statues and groups; the Palazzio Vecchio beyond.

consisting of arches of large span (12 and 15 feet) springing from the entablatures of coupled Doric columns.

LOGGIA DEI LANZI. At Florence; a very large open portico having three great arches fronting the northeast and the Piazza della Signoria, and one looking to the southeast and fronting on the court of the Uffizi. The

name signifies the portico of the Lansquenets. By common opinion it is the design of Andrea Orcagna and completed soon after his death, or about 1380. The building is the most perfect specimen of that later round-arched mediæval style peculiar to Italy, and which seems to have been developed by a few artists who objected to the adoption in Italy of the Gothic art of the North, and who were still wholly uninfluenced by, or unconscious of, the neoclassic feeling among scholars which was soon to lead to the classical Renaissance under Brunellesco.

LOGGIA DEI NOBILI. At Siena; an open arcade, in design not unlike that of the Loggia dei Lanzi, but much smaller. It dates from the beginning of the fifteenth century, and is ascribed to the architect Sano da Matteo.

LOGGIA DEL BIGALLO. At Florence; forming the entrance to an ancient hospital and house of charity of a now extinct fraternity. It was built about 1350, and is of the more florid class of that round-arched mediæval style of the fourteenth century (see Loggia dei Lanzi; also Certosa, that of Pavia).

LOGGIA DEL PAPA (of the Pope). At Siena; an open portico built at the expense of Pius II. about 1462. This building is not massive like the two, dei Lanzi and dei Nobili, with solid piers of masonry, but has slender columns with peculiarly elaborate capitals of generally Corinthian form.

LOGGIA DI S. PAOLO. At Florence; a portico and arcade of many arches not unlike, in general design, the Loggia degl' Innocenti. It has for its chief adornment a most remarkable piece of Della Robbia work, the meeting of S. Dominic and S. Francis. The two figures, clothed each in the gown of his order, are in high relief, and represented from the knees up, and about life size. They are in a lunette decorated in the spirit of the Renaissance. The spandrels are filled, like those of the Innocenti, by rondels with bas-reliefs. The design of this building is ascribed to Brunellesco, but it was probably not built during his life.

LOGGIE OF THE VATICAN. In the Vatican Palace; a system of galleries in three stories enclosing on three sides the Cortile di S. Damaso, in the southeast angle of the palace. The design is ascribed to Bramante. The second story gallery on the west side of the court is painted with arabesques enclosing scriptural pictures, for many of which Raphael furnished the cartoons; and this gallery is often called Loggie di Raffaello, which name is extended to the whole series.

LOG HOUSE. A house built of logs, usually of one story and a loft, but sometimes larger. The logs, with or without the bark, are notched and fitted near their ends to prevent spreading

letter A, and a corresponding notch was made in the under side of the logs that were to rest upon these. This operation was repeated to the top, 8 or 10 feet (see Fig. 3). Logs were sometimes notched on both sides.

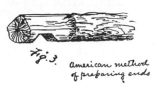

Fig. 3. american method of preparing ends

The rafters were made of poles. The chimney was generally outside, — the fireplace of stone, but the top often a stick chimney. The roof was sometimes thatched or of bark; but commonly it was of shingles or shakes split out and shaved smooth. Floors were made of split logs or of boards from a sawmill, or were merely the earth on which the house stood. Windows and doors were sawed out after the walls were up. The gable ends were closed by logs shortened to fit,

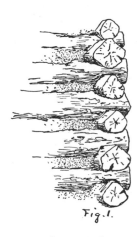

Fig. 1.

American exterior corner

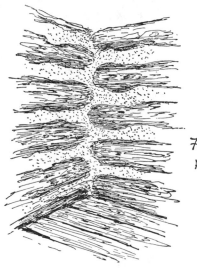

Fig. 2
American Interior Corner

and to bring their surfaces near together. Crevices due to imperfect contact were chinked in America with slats, sticks, stones, and mud, and pointed up outside and inside with mud or with lime and sand mortar (Figs. 1 and 2). The logs were often hewn smooth on the outside and inside, and sometimes they were squared up. In America the logs, properly cut in lengths, were hauled to the site of the proposed house, and then a "frolic" or "raising" was arranged, to which all the neighbouring men were invited. Two or four men, as the case might be, stationed themselves, axes in hand, at the corners, fitting the logs, and themselves rising with the work; the others passing the logs up, sliding them on poles, leaned against the completed portion as it grew in height. A space about a foot or 16 inches long at the ends of the first logs was shaped somewhat like a broad

or were of split logs or sawed boards placed vertically. The ends of logs were generally sawed or hewn perpendicularly. When the interior was plastered, the laths were nailed to furring strips attached vertically to the logs. Mud plaster was made by mixing with straw. The house from which Figs. 1, 2, and 3 were drawn was built in the Shawangunk Mountains, in New York, about 1862, by a man then about forty years old, who had built similar houses earlier, and whose father and grandfather had built them before him.

In Russian practice the log is hollowed throughout its length on the

Fig. 4   Fig. 5

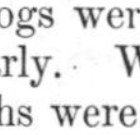

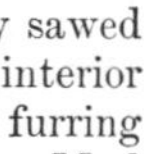

under side (Figs. 4 and 5), so that it somewhat conforms to the rounded upper side of the nether log, a layer of moss being laid on before the logs are adjusted; and this, being pressed between the two (Fig. 6), forms a tight joint superior to the American chinking method, though requiring more labour. Russian partitions are made of squared logs intricately fitted into the side logs (Fig. 7) to act as braces and ties. Figure 8 shows the outside corner of a Russian house, and Fig. 1 that

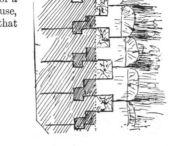

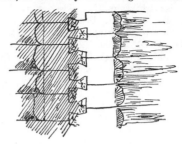

Fig. 6.

Fig. 7

Section on line of partition Russian method.

of an American one. Figure 9 shows the Russian method of preparing the end of the log, which is done before the building is begun. Russian log houses sometimes reached huge proportions, as in the noted Baranoff Castle that formerly stood at Sitka.

Building of this kind is the natural resort of

persons of small mechanical skill or of small means, in a country where large trees are abun-

Fig. 8. Russian outside corner with ends cut off.

dant. Vitruvius (Book II., Ch. 1) mentions them as having been in use in the Caucasus. In Russia, with the more slowly developing physical civilization of the country, such structures have lingered later, and have received a somewhat decorative treatment, in connection with which it is well to study the Swiss solid-timbered houses. (See Châlet; Switzerland, Architecture of.) — F. S. DELLENBAUGH.

Fig. 9. Russian method of preparing ends. a dressed log.

LOG HOUSE: FIG. 10. — THAT BUILT FOR THE RUSSIAN EXHIBITION AT VIENNA IN 1873.

787   788

LOHRE. (See Klaus von Lohre.)

LOMBARD ARCHITECTURE. *A.* That of the Lombards or Longobards or Langobards, a race of conquerers who invaded Italy and occupied a large tract of north Italy on both sides of the Po. Their strength lasted from the close of the sixth century to the conquest by the Franks in 774. It is now held by archæologists that the Lombards brought no art with them at all, and that what little was created during their supremacy was a mere remnant of the earlier Christian style. In the absence of a series of unaltered buildings, the sculptures that remain from those times show that the art of the fifth and of the first half of the sixth centuries was far superior to that of the centuries immediately following. The churches were almost invariably of the Latin basilica type, and the ornamentation Byzantine, the best of it executed by Greek workmen. — (J. S. F.)

B. That of Lombardy. In this sense the term is further qualified by other terms, as in Lombard Gothic, Lombard Renaissance, etc., the term architecture being understood. (See Italy, Part III.) — R. S.

LOMBARDESQUE ARCHITECTURE. That of, or influenced by, the architects whose surnames were Lombardo or Lombardi. There were a number of these, and among them two of the most prominent architects of the fifteenth and sixteenth centuries, who were of great weight in influencing the freer Renaissance of northern Italy. Buildings of the Certosa at Pavia and at Ravenna, Treviso, and Cividale were erected by Pietro Lombardo, but this architect and his son Tullio were especially successful in Venice, where they built a great number of the most important civic and religious buildings. Hence it is that the term *Lombardesco* constantly occurs in Italian writings concerning the architecture of Venice.

— R. S.

LOMBARDIC ARCHITECTURE. *A.* Same as Lombardesque Architecture. The term was, perhaps, introduced by John Ruskin. It is incapable of close definition because of the number of artists who bear the name.

B. Same as Lombard Architecture in either sense, *A* or *B*. By writers of the eighteenth century, and later, the term is confused with Lombardesque, and buildings are described without its being quite clear whether the term is used in the sense Lombard *B*, or in the sense given above, as belonging to the school of the architects named Lombardo. — R. S.

LOMBARDO, ANTONIO (SOLARO); architect and sculptor; d. 1516.

A son of Pietro Lombardo (see Lombardo, P.), whom he assisted in much of his work. In 1505 he finished one, the finest, of the reliefs in the Capella del Santo in Padua. After

1504 he was associated with Alessandro Leopardi (see Leopardi, A.), Alberghetto, and Campanato (see Campanato) in the erection of the altar and monument of the Cardinal Zeno in the church of S. Marco. In 1506 a payment of twenty gold ducats was made to Antonio on account of Alfonso d'Este, Duke of Ferrara, probably for the decoration of the Camerini d'Alabastro in his palace. Antonio spent the last eleven years of his life at Ferrara.

(For bibliography, see Lombardo, Pietro.)

LOMBARDO, PIETRO (PIETRO SO-LARO); architect and sculptor; b. about 1433; d. 1515.

The son of one Martino of Carona in Lombardy, probably also an architect. The earliest notice of Pietro Lombardo is in a document dated Sept. 8, 1479. He was probably employed on the Presbiterio and door of S. Giobbe at Venice, as well as the tomb of Cristoforo Moro in that church. The Palazzo Vendramin-Calergi, in Venice, is ascribed to Pietro. In the contract of March 4, 1481, for the erection of the church of the Miracoli, Pietro is mentioned as the architect of the monument of the Doge Pietro Mocenigo at the church of SS. Giovanni e Paolo, which was finished in 1481. In a manuscript quoted by Boni (op. cit.) an abstract is given of the contract made with Pietro, March 4, 1481, for the construction of the church of S. Maria dei Miracoli at Venice. The work was begun at once and finished in 1489. The little monument to Dante at Ravenna was erected by Pietro in 1482. May 1, 1489, the procuratori of the Scuola di S. Marco at Venice contracted with Pietro Lombardo and Giovanni Buora (see Buora) for the reconstruction of that building, which had been ruined by fire. After November, 1490, they were superseded by Mauro Coducci (see Coducci). Pietro also rebuilt the church of S. Andrea della Certosa, Venice, which was destroyed early in the nineteenth century. After the flight of Antonio Rizzo in 1498, Pietro was appointed *protomaestro* of the Doges' Palace, May 16, 1498. Owing to the loss of documents it is impossible to determine how much of the building was designed by him. In 1500–1506 he built the wings of the Torre dell' Orologio in the Piazza di S. Marco, Venice, and in 1502 rebuilt the duomo of Cividale in Friuli, which had fallen in. Pietro Lombardo conducted a botega in the quarter of S. Samuele, Venice, where a large business was done in decorative sculpture. The figures were usually cut by his sons, Antonio and Tullio (see Lombardo, Antonio and Tullio).

Alessandro Luzio and Ridolfo Renier, *Pietro Lombardo*, in *Archivio storico dell'Arte*, Vol. I.; Giacomo Boni, *Santa Maria dei Miracoli;* Paoletti, *Rinascimento;* Selvatico, *Sulla Architettura e sulla Scultura in Venezia;* Temanza, *Vite;* F. Sansovino, *Venezia*.

LOMBARDO, SANTO; architect.

A son of Tullio Lombardo (see Lombardo, T.). In 1524 he was chosen proto (with the coöperation of his father) of the Scuola di S. Rocco to supersede Bartolomeo Bono, Bergamasco (see Bono, B. B.), and held the place until May 12, 1527, when his accounts with the scuola were settled. The Palazzo Malipiero-Trevisan at Venice is attributed to Santo by Temanza (*Vite*). He is known as an architect only.

(For bibliography, see Lombardo, Pietro.)

LOMBARDO, TULLIO (SOLARO); architect and sculptor; d. Nov. 17, 1532.

A son of Pietro Lombardo (see Lombardo, P.). He assisted his father in many of his undertakings. Tullio made the bas-reliefs of the Apostles in the church of S. Giovanni Grisostomo in Venice. According to Temanza he assisted Leopardi (see Leopardi) on the monument to the Doge, Andrea Vendramini, in the church of SS. Giovanni e Paolo, Venice. The statuettes in niches under the sarcophagus are probably by him. He probably conducted the reconstruction of the cathedral of Cividale. The figures of the tomb of the Doge Giovanni Mocenigo in SS. Giovanni e Paolo are ascribed to him by Fr. Sansovino. In 1501, Tullio undertook two of the bas-reliefs in the Capella del Santo at Padua, which were not finished before 1525. Temanza ascribes to him the Capella del SS. Sacramento in the duomo, and the transept of the church of S. Maria Maggiore at Treviso. Oct. 29, 1507, he was associated with his father in the construction of the church of S. Salvatore in Venice. In 1523 he carved a door for the studiola of Isabella d' Este Gonzaga, in the Palazzo at Mantua.

(For bibliography, see Lombardo, Pietro.)

LONGHENA, BALDASSARE; architect; b. 1604; d. 1682.

The last architect of the great Venetian school. He formed himself on the work of Scamozzi, Palladio, and Jacopo Sansovino (see those names). His earliest important undertaking was the church of S. Maria della Salute, Venice, which was begun in 1631, but not finished until 1656. In 1640 he was appointed *Proto della procuratia di Sopra*, or state architect of Venice. The splendid church of S. Maria agli Scalzi, which Longhena built about 1646, is also famous for the ceiling of the nave by G. B. Tiepolo (see Tiepolo). Longhena built the Capella Vendramini in the church of S. Pietro di Castello, the ancient cathedral of Venice, and the great altar of the church of S. Francesco della Vigna. The most perfect expression of his skill is the Palazzo Pesaro, built about 1644. He built also the Palazzo Battaglia (now Belloni), the Palazzo Flangini, the

Palazzo Giustinian-Lolin, the Palazzo Zanne, near Sant' Agostino, the Palazzo Lezze, the Palazzo Morosini, near San Casciano, the Palazzo Marcello (now Papadopoli), near Santa Marina, and the Palazzo Widmann, near San Casciano. He built also the great stairway of the monastery of S. Giorgio Maggiore, and the monument to the Doge Giovanni Pesaro in the church of the Frari. All the work mentioned here is in Venice.

Gurlitt, *Geschichte des Barockstiles in Italien;* Ebe, *Spät-Renaissance;* Schütz, *Renaissance in Italien;* Cicognara, *Fabbriche di Venezia.*

LONG AND SHORT WORK. Building with, or arranging, stones, so as to present alternately parts projecting and receding along the face of the wall, as when the quoins of a building have some stones which are long horizontally, affording some hold as binders upon the wall. In what is known as Anglo-Saxon building in Great Britain, quoin stones are often set alternately vertical and horizontal and receive the above name. (See Saxon Architecture, *B.*)

LONG HOUSE. The peculiar dwelling of the Iroquois, called in their language ho-dé-no-sote, and from which came their tribal name Ho-dé-no-sau-nee (literally, they form a cabin), or the People-of-the-Long-house; the confederacy being likened to the structures in which they lived. It was built by placing poles in the ground, and binding them together by other poles running horizontally. Pole rafters were then adjusted in triangular or arched form. The frame was covered with sheets of bark, held in place by an outer frame of poles tied through to the inner one. The house was from 50 to 100 feet long, by about 16 wide. It was divided by transverse partitions into apartments 6 or 8 feet wide, opening on an aisle which ran the whole length of the building. In this open aisle were firepits between each four apartments. Holes in the roof let out the smoke. The occupants slept on raised bunks that ran around the walls of each apartment. (See Ganosote.) For full particulars see Morgan's *League of the Iroquois.* — F. S. D.

LONGLEAT HOUSE. A mansion built in 1578 upon an estate which is on the border between Wiltshire and Somersetshire, England. It is peculiar among the works of Elizabethan architecture, because of its decided classical character. It is very large for a private house, 220 feet long; it encloses two courts which have ambulatories, and is still a habitable and agreeable house. The interior was largely remodelled in the nineteenth century by that same Wyatville who did so much mischief at Salisbury Cathedral.

LONGUELUNE, ZACHARIE; architect; b. 1669; d. 1748.

He was a pupil of Lepautre (see Lepautre), and entered the service of Frederick I. of Prussia. He was employed also by the kings of Poland and Saxony. Longuelune erected numerous buildings in Warsaw, and designed in Dresden the Japanese palace, and probably also the *Blockhaus.*

Gurlitt, *Geschichte des Barockstiles in Deutschland; La Grande Encyclopédie;* Dr. Paul Schumann, *Barock und Rococo.*

LONJA. In Spain, an exchange; sometimes nearly the same as the French *bourse.* In some of the Spanish cities the Lonja is an important piece of neoclassic architecture.

LOOKOUT. *A.* A seat, platform, or more elaborate structure at a considerable height to afford an unobstructed view, as for a sentry. (For the architectural treatment of such structures see Echauguette.)

B. A short wooden Bracket or Cantilever, one end of which is secured in a wall so that it projects on the outside to support an overhanging portion of a roof, cornice, or the like. Generally concealed by the supported structure.

LOOKUM. A small roof, as a penthouse; used to shelter a hoisting wheel and its tackle.

LOOP. *A.* The crenel or open part of a battlement; the space between two merlons, usually having a low breast wall. Loop and crest is an old term for the whole battlement.

B. A loophole or loop window.

LOOPHOLE. In military structures, a small opening for the discharge of weapons; generally a long and narrow vertical aperture with splayed sides like an embrasure, forming an opening much larger inside than outside. (See Enclosure.) Those for bowmen were long slits, too narrow for the barrel of a firearm, and there exist some which have a wider central part, evidently meant for this later weapon.

LOOPHOLE FRAME. In modern buildings, a frame, as of wood, enclosing a door below and a window above, commonly as in a stable, or two or more windows in different stories: thus filling a high, windowlike opening in the outer wall.

LOOP WINDOW. A long and narrow window; more important than a loophole, although approaching such an aperture in form and perhaps intended often for the same purpose.

LOOSE BOX. An enclosed portion of a stable, larger than a stall of the usual size, to accommodate one or more horses, which are left free to move about within it.

LORENZO. A Roman architect and mosaicist. (See Cosmati.)

LORICULA. Same as Hagioscope.

LORRAIN, ROBERT LE; sculptor; b. 1666 (at Paris); d. 1743.

Le Lorrain was the preferred pupil of François Girardon (see Girardon). In 1689 he won the *Grand Prix de Rome* in sculpture. He was admitted to the *Académie Royale de peinture et sculpture* in 1702, was made professor of the Académie in 1717, and *recteur* in 1737. He was extensively employed at Versailles, especially in the decoration of the chapel of that palace (see Hardouin-Mansart, J.). The most remarkable of his creations is the bas-relief of the "Horses of the Sun" over the door of the stable of the old Hôtel de Rohan,

THE LOTUS IN SCULPTURE: THE OUTSIDE BORDER SHOWING ALTERNATELY THE BUD AND THE DEVELOPED FLOWER; THE SAME UNITS OF DECORATION USED IN THE PANELS. ASSYRIAN SCULPTURE FROM KOUYUNJIK.

Paris, now occupied by the *Imprimerie Nationale.*

Mariette, *Abecedario;* Gonse, *Sculpture Française.*

LOTUS. In art, the ornament supposed to be based upon one of several water plants, as a water lily of Egypt, or one of Mesopotamia. The lotus which is thought to have furnished the original theme for Egyptian design is not found now in Egypt, but in India (see Perrot and Chipiez, op. cit., Vol. I, *Égypte;* Balfour, *Cyclopœdia of India*). The Egyptian designs are, however, so perfectly adapted to purely decorative purposes, whether these are in pure sculpture, in sculpture enhanced by painting, or in flat coloured patterns, that the question of any natural plant disappears in the examination of the artistic purpose of the designs. So in Western Asia; the illustration, an Assyrian slab in the British Museum, while it is generally assumed that the border is composed of buds and open flowers of the Egyptian lotus, Layard is quoted (Perrot and Chipiez, op. cit., Vol. II., *Chaldée et Assyrie*) as believing that a red tulip, still common in Mesopotamia, is the more probable origin. Perrot and Chipiez point out that such design as this began in the imitation by the people of Western Asia of Egyptian ornament, in stuffs, metal work, and carving. Indeed, Flinders Petrie (op. cit.) points out that other flowers were confused with the lotus blossom in decoration. The lotus of Egyptian, Assyrian, and early Greek art is, then, not a close study of any natural form. The nearest approach to nature is probably in the carved masses resembling water lily buds, of which a cut is given under Capital (see Papyrus).

In the art of India, Farther India, Korea, China, and Japan, the lotus blossom is used in bronzework, carving, painting, and the like, and is in a special way identified with Buddhism. From this it passes into architectural carving and the like, especially in the peninsula of India.

Flinders Petrie, *Egyptian Decorative Art ;* Goodyear, *Grammar of the Lotus ;* Layard, *Nineveh and its Remains ;* Layard, *Discoveries in the Ruins of Nineveh and Babylon ;* Layard, *Monuments of Nineveh* (two series); Perrot et Chipiez, *Histoire de l'Art dans l'Antiquité,* Tome I, *Égypte ;* Tome II, *Chaldée et Assyrie ;* also translations of the same. (Also see bibliographies, Egypt, Architecture of ; Mesopotamia, Architecture of.)

— R. S.

LOUDON, JOHN CLAUDIUS; landscape gardener ; b. April 8, 1783 ; d. Dec. 14, 1843.

He was apprenticed to a nurseryman and landscape gardener. In 1803 he came to London, and in the same year published his first essay, *Observations on the Laying out of Public Squares.* In 1809 he rented a large farm and organized it as a school of agriculture, which was extremely successful. In 1818 he abandoned this scheme, and made a tour of Europe. His *Encyclopædia of Gardening* appeared in 1822, followed in 1825 by an *Encyclopædia of Agriculture,* and in 1829 by an *Encyclopædia of Plants.* From 1826 until his death he edited the *Gardener's Magazine.* In 1828 he began the *Magazine of Natural History.* In 1831 Loudon laid out the Birmingham Botanical Gardens. He published the *Encyclopædia of Cottage, Farm, and Villa Architecture* in 1832, and in 1834 established the *Architectural Magazine,* in which some of John Ruskin's earliest writings appeared. The *Arboretum or Fruticetum Britannicum* appeared in 1838.

Stephen Lee, *Dictionary of National Biography.*

LOUIS, LOUIS NICOLAS VICTOR; architect ; b. May 10, 1731 ; d. July 2, 1800.

Victor Louis was the son of a mason of Paris.

795

In 1746 he entered the *École royale d'Architecture.* In the competition for the *Prix de Rome* in 1755 he was granted a special prize with a gold medal and a *pension* at Rome. He returned to Paris in 1759. In 1765 Louis was appointed architect to Stanislas Auguste Poniatowsky, king of Poland, with permission to reside in Paris. He restored and decorated the royal palace at Warsaw, but left no monuments in Poland. His chief work is the great theatre of Bordeaux, built to replace one burned in 1755 ; this was inaugurated April 7, 1780. The main features of its arrangement have been adopted in the Grand Opera in Paris (see Garnier, C.). In 1780 Louis Philippe Joseph d'Orléans, Duke of Chartres, commissioned him to rebuild his residence, the Palais Royal in Paris, originally designed for the Cardinal Richelieu by Jacques Lemercier (see Lemercier, J.). The restoration included a new theatre to take the place of the old Salle de l'Opéra. This theatre, long celebrated as the Théâtre Français, has been recently injured by fire. Louis published a monograph on the *Salle de Spectacle de Bordeaux,* Paris, 1782.

Marionneau, *Victor Louis ;* Marionneau, *Douze lettres de Victor Louis ;* Detcheverry, *Histoire des théâtres de Bordeaux ;* Braquehaye, *Notes sur Louis Nicolas Louis.*

LOUIS QUATORZE ARCHITECTURE. In French, that of Louis XIV., the king who succeeded in 1643 and who died in 1715, after the longest reign in French history. The style called *L'Architecture Louis Quatorze* hardly developed itself until twenty years after the king's succession, previous to which time the style of the preceding reign continued (see Louis Treize). Under the influence of great ministers the church of the Sorbonne was built about 1650, a massive and costly chapel of great architectural interest, and a few years later the church of the Val-de-Grâce, the work of François Mansart. Cardinal Mazarin, who died 1661, left directions for the construction of college buildings which soon after became the Institute of France and still stand on the south bank of the Seine. That wing of the château of Blois which was built for Gaston d'Orléans, younger brother of Louis XIV., was built, as well as the building last named above, by François Mansart. After 1670, however, the king imposed upon the architects whom he employed the grand style which he especially affected ; and this, beginning in Levau's buildings, the Pavillon de Flore on the Seine, forming anciently the angle between the water gallery of the Louvre and the Tuileries, and the eastern front of the Louvre with its famous colonnade by Claude Perrault, soon went on to the vast constructions of Marly and Versailles. The Hôtel des Invalides, the design of Bruant, was begun in 1670, and the large church of S. Louis

796

was built with it ; but the famous southern part of the church, the Dôme des Invalides, is of the later years of this long reign. Interior decoration had a great share in the outlay of thought and money of this reign, its most triumphant structure being the Gallery of Apollo in the Louvre. Churches of great interest were built, of which the most important is the church of

expending its force in tasteless ornamentation ; but this common view can hardly be held by students of the whole body of building of this long reign. The years of the Regency, closing with the death of Philip, Duke of Orléans, in 1723, were indeed years rather of delicate design in private houses and their furniture than of grandiose public buildings ; but the noble build-

LOUIS XIV. ARCHITECTURE: FIG. 1.—INTERIOR OF CHAPEL, CHÂTEAU AT VERSAILLES.

S. Roch in Paris, all except its front, which is of a much later period. (Cut, cols. 799, 800.)
— R. S.

LOUIS QUINZE ARCHITECTURE. In French, that of Louis XV., the king who succeeded in 1715 (see Louis Quatorze) and reigned until 1774. The style known as *L'Architecture Louis Quinze* is often cited as trivial and as

ings of the Place de la Concorde in Paris, the work of Gabriel, the completion of the chapel of Versailles by Robert de Cotte, and the front of the church of S. Roch by the same artist, the châteaux of Nancy and Luneville in Lorraine by Boffrand, the church of S. Sulpice by Oppenord, completed by Servandoni, and the Panthéon of Paris by Soufflot, are buildings of

Louis XIV. Architecture: Fig. 2. — Salon; Destroyed Château at Bercy, Paris; the Work of François Mansart and Levau.

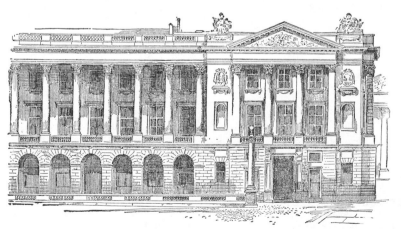

Louis XV. Architecture: Fig. 1. — Building, North Side of Place de la Concorde, Paris. Designed by Jacques Ange Gabriel, c. 1760.

LOUIS XV. ARCHITECTURE: FIG. 2.—FOUNTAIN AT ROUEN, JUNCTION OF THE SEINE
AND EURE.

such singular importance, and expressing so liberal and intelligent a spirit of originality in neoclassic design, that they may confidently be

LOUIS XV. ARCHITECTURE: FIG. 3. — PAVILION, HÔTEL SOUBISE, PARIS; c. 1730.
See interior of upper story below.

set against the similar buildings in any previous reign. (Cut, cols. 805, 806.) — R. S.

LOUIS SEIZE ARCHITECTURE. In French, that of Louis XVI., the king who succeeded in 1774 (see Louis Quinze) and was beheaded in 1793. The art known as the *Style Louis Seize* is expressed but in few important monuments, for the trouble of the whole reign, and that which brought the great Revolution to its first outbreak, was a threatening national bankruptcy. The delicate taste which marked the curious revival of severity and simplicity, as opposed to the overdone scrollwork and magnificence of the rocaille decoration common in the previous reign (see Rococo), is chiefly known to us by internal decoration, as in the panelling and painting of boudoirs and libraries in private houses and at Versailles and Fontainebleau, and in the exquisite furniture which was made for those rooms. Even in Paris only one complete building represents the taste of the

time, the palace in miniature, on the Quai, south of the Seine, which, built as a private hôtel, is now a part of the office and place of reception of the Legion of Honour. The theatre of Bordeaux by Louis is often pronounced by French students the noblest monument of this reign; but the mere addition to an otherwise utilitarian building of a dodecastyle portico of Corinthian columns can hardly be accounted as making up a building characteristic of a style.
— R. S.

LOUIS TREIZE ARCHITECTURE. In French, that of Louis XIII., the king who succeeded Henri IV. in 1610 and died 1643. The style known as *L'Architecture Louis Treize* is largely a continuation of that of Henri IV. Its best-known monument is the palace of the Luxembourg in Paris. (See Luxembourg, Palace of the.) Besides this building, De Brosse built in Paris the front of the church of S. Gervais, and important buildings which have since disappeared. The palace which the Cardinal Richelieu built and which afterward became the Palais Royal was designed by Jacques Lemercier, who also built at Fontainebleau the great perron in the Court of the White Horse, and at the Louvre those extensive additions to the famous square court, the "Cour du Louvre," properly so called, which made it four times as large as it had been in the Middle Ages, and as Pierre Lescot had left it. (See Louvre, I.) Many châteaux were built during this reign, among which was the old hunting lodge of brick and light-coloured stone, of which parts still remain in the very heart of the vast palace of Versailles. The Hôtel de Ville of Lyons, one of the most renowned buildings in the neoclassic style, is of 1636 and the following years, and, as the historian Chateau has pointed out, is still of the style of the preceding reign, although entirely built during the reign of Louis XIV. (Cuts, cols. 807, 808; 809, 810.) — R. S.

LOUNGING ROOM. In the United States, the same as Conversation Room. (See Club House.)

LOUVER. *A.* Originally, an outlet for smoke, as in a roof. Later, a lanternlike structure enclosing and covering such an outlet, the smoke escaping through openings in its sides. In modern times, such a structure serving for ventilation and having each opening filled with a series of horizontally fixed boards or slats sloping downward and outward. Each board laps over the one below, with an open space between, so as to permit the passage of air, while excluding rain. (Compare Lantern.)

B. By extension from the preceding definition, any opening arranged as above described; especially a belfry window, in which case the sloping boards serve also to throw outward and down-

PLATE XXVII

LOUVRE

The east front, including the famous colonnade of Perrault, which was built in 1665. The whole front, including the end pavilions, is nearly 600 feet long, wall, while a like projection at the south end was met by additions to the southern building. This additional length was probably given it from a fan-

ward the sound of the bells; (see Abat-sons). Written also Louvre, and in combination Luffer; as Luffer Board. — D. N. B. S.

LOUVER BOARD. One of the boards or slats of a Louver; written also Louvre and Luffer Board. (Compare Lever Board.)

LOUVERED. *A.* Furnished with Louvers.

of France from the time of Philip Augustus until the fall of the monarchy; since the Revolution, devoted to public purposes and containing at different times different departments of the government and always a museum of fine art; also, at intervals, the annual exhibitions of the *Salon*, and private studios.

LOUIS XV. ARCHITECTURE: FIG. 4. — INTERIOR OF PAVILION, HÔTEL SOUBISE, PARIS; c. 1730.
See exterior, Fig. 3.

B. Divided into or consisting of Louvers, as a louvered panel.

LOUVER SHUTTER. (See under Shutter.)

LOUVER WINDOW. A window opening arranged as a Louver in sense *B.*

LOUVRE (I.). (The term is of unknown origin and significance.) The royal château forming the centre and capital of the kingdom

The mediæval castle occupied a rectangle about 300 by 325 feet close to the north bank of the Seine.

At the beginning of the Renaissance movement in France, the old castle was taken in hand, and as early as 1554 the work at the southwest corner of the old square fortress was undertaken by Pierre Lescot. At the same time

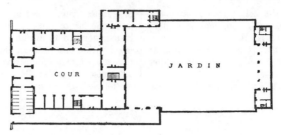

LOUIS XIII. ARCHITECTURE: FIG. 1.—PLAN OF HÔTEL DE SULLY, PARIS, RUE ST. ANTOINE.
Wheeled vehicles can enter the court (cour), and also the broad alley which leads to the garden (jardin). Stables are on the right as one enters the court.

LOUIS XIII. ARCHITECTURE: FIG. 2.—HÔTEL DE SULLY, PARIS, RUE ST. ANTOINE; FRONT ON COURT OF MAIN BUILDING. (SEE PLAN, FIG. 1.)

LOUIS XIII. ARCHITECTURE: FIG. 3. — PORTE-COCHÈRE RUE DES FRANCS-BOURGEOIS, PARIS.

ration, having the shape of an oblique parallelogram; usually one of a series. (Compare Diamond.)

L PLAN. A plan, as of a country house or other building, in which the general form or outline upon the ground is that of an L. (See L.)

LUCARNE. Same as Dormer Window.

LUCERNE. In Great Britain, a window in the roof, obviously a corruption of Lucarne. The term is sometimes applied to a window following the slope of a roof and not arranged vertically under a roof of its own, as is the dormer window.

LUCIANO DA LAURANA; architect; d. 1483.

Luciano came from Laurana or Lovrana, a little city in Istria, then Venetian territory. Frederico III., Count of Montefeltro and first Duke of Urbino, issued letters patent (now in the Vatican Library) dated June 10, 1468, creating Luciano chief architect and engineer of the palace which he had begun to erect at Urbino. According to Baldi (op. cit., p. 44,) Luciano had worked on the Poggio Reale, near Naples, and was recommended to Montefeltro by the Neapolitan court. Asso-

the south and west fronts on the court were entirely built up in the neoclassical taste. Under Louis XIII. the whole scheme was changed. What remained of the old castle was torn down, and nothing remains of it now except the foundations. The court was then enlarged to more than four times its original size, that which had been one side of the old square being now less than half of one side of the new square. Henri IV. completed the long gallery on the Quai, as far as the Pavilion of Flora (see Levau; Louis Quatorze), Louis XIII. and Louis XIV. devoted their attention to the buildings around the great court, and Louis XIV. built the great east front with the colonnade. (See Perrault.) It was left for Napoleon III. to complete the buildings of the château, which he did, clearing away all the previous encumbrances on the great square and making the plan, and in general, the appearance of the building, what it now is. (See Tuileries.) — R. S.

LOUVRE (II.). Same as Louver.

LOZENGE. A figure used in deco-

LOUIS XIII. ARCHITECTURE: FIG. 4. — CHURCH OF S. PAUL S. LOUIS, PARIS; 1627.

ciated with him were Baccio Pontelli (see Pontelli), and probably Francesco di Giorgio Martini (see Martini, F. di Giorgio). The principal sculptor employed was Barocci of Milan. (See Bramante.) The palace is also attributed to Luciano.

Friedrich Arnold, *Palast von Urbino*; Müntz, *Renaissance*; Baldi, *Memorie*.

LUDWIG, MEISTER; architect.

An important German architect of the Gothic period. From 1275 to 1306 he conducted the works at the cathedral of Regensburg (Ratisbon), in Bavaria. Associated with him were his sons Weichmann and Konrad.

Niedermayer, *Künstler und Kunstwerke der Stadt Regensburg*.

LUFFER BOARD. Same as Louver Board.

LUG. *A.* A short projecting portion of a member, usually as a means of attachment, or to keep another part in place. If such a projection also supports a weight, it usually is called a bracket.

B. In a sill, as for a door or window, that part at each end which has a horizontal top bed to receive the walling of a pier on either side; the wash of the sill stopping against an upright or a curve which forms the limit of the lug on the side toward the opening. Lugs are sometimes cut with a continuation of the mouldings of the jamb above; and these mouldings may stop against the slope of the wash or may even return along the front of the sill.

LUM. A chimney, the fireplace and flue being taken together. (Local English and Scotch.)

LUMBER. In the United States, in connection with building and manufacturing, wood as prepared for the market; whether in the log or in sawed or more elaborately dressed pieces. In Great Britain, such material is known simply as wood (which see for the classification there; see also Stuff).

As usually prepared for building purposes, lumber intended for the rougher operations of framing and the like is squared from the log in sawmills according to standard dimensions, but is otherwise undressed; while the lighter material, as for sheathing, ceiling, and other finish is commonly planed on one face and perhaps slightly moulded, as with a tongue and groove, a bead, or the like. The British system of classifying wood under definite names, according to its dimensions, is quite unknown in the United States, except in a very general way. Thus, squared pieces for framing and the like are commonly all designated as Scantling when not more than about 30 square inches in cross section; pieces of larger size being known as Timber, or more specifically Dimension Timber, with or without the article. Thus, a piece 5 inches by 6 inches in size has

been in the lumber trade more or less officially defined as a Scantling; a piece of 6 by 6 inches as a Dimension Timber. (See also Board; Plank; Veneer.) It is, therefore, in the United States, quite common to designate lumber by the use for which any given size may be primarily designed, as Studding, Furring, Sheathing, Veneer. (For the preparation of lumber, see Bastard Cut; Dress (v.); Heartwood; Quarter Sawed; Sapwood; Woodworking Machinery. See also Terra Cotta Lumber.) — D. N. B. S.

LUNATIC ASYLUM. (See Asylum.)

LUNCH ROOM. *A.* In a private house, a room which may be used for luncheon as distinguished from dinner. It may be one with the breakfast room, and in that case may take either title. The reason for separating it from the dining room is generally in its smaller size and in the less elaborate character of the meals served there.

B. A room or group of rooms in which a simple restaurant service is carried on; especially in the business quarters of great cities where usually only the midday meal is required by persons who are far away from their homes.

LUNETTE. That portion of a vertical surface beneath a vault which it intersects and bounded by the intrados and — approximately — by the springing line. When a solid wall it often receives mural painting, but is commonly filled with glass.

LUNG' ARNO. *A.* In Florence; the street along the river Arno on either side. It is commonly written in one word when combined with the local names; thus, the Lungarno Corsini extends from the Ponte S. Trinità to the Ponte Alla Carraja along the right or northern bank.

B. The street or quays similarly situated in Pisa; these are often called locally Lungo l' Arno.

LUNGHI, MARTINO (the elder); architect.

Architect of the school of Giacomo della Porta (see Giacomo della Porta) in Rome. He designed the church of S. Maria della Vallicella, the façade of S. Girolamo degli Schiavoni, after 1585, the Palazzo Ceri, and the Palazzo Altemps, all in Rome. Lunghi's most important work is the Palazzo Borghese, Rome, 1590.

Gurlitt, *Geschichte des Barockstiles in Italien*; Ebe, *Spät-Renaissance*; Strack, *Baudenkmäler Roms*.

LUNGHI, MARTINO (the younger); architect; d. 1657.

A son of Onorio Lunghi (see Lunghi, O.). He built about 1650 the church of SS. Vincenzo ed Anastasio near the fountain of Trevi for the Cardinal Mazarin, and the little church of S. Antonio de' Portoghesi, about 1652. Less important are the façades of S. Adriano and S. Maria dell' Orto and the altar of S. Carlo al Corso. All are in Rome.

Gurlitt, *Geschichte des Barockstiles in Italien*; Ebe, *Spät-Renaissance*.

LUNGHI, ONORIO; architect; b. 1516; d. 1619.

A son of Martino Lunghi the elder. He built the church of S. Maria Liberatrice, the Palazzo Verospo, now Torlonia, about 1616, and the church of S. Carlo al Corso, begun 1612, all in Rome.

Gurlitt, *Geschichte des Barockstiles in Italien;* Ebe, *Spät-Renaissance.*

LURAGO, ROCCO; architect; d. 1590.

In 1564 Lurago built the famous Palazzo Doria-Tarsi (del Municipio) in the Strada Nuova, Genoa. For Pius V. (Pope 1566–1572) he built the church and convent of the Dominicans at Bosco. (See Alessi, G.)

Milizia, *Memorie;* Reinhardt, *Genoa.*

LUXEMBOURG, PALACE OF THE. Built originally by Marie de Médicis (more properly, Maria dei Medici) widow of Henri IV. of France, during the years between 1615 and 1620. The greater part of the building remains as it was originally built, but the new fronts with projecting pavilions on the garden side were built during the reign of Louis Philippe. Under recent political systems the Chamber of Peers, afterward the Senate, has occupied a hall and rooms in the palace, and the well-known museum of the Luxembourg, devoted to the important works of living artists, has been contained in some of the galleries; but since 1890 the museum has been fixed in what was once the orangérie, and the senate has the whole palace proper. The garden of the Luxembourg is one of the public parks of Paris and is adorned with very interesting sculpture. — R. S.

LUZARCHES, ROBERT DE; architect.

The Carlovingian cathedral of Amiens, France, was burned in 1218. The bishop, Evrard de Fouilloy, determined to rebuild it at once on a magnificent scale. The plans for this building, the present cathedral, were made by a layman, Robert de Luzarches. At the death of Evrard in 1223, the foundations were completed. During the bishopric of his successor, Geoffroy d'Eu, the work was pushed with the greatest activity. Thomas de Cormont (see Cormont, T. de) succeeded Luzarches and built the nave and transept as far as the spring of the great vault according to the plans of his predecessor. In the labyrinth of the pavement of the cathedral, destroyed about fifty years ago, were to be seen the figures of Bishop Evrard and of the three architects, Luzarches, and Thomas and Renaud de Cormont with a commemorative inscription which is now in the Musée de Picardie.

Gonse, *L'Art Gothique;* Chapuy, *Vues pittoresques de la cathédrale d'Amiens.*

LYCEUM (Λύκειον). *A.* A place in Athens dedicated to Apollo Lukeios (the Wolf Apollo) and used mainly as a wrestling ground, palæstra, and the like. Nothing is known of the character of the buildings.

B. An institution of learning or of a literary

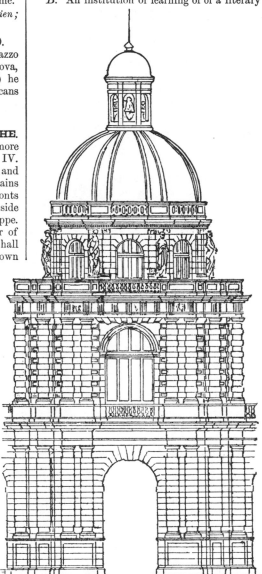

LUXEMBOURG, PALACE OF THE, PARIS: PAVILION OF ENTRANCE; C. 1620 A.D.

association, and hence the building erected for the purposes of such an institution. In the towns of the United States it was until recently the custom to have a lecture room and perhaps a library, reading room, or the like, in a building commonly called the Lyceum.

LYCH (and compounds). Same as Lich and compounds.

LYCHNITES. Same as Lychnites Marble, under Marble.

LYCHNOSCOPE. Same as Low Side Window.

LYCIA, ARCHITECTURE OF. That of the ancient state lying on the southern shore of Asia Minor close to the Syrian coast. It is but little known except in respect to the curious rock-cut tombs (for which see Asia Minor, Architecture of). In later times a pure Greek influence prevailed in this as in other parts of Asia Minor, and this has been partly described in the books cited below.

Fellows, *A Journal . . . in Asia Minor*, London, 1839 ; Fellows, *An Account of Discoveries in Lycia*, London, 1841 ; Spratt and Forbes, *Travels in Lycia*.
— R. S.

LYSIPPOS OF SICYONE ; sculptor.

An important Greek sculptor who was especially attached to the court of Alexander the Great (356–323 B.C.). His work differs from that of Polyclitus (see Polyclitus) in having greater refinement of proportion. His bronze statue of an Apoxyomenos, an athlete scraping himself with a strigil, which was placed by Agrippa in his baths at Rome, is represented by a splendid marble copy in the Braccio Nuovo of the Vatican, which was discovered by Canina (see Canina), in the Trastevere at Rome in 1849.

Collignon, *Histoire de la Sculpture Grecque ;* Plinius, *Historia Naturalis ;* Löwy, *Lysipp und seine Stellung in der Griechischen Plastik ;* Percy Gardner, *Types of Greek Coins ;* Stahr, *Torso*.

M

McCOMB, JOHN ; engineer and architect ; b. Oct. 17, 1763 (in New York) ; d. May 25, 1853.

His family were Scotch, and settled in New York. He designed the front of the old government house in New York, 1790, S. John's church, the Murray Street and the Bleecker Street churches, and many public and private buildings in New York, Philadelphia, and the Eastern states. McComb was supervising architect of the city of New York during the erection of the City Hall, and is supposed to have been its designer. (Wilde, op. cit.)

Wilde, *New York City Hall* in *Century Magazine*, Vol. XXVII.

MACELLUM. In Roman archæology, a market, especially for provisions. The only instance known to us where the plan can easily be made out is that of Pompeii. There, a tholos, really a twelve-sided enclosure, and apparently a mere roof supported on stone pillars, occupied the middle point, while all around the place was entirely open to the air, and the very

small shops which fronted on the open space were without windows or back rooms. A colonnade forming a cloister faced the open space on either side. Although the building is small and could never have had architectural pretensions, there are remains of paintings of great interest. (See Market.) — R. S.

MACHICOLATION. A projecting series of corbels often surmounting the walls of later mediæval fortifications, and carrying an overhanging portion of the stone floor of the rampart, the floor having openings between the corbels for the delivery of missiles on the enemy below. The parapet or battlement is constructed along the outer ends of the corbels. (See Castle ; Fortification.)

MACHICOLATION: A SIMPLE FORM; 13TH OR 14TH CENTURY.

The parapet wall, about 20 inches thick, rests upon a row of corbels, with an open space about 12 inches wide between the parapet and the face of the rampart.

MACHINERY SPACE. (See Engine Room.)

MACHUCA, PEDRO ; painter, sculptor, and architect.

He studied in Italy, and in 1526 or 1527 began the palace which the Emperor Charles V. undertook to build on the ruins of a part of the Alhambra (Granada, Spain).

Bermudez, *Diccionario*.

MACLAURIN ; architect.

The towers which Servandoni (see Servandoni) designed for the church of S. Sulpice (Paris) not being satisfactory to the authorities of the church, Maclaurin was commissioned in 1749 to rebuild them. His work was condemned, in turn. In 1777 Jean François Chalgrin rebuilt the northern tower. The southern tower is still as Maclaurin left it. (See Chalgrin.)

Bauchal, *Dictionnaire*.

MADELEINE, THE. (See Church of the Madeleine.)

MADERNA (MADERNO), CARLO ; architect ; b. 1556 ; d. 1629.

A Lombard architect, who followed his uncles, Domenico and Giovanni Fontana (see Fontana, D. and G.), to Rome. He was associated with them in their work, and completed several undertakings commenced by them, among others the Fontana dell' Acqua Paola. He was for many years the leading architect in Rome. His earliest independent work appears to be the façade of the church of S. Susanna (1595–1603). He built also the Palazzo Mattei di Giove (1602). The idea of applying the long nave of the church of Gesù, by Vignola (see Barozzio, G.), to the great church of S. Peter originated with Domenico Fontana. The execution of the scheme was the work of Carlo Maderna, who built also the façade as we now see it, the design for which was based on the model left by Michelangelo. The vestibule is one of Maderna's best works. The interior of the church of S. Maria della Vittoria dates from 1605. Maderna continued the construction of the Palazzo Quirinale (see Mascherino and Fontana, D.), designed the stairway of the Palazzo Chigi (1587) in the Piazza Colonna, and built the Palazzo Odescalchi in the Piazza dei SS. Apostoli. One of his most important works is the Palazzo Barberini (begun 1624), which was continued by Bernini (see Bernini) and Boromini (see Boromini). Maderna designed the fountains of the Piazza di San Pietro. All the works mentioned here are in Rome.

Gurlitt, *Geschichte des Barockstiles in Italien;* Ebe, *Spät-Renaissance;* H. Mosler, *Sansovino.*

MADERNA, STEFANO; sculptor; b. 1571; d. 1636.

His most important works are the reclining statue of S. Cecilia, in the church of that saint in the Trastevere, and decorative figures of children at the church of S. Maria Maggiore.

Marcel Reymond, *La Sainte Cécile de Stéphane Madérna;* Ebe, *Spät-Renaissance.*

MADHOUSE. A place for the care and medical treatment of the insane. (See Asylum; Hospital.)

MADISON SQUARE GARDEN. In New York City; a building erected about 1890, and containing a very large arena with seats for several thousand spectators; and also, under the same roof, a theatre, a concert hall which also serves as a ballroom, a smaller hall, and various minor rooms. The building fills the entire block 200 × 425 feet, and has a tower closely studied from the Giralda, capped by a vane with a statue of Diana modelled by Augustus St. Gaudens, and reaching a total height of 332 feet. The design is by McKim, Mead, and White. The building is almost wholly in brick and terra cotta, and there is an interesting arcade in three long stretches, of which the shafts are of polished granite.

MAENDER. Same as Meander.

MAGAZINE. A place of storage of any kind; especially, in modern use, of explosives and projectiles; an abbreviation of powder magazine.

MAGENTA, GIOVANNI AMBROSIO; architect.

An architect of the school of the Tibaldi (see Tibaldi), in Bologna. He built the fine nave of the cathedral of Bologna, which was remodelled by Alfonso Torrigiani in 1747, the church of S. Salvatore (1623), the church of S. Paolo (1611), etc., all in Bologna.

Gurlitt, *Geschichte des Barockstiles in Italien;* Ebe, *Spät-Renaissance.*

MAGISTER. In Latin, a chief, leader, master; in mediæval Latin, often an artisan or tradesman who had passed apprenticeship and was recognized as "master of his craft." (See Guild.)

MAGNA GRÆCIA (also Major Græcia). In Latin, Great Greece (Greater Greece). The southern part of Italy, so called from its general occupancy by Grecian colonists. The limits of the district so entitled are not accurately fixed; in modern times the term is applied rather to the far southeast, the shores of the Gulf of Taranto, or the Basilicata, with half of Apulia and half of Calabria. (See Italy, Parts XII., XIII., XIV., and Bibliography.)

MAGNE, AUGUSTE JOSEPH; architect; b. April 2, 1816; d. July 15, 1885.

Magne was a pupil of François Debret (see Debret) and of the *École des Beaux Arts.* He was *inspecteur divisionnaire* of the city of Paris from 1859 to 1869, and *architecte divisionnaire* from 1869 until his death. He built several of the churches, theatres, and markets of Paris. Magne published *Monographie du nouveau théâtre du vaudeville érigé par la ville de Paris* (1 vol. folio, Paris, 1873).

Bauchal, *Dictionnaire.*

MAGNET. (See Electrical Appliances.)

MAIANO, BENEDETTO DA. (See Benedetto da Maiano.)

MAIANO, GIULIANO DA. (See Giuliano da Maiano.)

MAIRIE. In France, the public building containing the offices of a *maire,* or chief officer, of a small city or part of a large city. There was a *maire* of Paris down to the time of the Revolution. Since then there have been twenty *arrondissements,* with a *maire* for each. The *mairies* in Paris and in the provincial cities are not large buildings; certain ceremonies have their proper place within them, and their most important room is generally the hall for marriages, in which, by French law, all marriages must take place, whether afterward celebrated by the church or not. (Cuts, cols. 819, 820.) — R. S.

MAISON CARRÉE. At Nîmes (Gard), in southern France. The most important Roman temple remaining. (See France, Architecture of; Roman Imperial Architecture; Temple.)

MAISON DIEU. Originally, in French, a hospital.

MAITANI, LORENZO; architect; b. about 1275; d. June, 1330.

In 1310 he appears first as *capomaestro* of the cathedral of Orvieto, Italy (begun in 1290). The façade was probably begun at this time. July 13, 1319, he was called to Perugia to superintend public works, especially the forti-

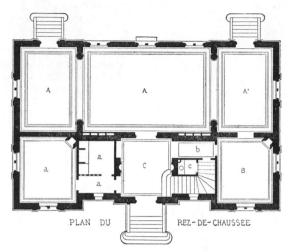

MAIRIE DE L'ISLE-ADAM (SEINE-ET-OISE). PLAN.

A, A. Halls for meetings and festivities, one of them serving for marriages ; the large room covered by a flat terrace roof (see exterior below). *A'.* Room for municipal council. *B.* Office of secretary. *C.* Vestibule. *a, a.* Residence of janitor. *b.* Passage. *c.* Toilet.

MAIRIE DE L'ISLE-ADAM (SEINE-ET-OISE). (SEE PLAN ABOVE.)

fications. The Porta di S. Fortunato at Todi is traditionally attributed to him. In 1322 he assisted as an adviser at the cathedral of Siena. Sept. 11, 1327, he was again at Perugia.

Fumi, *Duomo di Orvieto;* Luzi, *Duomo di Orvieto;* Mereu, *Le Dôme d'Orvieto;* Della Valle, *Duomo di Orvieto.*

MAITANI, VITALE; architect.

A son of Lorenzo Maitani. At his father's death in 1330, he succeeded him, with his brother Niccolò, in the superintendence of the construction of the cathedral of Orvieto. In 1350 he assumed complete direction of the works at the cathedral.

(For bibliography see Maitani, L.)

MAKSOORAH. A screen or partition in a mosque, and by extension the place enclosed by such a screen. There are two common uses of the term, (1) as denoting the reserved place of prayer (see Prayer Chamber), which is screened off from the rest of the mosque, and where conversation and free moving about of the crowd is prohibited; and (2) the enclosed space around a tomb in the few cases where a tomb is allowed within the roofed part of a structure.

MALACHITE. Carbonate of copper of a green colour, silky or velvety lustre, and pronounced concretionary structure. A little harder than common marble, but cuts to a sharp edge and acquires a good polish. To be had only in small pieces, and the table tops, vases and other works of art constructed from it are invariably patchwork veneers. The principal source of the commercial article is the Ural Mountains. — G. P. M.

MALATESTA CHAPEL. (See Tempio Malatestiano.)

MALAY ARCHITECTURE. That of the more civilized peoples of the Malay race; those who occupied the greater part of the Malay Peninsula (Malacca) with large tracts in the mainland of Farther India and in Sumatra and Java. Very little is known of the peninsula except on the seacoast; even the British possessions are only in part explored by European observers.

Of all architecture which can be called properly Malay, the most important is that of the ancient pagodas, in the heart of Java. The great temple called Borobodor, in the Kedu district, is a nearly solid structure like a Stupa, with platforms covered by small stone structures which rise one above another, forming six great terraces of generally rectangular shape. The topmost of these forms a platform from which rises a second moundlike structure of circular plan, carrying bell-shaped stone cupolas in three ranks, also rising step fashion, surrounding a great central cupola. The small stone buildings of the lower terraces are arranged along the edge; they are square in

plan, having niches worked into their sides, and seated statues in the niches; the bell-shaped cupolas of the upper and circular tiers are hollow and contain each a sacred figure, usually a complete statue. The height from the surrounding level of the ground is, to the great square platform, approximately 60 feet, and to the top of the dome which crowns the circular structure, 120 feet.

The temple at Brambanan is of more advanced character, constructionally speaking, as there are interiors of some importance provided in the central masses and also in the minor pavilions. The elaborate central pavilion has a square central tower rising to the height of two architectural stories, while the four square projections which form a Greek cross are only one architectural story in height. All these are roofed with octagonal pyramids and half pyramids, producing a most effective and well-imagined group, in all of which there is the most elaborate use of cut stone.

These buildings are of pre-Mohammedan date, and are to the present Moslem peoples that which the Buddhist, Jaina, or early Hindu buildings are to the modern half-Mohammedan peoples of northern Hindustan. It is, therefore, only in part that they are Malay in character. The only buildings which are strictly Malay are the modern dwellings, slight structures of bamboo and reed, such as are common in tropical islands. A careful study of these would be of the highest interest, but the materials for it do not exist. It is greatly to be desired that the scientific method of comparison should be applied to simple house building in the different tropical lands of Asia and the Pacific Ocean. — R. S.

MALL. A place for walking and taking the air. The name originates in the game of Pall Mall (balls struck by a malletlike implement), and from the epoch of its origin is generally taken as meaning a formal walk with straight rows of trees. (See Alameda.)

MALLEABLE CAST IRON. Cast iron which has been deprived of some of its carbon by heating to a red heat, together with some chemical compound having a strong affinity for carbon, and then allowing it to cool slowly. Such castings are not brittle in the sense that ordinary cast iron is brittle.

MALT HOUSE. A building for the malting of grain and similar preparations for brewers' work. (See bibliography under Brewery.)

MAMBAR. Same as Mimbar; a different transliteration.

MANDORAL. A figure of the general form of an almond; especially in Christian symbology a representation in art of the Vesica Piscis (which see).

MANETTI, ANTONIO (CIACCHERI); architect.

A Florentine architect who continued and completed several of the buildings undertaken by Brunellesco (see Brunellesco). He built the nave of the church of S. Lorenzo in Florence, after Brunellesco's death. He is not to be confounded with Antonio di Tuccio Manetti (see Manetti, A. di T.).

Geymüller, *Brunellesco* in Geymüller-Stegmann, *Die arch. der Renaissance in Toscana;* Müntz, *Renaissance.*

MANETTI, ANTONIO DI TUCCIO; historian and writer.

Manetti has been identified by Milanesi as the author of the anonymous contemporary life of Brunellesco (see Brunellesco), which was Vasari's chief source of information. It was first published by Moreni, *Vita di Filippo di Ser Brunellesco* (Florence, 1812). He is not to be confounded with Antonio Manetti, Ciaccheri (see Manetti, A., Ciaccheri), the architect.

Geymüller-Stegmann, *Die Arch. der Renaissance in Toscana*, art. *Brunellesco;* Manetti, *Vita di Filippo di Ser Brunellesco;* Müntz, *Renaissance.*

MANFREDI, FRA ANDREA; architect and military engineer.

Andrea built the church of S. Maria dei Servi at Bologna. He appears also to have assisted in designing the great basilica of S. Petronio in that city. (See Antonio di Vicenzo.) He assisted in the fortification of Bologna.

Archivio Storico dell' Arte, Vol. IV., p. 174.

MANGIN. (See **McCOMB, JOHN**.)

MANOR HOUSE. (See under House.)

MANSARD. (See Mansart.)

MANSARDE. In French, a dormer window. A term derived from Mansard or Mansart, the name or surname of several architects. The French term is extended to a roof lighted by such windows (*comble à la Mansarde*) and to the chambers within; in this sense expressing the same idea as the English Garret, a humble lodging in the roof.

MANSARD ROOF. (See Roof.)

MANSART DE JOUY, JEAN. (See Hardouin-Mansart, Jean.)

MANSART DE SAGONNE, JACQUES. (See Hardouin-Mansart, Jacques.)

MANSART, JULES HARDOUIN. (See Hardouin-Mansart, Jules.)

MANSART, NICOLAS FRANÇOIS; architect; b. Jan. 23, 1598; d. Sept. 23, 1666.

François was the son of one Absolon Mansart, a master carpenter. At the age of twenty-four he constructed the portal of the church of the Feuillants in the Rue Saint-Honoré (Paris), now destroyed. In 1632 he began the church of the convent of the Filles de la Visitation (Paris), which was dedicated in 1634 as Notre-Dame-des-Anges (now used as a Protestant church). In 1634 he began extensive additions to the Hôtel Carnavalet in Paris (see Goujon, Jean), and in 1635, built the hôtel of

the Marquis de la Vrillière, occupied by the Banque de France since 1811. In 1635, also, he was commissioned by Gaston, Duke of Orleans, to erect the great building at the rear of the court of the château of Blois (Loir-et-Cher). His scheme, interrupted by the death of Gaston, contemplated the entire reconstruction of the château. In 1645, Mansart began for Anne d'Autriche, queen of Louis XIII., the great church of the Val-de-Grâce (Paris). When the walls had reached a height of about 10 feet above the ground the work was transferred to Jacques Lemercier (see Lemercier, Jacques). Mansart afterward built for the château of Fresnes a chapel from the plans which he had made for the Val-de-Grâce, reduced to one third. At the invitation of Colbert (d. 1683), he made designs for the completion of the Louvre, but his intractable temperament prevented their execution (see Perrault, Claude). He built many residences in Paris, and châteaux in the provinces, which still exist. Many of his works are engraved in Marot (op. cit.).

Maurice du Seigneur in *La Grande Encyclopédie;* Ruprich-Robert, *Val-de-Grâce;* Abbé Lambert, *Histoire littéraire du siècle de Louis XIV;* Charles Perrault, *Les hommes illustres;* Brice, *Nouvelle description de la Ville de Paris;* Marot, *L'Architecture française.*

MANSDALE. (See Keldermans van Mansdale.)

MANSE. In North Britain, and in literary use elsewhere, the dwelling of a Protestant clergyman.

MANSION. A large, and usually costly and elegant, dwelling house.

MANSION HOUSE. The residence of the Lord Mayor of London, finished about 1750. It has an interesting hexastyle Corinthian portico.

MANTAPA; MANTAPPA. In Indian architecture, the porch or vestibule leading to a temple (see Choultry).

MANTEGAZZA, ANTONIO. (See Mantegazza, Cristoforo.)

MANTEGAZZA, CRISTOFORO; sculptor; d. about 1482.

Cristoforo and Antonio Mantegazza first appear at the Certosa of Pavia, Italy, in 1473. In an inventory of that date several works in the church of that monastery are mentioned. It is not supposed that Cristoforo did much work on the façade of the Certosa, as he died just as it was commenced. Antonio worked on the façade for eight years with Omodeo (see Omodeo).

Calvi, *Notizie;* Perkins, *Italian Sculptors;* Müntz, *Renaissance.*

MANTEGNA, ANDREA; painter; b. 1431; d. Sept. 13, 1506.

About 1474, the great painter Mantegna decorated the so-called Camera degli Sposi in the castle at Mantua, with frescoes illustrating

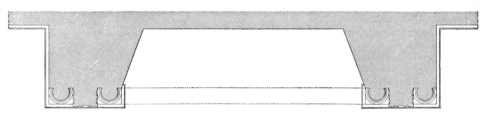

MANTELPIECE IN THE HÔTEL DE CLARY, TOULOUSE (HAUTE GARONNE); DATE ABOUT 1575.
Of peculiar local style.

the history of the Gonzaga family. For the Marquis Lodovico Gonzaga he designed also the "Triumph of Julius Cæsar," which was intended for a scene in a theatrical representation. It is now known only by cartoons, very much restored, and engravings.

Paul Mantz, *André Mantegna ;* Charles Yriarte, *Isabella d'Este et les Artistes de son temps ;* Carlo d'Arco, *Delle Arti e degli Artisti di Mantova.*

MANTEL. *A.* A projecting hood or cover above a fireplace to collect the smoke and guide it into the chimney flue above (see Chimney). *B.* Same as Mantelpiece ; a modern abbreviation.

MANTELBOARD. Same as Mantelshelf, when of wood.

MANTELPIECE. A structure forming a mantel, together with its supports ; a similar structure built against a chimney around and above a fireplace, either as a decorative finish or to afford one or more shelves above the fireplace.

MANTELSHELF. Originally, a shelf on a mantle and hence, a shelf over a fireplace; either independent or forming part of a Mantelpiece.

MANTELTREE. A beam to support a mantel; a wooden lintel over a fireplace.

MANUFACTORY. (See Factory.)

MARBLE. Any stone consisting essentially of carbonate of lime, or the carbonates of lime and magnesia, and of such colour and texture as to make it desirable for the higher grades of building, monumental, or decorative work.

The varying shades of gray and the black colours of marbles are due to the presence of carbonaceous matter; the yellow, brown and red colours to iron oxides, and the green to the presence of silicate minerals, as mica and talc. The veined and clouded effects are due to an unequal distribution of the colouring constituents throughout the mass of the stone.

The leading varieties of marble are described below. (See also section on Marbles in article Stone.)

Artificial Marble. (See Marbleizing.)

Bardiglio Marble. Bluish gray ground traversed by dark veins Obtained from Mont' Alto in southern Tuscany. In the variety *bardiglio fiorito* the veining gives a fancied resemblance to flowers. The *bardiglio 'scuro* is gray or bluish and saccharoidal, inferior to the above.

Belgian Black Marble. A well-known black marble from Golzines, near Dinant, and the provinces of Namur, Belgium.

Bird's-eye Marble. Any marble the uniformity of colour of which is broken by lighter or darker spots, fancied to resemble a bird's eye. Example: the bird's-eye griotte, of France.

Black and Gold Marble, called *Portor.* A compact brownish gray stone traversed by irregular veins and blotches of dull yellow. From the island of Palmaria in the Gulf of Spezia, and from Porto Venere.

Bougard Marble. A stone similar in general appearance to the Formosa, and from the same locality. Perhaps a trifle lighter in colour.

Breccia Marble. Any stone composed of angular fragments imbedded in a finer ground or paste. Among the best known of breccia marbles are the Egyptian breccia, many of the Numidian marbles, and the breccias of Gragnano and Serravezza, in Italy.

Breche Violette Marble. A coarse breccia of sharply angular white, pink, and red fragments in a dull red-brown paste.

Brocatelle Marble. (Italian Brocatello Antico.) A compact stone of dull yellowish and drab colour traversed by irregular veins and

blotches of dull terra cotta red. Often variegated by patches or spots of white crystalline calcite. Now brought from Catalonia in northern Spain.

Calico Marble; Potomac breccia. A marble composed of rounded and angular fragments, of varying sizes up to several inches in diameter, of limestone imbedded in a fine calcareous ground. From the Triassic formations near Point of Rocks in Maryland. Used in columns of Old Hall of Representatives in the Capitol in Washington.

Campan Marble. From the French Pyrenees, and of a variety of colours indicated by their trade names — Campan, *vert clair*, *vert foncé, isabelle, hortensia mélangé, mélangé*, and *rouge.*

Carrara Marble. A name given to the white and sometimes blue-gray veined and blotched saccharoidal marbles quarried at and near Carrara, in Italy.

Cipollino Marble. A white stone variegated with green and gray, called cipollino, from the Italian *cipolla*, an onion, owing to its fancied resemblance to a cross-section of an onion. Originally from the island of Eubœa in the Ægean Sea. Name now commonly applied to any white crystalline marble containing greenish mica, and especially the schistose varieties.

Egyptian Breccia Marble. A coarse breccia containing fragments of porphyry, basalt, quartz, and granite in a greenish or purplish ground. Said to be from quarries between Kossur and Koft in Egypt.

Fiorto Marble. A light chocolate and white mottled marble somewhat resembling the dark variegated varieties of Tennessee. From Italy. Called also *fiorto di Persico.*

Forest Marble. An impure limestone showing on a cut surface fanciful resemblances of forest landscapes. Also called Landscape Marble.

Formosa Marble. A dark gray and white mottled stone sometimes blotched with reddish; highly fossiliferous. From Nassau, Germany.

Giallo Antico Marble. (See Numidian Marble, below.)

Griotte Marble; French Red. A brilliant red, sometimes white-spotted compact marble found in the valley of the Barouse and other localities in the French Pyrenees. One of the best of red marbles.

Hymettian Marble. A blue-gray marble from Mt. Hymettus.

Irish Black Marble. A compact black marble occurring in counties Galway and Kilkenny in Ireland. One of the best of black marbles.

Kilkenny Marble. (See Irish Black Marble, above.)

Languedoc Marble; French Red. A compact marble of brilliant red colour blotched with white. Resembles the Griotte. From the Montagne Noire and other localities in the Pyrenees.

Lepanto Marble. A trade name given to a shell marble quarried near Plattsburg, New York.

Lisbon Yellow Marble. A compact yellow marble somewhat resembling that of Siena, but inferior. From Estremoz, Portugal.

Lucullan Marble. A black marble from the island of Malos. Named after Lucullus, a Roman consul.

Lumachelle Marble ; Shell Marble. Several varieties are recognized. The best known modern stone bearing this name is that from Bleiberg and Hall in the Tyrol. The ground is dark gray-brown interspersed with shells, which still retain their nacre or pearly lining.

Lychnites Marble. Probably the Parian marble.

Lyonaise Marble. A trade name for the coarsely mottled marble of Malletts Bay on Lake Champlain.

Madrepore Marble. A marble containing fossil madreporian corals.

Mischio Marble. A coarsely brecciated, very showy marble composed of whitish and pinkish fragments with a darker cement. From Serravezza, Italy. According to Delesse, it is identical, or at least but a varietal form, of the so-called Egyptian breccia.

Nero Antico Marble. A deep black marble with occasional white spots or lines, said to be found on the promontory of Tænarum in Greece.

Numidian Marble. This is found, not in Numidia proper, but in the Mountain of the Capes (Djebel-el-roos), in the provinces of Africa and Mauritania in Algeria. The colours range through shades of yellow, drab, and pink to deep red.

Onyx Marble. A compact form of travertine or stalagmite, and of a white, green, brown or red colour, often beautifully clouded and banded; translucent. Erroneously called alabaster.

Paonazzo Marble. A variety of the so-called Numidian marble. The name is probably a corruption of pavonazetta, since the description of the stones correspond to the last named.

Parian Marble ; *Greco duro.* A white granular saccharoidal marble used for statuary and also for building. From the island of Paros in the Ægean Sea. Called Lychnites, by Pliny.

Parmazo Marble. White or grayish crystalline granular marbles traversed by a very coarse network of black or blue veins. From the Miseglia, Pescina, and Bocca del Probli quarries in the Apuan Alps.

Pavonazetto Marble. White to isabelle yellow with purplish veins. Also known as Phrygian marble, because obtained at Phrygia in Asia Minor. Said to have been a favourite with the Emperor Hadrian.

Pentelic Marble ; *Marmor pentalicum, Greco fino.* A white to grayish crystalline granular stone from Mt. Penticulus, between Athens and Marathon, in Greece. Used in the construction of the Parthenon, at Athens.

Phengites Marble ; *Marmor phengite, Bianco e giallo.* A white, yellow-veined marble capable of receiving a very high polish. From Cappadocia.

Phrygian Marble. (See Pavonazetto Marble, above.)

Porta Santa Marble ; *Marmor Iassence.* A purplish red and white clouded stone from the island of Iasus or Caria, or, according to some authorities, the island of Chios. Used in the door jambs of the Porta Santa of S. Peter's church in Rome, hence the name. Also called Claudian stone, because a favourite with the Emperor Claudius.

Portor Marble. (Same as Black and Gold Marble, above.)

Purbeck Marble. A shell limestone found in the south of England. It is used in building since the 13th century. When polished it is dark gray, and is much used for interior shafts, especially in Gothic churches. It is not very durable.

Rosso Antico Marble ; *Marmor Tænarium.* A deep brick red, sometimes purplish marble from Cape Matapan in Laconia, Greece.

Rosso de Levanto Marble. A chocolate-red, mottled stone much resembling the Tennessee variegated varieties. From Spezia, Italy.

Rouge Antique Marble. Red antique marble. A red marble much used by the ancients, and found at Cynopolis and Damarestica in Greece.

Ruin Marble. A compact yellowish or drab limestone which has been shattered almost like so much glass and the fragments recemented with comparatively little displacement. Cut and polished slabs give a mosaic-like effect, representing ruins of buildings. From the Val di Sieve, environs of Florence, Italy.

Sarrancolin Marble. A breccia marble quarried near Sarrancolin in the French Pyrenees. The colours are extremely variable, gray, yellow, and red predominating.

Siena Marble. Yellow and drab marbles, often brecciated, from near Siena in Italy. A very compact stone of almost waxy lustre, and in great demand for interior work both at present and in the past. Has been used in America in the vestibule of the new library building in Boston, and the rotunda of the new library building in Washington.

Saint Anne Marble. A deep blue-black marble, variegated with short veins of white. From Saint Anne, Belgium.

Statuary Marble. Any white crystalline, granular, saccharoidal marble suitable for statuary purposes. Example : Parian and Carrara.

Tabrez Marble. A travertine, or "Onyx Marble," from near Lake Oroomiah in Persia. Mainly of a white colour.

Verdantique Marble. (Italian, *Verde Antico*: Antique Green.) A compact variety of serpentine used as a marble. (See Serpentine. See also Verdantique Marbles in article Stone.)

Winooski Marble. A reddish and brownish, variegated with white dolomitic, marble quarried near Winooski, in Chittenden County, Vermont.   — G. P. MERRILL.

MARBLEIZING. The art and practice of staining or coating a material, such as slate or cast iron, so as to resemble a surface of rich marble, the veins and cloudings being imitated by different expedients. Marbleized iron was formerly much used in the United States. This material was produced by a complete concealing of the surface, by a kind of paint in which the veins of marble were imitated. Recent work is done rather by staining the surface of inexpensive gray marble or slate, and some of the imitations are extremely truthful in appearance, and of decorative effect.

MARBLING. The art and practice of imitating or expressing the veins and colours of certain marbles ; whether this is done by painting of the usual sort, or by staining a plain marble, or by marbleizing. The above are the processes used in architectural work ; the marbling of paper is done in a wholly different way. (See Marbleizing.)

MARC D'ARGENT. (See Mardargent.)

MARCHAND, FRANÇOIS ; architect and sculptor ; b. about 1500 (at Orléans, France) ; d. about 1543.

Marchand appears to have been first employed to carve certain bas-reliefs for the façade of the château of Gaillon (Eure, France). A François Marchand, undoubtedly the same person, is mentioned in the records as associated with Pierre Bontemps (see Bontemps, Pierre) in the execution of the sculpture of the tomb of François I., at the church of S. Denis (near Paris).

Buzonnière, *Histoire Architecturale de la Ville d'Orléans* ; Gonse, *Sculpture Française*.

MARCHAND (MARCHANT), GUILLAUME ; architect and builder (*entrepreneur*); b. about 1530 ; d. Oct. 12, 1605.

In 1578 he was commissioned with Guillaume Guillain (see Guillain, G.), Thibaut Métezeau, (see Métezeau, T.), and Jean and François Petit (see Petit), to design and build the Pont-Neuf (Paris). He was charged by Henri IV. to continue the construction of the Pont-Neuf, which was not finished until 1608. Between 1594 and 1596, he was associated with others in the construction of the eastern half of the Grande Galerie of the Louvre. March 27, 1600, he undertook, with Pierre Chambiges

(see Chambiges, Pierre, II.) and others, the construction of the western half of the Grande Galerie. For Henri IV. he began the new château of Saint-Germain-en-Laye, which was finished in 1610 (destroyed about 1775).

Bauchal, *Dictionnaire* ; Palustre, *Renaissance* ; Berty, *Topographie*.

MARCHAND, LOUIS ; architect.

A son of Guillaume Marchand (see Marchand, G.). In 1604, Louis Marchand succeeded to his father's office of *maître général des œuvres de maçonnerie de la Viscomté de Paris*. He also continued the work at the château of Saint-Germain-en-Laye.

Bauchal, *Dictionnaire*.

MARCHANT. (See Marchand.)

MARCHIONESS. (See Slate.)

MARCILLA, GUGLIELMO DA. (See Marcillat, Guillaume de.)

MARCILLAT, GUILLAUME DE (Guglielmo da Marcilla) ; glass painter ; b. 1467 ; d. 1529.

The leading glass painter of the sixteenth century in Italy. The name is derived from the town of Marcillat in the department of Allier, France, where the family originated. Guillaume came to Rome during the pontificate of Julius II. (Pope 1503–1513), and painted glass at the Vatican under the direction of Bramante (see Bramante). He painted, also, the windows of the choir of S. Maria del Popolo (Rome) which still exist. Between 1515 and 1518 he painted in fresco the façade of the palace of the Cardinal Passerini at Cortona (Italy). Two windows which he painted for the church of the Pieve at Cortona, are now in the Museo Nazionale at Florence. Oct. 31, 1518, he first appears in the records of the cathedral of Arezzo. He was employed on the glass of the cathedral, and painted the window of the Spaderi family at the church of the Annunciata in Arezzo. The contract for his decoration in fresco of the vaults of the cathedral of Arezzo dates from Dec. 31, 1520. The work was not completed until 1526. His will is dated July 30, 1529.

Müntz, *Guillaume de Marcillat* ; Müntz, *Renaissance* ; Vasari, Milanesi ed. ; J. B. Waring, *Arts connected with Architecture in Central Italy*.

MARCO DA CAMPIONE. (See Frisone Marco.)

MARDARGENT (MARC D'ARGENT), JEAN ROUSSEL ; abbot and architect ; d. 1339. He became abbot of S. Ouen at Rouen in 1303. Mardargent augmented the revenues of the abbey and designed its church. He built the choir with its chapels, the pillars of the central tower, and began the transept and nave.

Deville, *Observations sur l'Achèvement de l'église de S. Ouen* ; De Jolimont, *Monuments de la ville de Rouen*.

MARGIN. *A.* Same as Bare.

B. The flat, unmoulded face of a rail or stile in panel work, especially of an outer one.

MARKEE. A tent or temporary awning, especially in Great Britain; apparently a mispronunciation of Marquise.

MARKET. In general, any place where merchandise is kept for sale. Napoleon I. established the public markets of Paris, and the erection of the famous *Halles Centrales* was commenced in 1811. London, Berlin, and other capitals of Europe followed with the erection of imposing structures. In the United States many cities have public market buildings. These are generally utilitarian structures, offering twofold advantages, viz. : market people and the public are protected against the weather, and the provisions are not damaged by rain, snow, heat, cold, or by street dust, and can be exposed to better advantage. Markets also facilitate the thorough inspection of the food supply by the sanitary police; and all waste material may be removed under official supervision. Covered market buildings afford also facilities for the storage of food products. Large cities in Europe have both wholesale and retail markets, the former located conveniently near to the traffic facilities, the railroads, river and canal transportation, harbour wharves, or the main roads leading from the surrounding country districts to the city. Markets for live cattle are generally located close to, or in connection with, the slaughtering establishments (see Slaughter House). Fish and oyster markets are located convenient to the harbour or docks.

Market buildings should be inexpensively designed, but substantially built, brick and stone, or iron and glass, structures. Plenty of floor space is essential. Many wide entrances and exits facilitate the market traffic. Wholesale markets require arrangements for loading and unloading, driveways for the carts and wagons, and rail connections for the freight coming from long distances.

The interior is usually a one-story lofty hall structure either with wide span roof trusses, or with smaller roof divisions, supported by intermediate columns. The latter may be utilized in the division of the sale stands. The interior is subdivided by several main and cross aisles. The buildings generally have cellars, for storage. For perfect cleanliness, the walls should be of non-absorbent material. The construction of the floor is of the greatest importance; should be waterproof, asphalted or cemented, or paved with asphalt paving blocks or hardburnt paving brick; sometimes mosaic tile floors are used. The driveways must be well paved and drained. There should be convenient cellar stairs and also cellar lifts. For the maintenance of a good sanitary condition a plentiful supply of water and also provisions for flushing are essential. Floors require welltrapped sewer-connected drainage openings. The market hall should be amply ventilated; and in winter time the building must be slightly heated. Some markets have special artificial refrigerating plants. Ample daylight illumination is essential, supplemented by gas or electric light. Rooms for the food inspectors may be provided in the divisions of the building. Condemned food and waste materials, pending transportation, should be stored in tight, covered, iron receptacles.

Handbuch der Architekur, Part IV., Vol. 3, 2 ; *Gebäude für Lebensmittel-Versorgung ;* Dr. Theodor Weyl, *Handbuch der Hygiene*, Vol. VI., *Markthallen ;* G. Osthoff, *Die Markthallen für Lebensmittel ;* Lindemann, *Die Markthallen Berlins ;* Bockelberg und Rowald, *Die städtische Markthalle zu Hannover ;* Behnke, *Die Markthalle in Frankfurt ;* Hennicke, *Mittheilungen über Markthallen in Deutschland, England, Frankreich, Belgien und Italien ;* Friedmann, *Entwürfe für den Bau von Hallen, Märkten und Lagerhäusern.*

— W. B. GERHARD.

MARKET HOUSE. A building prepared for the purposes of a market. The market houses of the Greeks have been identified by inscriptions, but as yet nothing positive is known of their form and character. (For those at Æge and at Alinda in Caria, see Asia Minor, Architecture of.) Of the Romans', we have only the Macellum (which see) at Pompeii. In Florence, the well-known church of Or San Michele was originally a market house, as the large open arches of the ground story (now filled with later tracery) plainly indicate. The market houses of Great Britain are among the most picturesque of the buildings in the smaller towns. They are sometimes octagonal, in one or two cases cruciform or nearly so, and sometimes of elaborately organized plan, as in the well-known instance of Rothwell in Northamptonshire, an unfinished building of excellent Elizabethan design. The most important market house in Europe is that in Paris known as the Halles Centrales (which see; see also Market).

MARLBOROUGH HOUSE. In London; the residence of the Prince of Wales from 1863 to his accession in 1901. It was designed by Sir Christopher Wren and built about 1710 for the Duke of Marlborough.

MAROT, DANIEL ; architect and engraver. Daniel was probably a son of Jean Marot (see Marot, Jean). He was a Protestant, and at the Revocation of the Edict of Nantes, Oct. 22, 1685, took refuge in Holland and became architect to the Prince of Orange, later King William III. of England. He went with William to England in 1688, and is supposed to have designed the gardens of the palace of Hampton Court. After the death of William, in 1702, Marot returned to Holland. He published *Œuvres de Sieur Daniel Marot, architecte de Guillaume III. de la Grande Bretagne*, Amsterdam, 1712.

Bauchal, *Dictionnaire;* Mariette, *Abecedario.*

MAROT, JEAN; architect and engraver; b. (at Paris) about 1620; d. Dec. 15, 1679.

Marot built the portal of the Feuillantines and numerous residences in Paris. With Lemercier (see Lemercier, J.), he made plans for the completion of the Louvre, which were never executed, but are engraved in his book. Marot is known by his architectural engravings, the greater part of which were collected in his *Architecture française ou Recueil des plans, élévations, coupes et profiles des églises, palais, hôtels et maisons particuliers de Paris*, etc. (The number of plates varies in different copies.) He published also *Le Magnifique château de Richelieu.*

Mariette, *Abecedario;* Bauchal, *Dictionnaire.*

MAROUFLAGE. In French, a process used in mural painting; canvas being secured to a wall by some adhesive material so as to become the permanent surface. (See Oil Painting.)

MARQUETRY. Inlay composed of thin veneers of hard wood, ivory, and other costly materials, usually fixed to a wooden backing. (See Inlaid Work.)

MARQUISE. In French, a roof put up out of doors to shelter the approach to a doorway, or the like; and less massive than that which forms part of a porch, cloister, or the like. By extension, the term may signify any out-of-door shelter which is somewhat unusual in character; thus, a carriage porch, which is not very common in France, is sometimes so called.

MARTINI; architect and military engineer; b. Sept. 23, 1439 (at Siena); d. 1502.

Besides his work on fortification, he was a student of antiquity; a manuscript of his translation of Vitruvius, bound up with other essays of his, is preserved in Florence. In 1476 he became attached to the court at Urbino, and from 1491 was in Naples. The only building of importance which is certainly by him is the church of the Madonna del Calcinaio, near Cortona, of which the first stone was laid in 1485; but this is one of the most valuable churches of the Renaissance. The cupola was added by Pietro di Domenico Nozzi.

MARTINO DA CRAPINA; architect.

In 1473 the monks of Santa Chiara di Murano (Venice) commissioned Martino da Crapina, *proto-maestro* of their church, to build for them a campanile like that of S. Michele di Murano. The accounts of S. Chiara show frequent payments to him of considerable amounts.

Paoletti, *Rinascimento in Venezia*, Vol. I.

MARTINUS; architect.

The fine Romanesque porch of S. Erasmo at Veroli (Italy) is signed by Martinus: EST MANIBVS FACTVS MARTINI QVEM PROBAT ARCVS. The work belongs to the middle of the twelfth century.

Frothingham, *Roman Artists of the Middle Ages.*

MARTYRIUM. A place where are deposited the relics of a martyr. In mediæval ecclesiology, now one and now another such place; a Shrine, a Sepulchre (which see in sense *B*), or a Crypt.

MARVILLE, JEAN DE; sculptor and architect.

A Flemish sculptor who appears first engaged on the church of S. Pierre at Lille. In 1383 he commenced the monument of Philippe le Hardi, which was continued by Claus Sluter (see Sluter), and completed by Claus de Werve (see Claus de Werve). It is now in the museum at Dijon.

Lami, *Dictionnaire des Sculpteurs français;* Gonse, *L'Art Gothique.*

MASCARON. A human or partly human face, or, more rarely, the front of a head of a lion or other beast, more or less caricatured; used as an architectural ornament, especially in the later neoclassic styles, as in the Italian work of the seventeenth century. The faces are apt to be highly grotesque, representing rather satyrs or fauns than men, and exaggerated modifications of animal heads. These are purely ornamental, and decorate keystones and the like. They should not be confounded with the lions' heads used as spouts or gargoyles.

MASCHERINO, OTTAVIO (OTTAVIANO); architect; b. about 1530; d. about 1610.

Mascherino rebuilt the church of S. Salvatore, Rome, which had been destroyed by fire in 1591. His most important work is the Palazzo Quirinale, Rome, which he designed for Paul V. (Pope 1605–1621). The façade on the Piazza di Monte Cavallo and the court are his work.

Gurlitt, *Geschichte des Barockstiles in Italien;* Ebe, *Spät-Renaissance.*

MASCHIO. Same as Donjon. The Italian term.

MASEGNE, GIACOMELLO DI ANTONIO DALLE; Venetian sculptor and architect of the late Gothic period.

His work shows Tuscan influence decidedly. In 1388 the Frati Minori of the church of S. Francesco at Bologna contracted with Masegne to make the great altar of that church. It is adorned with statuettes of the Virgin and saints, and bas-reliefs of the Coronation of the Virgin, and other subjects. In 1400 he made the tomb of Antonio Venier at the church of

SS. Giovanni e Paolo in Venice. A brother called Pietro Paolo dalle Masegne is stated to have worked with him. The Septo, or low screen enclosing the choir of S. Mark's church, Venice, with numerous statuettes, were made by the Masegne in 1394–1397.

Perkins, *Italian Sculptors*, 1868; Perkins, *Handbook of Italian Sculpture*, New York, 1883; Paoletti, *Rinascimento in Venezia*, Vol. I.

MASEGNE, PAOLO; Venetian sculptor and architect of the late Gothic period.

Paolo was the son of Giacomello dalle Masegne. His principal works are the monument of the Veronese condottiere Jacopo Cavelli (d. 1386) at the church of SS. Giovanni e Paolo in Venice, which has lost much of its sculpture and colour, and the sarcophagus of the famous General Prendiparte Pico, now in the museum of Modena, formerly at Mirandola.

(For bibliography, see **Masegne, Giacomello dalle.**)

MASHREBEEYEH. (See Meshrebeeyeh.)

MASK. A representation in art of the front part of the head of man, beast, or fantastic creature. In architecture, usually called Mascaron (which see).

MASONRY. The art and practice of building with stone, — natural or artificial, — with brick, and, by extension, with moulded earth, as in adobe and pisé; also, the work so produced. Stones and bricks are generally laid in mortar, but may be laid without it (dry

MASONRY OF RUBBLE BEDDED IN MORTAR, FACED WITH SQUARED RUBBLE AND HAVING BOND COURSES OF THIN BRICKS.

masonry), care being taken so to superimpose the materials as to bind or bond together those below them.

The front of the wall is called the face. The stones in the face of the wall are face stones;

those behind them are backing, and are generally of an inferior class of material. In architectural work, cut stones are generally backed with brick, or in very thick walls with rough rubble masonry. The upper and lower surfaces of a stone as laid are its beds. A stretcher is

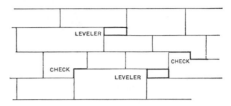

MASONRY: CUT TO ILLUSTRATE FACING OF STONE WALL.

a stone laid lengthwise with the face of the wall; a header is one laid across the wall, usually at right angles to the face, and binds the face stones to the backing. If the headers do not extend through the wall, others are placed in the rear face, the two series passing or overlapping each other (see Heart Bond, under Bond).

Stone masonry may be otherwise divided into three classes: Concrete (which see), Rubble Masonry (see subtitle), and dressed stone masonry, composed of squared stones with a greater or less degree of finish. This class may be subdivided into squared rubble and ashlar, which differ chiefly in the size of the stones. Ashlar, or cut stone masonry, is formed of large stones brought to regular shape with stone-cutting tools, with more or less fineness of joints and finish of face (see Ashlar).

In laying rough rubble, there should be some selection. Every stone should have at least one flat bed upon which it is to be laid. Any irregularities are to be filled with smaller stones or spalls laid in mortar to make a fair bed for the courses above. Care is to be taken that the stones are fitted to each other as far as possible. It is chiefly important that no voids be left in the wall, but that all vacant spaces be filled with mortar, into which spalls are driven. If the rubble is laid dry, without mortar, the stones must be larger and better shaped than for mortared masonry, and care must be taken that they are well bonded, so that each stone rests upon two or more of those below it, and by its weight and friction holds them in place. Dressed rubble and sometimes ashlar are laid as broken range work, the height of the courses being varied by checking or notching the thicker stone, or by levelling with small squared stones of a thickness equal to the difference in height of the adjacent courses.

The general principles to be followed in building stone masonry are: (1) to build with beds perpendicular, as nearly as may be, to the direction of the pressure upon them; (2) to lay the stones upon their natural beds; (3) to moisten the surface of dry or porous stones that they may not too rapidly absorb the water from the mortar; and, especially, (4) to fill all joints and vacant spaces between the stones with mortar alone or with mortar and spalls. It is very necessary, in dressed rubble as in ashlar, that the beds be truly parallel and set to a straight horizontal line, and the joints truly vertical.

Concrete properly made forms an artificial stone of great value in construction (see Concrete). It has been used chiefly for foundations; but with the progressive discoveries and improvements in the quality of the cements, it is applied to walls, arches, and other forms in which it can be placed in moulds. It is moulded into blocks for constructions under water, sometimes of enormous size, requiring special cranes (Titans) to handle them. The merits of concrete are chiefly that it can be made and put in place with unskilled labour, and that it can be made solid by ramming, solidity being very difficult to obtain in masonry made by hand. Yet the French masons are so successful in making solid work that some of their engineers prefer to use for their sea works blocks of rubble masonry rather than concrete, because of the smaller surface of mortar exposed to the action of sea water.

Stones for building must, above all, be sound. They must be sufficiently hard and strong to support any weight that may come upon them. They must be, as far as possible, non-absorbent, not liable to flake and crack with frost.

The stones most commonly used in masonry are the granites, gneiss, porphyry, the marbles, limestones, and sandstones. All these vary greatly in quality, durability, hardness, and the facility with which they can be worked.

Bricks of good quality laid in cement mortar make very strong and solid work, and may often with advantage take the place of stone. They are made in great variety both as to quality and form. They should be selected and inspected with care, and all underburned or salmon bricks, and all warped and twisted and broken bricks, must be rejected. Salmon bricks should only be permitted in the smallest and most temporary structures, and only the best of the class should be permitted in interior partitions in conjunction with harder material. When the face of the wall is of brick, a dense, smooth, well-shaped brick (front brick) is commonly used for the exterior, sometimes combined with cut stone or terra cotta. Brickwork is used to some extent for floor arches supported by steel beams, but in this respect it has been generally superseded by concrete and terra cotta.

The rules for the construction of brickwork are similar to those for stone masonry. The

bricks must be properly bonded and well bedded in mortar, all joints — both end and side joints — being filled. Where it is not necessary to consider appearances, the bricks are laid generally as stretchers, with now and then a course formed of headers (see American Bond; English Bond; under Bond). In building brick arches, they are laid as stretchers in separate rings, until the beds of two rings come fair, when a course of headers is introduced. Bricks should be wet before being laid in the mortar.

The mortar used in masonry construction is the binding material which renders the wall a solid mass. The Roman works are as a rule conglomerates, composed of pieces of stone in a matrix of pozzuolano mortar. In northern climates the causes of destruction are water and frost. It is necessary to keep out the water to prevent its freezing and dislocating the mass. This indicates the advantage of cement mortars and solid work. The lime mortars harden only by absorption of carbonic acid from the air, and in very thick walls they never harden. They answer for thin walls and small structures, but the much more valuable properties of the natural light-burned cements and their low price is causing their very general use in all structures of importance. These, again, are being superseded by the Portland cements, which are much heavier, are burned in manufacture to incipient vitrification, have greater strength, greater impermeability, and above all are less liable to injury by freezing. The sand to be combined with the limes or cements should be coarse, sharp, and, especially, it should be clean. Any mixture of organic matter injures the mortar made of it. The proportions of sand to the cement should depend upon the character of the work. Lime, which swells considerably in slaking, will bear being mixed with five or six times its bulk of sand; the light cements will rarely make good work with more than two measures of sand to one of cement, although a much larger proportion may be used in foundations where there is no tendency to lateral movement. The Portland cements will form a good coherent mass with three or four times their weight of sand. If the work is exposed to sea water, if it is to be water-tight, or if exposed to the weather, as in structures entirely of concrete, two and a half parts of sand to one of cement are required, and some constructors reduce this proportion to two. Specimens of mortars when tested indicate that the mortars made with as little water as possible are somewhat stronger than if mixed more moist; but in actual practice the mason will more easily make good beds, and fill all joints and spaces, with a soft mortar, than with one that is comparatively dry, and dry concrete is never so thoroughly compacted as that which is soft enough to permit the hard fragments to move under the rammer, and find places in contact with one another.

The strength of masonry depends not merely upon the strength of the stone or brick, but largely upon that of the mortar interposed. No fixed rule can be given, although, in good work, the mortar joints are frequently of greater strength than the brick. Walls of well-cut granite or other hard stone possess a strength far beyond that of the mortar between their beds. Common or rough rubble may exceed but little that of the mortar in which it is laid. Concrete and good brickwork made with Portland cement will safely bear two hundred pounds to the square inch.

Genuys, *Construction Maçonnerie*, 2 vols.; Merrill, *Stones for Building and Decoration;* Reid, *A Practical Treatise on Natural and Artificial Concrete;* Armstrong, *Chimneys for Furnaces, Fireplaces and Steam Boilers* (2d American ed., to which is appended an essay on High Chimneys, by Prof. L. Pinzger); R. M. and F. J. Bancroft, *Tall Chimney Construction; A Practical Treatise on the Construction of Tall Chimney Shafts.* (See also bibliography under Building; Vault.)

— W. R. HUTTON.

Adobe Masonry. (See Adobe and following titles.)

Ashlar Masonry. (See Masonry; also Ashlar and subtitles.)

Dry Masonry. That done without mortar. (See Masonry.)

Greek Masonry. Walling made of solid cut stone blocks laid without mortar; a term used by some moderns who copy a passage in Vitruvius. It has been pointed out by J. H. Middleton that the passage in Vitruvius (II., 8) signifies work done with blocks laid as stretchers, the whole thickness of the wall being formed of such stretchers, while other courses of headers or through stones alternate with the first.

Pisé Masonry. A cheap masonry of compressed earth. The most suitable solid for the purpose is a clayey, somewhat sandy, loam and vegetable earth. It is mixed with straw or hay to prevent it from cracking as it dries. After being screened, if necessary, it is moistened and thoroughly worked to mix in the straw. For very rough work the labourer puts it in place with an ordinary shovel, with which he dresses the face to lines. For careful work the wall is built in sections by means of a movable frame about 3 feet high and 10 feet' long, the two sides of which are of boards kept apart the thickness of the wall. This frame is placed on the wall, and between the sides the earth is rammed in and beaten in 4-inch layers. When this sort of box is full, it is taken apart and set up in another part of the wall. As the wall goes up, the keys in the cross pieces are driven in to make the box somewhat narrower and the wall thinner. The end of each block is sloped about sixty de-

grees, and care is taken that these joints do not come over those below them. The walls are generally low, but in some parts of France houses of two and three stories are built of pisé. The wall is strengthened by bedding withes or rods in it. When used for enclosing walls it is covered with thatch held in place by a cope of plastered earth which is renewed at intervals. The pisé is much stronger when it is mixed with a milk of lime instead of water. When the walls are dry they are plastered with one part of lime mixed with four parts of clay, with plasterers' hair. The foundations of walls of pisé should be of stone to a few inches above the ground. (See Pisé.)

Rubble Masonry. That made with stones smaller and less regular than ashlar, and what is called cut stone. (See Masonry; Rubble.)

MASSARI, GIORGIO; architect.

An architect of the eighteenth century in Venice. One of his most important works is the church of S. Maria del Rosario (called Gesuati) in Venice (1726–1743), which was decorated by G. B. Tiepolo (see Tiepolo, G. B.). He built also, in Venice, the upper order and staircase of the Palazzo Rezzonico (see Longhena, Baldassare).

Gurlitt, *Geschichte des Barockstiles in Italien;* Ebe, *Spät-Renaissance.*

MASSEGNE. (See Masegne.)

MASSEGNE, ANTONIO. (See Antonio di Pietro Paolo.)

MASTABA. In Egyptian archæology, a tomb of the more architectural sort; built above ground, having usually a very plain exterior, rectangular in form, with a flat roof, from which form has come the name, which signifies a bench. The exterior, therefore, is usually very plain, only the doorway having some slight architectural treatment, but there is sometimes great splendour of sculptured and painted decoration within. In most cases the mastaba has a shaft leading to a tomb chamber excavated in the rock at a considerable depth. Usually there is a small, narrow chamber, either entirely concealed in the masonry and without access, or having a very small passage. This chamber, the Serdab, was intended for a statue of the deceased, and the passage was probably to allow the smoke of incense to pass. See E. A. W. Budge, *The Mummy*, second edition (1894), pp. 316–326; and the papers by Mariette in the *Revue Archéologique*, referred to as the sources for that description. — R. S.

MASTIC. A pasty and adhesive compound hardening soon when exposed to the air, having no relation to the gum so called. It is somewhat used for plastering, but more often for filling gaps or cracks in cut stone, and for filling engraved or incised letters and ornamental patterns as in inscriptions and imitations of inlay. The distinction between mastic and putty is not carefully maintained, as each word is applied rather freely to compositions of this sort.

MAT (adj.). In painting, gilding, and the like, — flat, unpolished, whether from being left without polishing, or deadened or flatted, as when a coat of paint is dabbed with the brush.

MAT ROOM. A room whose size horizontally, and in each direction, depends upon the number of mats with which its floor is to be covered. Especially in Japan, rooms are so planned. The thick mats of rushes and rice straw, always of the same size (about three feet by six), serve as the unit of size, and each room is described as a ten mat room or the like.

MATCH (v.). To bring to equality, uniformity, or similarity. Thus the planks of a floor are required to be matched in thickness (See Thickness, verb) ; or in width, as is customary in all floors of any elegance or finish ; or in colour ; or in surface, as for greater smoothness or a coarser or finer grain.

By extension, and as applied to floor plank, sheathing, and the like, the term is held to include the working of tongues and grooves upon the edges ; so that flooring spoken of as matched is understood to be tongued and grooved.

MATHIAS (MATHIEU) D'ARRAS ; architect ; d. 1352.

Mathias d'Arras was brought from Avignon (France), by the Emperor Charles IV., to plan and construct the cathedral of Prague. He laid the foundations of the choir and built the surrounding chapels. The choir was completed, probably after his plans, by his successor, Pierre Arler or Peter Parler (see Parler).

Dr. J. Neuwirth, *Die Wochen-rechnungen des Prager Dombaues ;* Alfred Darcel, *Les architectes de la cathédrale de Prague ;* Bauchal, *Dictionnaire.*

MATHIAS VON BÖBLINGEN ; architect ; d. 1505.

Mathias von Böblingen appears to have succeeded Moriz von Ensingen (see Moriz von Ensingen) as architect of the cathedral of Ulm (Germany) about 1480. In 1492 the great tower at Ulm began to sink and part of the vaulting fell in. Probably on account of this accident Mathias retired to Ensingen in Switzerland.

Hassler, *Ulms Kunstgeschichte im Mittelalter.*

MATHIAS VON ENSINGEN ; architect ; d. 1463.

Mathias was the son of Ulrich von Ensingen (see Ulrich von Ensingen). In 1420 he was called to superintend the construction of the cathedral of Berne in Switzerland. In 1446 he went to Ulm, and in 1451 was made architect of the cathedral of that city. An inscription on the northern portal of the cathedral of

Ulm gives the date of his death. He was succeeded by his son Moriz von Ensingen (see Moriz von Ensingen).

Hassler, *Ulms Kunstgeschichte im Mittelalter ;* Gérard, *Les Artistes de l' Alsace.*

MATSYS, JOSSE ; ironworker (*serrurier*), architect, and sculptor ; b. 1463 (at Louvain, Belgium) ; d. 1530.

A brother of Quentin Matsys, the painter. He built the chapel of the Erpe family in the church of S. Pierre at Louvain. He began the tower of the church of S. Pierre in 1507, but did not complete it.

Biographie Nationale de Belgique.

MATTEO NUTI ; (see Nuti, Matteo).

MAUCH, JOHANN MATTHAUS VON ; draughtsman, engraver, architect, and painter ; b. 1792 (at Ulm, Germany) ; d. 1856.

A pupil of Schinkel (see Schinkel), in Berlin. He is best known by his works on the classical orders and on decoration.

Seubert, *Künstler-lexicon.*

MAUCH, KARL FRIEDRICH EDUARD ; draughtsman, engraver, and writer ; b. 1800 (at Ulm, Germany) ; d. Feb. 21, 1874.

He studied in Berlin and engraved plates for Schinkel's *Architektonischer Entwurfe.* He made a special study of the art and archæology of his native city. With Dr. C. Von Grüneisen he published *Ulms Kunstleben im Mittelalter.*

Seubert, *Künstler-lexicon.*

MAURICE. (See Mauritius.)

MAURITIUS ; Bishop of London ; d. 1107.

During his reign the old cathedral of S. Paul, London, was begun in place of an earlier building which was destroyed by fire in 1087. Old S. Paul's was burned in 1666 (see Wren).

Aiken, *S. Paul's Cathedral ;* Milman, *Annals of S. Paul's.*

MAURO. (See Coducci, Mauro, of Bergamo.)

MAUSOLEUM. A large and splendid tomb or cenotaph. The name was first applied to the building said by Pliny to have been erected in honour of King Mausoleus of Caria, in Asia Minor, in the fourth century B.C. Ruins of this building exist near Budrum. They were studied by Sir Charles Fellows (op. cit.), and attempted restorations have been made by several archæologists. The sculptures of this monument are partly in the British Museum.

Fellows, *Lycia, Caria, Lydia ;* Gardner, *Sculptured tombs of Hellas.*

MAUSOLEUM OF AUGUSTUS. In Rome, in the ancient Campus Martius, a gigantic circular structure which seems to have been of solid masonry with heavy vaulting below, and to have been heaped with earth above forming a vast conical mound planted with trees. It was nearly three hundred feet in diameter. The vaults below contained sculpture and historical monuments of extraordinary interest, some few of which have been preserved. What remains of the building itself is concealed by modern structures, but parts of it can be seen in the courtyards of certain palazzi between the river and the Corso near the Porto di Ripetta.

MAUSOLEUM OF HADRIAN. At Rome, on the right bank of the Tiber. It consisted originally of a great cylindrical drum raised upon a square podium, and crowned by a tapering roof probably made of receding steps. The building was entirely sheathed in marble, and had a great number of statues arranged around the top of the drum, and elsewhere about its exterior. All of this has disappeared, leaving only the massive core of cut stone and rubble masonry, and upon this mediæval additions have been placed. (See Castel S. Angelo.)

MAYA ARCH. That used by the Maya Indians of Yucatan, and kindred tribes. (See Corbel Arch.) — F. S. D.

MAYA ARCHITECTURE. That of the pre-Columbian inhabitants of Yucatan and adjacent regions. (See Mexico, Architecture of, § I.) — F. S. D.

MAZE. Same as Labyrinth.

MAZOIS, FRANÇOIS; architect and archæologist; b. Oct. 12, 1783 (at Lorient, France); d. Dec. 31, 1826.

Mazois was a student of the *École Polytechnique* in Paris and later entered the atelier of Charles Percier (see Percier). He was invited by Murat (made king of Naples, July 14, 1808) to restore the palace of Portici, Italy. Through the influence of the queen, Caroline, he was provided with a yearly pension of twelve thousand francs, which enabled him to undertake the great work on Pompeii with which his name is associated. The first volume was published in 1812 (reprinted in 1842).

In 1820 he was appointed *inspecteur général du conseil des bâtiments civils* in Paris. He published *Les ruines de Pompei, Le palais de Scaurus, ou description d'une maison romaine* (Paris, 1819 and 1822, 1 vol. 8vo.), and *Les ruines de Pæstum, Pouzzoles et d'Herculanéum*, etc.

Chevalier Artaud, *Notice biographique* in Mazois, *Ruines de Pompei;* Bauchal, *Dictionnaire.*

MEANDER. A bandlike ornament composed of right lines which meet one another at abrupt angles. The simplest form has the lines arranged perpendicularly with each other; but varieties of these are common in which the lines are diagonal with each other, forming, therefore, oblique angles with each other. Sometimes the pattern is continuous from end to end of the band; sometimes it is broken into short passages consisting, perhaps, of two squares or trapezoids each. (For similar orna-

mentation covering a surface indefinitely wide, see Fret, *B.*)

MEASURE. (For the measures of important buildings, see Size.)

MEASURE-UP; MEASURING-UP. (See Bill of Quantities.)

MECCHERINO. (See Beccafumi.)

MECHANIC'S LIEN. (See Legislation.)

MEDALLION. Properly a sculptured tablet, panel, or similar member, treated decoratively or forming part of a decorative composition of which it is the central or a prominent feature. By extension, such a decorative member, whether carved or flat, as in colour decoration. The term is usually restricted to mean a member approximately round or oval.

MEDITERRANEAN ISLANDS, ARCHITECTURE OF. That of Crete, Cyprus, and Sicily (see those terms); of Sardinia, Corsica, Malta, the Balearic Islands, and the Islands of the Archipelago and of the Ægean Sea (for which see also Greece, Architecture of). The small islands on the coast, as Elba, need not be considered apart from the mainland to which they belong.

Sardinia. This great island possesses the only specimens of the Noraghe (which see). Their epoch has never been settled; it has been noticed that in at least one instance a pier of unmistakable Roman building is based upon a ruined Noraghe, but whether they are of the third or fourth century B.C., or of a very much earlier epoch, is as yet undetermined. Megalithic monuments exist also in Sardinia, their character being generally not unlike the Cromlechs and Menhirs of Northern Europe. There are also enclosures of rude stones much resembling an enormous Cistvaen, their dimensions being from fifteen to forty feet in length, and of greater width than the cistvaen, properly so called. Cyclopean masonry exists in several places in the island, especially among the ruins of the ancient Tharros.

Roman remains are not common in the island, nor has anything of importance been learned as yet from their study. An amphitheatre partly excavated out of the rock exists in the neighbourhood of Cagliari, the principal town. There are also the ruins of a brick aqueduct, the bricks having Roman stamps, and there are tombs of interest. At the town of Pula there are ruins of waterside structures, such as quays, and fragments of these and other ancient buildings are built into the walls of subsequent structures. Here also is a small Roman theatre, of which the seats remain in great part intact.

The mediæval and later buildings of Sardinia are of sufficient interest to repay the student; but apparently little has been done to explore them. At Terranova, on the seashore, is a Romanesque basilica of importance, the nave and aisles being separated by columns and also by square piers, and the original roof of timber having been preserved. Here, and elsewhere in the island, granite is the common building material. Another basilica of still greater importance and of about the same epoch is at Porto Torres. This also has its original wooden roof, and is unrestored and in fair preservation, its most interesting feature being the presence of two apses, one at either end, and a very ancient crypt. Near Torralba is a church formerly a cathedral, and at a little distance inland is the church of the ruined city of Calmedia or Bosa. Each of these is Pisan Romanesque in architectural character, with large use of contrasting colour, some valuable sculpture, and a curious campanile of good Italian design. There are interesting mediæval fortresses ; castles which have been injured only by the carrying away of the material for building, so that those in the more open country are nearly intact. Of later buildings there is not much to attract attention. A very beautiful fountain at Sassari, built by Philip II. of Spain in 1605, would seem to be the most attractive thing of this epoch in the island.

Corsica. This island, extremely mountainous, and containing now not more than a quarter of a million inhabitants, can never have been thickly inhabited, and can hardly have possessed important monuments. The picturesqueness of towns closely built with narrow streets, and retaining many buildings of an early date, is almost the only artistic treasure which the island has to offer ; but those who have enjoyed to the full that charm in the small Italian towns and the ancient cities of the Riviera, will find it in the greatest perfection at Bonifacio. In this town also are several churches of Romanesque and of Gothic style, altogether Italian in their general character. In several of the villages among the mountains there are large houses belonging to the ancient nobility, but these are not villas in the true Italian sense, with abundant and richly adorned gardens ; they are rather palazzi like the simpler palazzi of Siena. Bastia, which was the capital during the seventeenth century, and Ajaccio, which is the principal town, and the capital of the French department, contain buildings of the seventeenth and eighteenth centuries which are not without interest from the use of local materials ; but their architecture possesses no individual character ; each building is a mere study of the Continental buildings of the controlling power, the Republic of Genoa, or France.

Malta. Prehistoric remains of unique character exist in the two larger islands of this group ; they are chiefly pieces of Phœnician

work (see Pelasgic), and the most celebrated collection of the ruins is that known as Hagier Kin, a term which is translated, "The Stone of Veneration." A similar ruin is at Mnidra near by. The plan of Hagier Kin as given by Dr. Caruana (op. cit.) is curiously made up of a series of ovals, and these arranged in two groups, although there are traces of what may have been a third similar group. Each of these ovals is from 40 to 60 feet long ; there are six of them in the largest group and two side by side in what was probably the gateway building to the large open court, also of general oval shape. The ruins present to cursory observation little beyond a formless mass of fallen stones.

Remains of a Greek villa are near to these two masses of earlier ruins, and a Roman villa is near Città Vecchia. To a student of military building the defences of Valletta, built during the sixteenth century, when the capital was fixed upon the peninsula which separates the arms of the curious double harbour which still remains the centre of the business of Malta, will be beyond measure instructive, illustrating as they do the earliest form of modern fortification. The later bastions and demilunes have not even replaced, but have rather surrounded and enclosed, the ancient fortifications.

There are several very curious churches. That of S. John of Jerusalem, begun in 1573, possesses one of the most interesting vaulted interiors in Europe, valuable for its constructional quality, and decorated with paintings by Matthias Preti which, though not of the greatest merit, individually, are valuable for their decorative quality. There are several splendid monuments in this church, especially those to the Grand Masters of the Knights of S. John. The chapels on either side of the nave are full of altars, altarpieces, and tombs of singular importance. The oldest church in Malta is also in the town of Valletta and contains some interesting paintings. The church of S. Lorenzo is of the last years of the seventeenth century, and has architectural merit. The church of S. Paul, the cathedral of the diocese, is not in Valletta, but in the little town called Città Vecchia, and is a building of the seventeenth century built after the complete destruction of the early church by an earthquake. The chapels contain most valuable works of art, but the building has been restored and altered.

Several of the civic buildings, erected in the seventeenth century, and serving for different purposes connected with the Order of S. John, remain intact, and are of great importance. Each one is called *auberge* (inn), the term reminding one of the Inns of Court (which see). The largest is the Auberge de Castille, serving in its time for the Knights of Castillian nationality, and this, though now acting as a kind of club house for the British garrison, has been allowed to preserve many of its ancient features. The auberges are all similar in general character to Italian palazzi.

The picturesqueness of effect which has been mentioned with regard to the towns of Corsica is exceptionally abundant in the steep streets of the Maltese towns, from Valletta to the smallest towns in the northern island of Gozo. The town of Rabato in Gozo (for there is a town of that name in each island) is singularly attractive in exterior appearance, the church crowning the massive cluster of stone buildings which rise one above another on the slopes of the hill.

Balearic Islands (Majorca or Mallorca and Menorca or Minorca). Certain megalithic monuments of not unusual character, bilithons and single standing stones, are found in both islands. These are sometimes disposed as if to mark avenues leading to the larger monuments mentioned below. The Talayot of Menorca resembles strongly the Noraghe of Sardinia, and is the only monument at all expressing the same idea or purpose or system of building. There are many of these in the island, some of them sixty feet in diameter, and nearly as high. They are built of dry stone. One form of monument is that exemplified by the Nau de Tudons near Ciudadela, the former capital of the island of Menorca, whose plan bears a curious resemblance to the horizontal form of a boat. It is about forty feet long and much narrower, built entirely of dry masonry, and containing within a chamber much resembling the ordinary cistvaen except in its size. There are several buildings of this form which are generally classed with the talayots. The island is so rich in these as yet insufficiently studied monuments that it is alone one of the most important regions of Europe for the archæologist.

Traces of Roman occupation, as in the foundations of villas, mosaic pavements, and the like, are known to exist, but they have been little studied. It is since the growth of Spanish power and the general Spanish control of the islands beginning with the fifteenth century that the architectural interest of the islands begins. The cathedral of Palma in Majorca is indeed earlier; a good piece of Spanish Gothic architecture, partly of the thirteenth century, and containing magnificent altars and a great reredos of carved wood of unique artistic value. In the same town (much the largest in the island) are another Gothic church, also the Lonja, of late Gothic style, not now used except for storage, a town hall of the seventeenth century, and some interesting palazzi of the old Spanish nobility.

The Greek Islands. Of these, the Sporades, or islands near the coast of Asia Minor, including Khios (Scio), Samos, and Rhodes; also in the far north, Thassos, Samothrace, and Lemnos, belong to the Turkish Empire; the Cyclades, including Andros and Naxos, belong to Greece. They are all Greek in history, and their ancient traditions and the remains of their ancient art are all Greek, as completely so as are the same features of the mainland of Greece. The most important ruins that have been explored are in Delos and Rhodes. Delos is almost uninhabited, and the French School at Athens has been able to make very elaborate studies here which have been published in the archæological periodicals. Plans for restoration of the ancient temple of Apollo have been made and reveal an architectural purpose different from that of similar buildings on the mainland. In all these islands, however, the discoveries of Greek statuary have been more important than the explorations of buildings of classical times, while they contain little architecture of any consequence of later periods. Rhodes alone, in which few of the Greek buildings have been traced, contains interesting buildings of the times of the Knights of S. John, who were expelled from the island by the Turks in 1523 after a famous siege. All the islands of these seas have suffered greatly from earthquakes, and it is on record that these were common in the earliest historical times. — R. S.

MEDRESSEH. In the Turkish empire and its former provinces, a college of Moslem law, especially in the sense of a mosque used in this way and planned especially for the purpose.

MEETING BAR. Same as Meeting Rail, or Meeting Stile.

MEETING HOUSE. Originally, and still in British usage, a building used as a place of worship for dissenters from the Established Church. In local United States, any church.

MEETING RAIL; MEETING STILE. That part of a frame of a door, sash, or the like which closely adjoins another similar part when the door or window is shut. Especially in sliding sash windows, the top rail of the lower sash or bottom rail of the other sash.

MEGALITHIC. Literally, consisting of great stones, a term applied to ancient monuments of prehistoric or of unknown date, and distinguished for the size of the rock masses. The most distinguished megalithic monument is Stonehenge in Salisbury Plain, in the south of England. The one which covers the most ground is, if the detached stones arranged in lines and circles be considered all together, that at Karnak, in Brittany. The monuments most generally described as megalithic are: —

Bilithon, which is any monument consisting of two stones only, or any part of a larger

MEGALITHIC MONUMENT: CROMLECH NEAR SAUMUR (MAINE-ET-LOIRE), FRANCE.

group consisting of two stones. One stone is laid flatwise or lengthwise upon top of a larger one, or a larger and approximately cylindrical stone is supported upon a smaller one, the whole bearing a resemblance to a mushroom.

Catstone. A form of Menhir. (See both terms.)

Cromlech. A large top stone supported tablewise upon several smaller ones. These

MEGALITHIC MONUMENT: MENHIR AT GRABUSSON
(ILE ET VILAINE, FRANCE).

851

latter may be of the nature of walls to an inner chamber of which the great stone forms the roof.

Cyclolith. A circle or several concentric circles of stones evidently intended to form all together a single monument.

Dolmen. Same as Cromlech; the Breton term, commonly used throughout France.

Galgal. Same as Cairn.

Loggan. A rough stone so supported on a small projection of its surface that it can be rocked slightly without moving from its place; called also Logan Stone from a misconception of the origin of the term, which appears to be in its capacity of having a rocking motion.

Menantol. A stone through which a hole has been bored. These are rather numerous in Ireland and Cornwall, and exist in many parts of the world. Such a stone may form part of a larger monument, a cromlech, or the like.

Menhir. A single stone set upright.

Ortholith. A single row of large stones.

Parallelith. Two rows of stones forming an avenue and, therefore, arranged nearly parallel one with another. It is rare to find more rows than two.

Peristalith. An arrangement of large stones around the outside of a mound and, therefore, if the mound is nearly circular, forming a kind of ring. The term is suggested by Peristyle and conveys the idea of columns around a sekos.

PLATE XXVIII

MEMORIAL ARCH.   PLATE I

That at Benevento in Campania, dedicated by the Senate and the People to Trajan, and covered with sculpture representing scenes in his life.   The arch is built of marble, and as it now stands is about fifty feet high, — a dimension interesting to note as illustrating the small scale and consequently moderate cost of these grandiose and effective monuments.

Trilithon. A group of three stones of monumental character. The monument of Stonehenge, as it is known to moderns, is composed mainly of trilithons. The Cairn and the Cistvaen or Kistvaen are sometimes included, but are not necessarily megalithic.

The study of megalithic monuments passes insensibly into that of other buildings of unknown date; thus the Kistvaen and the Cromlech were frequently the cores or central chambers of earth mounds.

J. B. Waring, *Stone Monuments;* Fergusson, *Rude Stone Monuments.*

— R. S.

MEGARON. In Greek archæology, the largest hall of an ancient residence such as the fortress palaces of Tiryns and Mycenæ. It is considered as equivalent to the Andron; the women's apartment being naturally smaller and more retired, while the megaron served for the assembly of soldiers and servants as well as the residents.

MEGHELEN, ROMBOUT; architect.
He built the castle of Vredenburg at Utrecht, Holland, for the Emperor Charles V., in 1528.

Kramm, *Hollandsche Kunstenaars.*

MEHRAB. Same as Mihrab.

MEIDAN. In some Moslem countries, as Persia, a Bazaar; especially, the large open square surrounded by shops, etc.

MEINHARDT, JOHANN GREGOR; architect and engineer; d. 1687.
Meinhardt was a Hollander who was made architect of the Electoral Court of Berlin, in 1650. He remodelled the city of Berlin and laid out the streets called *Unter den Linden* and the *Dorotheenstadt.* He began the *Schloss Oranienburg* (New Berlin) in 1651.

Gurlitt, *Barockstil in Deutschland.*

MEISSONIER, JUST-AURÈLE; jeweller, painter, sculptor, architect, and decorator; b. 1693 (at Turin); d. 1750 (in Paris).
From Louis XV. he received the title *dessinateur du cabinet et orfèvre du roi.* Meissonier built the tomb of Jean Victor de Besenval in the church of S. Sulpice (Paris). He designed the decorations of the many *fêtes* for the court. Many of the decorative plates engraved by him and preserved in the Bibliothèque Nationale and Bibliothèque de l'Arsenal (Paris) have been reproduced in a single volume, *Recueil des Œuvres de J. A. Meissonier* (1 vol. 4to, Paris, 1888.)

Guilmard, *Les Maîtres Ornemenistes;* Larousse, *Dictionnaire.*

MELANO, FRA; architect (*operarius*).
Employed on the present cathedral of Siena. The earliest documents of this building date from 1259. Fra Melano was ordered to vault the space between the last columns and the rear wall of the church. In the contract of

Sept. 29, 1266, with Niccolò da Pisa (see Niccolò da Pisa) for the pulpit in the cathedral of Siena, Fra Melano appears as the agent of the cathedral authorities. Nov. 6, 1268,

MEGALITHIC MONUMENT AT CARNAC (MORBIHAN), FRANCE.
The cross is comparatively recent.

Niccolò gave him a receipt in full for money paid for the pulpit.

Norton, *Church Building in the Middle Ages;* Norton, *Urkunden des Doms von Siena;* Milanesi, *Documenti.*

MELDAHL, FERDINAND; architect; b. March 16, 1827 (at Copenhagen, Denmark).
He was associated with Schinkel (see Schinkel) in Berlin. In 1860 he was appointed inspector of buildings at Copenhagen, Denmark. About 1875 he undertook the completion of the royal church in Copenhagen, begun by Eigtved (see Eigtved), and continued by N. H. Jardin (see Jardin).

Weilbach, *Nyt Dansk Kunstnerlexicon.*

MEMBRETTO. In Italian, a subordinate member, as of a building; in English, same as Alette. — (A. P. S.)

MEMORIAL ARCH. A building including one or more arched passages (see Arch, definition *A*), and erected as a commemorative monument. The memorial arch is a Roman creation; neither in form nor original purpose does it resemble the Greek propylæa. The term "triumphal arch," usually applied to this class of monuments, is misleading, as it correctly describes only a section within the class; there is no radical difference between the arches commemorating a triumph and those in honour of any peaceful event. There still remain, wholly or in part, over one hundred and fifty memorial arches scattered over nearly the entire Roman Empire — the Rhine province, Southern

Gaul, Spain, Italy, Greece and the islands, North Africa, Syria, and Asia Minor. Besides these there are records on coins, in inscriptions, and in literature of at least one hundred more, now destroyed or yet undiscovered.

These arches are not only the class of monuments best illustrating in unbroken historic sequence the six centuries of Roman architectural forms from the Gracchi to the fall of the empire, but they are also the best examples of the original manner in which the Romans married sculpture to architecture by developing that Roman specialty — the historic relief.

Memorial arches may be classified in two ways:

I. According to the persons erecting them.

II. According to the purpose of their erection.

I. *Classification by persons.*

(1) By private persons in honour of themselves, members of their family, or other private persons. Such works are rare because monumental arches did not become popular until the close of the Republic; and because, under the Empire, all facts to be commemorated were attributed to the emperor himself, as religious, political, and military chief, and private persons were allowed this glorification but seldom, and only after death and by authorization of the local magistrates. The arches of the Fabii (121 B.C.), of Stertinius (196 B.C.), of the Calpurnii, and of Scipio Africanus (190 B.C.), all in Rome, and that of Verres at Syracuse, were both personal and family memorials, as well as public monuments for the adornment of the city, during the time when private individuals were still allowed to erect arches to their own honour. But the arches of the Sergii at Pola, of the Julii at Saint-Remy, of the Campani at Aix-les-Bains, and of the Gavii at Verona, are works of the early Empire (Augustus to Trajan), and erected by private individuals as quasi-funerary memorials to deceased relatives. A number of other examples, now destroyed, are recorded in inscriptions; such as the arches of Rufinus (C. I. L.,[1] II, 3558) and of Bassus (C. I. L., III, 2922).

(2) By private persons as public monuments, or in honour of the emperor or some local official or benefactor. Such were, under the Republic, some of the "Janus" arches in Rome, Sinuessa, and other Roman colonies, especially in the forums; arches at the entrance of bridges (Pons Fabricius and Pons Æmilius), or of the city itself (Porta Carmentalis, Rome). Examples of the imperial period were the arch of Licinius Sura at Bara in Spain (107 A.D.), those of Donnius at Saint Chamas, and that of Sextilius (?) at Narbonne, both in France; and

[1] Corpus Inscriptionum Latinarum: the great collection of Latin Inscriptions, edited by Theodor Mommsen.

an enormous arch at Capara in Spain, all erected posthumously, by will (*ex testamento*), as public monuments. Many arches of this class are mentioned in inscriptions (C. I. L., II. 4282; VIII., 24, 98, 210, 937, 1309, 1310, 1320, add. 1478, 1858, 2372, etc.). An example of monuments erected to the memory of members of the imperial family is the double arch at Saintes, built by Rufus, priest of Rome and Augustus, under Nero, to the memory of Germanicus, Tiberius, and Drusus. An instance of an arch set up to an emperor by a private person is that of Aurelius Victor in Rome dedicated to Gallienus and his empress Solonina.

(3) By private associations or associated individuals. The silversmiths and other shopkeepers of the meat market in Rome (Forum Boarium) dedicated a flat "arch" to Septimius Severus, still standing. A group of private persons erected in 217, at Diana in Mauretania (now Lana, Algeria), an arch in honour of the accession of their compatriot, the Emperor Macrinus. Such arches were rare, as associations usually selected other kinds of honorary monuments, especially statues.

(4) By public officials as a record of their administrative acts. Such were the arches of Lentulus and Crispinus (2 A.D.) and of Dolabella and Silanus (10 A.D.), both in Rome and both connected with the city water supply.

(5) By public officials, or by a municipality or colony to the emperor. Sometimes this was done purely as a commemorative act, as in the case of the arch set up to Augustus by the municipality of Pisa in memory of the death of his grandsons, Caius and Lucius. But usually it was connected with important public works, like the building or rebuilding of the city walls, as by Marcus Aurelius, at Thasos. Such are the gates and arches at Nîmes and Vienne by Augustus, at Verona by Gallienus, at Grenoble by Diocletian and Maximianus, at Constantinople by Theodosius, at Thamugadi (Timgad in Algeria) by Trajan, and many other cities, especially in North Africa and Syria. Often the cost of the arch was borne by a single private individual or official: *e.g.*, by Sextilius Celsus in the arch to Antoninus Pius at Tuccaber (Tunisia); by Creperius Felicissimus in that to Gratian, Valentinian, and Theodosius at Gardimau near Carthage. In some cases the arch was dedicated by an individual official, but built probably from public funds; such was the tetrastyle arch to the Emperors Diocletian, Constans, and Maximian in Lesbos by Gennadius, governor of the island. In all imperial provinces, as distinguished from senatorial provinces, it was the duty of the officials governing in the emperor's name to provide for the erection and dedication of such public monuments. In Italy and the other senatorial provinces this devolved upon the Senate, except

in cases when it was undertaken by the colony or municipality itself. An interesting exceptional case is the arch at Susa, on the northern frontier of Italy, erected in honour of Augustus by the most prominent local chieftain turned into a Roman prefect, — M. Julius Cottius, — to celebrate the submission of the Alpine tribes. Sometimes a number of municipalities, colonies,

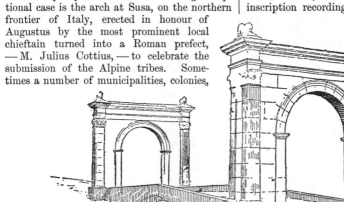

ceding class. Thamugadi, for example, in North Africa, had on its north gateway an inscription recording the founding of this col-

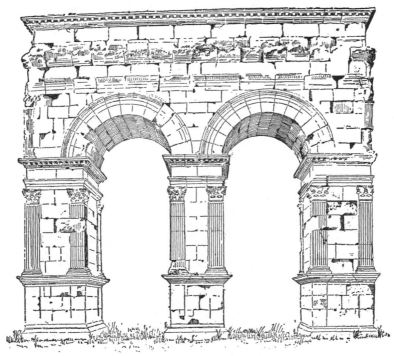

BRIDGE WITH MEMORIAL ARCHES AT SAINT-CHAMAS (BOUCHES DU RHÔNE), FRANCE.

or subject tribes clubbed together to build a monument; such was the bridge and arch of Trajan at Alcantara in Spain from the contribu-

ony by Trajan, in honour of his sister Marciana, by the hands of the Third Legion "Augusta," under the direction of the legate, L. Munatius

MEMORIAL ARCH AT SAINTES (CHARENTE INFÉRIEURE), FRANCE.
It has been removed piece by piece and rebuilt.

tions of about twenty "municipia" of Lusitania.
(6) By the army to the emperor. It is not always easy to distinguish this from the pre-

Gallus. It was rededicated to Antoninus Pius on its completion by L. Novius Crispinus, "patron" of the colony.

(7) By the Senate to members of the imperial family and others. As only the emperor was allowed arches during his lifetime, those in honour of generals were dedicated to the emperor: so also those to members of the imperial family, like those to Tiberius and Germanicus in Pannonia. Only the emperor's name appeared. But after death memorial arches could be and were dedicated by the Senate and emperor in honour of members of the imperial family. Such were the posthumous arches of Drusus and Germanicus placed by Tiberius on either side of the temple of Mars in the Forum of Augustus in Rome, the arch of Drusus at Moguntiacum in Germany, and those of Germanicus on the Rhine and in Syria (Mt. Amanus).

(8) By the Senate to the emperors. Beginning in the time of Augustus it was the privilege of the Senate to vote and erect honorary and triumphal monuments, not only in Rome itself, but throughout the provinces called senatorial, because they were under the direct civil jurisdiction of the Senate and not of the military rule of the emperor. We have seen that this was sometimes done even in these provinces by the local magistrates of the colony or municipality, but more often by the Senate. Hence the dedicatory formula, S P Q R, is widely found on memorial arches, and on the most important of them. The still existing great arches of Titus, Septimius Severus, and Constantine at Rome, and of Trajan at Benevento and Ancona, belong to this class. So did others of which fragments still remain; such as the arches of Claudius, of Drusus, of Marcus Aurelius, of Trajan, of Augustus, of Gordian III., and of Tiberius, all in Rome. The great majority were set up during the emperor's lifetime, but occasionally they were posthumous honours. Thus Claudius built in 41 A.D., in honour of Tiberius, an arch that had been voted him by the Senate during his lifetime, but never set up; also another arch to Drusus for his German victories. The arch of Titus was built under his brother and successor, Domitian. That to Septimius Severus († 211) at Theveste dates from 214.

(9) By the emperor. Not many arches could be technically said to be erected by the emperors, because, with rare exceptions, they were due to the decrees of the Senate or of local authorities, even when erected by the wish of, sometimes also at the expense of, the emperors. Apparently, one of these rare exceptions was an arch in honour of his favourite, which the sorrowing Hadrian built at Antinoë in Egypt, near where Antinous was drowned. Probably, also, it was the Emperor Vespasian himself, by the hands of his son Titus, who dedicated at Antioch the "Gate of the Cherubim," an arch on which he placed the bronze Cherubim from the temple at Jerusalem which he had just captured. Augustus, also, dedicated to his great-uncle Julius Cæsar an arch on the Palatine.

II. *Classification by purpose.*

(1) Commemorating military victories. Under Augustus there were arches: at Philippi for the victory over the republicans; at Merida and Tarragona for his conquests in Spain; at Rome for the defeat of Sextus Pompey; at Brundisium and Rome for Antony's defeat at Actium; at Susa for the submission of Alpine tribes; at Rome for Drusus's victories in Germany; and, also at Rome, for the recovery of the Roman standards from the Parthians.

Arches commemorated under Tiberius (Rome) the recovery of the standards of Varus from the Germans, and the victories of Germanicus; under Claudius the conquest of Britain; under Nero the victories of Corbulo over the Parthians; under Titus the conquest of the Jews; under Domitian, victories in the north of Europe; under Trajan the exploits in Dacia and the East; under Marcus Aurelius the conquests in Germany; and under Septimius Severus, the victorious campaigns in the East.

(2) Commemorating peaceful public events. Such events usually are: (*a*) the building of military roads with their bridges (Rimini, Benevento, Alcantara, Rome for Via Flaminia and Via Appia); (*b*) the building of city walls (Verona, Fano, Perugia, Nîmes, Vienne, Grenoble, Rome); (*c*) the opening or enlarging of ports (Ancona, Portus); (*d*) the erection of bridges (Rome for Fabrician and Æmilian bridges, Martorell and Alcantara in Spain, Saint-Chamas and Saintes in France, Antioch and Pyramus in the East); (*e*) the construction of aqueducts (Rome for Aquæ Julia, Marcia, Claudia, etc.; (*f*) the building of groups of monuments within a city, such as a quarter of Athens by Hadrian.

(3) Commemorating the entire life of an emperor; both peaceful and warlike events. For example, the arches of Titus in Rome and Trajan at Benevento.

(4) Commemorating the life of a private individual, as in the cases enumerated under I. 1; also, arch of Antinous (see I. 9), and probably the arches of Cavaillon and Vienne.

(5) As purely decorative monuments. Such were the arches at the entrances to forums (Rome, Forum of Trajan; Pompeii, Sidi-Amara); to temple enclosures or capitols (Damascus, Suffetula), to larger precincts (Olympia), as well as entrances to special buildings such as circuses (Circus Maximus and Circus Flaminius, Rome). Such were also the four-sided " Janus " arches at the intersection of the main streets (Latakia, Philippopolis, Gerasa, Lesbos, Tripolis, Theveste, Laodicea, Celenderis), and other arches standing free in squares and forums.

PLATE XXIX

MEMORIAL ARCH.   PLATE II

That built by Napoleon I. to the east of and very near the palace of the Tuileries.   The view shows the eastern front, and as the Tuileries have disappeared, the *Champs Elysées* are seen beyond.   The architects were Charles Percier and Pierre Fontaine ; the sculpture is by many different artists, the quadriga on top by François Bosio.   The design is closely studied from the Arch of Severus at Rome.

The inscriptions on the memorial arches are among the most monumental and perfect of all Latin inscriptions. These vary from extreme brevity to inflated pomposity. In the senatorial arches it was customary, as in the above, to give the imperial genealogy, followed by the imperial titles up to date, and finally, the special occasion for the erection of the arch.

occasions, would seem to be disproved by the fact that the earliest memorial arches (*e.g.* those of Stertinius and Scipio Africanus) were not connected with triumphs in any way.

Position. The position of the free-standing memorial — especially the triumphal — arches can best be studied in Rome because there they originated, were most numerous, and were

MEMORIAL ARCH IN THE FORUM, ROME, DEDICATED TO SEPTIMIUS SEVERUS.

Origin. Not a single arch is known to have been erected to do honour to the procession of the triumph it commemorated, and this counts against the common theory of their origin; nor is there anything to support the theory that the earliest monumental arches were permanent reproductions of temporary arches erected for the procession. The theory that the free-standing memorial arch was a reproduction of the city gates as they were temporarily decorated with inscriptions and trophies on triumphal

originally connected with the triumphal processions. We find that the triumphal arches were all placed at intervals along the road leading from the starting-point of the triumphal procession (outside the city, on the edge of the Campus Martius) to its goal, the temple of Jupiter on the Capitol. They spanned this road at every available point, being especially numerous in the Forum. During the later Empire they overflowed beyond the starting-point of the procession toward the Tiber.

Arches not of a triumphal nature were scattered elsewhere : those commemorating the building of roads were outside the city at the beginning of these roads or on bridges ; those recording the construction of aqueducts were openings in the aqueducts themselves as they passed over some main roadway entering the city ; those relating to ports were at the entrance to the quays ; and those connected with the construction of the walls were one or more of the city gates themselves, or free archways near the gates.

Under Augustus nearly all the various types of memorial arches appear. With the use of marble in their construction and the introduction of marble sculpture in their decoration, the arches were changed from mere monumental bases for statuary to works of art in themselves, which gradually overshadowed in artistic importance the statuary they supported. In their general scheme the Roman architects adopted the formula of the Etrusco-Latin arch, as constructive form, framed by the Greek architrave (and sometimes the pediment), as decorative form. This gave to the single imperial arches the appearance of a bay of a theatre or amphitheatre. Sculpture was used on the body of the arch in two ways : either in the form of statuary set in niches, or of reliefs carved on the surface of the arch itself. The niches were used especially in family arches (e.g. Aix-les-Bains) and Janus arches (e.g. Rome), to contain busts or statues of the persons honoured, and in some cases such portrait statuary was erected in front of the faces of the arch where no niches were provided. But a number of early Empire public arches belong to the niche type : For example, Nero's arch on the Capitol (coin), with its colossal statue of Hercules in one of the niches ; and other arches where the niches even contain groups of statues. It must have soon become evident to the best artists that this type was clumsy and inharmonious, for the better type, with only reliefs sculptured over the surface of the structure, after its erection, soon prevailed. It was brought to perfection between Titus (79–81) and Trajan (97–117). During the century from Cæsar to Titus the reliefs had been somewhat erratically disposed. At Saint-Remy (Cæsar) a few figures in high-relief like statuary, set, without framework, against the lower arch wall ; at Susa (Augustus) a narrow frieze only ; at Orange (Tiberius) most of the reliefs in the attic. Already under Claudius (41 A.D.) it would appear that the idea of setting elaborate quadrangular reliefs framed by columns and mouldings had been adopted. His reliefs, on two planes, foreshadow those of the arch of Titus. The highest perfection in combining the two arts was reached in the arches of Trajan in Rome (in Forum of Trajan and out-

side Porta Capena, part of whose sculptures remain, embodied in Constantine's arch), and that at Benevento. Broadly, the arrangement was : in the attic large reliefs flanking the central inscriptions ; under the cornice, over the opening, a continuous narrow triumphal frieze ; in the spandrils allegorical figures of Victories, River Gods, Seasons, etc. ; on either side of the arch several rows of narrow, historical compositions, about life size ; under the arch a similar composition on each jamb.

The symmetrical use of sculpture survived, with loss of life and force, through the reigns of Hadrian and the Antonines (Rome—Marcus Aurelius) ; but the ensuing decadence reigns in the triple arch of Septimius Severus in the Roman Forum (203 A.D.). In it such small figures as were arrayed in narrow bands on the columns of Trajan and Marcus Aurelius were flung confusedly over the surface. However, only a small proportion of the arches were sculptured, and these wholly in Italy, Gaul, and Spain ; throughout the Orient — both Africa and Asia — sculpture appears to be unknown except for detached statues. The Oriental arches were erected in regions where no schools of Greek or Roman figure sculpture existed, and here the arches were the work either of the architect-engineers who accompanied the Roman army of occupation, and directed the building of so many cities throughout the East, or else by native architects trained in the Greco-Asiatic schools that flourished under the successors of Alexander. This Hellenistic art even got a foothold in the official art of Italy under the leadership of such men as Apollodorus of Damascus, in the time of Trajan ; this is shown, for example, by the introduction, at that time, of free instead of engaged columns on either side of the archways of some of the more important memorial arches — an innovation due to Greco-Oriental influence ; such were at Rome, the arches of Drusus, Septimius Severus, and Constantine, and at Timgad, the arch of Trajan.

Probably the latest in date of memorial or monumental free-standing arches is one spanning the road leading to the great memorial church of S. Simon Stylites in Syria (about 500 A.D.), recently demolished.

     — ARTHUR L. FROTHINGHAM, JR.

In modern times the use of the memorial arch as a separate structure begins with the seventeenth century. The Porte S. Martin and Porte S. Denis were built under Louis XIV, and the Porte de Paris at Lille at about the same time ; the Porte de Pérau about 1690. The Arco delle Pace at Milan was begun under Napoleon ; the Brandenburgherthor at Berlin was built at the close of the eighteenth century ; the Marble Arch in London was first built by George IV, but was moved in 1850 to the corner of Oxford Street and Park Lane : and the Green Park arch, which has also been removed from its original site, is now at the head of Constitution Hill, close to Hyde Park corner. The Siegesthor at Munich was begun about 1840, and finished ten years later. (For Napoleon's arches in Paris, see Arc de Triomphe.) In the United States there is a memorial arch in Brooklyn, N.Y., and one in Hartford, Conn., and the Washington Arch in New York, which has never been completed by the proposed sculpture.   — R. S.

MEMORIAL BRASS. A plate of yellow metal engraved with an effigy or more than one, and with names, dates, texts from Scripture, prayers, or the like, set as the decorative and significant part of a tomb, sometimes vertically, as in a wall, sometimes as part of a pavement. The engraved characters are usually filled with black or red pigment. This form of memorial was very common in the Middle Ages, and in England great numbers remain. Dress and armour are represented in detail in connection with the figures, which are generally life size, or nearly so.

MEMORIAL COLUMN. A structure having approximately the form of a column, with capital, shaft, and base complete, but having no heavy superstructure and erected independently as a memorial. When Solomon built the temple at Jerusalem he had Hiram cast two high (30 cubits) brass lotiform columns to be placed in front of the temple, and called them Iachin and Boaz. These columns were reproduced in the reconstructed temple. That this erecting of a pair of twin columns was a common custom throughout the ancient East, seems proved by recent excavated remains at Telloh and Niffer in Babylonia (3000–2200 B.C.), and records on coins and elsewhere of Phœnician temples.

Leaving the Orient, we find that few examples seem known earlier than the archaic Greek period. On black-figured (sixth century B.C.) and red-figured (fifth and fourth centuries) Greek vases are frequent representations of such columns, apparently 12 to 20 feet high, used as supports for sculptured figures of emblematic birds, sphinxes, heroes, personifications (*e.g.* Nike) or divinities (*e.g.* Hera). It was a favourite Ionic custom. A number of such Ionic columns, with capitals having more projecting volutes than if they were intended to support architraves, originally stood on the Athenian Acropolis, were thrown down by the Persian invaders, used as building material, and lately recovered. One of them bore a piece of sculpture signed by Archermos. These were ex-votos. This impersonal was often changed to a personal memorial during the Hellenistic age; *e.g.* the column with statue of Isocrates († 86 B.C.) in

MEMORIAL COLUMN, NEAR S. MARIA NOVELLA, FLORENCE.

The work of Giovanni Pisano ; erected 1308, in memory of a theological movement. The capital shows emblems of the four evangelists.

the enclosure of the Olympian Zeus, Athens. Of remaining columns there are but two groups of this period, both in North Syria, and both decorating great funeral mounds. At Kara-Kusch are three groups of three columns (about 25 feet high) around the edge of a royal tumulus 110 metres in diameter and 20 metres high, in which were buried three female members of the family of Mithridates, king of Commagene (about 100 B.C.). In each group the central column carried a funeral stele (derived from Attic type) and each flanking column a statue of protecting animal — lion, eagle, or bull. There is a similar mound at Sesönk, with three groups of columns at regular intervals around the circumference. They bear eagles and seated statues, descendants of the archaic Branchidæ statues. Here the columns are joined by a common plinth on which the sculptures rest. In both cases the columns are of simple debased Doric, not monoliths, but built up. Presumably contemporary are groups of two columns at both ends of a bridge in the same region, near Kiakhta, used as the Romans occasionally used memorial arches in similar positions. That the use of columns in connection with sepulchres was general in Syria, would appear from three monuments of later date in Central Syria. At Bechindelayah, over the tomb of Sosandros (134 A.D.), rises a square pillar with two niches at its summit containing statuettes of Sosandros and his wife. At Sermeda, over a tomb of 130 A.D., stand two high columns joined part way up by a plinth on which a statue once stood. At Khatura two similar columns, joined by a plinth at the top, are over the tomb of Emilius Reginus († 195 A.D.).

The Romans put the column to several uses as a separate unit, and it became very common with them as a support for offerings and memorials, usually small statues. The Forum of the republic was crowded with statue-bearing columns of distinguished office-holders and military leaders. The consul Minucius (439 B.C.) was so honoured for services in provisioning famished Rome. On coins this memorial appears as a lofty Ionic column with bossed (?) drums, supporting a statue of Minucius holding a sceptre and a sheaf of wheat. But the column soon became connected with warlike triumphs. In the Campus Martius the *columna bellica* marked where war was declared and the symbolic spear cast. Earliest to commemorate a land victory was the column of the consul C. Mænius (327 B.C.) in the Forum, for his triumph over the Latins. Duillius's great naval victory over the Carthaginians (260 B.C.) was celebrated by his statue on a column decorated with six bronze beaks of the enemies' ships; of which Rostral Column (which see, under Column) there is a reproduction in the

Capitol Museum. Thus arose a special class of "beaked columns" for naval victories; e.g. those of M. Fulvius and Æmilius Paulus (254 B.C.) and others of imperial times, such as that of Augustus at Philippi. Sometimes not merely the decoration but the entire column was of bronze — plain or gilt; such were the four cast by Augustus in memory of Actium from the prows of Antony's ships, the column in the Hippodrome at Constantinople, and the golden milestone in the Roman Forum.

Unusual uses of the memorial column are illustrated by the twin columns in the harbour of Brindisi and the two columns of Egyptian granite surmounted by gilt Victories on either side of the great altar of Rome and Augustus erected in 12 B.C. by Drusus at Lyons. Among famous columns of the empire were: (1) one to Julius Cæsar, in the Roman Forum, after his death; (2) one of Theban granite surmounted by a statue of Tiberius, in the centre of the Forum of Antioch, in gratitude for the magnificent public structures of this emperor (especially the double columnar street colonnades); (3) one of porphyry at Antioch, erected under Caligula as a talisman against earthquakes; (4) one of uncertain date at Ancyra; (5) one of red granite, with sculptured base, to Antoninus Pius by his sons in front of his temple in Rome; (6) one of Alexander Severus at Antinoë; (7) a Corinthian granite column to Diocletian ("Column of Pompey") in Alexandria; (8) of marble and porphyry, 120 feet high, to Constantine in the forum at Constantinople; (9) one of immense size with a statue of Valentinian erected to him at Antioch by his brother Valens. All these were crowned by statues; so also were a few recorded under the Byzantine emperors of the succeeding centuries: (10) that to Justinian in Constantinople for his famous equestrian statue; and (11) that to Phokas, in the Forum, the last memorial of Byzantine dominion in Rome.

The Hellenistic innovation of sculpturing the lower drums or basements of columns as in the temple of Artemis at Ephesus (see Columna Cælata) was sometimes used in Roman memorial shafts, as at Cussy and Mertens in France. The Cussy column has a square foundation from which rises an octagonal base with figures encircling it and a shaft whose surface is covered with low relief patterns.

The creation of a new type of gigantic sculptured memorial column seems due to the famous architect of Trajan, Apollodorus of Damascus. It was called *columna cochlis* from its spiral internal staircase (see Column of Trajan). This column was part of Trajan's Forum in Rome, and was dedicated to him by the Senate in 113 A.D., in recognition of his having cut down the ridge between the Quirinal and Capitoline hills, establishing adequate communication between two sections of the city. The pedestal is decorated with trophies of Dacian arms. The shaft is entirely covered with about twenty-five hundred figures in low relief in twenty-two turns of an ascending spiral of decreasing height (4 to 3 ft.). They illustrate chronologically the incidents of Trajan's two Dacian wars, and are the most important artistic contribution to the study of the Roman army. The figures are so small and the relief so low as not to interfere with the outline of the column. Originally the reliefs were made bright by polychromy, traces of which were discovered by Semper in 1833.

An imitation of this masterpiece was erected in honour of Marcus Aurelius († 180 A.D.) in honour of his triumphs over Quadi and Marcomanni (see Column of Marcus Aurelius). This column has 20 spiral bands of reliefs; the greater size of the figures and increased relief diminish its apparent height, and their style shows the evident decadence of art. Both columns were surmounted by colossal gilt bronze statues of the emperors. They were called *columnæ centenariæ* from their height (100 Roman feet).

It was the aim of the Christian emperors to make Constantinople — the new Rome — as exact a duplicate as possible of the old Rome. So we find that there were there also two imperial columns of exactly the same type, erected to Theodosius and Arcadius. The column of Theodosius was erected in 386 A.D. and fell to the ground early in the sixteenth century, part of its spiral reliefs having previously been copied by Gentile Bellini. Its pedestal still remains, with elaborate figured compositions in relief unique as illustrating the decadence of sculpture. The column of Arcadius dates from 403 A.D. and was not destroyed by the Turks until 1720, when on the point of falling. It had thirteen spiral rows of reliefs and rested on a postament with four bands of reliefs. These were all drawn for the French ambassador in Constantinople about 1700. The subjects of the reliefs were apparently the victories of Theodosius and Arcadius over the Eastern Goths. There are also indications (Du Cange's drawing, 1680) of a third and smaller triumphal column with spiral reliefs in Constantinople.

The peculiar habits of the Stylite monks of living on the tops of columns led to special sanctity being attached to some of the columns after its hermit's death. This was especially the case with that of S. Simeon Stylites, around whose column in Central Syria, at Kal'at Seman, a memorial church of great magnificence was built (sixth century).

The use of the column as a memorial continued only where classic tradition survived. It died out in the Mohammedan East and was not adopted by the Germanic races. The best examples of the imitation of the columns of Trajan and Marcus Aurelius by mediaeval art are : (1) the bronze column with bands of reliefs erected about 1000 A.D. by Bishop Bernward in Hildesheim, after his return from Rome ; and (2) the marble column with similar reliefs set up in the fourteenth century in the cathedral square of Gaeta. A simple memorial shaft of the thirteenth century stands in a square of Piperno, resting on four animals ; another interesting early column is S. Ambrogio, Milan. A good Renaissance example is the column erected near Ravenna to commemorate the heroic Gaston de Foix, who died at the battle of Ravenna in 1512, leading the French against the Spaniards.

— A. L. FROTHINGHAM, JR.

MEMORIAL SLAB. A monument of a very simple kind, consisting of a slab of granite, marble, or the like, usually set against or built into a wall, and bearing an inscription, or, as is frequently the case, carrying a secondary slab or thin plate of metal upon which the inscription is engraved. Such slabs, costing but little and occupying but little space, are in modern times the most common memorials other than those erected immediately over graves.

MEMORIAL WINDOW. One which is so treated as to be a monument to a person, a number of persons, or a cause. Especially, a window of which the decorative glass is so treated as to furnish an inscription, a symbolical picture, or a decorative distribution of emblems and attributes.

MENAGERIE. A building or buildings for the safe keeping and exhibition of wild animals.

MENHIR. A stone monument of prehistoric or uncertain time, consisting of a single unhewn stone of great size set upright.

MENSA. The upper surface of an altar ; the stone slab or other piece forming the top of an altar.

MEO (BARTOLOMEO) DEL CAPRINO ; architect ; b. 1430 (at Settignano, Italy) ; d. 1501.

Although not mentioned by Vasari, Meo was undoubtedly one of the leading architects of his time in Italy. About 1462 he entered the service of Pius II. (Pope 1458–1464), and assisted in the construction of the loggia of the Benediction at the Vatican. He was employed by Paul II. (Pope 1464–1471), at the Vatican, and at the Palazzo di S. Marco, Rome. Meo built the cathedral of Turin, probably between 1471 and 1491.

Müntz, *Les arts à la cour des papes;* Müntz, *Renaissance;* Cittadella, *Notizie relative a Ferrara.*

MERCHANTS' HALL. *A.* A building or large room for the use of the merchants of a town, as in the great halls of the Middle Ages. (See Cloth Hall ; Town Hall ; also Exchange.)

B. In modern times, a building especially arranged for the sale of merchandise. Of these, the market house is much the most common form, but this would rarely be called a merchants' hall. In certain parts of Europe, however, a large building (as the *Halles* in a French town) is often a market in the usual sense, that is, a market for provisions, and also a bazaar for the sale of many kinds of goods.

MERLON. One of the higher portions of a battlement. (See Battlement; Castellate; Crenel.)

MERVEILLE, LA. At Mont Saint-Michel, on the coast of Normandy, an extraordinary structure of the Gothic epoch (finished about 1260), containing halls, cloisters, and chapels built of granite, and of an extremely elegant and graceful style. (See France, Part III.)

Corroyer, *Description de l'abbaye du Mont Saint-Michel.*

MESA DWELLING. A house built on the summit of a mesa, or tableland. The best modern examples are the dwellings of the Moki, in Arizona, and the Acoma, in New Mexico. Their construction is that of all Pueblo architecture. (See Communal Dwelling; Kiva; Pueblo.)

— F. S. D.

MESHREBEEYEH. In Moslem architecture, a latticed or grated window through which the air may draw freely while the inmates are concealed from view. The term is generally applied to members like bay windows or oriels of no great projection, which are supported on corbels or brackets along the walls facing the streets of Cairo and other towns of the Levant. These projecting windows are of all sizes, from a small polygonal cage hardly larger than a bird cage, to an oriel window with 2 feet projection and 8 or 10 feet of width in front; but they seldom reach the floor of the apartment, the floor of the bay window itself serving as a seat. The small cagelike projection is especially intended for the water bottle of porous clay, in which the water is cooled by evaporation, and this may project from the front of the larger bay window, or even from its sides. There is one instance in Cairo of a larger projecting window, having four of these polygonal cages projecting from its front and sides.

MESON. An inn; tavern; a rude sort of Mexican hotel. It is often unfurnished, with nothing more in the shape of a bedstead than a raised platform of clay or mud for the traveller to spread his own bed or blankets upon.

— F. S. D.

MESOPOTAMIA, ARCHITECTURE OF. That of the great plain between the rivers Tigris and Euphrates, which was the seat of a civilization perhaps as ancient as that of Egypt. The countries in which developed these two most ancient civilizations are in many respects strikingly similar. Both Egypt and Mesopo-

tamia are situated in the midst of deserts, and are, as it were, oases formed by the great rivers that run through them. In Egypt the cultivable area is a narrow ribbon following the Nile itself, which is without tributaries, and until the delta is reached is bordered by mountain ranges that form on either hand ramparts against the desert, and at the same time furnish excellent building stone in abundance. In Mesopotamia the fertile country is a broad plain between and about the Tigris and Euphrates and their many affluent streams. In both cases the civilization began at the mouth, on the rich alluvial delta, and ascended gradually toward the source.

The southern portion of the Mesopotamian plain, the alluvial portion, is absolutely level, its boundless horizon broken only by artificial mounds. It is without rocks, and even in ancient days, when the periodic floods were regulated by dykes and canals, and when the fertility was increased by a thorough system of irrigation, it bore but few trees except the palm. This is Chaldæa. Its principal cities in the earliest times were Ur (the Ur of the Chaldees of Scripture) and Larsam, and later the more northerly Babylon.

The northern portion of the country is gently undulating, mountains forming generally the northern and eastern boundary. This region is Assyria, whose capital in earliest times was Assur, and later Nineveh.

During all ancient history these two great divisions of the country were occupied by different and opposing, but related, nationalities, now independent, now one, and then the other, dominating its neighbour.

In the farthest period to which history has thus far with any certainty been able to penetrate we find Chaldæa, already civilized, in subjection to the less civilized Elamites, whose country lay to the eastward beyond the Tigris, and whose civilization seems to have been borrowed from that of Chaldæa. The earliest date that can be fixed even approximately is that of the conquest of Babylonia by the Elamites. It is variously given as 2280 and 2295 B.C. and the names of a number of Chaldæan monarchs have been found who belong to the period before the Elamite conquest, back to Sargon, about 3800 B.C., and there is reason to think that some Chaldæan remains may date back even to 5000 B.C., while many are of the pre-Elamite period. The earliest of these monarchs appears to be the king whose name is given as Ourcham. The supremacy of Elam or Susiana seems to have lasted about two hundred years. Then follows the first Chaldæan empire. This empire at its height included the whole of Mesopotamia, the Assyrian kings reigning as subjects of the Chaldæans. In the sixteenth century before Christ it was conquered by the Theban Pharaohs of

Egypt, and Chaldæan princes reigned at Babylon as vassals of the Thothmes and Ramses. It was at this period, especially, that the influence of Egyptian art was felt in Chaldæa, the evidences of which are so clearly to be seen in the later Assyrian art, and it was at this period also, in all probability, that the conquerors carried back into Egypt the Eastern — the Chaldæan — method of vaulting, which is to be seen in the stone chambers of the Ramesseum at Thebes, as well as in the drains of the palaces of the Assyrians, who doubtless inherited the method from the earlier Chaldæan art.

During this Egyptian ascendency Assyria had opportunity to develop and gather strength, freed, as it was, from the Chaldæan domination. It is at this time that Nineveh first comes into prominence; the Egyptians were gradually expelled, and by the fourteenth century the subjection of Chaldæa to Assyria seems complete. This is the period of the First Assyrian Empire. The Chaldæan kings at Babylon now build only as satraps of the Assyrian monarchs at Assur and Nineveh, the most important of whom were Shalmaneser I., who reigned about 1330, and founded Calah (the modern Nimrud), and Tiglath-Pileser I., one of the most warlike of these rulers (1120–1100 B.C.). Between 1060 and 1020 the Babylonian kings regained the ascendency, and put an end to the First Assyrian Empire. But after this brief half century of Chaldæan rule the vigorous race of Assyrian warrior kings established what has been called the Second Assyrian Empire, and made wide conquests. The most important of this great line of kings were Assurnazirpal (884–860 B.C.) and his son, Shalmaneser II. (860–824), Tiglath-Pileser III. (745–727), the conqueror of Egypt; and then follows the great Sargonide dynasty, beginning with King Sargon (722–705 B.C.), who conquered Samaria and defeated the Egyptians. His son Sennacherib follows (705–681). Essarhaddon (680–668 B.C.), who was ruler also over Upper and Lower Egypt and Ethiopia, marks the height of Assyrian power. The great grandson of Sargon is Assurbanipal (668–626), the last of the Sargonide kings. In his reign the downfall of Assyria begins. In the reigns of subsequent monarchs Scythian invaders were increasingly successful, the outlying vassal kingdoms fell away, and finally the combined attack of the Medes and Persians, under Cyaxares, and of the rebellious Babylonians, under Nabopalassar, resulted in 608 B.C.[1] in the taking of

[1] This date is sometimes given as 625 B.C., with corresponding changes in the dates previously quoted.

Nineveh, which was utterly destroyed, and the Assyrian kingdom, which was held together only by military prowess, fell to pieces immediately.

Upon the fall of Nineveh, the Babylonians in the south established what is generally

MESOPOTAMIA: PLAN OF THE PALACE OF SARGON.

referred to as the second Chaldæan or Neo-Babylonian Empire. Nebuchadnezzar (605–562 B.C.), the son of Nabopalassar, reconstructed and restored Babylon, and most of its present remains date from this comparatively late epoch. He was the conqueror of Judea and Phœnicia, and carried his arms into Egypt. Under the joint reign of his son Nabonidus and his grandson Belshazzar, Babylon was taken by the Persians under Cyrus in 536 B.C., and after this time Babylon gradually fell into ruin. Its walls were dismantled by Darius Hystaspes and its temples pillaged by Xerxes. In the time of Alexander the Great it was already in ruin, and the use of its materials in the construction of Seleucia, founded by Alexander's general, Seleucus Nicator, completed its destruction.

Chaldæan or Babylonian Architecture. In such a region as this we cannot expect to find an architecture in any way resembling that of the great monuments of Egypt, which was that of a post and lintel construction, an architecture of large material depending for its development on the use of stone. The absence of stone in Chaldæa forced the builders to the development of brick construction. So that we have here an architecture of small material depending for its development on the use of brick. Not only was sun-dried brick used, as in minor constructions in Egypt, the clay being generally mixed with straw, but in a very early age the Chaldæans discovered the art of making burnt bricks, which were cemented together with wet clay, lime mortar, or bitumen. As these bricks were frequently stamped with the name of the reigning monarch, the age of the ruins is in these cases not difficult to determine, since the writing in cuneiform character has been deciphered by Professor Grotefend, General Rawlinson, M. Oppert, and others. All the more important Chaldæan buildings, the temples and the palaces of the kings, seem to have been erected upon artificial platforms consisting of a construction of sun-dried brick (or of dividing walls of sun-dried brick filled with earth) faced on the outside with burnt bricks. These platforms were necessary, or at any rate desirable, in order to raise the building out of reach of the periodic floods and above the malarious vapours, and also to catch whatever breezes passed over the hot plains. The desire to obtain an extended view for the palaces and make them more secure against attack may also have had its influence.

Of the architectural form of these buildings we know only what little can be gleaned from the descriptions of Greek writers, — especially Herodotus, — from the somewhat crude representations on bas-reliefs, and by analogy from the better-preserved Assyrian monuments. To this knowledge the present formless ruins in lower Chaldæa can add but little except as to methods of construction. The temples seem to have been vast stepped pyramids, rising sometimes to a height comparable to that of the great Egyptian pyramids, if not higher, with a shrine at the top. Great ramps led from stage to stage of these structures, *zigurats*, as they are called in the Assyrian inscriptions. According to Herodotus and Strabo, the tower of the great temple of Bel at Babylon, rebuilt by Nebuchadnezzar, was in eight stages and measured a stadion (about 200 yards) across each side at the base and was a stadion high. Each stage was of a different colour. These towers were built of crude bricks faced with burnt bricks.

A plan drawn on a tablet which rests in the lap of a statue found at Tello in lower Chaldæa shows a fortress with towers similar to those of Assyrian bas-reliefs. The comparatively meagre remains of ancient Chaldæan art point to its practical identity with that of Assyria, which was borrowed from it.

The palaces were erected on great platforms, and consisted of a congeries of apartments about courtyards.

All these structures, built as they were of crude brick, having a facing only of burnt brick, crumbled to pieces as soon as they ceased to be repaired. The excellent fired bricks were frequently removed to do duty in the structures of later generations, and the core of unburnt clay has thus been exposed to the deluge of rain which at certain times of the year occasionally breaks over the Chaldæan plain. In the course of centuries all these structures have thus been reduced to shapeless mounds of earth, which have all the outward appearance of natural hills, their sides furrowed by the action of the weather and clothed with vegetation. The Birs-Nimrud, one of those mounds on the site of Babylon, is 198 feet high, and still bears on its summit a compact mass of brick 28 feet thick and 37 feet high.

A tomb at Magheir (Ur) shows in its interior a corbelled vault, and the recent excavations conducted by the University of Pennsylvania have proved, what had long been suspected, that the arch was employed in the very earliest times. The same expedition has found columns and colonnades which it is claimed are of the Babylonian period, though this does not seem to be entirely proved. Babylonian architecture, however, used the column freely, but it was generally of wood. As for stone, it was as easy to transport precious diorite and basalt as cheaper materials, and these costly stones were used for statues in the round, but not, as far as we know, for the buildings. Painting and enamelled tiles of rich colour were freely used.

Assyrian Architecture. Since the excavations in Assyria, which were begun at Khorsabad in 1843 by M. Botta, the French consul at Mosul, and by Sir A. H. Layard in 1845 at Kouyunjik, many of the main features of Assyrian architecture and most of the details are thoroughly well known, while the great bas-reliefs now in the British Museum, which once adorned the palaces of Sennacherib, of Esarhaddon, and of Assurbanipal present the everyday details of Assyrian life, in war, in the chase, and in the construction of monuments, as familiarly and vividly as events of yesterday.

Although building in a more hilly country, the Assyrians still continued to raise their palaces upon platforms of earth or crude brick as did the Chaldæans; but they faced these mounds with retaining walls of massive cut stone easily obtained and brought down the Tigris from the neighbouring mountains.

Their temples seem to have been similar in character, though smaller in scale, to the Babylonian temples above described. A fragment of such a temple was found in the palace at Khorsabad, the colour on its different stages still visible when it was first uncovered. But their chief buildings were the palaces of the kings. Of these the palace of King Sargon at Khorsabad, unearthed by Botta and Place, is the most complete and typical example.

The city of Sargon, the ruins of whose circuit walls are yet standing, was a rectangle measuring 5775 by 5547 feet, its corners set to the cardinal points. The walls at the base are nearly 80 feet thick. Ruins exist of several of the city gates, which were defended by a series of courts partly in the thickness of the walls. In one case M. Place found the great arch or barrel vault of the entrance still standing, flanked by alabaster figures of colossal man-headed bulls which carried the vault. He discovered also beautiful enamelled tiles decorated with figures and rosettes which ornamented its face. At intervals the defences were strengthened by towers which, as we know from the bas-reliefs, rose higher than the walls, and like them were surmounted by the stepped crenelations which are a marked feature of Assyrian architecture and which constantly appear in its decoration. The lower 4 feet of the wall was built of stone, above that it was of crude brick.

The palace occupied a position near the centre of the northwest side of the city. Its huge platform, 60 feet high to the top of its 5-foot parapet and covering an area of about 1,048,360 square feet, projected partly beyond the wall and partly into the city. This platform was built of crude brick faced with a retaining wall of coursed stonework nearly 10 feet in thickness, the blocks measuring about 6 feet 8 inches in width and thickness and 9 feet long. Like the city walls the platform was defended by towers. The side toward the city was approached by a great flight of steps and by ramps. The palace itself had a frontage of nearly 1000 feet, and its apartments were ranged around a series of courts large and small, of which the largest measures 315 by 280 feet. Its great gates are similar to those of the city, flanked on either side by colossal man-headed bulls which undoubtedly once carried arches. There were discovered in this palace 31 courts and 198 chambers. The apartments are long and narrow, and the walls are from 5 to 15 feet in thickness. In the principal apartments these walls are faced with carved slabs of alabaster or limestone, representing in bas-relief the exploits of the king, the figures having been originally coloured. Above them the walls, whose

core is of crude brick, were faced with burnt brick covered with stucco and decorated with colour. The minor apartments were similarly decorated in colour throughout their whole height. In some cases the lower part of the wall was decorated with enamelled bricks. The method by which these buildings were roofed is still uncertain. Most English investigators and theorists have supposed wooden roofs carrying a mud concrete to form a terrace, or have followed

MESOPOTAMIA: CONJECTURAL RESTORATION (CHIPIEZ AFTER STRABO) OF A GREAT TEMPLE SUCH AS THAT CALLED "THE OBSERVATORY" AT KHORSABAD.

Fergusson in supposing a series of open colonnades with wooden pillars. But Place found evidence in the excavations of the existence of barrel-vaulted roofs, which would give the most rational explanation of the narrow apartments and the enormously thick walls. That the Assyrian builders were thoroughly familiar with the vault is clear from the city gates and the vaulted drains beneath the palaces. The bas-reliefs show clearly that some of the palaces had colonnades on the top of the roof-terraces, probably of wood ornamented and protected by metal. The columns in some of these bas-reliefs show the rudimentary beginnings of Ionic and Corinthian capitals. The courts and platforms were paved with stone, sometimes carved into elaborate patterns, especially in the doorways. Colour was everywhere lavishly used in the decorations, and it is clear that the bas-reliefs and statues were also coloured. The principal elements in the decoration were the rosette, the palmetto, and the lotus, many of the borders especially showing the influence of Egyptian decoration.

In spite of the arguments in favour of there

having been wooden roofs over the Assyrian palaces, and in spite of the difficulties, especially with regard to the lighting, which stand in the way of a full acceptance of the theories of MM. Place and Thomas, it must still be admitted that these theories afford on the whole the best explanation of the facts so far discovered. We shall not then be far wrong, perhaps, in picturing to ourselves the narrow apartments of the palaces as covered with barrel vaults and filled in above with sun-dried brick to form level terraces. Above these ter-

races were, in some cases, open porticoes, built mainly of wood with wooden columns, protected and ornamented by plates of metal, and with wooden roofs.

No evidences of windows have anywhere been found, and the light was probably admitted by larger or smaller openings in the vaults themselves, or perhaps, in some cases, by leaving one end of the barrel vault open. Large hollow tubes of earthenware were found by Place in the ruins, which tubes he supposed to have been inserted in the vaulting to admit light. The vaults of the drains were laid of flat bricks, the length of the brick at right angles to the axis of the vault and the narrowest dimension in the direction of that axis. The successive courses or layers of which the vault was composed were often slightly inclined, in order to increase the stability while in process of construction. Such vaults were afterward used throughout the East, and could be built entirely without wooden centring, the use of which in a country not rich in timber had to be avoided. If this method was employed in vaulting the apartments of these palaces, it becomes easier to explain the existence of the great vaults of similar construction in Persia; and we get a glimpse of a continuous history of vault construction in the East from the time of the Assyrian to the time of the Byzantine empire: a system of construction radically different from that employed in the West. — H. LANGFORD WARREN.

META. One of the posts or columns placed at the ends of the spina of a Roman circus (see Circus).

METAGENES; architect.

Associated with Chersiphron (see Chersiphron) in the construction of the first temple of Artemis at Ephesus.

Brunn, *Geschichte der Griechischen Künstler.*

METAL WORK. *A.* Work done by melting metal and moulding or casting it in forms which can then be more or less finished by hand, as with cutting tools and files.

B. Work done by hammering and beating into shape metal either hot or cold.

The decoration of metal by means of inlay of different kinds is reducible to one of the two systems above named, except where it is a result of engraving, as in damascened work; but such ornamentation as this hardly enters into architectural practice of any period. The soldering of small parts together is common in jewellery, but only in rare cases in connection with building (see Roofing). The use of wire concerns only Lathing and such simple Railing as is used temporarily or in slight structures. Engraving upon metal is used in what is known as the Memorial Brass (which see), and the engraved lines were filled with some coloured material. Enamelling is used upon tombs, but chiefly in details of heraldry or of the costume of portrait statues.

The ornamental metal work of architecture proper is generally confined to bronze, which comes under definition *A*, and wrought iron, which comes under definition *B*. These will be treated below. Cast-iron is hardly to be recognized as of decorative value. (For structures of iron, their history and theory, see Iron Construction.)

Bronze. An alloy of copper and tin usually in the proportions of about nine parts of copper to one of tin; but the proportions vary, and the metal may still be called

METAL WORK: WROUGHT-IRON TENSION-ROD AND HINGE FROM GATE; ORVIETO CATHEDRAL.

structure; second, by the use, especially in modern times, of builders' hardware made of bronze instead of iron, brass, or other metal. (See Builders' Hardware.)

Wrought Iron. This is of peculiar importance, beyond that of any other hammered metal work, because partly of the abundance and the hardness of iron, but more especially on account of its power of being welded and forged. The whole system of ornamental wrought-iron work, by which the buildings of the Middle Ages of the Renaissance were made beautiful throughout Europe, depends upon this property, possessed by iron alone among metals, of adhering firmly one part to another

METAL WORK: WROUGHT-IRON HINGES AND LOCKS, 13TH CENTURY; ARMOIRE IN CATHEDRAL OF BAYEUX, NORMANDY.

bronze if some little lead or some little zinc enters into it. The term is used also, in combination, to give names to many modern alloys in which some other metal takes the place of tin. (See below.) The analysis of ancient and Oriental bronzes has given some surprising results, showing a much larger proportion of tin; and bell metal, coin metal, and the like, often contain the different ingredients in very different proportions.

In architecture, bronze is used in two special ways: first, by the addition to buildings of bronze bas-reliefs or inscribed statues or busts which are not intimately connected with the

when these are first heated to a certain temperature and are then hammered together. Thus,

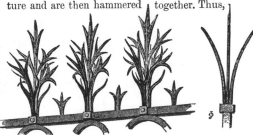

METAL WORK: SHEET- AND WROUGHT-IRON; CREST OF METAL RAILING, VERONA.

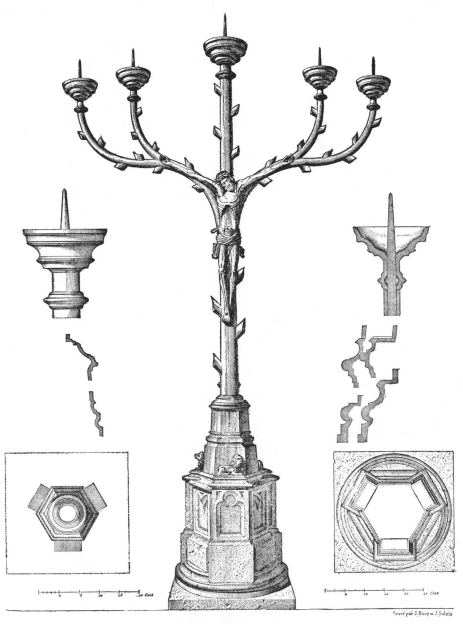

Gravé par J. Bury et J. Sulpis

METAL WORK: CANDELABRUM IN THE CHURCH OF S. CUNIBERT, COLOGNE.

METAL WORK: BRONZE ALTAR IN THE CATHEDRAL, BRUNSWICK.

when a hinge of wrought iron is to be made for a church door with deliberate decorative purpose, it is easy to terminate each strap by a series of branches, partly by cutting the strap iron itself and bending one sprig or branch away from

METAL WORK: MODERN; CAST AND MACHINE-WROUGHT: GRENELLE MARKET, PARIS. (SEE COL. 890.)

the others, and partly by forging other slender bars and the like, which can be welded to the original stem. The difficulty with such ironwork is, however, its extreme liability to rust and the consequent necessity of doing something to protect the surface. (See what is said of the painting of iron under Iron Construction.) It is in

this connection that gilding has become so common in the case of ironwork. Magnificent grilles of the eighteenth century and other modern imitations of equal refinement and elaboration, if of less original beauty, are commonly gilded in great part, and this extensive gilding often injures greatly their general effect. (Cuts, cols. 889, 890; 891, 892; 893, 894.) — R. S.

MÉTEZEAU, CLÉMENT (I.); architect; b. about 1479; d. about 1545.

He was master mason at Dreux (Eure-et-Loire), France, and founded a famous family of French architects and literary men. In 1514, with Jean des Moulins, he continued the construction of the Hôtel de Ville at Dreux, begun by Pierre Caron in 1512.

Genealogy of the architects of the Métezeau family: —

Clément (I.).
Jean.   Thibaut.
Louis.   Clément (II.).

Berty, *Les Grands architectes français.*

MÉTEZEAU, CLÉMENT (II.); architect; b. Feb. 6, 1581; d. 1652.

He was a son of Thibaut Métezeau, and grandson of Clément (I.). He enjoyed the protection of Marie de' Medici, queen of Henry IV. of France, and was associated with Salomon de Brosse (see Brosse) in the construction of the palace of the Luxembourg, Paris. In 1624 he had already become architect to Louis XIII. His name is especially associated with the great dike which was built across the harbour of La Rochelle, Charente-Inférieure, France, to secure the reduction of that city, besieged by Louis XIII. The dike was designed by Métezeau in association with Jean Thériot, an engineer, and built by Jean Thériot.

Berty, *Les Grands architectes français;* D'Argenville, *Vie des fameux architectes;* Bauchal, *Dictionnaire.*

MÉTEZEAU, LOUIS; architect; b. about 1559; d. Aug. 18, 1615. Louis was probably a son of Thibaut Métezeau, and grandson of Clément (I.). In an entry of the register of the city of Dreux (Eure-et-Loire), France, he appears as *architecte du roi et contrôleur des bâtiments royaux,* and in a receipt for marbles dated March 23, 1609, he describes himself as *concièrge et garde des meubles du palais des Thuillerys de sa Magesté.* Louis Métezeau was employed in the construction of the Petite and Grande Galeries at the Louvre.

Berty, *Les Grands architectes français;* Berty, *Topographie, Louvre et Tuileries.*

MÉTEZEAU, THIBAUT (THEOBALD); architect; b. Oct. 21, 1533; d. 1596.

Thibaut Métezeau was a younger son of Clément (I.) Métezeau. He seems to have lived and worked at Dreux, France, until 1569, when he went to Paris. According to Brice (op. cit.) he was an associate architect or contractor on the Pont Neuf, begun 1578. He was architect of the Duc d'Alençon in 1576, and of the king, Henry III. In 1570 and 1582 he was employed on the chapel of the Valois at Saint-Denis. Sauval (op. cit.) attributes to him the Salle des Antiques at the Louvre, and Berty (*Les Grands architectes*) ascribes to him the earliest plans for the Grande Galerie du Louvre.

Berty, *Les Grands architectes français;* Berty, *Topographie, Louvre et Tuileries;* Palustre, *La Renaissance en France;* Bauchal, *Dictionnaire;* Brice, *Description de Paris;* Sauval, *Antiquités de la Ville de Paris.*

METOPE. In a Doric entablature, that part of the front which is interposed between two triglyphs. The term implies, etymologically, the space between the triglyphs, whether open or closed; but in architecture it is applied almost exclusively to the slab or block of stone which fills this space, and this because we have no Grecian monument in which metopes have been left open. That they were so in early times appears from several passages in Greek literature. The metopes, considered as blocks of marble, were made the medium for very elaborate sculpture and painted decoration, and that from an early time. The painted metopes have generally lost their decoration to such an extent that they are no longer easily understood.

As the metope was of necessity a nearly square tablet, without constructional utility, it became natural to use an elaborate kind of sculpture for its decoration. Thus, in the Parthenon, the very highest relief is used — relief so high that the heads and limbs are sometimes detached from the background. The theme, or artistic subject, of each metope is generally limited to its own small surface, and a certain monotony of treatment follows the constant repetition of bodies of centaurs and warriors in violent action, or, as on the east front of the Theseion, the labours of Hercules. — R. S.

METROON. A shrine or sanctuary of the Great Mother, or Mother of the Gods; called also Basileia, or Queen, a deity of whom little has been ascertained by modern scholars. Such a sanctuary existed in Athens, and is called by Pliny (*Nat. Hist.*, XXXVI., 17), *Matris magni delubrum.* There are votive wreaths dedicated to her, but there is confusion between the Great Mother and Rhea.

MEWS. In Great Britain, anciently a place arranged for keeping hawks, usually in the open air, the term being derived from the mewing (*i.e.* the moulting) of birds. In modern times, generally, a court, street, or yard upon which open stables, carriage houses, and the like, especially in a city. The mews may be public, the stables opening upon the courtyard or street

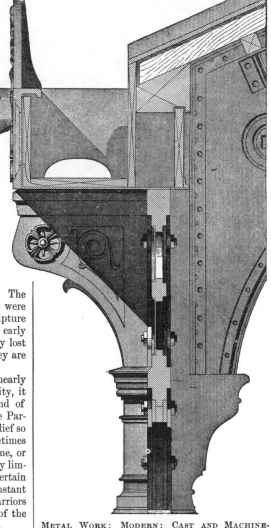

METAL WORK: MODERN; CAST AND MACHINE-WROUGHT; GRENELLE MARKET, PARIS. (SEE COL. 887.)

being occupied by different tenants, or the whole group of stables connected with a stately residence may be known by the same name. Thus, in London, the Royal Mews are south of Buckingham Palace.

MEXICAN ONYX. A travertine. (See Onyx Marble, under Marble.) — G. P. M.

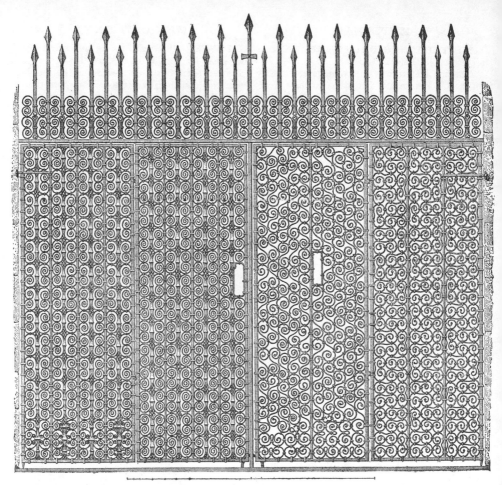

METAL WORK: WROUGHT-IRON SCREEN; CHURCH OF S. AVENTIN, FRANCE.

METAL WORK: WROUGHT-IRON GUARD FOR FANLIGHT; HOTEL, RUE S. PAUL, PARIS.

891   892

METAL WORK: APPARATUS OF WROUGHT AND PIERCED IRON, FOR RINGING A NUMBER
OF SMALL BELLS; 15TH CENTURY ABBEY CHURCH AT FULDA, GERMANY.

MEXICO, ARCHITECTURE OF. That of the Republic as it has existed since 1854.

§ **I. Precolumbian.** Within the borders of Mexico is contained almost the entire range of aboriginal American architecture. At one end of the scale are shelters of the rudest kind, and at the other the really impressive and extraordinary stone ruins of Yucatan. In the wide intervals are cliff-dwellings, houses of jacál, of pisé, of cajon, and of adobe bricks. The tendency of the Americans, discernible in the United States, to build on elevated ground and on artificial platforms and mounds, becomes more pronounced

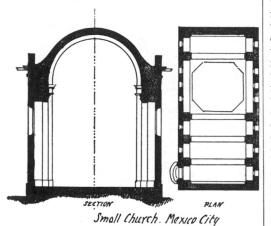

SECTION   PLAN

Small Church. Mexico City

MEXICO: FIG. 1.

toward the south, till in Yucatan and contiguous regions the majority of the important constructions are found on artificial substructures. In the extreme north are the great cajon houses, exemplified in the Casas Grandes ruins (though stone was also used there), and in the extreme south, the massive and more elaborate stone buildings like Uxmal, Mitla, and Palenque, while midway are remnants of the Aztec houses, which, in the day of their glory, gave such romantic colour to the Spanish conquest. In Yucatan, many buildings now in ruins were in the same condition when first seen by Europeans in the sixteenth century, while others were in possession of Maya Indians believed to have been their builders. In Central Mexico some of the ancient works have been ascribed to an uncertain race called Toltecs, whose existence is disputed by some authorities, but acknowledged by others equally good. By the latter they are said to have been a forerunner of the Aztecs. As there has undoubtedly been a succession of occupations of the different regions by various stocks, extending through a vast period of time, there is no reason for denying the existence of these Toltecs. They are described as a people of high intelligence and peaceful ways. There is nothing, however, to indicate that the

Toltecs, or any of the earlier stocks, were not members of the American race, like the latter, and distinct from other world races as known to-day. The art development alone seems sufficient to establish this isolation, for it is thoroughly American. Neither the sculptures, nor the architecture which they adorn, give any warrant for the endeavour, so often made, to find an origin for them in the Eastern Hemisphere. In their own way, ethnologically, archæologically, and artistically, they are of surpassing interest, exhibiting, as they do, one of the most extraordinary race developments in the world. The ages of the various ruin groups are still matters of doubt and discussion. Charnay holds them all to be quite modern, while others ascribe to some a great antiquity. It is not yet time to speak positively on this point. Goodman, from an inscription on the so-called Yucatec stone, obtains a date for it of 10,731 years from our time. But the strictly Aztec structures are fairly well established to have been comparatively modern. Tenochtitlan, their latest capital, which occupied the site of the present city of Mexico, is dated from 1325. Of its original buildings, which were of stone and adobe bricks, about two stories high, every trace has disappeared, the present buildings being entirely Spanish-Mexican. The common Aztec houses probably resembled, in their general features, more the buildings of the north than those of the south, the second story receding from the first in terrace form. They were speedily destroyed after the conquest. The florid descriptions of the conquerors make it difficult to arrive at a proper estimate of the character of the Aztec architecture. Morgan insisted that their buildings were no more than ordinary communal dwellings, such as still exist in New Mexico, while others maintain that they were palatial and luxurious. The truth is probably midway. The most important remaining structure of supposed Nahuatl erection is the temple of Xochicalco, not far southwest of Mexico City. The best preserved wall is 60 feet long and 13 feet high, the massive stones skilfully carved with representations of the feathered serpent, human figures, and other objects. Near this is another important ruin, the temple of Tepoztlan, a massive structure on a high cliff, containing an Aztec symbol corresponding to our year 1502.

According to Bandelier, some of the stone walls in New Mexico are fully as well laid as some he examined in ruins in the Aztec region. Proceeding southward from the old Aztec realm, the next important tribe of a different stock was the Tzapoteco, or Zapotec, about where the present state of Oaxaca lies, and where Zapotec Indians still live. This is a dry region with a sparse vegetation, and the remains are different from any others. The best known are the ruins of Mitla, in the state of Oaxaca,

PLATE XXX

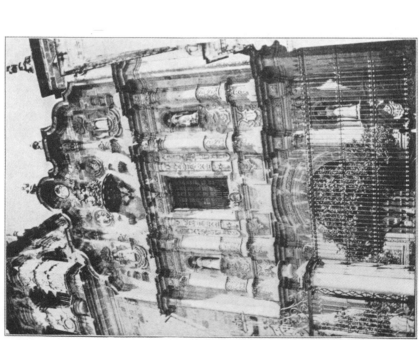

MEXICO.   ARCHITECTURE OF

The picture on the left is part of the front of a church at Guadalajara in northern Mexico ; that on the right is the front of the cathedral of Monterey. The three-storied bell tower in the second instance is well worthy of notice. The fantastic gable which in each case rises in front of and masks the actual roof of the nave is derived from sixteenth century Spanish work, a little less extravagant in taste but equally original, and forming a style quite apart from the architecture of northern Europe.

extensive stone structures with a mixture of adobe buildings, the former elaborately ornamented with geometrical designs. Human figures and animal forms, so abundant further southward, are absent. Saville, however, ascribes the Mitla structures, not to the Zapotecs, but to a tribe of Nahuatl stock; that is, allied to the Aztecs. The stone walls are 46 to 48 inches thick, and the adobe about the same. The former are of roughly broken stones laid in an abundance of adobe mortar, the outside being sheathed with slabs containing the ornamentation. Saville recently found in this district a new form of hieroglyph and also many mounds with sepulchral stone chambers containing elaborate terra cotta jars about 2½ feet high, modelled in human shape, and also some full-sized human figures in hollow earthenware, one being 150.9 centimeters in height, or about 5 feet. Recently, a remarkable cruciform tomb has been found by Saville, five miles from Mitla. It is composed of enormous blocks of stone brought from quarries about a mile distant. The entrance was never finished. The north, east, and south arms are exactly alike in dimensions, 11.7 feet long, 5.2 feet wide, and 7.5 feet deep. The entire length from the end of one arm to the other, inside, is 28.6 feet. The walls are decorated with the Mitla fret, carved in bas-relief, and there is no covering to them. The largest block of stone measures 12.5 feet by 3.3 by 3 feet wide. Eastward from here lie the celebrated ruins of extensive and elaborate buildings ascribed to the Mayas: Palenque, Uxmal, Copan, Mayapan, Chichen-Itza, Labna, Kabah, Menché, Aké, and others. The names, of course, are modern. These ruins are mainly of stone, but there are evidences of adobe buildings, and some mounds probably supported wooden structures. Lintels were of zapoté wood except when very short. The larger buildings were possibly devoted to religious and official purposes, though at present it is not safe to make a positive statement on this point. Many of them are stone-roofed, the rooms, generally very narrow, being vaulted in the corbel method, built over a core of masonry that was afterward removed. One building has been found where the core was still present, and Morgan assumed this a proof of recent construction; but it is clear that this is no indication of the time when the work was abandoned. Whether quicklime was used in the mortar of any of these buildings is not definitely settled. There were certainly cement and stucco which became very hard. ·In Yucatan, the peculiar earth called *zaccab* was used, but this was not found in the other regions, though the cement in the Aztec region appears the same as that in the Maya. Bandelier holds that the lime spoken of by the old chroniclers was pulverized carbonate. A chief principle pervading all the Yucatan buildings is the arrangement of three parallel walls with transverse walls forming two rows of rooms, the rear wall often being much thicker than any of the others. There are no windows, all light entering by the doorways. The masonry, of rudely squared blocks, was generally covered with a coating of stucco, which in turn was frequently coloured. Thick walls were of rubble, faced with the dressed stones. Many of the ornaments were of stucco, but others were carved in stone. Numerous examples of both are still in place. The human figure, the feathered serpent, and the hieroglyphs are the chief objects represented. Error has been created by the former reproduction of these sculptures in print through the medium of artists who, while faithfully reproducing their general forms, have often quite unintentionally, because of superior skill, disguised the crudity of the originals. To sum up, these sculptural and architectural remains, while rightfully challenging our admiration, are truly aboriginal, and their development appears

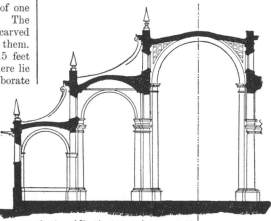

Section of Puebla Cathedral through Nave.

MEXICO: FIG. 2.

to have been entirely indigenous. (See Adobe; Cajon; Calli; Casa Grande; Casas Grandes; Central America; Communal Dwelling; Corbel Arch; Jacál; Mound; Pisé; Zahcab.)

Maudsley in *Biologia Centrali Americana;* Squier; Stephens; Bandelier; Viollet-le-Duc; Morgan; Saville; Charnay; Winsor's *Narrative History*, and others. The bibliography in H. H. Bancroft's *Native Races* furnishes a large number of references.
— F. S. DELLENBAUGH.

§ **II. Modern.** The architecture of Mexico has been developed in a dry, equable climate, necessitating protection from the sun rather than from cold or rain, by a race which mingles the polish and traditions of Europe with the barbaric taste of the Indian. Although stone serves for the best work, a native clay is most commonly used; as sun-dried brick it is known as adobe; it further serves when kiln-dried as terra cotta ornament, roofing tiles, brick, etc., and coloured glazed tiles are also made of it. It is often applied to masonry in the form of stucco and plaster, and such walls are frequently covered with coloured washes. Wrought iron in the form of balconies and grilles is common, but wood is scarce, and rarely employed in building.

With the advent of the Spaniards in 1521, the art and civilization of Spain, then the leading nation of Europe, were transplanted to the New World, and for a time all native feeling was crushed. It soon recovered, however, and, though it never took the first place again, after the two people had mingled for a generation, native taste began to influence the imported styles. The architecture thus produced is unique, and though sometimes crude and barbaric, it is often of a high character, and is always interesting. Entering a hitherto almost unstudied field, any classification of Mexican architecture must be subject to correction as new facts are made known. In general, however, Mexican work may be classified under five heads, each with the distinctive characteristics of a separate style.

(I.) The work of Cortez and his men was one of subjugation of the natives and settlement of the country. During the last half of the sixteenth century, however, the people of New Spain turned their attention toward making permanent their establishment on the Western Continent. But the natives did not submit to slavery without a struggle, and both churches and dwellings of this era had heavy walls, small windows, battlemented parapets, and other marks of defensive construction. Examples of such work are the church at Tula (1553), and S. Francisco of Durango (1556). The former has walls seven feet thick, towers at the four angles, and an entrance protected by a walled atrium.

(II.) Thee poch of conquest completed, the people turned directly to the forms in vogue in Spain, where the Renaissance had given way to the Jesuit style, and the last years of the sixteenth century saw the founding of several great churches designed in all the vulgarity of that period. Still, it must be admitted of the Jesuit work that, though usually vulgar and ugly, it is always strong in mass and studied in plan.

Colossal orders, heavy decorations, and debased details may be seen in the great cathedral of Guadalajara, consecrated in 1618, and elsewhere. Work on the cathedrals of Mexico and Zacaticas was begun, but fortunately they were finished at a later period.

(III.) There is hardly a finer class of modern work, — that is, of work since the fifteenth century, — than Mexican architecture during most of the seventeenth and the first half of the eighteenth centuries. It is full of originality and independence. The colossal orders and coarseness of the preceding epoch are replaced upon façades by orders and details in proper scale, while small volutes supplant the gigantic ones and serve to terminate buttresses and otherwise resist thrust. Columns and entablatures are in classic proportion, and the architectural lines are preserved unbroken. Ornament is refined, very original in character, and confined to panels, friezes, mouldings, etc. The Spanish temptation to overload with ornament, and to use fantastic forms and clumsy motives, is restrained in this period, and is merely a source of originality and freshness of design.

This style is exemplified in the superb cathedral of Puebla, about 1650, in parts of the cathedrals of Mexico (1573–1667), Zacaticas (1612–1752), and Durango (1695–1715, partly destroyed by fire), and the Church of the Profesa,[1] Mexico. The interiors of these churches are in a magnificent, pure Renaissance style, with bays of elegant proportions. The piers are a beautiful grouping of the Doric column and square pier, the fine vaulting is either coffered or frescoed, and an interesting composition of side chapels, aisles, and ambulatories produces a superb effect. The sacristy of Puebla, with its rich Ionic columns in the corners, its delicate rococo decoration, its brilliant colouring and enormous frescoes, is undoubtedly the finest room of the kind on the American continent. The exteriors of this epoch are often monotonous; witness the Federal Capitol (founded 1692).

Landowners now began to establish themselves in permanent "haciendas" on their country estates, usually first obtained under royal patents. These groups of buildings centre around the dwelling of the "administrador," and comprise a chapel, granaries, corrals, huts of the "peons," etc., generally picturesquely associated together.

(IV.) The common use of stucco and an easily baked clay must always be a temptation to overdecoration, because of the ease in elaborating detail and ornament with such a material. It is not surprising, therefore, that the fantastic style of work always common in Mexico, but especially so during the prolific eighteenth century, should for a time have overpowered the severer style. Moreover, the worker in clay properly feels that the legitimate artistic use of such material is to mould

[1] The writer is unable to ascertain the date of this church, but its interior would class it with Puebla.

it into free and elaborate detail. Finding it as cheap to be complicated as simple in his design, he drops the straight line and true arc, reduces the orders into service as mere applied ornament, and covers entire façades with heavy decoration. Cornices and mouldings are broken into a complication of angles and curves, with returns innumerable and having waving lines with broken pediments and spirals, while gables crowned with a series of curves and intersecting angles make extraordinary skylines. Arches of double curve, of broken straight lines, and of combinations of arc and angle, are favourite forms. Windows framed in thin, rich pilasters with fantastic pediments open on balconies of equally fantastic form, or, when small, take the shape of oval, hexagon, or star. Colour is used lavishly, and the heavy decoration almost invariably rests on a broad, flat surface of brick, tile, or tinted stucco. While lacking all qualities of a serious or monumental style, this work is light, gay, spirited, and full of the character of terra cotta.

Though this period is most prolific of churches, the light character of the style is not fitted for ecclesiastical work. Churches are usually overdecorated on the exterior and bald on the interior. For example, the Segrario (1749–1769) and the ancient church of the Guadaloupe (1709), both of Mexico City, are types of stucco work where the gable end of the plain exterior is covered with a meaningless mass of decoration, only redeemed by the emphasis of the vertical lines. Even such churches as the Paroquia of Chihuahua (1711–1789) and the churches of this epoch in Mexico ̀City are weak in the character of their details. The Guadaloupe of San Luis, built of rich red stone, has fine general proportions with dome, towers, and strong pilaster buttresses, but the profiles of its mouldings are poor. The same fault mars the exterior of S. Spirito of Puebla, with its walls laid up in brick herringbone pattern, though its buttresses and such details as the obelisks on its towers are interesting. The Chapel del Pocito at Guadaloupe near Mexico is a unique example of a double-domed church. The small dome covers the sacred spring in the vestibule, and the larger dome roofs the circular church. The thrust is resisted by continuing the walls upward above the spring of the domes. These walls are pierced with arched, rectangular, and star-shaped openings, some of which serve as belfries, while all the structure above the cornice is overlaid with blue and white tiles. The walls are red stucco with buff trimming.

There are many fine municipal buildings in this style, notably those of Aguas Calientes and Guadalajara. The latter is tinted pale violet with white stucco trimming, and is a fine mass with frothy detail. The portales or porticoes on public buildings and structures abutting on public squares are a feature of the work of this and the succeeding epoch, while dwellings have patios or courtyard with loggias on one or more sides.

Three dwellings in Puebla are a remarkable group in tile and stucco work. One of these is two stories in height, a plain balcony along the second floor level, and a cornice carried on a unique system of corbels having curved soffits between them. The wall surface is Indian red and the cornice and trim are white. The palace of Iturbide in Mexico City is not so successful, but it has some interesting loggias where, as in the court of the National Museum, the supports are capped with sawed corbels of

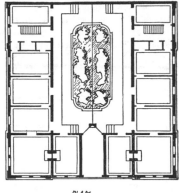

PLAN

SECTION

House. Mexico City. DWELLING FOR 2 FAMILIES

MEXICO: FIG. 3.

Moorish character. Two shops on opposite corners of a street near the National Museum, with stucco ornament in this style and wall surfaces coloured deep maroon, are perfect bazaar architecture. A charming example of this epoch in San Luis is a plain redstone dwelling, having as the only architectural feature of its façade a balcony of fantastic plan with a balustrade of vertical bars carrying light awning brackets.

(V.) Modern work in Mexico is original and independent in its character, and, while resembling modern work in Europe, it is still quite unlike anything that the present century has produced on the Continent. Its chief characteristic is the rapidity with which in late years it has seized new materials and new conditions of construction, and adapted the same to the solution of the problem in hand. Galvanized iron becomes a legitimate architectural material in the Mexican work of to-day.

The work of the years preceding and following 1800 is exemplified in the towers of Mexico cathedral (1791), the municipal palace of the capital, and the del Carmen (1803) of Tresguerras at Celaya. The last is a superb stone structure with a fine campanile uniquely placed in the centre of the gable façade. The Law School and the Segrario of Guadalajara (1803–1843), both weak, puny, and similar to much poor modern Italian work, are unfortunately a type of much of the modern architecture.

Mexico City has many small modern buildings, of suggestive design, and in general the use of wrought and sheet iron is simple and effective. Most successful of the modern work are the small villas, which have one side of the

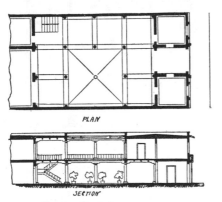

PLAN

SECTION

House Guadalajara

MEXICO: FIG. 4.

court open to the street and separated from it by a stone and iron barrier. Such a house, dating from the last century, is found in San Luis, while there are several charming examples which are full of originality in the outskirts of the capital.

The Hospicio of Guadalajara, which accommodates one thousand inmates, is a fine example of a pauper institution. The central feature is the large chapel, with a commonplace dome and a whitewashed interior. This stands upon the principal "patio," which is filled with trees and flowers and surrounded by an arcade. The laundry, culinary, industrial, and educational work of the institution has each its own courtyard with surrounding chambers. The ceilings are high; the twenty-three courtyards have flowers, shrubs, and basins of water, and in this climate nothing could be more admirably suited to its purpose than a building so planned.

Characteristics of Various Classes of Work: 1. *Churches.* At the base of Mexican church design is the fully developed cruciform plan common in Spain. With this as a basis, Mexican architecture has diversified the form into various types of plan to meet various needs. Commonly, the central motive is the dome, which rises on a low drum, carries a small lantern, and is either ribbed or overlaid with brilliant coloured glazed tiles. It covers the intersection of nave and transepts, though sometimes it occurs elsewhere, as in the case of Guadalajara cathedral, where it is over the choir at the end of the church. In chapels, the dome usually roofs the entire structure. Barrel vaulting, plain or with penetrations, is the commonest form, though ribbed intersecting vaults are sometimes used. The scanty rainfall is drained from the upper surface of the stone vault, along valleys which terminate in plain gargoyles. Side aisles are sometimes vaulted by shallow domes, or, as at Guadalajara, the vaulting of the three aisles is at the same level.

The belfry is universal in Mexican work, for the bell is a necessity in a clockless country. Its rudiment is found in the small parish church, where a portion of the wall of the plain façade is carried up, capped with a stone, and pierced with an opening in which the bell hangs. This "wall belfry" is often the only decorative feature on the little square adobe box that serves the small community; but it may be very elaborate, and carry several bells, as in the churches of Aguas Calientes. Another typical belfry is a square, one-storied tower, usually upon an angle of the façade, pierced with four openings, capped with a small dome, and either plain or decorated with pilasters, columns, conical roofs, etc. In plan it is often modified to circular, octagonal, and other forms. The typical parish church has two belfries, as in the chapel of Maximilian's hacienda at Bocas, the church of Cordoba, and others. In cities where churches are crowded between other buildings the belfry is often oddly placed on a long façade or on an angle.

Belfries are developed into towers by increasing the height by superposition. Some of the campanili, two or three stories high, thus formed, rank with the best examples of Renaissance church towers. The tower of del Carmen at Celaye, and that of the cathedral at Monterey, are among the finest in Mexico.

The use of iron grilles to enclose chapels and altars is a feature of the interior work. Puebla cathedral has fine ironwork enclosing that portion of the nave that is occupied by the choir stalls. The vertical spindles carry a horizontal moulded band with wrought-iron cresting; the chandeliers are superb metal work. Interiors are often richly decorated with frescoes; the churches of Celaye, with the works of Tresguerras, and Mexico cathedral and Puebla, with reputed Murillos, being the finest examples.

2. *Patios, Portales,* etc. The elementary plan of Mexican houses is an open, unroofed courtyard, partly or entirely surrounded by rooms. This plan, being familiar to the Indians in their pueblos and to the Spaniards in Spain, was naturally preserved by the mixed race. The simplest form is one or two adobe huts built against some convenient wall, thus forming an open square. The next step is to improve the huts, and form a complete enclosure; but this is usually accompanied by use of the portico, which may be considered to have developed naturally from a prolongation of the eaves. Examples of such simple method of shading the house walls are common throughout the country, and even as far north as Laguna, New Mexico. It is natural now to desire to deepen the shadow in the court, and sometimes on the street. The rafters are therefore projected until it is necessary to support them by a girder carried on posts, and thus a portico is formed. The drainage of the inner half of the roof and the entire court is carried down to a central covered cistern or ornamental basin.

Necessity for increased accommodation leads to the employment of secondary patios, or to the addition of one or two stories with porticoes on the court. Both of these modifications are used in hotels, *hospicios*, monasteries, etc., which are, therefore, only developed dwelling houses. The convents of Irapuato and of La Merced, in Mexico, are fine examples of such structures.

3. *Markets.* When porticoes are formed along street fronts of buildings, especially of such structures as face on public squares, they serve for the exposition of small wares, and become a species of market. Shops sometimes occupy the fronts of houses along the street level, and a second story is often carried over the portales. Markets proper are a development of the arcade idea. They are of two types: (*a*) the simpler form is a long shed with projecting eaves, covering a masonry platform several steps above the level of the street, and open at all sides with ventilation provided along the ridge. The San Luis market is of this type. (*b*) The more complex form, found at Puebla, Guadalajara, and elsewhere, also stands upon a masonry stylobate, and is square in plan, recalling the square plaza where produce was originally exposed. The exterior walls are of masonry, pierced with large arches, and having broad entrances with flights of steps at the angles. The roof is flat, carried on posts, and light and ventilation are admitted to the otherwise dark interior by omitting the roofing from certain of the rectangular spaces between the posts. A species of atrium is thus formed, and the centre of the open area thus provided is usually occupied with a large basin of water for the service of the market men. Small markets of square plan have only one such atrium.

4. *Government Buildings.* Primarily, the function of government was closely associated with the person of the officer, and for many years the viceroy's palace was the seat of judicial, legislative, and executive authority. It was natural, therefore, that governmental buildings in Mexico should be like developed dwelling houses. The municipal palace in Spain, moreover, was also of this type. The use of portales upon the exterior, arising from the necessity of protecting the crowd, which always surrounds the entrance to law courts and similar buildings, is a feature common to these structures. It is

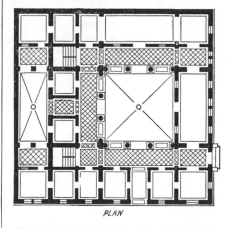

PLAN

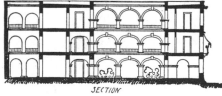

JECTION

Hotel. Monterey.

MEXICO: FIG. 5.

usual to extend the second story over the sidewalk, and this floor invariably has balconies, which recall the ancient custom of making public announcements by the crier from the governor's windows.

5. *Fountains, Landscape Architecture,* etc. In a dry climate like that of Mexico, the fountain is a source of water supply. Its form is almost universally an open basin, which receives the water from an ornamented central source, or from a spout in the wall.

The finest aqueduct in Mexico is that of Queretaro (1726), which spans a deep ravine with arches 100 feet in height, though the San Cosme aqueduct, from Chapultepec to the capital, is the longest.

Every town in Mexico has its plaza, with a central band stand, its alameda, or park, and its "paseo," or driveway. The "paseo" of the capital, having been laid out under French influence, may be called the *Champs Élysées* of the city. It is a superb driveway with four rows of trees and two sidewalks having four great circles, or "glorietas," nearly 400 feet in diameter, with statues in the centre and circular seats around them. The first "glorieta" contains an heroic equestrian statue of Charles IV., which, in the words of Humboldt, "may rank with the statue of Marcus Aurelius in Rome," while in the third "glorieta" the figure of Guatemoctzin advancing, spear in hand, rests upon a pedestal of three parts, with eight leopards at the base. It has a remarkably barbaric, and yet imposing, appearance. In general, barriers, which consist of iron grilles between stone posts, form a unique and interesting accompaniment to the architecture, and are very generally used in front of churches and modern dwellings in the cities. Two cemeteries in Puebla have gateways of funereal character with plain Doric columns.

Mexican architecture is unique in its boldness of colour and outline. It will bear close study, as being full of the character of the nation which produced it, and, in general, expressing frankly the originality and thought of the designer. The use of gorgeous tiles and coloured washes are its most interesting features, and yet colours are handled with a vigour and ease that show the Mexican to be an adept at such work, and an excellent master to any who would learn the use of colour in architecture.

— THORNTON F. TURNER.

MEZZANINE. A partial low story introduced in the height of a principal story; hence, any subordinate story intermediate between two main stories. (See Entresol.)

MEZZO RILIEVO. (See Relief.)

MIA MIA. In Australia, and the neighbouring islands, a hut made of the limbs of trees arranged around a circle and sloping or bent inward. These conical or dome-shaped huts were covered with grass and sometimes with turf in solid building, and they formed the most durable and permanent buildings of the aborigines. They were sometimes of such size that a fire being built in the middle, a ring of persons could sit on the ground around it.

Arch. Pub. Soc. Dictionary; J. G. Wood, *Natural History.*

MICHAEL OF CANTERBURY; architect or builder.

Magister Michael de Cantuaria cementarius contracted to build the Eleanor Cross (see Cross of Queen Eleanor) at East Cheap, London. During the years 1291, 1292 and 1293 he was paid £226 13s. 4d. for this work. No one else is mentioned in connection with it.

The construction of S. Stephen's chapel, Westminster, begun about 1292, burned in October, 1834, is also attributed to him. S. Stephen's, Westminster, was for a long period the Parliament House of Great Britain.

Hunter, *On the Death of Eleanor of Castille* in *Archæologia,* Vol. XXIX., p. 185.

MICHELANGELO BUONARROTI. (See Buonarroti-Simoni, Michelangelo.)

MICHELOZZI, MICHELOZZO DI BARTOLOMMEO DE'; architect and sculptor ; b. about 1396 ; d. 1472.

Michelozzo was trained as a goldsmith, and assisted Ghiberti (see Ghiberti) on both doors of the Florentine Baptistery. He built for Cosimo de' Medici the famous palace in the Via Larga, Florence, which was bought by the Riccardi in 1659, and, enlarged by them, is now the Prefetura. He built the library, finished 1441, and convent and cloister of S. Marco in Florence (1437–1452). About 1444 he began the works at the church of SS. Annunziata, Florence. He built the chapel, sacristy, *Chiostro del Antiporto,* and began the Tribuna or choir of this church. He remodelled the interior of the Palazzo Vecchio, Florence, especially the main court and the hall of the Two Hundred. At Milan he remodelled the palace of Cosimo de' Medici, now Vismara, and built the chapel of the Portinari at the church of S. Eustorgio, famous for frescoes by Vincenzo Foppa (both between 1456 and 1462). The arcade of the Palazzo Rettorale at Ragusa in Dalmatia is ascribed to him (Schmarsow, op. cit.). July 14, 1428, Michelozzo signed the contract for the exterior pulpit at Prato, the records of which still exist (Guasti, op. cit.). The sculpture is by Donatello. They also made together the Brancacci monument at Naples and that of ex-Pope John XXIII. at the Florentine Baptistery. The Aragazzi tomb at Montepulciano is ascribed to Michelozzo alone.

Geymüller-Stegmann, *Arch. der Renaissance in Toscana;* Müntz, *Renaissance in Toscana;* Müntz, *Renaissance;* A. Schmarsow, *Nuovi Studi intorno a Michelozzo;* Vasari, Blashfield-Hopkins ed.; Bocchi Cinelli, *Bellezze di Firenze;* Guasti, *Il Pergamo di Donatello.*

MIDDLE POST. Same as King-post (which see under Post).

MIHRAB. (The Arabic word used in Egypt and so generally transliterated ; Mehrab as written by Lane.) A niche in the wall of a mosque ; or sometimes a mere semblance of a niche, as a decorative panel or the like, indicating the direction of the Holy City of Mecca and the most sacred of all the Mohammedan shrines, the Kaaba.

MILIARIUM. Same as Miliary Pillar.

MILIARIUM AUREUM. The golden miliary pillar ; a column which stood in the Roman Forum, having been erected there by

PLATE XXXI

MINARET

Of the two examples that on the left belongs to the mosque of Sultan Kalaûn in Cairo, which is generally given as 193 feet high. The mosque is ruinous, but the beautiful minaret is one of the best pieces of Moslem art of the Middle Ages, about 1320 A.D. The one on the right is that of the mosque of El Bordei or El Bordenei, also in Cairo, and dates from the seventeenth century of our era.

Augustus, in 29 B.C., as a monument to the survey of the Roman world which had been undertaken, and partly or wholly completed at this time. It was of bronze and gilded, and stood upon a marble base which has been discovered in modern times.

MILIARY PILLAR. A Roman milestone; one of those pillars which were set up at intervals of 1000 paces along the Roman highroads in all parts of the Empire.

MILITARY ARCHITECTURE. (See Fortification.)

MILIZIA, FRANCESCO; architect and writer; b. 1725; d. 1798.

Milizia studied in Padua, Rome, and Naples. He is best known by his books, *Memorie degli Architetti più celebri* (2 vols. 8vo., Rome, 1768, Parma, 1781); *Del Teatro* (1772); *I Principi d'Architettura Civile* (3 vols. 8vo., 1781).

Arch. Pub. Soc. Dictionary.

MILL. *A.* Originally, a contrivance for grinding, as grain, and, hence, a building in which one or more sets of millstones are put up and prepared for such grinding.

B. Apparently, by deliberate extension of the significance *A*, a building in which any mechanical trade or manufacture is carried on, more especially one with a number of employees and a good deal of machinery. In this sense, frequently a very large building with a vast number of windows, so arranged as to throw daylight over all parts of each story with all the uniformity practicable. For this purpose windows are made with prismatic glass, the angles of the prisms being set especially to transmit daylight within, horizontally or nearly so. The construction of these buildings is also peculiar, generally of very solid timber and plank, and with precautions against the leaving of open spaces in which fire can be concealed, or can spread and run rapidly if once kindled. (See Slow Burning Construction.)

— R. S.

MILL-DRESSED. Same as Milled.

MILLED. Worked in the mill; as in the phrase "badly milled;" said of mill-worked boards, and the like.

MILLET, EUGÈNE LOUIS; architect; b. May 21, 1819; d. Feb. 24, 1879.

An associate of Viollet-le-Duc (see Viollet-le-Duc) and Henri Labrouste (see Labrouste). In 1847 he was appointed diocesan architect of Troyes and Châlons-sur-Marne, France, and restored the cathedral of Troyes. In 1855 he was made architect of the château of Saint-Germain-en-Laye, near Paris. Millet published *Monographie de la restoration du château de Saint-Germain-en-Laye* (Paris, 1892, 1 vol. folio).

L. Radoux, *Notice nécrologique* in *Revue Générale de l'Architecture.*

MILL-PLANED. (See under Plane, V.)

MILLS, ROBERT; architect.

After 1829, when Charles Bulfinch (see Bulfinch) retired, the office of supervising architect of the Capitol at Washington was vacant until July 6, 1836, when President Jackson appointed Robert Mills, a former assistant of Benjamin Latrobe (see Latrobe). He held the office until 1851.

Glenn Brown, *History of the United States Capitol.*

MILL-WORKED. Same as Milled.

MILNE. (See Mylne.)

MILON DE NANTEUIL; bishop.

Milon, the warrior-bishop of Beauvais, began the choir of his cathedral about 1226.

Desjardins, *Cathédrale de Beauvais.*

MIMBAR. (The Arabic word used in Egypt as transliterated by Lane; also Mambar; Minbar.) A pulpit in a mosque. The usual form is that of a very small standing place for the speaker, with a parapet of ordinary height enclosing it and a small canopy above, and a very narrow flight of steps leading to this platform, the whole forming one design. There is generally a gate at the foot of the stairs, which is usually kept shut, and this gate is sometimes hung between the jambs of the completed doorway, whose crowning decorative features rise as high as the platform of the pulpit, so that the sloping parapet of the stairs becomes a minor feature.

MINAH. In Indian architecture, a memorial tower built of masonry (compare Stamba), and so distinguished from a Lat.

MINAR. In Moslem architecture, a tower; usually, in English, equivalent to Minaret.

Kutub Minar. At Dehli (Delhi), in northern India (Punjab). It is a lofty and slender tower, probably intended as a minaret. As it now stands, its height is given as 238 feet, with the diameter of 47 feet at the base, but rapidly diminishing. The crowning cupola was thrown down by an earthquake.

MINARET. A tower attached to a mosque, and used only for the announcement by the *mueddin* of the hour of prayer. The Arabic term for such a tower, as transliterated by E. W. Lane, is *Mád'neh.* It is not known when these towers were first added to mosques. The earliest ones known are quadrilateral in their form, for at least the lower story, such as those of Sultan Hassan at Cairo, of Seville, in Spain (the Giralda, of which the plain lower story is very ancient), and of Ibn Tulun, Barkuk, and Kait Bey, all at Cairo, which are of the thirteenth and fourteenth centuries. The disposition to make the buildings very slender and fantastic in form was encouraged by the absence of any definite purpose in the towers beyond containing a very narrow staircase, or of any need for great solidity. The mosque at Ahmedahad, in the north of India, has a minaret which is studied from the pagodas of the early architecture of the Buddhists or Jainas. The minarets added by the Turks to S. Sophia, in Constantinople, are very slender, and this type is followed in many mosques. Also written menaret. (See Moslem Architecture.)

— R. S.

MINCH HOUSE. In parts of Great Britain, a place of shelter and rest; usually in the sense of a small inn.

MINERAL WOOL. A substance formed by reducing mineral slag to a fibrous condition. Commonly used as a deafener and as an insulator. Called also mineral cotton; slag wool.

MINO DA FIESOLE; sculptor; b. about 1430; d. 1484.

A Florentine sculptor of the school of Donatello. He made in Rome the monument of Paul II. (Pope 1464–1471), the sculpture of which is now in the vaults of the Vatican, the monument of Niccolò Forteguerra in the church of S. Cecilia in the Trastevere (1473), the monument of Pietro Riario in the church of SS. Apostoli (1474), etc. In much of his Roman work he was associated with Giovanni Dalmata (see Giovanni Dalmata). His Florentine works are better known : the monument of the Bishop Salutati·in the cathedral of Fiesole (1462), the monument to Bernardo Giugni in the Florentine Badia (1466), an altarpiece in the Florentine Badia (1470), the interior pulpit of the cathedral of Prato (1473), made in collaboration with Antonio Rossellino, etc. Mino's most important work is the monument of the Count Hugo (Ugo) von Andeburg in the Florentine Badia, which was begun about 1481.

Müntz, *Les Arts à la cour des Papes*; Vasari, Milanesi ed.; Hans Semper, *Hervorragende Bildhauer-Architekten der Renaissance*; D. Gnoli, *Le opere di Mino da Fiesole in Roma*; Perkins, *Tuscan Sculptors*; A. L. Tuckerman, *Renaissance in Italy*.

MINSTER. Originally, a conventual church; but, as the large churches of certain monasteries have been famous long after the other buildings have disappeared, therefore, a large and important church; the principal church of a town, whether a cathedral or not. Buildings known by this name especially are those of York and Beverley, in Yorkshire, England, and those of some Protestant cities on the Continent, as of Bonn on the Rhine and Basle in Switzerland.

MINT. A building in which money is coined. Such buildings have not commonly been of much architectural character; that of Paris (Hôtel des Monnaies, commonly called La Monnaie) is the most important. It was built in the last quarter of the eighteenth century, and has a front of over 600 feet on the Quai Conti. The exterior is not without merit as a piece of sim-

ple designing, with a portico of six columns decorating the middle of the façade. That of Venice is celebrated as a piece of neoclassic architecture (see Zecca). — R. S.

MINUTE. One division of a Module (which see).

MIQUE, RICHARD; architect; b. Sept. 18, 1728 (at Nancy, Meurthe-et-Moselle, France); d. July 8, 1794.

Mique was a pupil of Jacques François Blondel (see Blondel, J. F.), in Paris. In 1762 he was made chief engineer of the bridges and roads of Lorraine and Barrois. In 1766 Mique went to Paris, and was appointed *contrôleur général* of the buildings and gardens of the queen, Marie Antoinette. In 1785 he was appointed *premier architecte* of Louis XVI. During the French Revolution Mique was suspected of conspiring to liberate the queen. He was condemned, and executed July 8, 1794.

Lepage, *Archives de Nancy*; Lepage, *Palais ducal de Nancy*; Leroy, *Rues de Versailles*; Bauchal, *Dictionnaire*.

MIRADOR. A bay window, oriel window, loggia, or balcony arranged to command a prospect; hardly in use, except in describing Spanish architecture.

MIRROR. *A.* A reflecting surface so perfect that objects can be seen reproduced in it; especially, in architectural practice, a sheet of glass silvered on one side. The mirror enters into architectural design only in the way explained under Gallery of Mirrors, below.

B. A panel surrounded by a moulded or otherwise ornamented frame, and suggesting the idea of a mirror. Practically the same as a Cartouche, Rondel, or Medallion (see also Caisson; Lacuna); but the mirror, in this sense, is usually a detached panel and one of a series.

Gallery of Mirrors; Hall of Mirrors. A large room, into the decoration of which mirrors enter. In the eighteenth century, when the looking-glasses, originally coming from Venice, were esteemed, this feeble kind of decoration was put to use. The most important instance is the Galerie des Glaces at Versailles, a room 240 feet long, with large windows on one side and mirrors in casings, or frames, opposite them, the mirrors being not in large sheets, which at that time were not to be had, but arranged like the panes or lights of a window with sash bars.

MISERERE. A hinged seat in a choir stall, which, when turned up, affords a higher support as a resting place for a singer when standing. (See Stall.)

MISERICORD. In monastic architecture, a room, usually a separate building, devoted to meals of which flesh meat formed a part. It was not in all convents and monasteries that this was allowed at any time, and it seems never to have been served in the Frater or refectory.

H. J. Feasey, *Westminster Abbey historically described.*

MISSION (in Spanish, *mision*). A building or group of buildings composing a frontier or outpost settlement of one of the Spanish religious orders in America. At first these missions were rude huts, but they developed into extensive structures in the form of a quadrilateral building surrounding a court. There were church, hospital, workshops, schoolrooms, etc. The latter half of the eighteenth century saw the movement of the Franciscans from Mexico into California. In the missions built by Father Junipero and his friars may be recognized the artistic and constructive forms of Mexican architecture, modified by local conditions. (See Mexico, Architecture of.) Walls and piers were low and very heavy, built of adobe brick, and covered with stucco. Roofs were sometimes domed or vaulted, but more often tiles were laid on saplings, which were fastened with leather thongs to timber trusses. All this reflects the effort to prevent destruction by earthquakes ; but in spite of this many missions have been ruined from this cause. Plain, undecorated wall surfaces, fantastic gables, low belfries, walls pierced with arched openings to carry bells, as in S. Gabriel (1771) and S. Juan Capistrano (1776), roofs covered with large red clay tiles, and spacious cloisters with plain square piers carrying arches, as in S. Luis Rey (1798), S. Antonio (1770), and others, are the chief characteristics of this work. Some missions have a wooden architrave over the clustered piers bearing the roof rafters. This construction is used in S. Barbara (1786), which is one of the largest of the missions, and has a severe classic pediment and plain pilasters on the façade of the church. It has interesting window grilles made of turned wood spindles. A simple and decorative form of ceiling construction is found in S. Fernando Rey (1797), S. Ynez (1786), Dolores, and S. Miguel, where horizontal timbers are reënforced by flat carved corbels projecting out of the wall. One of the finest interiors is that of S. Buenaventura (1782). Large stone basins, which serve as fountains, are commonly found in the cloisters or near the entrance doorways of the missions. — THORNTON F. TURNER.

MITRE ; MITER. A bevel or oblique cut on each one of two parts which are to be joined end to end at an angle. (See Mitre Joint under Joint.)

MITRE BOX ; JACK. A carpenter's instrument for cutting mitres, and bevels, consisting of a small trough with upright sides and sawed cuts made in the sides. The moulding or strip to be mitred is laid in the trough and the saw is guided to the proper angle by the prepared cuts.

MNESIKLES ; architect.

According to Plutarch and other writers, Mnesikles built the Propylæa of the Acropolis at Athens, begun about 440 B.C., and finished in about five years. An inscription bearing his name has been found near the Propylæa.

Plutarch, *Life of Pericles.*

MOAT. A large trench ; especially one drawn around a building for defensive purposes. The moats of mediæval castles were of great importance, the height to the battlements being increased in this way by 30 or 40 feet, and approach to the base of the wall made almost impracticable. The sixteenth century châteaux of France had frequently moats which were intended to be filled with water and which enclosed both the house and also a certain surface of ground devoted to gardens, both for pleasure and for domestic purposes. In England the term moat house is not uncommon in local nomenclature as given to a manor house formerly, if not now, moated. — R. S.

MOAT HILL. A tumulus surrounded by a moat. These remains of prehistoric antiquity, though often called barrows, are more commonly remains of dwellings or fortifications.

MODEL. *A.* A pattern for something which is to be made ; and this may be either an exact working out, so far as form is concerned, of the intended utensil, piece of machinery, or work of art, so that it can be used to make a mould for casting in metal ; or it may be a similarly exact prestudy of the future work, to be followed closely by hammering or other mechanical process ; or, finally, it may be on a much smaller scale than the thing to be produced, and in this sense may be a study in clay or wax, on a very small scale, for a building of indefinitely great size. (For the use of the model in this last named direction, see Preliminary Study.)

B. A reproduction, usually in small, of an existing work of art, as a steamship or a building. Models in this sense have been made in the nineteenth century of singular elaborateness and finish ; thus one such of the new Hôtel de Ville at Paris was shown at the Paris Exhibition of 1878, in which the whole building was represented on a large scale (about $\frac{1}{100}$ of the actual structure), with all its accessories of sculpture, metal work, glass windows, and the like, and the benches on the sidewalk, lamp-posts near the building, and every accessory which could be thought of added with completely accurate reproduction of that quarter of the town. — R. S.

MODELLING. The art and practice of making a model in sense *A ;* especially the working a plastic material into a desired shape, as a step in the study of an artist's thought or in the way of commemoration of a form of which a memorandum is desired. Thus, a

modern sculptor makes a small model of his conception for a statue, then a larger one, and finally his full-size statue or group in wet clay : a plaster cast of which large model serves for the marble-worker or the bronze-founder in case the work of art is to be embodied in such resistant material. All the shaping of the plastic material is called modelling. Studies of furniture, pieces of jewellery, and keramic vessels may be made in wax or clay with equal ease.
— R. S.

Modelling in clay, or some other plastic material, is employed in the architectural schools to a limited extent, but not as fully as one might wish in consideration of the fact that the architect's art product is finally developed in solids. It is used very little by the architect in the study of his projected buildings, a fact which is much to be deplored. (See Preliminary Studies.)

Modelling at full size is employed in modern architectural practice, very generally, in determining the detail of important ornament; and all architects who use this means find it of great value in determining *in situ* the values of the ornament or sculpture which is to be applied to, or carved upon, their buildings. This practice is to be encouraged in every way, but it is well to note that there is a dangerous tendency observable in connection with this practice under the influence of the contract system now so generally in vogue. It has become almost habitual for the architect to be satisfied with inspection of the model, which, being accepted, is turned over for copying in stone to the mere artisan who has no artistic feeling, and whose sole object is the fulfilment of his contract in the shortest time, and with the least possible thought and labour and expense. The result is that in much of the architectural ornament seen, even in the best buildings of the day, we see reproduced in stone forms belonging properly only to soft clay. Such ornament appears too often as it would if cut in some substance of the consistency of butter or cheese. This defect is often most serious until Nature has applied her remedy, and has stained out, or eaten away, the imitation of a fine-grained, homogeneous, and soft material. This difficulty may be easily overcome by the architect, however, if he will but insist upon having the design shown in his model reproduced in stone by able carvers who feel an interest in their craft, and who will consult with the designer as they work upon the translation from clay into stone, which requires as nice an artistic feeling as does the translation of a poem from one language into another.
— Henry Rutgers Marshall.

MODILLION. One of a series of projecting corbels or bracket-like members supporting the corona of a cornice, especially in the Co-

rinthian and the Composite orders. While the distinction cannot always be made between modillion and console, where the latter is used in a series, yet the former term appears not to be applied to such a member used singly, nor to one not of a classic type. (See Console.)

MODULE. A standard, usually of length, by which the proportionate measurements of a building are supposed to be determined. Vitruvius (III., 3) says that the front of a Doric building, if columnar, is, when tetrastyle, to be divided into twenty-eight parts; if hexastyle, into forty-four parts; and that each of these parts is a "modulus," called by the Greeks ἐμβάτης (embates). He says, farther, that the thickness of a column (shaft) should be two moduli, the height with the capital, fourteen, the height of the capital alone, one module, and its width one and one-sixth; and he applies similar rules to the entablature. Starting from these loosely written chapters, which even its author could hardly have thought authoritative, or even exact, the writers of the Italian Renaissance and their imitators have laid down exact proportionate measurements for all parts of the order, dividing the module into parts called minutes, in English, twelve, eighteen, or thirty of them to a module; and taking the module itself, now a semidiameter, now a whole diameter, now the third of a diameter, now a fraction of the height of a column. (See Columnar Architecture; Intercolumniation.) — R. S.

MODULUS. *A.* A unit of measure assumed in determining the strength of materials as against stretching, bending, or rupture. (See Breaking Strain, under Strain.)

B. Same as Module.

MOGOTE. In southern Mexico, a certain kind of aboriginal mound. Some of these mounds examined by Seville were found to contain stone vaults with doorways facing the west, sealed by large stones. They were depositories for the bones of the dead. (See Mound.) — F. S. D.

MOGUL ARCHITECTURE. *A.* The architecture of the so-called Mogul empire, or of the Mogul dynasty. This was established in northwest India in the sixteenth century, with Agra as its chief seat. The characteristics of the architecture are very different from those of the purely Indian styles.

B. Loosely, and because of the little study which the Mohammedan architecture in India has received, any architecture of Mohammedan races or dynasties in India. (See India, Architecture of; Moslem Architecture.) — R. S.

MOHAMMEDAN   ARCHITECTURE. Same as Moslem Architecture.

MOITURIER, ANTOINE LE; sculptor; d. after 1497.

In 1464 he established himself at Dijon, Côtes d'Or, and completed the monument of

Jean Sans Peur, Duke of Burgundy, which had been abandoned by Jean de la Huerta (see Jean de la Huerta) in 1457. The splendid monument to Philippe Pot now in the Louvre is supposed to be by him.

Chabeuf, *Jean de la Huerta, Antoine le Moiturier*, etc. ; Chabeuf, *Dijon ;* Lami, *Dictionnaire des Sculpteurs français.*

MOLDAVIA, ARCHITECTURE OF. That of the region between the Dneister and the mouth of the Danube, on the Black Sea, formerly a province of the Turkish Empire, and now forming part of the kingdom of Roumania. This region is almost

which is strongly Byzantine in character, and which seems to be a result of Moldavian influences. A curious use of the separate bell tower is found in certain towns of this region. In some cases, even late neoclassic churches are treated in this way, and the result is a very interesting series of square towers of generally classic design.

Beside the buildings of masonry, wooden churches, some of great age, exist in this region. (Cuts, cols. 919, 920 ; 921.)

Romstorfer, *Die Moldauisch - Byzantinische Baukunst.*

MOLDING. Same as Moulding.

MOLE. Any massive structure. A word used very loosely, and generally in a poetical sense. "The Hadrian Mole," the mausoleum of Hadrian at Rome, now Castel S. Angelo. The term is hardly used with exactness except for a dike, jetty, pier, or quay. (Compare Molo.)

MOLDAVIA, ARCHITECTURE OF : FIG. 1.—CHURCH AT JASSY, CALLED BISERICA TREI ERARHI. PLAN.

MOLDAVIA, ARCHITECTURE OF : FIG. 2.—BISERICA TREI ERARHI IN JASSY. (SEE FIG. 1.)

wholly Byzantine in the character of its art, the earlier work being directly derived from the models existing in the Byzantine Empire, and the later buildings marked by an influence similar to that of Russia. The exceptions to this are in the occasional instances of detail of Western character, Romanesque, or Gothic ; or a late transition Gothic reminding one of the fifteenth century architecture of Spain. The churches with cupolas raised on high drums are of very great interest.

The architecture which is known as Moldavian spreads a little way beyond the border, and influences the Russian provinces of Bessarabia and Curson ; thus, at Odessa, is a church

MOLLER, GEORG ; architect, and writer on art.

Moller was court architect to the Grand Duke of Hessen, Germany, and published *Denkmäler der deutschen Baukunst,* 1815–1831.

Seubert, *Künstler-lexicon.*

MOLO. In Italian, a seawall, dam, or quay. In Venice, the broad quay in the Canale di S. Marco, and lying in front of the Ducal Palace and the piazzetta, with a narrow extension to the west in front of the library of S. Mark and the Zecca, or Mint. The Riva degli Schiavoni is its extension to the east. (For the meaning of the word, compare Mole.)

MOMENT. In mechanics, the quantity obtained by multiplying a force by the length

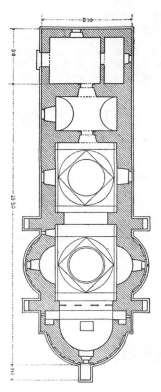

MOLDAVIA, ARCHITECTURE OF:
FIG. 3. — CHURCH AT BUR-
DUSCHENY (BURDUSENI).
PLAN.

MOLDAVIA, ARCHITECTURE OF: FIG. 4. — CHURCH AT BURDUS-
CHENY (BURDUSENI). (SEE FIG. 3.)

MOLDAVIA, ARCHITECTURE OF: FIG. 5. — WOODEN CHURCH AT KLOKUCZKA.

of a "lever arm," to which it is applied, the action of the force being considered with reference to a given point. The lever arm is the distance from the given point measured perpendicularly to the direction of the force.

Bending Moment. In the consideration of the strains produced in a loaded beam, the sum of the moments acting on one side of any section perpendicular to the neutral axis, the position of such section being assumed at pleasure for the purpose of investigation of the strains at any part of the beam. The bending moment is equal to the Couple formed by the sum of the forces producing tension and of those producing compression, on opposite sides of the neutral axis, respectively.

MOLDAVIA, ARCHITECTURE OF: FIG. 6. — WINDOW IN CHURCH AT RADAUTZ, SHOWING STRONG WESTERN INFLUENCE, AS OF THE 15TH CENTURY GOTHIC OF GERMANY.

MOMENT OF INERTIA. A quantity in constant use in computing the strength and deflection of a beam or a column. It is well known that when a beam is bent the fibres on the concave side are compressed, and on the convex side, extended, though all are not equally extended or compressed. If we suppose the section of a beam or of a column to be divided into infinitely small areas, and each area multiplied by the square of its distance from a line passing through the centre of gravity of the section, the sum of these products is the moment of inertia of the section, and, when multiplied by the strength of the fibre, represents the sum of the resistance of the different fibres to stress. The square of the radius of gyration, r^2, is the moment of inertia divided by the area of the section. It is the sum of the squares of the distances of the small areas from the axis about which the moment is taken.

If we represent each of these small areas by a, and the variable distance of each area from the centre line, or axis, by y, then the moment of inertia, $I = \int ay^2$, the sum of the small areas each by the square of y ($\int$ meaning "sum"). But the sum of the small areas equals A, the whole area of the section. If we call the sum of all the values of y^2, r^2, then $I = Ar^2$, which gives $\dfrac{I}{A} = r^2$, or the radius of gyration, $r = \sqrt{\dfrac{I}{A}}$. — W. R. HUTTON.

MONASTERY. A building or group of buildings arranged for the occupancy of members of a religious order, or of persons desiring religious seclusion. The term is commonly understood as meaning such a place for monks, as distinguished from a nunnery; but there appears to be no authority for this restriction, the term including properly the establishments of either sex, and thus being synonymous with convent. (See Abbey; Friary; Monastic Architecture; Nunnery; Priory.)

MONASTIC ARCHITECTURE. That of religious organizations having permanent rules of conduct and life, and divided into considerable bodies of men or women who devote themselves in common to a life of worship and labour. Many religions have recognized these religious bodies which, when in Christian nations, are called Orders of Monks and of Nuns; terms which are used also in an extended sense as applicable to similar communities in other religions. The present article deals only with the Christian religious orders.

The earliest convents, even those as late as of the seventh and eighth centuries, have disappeared except as relics of them exist in the stone building regions of the East. It was not before the ninth century that the recognized system of monastic building and the full plan of the monastery was fairly established in the West. A great cloister afforded the obvious means of communication from one building to another, of shelter for persons walking either in solitary meditation or in conversation, and a sheltered place for a garden with frequently a lavatory or a well. From the cloister the church was entered usually at two points along its south flank. The abbot's lodging, the Chap-

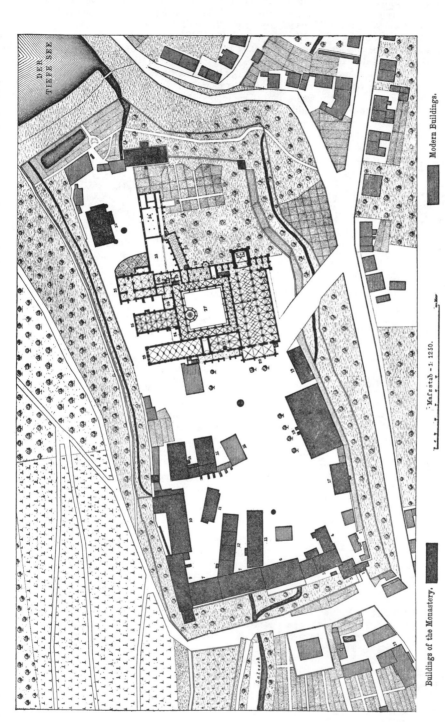

DER
TIEFE SEE

Mafsſtab - 1: 1250.

MONASTIC ARCHITECTURE: MONASTERY OF MAULBRONN, WURTEMBURG.

Buildings of the Monastery, ▮ Modern Buildings. ▮

1. Gate house for enclosure.
2. Formerly chapel.
3. Formerly inn for strangers.
4. Building for celebration of early morning mass.
5. Carriage house.
6. Forge.
7. Formerly steward's room.
8. Tower called the Witches' Tower.
9. Milking shed.

11. Formerly bake shop.
12. Storehouses.
13. Formerly blacksmith shop, now court of justice for the town.
14 15, 16. Kitchen and offices.
17. Office of the cellarer.
18. Storehouse for fruits.
19. Vintager's office.
20. Church.

23. Refectory for the lay brothers.
24. Kitchen.
25. Refectory.
26. Calefactory (which see under definition A).
27. Cloister, with well house.
28. Chapter house, with Chapel of S. John.
29. Room for penances

32. Parlour (auditorium).
33. Formerly residence of the abbot.
34. "Herrenhaus," probably lodgings of the lay feudal lord.
35. Ducal castle (a small building replacing a strong tower).
36. Hospital
37. Strong tower, called the Faustthurm.

923   924

ter House, the Lavatory, the Dormitory, and the lodgings for strangers opened upon this cloister, or, in large convents, upon one or two cloisters not far separated. (See the terms above cited; also plan of Westminster Abbey, under Abbey; also under Certosa.) It is to be noted that minor and yet important differences existed. Thus, in the Carthusian convent (see Certosa) there was no dormitory; in a Dominican convent there could hardly be said to be any separate cells, but the dormitory and the general lavatory and the church were everything.

The number of orders founded in Christianity between the fourth and the end of the nineteenth century is so very numerous that even a slight analysis of their peculiarities of plan and of building has proved hitherto unattainable. The

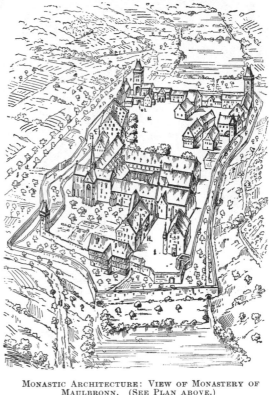

MONASTIC ARCHITECTURE: VIEW OF MONASTERY OF MAULBRONN. (SEE PLAN ABOVE.)

valuable papers and the few books devoted to this subject are far from achieving that result. There are, however, some few orders whose architecture is of singular importance to general architectural history.

The Cluniac or Clunisian monks had much influence in developing the Romanesque architecture of France (see Romanesque).

The Carthusian monks first established at the Chartreuse near Grenoble in France a monastery which came to be called La Grande Chartreuse (see Chartreuse and subtitle); they founded also the numerous Chartreuse of France and the establishments called Certosa (which see) in Italy.

The Cistercian monks came nearest of all the orders to creating a special style of

MONASTIC ARCHITECTURE: BUILDINGS OF THE MONASTERY AT CLUNY; ROMANESQUE TOWER OF SOUTH TRANSEPT.

MONASTIC ARCHITECTURE: FOUNTAINS ABBEY, YORKSHIRE; VIEW OF NAVE,
LOOKING WEST.

927   928

architecture. The spread of this order throughout Central Europe is contemporary with the full development of Gothic architecture, and it was the influence of this order which more than anything else tended to spread Gothic architecture southward and eastward from Burgundy into the other countries of Europe, and especially into Italy. They built skilfully, kept the French traditions of the Burgundian school, and in a church, a chapter house or a refectory like that at Fossanova (see Italy, Part IX., Latium) constructed vaults and the accessories and substructures of those vaults almost exactly as similar work was done in the North at the same time. The monasteries of the Cistercians have existed in great numbers

mentation, which, indeed, they seem always to have avoided. In later times the Dominicans, who retained their weight and influence to a remarkable degree, followed the style of the period, and some of the most remarkable conventual buildings in Europe of Renaissance and post-Renaissance architecture are of their building. (See Cistercian, above.)

The Carmelites, founded in Jerusalem in the fifth century, built many churches in the fourteenth and fifteenth centuries in Italy.

The Gesuati or Jesuat monks built little, but their buildings are interesting. (See Jesuat Architecture.)

The Jesuits, one of the latest of the great orders, seem not to have developed a new plan

MONASTIC ARCHITECTURE: CHAPTER HOUSE AT FOSSANOVA, LATIUM, ITALY.

throughout central and eastern France, Germany, Italy, and the British Isles; but the order decayed at an early time, the buildings have been destroyed or have passed into vulgar uses, and it is only in very recent times that the important Italian ruins have been investigated (see especially Enlart, op. cit.). The Cistercian monasteries in England and Scotland are nearly all in ruins, but as ruins they have been much admired and somewhat studied (see Abbeys of Scotland; Abbeys of Yorkshire).

The Dominican monks, called also Cordeliers, the Preaching Friars, and, at a later time, Jacobins, are an order of later foundation, originating in the twelfth century. They built excellent Gothic buildings, thorough in construction and intelligent in constructional design, but without sculpture and similar orna-

or a new arrangement of monastery, but their churches in towns arranged for purposes of preaching are of peculiar importance in the history of the sixteenth and seventeenth centuries. (See Jesuit Architecture.)

The Trappist order, or Monks of La Trappe, are peculiarly interesting for their latest revival in building, this community having built several great monasteries in the second half of the nineteenth century, one of which, in Normandy, is an enormous institution with most interesting modern Gothic buildings. (See France, Part III.)

The buildings of the military orders have peculiar value to students of early fortification. The castles of the Templars and of the Knights of S. John in Syria have only within a few years received some part of the attention which they deserve; but in Europe these orders can hardly be said to have altered in any important sense the progress of architectural design. (See, for the Knights of S. John, Malta, under Mediterranean Islands; and for the Templars, Commandery; Preceptory; Temple.)

up establishments so large that they resemble rather small cities than single monasteries; and this appearance is increased by their precautions against attack. These, however, are not of the nature of fortification considered as an elaborate science or a highly developed art of military building, but are rather the surrounding of towns on a plain by lofty walls sufficient to guard against sudden attacks from robbers, and in mountain countries of the selection of inaccessible and difficult sites. (See Curzon, op. cit.) (Cut, cols. 933, 934.)

Enlart, *Origines françaises de l'architecture gothique en Italie;* Lenoir, *Architecture monastique* (2 vols.) ; Curzon, *The Monasteries of the Levant.*
— R. S.

MONASTIC ARCHITECTURE: REFECTORY AT FOSSANOVA. (SEE CHAPTER HOUSE, ABOVE.)

MONEGRO, JUAN BATTISTA; sculptor and architect.

In 1587 he was appointed supervising architect of the Alcazar at Toledo. He made much of the sculpture of the church and palace of the Escorial. He was later appointed supervising architect of the cathedral of Toledo.

Bermudez, *Diccionario.*

MONKEY. Same as Ram, *A.*

MONOCHROMY. The use of one colour in a design, as distinguished from work in many colours; the production of unicoloured instead of multicoloured designs. This is generally held to signify not the use of several different blues (as Cobalt Blue, Prussian Blue, and the like), or of several different reds in one composition, but rather the use of colour of single character, made darker and lighter either by the mixture of white or black with the original tint, or, when transparent colours are

In the regions influenced by Byzantine architecture the monasteries existing from great antiquity, without apparently serious changes in their plan or in the structure of their separate buildings, offer interesting instances of Byzantine architecture in its simpler forms. These humble buildings sometimes go to make

MONASTIC ARCHITECTURE: MONT SAINT-MICHEL, NORMANDY.

The most imposing group of conventual buildings in Europe.

used, the putting on of a colour in fewer or more numerous coats.

The term is much more commonly employed for decorative work in gray or some other neutral colour. (See Grisaille.) When light and shade is considered by itself without reference to the local colours of the objects viewed in light, in shade, and in shadow, the result is usually a work in monochromy.

MONOGRAM FROM A NE-
CROPOLIS AT EL-BARAH,
SYRIA.

X P for Christos, with alpha (to
right) and omega.

MONOGRAM. A combination of two or more letters, which, when so combined, stand for a word or phrase; usually, a single word, as a proper name. (See I H S.) Combinations of letters which form the initials of different names, as when a piece of silver is marked with the initials of the owner, are not monograms, but ciphers.

MONOLITH. An architectural member, as an obelisk, the shaft of a column, or the like, when consisting of a single stone. Monoliths in unusual conditions are especially described by this term, as the roof of the tomb of Theodoric at Ravenna. (See Tomb.)

MONOLITHIC ARCHITECTURE. *A.* That depending upon rock-cutting, as in the temples of India (for which, see Buddhist Architecture; India, Architecture of; Jaina).

B. That depending upon building with material which is put together in a semiliquid form, and hardens in the place which it is to occupy permanently. This is usually done with artificial stone made of cement and sand and other materials, the mixture being thrown into a trench, either made in the ground or into a box made of plank, or the like, which box is carried up as the walls rise. All work in concrete is monolithic; but concrete, in the usual sense, is generally reserved for foundations, and the like. In countries where good building stone is rare, and where good clay for bricks is not found, monolithic building naturally suggests itself, and an architecture based upon it existed in Syria on the seacoast during the supremacy of the Phœnicians. Recent buildings in California and the neighbouring states are monolithic in character, and a very interesting system of design based upon ancient Spanish-American architecture seems to be developing itself from this.

MONOPODIUM. The solid and permanent part of a Roman table, as in a triclinium. This was commonly of masonry or cut stone, and different table tops seem to have been brought in and taken away with the dishes, much as in modern times we use large trays. These supports for tables are found in houses at Pompeii. (Compare Table.)

MONOPTERAL. Constructed or formed as a Monopteron; pertaining to a Monopteron.

MONOPTERON; MONOPTEROS. In Greek architecture, a circular peripteral building, as a temple, having only a single row of columns.

MONOSTYLE. Having but a single shaft; said of a pier, as in a church, and in distinction to compound; thus, the nave piers of Notre Dame, in Paris, are monostyle; that is to say, are single round columns with capital and base, whereas those of Reims cathedral are clustered piers.

MONOTRIGLYPHIC (adj.). In the Doric order, having one triglyph over the space between two columns, the space between the centres of two adjoining columns being equal to the width of two triglyphs and two metopes.

MONSTRANCE. In ecclesiology, a receptacle of any kind in which the Host is displayed, as distinguished from a vessel in which wafers are kept for security. In modern practice, the term is used exclusively for small and portable vessels of the sort.

MONTACUTE HOUSE. An English mansion in Yeovil, Somersetshire, the name being taken from an ancient priory whose ruins are late Gothic in character. The mansion is Elizabethan, the ground plan being in the form of an H; and the gardens, still preserving the ancient disposition, are excellent examples of the formal garden of the sixteenth century.

MONTANT. A slender, vertical member. The term is French, and, in its adapted use, of uncertain significance; perhaps most generally used as the equivalent of mullion, or muntin.

MONTELUPO, RAFFAELLO DA. (See Raffaello da Montelupo.)

MONTEREAU, EUDES DE. (See Montreuil, Eudes de.)

MONTEREAU, PIERRE DE. (See Montreuil, Pierre de.)

MONTEROULT, PIERRE DE. (See Grappin, Jehan, I.)

MONTFERRAND, AUGUSTE RICARD DE; architect; b. Jan. 24, 1786 (at Paris); d. July 14, 1859 (at Saint Petersburg, Russia).

De Montferrand was a pupil of Charles Percier (see Percier). In 1816 he went to Saint Petersburg, and assumed the position of architect of the Czar Alexander I. In 1817 he was successful in a competition for the reconstruction of the old cathedral of S. Isaac at Saint Petersburg. The present cathedral was designed by him, and completed in about forty years. He published *L'église cathédrale de Saint Isaac, description architecturale*, etc. (Paris and Saint Petersburg, 1845, folio.)

Lance, *Dictionnaire*.

MONTORSOLI, FRA GIOVANNI AN-GIOLO DA; sculptor and architect; b. 1507; d. August, 1563.

He received his name from the village of Montorsoli, near Florence, where he was born. He was attached to the works at S. Peter's, where he attracted the attention of Michelangelo, whom he assisted in the completion of the Medici tombs in the new sacristy of S. Lorenzo at Florence. The statue of S. Cosimo, now in the sacristy, was made by him. In October, 1530, he entered the religious order of the Servi dell' Annunziata, in Florence. Returning to Rome, he was employed by Clement VII. (Pope 1523–1534), to restore antique statues at the Belvedere, Vatican. Montorsoli also assisted Michelangelo on the tomb of Julius II. A visit to Paris was without important results. About 1543, for the great admiral, Andrea Doria, he began the decoration of the church of S. Matteo, Genoa, including the altar and the tomb of the admiral. He assisted also in the decoration of the Doria palace. In September, 1547, Montorsoli was called to Messina, Sicily, to construct the great fountain of the Piazza del Duomo. This was followed by the fountain of the port of Messina.

Vasari, Milanesi ed.; Müntz, *Renaissance;* Perkins, *Tuscan Sculptors;* Hittorff and Zanth, *Architecture moderne de la Sicile.*

MONTREUIL (MONTEREAU), EUDES DE; architect; d. 1289.

Probably related to Pierre de Montreuil (see Montreuil, P. de). In 1248 he went with King Louis IX. of France (S. Louis) on the seventh crusade, and assisted in the fortification of the city of Jaffa, in Palestine. On his return, in 1254, he built the church of the great asylum for the blind, established by S. Louis, which was called the Hospice des Quinze Vingts (destroyed 1779). He built also, in Paris, the churches of the Blancs Manteaux, of the Val des Écoliers, of the Mathurins, of the Cordeliers, of S. Catherine, and of the Hôtel Dieu. His epitaph was to be seen in the church of the Cordeliers until its destruction in 1580.

Decloux et Doury, *Sainte-Chapelle;* Bauchal, *Dictionnaire.*

MONTREUIL, PIERRE DE; architect.

A layman, and the principal architect of Louis IX. (S. Louis). The Sainte-Chapelle of the château of Saint-Germain-en-Laye, near Paris, is supposed to have been one of his earlier works; but the attribution is discredited by Viollet-le-Duc and Gonse (op. cit., p. 242). He built the refectory (1239–1244) and the Chapelle de la Vierge (begun 1244) at the monastery of S. Germain des Prés, Paris, which were destroyed during the Revolution. Some of the glass of the chapel has been placed in the church of S. Germain des Prés; the carved doorway with the statue of the Madonna

is in the church of Saint Denis, near Paris. The tomb of Montreuil existed in the chapel of S. Germain des Prés until the Revolution. In 1240 Montreuil was commissioned by S. Louis to build the Sainte-Chapelle of the royal palace (now in the Palais de Justice), Paris. This building, one of the finest works of the thirteenth century, was built to contain the Crown of Thorns, a fragment of the true Cross, and other relics, which were secured from Baudouin de Courtenay, Emperor of Constantinople. It was dedicated April 25, 1248. The chapel of the château of Vincennes, near Paris, is also attributed to Pierre de Montreuil.

Decloux et Doury, *Histoire de la Sainte-Chapelle;* Gonse, *L'art gothique;* Viollet-le-Duc, *Dictionnaire de l'architecture française;* Édouard Fournier, in *Hoffbauer, Paris à Travers les âges;* Éméric-David, *Sculpture française.*

MONUMENT. *A.* A building considered as notable for its beauty, its size and grandeur, or the purpose it serves as a memorial, or as dedicated to worship, or the like. Buildings which have no purpose except that of commemoration or devotion are often called monuments, in contradistinction to buildings of utility; and memorials, more especially tombs and cenotaphs, are often called monuments without qualifying term. The term does not generally cover slabs in the floor, or even incrusted in the wall, unless unusually enriched with sculpture; nor altar tombs unless these have canopies.

B. Any more or less permanently fixed and immovable object serving to indicate a particular point of a survey or piece of land. It may be a natural object, as a tree or rock, or a masonry structure erected for the purpose. The exact location of the point is commonly indicated by marks on the monument.

(See Cenotaph; Mausoleum; Memorial Arch; Memorial Column; Pyramid; Tomb. See also general treatment, below, of the Monument considered as a Memorial.)

In Egypt, the most usual form of memorial monuments was the obelisk, of which there is a long series from the fifth dynasty to Cleopatra. The temples sometimes served as royal memorials, their sculptures detailing the life and exploits of the king who built them; for example, the temple of Rameses at Karnak, with its battle scenes, processions of captives, and trophies. Unique in form, and specifically a memorial, was the temple of Hatasu at Deir-el-Bahari. The pyramid of the Ancient Empire and the rock tomb of the New Empire were more memorials than mere tombs.

Concerning Western Asia: in Assyria, the palace which nearly every king erected took the place of the temple as a memorial; the king's life and exploits were detailed in long friezes of reliefs lining its halls and passages.

Obelisks, much smaller than the Egyptian, were covered, not merely with inscriptions, but with reliefs ; for instance, the obelisk of Shalmaneser. The Babylonian Elamite and Assyrian kings also left memorials of victory in foreign lands in the shape of rock-cut sculptures and free-standing carved steles, such as those of Assurnazirpal and Sargon.

In Greece, temples, though often erected with the spoils of war, were never memorials ; neither were there memorial palaces. Though the trophy, and later the column with its sculpture, and still later the mausoleum, were used, the personal element, conspicuous in corresponding Oriental and later Roman works, was lacking, being replaced by glorification of the state. Most representative of this tendency were the buildings called " Treasuries," erected by each important Hellenic state in the enclosures of the great national shrines, such as Olympia and Delphi, a number of which have been discovered. These monuments, in the sculptures and inscriptions outside and the votive offerings within, were microscopic memorials of each Greek state, records of their glory, wealth, and devotion to the gods.

In Rome, glorification of the state found unexampled monumental expression, beginning in the kingly period. It was at first closely associated with religion. Such were, in Rome, the temples of Jupiter Feretrius (treasury for military spoils), of Jupiter Victor (for victory over Samnites in 294 B.C.), and of Victory ; and under the Empire the temple of Mars in the Forum, of Augustus and the Neptunium, representative, respectively, of military and naval achievements. The memorial temples built everywhere to the deified emperors, such as Julius Cæsar, Augustus, Claudius, Vespasian, Trajan, Marcus Aurelius, and members of their families, were characteristic of the Roman subordination of religion to politics.

Memorial arches, columns, and trophies were erected to commemorate warlike and peaceful events. (See Memorial Arch ; Memorial Column ; Pax Romana ; Trophy.) The great mausolea, especially those erected by Augustus and Hadrian, combine as memorials

early Etruscan and Hellenistic traditions. (See Tomb.)

In the early days of Christianity, religious memorials overshadowed all others : (1) Memorials of the life of Christ : such were the build-

MONUMENT AT S. REMY (BOUCHES DU RHÔNE) ; PROBABLY OF THE 3D CENTURY, A.D.

ings erected throughout Palestine, at Bethlehem (Nativity), Nazareth, Jerusalem (Dome of the Rock, Holy Sepulchre), or those to contain some relic, like that of the cross (S. Croce, Rome). (2) Memorials of the apostles and of saints and martyrs (churches over their tombs, relics, or places of martyrdom). (3) Memorials of prominent lay persons, such as the mausolea of Helena and Constantina, in Rome, of Theodoric and Galla Placidia, in Ravenna. The unique memorial church connected with the column of S. Simeon Stylites, in Syria, apparently cruciform, is really a basilica on the east of the column, from which, as from a centre, extend to the north, south, and west three groups of triple colonnades corresponding to the church.

Columns were used as memorials until the seventh century, but mosaic pictures began to replace them with the decline of sculpture in the sixth century (mosaics of Theodoric and Justinian), and arches had been discontinued in the fifth century. Mosaic and fresco painting were almost exclusively employed henceforth to record the same facts previously commemorated by a combination of architecture and sculpture.

— A. L. FROTHINGHAM, JR.

In the later Middle Ages few monuments were erected except the tombs of deceased persons of importance. There were, however, buildings of some utility which were erected for votive or dedicatory purposes (see Memorial Cross, Wayside Cross, etc., under Cross; Fountain; Lantern of the Dead), and the few that remain of these buildings are among the most attractive works of art known to us. (For memorials of the dead, both in the churches and standing freely out of doors, often of surprising variety and beauty, see Tomb. For the rude stone monuments of the northern nations, see Megalithic, and references.)

With the classical revival in Southern Europe the desire to imitate the Romans in the erection of monuments became strong, and in the cities of Italy equestrian and other statues mounted on pedestals, often richly adorned, were set up in the streets and squares to do honour to some person who might still be alive. Thus, the statue of Gatamelatta, in Padua, by Donatello, and that of Colleone, in Venice, by Verrocchio, are instances of a kind of monument which the princes and communities of the Renaissance erected here and there, in feeble imitation of the vast accumulation of such memorials which existed in the cities of the great empire. The wealthier communities of later times acted still in partial imitation of the traditional Roman method. Thus, the monument which commemorates the great fire of London, designed by Sir Christopher Wren, and erected at the head of Fish Street Hill, and the memorial gateway of King Ferdinand attached to the Castello del Ovo at Naples, are instances of a sort of monument which has become much more frequent as the nations have grown larger and public wealth greater. In the nineteenth century such monuments as the Column of July,

in Paris, the equestrian and other statues, in Saint Petersburg, London, Berlin, Munich, and Paris; the imitation of Roman triumphal arches, of which there are two in London, two in Paris, — excluding those gateways dating from the time of Louis XIV., — one in Milan, one in Munich; and the gateways of more strictly Grecian style, of which there are several of quite recent date, are all monuments in the strict sense of the word. (See Memorial Arch; Memorial Column.) In the United States monuments have been erected to Washington, — such as the classical column in Baltimore, which is 130 feet high to the feet of the statue which crowns it, — and to Lincoln, in many of the cities of the Union; statues, usually in bronze, have been put up in Boston, New York, Chicago, and especially in Washington, in memory of the national heroes of war and peace; and of late some slight beginning has been made in the way of triumphal arches. One of the most original monuments existing is that in Boston, in memory of Colonel Robert Gould Shaw and the coloured soldiers of his regiment; this consists of a very large alto-relief in bronze, by Augustus Saint Gaudens, which is supported by a granite structure forming a background and canopy. (Cuts, cols. 943, 944; 945, 946.)

— R. S.

Igel Monument. A Roman pillar at the little village of Igel near Trèves (Trier), Rhenish Prussia. The building is a square upright shaft 70 feet high, originally covered with sculpture, but now so defaced that its original purpose is in dispute.

Nereid Monument. A building at Xanthos, in Lycia, Asia Minor, having a solid basalt structure, still existing, 22 feet wide and 32 feet long, built of solid blocks of stone. The fragments of architecture and sculpture found in its immediate vicinity seem to confirm the belief of its discoverer, Sir Charles Fellows, that the high base carried a temple-like building with sixteen Ionic columns and with sculptures standing upon a krepidoma between the columns. It is known that bas-reliefs of importance were built into the basement.

The name Nereid Monument comes from the draped statues which are thought to have been between the columns, and which are taken as representing sea goddesses.

MONUMENT OF LYSIKRATES. (See Choragic Monument.)

MONUMENT OF PHILOPAPPOS. At Athens, Greece. Erected in the second century A.D.; now much ruined. A restoration is given in Stuart and Revett, Vol. III.; and this is generally accepted as approximately correct.

MONUMENT OF THRASYLLOS. (See Choragic Monument.)

MONUMENTS HISTORIQUES. In French, the buildings which have been regis-

MONUMENT TO THE FRENCHMEN WHO FELL AT NUITS IN 1870.

MONUMENT; CEMETERY OF MONTPARNASSE, PARIS.

MOORISH ARCHITECTURE: BRICK ARCADE ON EX-
TERIOR OF THE GIRALDA, SEVILLE, SPAIN.

in a minority in every part of Spain except the extreme south, and the traditions of massive and elaborate building remained with their subjects, the Christianized Spaniards, far more than with the more scattered and more completely subjugated tribes of the north of Africa. It appears, too, that at no time were the Moslem states of North Africa possessed of much wealth. The tendency of Islam to discourage industry and the growth of material prosperity had unchecked sway in the states which we now call Morocco, Algiers, Tunis, and Tripoli; whereas in Spain it had but little comparative effect, and the Moors of the Peninsula were able to indulge in a splendour which those of North Africa did not dream of.

tered and reserved in all parts of France, and over which the government has a certain control. This control is exercised by the *Commission des Monuments Historiques*. (See Historical Monuments.)

MOORISH ARCHITEC-TURE. That of the Mohammedan races of North Africa and of the kingdoms which they established in Spain. The work of these last-named states may be designated Hispano-Moresque. It does not appear that the Mohammedan conquerors of North Africa developed at any time an architecture or a decorative art at all comparable to that which took shape under somewhat similar conditions in Syria and in Egypt. It is probable that the natural incapacity of the Arab for thinking in terms of fine art found in North Africa no race superior in constructive and decorative skill which it could employ. The architecture of Cairo or of Damascus is that of Persians and Byzantines working for their conquerors, the Mohammedans of Arabia, and their allies; and it is clear that no race of workmen at all comparable to the above-named were to be found in North Africa in the seventh century and thereafter. The conquerors of Spain found, however, somewhat better conditions existing: a race which had been highly civilized under the dominion of Rome, and which under the Visigoths had begun the development of a mediæval civilization of some artistic power. Moreover, the Mohammedan conquerors must always have been

MOORISH ARCHITECTURE: VERY EARLY STYLE ;
MOSQUE, CORDOVA, SPAIN.

MOORISH ARCHITECTURE: MOSQUE (NOW CATHEDRAL) OF CORDOVA, SPAIN.

The result of these tendencies is seen in the comparatively humble character of the building of North Africa, while in the matter of intelligent and interesting design those buildings are equal to the buildings of Spain. The mosques, towers, and tombs of Tlemcen, Constantine, and Algiers in Algeria are the equal in good taste, in judicious planning, and in variety and sprightliness of detail to the vastly more expensive, costly, and permanent structures of the Spanish Peninsula. The buildings of Morocco are less known, and the existence for many centuries of a benighted despotism seems to have told against the preservation of even what few Mohammedan buildings of importance may have once existed.

In Spain, on the other hand, mosques of great size were built at an early period, and these were continually enlarged and enriched by subsequent sovereigns. Fortress palaces (see Alcazar) were erected, which contained within their defensive exterior walls much splendour of arrangement in the way of courtyards, fountains, covered galleries, and reception halls, and a wealth of decoration in glazed and coloured tiles, moulded, painted, and gilded plaster, and carved wood. Decoration of more permanent character was given to the exteriors of a few monuments. The peculiar ornamentation, com-

MOORISH ARCHITECTURE: DOORWAY, TARRAGONA, SPAIN.

posed of a constantly repeated unit of diaper, which, for the Mohammedans, replaced the spirited and naturalistic carving of Christian Europe, lent itself to the semi-mechanical reproduction, yard after yard, with but little change ; and the result was speedily seen in a monotony

951

and dulness of effect which was relieved only by that natural inequality of the material which, in all ancient keramic work, is so fortunate for the decorative artist. In this way it has happened that Moslem decoration, by means of glazed tiles, is generally valuable and attractive; while that in stamped, moulded, and painted plaster is of but little interest. These peculiarities are very noticeable in the Moorish architecture of Spain.
— R. S.

MOORISH ARCHITECTURE: SCROLL PATTERN FROM THE ALHAMBRA.

MOPBOARD. Same as Base Board.

MORARD ; abbot and architect ; d. 1014.

Morard was elected abbot of the monastery of S. Germain des Prés, Paris, in 990. He rebuilt the church of his abbey, which had been repeatedly sacked by the Normans. Of his work only the interior porch and the base of the tower remain. The rest of the church belongs to the second half of the eleventh and first half of the twelfth century. It was consecrated April 21, 1163.

Berty, *Topographie, Région du Bourg Saint-Germain.*

MORESQUE (properly same as Moorish). Moresque design or composition ; decoration by means of more or less geometrical figures and interlacing bands, flat or in slight relief, and commonly in brilliant colour, as that of the Alhambra (which see ; and compare Arabesque).

MOREY, PEDRO ; sculptor and architect ; d. 1394.

A native of the island of Majorca, he built the portal called the Miramar of the cathedral of Palma, Majorca. (See Mediterranean Islands.)

Viñaza, *Adiciones.*

MORGUE. Same as Dead House (I.).

MORIN, CHARLES ALEXANDRE FRANÇOIS; architect; b. 1810; d. Oct. 9, 1898.

A pupil of Huyot (see Huyot), he won a first-class medal at the *École des Beaux Arts* in 1831. Morin held the office of chief architect of the *département du Bas Rhin* for thirty years, and under the second Empire was made architect of the crown for the city of Strasburg. During the siege and bombardment of Strasburg, with his son, Georges Morin, at the peril of his life, he did what could be done to protect the cathedral and other monuments.

952

In 1871 the German government desired to retain him in his position, but he settled in Paris.

Ch. Lucas, in *Construction Moderne*, Oct. 23, 1898.

MORIZ VON ENSINGEN; architect.

Moriz succeeded his father, Mathias von Ensingen (see Mathias von Ensingen), as architect of the cathedral of Ulm, Germany. His mason's mark is found on the great vault and main portal of the cathedral. Between 1470 and 1480 he was consulted about the construction of the *Frauenkirche* in Munich.

Hassler, *Ulms Kunstgeschichte im Mittelalter.*

MORNING ROOM. In Great Britain, in the more pretentious residences, a parlour or subordinate sitting-room for the general family use, especially during the day, while the drawing-room proper is reserved for entertainment and the more formal functions of the evening. It is thus nearly the equivalent of the sitting room of the United States. (Compare Breakfast Room.)

MOROCCO, ARCHITECTURE OF. (See North Africa, Architecture of.)

MORO LOMBARDO. (See Coducci, Mauro.)

MORO, LUIGI DEL; architect; b. 1845 (at Livorno, Italy); d. 1897.

Moro was president of the Academy of Fine Arts in Florence, Italy, director of the bureau for the preservation of the monuments of Tuscany, and member of the Superior Commission of the Fine Arts. He studied architecture at Florence under Émile De Fabris, and replaced him as architect of the new façade of the cathedral of Florence designed by De Fabris. Del Moro published *La Facciata di Santa Maria del Fiore* (Florence, 1888, folio).

Alfredo Melani, in *Construction Moderne* for Oct. 9, 1897.

MORTAGNE, ÉTIENNE DE; architect.

Mortagne was *maître d'œuvre* (supervising architect) of the cathedral of Tours, Indre-et-Loire, France, from 1279 until about the close of the century. Bauchal conjectures that he is identical with the *magister Stephanus* who, according to an inscription, built the church of Marmoutier.

Grandmaison, *Tours Archéologiques;* Bauchal, *Dictionnaire.*

MORTAR. A mixture of lime or of cement, or of both, with sand and water, or, more rarely, of those materials with some other, such as plaster of Paris. Ordinary mortar is made with lime and sand alone; that made with cement is generally called cement mortar, and that with plaster of Paris is called gauge mortar. By extension, bitumen, Nile mud, adobe clay, etc., are called by this name.

The use of mortar in building is not primarily to act as an adhesive mixture and to hold two masses of stone, brick, or the like together, but to interpose its soft and yielding, but soon hardening, mass between courses of stone or brick, and thus enable the uppermost one to take a more perfect bearing or bed upon the surface below. Its secondary purpose is to afford an artificial matrix, in which small materials may be so bedded that, when the whole mass of mortar is hardened, the wall, pier, or the like forms a solid homogeneous mass. This object is gained in one of two ways: first, by laying the mortar in quantity upon the upper surface of the masonry already completed and bedding the bricks or small stones upon it while it is still soft (see Bath of Mortar); second, by mingling the mortar with the small materials, as broken stone, brick, and the like, and throwing the whole mass together into the place to be filled by it (see Concrete). The Greeks seem not to have used mortar after the Mycenæan period. The temples which we admire were built entirely of solid blocks of stone fitted one upon another with dry beds, the surfaces being made to correspond accurately; in some cases, at least, by grinding one upon the other. Among the Romans, in the immense works carried out by the engineers of the Empire, mortar was unknown in cut-stone walling, and even in vaulting when composed of large blocks of stone; but the great masses of Roman vaulting, walling, etc., after the time of Augustus, were commonly built of small roughly shaped blocks of stone bedded in quantities of strong cement mortar, and the whole surface faced with flat, thin bricks or tiles. Wherever brickwork was used in antiquity it was of necessity used with some adhesive material; thus, even the Egyptians of very early time used Nile mud, and the builders of Mesopotamia used bitumen (called slime in Genesis), although the unbaked bricks most in use in this region were cemented together by the powdered clay of which they were made, mixed with water and with a little chopped straw. Mortar in the strict sense was not in use in this early time; even the Mycenæan Greeks seem to have used only soft bituminous clay to close the open joints of rough stone work. Since the fall of the great Roman Empire, building has been commonly done with mortar, whether the chief material is cut stone, rough stone, or brick. The vaults of the earlier Middle Ages (see Romanesque Architecture) were built of rubble stone made to adhere by mortar used in great abundance, and the thick walls of that time had little coherence except that afforded by the mortar in which the stones were bedded. In modern bricklaying, mortar serves almost exactly the same purpose. The bricklayer spreads the mortar in a thick bed upon the surface below, and lays half a dozen bricks rapidly upon this mortar, forcing the soft material upward in the vertical joints as he does so (see Shove Joint under Joint). One of the chief requirements in good brickwork, and which distinguishes it from inferior work of the same kind, is the use of mortar in great abundance, filling up the whole of the solid mass, and not allowing irregular openings, large or small, between its two faces.

Brick Dust Mortar. Mortar reddened with brick dust. (See Brickwork.)

Cement Mortar. Mortar into which there enters a considerable proportion of cement. One advantage of building with this material is that it sets rapidly, and that therefore walls can be carried up in freezing weather, because the frost will not have time to affect the mortar before it hardens. Its resistance to moisture is, however, its most valuable quality. In ordinary building above ground, mortar is rarely made of cement and sand alone, but the mixture of half cement and half lime, or one-third cement and two-thirds lime, is made, and this then is mixed with the amount of sand thought expedient. (See Béton ; Concrete ; Mortar ; Rough Cast ; Stucco.) — R. S.

Gauge Mortar. That which is prepared for rapid setting and which is in this way valuable in many cases where slow-drying mortar would cause settling or cracks. It is usually made with plaster of Paris, either used pure or combined with lime, or lime and sand.

Mud Mortar. A mixture of earth, preferably argillaceous, and water used in arid regions as a mortar. (See also Adobe Mortar.)

MORTAR COLOUR;—STAIN. Pigment of any kind intended for colouring mortar for the joints of masonry ; sometimes ground coal or powdered brick, now more often a special preparation marketed in many different tints.

MORTICE ; MORTISE. A hole or recess, rather long and narrow, and usually with parallel sides, formed in one piece of a structure to receive and hold securely another corresponding part : as a tenon in wood framing ; the lock of a door.

Chase Mortice. One which is extended on one side by a chase or groove of the same width, the bottom of the chase made sloping, so as to form an incline from the bottom of the mortice to the surface. It may be formed in one or both of two opposite immovable parts for the insertion of a beam or other crosspiece. One end of the latter being inserted, the other may be revolved so as to pass along the chase and enter the mortice proper.

Pulley Mortice. *A.* A mortice to contain a pulley in a Cased Frame.

B. Same as Chase Mortice.

Stub Mortice. A shallow mortice hole

which does not pass through the entire thickness of the timber in which it is made.

Through Mortice. A mortice passing through the timber.

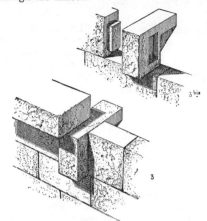

MORTISE PUT TO UNUSUAL SERVICE: TO HOLD A CORBEL FIRMLY IN PLACE IN SOLID CUT-STONE MASONRY; SYRIA, 5TH CENTURY, A.D.

MORTUARY CHAPEL, etc. (See the nouns.)

MOSAIC. The decoration of surfaces by means of inlaid substances. In an architectural sense it denotes the decoration of pavements, wall surfaces, and fixed furniture by means of coloured marbles, glass, or other durable materials. It has various subdivisions corresponding to the matter and manner employed. Thus, *Opus Lithòstratum* signifies all sorts of *stone* mosaic, such, for example, as marble pavements in large patterns : *Opus Sectile*, any mosaic in which the material is *cut* into regular pieces ; *Opus Tesselatum* (checkered), a variety of *Opus Sectile* in which the geometrical patterns formed by straight lines are used ; while *Opus Vermiculatum* (imitating the track of worms) includes the representation of the more varied forms of animate and inanimate nature. *Opus Alexandrinum* is another form of *Opus Sectile*, where but few colours are used, such as white and black, or dark green on a red ground, or *vice versa*. This term is particularly employed to designate a species of geometrical mosaic, found in combination with large slabs of marble, much used on the pavements of mediæval Roman churches and even in Renaissance times, as, for instance, on the pavements of the Sistine Chapel and the stanza of the Segnatura. *Cosmati Work* (which see) is frequently associated with pavements of *Opus Alexandrinum*. It takes its name from the family of the Cosmati, which flourished in Rome during the twelfth and thirteenth centuries and practised the art of mosaic. The Cosmati work has this peculiarity, that it is a glass mosaic used in combination with marble. At times it is inlaid on the white marble architraves of doors, on the friezes of cloisters, the flutings of columns, and on sepulchral monuments. Again, it frames panels, of porphyry or other marbles, on pulpits, episcopal chairs, screens, etc., or is itself used as a panel. The colour is brilliant, — gold tesseræ being freely used. While more frequent in Rome than elsewhere, its use is not confined to that city. Among other places it is found in the Capella Palatina in Palermo. Just what its connection may be with the southern art of Sicily has yet to be determined.

Specifically, the term "mosaic" is used to designate either figure pictures or ornament composed of small cuboids called tesseræ, applied either to pavement, wall, vault, or interior fittings. It is in this limited acceptation of the term that the art of mosaic will now be considered.

The origin of mosaic is unknown. It was used by the Eastern nations in very early times, and later by the Greeks and Romans. What we know of the ancient mosaics is chiefly gathered from the Roman remains found in Italy and the colonies. While the Romans occasionally used it for the minor decorations of fountains, columns, and the like, as well as on walls and possibly on ceilings, most of the examples that have come down to us are of pavements, and there can be but little doubt that its chief employment was for the floor. It remained for the Church to develop it as a mural decoration. Not only simple geometrical patterns in equally simple colour were used for pavements, but elaborate figure compositions as well, such, for example, as the "Battle of Arbela" at Pompeii, the Nereids and Centaurs in the Sala Rotunda, at the Vatican, the "Triumph of Neptune and Amphitrite" at Condiat-Aty. To place such elaborate figure composition on the floor may be deemed questionable taste; but, as the decorative unit, or architectural conditions of the *ensemble* are wanting, possibly it is unjust to condemn this custom. In mosaic pictures like the "Doves of Pliny," at the Capitol Museum, — not to mention a great deal of modern work at the Vatican, — where glass and stone are made to do the work of brush and paint — in other words, where painting is *imitated*, — the material is improperly forced. The only excuse for these *tours de force* is the preservation of otherwise perishable compositions. For architectural purposes such work is out of the question, being far too costly, and deficient in decorative quality.

As to arrangement and colour scheme, the Greek and Roman mosaics were not dissimilar to their mural paintings. Generally the composition was developed in brilliant hues on a white ground, or white was freely used in the border to clean up the picture, the whole thoroughly in harmony with the furniture and

wall surfaces. This, too, is the scheme of the early Christian mosaics. Thus, all the vaultings of S. Costanza (fourth century A.D.) are thoroughly classic in taste. The fine apsidal mosaic in S. Pudenziana (also of the same century, but a little later) is replete with classic feeling, and is, in some respects, the most remarkable early Christian mosaic that has come down to us. The domical mosaic in S. George at Thessalonica, of the fourth century, is Pompeian in feeling. Shortly after, a new style of coloration was introduced, or, more properly speaking, was developed. Richer tonalities were demanded. In the baptistery of S. Giovanni in Laterano, there is a simple but beautiful composition of greenish floriated forms heightened by gold on a blue ground. It dates, probably, from the latter part of the fourth, or the early part of the fifth century. Immediately following we have many specimens of this richer method in the Roman basilicas, and especially at Ravenna whither the seat of government was moved from Rome by Honorius. It is here that the regent, Galla Placidia, wife of Constantine II., established her residence in 425. To her we are indebted for the beautiful mosaics that decorate the mausoleum which bears her name, as well as for those of the baptistery of S. Giovanni in Fonte. Quiet but rich harmonies in blue, green, and gold dominate in these monuments. The execution is excellent, and while the figures are less correctly drawn than in the earlier work of the apsidal mosaic in S. Pudenziana, they have a noble mien. Decoratively these mosaics are admirable, and mark the transition between those of Rome and Byzantium. Mosaic might almost be called *the* pictorial medium of Byzantine mural decoration in the Empire's best days, before political decadence and lack of means substituted "fresco." Byzantium was nothing if not splendid. The gleaming opulence of mosaic, its barbaric gorgeousness, if you will, accorded with the religious and social sumptuousness of the church and court. It was admirably suited to the architecture, an architecture that offered broad, flat surfaces free from projections, and that counted largely on colour for effect. No pigment could compete with the glistening cubes of glass. Nor was the use of mosaic confined to the churches. Palaces blazed with it too, if we may trust the historians. While Byzantine art is always splendid, it varies in excellence according to the epoch. That of Justinian (483–565) is, perhaps, the best, being nearer the classic days. The drawing is more correct, more lifelike, and less hieratic, the draperies especially showing the influence of the antique. True, the anatomy is characterized by ignorance, the figures are stiff, conventional, and lacking in dramatic force. On the other hand, they are wonderfully calm, solemn, and impressive, and their scale well calculated. The very limitation of mosaic lends them dignity. Had not S. Sophia been mutilated by the Turks, it would have afforded us the best example of Byzantine mosaic during the reign of Justinian. As it is, we must turn to the almost synchronous church of S. Vitale at Ravenna, which affords an admirable *ensemble* of Byzantine mosaics of the epoch, though they are slightly affected by Italian influence. Gold is more freely used than in the earlier time of Galla Placidia, and altogether the effect was more sumptuous. After a gradual decline, there was a revival of Byzantine art under the Macedonian dynasty (867–1057), which lasted till the thirteenth century. To this revival belong the mosaics of S. Luke's in

MOSAIC FLOOR: MONASTERY CHURCH AT ARN-
STEIN, RHENISH PRUSSIA.

Phocis, S. Mark's in Venice, and the Sicilian churches. Those of S. Luke's (eleventh century) offer a splendid decorative whole. The figures are less majestic than those of the sixth century at Ravenna, but the attitudes and compositions are good, and there is still discernible a flavour of ancient Greek inspiration. While decorative methods in the disposition of the tesseræ are still in vogue, a tendency to use smaller cubes is noticeable, thus approximating the execution to that of painting, which, as we know, ultimately replaced mosaic. There are many points of contact between the decoration of S. Luke's and that of the Byzantine S. Mark's at Venice, which offers beautiful examples of mosaics on gold grounds. The Sicilian churches of the twelfth century, such as the Capella Palatina at Palermo, the cathedrals of Monreale and Cefalu, while Byzantine

in the character of their mosaic decorations, are somewhat touched by Arabic, Norman, and Italian influences. Here, as at S. Mark's, the pavements and lower parts of the wall are covered with marbles, and the whole upper portion sheathed with mosaics, including the soffits, reveals of the windows, etc., the angles being rounded in accordance with sound mosaic laws. These Greek, Venetian, and Sicilian interiors are literally enveloped in mosaic of one form or another, and are splendid beyond compare.

While Rome cannot offer such sumptuous decorative *ensembles* as these, there is no place where the comparative historical study of mosaic can be made to greater advantage. If the environs also be taken into account, it offers examples of the art from the times of the ancients down to the present day. Not a century is missing. Unfortunately, these examples are often fragmentary, and therefore cannot be judged as decorative concomitants in their present altered surroundings. Frequently they are restored. Then, too, the Latin influence is always dominant; yet this same Latin influence, more observant of nature, revived the moribund Byzantine art after its last splendid manifestations in the twelfth century, and greatly contributed to the Renaissance of the sister art of painting in Giotto's time. Reference has already been made to the classic mosaics of the fourth century in S. Costanza, S. Pudenziana, and S. Giovanni in Laterano. As the distance from classic times increases, so correction and power of delineation decreases. From century to century the mosaics become more barbaric in form; in colour there is no loss — if anything, a gain in mere splendour. About the ninth century art, as a whole, had pretty nearly touched bottom; from the academic point of view, nothing could be more grotesque, for instance, than the figures in the apse of S. Prassede, or in the "Orto del Paradiso" of the same church. Yet the composition is simple and monumental, the scale good, the colour very impressive, and the laws of architectural decoration everywhere observed. The same may be said of the other mosaics of this century, ludicrous as they may appear from an expressional point of view. With Innocent II. (Pope 1130–1143) the art received a fresh impulse. The mosaics ordered by him that decorate the façade, the triumphal arch, and the apse of S. Maria in Trastevere show a marked advance in correction of form. The mosaicists of this epoch began to study life. As Gerspach remarks, these forgotten artists of the twelfth century are not sufficiently appreciated. In the latter part of the thirteenth century, and the beginning of the fourteenth, the great art of mosaic culminated. From the decorative and monumental point of view, nothing superior can be found to Jacopo Torriti's mosaics in the apses of

S. Giovanni in Laterano, and S. Maria Maggiore, both ordered by Nicholas IV. (1285–1294). There are still vestiges of linear archaism, which help, rather than mar, the decorative effect. Unfortunately, at a later epoch, when art had mastered the human form, in the insolence of its triumph, it substituted too free a movement for the necessarily constrained and majestic figures of the period we are now considering. The apse of S. Giovanni in Laterano has been much, but cleverly, restored. The colour scheme, however, the architectural subdivisions, and the scale of the figures are the same. It is particularly agreeable to us moderns on account of its openness and feeling for space, without the frequent overcrowding in mosaic compositions. Every one interested in mosaics should study the works of Torriti. His use of gold tesseræ, not only to enliven otherwise monotonous tones but at times to define the forms, instead of a dark line, is very artistic. Generally speaking, the surfaces of the early mosaics are rough. The vitreous tesseræ glisten wonderfully, and even the opaque cubes radiate light. The use of white in spots (not for the ground, as the Romans used it) is very judicious, cleaning up the deep colours of the pictures. Tones apparently uniform are much broken by the subtle introduction of other tones, and even by occasional gold tesseræ. Thus, a blue ground representing the sky is not graded, but is varied by cognate tones, just as the water-colour painter gives "quality" to a wash by breaking it. The palette — if the term may be applied — is not an extended one, nor should it be. The far greater range of coloured tesseræ in later times was a positive drawback, increasing the temptation to imitate nature and paintings. Nor are the tesseræ set close together, as was frequently the case when mosaic became too naturalistic. The interstices of gray or white tie the colour together, and lend great harmony to the whole. While glass tesseræ predominate, those of opaque material are sometimes used in combination. The art of mosaic declined as the Renaissance advanced. As before stated, it became too pictorial. Luigi della Pace's mosaics (1516), from Raphael's cartoons in the Chigi chapel, S. Maria del Popolo, are not decoratively successful, notwithstanding the elegance and nobility of the drawing. The scale of the figures is too small, and the colour garish. The ceiling mosaic in S. Maria in Gerusalemme, attributed to Baldassare Peruzzi (1481–1536?), is rich in colour, but too pictorial in treatment. The apsidal mosaic in S. Maria Scala Cœli, by F. Zucchio, from designs by Giovanni da Vecchi (1536–1614), though decadent in taste are not without merit, the figures being monumentally grouped in the early manner, but lacking in simplicity of movement and overmodelled.

In the basilica of S. Peter is written, says Gerspach, the history of mosaic during the seventeenth and eighteenth centuries. From 1576 to 1727 there was no government atelier. The mosaicists were taken from the many private workshops in Rome and Venice. In 1727 Benedict XIII. founded the pontifical atelier, which is still active at the present day, and has been the mother, as it were, of the many foreign workshops established in other lands. The imitated pictures in mosaics to be found in S. Peter's have no decorative or architectural interest. As before remarked, they are *tours de force*, produced at enormous expense. The decorative mural mosaics, however, are worthy of study. Take, for instance, those of the dome and its pendentives. The art of the epoch is certainly decadent ; but, putting aside the question of style, the decorative *ensemble* is fine, and the figures correct in scale. The surfaces are rough and brilliant. The Evangelists in the pendentives are large in feeling and have a fine movement. They were executed by M. Provenzale and others, from cartoons by Giovanni da Vecchi. After these works there is but little to commend in decorative mosaic until the present time. It has always been, and still is, a popular art in Italy, where it is practised with great mechanical success. Government ateliers have been established during the present century in France and Russia, the personnel being largely recruited from the Italian workshops. Private ateliers are now numerous both in Europe and America. Many interesting works have been recently executed both in the Old World and in the New, where the art seems to have a future ; but it is the task of posterity, not ours, to estimate these undertakings. Technically, it may be said that no progress has been made since the days of the ancients, with the exception of the invention of certain coloured tesseræ with a metallic base, and the discovery of oil mastic by Muziano da Brescia (1528–1592) as a substitute for the usual plaster. The oil cement sets less rapidly, and allows the mosaicist to work more leisurely. Nor can there be any doubt that the ancient method of working directly on the wall, like all other direct processes, is the best. Moreover, it is probable that in pre-Renaissance times the mosaicist and artist was one and the same person. Thus a liberty of interpretation was allowed most advantageous to the artistic result, and much useless elaboration was saved on the cartoon.

There is a tendency in all modern decoration to divorce the artist from the artisan, the designer conceiving a work from the mechanic executing it. Hence a discrepancy between the original design and the finished product, to the disadvantage of the latter. Hence, too, a certain hard and disagreeably mechanical technic.

Personality is one of the greatest charms in art, and much of this is sacrificed when the execution of the work is delegated to others. The individuality of touch is quite as important as individuality of conception. There are two methods now in vogue for the execution of monumental mosaics, both indirect, but one much more so than the other. Of these, the best is called *a rivoltatura*, by which the design is executed *face upward*, in portable compartments, the tesseræ being temporarily inserted into wet sand, or the like. Paper or linen is glued over the surface, and the section then transferred to the wall, being set into the cement previously prepared for its reception. The paper or linen is afterward removed. This is the method practised in the Vatican ateliers. By the other and inferior process, much used by the modern Venetians, the tesseræ are glued *face downward* to the paper design, and then transferred to the wall in a manner similar to that just described. The latter is the cheaper method, but has the disadvantage that the artisan does not see his work as it progresses, nor is the surface so brilliantly irregular. Moreover, this process is said to be less durable. It is claimed for the *rivoltatura* method that it is cheaper than direct mural work. Possibly it may be so for equal quantities of work executed, respectively, on the wall and in the shop, but it invariably happens with indirect work that there is a great sacrifice of labour. On the wall itself the artist knows just what *not* to do. In conclusion, it should be borne in mind that while mosaic is a sumptuous decorative medium, barbaric gorgeousness should never replace simple, noble, and monumental design. — FREDERIC CROWNINSHIELD.

Florentine Mosaic. An inlay of fine and delicately coloured stones usually in a surface of marble, white, black, or of some other flat and uniform tint, but sometimes covering the whole surface with a continuous pattern, and without background which can be specially indicated. As early as the middle of the sixteenth century the work had received a great development, and in 1604–1606 the chapel of the Princes, or Medicean chapel, attached to the church of S. Lorenzo, at Florence, was built, the walls being entirely sheathed within with an elaborate inlay of very precious materials. Table tops, altar fronts, and the like made of this material are rather abundant in central Italy, and are often very beautiful. This work is generally perfectly flat, but there are some instances in which a slight relief is given to parts of the design ; thus, cherries are represented by precious agates of a chosen colour, and are in relief nearly half their diameter.
— R. S.

MOSLEM ARCHITECTURE. The architecture of the Mohammedans, particularly of the

Arab conquerors in Syria and Egypt, of the Moors in North Africa and Spain, of the Persians, of the Mohammedans of India, and of the Turks. These five divisions comprise all that is important in Mohammedan architecture. It is necessary, in the present article, only to sketch broadly the general course of their historical development, and their chief characteristics and relations.

Except in Persia, Moslem architecture has everywhere begun with Christian models. The Arabs who conquered the Mediterranean littoral in the seventh century were no artists, neither were the Osmanli Turks, nor the Mongols who overran India and Persia. Bringing with them no artistic traditions and no established types, they employed Coptic, Syrian, Greek, and Byzantine builders to erect and decorate their mosques and palaces in the prevailing local styles. Civilized in time by their contact with the Western world, they developed, in the course of the centuries, decided predilections and aptitudes in design, by which their art was given a form and spirit wholly unlike those of the arts on which it was based, emphatically Oriental in character. During the Dark Ages, while Europe was plunged in social and political chaos, Bagdad, Cairo, Cordova, and Toledo were centres of a brilliant artistic and intellectual activity, and of a material splendour almost beyond belief. Yet this brilliant productivity was not lasting ; Islam, with all its unity of creed and intense fanaticism, has never been a constructive force. It has flourished only upon the weaknesses of Christian peoples, and its arts have never exerted any reflex vitalizing influence on Western design.

Historical Summary. The beginnings of Mohammedan architecture were made under the Arab dominion, which, during the first century after the Hegira (622–722 A.D.), extended over Syria (Damascus, Jerusalem, Aleppo, Antioch, 634–641), Persia (Madain captured 642 ; Sassanid dynasty overthrown), Armenia and Mesopotamia (644), Rhodes (655), and northern Africa (Cyrene or Kairouan, 655 ; Carthage, 692) and Spain (710–713). Sicily and southern Italy were subjugated early in the ninth century. As early as 637 the conqueror Omar erected a magnificent mosque on the temple site in Jerusalem. This was purely Byzantine in style, and has wholly perished. The mosque of Amru, at Fostat, near the modern Cairo, built a few years later, was a purely Coptic design ; a few vestiges of it still exist. Other edifices in Jerusalem (El Aksah, Kubbet Yakub, Mehd Isa, Djaim, etc.) and in Arabia were either Coptic or Byzantine in style ; so also the mosque of El Walid and the Maristan at Damascus (705). Shortly after this the khalifate was transferred from Damascus to Bagdad, under the Abbasid line. The expelled

PLATE XXXII

MOSLEM ARCHITECTURE

The detail of the mosque of Kait Bey, in Cairo, Egypt. The use of scroll patterns and interlacing patterns in low relief and in cut stone is very interesting. This is the kind of decoration which was imitated in the plaster work of the Alhambra. This mosque, within the city of Cairo, was built in the fifteenth century of the Christian era ; it must not be confounded with the tomb of Kait Bey.

Ommyads, fleeing to North Africa, established the independent khalifate of the Moghreb (Morocco), which rapidly rose in power and civilization, and overran Spain, where in time the khalifate of Cordova surpassed the splendours of Kairouan and the Moghreb. The ninth and tenth centuries were the most brilliant era of Moslem civilization. This period covers the splendid reigns of El Mansur, Haroun-el-Rashid, and El Mamoun, in the East, under whom Bagdad was adorned with mosques and palaces of almost fabulous magnificence. It witnessed the complete subjugation of the Copts and the establishment in Egypt of the Turcoman Toulunid dynasty, the erection of the mosque of Ibn Toulun (876), of the great mosque of Kairouan, and of the greater part of the great mosque of Cordova (begun 786, enlarged 876, completed by El Mansur 976). The latter part of this period was marked by a remarkable architectural activity in North Africa and Spain, and by the continued triumphs of the Moghrebi (Moorish) arms in Sicily, Sardinia, Malta, and Egypt. In 969 the Moghreb general, Djouhar, overthrew the Toulunid sultans, established the Fatimite dynasty on the throne, founded the present city of Cairo (El Kahireh), and built the mosque of El Azhar. It was under the Fatimites that vaulting and domes began to figure as important elements of the Egypto-Arabic style. The remarkable group of domical shrines and tombs of the Karafah, miscalled "Tombs of the Khalifs," was begun in the reign of El Hakim. During the four centuries following, under the Ayub dynasty and the Mameluke sultans of the Baharite (1250–1381) and the Borgite lines, Cairo was the centre of a remarkable architectural activity, to which we owe the further embellishment of the Karafah and the majority of those beautiful mosques which are the glory of that city, e.g., of Kalaoun (1284), Hassan (1356–1379), Barkuk (1384), Muayyad (1415), Kaït Bey (1465), besides many others, and many fountains and palaces which no longer exist. During this period, corresponding with that of the Gothic styles in Europe, were developed the geometric and stalactite ornamentation, the square or polygonal minaret, and the pointed dome, which characterize the Cairene style.

While Egypt was thus prosperous, the Hispano-Moresque empire was disintegrating, first by breaking up into the separate kingdoms of Cordova, Toledo, Granada, Valencia, etc., and then by successive losses of territory to the Christians, culminating in the fall of Granada in 1482. Yet it was during this period of disintegration — especially in the thirteenth and fourteenth centuries — that some of the most notable monuments of Hispano-Moresque art were erected. The "Giralda" tower at Seville dates from 1160; the Alcazars of Seville

and Malaga, 1181, 1225–1300; the Alhambra at Granada, begun by Mohammed-ben-al-Hamar (the Red) in 1248, was completed in 1306. (See Moorish Architecture.)

During these same centuries, — from the twelfth to the sixteenth, — while European Christendom was developing Gothic architecture to its final perfection of structural design, the Moslems of Persia and India were likewise giving shape to their own styles in a series of remarkable buildings. Of the earlier Moslem style of Persia, which one may suppose was based chiefly on Sassanian traditions with an admixture of Byzantine elements, the long series of Mongol invasions, from Toghrul Bey (1030) to Genghis Khan (1250), left almost nothing standing; and the late style, which developed first under the weak Persian Ilkhan dynasty and reached its culmination under the Sufi, or Sefi, shahs, is often called the Mogul (Mongol) style. Among its earliest monuments are the ruined mosque at Tabriz (1300) and the beautiful tomb of Oljaitou Khodabendeh at Sultanieh (1313). The style culminated in a veritable Renaissance under the Sufis, who came into power in 1478, and to whom we owe the Meidan at Ispahan (Isfan), the Great Mosque, college of Hossein, and Palace of Mirrors, at the same place, the Caravanserai at Aminabad, and other important buildings at Ispahan, Hamadan, Shiraz, etc. These are all of domical design, and revetted externally with glazed tiles of brilliant colours — a branch of keramic art which the Persians carried into Spain, Turkey, and India, and developed to a high state of perfection. The Persians built preferably of brick, and their forms of dome, arch, and minaret were carried into India by the Mogul conquerors, and formed the basis of the Indo-Moslem style. (See Persian Architecture, Part III., Moslem Architecture.)

The Mohammedans first invaded India in the eighth century, but effected no permanent conquest until 1192 in the Pathan region of northern India. The early Pathan monuments are all more or less affected by the Hindu influence (Kutub Minar, tomb of Altumsh, ruined mosque at old Delhi, mosque at Ajmir). Various local styles flourished between the twelfth and sixteenth centuries, as in Jaunpur and Gujerat, in Scinde, Kalburgah, and Bijapur; but these were all absorbed or overborne by the style of the Moguls (1494–1706), in which Persian traditions prevailed over the Hindu and Jaina forms. The Jaina bracket columns, the corbelled arches and horizontal-coursed domes of the Pathan and Gujerati styles, disappeared in favour of the Persian bulb dome, compartment vaulting, round minarets, and huge niche portals. The mosque and the tomb of Mahmud, at Bijapur, — the latter with a noble dome 137 feet in diameter, — were an earnest of the style under the Moguls. Delhi, Gwalior, the new city of Fattehpur-Sikhri, Lahore, and Agra were adorned with an extraordinary series of palaces, tombs, gates, and audience halls, on a vast scale, and lavishly decorated. Among them none is more celebrated than the mausoleum of Shah Jehan at Agra (1650), known as the Taj Mahal, of white marble and alabaster, of exquisite workmanship, and set in beautiful surroundings of gardens, towers, and terraces. (See India, Architecture of.)

The latest of the five styles is that of Turkey. The victorious Osmanli Turks, whose career began in 1299 with the occupation of Bithynia, invaded Europe in the fourteenth century, capturing Adrianople in 1361, and Constantinople in 1453. The most important monuments of their style, based wholly on Byzantine precedents at the outset, are chiefly confined to these two cities, though Brusa, in Bithynia, possesses, in the green mosque, Yeshil Djami (1350), a structure of great elegance, adorned with Persian faience of remarkable beauty. While the earlier mosques of Constantinople were of Greek Byzantine architects, those of later date were, in most cases, of Turkish design ; and the architect Sinan, who built the mosque of Selim I. at Adrianople (1515) and that of Soliman I. at Constantinople (1553), deserves to rank among the world's great architects by reason of the extraordinary number and great merit of his works. The Turkish mosques are nearly all based on variants of the plan of Hagia Sophia, and alone, among Moslem domical buildings, employ the Byzantine pendentive and half dome ; but they display many innovations and improvements on their Byzantine prototypes. Selim I. conquered Egypt in 1517, and many of the later mosques of Cairo are Turkish in style, e.g., that of Mohammed Ali in the citadel (cir. 1820). One of the most interesting examples of Turkish architecture is the mosque of Sinan Pasha at Cairo (1468) ; contemporary with the mosque of Kaït Bey, it offers a striking contrast to it, with its broad spherical dome on pendentives and its Turkish minarets.

Characteristics of Moslem Architecture. Underlying all the specific differences between the above five styles, due partly to the racial distinctions between the Semitic Arabs, the Moors, the Tartar, or Turanian, Turks, and the Aryans of Persia and India, and partly to local environment, there are certain characteristics common to them all. Moslem art is preeminently Asiatic in its decorative spirit, delighting above all in superficial ornament of minute elements, and in brilliant colours broken up into small units mingling harmoniously over broad areas. In this connection the use of Arabic letters in a decorative way should be noted (see Lettering). In general the decorative pre-

vails over the constructive spirit ; but this predominance is not universal, and in Persia, Turkey, and India there are many monuments worthy of comparison, on the structural side, with the finest contemporary works of Christendom. Pictorial art and sculpture have no place whatever in Mohammedan architecture, not because of any hieratic prohibition, but because of a general aversion to forms of art associated with idolatry. The Eastern forms of Christianity often rejected all representation of the human figure, and Christian image worship and Christian religious decoration were associated with the hated Latin Church — a feeling which seems to have influenced the Moslems. Restricted thus to purely conventional forms, the early Arabic decorators, naturally inclined by temperament toward mathematics and philosophy rather than toward practical construction, developed a marvellous system of geometric decoration, in which an intricate interlacing network of lines proceeding from various star centres, formed the dominant motive. Whether the stalactite ornamentation so characteristic of Arabic, Persian, and Moorish design, and to some extent found in Turkish and Indian architecture, was primarily of Arabic or Persian origin, is a disputed point. There is no question, however, as to the origin of the Moslem system of decorative inscriptions : it originated with the Arabs in Egypt, and served as a substitute for pictorial symbolism. From Egypt it spread to North Africa and Spain, and also to Persia, where it was executed in colour on tiles instead of being stamped in stucco or carved in stone. These decorative inscriptions are rare in Turkish architecture, and in India are most frequent in the early Pathan style ; nowhere else, indeed, are they as important or as beautiful as in Egypto-Arabic and Moorish buildings.

Distinctions of Style. The Egypto-Arabic style employs almost exclusively the pointed arch, nearly equilateral ; the pointed dome externally decorated in relief, and the square or polygonal minaret in diminishing stages ; its buildings are usually of moderate scale, though often covering large areas ; stalactite decoration, geometric panelling, inlays, and vestments of coloured marble abound. The Moorish style is characterized by the horseshoe arch, often cusped ; by the general absence of domical or vaulted construction and of lofty features (except a few isolated towers) ; and by a showy system of internal decoration in stamped plaster and mosaic of tiles. Secular buildings abound among its remains in larger proportion than in any other Moslem style except that of India. Persian architecture is distinguished by its bulb domes, huge niche portals, round minarets, external colour decoration in figured tiles, and by the use of a four-centred arch something like those of the Tudor style. Indo-Moslem buildings are mostly of stone, which gives them a dignity of external aspect often wanting in Arabic and Persian edifices. In constructive science they rank high, and are further dignified by their beautiful settings and approaches. The bulb dome and round minaret are found in India as in Persia; but the ogee arch is more common, and ornate carving in stone is especially characteristic of the Indian buildings. Turkish architecture alone employs the Byzantine dome, half dome and pendentive, and the round minaret with conical spire. It is the most sparingly decorated of all the Mohammedan styles, especially in its total lack of external colour; on the other hand its great monuments have a picturesqueness of mass and a scientific excellence of construction which partly atone for their coldness and bareness. (Compare Balkan Peninsula; Mosque.)

Bourgoin, *Les Arts Arabes;* Fergusson, *Indian and Eastern Architecture;* Franz Pasha, *Die Baukunst des Islam* (in the Darmstadt *Handbuch der Architektur*); Gayet, *L'Art Arabe, l'Art Persan;* Owen Jones, *The Alhambra;* Coste, *Monuments Modernes de la Perse;* Parvillée, *L'Architecture Ottomane;* Prisse d'Avennes, *L'Art Arabe;* Texier, *Description de l'Arménie, la Perse, etc.;* Gustave Le Bon, *La Civilisation des Arabes, Les Civilisations de l'Inde, Les Monuments de l'Inde;* Choisy, *Histoire de l'Architecture.*

— A. D. F. HAMLIN.

MOSQUE. The building which for Mohammedans takes the place of the church among Christians and the synagogue among Hebrews; that is to say, a specially appointed place for prayer and exhortation. Attendance there is enjoined by the law of Islam. (See Egypt, Architecture of; Mihrab; Moslem Architecture.) (Cuts, cols. 971, 972.)

MOSQUE EL–AKSA. (See El-Aksa.)

MOSQUE OF AYA SOPHIA (HAGIA SOPHIA). (See Church of S. Sophia.)

MOSQUE OF OMAR. In Jerusalem; a building of late Byzantine or perhaps of the earliest Mohammedan period in Syria. The mixed character of the architectural details has caused great controversy as to its origin.

MOSUNG, DIEBOLT; architect. In 1454 Mosung built the existing choir of the church of S. Nicolas at Strasburg, Alsace, Germany, and a tower for this church which has been destroyed.

Gérard, *Les Artistes de l'Alsace.*

MOTIVE. In fine art, primarily, the subject of a work of art, as when it is said that the motive of a wall painting in a church is biblical, or legendary, or drawn from the history of a saint or other personage. By extension, and more commonly, the peculiar character of a work of art, either considered in its entirety or in its details. Thus, it may be said that the motives of Gothic sculpture are rather vigorous action, portraiture, grotesque imaginings of

monsters, or the like, than religious representation. So it is often said of a building of one epoch or style that it has some motives drawn from another and earlier style. A person who denies to Italian Gothic the character of true Gothic architecture may yet say that it offers admirable Gothic motives.

MOTOR. (See Dynamo, under Electrical Appliances.)

MOUCHARABY. Same as Meshrebeeyeh. The attempt to apply this term written in this or any other way to overhanging or projecting members in other than Moslem architecture is unwarranted.

MOULD. *A.* A form used to guide a workman, whether a solid object requiring to be exactly copied or reproduced by casting, or a profile cut out of a board or piece of sheet metal. In the second of these characters the mould is used for running plaster mouldings and the like. (Compare Pattern; Templet.)

B. The hollow into which melted metal, liquid plaster, or the like is poured in the process of casting. Such a mould is itself a direct cast or impression of a mould in sense *A.*

C. Same as moulding; a common abbreviation used by the trades in composition, as bed mould.

Face Mould. (See under F.)

Falling Mould. (See under F.)

MOULDING. *A.* The plane, curved, broken, irregular, or compound surface formed at the face of any piece or member by casting, cutting, or otherwise shaping and modelling the material, so as to produce modulations of light, shade, and shadow. The term is generally understood as meaning such a surface when continued uniformly to a considerable extent, as a continuous band or a series of small parts.

B. By extension, a piece of material worked with a moulding or group of mouldings, in sense *A,* on one or more sides; the piece being usually just large enough to receive the moulding so worked and to afford one or two plane surfaces by which it is secured in place for decorative or other purpose.

C. From the common use of wooden mouldings made separate and very cheaply, in the moulding mill, any slender strip of material planed and finished, used for covering joints, concealing wires, and the like. (For the use in electric wiring, see under Electrical Appliances.)

NOTE. — Mouldings having specific names descriptive of their particular forms are not defined here because the use of the attributive term is self-explanatory, as in Cove Moulding, Drip Moulding.

(See Apophyge; Bead; Beak; Casement; Cavetto; Chamfer; Congee; Cove; Cyma; Dentil; Drip; Echinus; Fillet; Flat; Fluting; Fret; Keel; Lamb's Tongue; Lip; List; Ogee; Ovolo; Quirk; Rabbet; Reeding; Scape; Scotia; Spring; Talon; Torus; Trochilus.)

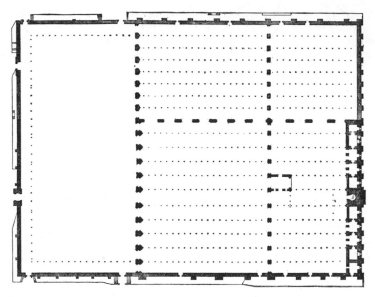

MOSQUE OF CORDOVA: PLAN.

On the left is the open court.   (See interior view below, and exterior under Moorish Architecture.)

MOSQUE OF CORDOVA: INTERIOR VIEW.

(See plan above.)

Annular Moulding. Any moulding, of whatever section, which forms a ring about a surface of revolution, as a shaft, base, or capital. The fillet, torus, etc., of a classic base, the astragal of the necking, the echinus and annuli of the capital, are all annular mouldings.

Anthemion Moulding. One decorated by anthemions. (See Anthemion Band.)

Back Moulding. Same as Wall Moulding, especially as applied at the back of the trim around a window or the like.

soffit of a cornice or a similar projecting surface. In the Ionic and Corinthian cornices, in particular, the mouldings below the dentil band.

Belection Moulding. Same as Balection Moulding.

Billet Moulding. One composed wholly or in part of one or more series of Billets, that is of small cylindrical or prismatic members placed at regular intervals, so that their axes and that of the entire series is parallel to the general direction of the moulding.

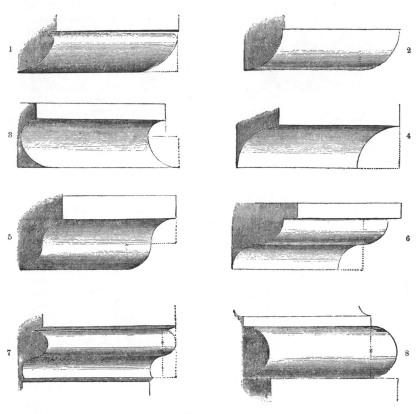

MOULDING:

1. Ovolo moulding from the Doric Temple, Corinth.
2. Ovolo moulding from the Theatre of Marcellus, Rome.
3. Scotia, or Trochilus, Baths of Diocletian, Rome.
4. Cavetto.
5. Cyma Recta.
6. Cyma Reversa.   (5 and 6 are forms of the Ogee.)
7. Ogee of late Roman work.
8. Torus, from Palladio's works.

Balection Moulding. In panelled work, a moulding next the stiles and rails and projecting beyond the plane of their face. (Rare in the United States.)

Band Moulding. In carpentry, any moulding applied to a flat surface as a band.

Base Moulding. In general, any horizontal moulding forming a base or part of a base. In particular, the moulding at the top of a baseboard or other similar member.

Bed Moulding. The moulding or group of mouldings immediately beneath the projecting

Bird's Beak Moulding. A moulding having a profile like a bird's beak; convex on the upper or outer face and concave on the lower or inner face.

Bolection Moulding. Same as Balection Moulding.

Brace Moulding. A moulding composed of two ogees, each the reverse of the other, having the general outline of a printer's brace or bracket. (See Keel.)

Cable Moulding. A form of moulding resembling a rope or cable, used occasionally in the Romanesque or round-arched period of mediæval architecture (twelfth century) in the decoration of arches. The slender twisted shafts of late Gothic architecture in Florence and Venice, as applied to the angles of buildings, are sometimes called cable mouldings.

MOULDING: 12TH CENTURY; FROM S. EBBE'S CHURCH, OXFORDSHIRE, AND FROM LINCOLN CATHEDRAL.

Calf's Tongue Moulding. One formed by a series of pendant, pointed, tongue-like members relieved against a plane or, more usually, a curved surface. This decoration is commonly found in archivolts of early mediæval British architecture, the tongues, in such cases, radiating from a common centre.

Cant Moulding. A bevelled moulding; either one having a bevelled back, for nailing into a corner or angle, as between a wall and ceiling, or one whose face or profile is chiefly a cant or oblique surface.

Chain Moulding. A moulding in the form of a chain with links; occasionally met with in Norman and Romanesque buildings (twelfth century).

Chinbeak Moulding. A moulding common in Renaissance and modern work, consisting of a convex followed below by a concave profile, with or without a fillet below or between, as an inverted ogee, or an ovolo, fillet, and cove. (Compare Bird's Beak Moulding.)

Crown Moulding. Any moulding serving as a corona or otherwise forming the crowning or finishing member of a structure or of a decorative feature; especially, in the trades, a moulding having the form of the cyma recta.

MOULDING: 12TH CENTURY; CHURCH OF SAINT CROSS, HANTS.

Edge Moulding. A moulding whose general form is rounded convexly, the curves being interrupted by a fillet or concave curve making a sharp edge at about its centre line. Typically, it has a quarter round above, then a horizontal fillet, then a quarter round of smaller radius.

Many modifications of this form are, however, designated by the term.

Head Moulding. Same as Hood Moulding.

Hood Moulding. Any moulding having the form of a miniature Hood; especially the moulding or group of mouldings which, in mediæval architecture, is often carried in projection above the opening of a door or window, and which commonly follows and is parallel to the lines of the opening. This feature is very common in English domestic architecture,

MOULDING: VENETIAN; 14TH CENTURY; A VARIETY OF DENTIL MOULDING.

and the hood moulding is either in the form of a pointed arch or in the familiar form of a straight bar terminating the lintel or flat arch at top and having vertical returns carried downward. (See Label.) — R. S.

Nebuly Moulding. An overhanging band whose lower, projecting edge is shaped to a continuous undulating curve. The term is evidently derived from the heraldic adjective nebulée or nebuly, while the member so described is hardly to be considered as a moulding. Common in Romanesque architecture and perhaps derived from the so-called Wave Moulding.

MOULDING: VENETIAN; WITH GEOMETRICAL FIGURES IN RELIEF.

Ox-eyed Moulding. A concave moulding assumed to be less hollow than the Scotia but deeper than the Cavetto.

Pearl Moulding. (See Paternoster.)

Pellet Moulding. In Romanesque architecture, a fillet or small fascia ornamented with small hemispherical projections. Pellet ornamentation is the treatment of any surface with similar projections arranged geometrically or in patterns; especially used in pottery. The ornamentation of fasciæ with a succession of flat disks in Romanesque architecture is sometimes called pellet moulding. (Compare Bezant.)

MOULDING: HOOD-MOULDING OF WINDOW, FROM WITNEY, OXON.

Picture Moulding. A continuous moulding of wood from $1\frac{1}{2}$ to $2\frac{1}{2}$ or 3 inches wide, nailed near the top of the wall of a room, sometimes forming the lower member of the cornice, or serving itself as a cornice, or to separate the frieze from the wall field below; adapted to receive easily adjustable picture hooks from which pictures may be hung.

Quirk Moulding. Any moulding characterized or accentuated by one or more quirks, as the beads worked along the edges of common sheathing.

Raised Moulding. Same as Balection Moulding.

Raking Moulding. *A.* Any moulding adjusted to a rake or ramp.

B. Any overhanging moulding having a soffit which has a rake or slope downward and outward.

Roll and Fillet Moulding. (See next term.)

Roll Moulding. Any convex, rounded moulding, approaching wholly, or in part, a cylindrical form. The term has no absolute meaning and may be applied to a simple round, as a Torus or Bowtell, or to a more elaborate form, as an Edge Moulding. A common form is semicylindrical, interrupted at about its centre line with a vertical projecting fillet. This and any other kindred form is frequently known as a Roll and Fillet Moulding.

Sprung Moulding. In carpentry, a moulding, or group of mouldings, to which is given a considerable projection, with a minimum use of material, by being worked along one face of a board whose width corresponds to the sloping dimension of the mouldings from edge to edge. The board is then set at a slope following the general direction of the projection.

Star Moulding. In Romanesque architecture, a moulding whose surface is carved into a succession of projecting starlike shapes.

Thumb Moulding. In carpentry, a moulding having a cross section supposed to resemble the lateral profile of the end of a thumb.

Wall Moulding. A moulding in sense *B*, used to conceal the joint between a trim and the wall behind by being closely fitted into the angle.

Wave Moulding. A decoration for flat members, as a fascia, composed of a succession of similar undulations somewhat resembling curling waves, first used in Greek architecture and common in all derived styles. (See Nebuly Moulding; Vitruvian Scroll, under Scroll.)

Weather Moulding. Any moulding which is weathered so as to throw off water to protect the structure below, as a hood, drip, or water table.

Zigzag Moulding. (See Bâtons Rompus; Chevron.)

MOULDING MILL. A mill in which primarily wooden mouldings are manufactured by power machines. (See Woodworking Machinery.)

MOUND. A heap of any material, especially of permanent character and more or less symmetrical shape. (See Barrow; Tumulus.)

In America there are two classes of mounds: first, those which are simply of earth heaped up, and, second, those which are wholly or partly of masonry. To the latter the term "pyramid" has been applied. They are all the work of the American Indian or red race. Earthwork mounds, the principal region for which is the Mississippi Valley eastward from the river, have been attributed to a prehistoric mysterious race called Mound Builders, but there is nothing to prove its existence. The mounds are generally not high, but are often extensive.

Masonry mounds are numerous in the Mexican country and southward, and are frequently of great magnitude. They were constructed of adobe brick, of rubble, and of rough or dressed stone, or all combined, usually plastered over with a layer of stucco. It is not certain that they were always wholly artificial. They were built as raised platforms to support other buildings, something in the fashion of the palace temples of Mesopotamia. (See Mexico, Architecture of, § I; Mogote.)

Bandelier's *Archæological Tour in Mexico;* the writings of Lewis Morgan, Cyrus Thomas, Charnay, Stephens, Saville, and Maudsley.

— F. S. DELLENBAUGH.

MOVING. In the technical sense, the process of shifting a building from one site to another. (For a full treatment of the subject, see under Shoring.)

MOXO, EL. (See Herrera, Francisco.)

MUD BRICK. (See Adobe; Adobe Brick.)

MUD BUILDING. Building done with natural materials mixed with water, as distinguished from that monolithic work which is made with cement or other prepared material. Pisé work and adobe are strictly mud building. This kind of work was done largely in ancient Egypt, and it is evident that many of the forms of the massive stone building of later times were derived directly from the older use of the skeleton frame of light reeds, and the like, covered with mud probably applied in many successive coats.

MUDEJAR ARCHITECTURE. That which in Spain shows strong Moorish influence, while yet following in its main lines the style of the European building of the time. The name is principally given to that of the four-

MUDEJAR ARCHITECTURE: HOUSE AT SEVILLE, BEGUN ABOUT 1500.

teenth and following centuries. (See Spain, Architecture of.)

MUET, PIERRE LE; architect and engineer; b. Oct. 7, 1591 (at Dijon); d. 1669.

He was attached to the works at the church of Val-de-Grâce, Paris, from the beginning (see Mansart, N. F.), and by brevet of March 5, 1655, succeeded Jacques Lemercier (see Lemercier, J.) as architect of that edifice. The walls had at this time reached the cornice of the great order of pilasters. After 1666 he was superseded by his associate Gabriel Le Duc (see Duc, Gabriel le). Le Muet published *Manière de bien bâtir pour toutes sortes de personnes* (folio, Paris, 1623).

Ruprich-Robert, *L'Église de Val-de-Grâce.*

MULLET, A. B.; architect; d. October, 1890.

Mullet came to Washington from Ohio soon after the close of the Civil War, at the invitation of Secretary Chase, and was made supervising architect of the Treasury. An immense number of public buildings were carried out under his administration in New York, Boston, Chicago, Cincinnati, and other great cities of the United States.

American Architect, Vol. XXX, p. 45.

MULLION. A slender, vertical, intermediate member forming part of a framework, or serving to subdivide an opening or the like. The term is, perhaps, to be considered as referring to an accessory piece introduced for ornament or for some subordinate

MULLION IN FORM OF A FREE COLUMN; HOUSE OF THE 6TH CENTURY, REFADI, SYRIA.

purpose, rather than to a supporting member forming part of the general construction. (Compare Muntin.)

MULTIFOIL. (See Foil.)

MUNICIPAL BUILDING. A building containing offices for the administration of the affairs of a municipality, — that is, a corporate city, — and hence applied to such a building of any large and important community. (See Broletto; Capitole; Casa de Ayuntamiento; City Hall; Hôtel de Ville; Mairie; Palazzo Publico; Rathhaus; Stadhuis; Town Hall; Village Hall.)

MUNIMENT ROOM. A room arranged for the keeping of documents of importance, as,

MULLION: CATHEDRAL AT PISA, TUSCANY, IN FORM OF A FREE COLUMN, CARRYING SUBORDINATE ARCHES.

PLATE XXXIII

MURAL PAINTING

That of the Sistine Chapel, in the Vatican. The north wall on the right has, nearest the altar, Perugino's Baptism of Christ, second, Botticelli's Temptation of Christ, third, Ghirlandajo's Calling of Andrew and Peter. The west wall has Michelangelo's Last Judgment, and about one third of his paintings on the vault are visible. This is a perfectly bare room, with no architectural decoration.

in a dwelling house, title deeds, marriage settlements, and the like; or, in a monastery, its charters and laws.

MUNNION. Same as Mullion; most often used, however, in the more restricted sense of muntin.

MUNTIN. A small, slender mullion in light framing, as a sash bar, a middle stile of a door.

MURAL PAINTING. In its literal sense, the painting of wall surfaces and ceilings with patterns or subjects. The discussion of this subject falls conveniently under certain separate headings, which, however, cannot be entirely kept apart, but to an extent include each other.

Media and Methods used. (For media, see Encaustic Painting; Fresco Painting; Kalsomine; Mosaic; Oil Painting; Water Colour; Water Glass; Wax Painting.)

Methods in Practising. In painting a decoration, a small rough sketch is usually made first, in black and white, or colour, or both; then a larger and more elaborate sketch in colour follows. Careful drawings are next made. These latter are enlarged to the full size to be adopted. The enlargement is usually made by dividing the drawing into many squares and triangles by ruled lines, and then enlarging these latter mathematically together with the figures which the lines subdivide. Sometimes the modern artist photographs his drawings and enlarges them by means of a lantern throwing the picture upon a flat surface (curved surfaces distort the lines), and then tracing these pictured lines with charcoal or other drawing material. Enlargements are usually made upon paper, and this drawing made to full scale is generally called the cartoon. The lines of this cartoon may be transferred to the wall: (1) By means of coloured impression paper; this can be used conveniently only in small work. (2) The direct pressure of the stylus along the lines of the drawing. This method can be used only when the surface of the wall is soft enough to take an impression. (3) By pricking with a sharp instrument along the lines of the drawing and then pouncing the lines with coloured powder, which penetrates the paper and leaves a pattern on the wall. All these methods injure and often practically destroy the cartoon.

Scaffolding. Scaffolding is required in nearly all mural work and is more or less rough, or ingenious. The best scaffolding is the one which cuts off least light from the worker, since in some cases nearly all the light is obscured by the platforms of planks, and the artist works wholly by calculation. In such cases, this platform must occasionally be in part removed and replaced to enable the worker to correct errors of judgment caused by the dark-

ness. In lofty churches the Italians frequently use movable towers, suggesting the "city taking" war machines of the ancients. Probably one of the most ingenious scaffolds ever made was that constructed by Mr. Bernard R. Green, the engineer of the Congressional Library in Washington. It consisted of an enormous steel truss hung from a steel pin in the eye of the lantern at 125 feet from the pavement, and resting below upon wheels which travelled on a rail around the cornice at the spring of the dome, which was at about 70 feet from the ground below. The immense advantage of this scaffold or "traveller" was that by moving it from the place on which he had been working, the artist going down to the pavement could look up and see exactly what he had done and what changes he must make.

When the artist has his scaffold and has transferred his cartoon to the wall, he works much as does the painter upon the canvas, except that the physical conditions are apt to be less comfortable. For the actual application of colour see under the head of the various Media.

The first and last essential of mural painting is *harmony;* harmony of the painted work with its architectural surroundings and light. The painting must be consistent with its environment, otherwise you may have good architecture and good painting, but you will have a bad effect, that is to say, bad decoration. A consideration of this *harmony* may cover the whole field by subdivision into harmony of composition, of scale, of line, colour, modelling, masses, lighting, perspective, since composition is the art which all these are made to act together in by homogeneous effect upon the eye of the spectator.

Scale. In an easel picture the scale may vary from miniature to the size of life; in mural painting these variations are included and are often exceeded, the scale of the figures attaining a heroic or even a colossal proportion. This scale is determined primarily by the distance from the eye at which the painting is placed. Thus the figures in the ceiling of a drawing-room 16 feet high would but little exceed the size of life, whereas the figures painted upon the vaulting of a chapel 60 feet high or upon a dome at 150 feet would necessarily be of much greater size.

A second determinative influence upon scale of figures in mural painting is that of the architectural members or architectural ornament juxtaposed to the painted work. The safest method for determining scale is to fasten experimentally to the surface to be painted cartoons of figures executed to various scales.

The composition of lines, in mural painting, must be influenced by the surrounding architectural forms and the shape of the painting itself. Thus, in a medallion or lunette the

MURAL PAINTING, POMPEII: CEILING OF BATHS NEAR THE PORTE STABIANA.

effect is enhanced if certain main lines in the composition reëcho the form of the entire subject. For fine examples see Raphael's lunettes in the Vatican Stanze and Del Sarto's "Madonna del Sacco." Lines directly contradicting the surrounding forms are also useful at times, and the apparent height or width of a painting may be increased by the skilful use of lines.

In the *composition of masses* the same rules apply, since a mass is in a measure circumscribed by an imaginary line. The size and number of the masses are, however, greatly influenced by the surrounding architecture, since the eye demands in certain spaces the repose produced by large simple masses, and in other spaces an effect in greater complexity. See Giotto and also Raphael as masters of simplicity in masses, and among modern painters, Jean Paul Laurens as one who has specially used the contrast of simplicity and complexity in the distribution of masses.

Composition of lighting, of modelling, of colour, are so interdependent that they cannot be separated. All should work together to produce that relative flatness which is essential to anything mural, since a mural painting must cling to the wall surface, must not make a hole in it nor start forth from it, must not focus its effect stereoscopically, but must tell as one piece from corner to corner.

The modelling, in a decorative painting, in order that the mural quality of relative flatness shall be preserved, must be far simpler than in an easel picture. Again, distance affects modelling. A heroic or colossal head which appears right in a studio may at 150 feet of height, if too much modelled, be nothing but a confused spot. The attainment of a proper medium between too much and too little modelling in decoration is one of the greatest difficulties of the artist. For almost complete elimination of modelling see Greek vases; for *naïf* simplicity see Giotto; for modelling, still relatively flat but complicated by detail, see the late fifteenth century Tuscans; for a return to relative simplicity governed by science see Raphael's Stanze; for modelling pushed further in mural work, see Tintoretto, Veronese, and later men.

Colour in decoration is subject to some of the laws that govern modelling. Colours are less affected by distance as they approach blue. All artificial light alters colour, electricity somewhat less than gas or candlelight. Blues are especially troublesome under artificial light, as are also blue purples; greens and yellows are less difficult to manage. Sunlight, pure north light as required in the northern hemisphere, twilight, all essentially affect colour, which, indeed, is the creature of light and may be created or destroyed by it. Again, inequality of lighting has an important effect on colour. Parts of any large decoration are sure to be nearer the light of door or window than other parts. The artist must heighten his key in the less lighted portions of the picture. Decorations are also subject to reflections; thus one receiving reflected light from cool greensward requires different treatment from one which receives warm yellow sunlight from a pavement.

Linear Perspective. In the mural painting of vertical surfaces raised to a considerable distance above the ground, and especially in the painting of ceilings, certain tricks, or at least *tours de force*, of perspective were achieved in the fifteenth century by the Italians and developed to an extraordinary extent in the eighteenth. In this treatment, called "di sotto in su" (from below, upward), the attempt was made by the use of violent perspective to make things painted on ceilings appear as they really

would if seen from below. The attempt never wholly succeeded. To begin with, architecture thus painted in perspective can look right only when seen from one single place in the room, or, as a critic has said, can only appear right to one man with one eye in one place.

Again, the human figure, when violently foreshortened from underneath, becomes unbeautiful. The cleverest artist cannot make the head spring gracefully from the centre of the body, or a face show, advantageously, only the under part of

MURAL PAINTING: 12TH AND 13TH CENTURIES; CHURCH OF S. FRANCIS ASSISI; SECTION SHOWING ONE BAY OF UPPER AND OF LOWER CHURCH.

the chin and the point of the nose. Some of the most skilful masters avoided these difficulties by being illogical and violating truth. Mantegna and Melozzo da Forli, the first to introduce violent ceiling perspective, met the difficulties honestly and the result was almost always ugly. Compare for proof of this the foreshortened figures which lean over the balustrade in the ceiling of Mantegna's "Camera degli Sposi" (Ducal Palace of Mantua) with the marching

Romans of his "Triumph of Cæsar" (Hampton Court Palace) and see how the latter exceed the former in grace.

When the attempt is limited to making figures upon a *vertical* surface, raised high above the head of the spectator, appear as they really would when seen from below, the result is more successful. See, as instance, some of Mantegna's wall frescoes. But even here the effect is rather suggested than logically carried out, since upon any plane placed high above one's head and abutting upon a vertical surface, the figures would soon disappear from view, concealed by the ground which gave them footing.

Entertaining and skilful effects of suggested foreshortening have frequently been achieved on vertical surfaces and surfaces sloping slightly inward as they rise, such as pendentives to cupolas. See especially the pendentives painted by Correggio in the cathedral of Parma.

Correggio was the first to attack the problem of "di sotto in su" perspective on a tremendous scale in this same cathedral, and he probably carried out his scheme as logically as was possible to any painter who proposed to combine beauty with truth. To begin with, he chose for the portion of his masonry which was to come directly above the head, the *only* possible logical scheme, that of figures flying freely in the air and therefore susceptible of *any* variation of attitude. Below these figures, representing the Assumption of the Virgin, he set about the vertical octagon supporting the cupola, figures leaning against a simulated balustrade and looking upward. The best proof of the ugliness of violent foreshortening is that even when the work is in the hands of so consummate a master as Correggio, by far the least beautiful portion of the whole decoration is found where the foreshortening is most violent, that is to say, in the group supporting the Virgin and especially in the Madonna herself.

When we come to flat ceilings the problem is more difficult still, and it is perhaps impossible to find a single case among the later masters in which the conditions have been logically met. Veronese, perhaps the most skilful painter of the Italian Renaissance, greatly enjoyed performing tricks of perspective; but in his finest ceilings he is utterly and audaciously illogical, for after foreshortening two or three figures violently to show how clever he can be, he leaves other figures (nearly always his central or principal figures, the ones in fact in which he most desired to have beauty and grace) quite unforeshortened, so that they would pitch headforemost from the ceiling if they were real people. As an instance see the great "Triumph of Venice" in the Ducal Palace, where the horseman in the foreground is carefully foreshortened, while the ladies in the balcony above are hardly foreshortened at all. A

still more curious example is that of the "Crowning of the Virtues" (No. 1197) in the Louvre.

Tiepolo, who loved *tours de force* more and dignity less than did the Veronese, has gone even farther than the latter in his tricks of perspective.

To resume all. These foreshortened ceilings suggest skill, and are often eminently entertaining. They are never quite logical, but as all pictorial art is conventional, they are legitimate. They astonish and impress the average spectator, and no question is more common than "Is it not terribly difficult to paint a ceiling because of the foreshortening?"

To this the answer is "No; to a trained and skilful artist, foreshortening figures is not especially difficult." The difficulty, and it amounts perhaps to *impossibility*, is to make violently foreshortened figures as beautiful as figures in simpler attitudes.

This difficulty is heightened when many figures are grouped together, so that a ceiling abounding in pronounced foreshortening, while it may be entertaining in a *salôn*, is less suitable to a room making distinct pretensions to dignity. No man loved foreshortening better than did Michelangelo, no one performed it with more ease; yet he instinctively felt (as did Raphael) its lack of dignity when used in the "di sotto in su" manner, and among some three hundred figures that crowd the vaulting of the Sistine Chapel only one, the Jonah, even suggests this trick perspective.

It must be remembered that we speak here only of foreshortening from underneath. Since pictorial art represents round figures upon flat surfaces, *every* figure is necessarily foreshortened; it is only when the "di sotto in su" problem is confronted, and the figure is seen, as it were, from the soles of the feet upward, that foreshortening becomes incompatible with beauty.

Tiepolo in the eighteenth century pushed the use of this foreshortening farther than any other master; but his title to fame by no means rests here, but rather in his consummate use of colour and of broad, flat, clean-edged *planes* of colour.

Mural flatness is such an important factor in decoration that its discussion becomes in a measure a short history of decorative painting.

The wall paintings and coloured reliefs of Egyptian and Assyrian art are made absolutely mural by their lack of perspective, linear or atmospheric. The same may be said of Etruscan wall painting. In the decorations upon the walls of Pompeian houses there is much more attempt at perspective illusion, but even here no real perspective depth, no realistic variety of atmospheric planes, is obtained. There is little, if any, subtle modulation of tints. The æsthetic sense of the Greco-Roman work-

MURAL PAINTING: UPPER CHURCH OF S. FRANCIS AT ASSISI, ITALY.

men, fortified by centuries of tradition, demanded
a flat mural treatment, even when background
and middle ground objects had some importance
in the decoration.   This sentiment of decorative
flatness subsisted for many centuries.   In the
mosaics of the Byzantine Greeks, the figures of
men, women, and animals are in the main coloured patterns upon flat coloured ground.
Where accessories are introduced, they also are
treated flatly, and are intended either to sym-

bolize, to help out a story, or simply to fill
space as decorative spots, never to appear as
real objects, set deeply enough into the background to justify their small size as compared
with the human figures.   This is to say, in a
word, that they have no atmospheric perspective.
As instances, one may note the little "Palatium" of Theodoric, or the tiny "Portus Classis"
in the mosaics of S. Apollinare Nuovo at Ravenna; here the saints and virgins, the palace

and the gallery, all stand in a frieze of equal height; columns and ships do not overtop the men and women, yet all are on exactly the same atmospheric plane.

All that play of light and modulation which comes in an absolutely realistic treatment of

MURAL PAINTING: 14TH CENTURY; ONE BAY OF NAVE OF S. ANASTASIA AT VERONA.

nature was left out of these mosaics, and was replaced by the play of light upon the uneven surface made by the cubes or tesseræ, the decorative arrangement of lines, the use of purely ornamental forms, and the subtile variations of tone in masses of cubes, which when seen from a distance appeared to form flat patterns.

All this was in strict comprehension of the laws of decoration. In later mosaics, such as those of the Capella Reale at Palermo, of Monreale, or of the earlier works in S. Marco, such changes from the Ravennese treatment as occur are not in the direction of loss of flatness, but rather in the direction of complication. The decorations are more broken up into smaller and more numerous parts, that is to say, the artists who worked for Roger of Sicily or for the crusading Doges thought and composed less simply than did the men who worked for Justinian and Theodoric. In the north of Europe, where mosaic was little used, the same decorative flatness prevailed throughout all of what we call Gothic art, and a man painted a miracle or a battle upon the walls of a church or in the miniatures of a manuscript exactly as he painted a blazon upon a shield. Approximately, the same treatment was applied to tapestries and subsisted in this branch of art (owing to certain mechanical conditions, which see later) much longer than it did in wall painting.

Indeed, realism in textile art hardly obtained at all until the late seventeenth century, and this in great part is why the tapestries of the eighteenth century are artistically so inferior to those of earlier times, since they are not only less dignified in design, but are usually far less flat in treatment.

The change from flat to realistic treatment in Italian mural painting was gradually effected between the middle fifteenth and the middle sixteenth centuries. This change was very prejudicial to true decoration, but it was a necessary phase in the evolution of modern art, and was, in fact, the direct result of increased (though still immature) knowledge in the artist. Three factors especially enter into the evolution of this change of treatment: first, the knowledge of anatomy and modelling; secondly, the knowledge of linear and atmospheric perspective; thirdly, the use of oil as a medium instead of fresco. Giotto did not know how to model, and his figures stand up in flat decorative silhouette. Pollajuolo and his contemporaries, studying anatomy enthusiastically, fell too much in love with it to forfeit a single detail, so that collar-bone and ribs, muscles of back and breast, unduly accentuated, painted for their own sakes and not for the general effect, broke up the silhouette of the body. This complicated the decoration, "made holes in it," in artist's parlance; but a far greater blow to the decorative flatness of mural painting was given by the achievement of atmospheric perspective. Paolo Uccello, Brunellesco, and others, dissatisfied with our "Palatium" or "Portus Classis" of Ravenna, wished a house to have four sides; to be capable of standing up by itself, not as flat cardboards, but as a solid.

They worked hard at linear perspective until all the lines were correct; but even then, although the house might look right to many Florentines, or to Mantegna in Padua, in fact, to the men who had no feeling for atmosphere, it did *not* look right to Giorgione, Cima, Titian. They pushed the house back into the depths of the picture by the atmospheric planes, golden or brown or gray, that lay between it and the foreground figures of their picture. *Picture* now becomes the word, for the more truly mural decoration of the early time, the works of Giotto and Masaccio, are replaced by the magnificent pictures of Titian, Veronese, Tintoretto. The third factor in this evolution, namely, the use of oil as a medium, had great influence in determining the new realism, because it facilitated the expression of atmospheric planes and what artists call envelopment. With this change in treatment came a change in the setting of the pictorial decoration. The Tuscans during the fourteenth and fifteenth centuries habitually vaulted their rooms, and the tendency of this architectural arrangement was to give the more important decorative subjects to the walls, and to cover the vaulting, pendentives, lunettes, etc., with minor subjects or pure ornament. These subjects were surrounded with flat painted borders, which also followed the intersections of the vaulting. Such is the general arrangement of many of the most famous cycles of Tuscan decoration, of the Giottos, of the Masaccios, the frescoes of Perugino in the Cambio at Perugia, of Signorelli at Orvieto, Ghirlandajo in Florence, in fact of the typical fifteenth century wall painting of central Italy. We have said that the Tuscan realists and idealists alike in the fifteenth century detracted from the flatness and simplicity of their work by complication and overloading.

The great Tuscans and Umbrians of the cumulative period, the beginning of the sixteenth century, had learned the lesson of all this; they simplified their anatomy, treating the body more

freely, rejected much of the decorative detail, and Raphael in his Stanze of the Vatican said the ultimate word in monumental mural painting. With all of these men fresco was the medium used, and fresco is the ideal medium for the decorator, since there is a sort of silvery grayness inherent in it which keeps the work upon the surface of the wall.

As an instance of this difference between true fresco and other media, compare Andrea del Sarto's frescoes in the portico of the Annunziata of Florence with the beautiful frieze painted

MURAL PAINTING: PART OF TRIFORIUM OF NAVE OF S. FRANCESCO AT ASSISI.

by Carpaccio in the little church of S. Giorgio degli Schiavoni at Venice. In the cycle of Andrea both linear and atmospheric perspective are adequate, and the composition is filled with objects upon many different atmospheric planes; nevertheless there is a certain mural flatness about it all largely due to the medium, fresco, and differing widely from the atmospheric depth given by Carpaccio to, for instance, his study chamber of S. Jerome, in the S. Giorgio frieze. The period of the change of medium from fresco to oil coincided with an architectural change in rooms. There had always been some flat ceilings in Tuscany, but large rooms were usually vaulted; now even great halls received the beamed ceilings with caissons. For a while the mouldings of such were delicate and suited to a flat treatment of the pictures, but soon these mouldings in relief, which had superseded the painted borders of the quattrocentisti, grew large and ponderous, oval and round medallions were surrounded by such heavy wreaths, caissons were filled with such high relief of stucco and wood, that a richer and more realistically modelled treatment of the pictured surface suited them, while the depth of the oil painting seemed to harmonize with the masses of gold and the deep shadows resulting from the heavy carving of the framing. The artists now forgot all about making their work mural, that is to say, keeping in the mind of the spectator the feeling that there was a wall behind their painting. Raphael in his Stanza della Segnatura had résuméd all the lessons of Italian mural painting, and had brought to his résumé consummate artistic science. Upon the four walls of his room he placed his principal subjects, medallions and minor subjects decorate his vaulting; he rejects at once the overemphatic anatomy of Pollajuolo and the complicated decorative paraphernalia of Pinturicchio. In the "Stanze" there is little or no gold, few brocaded patterns, or minute details of armour or costume. In the "Disputa," the "School of Athens," the "Jurisprudence," figures, draperies, and architecture are treated simply and with a breadth which takes us back to the days of Giotto and Masaccio. Andrea del Sarto in his cloister of the Scalzo follows the same broad path. In the Stanze of Raphael and in many other decorations of the time we have painted architecture instead of the borders painted *upon* architecture which had gone before, and upon the vaulting of the Sistine Chapel Michelangelo painted all about his pictures and his prophets a tremendous architectural framework, a sort of painted hypæthral illusion, whch is fine *because it is Michelangelo's*, and because it binds together such tremendous creations. Painted architecture became common in Tuscany wherever there were plaster walls in the great rooms, but much space was given to real pilasters, engaged columns, friezes in relief and niches; for the direct imitation of antique architecture had grown apace.

The domes which followed those of Brunellesco and Michelangelo gave a field for decoration of a most imposing character, but few of the works executed justify the opportunity offered.

The finest and most typical example is that given by Correggio in his wonderful cupola of Parma, where the artist breaks straight through his dome surface and shows us figures flying freely in the sky above a painted balustrade which, with foreshortened figures against it, surrounds the octagon that supports the cupola. In this work the medium is fortunately fresco, which helps to preserve an atmospheric feeling throughout the dome; and if Correggio breaks with some of the traditions of decoration, he atones for their violation by the beauty of his types, the power and sweep of his conception and execution. Except for the domes, flat ceilings instead of vaulting were now the rule, and the caisson openings were usually filled with vast canvases, fastened upon stretchers, or whiteleaded to the walls. Oil had become the medium used, and this was the epoch of the splendid paintings of Titian, Veronese, and Tintoretto, which cover the walls and ceilings of Venice. The artist, as has been said before, had wholly forgotten that any restraint can exist for the mural painter, any limitations in the direction of flatness, or simplicity, or emphasis of silhouette; and he now painted upon a church wall exactly as he would the same scene in an easel picture, that is to say, realistically, with focussed effect, with depth of perspective, with richest and deepest colours whenever he wished them.

Let us compare Raphael's Segnatura Hall with Tintoretto's upper hall in the Scuola di S. Rocco. We know what the former was with its vaulting, its frescoed walls, its flat painted architecture, which represented hardly more than borders to the subjects. In the hall in the Scuola we leap from Raphael and central Italy in the beginning of the sixteenth century to Tintoretto and Venice fifty years later. The whole architectonic character of a decorative setting has changed. A vast hall is surrounded by richly carved benches and dado in very high relief; terminal figures abound with their heads cut clear from the wall. The windows are loaded with heavy sculpture; everywhere there is sally and jut; the ceilings hold ponderous caissons. Between the windows and in the caissons are the decorations of Tintoretto. To make a comparison, one feels that in the Stanze of the Vatican Raphael took a simple empty room, with four brick walls, and *truly decorated it;* that in the Scuola the architect built a gorgeous hall, the sculptor enriched it, and that then Tintoretto came along and turned it into a *picture gallery.*

These great canvases of Tintoretto, Veronese, and Titian are in one sense not decorations at all; that is to say, they are not mural because they are not flat. Their atmospheric perspective "makes a hole " in the wall. They are in fact huge pictures framed in architecture, and are not easel pictures only because they are too large to go upon any easel or to find floor space if movable. On the other hand, certain pictorial subjects are suited only to very large canvases, and when such men as Veronese and Tintoretto paint them we are glad indeed to have the result, even if it is not in accordance with the canons of decoration, canons which the artistic temperament of these men could not have conformed to without loss to their work. In considering how much latitude may be allowed to temperament in mural painting, this at least can be said, that although vast realistic pictures *may* be accepted upon flat wall or flat ceiling, they are utterly inadmissible upon such portions of wall as especially suggest construction, — the interstitial spaces of vaulting, for instance. Taking into account all this, the general fact remains that, splendid as were the later painters, especially the Venetians, the earlier painters were truer decorators ; and as muralist, pure and simple, the great Veronese or the gorgeous Tiepolo must bow to the grave and simple Giotto. — EDWIN HOWLAND BLASHFIELD.

F. Crowninshield, *Mural Painting*, Boston, 1887; Vasari, Blashfield-Hopkins ed., especially the notes in which the principles of mural painting are discussed; works on painting for those epochs especially devoted to mural painting, as the books of Crowe and Cavalcaselle on Italian art, and biographies, whether in separate works or in dictionaries of biographies of painters who have been eminent, as Ricci's *Correggio*, Michel's *Rubens*, Müntz's *Leonardo da Vinci*, Dilke's *French Painters of the Eighteenth Century*, Havard's *Vie de J. P. Galland*, Rhys's *Sir Frederick Leighton*, (quarto, 1895), and *Frederick, Lord Leighton* (octavo, 1900). — R. S.

MURPHY, JAMES CAVANAH ; architect ; d. Sept. 12, 1814.

Murphy practised in Dublin in 1786. In 1788 he went to Portugal to make the illustrations for *Plans, Elevations, Sections, and Views of the Church of Batalha* (London, 1793–1795, folio). His chief work is *The Arabian Antiquities of Spain, with description by T. H. Horne* (London, folio, 1813–1816).

Arch. Pub. Soc. Dictionary.

MUSÉE CARNAVALET. In Paris, a museum of antiquities and history of the city, occupying the Hôtel de Carnavalet.

MUSÉE DE CLUNY. (See Hôtel de Cluny ; also Lenoir, A. A.)

MUSÉE DES MONUMENTS FRANÇAIS. A collection formed under the first French Republic and the Empire by Marie Alexandre Lenoir (see Lenoir, M. A.), with official sanction. It contained monuments taken from desecrated churches, portions of buildings which had been sold and were in process of destruction, and many precious antiquities which were likely to disappear in more ordinary ways. After the Restoration it was broken up, but the more bulky monuments remained in the building on the Quai Malaquais, and still remain now that that building is used for the *École des Beaux Arts*.

MUSÉE DES PETITS-AUGUSTINS. Same as Musée des Monuments Français ; so called from the ancient monastery in which the collections were deposited.

MUSÉE DU LUXEMBOURG. In Paris, the chief national collection of works by living artists, occupying galleries and other rooms in the palace of the Luxembourg.

MUSÉE GALLIERA. In Paris, a private foundation occupying a very interesting building designed for the museum and built about 1890.

MUSÉE GUIMET. In Paris, a private foundation occupying a modern building of neoclassical design.

MUSEO CORRER. In Venice, of which the name, belonging properly to the collection of Teodoro Correr, has been extended to the whole foundation; occupies the Fondaco dei Turchi.

MUSEO NAZIONALE. In Italian, a National Museum, especially so called. That of Florence occupies the Bargello, to which it has given its name. That of Palermo occupies buildings which were once a convent. That of Naples fills a very large and important building, built in the sixteenth century, but often altered, and used for a museum only since 1790 ; and, from soon after that time until 1861, under the name Museo Real Borbonico. The very beautiful staircase and the uppermost story date from about 1790. The building is throughout plain and roughly finished, but is well adapted for its present purpose, and is a dignified structure.

MUSEUM. A building or group of buildings arranged to contain collections of any kind for public inspection or for special study, or both. Specimens in natural history, anatomical and other preparations, and specimens used in medical study, works of fine art, models, and objects gathered for archæological study are all stored and exhibited in museums. Picture galleries and sculpture galleries for permanent storage and exhibition as distinguished from those prepared for annual or less frequent temporary exhibitions are also museums in the above sense.

The museums of Europe and America are either (1) old buildings intended for a different purpose, or (2) old buildings to which important alterations have been made, or (3) buildings erected especially as museums.

(1) The Museo Nazionale in Florence is the old Bargello, the large halls and open galleries of which are used without alteration, the light being admitted through the ancient windows. The halls of the Pitti Palace are used in exactly the same way. Of similar character were most of the galleries of the Luxembourg until the recent removal of the collections to an outside building, and all the ground floor galleries of

the vast Louvre Museum as well as many of those in the upper stories. Where side light is acceptable these arrangements are not necessarily bad; but in these more than in others the supposed necessity of architectural effect interferes with the proper lighting of objects exposed.

(2) In ancient palaces, halls reserved for museum purposes have had skylights opened, and in many cases long galleries have been built, even to the extent of an additional upper story, as in the Uffizi at Florence, where what was once an open loggia has been enclosed and has had skylights opened; or, as in the Belvedere Museum, formerly the principal one in Vienna; or, as in the great galleries of the Louvre, where the uppermost story has been partly built for the purpose and partly altered so as to furnish the pictures with top light. The Museo Nazionale at Naples is one of the best instances of this class; here an immense palace-like building, built originally for a university and used at different times for different purposes, was finally established as a museum about 1816, the change of destination involving the building of top-lighted galleries. The minor or special collections of many European capitals are often provided with exhibition rooms; in this way the lower halls of a great palace, as in the Lateran Palace at Rome, in the Doge's Palace at Venice, the Grüne Gewölbe at Dresden, were used; but these, though often called "museum" or by an equivalent term in the language of the country, are not museums in the sense here given to that term.

(3) The old museum at Berlin was finished in 1828, and remains as useful a building as any of its successors. The Glyptothek at Munich, finished in 1830, is a singularly elaborate structure with a plan involving great variety in the different rooms and halls. This, though providing top light for sculptures and in so far less perfectly successful than if a different system had been followed, is yet one of the best museums in Europe. The old Pinakothek of Munich, though not finished till 1836, seems to have been planned before either of the museums above named. In this a very serious attempt was made to combine everything which a museum of art should provide (see Pinakothek). The London National Gallery was finished in 1838. The British Museum, begun in 1823, was continued at different epochs, and some of the changes have been so great as almost entirely to renew the building, so that the actual date of its present arrangement is hard to fix. The picture gallery of Dresden was built about 1850, the new Pinakothek at Munich was finished in that year, the new museum at Berlin in 1855, the National Museum at Munich in 1866, the Vienna Mu-

seum of Art and Industry was finished in 1871; the Museum of Fine Arts in Boston was begun at about that time, and finished in its original form two years later.

It is noticeable that no special pains have been taken by the directors, guardians, or builders of museums to agree as to the essential characteristics of those buildings. Such agreement as the librarians of Europe and the United States have sought to reach (see Library) might have proved of great benefit to the managers and to the public. The earliest museums especially built for that purpose are as good as the latest. Private picture galleries and the like have received no more consistent study than museums, and the latest built ones are as likely to prove failures as those of half a century ago. (See Gallery; Lighting; Skylight.)

It is the experience of those who have had works of art to show in temporary exhibitions, or those who have had temporary buildings to provide as the commencement of permanent museums have found, that a very plain shed, possibly of fireproof material, is easy to arrange; but that the demands sure to be made upon the managers to allow of great architectural splendour in the permanent structure have generally interfered greatly with the proper lighting and showing of the objects exposed. It is on this account the more necessary that a body of rules should be accepted as binding upon all builders of museums. Certain formulæ for the section through the room, for the placing and comparative size of the windows, or skylights, for the protection of the objects within from the direct glare of the sun, or the like, might be adopted and the existence of these rules, even if not binding upon the planners of new museums, might be useful.

The National Museum at Athens, of which a part was finished and occupied before 1880, is a building in which perfect simplicity was combined with incombustible structure. As there were no pictures to be exhibited, side light was used exclusively, and the openings placed high in the wall with excellent results. The Natural History Museum in London, built 1882–1883, is largely sacrificed to the very stately and effective entrance hall. The most recent great museums are the two buildings on the Burg Ring at Vienna, finished in 1889, and the National Portrait Gallery in London, finished 1895; while the Metropolitan Museum of Art and the American Museum of Natural History, both in New York, have additions made to them rather frequently. — R. S.

British Museum. The chief national museum of art and science of Great Britain. The natural history collections have been removed to a building at South Kensington, and the building on Bloomsbury Square, London, which still retains the name British Museum, is now devoted to antiquities and fine arts alone. The building, with its remarkable colonnade, was finished about 1850 ; but the circular reading-room, covered by a great dome, is of later erection.

Capitoline Museum. At Rome ; opposite the palace of the Conservators. (See Campidoglio.)

MUSHREBEEYEH. (See Meshrebeeyeh.)

MUSIC HALL. A large room arranged for the giving of musical entertainments, usually public. The smaller halls used for this purpose are commonly called recital halls, or temporarily by other names. The larger music halls resemble theatres in most of the details of arrangement, etc. The smaller are apt to resemble lecture rooms, in having only one floor or a floor with one set of galleries.

The following maxims for the proper arrangement and finishing of the music hall have reference only to the transmission of sound from the orchestra or singer to the audience. They should be compared with the scientific treatment of the same subject under Acoustics, and as referred to under that term.

(1) Soft wood should be used to cover or line the walls throughout, replacing plaster. Under no circumstances should there be anywhere a brick wall not covered and concealed by wood sheathing ; nor should the podium or front wall of the stage be of brick. The music hall is to be considered as a separate internal structure, built within and separated from the outer walls and roof of the building. The spaces between may be used for foyers, passages, staircases, etc., as is usual.

(2) It is necessary that the walls and ceiling back of the stage should be connected by a continuous curve, which will allow the sound waves to move unhindered, and fast enough not to be caught by new waves. A similar, if not the same, curve should be used with the side walls and also with the wall opposite the stage. It is often good to have the ceiling of the entire hall slope gradually downward toward the stage. The height of the highest point over the auditorium is perhaps indifferent, but its lowest point, where it joins the wall back of the stage, or where the curve connecting it with that wall begins, should not exceed 35 feet, and should be less than this in small rooms. The object of limiting the height above the stage is to preserve the integrity of the tone. If the ceiling is too high, the tone loses something before it reaches the audience ; and also, in orchestral performances, the various choirs cannot blend if the space is too ample. A stage should never be arranged in an alcove ; that is to say, like the apse of a church, having a semicircular wall with a semi-dome as ceiling.

(3) A music hall should not be built on a rock foundation. Moreover, it should never have another hall beneath it, as the large empty space below causes too much vibration and acts on the principle of a drum. An ordinary cellar, without flooring and on a soft soil, gives the best substructure.

(4) A modern orchestra has a large choir of brass and one of percussion instruments. These can only be placed behind the string choir and the wood wind choir. For this reason, and in order to be in connection with the conductor, their seats must be on raised platforms. Now, neither a brass wind instrument nor a drum expresses its true character unless played with a certain freedom. In order that the wall at the back of the stage shall not give too great a resonance for these instruments, the floors must be set at some distance in front of that wall. Other means for diminishing the too great brilliancy of the brass and percussion instruments may be employed : thus, a permanent stage for the chorus may be built behind the stage for the orchestra ; or, in place of the stage, a system of platforms or bench seats rising one above another in the usual way, but established permanently. If the chorus seats cannot be established here, there may be an opening between the orchestra and the rear wall of the stage, above or on each side, or both, to reduce the superfluous force of the brass and percussion instruments, and to enable them to blend with, instead of overpowering, the other instruments. Resort to this method has been found necessary when, as in the ordinary theatre, the orchestra stage is cased with canvas scenery and ceiling : the curtain or drop scene at the rear has to be moved back from 6 to 10 feet behind the orchestra, and the canvas ceiling is also cut off before it reaches the point above the platforms where the brass and percussion instruments are placed. In a permanent structure care must be taken that no draught can come through these openings over the back of the stage, as the effect of draught on instruments makes a good performance impossible.

(5) The sounding-board is only useful in the open air or in a very large building or theatre, its purpose being to throw the tone directly toward the auditorium. Apart from this it is objectionable, for it affects the tone quality because it forces it. The summer concerts in the Chicago Exposition building of 1893, a vast room two blocks long, were very satisfactory, although there was an orchestra of only from fifty to sixty performers. This was accomplished by means of a sounding-board made of thin wood, which has been copied several times, but unsuccessfully, because the angle was not observed. It should be observed that there is an opening behind the stage at the lower end of the sounding-board.

(6) An escape for the sound through the roof is not practicable, because the tone waves mov-

ing from the stage should travel undisturbed throughout the whole building. A high and deep gallery is good, because the tone waves can run out and disappear gradually, as the Rhine loses itself in the sand. It must not be forgotten, though, that the seats under the gallery are never good for hearing the music, and, consequently, the upper gallery should be an extension to the hall, in fact, a carrying of the isacoustic curve of the floor upward, and with a greater or smaller podium dividing the upper from the lower parts of the curve. The bare wall above the gallery is, however, very apt to throw the sound back into the seats of the parquet, or even as far as the stage, and this causes great confusion. This wall, if it must exist, might be covered by a soft stuff which would take up the sound and not allow the resilience of the tone waves even in a slight degree. This, however, is the only way in which a sound-absorbing stuff could be used to advantage. The audience in their seats should always constitute a sufficiently absorbent medium. Certainly no hanging should be put above the stage, where it would of necessity influence the life and quality of the tone.

(7) A hall may be good for vocal music or for instrumental solos, and yet absolutely bad for orchestral music. The modern orchestra has endless resources in colour and rhythmical combination, partly in consequence of its numerical strength. Where Mozart, or even Beethoven, used only one or two flutes, the modern composer uses three or four, thereby establishing an independent choir of flutes alone, and enabling him to give the full harmony to instruments of the same tone quality. It is the same with all the other instruments. It can be seen that, when a separate choir can be formed of each individual kind of instrument, there must be many distinct tone colours, independent of the mixtures produced by combining the different choirs. This possible independence of the choirs, each of the other, allows many different rhythms to be used at the same time, giving a certain undercurrent of life. Too much vibration in a hall will prevent rhythmical combinations from being audible. The modern orchestra therefore represents polophony as opposed to the homophony represented by the soloist.

(8) An empty hall should have much resonance, but no echo. It is advisable always to have a number of alleys or passageways in the parquet, the floors of which should be covered with a thin carpet, and which should be always kept unoccupied by the audience. There is scarcely anything which takes so much brilliancy from the tone as a packed parquet without open passages.

To the above considerations there should be added the historical distinction between the

instrumentation of the time of Mozart and Beethoven (see above, section 7) and that of the present day. It is probable that nothing could be done for music more instructive in the best sense than the building and careful preparation of a small music hall and the organization of an orchestra exactly such as Mozart is known to have used. To this orchestra should be intrusted the rendering of the classical music exactly as it was first composed. The performance of the music of the great masters of the eighteenth century by the full modern orchestra is of necessity a translation from one language into another, although a kindred language. A similar change in the interpretation of music is made when that which was written for the spinet is performed upon the grand pianoforte tuned to concert pitch. — R. S.

NOTE. — For the essential parts of the above statement of conditions, the writer is indebted to Mr. Theodore Thomas, whose invaluable contribution he acknowledges with gratitude.

MUSIC ROOM. A room in a private house, a hotel, or the like, supposed to be devoted to the giving of musical entertainments, private or semipublic. There are no particular characteristics in the fittings or architectural decoration of such rooms; they are usually marked by being nearly devoid of furniture except light chairs and the musical instruments themselves, so far as these are heavy and need a permanent place of deposit. In fact, the music room is usually one of a suite of drawing-rooms, but kept in a condition supposed to be more resonant and more fit for the transmission of sound. On the other hand, the room may be especially adapted for musical performances, other things being sacrificed to that end; the conditions are those of a Music Hall (which see; see also Acoustics and the references).

MUTIUS, CAIUS; architect.

Mutius is mentioned by Vitruvius as having built the temple of Honos and Virtus in Rome with great skill.

Vitruvius, Marini ed.

MUTUAL GABLE. In Scottish law, same as Party Wall. The use of the term should be compared with that of Gable Wall in sense B, the American use applying generally to any side wall, as in a city house, while the Scottish use is limited to the wall which separates two houses.

MUTULE. A flat member slightly projecting from the soffit of the Doric cornice, placed one over each triglyph and one over each metope, and of about the width of the former.

MYCENÆAN ARCHITECTURE. That of the mainland of Greece of the age to which belong the decorative objects, the inlays, the painting, and the general plan and arrangement of the palace fortress at Mykenai or Mycenæ, and its appendages, and of Tiryns. By extension, the architecture having similar characteristics in the Greek islands or elsewhere ; but of this very little has as yet been brought to light. The period now given by most scholars to the Mycenæan age is one anterior to the time of Homer. Messrs. Perrot and Chipiez place it between the years 1500 and 1100 B.C. Drs. Tsountas and Manatt put its commencement some two hundred years earlier. It is assumed that from about 1000 B.C. until historic time there was but little building or original art in Greece, and that the Mycenæan art belonging to an earlier time, and representing a civilization which had then disappeared, retained its influence. (See Grecian Architecture ; Greece, Architecture of.)

Perrot and Chipiez, *Histoire de l'Art dans l'Antiquité;* Tsountas and Manatt, *The Mycenæan Age* (see also Bibliography under the articles cited above). — R. S.

MYLNE (MILNE), JOHN ; architect.

Mylne is the name of a large family of builders and architects who were master masons to the kings of Scotland. John (I.) was appointed by James III. about 1481. John (II.) (d. 1621) and John (III.) (d. 1657) succeeded to the office. John (IV.) (b. 1611, d. Dec. 24, 1667) succeeded his father, John (III.), as principal master mason, and was made master mason of the city of Edinburgh.

Arch. Pub. Soc. Dictionary; Mylne, *The King's Master Masons.*

MYLNE, ROBERT, F. R. S. ; architect and engineer ; b. Jan. 4, 1734 ; d. May 5, 1811.

He was a descendant of John (IV.) Mylne. Mylne travelled in France and Italy, and in 1758 won the gold and silver medals in architecture at the Academy of S. Luke in Rome. He competed successfully for the construction of Blackfriars' Bridge in London, of which he was appointed architect Feb. 28, 1760. This structure was removed in 1868. In 1767 he was appointed surveyor to Canterbury cathedral.

Arch. Pub. Soc. Dictionary; Mylne, *The King's Master Masons.*

N

NAHUATL ARCHITECTURE. That of the American Indians of the Nahuatl stock, whose highest representatives were the Aztecs. Written also Nahua. (See Mexico, Architecture of, § I.) — F. S. D.

NAIL. A slender and small piece of material, usually metal, intended to be driven into anything, especially a board, plank, joist, or other wooden member, for the purpose of holding fast, usually by the elastic force of the wood pressing against it. The term is usually confined to the above described form, but in composition (as in Tree Nail or Trenail) a different signification is implied, which does not generally concern the architect or builder.

Cut Nail. One cut by a machine, as distinguished from wrought and wire nails. The invention of the cut nail machine, together with the increase of woodworking machinery, producing cheap clapboards, shingles, etc., was largely instrumental in developing the wooden building of the United States (see Wood, Construction in, Part II.). The metal of the cut nail is compressed by the machine so much that it is too brittle to be clinched; but it is practicable to soften it sufficiently by heating and allowing it to cool slowly.

Tree Nail. Same as Trenail.

Wire Nail. One cut from a wire, and having a cylindrical shank, a sharp point, and a head made by flattening the metal. These are the nails commonly used in France and over large parts of the Continent of Europe. They have been much used in the United States for certain delicate kinds of cabinet work, as for planting separate mouldings on to rails and stiles, etc., and they have recently been imported and manufactured in considerable quantities, even in the larger sizes. They are usually capable of clinching.

Wrought Nail. Anciently, a nail worked by hand, each piece having been forged separately. Long after the introduction of the cut nail, wrought nails were still used where clinching was thought desirable. They are not now common, except when it is desirable to complete decorative wrought-iron work by having the visible nailheads also finely designed. There is then an infinite variety of simple and effective patterns into which the heads can be worked.

NAILHEAD. A small projecting feature, usually ornamental and common in Romanesque sculpture, thought to resemble the projecting head of an old-fashioned wrought nail ; as a rough four-sided pyramid. (See Wrought Nail under Nail ; also compare Dog Tooth.)

NAILING. The operation of securing by means of nails ; the result of such operation. (See Nail and subtitles.)

Blind Nailing. In flooring, and the like, the securing of planks or boards to the beams or other supports by driving the nails diagonally into the edge, so that each plank, when put into place, conceals the heads of the nails in the adjoining plank. The object of this is partly the smoother appearance of the floor, but chiefly the avoidance of the risk of the nails drawing out as the planks tend to warp.

Secret Nailing. Same as Blind Nailing above.

Skew Nailing. Securing by means of nails driven obliquely to the surface or joint ; either to conceal the nailhead, as in blind nailing, or where the nail cannot be driven perpendicularly through the first or outer piece, as where an upright is to be secured to a horizontal.

Tosh Nailing. Same as Blind Nailing above.

NAKHON WAT. A temple near Angkor in Cambodia. (See Farther India, Architecture of.)

NANNI D'ANTONIO DI BANCO; sculptor.

Nanni was the son of one Antonio di Banco, a sculptor in Florence, and was associated with his father and Nicolò di Piero Lamberti (see Lamberti) in decorating the Porta della Mandorla at the cathedral of Florence. The angels which he made for this portal are especially fine.

Vasari, Milanesi ed.; Müntz, *Renaissance*.

NANTEUIL. (See Milon de Nanteuil.)

NAOS. Same as Cella in both senses.

NAPKIN PATTERN. Same as Linen Pattern.

NARTHEX. In early Christian and Byzantine architecture, the great porch or vestibule at the end farthest from the altar and sanctuary, and therefore just within the main entrance to the church. In the simplest, early buildings it was merely a part of the church screened or railed off, and often an aisle carried athwart the church as in pre-Christian basilicas, but in the larger buildings it is a separate room. The familiar type of narthex is a room as long as the combined width of the naves and aisles, having a door into each of these divisions, and corresponding doors to the outer air. The term has been extended in use to all church vestibules having this form and character. Thus, the great entrance porch of S. Peter's at Rome is often called the narthex. The term is also used loosely for any enclosed vestibule of entrance to a religious building.

As to the original use of the narthex, when persons not fully admitted to Christian fellowship were separated from the members of the church, distinctions were made by which some were admitted to the church proper, others not beyond the narthex, and others again not beyond the atrium and its porticoes. It is also asserted that in some instances the women of the congregation occupied the narthex, but this may be a mistake for the gallery over the narthex, which, with the other galleries of a church, was often appropriated to the women. — R. S.

NASH, SIR JOHN; architect; b. 1752; d. May 13, 1835.

He was a pupil of Sir Robert Taylor. His name is especially associated with the transformation of the old Marylebone region in London into the modern Regent's Park, with its terraces and surrounding streets, which was begun in 1811. Regent Street, Park Crescent and Square, Albany, and other adjoining streets were laid out and built from Nash's designs.

He completed Saint James's Park and transformed Buckingham House into Buckingham Palace.

Stephen, *Dictionary of National Biography*; Gwilt-Papworth, *Encyclopedia of Architecture*.

NASH, JOSEPH; draftsman and lithographer; b. Dec. 17, 1809; d. Dec. 19, 1878.

He studied architecture with Augustus Pugin (see Pugin, A.), whom he assisted in the illustration of his works. In 1834 he was elected associate, and in 1842 a full member, of the Society of Painters in Water Colours. He won his reputation by his lithographs of architectural subjects accompanied with figures. Nash published *Architecture of the Middle Ages* (1838); *Mansions of England in the Olden Time*, his chief work; *Views of the Exterior and Interior of Windsor Castle* (1848); and other works.

Stephen, *Dictionary of National Biography*.

NAVE. *A.* Anciently, that part of a church which was nearest to the common entrance, and which was appropriated to the general congregation of the laity, while the choir and transepts were reserved for the clergy and others. In this sense the term includes the central and side portions alike, or the nave in sense *B* with its adjacent aisles.

B. The chief division of a building, especially of such a building as contains but one very large room divided by piers or columns. Thus, in a church, the middle, and usually highest, part is called the nave where there are aisles on both sides. The term "nave," then, denotes the whole space between the two rows of piers or columns and from floor to roof, including the height of the clearstory.

As there is no special term, other than nave, for the central and highest part of the choir or chancel, or of the transept, when there are aisles to such part of the church, we may say, the nave and aisles of the choir. This is strictly in accordance with definition *B*, above, but it is rarely used, and a circumlocution replaces it. (Compare Clearstory, which is the uppermost part (Étage) of the nave in sense *B* for choir and transept as well as for the nave in sense *A*. — R. S.

NECK. A part of a column considered as interposed between the spreading or ornamental part of the capital and the shaft. This is sometimes enclosed between two neck mouldings and may even receive a separate decoration.

NECKING. *A.* Same as Neck.

B. A moulding or group of mouldings separating the capital from the shaft.

C. In a general sense, any ornamental member at the lower part of a capital. Called also Gorgerin.

NECK MOULDING. A necking which takes the form of a moulding of any sort.

PLATE XXXIV

NEOCLASSIC ARCHITECTURE

Outer portico of the chapel of the Pazzi, adjoining the church of S. Croce in Florence. This chapel was built by Brunellesco in 1420 and the following years, and is the first modern building in which classical details were freely used, though Roman examples were not followed closely.

NECROPOLIS. A city of the dead; applied generally to collections of ancient graves or tombs, considered as the objects of exploration; rarely used for a modern cemetery.

NEEDLE. In shoring, underpinning, and the like, a stout piece of timber, or a steel or iron beam, which is passed through a hole in the wall and supported by shoring or the like; and upon which the load of the wall above the hole is carefully disposed in order that the wall around or below may be removed. (See Shoring.)

NEEDLE LATCH;
LOCK. One in which steel needles hung on pivots are moved by a key so as to pass through holes in a metal plate, allowing the lock to open; the device being a substitute for the usual tumblers. (Compare Cylinder Lock, under Lock.) — (A. P. S.)

NECROPOLIS AT MYRA IN LYCIA, ASIA MINOR: TOMBS CUT IN THE CLIFF OF SOFT STONE.

NEHRING, JOHANN ARNOLD; architect; d. 1695.

Nehring probably came to Berlin from Holland, and was associated with Matthias Smids (see Smids). Among his important buildings are the Reichsbank (National Bank) in Berlin, and the Schloss at Oranienburg. He began the construction of the Zeughaus in Berlin, which was continued by Jean de Bodt (see Bodt). The designs for this fine building are supposed to have been made by François Blondel (see Blondel).

Borrmann, *Denkmäler von Berlin;* Borrmann, *Nehring* in *Deutsche Bauzeitung,* 1894.

NEOANTIQUE. *A.* Same as Neoclassic.

B. Characterizing any special movement in modern architecture involving the study of ancient architecture, such as the attempt, during and since the French Revolution, to study afresh the forms of Greco-Roman architecture without reference to the Renaissance and post-Renaissance styles. (See Neo-Grec.)

NEOCLASSIC ARCHITECTURE. That of modern times beginning with the Italian Renaissance of the fifteenth century; and especially that which is carefully studied from Greco-Roman examples.

The classic transformation of architecture at the period of the Renaissance was not a sudden and unprepared change, as is often supposed; it was the revival in Italy of a tradition long neglected, but never entirely forgotten or without influence. The Lombard Romanesque style and the Italian Gothic had overspread in the Middle Ages those parts of Italy which came under a prevailing German influence; and Byzantine architecture had left its mark on those that were under control of the Eastern Empire. But in Rome and Tuscany there was always a residuum of the Roman classical spirit. Rome was poor and depopulated during the Middle Ages (but see Latin Architecture); and Romanesque and Gothic architecture hardly appeared there, except spasmodically, brought in by colonies of monks. A slight architectural impulse at the beginning of the thirteenth century showed in building that was in strong contrast to what was going on throughout Italy, being distinctly classic in aim, though uninstructed — the porches, for instance, added to S. Lorenzo fuori le Mura, and to S. Maria Maggiore (since removed), and to the cathedral of the near town of Città Castellana, the cloisters of S. John Lateran and the basilica of S. Paul outside the Walls, with other work of the so-called Cosmati style, and, as some authorities think, the rebuilding of S. Maria in Trastevere. In Tuscany, the lower part of the front of the cathedral at Empoli, dated 1093, and at Florence, the façade of S. Miniato, the Baptistery, the porch of the little church of S. Jacopo, and parts of SS. Apostoli show the same classical effort under their parti-coloured marbles. Even the usual Tuscan Romanesque of later date displays a classic feeling for horizontal lines and pediments, for columns of quasi-classic type and proportion, for lintels and entablatures under arches. The introduction of Italian Gothic into Tuscany, the banishment of the papal court to Avignon, and the further decadence of Rome interrupted these tendencies. When the interruptions were past, it was in Florence that what we call Neoclassic architecture, the architecture of the Renaissance, first showed itself; in Rome, chiefly, that it was developed and shaped.

The beginning of the fifteenth century may count as the beginning of the Neoclassic movement in architecture, and Brunellesco as its first leader. His journey to Rome in 1403, where he was the first real student of the remains of classic architecture, has been taken for an epoch. The dome of the cathedral of Florence, his greatest achievement, has no classic

the new choir of S. Annunziata, and the new façade of S. Maria Novella.

It was not the men who were bred to architecture that imported the classic revival into it. Brunellesco, first a goldsmith, then a sculptor, was tempted into it by the engineering problem of the dome; it was only by virtue of a commanding genius and an unequalled opportunity that he held his place. Alberti was an aristocrat, a scholar, and a universal genius; begin-

NEOCLASSIC: EARLIEST FORM, ITALIAN RENAISSANCE; CHURCH OF S. FANTINO, VENICE.

character except in some exterior details of the drum and lantern; but other works, designed while he was busy with this,—the Pazzi chapel, the great churches of S. Lorenzo and S. Spirito, the hospital of the Innocenti, the Pitti palace, —set the examples for the chief applications of classic forms to the buildings of his day. Alberti, the second great Florentine innovator, after visiting Rome like Brunellesco, embodied his studies in his famous treatise *De Re Ædificatoria*, and in the Rucellai palace and loggia,

ning as a literary man, then as a painter, but never a thoroughly qualified architect, only by his own individuality and by being on the crest of the new wave was he made a leader in the Renaissance. The two were, in fact, enthusiastic amateurs, without habits or prepossessions that bound them to the old ways of building; their only inward restraint was in their imperfect knowledge of classical art. Brunellesco had no guide but his own observation and instinct; his work was visibly tentative; his lean entablatures and starved orders and bald detail contrast notably with the freshness and nobility of his ideas and their classic intention. He and Alberti felt from the beginning that the secret of classic architecture lay in subjecting a whole composition to a scheme of well-adjusted proportions, and carefully adapting every part. Alberti, with the newly found treatise of Vitruvius to help him, tried to recover the scheme of ratios by which the Romans had undertaken to regulate this harmony, and his orders were the first to put on the classic look. He recorded his deductions from Vitruvius and his own observations in *De Re Ædificatoria ;* and that was the gospel of the new style till the translation of Vitruvius himself in the next century in a measure superseded it. In his façade for S. Francesco at Rimini, and in the ordinance of S. Andrea at Mantua, his greatest design, he came nearer than any of his contemporaries to that authenticity of classic style which was his great aim.

The task of the Renaissance architects was to restore the supremacy of the order, and this involved complete subversion of those relations of column and arch on which mediæval architecture was based ; it meant therefore a revolution in the artistic habit and ways of thought of builders. It is not strange, then, that the new movement met with opposition, instinctive if not deliberate. Outside Tuscany and Rome, — in Lombardy and middle Italy, where mediæval traditions of building were strong, — though the new style made its way fast, it was by admixture with the old, not by at once displacing it. Details of classic ornament appear first in buildings whose general design does not differ greatly from the old manner, — finely wrought arabesques, strings and cornices of classic profile, delicate pilasters, pediments, and orders refined away from the robust self-assertion of the classic types, a great profusion of surface ornament and colour. This is conspicuous in Lombardy during the fifteenth century, and even later in Venice, where the Byzantine feeling for polychrome material and surface decoration lingered. Characteristic examples are the Loggia del Consiglio by Fra Giocondo at Verona, the oratory of S. Bernardino at Perugia, the church of S. Maria dei Miracoli, the Dario palace, and other works of the Lombardi at Venice. There was in this transitional work the work of builders who inherited the mediæval feeling and traditions, yet caught with enthusiasm at so much of classic forms as would enter naturally into

their own conceptions, — a rare charm of delicate abundant fancy, of picturesqueness, grace, and freedom. It could not last, however. The progress of the revival was inevitable, leading directly back to the formalism of that Roman architecture which it was the object of the reformers to reëstablish.

Both Brunellesco and Alberti had been too much occupied with this main object to give their best thought to details, and neither was fitted by training to design them. Hence the baldness and primness of their detail, and the lack of the charm which a free invention gave

NEOCLASSIC OF THE ITALIAN CINQUE CENTO: CHURCH OF THE REDEEMER AT VENICE, ITALY.

to that of the men who were trained to building. Bramante, the third of the great classicists, was of this last kind. Beginning as a mural painter and decorator of the walls of many churches and palaces, he gravitated naturally into architecture. The sacristy of S. Satiro and the choir which he added to S. Maria delle Grazie, both at Milan, and the many churches in other Lombard cities which are ascribed to him, show the free handling of classic forms, the exuberance and picturesqueness that belong to the Renaissance of Lombardy. When he came to Rome in 1500 to give himself to stricter study of classic building, matured and long-practised in architecture, he soon changed his style, turning to simplicity and grandeur of design, and following the Roman models. He took up by order of Julius II. the building of S. Peter's, begun fifty years before under Alberti and Rossellino, but soon interrupted, making for it a new design to which, though overbuilt by many other hands, the building still owes its scale and grandeur.

It was the effort of these men of the early Renaissance to meet the practical wants of their day with an architecture which had the style and the proportions of the Romans; they tried to apply the Roman forms to their own constructions. At first, they used the forms with great freedom, adapting them to their position in the general design as mediæval forms had been adapted. The subdivision of stories was maintained, the cornice at the top and the base at the bottom were the cornice and the base of the whole façade, and must be proportioned accordingly. An order was the decoration of a story, and must be correspondingly subordinated. Hence the great cornices which we admire in the Riccardi, Strozzi, and Farnese palaces (see Cornicione); hence the starved lower entablatures and delicate pilasters of the Rucellai palace and the Cancelleria. But the study of Vitruvius soon showed that the proportions of the order were sacred, and its position royal. We have already noted that the restoration of it was logically the central task of the Renaissance architects, and that the traditions of mediæval building were opposed to it. A further obstacle was the close union of the arch and column which had become habitual in the Middle Ages, in which the column was always the subordinate. The restoration of the supremacy given by the Romans to the order and the column was slow. Even Brunellesco did not go so far as to put the arch beneath the order in Roman fashion. In the Capella Pazzi he set his vaults over a continuous order. In S. Lorenzo and S. Spirito he followed the method of the later Roman baths and the Basilica of Constantine in carrying his arches on blocks of entablature over single columns. In less monumental compositions, as in the loggia of the Innocenti and the cloister of S. Croce, he set his arches directly on his capitals in the mediæval way, which continued to prevail all through the Renaissance in the galleries of courts and cloisters. Indeed, in the earlier Renaissance the column was chiefly reserved for this use and for the dignifying of doorways; and the pilaster, sparingly used by the Romans, but characteristic in a simpler form of Lombard architecture, was preferred for decorative uses. Alberti, a more complete classicist than his fellows, free from mediæval influence, grew into a thoroughly classical appreciation of the column and of the entablature. Though he caged the Rucellai palace in pilasters, he was the first to use the engaged column with the entablature broken over it (see Ressaut),

and to set the order over the arch, in his façades at Rimini and at Mantua.

It took half a century to bring the arch back into Roman subserviency under the order, as we see it in the lower arcades of the Palazzo Communale at Brescia, and still more in the loggia of the cathedral of Spoleto, one of the most perfect works of the neoclassic and commonly ascribed to Bramante, but believed to be the work of Ambrozio and Pippo d'Antonio, in 1491. Bramante, once in the presence of classical architecture at Rome, was possessed by this idea, carrying it out more logically than Brunellesco or even Alberti had done. His little round chapel or Tempietto in the cloister of S. Pietro in Montorio (1502) was his first embodiment of it, and made an epoch, as Brunellesco's Pazzi chapel had done eighty years before. The study of the Roman orders was taken up with new zeal and minuteness. Vitruvius's treatise, translated and commented on by Fra Giocondo and others, gave decisive formulæ for constructing them. The orders, thus made dominant, gradually changed the character of the new architecture. Hitherto the effort had been to adapt, as has been said, the forms of classic architecture to the constructions of the day; now it began to be to adapt the whole architectural scheme to these forms, with as little violence to them as possible. Bramante and his immediate followers, Peruzzi, Raphael, San Gallo, Sansovino, used their material with a freedom and novelty which preserved to their work a character of inspiration; but the inevitable tendency was to formalism, resulting in a style that aimed at vigorous reproduction of Roman architecture, and that may reasonably be called the Pseudoclassic.

With the leaders of the Renaissance in all its branches there was a progressive effort for the simplicity and largeness of treatment that belonged to classic art and literature. The underlying idea in that architecture, never forgotten by the Greeks (whose work, to be sure, was practically unknown to the men of the Renaissance), and recognized by the Romans in their most monumental work, was that a single order constituted the monument, and the larger the better. A greater building was to be designed, not by multiplying parts, but by increasing the scale of them. This was the pervading Florentine feeling, notably instanced in the cathedral of Florence, and the buildings of old Rome enforced it on every student. There was a steady tendency to make a single order, as in the classical temple, the material for the whole design. This tendency culminated in Bramante's design for S. Peter's, where, as it seems, he used a single great order to cover the whole building, outside and in, as indeed Alberti had done, though on a much smaller scale, at Mantua. His more timid successor, Antonio San

Gallo, proposed to substitute two stories of orders; but Michelangelo, declaring that this multiplication of parts would make a Gothic building instead of a classic one, restored the single order on a scale that had never been equalled, making it a hundred feet high and grouping the windows of two and even four stories under it. This treatment was too obviously the logical outcome of a devout classic revival not to prevail. The great order, once seen on an imposing scale, was generally admired and imitated. In churches it grew to a prevailing fashion from that time, especially within; and even in secular buildings it soon became a habit to put two or three stories under one great order. Neither Greek nor Roman had done this; yet the stories must be provided, and the single order was clearly the most characteristic presentation of classic architecture. Stateliness as well as novelty recommended it. The habit spread rapidly over Italy, and more slowly over the rest of Europe, where on the average the new style had established itself nearly a century later than in Italy. It made the culmination of what we have called the pseudoclassic, distinguished by high orders, colonnades, great pediments, horizontal eaves, straight entablatures, low pitched roofs, and rigorous classicism in detail. Familiar examples are the great colonnade of the Louvre in Paris and most of the French buildings of the time of Louis XIV., the Caserta near Naples, the Escorial in Spain, the Schloss in Berlin, the work of Wren and his followers in England. Further we might add, perhaps, the majority of modern parliament houses and almost every statehouse in the United States.

The system of Vitruvius, once recovered or imitated, gave great facilities for designing. The orders, each reduced to a stereotyped form, could be handled in mass by the architect like building blocks. The great architects of the latter half of the sixteenth century gave laws in their turn; Vignola, Serlio, Scamozzi, Palladio, and then the innovators in France, Germany, and the Netherlands, wrote each his treatise, and minutely regulated the proportions of the orders for himself and his followers. Only in this way, perhaps, by using predetermined types and making every part repeat every corresponding part, could they have accomplished the immense amount of work which they produced on a large scale. It must be said that, while they strained Roman architecture to uses which were foreign to it, these men were far better artists than the Romans had been. They gave to their orders and their decoration a refined beauty of which the Romans had no conception. Their combinations were richer, finer, more varied. They invented a host of new details, — door and window coverings, consoles, capitals, balustrades, and the like. They and the sculptors who worked with them carried

the art into lesser structures, tombs, altars, shrines, sarcophagi, and countless furnishings, thus developing a decorative art of unexampled richness and fertility, founded on Roman models which it far surpassed. The great development of vaulting in mediæval architecture helped them. They found in it hints for vaults of a great variety of shapes, and especially the dome, which set the keynote for their most magnificent designs. If their architecture could not outdo the Roman in scale and majesty, it far surpassed it in variety, elegance, and refinement.

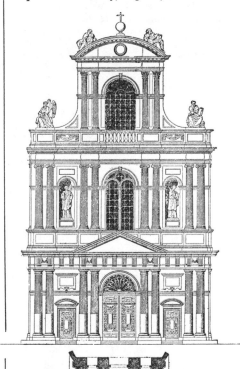

NEOCLASSIC OF THE STYLE LOUIS TREIZE; CHURCH OF S. JERVAIS AND S. PROTAIS, PARIS.

The architects of the seventeenth century, however, tired of the formality of the pseudoclassic. The desire for freedom and novelty revived. Then came the season of proportions relaxed, of details lawlessly and picturesquely handled, which has been called the Baroco, and soon the time when every license prevailed, — of columns contorted, pediments broken, warped, and reversed, of crooked cornices, mouldings and brackets upside down, writhing skylines, overloaded ornament, and all the extravagance which made up the Rococo.

From its beginning in Italy the neoclassic movement had gradually spread over all Europe, displacing the Gothic style, which after three or four centuries of supremacy was falling into decadence. In France it naturally found more obstacles than in Italy, for France was the home of the Gothic, and the Renaissance was there a foreign fashion. Her builders had been the most skilful and inventive in Europe, her architectural traditions the clearest. Some foundation for the Renaissance had been laid during the residence of the popes at Avignon, and later by a considerable influx of cultivated Italian churchmen, who, if they had not had any influence on architecture, had affected the decorative arts and helped to introduce connoisseurship in ancient art. France had her Roman monuments in the south and along the

Italy, and brought back, we are told, painters, jewellers, joiners, and gardeners, yet no architects. The beginning of the Renaissance in France has been ascribed to the visit of Fra Giocondo under Louis XII., and especially to the importation of Rosso and Serlio by Francis I.; but examination shows that the French builders had adopted the new style, slowly indeed, being more than half a century behind the Italians, yet had fairly entered upon it before the appearance of Rosso and Serlio at Fontainebleau. But though the French architects gradually accepted the neo-

NEOCLASSIC OF THE ITALIAN CLASSICISMO: COLONNADE IN PIAZZA OF S. PIETRO, ROME; BEGUN 1667.

Rhine to claim study when the cultivated world turned to the antique. Italian architects, Giuliano San Gallo and later Vignola and Palladio, it is said, travelled about to record them; but she seems to have owed her classical Renaissance, when it came, to her own builders. Sculptors and decorators were imported by resident Italians and by Frenchmen who had become enamoured of Italian art, and the new movement showed itself first in smaller works, in tombs, altars, and the like. Charles VIII. came back from his conquest of Naples (1495) in love with

classic, they were too fixed in their habits and tastes to give themselves up to it unreservedly. They kept their fondness for the high roofs, the tall dormers, turrets, chimneys, and pinnacles of the Gothic, as their châteaux of the sixteenth and seventeenth centuries showed, — the wing of Louis XII. at the château of Blois, for instance, the château of Gaillon (impossibly attributed to Fra Giocondo), of Azay-le-Rideau, Chenonceaux, Chambord, and a hundred others. In church building the conservatism was greater. The builders clung long to the ribbed vault, the

NEOCLASSIC OF THE NINETEENTH CENTURY: PALAIS DE JUSTICE, PARIS.

elongated vertical lines, the grouped pier, and pinnacled buttress, — even the flying buttress, — which appear conspicuously in S. Eustache at Paris and the choir of S. Pierre at Caen. There was not in France a body of painters or of eager amateurs to offer themselves for architects and lead in the new direction, as there had been in Italy ; though we hear of the magistrate Pierre Lescot, and in a later generation of the physician Claude Perrot, by way of exception. The architects of France were her master builders, thoroughly trained in her earlier style, and ready only for a gradual engrafting of the new upon the old, not for a sudden out-and-out change of fashion. It was near the middle of the sixteenth century, in the reign of Francis I., that architects began to disengage themselves from the mass of builders, and be conspicuous in history.. Hence the Renaissance of France retained a free handling, a pervading picturesqueness, and an upward tendency of lines which were entirely un-Italian as well as un-Roman. The relief and play of light and shade which the Italians got by the deeply shadowed galleries in their arcaded courts the French secured by their broken roofs and salient dormers, in as unclassic a fashion as could well be devised, and each held to his own way. Not until the pseudoclassic of Louis Quatorze had the pressure of discipline brought in such a submission to Roman precedent as would have satisfied the Italian leaders, and brought French architecture down to the formal level of the rest of Europe ; even then the high roof held its place obstinately. By 1550, however, the order had won primacy as the chief element in design ; Jean Bullant early introduced the single great order, covering two or more stories, but still the French idiosyncrasy asserted itself. Bullant's great order in the little château at Chantilly is bolstered up between lower windows and cut through in its whole entablature by upper windows in a hopelessly unclassic manner. Philibert de l'Orme, the French lawgiver of the style, who after studying in Italy had come back to write a treatise on architecture like the masters there, took a liberty on which these would never have dreamed of venturing, by devising a new kind of column, with banded and rusticated shaft, which he called the French column. It was familiar to us in his palace of the Tuileries before that was destroyed, and .has not yet lost its place in French architecture. After the stilted dignity of the style of Louis XIV. came a lapse into that variation of the Rococo which the French call the style Louis Quinze, a variation which was capricious and irrational enough, yet did not fall into the wild extravagance of the Rococo of the North nor even the recklessness of the Italian, but kept a certain measure and grace which were characteristically French. (See France, Architecture of.)

In Germany and the Netherlands the new style was handled with more freedom than anywhere else, or, if we please, with more recklessness. We see its picturesqueness in the castle of Heidelberg, the Rathhaus of Bremen and of Cologne, the bishop's palace at Liège. After reaching a climax of dulness in the pseudoclassic period, it fell away into the vagaries of that Rococo which Germans call the Zopfstyl, or pigtail style — the wildest and most whimsical version of the Rococo that has been seen. (See Germany, Architecture of.) England was held back from the new movement not only by her remoteness, but by the development at the beginning of the sixteenth century of a new and striking variation of the Gothic style, the Tudor, which with its admired invention of fanvaulting held possession of the country for half a century. It was not till Elizabeth's reign that Shute, Thorpe, and others succeeded in introducing that distinctive version of the Renaissance which we call Elizabethan, and of which many famous country seats, Wollaton, Longleat, Hatfield, etc., are well-known examples. This was followed under the Stuarts by the pseudoclassic of Inigo Jones and Wren, in exotics that never attained the elegant inventiveness of the Italian which it emulated, and soon withered into the license of the so-called Jacobean. (See England, Architecture of.)

In Spain and Portugal, also, isolation and the peculiar condition of the arts were barriers to the Renaissance movement. The Gothic art of the Spaniards, gathered eclectically from France, Germany, and the Netherlands, and their predilection for Moorish decoration embodied in the Mudejar style which they amalgamated with the Gothic, would seem to have bred in them incapacity for the purity and reserve of style which were the aim of the revival. Their great leader in the Renaissance, Berruguete, went to Rome at about the same time with Bramante, and, returning to Spain after Bramante's death, built in the classic manner for Charles V. the Alcazar of Toledo, and that grandiose addition which, still unfinished, is so conspicuous an excrescence on the Alhambra at Granada. But the Spanish taste reverted in spite of this example to the license of its earlier ways, and fell into a mixed fashion which, from its analogy to jeweller's work, is called the Plateresque, or silversmith's style, and whose peculiarity is a lavish incrustation of sculptured ornamentation, mainly Gothic in spirit but of classic detail, tinctured with Gothic and Moresque feeling. Though Philip II. followed his father's lead, building the Escorial in the most rigid pseudoclassic style, his example did not prevail. The new sacristy of the cathedral of Seville was built in the old confused pseudo-Gothic style ; the cathedrals of Granada and Segovia and many other buildings were adorned, enlarged, or

built with all the lavishness of the Plateresque. Thus in Spain the usual growth of the Renaissance was reversed, and its development was backward rather than forward. In Portugal its progress was very similar ; a style analogous to the Plateresque disputed the ground with the neoclassic — the church and monastery of Belem show us examples of both. (See Spain, Architecture of ; Portugal, Architecture of.)
— W. P. P. LONGFELLOW.

NEO–GOTHIC. In a style based upon ancient Gothic ; said of the results of the Gothic revival in parts of Europe and its further extension in America. The term has been generally used as one of reproach by those who note the absence from the modern structures of some of the most important characteristics of the ancient art.

NEO–GREC (adj.). In French, modern, but imitating or studied from work of the Greeks of antiquity ; Greek or supposed Greek in style : said especially of a few buildings erected in France during the years following 1827, the year of the battle of Navarino, though the term does not appear in French writing until 1860 or later. The attempts at Greek work of the time of the French Revolution are hardly classed under this head, though they were marked by a careful study of the buildings of Greece and of Pæstum, especially by a few students, such as Jean David Leroy and Dufourny, and which resulted in but few and small buildings of detail studied from the Grecian Doric style, such as the buildings of the Octroi at the old Barriers of Paris, and a few private houses in the same city. The neo-Grec movement is generally credited to Duc, L. T. J. Visconti, J. F. Duban, A. L. T. Vaudoyer, Constant-Dufeux, Alexis Paccard, and especially Henri Labrouste, and began in the reign of Louis Philippe. There was much help given by the archæologists, Blouet and Hittorff. The principles of this new school were deliberately formed and carefully considered ; they enjoined a most careful studying of design based upon the materials of the structure, and of decoration strictly rational and called for by the forms themselves. In this way it partook of mediæval as well as neoclassic character ; indeed, it was chiefly in mouldings and other details that Greek feeling appeared ; and the building which is often quoted as the best type of neo-Grec, the Bibliothèque S. Geneviève, in Paris, has much ironwork exposed to view, a high roof, and detail carefully studied afresh without close reference to antiquity. The openings, moreover, are arched ; and in no sense of the word is the building Greek in its structure or its system of design.

Other buildings which are classed as works of this school are Visconti's Tomb of Napoleon under the Dome of the Invalides, Duc's great

Palais de Justice on the Island of the Seine, Duban's new buildings for the *École des Beaux Arts,* and the *Cirque d'Hiver.*
— ALEXANDRE SANDIER.

NEO–ROMAN. Roman of the new or later time as contrasted with antiquity ; applied either to the Rome of the Middle Ages, of the classical Renaissance, of the fifteenth century (see Cinquecento), or of the Rome of to-day. The term is used also as a direct translation of the French *Néo-Romain,* which is applied to that more showy style of about 1860–1870, which succeeded the Neo-Grec.

NEPHRITE. Jade ; *Lapis nephriticus ;* kidney stone. An exceedingly dense and tough variety of amphibole of white or green colour ; translucent. Used by many aboriginal tribes for making knives and ornaments, and by the Chinese and Russians for vases and other works of art. The known sources are Brittany, Switzerland, Silesia, New Zealand, New Caledonia, China, Turkestan, Siberia, and Alaska.
— G. P. M.

NERO ANTICO. Same as Nero Antico Marble (which see, under Marble).

NEPVEU, PIERRE (PIERROT), called **TRINQUEAU ;** architect ; d. 1538 (Félibien op. cit.).

Pierre Nepveu appears to have come from Amboise (Indre-et-Loire), France. After the return of François I. from his Spanish captivity, in 1526, Nepveu was associated with Antoine de Troyes in the construction of the château of Chambord (Loir-et-Cher), France. It was probably designed by Nepveu, who, in an act of 1536 in the *régistre de la baronnage d'Amboise,* is called *honneste homme Pierrot Nepveu, dit Trinqueau maistre de l'œuvre de maçonnerie du chastel de Chambord.*

De la Saussaye, *Le château de Chambord ;* Storelli, *Les châteaux du Blaisois ;* Félibien, *Maisons royales et bâtiments de France ;* Loiseleur, *Résidences royales des bords de la Loire.*

NERVURE. Same as Rib in Gothic vaulting ; the French term sometimes used in English.

NETHERLANDS, ARCHITECTURE OF. That of the low-lying country at the mouth of the Rhine, where this river and the Meuse unite, and also divide and subdivide into many branches. It is called officially the kingdom of the Netherlands, and its more common name among foreigners is Holland, which is properly the name of the largest and wealthiest of the little states of which it was formerly composed.

The inhabitants of the kingdom now number less than five millions. This small community of agriculturists and merchants have inevitably followed closely the immensely powerful impulse given by the architecture of the French lands lying not far to the south. The Protestant Reformation, which in the sixteenth century divided the state as above described from Belgium, came too late to affect the growth of architecture in those styles which were swayed by religious enthusiasm and guided by religious unity; and the more civic architecture of the sixteenth and later centuries took no further modification in the Netherlands than it did in Germany, — that is to say, the Italian influence was only partially felt, being turned aside and partly neutralized by the strong feeling for domesticity, which led to results not unlike those found in Great Britain. As in Great Britain, so here, there is no Renaissance architecture in any true sense, the mingled influences of domestic feeling and of the northern climate making a Dutch seventeenth century architecture of unique and altogether national character. Still, in the great city of Amsterdam, there was never a very powerful architectural school. The most attractive thing to the student is to be found in the long rows of private dwellings; the simplest buildings five stories high with gables fronting on the Nieuwmarkt; the somewhat more recent houses in the newer quarters with shops in their ground stories; the warehouses on the Voorburgwal, and here and there a public building designed on precisely the same lines as the private houses with a great gable on the narrow street — in this is the lesson which the travelling architect may learn from Amsterdam. The very interesting royal palace built between 1648 and 1655, and intended originally for a town hall, is, in character, as sober, as tranquil, and as free from any Southern influence as the dwelling houses themselves, although it is without their high-pitched gables. It has an excellent belfry lantern, which serves at once as a bell chamber and clock house. The most important church in Holland is the cathedral of S. Hertogenbosch, called by the French Bois-le-Duc. It is of very late and florid Gothic, and not to be compared for charm to the buildings of the same epoch in the heart of France, but full of spirited elements of design, and it is adorned with sculpture, especially statues, of great importance. The interior is filled with curious and valuable art treasures, wood carvings, glass, and metal work. Another important church is the great church of Breda, which is interesting in itself and doubly so on account of the extraordinary wealth of carved choir stalls, fonts, tabernacles, and tombs. Some of the latter are as magnificent as anything in the north of Europe, and they are of great variety. The cathedral at Utrecht is partly in ruins, the nave having almost entirely disappeared, but there is a magnificent tower and extensive cloisters. In Leyden, the church of S. Pancras, of the fifteenth century, and the church at Kampen are also important, late Gothic work passing into Renaissance. The

attraction in all the country is, however, nearly the same as in Amsterdam itself, namely, the fascinating private houses, town halls, weighing houses, and the like. At Alkmaar, Bergen-op-Zoom, Bolswaert, Bois-le-Duc, Breda, Delft, Dordrecht, Haarlem, The Hague, Kampen, Leeuwarden, Leyden, Middelburg, Naarden, Nymwegen, Utrecht, and Veere, buildings of this general character are to be found, simply and tastefully designed, built of brick and stone with but little elaboration of sculpture, and always simple in construction. For the study of such architecture as this, domestic and civic of the simpler kind, no country in Europe surpasses the Netherlands. (See West Indies, Architecture of.) — R. S.

Van Ysendyck, *Documents classés de l'art dans les Pays-bas du 10ᵉ au 18ᵉ siècle.*

NEUMANN, JOHANN BALTHAZAR; architect; b. 1687; d. 1753.

In 1711 he entered the artillery service in Würzburg, Germany. He attracted the attention of the prince-bishop, Johann von Schönborn, who sent him to Italy, France, and the Netherlands to study. Neumann built the fine palace at Würzburg decorated by Tiepolo (see Tiepolo, G. B.), and the palaces of Bruchsal and Werneck.

Gurlitt, *Barockstil in Deutschland;* Seubert, *Künstler-lexicon.*

NEVEU, PIERRE. (See Nepveu, Pierre.)

NEWEL. A continuous vertical member forming the axis of a turning stair, either a post, pier, or other upright to support the inner ends of the steps, or built up of a series of circular projections, each worked in one piece with a solid step, as is common in such a stair when of stone. The term applies equally to a comparatively slender cylinder of stone as well as to a square or rectangular pier of considerable extent. By extension, an upright member set at any turning-point of a stair, or at the top or bottom of a flight; commonly forming part of the framing of the stairs, when of wood, and serving to connect, and perhaps support, the strings; and also to support the hand rails at a turn or at an end. — D. N. B. S.

Close; Closed Newel. The central shaft of a turning stair when constructed as a continuous enclosing wall, either hollow or solid. Hence, the term is used to qualify any stair returning sharply on itself so as to leave no well, as a dog-legged stair.

Hollow Newel. The newel or central shaft of a winding stair when constructed as a hollow cylinder, as sometimes in circular masonry stairs. Sometimes erroneously applied to the open well in such a stair when constructed without a newel, and which is properly an open newel. The best-known instance of the use of a hollow newel in the former strict sense is in the central

NEWEL AT TOP OF STAIRCASE, BUILDING OF LOUIS XII., IN THE CHÂTEAU, BLOIS, FRANCE;
ABOUT 1500 A.D.

This newel is a massive compound pier and carries the vaulting of the roof.

staircase of the château of Chambord. Here, the space inside the newel is occupied at its upper end by a secondary circular stair.

NEWEL OF STAIRCASE, HOSPITAL DE LA CRUZ, TO-LEDO, SPAIN ; EARLY YEARS OF 16TH CENTURY.

Open Newel. See Hollow Newel. Used most often attributively, as in the phrase, open newel stairs, which are spiral stairs built without a newel, the stones supporting one another, and having their outer ends built into the cylindrical wall. (Cut, cols. 1033, 1034.)

NEWEL POST. A post or postlike structure, used as a newel, in the derived secondary meaning given above. It may be a small, simple piece of scantling, forming a part of the structural framing of the stair ; or a large and elaborate pillar forming a decorative feature, as at the foot of an important principal flight.

NEW ZEALAND, ARCHITECTURE OF. That of the group of two large islands so called. A peculiar civilization existed among the natives which has been the subject of investigation by expert writers. Dress and personal ornamentation were carried to a certain development.

Roofed houses were built of considerable size ; thus, it is not unusual to find a native house covering 500 square feet of ground, that is to say, 20×25 feet, or thereabout, the walls being from 4 to 5 feet high at the eaves, and the roof rising to a ridge, giving two gable walls each 10 or 12 feet high at the point. The construction is chiefly the attaching of poles and rods to one another by means of ropes and cords made of fibrous leaves and the like, which are twisted with some skill and prove durable. The only limit to the size of a house seems to be the length of the poles which it is convenient to cut and transport. The lashings at the crossings of the upright and horizontal poles are so wound and knotted as to produce a very decorative effect. On the other hand, heavy timbers are in some cases used, and these, generally, in the roofs and protecting gables which form verandas outside of the gable walls. These timbers are sometimes elaborately carved, — the uprights into the semblance of men, but monstrous, distorted, and savage-looking. Such characteristics are the result, not necessarily of a lack of interest in, or power over, decoration, but are supposed to give certain moral characteristics, such as bravery or ferocity in war, to the figures. In the houses of chiefs, where alone such carved work is common, the door openings and the occasional window openings are sometimes framed about with timbers carved in a similar way, heads and hands so combined with elaborate scrollwork that a distant resemblance to humanity is given to each upright piece. The *tiki* or *teekee*, which is a

NEWEL SERVING AS A PILLAR TO CARRY A VAULTED ROOF ; ÖESTERLÄNGATAN, 17TH CENTURY.

figure terminating in a characteristic human head with protruding tongue, which is repeated in the heads or handles of war clubs and pro-

NEWEL, PALAIS DE JUSTICE, PARIS; 19TH CENTURY.
A massive block of masonry, having no purpose beyond steadying the hand rail and parapet.

cessional spears, furnishes a model for the decoration of houses also.

Houses were built easily and without much labour, and there were many of the natives who understood this character of architecture very perfectly. Besides the dwellings and the remains of temples, a curious institution called the battle house or war house was built in honour of some tribal victory, and this was the recipient of the most elaborate carving. The *pah* or *pa* was a defensible enclosure of strong, upright stakes, and such a stockade usually surrounded each one of these war houses.

The modern dwellings of the natives are made to resemble the houses of white men as much as possible. On the other hand, the white men's houses in the country have a certain picturesque character which is pleasant to see. There has been no time to develop a local style; it is not yet fifty years since white settlements became at all common, and even at the present day this great region, larger than the island of Great Britain or than the states of New York and Pennsylvania taken together, contains only about 800,000 inhabitants in all. Auckland was founded in 1840, and has 65,000 inhabitants including its suburbs. The business part of the city is built up with structures three or four stories high, but the residences are less citylike, having rather the air of suburban cottages even when large. The town of Christchurch, the capital, is a small place, but the government buildings, as yet unfinished, are elaborately planned in an English collegiate Gothic style, and are to be faced with stone. The private buildings here are generally unimportant, but there is a partly finished cathedral of considerable pretensions. Dunedin, a Scotch settlement, with 50,000 inhabitants, is built up with stone-faced houses. — R. S.

NICCOLO DA PISA; architect and sculptor; b. about 1207; d. 1278.

At about fifteen, he went with Emperor Frederic II. to Naples, where he was employed on the Castel Capuano and Castel del Ovo. In 1233 he made the bas-relief of the "Deposition" over one of the side doors of the cathedral of S. Martino at Lucca. Niccolò's chief works are the pulpits of the Baptistery at Pisa, and the cathedral of Siena. The Pisan pulpit is signed *Nicola Pisanus*, with the date 1260. It is the first important work of modern sculpture which is based on a study of the antique. The models were found in certain Roman remains at Pisa. About 1265 Niccolò began the Arca di S. Domenico at Bologna. (See Agnelli, G., Niccolò dell' Arca, and Buonarroti.) The contract for the great pulpit of the cathedral of Siena is signed Sept. 29, 1266. In 1274 Niccolò went to Perugia to design the fountain of the piazza. (See Giovanni Pisano.) The twenty-four statuettes about the basin are

attributed to him. Many important buildings are ascribed to Niccolo by Vasari without corroboration.

Vasari, Blashfield-Hopkins ed.; Marcel Reymond, *Sculpture Florentine;* Massari e Vermiglioli, *Fontana di Perugia;* Milanesi, *Documenti dell' Arte Senesi.*

NICCOLO D' AREZZO. (See Lamberti, Niccolò di Piero.)

NICCOLO DE BONAVENTURI. (See Bonaventuri, Niccolò de.)

NICCOLO DEL ABBATE; painter.

An Italian painter who came to France about 1552 and worked under the direction of Primaticcio (see Primaticcio). His most important work was the decoration of the gallery of Henri II. at Fontainebleau.

Palustre, *Renaissance en France;* Mariette, *Abecedario.*

NICCOLO DELL' ARCA; sculptor; b. about 1469; d. 1483.

Niccolò was born at Bari in southern Italy. He worked at first in Naples, and established himself in Bologna when quite young. He formed himself especially on the sculpture of Giacomo della Quercia (see Giacomo della Quercia). His earliest known work is the equestrian bas-relief of Annibale Bentivoglio in the church of S. Giacomo Maggiore at Bologna. He derived his name from the *Arca* or tomb of S. Domenico in the church of that saint at Bologna, of which he was the principal sculptor. It was begun by Niccolò da Pisa. (See Niccolò da Pisa.)

Müntz, *Renaissance.*

NICCOLO GROSSO. (See Caparra.)

NICCOLO DI PIERO LAMBERTI. (See Lamberti, Niccolò di Piero.)

NICCOLO PISANO. (See Niccolò da Pisa.)

NICHE. A recess or hollow in the upright face of a wall or pier, or a structure resembling, or in imitation of, such a form. Generally, such a feature when entirely open to the front, — intended to receive a statue or other decorative object. (Cuts, cols. 1037, 1038.)

NICHOLSON, JAMES; glass painter.

Nicholson was much employed in England in the sixteenth century. He was one of four who contracted to paint eighteen windows in the upper story of King's College Chapel, Cambridge, in the reign of Henry VIII.

Redgrave, *Dictionary of Artists.*

NICHOLSON, PETER; architect; b. July 20, 1765; d. June 18, 1844.

Nicholson is known as a writer on practical architectural subjects. He published *The Carpenter's Guide* (1792, 4to), *Principles of Architecture* (1795–1798, 8vo), *The Architectural Dictionary* (1812–1819, 2 vols. 4to), *Student's Instructor in Drawing* (1837, 8vo), *New and Improved Practical Builder and*

Workman's Companion (1848, 4to), and other works.

Arch. Pub. Soc. Dictionary.

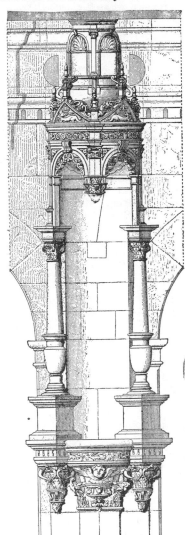

appears that Nicole de l'Escluse was supervising architect of the cathedral of Le Mans in July, 1420. It is supposed by Hucher that he designed the northern transept with its immense rose window, one of the finest in France (but see Dammartin, Jean).

Hucher, *Calques des vitraux de la cathédrale du Mans;* Esnault, *Le transept septentrional de la cathédrale du Mans;* Piolin, *Histoire de l'Église du Mans.*

NIDGE (v.). Same as Nig (local).

NIESENBERGER, HANS (HANS VON GRAETZ); architect.

Niesenberger was appointed architect of the cathedral of Freiburg, Baden, Germany, and took up the construction of the choir of that church begun in 1354 by Hans von Gmünd. It was not finished until 1513. He is supposed to have been a pupil of Jost Dotzinger (see Dotzinger) and to have worked on the cathedral of Strasburg.

Gérard, *Les Artistes de l'Alsace.*

NIG (v.). To dress with the hammer, as stone. (See Hammer; Stone Dressing.)

NIMBUS. (See Aureole; Glory; Vesica Piscis.)

NINEPIN ALLEY. (See Bowling Alley.)

NICHE: ONE ON THE LEFT FOR A PISCINA.
The three openings of the sedilia are also called niches, by an easy extension of the meaning.

NICHE OF THE GRAND STAIRCASE, CHÂTEAU OF CHAMBORD; WORK OF THE FRENCH RENAISSANCE; TIME OF FRANCIS I.

NICOLE DE L'ESCLUSE; architect.

From a document preserved in the *archives départementales* of La Manche, France, it

NINO DI ANDREA (PISANO); sculptor and architect; d. about 1357.

A son of Andrea da Pisa (see Andrea da Pisa). He assisted his father on the first door of the Baptistery at Florence and at the cathedral of Orvieto. He succeeded Andrea as *capomæstro* at Orvieto. Reymond supposes that he worked on the *Genesis* reliefs of the

Orvieto façade. Nino made the Saltarelli monument at Pisa.

Marcel Reymond, *La Sculpture Florentine.*

NOBBLE. To shape a stone roughly; usually at the quarry, so as to save the handling of unnecessary weight.

NOBILE, PETER VON; architect; b. 1774; d. 1854.

Educated in Rome, and devoted himself especially to the classic architecture of Vignola and Palladio (see Barozzio and Palladio). Among his important buildings are the *Burgthor* and *Canal Brücke* in Vienna and the lighthouse in Triest. He was *Hofbaurath* and director of the architectural school in the academy of Vienna.

Seubert, *Künstler-lexicon.*

NOG; NOGGING. A piece of wood, usually one of many, cut in between the upright and other timbers of a frame or a half-timbered construction. The brickwork is filled in between these noggings, which thus serve at once to steady the wooden frame and to retain the brick filling in place. (Called also Nogging Piece; see Brick Nogging.)

NOOK SHAFT. A column or colonnette set in a square break, as at the angle of a building, or where the jamb of a doorway meets the external face of the wall. It differs from an angle shaft in standing well within the projecting corners of the wall, and usually in standing free, not as an engaged column. Sometimes there are two shafts close together, and frequently the jamb of a Romanesque or Gothic doorway has a series of shafts adorning the splay, which, if not engaged shafts, will be nook shafts in the proper sense.

NORAGHE. One of a class of buildings existing in Sardinia and unknown elsewhere. They are sometimes towers in the form of a truncated cone, and containing from one to four small rooms hollowed in the mass of rough masonry, or they are rudely triangular in plan, or, finally, they are large buildings not unlike mediæval strong castles, produced by the constant repetition of the forms mentioned above, triangular and circular. The largest one known is that called Ortu in the province of Iglesias, of which a plan and restoration are offered by Chipiez (op. cit.). It consists of a central conical tower, with a kind of outwork enclosing three much smaller towers, and this whole mass surrounded by an outer wall with six towers, all these being conical, and the curtain walls themselves battered or sloping inward. Their purpose has been matter of dispute, and it is probable that defence on occasion of a sudden attack, and the frequent necessity of an outlook over the country, were the main reasons for their construction. — R. S.

Perrot and Chipiez, *Histoire de l'art dans l'antiquité,* vol. IV.

NORMAN ARCHITECTURE. *A.* That of the people of Normandy; that is to say, of the descendants of the Norwegian predatory and conquering invaders who settled on both sides of the river Seine from Rouen to the mouth of the river, during the eighth and ninth centuries, or of that district. The term covers the architecture developed under the control of Norman conquerors in other lands than Normandy, as that of England, where the Norman influence was felt even before the Conquest of 1066; that of south Italy, where the Norman invasions began about 1040; and that of Sicily, originating about 1061. These buildings belong to the Romanesque style. It would be well to use the term English Romanesque for that branch or school of it which prevailed in England from 1066 for about one hundred years. The old division, especially popularized by Rickman, of English mediæval architecture, as successively Norman, Early English, Decorated, and Perpendicular, loses its value when the English styles are compared with those of the Continent; and in the present work the terms named will be used for reference only. (See England, Architecture of; France, Architecture of; Italy, Architecture of, Parts XI to XIV; Sicily, Architecture of.)

B. That of the region known as Normandy (see France, Architecture of, Part III), and of any epoch. The Norman Gothic was peculiar, and had a great influence on English art (see England, Architecture of; Gothic Architecture in England). — ? S.

Delhi, *Norman Monuments, Palermo and Environs;* Ruprich-Robert, *L'Architecture Normande aux XIe et XIIe Siècles en Normandie et en Angleterre;* Huillard-Bréholles, *Recherches sur les Monuments et l'Histoire des Normands et de la Maison de Souabe dans l'Italie Méridionale.*

NORMAND, CHARLES PIERRE JOSEPH; architect; b. Nov. 25, 1765 (at Goyencourt, Somme, France); d. Feb. 13, 1840.

In 1791 he won the *Premier Grand Prix de Rome* in architecture, which entitled him to a stay of five years in Italy. This course of study being interrupted by the French Revolution, he devoted himself to the art of architectural engraving, and produced an enormous number of plates. He was employed upon nearly all the great illustrated architectural books of his time. Normand was also interested in the production of practical works for the assistance of architects and mechanics employed in architecture, such as *Nouveau parallèle des ordres d'Architecture,* (Paris 1819, folio); *La Vignole des ouvriers* (Paris, 1835, 4to); etc.

NORSE AMERICAN ARCHITECTURE. That in the western hemisphere which shows Scandinavian influence. A few examples of early Norse buildings are found in ruins in southern Greenland, and there are traces in Labrador. Nothing authentic has ever been discovered in the limits of the United States, the round tower at Newport, long ascribed to the Northmen, having been a windmill erected by one of the early governors of Rhode Island. (See Greenland, Architecture of.) — F. S. D.

NORTH AFRICA, ARCHITECTURE OF. That of the vast tract of country bordering on the Mediterranean, comprising Tripoli, Tunisia, Algeria, and Morocco. The last forty years have witnessed the labours of many distinguished archæologists, especially those associated with the *service des monuments historiques*, resulting in a mass of valuable information at the disposal of any future historian. Notwithstanding this flood of antiquarian literature, there cannot be said to be any continuous history of North Africa, as recorded by its monuments. Westward of the land of Egypt, and separated from it by the sandy region of Marmarica, lay the little kingdom of Cyrenaica, peopled by colonists from Greek islands. This territory now forms part of the present Beylik of Tripoli, which has a seaboard of about 800 miles (see Barca). Continuing westward, past the island of Djerba, and then northward to the headland known as Cape Bon, with a farther stretch of seaboard some 200 miles westward, was the territory of the Carthaginians, whose stronghold and capital was Carthage. The boundaries of this region, afterward known as Africa Provincia, corresponded, or nearly so, with those of modern Tunisia. Still farther westward was the land of the Numidæ, which now forms the eastern half of the French colony of Algeria. Again farther westward and round the shores of the Atlantic, stretching far inland into the Great Desert, was the ancient Mauretania, divided by the Romans into two provinces, M. Cæsariensis and M. Tingitana, the latter now known as Morocco.

The province of Tripoli, with its three cities, Oea, Leptis, and Sebrata, which attained so high a degree of prosperity under the Antonines, has also little to show for its long record. The only monument of note is the half-buried quadrifrontal arch in the northeast quarter of the town of Tripoli (formerly Oea). It is dedicated to Marcus Aurelius and L. Aurelius Verus. The form of the monument is a rectangle measuring about 41 feet by 33 feet. Its height is difficult to state, as only the upper part, about 23 feet, is visible above the ground. The structure is entirely of marble, beautifully put together with large blocks, without cement at the joints. The surfaces are covered with busts, architectural ornament of great excellence, and groups of life-size figures. The coffering of the arches with their enrichments will bear comparison with any similar work in Rome itself.

Carthage became the metropolis of a widespread kingdom and one of the wealthiest cities of the world. But prosperity was mainly due to its central position as the most convenient outlet for the vast products of North Africa. Temples and stately edifices adorned its streets, and the remains of great structural works still attest the solid grandeur of the city; but the architecture was the work of Greek and not of Punic artists; and the few sculptures of note, which may be assigned to a period anterior to the last Punic war, 146 B.C., have nothing in common with the rude carvings that bear the impress of Carthaginian origin. The close relation that existed so long between Carthage and Sicily gave the Carthaginians the benefit of Greek tastes and culture, and it is reasonable to infer that public buildings, the better class of houses, and the general embellishment of the principal cities were the work of Sicilian Greeks and not of natives. Certainly every exploration, either on the site of the city, or of the numerous emporia on the coast, favours the assertion that the fine arts never flourished in Carthage. The consideration of the architecture of the Carthaginians may therefore be dismissed, although the paved streets of the metropolis, some 40 feet below the present surface, still await the spade of the explorer.

The long interval of nearly 250 years, which elapsed between the destruction of Carthage and its entire reconstruction by the Romans, is frequently lost sight of. It is true that an imperial edict for rebuilding the city was issued by Julius Cæsar, but many generations passed away before it became of sufficient importance to be regarded as the capital of the great colony of Africa Provincia. With the advent of the Flavian emperors commenced an era of distinction, and the favours showered on the inhabitants by Trajan and Hadrian, and by their successors, the Antonines, are attested by the numerous monuments bearing their honoured names. A still further impetus was given to the construction of works of public utility and embellishment during the subsequent rule of Septimius Severus, an African by birth. The Carthage of the Romans, built on the site of the older city, but occupying a smaller area and enclosed by a wall having a circuit of about twenty miles, contained (according to Strabo, a writer of the first century) a population of 700,000. Some idea of its magnificence can be obtained from the remains of marble and porphyry, which still enrich the mosques and palaces of North Africa, which help to make Cordova one of the wonders of the Western world, and to which the sumptuousness of Pisa is chiefly due.

After the destruction of Punic Carthage in 146 B.C., Utica became the metropolis of Roman Africa, and remained so for more than two centuries. It was built on a promontory and was girt, like Carthage, with walls of great solidity. The city had a large war harbour with a palace for the admiral or governor in the centre (similar to the *cothon* at Carthage and other coast towns), a citadel of great strength, a vast amphitheatre, a spacious theatre, temples, and an immense arsenal. Parts of the city walls still remain. They are of solid rubble, having the appearance of concrete, owing to the small-ness of the stones. As the lime was made from the same stone and is of the same colour, it is difficult to distinguish one from the other. The remains of Utica, as well as of other towns on the coast, present opportunities of comparing the Punic and Roman methods of building, in

arched doorways with their delicate carvings in stone and marble, its wilderness of shops, their wooden columns painted with spiral bands in gaudy colours of blue, red, and green, has much to charm the eye, and colouring enough to bal-ance the wearying monotony of whitewash. Very curious too and characteristic are the wooden doors of ordinary Moorish houses, with their quaint devices in round-headed nails. Crescents and crosses, graceful curves, and crude imitations of symbols of deities of long-forgotten Phœnician origin are mixed together in endless variety. Few of the buildings, pub-lic or private, have any striking architectural merit. Exceptions may be made in favour of the Bishia mosque with its graceful minaret, the Djamaa-ez-Zeitouna, with its imposing en-trance and arcaded loggia, and the façade of the town palace, the Dar-el-Bey. Tunis is essentially an Eastern city. The over-throw of the Moors in Sicily in the thirteenth century, and their expulsion from Spain two centuries later, brought to the towns of North Africa a people renowned in art, and possess-ing a culture far in advance of other nations on the shores of the Mediterranean. The arts of Tunis originated with these Moors, and are feebly ap-parent at the present day. As decorative work the domed ceilings in the Bardo palace are worthy of note, and the rich plas-terwork and gild-

NORTH AFRICA: ROMAN PRÆTORIUM OF 2D CENTURY A.D., AT LAMBESE, ALGERIA.

the use of stone and rubble, and the application of concrete or rammed earth commonly known as pisé. At Utica the distinction is very marked. The earliest walls are entirely of rubble and without facing. The vaulting of Punic times is done with the same materials. The inner surfaces appear to have been thinly coated with lime, and from the absence of cut stones and the bold rounding of angles, it would seem that implements for dressing and squaring were unknown. The admiral's palace, the re-mains of which form a conspicuous mass, is a good example of this kind of building.

In spite of a dearth of architectural monu-ments, Tunis, the successor of these cities of antiquity, with its labyrinth of streets, its flying arches across the narrow thoroughfares, its

ed ornamentation of the chief apartments of the Dar el-Bey, done so recently as the beginning of the nineteenth century, will compare favour-ably with similar work at Seville or Granada.

The Roman road that connected Utica with Carthage continued northward to Hippo-Zary-tus, called by the Arabs Benzerte, but known in Europe as Bizerta. There is no architecture here worth noting, the Roman monuments hav-ing been destroyed by the Arabs. The next coast town of any importance from an architec-tural point of view is Thabraca or Tabarca. This appears to have been a large commercial port in Roman times, but the interest of the place is now centred on a small rocky island, about one third of a mile from the shore, where, at a height of nearly 400 feet, rises an immense ruined citadel, built by the Genoese under Charles V., after his memorable expedition to Tunis in 1535.

On descending the southern slopes of the mountains, which separate the coast from the plains, and arriving at the great highway which led from Carthage to Hippone, the modern Bone, ruined towns and villages, that once sheltered a vast population, greet the eye on every side. Bulla Regia, for instance, now called Beni-Mazeu, for many centuries the residence of Numidian kings, has not at the present day, so far as the site has been explored, a single architectural monument standing. An inexcusable and thoughtless concession of the stone of the district, for the purposes of the Tunisian railway, resulted in the destruction of existing edifices, including a number of inscribed stones which might have thrown some light on the early history of this royal city. The thermæ, during the Roman occupation, must have been on a large scale, judging from the extent of their remains, and the theatre, the walls of which are still intact, was built with great blocks of finely dressed stone. Some idea of the alteration of the surface since the final destruction and abandonment of Bulla Regia by the Arabs in the seventh century may be gathered from the fact that the ground now rises to a level with the top of the proscenium wall of the theatre. The amphitheatre is only indicated by undulations, and the entire site of the city, nearly a mile long, is so choked with weeds and undergrowth that recognition of the different public buildings is almost impossible. Simittu, or Chemtou, one day's journey westward, also awaits systematic exploration. The monumental remains of Simittu are in complete ruin, but the quarries, after an interval of twelve centuries, have recently been in full work and their beautiful products shipped to all parts of Europe. A stately line of piers and arches crosses the Medjerda valley about a hundred miles lower down, bringing the waters of Mt. Zaghouan and Mt. Djougar to the hill of Carthage ; and there is no structure now standing within the vast area of the old Roman Empire which bears in so high a degree the impress of imperial will, or attests so visibly the strength of Roman character, as this so-called aqueduct of Carthage. It was commenced by Hadrian, as a work of necessity, after his first visit to Africa, 123 A.D., and there is reason to believe that the work was not finally completed till the reign of Septimius Severus, seventy years later. The greater part of its length, which is estimated at sixty-one miles, is subterranean, but where it passes over the plains it is carried on a series of arches rising 60 or 70 feet, some of them having two tiers with a total height of more than 120 feet. The actual duct or channel was about 3 feet wide and 6 feet high, arched over,

with openings at intervals for inspection and ventilation. The springs from the two mountains were (and are still, it is said) capable of supplying eight millions of gallons in twenty-four hours. The construction varies in different portions. That nearest to Zaghouan is beautifully built with courses of finely cut stone, each course being 20 inches high. The piers average 12 feet in width and 15 feet in thickness, the span of the arches averaging 15 feet. A roll moulding 20 inches thick forms the impost. The voussoirs are carefully cut, and the duct over them is built entirely with rubble. The most interesting portion, as a building construction, is that which crosses the Medjerda plain some ten miles from Tunis. This is built of pisé, being simply the clay of the district mixed with a certain portion of lime. The foundations consist of several courses of cut stone, and the superstructure is built up in sections 3 feet 8 inches high. On the upper surface of each section are channels 6 inches square and 2 feet 3 inches long. There are five such channels on the face of each pier and three generally in the thickness. In these were placed strips of olive wood 1 inch or more thick and 6 inches wide. When the material was well consolidated, strong mortar $2\frac{1}{2}$ inches thick, containing a large admixture of wood ashes, was laid over the entire surface, filling up the channels. Wood pegs were driven in at intervals in order to ascertain and secure a perfectly level bed for the next section, and so on up to the top, 60 or more feet from the ground. There is a course of stone at the springing of the arches, the voussoirs being 2 feet on the face, but of two or more stones in depth. The stability of the construction is shown by the excellent condition of the aqueduct, in spite of repeated earthquakes. It is supposed that the Carthaginians found this kind of construction prevalent among the earlier inhabitants of Africa and transmitted it to their successors. At Dimas, for instance, the ancient Thapsus, where Julius Cæsar landed with his army, there are remains of the old Punic sea wall nearly a quarter of a mile long, built in frames with small pebbles and mortar, like modern concrete construction.

The system of water supply, which the Carthaginians had brought to perfection, was continued by their successors. The great reservoirs, now in ruins, were restored for the service of the aqueduct, and another range called the small cisterns, of which there were eighteen, each measuring 93 feet by 19 feet 8 inches and 27 feet 6 inches high to the crown of the vault, were built by the Romans for the storage of rainwater. These are constructed with rubble and remarkably hard mortar, with a thin coating of cement apparently made with marble dust. Some of these cisterns are in fair preservation and are still used by the peasantry.

A day's journey from Tunis may be seen the source of supply to the great aqueduct, indicated by the remains of an architectural monument of noble proportions. Under a spur of Mt. Zaghouan is a small ruined temple with wings in the form of a vaulted semicircular colonnade, recalling, on a much smaller scale, the portico of S. Peter's at Rome with its adjuncts. The width of the colonnade is 15 feet, having a wall at the back with niches in alternate inter-columniations. The columns, of which there are twelve on either side of the central edifice, are of the Corinthian order, and the entire area in front, which was paved with stone, is 94 by 86 feet. The spring flowed under this area, the water passing into a basin of double horseshoe form, to which there was access by a flight of steps at each end. Here commenced the conduits which served to irrigate the adjacent land as well as to supply the great aqueduct. The shafts and their capitals have all been removed. They will be found in neighbouring mosques, misapplied as usual, covered with whitewash, and wedged up to support some flimsy Arab roof. From the same source, supplemented by an extension to Djougar about twenty miles farther south, the city of Tunis is still supplied, but through a more prosaic channel than the stately duct which terminated in Roman Carthage.

Between Carthage and Hadrumetum, the modern Soussa (a distance of about eighty miles), are the remains of a continuous line of towns and villages, mostly situated on rising ground near the seashore. Among them Aphrodisium must have been conspicuous. It is now a confused mass of stone and rubble. A large circular tomb or mausoleum in the vicinity attracts notice, resembling that of Cæcilia Metella, or of the Plautian family near Tivoli, but of smaller dimensions. Its diameter is about 48 feet, and its present height 34 feet. It was faced with large blocks of cut stone 20 inches high, had a cornice and probably an attic. It had three inscribed slabs on the face, but these have entirely disappeared. To the Arabs this monument is known as Kasr-el-Menara, signifying a lighthouse. Amongst other ruined towns in this part of the country Uthina deserves passing record, covering the surface for more than a mile. At the present day it has no direct approach. Theatres and baths, the great basilica, and the arcades of the amphitheatre have long since been overthrown and despoiled, and are now the home of the jackal, or a rough shelter for some dozen of Bedouin families.

Soussa possesses little interest to the architect. Even the principal mosque, with its misapplied Roman shafts, may be passed by unobserved. Some of the koubbas (tombs of saints) are curious, and the doorways of many of the larger houses are worth noticing. They differ in design in different towns of North Africa, favouring the supposition that, during a certain period, traditional treatment was observed.

The Roman road southward from Soussa has a special interest. At a distance of about forty miles stand the magnificent remains of the amphitheatre of El-Djem, the ancient Thysdrus, second only in size to the Coliseum at Rome, and possessing considerable architectural pretensions. History is almost silent as to its origin, but there is little doubt that it was conceived by the elder Gordian, and continued by his successor. The dimensions and arrangements have no distinctive features, having externally the usual open arcades, each presenting a complete order. The first and third stories are Corinthian, and the second Composite. Whether the attic was Corinthian or not we have no means of judging, as only a portion of its inner wall remains. There are many indications that this colossal edifice was built very hurriedly. The major axis may be estimated at 489 feet, and the minor axis 403 feet. The height of the first order is 26 feet 6 inches, of the second 32 feet 10 inches, and of the third 29 feet 8 inches. Assuming that the attic was intended to be of the same proportionate height as its prototype in Rome, the total height of its external wall would have been 124 feet 6 inches. The construction possesses considerable merit. It is built entirely with a shelly limestone from the quarries at Sallecta, some twenty miles distant. The courses are nearly all of the same height, almost 20 inches, and the lengths of the stones average 38 inches. There is every reason to suppose that the structure was never finished. The short rule of the three Gordians, 236–244 A.D., with whose memory it was intimately associated, was followed by another dynasty which had no interest in an obscure town so far distant from the coast.

The road leading westward from Soussa is the old Arab highway to the sacred walled city of Kairouan. This is one of the few towns of importance in North Africa that is of Arab origin. As there was no stone within a reasonable distance, brick was the material mostly used, — a manufacture still carried on in the vicinity. The great mosque, known as Djamaa-el-Kebir, was built, according to tradition, by Sidi-Okbar, the companion of the Prophet and the founder of the creed in North Africa. But this is open to doubt. The arrangements, as they now exist, differ little from those at Damascus, or the greater work at Cordova, of which it was the undoubted prototype. But any one intimate with the mosque at Cordova will experience a feeling of disappointment in treading the prayer chamber of the African mosque. The noble shafts of marble and porphyry, with their varied capitals of white marble, are not wanting ; but of the delicate stucco ornament, the *nuksh hadida* of the Arabs, so beautiful at Cordova, there are no traces here. The mihrab is on a small scale, and the tilework, of which there are a few exquisite specimens, has been so injured through frequent reconstruction that the beauty of the whole suffers accordingly. Mention must be made of the tomb of Sidi Sahab, the holy companion and friend of the Prophet, sometimes styled "The Mosque of the Barber." Round this sepulchre are clustered a remarkable group of buildings embracing a medrassen (see Medresseh) or college for instruction in the Koran. The original stucco and tilework have been sadly defaced, but the wooden sarcophagus of "The Companion," with its velvet pall decorated with native ostrich eggs, gilt balls of earth from Mecca, and richly bespangled banners, is very impressive. This tomb and its surroundings are characteristic specimens of native architecture and its adornments.

Turning back to Carthage and following the other great highway into the interior which skirted the southern bank of the Bagradas, the modern Medjerda, the remains of a long succession of towns are visible. Thugga, now known as Dougga, is the first town having any architectural monuments worth noting. Among the most conspicuous of its remains is the tetrastyle portico of a basilica of the Corinthian order, which, for general design, justness of proportion, and refinement of detail, will compare favourably with any similar work in Rome itself. It was built during the reign of M. Aurelius and his colleague, L. Verus, 161–169 A.D., at the expense of two brothers of the family of Marcus, and was dedicated to Jupiter and Minerva. The shafts, 33 feet high, are fluted, and, with one exception, are monoliths. The moulded door jambs, 27 feet high, and the lintel, 22 feet long, are also monoliths. The other remains of the city comprise a similar portico in a more ruined condition, three triumphal arches, two fountains, and several cisterns similar in form to those at Carthage. One monument deserves special notice. It is a mausoleum commemorative of a distinguished Numidian, and is supposed to have been erected in the fourth century B.C. It consists of two stories, the lower one nearly 22 feet square standing on a broad base of five steps, the whole being crowned by a graduated pyramid. The general design is of the Ionic order of an early Greek type, the lotus-shaped leaves in some of the capitals betraying Egyptian and possibly other influences. The sad story of its demolition is a matter of recent history and may be passed over in silence. It is sufficient to state that two dedicatory slabs, bearing an inscription in the Libyan and Punic tongues, may be studied in the British Museum.

A few miles south of Thugga are the conspicuous remains of an immense fortress with square towers at the angles. Such edifices, square or oblong in plan, are a marked feature

in this country, and have a peculiar interest as the prototype of the mediæval castle. They were erected during the Byzantine occupation in the fifth century, partly as a defence against the Moors and desert tribes, and partly as convents for the shelter and protection of soldier monks, the originals of a class so celebrated in the Middle Ages. The walls are mostly built with the materials of Roman structures, of coursed rubble bonded with long and short work.

Continuing the track, which, it may be observed, follows the old Roman road so closely that distinct traces of the pavement are frequently visible, and skirting the hillside which overlooks the fatal plain of Zama, the ruins of Zanfour, the ancient Assuras, stand up conspicuously on the banks of a precipitous ravine. A lower road or track leads to Mactar, a city of ruins, and an upper one to El-Kef, perched so high on its rocky site as to look like a city in the skies. Among its numerous remains there is not one architectural monument, but there is sufficient evidence, from the character of the masonry, that the town must have flourished about the time of Diocletian. An extraordinary number of inscribed stones built into the walls of Arab houses makes El-Kef a treasury of delight to the epigraphist. The Roman road southward of Mactar is difficult to trace, but it passed through Sufes, bearing the modern name of Sbiba. "We arrived at Sbiba," says El-Bekri, in the eleventh century, "a town of great antiquity, built of stone, and containing a college and several baths." It is now a wilderness. Two days' journey westward are the ruins of Ammœdara, abbreviated to Haidra, where Roman work is not remarkable either for design or construction ; and two days' journey southward lies Sufetula, corrupted by the Arabs into Sbeitla. The whole of this part of North Africa was thickly peopled during the Roman occupation, remains of towns and villages dotting the plains and hillsides wherever the eye wanders. To the architect the ruins of Sufetula have an interest second to none in North Africa. They offer to the student admirable examples of Roman architecture before its decline, and present a variety only to be found at two other places in the country, Lambessa and Timgad. The most conspicuous monument comprises three temples, side by side, forming a portion of the northwest side of a rectangular walled enclosure, measuring 238 feet by 198 feet. The principal approach is through a monumental gateway on the southeast side, which is not in the axis of the central temple, but is fully 20 feet on one side of it. The three edifices are tetrastyle prostyle, the middle one being of the Composite order of great elegance of proportion, and higher than the side ones, which are of the

Corinthian order. Taking the three porticoes together, there were eighteen columns, the height of the shafts of the central temple being 29 feet, and the others 25 feet 3 inches. They all stood on lofty stylobates, constructed with huge blocks of stone. The side and back walls of the central building were ornamented with engaged shafts, projecting a full half diameter. Those of the side temples were decorated with pilasters. Most of these are still standing, but the porticoes are entirely overthrown. The broken shafts, which were monoliths, the capitals, fragments of enriched cornices, and other embellishments lie piled up on the ground. So much material is buried beneath the surface that it is impossible to say whether the pediments were adorned with sculpture. The decorative character of the entablature favours the supposition that they were not devoid of sculptured ornament of some kind. The enclosure was paved with large slabs of stone, some of which are nearly 8 feet long. The monumental gateway, before referred to, consists of a large central arch and two lateral ones. It has four engaged Corinthian shafts on the outer face, not fluted, but having a projection that has all the appearance of rustication. Within the gateway was a portico communicating with a colonnade which continued round the enclosure on three sides. A range of shops stood against one of the side walls, but these were probably of a later erection than the original enclosure. This gateway was dedicated to Antoninus Pius, as recorded on an inscription in the frieze, and the temples were probably built under the same emperor. There are many points of resemblance in the details of all these monuments. There is also a triumphal arch to the south of the city, more remarkable for its mass than for any features of special merit. The remains of a theatre may still be seen on the banks of the river that skirted the southeast side, now known as the Oued Sbeitla. It appears to have been constructed during the reign of Diocletian. The fragments of sculpture strewn over the site of the theatre do not exhibit much refinement of design or skill in workmanship. The aqueduct which supplied the city from the adjacent range of hills, crossing the river at considerable altitude, is a marked feature in the landscape. It was built 145 A.D., and is still in fair preservation. The plans of several Christian churches, with nave, apse, and aisles, can be easily traced, but their architectural features have mostly disappeared. There is sufficient evidence to show that their vaulting was formed with hollow terra-cotta tubes, each piece measuring 6 inches by $2\frac{1}{2}$ inches. The city, which had been for a long period one of the strongholds of Christianity in North Africa, was the last to resist the Arab invasion. It was besieged and razed to the ground

646 A.D. The remote position of the city has been the best protector of its monuments. About twenty miles westward lie the remains of Kasrin, the ancient Scillium, more remarkable for beauty of site than for architectural excellence. A triumphal arch, of great excellence of construction, but unsatisfactory in general design and detail, stands conspicuously on the edge of a precipitous ravine. No date can be assigned to this monument, which was probably erected at a late period of the Empire. There are the remains of three mausolea, one only being in good preservation. This building, three stories in height, is erected on a pyramid of steps now mostly under the surface. The lowest story, 12 feet square, is of plain masonry, with two small entrances 3 feet square. The middle story, slightly receding from the bottom one, is decorated on each face with four fluted Corinthian pilasters of great delicacy of workmanship, the two central ones on one face being spaced a little farther apart in order to find room for a lengthy inscription. The top story consists at present of a large niche, without any traces of ornamentation. The statue that undoubtedly filled it has long since disappeared. The height of the mausoleum, in its present state, may be estimated at 50 feet. The monument was erected by M. Flavius Secundus, in honour of his parents and other members of his family, who are fully described in lengthy inscriptions nearly covering one face. In addition, there are no less than ninety hexameters and twenty elegiacs, in which the charms of the city of Scillium and its surroundings are portrayed by a local poet. The greatest length of the city may be estimated at one and a half miles, but there are no indications of an enclosing wall. Farther south no monuments of architectural interest have been noted. Nor is it necessary to make more than passing mention of such remote towns as Feriana, Capsa, or Tozer, where outlying military posts established by the Romans are now occupied by French soldiers.

With few exceptions the remaining towns on the southern shores of the Mediterranean have little architectural interest. Conspicuous among them is the very modern town of Bona, once the Ubba of the Carthaginians, the Hippone of the Romans, and the scene of the life-long labours of S. Augustine. What the Vandals did not destroy the Arabs did two centuries later, and with the stones of the Roman city this busy little seaport town, some mile and a half distant, was constructed. At Philippeville, farther west, the Thapsus of the Carthaginians and Rusicada of the Romans, destruction was almost as complete, little remaining beyond the ruined theatre, the walls of the old cisterns, and structural portions of an amphitheatre. In the cavea of the theatre are stored some interesting fragments, two or more sculptured reliefs being good specimens of Roman art.

There are few spots in North Africa possessing more interest than Cherchel, the site of Jol of the Old World, afterward Julia Cæsarea of the Romans, and occupying a headland seventy-one miles west of Algiers. Juba II., the last of the Numidian kings, and ruling under the suzerainty of the Emperor Claudius, built himself a city which he embellished with magnificent works from Greece and Rome. Sacked by Firmus in the fourth century, it was razed to the ground by Vandals a century later. Under Barbarossa, the city regained something of its former splendour, but it was overthrown by an earthquake in 1738. Wherever excavations have been made architectural fragments have been discovered. Some of them are still to be seen in the little museum at Cherchel, giving evidence of the splendour of Juba's capital and his appreciation of the works of Greek artists. Like other Old World potentates, the distinguished Numidian built himself a lordly tomb some ten miles east of the city, still forming the chief attraction of this part of North Africa, and taking rank as one of the great sepulchral monuments of the world. This edifice is apparently of circular form at the base, but is, in fact, polygonal. Its diameter is 198 feet, and its original height was 130 feet. The base forms an encircling podium, presenting a decorative wall 36 feet high with sixty engaged colums of the Ionic order, having capitals of a Greek type, but archaic in form, and surmounted by an entablature of simple outline. At the cardinal points of this encircling colonnade were false stone doors, each in four panels. The imitation of framing was taken by the Arabs to represent a cross, and gave rise to various legends resulting in the mausoleum being designated as the *Tombeau de la Chrétienne*. It retains this name to the present day. Above the order rises a series of thirty-three stone steps which gradually decrease in circular area, giving the structure the appearance of a truncated cone. In the centre of the mass are two sepulchral vaulted chambers, 12 feet 4 inches long, and 9 feet 3 inches and 9 feet 7 inches wide, respectively, separated from each other by a short passage, at one end of which are stone doors in the form of a portcullis. These doors form the termination of a winding gallery 483 feet in length, 7 feet 5 inches in height, and of varying width, which communicates with the external face of the monument. The access to the gallery, which was not discovered till 1866, is not by one of the four panel-doors above referred to, but by a concealed stone door under the one facing east. Along the gallery at intervals are niches in the wall intended for lamps. The entire monument stands on a raised stone platform 210 feet square. The marked

resemblance of this tomb, both in form and construction, to the Medrassen, or tomb of the Numidian kings, which lies between Theveste and Diana Veteranorum, favours the presumption that Juba's respect for his ancestors prompted him to erect a similar resting place for himself and his successors. The older monument, which probably contained the ashes of Masinissa, the hero of Numidian history, was built about 150 B.C. Its cylindrical base is 193 feet in diameter, and the encircling wall is decorated with sixty attached Doric columns four diameters in height, resting on three stone steps and surrounded by an entablature of cavetto form, as if of Egyptian origin. The conical portion is formed by a series of steps averaging 37 inches tread and 22 inches rise. The apex of the cone has long since been destroyed. The name of Juba is historic. His wife was the offspring of Antony and Cleopatra, and their only daughter was Drusilla, the wife of Felix, governor of Judæa, before whom Paul was arraigned. A few miles east of Cherchel are the scattered ruins of Tipasa, which still retains its Roman name. From the appearance of its sculptured remains, which show great refinement of detail, it may be assumed that the same colony of artists worked in both towns.

The occupation of Numidia by the Romans gave a great impetus to building operations. Cirta, its capital, known in Punic times as Cartha, *i.e.* Civitas, and since the fourth century as Constantine, was, according to Strabo, a magnificent city adorned with numerous palaces. It attained the height of prosperity in the peaceful reign of Micipsa, just after the close of the third Punic War, 146 B.C., and maintained its position with almost uninterrupted success till the Arab invasion of the seventh century. The architectural remains are few and need no special notice. About sixteen miles northwest of the city is a tomb of cylindrical form, of the time of Hadrian, and twelve miles south another ruined memorial called by the Arabs Es-Soumah, signifying "a minaret." It is an architectural composition of considerable merit, consisting originally of two stages, the upper one being of the Doric order. The monument may be assigned to the first century. The attractions of Cirta, surpassed by few cities in the world for grandeur of situation, and the extraordinary fertility of the adjacent country, resulted in the growth of a number of towns which, judging by their monumental remains, must have been centres of refinement as well as of wealth. At Calama, the modern Guelma; Tibilis, better known by its Arabic name of Announa; Thubursicum, renamed Khamisa; and Medaura and Tipasa, the former celebrated as the birthplace of Apuleius, there are monuments still standing which claim, even in their present mutilated beauty, the respect and admiration of all students of Roman architecture. Farther south, on the high road between Diana Veteranorum, now abbreviated to Zana, and Theveste is a tomb of gigantic dimensions already referred to as the Medrassen. The burial chamber in the centre of this monumental edifice measures about 10 feet by 4 feet.

In recent years the investigations of French archæologists have been largely devoted to three cities south of the plains and fringing the slopes of some of the spurs of the Aures Mountains. The student of Roman architecture will find among the remains of Lambæsis, Thamugas, and Theveste a larger amount of material for his notebook than anywhere else out of Italy, besides acquiring from well-preserved inscriptions an insight into civic life and customs during a period of three or more centuries. Lambæsis, commonly known as Lambessa, appears to have been built early in the second century, having been selected as the seat of military government, Carthage being the centre of civil government. It owed its development and subsequent splendour to its being the headquarters of the camp of the Third Augustan Legion. A decree of Septimius Severus accorded to the soldiers the privilege of residing with their wives, and numerous inscriptions show that the legion had in its ranks sculptors, skilled architects, and experienced artificers. The town covered an area of about 1500 acres. When visited by Peyssonnel in 1740, there were forty triumphal arches noticeable and fifteen were standing. At the present day there are only two, both dilapidated. The site of the forum has been unearthed, and a large octostyle temple on the west side is sufficiently defined to give an idea of the scale and proportions. There is also an Ionic temple dedicated to Æsculapius and Health, during the reign of M. Aurelius, with an atrium in front of it 200 feet long, and a series of chapels on either side, approached by broad flights of steps. Numerous monumental remains and decorative fragments offer a great field for still further research. The most conspicuous ruin is that of a large structure called the Prætorium, the headquarters of the Legion, built during the reign of the Emperor Gallien, 268 A.D. It consists of two stories externally, and probably had an attic in addition. Internally it is one vast hall, the great shafts attached to the walls reminding one of the interior of some ' Norman keep. Numerous mosaic pavements have been discovered. These have been carefully put together and stored in the local museum. Other objects have been deposited in the Louvre.

About fourteen miles eastward of Lambessa are the still more remarkable ruins of another city, which has not inaptly been termed the Pompeii of North Africa. Like most towns in this country, Thamugas, noted in the itinerary of Antonine as Thamugadas, but now known as Timgad, suffered from earthquakes, and, like Lambæsis, its present condition is due rather to neglect and abandonment than to any other cause. The general plan is defined and a greater part of the walls are still entire, but it is doubtful whether Thamugas was ever fortified. It was essentially a Roman city, as attested by numerous inscriptions, and still further it was a city of delight, the fertility of the soil, the beauty of the mountain scenery, and abundant water supply attracting citizens of wealth from other parts of the colony. The attention of the French government was directed more than thirty years ago to these remarkable ruins, and the immediate result was a partial exploration by skilled officers attached to the *Commission des monuments historiques*. Since that time the city has been systematically unearthed, and now offers to the student of Roman architecture an exceedingly valuable field for research. An admirable monograph, entitled *Timgad, une Cité Africaine*, was commenced as far back as 1891, and its authors, MM. Boeswillwald and Cagnat, have given reliable information upon the discovered remains, illustrated by photographs and measured drawings of the principal monuments. Similar praise is due to M. A. Ballu for his work entitled *Les ruines de Timgad*, published in 1897. Of the history of Timgad little is known beyond what may be deciphered from inscribed stones. Its prosperity, which apparently culminated under Trajan and his immediate successors, must have continued till the fall of the Empire, because the capitol, dedicated to Jupiter Capitolinus, was rebuilt during the reign of Valentinian I. The remains, which cover a large area, are of gigantic proportions, the shafts of the order being about 50 feet high. Ruin and destruction overtook the city when the Vandals swept like a whirlwind over the land in the fifth century.

It is impossible, in a short notice, to give a just description of the numerous buildings and fragments of architectural sculpture which cover the entire area of this interesting Old World city. One edifice alone deserves special mention, on account of merit as an architectural composition and great elegance of form and proportion. It is the arch of Trajan, erected between 100 and 112 A.D. in honour of the emperor, who laid the foundations of the city of Thamugas and bestowed many favours upon its inhabitants. Like many of the Roman triumphal arches, it has three openings. The central one is 13 feet 8 inches wide and 22 feet 8 inches high. The lateral ones are 7 feet 2 inches wide and of proportionate height. The monument is of the Corinthian order, each face being ornamented with four fluted detached columns 19 feet 6 inches high, and with corresponding pilasters against the face of the walls, both standing on lofty, well-proportioned stylobates. The most interesting part of the composition is the adornment of the rectangular niches over the lateral openings. These are flanked by small columns resting on beautifully carved corbels, and surmounted by separate entablatures, which are made to mitre with the frieze and architrave of the main cornice. The main entablature is horizontal over the central opening, but forms a curved pediment over each of the lateral ones, being set back in the middle and mitred over each of the principal columns. The two façades are identical, except that the two capitals of the two middle columns on the west front have eagles instead of the ordinary volutes. The attic appears to have extended over the whole of the structure. No statuary has yet been brought to light, but it is fair to assume that the four lateral niches were filled with figures or busts of the emperor and his family, or of his successors. The mass of the edifice is built of sandstone, having all the appearance of marble. The small columns which flank the lateral niches are marble.

The next Roman settlement, of which there are remains, was Mascula, now known as Ain-Khenchla. It was a garrison town, built early in the second century. Greater interest is attached to the still remote city of Theveste, modernized into Tebessa. No mention is made of it in old Latin authors, the name first appearing in the geography of Ptolemy. The oldest inscriptions are of the reign of Vespasian. Among the remains which may be found scattered over many miles, a quadrifrontal arch, erected to the memory of Caracalla and his brother Geta, is one of the most conspicuous. The chief peculiarity of this monument is the absence of an attic and the substitution of two tetrastyles, enclosing statues of the two emperors, as crowning features of the edifice. The material is hard limestone, the sixteen columns of the Corinthian order being of marble. As an architectural work it merits special notice, because it shows considerable departure from the recognized treatment and proportions of a classic order. Of equal importance are the extensive remains of the basilica. Built not later than the end of the first century, it appears to have been almost destroyed during the incursions of the Moors and the wild tribes of the Aures. When Solomon, the successor of Belisarius, arrived at the gates of Theveste, he found the city in ruins, and we learn from an inscription in the reign of Justinian, 539 A.D., that *Theveste civitas a fundamentis oedificata est.* The Roman basilica stood on the north side of a forum, approached through two lofty gateways, the arch of one of them still standing. A broad flight of steps, now partly destroyed, gave access to the building, which has

a nave with an apse and two aisles. The nave and aisles were separated by piers and engaged shafts in two superimposed orders, the whole being arcaded and the aisles having galleries. The material is a finely grained limestone in regular courses about 20 inches thick, of large stones bedded in very thin mortar. The columns are of granite and gray marble, not fluted, and the capitals of the Corinthian order of white marble, showing great refinement of form and leafage. There are no archivolts, and the surfaces of the masonry are polished like marble. The Byzantine restoration and additions appear to have been commenced during the same year in which Justinian laid the foundations of S. Sophia. The additions are easily distinguishable, the masonry being of a different character, specially noticeable in the trefoil chapel on the east side. Round three sides of the edifice were shops or small dwellings, the walls of which are still standing. The whole was enclosed with a wall about 25 feet high, strengthened with twelve towers. What was the object of this inner fortification, when a large part of the city was girt with a high wall with ramparts, and a citadel of great strength in the centre? Procopius, the contemporary historian, throws light upon the subject. "Inside the walls of Carthage is a church, under the charge of men devoted to the service of God, whom we call monks. Solomon, who had built this church a little time before, surrounded it with walls in order that, in case of necessity, it might serve as a fortress." One may assume that in case of siege the fortified basilica, or monastery, would serve as an additional refuge for the inhabitants of a city so remotely situated as Theveste.

History is almost silent on the subject of Roman towns in the western provinces of North Africa. It is probable that, with the exception of towns on the coast, which Rome inherited from Carthage, the settlements were mostly military stations. The absence of fragments of ornament, such as are usually found in all public buildings of Roman origin, favours this assumption. Pomaria, for instance, was a headquarters, on account of its commanding position; Tlemcen, rising from its ashes, became in the twelfth and thirteenth centuries one of the chief Mohammedan cities of the West, a rival of Granada, a seat of wealth and commerce, and the home of civilization, art, and philosophy. The place has still abundant interest for the architect, and presents, in the mosques of Sidi Ahmed Bel Hassan el-Ghomari and of Sidi-Abrahim, exquisite specimens of Moorish art. Outside the walls are the mosque of Sidi-el-Halawi, with its columns of onyx and its ceiling of cedar, well worthy of study, and the koubba of Sidi Bou Medin, with its beautiful entrance. About one and a half miles farther

west are the remains of Mansoura, a walled city of great strength and importance in the fourteenth century. There is little left to tell of its former greatness, except the beautiful minaret of the mosque, which may be classed among the chief architectural monuments of Moorish art. One other town in the extreme west of North Africa, mentioned by ancient writers as occupied by the Romans, was Volubilis, called by the Moors Oualili. The ruins of a triumphal arch and the gateway of the old basilica, both of late Roman type, are the sole memorials of its ancient rulers. The town of Mequinez, some twelve miles distant, is built with the materials of this Roman city. The student of Moorish ornament and decorative art will find in other towns in the western provinces of North Africa many examples worthy of study, and traces of that refinement and beauty of execution which are so conspicuous in the greater edifices at Cordova and Granada.
— ALEXANDER GRAHAM.

NORTH SIDE. (See Orientation.)

NORWAY, ARCHITECTURE OF. (See Scandinavia, Architecture of.)

NOSE. A projecting edge or angle; a general term. (See Bull's Nose; Nosing.)

NOSING. A projection formed by a horizontal edge which extends beyond an upright face below; as the projection of a tread beyond the riser.

NOTCH BOARD. In Great Britain, the string of a flight of stairs, especially when horsed out, so as to show a series of right-angled notches on the upper edge.

NOTCH ORNAMENT. An ornament produced by notching the edges of a band, fillet, or

NOTCH ORNAMENT IN WOOD: THE PLANKSHEER OF A VENETIAN BOAT.

listel. If the edge of a shelf be cut with notches alternating on the upper and the lower edges, a simple pattern of considerable effectiveness results; and this can be varied in many ways. In the simple decoration applied to the marble work of Venetian domestic architecture, this ornament is found in connection with the Venetian Dentil.

NOTRE DAME. In French, "Our Lady"; a common dedication of French churches, and giving the popular name to more cathedrals than any other ecclesiastical title. The cathedrals of Paris, Chartres, Amiens, Reims, Rouen, Laon, Soissons, Senlis, Coutances, are each called Notre Dame; but the building most commonly understood by this title among foreigners is the cathedral of Paris.

NOTCH ORNAMENT: A MARBLE MOULDING FROM TOMB OF DOGE ANDREA DANDOLO, S. MARK'S CHURCH, VENICE.

NOVELTY SIDING. (See Siding.)

NOYER. (See Geoffroi du Noyer.)

NULL, EDWARD VAN DER; architect; b. Jan. 9, 1812; d. April 3, 1868.

In 1844 he was appointed professor of ornament in the academy of Vienna. In association with August Siccard von Siccardsburg (see Siccard von Siccardsburg), he built the new opera house in Vienna and other important buildings.

Seubert, *Künstler-lexicon;* Niemann-Feldegg, *Theophilos Hansen.*

NUMMULITIC LIMESTONE. A limestone composed largely of fossil nummulites. The pyramid of Cheops is largely of this stone.
— G. M. P.

NUNNERY. A convent for females, the arrangements for which do not differ essentially from a religious house of the same epoch for men. (See Monastic Architecture.)

NURAGHE. Same as Noraghe.

NUT. A polygonal piece of wood or metal pierced by a screw-threaded hole to fit the screw end of a bolt, rod, or the like.

NYMPHÆUM. A place or building dedicated to the worship of a nymph, or the nymphs, of a river, a forest, or the like. The most famous existing building of the kind is that at Nîmes in southern France. The name is given also to a room, as in a large house, fitted with an ornamental basin, statues of nymphs, and the like. The word is classical, but its meaning has been extended by modern archæologists.